THE AMERICAN PROMISE

A HISTORY OF THE UNITED STATES

Second Edition

Vancouver
Island
Strait of Juan de Fuca
Cape Flattery

Mt. Rainier
(14,410 ft.; 4,392 m) ▲
Mt. St. Helens
(8,366 ft.; 2,550 m) ▲

Columbia River

COASTAL RANGES

CASCADE RANGE

COLUMBIA PLATEAU

Columbia River

BITTERROOT RANGE

Salmon River

SNAKE RIVER PLAIN

Snake River

Missouri River

Yellowstone River

Little Missouri River

James River

BADLANDS

BLACK HILLS

GREAT

Pt. Reyes
San Francisco Bay

Monterey Bay

SIERRA NEVADA

CENTRAL VALLEY

San Joaquin River

Mt. Whitney
(14,494ft.; 4,418 m) ▲

GREAT
BASIN

Great
Salt
Lake

GREAT
SALT LAKE
DESERT

GREAT
DIVIDE
BASIN

ROCKY

Mt. Elbert
(14,433 ft.; 4,399 m) ▲

Pikes Peak
(14,110 ft.; 4,301 m) ▲

N. Platte River

Platte River

S. Platte River

Arkansas River

P
L
A
I
N
S

Pt. Conception

CHANNEL
ISLANDS

MOJAVE DESERT

Colorado River

COLORADO
PLATEAU

M
O
U
N
T
A
I
N
S

Canadian River

LLANO
ESTACADO

PACIFIC
OCEAN

SONORAN
DESERT

Gila River

Rio Grande

Pecos River

Colorado River

EDWARDS
PLATEAU

Nueces River

ARCTIC OCEAN

Chukchi
Sea

RUSSIA

NORTH SLOPE
BROOKS RANGE

SEWARD
PENINSULA

St.
Lawrence
Island

Mt. McKinley
(20,320 ft.; 6,194 m) ▲

ALASKA RANGE

Mackenzie River

Yukon River

CANADA

CHUGACH MTS.

Nunivak
Island

Bering
Sea

Gulf of Alaska

ALASKA
PENINSULA

Kodiak
Island

ALEUTIAN
ISLANDS

| 0 | 250 | 500 miles |
| 0 | 250 | 500 kilometers |

Kauai

Niihau

Kauai
Channel

Oahu

Kaiwi Channel

Molokai

Lanai

Maui

Kahoolawe

Alenuihaha Channel

PACIFIC
OCEAN

| 0 | 50 | 100 miles |
| 0 | 50 | 100 kilometers |

Hawaii

M E X I C O

CANADA

Lake Superior

Lake Michigan

Lake Huron

Lake Ontario

Lake Erie

St. Lawrence River

Mt. Washington
(6,288 ft.; 1,917 m)

Gulf of Maine

Cape Cod

Connecticut River

Hudson River

Long Island

Missouri River

Des Moines River

*C E N T R A L
L O W L A N D*

Wabash River

Illinois River

Ohio River

APPALACHIAN PLATEAU

APPALACHIAN MOUNTAINS

Potomac River

Susquehanna River

Delaware River

James River

Chesapeake
Bay

N
W   E
S

*OZARK
PLATEAU*

Mississippi River

Cumberland River

Mt. Mitchell
(6,684 ft.; 2,037 m)

BLUE RIDGE MTS.

P I E D M O N T

Roanoke River

Cape
Hatteras

ATLANTIC
OCEAN

Red River

Tennessee River

Chattahoochee River

Savannah River

C O A S T A L

P L A I N

Cape
Fear

THE
UNITED STATES

Elevation

Feet	Meters
Over 13,001	Over 3,001
6,561-13,000	2,001-3,000
3,281-6,560	1,001-2,000
1,641-3,280	501-1,000
661-1,640	201-500
0-660	0-200
Below sea level	Below sea level

Alabama River

*OKEEFENOKEE
SWAMP*

Cape
Canaveral

Brazos River

*Mississippi
River Delta*

Gulf of Mexico

Lake
Okeechobee

*THE
EVERGLADES*

B A H A M A S

*ATLANTIC
OCEAN*

*VIRGIN
ISLANDS*

**PUERTO
RICO**

Caribbean Sea

0   50   100 miles

0   50   100 kilometers

*FLORIDA
KEYS*

0   150   300 miles

0   150   300 kilometers

CUBA

For a series of maps showing the territorial growth of the
United States, see pages M–2 to M–9 at the back of this book.

THE CONTEMPORARY WORLD

80°N

Greenland
(Den.)

ICELAND

Alaska

60°N

CANADA

UNITED
KINGDOM

IRELAND

FRANCE

SPAIN

40°N

PORTUGAL

UNITED STATES

Azores
(Port.)

ATLANTIC
OCEAN

MOROCCO

Canary Is.
(Sp.)

Western Sahara
(Mor.)

20°N

Hawaii

MEXICO

BAHAMAS
DOMINICAN
REPUBLIC

HAITI

Puerto Rico (U.S.)

CUBA
JAMAICA

BELIZE

ST. KITTS AND NEVIS
ANTIGUA AND BARBUDA
DOMINICA

Guadeloupe (Fr.)
Martinique (Fr.)
ST. LUCIA

ST. VINCENT AND THE GRENADINES
BARBADOS

GUATEMALA
EL SALVADOR

HONDURAS

NICARAGUA

GRENADA
TRINIDAD AND TOBAGO

COSTA RICA

PANAMA

VENEZUELA

GUYANA

SURINAME

French Guiana (Fr.)

MAURITANIA

CAPE
VERDE

SENEGAL
GAMBIA

GUINEA-BISSAU

MALI

GUINEA
SIERRA LEONE

LIBERIA
CÔTE D'IVOIRE

COLOMBIA

BURKINA FASO
GHANA

PACIFIC OCEAN

0°

Equator

Galápagos Is.
(Ec.)

ECUADOR

PERU

BRAZIL

SAMOA

20°S

TONGA

BOLIVIA

PARAGUAY

Easter I.
(Chile)

CHILE

ATLANTIC
OCEAN

URUGUAY

0   1,500   3,000 miles

ARGENTINA

0   1,500   3,000 kilometers

40°S

Falkland Is.
(U.K.)

60°S

80°S

160°W   140°W   120°W   100°W   80°W   60°W   40°W   20°W

ARCTIC OCEAN

NORWAY
SWEDEN
FINLAND
ESTONIA
LATVIA
LITHUANIA
DEN.
NETH.
BELARUS
GERMANY
POLAND
BE-
LUX. CZ. REP.
SLK.
UKRAINE
AUS.
HUNG.
MOLDOVA
SLN.
ROMANIA
SWITZ.
CR.
YUG.
BULGARIA
B.H.
MAC.
GEORGIA
ALB.
GREECE
TURKEY
ARMENIA
AZERBAIJAN
TUNISIA
MALTA
CYPRUS
LEBANON
SYRIA
ISRAEL
IRAQ
JORDAN
IRAN
KUWAIT
ALGERIA
LIBYA
EGYPT
SAUDI ARABIA
QATAR
BAHRAIN
UNITED ARAB
EMIRATES
OMAN
NIGER
CHAD
SUDAN
YEMEN
NIGERIA
ERITREA
DJIBOUTI
BENIN
CENTRAL
AFRICAN REP.
ETHIOPIA
SOMALIA
TOGO
CAMEROON
EQ.
GUINEA
UGANDA
GABON
RWANDA
KENYA
CONGO
DEM. REP. OF
THE CONGO
SÃO TOMÉ
& PRÍNCIPE
BURUNDI
TANZANIA
COMOROS
SEYCHELLES
ANGOLA
ZAMBIA
MALAWI
NAMIBIA
ZIMBABWE
MADAGASCAR
MAURITIUS
BOTSWANA
MOZAMBIQUE
SOUTH
AFRICA
SWAZILAND
LESOTHO

RUSSIAN FEDERATION

KAZAKHSTAN
MONGOLIA
UZBEKISTAN
KYRGYZSTAN
TURKMENISTAN
TAJIKISTAN
AFGHANISTAN
PAKISTAN
CHINA
N. KOREA
S. KOREA
JAPAN
BHUTAN
NEPAL
BANGLADESH
TAIWAN
INDIA
MYANMAR
(BURMA)
LAOS
VIETNAM
THAILAND
CAMBODIA
MALDIVES
SRI
LANKA
PHILIPPINES
BRUNEI
PALAU
MALAYSIA
SINGAPORE
FEDERATED STATES
OF MICRONESIA
INDONESIA
PAPUA
NEW
GUINEA
NAURU

PACIFIC OCEAN

Mariana Is.
(U.S.)
Guam
(U.S.)
MARSHALL
IS.
KIRIBATI
TUVALU
SOLOMON
IS.
VANUATU
FIJI
New Caledonia
(Fr.)

INDIAN OCEAN

AUSTRALIA

NEW
ZEALAND
Tasmania
(Aust.)

ABBREVIATIONS	
ALB.	ALBANIA
AUS.	AUSTRIA
BEL.	BELGIUM
B.H.	BOSNIA AND HERZEGOVINA
CR.	CROATIA
CZ. REP.	CZECH REPUBLIC
DEN.	DENMARK
HUNG.	HUNGARY
LUX.	LUXEMBOURG
MAC.	MACEDONIA
NETH.	NETHERLANDS
SLK.	SLOVAKIA
SLN.	SLOVENIA
SWITZ.	SWITZERLAND
YUG.	YUGOSLAVIA

ANTARCTICA

20°E   40°E   60°E   80°E   100°E   120°E   140°E   160°E

THE
AMERICAN
PROMISE

A HISTORY OF THE UNITED STATES

Second Edition

UNITED FARM WORKERS' UNION MARCH © *George Ballis/Take Stock.*

THE AMERICAN PROMISE

A HISTORY OF THE UNITED STATES

Volume II: From 1865

Second Edition

JAMES L. ROARK
Emory University

MICHAEL P. JOHNSON
Johns Hopkins University

PATRICIA CLINE COHEN
University of California at Santa Barbara

SARAH STAGE
Arizona State University West

ALAN LAWSON
Boston College

SUSAN M. HARTMANN
The Ohio State University

BEDFORD / ST. MARTIN'S
Boston • New York

FOR BEDFORD/ST. MARTIN'S

Publisher of History: Patricia A. Rossi
Senior Development Editor: Elizabeth M. Welch
Production Editor: Ara Salibian
Senior Production Supervisor: Catherine Hetmansky
Art Editors: Tina Samaha and Coleen O'Hanley
Marketing Manager: Jenna Bookin Barry
Associate Editor: Sarah Barrash
Editorial Assistant: Brianna R. Germain
Production Assistants: Coleen O'Hanley and Arthur Johnson
Copyeditors: Barbara G. Flanagan, Janet Renard, and Joy Sobeck
Proofreaders: Pauline Chin and Janet Cocker
Text Design: Wanda Kossak
Photo Research: Pembroke Herbert / Sandi Rygiel, Picture Research Consultants & Archives, Inc.
Cartography: Mapping Specialists Limited
Indexer: Maro Riofrancos
Cover Designer: Donna Lee Dennison
Composition: TechBooks East
Printing and Binding: RR Donnelley & Sons Company

President: Charles H. Christensen
Editorial Director: Joan E. Feinberg
Director of Marketing: Karen Melton
Director of Editing, Design, and Production: Marcia Cohen
Managing Editor: Elizabeth Schaaf

Library of Congress Control Number: 2001131214

Manufactured in the United States of America.

6 5 4 3 2 1
f e d c b a

For information, contact: Bedford/St. Martin's, 75 Arlington Street, Boston, MA 02116
617-399-4000
www.bedfordstmartins.com

ISBN: 0–312–39124–2 (hardcover)
ISBN: 0–312–39419–5 (paperback Vol. I)
ISBN: 0–312–39418–7 (paperback Vol. II)

Cover art: 1920s New York City hatbox: Picture Research Consultants & Archives. TV—*Father Knows Best:* Culver Pictures and Picture Research Consultants & Archives. Vietnam vet hat: Picture Research Consultants & Archives. Roosevelt New Deal Prosperity Needle Book: Collection of Janice L. and David J. Frent.

BRIEF CONTENTS

CONTENTS

APPENDICES

MAPS, FIGURES, AND TABLES

Maps

Figures

Tables

SPECIAL FEATURES

PREFACE

The American Promise grew out of the authors' experience as longtime teachers of the survey course. Collectively, we have logged more than a century in introductory American history classrooms in institutions that range from community colleges and state universities to private colleges and research institutions. We know firsthand that the survey course is the most difficult to teach and the most difficult to take. Our goal was an ambitious one: to publish the most teachable and readable textbook available.

Most survey texts emphasize either a social or political approach to history; by focusing on one, they inevitably slight the other. In our classrooms, students need **both** the structure a political narrative provides and the insights gained from examining social and cultural experiences. To write a comprehensive, balanced account of American history, we focused on the public arena—the place where politics intersects social and cultural developments—to show how Americans confronted the major issues of their day and created far-reaching historical change.

> *Our title,* The American Promise, *reflects our emphasis on human agency and our conviction that American history is an unfinished story.*

We thought hard about the concerns most frequently voiced by instructors: that students often find history boring, unfocused, and difficult. How could our text help introductory students see and remember American history's main events and developments? We decided to explore fully the political, social, economic, and cultural changes that students need to understand, at the same time avoiding unnecessary detail that threatened to befuddle rather than inform them. We organized each chapter to emphasize the essential people, events, and themes of the period. To portray the power of human agency and the diversity of the American experience, we stitched into the narrative the voices of hundreds of contemporaries—from presidents to pipefitters—whose ideas and actions shaped their times and whose efforts still affect our lives. By incorporating a rich selection of authentic American voices, we sought to create a vivid and compelling narrative that captures students' interest and sparks their historical imagination.

Our title, *The American Promise,* reflects our emphasis on human agency and our conviction that American history is an unfinished story. For millions, the nation held out the promise of a better life, unfettered worship, representative government, democratic politics, and other freedoms seldom found elsewhere on the globe. But none of these promises came with guarantees. And promises fulfilled for some meant promises denied to others. As we see it, much of American history is a continuing struggle over the definition and realization of the nation's promise. Abraham Lincoln, in the midst of what he termed the "fiery trial" of the Civil War, pronounced the nation "the last best hope of Earth." That hope, kept alive by countless sacrifices, has been marred by compromises, disappointments, and denials, but it lives still. Ideally, *The American Promise,* Second Edition, will help students become aware of the legacy of hope bequeathed to them by previous generations of Americans stretching back nearly four centuries, a legacy that is theirs to preserve and to build upon.

Features

Because students learn best when they find a subject engaging, we have made a special effort to incorporate features that bring American history to life and make it memorable. **Chapter-opening vignettes** invite students into the narrative with vivid accounts of individuals or groups who embody each chapter's main themes. Vignettes new to this edition include Andrew Carnegie's peace movement during World War I and Fannie Lou Hammer's civil rights struggles. **Two-tiered running heads** on every page remind students where the reading falls chronologically. Innovative **call-outs**—key points pulled from the main narrative and set in larger type—catch the student's eye and highlight the text's narrative power. At the close of each chapter, strengthened **conclusions** revisit central ideas and provide a bridge to the next chapter; annotated **chronologies** review the key events and developments explored in the chapter; and extensive **bibliographies,** updated to include recent studies, provide students with detailed suggestions for reading and research beyond the boundaries of the textbook. We have retained the well-received **appendices,** adding to our comprehensive collection of reference materials such important documents as the Articles of Confederation, the Seneca Falls Resolution, the Confederate Constitution, and Martin Luther King Jr.'s "I Have a Dream" speech; we have also expanded the section on research resources to include more information on Internet sites. Throughout the text **cross-references to the new Online Study Guide** encourage mastery of the text material and development of critical-thinking skills.

An enriched array of special features reinforces the narrative and offers teachers more points of departure for assignments and discussion. By adding new selections to the feature program, we now provide in every chapter two distinctive special features that captivate students' attention while helping them understand that history is both a body of knowledge and an ongoing process of investigation. **Documenting the American Promise** features (formerly "Texts in Historical Context") combine three or four primary documents that dramatize the human dimension of major events and controversies with brief interpretive commentary. For this edition we nearly doubled the number of primary-source selections, adding such topics as "Rockefeller and His Critics," "The Emerging Cold War," and "Student Protest." Questions for Analysis and Debate now follow the documents to help students analyze and squeeze meaning from primary sources. Illustrated **Historical Questions** pose and interpret specific questions of continuing interest so as to demonstrate the depth and variety of possible answers, thereby countering the belief of many beginning students that historians simply gather facts and string them together into a chronological narrative. New Historical Questions include "What Sank the *Maine*?," "Was Prohibition a Bad Idea?," and "Why Did the ERA Fail?" **The Promise of Technology** features (formerly "Technology in America") examine the ramifications—positive and negative—of technological innovations in American society and culture. We have revised substantially

all these illustrated essays to provide additional context and analysis, and again, we have nearly doubled the number of topics to include such significant technologies as the military helicopter and the Internet.

We take great pride as well in our full-color design and rich art program. We have preserved the **award-winning design** and added many new **illustrations** to make *The American Promise* a visual feast. In all, more than 200 images, many in full color and all large enough to study in detail, reinforce and extend the narrative. To emphasize visually the text's sustained treatment of Western history, all chapters offer one or more images of the West. An illustration accompanies each chapter-opening vignette, providing a visual supplement to the narrative portrait that opens every chapter. All pictures are contemporaneous with the period of the chapter, with **comprehensive captions** that draw students into active engagement with the images and help them unpack the layers of meaning. Full-page **chapter-opening artifacts** combine with many other illustrations of artifacts to emphasize the importance of material culture in the study of the past.

Finally, we have extended and expanded our highly regarded **map program** to offer the most effective set of maps available in a survey text. Each chapter offers, on average, four **full-size maps** showing major developments in a wide range of areas, from environmental and technological issues to political, social, cultural, and diplomatic matters. New maps reflect this edition's increased attention to Native American peoples and to a sustained continental perspective. Each chapter includes as well two or three new **"spot maps,"** small, single-concept maps embedded in pertinent passages of the narrative to increase students' grasp of crucial issues. Unique to our text, the spot maps highlight such topics as the Dust Bowl, the creation of Israel, and the breakup of Yugoslavia. In addition, critical-thinking map exercises—one per chapter—combine for an **embedded map workbook.** Another unique feature is our **mini-atlas,** a series of full-color maps at the end of each volume that reveals the changing cartography of America and its role in the world.

Textual Changes

A new edition of a textbook is cause for celebration, for it proudly announces the successful reception of the previous edition. But as authors, we found little time for complacency, for we welcomed this opportunity to reconsider the original text, to take stock of what worked and what could be improved. In addition to the many changes already mentioned, we made several major revisions in organization and coverage.

To mesh better with most course calendars, we reduced the number of chapters from seventeen to sixteen, in the process highlighting a stronger thematic development. Specifically, coverage of the closing decades of the twentieth century has been recast from three chapters into two in order to spotlight social and cultural themes as brightly as diplomacy and politics. The final chapters have also been thoroughly updated to treat the second term of the Clinton administration, developments in the Middle East and the former Yugoslavia, and the controversy surrounding the 2000 presidential election. Throughout the text we have incorporated the most important recent scholarship, as reflected in chapter bibliographies.

Shortening the text by 15 percent permitted us to eliminate excessive political detail and to achieve a clearer, more focused narrative. To provide an even more dynamic and memorable narrative while reinforcing the text's central theme, we expanded the number of historical actors whose interpretations of "the American promise"—sometimes shared, often competing—drove historical change. More succinct coverage of politics also permitted us to expand discussion of cultural and social topics such as the drive for woman suffrage and the rise of the civil rights movement. We have also made an effort to better place American history in a global context. Discussions of expanded accounts of American imperialism and the rise of the global economy, for example, strengthen the text's balanced, braided coverage, contributing to our effort to provide the introductory classroom the most teachable and readable text available.

Supplements

Thoroughly revised to reflect changes in the new edition, our comprehensive collection of print and electronic supplements provides a wide range of resources for students and teachers. We are especially pleased to welcome the groundbreaking Online Study Guide to our broad and integrated program of teaching and learning.

For Students

***Reading the American Past: Selected Historical Documents,* Second Edition.** This highly regarded primary-source collection, edited by Michael Johnson (Johns Hopkins University), one of the authors of *The American Promise,* complements the textbook by offering 4 or 5 documents for each chapter. The new edition provides a host of compelling features while retaining its low cost and brevity: a rich selection of over 125 documents (one-quarter of them new to this edition), balancing accounts by well-known figures with the voices of ordinary people; a wide array of sources that vividly illustrate the diversity of materials with which historians work; and user-friendly editorial apparatus such as chapter introductions, headnotes, questions, and an Introduction for Students on the goals and methods of source analysis.

Study Guide. For each chapter, this essential supplement for students, prepared by Rachel Standish (Foothill College), offers a summary; an annotated chronology followed by multiple-choice questions; a term-matching exercise; multiple-choice and short-answer questions; and map, illustration, and source exercises that help students synthesize the material they have learned as well as understand the skills historians use to make sense of the past. Answers for all exercises are provided, with cross-references to relevant discussion in the textbook.

Online Study Guide www.bedfordstmartins .com/tap. For each chapter, our free Online Study Guide offers an initial multiple-choice test that allows students to assess their comprehension of the material and a Recommended Study Plan that suggests specific exercises on the subject areas students still need to master. Two follow-up multiple-choice tests per chapter help students judge their command of the material. Additional exercises encourage students to think about chapter themes as well as help them develop skills of analysis. Results of multiple-choice tests can be e-mailed to instructors.

The Bedford Series in History and Culture. Over fifty American titles in this highly praised series combine first-rate scholarship, historical narrative, and important primary documents for undergraduate courses. Each book is brief, inexpensive, and focused on a specific topic or period. Package discounts are available.

Historians at Work Series. Brief enough for a single assignment yet substantive enough to provoke thoughtful discussion, each volume in this series combines the best thinking about an important historical issue with helpful learning aids. Selections by distinguished historians, each with a differing perspective, provide a unique structure within which to examine a single question. With headnotes and questions to guide their reading and the complete original footnotes, students are able to engage in discussion that captures the intellectual excitement of historical research and interpretation. Package discounts are available.

For Instructors

Instructor's Resource Manual. This popular manual by Sarah E. Gardner (Mercer University) offers extensive information for each chapter in the textbook: outlines of chapter themes and topics, lecture and discussion strategies, multiple-choice questions for quizzing, video and film resources, and advice on outside readings. The new edition offers as well suggestions on how to incorporate all the supplements to *The American Promise,* including the volumes in the Bedford Series relevant to each chapter, into teaching plans; "Using the Internet" exercises that reinforce and extend the text; and a wealth of practical offerings for first-time teaching assistants, ranging from suggestions on running discussion sections and designing assignments to advice on dealing with difficult students.

Online Instructor's Resource Manual www .bedfordstmartins.com/tap. For each chapter in the textbook, the Online Instructor's Resource Manual provides chapter outlines; lecture and discussion strategies; suggestions on how to incorporate all the supplements to *The American Promise,* including relevant volumes in the Bedford Series, into teaching plans; multiple-choice questions for quizzing; advice on outside readings; "Using the Internet" exercises, with links; and video and film resources. In addition, the Online Instructor's Manual offers annotated Web links for each chapter, PowerPoint slides for lectures, syllabus hosting, and the ability to track student work.

Test Bank. This thoroughly revised test bank by Norman C. McLeod (Dixie State College) and Valerie Hinton (Richland College) includes for each chapter in the text fifty multiple-choice questions (ranked as easy, medium, or difficult), an exercise in which students match important terms with definitions or examples, a chronology exercise, ten short-answer questions, four essay questions, and a two-part map exercise. Answers for objective questions are provided.

Computerized Test Bank CD-ROM for Windows or Macintosh provides easy-to-use software to create and administer tests on paper or over a network. Instructors can generate exams and quizzes from the print test bank or write their own. A grade-management function helps keep track of student progress.

Map Transparencies. Full-color transparencies of all full-size maps in the text help instructors present the materials and teach students important map-reading skills.

Presentation Manager Pro. This CD offers all the maps and chapter-opening artifacts as well as numerous other illustrations from the text in an electronic format designed to enhance class presentations. Extended captions for many of the maps and artifacts provide additional background information as well as suggestions for discussion.

Using the Bedford Series in the U.S. History Survey. This short guide by Scott Hovey (Boston University) gives practical suggestions for using more than sixty volumes from the Bedford Series with a core text in the survey classroom. The guide not only supplies links between the text and the supplements but also provides ideas for starting discussions focused on a single primary-source volume.

Map Central   www.bedfordstmartins.com
/mapcentral. Bedford/St. Martin's is proud to announce Map Central, a database of the more than 450 maps that appear in *The American Promise* and its other history survey texts. Designed to help instructors create more effective lecture presentations, Map Central is easily searchable by specific chapter or by keyword. Maps are in full color and downloadable for use in PowerPoint or other presentation software.

Videos. Available to all adopters of the text are segments drawn from the award-winning telecourse "Shaping America," developed and distributed by the LeCroy Center for Educational Telecommunications, Dallas County Community College District. Bedford/St. Martin's is proud to announce that *The American Promise: To 1877,* Second Edition, has been selected for use in this distinguished long-distance learning program.

Acknowledgments

We gratefully acknowledge all of the helpful suggestions that have come from those who have read and taught the first edition of *The American Promise,* and we hope that our many classroom collaborators will see their influence in this revision. In particular, we wish to thank the talented scholars and teachers who gave generously of their time and knowledge to review our manuscript; their critiques and suggestions have contributed greatly to the published work: Robert Allison, *Suffolk University;* Edward Baptist, *University of Miami;* Manuel Callahan, *University of Texas;* Marvin Cann, *Lander University;* Robert Cormier, *Shrewsbury High School;* Dolores Davison Peterson, *Foothill College;* Randy Finley, *Georgia Perimeter College;* Valerie Hinton, *Richland College;* Jill Lepore, *Boston College;* Barbara Loomis, *San Francisco State University;* Norman Love, *El Paso Community College;* Joanne Maypole, *Front Range Community College;* Tom Nierman, *University of Kansas;* Robert Olwell, *University of Texas at Austin;* Terry Perrin, *Austin Community College;* Peggy Renner, *Glendale Community College;* James Schick, *Pittsburgh State University;* Michael Searles, *Augusta State College;* Rebecca Shoemaker, *Indiana State University;* Rachel Standish, *Foothill College;* Thomas Winn, *Austin Peay State University.*

A project as complex as this requires the talents of many individuals. First, the authors would like to acknowledge our families for their support, forbearance, and toleration of our textbook responsibilities. Pembroke Herbert and Sandi Rygiel of Picture Research Consultants, Inc., contributed their imagination and research to make possible the extraordinary illustration program. Thanks are also due to Louise Townsend, whose accomplished editing greatly improved the manuscript.

We would also like to thank the many people at Bedford/St. Martin's who have been crucial to this project. No one has done more than our friend, Senior Editor Elizabeth M. Welch, whose intelligence, knowledge of American history, commitment to excellence, and unfailing good judgment guided our every step. We thank as well Patricia Rossi, Publisher for History, and Jenna Bookin Barry, Marketing Manager, for their tireless efforts in marketing the book. With great skill and professionalism, Ara Salibian, Production Editor, pulled all the pieces together with the assistance of Arthur Johnson, Coleen O'Hanley, and Kerri Cardone, as well as the invaluable guidance of Project Consultant Tina Samaha. Managing Editor Elizabeth Schaaf, Assistant Managing Editor John Amburg, and Senior Production Supervisor Catherine Hetmansky oversaw production of the book, and Sarah Barrash and Brianna Germain helped with countless editorial tasks. Our original copyeditor, Barbara Flanagan, returned to the project, and her sharp eye improved our best efforts. Charles H. Christensen, President, and Joan E. Feinberg, Editorial Director, have taken a personal interest in *The American Promise* from the start and have guided all its editions through every stage of development.

ABOUT THE AUTHORS

James L. Roark

Born in Eunice, Louisiana, and raised in the West, James L. Roark received his B.A. from the University of California, Davis, in 1963 and his Ph.D. from Stanford University in 1973. His dissertation won the Allan Nevins Prize. He has taught at the University of Nigeria, Nsukka; the University of Nairobi, Kenya; the University of Missouri, St. Louis; and, since 1983, Emory University, where he is Samuel Candler Dobbs Professor of American History. In 1993, he received the Emory Williams Distinguished Teaching Award. He has written *Masters without Slaves: Southern Planters in the Civil War and Reconstruction* (1977). With Michael P. Johnson, he is author of *Black Masters: A Free Family of Color in the Old South* (1984) and editor of *No Chariot Let Down: Charleston's Free People of Color on the Eve of the Civil War* (1984). He has received research assistance from the American Philosophical Society, the National Endowment for the Humanities, and the Gilder Lehrman Institute of American History. Active in the Organization of American Historians and the Southern Historical Association, he is also a fellow of the Society of American Historians. He will be the Pitt Professor of American Institutions at Cambridge University for 2001–2002.

Michael P. Johnson

Born and raised in Ponca City, Oklahoma, Michael P. Johnson studied at Knox College in Galesburg, Illinois, where he received a B.A. in 1963, and at Stanford University in Palo Alto, California, earning a Ph.D. in 1973. He is currently professor of history at Johns Hopkins University in Baltimore, having previously taught at the University of California, Irvine, San Jose State University, and LeMoyne (now LeMoyne-Owen) College in Memphis. He is the author, co-author, or editor of *Toward a Patriarchal Republic: The Secession of Georgia* (1977); *Black Masters: A Free Family of Color in the Old South* (1984); *No Chariot Let Down: Charleston's Free People of Color on the Eve of the Civil War* (1984); *Reading the American Past: Selected Historical Documents* (1998); and *Abraham Lincoln, Slavery, and the Civil War: Selected Speeches and Writings* (2000); and articles that have appeared in the *William and Mary Quarterly,* the *Journal of Southern History, Labor History,* the *New York Review of Books,* the *New Republic,* the *Nation,* and other journals. Johnson has been awarded research fellowships by the American Council of Learned Societies, the National Endowment for the Humanities, and the Center for Advanced Study in the Behavioral Sciences. He directed a National Endowment for the Humanities Summer Seminar for College Teachers and has been honored with the University of California, Irvine, Academic Senate Distinguished Teaching Award and the University of California, Irvine, Alumni Association Outstanding Teaching Award. He is an active member of the American Historical Association, the Organization of American Historians, and the Southern Historical Association.

Patricia Cline Cohen

Born in Ann Arbor, Michigan, and raised in Palo Alto, California, Patricia Cline Cohen earned a B.A. at the University of Chicago in 1968 and a Ph.D. at the University of California, Berkeley in 1977. In 1976, she joined the history faculty at the University of California at Santa Barbara. Cohen has written *A Calculating People: The Spread of Numeracy in Early America* (1982; reissued 1999) and *The Murder of Helen Jewett: The Life and Death of a Prostitute in Nineteenth-Century New York* (1998). She has also published articles on numeracy, prostitution, sexual crime, and murder in journals including the *Journal of Women's History, Radical History Review,* the *William and Mary Quarterly,* and the *NWSA Journal.* Her scholarly work has received support from the National Endowment for the Humanities, the National Humanities Center, the Mellon Foundation, the American Antiquarian Society, the University of California President's Fellowship in the Humanities, the Schlesinger Library, and the Newberry Library. She sits on the council for the Omohundro Institute of Early American History and Culture and on the advisory council of the Society for the History of the Early American Republic. She has served as chair of the Women's Studies Program and as acting dean of the humanities and fine arts at the University of California at Santa Barbara.

Sarah Stage

Sarah Stage was born in Davenport, Iowa, and received a B.A. from the University of Iowa in 1966 and a Ph.D. in American studies from Yale University in 1975. She has taught U.S. history for more than twenty-five years at Williams College and the University of California, Riverside. Currently she is professor of Women's Studies at Arizona State University West, in Phoenix. Her books include *Female Complaints: Lydia Pinkham and the Business of Women's Medicine* (1979) and *Rethinking Home Economics: Women and the History of a Profession* (1997). Among the fellowships she has received are the Rockefeller Foundation Humanities Fellowship, the American Association of University Women dissertation fellowship, a fellowship from the Charles Warren Center for the Study of History at Harvard University, and the University of California President's Fellowship in the Humanities. She is at work on a book entitled *Women and the Progressive Impulse in American Politics, 1890–1914.*

Alan Lawson

Born in Providence, Rhode Island, Alan Lawson received his B.A. from Brown University in 1955 and his Ph.D. from the University of Michigan in 1967. Since winning the Allan Nevins Prize for his dissertation, Lawson has served on the faculties of the University of California, Irvine, Smith College, and, currently, Boston College. He has written *The Failure of Independent Liberalism* (1971) and coedited *From Revolution to Republic* (1976). While completing the forthcoming *The New Deal and the Mobilization of Progressive Experience,* he has published book chapters and essays on political economy and the cultural legacy of the New Deal. He has served as editor of the *Review of Education and the Intellectual History Newsletter* and contributed articles to those journals as well as to the *History Education Quarterly.* He has been active in the field of American studies as director of the Boston College American studies program and as a contributor to the *American Quarterly.* Under the auspices of the United States Information Agency, Lawson has been coordinator and lecturer for programs to instruct faculty from foreign nations in the state of American historical scholarship and teaching.

Susan M. Hartmann

Professor of history and women's studies at Ohio State University, Susan M. Hartmann received her B.A. from Washington University in 1961 and her Ph.D. from the University of Missouri in 1966. After specializing in the political economy of the post–World War II period and publishing *Truman and the 80th Congress* (1971), she expanded her interests to the field of women's history, publishing many articles and three books: *The Home Front and Beyond: American Women in the 1940s* (1982); *From Margin to Mainstream: American Women and Politics since 1960* (1989); and *The Other Feminists: Activists in the Liberal Establishment* (1998). She has won research fellowships from the Rockefeller Foundation, the National Endowment for the Humanities, and the American Council of Learned Societies. Hartmann has taught at the University of Missouri, St. Louis, and Boston University, and she has lectured on American history in Greece, France, Austria, Germany, Australia, New Zealand, and Nepal. She has served on book and article award committees of the American Historical Association, the Organization of American Historians, and the American Studies Association. At Ohio State she has served as director of women's studies, and in 1995 she won the Exemplary Faculty Award in the College of Humanities.

THE
AMERICAN
PROMISE

A HISTORY OF THE UNITED STATES

Second Edition

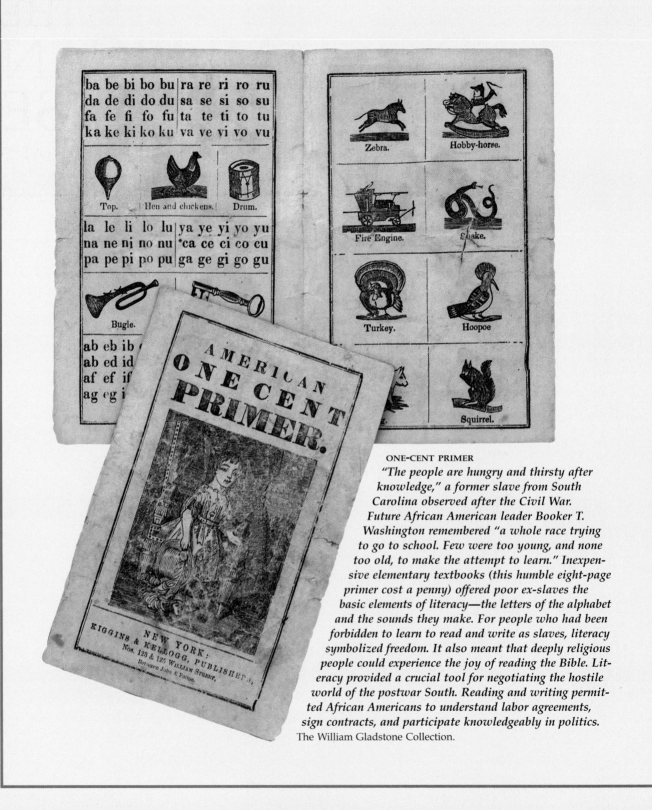

ONE-CENT PRIMER

"The people are hungry and thirsty after knowledge," a former slave from South Carolina observed after the Civil War. Future African American leader Booker T. Washington remembered "a whole race trying to go to school. Few were too young, and none too old, to make the attempt to learn." Inexpensive elementary textbooks (this humble eight-page primer cost a penny) offered poor ex-slaves the basic elements of literacy—the letters of the alphabet and the sounds they make. For people who had been forbidden to learn to read and write as slaves, literacy symbolized freedom. It also meant that deeply religious people could experience the joy of reading the Bible. Literacy provided a crucial tool for negotiating the hostile world of the postwar South. Reading and writing permitted African Americans to understand labor agreements, sign contracts, and participate knowledgeably in politics.

The William Gladstone Collection.

RECONSTRUCTION
1863–1877

Y ORK DISAPPEARED on yesterday morning," David Golightly Harris noted in his journal on June 6, 1865. "I suppose that he has gone to the yankey. I wish they would give him a good whipping & hasten him back." York, a black field hand, had once belonged to Harris, a white slaveholder in Spartanburg District, South Carolina. When York "disappeared," however, the war had been over for two months, and York was a free man. In Harris's mind, however, simply declaring York free did not make him so. In July, Harris noted that another field hand, Old Will, had left "to try to enjoy the freedom the Yankey's have promised the negroes." Two weeks later black freedom still seemed in doubt. "There is much talk about freeing the negroes. Some are said already to have freed them," Harris declared. But Harris had not freed anyone. He did not inform his former slaves of their freedom until federal military authorities required him to. *Freed the Negroes,*" he announced on August 16, four months after Appomattox.

Like many ex-slaveholders, Harris had trouble coming to grips with emancipation. "Family well, Horses well, Cattle well, Hogs well & everything else are well so far as I know, if it was not for the free negroes," Harris wrote on September 17. "On their account everything is turned upside down. So much so that we do not know what to do with our land, nor who to hire if we want it worked. . . . We are in the midst of troublesome times & do not know what will turn up." Harris had owned ten slaves, and emancipation cost him more than $10,000 in lost capital, but the future concerned him more than the past. He faced what seemed to him an insoluble problem. He needed black labor to cultivate his farm, but like most whites he did not believe that blacks would work much when free. Some kind of compulsion would be needed. But slavery was gone, leaving the South upside down. Some white men in Harris's neighborhood sought to put it right again. "In this district several negroes have been badly whipped & several have been hung by some unknown persons," he noted in November. "This has a tendency to keep them in their proper bounds & make them more humble." But the violence did not keep ex-slaves from acting like free people. On Christmas Day 1865, Harris recorded, "The negroes leave today to hunt themselves a new home while we will be left to wait upon ourselves."

Across the South, ex-masters predicted that emancipation would mean economic collapse and social anarchy. Carl Schurz, a Union general who undertook a fact-finding mission to the ex-Confederate states in the summer of 1865, encountered this dire prediction often enough to conclude that the Civil War was a "revolution but half accomplished." Northern victory had freed the slaves, but it had not changed former slaveholders' minds about the need for slavery. Left to themselves, Schurz believed, whites would "introduce some new system of forced labor, not perhaps exactly slavery in its old form but something similar to it." To defend their freedom, blacks would need federal protection, land of their own, and voting rights, Schurz concluded. Until whites "cut loose from the past, it will be a dangerous experiment

**BLACK WOMAN IN COTTON FIELDS,
THOMASVILLE, GEORGIA**

Few images of everyday black women during the era of reconstruction survive. This photograph was taken in 1895, but it nevertheless goes to the heart of the labor struggle after the Civil War. As slaves, black women worked in the fields, and white landlords wanted them to continue working there after emancipation. Freedom allowed some women to escape field labor, but not this Georgian, who no doubt worked to survive. Despite her plight, the photograph reveals a strong person with a clear sense of who she is. Although worn to protect her head and body from the fierce heat, her intricately wrapped headdress dramatically expresses her individuality.

Vanishing Georgia Collection, Georgia Department of Archives and History, Atlanta, Georgia.

to put Southern society upon its own legs." The end of the war did not mean the beginning of peace. Instead, the nation entered one of its most chaotic and conflicted eras—Reconstruction.

It was not that the Civil War failed to resolve anything. Northern victory doomed secession and slavery, but out of the war emerged two new divisive questions. First, what was the status of the defeated South within the Union? Would the eleven ex-Confederate states be quickly and forgivingly welcomed back, or would they be held at arm's length and required to reform before resuming their former places? Second, what would freedom mean for ex-slaves? Would they be left to make their place in the South on their own, or would the federal government guarantee free labor, full citizenship, and equality?

The political part of the debate took place in the nation's capital and in the state legislatures and county seats of the South. Politics was never simply a debate between whites. Blacks emerged from slavery with their own ideas, and they became active agents in the struggle to define freedom. The struggle also had social and economic dimensions. On farms and plantations from Virginia to Texas, ex-slaves like York and Old Will strove to escape bondage and to become free laborers and free people, while whites like David Golightly Harris resisted letting go of the Old South. In the midst of the flux and chaos, a small band of crusading women sought to achieve gender equality. The years of reconstruction witnessed an enormous contest to determine the consequences of Confederate defeat and emancipation. In the end white Southerners prevailed. They declared a "New South," but it was a very different South from the one Harris wished to return.

Wartime Reconstruction

Reconstruction did not wait for the end of war. As the odds of a northern victory increased, thinking about reunification quickened. Immediately, a question arose: Who had authority to devise a plan of reconstruction? The Founders had not anticipated such a problem, and so the Constitution stood silent. Lincoln believed firmly that reconstruction was a matter of executive responsibility. Congress just as firmly asserted its jurisdiction. Fueling the argument about who had authority to set the terms of reconstruction were significant differences about the terms themselves. Lincoln's primary aim was the restoration of national unity, which he sought through a program of speedy, forgiving political reconciliation. Congress feared that the president's program amounted to restoring the old southern ruling class to power. It wanted greater assurances of white loyalty and greater guarantees of black rights.

In their eagerness to formulate a plan for political reunification, neither Lincoln nor Congress gave much attention to the South's land and labor problems. But the war rapidly eroded slavery and traditional plantation agriculture, and Yankee military commanders in the Union-occupied areas of the Confederacy had no choice but to oversee the emergence of a new labor system. With little guidance from Washington, northern officials felt their way along, bumping heads with both planters and freedmen.

"To Bind Up the Nation's Wounds"

On March 4, 1865, President Abraham Lincoln delivered his second inaugural address. His words blazed with religious imagery as he surveyed the history of the long, deadly war and then looked ahead to peace. "With malice toward none; with charity for all; with firmness in the right, as God gives us to see the right," Lincoln said, "let us strive on to finish the work we are in; to bind up the nation's wounds . . . to do all which may achieve and cherish a just, and a lasting peace." Lincoln had contemplated reunion for nearly two years. Deep compassion for the enemy guided his thinking about peace. But kindness is not the key to understanding Lincoln's program. His reconstruction plan aimed primarily at shortening the war and ending slavery.

In his Proclamation of Amnesty and Reconstruction, issued in December 1863, when Union forces had finally gained the upper hand on the battlefield, Lincoln offered a full pardon to rebels willing to renounce secession and to accept the abolition of slavery. (Pardons were valuable because they restored all property, except slaves, and full political rights.) His offer excluded several groups of Confederates, such as high-ranking civilian and military officers, but the plan called for no mass arrests, no trials for treason, and no executions. Instead, when only 10 percent of men who had been qualified voters in 1860 had taken an oath of allegiance, they could organize a new state government. Lincoln's plan did not require ex-rebels to ex-

tend social or political rights to ex-slaves, nor did it anticipate a program of long-term federal assistance to freedmen. Clearly, the president sought to restore the broken Union, not to reform it.

Lincoln's easy terms enraged abolitionists like Bostonian Wendell Phillips, who charged that the president "makes the negro's freedom a mere sham." He "is willing that the negro should be free but seeks nothing else for him," Phillips declared. He compared Lincoln to the most passive of the Civil War generals: "What McClellan was on the battlefield—'Do as little hurt as possible!'—Lincoln is in civil affairs—'Make as little change as possible!'" Phillips and other northern radicals called instead for a thorough overhaul of southern society. Their ideas proved to be too drastic for most Republicans during the war years, but Congress agreed that Lincoln's plan was inadequate. In July 1864, Congress put forward a plan of its own.

As General William T. Sherman was marching on Atlanta, Congressman Henry Winter Davis of Maryland and Senator Benjamin Wade of Ohio jointly sponsored a bill that threw out Lincoln's "10 percent plan" and demanded that at least half of the voters in a conquered rebel state take the oath of allegiance before reconstruction could begin. Moreover, the Wade-Davis bill banned ex-Confederates from participating in the drafting of new state constitutions. Finally, the bill guaranteed the equality of freedmen before the law. Congress's reconstruction would be neither as quick nor as forgiving as Lincoln's. Still, the Wade-Davis bill angered radicals because it did not include a provision for black suffrage. When Lincoln exercised his right not to sign the bill and let it die instead, Wade and Davis published a manifesto charging the president with usurpation of power. They warned Lincoln to confine himself to "his executive duties—to obey and execute, not make the laws—to suppress by arms armed rebellion, and leave political organization to Congress."

Clearly, the president sought to restore the broken Union, not to reform it.

Undeterred, Lincoln continued to nurture the formation of loyal state governments under his own plan. Four states—Louisiana, Arkansas, Tennessee, and Virginia—fulfilled the president's requirements, but Congress refused to seat representatives from the "Lincoln states." In his last public address in April 1865, Lincoln defended his plan but stressed his willingness to be flexible. For the first time he expressed publicly his endorsement of suffrage for southern blacks, at least "the very intelligent, and . . . those who serve our cause as soldiers." The announcement demonstrated that Lincoln's thinking about reconstruction was still evolving. Four days later, he was dead.

Land and Labor

Of all the problems raised by emancipation, none proved more critical than the transition from slave to free labor. Slavery had been, at bottom, a labor system, and while Republicans agreed that free labor would replace forced labor, they disagreed about what free labor would mean in the South. As federal armies proceeded to invade and occupy the Confederacy during the war, hundreds of thousands of slaves became free workers. Moreover, northern occupation meant that Union armies controlled vast territories where legal title to land had become unclear. The wartime Confiscation Acts punished "traitors" by taking away their property. What to do with federally occupied land and how to organize labor on it engaged former slaves, former slaveholders, Union military commanders, and federal government officials long before the war ended.

Up and down the Mississippi valley, occupying federal troops announced a new labor code. The code required planters to sign contracts with ex-slaves and to pay wages. It also obligated employers to provide food, housing, and medical care. It outlawed whipping and other forms of physical punishment, but it reserved to the army the right to discipline blacks who refused to work. The code required black laborers to enter into contracts, work diligently, and remain subordinate and obedient. Military leaders clearly had no intention of promoting a social or economic revolution. Instead, they sought to end coerced labor and to restore plantation agriculture with wage labor. The effort resulted in a hybrid system of "compulsory free labor" that satisfied no one. Depending on one's point of view, it either provided too little or too much of a break with the past.

Planters complained because the new system fell short of slavery. Blacks could not be "transformed by proclamation," a Louisiana sugar planter warned. Yet under the new system, blacks "are ex-

pected to perform their new obligations without coercion, & without the fear of punishment which is essential to stimulate the idle and correct the vicious." Without the right to whip, he concluded, the new labor system did not have a chance.

African Americans found the new regime too reminiscent of slavery to be called "free labor." Of its many shortcomings, none disappointed ex-slaves more than the failure to provide them land of their own. "What's the use of being free if you don't own land enough to be buried in?" one man asked. Freedmen believed they had a moral right to land because they and their ancestors had worked it without compensation for more than two centuries. Moreover, several wartime developments seemed to indicate that the federal government planned to link black freedom and landownership.

In January 1865, General Sherman had set aside for black settlement part of the coast south of Charleston. He devised the plan to relieve himself of the burden of thousands of impoverished blacks who trailed desperately after his army. By June 1865, some forty thousand freedmen sat on 400,000 acres of "Sherman land." In addition, in March 1865, Congress established the Bureau of Refugees, Freedmen, and Abandoned Lands. The Freedmen's Bureau, as it was called, distributed food and clothing to destitute Southerners and eased the transition of blacks from slaves to free persons. Congress also authorized the agency to divide abandoned and confiscated land into 40-acre plots, to rent them to freedmen, and eventually to sell them "with such title as the United States can convey." By June 1865, the bureau had situated nearly ten thousand black families on a half million acres that had been abandoned by fleeing South Carolina and Georgia planters. Hundreds of thousands of other ex-slaves eagerly anticipated farms of their own.

Despite the flurry of activity, wartime reconstruction had settled nothing. Two years of controversy had failed to produce agreement about whether the president or Congress had the authority to devise and direct policy or what proper policy should be. Lincoln had organized several new state governments, but Congress had not readmitted a single "reconstructed" state into the Union. There were hints of a revolution in landholding, but the "compulsory free labor" system that emerged on southern plantations suggested more continuity with antebellum traditions. Clearly, the nation faced dilemmas and difficulties almost as burdensome as those of the war.

The African American Quest for Autonomy

Although white politicians had difficulty agreeing, ex-slaves never had any doubt about what they wanted freedom to mean. They had only to contemplate what they had been denied as slaves. (See "Documenting the American Promise," page 542.) Slaves had to remain on their plantations; freedom allowed blacks to go wherever they pleased. Thus, in the first heady weeks after emancipation, freedmen often abandoned their plantations just to see what was on the other side of the hill and to feel freedom under their feet. Slaves had to be at work in the fields by dawn; freedom permitted blacks to taste the forbidden pleasure of sleeping through a sunrise. Slaves had to defer to whites; freedom saw them test the etiquette of racial subordination. "Lizzie's maid passed me today when I was coming from church *without speaking to me*," huffed one plantation mistress.

To whites, it looked like pure anarchy. Without the discipline of slavery, they said, blacks had reverted to their natural condition: lazy, irresponsible, and wild. Actually, former slaves were experiment-

WASHINGTON MILLER AND FAMILY
After the Civil War, thousands of ex-slaves whose marriages had no legal standing under slavery rushed to formalize their unions. Natchez, Mississippi, home of cotton millionaires before the war, became the home of many black families after the war. Most ex-slaves worked as house servants, laundresses, gardeners, cooks, and day laborers, but some gained real economic independence. The proud and respectable Washington Miller family represents the achievement of middle-class African Americans. This sensitive photograph is the work of Henry C. Norman, a white Georgian who arrived in Natchez about 1870. Over the next four decades Norman made thousands of photographs of the black and white citizens who visited his studio.
Collection of Thomas H. Gandy and Joan W. Gandy.

The Meaning of Freedom

*O*n New Year's Day 1863, President Abraham Lincoln issued the Emancipation Proclamation. It stated that "all persons held as slaves" within the states still in rebellion "are, and henceforward shall be, free." Although it did not in and of itself free any slaves, it transformed the character of the war. Despite often intolerable conditions, black people focused on the possibilities of freedom.

DOCUMENT 1. Letter from John Q. A. Dennis to Edwin M. Stanton, July 26, 1864

John Q. A. Dennis, formerly a slave in Maryland, wrote to Secretary of War Edwin M. Stanton to ask his help in reuniting his family.

Boston

Dear Sir I am Glad that I have the Honour to Write you afew line I have been in troble for about four yars my Dear wife was taken from me Nov 19th 1859 and left me with three Children and I being a Slave At the time Could Not do Anny thing for the poor little Children for my master it was took me Carry me some forty mile from them So I Could Not do for them and the man that they live with half feed them and half Cloth them & beat them like dogs & when I was admitted to go to see them it use to brake my heart & Now I say again I am Glad to have the honour to write to you to see if you Can Do Anny thing for me or for my poor little Children I was keap in Slavy untell last Novr 1863. then the Good lord sent the Cornel borne [federal Colonel William Birney?] Down their in Marland in worsester Co So as I have been recently freed I have but letle to live on but I am Striveing Dear Sir but what I went too know of you Sir is it possible for me to go & take my Children from those men that keep them in Savery if it is possible will you pleas give me a permit from your hand then I think they would let them go. . . .

Hon sir will you please excuse my Miserable writeing & answer me as soon as you can I want get the little Children out of Slavery, I being Criple would like to know of you also if I Cant be permited to rase a Shool Down there & on what turm I Could be admited to Do so No more At present Dear Hon Sir

SOURCE: Ira Berlin, Joseph P. Reidy, and Leslie S. Rowland, eds., *Freedom: A Documentary History of Emancipation, 1861–1867*, ser. 1, vol. 1, *The Destruction of Slavery* (Cambridge: Cambridge University Press, 1985), 386.

DOCUMENT 2. Report from Reverend A. B. Randall, February 28, 1865

Freedom also prompted ex-slaves to seek legal marriages, which under slavery had been impossible. Writing from Little Rock, Arkansas, A. B. Randall, the white chaplain of a black regiment, in a report of February 1865 to the adjutant general of the Union army, affirmed the importance of marriage to freed slaves and emphasized their conviction that emancipation was just the first step toward full freedom.

Weddings, just now, are very popular, and abundant among the Colored People. They have just learned, of the Special Order No. 15. of Gen Thomas [Adjutant General Lorenzo Thomas] by which, they may not only be lawfully married, but have their Marriage Certificates, Recorded; in a book furnished by the Government. This is most desirable. . . . Those who were captured . . . at Ivy's Ford, on the 17th of January, by Col Brooks, had their Marriage Certificates, taken from them; and destroyed; and then were roundly cursed, for having such papers in their posession. I have married, during the month, at this Post; Twenty five couples; mostly, those, who have families; & have been living together for years. I try to dissuade single men, who are soldiers, from marrying, till their time of enlistment is out: as that course seems to me, to be most judicious.

The Colord People here, generally consider, this war not only; their exodus, from bondage; but the road, to Responsibility; Competency; and an honorable Citizenship—God grant that their hopes and expectations may be fully realized.

SOURCE: Ira Berlin, Joseph P. Reidy, and Leslie S. Rowland, eds., *Freedom: A Documentary History of Emancipation, 1861–1867,* ser. 2, *The Black Military Experience* (Cambridge: Cambridge University Press, 1982), 712.

DOCUMENT 3. Petition "to the Union Convention of Tennessee Assembled in the Capitol at Nashville," January 9, 1865

Early efforts at political reconstruction prompted petitions from former slaves demanding civil and political rights. In January 1865, black Tennesseans petitioned a convention of white Unionists debating the reorganization of state government.

We the undersigned petitioners, American citizens of African descent, natives and residents of Tennessee, and devoted friends of the great National cause, do most respectfully ask a patient hearing of your honorable body in regard to matters deeply affecting the future condition of our unfortunate and long suffering race.

First of all, however, we would say that words are too weak to tell how profoundly grateful we are to the Federal Government for the good work of freedom which it is gradually carrying forward; and for the Emancipation Proclamation which has set free all the slaves in some of the rebellious States, as well as many of the slaves in Tennessee. . . .

We claim freedom, as our natural right, and ask that in harmony and co-operation with the nation at large, you should cut up by the roots the system of slavery, which is not only a wrong to us, but the source of all the evil which at present afflicts the State. For slavery, corrupt itself, corrupted nearly all, also, around it, so that it has influenced nearly all the slave States to rebel against the Federal Government, in order to set up a government of pirates under which slavery might be perpetrated.

In the contest between the nation and slavery, our unfortunate people have sided, by instinct, with the former. We have little fortune to devote to the national cause, for a hard fate has hitherto forced us to live in poverty, but we do devote to its success, our hopes, our toils, our whole heart, our sacred honor, and our lives. We will work, pray, live, and, if need be, die for the Union, as cheerfully as ever a white patriot died for his country. The color of our skin does not lessen in the least degree, our love either for God or for the land of our birth. . . .

We know the burdens of citizenship, and are ready to bear them. We know the duties of the good citizen, and are ready to perform them cheerfully, and would ask to be put in a position in which we can discharge them more effectually. . . .

This is a democracy—a government of the people. It should aim to make every man, without regard to the color of his skin, the amount of his wealth, or the character of his religious faith, feel personally interested in its welfare. Every man who lives under the Government should feel that it is his property, his treasure, the bulwark and defence of himself and his family, his pearl of great price, which he must preserve, protect, and defend faithfully at all times, on all occasions, in every possible manner.

This is not a Democratic Government if a numerous, law-abiding, industrious, and useful class of citizens, born and bred on the soil, are to be treated as aliens and enemies, as an inferior degraded class, who must have no voice in the Government which they support, protect and defend, with all their heart, soul, mind, and body, both in peace and war. . . .

The possibility that the negro suffrage proposition may shock popular prejudice at first sight, is not a conclusive argument against its wisdom and policy. No proposition ever met with more furious or general opposition than the one to enlist colored soldiers in the United States army. The opponents of the measure exclaimed on all hands that the negro was a coward; that he would not fight; that one white man, with a whip in his hand could put to flight a regiment of them; that the experiment would end in the utter rout and ruin of the Federal army. Yet the colored man has fought so well, on almost every occasion, that the rebel government is prevented, only by its fears and distrust of being able to force him to fight for slavery as well as he fights against it, from putting half a million of negroes into its ranks.

The Government has asked the colored man to fight for its preservation and gladly has he done it. It can afford to trust him with a vote as safely as it trusted him with a bayonet.

SOURCE: Ira Berlin, Joseph P. Reidy, and Leslie S. Rowland, eds., *Freedom: A Documentary History of Emancipation, 1861–1867,* ser. 2, *The Black Military Experience* (Cambridge: Cambridge University Press, 1982), 811–16.
(Continued)

Document 4: Interview with Henry Baker, 1938

Henry Baker was born a slave in Alabama in 1854. In 1938, Thomas Monroe Campbell, a graduate of Tuskegee Institute and a black farm demonstration agent for the U.S. Department of Agriculture, visited Baker and recorded the interview. Here, Baker remembers his brush with formal education when he was a young man during Reconstruction.

'Gardin' muh education, I went tuh school once. It wuz de time dat I wuz workin' es wage han' fer ole man B. It wuz layin' by time en he sed ter me, "Now Henry yuh kin go 'head I haven't got enythin' fer yuh tuh do 'til time tuh start gatherin' de crops." This wuz all 'fore I mar'ied. So I 'cided tuh use dis time en goin' tuh school. So dere wuz er white man, named John Bradley. He wuz teachin' de "nigger" school. I went ter see him en he wuz glad tuh let me in. I went tuh school five days en muh landlord he'rd dat I wuz gwine tuh school so he sent fer me en tole me he had a job right away en he put me back tuh work. Yasser took me right outter school. 'Coase aftuh I mar'ed I did go tuh school three weeks dat wuz all. I wus a renter en uv coase I had so many obligations I couldn't keep up muh school work en look aftuh muh farm so I had tuh give hit up. So I went ter school in muh life, in all, three weeks en five days. I wuz not satisfied so I determined tuh better muh condition so I turned tuh Jesus Christ. . . . He'll teach yuh enythin yuh want ter know. He sho will.

SOURCE: John W. Blassingame, ed., *Slave Testimony: Two Centuries of Letters, Speeches, Interviews, and Autobiographies* (Baton Rouge: Louisiana State University Press, 1977), 667.

QUESTIONS FOR ANALYSIS AND DEBATE

1. How does John Q. A. Dennis interpret his responsibility as a father?
2. Why do you think ex-slaves wanted their marriages legalized?
3. Why, according to the Union Convention of Tennessee, did blacks deserve voting rights?
4. How would you characterize Henry Baker's attitude toward education?

---

ing with freedom, in both trivial and profound ways. But poor black people could not long afford to roam the countryside, neglect work, and casually provoke whites. Soon, most were back on plantations, at work in the fields and kitchens.

Ex-slaves never had any doubt about what they wanted freedom to mean. They had only to contemplate what they had been denied as slaves.

But other items on ex-slaves' agenda of freedom endured. Freedmen did not easily give up their quest for economic independence. In addition, slavery had deliberately kept blacks illiterate, and freedmen emerged from slavery eager to read and write. Moreover, bondage had denied slaves secure family lives, and the restoration of their families became a persistent black aspiration. Although slave marriages and family relations had existed only at the master's whim, slaves had nevertheless managed to create deep, enduring family ties. Still, slave sales had often severed family connections. As a consequence, thousands of black men and women took to the roads in 1865 to look for relations who had been sold away. One northern journalist encountered a ragged freedman who had walked six hundred miles to North Carolina, where he had *heard* that his wife and children had been sold. Couples who emerged from slavery with their marriages intact often rushed to northern military chaplains to legalize their unions.

Another hunger that freedom permitted African Americans to satisfy was independent worship. Under slavery, blacks had often, like it or not, prayed with whites in biracial churches. Intent on religious independence, blacks greeted freedom with a mass exodus from white churches. Some joined the newly established southern branches of all-black northern churches, such as the African Methodist Episcopal Church. Others formed black versions of the major southern denominations, Baptists and Methodists. Slaves had viewed their tribulations through the lens of their deeply felt Christian faith, and freedmen comprehended the events of the Civil War and reconstruction as people of faith. It was not surprising that ex-slaves claimed Abraham Lincoln as their Moses.

Presidential Reconstruction

Abraham Lincoln died on April 15, 1865, just hours after John Wilkes Booth had shot him at a Washington, D.C., theater. Chief Justice Salmon P. Chase immediately administered the oath of office to Vice President Andrew Johnson. Lincoln's assassination thrust the Tennessean into leadership at a time of grave national crisis. Moreover, Congress had adjourned in March, which meant that legislators were away from Washington when Lincoln was killed. They would not reconvene until December. Throughout the summer and fall, therefore, the "accidental president" made critical decisions about the future of the South. Like Lincoln, Johnson believed that responsibility for restoring the Union lay with the president. With dizzying speed, he drew up and executed a plan of reconstruction.

Congress returned to the capital in December to find that, as far as the president and former Confederates were concerned, reconstruction was over. To most Republicans, Johnson's modest demands of ex-rebels made a mockery of the sacrifice of Union soldiers. In an 1863 speech dedicating the cemetery at Gettysburg, Lincoln had spoken of the "great task remaining before us . . . that we here highly resolve that these dead shall not have died in vain—that this nation, under God, shall have a new birth of freedom." Instead, Johnson had acted as midwife to the rebirth of the Old South. He had achieved political reunification at the cost of black liberty. To let his program stand, Republican legislators said, would mean that the North's dead had indeed died in vain.

Johnson's Program of Reconciliation

Born in 1808 in Raleigh, North Carolina, Andrew Johnson was the son of poor, illiterate parents. Un-

able to afford to send her son to school, Johnson's widowed mother apprenticed him to a tailor. Self-educated and ambitious, the young man ran away before completing his indenture and headed for Tennessee. There he worked as a tailor, accumulated a fortune in land, acquired five slaves, and built a career in politics championing the South's common white people and assailing its "illegitimate, swaggering, bastard, scrub aristocracy." The only senator from a Confederate state to remain loyal to the Union, Johnson held no grudge against the South's rebel yeomen. He believed they had been hoodwinked by slaveholding secessionists. Less than two weeks before he became president, he made it clear what he would do to the rascals if he ever had the chance: "I would arrest them—I would try them—I would convict them and I would hang them."

No wonder the South's elite trembled when Lincoln died. In reality, however, Johnson was no friend of northern radicals. A Democrat all his life, Johnson occupied the White House only because the Republican Party in 1864 had needed to broaden its appeal to loyal, Union-supporting Democrats. As a Tennessee congressman and senator, Johnson had favored traditional Democratic causes, vigorously defending states' rights (but not secession) and opposing Republican efforts to expand the power of the federal government, especially in the economic realm. He had voted against almost every federal appropriation, including a bill to pave the streets of Washington.

Moreover, Johnson had been a steadfast defender of slavery. He had owned slaves until 1862, when Tennessee rebels, angry at his Unionism, confiscated them. He only grudgingly accepted emancipation. When he did, it was more because of his hatred for slaveholders than sympathy for slaves. "Damn the negroes," he said. "I am fighting those traitorous aristocrats, their masters." At a time when the nation faced its moment of truth regarding black Americans, the new president harbored unshakable racist convictions. Africans, Johnson said, were "inferior to the white man in point of intellect—better calculated in physical structure to undergo drudgery and hardship." On the eve of his inauguration as vice president, he had reiterated his belief in a white man's government.

Johnson presented his plan of reconstruction as a continuation of Lincoln's plan, and in some ways it was. Like Lincoln, he stressed reconciliation between the Union and the defeated Confederacy and rapid restoration of civil government in the South. He offered to pardon most ex-rebels. Like Lincoln, Johnson excluded high-ranking ex-Confederates, but he also excluded all ex-rebels with property worth more than $20,000. The Tennessee tailor was apparently taking aim at his old enemy, the planter aristocrats. Wealthy individuals would have to apply directly to the president for pardons. Johnson recognized the state governments created by Lincoln and set out his own requirements for restoring the rebel states to the Union. All that the citizens of a state had to do was to renounce the right of secession, deny that the debts of the Confederacy were legal and binding, and ratify the Thirteenth Amendment abolishing slavery, which became part of the Constitution in December 1865. Johnson's plan ignored Lincoln's acceptance near the end of his life of some form of limited black voting.

Johnson's eagerness to normalize relations with southern states and his lack of sympathy for blacks also led him to instruct military and government officials to return to pardoned ex-Confederates all confiscated and abandoned land, even if it was in the hands of freedmen. Reformers were shocked. They had expected the president's vendetta against planters to mean the permanent confiscation of the South's plantations and the distribution of the land to loyal freedmen. Instead, his instructions canceled the promising beginnings made by General Sherman and the Freedmen's Bureau to settle blacks on land of their own. As one freedman observed, "Things was hurt by Mr. Lincoln getting killed."

Southern Resistance and Black Codes

In the summer of 1865, delegates across the South gathered to draw up the new state constitutions required by Johnson's plan of reconstruction. While they had been defeated, clearly they had not been subdued. Rather than take their medicine, delegates choked on even the president's mild requirements. Refusing to declare their secession ordinances null and void, the South Carolina and Georgia conventions merely "repudiated" their ordinances, preserving in principle their right to secede. In addition, every state convention wrangled over the precise wording of the constitutional amendment ending slavery. In the end, Mississippi rejected the Thirteenth Amendment outright, and Alabama rejected it in part. Finally, South Carolina and Mississippi refused to repudiate their Confederate war debts. Despite these defiant acts, Johnson did not demand that Southerners comply with his lenient terms. By failing to draw a hard line, he rekindled southern

THE BLACK CODES
Entitled **Selling a Freeman to Pay His Fine at Monticello, Florida,** *this 1867 drawing from a northern magazine equates the black codes with the reinstitution of slavery. The laws stopped short of reenslavement, but they did sharply restrict blacks' freedom. In Florida, as in other southern states, certain acts, such as breaking a labor contract, were made criminal offenses, the penalty for which could be involuntary plantation labor for a year.*
Library of Congress.

resistance. White Southerners began to think that by standing up for themselves they—not victorious Northerners—would shape the transition from slavery to freedom. In the fall of 1865, newly elected southern legislators set out to reverse the "retreat into barbarism" that followed emancipation.

Under the mantle of protectors of the freedmen, state governments across the South adopted a series of laws known as the *black codes.* While emancipation had brought freedmen important rights that they had lacked as slaves—to own property, to make contracts, to marry legally, and to sue and be sued in court—the black codes made a travesty of freedom. They sought to keep blacks subordinate to whites by subjecting blacks to every sort of discrimination. Several states made it illegal for blacks to own a gun. Mississippi made insulting gestures and language a criminal offense. Blacks were barred from jury duty. Not a single southern state granted any black—no matter how educated, wealthy, or refined—the right to vote.

At the core of the black codes, however, lay the matter of labor. Faced with the death of slavery and the disintegration of plantations, legislators sought to hustle freedmen back into traditional tasks. South Carolina attempted to limit blacks to either farmwork or domestic service by requiring them to pay annual taxes of $10 to $100 to work in any other occupation. Mississippi declared that blacks who did not possess written evidence of employment could be declared vagrants and be subject to fines or involuntary plantation labor. Most states allowed judges to bind black children—orphans and others whose parents they deemed unable to support them—to white employers. Under these so-called apprenticeship laws, courts bound out thousands of black children to planter "guardians." Legislators made every effort to resuscitate the traditional plantation economy and resurrect as nearly as possible the old regime.

While emancipation had brought freedmen important rights that they had lacked as slaves—to own property, to make contracts, to marry legally—the black codes made a travesty of freedom.

Johnson refused to intervene decisively. A staunch defender of states' rights, he believed that the citizens of every state, even those citizens who had attempted to destroy the Union, should be free to write their own constitutions and laws. Moreover, since Johnson was as eager as other white Southerners to restore white supremacy and black subordination, the black codes did not offend him.

But Johnson also followed the path he believed offered him the greatest political return. A conservative Tennessee Democrat at the head of a northern Republican Party, he began to look southward for political allies. Despite tough talk about punishing traitors, he issued more than fourteen thousand special pardons to wealthy or high-ranking ex-Confederates. By pardoning planters and Confederate officials, by acquiescing in the South's black codes, and by accepting the new southern governments even when they failed to satisfy his minimal demands, he won useful allies.

If Northerners had any doubts about the mood of the South, they evaporated in the elections of 1865. To represent them in Congress, white Southerners chose former Confederates, not loyal Unionists. Of the eighty senators and representatives they sent to Washington, fifteen had served in the Confederate army, ten of them as generals. Another sixteen had served in civil and judicial posts in the Confederacy. Nine others had served in the Confederate Congress. One—Alexander Stephens—had been vice president of the Confederacy. In December, this remarkable group arrived on the steps of the nation's Capitol building to be seated in Congress. As one Georgian later remarked: "It looked as though Richmond had moved to Washington."

Expansion of Black Rights and Federal Authority

Southerners had blundered monumentally. They had assumed that what Andrew Johnson was willing to accept, the northern public and Congress would accept as well. But southern intransigence compelled even moderate Republicans to conclude that ex-rebels were a "generation of vipers," still dangerous and untrustworthy.

The black codes in particular soured moderate Republicans on the South. The codes became a symbol of southern intentions not to accept the verdict of the battlefields, but instead to "restore all of slavery but its name." Northerners were hardly saints when it came to racial justice, but black freedom had become a hallowed war aim. "We tell the white men of Mississippi," the *Chicago Tribune* roared, "that the

THE LOST CAUSE
While politicians in Washington, D.C., debated the future of the South, white Southerners were coming to grips with their emotions and history. They began to refer to their failure to secede from the Union as the "Lost Cause." They enshrined the memory of certain former Confederates, especially Robert E. Lee, whose nobility and courage represented the white South's image of itself. This quilt from about 1870, with Lee stitched in the center, illustrates how common whites incorporated the symbols of the Lost Cause into their daily lives. The maker of the quilt, a woman whose name is unknown, also included miniature Confederate flags and memorial ribbons. Valentine Museum, Cook Collection.

men of the North will convert the State of Mississippi into a frog pond before they will allow such laws to disgrace one foot of the soil in which the bones of our soldiers sleep and over which the flag of freedom waves."

Moderates represented the mainstream of the Republican Party and wanted only assurance that slavery and treason were dead. They did not seek a revolution of the entire southern social order. They did not champion black equality or the confiscation of plantations or black voting, as did the Radicals, a minority faction within the Republican Party. In

December 1865, however, when Congress convened in Washington, it became clear that events in the South had succeeded in forging unity (at least temporarily) among Republican factions. Exercising Congress's right to determine the qualifications of its members, the moderate majority and the Radical minority came together to refuse to seat the southern representatives. Rather than accept Johnson's claim that the "work of restoration" was done, Congress countered his executive power. Congressional Republicans enjoyed a three-to-one majority over the Democrats, and if they could agree on a program of reconstruction, they could easily pass legislation and even override presidential vetoes.

The moderates took the initiative. Senator Lyman Trumbull of Illinois declared that the president's policy of trusting southern whites proved that the ex-slave would "be tyrannized over, abused, and virtually reenslaved without some legislation by the nation for his protection." Early in 1866, the moderates produced two bills that strengthened the federal shield. The first, the Freedmen's Bureau bill, prolonged the life of the agency established by the previous Congress. Since the end of the war, it had distributed food, supervised labor contracts, and sponsored schools for freedmen. Arguing that the Constitution never contemplated a "system for the support of indigent persons," President Andrew Johnson vetoed the Freedmen's Bureau bill. Congress failed by only a narrow margin to override the president's veto.

Johnson's shocking veto galvanized nearly unanimous Republican support for the moderates' second measure, the Civil Rights Act. Designed to nullify the black codes, it affirmed the rights of blacks to enjoy "full and equal benefit of all laws and proceedings for the security of person and property as is enjoyed by white citizens." Modest on its surface, the act boldly required the end of legal discrimination in state laws and represented an extraordinary expansion of black rights and federal authority. The president argued that the civil rights bill amounted to an "unconstitutional invasion of states' rights" and vetoed it. In essence, he denied that the federal government possessed authority to protect the civil rights of blacks.

Had Johnson's veto stood, reconstruction would have been over, and the president would have had the final word. But in April 1866, a thoroughly aroused Republican Party again pushed a civil rights bill through Congress and overrode another presidential veto. In July, it sustained another Freedmen's Bureau Act. For the first time in American history, Congress had overridden presidential vetoes of major legislation. As a worried South Carolinian observed, Johnson had succeeded in uniting the Republicans and probably touched off "a fight this fall such as has never been seen."

Congressional Reconstruction

By the summer of 1866, President Andrew Johnson and Congress had dropped their gloves and stood toe to toe in a bare-knuckled contest unprecedented in American history. Johnson had made it clear that he would not budge on either constitutional questions or policy. Moderate Republicans made a major effort to resolve the dilemma of reconstruction by amending the Constitution, but the obstinacy of Johnson and white Southerners pushed Republican moderates ever closer to the Radicals and to acceptance of additional federal intervention in the South.

Congressional reconstruction evolved haltingly and unevenly, but through it all black suffrage acted like a powerful magnet that steadily drew discussion its way. In time, white men in Congress debated whether to give the ballot to black men. Outside of Congress, blacks raised their voices on behalf of color-blind voting rights, while women argued to make voting sex-blind as well.

The Fourteenth Amendment and Escalating Violence

In April 1866, Republican moderates introduced the Fourteenth Amendment to the Constitution, which both houses of Congress approved in June by the necessary two-thirds majority. The amendment then went to the states for ratification. Although it took two years to gather approval from the required three-fourths of the states, the Fourteenth Amendment had immediate consequences.

The most important provisions of this complex amendment made all native-born or naturalized persons American citizens and prohibited states from abridging the "privileges and immunities" of citizens, depriving them of "life, liberty, or property without due process of law," and denying them "equal protection of the laws." Lawyers have battled ever since about the meaning of this broad

language, but by making blacks national citizens the amendment nullified the *Dred Scott* decision of 1857 and provided a national guarantee of equality before the law. In essence, it protected the rights of citizens against violation by their own state governments.

The Fourteenth Amendment also dealt with voting rights. Republicans revealed that while genuinely committed to black freedom, they were also alert to partisan advantage. Rather than explicitly granting the vote to blacks, as Radicals wanted, the amendment gave Congress the right to reduce the congressional representation of states that withheld suffrage from some of its adult male population. In other words, white Southerners could either allow their former slaves to vote or see their representation in Washington slashed.

By making blacks national citizens, the Fourteenth Amendment provided a guarantee of equality before the law. In essence, it protected the rights of citizens against violation by their own state governments.

The Republicans drafted the Fourteenth Amendment in such a way that they could not lose. If southern whites caved in and granted voting rights to freedmen, the Republican Party, entirely a northern party since its birth, would gain valuable black votes, establish a wing in the South, and secure its national power. But if whites refused, southern representation in Congress would plunge, and Republicans would still gain immunity from southern Democratic political power. The Fourteenth Amendment's voting provision included northern states, where whites were largely hostile to voting rights for black Northerners. But northern states could continue to withhold suffrage and not suffer in Washington, for their black populations were too small to count in figuring representation. Radicals labeled the Fourteenth Amendment's voting provision "hypocritical" and a "swindle," but they understood that it was the best they could get at the time.

Tennessee approved the Fourteenth Amendment in July, and Congress promptly welcomed its representatives and senators back. Had Johnson counseled other southern states to ratify this relatively mild amendment and warned them that they

MEMPHIS RIOTS, MAY 1866

On May 1, 1866, two carriages, one driven by a white man and the other by a black man, collided on a busy Memphis street. This minor incident spiraled into three days of bloody racial violence in which dozens of blacks and two whites died. Racial friction was common in postwar Memphis, and white newspapers routinely heaped abuse on black citizens. "Would to God they were back in Africa, or some other seaport town," the Memphis **Argus** *shouted two days before the riot erupted, "anywhere but here." South Memphis, pictured in this lithograph from* **Harper's Weekly,** *was a shantytown where the families of black soldiers stationed at nearby Fort Pickering lived. The army commander refused to send troops to protect the soldiers' families and property, and white mobs ran wild.*
Library of Congress.

faced the fury of an outraged Republican Party if they refused, they might have listened. Instead, Johnson advised Southerners to reject the Fourteenth Amendment and to rely on him to trounce the Republicans in the fall congressional elections.

Johnson had decided to make the Fourteenth Amendment the overriding issue of the 1866 congressional elections and to gather its white opponents into a new conservative party, the National Union Party. In August, his supporters met in Philadelphia. Democrats came, but the slim Republican turnout made it clear that rather than drawing disgruntled Republicans to him, Johnson had united nearly the entire Republican Party against him.

The president's strategy had already suffered a setback two weeks earlier when whites in several southern cities went on rampages against blacks. It was less an outbreak of violence than an escalation of the violence that had never ceased. In New Orleans, a mob assaulted delegates to a black suffrage convention, and thirty-four blacks died. In Memphis, white mobs hurtled through the black sections of town and killed at least forty-six people. The slaughter shocked Northerners and renewed skepticism about Johnson's claim that southern whites could be trusted. "Who doubts that the Freedmen's Bureau ought to be abolished forthwith," a New Yorker observed sarcastically, "and the blacks remitted to the paternal care of their old masters, who 'understand the nigger, you know, a great deal better than the Yankees can.'"

In a last-ditch effort, Johnson took his case directly to the people. In August, he made an ill-fated "swing around the circle," which took him from Washington to Chicago and St. Louis and back to Washington. However, the president embarrassed himself and his office. When hostile crowds hurled insults, he gave as good as he got. It was Johnson at his worst—intemperate, crude, undignified. Even a friend agreed that he had "made an ass of himself." Johnson's reception on the campaign trail foretold the fate of the National Union movement in the elections. Rather than witnessing the birth of a new conservative party, the elections pitted traditional rivals: Democrats (who lined up with Johnson) against Republicans (who lined up against him). The result was an overwhelming Republican victory in which the party retained its three-to-one congressional majority.

Johnson had bet that Northerners would not support federal protection of black rights. He expected a racist backlash to defeat the Fourteenth Amendment and blast the Republican Party. But the cautious (and ingenious) amendment was not radical enough to drive Republican voters into Johnson's camp. Besides, the war was still fresh in northern minds. As one Republican explained, southern whites "with all their intelligence were traitors, the blacks with all their ignorance were loyal."

Radical Reconstruction and Military Rule

The elections of 1866 should have taught southern whites the folly of relying on Andrew Johnson as a guide through the thicket of reconstruction. But when Johnson continued to urge Southerners toward rejection of the Fourteenth Amendment, one by one every southern state except Tennessee voted it down. "The last one of the sinful ten," thundered Representative James A. Garfield of Ohio, "has flung back into our teeth the magnanimous offer of a generous nation." In the void created by the South's rejection of the moderates' program, the Radicals seized the initiative.

Each act of defiance by southern whites had boosted the standing of the Radicals within the Republican Party. At the core was a small group of men who had cut their political teeth on the antebellum campaign against slavery, who had goaded Lincoln toward making the war a crusade for freedom, and who had carried into the postwar period the conviction that only federal power could protect the rights of the freedmen. Except for freedmen

themselves, no one did more to make freedom the "mighty moral question of the age." Men like Senator Charles Sumner, that pompous but sincere Massachusetts crusader, and Thaddeus Stevens, the caustic, cadaverous representative from Pennsylvania, did not speak with a single voice, but they united in calling for civil and political equality. They insisted on extending to ex-slaves the same opportunities that northern working people enjoyed under the free-labor system. The southern states were "like clay in the hands of the potter," Stevens declared in January 1867, and he called on Congress to begin reconstruction all over again.

In March 1867, after exhaustive debate, moderates joined the Radicals to overturn the Johnson state governments and initiate military rule of the South. The Military Reconstruction Act (and three subsequent acts) divided the ten unreconstructed Confederate states into five military districts. Congress placed a Union general in charge of each district and instructed him to "suppress insurrection, disorder, and violence" and to begin political reform. After the military had completed voter registration, which would include black men and exclude all those barred by the Fourteenth Amendment from holding public office, voters would elect delegates to conventions that would draw up new state constitutions. Each constitution would guarantee black suffrage. When the voters of each state had approved the constitution and the first legislature had ratified the Fourteenth Amendment, the state could submit its work to Congress. If Congress approved, the state's senators and representatives could be seated and political reunification would be accomplished.

Radicals proclaimed the provision for black suffrage "a prodigious triumph." The doggedness of the Radicals and of African Americans, along with the pigheadedness of Johnson and the white South, had swept the Republican Party far beyond the limited suffrage provisions of the Fourteenth Amendment. Republicans finally agreed with Sumner that only the voting power of ex-slaves could bring about a permanent revolution in the South. Indeed, suffrage provided blacks with a powerful instrument of change and self-protection. When combined with the disfranchisement of thousands of ex-rebels, it promised to cripple any neo-Confederate resurgence and guarantee Republican governments in the South.

Despite its bold suffrage provision, the Military Reconstruction Act of 1867 disappointed those who advocated the confiscation and redistribution of southern plantations. No one in Washington was more distressed than Thaddeus Stevens. Unlike Sumner, who conceived of reconstruction primarily in political terms, Stevens believed it was at bottom an economic problem. He agreed wholeheartedly with the ex-slave who said, "Give us our own land and we take care of ourselves, but without land, the old masters can hire us or starve us, as they please." But Johnson's offers of amnesty and pardon had reversed the small program of land transfer begun during the war. By early 1867, nearly all of the land had been returned to its ex-Confederate owners. Most Republicans believed they had already provided blacks with the critical tools: equal legal rights and the ballot. If blacks were to get forty acres, they would have to gain it themselves.

The doggedness of the Radicals and of African Americans, along with the pigheadedness of Johnson and the white South, had swept the Republican Party far beyond the limited suffrage of the Fourteenth Amendment.

Declaring that he would rather sever his right arm than sign such a formula for "anarchy and chaos," Andrew Johnson vetoed the Military Reconstruction Act. Congress overrode his veto the very same day, dramatizing the shift in power from the executive to the legislative branch of government. With the passage of the Reconstruction Acts of 1867, congressional reconstruction was virtually completed. Congress had left white folks owning most of the South's land, but in a radical departure it had given black men the ballot. More than any other provision, black suffrage justifies the term "radical reconstruction." In 1867, the nation began an unprecedented experiment in interracial democracy—at least in the South, for Congress's plan did not touch the North. Soon the former Confederate states

Reconstruction Military Districts, 1867

would become the primary theater for political struggle. But before the spotlight swung away from Washington, the president and Congress had one more scene to play.

Impeaching a President

Although Johnson had lost the support of the northern people and faced a hostile Republican majority in Congress, he had no intention of yielding control of reconstruction. As president, he was responsible for enforcing the laws that Congress enacted. As commander in chief, he oversaw the military rule of the South that Congress instituted. Yet in a dozen ways he sabotaged Congress's will and encouraged white belligerence and resistance. He issued a flood of pardons to undermine efforts at political and economic change. He waged war against the Freedmen's Bureau by removing officers who sympathized too fully with ex-slaves. And he replaced Union generals eager to enforce Congress's Reconstruction Acts with conservative men who were eager to defeat them. Johnson claimed that he was merely defending the "violated Constitution." At bottom, however, the president subverted congressional reconstruction to protect southern whites from what he considered the horrors of "Negro domination."

When Congress learned that overriding Johnson's vetoes did not ensure victory, it attempted to tie the president's hands. Congress required that all orders to field commanders pass through the General of the Army, Ulysses S. Grant, who Congress believed was sympathetic to southern freedmen, Unionists, and Republicans. It also enacted the Tenure of Office Act in 1867, which required the approval of the Senate for the removal of any government official who had been appointed with Senate consent. Republicans were seeking to protect Secretary of War Edwin M. Stanton, the lone cabinet officer who supported congressional policies. Some Republicans, however, believed that nothing less than removing Johnson from office could save reconstruction, and they initiated a crusade to impeach the president. According to the United States Constitution, the House of Representatives can impeach and the Senate can try any federal official for "TREASON, BRIBERY, or other high CRIMES and MISDEMEANORS."

As long as Johnson refrained from breaking a law, however, impeachment languished. Moderates interpreted "high CRIMES and MISDEMEANORS" to

ANDREW JOHNSON, WITH ADDITIONS
This dignified portrait by Currier and Ives of President Andrew Johnson appeared in 1868, the year of his impeachment trial. The portrait was apparently amended by a disgruntled citizen. Johnson's vetoes of several reconstruction measures passed by Congress caused his opponents to charge him with arrogant monarchical behavior. Johnson preferred the unamended image—that of a plain and sturdy statesman.
Museum of American Political Life.

mean violation of criminal statutes, and they did not believe that the president had committed an actual crime. Radicals argued that Johnson's abuse of constitutional powers and his failure to fulfill constitutional obligations were impeachable offenses. But in August 1867, Johnson suspended Secretary of War Stanton from office. As required by the Tenure of Office Act, he requested the Senate to consent to dismissal. When the Senate balked, the president removed Stanton anyway. "Is the President crazy, or only drunk?" asked a dumbfounded Republican moderate. "I'm afraid his doings will make us all favor impeachment."

News of Johnson's open defiance of the law did indeed convince every Republican in the House to vote for a resolution impeaching the president. Chief Justice Salmon Chase presided over the Senate trial, which lasted from March until May 1868. Chase refused to allow Johnson's opponents to raise the broad issues of misuse of power, his "high crimes," and forced them to argue their case exclusively on the narrow legal grounds of Johnson's removal of Stanton. Johnson's lawyers argued that he had not committed a criminal offense, that the Tenure of Office Act was unconstitutional, and that in any case it did not apply to Stanton, who had been appointed by Lincoln. When the critical vote came, seven moderate Republicans broke with their party and joined the Democrats in voting not guilty. With thirty-five in favor and nineteen opposed, the impeachment forces fell one vote short of the two-thirds needed to convict.

Republicans had put Johnson on trial because he threatened their efforts to remake the South. But some, including Chief Justice Chase, feared that impeachment for insufficient cause would permanently weaken the office of president. So Johnson survived, but he did not come through the ordeal unscathed. After his trial he called a truce, and for the remaining ten months of his term reconstruction proceeded unhindered by presidential interference.

The Fifteenth Amendment and Women's Demands

In February 1869, Republicans passed the Fifteenth Amendment to the Constitution. The amendment prohibited states from depriving any citizen of the right to vote because of "race, color, or previous condition of servitude." The Reconstruction Acts of 1867 had already required black suffrage in the South, but the Fifteenth Amendment extended black voting to the entire nation. Some Republicans felt morally obligated to do away with the double standard between North and South. Others believed that the freedman's ballot required the extra armor of a constitutional amendment to protect it from white counterattack. But partisan advantage also played an important role in the amendment's passage. Gains by northern Democrats in the 1868 elections worried Republicans, and black voters now represented the balance of power in several northern states. By giving ballots to northern blacks, Republicans could lessen their political vulnerability. As one Republican congressman observed, "Party expediency and exact justice coincide for once."

Some Republicans, however, found the final wording of the Fifteenth Amendment "lame and halting." Rather than absolutely guaranteeing the right to vote, the amendment merely prohibited exclusion on grounds of race. The distinction would prove to be significant. In time, inventive white Southerners would devise tests of literacy and property and other apparently nonracial measures that would effectively disfranchise blacks and yet not violate the Fifteenth Amendment. But an amendment that guaranteed the right to vote courted defeat in the North. Rising antiforeign sentiment—against the Chinese in California and against European immigrants in the Northeast—caused states to resist giving up control of suffrage requirements. In March 1870, after three-fourths of the states had ratified it, the Fifteenth Amendment became part of the Constitution. Republicans generally breathed a sigh of relief, confident that black suffrage had been "the last great point that remained to be settled of the issues of the war."

But the Republican Party's reappraisal of suffrage had ignored completely the small band of politicized and energized women who had emerged from the war demanding "the ballot for the two disenfranchised classes, negroes and women." Founding the Equal Rights Association in 1866, Susan B. Anthony and Elizabeth Cady Stanton lobbied for "a government by the people, and the whole people; for the people and the whole people." They felt betrayed when their old antislavery allies, who now occupied positions of national power, proved to be fickle and refused to work for their goals. "It was the Negro's hour," Frederick Douglass later explained. The Republican Party had to avoid anything that might jeopardize black gains, Charles Sumner declared. He suggested that woman suffrage could be "the great question of the future."

SUSAN B. ANTHONY

Like many outspoken suffragists, Anthony, depicted here in 1852, had begun her public career working on behalf of temperance and abolition. But she grew tired of laboring under the direction of male clergymen—"white orthodox little saints," she called them—who controlled the reform movements and who routinely dismissed the opinions of women. Anthony's continued passion for other causes—improving working conditions for labor, for example—led some conservatives to oppose women's political rights because they equated the suffragist cause with radicalism in general. Women could not easily overcome such views, and the long struggle for the vote eventually drew millions of women into public life.
Susan B. Anthony House, Inc.

> *The Republican Party's reappraisal of suffrage had ignored completely the small band of politicized and energized women who had emerged from the war demanding "the ballot for two disenfranchised classes, negroes and women."*

It was not the first time women's expectations had been dashed. The Fourteenth Amendment had provided for punishment of any state that excluded voters on the basis of race but not on the basis of sex. It had also introduced the word *male* into the Constitution when it referred to a citizen's right to vote. Stanton had predicted that "if that word 'male' be inserted, it will take us a century at least to get it out." The Fifteenth Amendment proved to be no less disappointing. Although women fought hard to include the word *sex*, the amendment denied states the right to forbid suffrage only on the basis of race. Stanton and Anthony condemned the

Republicans' "negro first" strategy and concluded that woman "must not put her trust in man."

In a single decade, abolitionist William Lloyd Garrison declared, blacks had progressed from "the auction-block to the ballot-box." The Fifteenth Amendment, Congressman James A. Garfield of Ohio proclaimed, "confers upon the African race the care of its own destiny. It places their fortunes in their own hands." Even Wendell Phillips, that uncompromising crusader for equality, argued that the black man held "sufficient shield in his own hands. . . . Whatever he suffers will be largely now, and in future, his own fault." In essence, northern Republicans declared victory and scratched the "Negro question" from the agenda of national politics.

The Struggle in the South

While Northerners believed they had discharged their responsibilities with the Reconstruction Acts and the amendments to the Constitution, Southerners knew that the battle had just begun. Black suffrage and large-scale rebel disfranchisement that came with congressional reconstruction had destroyed traditional southern politics and established the foundation for the rise of the Republican Party. Gathering together outsiders and outcasts from traditional society, the Republicans in the South won elections, wrote new state constitutions, and formed new state governments.

Challenging the established class for political control was dangerous business. Equally dangerous were the confrontations that took place on farms and plantations from Virginia to Texas. In the countryside, blacks sought to give practical, everyday meaning to their newly won legal and political equality. But ex-masters like David Golightly Harris and other whites had their own ideas about the social and economic arrangements that should replace slavery. Freedom remained contested territory, and Southerners fought pitched battles with one another to determine the boundaries of their postemancipation world.

Freedmen, Yankees, and Yeomen

African Americans made up the majority of southern Republicans. Freedmen emerged from bondage illiterate and politically inexperienced, but they understood their own interests. They realized that without the ballot they were almost powerless, and they threw themselves into the suffrage campaign.

Southern blacks gained voting rights in 1867, and within months virtually every eligible black man had registered to vote. Blacks (like whites) did not have identical political priorities, but almost all voted Republican, and they united in their desire for education and equal treatment before the laws.

Northern whites who decided to make the South their home after the war were a second element of the South's Republican Party. Conservative white Southerners called any northern migrant a "carpetbagger," a man so poor that he could pack all his earthly belongings in a single carpet-sided suitcase and swoop southward like a buzzard to "fatten on our misfortunes." Some Northerners who moved south were scavengers, but most were restless, relatively well educated young men, often former Union officers and Freedmen's Bureau agents who looked upon the South as they did the West—as a promising place to make a living. Northerners in the southern Republican Party consistently supported programs that encouraged vigorous economic development along the lines of the northern free-labor model.

Southern whites made up the third element of the Republican Party in the South. Approximately one out of four white Southerners voted Republican. The other three cursed those who did. They condemned southern-born white Republicans as traitors to their region and their race and called them "scalawags," a term for runty horses and low-down, good-for-nothing rascals. Yeoman farmers in the piedmont accounted for the vast majority of white Republicans in the South. Many were Unionists who emerged from the war with bitter memories of Confederate persecution. Some small farmers also nursed long-standing grievances against planter domination and welcomed the Republican Party because it promised to end favoritism toward plantation interests. Yeomen usually supported initiatives for public schools and for expanding economic opportunity within a reinvigorated southern economy.

The Republican Party in the South, then, was made up of freedmen, Yankees, and yeomen—an improbable coalition. The mix of races, regions, and classes inevitably meant friction as each group maneuvered to define the party. Despite the stress and strain, reconstruction represents an extraordinary moment in American politics: Blacks and whites joined together to pursue political change. The Republican Party defended the political and civil equality of black Southerners and struggled to bring the South into the mainstream of American social and economic development. Formally, of course, only men participated in politics—casting ballots and holding offices—but women also played parts in the political struggle. Women joined in parades and rallies, attended stump speeches, and even campaigned. In 1868, black maids in Yazoo, Mississippi, shocked their white employers when they showed up for work boldly wearing buttons depicting the Republican candidate for president: Ulysses S. Grant.

Despite the stress and strain, reconstruction represents an extraordinary moment in American politics: Blacks and whites joined together to pursue political change.

Reconstruction politics was not for cowards. Any political act, even wearing a political button, took courage. Congress had introduced hundreds of thousands of ex-slaves into the southern electorate against the will of the white majority. Then, according to one Democrat, the Republican Party herded them to the polls like "senseless cattle." Most whites in the South condemned the entire political process as illegitimate and felt justified in doing whatever it took to stamp out Republicanism. Violence against blacks—the "white terror"—took brutal institutional form in 1866 with the formation of the Ku Klux Klan, a social club of Confederate veterans that quickly developed into a paramilitary organization armed against Republicans. The Klan went on a rampage of whipping, hanging, shooting, burning, and throat-cutting to defeat reconstruction and restore white supremacy. (See "Historical Question," page 558.) Rapid demobilization of the Union army after the war left only twenty thousand troops to patrol the entire South, a vast territory. Without effective military protection, southern Republicans had to take care of themselves.

Republican Rule

The Reconstruction Acts required southern states to draw up new constitutions before they could be readmitted to Congress. Beginning in the fall of 1867, states held elections for delegates to constitutional conventions. About 40 percent of the white electorate stayed home, either because they had been disfranchised or because they were boycotting

CONGRESSMAN JOHN R. LYNCH
Although whites almost always maintained control of reconstruction politics, over six hundred blacks served in legislatures in the South. Ex-slaves made up the majority of the black legislators. The Union Army freed John R. Lynch of Mississippi, and he gained an education at a Natchez freedmen's school. Lynch achieved power at an extraordinary age. He was only twenty-four when he became speaker of Mississippi's House. In 1872, he joined six other African Americans in Congress in Washington, D.C., where in support of civil rights legislation he told stories from his personal experience of being forced to occupy railroad smoking cars with gamblers and drunks. After reconstruction ended, Lynch practiced law and fought for an honest history of reconstruction legislatures, which he argued were the "best governments those States ever had." Natchez photographer Henry C. Norman took this powerful photograph, probably in the early 1870s.
Collection of Thomas H. Gandy and Joan W. Gandy.

politics. Republicans won three-fourths of the seats. About 15 percent of the Republican delegates were Northerners who had moved south, 25 percent were African Americans, and 60 percent were white

Southerners. As a British visitor observed, the elections reflected "the mighty revolution that had taken place in America." But Democrats described the conventions as zoos of "baboons, monkeys, mules . . . and other jackasses." David Golightly Harris despaired and asked, "What can be expected of a government framed by . . . black and ignorant negroes[?]" In fact, the conventions brought together serious, purposeful men who hammered out the legal framework for a new order.

The reconstruction constitutions introduced extensive changes into southern life. In general, changes fell into two categories: those that reduced aristocratic privilege and increased democratic equality and those that expanded the state's responsibility for the general welfare. In the first category, the constitutions adopted universal male suffrage, abolished property qualifications for holding office, and made more offices elective and fewer appointive. In the second category, they enacted prison reform; made the state responsible for caring for orphans, the insane, and the deaf and mute; and aided debtors by exempting their homes from seizure.

These forward-looking constitutions provided blueprints for a new South. But they stopped short of the specific reforms advocated by particular groups within southern Republicanism. Despite the wishes of virtually every former slave, no southern constitution confiscated and redistributed land. And despite the prediction of Unionists that unless all former Confederates were banned from politics they would storm back and wreck reconstruction, no constitution disfranchised ex-rebels wholesale.

But Democrats were blind to the limits of the Republican program. In their eyes, they stared at wild revolution. According to Democrats, Republican victories initiated "black and tan" (ex-slave and mulatto) governments. But the claims of "Negro domination" had almost no validity. Four out of five Republican voters were black men, but more than four out of five Republican officeholders were white. Southerners sent fourteen black congressmen and two black senators to Washington, but only 6 percent of Southerners in Congress during Reconstruction were black (Figure 15.1). With the exception of South Carolina, where blacks briefly held a majority in one house of the legislature, no state experienced "Negro rule," despite black majorities in the populations of three states.

In almost every state, voters ratified the new constitutions and swept Republicans into power. After they ratified the Fourteenth Amendment, the

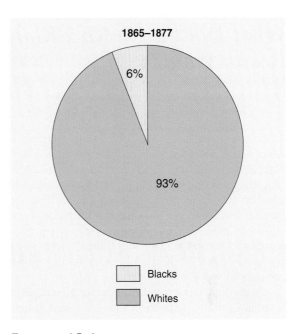

1865–1877

6%

93%

☐ Blacks

☐ Whites

FIGURE **15.1**
Southern Congressional Delegations
The statistics contradict the myth of black domination of congressional representation during reconstruction.

former Confederate states were readmitted to Congress. Southern Republicans then turned to a staggering array of problems. Wartime destruction still littered the landscape. The South's share of the nation's wealth had fallen from 30 percent to only 12 percent. Manufacturing limped along at a fraction of prewar levels, agricultural production remained anemic, and the region's railroads had hardly advanced from the devastated condition in which Sherman had left them. Without the efforts of the Freedmen's Bureau, people would have starved. Moreover, reactionary violence and racial harassment dogged Southerners who sought reform. In this desperate context, Republicans struggled to breathe life into their new state governments.

Activity focused on three major areas. First, every state inaugurated a system of public education and began building schools and training teachers. Before the Civil War, whites had deliberately kept slaves illiterate, and planter-dominated governments rarely spent tax money to educate the children of yeomen. By 1875, half of Mississippi's and South Carolina's eligible children (the majority of whom were black) attended school. Persistent underfunding meant too few schools, dilapidated

What Did the Ku Klux Klan Really Want?

IN THE SUMMER OF 1866, six Confederate veterans in Pulaski, Tennessee, founded the Ku Klux Klan. Borrowing oaths and rituals from a college fraternity, the young men innocently sought fun and fellowship in a social club. But they quickly tired of playing pranks on one another and shifted to more serious matters. By the spring of 1868, when congressional reconstruction went into effect, new groups or "dens" of the Ku Klux Klan had sprouted throughout the South.

According to former Confederate general and Georgia Democratic politician John B. Gordon, the Klan owed its popularity to the "instinct of self-preservation . . . the sense of insecurity and danger, particularly in those neighborhoods where the Negro population largely predominated." Everywhere whites looked, he said, they saw "great crime." Republican politicians organized ignorant freedmen and marched them to the polls, where they blighted honest government. Ex-slaves drove overseers from plantations and claimed the land for themselves. Black robbers and rapists made white women cower behind barred doors. It was necessary, Gordon declared, "in order to protect our families from outrage and preserve our own lives, to have something that we could regard as a brotherhood—a combination of the best men of the country, to act purely in self-defense." According to Gordon and other conservative white Southerners, then, Klansmen were good men who stepped forward to do their duty, men who wanted nothing more than to guard their families and defend decent society from the assaults of degraded ex-slaves and a vindictive Republican Party.

Behind the Klan's high-minded and self-justifying rhetoric, however, lay another agenda. It was revealed in their actions, not their words. Klansmen embarked on a campaign to reverse history. Garbed in robes and hoods, Klansmen engaged in hit-and-run guerrilla warfare against free labor, civil equality, and political democracy. They aimed to terrorize their enemies—ex-slaves and white Republicans—into submission. As the South's chief terrorist organization between 1868 and 1871, the Klan whipped, burned, and shot in the name of white supremacy. Changes in four particular areas of southern life proved flash points for Klan violence: racial etiquette, education, labor, and politics.

The Klan punished those blacks and whites guilty of breaking the Old South's racial code. The Klan considered "impudence" a punishable offense. Asked to define "impudence" before a congressional investigating committee, one white opponent of the Klan responded: "Well, it is considered impudence for a negro not to be polite to a white man—not to pull off his hat and bow and scrape to a white man, as was done formerly." Klansmen whipped blacks for crimes that ranged from speaking disrespectfully and refusing to yield the sidewalk to raising a good crop and dressing well. Black women who "dress up and fix up like ladies" risked a midnight visit from the Klan. The Ku Klux Klan sought to restore racial subordination in every aspect of private and public life.

Klansmen also took aim at black education. White men, especially those with little schooling, found the sight of blacks in classrooms hard to stomach. Schools were easy targets, and scores of them went up in flames. Teachers, male and female, were flogged, or worse. Klansmen drove northern-born teacher Alonzo B. Corliss from North Carolina for "teaching niggers and making them like white men." In Cross Plains, Alabama, the Klan hanged an Irish-born teacher along with four black men. But not just ill-educated whites opposed black education. Planters wanted ex-slaves back in the fields, not at desks. Each student meant one less laborer. In 1869, an Alabama newspaper reported the burning of a black school and observed that it should be "a warning for them to stick hereafter to 'de shovel and de hoe,' and let their dirty-backed primers go."

Planters turned to the Klan as part of their effort to preserve plantation agriculture and restore labor discipline. An Alabama white admitted that in his area, the Klan was "intended principally for the negroes who failed to work." Masked bands "punished Negroes whose landlords had complained of

KU KLUX KLAN ROBE AND HOOD
The white robes that we associate with the Ku Klux Klan are a twentieth-century phenomenon. During reconstruction, Klansmen donned robes of various designs and colors. It is unlikely that the man who wore this robe about 1866—with its eye holes carefully trimmed with blue fabric—sewed it himself. Women did not participate in midnight raids, but mothers, wives, and daughters of Klansmen often shared their reactionary vision and did what they could to bring about the triumph of white supremacy.
Chicago Historical Society, Hope B. McCormick Center. Worn by Joseph Boyce Stewart, Lincoln County, Tenn., c. 1866. Gift of W. G. Dithmer.

them." Sharecroppers who disputed their share at "settling up time" risked a visit from the night riders. Klansmen murdered a Georgia blacksmith who refused to do additional work for a white man until he was paid for a previous job. It was dangerous for freedmen to consider changing employers. "If we got out looking for some other place to go," an ex-slave from Texas remembered, "them KKK they would tend to Mister negro good and plenty." In Marengo County, Alabama, when the Klan heard that some local blacks were planning to leave, "the disguised men went to them and told them if they undertook it they would be killed on their way." Whites had decided that they would not be "deprived of their labor."

Above all, the Klan terrorized Republican leaders and voters. Klansmen became the military arm of the Democratic Party. They drove blacks from the polls on election day and terrorized black officeholders. Klansmen gave Andrew Flowers, a black politician in Chattanooga, a brutal beating and told him that they "did not intend any nigger to hold office in the United States." Jack Dupree, president of the Republican Club in Monroe County, Mississippi, a man known to "speak his mind," had his throat cut and was disemboweled while his wife was forced to watch.

Between 1868 and 1871, political violence reached astounding levels. Arkansas experienced nearly three hundred political killings in the three months before the fall elections in 1868, including Little Rock's U.S. congressman, J. M. Hinds. Louisiana was even bloodier. Between the local elections in the spring of 1868 and the presidential election in the fall, Louisiana experienced more than one thousand killings. Political violence often proved effective. In Georgia, Republican presidential candidate Ulysses S. Grant received no votes at all in 1868 in eleven counties, despite black majorities. The Klan murdered three scalawag members of the Georgia legislature and drove ten others from their homes. As one Georgia Republican commented after a Klan attack: "We don't call them democrats, we call them southern murderers."

It proved hard to arrest Klansmen and harder still to convict them. "If a white man kills a colored man in any of the counties of this State," observed a Florida sheriff, "you cannot convict him." By 1871, the death toll had reached thousands. Federal intervention—in the Ku Klux Klan Acts of 1870 and 1871—signaled an end to much of the Klan's power but not to counterrevolutionary violence in the South. Other groups continued the terror.

facilities, and poorly trained teachers, but literacy rates rose sharply, nevertheless. Although public schools were racially segregated, education remained for many blacks a tangible, deeply satisfying benefit of freedom and Republican rule.

Second, states attacked racial discrimination and defended civil rights. Republicans especially resisted efforts by whites to establish separate facilities for blacks in public transportation. Texas replaced its law requiring segregation in its railroads with one that outlawed seating by race. Mississippi went further, levying fines of up to $1,000 and three years in jail for railroads, steamboats, hotels, and theaters that denied "full and equal rights" to all citizens. But passing color-blind laws was one thing; enforcing them was another. Segregation—the separation of blacks and whites in public places—developed at white insistence despite the law and became a feature of southern life long before the end of reconstruction.

Third, Republican governments launched ambitious programs of economic development. They envisioned a South of diversified agriculture, roaring factories, and booming towns. Republican legislatures chartered scores of banks and industrial companies, appropriated funds to fix ruined levees and to drain swamps, and went on a railroad-building binge, repairing old lines and adding some seven thousand miles of track. The mania for railroads and state-sponsored economic development fell far short of solving the South's economic troubles, however. Republican spending to stimulate economic growth also meant rising taxes and enormous debt that drained funds from schools and other programs.

Segregation developed at white insistence despite the law and became a feature of southern life long before the end of reconstruction.

The southern Republicans' record, then, was mixed. To their credit, the biracial Republican coalition had taken up an ambitious agenda to change the South. Success would have been difficult under the best circumstances. As it was, money was scarce. In addition, Democrats kept up a constant drumbeat of harassment, while factionalism threatened the party from within. Moreover, corruption infected Republican governments in the South. Public morality reached new lows everywhere in the nation after the Civil War, and the chaos and disruption of the postwar South proved fertile soil for bribery, fraud, and influence peddling. Despite all of its problems and shortcomings, however, the Republican Party made headway in its efforts to purge the South of aristocratic privilege and racist oppression.

White Landlords, Black Sharecroppers

Reconstruction politics did not arise within a vacuum. Sharp dissatisfaction with conditions in the southern countryside politicized blacks and fueled political upheaval. Clashes occurred daily between ex-slaves who wished to take control of the conditions of their own labor and ex-masters who wanted to reinstitute old ways.

The system of agricultural labor that emerged in 1865 grew out of the labor program begun during the war by the federal military. When the war ended, supervision shifted to the Freedmen's Bureau, which renewed the army's campaign to restore production by binding black laborers and planters with wage contracts. Except for having to put down the whip and pay subsistence wages, planters were not required to offer many concessions to emancipation. Instead, they moved quickly to restore the antebellum world of work gangs, white overseers, field labor for black women and children, clustered cabins, minimal personal freedom, and even corporal punishment whenever they could get away with it.

Ex-slaves resisted every effort to roll back the clock. Land of their own would do much to end planters' involvement in their personal lives. They wanted, for example, to make their own decisions about whether women and children would labor in the fields. Indeed, within months after the war, perhaps one-third of black women abandoned field labor and began working full time within their own households. Whites claimed that black women were "acting the lady," but what whites meant was that black women were not acting like slaves. Instead, they behaved like free mothers and housewives, occupied with the same arduous domestic chores as poor white women. Moreover, hundreds of thousands of black children enrolled in school.

The freedmen's dream of landownership never came true. Congress and southern legislatures refused to confiscate the planters' land, and without political intervention, landownership proved to be beyond the reach of all but a small fraction of blacks. Without land, ex-slaves would have little choice but to work on plantations.

Although blacks were forced to return to the planters' fields, freedmen resisted efforts to restore slavelike conditions. In his South Carolina neighborhood, David Golightly Harris discovered that few freedmen were "willing to hire by the day, month or year." Instead of working for wages, "the negroes all seem disposed to rent land." By rejecting wage labor, by striking, and by abandoning the most reactionary employers, blacks sought to force concessions. A tug-of-war between white landlords and black laborers took place on thousands of farms and plantations and out of it emerged a new system of southern agriculture.

Sharecropping was a compromise that offered both ex-masters and ex-slaves something but satisfied neither. Under the new system, planters divided their cotton plantations into small farms of twenty-five to thirty acres that freedmen rented, paying with a share of each year's crop, usually half. Sharecropping gave blacks more freedom than wages and labor gangs and released them from the day-to-day supervision of whites. Black families abandoned the old slave quarters and scattered over plantations, building separate cabins on the patches of land they tilled (Map 15.1). David Golightly Harris reported in late 1867 that "much moveing is being done" and that "few negroes remain in their old homes." Black families now decided who would work, for how long, and how hard. Still, most blacks remained dependent on the white landlord, who retained the power to expel them at the end of each

MAP 15.1

A Southern Plantation in 1860 and 1881

The maps of the Barrow plantation in Georgia illustrate some of the ways that ex-slaves expressed their freedom. Former slaves deserted the clustered living quarters behind the big house, scattered over the plantation, built new family cabins, and farmed rented land. These ex-slaves also worked together to build a school and a church.

season. For planters, sharecropping offered a way to resume agricultural production, but it did not allow them to reinstitute the unified plantation system or to administer what they considered necessary discipline.

Sharecropping was a compromise that offered both ex-masters and ex-slaves something but satisfied neither.

Sharecropping also introduced a new figure—the country merchant—into the agricultural equation. While landlords supplied sharecroppers with land, mules, and tools, blacks needed someone to extend essential food and clothing on credit until they harvested their crops. Thousands of merchants at small crossroads stores sprang up to provide this service. Under an arrangement called a crop lien, local merchants advanced goods to sharecroppers in exchange for a lien, or claim, on the farmer's crop. Merchants sometimes charged exorbitant interest, as much as 60 percent, on the goods they sold—from seeds to needles to slabs of bacon. At "settling up time," after the landlord took half of the farmer's crop for rent, the merchant consulted his ledger. Invariably, the farmer's expenses exceeded the income from his half of the crop. It was a rare cropper who had two nickels to rub together at the end of a season. Empty-handed, he had no choice but to begin the cycle all over again.

An experiment at first, sharecropping spread quickly throughout the cotton South. While it never became the only system of agricultural labor, sharecropping soon dominated. By 1870, the old gang system, direct white supervision, and clustered black living quarters were fading memories. Soon, sharecropping ensnared small white farmers as well as black farmers.

Reconstruction Collapses

By 1870, Northerners looked forward to putting "the southern problem" behind them. They had written into the Constitution guarantees of civil and political rights for blacks and enacted a program of political reunification that had restored ex-Confederate states to the Union. Now, after a decade of engagement with the public issues of war and reconstruction, they wanted to turn to their own affairs. Increasingly, practical business-minded men came to the forefront of the Republican Party, replacing the band of reformers and idealists who had been prominent in the 1860s. While northern resolve to defend black freedom withered, southern commitment to white supremacy intensified. Without northern protection, southern Republicans were no match for the Democrats' economic coercion, political corruption, and bloody violence. One by one, Republican state governments fell. The election of 1876 both confirmed and completed the collapse of reconstruction.

The Grant Regime: Cronies, Corruption, and Economic Collapse

Ulysses S. Grant was the obvious choice for the Republican Party's presidential nomination in 1868. When the Civil War ended, the general who beat Lee was easily the most popular man in the nation, at least north of the Mason-Dixon line. Radicals preferred someone with a deeper moral commitment to black equality, but Grant supported congressional reconstruction and that was enough for the Republican convention. The Democrats chose Horatio Seymour, former governor of New York. Their platform blasted congressional reconstruction as "a flagrant usurpation of power . . . unconstitutional, revolutionary, and void." Republicans answered by "waving the bloody shirt"; that is, they reminded voters that the Democrats were "the party of rebellion," the party that stubbornly resisted a just peace. During the campaign, the Ku Klux Klan erupted in another reign of terror, murdering hundreds of southern Republicans. Terrorist tactics cut into Grant's tally, but he gained a narrow 300,000-vote margin in the popular vote and a substantial victory (214 votes to 80) in the electoral college.

Grant understood that most Northerners had grown weary of reconstruction. Conservative business-minded Northerners had become convinced that recurrent federal intrusion was itself a major cause of instability. Eager to invest in the South and especially to resume the profitable cotton trade, they sought order, not disruption. A growing number of northern Republican leaders began to question the wisdom of their party's alliance with the South's lower classes—its small farmers and sharecroppers. Grant's secretary of the interior, Jacob D. Cox of Ohio, proposed allying with the "thinking

"I BEG TO REPEAT THAT THESE FRAUDS ON THE GOVERNMENT SHALL BE PROBED TO THE VERY BOTTOM."

TAMMANY RING.
CANAL RING.
WHISKEY RING.
INDIAN RING.
PRESS RING.
STATE RING.
COUNTY RING.
TOWN RING.
WARD RING.

BELKNAP.
FRAUD CLAIMS.
BACK PAY GRAB
GEMMA MINE
WHISKEY FRAUDS
BRIBERY

GRANT AND SCANDAL
This anti-Grant cartoon by the nation's most celebrated political cartoonist, Thomas Nast, shows the president falling headfirst into the barrel of fraud and corruption that tainted his administration. During Grant's eight years in the White House, many in his administration failed him. Sometimes duped, sometimes merely loyal, Grant stubbornly defended wrongdoers, even to the point of perjuring himself to keep an aide out of jail.
Library of Congress.

www.bedfordstmartins.com /tap SEE THE ONLINE STUDY GUIDE for more help in analyzing this image.

and influential native southerners . . . the intelligent, well-to-do, and controlling class."

The talents Grant had demonstrated on the battlefield—decisiveness, clarity, and resolution—deserted him in the White House. Unclear about his objectives, he grew tentative, unsure of himself, almost bewildered. Able advisers might have helped, but Grant surrounded himself with fumbling kinfolk and old cronies from his army days. He also made a string of dubious appointments that led to a series of damaging scandals. Charges of corruption tainted his vice president, Schuyler Colfax, and brought down his secretary of war and secretary of the navy as well as his private secretary. Grant's dogged loyalty to liars and cheats only compounded the damage. While never personally implicated in any scandal, Grant was aggravatingly naive and his administration filled with rot.

In 1872, disgusted anti-Grant Republicans bolted and launched a third party, the Liberal Republicans. The Liberals promised to create a government "which the best people of this country will be proud of." They condemned the Grant regime as a riot of vulgarity—crude graft, tasteless materialism, and blatant anti-intellectualism. To clean up the mess, they proposed ending the spoils system, by which victorious parties rewarded loyal workers with public office, and replacing it with a nonpartisan civil service commission that would oversee competitive examinations for appointment to office. Moreover, they demanded that the government remove federal troops from the South and restore "home rule." Democrats especially liked the southern policy of the Liberals, and the Democratic Party endorsed the Liberal presidential candidate, Horace Greeley, the longtime editor of the *New York Tribune*. Despite Grant's problems, however, the nation still felt enormous affection for the man who had saved the Union. In the 1872 election, voters gave him 56 percent of the popular vote, the most lopsided victory since Andrew Jackson swept into the White House forty-four years earlier.

In 1872, disgusted anti-Grant Republicans bolted and launched a third party, the Liberal Republicans. The Liberals promised to create a government "which the best people of this country will be proud of."

Grant was not without accomplishments during his eight years as president. Ironically, he scored his greatest triumph on an issue he cared little about: the settlement of the U.S. claim against Great Britain for wartime damages caused by British-built Confederate ships. When Britain denied any wrongdoing, tempers flared. But in 1872, Hamilton Fish, Grant's able secretary of state, skillfully orchestrated a peaceful settlement that paid the United States $15.5 million in damages.

Grant's great passion in foreign affairs—annexation of Santo Domingo in the Caribbean—ended in utter failure. Grant argued that the acquisition of this tropical land would permit the United States to expand its trade in the Caribbean and simultaneously provide a new home for the South's blacks, who were so desperately harassed by the Klan. Aggressive foreign policy had not originated with the Grant administration. Lincoln and Johnson's secretary of state, William H. Seward, had thwarted French efforts to set up a puppet empire under Maximilian in Mexico, and his purchase of Alaska ("Seward's Ice Box") from Russia in 1867 for only $7 million had fired Grant's imperial ambition. But the Republican Party split over the president's scheme to acquire Santo Domingo, and in the end Grant could not marshal the votes needed to approve the treaty of annexation.

Grant's Proposed Annexation of Santo Domingo

The Grant administration was caught up in a tangle of complicated problems, including a devastating economic depression that began in 1873. Railroads, which had fueled the postwar boom, led directly to the bust. A major Philadelphia bank, headed by Jay Cooke, had poured enormous sums into railroads, become overextended with debt, and

gone under, initiating the panic of 1873. Like dominoes, other companies failed, and soon the nation sank into its most severe depression to that time. More than eighteen thousand businesses collapsed in two years, and more than one million workers lost their jobs. Desperate times arrived at the doorsteps of most working people. Workers battled owners as industrial violence kept pace with economic hardship. The violence subsided as men and women returned to work, but only at the end of the decade did the depression lift. By then, southern Republican governments had fallen, and the experiment of reconstruction had ended.

Northern Resolve Withers

Although Northerners wanted desperately to shift their attention to the new issues, the old ones would not go away. When southern Republicans pleaded for federal protection from Klan violence, Congress enacted three laws in 1870 and 1871 that were intended to break the back of white terrorism. The severest of the three, the Ku Klux Klan Act, made interference with voting rights a felony and authorized the use of the army to enforce it. Intrepid federal marshals arrested thousands of suspected Klansmen. While the government came close to destroying the Klan, it did not end terrorism against blacks. Congress also passed the Civil Rights Act of 1875, which boldly outlawed racial discrimination in transportation, public accommodations, and juries. But federal authorities did little to enforce the law, and segregated facilities remained the rule throughout the South.

In reality, the retreat from reconstruction had begun in 1868 with Grant's election. Grant genuinely wanted to see blacks' civil and political rights protected, but he felt uneasy about an open-ended commitment that seemed to ignore constitutional limitations on federal power. Like his predecessor, he distributed pardons liberally and encouraged the passage of a general amnesty. In May 1872, Congress obliged and restored the right of officeholding to all but three hundred ex-rebels. Radicals did what they could to stiffen the North's resolve, but by the early 1870s reform had lost its principal spokesmen to death or defeat at the polls. Many Republicans had washed their hands of reconstruction, concluding that the quest for black equality was mistaken or hopelessly naive. Those who bolted to the Liberal Republican Party, for example, welcomed the South's "best people" back to power.

Traditional white leaders, it seemed to them, offered the best hope for honesty, order, and prosperity.

The North's abandonment of reconstruction rested on more than weariness, greed, and disillusionment. Underlying everything was unyielding racial prejudice. Emancipation failed to uproot racism in either the South or the North. During the war, Northerners had learned to accept black freedom, but deep-seated prejudice prevented many from equating freedom with equality. Even the actions they took on behalf of blacks often served partisan political advantage. Whether they expressed it quietly or boisterously, Northerners generally supported Indiana Senator Thomas A. Hendricks's declaration that "this is a white man's Government, made by the white man for the white man." Increasingly, when Radicals asked Northerners to remember reconstruction's victims, northern sympathy went out to white Southerners.

The U.S. Supreme Court also did its part to undermine reconstruction. From the first, Republicans had feared that the conservative Court would declare their southern policies unconstitutional. In the 1870s, a series of Court decisions significantly weakened the federal government's ability to protect black Southerners under the Fourteenth and Fifteenth Amendments. In the *Slaughterhouse* cases (1873), the Court distinguished between national and state citizenship and ruled that the Fourteenth Amendment protected only those rights that stemmed from the federal government, like voting in federal elections and interstate travel. Since the Court decided that most rights derived from the states, it sharply curtailed the federal government's authority to protect black citizens. Even more devastating, the *United States v. Cruikshank* ruling (1876) said that the reconstruction amendments gave Congress power to legislate only against discrimination by states, not by individuals. The "suppression of ordinary crime," such as assault, remained a state responsibility. The Supreme Court did not declare reconstruction unconstitutional, but it gradually undermined its legal foundation.

The mood of the North found political expression in the election of 1874, when for the first time in eighteen years the Democrats gained control of the House of Representatives. Voters blamed the Grant administration for the economic hard times that had begun the previous year, but they also sent a message about reconstruction. As one Republican observed, the people had grown tired of the "negro question, with all its complications, and the recon-

struction of the Southern States, with all its interminable embroilments."

Reconstruction had come apart in the North, and Congress gradually abandoned it. President Grant grew increasingly unwilling to enforce it. The Supreme Court busily denied the constitutionality of significant parts of it. And the people sent unmistakable messages that they were tired of it. Rather than defend reconstruction from its southern enemies, Northerners steadily backed away from the challenge. After the early 1870s, southern blacks faced the forces of reaction largely on their own.

White Supremacy Triumphs

Republican governments in the South attracted more bitterness and hatred than any other political regimes in American history. In the eyes of the majority of whites, each day of Republican rule produced fresh insults: Black militiamen patrolled town streets, black laborers negotiated contracts with former masters, black maids stood up to former mistresses, black voters cast ballots, and black legislators enacted laws. The northern retreat from reconstruction permitted southern Democrats to harness this white rage to politics. Taking the name "Redeemers," they promised to replace "bayonet rule" (some federal troops continued to be stationed in the South) with "home rule" (white southern control). They branded Republican governments a carnival of extravagance, waste, and fraud and promised that honest, thrifty Democrats would supplant the irresponsible tax-and-spend Republicans. Above all, Redeemers swore to save southern civilization from a descent into African "barbarism" and "negro rule." As one man put it, "We must render this either a white man's government, or convert the land into a Negro man's cemetery."

By the early 1870s, Democrats understood that race was their most potent weapon. They adopted a two-pronged racial strategy to overthrow Republican governments. First, they sought to polarize the parties around color, and, second, they relentlessly intimidated black voters. They went about gathering all the South's white voters into the Democratic Party, leaving the Republicans to depend on blacks. The "straight-out" appeal to whites promised great advantage because whites made up a majority of the population in every southern state except Mississippi, South Carolina, and Louisiana.

Democrats employed several devices to dislodge whites from the Republican Party. First and foremost, they fanned the flames of racial prejudice. In South Carolina, a Democrat crowed that his party appealed to the "proud Caucasian race, whose sovereignty on earth God has proclaimed." Ostracism also proved effective. Local newspapers published the names of whites who kept company with blacks. So complete was the ostracism that one of its victims said, "No white man can live in the South in the future and act with any other than the Democratic party unless he is willing and prepared to live a life of social isolation."

> *Above all, Redeemers swore to save southern civilization from a descent into African "barbarism" and "negro rule."*

In addition, Democrats exploited the small white farmer's severe economic plight by blaming it on Republican financial policy. Government spending soared during reconstruction, and small farmers saw their tax burden skyrocket. Farms in Mississippi were taxed at four times the prewar level. When cotton prices fell by nearly 50 percent in the 1870s, yeomen farmers found cash in short supply. To pay their taxes, one man observed, "people are selling every egg and chicken they can get." In South Carolina, David Golightly Harris observed, "This is tax time. We are nearly all on our head about them. They are so high & so little money to pay with." He scraped together the $81.57 he owed, but those unable to pay lost their land. In 1871, Mississippi reported that one-seventh of the state's land—3.3 million acres—had been forfeited for nonpayment of taxes. The small farmer's economic distress had a racial dimension. Because few freedmen succeeded in acquiring land, they rarely paid taxes. In Georgia in 1874, blacks made up 46 percent of the population but paid only 2 percent of the taxes. From the perspective of the small white farmer, Republican rule meant not only that he was paying more taxes but that he was paying them to aid blacks. Democrats asked whether it was not time for hard-pressed yeomen to join the white man's party.

If racial pride, social isolation, and Republican financial policies proved insufficient to drive yeomen from the Republican Party, Democrats turned to terrorism. "Night riders" targeted scalawags as well as blacks for murder and assassination. By the early 1870s, then, only a fraction of southern whites any

IS THIS A REPUBLICAN FORM OF GOVERNMENT?
This powerful 1876 drawing by Thomas Nast depicts the end of reconstruction as the tragedy it was. As white supremacists in the South piled up more and more bodies, supporters of civil rights accused the Grant administration of failing to protect black Southerners and legitimately elected governments. They pointed specifically to the constitutional requirement that "[t]he United States shall guarantee to every State in this Union a Republican Form of Government, and shall protect each of them . . . against domestic violence" (Article IV, section 4). Library of Congress.

longer professed allegiance to the party of Lincoln. Racial polarization became a reality. Rich and poor whites united. Yeoman defection to the Redeemers proved a heavy blow to southern Republicanism.

The second prong of Democratic strategy—intimidation of black voters—proved equally devastating. Antiblack political violence escalated to unprecedented levels. In 1873 in Louisiana, a clash between black militiamen and gun-toting whites killed two white men and an estimated seventy black men. Half of the black men were slaughtered after they had surrendered. Although the federal government indicted more than one hundred white men, local juries failed to convict a single one of them.

Even before adopting the all-out white supremacist tactics of the 1870s, Democrats had already captured Virginia, Tennessee, and North Carolina. The new campaign brought fresh gains. The Redeemers retook Georgia in 1871, Texas in 1873, and Arkansas and Alabama in 1874. In 1876, Mississippi fell. The story in Mississippi was one of open, unrelenting, and often savage intimidation of black voters and their few remaining white allies. In a rampage by whites in Vicksburg, Mississippi, thirty-five blacks and two whites lost their lives. As the state election approached in 1876, Governor Adelbert Ames appealed to Washington for federal troops to control the violence, only to hear from the attorney general that the "whole public are tired of these annual autumnal outbreaks in the South." Abandoned, Mississippi Republicans succumbed to the Democratic onslaught in the fall elections. By 1876, only three Republican state governments—in Florida, Louisiana, and South Carolina—survived (Map 15.2).

An Election and a Compromise

The centennial year of 1876 witnessed one of the most tumultuous elections in American history. Its chaos and confusion provided a fitting conclusion to the experiment known as reconstruction. The election took place in November, but not until

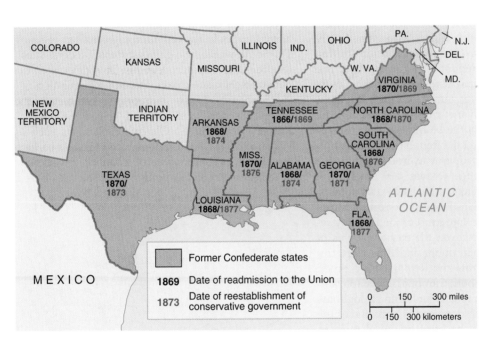

MAP 15.2

The Reconstruction of the South

Myth has it that Republican rule of the former Confederacy was not only harsh but long. In most states, however, conservative southern whites stormed back into power in only a matter of a few months or a very few years. By the election of 1876, Republican governments could be found in only three states. And they soon fell.

READING THE MAP: List in chronological order the readmission of former states to the Union. Which states reestablished conservative governments most quickly?

CONNECTIONS: What did the former Confederate states need to do in order to be readmitted to the Union? How did reestablished conservative governments react to reconstruction?

www.bedfordstmartins.com/tap   SEE THE ONLINE STUDY GUIDE for more help in analyzing this map.

March 2 of the following year, at 4 A.M., did the nation know who would be inaugurated president on March 4. For four months the country suffered through a constitutional and political crisis that jeopardized the peaceful transfer of power from one administration to the next. Sixteen years after Lincoln's election, Americans feared that a presidential contest would again precipitate civil war.

The centennial year of 1876 witnessed one of the most tumultuous elections in American history, a fitting conclusion to the experiment known as reconstruction.

The Democrats had nominated New York's reform governor, Samuel J. Tilden, who immediately targeted the corruption of the Grant administration and the despotism of Republican reconstruction. The Republicans put forward a reformer of their own, Rutherford B. Hayes, governor of Ohio. Privately, Hayes considered "bayonet rule" a mistake, but he concluded that waving the bloody shirt, as threadbare as it was, remained the Republicans' best political strategy." It leads people away from 'hard times,' which is our deadliest foe," Hayes said lamely.

On election day, Tilden tallied 4,284,000 votes to Hayes's 4,036,000. Yet in the all-important electoral college, Tilden fell one vote short of the majority required for victory. However, the electoral votes of three states remained in doubt and thus were uncounted. Both Democrats and Republicans claimed the nineteen votes of South Carolina, Louisiana, and Florida, the only remaining Republican strongholds in the South. To win, Tilden needed only one of the contested votes. Hayes had to have all of them to take the election. The two parties traded charges of fraud and intimidation. To be sure, Republicans had stuffed some southern ballot boxes, but stepped-up violence by the Democrats had kept hundreds of thousands of Republicans from the polls.

Congress had to decide who had actually won the elections in the three southern states and thus who would be president. The Constitution provided little guidance. Moreover, Democrats controlled the House, and Republicans the Senate. To break the deadlock, Congress created a special electoral commission to arbitrate the disputed returns. An odd and cumbersome compromise, the commission was made up of five representatives (two Republicans,

three Democrats), five senators (two Democrats, three Republicans), and five justices of the Supreme Court (two Republicans, two Democrats, and one justice who was considered an independent). But before the commission could meet, the Illinois legislature elected the independent justice to the Senate, and his place was filled with a Republican. The commissioners all voted the straight party line, giving every state to the Republican Hayes and putting him over the top in electoral votes (Map 15.3).

Some outraged Democrats vowed to resist Hayes's victory. But the impasse was broken when negotiations behind the scenes between Hayes's lieutenants and some moderate southern Democrats resulted in an informal understanding, known as the Compromise of 1877. In exchange for a Democratic promise not to block Hayes's inauguration and to deal fairly with the freedmen, Hayes vowed not to use the army to uphold the remaining Republican regimes. The South would also gain substantial federal subsidies for internal improvements. Two days later, the nation celebrated Hayes's peaceful inauguration.

Stubborn Tilden supporters bemoaned the "stolen election" and damned "His Fraudulency," Rutherford B. Hayes. Old-guard Radicals such as William Lloyd Garrison denounced Hayes's bargain as a "policy of compromise, of credulity, of weakness, of subserviency, of surrender." But the nation as a

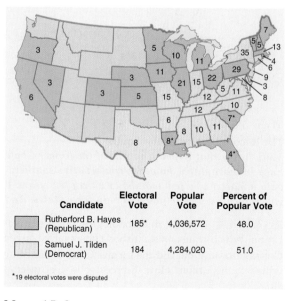

Candidate	Electoral Vote	Popular Vote	Percent of Popular Vote
Rutherford B. Hayes (Republican)	185*	4,036,572	48.0
Samuel J. Tilden (Democrat)	184	4,284,020	51.0

*19 electoral votes were disputed

MAP 15.3
The Election of 1876

whole celebrated, for the Republic had weathered a grave crisis. The Compromise of 1877 confirmed the conservatism that had been growing in the North for years. Even without a deal, Hayes would probably have withdrawn the troops. The last three Republican state governments fell quickly once Hayes abandoned them. Reconstruction had ended.

The nation's solution to the crisis of 1877 marked a return to the antebellum tradition of sectional compromise. As in previous crises, whites had found a way to bridge their differences and retain the peace, and again blacks had paid the price. Republicans followed a path of expediency and gained the presidency. Southern Democrats got home rule and a free hand in racial matters. Black Southerners were not completely subordinated to whites in 1877, but their prospects in the New South looked bleak.

Conclusion: "A Revolution but Half-Accomplished"

In 1865, when General Carl Schurz visited the South, he discovered "a revolution but half-accomplished." Defeat had not prepared the South for an easy transition from slavery to free labor, from white racial despotism to equal justice, and from white political monopoly to biracial democracy. Ex-masters like David Golightly Harris had trouble seeing former slaves like York and Old Will as free people. The old elite wanted to get "things back as near to slavery as possible," while ex-slaves and whites who had lacked power in the slave regime were eager to exploit the revolutionary implications of defeat and emancipation.

The northern-dominated Congress pushed the revolution along. Although it refused to provide an economic underpinning to black freedom, it required defeated Confederates to accept legal equality and share political power. But conservative whites fought ferociously to recover their power and privilege. When they regained control of politics, they used the power of the state, along with private violence, to wipe out many of the gains of reconstruction. So successful were the reactionaries that one observer concluded that the North had won the war but the South had won the peace.

But the Redeemer counterrevolution did not mean a return to slavery. Northern victory in the Civil War ensured abolition, and ex-slaves gained the freedom to not be whipped or sold, to send their children to school, to worship in their own churches, and to work independently on their own rented farms. The lives of impoverished sharecroppers overflowed with hardships, but even sharecropping provided more autonomy and economic welfare than bondage had. It was limited freedom, to be sure, but it was not slavery.

Emancipation set in motion the most profound upheaval in the nation's history, and nothing whites did entirely erased its revolutionary impact. War destroyed the richest and largest slave society in the New World. It cost masters $3 billion in lost property and destroyed the foundation of planter wealth. Abolition overturned the social and economic order that had dominated the region for nearly two centuries. The world of masters and slaves succumbed to that of landlords and sharecroppers. Even today, some Southerners divide history into "before the war" and "after the war."

The Civil War and emancipation mark a watershed not just in the South's history but in that of the entire nation. War served as midwife for the birth of a modern nation-state, and for the first time sovereignty rested uncontested in the federal government. Moreover, the South returned to the Union, but as a junior partner. The victorious North now possessed the power to establish the nation's direction, and it set its compass toward the expansion of industrial capitalism. War laid the foundation for the power of big business and its captains in postwar America.

Still, in one significant respect, the Civil War remained only a "half-accomplished" revolution. As such, reconstruction represents a tragedy of enormous proportions. The nation did not fulfill the promises that it seemed to hold out to black Americans at war's end. The revolution raced forward, halted, and then slipped back, coming to rest far short of equality and justice. The failure had enduring consequences. Almost a century after reconstruction, the nation would embark on what one observer called a "second reconstruction," another effort to fulfill nineteenth-century promises. The solid achievements of the Thirteenth, Fourteenth, and Fifteenth Amendments to the Constitution would provide a legal foundation for the renewed commitment. It is worth remembering, though, that it was only the failure of the first reconstruction that made a modern civil rights movement necessary.

www.bedfordstmartins.com/tap   SEE THE ONLINE STUDY GUIDE to test your mastery of the material covered in this chapter.

CHRONOLOGY

1863 December. Lincoln issues Proclamation of Amnesty and Reconstruction.

1864 July. Congress offers more stringent plan for reconstruction, Wade-Davis bill.

1865 January. General William T. Sherman sets aside land in South Carolina for black settlement.

March 4. Lincoln sworn in for second term as president of United States.

March. Congress establishes Freedmen's Bureau.

April 14. Lincoln shot, dies on April 15, succeeded by Vice President Andrew Johnson.

Fall. Southern legislatures enact discriminatory black codes.

December. Thirteenth Amendment abolishing slavery becomes part of U.S. Constitution.

1866 April. Congress approves Fourteenth Amendment making native-born blacks American citizens and guaranteeing all American citizens "equal protection of the laws." Amendment becomes part of Constitution in 1868.

April. Congress passes Civil Rights Act over President Johnson's veto.

May. Susan B. Anthony and Elizabeth Cady Stanton found Equal Rights Association to lobby for vote for women.

July. Congress extends Freedmen's Bureau over President Johnson's veto.

Summer. Ku Klux Klan founded in Tennessee.

November. Republicans triumph over Johnson's Democrats in congressional elections.

1867 March. Overriding Johnson's veto, Congress passes Military Reconstruction Act imposing military rule on South and requiring states to guarantee vote to black men.

1868 March–May. Senate impeachment trial of President Johnson results in acquittal.

November. Ulysses S. Grant elected president of the United States.

1869 February. Congress approves Fifteenth Amendment prohibiting racial discrimination in voting rights. Amendment becomes part of Constitution in 1870.

1871 April. Congress enacts Ku Klux Klan Act in effort to end white terrorism in South.

1872 November. President Grant reelected.

1873 Economic depression sets in for remainder of decade.

1874 November. Elections return Democratic majority to House of Representatives.

1875 February. Civil Rights Act of 1875 outlaws racial discrimination, but federal authorities do little to enforce law.

1877 March. Special congressional committee awards disputed electoral votes to Republican Rutherford B. Hayes, making him president of United States; Hayes agrees to pull military out of South.

BIBLIOGRAPHY

GENERAL WORKS

David Herbert Donald, Jean H. Baker, and Michael F. Holt, *The Civil War and Reconstruction* (2000).

W. E. B. Du Bois, *Black Reconstruction, 1860–1880* (1935).

Eric Foner, *Reconstruction: America's Unfinished Revolution* (1988).

John Hope Franklin, *Reconstruction after the Civil War* (1961).

James M. McPherson, *Ordeal by Fire: The Civil War and Reconstruction* (3rd ed., 2000).

Kenneth M. Stampp, *The Era of Reconstruction, 1865–1877* (1965).

WARTIME RECONSTRUCTION

Richard H. Abbott, *The Republican Party and the South, 1855–1877: The First Southern Strategy* (1986).

Herman Belz, *Emancipation and Equal Rights: Politics and Constitutionalism in the Civil War Era* (1978).

Louis S. Gerteis, *From Contraband to Freedman: Federal Policy toward Southern Blacks, 1861–1865* (1973).

William S. McFeely, *Yankee Stepfather: General O. O. Howard and the Freedmen* (1968).

James M. McPherson, *The Struggle for Equality: Abolitionists and the Negro in the Civil War and Reconstruction* (1964).

Willie Lee Rose, *Rehearsal for Reconstruction: The Port Royal Experiment* (1964).

Brooks D. Simpson, *Let Us Have Peace: Ulysses S. Grant and the Politics of War and Reconstruction, 1861–1868* (1991).

THE MEANING OF FREEDOM

James D. Anderson, *The Education of Blacks in the South, 1860–1935* (1988).

Ira Berlin et al., eds., *Freedom: A Documentary History of Emancipation, 1861–1867,* 4 vols. to date (1982–).

Edmund L. Drago, *Black Politicians and Reconstruction in Georgia: A Splendid Failure* (1982).

Russell Duncan, *Freedom's Shore: Tunis Campbell and the Georgia Freedmen* (1986).

Barbara J. Fields, *Slavery and Freedom on the Middle Ground: Maryland during the Nineteenth Century* (1985).

Michael W. Fitzgerald, *The Union League Movement in the Deep South: Politics and Agricultural Change during Reconstruction* (1989).

Eric Foner, *Nothing but Freedom: Emancipation and Its Legacy* (1983).

Janet Sharp Hermann, *The Pursuit of a Dream* (1981).

Thomas C. Holt, *Black over White: Negro Political Leadership in South Carolina during Reconstruction* (1977).

Peter Kolchin, *First Freedom: The Responses of Alabama's Blacks to Emancipation and Reconstruction* (1972).

Leon F. Litwack, *Been in the Storm So Long: The Aftermath of Slavery* (1979).

William E. Montgomery, *Under Their Own Vine and Fig Tree: The African-American Church in the South, 1865–1900* (1992).

Lynda J. Morgan, *Emancipation in Virginia's Tobacco Belt, 1850–1870* (1992).

Robert Morris, *Reading, 'Riting and Reconstruction* (1981).

Howard N. Rabinowitz, *Race Relations in the Urban South, 1865–1890* (1978).

Roger L. Ransom and Richard Sutch, *One Kind of Freedom: The Economic Consequences of Emancipation* (1977).

C. Peter Ripley, *Slaves and Freedmen in Civil War Louisiana* (1976).

Julie Saville, *The Work of Reconstruction: From Slave to Wage Laborer in South Carolina, 1860–1870* (1994).

Clarence E. Walker, *A Rock in a Weary Land: The African Methodist Episcopal Church during the Civil War and Reconstruction* (1982).

Joel Williamson, *After Slavery: The Negro in South Carolina during Reconstruction, 1861–1877* (1965).

Joel Williamson, *The Crucible of Race: Black/White Relations in the American South since Emancipation* (1984).

THE POLITICS OF RECONSTRUCTION

Michael Les Benedict, *The Impeachment and Trial of Andrew Johnson* (1973).

Michael Les Benedict, *A Compromise of Principle: Congressional Republicans and Reconstruction* (1974).

Richard F. Bensel, *Yankee Leviathan: The Origins of Central State Authority in America, 1859–1877* (1990).

Michael Kent Curtis, *No State Shall Abridge: The Fourteenth Amendment and the Bill of Rights* (1986).

David H. Donald, *Charles Sumner and the Rights of Man* (1970).

Ellen Carol DuBois, *Feminism and Suffrage: The Emergence of an Independent Women's Movement in America* (1978).

William Gillette, *The Right to Vote: Politics and the Passage of the Fifteenth Amendment* (1965).

Victor B. Howard, *Religion and the Radical Republican Movement, 1860–1870* (1990).

Harold M. Hyman, *A More Perfect Union: The Impact of the Civil War and Reconstruction on the Constitution* (1973).

Michael L. Lanza, *Agrarianism and Reconstruction Politics: The Southern Homestead Act* (1990).

William S. McFeely, *Grant: A Biography* (1981).

Eric L. McKitrick, *Andrew Johnson and Reconstruction* (1960).

James C. Mohr, ed., *Radical Republicans in the North: State Politics during Reconstruction* (1976).

David Montgomery, *Beyond Equality: Labor and the Radical Republicans, 1862–1872* (1967).

William E. Nelson, *The Fourteenth Amendment: From Political Principle to Judicial Doctrine* (1988).

James E. Sefton, *Andrew Johnson and the Uses of Constitutional Power* (1980).

Joel H. Sibley, *A Respectable Minority: The Democratic Party in the Civil War Era, 1860–1868* (1977).

Hans L. Trefousse, *Andrew Johnson: A Biography* (1989).

THE STRUGGLE IN THE SOUTH

Stephen V. Ash, *Middle Tennessee Society Transformed, 1860–1870: War and Peace in the Upper South* (1988).

Dwight B. Billings Jr., *Planters and the Making of a "New South": Class, Politics, and Development in North Carolina, 1865–1900* (1979).

Randolph B. Campbell, *A Southern Community in Crisis: Harrison County, Texas, 1850–1880* (1983).

Dan T. Carter, *When the War Was Over: The Failure of Self-Reconstruction in the South, 1865–1867* (1985).

Barry A. Crouch, *The Freedmen's Bureau and Black Texans* (1992).

Richard N. Current, *Those Terrible Carpetbaggers: A Reinterpretation* (1988).

Jane E. Dailey, *Before Jim Crow: The Politics of Race in Postemancipation Virginia* (2000).

Laura F. Edwards, *Gendered Strife and Confusion: The Political Culture of Reconstruction* (1997).

W. McKee Evans, *Ballots and Fence Rails: Reconstruction on the Lower Cape Fear* (1966).

Gaines Foster, *Ghosts of the Confederacy: Defeat of the Lost Cause and the Emergence of the New South, 1865 to 1913* (1987).

Steven Hahn, *The Roots of Southern Populism: Yeoman Farmers and the Transformation of the Georgia Upcountry, 1850–1890* (1983).

William C. Harris, *Day of the Carpetbagger: Republican Reconstruction in Mississippi* (1979).

Elizabeth Jacoway, *Yankee Missionaries in the South: The Penn School Experiment* (1980).

Jacqueline Jones, *Soldiers of Light and Love: Northern Teachers and Georgia Blacks, 1865–1873* (1980).

Robert C. Kenzer, *Kinship and Neighborhood in a Southern Community: Orange County, North Carolina, 1849–1881* (1987).

Richard G. Lowe, *Republicans and Reconstruction in Virginia, 1865–1870* (1991).

Scott Reynolds Nelson, *Iron Confederacies: Southern Railways, Klan Violence, and Reconstruction* (1999).

Donald G. Nieman, *To Set the Law in Motion: The Freedmen's Bureau and the Legal Rights of Blacks, 1865–1868* (1979).

Michael Perman, *Reunion without Compromise: The South and Reconstruction, 1865–1868* (1973).

Michael Perman, *The Road to Redemption: Southern Politics, 1869–1879* (1984).

Lawrence N. Powell, *New Masters: Northern Planters during the Civil War and Reconstruction* (1980).

George C. Rable, *But There Was No Peace: The Role of Violence in the Politics of Reconstruction* (1984).

Philip N. Racine, ed., *Piedmont Farmer: The Journals of David Golightly Harris, 1855–1870* (1990).

James L. Roark, *Masters without Slaves: Southern Planters in the Civil War and Reconstruction* (1977).

Crandall A. Shifflett, *Patronage and Poverty in the Tobacco South: Louisa County, Virginia, 1860–1900* (1982).

Mark W. Summers, *Railroads, Reconstruction, and the Gospel of Prosperity: Aid under the Radical Republicans, 1865–1877* (1984).

Allen Trelease, *White Terror: The Ku Klux Klan Conspiracy and Southern Reconstruction* (1971).

Ted Tunnell, *Crucible of Reconstruction: War, Radicalism, and Race in Louisiana, 1862–1877* (1984).

Peter Wallenstein, *From Slave South to New South: Public Policy in Nineteenth-Century Georgia* (1987).

Michael Wayne, *The Reshaping of Plantation Society: The Natchez District, 1860–1880* (1983).

Jonathan M. Wiener, *Social Origins of the New South, 1860–1885* (1978).

Sara Woolfolk Wiggins, *The Scalawag in Alabama Politics, 1865–1881* (1977).

Gavin Wright, *Old South, New South: Revolutions in the Southern Economy since the Civil War* (1986).

THE COLLAPSE OF RECONSTRUCTION

William Gillette, *Retreat from Reconstruction, 1869–1879* (1979).

Otto H. Olsen, ed., *Reconstruction and Redemption in the South: An Assessment* (1980).

Ian Polakoff, *The Politics of Inertia: The Election of 1876 and the End of Reconstruction* (1973).

Terry L. Seip, *The South Returns to Congress: Men, Economic Measures, and Intersectional Relationships, 1868–1879* (1983).

John G. Sproat, *"The Best Men": Liberal Reformers in the Gilded Age* (1968).

Mark W. Summers, *The Era of Good Stealings* (1993).

Margaret S. Thompson, *The "Spider Web": Congress and Lobbying in the Age of Grant* (1985).

C. Vann Woodward, *Reunion and Reaction: The Compromise of 1877 and the End of Reconstruction* (1951).

KANSAS QUILT C. 1880S

This carefully hand-stitched quilt, made from pieces of leftover wool clothing and blankets, shows how a woman named Nancy Miller Grider responded creatively to the challenges of her life in Russell County, Kansas, in the 1880s. Historically, women have produced quilts as a visual language, to tell something about themselves by using materials at hand. The circular pattern in Grider's quilt may represent the spokes of a wheel— a fitting symbol not only of her own migration west but of the mass migrations taking place after the Civil War, when restless Americans on the move peopled the West and fed the growth of the big cities.

Collection of the Kentucky Quilt Project, photograph courtesy of the Kentucky Quilt Project, Inc., Louisville, Ky.

AMERICANS ON THE MOVE: THE WEST AND THE CITY

1870–1900

A MISSOURI HOMESTEADER REMEMBERED PACKING as the family pulled up stakes and headed west to Oklahoma:

> We were going to God's Country. Eighteen hundred and 90. . . . It was pretty hard to part with some of our things. We didn't have much but we had worked hard for everything we had. You had to work hard in that rocky country in Missouri. I was glad to be leaving it. We were going to God's Country. . . . We were going to a new land and get rich.

In the Dakotas an Oglala Sioux recalled moving with his family as a child:

> The snow was deep and it was very cold, and I remember sitting in another pony drag beside my father and mother, all wrapped up in fur. We were going away from where the soldiers were, and I do not know where we went, but it was west.

In the Midwest a young man turned his face to the city, leaving his hometown behind:

> He saw again in his mind's eye, as he tramped the road, a picture of the map on the wall of the railway station—the map with a picture of iron roads from all over the Middle West centering in a dark blotch in the corner. . . .
> "Chicago!" he said to himself.

And in Russia a young girl on her way to America bid good-bye to her village:

> I remember how the women crowded around mother . . . how, finally, the ringing of the signal bell set them all talking faster and louder than ever, in desperate efforts to give the last bits of advice, deliver the last messages, and, to their credit let it be said, to give the final, hearty, unfeigned good-bye kisses, hugs, and good wishes.

America in the nineteenth century witnessed a massive movement of peoples as men and women searched for jobs, land, and opportunity. American Indians sought a place where they might live their traditional life in peace. In the last three decades of the century, this movement took many forms and went in many directions. The trek to the West continued apace as homesteaders, ranchers, and miners sought their fortunes. They in turn pushed Native Americans off the land and farther toward the sunset.

At the same time, the pull of the great industrial centers in the Northeast counterbalanced the westward migration. Farmers left the country to seek jobs in industrial centers like Chicago, New York, Pittsburgh, and Detroit. African Americans from the South began a migration to the northern cities, and Canadians crossed the border to work in the factories and mill towns of New England.

Fourteen million immigrants braved the Atlantic to come to America from Europe, creating the great migration that we think of as part of a worldwide westward movement. But the movement of peoples was by no means limited to one direction. Immigrants from Mexico and Latin America journeyed to "El Norte." Canadians headed south. Asians voyaged east across the Pacific to work on the "gold mountain" of California. It is not an exaggeration to say that the decades surrounding the turn of the twentieth century witnessed a migration unmatched in the history of the world.

By the end of the nineteenth century, Americans on the move had peopled a continent and created the outlines of modern America. As industrial capitalism transformed the nation from a rural agrarian economy into an increasingly urban, industrial society, it changed life not just in the burgeoning cities but also on the plains of the Dakotas, in the mines of Colorado, and on the farms of Texas and California. Iron rails and a national market economy inextricably linked the country and the city. The settlement of the West and the rise of the city occurred simultaneously and witnessed many of the same economic, social, and political manifestations—the rise of big business combinations, growing ethnic and racial tensions, and the exploitation of labor and natural resources. It makes more sense to look at the West not as separate and unique, but as an important part of a nationwide transformation that took place in the last three decades of the nineteenth century.

RAILROAD LOCOMOTIVE
In the years following the Civil War, the locomotive replaced the covered wagon, enabling settlers to travel from Chicago or St. Louis to the West Coast in two days. By the 1890s, more than 72,000 miles of track stretched west of the Mississippi River. In this photograph, men and women hop aboard a locomotive to celebrate the completion of a section of track.
Library of Congress.

Western Land Fever

Americans by the hundreds of thousands packed up and moved, pinning their hopes and ambitions on the American West. In the three decades following 1870, this westward stream of migration swelled into a torrent, spilling across the prairies, moving on to the Pacific coast, and eventually flooding back onto the Great Plains. During this brief span of time, more land was settled than in all the previous history of the country. Between 1876 and 1900, eight new states entered the Union—Colorado, Montana, North and South Dakota, Washington, Idaho, Wyoming, and Utah—leaving only three territories—Oklahoma, New Mexico, and Arizona—in the continental United States.

Two factors stimulated the rapid settlement of the trans-Mississippi West. The Homestead Act of 1862 promised 160 acres free to any citizen or prospective citizen, male or female, who settled on the land for five years. And railroads opened up new areas and actively recruited people who set their sights westward. In the 1870s, the promise of land lured thousands west across the plains in covered wagons, a hard journey that took many months and cost many lives. With the completion of a transcontinental railroad system in the 1880s, settlers could choose from four competing rail lines and make the trip in less than a week. Those who took advantage of the government's offer of free land were called homesteaders, as distinguished from "settlers," who purchased their land from private parties. Often they bought from speculators who took up land with an eye to profit, never intending to live on it.

While the country was rich in land and resources, not all who wanted to own their own land were able to do so. Land prices soared to dizzying heights as speculation drove up prices. At the same time, large landowners, often foreign investors, gobbled up huge ranches in California and the Southwest. In the South, still reeling from the economic impact of the Civil War, the old plantation system gave way to tenancy and peonage. A growing number of Americans found themselves dispossessed, forced to work for wages on land they would never own.

Moving West: Farmers, Ranchers, and Speculators

Families who ventured west searching for "God's country" faced hardship, loneliness, and deprivation. To carve a farm from the raw prairie of Iowa, the plains of Nebraska, or the forests of the Pacific Northwest took more than fortitude and back-breaking toil. It took luck. Blizzards, tornadoes, grasshoppers, hailstorms, drought, prairie fires, accidental death, and disease were only a few of the catastrophes that could befall even the best farmer. Homesteaders on "free" land needed as much as a thousand dollars for a house, a team of farm animals, a well, fencing, and seed. Poor farmers, called "sodbusters," did without even these basics, living in dugouts carved in the land and using muscle instead of machinery.

Americans by the hundreds of thousands packed up and moved, pinning their hopes and ambitions on the American West.

"Father made a dugout and covered it with willows and grass," one Kansas girl recounted. When it rained, the dugout flooded and "we carried the water out in buckets, then waded around in the mud until it dried." Rain wasn't the only problem. "Sometimes the bull snakes would get in the roof and now and then one would lose his hold and fall down on the bed, then off on the floor. Mother would grab the hoe . . . and after the fight was over Mr. Bull Snake was dragged outside."

For women on the frontier, simple daily necessities like obtaining water and fuel meant back-breaking labor. Out on the plains, where water was scarce, women often had to trudge to the nearest creek or spring. "A yoke was made to place across the shoulders, so as to carry at each end a bucket of water," one daughter recollected, "and then water was brought a half mile from spring to house." Gathering fuel was another heavy chore. Without ready sources of coal or firewood, settlers on the prairies and plains turned to what substitutes they could scavenge. Anything that would burn—twigs, tufts of grass, old corncobs, sunflower stalks—was used for fuel. But by far the most prevalent fuel used for cooking and heating were "chips," which were chunks of dried cattle and buffalo dung found in abundance on the plains and grasslands.

Many farmers succeeded in building comfortable lives. The sod hut made way for a more substantial house; the log cabin yielded to a white clapboard home with a porch. And the type and quality

OUR HOME

A mother and her children pose in front of their dugout near McCook, Nebraska, in the 1890s. With its real roof, glass windowpanes, and solid door, their dugout is more substantial than most.

Nebraska State Historical Society.

of the family diet improved. "Our living at first was very scanty," recalled one Kansas woman, "mostly corn coarsely ground and made into hominy." Then the family raised a crop of wheat and ground it into flour. "We would invite the neighbors proudly telling them we have 'flour doings.'" When the farm wife began to raise chickens, the family added "chicken fixings" to its diet, "and when we could have 'flour doings' and 'chicken fixings' at the same meal we felt we were on the road to prosperity."

Cattle ranching gave rise to a culture unto itself. Texas longhorns, a hardy breed ideally suited for life on the plains, grazed on public lands. Ranchers needed little capital to start—calves cost $4 a head and overhead consisted of a dugout, a rude corral, and a few cowboys. With open grazing, few ranchers bothered to buy the land they grazed on. Once a year cowboys drove the herd along the Chisholm Trail, through Indian Territory, to railheads in Abilene, Kansas, and later as railroads expanded, to other cattle towns like Wichita and Dodge City. As the nation emerged from the depression of the 1870s the market for beef skyrock-

eted. At the apex of the cattle boom, ranchers turned a 40 percent profit on their herds. Lust for profits, however, soon led to overgrazing. By 1880 over 7.5 million head of cattle grazed on the Great Plains north of Texas and New Mexico—an economic and ecological disaster in the making.

While farmers and ranchers succeed through hard work, speculators who did no physical labor at all also reaped profits in the West. For many who sought to homestead or buy land, the opportunities of the West failed to materialize. Already by the 1870s, much of the best land had been taken, given to the railroads as land grants or to the states to finance education. Too often, homesteaders found that only the least desirable tracts were left—poorer lands, far from markets, transportation, and society. Land speculators took the lion's share of the remaining land. "There is plenty of land for sale in California," one migrant complained in 1870, but "the majority of the available lands are held by speculators, at prices far beyond the reach of a poor man."

Areas Settled before 1862

The railroads were by far the biggest winners in the scramble for western land. To encourage railroad building in the decades after the Civil War, the federal government and the states gave public lands to the railroads. Together the land grants totaled approximately 180 million acres—an area almost one-tenth the size of the United States (Map 16.1). Farmers who went west to homestead often ended up buying land from the railroads or from the speculators and land companies that quickly followed the railroads into the new territories. Of the 2.5 million farms established on public lands between 1860 and 1900, homesteading accounted for only one in five; the vast majority of farmland sold for a profit.

As land for homesteading grew scarce on the prairie in the 1870s, farmers began to push farther westward, moving into western Kansas, Nebraska,

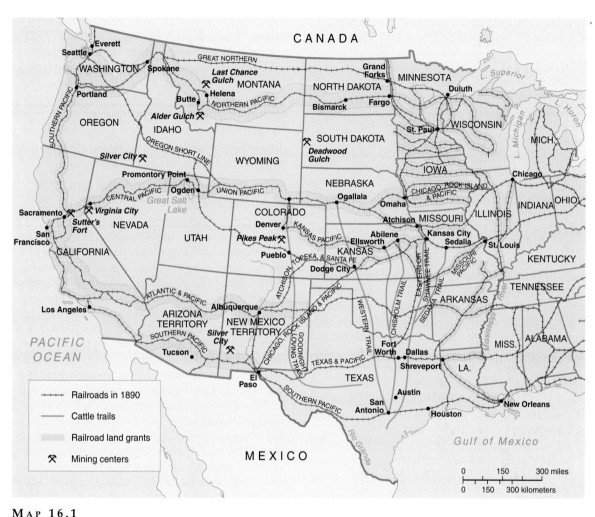

MAP 16.1

Federal Land Grants to Railroads and the Development of the West, 1850–1900
Generous federal land grants meant that railroads could sell the desirable land next to the track at a profit or hold it for speculation. Railroads received more than 180 million acres, an area equal to the size of Texas. Note how the cattle trails connect with major railheads in Dodge City, Abilene, and Kansas City and to mines in Montana, Nevada, Colorado, and New Mexico.

and eastern Colorado—the land called the Great American Desert by settlers who had passed over it on their way to California and Oregon. Although many agricultural experts warned that the semiarid land (where less than twenty inches of rain fell annually) should be reserved for grazing, their words of caution were drowned out by the extravagant claims of western promoters. "Rain follows the plow" became the slogan of western boosters, who insisted that cultivation would alter the climate of the region and bring more rainfall.

It would have been more accurate to say that drought followed the plow. Periodic droughts at roughly twenty-year intervals were a fact of life on the Great Plains. Plowed up, the dry topsoil blew away in the wind. A period of relatively good rainfall in the early 1880s encouraged farming, but a protracted drought in the late 1880s and early 1890s sent starving farmers reeling back from the plains. Hundreds of thousands retreated from western Kansas and Nebraska, some in wagons carrying the slogan "In God we trusted, in Kansas we busted."

A popular ballad bitterly summed up the plight of the worst off, those too poor to leave:

How happy I am on my government claim,
Where I've nothing to lose and nothing to gain,
Nothing to eat and nothing to wear,
Nothing from nothing is honest and square.
But here I am stuck and here I must stay
My money's all gone and I can't get away;
There's nothing will make a man hard and profane
Like starving to death on a government claim.

The fever for fertile land set off a series of spectacular land runs in Oklahoma. When the government took over two million acres of Indian territory and opened it to settlement in 1889, thousands rushed to grab a piece. Federal troops kept order as the homesteaders massed on the border. On April 22 at noon, pistol shots signaled the opening, and they were off. "Along the line as far as the eye could reach, with a shout and a yell the swift riders shot out, then followed the light buggies or wagons and last the lumbering prairie schooners and freighters' wagons," a reporter wrote. "Above all a great cloud of dust hover[ed] like smoke over a battlefield." By the end of the day, hundreds of homesteaders had staked claims, and Oklahoma boasted two tent cities with more than 10,000 residents.

Four years later, in a frenzied land rush on the Cherokee strip in Oklahoma Territory, more competed for 40,000 claims. Several settlers were killed in the stampede, and nervous men guarded their claims with rifles. As public lands grew smaller, the hunger for land grew fiercer.

The Dispossessed: Tenants, Sharecroppers, and Migrants

Landownership, the symbol of the American dream in the nineteenth century, remained an elusive goal for many Americans—freed slaves, immigrants from Europe and Asia, and Mexicans on the Texas border. In the post–Civil War period, as agriculture became a big business tied to national and global markets, an increasing number of dispossessed laborers worked land that they would never own.

In the southern United States, the farmer labored under particularly heavy burdens. The Civil War wiped out much of the region's capital, which had been invested in slaves, and crippled the plantation economy. The newly freed slaves rarely managed to obtain land of their own. Instead, they soon found themselves reduced to propertyless farm laborers. "The colored folks stayed with the old boss man and farmed and worked on the plantations," a black Alabama sharecropper observed bitterly. "They were still slaves, but they were free slaves."

Landownership, the symbol of the American dream in the nineteenth century, remained an elusive goal for many Americans—freed slaves, immigrants from Europe and Asia, and Mexicans on the Texas border.

Tenancy and sharecropping became a way of life for poor blacks and whites alike. The tenant rented land; the sharecropper worked someone else's land for a share of the proceeds. Even those who owned their own land faced enormous difficulties. In the states of the old Confederacy, both money and credit were in short supply. In desperation, southern farmers turned for credit to country merchants, some of whom were former masters who opened stores on their plantations. Under an arrangement called crop lien, local merchants supplied goods to the farmers on credit; in return, the farmers put up their next year's crop as collateral. The merchants charged exorbitant interest, up to 60 percent, on the goods they sold—from seed to a slab of bacon. At "settling up time," after the landlord took half the farmer's yield, the merchant consulted the debt ledger. Invariably, the farmer's expenses exceeded the income from his half of the cotton crop, and the cropper went home empty-handed, only to begin the cycle all over again.

There was no escape. Indebtedness bound the sharecroppers to the landlords and the merchants by prohibiting them from moving or buying from another store. Even small farmers who owned their own land suffered under the crop lien system. After seven years, farmers who did not "pay out" lost their land. Across the South the merchant became known as the "furnishing man." Black farmers called him simply "the man." By the beginning of the twentieth century, a majority of white farmers had become landless sharecroppers, outnumbering even the freedpeople caught in the system.

In Texas, the coming of the railroads at the end of the nineteenth century made cattle ranching big business, undermining the free-range ranch culture. As early as the 1860s, the large ranchers had begun to enclose the open range with barbed-wire fences. As one old-timer observed, "Those persons, Mexicans and Americans, without land but who had cattle were put out of business by fencing." Fencing eliminated those cattle and sheep ranchers who had grazed their herds on the open range, and forced small-time landowners who could not afford to buy barbed wire or to sink wells to sell out for the best price they could get. The displaced ranchers, many of them Mexican, ended up as wageworkers on the huge spreads owned by Anglos or by European syndicates.

Cattle Trails, 1860–1890

After the heyday of cattle ranching ended in the late 1880s came the rise of cotton production in the southeastern regions of Texas. Ranchers turned their pastures into sharecroppers' plots and hired displaced cowboys, most of them Mexican, as seasonal laborers for as little as seventy-five cents a day. Within the space of ten years, ranch life in southern Texas gave way to a growing army of agricultural wageworkers.

In California, a pattern of land monopoly and large-scale farming fostered tenancy and migratory labor. By the 1870s, less than one percent of the population owned half the state's available agricultural land. The rigid economics of large-scale commercial agriculture and the seasonal nature of the crops spawned a ragged army of migratory agricultural laborers. Derisively labeled "blanket men" or "bindle stiffs," these homeless and landless transients worked the fields in the growing season and wintered in the flophouses of San Francisco. Bonanza wheat farming in California in the 1870s and 1880s exhausted the land and was replaced, with the introduction of irrigation, by fruit and sugar beet farming. Most of the California farm laborers were Chinese immigrants, until the enactment of Chinese exclusion in 1882 forced big growers to look to other groups, including Mexicans, Filipinos, and Japanese, for farm labor.

The Changing Face of Rural America

In the late nineteenth century, America's population remained overwhelmingly rural. The 1870 census showed that nearly 80 percent of the nation's people lived on farms and in villages of less than eight thousand inhabitants. In 1900, the figure had dropped to 66 percent (Figure 16.1). But while the percentage of rural inhabitants fell, the number of farms grew—from 2 million in 1860 to over 5.7 million in 1900. Rapid growth in the West accounted for the rise in the number of farms, but not all the nation's farmers lived in the West. The rural population spread evenly across the country, with rural inhabitants outnumbering city dwellers even in industrial states like Pennsylvania and New York as late as 1880.

Like all aspects of American life, farm life changed rapidly in the last decades of the nineteenth century. With the rise of industrialization and the

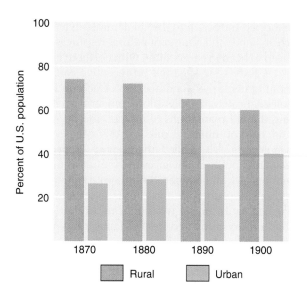

FIGURE **16.1**

Changes in Rural and Urban Populations, 1870–1900
Between 1870 and 1900 not only did the number of urban dwellers increase, but the number of rural inhabitants fell. Mechanization made it possible to farm with fewer hands and fueled the exodus from farm to city throughout the second half of the nineteenth century.

growth of big cities, many farmers gave up their farms and moved to towns and cities. Those who stayed behind increasingly adopted new technologies, making farming less a way of life and more a business venture. In the states of the old Confederacy, cotton remained king, and the region's emphasis on a cash-crop economy signaled a nationwide trend away from family farming and toward agribusiness.

The Colonial Economy of the New South

In the decades following the Civil War, the South struggled to regain its economic footing. The region's economy, devastated by the war and altered forever by the abolition of slavery, foundered at the same time the North experienced an unprecedented industrial boom. No wonder some Southerners called for a New South, modeled on the industrial North. Henry Grady, the ebullient young editor of the *Atlanta Constitution,* used his paper's substantial influence (it boasted the largest circulation of any weekly in the country) to extol the virtues of a new industrial South. Part bully, part booster, Grady exhorted the South to use its natural advantages— cheap labor and abundant natural resources—to go head to head in competition with northern industry.

Grady's message fell on receptive ears. Many Southerners, men and women, black and white, joined the national migration from farm to city, leaving the old plantations to molder and decay. With the end of military rule in 1877, the southern Democrats, who called themselves "Redeemers," regained political power in the southern states and enthusiastically embraced northern promoters who promised prosperity and profits. Northern capital rushed south in the waning years of the 1870s as the country recovered from the hard times precipitated by the panic of 1873.

The railroads came first, opening up the region for industrial development. Railroad mileage grew fourfold from 1865 to 1890 (see Map 16.1). The number of cotton spindles also soared, as textile mill owners abandoned New England in search of the cheap labor, low taxes, and proximity to raw materials promised in the South. By 1900, the South had become the nation's leading producer of cloth, and more than 100,000 Southerners, many of them women and children, had traded agricultural labor for work in textile mills.

The extractive industries, mining and lumber, also experienced a boom in the New South, but with devastating results. Coal from Appalachia could now be transported by rail to fuel the blast furnaces and factories of the nation. In the race to exploit the South's coal reserves, whole mountains were eaten up, often with catastrophic environmental and human costs. Investors in the North and abroad, not Southerners, reaped the lion's share of the plunder. The miners themselves violently protested their poor wages and dangerous working conditions in a series of strikes that gave one county in Kentucky the name "Bloody" Harlan. In the lumber industry, the demand for southern wood led to untrammeled expansion. Twenty years of milling resulted in what one contemporary forestry expert called "probably the most rapid and reckless destruction of forests known in history."

The New South was proudest of its iron and steel industry, which grew up in the area surrounding Birmingham, Alabama. Soon the smokestack replaced the white-pillared plantation as the symbol of the South. Pennsylvania iron magnate Andrew Carnegie toured the region in 1889 and observed, "The South is Pennsylvania's most formidable industrial enemy." But as long as control of southern industry remained in the hands of northern investors, Pennsylvania had nothing to fear. Whatever the South's natural advantages, northern bankers and investors had no intention of letting the South beat the North at its own game. Elaborate mechanisms rigged the price of southern steel, inflating it, as one northern insider confessed "for the purpose of protecting the Pittsburgh mills and in turn the Pittsburgh steel users."

In only one industry did the South truly dominate—tobacco. Capitalizing on the invention of a machine for rolling cigarettes, the Duke family of Virginia eventually dominated the industry with their American Tobacco Company. The new popularity of cigarettes, which replaced chewing tobacco among American's growing urban population, provided a booming market for Duke's "ready-made" cigarettes. Soon the company was selling 400,000 cigarettes a day.

In practical terms, the industrialized New South proved an illusion. Instead of thriving, the South found itself reduced to the status of an economic colony of the North. Just as today's colonial economies the world over feature cheap labor, extractive industries, and exported raw materials, so

BIRMINGHAM, ALABAMA, 1885
A symbol of the New South, Birmingham, Alabama, was founded after the Civil War in 1871. With rich coal and iron deposits nearby, Birmingham soon became the iron and steel capital of the region. An economic boom took the city from 3,000 inhabitants to more than 26,000 in the decade of the 1880s. The smokestack, that symbol of the new industrial South, is prominently featured in these illustrations published in 1885.
Library of Congress.

too did the economy of the New South. Similarly, the region experienced low wages, absentee ownership, and little control over policy or pricing—key determinants of colonial status.

In practical terms, the industrialized New South proved an illusion. Instead of thriving, the South found itself reduced to the status of an economic colony of the North.

Agriculture in the New South fared no better. Dependence on cotton increased rather than decreased in the postbellum period. Landlords and merchants alike demanded that sharecroppers grow more cotton, which they considered an easily marketable cash crop. Before the end of the nineteenth century, the South was producing nearly three times as much cotton as it had before the Civil War. Unfortunately, the South's vastly increased production, combined now with millions of bales from Egypt and India, coincided with a slowdown in world demand. Cotton prices plummeted. Further, relentless cotton cultivation exhausted the soil and eroded the countryside. Although a few merchants and landowners managed to hold on and even profit, the majority of Southerners succumbed to the numbing poverty that settled over the rural South. Dissatisfaction with this state of affairs would fuel the populist movement in the 1890s.

From the Family Farm toward Agribusiness

The promise of cheap land lured many settlers west at the same time the growing cities acted as powerful magnets, particularly to young people, pulling them off the farm. In the 1870s and 1890s, crop failures and economic depression forced many farmers into foreclosure and off the land. By the 1890s, rural depopulation caused a growing chorus of alarm. "One by one, family by family, [the] inhabitants slip away in search of other homes," a New England writer lamented. The loss of population was by no means limited to New England. More than half the rural townships of Ohio, Indiana, and Illinois lost population between 1880 and 1890, and the rate in Iowa was not far behind. Alarmed observers wondered who would be left to feed the growing urban population if all the farmers left for the cities.

They needn't have worried. Despite the loss in population, farming itself was thriving as an agricultural revolution transformed American farm life. New plows and reapers halved the time and labor cost of production and made it possible to farm vast tracts of land. Industrialization and urbanization provided farmers with expanding markets for their produce, and railroads carried farmers' crops to markets thousands of miles away. The diversified family farm of the past began to give way to specialized, commercial farming. Even before the opening of the twentieth century, American agriculture had entered the era of what would come to be called "agribusiness"—farming as a big business.

Business became the order of the day. Instead of extolling the virtues of the self-sufficient farmer, farm journals, agricultural societies, and educators pushed farmers to act more like businessmen, to specialize and to consolidate. Together they helped to create a striking new image of what constituted successful farming. "Farming for business, not for a living—this is the motif of the New Farmer," announced one agricultural writer. The message was clear: The job of the up-to-date farmer was to produce money, not just crops.

As farming moved onto the prairies and plains, mechanization took command. Steel plows, reapers, mowers, harrows, seed drills, combines, and threshers replaced human muscle on the farm. Horse-drawn implements gave way to steam-powered machinery. By 1880, a new harvester could reap and shock twenty acres of wheat in a day, and a single combine could do the work of twenty men. Machines enabled farmers to vastly increase their acreage. Two men with one machine could cultivate 250 acres of wheat. Production soared. Mechanization spurred the growth of huge bonanza wheat farms, some over 100,000 acres, in California and the Red River valley of North Dakota and Minnesota. The agricultural revolution meant that Americans raised more than four times the corn, five times the hay,

IOWA FARMHOUSE
This farmhouse in Clay County, Iowa, was built in the 1870s to replace the log cabin at the left where the homesteaders had lived when they first migrated from upstate New York. The rocking chair on the porch hints at the leisure the family could now occasionally enjoy. As some farmers prospered, they were able to construct white clapboard houses like this one, replicating the homes they had known back east.
Collection of Julia Booth.

and seven times the wheat and oats they had before the Civil War.

The Tariff and the World Market

The farmer existed in a web of dependence, not only on weather and credit but increasingly on a world market. American foodstuffs fed people as far away as England and Germany. Like the cotton farmer in the South, northern grain and livestock farmers increasingly depended on foreign markets for their livelihood. Farmers exported 217 million bushels of wheat and 212 million bushels of corn by 1897. A fall in commodity prices meant that a farmer's entire crop went to pay off debts. In periods of de-

pression, many heavily mortgaged farmers lost their land to creditors.

The protective tariff, endorsed by every Republican president from Abraham Lincoln to William Howard Taft, further hurt the farmer. The tariff, designed to protect "infant industries," prevented foreign competition and effectively raised the price of manufactured goods. Almost everything the farmer purchased, from plows and reapers to kerosene and calico, cost more because of the tariff. Habitual debtors, farmers also suffered from the government's tight monetary policy. The gold standard caused a steady deflation, which forced debtors to repay loans with money worth much more than the money they had originally borrowed. Or, put in

MECHANICAL CORN PLANTER
The Farmer's Friend Manufacturing Company of Dayton, Ohio, advertised its lever and treadle corn planter in this colorful advertisement in the early 1880s. Mechanical planters came into use in the 1860s. Although the 1880 planter featured attachments for grain drilling and fertilizing, it appears designed to be drawn by farm animals. Steam-powered farm implements would soon replace animal power. Notice how the idealized, bucolic farm life pictured in the advertisement gets a dose of reality in the illustration of the company's impressive factory in Dayton.
Ohio Historical Society.

terms of labor, a farmer who had borrowed a thousand dollars in 1868 had to grow twice as much wheat in 1888 than he would have had to grow twenty years earlier to pay back his loan. Farmers also resented the profits made by bankers and mortgage lenders and by the owners of grain elevators, who often made more money storing the farmers' grain than the farmers made when they sold it. "By the time the World Gets their Liveing out of the Farmer as we have to Feed the World," a Texas cotton farmer complained in the 1890s, "we the Farmer has nothing Left but a Bear Hard Liveing."

The farmer existed in a web of dependence, not only on weather and credit but increasingly on a world market.

Since the days of Thomas Jefferson, farming had been linked with the highest ideals of a democratic society. Now agrarianism itself had been transformed. The farmer was no longer the self-sufficient yeoman, but a businessman on the one hand or a dispossessed wage laborer on the other, both tied to a global market. And even as farm production soared, industrial production outstripped it. More and more farmers left the fields for the factories. Now that the future seemed to lie with the cities, was democracy itself at risk? This question would ignite a farmers' revolt in the 1880s and dominate political debate in the 1890s.

The American West: A Clash of Cultures

In the movies, the American West is often portrayed in mythic terms as a picturesque landscape where strong-jawed heroes square off against villains. The good guys are always white, even their hats. Often the bad guys are red—Indians, the name Columbus mistakenly gave to Native Americans. In this masculine tableau the setting is so timeless that it is easy to forget that the action takes place at roughly the same time that waves of new immigrants sailed past the Statue of Liberty, engineers built the Brooklyn Bridge, and men like John D. Rockefeller consolidated their empires in emerging industrial America. The mythi-cal West exists away from all of this, out of time. Once the West is situated within its historical context, however, once it is seen as a particular place at a particular time, reality supersedes myth, and the West appears to be not so different from the rest of the country. The problems and issues facing the nation at the beginning of the twentieth century—the growing power of corporations, ethnic and racial animosity, the exploitation of labor and of natural resources—all played themselves out under western skies.

The Peoples of the Great Plains and the Far West

"West" has always been a relative term. Until the gold rush of 1849 focused attention on California, the West for settlers lay beyond the Appalachians, east of the Mississippi in the lands drained by the Ohio River—a part of the country that we now call the Old Northwest. But by 1870, "West" increasingly referred to the land across the Mississippi, from the Great Plains to the Pacific Ocean.

The West of the late nineteenth century was a polyglot place, as much so as the big cities of the East. An illustrator on his way to the California goldfields deftly depicted the mix: "The stranger as he ascends the mountains towards the mining towns . . . notices the contrast in the scenes around him to anything he ever saw before. Indians are met in groups. . . . Strings of Chinamen pass, and greet you in broken English. . . . Next comes a Negro, with a polite 'good morning, sar' or Chileno, Mexican, or Kanaka."

The parade of peoples who came to the West included immigrants from Europe, Asia, and Canada, not to mention New Englanders, Mormons, African Americans, Mexicans, Latinos, and numerous Indian tribes removed by the government. The sheer number of races that came together and mingled in the West produced a complex racism. One historian has noted, not entirely facetiously, that there were at least eight oppressed races in the West—Indians, Latinos, Chinese, Japanese, blacks, Mormons, strikers, and radicals. The Chinese suffered brutal treatment at the hands of employers and other laborers. Fearful of competition, workingmen rioted in the 1870s and fought to keep the Chinese out of the United States. African Americans who ventured out to the territories faced hostile settlers determined to keep the West "for whites only." And Native Americans, who once warred with one another, increasingly united to fight off white encroachment.

Hispanic peoples had lived in Texas and the Southwest since Juan de Oñate led his pioneer settlers up the Rio Grande in 1598 and had occupied the Pacific coast since San Diego was founded in 1769. Overnight they were reduced to a "minority" after the United States annexed Texas and took California in the Mexican War of the 1840s. Initially the Hispanic owners of large ranchos in California, New Mexico, and Texas along with claimants of land grants from the Mexican and Spanish governments greeted conquest as an economic opportunity—new markets for their livestock and buyers for their lands. But racial prejudice soon put an end to their optimism. *Californios,* granted American citizenship by the Treaty of Guadalupe Hidalgo (1848), soon found themselves discriminated against by whites who sought to keep them out of California's mines and commerce. Whites illegally squatted on rancho lands while protracted litigation over Spanish and Mexican land grants forced the rancheros into court to fight for their land. Although the Supreme Court eventually validated most of their claims, it took so long that many had to sell their property to pay taxes and heavy legal debts. Today's city of Oakland, California, sits on what was once a 19,000-acre ranch owned by the Peralta family. Swindle, chicanery, and intimidation dispossessed scores of Hispanics. Many ended up in city barrios—segregated ghettos—in their own homeland. In California their population declined from 82 percent in 1850 to 19 percent by 1880. A similar fate befell Hispanic people in New Mexico and Texas. In these states Hispanics remained the majority, but they became an increasingly impoverished one.

The Mormons, followers of Joseph Smith, the founder and prophet of the Church of Jesus Christ of Latter-Day Saints, fled west to avoid religious persecution. They believed that they had a divine right to the land, and their messianic militancy contributed to making them outcasts. Although they were not the only religious sect of this period to practice plural marriage, the Mormons' polygamy (taking more than one wife) became a convenient point of attack for those who hated and feared the group. After Smith was killed by an Illinois mob in 1844, Brigham Young led the flock, which numbered more than twenty thousand, over the Rockies to the valley of the Great Salt Lake in Utah. The Utah land that they

settled was a virtual desert, but the Mormons quickly set to work irrigating it. Lacking foreign or eastern capital to back them, they relied on cooperation and communalism. The church established and controlled water supplies, stores, insurance companies, and later factories and mining smelters. By 1882, the Mormons had built a thriving city of more than 150,000 residents in Salt Lake City. Not until 1896, however, when the church discontinued the traditional practice of polygamy, did Congress grant Utah statehood.

One historian has noted, not entirely facetiously, that there were at least eight oppressed races in the West—Indians, Latinos, Chinese, Japanese, blacks, Mormons, strikers, and radicals.

Prospectors and cowboys have a special place in the folklore of the West. Yet by the 1870s, both mining and cattle had become big business. (See "The Promise of Technology,"page 588.) The colorful prospector, with his pan and his burro, gave way to huge underground operations and quartz mines in which rock was crushed to extract gold and base metals. Corporate control of the industry replaced individual prospecting, and New York replaced San Francisco as the center of speculation in mining stock.

The story of mining in the West is a tale of one rush after another in lands rich with gold, silver, lead, zinc, and copper. Boomtown to ghost town in a matter of years was a pattern common in western mining, a pattern that left an ominous legacy of reckless exploitation. Labor as well as land was harshly treated. Miners in the West, like their counterparts in Kentucky, worked for low wages in dangerous conditions. In a scenario familiar in the East, desperate miners in Coeur d'Alene, Idaho, struck for union recognition in 1892, only to be put down by state troops.

Like mining, cattle ranching became a big business in the 1870s. On the range, the cowboy gave way to the cattle king. Cattle ranchers followed the railroads onto the plains, establishing between 1865 and 1885 a cattle kingdom from Texas to Wyoming. By 1886, cattle overcrowded the range. Severe blizzards during the next two winters decimated the

Hydraulic Mining

INDIVIDUAL PROSPECTORS WHO MADE the first gold strikes in California in 1849 employed a simple process known as placer mining. "No capital is required to obtain this gold, as the laboring man wants nothing but his pick and shovel and tin pan with which to dig and wash the gravel." But when the easy pickings along the rivers and streams gave out, a good deal of gold still remained trapped in quartz or buried deep in the earth, extractable only by methods far beyond the means and capacity of the average prospector.

Soon technology and capital invaded the diggings. As early as 1853 a French Canadian sail maker, Antoine Chabot, hoping to avoid the cost and labor of digging a long feeder ditch to get water to his claim, stitched together heavy strips of canvas and made a 100-foot length of hose. Building on this invention, a Connecticut forty-niner named Edward Matteson marveled at the power of the new technology he called "hydraulicking." "Ten men who own a claim are enabled . . . by directing streams of water against the base of a high bank to cut away such an extent as to cause immense slides of earth which often bring with them large trees and heavy boulders." Tons of fallen earth "are carried away through the sluices with almost as much rapidity as if they were a bank of [melting] snow."

The speed and efficiency of hydraulic mining promised more gold in less time for less work and consequently with fewer workers. With water doing the labor formerly provided by pick and shovel, prospectors who came to the goldfields to make a fortune ended up settling for four dollars a day, a decent wage for the time, but no way to get rich quick.

Hydraulic mining industrialized gold mining, introducing what amounted to a form of mass production that involved all the features of modern, capital-intensive industry: corporations trading shares on an international market, engineers installing large and expensive works and equipment, and wage laborers replacing prospectors. By the 1880s the Army Corps of Engineers estimated that some $100 million had been spent to build California's hydraulic mining system. The results proved worth it for the mine owners. Hydraulic mining produced 90 percent of California's gold.

Eager to make a quick profit, the purveyors of this new technology gave little thought to its impact on the environment. Hydraulic mining used a prodigious amount of water—two large nozzles could shoot out 1,700,000 gallons a day. These huge water cannons demolished entire mountains, devastating streambeds and creating heaps of rubble. Thomas Starr King, a young Unitarian minister visiting hydraulic mining operations near Nevada City, California, was appalled by the sight that greeted him. Huge nozzles blasted water, "tearing all the beauty out of the landscape and setting up 'the abomination of desolation' in its place." He grimly predicted, "If the hydraulic mining method is to be infinitely used, without restraint, upon all the surface that will yield a good return, then California of the future will be a waste more repulsive than any denounced in prophecy. . . ."

Angry farmers protested that hydraulic mines discharged tailings (debris) that filled channels and forced rivers out of their banks, causing devastating floods. Farms were swept away and cattle herds. "A whole generation of cowmen," wrote one chronicler, "went dead broke." After the crash in 1887, cattle ranching, like mining, became largely a corporate business with distant boards of directors in the East and wage-earning workers on the range.

The cowboy, that symbol of American independence, became, like the miner, a wage laborer. Though the cowboy was more colorful than his eastern counterparts in the factory, his life was no easier. Many cowboys were African Americans and Mexicans, although western literature chose to ignore that fact and transformed the black cowboy Deadwood Dick into a white man. Like many other dissatisfied workers, cowboys organized labor unions in the 1880s and mounted strikes in both Texas and Wyoming.

The American West in the nineteenth century witnessed more than its share of bloodshed. Vio-

HYDRAULIC MINING AND THE ENVIRONMENT

Hydraulic mining of California's gold ripped up the landscape, creating waterfalls, as seen in this picture. The pipes connected to the huge hoses, capable of washing away entire hills. The debris filled the rivers and led to devastating floods that wiped out entire farms.

California History Section, California State Library.

drowned. Millions of cubic yards of silt from the hydraulic tailings washed down and covered farms with a muddy sand—slickens—two to seven feet deep, destroying all hopes of vegetation. Orchards and fields disappeared each year under new layers of mining debris.

In 1875, farmers organized. But after four years of litigation the California Supreme Court ruled in favor of the miners. Gold remained king in California. Through the 1880s silver as well as gold drew miners to Nevada and Colorado. As mining moved on, so went the new technology. Between 1860 and 1880 mechanized mining took $300 million in gold and silver from Nevada's Comstock Lode alone. Not until the mid-1880s, when California's economy tilted from mining to agriculture and wheat became California's new gold, did farmers finally succeed in winning a court injunction against hydraulic mining. Renegade miners continued to use hydraulic methods until the 1890s, when more aggressive enforcement finally silenced the great hoses. The sounds of nature eventually returned to the California foothills and the rivers began to run clear.

lence broke out between cattle ranchers and sheep ranchers, between ranchers and farmers, between strikers and bosses, between rival Indian groups, and between whites and those whom they judged "lesser breeds." At issue was who would control the vast resources of the emerging region. Each group claimed the public domain as its own, and each group was prepared to fight for it. In the ensuing struggle for preeminence, the biggest losers with the most broken promises were those with the best claim to the land, the Americans who had been living on it since before Columbus or Coronado or de Soto arrived.

The Final Removal of the Indians

In the 1830s, President Andrew Jackson initiated the policy of Indian removal by pushing the Cherokee,

Choctaw, Chickasaw, Creek, and Seminole tribes off their lands in the southern United States. Jackson's Indian removal forced thousands of men, women, and children to leave their homes in Georgia and Tennessee and walk hundreds of miles to lands across the Mississippi River. So many died of hunger, exhaustion, and disease along the way that the Cherokees called their path "the trail on which we cried." At the end of this trail of tears stood the Great Plains. Here, the government promised the Indians, they could remain "as long as grass shall grow."

But in the 1840s, the gold rush in California, the Mexican War, and Oregon land fever put an end to the promise. Settlers repeatedly trespassed onto Indian land and then were surprised when they encountered hostility. Indignantly, they demanded protection from the U.S. army. The result was thirty years of Indian wars that culminated in a final removal of the Indians.

The Indian wars on the plains lasted from 1861 until 1890. By the time they ended, only 250,000 Native Americans remained of the estimated 2.5 million who had lived on the continent when Columbus landed. To Americans filled with theories of racial superiority, the Indian constituted, in the words of a Colorado militia major, "an obstacle to civilization." Testifying before a congressional com-

mission in 1864, the major concluded that they "should be exterminated." The federal government, acting through the army, adopted a different policy, succinctly summed up by General William T. Sherman: "Rather remove all to a safe place and then reduce them to a helpless condition." The government herded the Indians into ever dwindling reservations where the U.S. Bureau of Indian Affairs, a badly managed, weak agency, often acting through corrupt agents, supposedly ministered to their needs (Map 16.2).

On the plains, the Sioux, Cheyenne, Arapaho, Nez Perce, Comanche, Kiowa, Ute, Apache, and Navajo nations put up a determined resistance. The Indian wars involved violence and atrocities on both sides. (See "Historical Question," page 592.) In 1864 at Sand Creek, Colonel John M. Chivington, leader of the local Colorado militia, slaughtered an entire village of Cheyenne. An upright Methodist elder, Chivington watched as his men mutilated their hapless victims and later justified the killing of Indian children with the terse remark "Nits make lice." The city of Denver treated Chivington and his men as heroes, but after a congressional inquiry he was forced to resign his commission to avoid court-martial.

Two years later, the Cheyenne united with the Sioux and retaliated on the Bozeman Trail in

INDIANS
Sevara, identified as a Ute chieftain, poses with three generations of his family in this photograph. Pictures like this one depict a way of life that by the end of the nineteenth century was already becoming extinct. Only in posed photographs carefully crafted for public consumption did the proud history of Native Americans seem able to survive.
From *The Birth of a Century,* KEA Publishing Services, Ltd.

MAP 16.2

The Loss of Indian Lands, 1850–1890

By 1890, western Indians were isolated on small, scattered reservations. Native Americans struggled to retain their land in major battles, from the Santee uprising in Minnesota in 1862 to the massacre at Wounded Knee, South Dakota, in 1890.

Montana and Wyoming. Captain William Fetterman, who had boasted that with eighty men he could ride through the Sioux nation, was killed, along with all eighty-one of his troops. The Sioux's impressive victories led to a treaty in 1868, under which the government promised to give the Indians lands stretching from the Missouri River to the Black Hills in western South Dakota in return for their promise to stop fighting. The great chief Red Cloud led many of his people onto the new reservation. But several young chiefs, among them Crazy Horse of the Oglala band and Sitting Bull of the Hunkpapa, refused to go. Crazy Horse said that he wanted no part of the "piecemeal penning" of his people. Renegade bands of Sioux continued to roam the plains, hunting buffalo.

The buffalo had a more dangerous enemy than the Indian—the railroad. To the Sioux and the Kiowa the buffalo constituted a way of life; they were the source of food, fuel, and shelter and a

Did Whites Teach Indians to Scalp?

IN 1879, JUST THREE YEARS AFTER CUSTER and his troops were massacred at the Little Bighorn, Susette La Flesche, a member of the Omaha tribe, made a national tour to promote justice for Native Americans. Using her Indian name, Bright Eyes, La Flesche made a fascinating spokesperson for Indian rights. Her father, one of the best known of the Omaha chiefs, was of mixed blood, as was his wife. The La Flesche family embraced Christianity and advocated "progressive" Indian policy. Working closely with Presbyterian missionaries, they attacked the use of alcohol and urged Indians to take up farming. Susette grew up in the first frame house on the reservation in Nebraska. All the La Flesche children attended Presbyterian mission school at the Omaha agency. Later Susette and her sisters were sent to boarding school in New Jersey. Susette's sister Susan La Flesche Picotte became the first Indian woman to receive a medical degree, and her brother Francis became the first Indian anthropologist employed by the Smithsonian Institution. To Victorian society, the remarkable La Flesche family offered an inspiring example of the transition from "savagery" to civilization.

Susette La Flesche's East Coast tour was intended to publicize the plight of the Ponca Indians, who had lost their land in one of the many swindles perpetrated by the federal government. Boston audiences expecting an Indian "princess" dressed in deerskin encountered instead an educated young woman in a black velvet bonnet. But for all her modest demeanor, La Flesche did not hesitate in pointing out the routine barbarity of the U.S. army in its treatment of the Plains tribes. In Chicago, she was accosted by a reporter who chided her, pointing to the Indians' "barbarous . . . acts of atrocity upon captives and the bodies of the dead." La Flesche shot back, "Scalping, you mean, I suppose. Don't you know that the white man taught Indians that?" She insisted that "scalping was first practiced in New England on the Penobscot Indians." The General Court of the province of Massachusetts, she informed the reporter, "offered a bounty of forty pounds for every scalp of a male Indian brought in as evidence of his being killed, and for every scalp of a female or male Indian under twelve years, twenty pounds."

A hundred years later, La Flesche's charge that European colonists in New England had taught the Indians to scalp was well on its way to becoming accepted wisdom. Native American author Vine Deloria, in his widely read manifesto *Custer Died for Your Sins* (1969), echoed the belief that eighteenth-century European settlers with their bounty laws had introduced the practice of scalping among the eastern tribes.

Certainly scalping became synonymous with Indian barbarity. Europeans might draw and quarter, burn at the stake, and introduce the tortures of the rack, but Indian mutilation of the dead remained the quintessential symbol of "savagery." Not surprisingly, La Flesche's effort to rehabilitate the popular image of the Indian in 1879 and Deloria's similar effort a century later began by calling into question the Indian origin of scalping. If whites had taught Indians to scalp, who then was the "savage"? As scholars became more sympathetic to the dispossession of American Indians and sought to rehabilitate the stereotype of the fiendish savage, the charge that scalping was a white invention gained wide acceptance. But was it factual? Had the European settlers, with their bounties on scalps, introduced the practice?

Historian James Axtell set out to find the answer. But what sources would provide proof? Axtell drew on the records of early explorers and settlers and on the work of ethnohistorians, who study "primitive" peoples, and archaeologists. All the evidence seemed

SUSETTE LA FLESCHE
Susette La Flesche toured the country in 1879 using her Indian name, Bright Eyes, to publicize the plight of the Ponca Indians. It was La Flesche who alleged that whites had taught the Indians to scalp.
Nebraska State Historical Society.

SCALPED DEAD MAN
A scout and a cavalry officer kneel beside the body of a man who has been killed and scalped. Notice that only the top part of the hair above the forehead has been taken. Indians used a sharp knife to loosen the scalp and then tugged, pulling until the scalp came free with a sound one observer likened to that of a watermelon being split open.

Collection of the J. Paul Getty Museum, Malibu, Calif. *Ralph Morrison, Scalped Hunter near Fort Dodge, Dec. 7, 1868,* by W. S. Soule, albumen, 513/32 3 711/16.

to point in the opposite direction from Susette La Flesche's confident assertion. Among the earliest visitors to American shores, Jacques Cartier in 1535 described "skins of five men's heads, stretched on hoops, like parchment." The practice was widespread, noted by Cartier in the North and by Hernando de Soto's men in Florida and the Southeast. As Axtell carefully demonstrated, "the list of Europeans who found scalping among the eastern Indians in the earliest stages of contact could be extended almost indefinitely."

Furthermore, although Europeans practiced many barbarities during the sixteenth and seventeenth centuries, nowhere was there evidence that they ever scalped their victims. The European languages did not even have a word to describe the practice. Archaeological evidence, too, pointed away from La Flesche's claim. Pre-Columbian skulls collected by early anthropologists showed distinct evidence of scalping.

What role, then, did scalping play in Indian culture? According to ethnohistorians and their Indian subjects, the practice, while widespread, varied markedly from tribe to tribe. Often the scalp served as more than physical proof of valor. The Iroquois believed that after death the soul hovered by the body. To take the scalp, they believed, was to take the spiritual life of the enemy. However, the practice of scalping took on a different character during the French and Indian War when both sides offered their Indian allies bounties for scalps, sometimes as much as one hundred pounds (roughly two hun-

dred dollars) for every scalp of an adult male. Soon the trading of scalps became part of the complex web that bound Indians and whites in colonial commerce. In Salem, Massachusetts, scalps that had been redeemed for bounties decorated the walls of the town courthouse until it was torn down in 1785.

By the nineteenth century, bounties had long been outlawed, and scalping existed among the Plains Indians in the context of tribal practice. Black Elk, an Oglala Sioux, recounted how he took his first scalp and proudly presented the trophy to his mother for her approval.

One final intriguing piece of the puzzle is the question of how Custer escaped scalping. Well known for his flowing locks, Custer, by all accounts, was not scalped after the battle, as were many of his men. Although no soldier lived to describe the battle scene, Indian accounts are unanimous in their assertion that Custer's body was not mutilated, except for one fingertip and a pierced eardrum. Why did the Indians not take his scalp for a trophy? In large part the answer has changed as Custer's fortunes with historians and the public have waxed and waned. At the time of his death, when Custer was viewed as a brave martyr, writers conjectured that his Indian foes respected his bravery and refused to mutilate the man they called Pahuska, or Long Hair. As Custer's reputation sank to low ebb in the mid-twentieth century, writers became more skeptical. One author guessed that Custer, who was balding by 1879 and had cut his hair right before the battle, was spared because from a warrior's point of view his scalp made a poor trophy.

central part of religion and ritual. To the railroads the buffalo were a nuisance, at best a target for sport and a source of cheap meat for the workers. Buffalo hunters hired by the railroads decimated the great herds; sport hunters fired at random from railroad cars just for the thrill of it. In the heyday of buffalo hunting in the 1880s, hunters sold as many as fifty thousand hides at a time to tanneries in the East. In thirty years, more than sixty million animals were slaughtered. General Philip Sheridan applauded the hunters for "destroying the Indians' commissary." The army took credit for subduing the Indians, but their defeat came about more as a result of the decimation of the buffalo herds.

In 1876, rumors of gold in the Black Hills effectively nullified the government's promise to Red Cloud. Miners began pouring into the area, and the Northern Pacific Railroad made plans to build tracks. Lt. Col. George Armstrong Custer fed the fever by trumpeting news of the first gold strikes. Under the leadership of Crazy Horse and Sitting Bull, the Sioux tribes massed to resist the incursion. In June, Custer led the two hundred men of the Seventh Cavalry into the largest group of Indians ever assembled in one place on the plains. At the Little Bighorn River in Montana Territory, four thousand Sioux warriors set upon them. No federal soldier lived to tell the story, but Crazy Horse, Sitting Bull, and others recounted the killing of Pahuska or Long Hair, as the Indians called the dashing Custer. Their victory was short-lived. In the next year, Crazy Horse was killed and Sitting Bull surrendered. Chief Joseph of the Nez Perce resisted removal and fled toward Canada. Just forty miles from freedom, federal troops caught up with his band. With his people cold and starving, the chief surrendered. His speech stands as an eloquent statement of the plight of the Indians: "I am tired of fighting. Our chiefs are killed. . . . It is cold and we have no blankets. The little children are freezing to death. My people, some of them, have run away to the hills, and have no blankets, no food; no one knows where they are—perhaps freezing to death. I want to have time to look for my children and see how many I can find. Maybe I shall find them among the dead. Hear me, my chiefs, I am tired; my heart is sick and sad. From where the sun now stands, I will fight no more forever."

The policy of rounding up Indians and herding them onto reservations gained momentum. After

Custer's Last Stand, as the battle in 1876 came to be called, policy toward the Indians toughened. Even the most philanthropic Americans seemed convinced that the Indian way of life must go. Instead of remaining American Indians, they had to become Indian Americans. When Indians resisted, their children were taken off the reservations and sent to special schools to learn white ways—to play the piano, to farm, to act like white Americans.

After Custer's Last Stand, policy toward the Indians toughened. Even the most philanthropic Americans seemed convinced that the Indian way of life must go.

In 1887, Congress passed the Dawes Act, breaking up the reservations and giving each Indian an allotment of land. The act effectively reduced Indian lands from 138 million acres to a scant 48 million, making it, in the words of one critic, "a bill to despoil the Indians of their lands and to make them vagabonds on the face of the earth." The surplus land was then opened to white settlement, setting off the great land rushes in Oklahoma. Well-meaning philanthropists viewed the Dawes Act as a way to foster individualism among the Indians and to extend to them the rights of citizenship. The result of this legislation, however, was the further destruction of Indian culture.

Indian Resistance

Faced with the extinction of their entire way of life and means of livelihood, different groups of Indians responded in different ways. Outright violent resistance was perhaps best embodied in the Apaches of the Southwest, while nonviolent resistance was exemplified in the Ghost Dance religion, a movement that swept the Plains in the 1890s. Both met with the same brutal military repression.

The Apache tribes who roamed the Sonoran desert of southern Arizona and northern Mexico never combined as the Plains Indians had done so successfully at the Little Bighorn. Instead they operated in small raiding parties, perfecting a hit-and-run guerrilla warfare that terrorized white settlers and deviled the army in the 1870s and 1880s. General George Crook, a skilled Indian fighter, combined a policy of dogged pursuit with judicious diplomacy. Convinced that white troops could not fight the Apaches on their home ground, Crook relied on Indian scouts, recruiting nearly two hundred, to hunt down the Apaches. The Indians welcomed a release from the boredom of reservation life and joined up with Crook. Trained to a life of hunting, tracking, and raiding, even some Apaches proved willing to track their own people. Eventually Crook was able to persuade most of the renegades to surrender. By 1882, the Apaches had settled on the San Carlos reservation in Arizona territory.

Reservation life was particularly difficult for the nomadic Apaches. Geronimo, a recalcitrant chieftain, repeatedly led raiding parties of renegades off the reservation. They were fierce warriors who raided ranches, killing the ranchers and stealing their cattle and horses. In the spring of 1885, Geronimo went on a ten-month rampage, moving from his sanctuary in the Sierra Madre to raid and burn ranches and towns on both sides of the Mexican border. General Crook caught up with Geronimo in the fall, only to have him slip away with a small band on the way back to the San Carlos reservation. Chagrined, Crook resigned his post. General Nelson Miles, Crook's replacement, determined to put an end to Geronimo once and for all, adopted a policy of hunt and destroy.

There were only thirty-three Apaches still at large, thirteen of them women, but they eluded Miles's troops for more than five months. Throughout the blistering summer, the Indians, constantly on the move, kept one step ahead of the army. In the end this small band of Apaches fought two thousand soldiers to a stalemate. Miles, who believed in the superiority of white troops over any Indian, watched as his spit-and-polish cavalry, after months of tracking the elusive Apaches, became barely recognizable as soldiers. Lt. Leonard Wood, one of only two white soldiers who rode with the scouts to the end, discarded his horse and most of his clothes. Reduced to wearing nothing "but a pair of canton flannel drawers, and an old blue blouse, a pair of moccasins and a hat without a crown," Wood had trouble convincing one Indian party that he was a soldier at all.

Eventually the scouts tracked down Geronimo and his band. Caught between Mexican regulars and the American army, the chieftain agreed to march north with the soldiers and negotiate a set-

tlement. "We have not slept for six months," Geronimo admitted, "and we are worn out." He met with General Miles to negotiate a peace, but, as in the past, the Indians did not get what they were promised.

Fewer than three dozen Apaches had been hostile when General Miles induced them to surrender, yet the government gathered up nearly five hundred Apaches and sent them as prisoners to Florida, including the scouts who had helped track Geronimo. By 1889, more than a quarter of them had died, some by illness contracted in the damp, lowland climate and some by suicide. Their plight roused public opinion and eventually, in 1892, they were moved to Fort Sill in Oklahoma and later to New Mexico.

Geronimo lived to become something of a celebrity. He appeared at the St. Louis Exposition in 1904, where he sold pictures of himself for twenty-five cents apiece, and rode in President Theodore Roosevelt's inaugural parade in 1905. In a newspaper interview he confessed, "I want to go to my old home before I die. . . . Want to go back to the mountains again. I asked the Great White Father to allow me to go back, but he said no." None of the Apaches were permitted to return to Arizona; when Geronimo died in 1909, he was buried in Oklahoma.

On the plains many different tribes turned to a nonviolent form of resistance—a compelling new religion, the Ghost Dance. The Paiute shaman Wovoka, drawing on a cult that had developed in the 1870s, combined elements of Christianity and traditional Indian religion to found the Ghost Dance religion in 1889. Wovoka claimed that he had received a vision in which the Great Spirit spoke through him to all Indians, urging them to unite and promising that whites would be destroyed in an apocalypse. The Indian warriors slain in battle would return to life, and buffalo once again would roam the land unimpeded.

This religion of despair with its message of hope spread like wildfire over the plains. It was danced in Idaho, Montana, Utah, Wyoming, Colorado, Nebraska, Kansas, the Dakotas, and Oklahoma Territory by tribes as diverse as the Arapaho, Cheyenne, Pawnee, and Shoshone. Various tribes developed different forms of the dance, but all dances were held in a circle. Often dancers went into hypnotic trances. Some danced until they dropped from sheer physical exhaustion.

GHOST DANCE DRESS
This deerskin dress was worn by an Arapaho woman during the Ghost Dance fervor of the 1880s in Oklahoma. Decorated with stars and eagles, it evoked powerful magic to protect its wearer.
National Museum of the American Indian.

In December 1889, when Sitting Bull sought permission to go to the Pine Ridge reservation to meet with Wovoka, the local Indian agent laid a trap for him, and Sitting Bull was shot. His people, fleeing the scene, were apprehended by the Seventh Cavalry, Custer's old regiment, near Wounded Knee Creek, South Dakota. As the Indians laid down their arms, a shot rang out and the army opened fire. In the ensuing melee, Indian warriors stormed the troops, killing more than thirty soldiers. But they were badly outgunned. Men, women, and children were mowed down in minutes by the army's brutally efficient Hotchkiss machine guns. More than two hundred Sioux lay dead or dying in the snow. Settler Jules Sandoz surveyed the scene the day after the massacre. "Here in ten minutes an entire community was as the buffalo that bleached on the plains," he wrote. "There was something loose in the world that hated joy and happiness as it hated brightness and color, reducing everything to drab agony and gray."

Although the massacre at Wounded Knee did not end the story of Native Americans, it did eliminate their way of life. The Indian population would gradually recover; the 1990 census showed 1.9 million Native Americans. But their culture sustained a crushing blow. In the words of the visionary Black Elk, "The nation's hoop is broken and scattered. There is no center any longer, and the sacred tree is dead."

The West of the Imagination

Even as the Old West was dying, the myth of the West was being created. The dime novel, a precursor of today's paperback, capitalized on western heroes like Kit Carson, Wild Bill Hickok, Calamity Jane, and Deadwood Dick to entertain eastern readers seeking escapist fare. Published in the East and sometimes written by tenderfeet who had never ventured beyond the Hudson River, dime novels sold at a prodigious rate.

The prince of the dime novel heroes was Buffalo Bill, featured in more than two hundred titles. Born William F. Cody, the real-life Buffalo Bill had panned for gold, ridden for the Pony Express, scouted for the army, and earned his nickname hunting buffalo for the railroad. A masterful showman, he capitalized on his success and formed the touring Wild West Company in 1883. Part circus, part theater, the Wild West extravaganza featured

Ghost Dances were generally nonviolent, but among the Sioux, especially the Oglala, Blackfeet, and Hunkpapa, the dance took on a more militant flavor. Sioux disciples of the Ghost Dance religion taught that the wearing of white ghost shirts made Indians immune to the bullets of the soldiers. Their message frightened whites, who began to fear an uprising. "Indians are dancing in the snow and are wild and crazy," wrote the Bureau of Indian Affairs agent at the Pine Ridge reservation in South Dakota. Frantic, he pleaded for reinforcements. "We are at the mercy of these dancers. We need protection, and we need it now." President Benjamin Harrison dispatched several thousand federal troops to Sioux country to handle any outbreak.

BUFFALO BILL POSTER
Buffalo Bill Cody used colorful posters to publicize his Wild West Show during the
1880s and 1890s. One of his most popular features was the reenactment of Custer's Last
Stand, which he performed for Queen Victoria in London and at the World Columbian
Exposition in Chicago.
Buffalo Bill Historical Center, Cody, Wyoming.

exhibitions of riding, shooting, and roping and presented dramatic reenactments of great moments in western U.S. history. The star of the show was Phoebe Moses Butler, whose stage name was Annie Oakley. Dubbed "Little Miss Sure Shot," she delighted the crowd by shooting a dime out of her husband's hand. The centerpiece of Buffalo Bill's Wild West Show was the reenactment of Custer's Last Stand, in which Indians in war paint and bonnets massacred the hapless Custer and his men. At the end, Buffalo Bill galloped in with a cloud of dust and dramatically mouthed the words "Too late!"

The Wild West that Buffalo Bill presented indiscriminately mixed the authentic with the romantic until reality itself blurred in the popular mind. Cody had not arrived too late at the Little

Bighorn. But some of the Indians in his troupe had been there and knew their parts firsthand. During the 1885 season, Sitting Bull, a veteran of the Little Bighorn, toured with Buffalo Bill. The rapid demise of the Wild West that Buffalo Bill enshrined in his show may perhaps best be comprehended if we juxtapose Cody with historian Frederick Jackson Turner. At the 1893 Columbian Exposition in Chicago, Turner addressed the American Historical Association on "The Significance of the Frontier in American History." Turner postulated that the frontier had vanished, that by 1890 American settlers had filled the map of the West so that no clear frontier line could be discerned. Later historians would take issue with Turner's thesis that what made America unique was some fixed, retreating frontier.

But the sense of an old world passing that Turner summed up in his speech was perhaps nowhere better demonstrated than across the Chicago fairground in the spectacle of Buffalo Bill's Wild West Show performing to sellout crowds in the bleachers. The high drama of the struggle for the West by 1893 had become no more than a thrilling but harmless entertainment.

The Wild West that Buffalo Bill presented indiscriminately mixed the authentic with the romantic until reality itself blurred in the popular mind.

The West of the imagination, the West of Buffalo Bill, of artists Frederic Remington and Albert Bierstadt, of novelists Owen Wister and Zane Grey, shrouded the region in myth. Yet the historical reality was every bit as dramatic as the fictions it sparked: By the 1890s, the American West had been transformed. More than seven-tenths of the farmland west of the Mississippi River was owned by investors who neither farmed nor ranched the land themselves. The shift from farming and ranching to agribusiness, not the disappearance of some magical frontier line, marked the end of an era in America. Far from being a mythic landscape out of place and time, the West was linked inextricably to the urban East by capital investment and iron rails that carried western goods to world markets.

The Rise of the City

Although much of the nation remained heavily rural, the last decades of the nineteenth century witnessed an urban explosion. Cities and towns grew more than twice as rapidly as the total population, far outstripping rural growth. Patterns of global migration contributed to the ascendancy of urban America. In the port cities, immigrants from southern and eastern Europe lived in dense ghettos where the English language was rarely heard. The word *slum* entered the American vocabulary during these years and with it a growing concern over the gap between the rich and the poor, a gap only widened by the changing social geography of the cities.

The Urban Explosion, a Global Migration

"We cannot all live in cities, yet nearly all seem determined to do so," New York editor Horace Greeley complained. The astonishing growth that occurred in the nation's cities between 1870 and 1900 came about not from the natural increase of the city population but from the internal and international movement of people. The percentage of people living in towns and cities leapt from 20 percent in 1870 to 33 percent by 1900. Growth in the urban population was actually divided about evenly between large and small cities. But the emergence of the modern metropolis marked the most dramatic demographic development of the period. The number of cities with more than 100,000 inhabitants jumped from eighteen in 1870 to thirty-eight by 1900. As the twentieth century began, the United States could boast three cities with more than a million inhabitants—New York, Chicago, and Philadelphia.

Railroad growth stimulated urban development. Cities like Reno, Butte, and Cheyenne sprang up along the tracks long before the surrounding countryside was settled. The transcontinental rail lines set off booms in Kansas City, Omaha, and Salt Lake City.

The astonishing growth that occurred in the nation's cities between 1870 and 1900 came about not from the natural increase of the city population but from the internal and international movement of people.

Urbanization went hand in hand with industrialization. As workers left the farm for the factory, the growth of the urban population fueled a constantly expanding market. In a process that economists call the multiplier effect, the growing market in turn stimulated greater and greater production, creating more jobs in an expanding spiral. The emergence of a mass consumer market enabled cities to become centers for wholesaling and retailing, not just manufacturing and industry. Chicago, with its mail order houses like Montgomery Ward and Sears, Roebuck, along with its great department stores, Marshall Field and Carson Pirie Scott, led the country as an urban marketing center.

The United States grew up in the country and moved to the city, or so it seemed by the twentieth century. Hundreds of thousands of farm boys and girls ran away to the city looking for jobs in the burgeoning industrial centers and hoping to make their fortunes. But for at least one group, the move to the city promised something more. African Americans came north looking not just for economic opportunity. Restrictive laws that segregated blacks, called Jim Crow laws, became common throughout the South in the decades following reconstruction. The South's efforts to segregate and subordinate African Americans gained federal endorsement when in 1896 the United States Supreme Court, in the landmark case *Plessy v. Ferguson,* upheld the legality of segregated facilities under the doctrine of "separate but equal." Intimidation and lynching, justified by white Southerners as necessary to "keep the Negro in his place," also became increasingly common throughout the South. "To die from the bite of frost is far more glorious than at the hands of a mob," proclaimed the *Defender,* Chicago's largest African American newspaper. As early as the 1890s, many blacks agreed. They moved North, settling for the most part in the growing cities. Racial discrimination and poverty limited blacks' options in the North, just as they had in the South. Yet by 1900, New York, Philadelphia, and Chicago contained the largest black communities in the nation. Although the greatest African American migration out of the South would occur during and after the end of World War I, the great exodus was already under way.

Rural migrants to the cities were by no means limited to American farmers and southern blacks. Worldwide in scope, the movement from rural areas to industrial centers attracted to the United States more than fourteen million Europeans in the waning decades of the nineteenth century. That migration came in two distinct waves that have been called the old and the new immigration. (See page A-61 in the appendix.) Before 1880, the bulk of the new arrivals came from northern and western Europe, with the Germans, Irish, English, and Scandinavians making up approximately 85 percent of the newcomers.

After 1880, the pattern shifted, with more and more immigrant ships carrying passengers from southern and eastern Europe. Italians, Hungarians, eastern European Jews, Turks, Armenians, and Poles, Russians, and other Slavic peoples accounted for more than 80 percent of all the immigrants by 1896 (Figure 16.2). Alongside the tide of new European immigrants streamed Japanese coming east from Asia, French Canadians flowing south to work in New England's mill towns, and Mexicans and other Latin Americans heading north to settle in California and the Southwest (Map 16.3).

In sheer numbers, the new immigration was unprecedented. In 1888 alone, more than half a million Europeans came to America, 75 percent landing in New York City. The Statue of Liberty, a gift from the people of France erected in 1886, stood sentinel in the harbor. A young Jewish girl named Emma Lazarus penned the verse at Liberty's base:

> Give me your tired, your poor,
> Your huddled masses yearning to breathe free,
> The wretched refuse of your teeming shore,
> Send these, the homeless, tempest-tost to me,
> I lift my lamp beside the golden door!

IMMIGRANTS

Dressed in the clothing of the old country (cap and collarless shirt, apron and shawl), this immigrant couple carries their meager possessions, bedding in his bundle, food and utensils in her basket, and two umbrellas tied together. Note how the man gazes confidently, almost defiantly, into the camera, while the woman, looking miserable, averts her eyes. What do their postures tell about whose decision it was to come to America and about their hopes and apprehensions?

Wide World Photos, Inc.

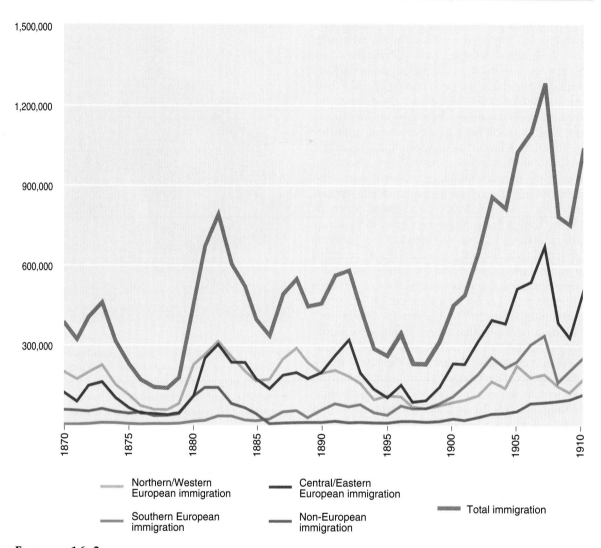

FIGURE 16.2

The Old and the New Immigration, 1870–1910
Southern and eastern Europeans dominated the immigration of the 1880s. Before 1880, over 85 percent of immigrants had come from Western Europe—Germany, Ireland, England, and the Scandinavian countries. After 1880, 80 percent of the new arrivals came from Italy, Turkey, Hungary, and Armenia and Poland, Russia, and other Slavic countries.

The tide of immigrants soon swamped the immigrant office at Castle Garden in lower Manhattan. An imposing new brick facility opened on Ellis Island in New York harbor in 1900. Able to handle 5,000 immigrants a day, it was already inadequate by the time it opened. By 1907, the peak year of immigration, more than one million immigrants passed through the gates at Ellis Island, and on a record day inspectors processed more than 11,700.

New Immigrants and the Call for Immigration Restriction

The new wave of immigration at the turn of the twentieth century resulted from a number of fac-

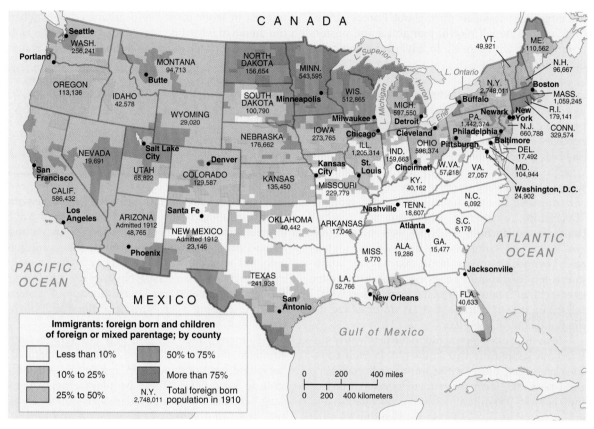

MAP 16.3

The Impact of Immigration to 1910
Immigration flowed in all directions—south from Canada, north from Mexico, east from Asia to the port cities of Seattle and San Francisco, and west from Europe to ports in Boston and New York.

READING THE MAP: What states have high percentages of immigrants? Which cities drew the most immigrants? Which cities the least?
CONNECTIONS: Why did most immigrants gravitate toward cities? Why do you think the South drew such a low percentage of immigrants?

www.bedfordstmartins.com/tap SEE THE ONLINE STUDY GUIDE for more help in analyzing this map.

tors. Improved economic conditions in western Europe, as well as immigration to Australia and Canada, cut down on the flow of "old" immigrants to the United States. At the same time, a protracted economic depression in southern Italy, the religious persecution of Jews in eastern Europe, and a general desire to avoid conscription into the Russian army led many in southern and eastern Europe to move to the United States. (See page A-62 in the appendix.)

Economic factors in the United States also played a role. The need of America's industries for cheap, unskilled labor stimulated immigration during good times. In the depressions following the economic panics of 1873 and 1893, immigration slowed, only to pick up again when prosperity returned. Although the U.S. government did not offer direct inducements to immigrate, the steamship companies courted immigrants, who provided a highly profitable, self-loading cargo. Agents from the large lines traveled throughout Europe drumming up business. Colorful pamphlets and posters mingled fact with fantasy to advertise America as the land of promise.

Would-be immigrants eager for information about America relied on letters, advertisements, and word of mouth—sources that were not always dependable or truthful. Even photographs proved deceptive—American workers dressed in their Sunday best looked more prosperous than they actually were to the eyes of relatives in the old country, where only the very wealthy wore white collars or silk dresses. As one Italian immigrant recalled, "Everything emanating from America reached [Italy] as a distortion. . . . News was colored, success magnified, comforts and advantages exaggerated beyond all proportions." No wonder immigrants left for America believing "that if they were ever fortunate enough to reach America, they would fall into a pile of manure and get up brushing the diamonds out of their hair."

In at least one respect, life in the new world differed markedly from that in the old. In their countries of origin, most of the immigrants had been rural peasants, farmers, and villagers. In America they became urbanites, both out of inclination and out of necessity. By 1900, almost two-thirds of the country's immigrant population resided in cities, drawn by the availability of jobs in the nation's industrial centers at the same time poverty limited their ability to buy land in the West. Although nowhere did the foreign-born population outnumber the native-born population, taken together foreign immigrants and their American-born children did constitute a majority in many of the nation's largest cities. Fifty percent of Philadelphia's population was foreign-born or born of foreign parents, and the percentages were even higher in other cities: 66 percent in Boston, 75 percent in Chicago, and an amazing 80 percent in New York City.

Not all the newcomers came to stay. Perhaps eight million, mostly young men, worked for a year or a season and then returned to their homelands. American immigration officers referred to these young male immigrants as "birds of passage" because they followed a regular pattern of migration to and from the United States. By 1900, almost 75 percent of the new immigrants were single young men. Intent on making money as quickly as possible, they were willing to accept conditions that other workers regarded as intolerable. They showed little interest in labor unions and organized only when the dream of returning home faded, as it did for millions who ultimately remained in the United States.

In their countries of origin, most of the immigrants had been rural peasants, farmers, and villagers. In America they became urbanites, both out of inclination and out of necessity.

Jews from eastern Europe most often came with their families and came to stay. In the 1880s, a wave of violent pogroms, or persecutions, in Russia and Poland led to the departure of more than a million Jews in the next two decades. They settled mostly in the port cities of the East. New York City's Lower East Side replicated the Jewish ghettos of eastern Europe, teeming with street peddlers and pushcarts.

To many Americans, the new immigrants from southern and eastern Europe seemed uneducated, backward, and outlandish in appearance—impossible to assimilate. "These people are not Americans," editorialized the popular journal *Public Opinion*, "they are the very scum and offal of Europe." Terence Powderly, head of the labor organization the Knights of Labor, complained that the newcomers "herded together like animals and lived like beasts." Convinced that the new immigrants were undesirable, groups began to call for measures to limit immigration.

Old-stock aristocrats such as Senator Henry Cabot Lodge of Massachusetts formed an unlikely alliance with organized labor to press for immigration restriction. A precedent for keeping out "undesirable" immigrants had been established in 1882, when labor agitation and racism in California led to passage of the Chinese Exclusion Act. On the East Coast, Lodge and his followers championed a literacy test, a device designed to limit immigration from Italy and eastern Europe by requiring immigrants to demonstrate the ability to read and write in their native language. Since the vast majority of Italian and Slavic peasants had no schooling, it was assumed that few would be able to pass the test. In 1906, Congress approved a literacy test for immigrants, but President Theodore Roosevelt promptly vetoed it. "It is said," the president reminded Congress, "that the quality of recent immigration is un-

STUDIO PORTRAIT OF IMMIGRANTS
Studio portraits of immigrant families, like this one of a Russian Jewish family taken at the turn of the century, showed everyone dressed in their finest clothes—the men in starched shirts and collars, the women in silk dresses or lacy shirtwaists. Mailed back to relatives in Europe, these pictures provided a tantalizing but not always entirely accurate picture of the promise of America.
Collection of Sharon Salinger.

desirable. The time is quite within recent memory when the same thing was said of immigrants, who, with their descendants, are now numbered among our best citizens." Roosevelt's veto forestalled immigration restriction but did not stop the forces seeking to close the gates. They would continue to press for restriction until they achieved their goal in the 1920s.

The Social Geography of the City

In the 1870s, Cleveland, Ohio, was a small city, in both population and geographical area. Oil magnate John D. Rockefeller could, and often did, walk from his large brick house on Euclid Avenue to his office downtown. On his way he passed the small homes of his clerks and other middle-class families. Behind these homes ran miles of alleys crowded with the dwellings of Cleveland's working class. Farther out, on the shores of Lake Erie, close to the factories and foundries, clustered the shanties of the city's poorest laborers.

Within two decades, the Cleveland that Rockefeller knew no longer existed. The coming of mass transit transformed the walking city. In its place emerged a central business district surrounded by concentric rings of residences graded by ethnicity and income. First the horsecar in the 1870s and then the electric streetcar in the 1880s made it possible to commute to work. City workers could enjoy single-family homes with lawns, gardens, and trees and still travel to work downtown for as little as five cents a day. By the early twentieth century, more than half of Cleveland's residents rode the streetcars to work. This pattern of development was repeated throughout the country as urban congestion and suburban sprawl forever altered the social geography of the city.

The city's poor, unable to afford even the few cents for trolley fare, crowded into the inner city or lived "back of the yards" near the factories where they worked. The term *slum* came into common use by the mid-nineteenth century, coinciding with the increased clustering of the poor in the least desirable areas of the city. This social segregation—rich and poor, ethnic and old-stock Americans—was one of the major social changes engendered by the rise of the industrial metropolis, and it occurred not only in Cleveland but in cities across the nation.

Race and ethnicity affected the way in which cities evolved. Newcomers to the burgeoning cities, whether Jews and Italians "just off the boat" or African Americans up from the South, sought out their kin and countryfolk and struggled to maintain their culture in distinct neighborhoods that often

HOW BOTH HALVES LIVED
The gap between the rich and poor documented so successfully in Jacob Riis's **How the Other Half Lives** *(1890) is underscored here by juxtaposing the photographs of two women. Riis took the photograph above left of a "scrub" or washer woman in one of the notorious Police Station lodging houses, the shelters of last resort for the city's poor. Notice how large and misshapen her hands are from her heavy work. To the right is Alice Vanderbilt as she appeared as "The Spirit of Electricity" at the Vanderbilt costume ball in 1883. Her gown, by the French designer Worth, was no doubt inspired by Thomas Edison's triumphant lighting of lower Manhattan six months earlier. Silk satin, velvet-trimmed with gilt metallic bullion and diamonds, the gown epitomized what political economist Thorstein Veblen would call "conspicuous consumption."*
Riis photograph courtesy of the Museum of the City of New York. Vanderbilt photograph courtesy of the Collection of the New-York Historical Society.

formed around the synagogue or church. Blacks typically experienced the greatest residential segregation, but every large city had its ethnic neighborhoods, its Little Italy, Chinatown, Bohemia Flats, or Germantown, where one could walk for blocks without hearing a word of English.

In 1890, a young police reporter named Jacob Riis took his notebook and his camera into the tenements of New York's Lower East Side; the result was the best-selling book *How the Other Half Lives.*

Riis invited his audience into a Cherry Street tenement:

Be careful please! The hall is dark and you might stumble over the children pitching pennies back there. . . . Close? Yes! What would you have? All the fresh air that ever enters these stairs comes from the hall door and it is forever slamming, and from the windows of dark bedrooms that in turn receive from the stairs their sole supply of the elements God meant to be free, but man deals out with such niggardly hand. . . .

Here is a door. Listen! That short hacking cough, that tiny, helpless wail—what do they mean? They mean that the soiled bow of white you saw on the door downstairs will have another story to tell—Oh! a sadly familiar story—before the day is at an end. The child is dying with measles. With half a chance it might have lived; but it had none. That dark bedroom killed it.

As Riis discovered, poverty, crowding, dirt, and disease constituted the daily reality of New York's poor. Riis's book, like his photographs, presented a world of black and white. There were many layers to the population Riis labeled "the other half," distinctions furthered by ethnicity, religion, race, and gender. *How the Other Half Lives* must be read more as a social reformer's call to action than as an accurate portrayal.

Jacob Riis's audience shivered at his revelations about the "other half." But middle-class Americans worried equally about excesses of the wealthy and class antagonism fueled by the growing chasm between rich and poor. Many people shared Riis's view that "the real danger to society comes not only from the tenements, but from the ill-spent wealth which reared them."

Jacob Riis's audience shivered at his revelations about the "other half." But middle-class Americans worried equally about excesses of the wealthy and class antagonism fueled by the growing chasm between rich and poor.

The excesses of newly minted millionaires in the decades following the Civil War were nowhere more visible than in the lifestyle of the Vanderbilts. "Commodore" Cornelius Vanderbilt, the uncouth ferryman who built the New York Central Railroad, died in 1877, leaving his son $90 million. William Vanderbilt doubled that sum and his two sons proceeded to spend it on Fifth Avenue mansions and on "cottages" in Newport, Rhode Island, which, with their marble and gold leaf, sought to rival the palaces of Europe. In 1883, Alva Vanderbilt (Mrs. William K. Vanderbilt I) determined to gain admittance to old New York society, which had resisted the inclusion of the *nouveaux riches* (newly rich). She threw a costume party so lavish that no one could

resist an invitation. Dressed as a Venetian princess, the hostess greeted her twelve hundred guests. But her sister-in-law capped the evening, appearing in costume as that miraculous new invention, the electric light, resplendent in a white satin evening dress studded with diamonds. Many costumes cost as much as $1,500 apiece, three times the average yearly wage of a worker. The New York *World* speculated that the party cost over a quarter of a million dollars. Alva got her money's worth. One guest observed that the ball had placed the Vanderbilts "at the top of the heap in what is recognized as good society in New York."

Such ostentatious displays of wealth became even more alarming when they were coupled with disdain for the general welfare of the people. When a reporter in 1882 asked William Vanderbilt whether he considered the public good in running his railroads, he shot back, "The public be damned." The fear that America had become a plutocracy—a society ruled by the rich—gained credence from the fact that the wealthiest one percent of the population owned more than half the real and personal property in the country (a century later, the top one percent controlled less than a quarter).

City Life and City Images

In America, private enterprise built the cities. Boosters, builders, businessmen, planners, and politicians all had a hand in creating the modern city. With a few notable exceptions, such as Washington, D.C., there was no such thing as a comprehensive city plan. Cities simply mushroomed, formed by the dictates of private enterprise and the exigencies of local politics. With the rise of the city came the need for public facilities, transportation, and services that would tax the imaginations of America's architects and engineers and set the scene for the rough-and-tumble story of big-city government, politics, and politicians.

Big-City Government and the "Bosses"

The physical growth of the cities required the expansion of public services and the creation of entirely new facilities: streets, subways, elevated trains, bridges, docks, parks, sewers, and public utilities. There was work to be done and money to be made. The professional politician—the colorful big-city boss—became a phenomenon of nineteenth-century urban growth. Although corrupt and often criminal, the boss saw to the building of the city and provided needed social services for the new residents. Yet not even the big-city boss could be said to rule the unruly city. The governing of America's cities resembled more a tug-of-war than boss rule.

The most notorious of all the city bosses was William Marcy Tweed of New York. At midcentury, Boss Tweed's Democratic Party machine held sway. A machine was really no more than a political party organized on the grassroots level. It existed to win elections and reward its followers with jobs on the city's payroll. New York's citywide Democratic organization, Tammany Hall, consisted of an army of party functionaries. At the bottom were the district captains. In return for votes, they provided services for their constituents, everything from a scuttle of coal in the winter to housing for an evicted family. At the top were the powerful ward bosses who distributed lucrative franchises for subways and streetcars. They formed a shadow government, more powerful than the city's elected officials. Tweed held the official title of alderman. But as a ward boss and chairman of the Tammany general committee, he wielded more power than the mayor. Through the use of bribery and graft, he held the Democratic Party together and ran the city.

The cost of Tweed's rule was staggering. The construction of New York City's courthouse, budgeted at $250,000, ended up costing the taxpayers $14 million. The inflated sum represented bribery, kickbacks, and the greasing of many palms. The excesses of the Tweed ring soon led to a clamor for reform and cries of "Throw the rascals out." Cartoonist Thomas Nast pilloried Tweed in the pages of *Harper's Weekly*. His cartoons, easily understood even by those who could not read, did the boss more harm than hundreds of outraged editorials. Tweed fled to Europe in 1871 to avoid prosecution, but eventually he was tried and convicted and died in jail.

New York was not the only city to experience bossism and corruption. The British visitor James Bryce concluded in 1888, "There is no denying that the government of cities is the one conspicuous failure of the United States." More than 80 percent of the nation's thirty largest cities experienced some form of boss rule in the decades around the turn of the twentieth century.

Infighting among powerful ward bosses was more typical in municipal government than domination by one big-city boss. "Czar" Martin Lomasney in Boston and Chicago's "Bathhouse" John Coughlin and Michael "Hinky Dink" Kenna exemplified the breed. Their colorful nicknames signaled their distance from respectable society and hinted at unsavory connections with an underworld of crime and vice. The power they wielded belied the charge that any single boss enjoyed hegemony in the big cities.

Occasionally, a political strategist of more than ordinary skill emerged to become a bona fide boss. Less notorious but more powerful than Boss Tweed was Richard Croker of New York. Croker, who ruled Tammany Hall beginning in 1886, relied more on bureaucracy than boodle (bribery). He directed the distribution of lucrative construction contracts, con-

TAMMANY BANK
This cast-iron bank, a campaign novelty, is named after the New York City Democratic machine. It tells its political reform message graphically: When you put a penny into the politician's hand, he puts it in his pocket. Tammany Hall dominated city politics for more than a century, dispensing contracts and franchises worth millions of dollars. Some of those dollars invariably found their way into the pockets of Tammany politicians.
Collection of Janice L. and David J. Frent.

trolled franchises for street railways and public utilities, and made sure these plums went to men who supported the party machine. Like Tweed, Croker held no elective office. As boss, he did not want to govern; he simply wanted to ensure that he and his supporters benefited from government. Unlike Tweed, who died in jail, Croker retired in 1901 to Wantage, his country estate in Ireland, a move that led one of his critics to quip,"New York's wastage is Croker's Wantage."

In the late nineteenth century, urban reformers and proponents of good government (derisively called "goo goos" by their rivals) challenged machine rule and sometimes succeeded in electing reform mayors. But the reformers rarely managed to stay in office for long. Their detractors called them "mornin' glories," observing that they "looked lovely in the mornin' and withered up in a short time." New York's William Strong is a fair example of the breed. A businessman, he won office in 1894 on the basis of his reputation for honesty and integrity. But Strong lacked the political skills needed to win reelection.

The bosses enjoyed continued success over the reformers for one main reason: the help the urban political machine handed out to the cities' immigrants and poor. In return for votes the machine provided legal aid, jobs, fuel, temporary shelter, and a host of small favors. The ability to combine philanthropy and politics was a hallmark of the urban boss. "What tells in holding your district is to go right down among the poor and help them in the different ways they need help," a Tammany ward boss observed. "It's philanthropy, but it's politics, too—mighty good politics." For the social services they received (and not because they were ignorant or undemocratic, as critics charged), the urban poor remained the bosses' staunchest allies.

Some reform mayors managed to achieve success and longevity. In cities where they sponsored public services and championed the working class, reformers proved as unbeatable as any boss. Hazen S. Pingree of Detroit exemplified the successful reform mayor. A businessman who went into politics in the 1890s, Pingree, like most good-government candidates, promised to root out dishonesty and inefficiency. He did, but he also tangled with business interests when he tried to lower streetcar fares and utility rates. When the depression of 1893 struck, Pingree emerged as a champion of the working class and the poor. He hired the unemployed to build schools, parks, and public baths. And he fought for

and got public ownership of electric utilities. By providing needed services, he built a powerful political organization based on working-class support. Detroit's voters kept him in the mayor's office for four terms and then helped elect him governor twice.

The bosses enjoyed continued success over the reformers for one main reason: the help the urban political machine handed out to the cities' immigrants and poor.

While most good-government candidates harped on the Sunday closing of saloons and attacked vice and crime, Pingree demurred. "The most dangerous enemies to good government are not the saloons, the dives, the dens of iniquity and the criminals," but "the temptations which are offered to city officials when franchises are sought by wealthy corporations, or contracts are to be let for public works."

As Pingree shrewdly observed, not only the urban poor but the business class benefited from bossism and corruption. The boss could juggle tax assessments for property owners and provide lucrative franchises. Through the skillful orchestration of rewards, an astute political operator like Croker exerted powerful leverage and lined up support for his party from a broad range of constituents, from the urban poor to wealthy industrialists. When journalist Lincoln Steffens began *The Shame of the Cities* in 1902, a series of articles exposing city corruption, he found that business leaders who fastidiously refused to mingle socially with the bosses nevertheless struck deals with them. "He is a self-righteous fraud, this big businessman," Steffens concluded. "I found him buying boodlers [bribers] in St. Louis, defending grafters in Minneapolis, originating corruption in Pittsburgh, sharing with bosses in Philadelphia, deploring reform in Chicago, and beating good government with corruption funds in New York."

The complexity of big-city government, apparent in the levels of corruption Steffens uncovered, pointed to one conclusion: For all the color and flamboyance of the big-city boss, he was simply one of many actors in the drama of municipal government. The successful boss was not an autocratic ruler but a power broker. Old-stock aristocrats, new professionals, saloon keepers, pushcart peddlers, and politicians all fought for their interests in the hurly-burly of city government. They didn't much like each other and they sometimes fought savagely. But they learned to live with one another. Compromise and accommodation—not boss rule—best characterized big-city government by the turn of the twentieth century.

Building Cities of Stone and Steel

"A town that crawled now stands erect," boasted an ironworker. "And we whose backs were bent above the [open] hearths know how it got its spine." Technology transformed the urban landscape in the late nineteenth and early twentieth centuries. Where once wooden buildings had stood rooted in the mire of unpaved streets, new cities of stone and steel sprang up. The skyscrapers and mighty bridges dominated the imagination and the urban landscape at the turn of the century. Less imposing, but no less significant, were the paved streets, the parks and public libraries, and the subways and sewers. In the late nineteenth century, Americans rushed to embrace new technology, making their cities the most modern in the world.

The Brooklyn Bridge opened in May 1883 and was quickly proclaimed "one of the wonders of the world." The world's longest suspension bridge soared over the East River in a single mile-long span connecting Brooklyn and Manhattan. Begun in 1869 during the days of Boss Tweed, the great bridge was the dream of builder John Roebling, who never lived to see it completed. His son, Washington Roebling, carried on the great work. The building of the Brooklyn Bridge called forth heroic effort. It took fourteen years and cost the lives of twenty men. To sink the foundation deep into the riverbed, laborers tunneled down through the mud and debris, working in reinforced wooden boxes called caissons, which were open at the bottom and pressurized to keep the water from flooding in. When the men emerged after a hard day's work, they often came up too quickly and suffered from the crippling effects of "the bends," a painful, debilitating condition caused by nitrogen bubbles forming in the blood. Washington Roebling himself fell victim to this disorder and ended up an invalid. He directed the completion of the bridge from his window in Brooklyn Heights through a telescope while his wife, Emily Warren Roebling, acted as site superintendent and general engineer of the project. When

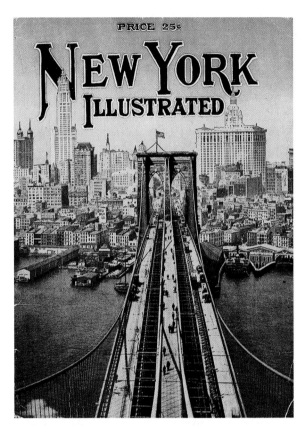

BROOKLYN BRIDGE
Arching 130 feet above the East River, the Brooklyn Bridge has proven not only aesthetically pleasing but remarkably functional for more than a century. A raised walkway allows pedestrians to enjoy their view above the traffic. John Roebling succeeded in his goal—to create "a great work of art" as well as "a successful specimen of advanced Bridge engineering."
Picture Research Consultants & Archives.

www.bedfordstmartins.com/tap SEE THE ONLINE STUDY GUIDE for more help in analyzing this image.

the bridge was dedicated in 1883, Roebling turned to his wife and said, "I want the world to know that you, too, are one of the Builders of the Bridge."

Skyscrapers as well as bridges changed the cityscape. Competition for space in Manhattan pushed the city up into the air even before the use of steel. The invention of Elisha Otis's elevator (called a "safety hoister") in the 1850s led to the construction of cast-iron buildings with elevators that carried passengers as high as ten stories. In 1890, the Pulitzer Building climbed to 349 feet, the tallest office building in the world. But until the advent of structural steel, no building in Manhattan topped the spire of Wall Street's Trinity Church.

Chicago, not New York, gave birth to the modern skyscraper. Rising from the ashes of the Great Fire of 1871, Chicago offered a generation of skilled architects and engineers the chance to experiment with new technologies. Commercial architecture became an art form at the hands of a skilled group of architects who together constituted the "Chicago school." Men of genius such as Louis Sullivan and John Wellborn Root gave Chicago some of the world's finest commercial buildings. Employing the dictum "form follows function," they built startlingly modern structures. The massive commercial buildings, in Root's words, "carried out the ideas of modern business life, simplicity, breadth, dignity." A fitting symbol of modern America, the skyscraper expressed and exalted the domination of corporate power.

Alongside the skyscrapers rose new residential apartments for the rich and middle class. The "French flat" gained popularity in the 1880s as city dwellers overcame their distaste for multifamily housing (which carried the stigma of the tenement) and gave in to "flat fever." Fashionable new apartments, built for affluent tenants, boasted such modern luxuries as electricity, telephones, central heating, elevators, and modern plumbing. The convenience of apartment living appealed particularly to women. "Housekeeping isn't fun," cried one New York woman. "Give us flats!" In 1883 alone, more than one thousand new apartments went up in Chicago.

A fitting symbol of modern America, the skyscraper expressed and exalted the domination of corporate power.

Throughout the United States, municipal governments undertook public works on a scale unknown in European cities. They paved streets with asphalt, built sewers and water mains, replaced gas lamps with electric lights, ran trolley tracks on the old horsecar lines, and dug underground to build subways, tearing down the unsightly elevated tracks that had clogged the city streets. In San Francisco, Andrew Smith Hallidie mastered the city's hills, building a system of cable cars in 1873. Montgomery, Alabama, became the first city in the coun-

try to install a fully electrified streetcar system in 1886. Boston completed the nation's first subway system in 1897, and New York and Philadelphia soon followed.

Cities became more beautiful as planners created urban public parks. Much of the credit for America's public parks goes to one man—landscape architect Frederick Law Olmsted. Olmsted designed parks in cities from Atlanta, Brooklyn, and Hartford to Detroit, Chicago, and Louisville. The indefatigable Olmsted also laid out the grounds for the U.S. Capitol and planned an entire city, Riverside, Illinois. The Boston park system, a seven-mile ring of green that Olmsted called the city's "emerald necklace," was his most ambitious and successful project. But he is best remembered for the creation of New York's Central Park. He and his partner, Calvert Vaux, directed the planting of more than five million trees, shrubs, and vines to transform the eight hundred acres between 59th and 110th Streets into an oasis for urban dwellers. "We want a ground to which people may easily go after their day's work is done," he wrote, "where they may stroll for an hour, seeing, hearing, and feeling nothing of the bustle and jar of the streets."

Olmsted intended his parks for contemplation, but in the 1880s and 1890s, parks became playgrounds for the people. Lincoln Park in Chicago offered baseball diamonds, tennis courts, a zoo, bicycle and bridle paths, and a band shell. San Francisco's Golden Gate Park, built on a sandy waste, by 1900 stood as a magnificent recreational area complete with a Japanese tea garden and a herd of grazing buffalo.

American cities did not overlook the mind in their efforts at improvement. They created a comprehensive free public school system that educated everyone from the children of urban professionals to the sons and daughters of immigrants. The exploding urban population strained the system and led to crowded and inadequate facilities, but no one was turned away. In 1899, more than 544,000 pupils attended school in New York's five boroughs. Schools in Boston, New York, Chicago, and Detroit as well as other cities and towns provided the only classrooms in the world where students could attend secondary school free of charge.

In addition to schools, the cities built libraries to educate their citizens. American cities in the late nineteenth century created the most extensive free public library system in the world. In 1895, the Boston Public Library opened its bronze doors

MOONLIGHT SKATING—CENTRAL PARK, THE TERRACE, AND LAKE

After the Civil War, Frederick Law Olmsted and Calvert Vaux put the finishing touches on New York City's Central Park. As the centerpiece of the entire design, Bethesda terrace stood with its central fountain dedicated as a monument to the Union navy's dead. Sculptor Emma Stebbins designed Angel of the Waters, the graceful bronze figure which tops the fountain. Vaux considered the grand terrace "the drawing room" of the park and by the 1870s it had become one of the most popular gathering places in the city. Shown here in an 1878 painting by John O'Brien Inman, Bethesda terrace shines in the moonlight as skaters take a turn on the pond while bustled Victorian ladies converse with top-hatted gentlemen on the shore in the foreground. The Angel of the Waters, with uplifted wings, can be glimpsed in the center background.

Museum of the City of New York.

under the inscription "Free to All." Designed in the style of a Renaissance palazzo, with more than 700,000 books on the shelves ready to be checked out, the library earned the description "a palace of the people." Across the United States, other cities participated in the public library movement. Cincinnati, Detroit, St. Louis, Chicago, and Cleveland sponsored libraries in the 1870s. And in New York, Philadelphia, and Buffalo, the city stepped in with support when private libraries faltered in the 1890s.

Despite the Boston Public Library's legend "Free to All," the poor did not share equally in the advantages of city life. The parks, the libraries, and

even the subways and sewers benefited some city dwellers more than others. Few library cards were held by Boston's laborers, who worked six days a week and found the library closed on Sunday. And in the 1890s, there was nothing central about New York's Central Park. It was a four-mile walk from the tenements of Hester Street to the park's entrance at 59th Street and Fifth Avenue. Cities spent more money on plumbing improvements for affluent apartment dwellers than on public baths and lodging houses for the down and out. Even the uniform subway fare, which enabled Boston and New York riders to travel anywhere in the system for five cents, worked to the advantage of the middle-class commuter and not the downtown poor. Then, as now, the comfortable majority, not the indigent minority, reaped a disproportionate share of the benefits in the nation's big cities.

Any story of the American city, it seems, must be a tale of two cities—or, more correctly, given the great diversity, a tale of many cities within each metropolis. At the turn of the twentieth century a central paradox emerged: The enduring monuments of America's cities—the bridges, skyscrapers, parks, and libraries—stood as the undeniable achievements of the same system of municipal government that many reformers dismissed as boss ridden, criminal, and corrupt.

White City or City of Sin?

Americans have always been of two minds about the city. They boast of its skyscrapers and bridges, its culture and sophistication, and they pride themselves on its bigness and bustle. At the same time they fear it as the city of sin, the home of immigrant slums, the center of vice and crime. Americans in the late nineteenth century experienced the same ambivalence. Nowhere did the divided view of the American city take form more graphically than in Chicago in 1893.

In that year, Chicago hosted the Columbian Exposition, the grandest world's fair in the nation's history. The fairground, nicknamed the White City and built on the shores of Lake Michigan to honor the four hundredth anniversary of Columbus's voyage to America, offered a lesson in what Americans on the eve of the twentieth century imagined a city might be. Only five miles down the shore from Chicago, the White City seemed light-years away. Its very name celebrated a harmony, a uniformity, and a cleanliness unknown in Chicago, with its stockyards, slums, and bustling terminals. "Formal," "academic," and "monumental" are words that best described the city built for the Columbian Exposition. Frederick Law Olmsted and architect Daniel Burnham supervised the transformation of a wasteland into a pristine paradise of lagoons, fountains, wooded islands, gardens, and imposing white buildings. "Here," wrote the novelist Theodore Dreiser, "hungry men, raw from the shops and fields, idylls and romances in their minds, built them an empire crying glory in the mud."

What did it mean, this harmony, this White City, juxtaposed against the big-shouldered, brash Chicago? To Henry Adams, one of the more astute observers of his time, the fair offered not so much a lesson as a riddle. "Chicago," Adams wrote, "asked in 1893 for the first time the question whether the American people knew where they were driving." To Louis Sullivan, whose Transportation Building was judged the most innovative of the main buildings, the very harmony of the White City marked a triumph of uniformity over invention. Sullivan branded the fair a blight, a

FIRE AT THE WHITE CITY, CHICAGO
Spectators watch as the White City goes up in smoke in July 1894. After the World Columbian Exposition closed in 1893, the grounds became home to growing numbers of homeless unemployed thrown out of work following the panic of 1893. Unsure of what to do with the buildings, city officials may have been relieved by the fire, which broke out in a clash between federal troops and striking railway workers.
Chicago Historical Society.

"virus." Its celebration of the neoclassical and Renaissance styles, he argued, set back modern architecture a generation.

But the average American delighted in the classical beauty of the White City. "Sell the cookstove and come," the novelist Hamlin Garland wrote to his parents on the farm. "You must see this fair." And come they did, in spite of the panic and depression that broke out only weeks after the Columbian Exposition opened in May 1893. More than 27 million people attended the fair. They marveled at the art and architecture, strolled the elaborate grounds, visited the exhibits—everything from an eleven-ton cheese to the gigantic Yerkes telescope—and were by turns educated and entertained. Half carnival, half culture, the great fair offered something for everyone. On the Midway Plaisance, a separate concession away from the White City proper, crowds thrilled to the massive wheel built by Mr. Ferris and watched agog as Little Egypt danced the hootchy-kootchy.

In October the fair closed its doors in the midst of the worst depression the country had seen. The depression turned the decaying White City into a city of the poor and unemployed. During the winter of 1894, Chicago's homeless took over the grounds, vandalized the buildings, and frightened the respectable population. When Daniel Burnham was asked what should be done with the moldering remains of the White City, he responded, "It should be torched." And it was. In July 1894, in a clash between federal troops and striking railway workers, incendiaries set fire to the great buildings. In a matter of hours, nothing remained but a mass of rubble and twisted girders.

In the end, the White City remained what it had always been, a dreamscape. Buildings that looked like marble from a distance began to crumble even before fire destroyed the fairgrounds. Some had talked of preserving the vision, of building a permanent landmark for the city. But times were hard, and money was scarce. With the exception of the Arts Building, erected to house the Museum of Science and Industry, the White City remained a fantasy, never destined to endure. Perhaps it was not so strange that the legacy of the White City was felt most clearly on Coney Island, where two new amusement parks, Luna and Dreamland, sought to combine in a cheapened form the beauty of the White City with the thrill of the Midway Plaisance.

Conclusion: The City and the Country

Those like Henry Adams who pondered the riddle of where the country was heading as the nineteenth century gave way to the twentieth would have been better advised to leave the White City and look to Chicago. There in the young metropolis, with its stockyards, terminals, and railyards, the answer could be found. Americans on the move had populated a continent and, along with a host of newcomers from around the world, filled the cities, doubling Chicago's population each decade.

The story of Chicago was the story of America, where it had been and where it was heading. In the three decades between 1870 and 1900, the United States had filled out the map of the continent all the way to the Pacific Ocean as settlers pushed into the trans-Mississippi West, forcing the Native Americans onto reservations and establishing eight new states and territories. A mass migration of peoples, global in scope, transformed both rural and urban life. As settlers moved out onto the plains, agriculture became increasingly commercial, with bonanza farms totaling thousands of acres tilled by machine, not muscle. In urban America mass transportation and the development of the skyscraper transformed the cityscape at the same time that millions of new immigrants arrived on the shores. Municipal governments, straining to build the new cities, experienced the rough-and-tumble of machine politics as bosses and their constituents looked to profit from city growth.

An American contemplating a map of the nation in 1900 saw a spiderweb of railway tracks crisscrossing the continent, linking the burgeoning cities to the orange groves in California, the cotton fields of Texas, and the cattle ranches of Montana. No longer a set of isolated entities, the farms, the villages and towns, and the cities of the United States were by the twentieth century part of a vast network, linked to a global market and tied together by rails of steel.

www.bedfordstmartins.com/tap SEE THE ONLINE STUDY GUIDE to assess your mastery of the material covered in this chapter.

CHRONOLOGY

1860– **1900**	2.5 million farms established on public lands.
1862	Homestead Act promises 160 acres of western land to anyone who settles on land for five years.
1870	80 percent of population lives in rural areas, according to U.S. census.
1871	William Marcy Tweed's rule in New York ends. Fire ravages Chicago and leads to architectural innovation.
1873	Panic on Wall Street leads to nation-wide economic depression.
1876	Custer's cavalry forces killed by Indians near Little Bighorn River in Montana Territory. Statehood granted to Colorado.
1880– **1890**	Rural areas of New England and Midwest suffer depopulation.
1880s	Immigration patterns shift as more people arrive from southern and eastern Europe.
1882	Chinese Exclusion Act.
1883	Buffalo Bill Cody begins to tour with his Wild West Company. Brooklyn Bridge opens.
1886	Statue of Liberty, a gift from France, dedicated in New York harbor. Severe blizzards in Dakotas devastate cattle ranching. Geronimo surrenders.
1887	Congress passes Dawes Act, breaking up Indian lands. Massive droughts defeat home-steaders on Great Plains.
1889	Rise of Ghost Dance religion.

Sitting Bull killed by U.S. soldiers at Pine Ridge reservation.

Government opens two million acres of former Indian territory in Oklahoma to settlement.

Statehood granted to Montana, North Dakota, South Dakota, and Washington.

1890	Last remnant of Sioux surrenders, and army troops kill 200 Indians at Wounded Knee, South Dakota. Jacob Riis's *How the Other Half Lives* published. Statehood granted to Idaho and Wyoming.
1890s	First wave of African American migration from South to North begins.
1893	Columbian Exposition opens in Chicago to celebrate four hundredth anniversary of Columbus's arrival in the New World. Panic on Wall Street touches off major economic depression. Frenzied land rush takes place on Cherokee strip in Oklahoma Territory.
1895	Boston Public Library opens.
1896	Statehood granted to Utah.
1900	Ellis Island opens in New York harbor to process newly arrived immigrants. Census finds that 66 percent of population live in rural areas, compared with 80 percent in 1870. Three cities—New York, Chicago, and Philadelphia—top one million inhabitants.

BIBLIOGRAPHY

GENERAL WORKS

Edward L. Ayers, *The Promise of the New South: Life after Reconstruction* (1992).

John B. Boles, *The South through Time* (1995).

William Cronin, *Nature's Metropolis: Chicago and the Great West* (1991).

Allan Dawley, *Struggles for Justice: Social Responsibility and the Liberal State* (1991).

Robert V. Hine and John Mack Faragher, *The American West: A New Interpretive History* (2000).

Nell Irvin Painter, *Standing at Armageddon, The United States, 1877–1919* (1984).

Richard White, *"It's Your Misfortune and None of My Own": A History of the American West* (1991).

RURAL AMERICA AND THE WEST

Hal S. Barron, *Those Who Stayed Behind: Rural Society in Nineteenth-Century New England* (1984).

James H. Beckstead, *Cowboying: A Tough Job in a Hard Land* (1991).

Sucheng Chan, *This Bittersweet Soil: The Chinese in California Agriculture, 1860–1910* (1986).

Cletus E. Daniel, *Bitter Harvest: A History of Farmworkers, 1870–1941* (1981).

David Dary, *Cowboy Culture* (1981).

Sarah Deutsch, *No Separate Refuge* (1987).

Richard Drinnon, *Facing West: The Metaphysics of Indian-Hating and Empire Building* (1980).

Deborah Fink, *Agrarian Women: Wives and Mothers in Rural Nebraska, 1880–1940* (1992).

Neil Foley, *The White Scourge: Mexicans, Blacks, and Poor Whites in Texas Cotton Culture* (1999).

Manuel G. Gonzales, *Mexicanos: A History of Mexicans in the United States* (1999).

J. S. Holliday, *Rush for Riches: Gold Fever and the Making of California* (1999).

Kenneth L. Holmes, ed., *Covered Wagon Women: Diaries and Letters from the Western Trails, 1879–1903* (2000).

Andrew C. Isenberg, *The Destruction of the Bison: An Environmental History, 1740–1920* (2000).

Elizabeth Jameson and Susan Armitage, *Writing the Range: Race, Class, and Culture in the Women's West* (1997).

Julie Roy Jeffrey, *Frontier Women: The Trans-Mississippi West, 1840–1880* (1979).

Patricia Nelson Limerick, *The Legacy of Conquest: The Unbroken Past of the American West* (1987).

H. Elaine Lindgren, *Land in Her Own Name: Women as Homesteaders in North Dakota* (1996).

Valerie Matsumoto and Blake Allmendinger, eds., *Over the Edge: Remapping the American West* (1999).

Gerald McFarland, *A Scattered People: An American Family Moves West* (1985).

Sally McMurry, *Families and Farmhouses in Nineteenth-Century America: Vernacular Design and Social Change* (1988).

Larry McMurtry, *Crazy Horse* (1999).

Eric H. Monkkonen, ed., *Walking to Work: Tramps in America, 1790–1935* (1984).

David Montejano, *Anglos and Mexicans in the Making of Texas, 1836–1986* (1989).

Sandra J. Myres, *Westering Women and the Frontier Experience, 1800–1915* (1982).

Rodman W. Paul, *The Far West and the Great Plains in Transition, 1859–1900* (1988).

Paula Petrik, *No Step Backward: Women and Family on the Rocky Mountain Mining Frontier* (1987).

Paul Reddin, *Wild West Shows* (1999).

Glenda Gates Riley, *A Place to Grow: Women in the American West* (1992).

William G. Robbins, *Colony and Empire: The Capitalist Transformation of the American West* (1994).

Lillian Schlissel, Byrd Gibbens, and Elizabeth Hampsten, *Far from Home: Families of the Westward Journey* (1989).

Nancy Shoemaker, *American Indian Population Recovery in the Twentieth Century* (1999).

Richard Slatta, *Cowboys of the Americas* (1990).

Paul F. Starrs, *Let the Cowboy Ride: Cattle Ranching in the American West* (1998).

Joanna L. Stratton, *Pioneer Women: Voices from the Kansas Frontier* (1981).

Russell Thornton, *American Indian Holocaust and Survival: A Population History since 1492* (1987).

Dan L. Thrapp, *The Conquest of Apacheria* (1967).

Alf H. Walle, *The Cowboy Hero and Its Audience: Popular Culture as Market-Derived Art* (2000).

Elliott West, *The Contested Plains: Indians, Goldseekers, and the Rush to Colorado* (1998).

C. Vann Woodward, *The Origins of the New South* (1951).

Donald Worster, *Under Western Skies* (1992).

William Wyckoff, *Creating Colorado: The Making of a Western American Landscape, 1860–1940* (1999).

THE RISE OF THE CITY

Reid Badger, *The Great American Fair: The World's Columbian Exposition and American Culture* (1979).

Gunther Barth, *City People: The Rise of Modern City Culture in Nineteenth-Century America* (1980).

Edwin G. Burrows and Mike Wallace, *Gotham: A History of New York City to 1898* (1999).

Charles W. Cheape, *Moving the Masses: Urban Public Transport in New York, Boston, and Philadelphia, 1880–1912* (1980).

Elizabeth Collins Cromley, *Alone Together: A History of New York's Early Apartments* (1990).

Mona Domosh, *Invented Cities: The Creation of Landscape in Nineteenth-Century New York and Boston* (1996).

Robert Fishman, *Bourgeois Utopias: The Rise and Fall of Suburbia* (1987).

William D. Griffin, *The Book of Irish Americans* (1990).

David C. Hammack, *Power and Society: Greater New York at the Turn of the Century* (1982).

Elizabeth Hawes, *New York, New York: How the Apartment House Transformed Life in the City, 1869–1930* (1993).

Melvin G. Holli, *The American Mayor* (1999).

Kenneth T. Jackson, *Crabgrass Frontier: The Suburbanization of the United States* (1985).

Lawrence Karsen, *The Rise of the Urban South* (1985).

Donald A. Mackay, *The Building of Manhattan* (1987).

Carolyn Marvin, *When Old Technologies Were New: Thinking About Electric Communication in the Late Nineteenth Century* (1988).

David McCullough, *The Great Bridge* (1972).

Donald L. Miller, *City of the Century: The Epic of Chicago and the Making of America* (1996).

Raymond A. Mohl, *The New City: Urban America in the Industrial Age, 1860–1920* (1985).

Eric H. Monkkonen, *America Becomes Urban* (1988).

David E. Nye, *Electrifying America: Social Meanings of a New Technology, 1880–1940* (1990).

Kathy Peiss, *Cheap Amusements: Working Women and Leisure in Turn-of-the-Century New York* (1986).

Henry Petroski, *Engineers of Dreams* (1994).

Harold L. Platt, *The Electric City: Energy and Growth of the Chicago Area, 1880–1930* (1991).

Samuel H. Preston and Michael R. Haines, *Fatal Years: Child Mortality in Late-Nineteenth-Century America* (1991).

Roy Rosenzweig, *Eight Hours for What We Will: Workers and Leisure in an Industrial City, 1870–1920* (1983).

Roy Rosenzweig and Elizabeth Blackmar, *The Park and the People: A History of Central Park* (1992).

Witold Rybczynski, *A Clearing in the Distance: Frederick Law Olmsted and America in the Nineteenth Century* (1999).

Luc Sante, *Low Life: Lures and Snares of Old New York* (1991).

Carl Smith, *Urban Disorder and the Shape of Belief* (1995).

John R. Stilgoe, *Borderland: Origins of the American Suburb, 1820–1939* (1988).

Jon C. Teaford, *City and Suburb: The Political Fragmentation of Metropolitan America, 1850–1970* (1979).

John Emerson Todd, *Frederick Law Olmsted* (1982).

Alan Trachtenberg, *Brooklyn Bridge: Fact and Symbol* (1965).

David B. Tyack, *The One Best System: A History of American Urban Education* (1974).

Oliver Zunz, *The Changing Face of Inequality* (1982).

IMMIGRANTS

Glenn C. Altschuler, *Race, Ethnicity, and Class in American Social Thought, 1865–1919* (1982).

John Bodnar, *The Transplanted: A History of Immigration in Urban America* (1985).

Roger Daniels, *Coming to America: A History of Immigration and Ethnicity in American Life* (1991).

Leonard Dinnerstein and David M. Reimers, *Ethnic Americans: A History of Immigration* (1999).

Andrew Gyory, *Closing the Gate: Race, Politics, and the Chinese Exclusion Act* (1999).

John Higham, *Send These to Me: Jews and Other Immigrants in Urban America* (1975).

Matthew Frye Jacobson, *Whiteness of a Different Color: European Immigrants and the Alchemy of Race* (1998).

Alan M. Kraut, *The Huddled Masses: The Immigrant in American Society, 1880–1921* (1982).

Dusanka Miscevic and Peter Kwong, *Chinese Americans: The Immigrant Experience* (2000).

Humbert S. Nelli, *The Italians in Chicago, 1860–1920* (1970).

Thomas M. Pitkin, *Keepers of the Gate: A History of Ellis Island* (1975).

David M. Reimers, *Unwelcome Strangers* (1998).

Ronald Takaki, *Strangers from a Different Shore: A History of Asian Americans* (1998).

HAYES CAMPAIGN LANTERN, 1876

Republicans employed this lantern in the campaign of 1876. Designed for nighttime rallies, the lantern featured paper transparencies that allowed light to shine through the stars and illuminate the portrait of candidate Rutherford B. Hayes. Marching men with lighted lanterns held aloft must have made a dramatic scene in small towns across the country. Nevertheless, Hayes did not win the popular vote and came to power in a contested election that led Democrats to question his legitimacy and dub him "Rutherfraud."
Collection of Janice L. and David J. Frent.

BUSINESS AND POLITICS IN THE GILDED AGE 17
1870–1895

ONE NIGHT AT DINNER, the humorist and author Mark Twain and his friend Charles Dudley Warner, editor of the Hartford *Courant,* teased their wives about the popular novels they read—the sentimental, domestic fiction lambasted as the product of "female scribblers." Challenged in return to write something better, the two men set to work. Warner supplied the sentimental melodrama, while Twain "hurled in the facts." The result was a runaway best-seller, uneven as fiction but offering a savage satire of the speculative mania of the era that forever after would be known by the book's title, *The Gilded Age* (1873).

Twain left no one unscathed in the novel—political hacks, Washington lobbyists, Wall Street financiers, small-town boosters, wildcat miners, and the "great putty-hearted public" that tolerated the plunder. The author had witnessed up close the corrupt partnership of business and politics in the administration of Ulysses S. Grant. Drawing on his experience, Twain described how a lobbyist could get an appropriation bill through Congress:

> Why the matter is simple enough. A Congressional appropriation costs money. Just reflect, for instance. A majority of the House Committee, say $10,000 apiece—$40,000; a majority of the Senate Committee, the same each—say $40,000; a little extra to one or two chairmen of one or two such committees, say $10,000 each—$20,000; and there's $100,000 of the money gone, to begin with. Then, seven male lobbyists, at $3,000 each—$21,000; one female lobbyist, $3,000; a high moral Congressman or Senator here and there—the high moral ones cost more, because they give tone to a measure—say ten of these at $3,000 each, is $30,000; then a lot of small fry country members who won't vote for anything whatever without pay—say twenty at $500 apiece, is $10,000 altogether; lot of jimcracks for Congressmen's wives and children—those go a long way—you can't spend too much money in that line—well, those things cost in a lump, say $10,000—along there somewhere;—and then comes your printed documents. . . . Oh, my dear sir, printing bills are destruction itself. Ours, so far amount to—let me see— . . . well, never mind the details, the total in clean numbers foots up $118,254.42 thus far!

The Gilded Age seemed to tarnish all who touched it. No one would learn that lesson better than Twain, who, even as he attacked it as an "era of incredible rottenness," fell prey to its enticements. Born Samuel Langhorne Clemens in a rough Mississippi river town, he first became a journeyman printer and then a riverboat pilot. Taking the pen name Mark Twain, he moved west and gained fame as a chronicler of California's gold rush. In 1866 he came east to launch a career as an author, public speaker, and itinerant humorist. Twain played to packed houses, but his work was judged too vulgar for the genteel tastes of the time because he wrote

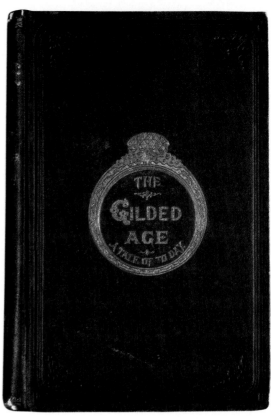

MARK TWAIN

Popular author Mark Twain (Samuel Langhorne Clemens) wrote acerbically about the excesses of the Gilded Age. No one knew the meretricious lure of the era better than Twain, who succumbed to a get-rich-quick scheme that left him virtually bankrupt.

Left: Beinecke Rare Book and Manuscript Library, Yale University. Right: Newberry Library.

about common people and used common language. *The Adventures of Huckleberry Finn,* his masterpiece of American realistic fiction, was banned in Boston when it appeared in 1884.

Huck Finn's creator eventually stormed the citadels of polite society, hobnobbing with the wealthy and living in increasingly expensive and elegant style. He built an ornate Victorian mansion in Hartford, Connecticut, and maintained a townhouse off Fifth Avenue in New York City. Succumbing without much of a struggle to the money fever of his age, Twain plunged into one scheme after another in the hope of making millions. The Paige typesetting machine proved his downfall. This elaborate invention (it had more than eighteen thousand parts) promised to mechanize typesetting, replacing human labor with machine. The idea was a good one—German-born inventor Ottmar Mer-

genthaler soon successfully patented his own typesetting machine, the Linotype. But the Paige machine proved much too temperamental to be practical, and its investors lost out. By the 1890s, Twain faced bankruptcy. Only the help of Standard Oil millionaire Henry H. Rogers enabled him to begin his dogged climb out of debt. Twain's tale was a common one in an age when the promise of wealth led as many to ruin as to riches.

A child of his age, Twain knew intimately the allure of money and power and the giddy rise and fall of fortune. The indictment of his times in *The Gilded Age* was not so much the detached disdain of an observer as the rueful recognition of a man deeply mired in the gaudy, meretricious era he so aptly named. In the Gilded Age great fortunes were made (and lost) with dizzying frequency. Wall Street panics, like the one in 1873, periodically interrupted the boom times and led to nationwide depressions. But with railroads to be built, cities demanding bridges, buildings, and mass transportation, and industry expanding on every level, the mood of the country remained buoyant. Hand in hand with the chances for riches went opportunities for graft and corruption. The interplay between business and politics, which Twain so deftly satirized in *The Gilded Age,* raised serious questions about the future of democracy.

The rise of industrialism in the United States and the interplay of business and politics strike the key themes in the Gilded Age, the period from the 1870s through the 1890s. In these three decades, the transition from a rural, agricultural economy to urban industrialism proved a deeply unsettling experience. The hopes and fears that industrialism inspired can be seen in the public's attitude toward the great business moguls of the day, men like Jay Gould, Andrew Carnegie, John D. Rockefeller, and J. P. Morgan. These larger-than-life figures not only dominated business but also sparked the popular imagination as the heroes and villains in the high drama of industrialization. At no other period in U.S. history would the industrial giants and the businesses they built (and sometimes wrecked) loom so large in American life.

Old Industries Transformed, New Industries Born

In the years following the Civil War, the scale and scope of American industry expanded dramatically. Old industries became modern big businesses, while discovery and invention stimulated new industries such as oil and electric power. The rise of the railroad played the key role in the transformation of the American economy, creating a national market that enabled businesses to expand from a local to a nationwide scale. Needing more and better rails to carry freight, the railroad radically changed the iron industry by speeding the transition from iron to steel.

The Railroads, America's First Big Business

In the decades following the Civil War, the United States built the greatest railroad network in the world and in the process created America's first big business. America's first transcontinental railroad system was completed in 1869 when the Union Pacific and Central Pacific tracks came together in Promontory Point, Utah, and a golden spike was driven to commemorate the occasion. Between 1870 and 1880, the amount of track laid in the country doubled, and it nearly doubled again in the following decade. By 1900, the country boasted over 193,000 miles of track, more than in all of Europe and Russia combined (Map 17.1).

By 1900, the country boasted over 193,000 miles of track, more than in all of Europe and Russia combined.

To understand how the railroads developed and came to dominate American life, there is no better study than the career of Jay Gould, a man who came to personify the Gilded Age. Jason "Jay" Gould bought his first railroad before he was twenty-five years old. It was only sixty-two miles long, in bad repair, and on the brink of failure. But within two years, he had sold it at a profit of $130,000. Thus began the career of the man who would pioneer the development of America's railway system and become the era's most notorious speculator.

Gould, by his own account, knew little about railroads and cared less about their operation. Nevertheless, he became a master of corporate expansion, the architect of the vast railway systems that developed in the 1870s. The secretive Gould operated in the stock market like a shark, looking for vulnerable railroads, buying enough stock to take control, and threatening to undercut his competitors until they bought him out at a high profit. The railroads that fell into his hands fared badly and often went bankrupt, but Gould's genius lay in cleverly buying and selling railroad stock, not in providing transportation.

Jay Gould's power and success underscored the haphazard development of the American railway system. To encourage railroad building, the federal and state governments provided the railroad companies with generous cash subsidies and grants of land. States and local communities clamored to offer inducements to railroad builders, knowing that towns and villages along the tracks would grow and

MAP 17.1

Railroad Expansion, 1870–1890

Railroad mileage nearly quadrupled between 1870 and 1890, with the greatest growth coming in the trans-Mississippi West. New transcontinental lines—the Great Northern, the Northern Pacific, the Southern Pacific, and the Atlantic and Pacific—were completed in the 1880s. Small feeder lines like the Oregon Short Line and the Atchison, Topeka, and Santa Fe fed into the great transcontinental systems, knitting the nation together.

READING THE MAP: Where were most of the railroad lines located in 1870? What cities were the major railroad centers? What was the endpoint of the only western route?
CONNECTIONS: Why were so many rails laid between 1870 and 1890? How did the railroads affect the nation's economy?

www.bedfordstmartins.com/tap   SEE THE ONLINE STUDY GUIDE for more help in analyzing this map.

flourish. The federal government held vast tracts of public land in the West, and Congress did not hesitate to give it away to promote railroad building. The railroads received not only land for rights-of-way but also liberal sections on alternating sides of the track to do with as they pleased, most often to sell to the settlers who followed the railroads into the West. Over the years, the federal government

alone granted the railroad builders a total of 180 million acres, an area larger than the state of Texas. But the lion's share of capital for the railroads came from U.S. and foreign investors.

Lack of planning soon led to overbuilding. Already by the 1870s, the railroads competed fiercely for business on the eastern seaboard. A manufacturer who needed to get goods to the market and

JAY GOULD AS A PIRATE
In this 1885 political cartoon, Jay Gould is portrayed as the pirate of Wall Street, sailing under the skull and crossbones while afloat on the sea of speculation in a raft of watered stock. "Out of His Reach" is the Baltimore and Ohio stock he seeks to gain using the hook of his monopoly of Western Union.
Granger Collection.

who was fortunate enough to be in an area served by a number of competing railroads could get a substantially reduced shipping rate in return for promising the chosen railroad steady business. Because railroad owners lost money through this kind of competition, they tried to set up agreements or "pools" to divide up territory and set rates. But these informal combinations invariably failed because they had no legal standing and because men like Jay Gould were intent on undercutting all competitors.

In the 1880s, Gould moved to put together a second transcontinental railroad to compete with the Union Pacific/Central Pacific. His decision meant that other railroads had no choice but to defend their interests by adopting his strategy of expansion and consolidation. By the 1890s, large railway systems—including the Southern Pacific, the Northern Pacific, and the Atchison, Topeka, and Santa Fe—dominated American rail travel.

Not all the early railroad builders were as unscrupulous as Gould. James J. Hill built the Great Northern and built it well. Without benefit of land grants or subsidies, Hill had to plan carefully and calculate which areas would best be served by the railroad in order to maximize returns to his investors. As a result, the Great Northern was one of the few major railroads able to weather the hard times of the 1890s. In contrast, speculators like Daniel Drew and James Fisk, Gould's partners at the Erie Railroad, could more accurately be described as wreckers than as builders. They ruined the Erie by gambling with its stock to line their own pockets. In the West, the Big Four railroad builders—Collis P. Huntington, Richard Crocker, Leland Stanford, and Mark Hopkins—became so powerful that critics claimed the Southern Pacific held California in the grip of an "octopus."

The public's alarm at the control wielded by the new railroads provided a barometer of attitudes toward big business itself. When Jay Gould died in 1892, the press described him as "the world's richest man," estimating his fortune at over $100 million. His competitor "Commodore" Cornelius Vanderbilt, who built the New York Central Railroad, judged Gould "the smartest man in America." But to the public, who found in Gould a symbol of all that most troubled them about the rise of big business, he was, as he himself admitted shortly before his death, "the most hated man in America."

Andrew Carnegie and Vertical Integration

Railroad building led directly to the development of a second major industry—steel. The first railroads ran on iron rails, which cracked and broke with alarming frequency. Steel, both stronger and more flexible than iron, remained too expensive for use in rails until the 1850s, when an Englishman named Henry Bessemer developed a way to make steel from iron. After the Civil War, with the discovery of rich iron ore deposits near the Great Lakes, the Bessemer process came into use in America. Andrew Carnegie, among the first to champion the new "King Steel," came to dominate the emerging industry.

If Jay Gould was the man Americans loved to hate, Andrew Carnegie was one of America's heroes. The infamy of the one man and the popularity of the other testified to the country's ambivalent reaction to industrialism. Carnegie, a Scottish immigrant, landed in New York in 1848 at the age of twelve. He rose from a job cleaning bobbins in a textile factory to become one of the richest men in America. Before he died, he gave away more than

ANDREW CARNEGIE
Andrew Carnegie, shown here in 1861, made a small fortune as a young man. In 1868, he totaled his assets. "Thirty three and an income of $50,000 per annum," he recorded. "Beyond this never earn—make no effort to increase fortune, but spend the surplus each year for benovelent [sic] purposes." Carnegie didn't stick to his plan. In 1872, he founded Carnegie Steel and went on to become one of the richest men in America, giving away an estimated $300 million to charitable causes before his death in 1919.
Carnegie Library.

"My preference was always manufacturing," he wrote. "I wished to make something tangible." By applying the lessons of cost accounting and efficiency that he had learned from twelve years with the Pennsylvania Railroad, Carnegie turned steel into the nation's first manufacturing big business.

In Braddock, on the outskirts of Pittsburgh, Pennsylvania, in 1872 he built the most up-to-date Bessemer steel plant in the world and began turning out steel at a furious rate. At that time, steelmakers were able to produce about seventy tons a week. Within two decades, Carnegie's blast furnaces poured out an incredible ten thousand tons a week (Figure 17.1). He soon cut the cost of making rails by more than half, from $58 to $25 a ton. Carnegie's formula for success was simple: "Cut the prices, scoop the market, run the mills full; watch the costs and profits will take care of themselves." And they did. By 1900, Carnegie Steel earned $40 million a year.

> *By applying the lessons of cost accounting and efficiency that he had learned from twelve years with the Pennsylvania Railroad, Carnegie turned steel into the nation's first manufacturing big business.*

To guarantee the lowest costs and the maximum output, Carnegie pioneered a system of business organization called vertical integration. All aspects of the business were under Carnegie's control. From the mining of iron ore to its transport on the Great Lakes to the production of steel, vertical integration meant, in the words of one observer, that "from the moment these crude stuffs were dug out of the earth until they flowed in a stream of liquid steel in the ladles, there was never a price, profit, or royalty paid to any outsider."

Always, Carnegie kept his eyes on the account books, looking for ways to cut costs. The great productivity he encouraged came at a high price. He deliberately pitted his managers against one another, firing the losers and rewarding the winners with small shares in the company. His workers achieved the high productivity Carnegie demanded by enduring long hours, low wages, and dangerous working conditions. Steelworkers toiled twelve hours a day in his plants, and when the shift changed every other week, they worked twenty-four hours straight.

$300 million of his fortune, most notably to public libraries. His generosity, combined with his own rise from poverty, gave him a positive public image. But he had another side—that of a harsh taskmaster who made nearly inhuman demands on those who worked for him.

When Carnegie was still a teenager, his skill as a telegraph operator caught the attention of Tom Scott, superintendent of the Pennsylvania Railroad. Scott hired Carnegie, soon promoted him, and lent him the money for his first investments. A millionaire before he turned thirty, Carnegie struck out on his own to reshape the iron and steel industries.

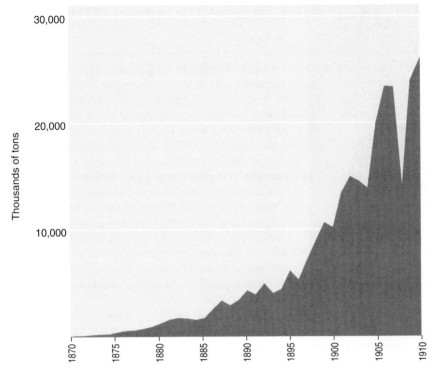

FIGURE 17.1

Iron and Steel Production in the United States, 1870–1910
Iron and steel production in the United States grew from virtually nonexistent to ten million tons a year by 1900. In steel production, the secrets to the great increase were the use of the Bessemer process and the vertical integration pioneered by Andrew Carnegie. By 1900, Carnegie's mills alone produced more steel than all of Great Britain. With corporate consolidation after 1900, the rate of growth in iron and steel production was even more spectacular.

Andrew Carnegie built Carnegie Steel into an industrial giant, the largest steel producer in the world. Carnegie's steel supported the elevated trains in New York and Chicago, formed the skeleton of the Washington Monument, supported the first steel bridge to span the Mississippi, and girded America's first skyscrapers. By 1900, Andrew Carnegie had become the best-known manufacturer in the world and the age of iron had yielded to an age of steel.

Standard Oil and the Trust

Edwin Drake's discovery of oil in Pennsylvania in 1859 sent thousands rushing to the oil fields in search of "black gold." In the days before the automobile and gasoline, crude oil was refined into lubricating oil for machinery and kerosene for lamps, the major source of lighting in nineteenth-century houses before the advent of gas lamps or electric lighting. The amount of capital needed to buy or build an oil refinery in the 1860s and 1870s remained relatively low: less than $25,000, or roughly what it cost to lay one mile of railroad track. With investment cost so low, the story of the new petroleum industry was one of riotous competition

among many small refineries. Ultimately, one company came to dominate oil refining through the use of a new organizational strategy, called the trust. That company, Standard Oil, founded by John D. Rockefeller, eventually succeeded in controlling nine-tenths of the oil refining business.

John D. Rockefeller grew up the son of a shrewd Yankee who peddled quack cures for cancer. Under his father's rough tutelage, he learned how to drive a hard bargain. "I trade with the boys and skin 'em and I just beat 'em every time I can," Big Bill Rockefeller boasted. "I want to make 'em sharp." John D. learned his lessons well. He owned his own business by the time he turned twenty-one. A taciturn young man with a devouring passion for business, Rockefeller hired a substitute to fight for him during the Civil War, as did Gould, Carnegie, and J. P. Morgan. By the time the fighting ended, John D. Rockefeller had become a wealthy man.

In 1865, Rockefeller bought out his partner with borrowed money and took control of the largest oil refinery in Cleveland. Like a growing number of business owners, Rockefeller abandoned partnership or single proprietorship to embrace the corporation as the business structure best suited to maximizing profit and minimizing personal liability. In

JOHN D. ROCKEFELLER
Like Andrew Carnegie, John D. Rockefeller made his fortune at a young age. Shown here in 1884, the year he moved his Standard Oil offices from Cleveland to New York City, Rockefeller was already a million-aire many times over. Nevertheless, as a newcomer to the big city, he looks at once wary and diffident.
Courtesy Rockefeller Archive Center.

1870, he incorporated his oil business, founding the Standard Oil Company, the precursor of today's ExxonMobil Corporation.

As the largest refiner in Cleveland, Standard Oil demanded secret rebates, or refunds, from the railroads. These rebates enabled Rockefeller to undercut his competitors. The railroads wanted his business so badly that they not only gave him rebates on his own shipping fares but also granted him a share of the rates paid by his competitors. As an official with the Pennsylvania Railroad later confessed, Rockefeller extracted such huge rebates that the railroad literally ended up paying Standard Oil

to transport its oil. Using this kind of leverage, Rockefeller pressured competing refiners to sell out or face ruin.

To gain legal standing for Standard Oil's secret deals, Rockefeller in 1882 pioneered a new form of corporate structure—the trust. The trust was a form of horizontal integration, which differed markedly from Carnegie's vertical approach in steel. Instead of attempting to control all aspects of the oil business, from the well to the consumer, Rockefeller moved horizontally to control only the refining process. Several trustees held stock in the various refineries "in trust" for Standard's stockholders. This elaborate stock swap created a union not of corporations but of stockholders, ensuring that the companies could act in concert without running afoul of the law. The new enterprise, valued at $70 million, gave Rockefeller a virtual monopoly of the oil refining business with the unsuspecting public knowing nothing about it.

When the government threatened to outlaw the trust as a violation of free trade, Standard Oil changed its tactics and organized into a holding company. This new type of company operated to control competition in much the same way as trusts but had the advantage of being legal. Instead of stockholders in competing companies acting through trustees to set prices and determine territories, the holding company simply combined competing companies under one central administration. New Jersey facilitated the development of the holding company by passing a law in 1889 that allowed corporations chartered in the state to hold stock in out-of-state ventures. Other businesses soon imitated Standard Oil's tactics. By the 1890s, New Jersey had become the home of a number of holding companies, the largest of which was Standard Oil.

Rockefeller began to integrate vertically, even as Standard Oil expanded horizontally. As the company's empire grew, central control became essential. Rockefeller ended the independence of the refinery operators and closed inefficient plants. Next he moved to control sources of crude oil and took charge of the transportation and marketing of petroleum products. By the 1890s, Standard Oil ruled more than 90 percent of the oil business. Rockefeller's company controlled twenty thousand oil wells, employed a hundred thousand people, and was the biggest, richest, most feared and admired business organization in the world.

"WHAT A FUNNY LITTLE GOVERNMENT"
The power wielded by John D. Rockefeller and his Standard Oil Company is captured in this political cartoon that appeared in the January 22, 1900, issue of **The Verdict.** *Rockefeller is pictured holding the White House and the Treasury Department in the palm of his hand while in the background the U.S. Capitol has been converted into an oil refinery. Standard Oil epitomized the gigantic trusts that many feared threatened democracy in the Gilded Age.*
Collection of The New-York Historical Society.

www.bedfordstmartins.com/tap   SEE THE ONLINE STUDY GUIDE for more help in analyzing this image.

John D. Rockefeller enjoyed unequaled business success. Before he died in 1937, at the age of ninety-eight, he had become the country's first billionaire. But despite his modest habits, his pious Baptist faith, and his many charitable gifts, he never shared in the public affection that Carnegie enjoyed. John D. Rockefeller served as a lightning rod for the nation's fear of industrial consolidation. Americans vilified him because they felt helpless against the vast power of the Standard Oil trust. With its iron control of the market, its own secret codes and spy system, and its ruthless suppression of competition, the company Rockefeller created earned the title "sovereign state of Standard Oil." To many Americans Standard Oil came not only to symbolize all the disquieting forces reshaping America but also to represent a danger to democracy itself.

John D. Rockefeller served as a lightning rod for the nation's fear of industrial consolidation. Americans vilified him because they felt helpless against the vast power of the Standard Oil trust.

Editor and journalist Ida M. Tarbell, whose *History of the Standard Oil Company* ran for three years (1902–1905) in serial form in *McClure's Magazine,* largely shaped the public's harsh view of Rockefeller. She had grown up in the Pennsylvania oil region, and her father had owned one of the small refineries gobbled up by Standard Oil. Her devastatingly thorough history chronicled the methods

IDA TARBELL AND *MCCLURE'S*
Ida Tarbell's **History of the Standard Oil Company** *ran in* **McClure's Magazine** *for three years. Her revelations of the ruthless practices Rockefeller used to seize control of the oil industry convinced readers that it was time for economic and political reforms to curb the power of big business. She grew up in the Pennsylvania oil region and knew firsthand how Standard Oil forced out its competitors.*
Culver Pictures; Corbis.

Rockefeller had used to gain control of the oil industry. By the time she finished publishing her story, Rockefeller slept with a loaded revolver by his bed in fear of would-be assassins. Standard Oil and the man who created it had become the symbol of a heartless monopoly. (See "Documenting the American Promise," page 628.)

Electricity and the Telephone

Although Americans frequently disliked industrial giants like Rockefeller, they admired inventors. The second half of the nineteenth century was an age

of invention, and men like Thomas Alva Edison and Alexander Graham Bell became folk heroes (Table 17.1). But no matter how dramatic the inventors or the inventions themselves, the new electric and telephone industries they pioneered soon eclipsed their inventors and fell under the control of the bankers and the industrialists.

Alexander Graham Bell came to America from Scotland at the age of twenty-four with a passion to find a way to teach the deaf to speak; instead, he developed a way to transmit voice over wires—the telephone. The emperor of Brazil, dumbfounded by the telephone on display at the Philadelphia Cen-

TABLE 17.1
NOTABLE AMERICAN INVENTIONS, 1850–1900

Year	Invention
1851	Ice-making machine
1852	Elevator brake
1855	Gas burner
1857	Sewing machine
1860	Repeating rifle
1865	Web printing press
1865	Railroad sleeping car
1867	Typewriter
1867	Barbed wire
1868	Railroad refrigerator car
1869	Oleomargarine
1870	Stock ticker
1876	Telephone
1877	Phonograph
1879	Cash register
1882	Electric fan
1885	Adding machine
1886	Coca-Cola
1888	Kodak camera
1889	Kinetoscope
1890	Electric chair
1891	Zipper
1895	Kellogg's Corn Flakes
1895	Safety razor
1896	Electric stove
1896	Ice cream cone
1899	Tape recorder
1900	Alkaline storage cells

THE TELEPHONE IN THE HOME
The telephone achieved spectacular success, despite the daunting technical and marketing problems posed by a new technology that called for linking towns and cities by electrical wires to transmit voice. The number of phones soared from 310,000 in 1895 to over 1.5 million by 1900.

Corbis.

tennial Exposition in 1876, cried out, "My God, it talks!" American Bell, the company formed by the inventor in 1880, marketed the telephone under the skilled direction of a professional manager named Theodore N. Vail. Vail pioneered long lines, or long-distance telephone service, creating American Telephone and Telegraph (AT&T) as a subsidiary. In 1900, AT&T became the parent company of the system as a whole, controlling Western Electric, which manufactured and installed the equipment, and coordinating the Bell regional divisions. In practical terms, this complicated organizational structure meant that Americans could communicate not only locally in their cities but across the country as well. The telephone connected parties immediately and privately, contributing greatly to speed and efficiency in business.

Rockefeller and His Critics

No one inspired the nation's fear of industrial consolidation more than John D. Rockefeller, creator of the Standard Oil trust. To many Americans Rockefeller and "the sovereign state of Standard Oil" came to represent a danger to democracy itself.

DOCUMENT 1. "The Smokeless Rebate" from Henry Demarest Lloyd's *Wealth v. Commonwealth*, 1894

As early as 1881 Henry Demarest Lloyd introduced Rockefeller to a national audience by attacking Standard Oil and its founder in "The Story of a Great Monopoly," published in the February issue of Atlantic Monthly. *The public eagerly snapped up the exposé — the issue went through six printings. Convinced that Standard Oil posed a threat to democracy, Lloyd embarked on a full-scale exposé of the company, published in 1894 under the title* Wealth v. Commonwealth. *To avoid charges of libel Lloyd used no names, but his readers knew he referred to Rockefeller and Standard Oil when he charged that the "oil combination" controlled two U.S. senators and had "done everything with the Pennsylvania legislature except to refine it." Here Lloyd describes how Rockefeller used illegal railroad rebates to best his competitors.*

With searching intelligence, indomitable will, and a conscience which makes religion, patriotism, and the domestic virtues but subordinate paragraphs in a ritual of money worship, the mercantile mind flies its air-line to business supremacy. That entirely modern social arrangement—the private ownership of [railroads]—has introduced a new weapon into business warfare which means universal dominion to him who will use it with an iron hand.

This weapon is the rebate, smokeless, noiseless, invisible, of extraordinary range, and the deadliest gun known to commercial warfare. It is not a lawful weapon. . . . It has to be used secretly. All the rates he got were a secret between himself and the railroads. "It has never been otherwise," testified one of the oil combination.

. . . The gentlemen who employ it give no evidence of being otherwise engaged than in their ordinary pursuits, hands empty of all tools of death. But all about them as they will, as if it were only by wish of theirs which attendant spirits hastened to execute, the rivals are blown out of the highways, busy mills and refineries turn to dust, hearts break, and strong men go mad or commit suicide or surrender their persons and their property to the skilful artillerists. . . .

The smokeless rebate makes the secret of success in business to be not manufacture, but manufracture—breaking down with a strong hand the true makers of things. To those who can get the rebate it makes no difference who does the digging, building, mining, making, producing the million forms of wealth they covet for themselves. They need only get control of the roads. . . . To succeed, ambitious men must make themselves refiners of freight raters, distillers of discriminations, owners not of lands, mines, and forests—not in the first place, at least—but of the railway officials through whose hands the produce must go to market. Builders, not of manufactories, but of privileges; inventors only of schemes . . . , contrivers, not of competition, but of ways to tax the property of their competitors into their pockets. They need not make money; they can take it from those who have made it.

SOURCE: Henry Demarest Lloyd, *Wealth v. Commonwealth* (Harper & Brothers, 1894), 474–75, 488.

DOCUMENT 2. Ida M. Tarbell, "The Oil War of 1872"

Editor and journalist Ida Minerva Tarbell, whose "History of the Standard Oil Company" ran for three years (1902–1905) in serial form in McClure's Magazine, *proved Rockefeller's most damaging critic. Tarbell grew up in the Pennsylvania oil region, and her father had owned one of the small refineries gobbled up by Standard Oil. Her devastatingly thorough history chronicled the underhanded methods Rockefeller employed to gain control of the oil refining industry. By the time she finished her story, Rockefeller slept with a loaded revolver by his bed in fear of would-be assassins.*

Here she portrays a critical chapter in the history of Standard Oil. In 1879, Rockefeller's first attempt to consolidate the oil industry through the use of illegal rebates had failed.

If Mr. Rockefeller had been an ordinary man the outburst of popular contempt and suspicion which suddenly poured on his head would have thwarted and crushed him. But he was no ordinary man. He had the powerful imagination to see what might be done with the oil business if it could be centered in his hands—the intelligence to analyze the problem into its elements and to find the key to control. He had the essential element to all great achievement, a steadfastness to a purpose once conceived which nothing can crush. The Oil Regions might rage, call him a conspirator and those who sold to him traitors; the railroads might withdraw their contacts and the legislature annul his charter; undisturbed and unresting he kept at this great purpose. . . .

He got a rebate. . . . How much less a rate than $1.25 Mr. Rockefeller had before the end of April the writer does not know. Of course the rate was secret and he probably understood now, as he had not two months before, how essential it was that he keep it secret. His task was more difficult now, for he had an enemy active, clamorous, contemptuous, whose suspicions had reached that acute point where they could believe nothing but evil of him— the producers and independents of the Oil Regions. It was utterly impossible that he should ever silence his enemy, for their points of view were diametrically opposed.

They believed in independent effort—every man for himself and fair play for all. They wanted competition, loved open fight. They considered that all business should be done openly—that railways were bound as public carriers to give equal rates— that any combination which favored one firm or one locality at the expense of another was unjust and illegal. . . .

Those theories which the body of oil men held as vital and fundamental Mr. Rockefeller and his associates either did not comprehend or were deaf to. This lack of comprehension by many men of what seems to other men to be the most obvious principles of justice is not rare. Many men who are widely known as good, share it. Mr. Rockefeller was "good." There was no more faithful Baptist in Cleveland than he. Every enterprise of that church he had supported liberally from youth. He gave to its poor. He visited its sick. He wept with its suffering. Moreover, he gave unostentatiously to many outside charities of whose worthiness he was satisfied. He was simple and frugal in his habits. He never went to the theater, never drank wine. He was a devoted husband, and he gave much time to the training of his children, seeking to develop in them his own habits of economy and of charity. Yet he was willing to strain every nerve to obtain for himself special and illegal privileges from the railroads which were bound to ruin every man in the oil business not sharing them with him. Religious emotion and sentiments of charity, propriety and self-denial seem to have taken the place in him of notions of justice and regard for the rights of others.

SOURCE: Ida M. Tarbell, "The Oil War of 1872," in Ellen F. Fitzpatrick, ed., *Muckraking: Three Landmark Articles* (Bedford Books of St. Martin's Press, 1994), 77–79.

DOCUMENT 3. Matthew Josephson, *The Robber Barons*, 1934

The historian Matthew Josephson, writing in 1934 in the trough of the depression, took a dim view of the great capitalists of the Gilded Age in his book The Robber Barons. *Noting that Rockefeller, Gould, and Morgan had avoided fighting in the Civil War by hiring substitutes, Josephson described them as follows.*

But besides the young men who marched to Bull Run, there were other young men of '61 whose instinctive sense of history proved to be unerring. Loving not the paths of glory they slunk away quickly bent upon business of their own. They were warlike enough and pitiless yet never risked their own skin: they fought without military rules or codes of honor or any tactics or weapons familiar to men: they were the strange, new mercenary soldiers of economic life. The plunder and trophies of victory would go neither to the soldier nor the statesman, but to these other young men of '61, who soon figured as "massive interests moving obscurely in the background" of wars. Hence these, rather than the military captains or tribunes are the subject of this history. *(Continued)*

Josephson's portrait of the young John D. Rockefeller is a caricature of the bloodless miser:

In his first position, bookkeeper to a produce merchant at the Cleveland docks, when he was sixteen, he distinguished himself by his composed orderly habits. Very carefully he examined each item on each bill before he approved it for payment. Out of a salary which began at $15 a month and advanced ultimately to $50 a month, he saved $800 in three years, the lion's share of his total earnings! This was fantastic parsimony. . . .

He was given to secrecy; he loathed all display. When he married a few years afterward, he lost not a day from his business. His wife, Laura Spelman, proved an excellent mate. She encouraged his furtiveness, he relates, advising him always to be silent, to say as little as possible. His composure, his self-possession was excessive. . . . He was a hard man to best in a trade, he rarely smiled and almost never laughed, save when he struck a good bargain. Then he might clap his hands with delight, or he might even, if the occasion warranted, throw up his hat, kick his heels, and hug his informer. One time he was so overjoyed at a favorable piece of news that he burst out: "I'm bound to be rich! *Bound to be rich!*"

Source: Excerpt (pp. 4, 48–49) from *The Robber Barons* by Matthew Josephson. Copyright © 1934 Harcourt, Brace and Company. Reprinted with permission.

QUESTIONS FOR ANALYSIS AND DEBATE

1. Henry Demarest Lloyd and Ida Tarbell agree that Rockefeller gained control of the oil industry through illegal methods. What was his primary weapon and how did it operate?

2. Compare Henry Demarest Lloyd's style to that of Ida Tarbell. Which is the more effective and why? Do you think Tarbell is an impartial observer?

3. Rockefeller never responded to his critics. Although in private he referred to the author as "Miss Tarbarrel," he pointedly refused to respond, even to point out factual errors in her history. "If I step on that worm I will call attention to it," he said. "If I ignore it, it will disappear." Do you think Rockefeller's silence was a good strategy? Why or why not?

4. By the time Matthew Josephson wrote his unflattering portrait of Rockefeller in *The Robber Barons*, Rockefeller was long retired, Standard Oil had been broken up by an edict from the Supreme Court, and oil discoveries in Texas and Oklahoma had eclipsed the Oil Regions in Pennsylvania and Ohio. What do you think motivated Josephson's attack on the "robber barons" in 1934?

Thomas Alva Edison embodied the old-fashioned virtues of Yankee ingenuity and rugged individualism that Americans most admired. A self-educated dynamo, he worked twenty hours a day in his laboratory in Menlo Park, New Jersey, vowing to turn out "a minor invention every ten days and a big thing every six months or so." He almost made good on his promise. At the height of his career, he averaged a patent every eleven days and invented such "big things" as the phonograph, the motion picture camera, and the electric light-bulb.

By the turn of the twentieth century, electricity had become a part of American urban life. It powered trolley cars, subways, and factory machinery. It lighted homes, apartments, factories, and office buildings. Indeed, electricity became so prevalent in urban life that it symbolized the city, whose bright lights contrasted with a rural America, left largely in the dark. As late as the 1930s, only 10 percent of the nation's farms had electricity.

While Americans thrilled to the new electric cities, the day of the inventor quietly yielded to the heyday of the corporation. (See "The Promise of Technology," page 632.) In 1892, financier J. P. Morgan consolidated the electric industry, selling Edison General Electric out from under its inventor and dropping Edison's name from the title. The new General Electric Company soon dominated the market.

AN UNRESTRAINED DEMON.

FEARS OF ELECTRICITY
Electricity was by no means a technology easy to sell, as this 1889 cartoon shows. Innocent pedestrians are electrocuted by the wires, a woman swoons, presumably as a result of the buzzing current, a horse and driver have collapsed, and a policeman runs for help. The skull in the wires attached to the electric lightbulb warns that this new technology is deadly. Both an urban sophisticate in a top hat and a cowboy in boots have succumbed to the deadly wires. Edison had to develop an entirely new system of marketing that relied on skilled engineers to sell electric light and power.
The Granger Collection, New York.

From Competition to Consolidation

Even as Rockefeller and Carnegie built their empires, the era of the industrial giant was coming to a close. Business increasingly developed into the anonymous corporate world of the twentieth century as the corporation became the dominant form of business organization and as corporate mergers restructured American industry.

Banks and financiers played a key role in this consolidation, so much so that individual entrepreneurship yielded to finance capitalism—investment sponsored by banks and bankers. The great banker J. P. Morgan took the lead in reshaping American business at the turn of the twentieth century, con-

solidating several major industries, including the railroads and steel. During these years, a new social philosophy based on the theories of Charles Darwin helped to justify consolidation and to inhibit state or federal regulation of business. The Supreme Court, a bastion of conservatism in this period, further proscribed attempts to control business by consistently declaring unconstitutional any legislation designed to regulate railroad rates or to outlaw trusts and monopolies.

J. P. Morgan and Finance Capitalism

The prominent business leaders of the late nineteenth century loathed competition and sought whenever possible to substitute consolidation and central control. None had a greater passion for

Vertical Transport: The Elevator

I N 1890, FOR THE FIRST TIME a building in New York City reached higher than the spire of Trinity Church in lower Manhattan. The new Church Building gave New York its first skyscraper, a feat that would have been impossible without the development of vertical transport—that is, the invention of the elevator.

The concept of the elevator was not new. As early as the Renaissance, Leonardo da Vinci had plans for one among his drawings. By the mid-nineteenth century power elevators, often operated by steam, were used to convey materials in factories, mines, and warehouses. But not until Elisha Graves Otis perfected the "safety hoister" and patented it in the 1860s did the elevator become safe enough for people to use. Otis, a master mechanic in a bed factory, was an ambitious inventor who pioneered the safety elevator in a warehouse in Yonkers, New York. Otis devised an ingenious mechanism consisting of two metal pieces fastened to the elevator platform. If the rope or cable supporting the elevator broke, the metal pieces would spring out and stop the downward motion. In a dramatic demonstration in the Crystal Palace Exposition in New York in 1854, Otis cut the cable and proved the safety of his elevator.

Otis designed his first elevator to carry freight, but it was as a people mover that the elevator came into its own. The Otis elevator transformed the value of urban real estate, making it possible to build into the air. In the 1870s, steam elevators gave way to hydraulic mechanisms powered by water operating under the force of gravity. To move the car upward, the operator opened a valve that filled a bucket, causing it to rise while simultaneously allowing the car to descend under its own weight. When the car reached the bottom floor, pumps filled the bucket for the next trip. Movement up and down was smooth, fast, and economical—but also dangerous: The car was controlled only by its brake, which could (and sometimes did) fail. As buildings became taller and taller, the risk increased. In 1896, an elevator in the twenty-three-story American Tract Society Building dropped from the nineteenth floor to the bottom of the shaft, killing both occu-

Archive United Technologies Corporation, Hartford, CT 06101.

pants. The accident underscored the necessity of employing highly trained technical personnel in the maintenance of big office buildings, and the necessity for routine inspection of elevators to maintain safety.

As Elisha Otis's son Charles later wrote, "I do not suppose that my father had the slightest conception at the time of what the outcome of his invention would be." Otis died in 1861 before his invention made him a fortune. His sons, who proved to be astute businessmen as well as skilled mechanics, founded the Otis Elevator Company and continued to pioneer vertical transportation, developing the escalator in 1900. In 1898, Otis Elevator, capitalized at $11 million, was formed through the merger of eight other elevator companies. The company went on to become one of the greatest industrial enterprises in America as well as one of the first multinational corporations.

J. P. MORGAN, PHOTOGRAPH BY EDWARD STEICHEN

Few photographs of J. P. Morgan exist. Morgan, who suffered from a skin condition that left him with a misshapen strawberry of a nose, rarely allowed his picture to be taken. But it was his eyes that people remembered—eyes so piercing that Edward Steichen, who took this photograph, observed that "meeting his gaze was a little like confronting the headlights of an express train."

Courtesy of George Eastman House. Reprinted with permission of Joanna T. Steichen.

order, predictability, and profit than John Pierpont Morgan, the Wall Street banker who became the architect of business consolidation (Figure 17.2). J. P. Morgan dominated the financial world of Wall Street. Aloof and silent, he looked down on the climbers and the speculators with a haughtiness that led his rivals to call him "Jupiter," after the ruler of all the Roman gods. At the turn of the twentieth century Morgan exerted an influence so powerful that his critics charged that he controlled a vast "money trust."

Morgan acted as a power broker in the reorganization of the railroads and the creation of industrial giants like General Electric and U.S. Steel. When the railroads fell on hard times in the 1890s, Morgan, with his passion for order and his access

to capital, took them in hand. He eliminated competition by creating what he called "a community of interest" among the managers, men he handpicked. Often, Morgan's partners sat on the boards of competing firms, forming interlocking directorates. By the time Morgan was finished reorganizing the railroads, seven major groups controlled two-thirds of the nation's track.

Banker control of the railroads rationalized, or coordinated, the industry. But peace came at a high price. Morgan heavily "watered" the stock of the railroads, issuing new stock lavishly to keep old investors happy and to guarantee huge profits. J. P. Morgan & Co. made millions of dollars from commissions and from blocks of stock acquired through reorganization. The flagrant overcapitalization created by the watered stock hurt the railroads in the long run, saddling them with enormous debts. Equally harmful was the management style of the Morgan directors who ran the railroads. They were not railroad men. They were bankers who looked at the railroads as little more than "a set of books." Their conservatism discouraged the continued technological and organizational innovation needed to run the railroads effectively.

F I G U R E 17.2

Merger Mania, 1895–1905

The depression that began with the panic of 1893 fueled a "merger mania," as businesses consolidated and reorganized, often at the prompting of finance capitalists like J. P. Morgan. The number of mergers peaked in 1899 but high rates of consolidation continued into the first decade of the twentieth century.

In 1898, Morgan moved into the steel industry. His acquisition of Carnegie Steel exemplifies the passing of one age and the coming of a new one. Carnegie represented the old entrepreneurial order, Morgan the new corporate system. As he began to challenge Carnegie's control, Morgan supervised the mergers of several smaller steel companies, which soon began to integrate vertically by moving from the manufacture of finished goods into steel production. Carnegie, who for decades had controlled the production of steel, countered by creating a new plant for the manufacture of finished products such as tubing, nails, wire, and hoops. A pugnacious Carnegie cabled his partners in the summer of 1900: "Action essential: crisis has arrived . . . have no fear as to the result; victory certain."

The press trumpeted news of the impending fight between the feisty Scot and the haughty Wall Street banker, but what the papers called the "battle of the giants" in the end proved little more than the wily maneuvering of two businessmen so adept that even today it is difficult to say who won. For all his belligerence, the sixty-six-year-old Carnegie yearned to retire to Skibo Castle, his home in Scotland, and may well have invited Morgan's bid for power, knowing that only Morgan could command the capital to buy him out. Morgan, who disdained haggling, agreed to pay Carnegie's asking price, $480 million (the equivalent of about $9.6 billion, in today's currency). Carnegie's personal share alone amounted to more than $250 million. According to legend, when Carnegie later teased Morgan, saying that he should have asked $100 million more, Morgan replied: "You would have got it if you had."

Carnegie represented the old entrepreneurial order, Morgan the new corporate system.

Morgan quickly moved to pull together Carnegie's chief competitors to form a huge new steel corporation, United States Steel, known today as USX. Capitalized (some said grossly overcapitalized) at $1.4 billion, U.S. Steel was the largest corporation in the world. Yet for all its size, it did not hold a monopoly in the steel industry. Significant small competitors such as Bethlehem Steel remained independent, creating a competitive system

HOMESTEAD STEEL WORKS
The Homestead steel works outside of Pittsburgh, Pennsylvania, pictured shortly after J. P. Morgan bought out Andrew Carnegie and created U.S. Steel, the precursor to today's USX. Try to count the smokestacks in the picture—it is no wonder that trees and plants would not grow in Homestead.
Library of Congress.

called an oligopoly, in which several large combinations, not one alone, control production. Other industries, such as electricity and meatpacking, were also oligopolies. Businesses in this system seldom competed by cutting prices, as older businesses had done. Instead, the smaller firms simply followed the lead of giants like U.S. Steel in setting prices and dividing the market so that each business held a comfortable share. Although oligopoly did not entirely eliminate competition, it did effectively blunt it.

When J. P. Morgan died in 1913, his estate totaled $68 million, not counting an estimated $50 million in art treasures. Andrew Carnegie, who gave away more than $300 million before his death six years later, is said to have quipped, "And to think he was not a rich man!" But Carnegie's gibe missed the mark. The quest for power, not wealth, characterized J. P. Morgan, and his power could best be measured not in the millions he owned, but in the billions he controlled. Morgan, even more than Carnegie or Rockefeller, left his stamp on twentieth-century America.

Social Darwinism and the Gospel of Wealth

John D. Rockefeller Jr., the son of the founder of Standard Oil, once told the Brown University YMCA that the Standard Oil Company, like the American Beauty rose, resulted from "pruning the early buds that grew up around it." The elimination of smaller, inefficient units was, he said, "merely the working out of a law of nature and a law of God." The comparison of the business world to the natural world formed the backbone of a new theory of society based on the "law of evolution" formulated by British scientist Charles Darwin. In his monumental work *On the Origin of Species,* published in 1859, Darwin theorized that in the struggle for survival, the process of adaptation to environment triggered a natural selection process among species that led to evolutionary progress. In the late nineteenth century, Herbert Spencer in Britain and William Graham Sumner in the United States developed a theory called social Darwinism. Crudely applying Darwin's teachings to human society, the social Darwinists concluded that progress came about as a result of relentless competition in which the strong survived and the weak died out.

In social terms, the doctrine of "survival of the fittest" had profound significance, as Sumner, a pro-

fessor of political economy at Yale University, made clear in his 1883 book *What Social Classes Owe to Each Other*. "The drunkard in the gutter is just where he ought to be, according to the fitness and tendency of things," Sumner insisted. Any efforts by one class to aid another only tampered with the rigid laws of nature and slowed down evolution. Social Darwinism's claim that human interference hampered evolutionary progress acted as a strong curb to reform at the same time that it glorified great wealth. In an age when men like Rockefeller and Carnegie amassed hundreds of millions of dollars (billions in today's currency) while the average worker earned $500 a year (the equivalent of about $8,800 today), social Darwinism justified economic inequality.

Andrew Carnegie softened some of the harsher features of social Darwinism in his "Gospel of Wealth," published in 1889. The millionaire, Carnegie wrote, acted as a "mere trustee and agent for his poorer brethren, bringing to their service his superior wisdom, experience, and ability to administer, doing for them better than they could or would do for themselves." Carnegie preached philanthropy and urged the rich to "live unostentatious lives" and "administer surplus wealth for the good of the people." But although his Gospel of Wealth earned much praise, it won few converts. Most millionaires followed the lead of J. P. Morgan, who amassed private treasures in his marble library rather than distributing his wealth as Carnegie counseled.

In an age when men like Rockefeller and Carnegie amassed hundreds of millions of dollars while the average worker earned $500 a year, social Darwinism justified economic inequality.

Social Darwinism and the Gospel of Wealth suited an age in which the baffling changes accompanying industrialization seemed to cry out for some rational explanation. According to social Darwinism, even as refined by Carnegie, the success of huge industries and great industrialists was a sign of their superiority and therefore inevitable. This belief assuaged the wealthy individual's conscience and made it possible to neglect the poor in the name of "race progress." When the poor were of a different race or ethnicity from the wealthy—as they so often were—social Darwinism smacked of racism. This ugly aspect was never far from social Darwinist ideology, which judged Anglo-Saxons superior to all other groups. Social Darwinism provided a perfect rationale for the status quo.

Laissez-faire and the Courts

At first glance it seems ironic that William Graham Sumner, who so often sounded like an apologist for the rich, incurred the wrath of wealthy Yale alumni. But in 1890, they almost succeeded in getting him fired. The problem was that strict social Darwinists like Sumner insisted absolutely that the government ought not to meddle in the economy, subscribing to a doctrine called *laissez-faire* (French for "let it alone"). Sumner therefore opposed protective tariffs, which levied duties on imported goods to raise their prices so that they could not compete effectively with American products. His sharp attacks on the high tariffs angered Yale's alumni who championed protection. This discontinuity between theory and practice underscores that while in theory laissez-faire constrained the government from playing an active role in business affairs, in practice businessmen fought for government favors—whether tariffs, land grants, or subsidies—that helped business. Only when it came to taxes or regulation were they quick to cry laissez-faire.

Business found a strong ally in the U.S. Supreme Court. During the 1880s and 1890s, the Court increasingly reinterpreted the Constitution to protect business from taxation, regulation, labor organization, and antitrust legislation. In a series of landmark decisions, the Court used the Fourteenth Amendment, originally intended to protect freed slaves from state laws violating their rights, to protect corporations. The Fourteenth Amendment declares that no state can "deprive any person of life, liberty, or property, without due process of law." By defining corporations as "persons" under the law, the Court determined that legislation designed to regulate corporations deprived them of "due process." Using this reasoning, the Court struck down state laws regulating railroad rates, declared income tax unconstitutional, and judged labor unions a "conspiracy in restraint of trade."

Faced with the host of economic and social dislocations caused by industrialism, the Court insisted on elevating the rights of property over the rights of people. According to Justice Stephen J. Field, the Constitution "allows no impediments to the acquisition of property." Field, born to a wealthy New England family, spoke with the bias of the privileged class to whom property rights were sacrosanct. Imbued with this ideology, the Court refused to impede corporate consolidation and did nothing to curb the excesses of corporate capitalism.

Party Politics in an Age of Enterprise

Writing of the late-nineteenth-century presidents, the modern novelist Thomas Wolfe observed, "Garfield, Arthur, Harrison, and Hayes, for me they were the lost Americans: Their gravely vacant and bewhiskered faces mixed, melted, swam together in the sea depths of a past intangible, immeasurable, and unknowable." Why do the great industrialists like Rockefeller, Morgan, and Carnegie jump vividly from the pages of the past while the presidents of that period remain so pallid?

The presidents from Rutherford B. Hayes (1877–1881) to William McKinley (1897–1901) are indeed forgotten men, largely because so little was expected of them. Until the 1890s, few Americans thought the president or the national government had any role in addressing the problems accompanying the industrial transformation of the nation. The dominant creed of laissez-faire, coupled with the dictates of social Darwinism, warned government to leave business alone: Intervention to soften even the harshest evils of industrialization would only slow evolutionary progress. This crippling view of its rights and responsibilities in the economy and in society reduced the federal government to something of a sideshow. The real action took place elsewhere—in party politics on the local and state levels and in the centers of business and industry.

Politics and Culture

It is somewhat ironic that the voters of the day swarmed to the polls in record numbers to elect presidents who today seem so colorless. Voter turnout in the last three decades of the nineteenth century averaged a hefty 77 percent, compared with an average turnout of 54 percent from 1968 to 2000 (Figure 17.3). Why were voters then so eager to cast their ballots? The answer lies in the role politics played in the culture of the late nineteenth century. Politi-

*Decrease because of expansion of eligibility with the enfranchisement of 18- to 21-year-olds.

FIGURE 17.3

Voter Turnout, 1868–1900 and 1968–2000
Despite the weakness of the presidency and the largely undistinguished men who filled the office, voters turned out in record numbers to vote in the late-nineteenth-century elections. Compare the robust rate of participation to the anemic turnout in the late-twentieth-century elections. What factors do you think account for the change?

cal parties used state, local, and federal jobs to reward voters for their support. Many voters owed their livelihood to party bosses. Political affiliation also provided a sense of group identity for many participants proud of their loyalty to the Democrats or the Republicans. Moreover, politics constituted one of the chief forms of entertainment for voters and nonvoters alike in an age before mass recreation and amusement. Political parties sponsored parades, rallies, speeches, picnics, torchlight processions, and Fourth of July fireworks, attracting millions of Americans. Outside the big cities, only religious revivals and traveling shows could compete.

Politics constituted one of the chief forms of entertainment for voters and nonvoters alike in an age before mass recreation and amusement.

After the end of reconstruction, the old Confederate South voted Democratic in every election

for the next seventy years. Opposing the "solid South" was the Republican Northeast, with nearly enough electoral votes to guarantee control of the presidency. To preserve Republican rule, the party had to carry key states such as Ohio, Indiana, and New York and had to prevent an alliance from developing between the agricultural South and the West. Republican politicians, like their Democratic rivals, encouraged sectional divisions by emotional appeals that evoked the Civil War, a tactic known as "waving the bloody shirt." Strong Unionist states in the Midwest responded by voting consistently Republican. "Iowa will go Democratic," one observer joked, "when Hell goes Methodist."

Religion and ethnicity also played a significant role in politics. In the North, Protestants from the old-line denominations, particularly Presbyterians and Methodists, were drawn to the Republican Party, which championed a series of moral reforms such as temperance (the campaign against alcoholic beverages). The Democratic Party courted immigrants and attracted Catholic and Jewish voters by consistently opposing laws to close taverns and other businesses on Sunday, the only day workers had off, and by charging that crusades against liquor only masked attacks on immigrant culture.

Participating in electoral politics, like chewing tobacco, remained exclusively a male pursuit. Women could not vote anywhere in the United States until the 1890s and then in only four western states: Wyoming (1890), Colorado (1893), and Utah and Idaho (1896). Elsewhere, they continued to fight for suffrage by campaigning for state referenda across the nation. And increasingly in the 1890s, politics became limited to white males only. Although black men gained the vote during reconstruction, the withdrawal of federal troops from the South in 1877 led to a massive deterioration in black voters' franchise.

The power of the two major parties remained about equally divided from the 1870s into the 1890s. Although the Republicans captured the White House in four out of five elections, they rarely controlled the Congress. The Democrats, noted more for their local appeal than for their national unity, generally dominated the U.S. House of Representatives.

During this period, senators were not directly elected by the voters but were selected by state legislatures. In an era noted for its tolerance of all but the most flagrant bribery and corruption, state legislatures frequently came under the influence of powerful business interests. In *Wealth Against Commonwealth* (1894), his denunciation of the Standard Oil Company, journalist Henry Demarest Lloyd wrote, "The Standard has done everything with the Pennsylvania legislature except to refine it." Senators were often closely identified with business interests, as in the case of Nelson Aldrich, the powerful Republican from Rhode Island. Aldrich, whose daughter married John D. Rockefeller Jr., did not object to being called "the senator from Standard Oil."

Corruption and Party Strife

The political corruption and party factionalism that characterized the administration of Ulysses S. Grant (1869–1877) continued to trouble the nation in the 1880s. The spoils system—the awarding of jobs for political purposes—remained the driving force of party politics. The concept of ethics in government, precluding private individuals from getting rich from public office, remained an issue raised only among a small band of reformers during this period. Most respectable Americans viewed politics as a sordid business; corruption at the ballot box and in public office came to be taken for granted.

President Rutherford B. Hayes, whose disputed election in 1876 signaled the end of reconstruction in the South, proved to be a hardworking, well-informed executive who wanted peace, prosperity, and an end to party strife. Although he was ridiculed by the Democratic press as "Rutherfraud" and "His Fraudulency," Hayes was a figure of honesty and integrity who seemed well suited to his role as a national leader. But it was not an easy task. The Republican Party remained divided into factions led by strong party bosses who boasted that they could make or break a president.

The three Republican factions bore the colorful names Stalwarts, Half-Breeds, and Mugwumps. The Stalwarts, led by Senator Roscoe Conkling of New York, remained loyal to Grant and consequently carried the taint of corruption from the scandals of his administration. Opposing them were the Half-Breeds, led by Senator James G. Blaine of Maine, who decried the flagrant corruption of the Stalwarts but drew no fine distinction between public service and private gain; Blaine was himself tarnished by certain shady dealings in railroad bonds. Standing against both factions was a small but prominent group of liberal Republican reformers, mostly from Massachusetts and New York, whose critics later dubbed them Mugwumps. The name came from an Indian chief of the Algonquian but was used derisively by those who insisted that the Mugwumps straddled the fence on issues of party loyalty, "with their mug on one side and wump on the other." Often Mugwumps were men of influence like former abolitionist and Union general Carl Schurz and E. L. Godkin, editor of the *Nation*. They were eager to put government in the hands of competent, honest men like themselves. In their pursuit of reform, they largely evaded the complex and divisive economic issues of the day and called instead for the purification of the government through civil service reforms designed to set standards for officeholders and put an end to the spoils system.

The power of party bosses like Blaine and Conkling more than matched the limited power of the president. Fiery and dynamic leaders, they dominated national politics. Conkling, a master spoilsman, ridiculed civil service as "snivel service" and tried his best to get the Republicans to run Grant again for president in 1880. His archrival Blaine coveted the nomination and worked to block Grant and oust Hayes.

President Hayes, despite his virtues, soon managed to alienate all three factions in his party. A realist, he used federal patronage to build Republican strength by filling government jobs with, if not the best men, the best Republicans he could find. To the Stalwarts, who wanted more positions, his action constituted betrayal; to the Mugwumps, it smacked too much of the spoils system. Hayes soon found himself a man without a party and announced that he would not seek reelection in 1880, much to the delight of Blaine and the Half-Breeds.

The power of party bosses like Blaine and Conkling more than matched the limited power of the president. Fiery and dynamic leaders, they dominated national politics.

But the Republicans did not pick Blaine as their presidential nominee. To avoid choosing sides, they nominated instead a dark-horse candidate, Representative James A. Garfield from Ohio. To appease Conkling, they picked a Stalwart, Chester A. Arthur of New York, as the vice presidential candidate. The Democrats made an attempt to break down sectionalism and establish a national party by selecting as their presidential standard-bearer the old Union general Winfield Scott Hancock. But as one observer noted, "It is a peculiarly constituted party which sends rebel brigadiers to Congress because of their rebellion, and which nominated a Union General as its candidate for president because of his loyalty." Although the popular vote was close, Garfield won 214 electoral votes to Hancock's 155.

Garfield's Assassination and Civil Service Reform

Government bureaucracy grew in the years following the Civil War until nearly 150,000 jobs existed on the federal payroll. The spoils system proved a poor way to select qualified individuals to serve as the clerks, civil engineers, and trained professionals needed in the new government posts. Politicians from the president down were tormented by a steady stream of office seekers. Critics soon called for civil service reform designed to mandate examinations and establish a merit system to screen applicants for government jobs. The struggle for civil service reform would come to a head with the assassination of President James Garfield.

"My God," Garfield swore after only a few months in office, "what is there in this place that a man should ever want to get into it?" Garfield, like Hayes, faced the difficult task of remaining independent while pacifying the bosses and placating the reformers. Thousands of office seekers swarmed to the nation's capital, each clamoring for a place, and in the days before Secret Service protection, the White House door stood open to all comers. Garfield took a fatalistic view. "Assassination," he told a friend, "can no more be guarded against than death by lightning, and it is best not to worry about either."

On July 2, 1881, less than four months after taking office, Garfield was shot in the back at a Washington, D.C., railroad station while catching a train. His assassin, Charles Guiteau, though clearly insane, was a disappointed office seeker who claimed to be motivated by political partisanship. He told the police officer who arrested him, "I did it; I will go to jail for it; Arthur is president, and I am a Stalwart." Garfield lingered on through the hot summer while the nation held a long deathbed vigil. He died on September 19, 1881.

The press almost universally condemned the Stalwarts, if not for inspiring Guiteau, then for creating the political climate that produced him. Conkling's influence waned, as did his hopes for the White House. Attacks on the spoils system increased, and the public clamored for reform. But though Garfield's death crystallized the desire for civil service reform, the debate was long and hard. Many of those who opposed reform recognized that civil service had built-in class and ethnic biases. They knew that when Mugwumps spoke of government run by the "best men," they meant men of their own class and ethnicity. Just as Irish Americans were beginning to carve out a place for themselves in local and state politics, civil service threatened to turn government back over to an educated Yankee elite. At a time when few men had more than a grammar school education, office seekers did not relish the prospect of written civil service examinations. One opponent argued, "George Washington could not have passed examination for a clerkship," observing that "in his will written by his own hand, he spells clothes, cloathes."

The legislation that established civil service reform—the Pendleton Act—passed in 1883, after more than a year of congressional debate and compromise. Both parties claimed credit for the act, which established a permanent Civil Service Commission of three members, appointed by the president. Some fourteen thousand jobs were placed under a merit system that required examinations for office and made it impossible to remove jobholders for political reasons. Half of the postal jobs and most of the customhouse jobs, the lion's share of the spoils system's bounty, passed to the control of the Civil Service Commission. The new law sought to prohibit federal jobholders from contributing to political campaigns, thus drying up a major source of the party bosses' revenue. Soon business interests replaced officeholders as the nation's chief political contributors. Ironically, civil service reform thus gave business an even greater influence in political life than it already had.

"Chet Arthur, president of the United States! Good God!" incredulous men exclaimed on hearing of Garfield's death. Surely little in his background made Chester A. Arthur seem like a man suited for the highest office in the country. Only four years earlier, he had been dismissed from his position in the customhouse in New York City because of his close association with corrupt politicians. But as president, he quickly dispelled the nation's fears and acted independently, signing the Pendleton Act, which his fellow Stalwarts had so long opposed. Arthur himself had little faith in reform but knew enough of politics not to stand in the path of public sentiment. Arthur surprised his critics by turning out to be a competent president, but his was a lackluster administration. The Republicans quickly looked to Blaine to bear the party standard in 1884.

The Political Circus: The Campaign of 1884

With the downfall of the Stalwarts, James G. Blaine assumed leadership of the Republican Party and at long last captured the presidential nomination in 1884. A magnetic Irish American politician whose followers dubbed him the "Plumed Knight," Blaine inspired such devotion that his supporters were called Blainiacs. But to many reformers, Blaine personified corruption. Led by Carl Schurz, who insisted that Blaine "wallowed in spoils like a rhinoceros in an

African pool," the Mugwumps bolted the party and embraced the Democratic presidential candidate, the stolid Grover Cleveland, reform governor of New York. The burly, beer-drinking Cleveland distinguished himself from an entire generation of politicians by the simple motto "A public office is a public trust." First as mayor of Buffalo and later as governor of New York, he built a solid reputation for honesty, economy, and administrative efficiency. He soon alienated the Tammany Hall political machine; but with reform in the air, the enemies he made only added to his appeal. The Democrats, who had not won the presidency since 1856, rushed to nominate him. As was expected, Cleveland received the enthusiastic endorsement of the Mugwumps, who announced that "the paramount issue this year is moral rather than political."

They would soon regret their words. The 1884 contest degenerated so far into nasty mudslinging that one disgusted journalist styled it "the vilest campaign ever waged." Grover Cleveland, whatever his reform virtues, made an easy target. In July, his hometown paper, the Buffalo *Telegraph,* dropped the bombshell that the bachelor candidate had fathered an illegitimate child in an affair with a widow named Maria Halpin. The crestfallen Mugwumps tried to argue the difference between public and private morality. But robbed of their moral righteousness, they lost much of their enthusiasm. "Now I fear it has resolved itself into a choice of two evils," one weary reformer confessed.

At public rallies, Blaine's partisans taunted Cleveland, chanting:

Ma, ma, where's my pa?
Going to the White House
ha! ha! ha!

The stoic Cleveland accepted responsibility for the child, who may in fact have been fathered by his business partner. It is said Cleveland wished to spare his partner's reputation because he had fallen in love with the man's daughter. Silent but fuming, Cleveland waged his campaign in the traditional fashion—by staying home. Blaine broke precedent by making a national tour. On a last-minute stop in New York, the exhausted candidate overlooked a remark by a local clergyman—and may have lost the election as a result. While introducing Blaine, the Reverend Samuel Burchard blasted the Democrats as the party of "Rum, Romanism, and Rebel-

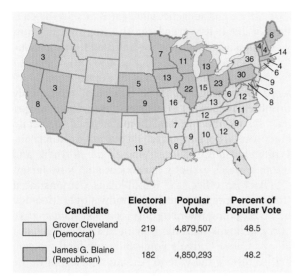

Candidate	Electoral Vote	Popular Vote	Percent of Popular Vote
Grover Cleveland (Democrat)	219	4,879,507	48.5
James G. Blaine (Republican)	182	4,850,293	48.2

M A P **17.2**
The Election of 1884

lion." An Associated Press correspondent hurriedly filed his story, crying, "If anything will elect Cleveland, these words will do it." By linking drinking and Catholicism, Burchard cast a slur on Irish Catholic voters, who had been counted on to desert the Democratic Party and support Blaine because of his Irish background.

With less than a week to go until the election, Blaine had no chance to recover from the negative publicity. He lost New York State by less than twelve hundred votes and with it the election. In the final tally, the Democrats ended twenty-five years of Republican rule, defeating Blaine by a scant 29,214 votes nationwide, but winning 219 electoral votes to 182 (Map 17.2). Cleveland's followers had the last word:

> Hurrah for Maria! Hurrah for the kid!
> I voted for Cleveland,
> And Damned glad I did!

Economic Issues and Party Realignment

Four years later, in the election of 1888, fickle voters would turn Cleveland out, electing Republican Benjamin Harrison, the grandson of President William Henry Harrison. Then, in the only instance in America's history when a president who had once been defeated at the polls was returned to office, the voters brought Cleveland back in the election of 1892. What factors account for such a surprising turnaround? The strengths and weaknesses of the men themselves partially determined the outcome. The stubborn Cleveland, newly married to his partner's daughter, Frances Folsom, resented demands on his time and refused to campaign in 1888. Although he won more popular votes than Harrison, he lost the electoral college. Once in office, Harrison proved to be a cold and distant leader, prompting critics to call him "the human iceberg."

ANTI-CLEVELAND POSTER, 1888
In this early example of negative campaign advertising, Republicans pillory Democratic President Grover Cleveland as an advocate of free trade, while dredging up the image of his illegitimate child, which had proved such a scandal in the 1884 campaign. The bottom lines echo the earlier campaign ditty "Ma, Ma, Where's My Pa?" In this election the tariff became a potent issue, winning support from business and labor and helping to elect Republican Benjamin Harrison.

Collection of David J. and Janice L. Frent.

But issues as well as personalities increasingly swayed the voters. The 1880s witnessed a remarkable political realignment as a new set of economic concerns replaced the Civil War rhetoric of carpetbaggers, rebels, and the bloody shirt. The tariff, federal regulation of the railroads and trusts, and the campaign for free silver restructured American politics.

The Tariff and the Politics of Protection

The concept of a protective tariff to raise the price of imported goods and stimulate American industry dated back to Alexander Hamilton in the founding days of the Republic. Congress enacted the first tariff following the War of 1812. The Republicans turned the tariff to political ends in 1861 by enacting a measure that simultaneously raised revenues for the Civil War and rewarded their industrial supporters who wanted protection from foreign competition. After the war, the Republicans continued to revise and enlarge the tariff at the prompting of northeastern industrialists. By the 1880s, the tariff posed a threat to prosperity. The huge surplus engendered by the tariff sat in the Treasury's vaults, depriving the country of money that might otherwise have been invested to create jobs and products, while the government argued about how (or even whether) to spend it.

To many Americans, particularly southern and midwestern farmers who sold their crops in a world market yet had to buy goods priced artificially high because of the protective tariff, the answer was simple: Reduce the tariff. Advocates of free trade and moderates agitated for tariff reform. But those who benefited from the tariff—industrialists like Andrew Carnegie who insisted that America's "infant industries" needed protection and westerners producing protected raw materials such as wool, hides, and lumber—firmly opposed lowering the tariff. Many workers, too, believed that the tariff protected American wage levels by giving American products a competitive edge over goods imported from other countries.

The Republican Party seized on the tariff issue to forge a new national alliance. Blaine shrewdly recognized its potent political uses. "Fold up the bloody shirt and lay it away," he advised a colleague in 1880. "It's of no use to us. You want to shift the main issue to protection." By encouraging an alliance among industrialists, labor, and western producers of raw materials, Blaine hoped to solidify the North and West against the solidly Democratic South.

Although the tactic failed for Blaine in the election of 1884, it worked for the Republicans four years later. Cleveland, who straddled the tariff issue in the election of 1884, startled the nation in 1887 by calling for tariff reform. The Republicans countered by arguing that "tariff tinkering" would only unsettle prosperous industries, drive down wages, and shrink the farmers' home market. Benjamin Harrison, who supported the tariff, captured the White House in 1888, carrying all the northern and western states except Connecticut and New Jersey.

Back in office, the Republicans demonstrated their new commitment to economics over ideology by abandoning their support for freed slaves while currying favor with the new industrialists. Senator Henry Cabot Lodge's Force Bill, a federal election law to restore the vote to African Americans in the South, died in the same Republican Congress that passed the highest tariff in the nation's history in 1890. The new tariff sponsored by Representative William McKinley of Ohio stirred a hornet's nest of protest. The American people had elected Harrison to preserve protection, but not to enact a higher tariff. The McKinley tariff set about solving the vexing problem of too much revenue by raising duties so high that foreign producers no longer wanted to sell their goods to Americans.

Democrats condemned the McKinley tariff and labeled the Republican Congress that passed it the "Billion Dollar Congress" for its carnival of spending. The Fifty-first Congress earned its nickname by spending the nation's surplus on a series of "pork barrel" programs—legislation shamelessly designed by senators and representatives to bring federal money to their own constituents. In the congressional election of 1890, angry voters swept the hapless Republicans, including tariff sponsor McKinley, out of office. Two years later, Harrison himself was defeated. Grover Cleveland, whose call for tariff revision had lost him the election in 1888, triumphantly returned to the White House vowing to lower the tariff. Such were the changes in the political winds whipped up by the tariff issue.

The Railroads, the Trusts, and the Federal Government

American voters may have divided on the tariff, but increasingly they agreed on the need for federal regulation of the railroads and federal legislation against the trusts. As early as the 1870s, angry farmers had organized to attack the railroads. The Pa-

THE CORRUPTION OF GOVERNMENT BY BIG BUSINESS
In this **Puck** *cartoon, a gullible Uncle Sam is being led by trusts and monopolies, satirically styled as "his philanthropic friends." Concern over the power of big business led in 1890 to the passage of the Sherman Antitrust Act, the first attempt to regulate business by making it illegal to restrict competition.*
Picture Research Consultants & Archives.

American voters may have divided on the tariff, but increasingly they agreed on the need for federal regulation of the railroads and federal legislation against the trusts.

Anger over the *Wabash* decision finally led to the passage of the first federal law to regulate the railroads, the Interstate Commerce Act, passed in 1887 during Cleveland's first administration. The act established the nation's first federal regulatory agency, the Interstate Commerce Commission (ICC). In its early years, the ICC was never strong or sure enough to pose a serious threat to the railroads. It proved more important as a precedent than effective as a watchdog.

Concern over the growing power of the trusts led Congress to pass the Sherman Antitrust Act in 1890. The act outlawed pools and trusts, ruling that businesses could no longer enter into agreements to restrict competition. It did nothing to restrict huge holding companies like Standard Oil, however, and proved to be a weak sword against the trusts. In the decade after passing the Sherman Antitrust Act, the government successfully struck down only six trusts. However, the act was used four times against labor by outlawing unions as a "conspiracy in restraint of trade." Then, in 1895, the Supreme Court dealt the law a crippling blow in *United States v. E. C. Knight Company*. The decision in this case drastically narrowed the law by allowing the American Sugar Refining Company, which had bought out a number of other sugar companies (including E. C. Knight) and thus controlled 98 percent of the production of sugar, to continue its virtual monopoly on the grounds that "manufacture" did not constitute "trade."

Both the ICC and the Sherman Antitrust Act testified to the nation's concern about the big business's abuses of power and to a growing willingness to use federal measures to intervene on behalf of the public interest. Yet not until the twentieth century would more active presidents sharpen and use these weapons against the large corporations.

The Fight for Free Silver

The silver issue stirred passions like no other issue of the day. On one side stood those who believed that gold constituted the only honest money. Although

trons of Husbandry, or the Grange, founded in 1867 as a social and educational organization for farmers, soon became an independent political movement. By electing Grangers to state office, farmers made it possible for several midwestern states to pass laws regulating the railroads. At first the Supreme Court ruled in favor of regulation (*Munn v. Illinois*, 1877). But in 1886, the Court reversed itself, ruling that because railroads crossed state boundaries, they fell outside state jurisdiction (*Wabash v. Illinois*). With more than three-fourths of railroads crossing state lines, the Supreme Court's decision effectively quashed the states' attempts at railroad regulation.

U.S. CURRENCY

While gold remained the nation's standard currency, silver supporters, including farmers and western mining interests, demanded the minting of silver coins and the issuance of silver certificates like those pictured on the right. In the center is a gold piece.

The American Numismatic Assn.; Picture Research Consultants & Archives.

other forms of currency circulated, notably paper money like banknotes and greenbacks, the government's support of the gold standard meant that all currency could be redeemed for gold. Many who supported the gold standard were eastern creditors who did not wish to be paid in devalued dollars. On the opposite side stood a coalition of silver barons and poor farmers. The mining interests, who had seen the silver bonanza in the West drive down the price of silver, wanted the government to buy the metal and mint silver dollars to help jack up the price. Farmers from the West and South who had suffered economically during the 1870s and 1880s hoped that increasing the money supply with silver dollars would give them some relief, enabling them to pay off their debts with devalued dollars.

The silver issue stirred passions like no other issue of the day. On one side stood those who believed that gold constituted the only honest money. . . . On the opposite side stood a coalition of silver barons and poor farmers.

Advocates of silver pointed out that until 1873 the country had enjoyed a system of bimetallism, with both silver and gold minted into coins. In that year, at the behest of those who favored gold, Congress voted to demonetize (stop buying and minting) silver, an act advocates of bimetallism de-

nounced as the "crime of '73." In 1878, Congress took steps to appease advocates of silver by passing the Bland-Allison Act over President Hayes's veto. The measure required the government to buy silver and issue silver certificates. The Bland-Allison Act helped mine owners, who now had a buyer for their ore, but it had little inflationary impact.

Pressures for inflation continued, but the silver advocates were unable to make any headway until 1890, when in return for their support of the McKinley tariff, Congress passed the Sherman Silver Purchase Act, increasing the amount of silver the government bought. Once again, the measure failed to produce the desired inflationary effect, and advocates began to call for "the free and unlimited coinage of silver," a plan whereby virtually all the silver mined in the West would be minted into silver coins circulated at the rate of sixteen ounces of silver to one ounce of gold.

The silver issue crossed party lines, but the Democrats hoped to use it to achieve a union between western and southern voters. Unfortunately for them, Grover Cleveland, a conservative in money matters and a strong supporter of the gold standard, sat in the White House. Cleveland called a special session of Congress in August 1893 and bullied the legislature into repealing the Sherman Silver Purchase Act. Repeal only divided the country, making the Mississippi River for a time as potent a political boundary as the Mason-Dixon line. Angry farmers warned Cleveland not to travel west of the river if he valued his life.

The year 1893 marked a black time in the nation's economic history. In the spring a panic on Wall Street touched off a deep economic depression that would last for several years. In the winter of 1894–95, Cleveland walked the floor of the White House, sleepless over the prospect that the United States might go bankrupt. The Treasury's gold reserves had dipped so low that unless gold could be purchased abroad, the unthinkable might happen— the U.S. Treasury might not be able to meet its obligations.

At this juncture J. P. Morgan stepped in and suggested a plan whereby a private group of bankers would purchase gold abroad and supply it to the Treasury. Cleveland knew only too well that such a scheme would touch off a thunder of protest from citizens and politicians already suspicious of the power the influential bankers wielded. Yet to save the gold standard, the president turned to Morgan for help. A storm of controversy erupted over the deal. The press claimed that Cleveland lined his own pockets and rumored that Morgan had made $8.9 million on profits. Neither was true. Cleveland had not profited a penny, and Morgan made about $300,000 on the deal—far less than the millions his critics claimed.

Yet the passions stirred by Cleveland's action in 1895 cannot be dismissed lightly. Undoubtedly Morgan saved the gold reserves. But if President Cleveland's action managed to salvage the gold standard, it did not save the country. The winter of 1894–95 was one of the hardest in American history. People faced unemployment, cold, and hunger. It never occurred to Cleveland that his great faith in gold prolonged the depression, favored creditors over debtors, and caused immense hardship for millions of Americans.

Conclusion: The Gilded Age Reconsidered

The deal between J. P. Morgan and Grover Cleveland underscored the ties between business and politics in the Gilded Age. Mark Twain's label has stood for more than a century as a fair representation of an era that spawned greed, corruption, and vulgarity on a grand scale, when speculator/industrialists like Jay Gould could not only build or wreck businesses to turn paper profits but also boast openly of buying politicians who lined their pockets at the public's expense. Nevertheless, the era was not without its share of solid achievements. In these years, America made the leap into the industrial age. Factories and mills poured out American goods in unprecedented numbers. In the offices and boardrooms of business, men like Carnegie, Rockefeller, and Morgan consolidated American industry. By the end of the nineteenth century, the country had achieved industrial maturity. No other era in the nation's history witnessed such a transformation.

But whether or not the nation could solve the problems accompanying industrialization and curb the power of the financiers and corporations remained to be seen. By the 1890s, the United States faced a crisis. Agrarian discontent, labor unrest, depression, unemployment—problems that were not only economic but also social and political—cried out for solutions. In the grim winter of 1894–95, men and women talked of revolution, some of them in fear and some of them in anger.

www.bedfordstmartins.com/tap SEE THE ONLINE STUDY GUIDE to assess your mastery of the material covered in this chapter.

CHRONOLOGY

1869   Completion of first transcontinental railroad.

1870   John D. Rockefeller incorporates Standard Oil Company in Cleveland.

1872   Andrew Carnegie builds nation's largest Bessemer process steel plant near Pittsburgh.

1873   U.S. government decides to stop minting silver dollars.

Panic on Wall Street leads to major economic depression.

Mark Twain and Charles Dudley Warner publish *The Gilded Age,* a novel satirizing the speculative mania of the age.

1876   Alexander Graham Bell demonstrates telephone at Philadelphia Centennial Exposition.

1877   Rutherford B. Hayes sworn in as president of United States after disputed election.

U.S. Supreme Court upholds right of states to regulate railroads in *Munn v. Illinois.*

1879   Congress votes to resume gold standard.

Thomas Alva Edison perfects filament for incandescent lightbulb.

1880s   Jay Gould becomes architect of a transcontinental railway system.

1880   Dark-horse Republican candidate James A. Garfield elected president of United States.

1881   President Garfield assassinated; Vice President Chester A. Arthur becomes president.

1882   Standard Oil develops the trust.

1883   Congress passes Pendleton Act, establishing civil service reform.

1884   Grover Cleveland wins presidency; first Democratic president since before the Civil War.

Mark Twain's *Adventures of Huckleberry Finn* published (and subsequently banned in Boston).

1886   In *Wabash* case, U.S. Supreme Court reverses itself and disallows state regulation of railroads that cross state lines.

1887   Congress passes Interstate Commerce Act, creating the first federal agency designed to regulate railroads.

1888   Benjamin Harrison elected president of United States.

1890   Congress passes McKinley tariff and Sherman Silver Purchase Act.

Congress passes Sherman Antitrust Act.

1893   Panic devastates financial markets and touches off national depression.

1895   J. P. Morgan bails out U.S. Treasury and saves country's gold reserves.

1901   J. P. Morgan buys out Carnegie Steel and creates U.S. Steel, first billion-dollar corporation in United States.

BIBLIOGRAPHY

GENERAL

Sean Dennis Cashman, *America in the Gilded Age: From the Death of Lincoln to the Rise of Theodore Roosevelt* (1993).

Alan Dawley, *Struggles for Justice: Social Responsibility and the Liberal State* (1991).

Vincent P. DeSantis, *The Shaping of Modern America, 1877–1920,* 2nd ed. (1989).

Nell Irwin Painter, *Standing at Armageddon: The United States, 1877–1919* (1987).

BUSINESS

David Haward Bain, *Empire Express: Building the First Transcontinental Railroad* (1999).

Kathleen Brady, *Ida Tarbell: Portrait of a Muckraker* (1984).

Stuart Bruchey, *Growth of the Modern American Economy* (1975).

Vincent P. Carosso, *The Morgans: Private International Bankers, 1854–1913* (1987).

Edward Chancellor, *Devil Take the Hindmost: A History of Financial Speculation* (1999).

Alfred D. Chandler Jr., *The Railroads, The Nation's First Big Business: Sources and Readings* (1965).

Alfred D. Chandler Jr., *The Visible Hand: The Managerial Revolution in American Business* (1977).

Alfred D. Chandler Jr., *Scale and Scope: The Dynamics of Industrial Capitalism* (1990).

Ron Chernow, *The House of Morgan: An American Banking Dynasty and the Rise of Modern Finance* (1990).

Ron Chernow, *Titan: The Life of John D. Rockefeller, Sr.* (1998).

Louis Galambos, *The Public Image of Big Business in America, 1880–1940: A Quantitative Study in Social Change* (1974).

John A. Garraty, *The New Commonwealth, 1877–1890* (1968).

David Freeman Hawke, *John D.: The Founding Father of the Rockefellers* (1980).

Robert L. Heilbroner and Aaron Singer, *The Economic Transformation of America* (1977).

David H. Howard, *People, Pride, and Progress: 125 Years of the Grange in America* (1992).

Jonathan Hughes, *The Vital Few: The Entrepreneur and American Economic Progress* (1986).

Edward C. Kirkland, *Industry Comes of Age: Business, Labor, and Public Policy, 1860–1897* (1961).

Maury Klein, *Unfinished Business: The Railroad in American Life* (1994).

Maury Klein, *The Life and Legend of Jay Gould* (1997).

Maury Klein, *The Life and Legend of E. H. Harriman* (2000).

James T. Kloppenberg, *Uncertain Victory: Social Democracy and Progressivism in European and American Thought, 1870–1920* (1986).

Peter J. Lewty, *To the Columbia Gateway: The Oregon Railway and the Northern Pacific, 1879–1884* (1987).

Harold C. Livesay, *Andrew Carnegie and the Rise of Big Business* (1975).

Robert D. Marcus, *Grand Old Party: Political Structure in the Gilded Age, 1880–1896* (1971).

Albro Martin, *James J. Hill and the Opening of the Northwest* (1991).

Albro Martin, *Railroads Triumphant: The Growth, Rejection, and Rebirth of a Vital American Force* (1992).

Carol Marvin, *When Technologies Were New* (1988).

Richard O'Connor, *Gould's Millions* (1962).

Glenn Porter, *The Rise of Big Business, 1860–1910* (1973).

Andrew Sinclair, *Corsair: The Life of J. Pierpont Morgan* (1980).

Jean Strouse, *Morgan: American Financier* (1999).

George Rogers Taylor and Irene D. Neu, *The American Railroad Network, 1861–1890* (1956).

William G. Thomas, *Lawyering for the Railroad: Business, Law, and Power in the New South* (1999).

Joseph Frazier Wall, *Andrew Carnegie* (1970).

Thomas Weiss and Donald Schaefer, eds., *American Economic Development in Historical Perspective* (1994).

Elmus Wicker, *Banking Panics of the Gilded Age* (2000).

John Hoyt Williams, *The Great and Shining Road: The Epic Story of the Transcontinental Railroad* (1988).

LAW

William E. Forbath, *Law and the Shaping of the American Labor Movement* (1991).

Morton J. Horowitz, *The Transformation of American Law, 1870–1960* (1992).

Paul Kens, *Justice Stephen Field: Shaping Liberty from the Gold Rush to the Gilded Age* (1997).

Robert Green McCloskey, *American Conservatism in the Age of Enterprise, 1865–1910* (1951).

Arnold M. Paul, *Conservative Crisis and the Rule of Law: Attitudes of the Bar and Bench, 1887–1895* (1965).

Charles E. Rosenberg, *The Trial of the Assassin Guiteau: Psychiatry and the Law in the Gilded Age* (1968).

POLITICS

Alyn Brodsky, *Grover Cleveland: A Study in Character* (2000).

John M. Dobson, *Politics in the Gilded Age: A New Perspective on Reform* (1972).

Michael L. Goldberg, *An Army of Women: Gender and Politics in Gilded Age Kansas* (1997).

Lewis L. Gould, *William McKinley: A Biography* (1988).

Ari Hoogenboom, *Rutherford B. Hayes: Warrior and President* (1995).

David H. Howard, *People, Pride, and Progress: 125 Years of the Grange in America* (1992).

H. Paul Jeffers, *An Honest President: The Life and Presidencies of Grover Cleveland* (2000).

David M. Jordan, *Roscoe Conkling of New York: Voice in the Senate* (1986).

Matthew Josephson, *The Politicos, 1865–1896* (1938).

James. A. Kehl, *Boss Rule in the Gilded Age: Matt Quay of Pennsylvania* (1980).

Paul Kleppner, *The Cross of Culture: A Social Analysis of Midwestern Politics, 1850–1900* (1970).

John F. Marszalek, *Grover Cleveland* (1988).

Gerald W. McFarland, *Mugwumps, Morals & Politics, 1884–1920* (1975).

Michael E. McGerr, *The Decline of Popular Politics: The American North, 1865–1928* (1986).

H. Wayne Morgan, *From Hayes to McKinley: National Party Politics, 1877–1896* (1969).

D. Sven Nordin, *Rich Harvest: A History of the Grange, 1867–1900* (1974).

Allan Peskin, *Garfield: A Biography* (1998).

Thomas C. Reeves, *Gentleman Boss: The Life of Chester Alan Arthur* (1991).

Joanne R. Reitano, *The Tariff Question in the Gilded Age* (1994).

David J. Rothman, *Politics and Power: The United States Senate, 1869–1901* (1966).

Milton Rugoff, *America's Gilded Age: Intimate Portraits from an Era of Extravagance and Change, 1850–1890* (1989).

John G. Sproat, *The Best Men: Liberal Reformers in the Gilded Age* (1968).

Mark Wahlgren Summers, *Rum, Romanism, and Rebellion: The Making of a President, 1884* (1999).

David M. Tucker, *Mugwumps: Public Moralists of the Gilded Age* (1998).

Rexford Tugwell, *Grover Cleveland* (1968).

Lynette Boney Wrenn, *Crisis and Commission Government in Memphis: Elite Rule in a Gilded Age City* (1998).

CULTURE

Louis Auchincloss, *The Vanderbilt Era: Profiles of a Gilded Age* (1989).

Mary Warner Blanchard, *Oscar Wilde's America: Counterculture in the Gilded Age* (1998).

William A. Bullough, *Cities and Schools in the Gilded Age* (1974).

Charles. W. Calhoun, ed., *The Gilded Age: Essays on the Origins of Modern America* (1995).

John G. Cawelti, *Apostles of the Self-Made Man: Changing Concepts of Success in America* (1965).

John Foreman, *The Vanderbilts and the Gilded Age* (1991).

Gene M. Greesley, *West by East: The American West in the Gilded Age* (1972).

Judy Arlene Hilkey, *Character Is Capital: Success Manuals and Manhood in Gilded Age America* (1997).

Wilbert Jenkins, *Seizing the Day: African Americans in Post–Civil War Charleston* (1998).

Justin Kaplan, *Mr. Clemens and Mark Twain* (1966).

Paulette D. Kilmer, *The Fear of Sinking: The American Success Formula in the Gilded Age* (1996).

Susan Levine, *Labor's True Woman, Carpet Weavers, Industrialization, and Labor Reform in the Gilded Age* (1984).

Donald B. Marti, *Women of the Grange* (1991).

Gloria Moldow, *Women Doctors in Gilded-Age Washington: Race, Gender and Professionalization* (1987).

Frederick Platt, *America's Gilded Age: Its Architecture and Decoration* (1976).

Robert A. M. Stern, *New York 1880: Architecture and Urbanism in the Gilded Age* (1999).

John L. Thomas, *Alternative America: Henry George, Edward Bellamy, Henry Demarest Lloyd and the Adversary Tradition* (1983).

John Tomsich, *A Genteel Endeavor: American Culture and Politics in the Gilded Age* (1971).

Alan Trachtenberg, *The Incorporation of America: Culture and Society in the Gilded Age* (1982).

DINNER PAILS

The dinner pail or lunch bucket, the universal symbol of the working class, took many sizes and shapes. Designed to carry a midday meal for workers who did not have time to go home to eat, it might hold bread, leftovers, a sandwich, coffee, or whatever else fit easily into the container. Some cities such as Riverside, California, prohibited workers from carrying dinner pails on downtown streets. Presumably sidewalks were meant only for the middle class and well to do.

Anthracite Heritage Museum.

AMERICA THROUGH THE EYES OF THE WORKERS 18

1870–1890

F OR TWO WEEKS DURING THE SUMMER of 1877, President Rutherford B. Hayes faced an insurrection greater than any since the Civil War. Hayes met daily with his cabinet to plan military strategy and sat up late into the night receiving reports from his generals. He dispatched federal troops to nine states, ordered warships to protect the nation's capital, and threatened to declare martial law. Not since the Confederates fired on Fort Sumter had the nation witnessed such an alarm. Who posed this threat to the Republic? Not former rebels or foreign armies, but American workers engaged in the first nationwide labor strike in the country's history.

Economic depression following the panic of 1873 had thrown as many as three million people out of work. Those who were lucky enough to keep their jobs watched as pay cuts eroded their wages until they could no longer feed their families. When a Cincinnati cigar worker with a wife and three children was asked how he lived on $5 a week, he replied, "I don't live. I am literally starving. We get meat once a week, the rest of the week we have dry bread and black coffee."

The burden of the depression fell disproportionately on the backs of the country's working class. So that they could continue paying dividends to their shareholders, corporations laid off workers and cut wages. When the Baltimore and Ohio (B&O) Railroad announced a 10 percent wage reduction in the summer of 1877 at the same time it declared a 10 percent dividend to its stockholders, the brakemen in West Virginia, whose wages had already fallen from $70 to $30 a month, walked out on strike. One B&O worker described the hardship that had driven him to take such desperate action: "We eat our hard bread and tainted meat two days old on the sooty cars up the road, and when we come home, find our children gnawing bones and our wives complaining that they cannot even buy hominy and molasses for food."

The strike by brakemen in West Virginia touched off the Great Railroad Strike, a nationwide uprising that spread rapidly to Pittsburgh and Chicago, St. Louis and San Francisco. Within a few days, nearly 100,000 railroad workers went out on strike. The spark of rebellion soon fired other workers to action. An estimated 500,000 laborers joined the striking train workers. Steelworkers, longshoremen, workers from all industries, often with their wives and children, made common cause with the railroad strikers. Violence erupted as the strikers clashed with state militia. President Hayes, after hesitating briefly, called up federal troops. In three weeks it was over. "The strikes have been put down by force," Hayes noted in his diary on August 5. "But now for the real remedy. Can't something be done by education of the strikers, by judicious control of the capitalists, by wise general policy to end or diminish the evil? The railroad strikers, as a rule, are good men, sober, intelligent, and industrious."

THE GREAT RAILROAD STRIKE
The August 11, 1877 cover of Harper's Weekly *featured an illustration of the great railroad strike depicting the sixth Maryland regiment firing its way through Baltimore. Notice the fixed bayonets of the soldiers and the brick-throwing strikers fighting in close quarters. Such scenes of violence frightened many middle-class Americans who initially had sympathized with the strikers. Public opinion shifted as a result of news coverage as many blamed the strikers for the bloodshed and damage to property that accompanied the strike.*

Harper's Weekly, August 11, 1877.

The uprising of the workers in 1877 underscored the tensions produced by rapid industrialization and pointed to many legitimate grievances on the part of labor. The unprecedented industrial growth that occurred after the Civil War came about as a result of the labor of millions of men, women, and children who toiled in workshops and factories, in sweatshops and mines, on the railroads and construction sites across America. Their stories provide a different perspective from that of the great industrialists and the politicians. Through their eyes it is possible to gauge how corporate capitalism transformed old work patterns and affected the social and cultural—as well as the economic and political—life of the United States.

America's New Industrial Workers

America's industrial growth in the years following the Civil War brought about a massive redistribution of population as agricultural workers moved to the city and became recruits in the industrial labor force. Burgeoning industrial centers such as

Pittsburgh, Chicago, New York, and Detroit acted like giant magnets, attracting workers from the countryside (Map 18.1). The movement from the rural periphery to industrial centers was not just American in scope. Farm boys and girls from western Pennsylvania who left for the mills of Pittsburgh were part of a global migration that included rural immigrants from Ireland, southern Italy, Russia, Japan, and China. As labor historian David Montgomery has pointed out, "The rural periphery of the nineteenth century industrial world became the primary source of supply for 'human machines.'"

Workers from the Rural Periphery

By the 1870s, the world could be seen as divided into three interlocking geographic regions forming roughly concentric circles (Map 18.2). At the center stood an industrial core bounded by Chicago and St. Louis in the west; Toronto, Glasgow, and Berlin

MAP 18.1

Industrialization, 1865–1900

Industrial development between 1865 and 1900 shows the clustering of industry in the Northeast and Great Lakes states. Only in these regions did industry employ 25 percent or more of the labor force. The West supplied raw materials—oil, minerals, and timber— while in the South and the Midwest agriculture and attendant industries such as tobacco processing and meatpacking dominated. Note, however, the concentration of textile manufacturing in the South.

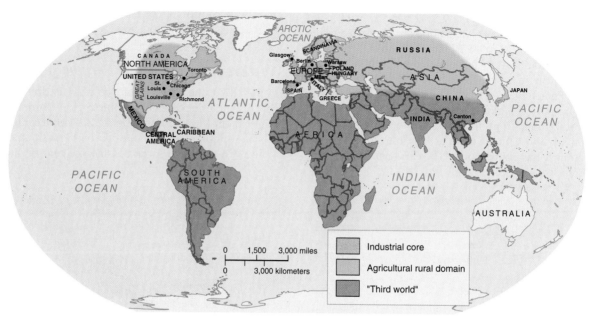

MAP 18.2

Economic Regions of the World
The global nature of the world economy at the turn of the twentieth century is indicated by three interlocking geographic regions. At the center was the industrial core—western Europe and the northeastern United States; the agricultural periphery (rural domain) supplied immigrant laborers to the industries in the core. Beyond these two regions lay a "third world" tied economically to the industrial core by colonialism.

READING THE MAP: What parts of the world did not belong to one of these three economic regions? Where did the United States fit in this economic division of the globe?

CONNECTIONS: What does this characterization of the United States say about its stage of economic development in the late nineteenth century? How would you characterize the areas outside the economic regions specified?

www.bedfordstmartins.com/tap   SEE THE ONLINE STUDY GUIDE for more help in analyzing this map.

in the north; Warsaw in the east; and Milan, Barcelona, Richmond, and Louisville in the south. Surrounding the industrial core and its urban outposts lay a vast agricultural domain encompassing Canada, much of Scandinavia, Russia and Poland, Hungary, Greece, Italy and Sicily, southern Spain, the defeated Confederate states and the Great Plains of America, central and northern Mexico, the hinterlands of Canton, China, and later the southern islands of Japan. Capitalist development in the late nineteenth century shattered traditional patterns of economic activity in this rural periphery. As old patterns broke down, the rural areas exported, along with other raw materials, new recruits for the industrial labor force.

Farm boys and girls from western Pennsylvania who left for the mills of Pittsburgh were part of a global migration that included rural immigrants from Ireland, Italy, Russia, Japan, and China.

Beyond this second circle lay an even larger area including the Caribbean, Central and South America, the Middle East, Africa, India, and most of Asia. This third area too became increasingly tied to the industrial core in the late nineteenth century, but its peoples largely stayed put. They worked on the plantations and railroads, in the mines and ports as part of a huge export network managed by foreign powers that staked out spheres of influence and colonies, often with gunboats and soldiers.

Beginning in the 1870s, railroad expansion and low steamship fares gave the world's peoples a newfound mobility that enabled industrialists to draw on a worldwide population for cheap labor. The Carnegie steel mills outside Pittsburgh provide a good example. When Andrew Carnegie opened his first mill in 1872, his superintendent hired workers he called "buckwheats"—young American boys just off the farm. By the 1890s, however, Carnegie's workforce was liberally sprinkled with other rural boys—Hungarians and Slavs who had migrated to the United States, willing to work for low wages. The ability to draw on cheap labor on a global scale helps explain why, in spite of the soaring demand for laborers after the Civil War, the wages of unskilled workers in the United States remained relatively stagnant. Their pay fell dramatically during the depressions of 1873–1878 and 1893–1896, and did not regain 1872 levels before the end of the century.

Immigration, Ethnic Rivalry, and Racism

Ethnic diversity played a role in dividing skilled workers (those with a craft or specialized ability) from the unskilled (those who supplied muscle and brawn). As managers increasingly mechanized to replace skilled craftsworkers with lower-paid, unskilled labor, they drew on immigrants from southern and eastern Europe. The skilled workers, mostly from northern or western Europe, found it easy to criticize the newcomers. As one Irish worker complained, "There should be a law . . . to keep all the I-talians from comin' in and takin' the bread out of the mouths of honest people."

The Irish worker's resentment of the new Italian immigrants brings into focus the importance of the ideology and practice of racism in the experience of America's immigrant laborers. Throughout the nineteenth century, members of the educated elite as well as workers viewed ethnic and even religious differences as racial characteristics—referring to the Polish "race" or the Jewish "race." Each wave of newcomers was seen as being somehow inferior to the established residents. The Irish who judged the Italians so harshly had themselves been

THE COMPETITION OF CHEAP LABOR
Big business looks on approvingly as cheap immigrant labor outweighs American workers in this political cartoon published in the weekly **Judge** *in 1888. "As long as I am plentifully supplied with Immigrant Labor," says the portly manufacturer, "I shall be deaf to the demands of the native workingman." Cartoons like this one underscored organized labor's concern with the number of foreign workers entering the country in the 1880s—nearly eight million, twice the number of the previous decade. Not only did the seemingly unlimited supply of immigrant laborers keep wages low, but the new recruits, who knew nothing of labor's struggles, often took work as strikebreakers.*
Judge, February 11, 1888.

www.bedfordstmartins.com/tap   SEE THE ONLINE STUDY GUIDE for more help in analyzing this image.

seen as a subhuman species just a generation before. Immigrants not only brought their own religious and racial prejudices to the United States but also absorbed the popular prejudices of American culture. Social Darwinism, with its strongly racist overtones, decreed that whites stood at the top of the evolutionary ladder. But who was "white"? The social construction of race is nowhere more apparent than in the testimony of an Irish dockworker, who boasted that he hired only "white men" to load cargo, a category that he insisted excluded "Poles and Italians."

Racism took its most blatant form in the treatment of African Americans and Asians. Like other migrants from the rural periphery, African American men in the South, former slaves and the children of slaves, found work as human machines. The labor gang system used in many industries was most extreme and brutal in the South, where private employers contracted prison labor, mostly African Americans jailed for such minor crimes as vagrancy. Shackled together by chains as they worked under the watchful eyes of armed guards, these workers formed the bottom rung on labor's ladder. A Georgia man who escaped the brutal chain gang system remarked, "Call it slavery, peonage, or what not, the truth is we lived in a hell on earth."

On the West Coast, Asian immigrants became the scapegoats of the changing economy. Workers vigorously attacked the Chinese and later the Japanese as the "tools of corporate interest" recruited by the bosses to undercut wages and threaten "white society." The labor movement played a key role in excluding Asians from American life. Labor unions practiced exclusionary policies against both Chinese and Japanese workers and championed the 1882 Chinese Exclusion Act, which prohibited the immigration of Chinese to the United States.

America's Diverse Workers

Throughout the nineteenth century, America's industrial workers toiled in a variety of settings. Skilled craftsworkers and artisans still worked in small workshops or alone. But with the rise of corporate capitalism, large factories, mills, and mines increasingly dotted the landscape. Sweatshops and outwork, the contracting of piecework performed in the home, provided a different work experience from that of the factory operative (machine tender) or the industrial worker. Pick-and-shovel labor, whether on the railroads or in the building trades, constituted another kind of work. The best way to get a sense of the diversity of workers and workplaces is to look at five distinct types of industrial work: common labor, skilled work, factory work, sweatshop labor, and mining.

Common laborers formed the backbone of the American labor force throughout the nineteenth century. They built the railroads and subways, tunneled under New York's East River to anchor the Brooklyn Bridge, and helped to lay the foundation of industrial America. In her book *China Men*, Maxine Hong Kingston tells the story of Ah Goong, one of the *gam saan haak* ("travelers to the gold mountain") who came to California in 1863 and went to work for the Central Pacific Railroad. For less than a dollar a day, Ah Goong hung in a basket on the cliffs above the American River, setting black powder in crevices and firing the fuses to blast a path through the mountains. In 1869, when the railroad experimented with nitroglycerin, he sometimes risked his life to earn an extra dollar by going back into the tunnel to investigate when the temperamental nitro failed to explode. Working in the dark tunnel, Ah Goong toiled on eight-hour shifts seven days a week. When the railroad tried to increase the shift to ten hours, Ah Goong and ten thousand of his fellow workers went on strike in 1867. They demanded the same wages paid to the white, mostly Irish gangs, who earned $40 a month compared with Ah Goong's $30. Construction superintendent Charles Crocker broke the strike, but in the end he raised the wages of the Chinese workers to $35 a month.

Common laborers built the railroads and subways, tunneled under New York's East River to anchor the Brooklyn Bridge, and helped to lay the foundation of industrial America.

Life was cheap on the Central Pacific. Men died on the cliffs when they failed to scramble out of the way before a blast or when the ropes to the baskets broke. Men died in the tunnels when the nitroglycerin exploded without warning. Ah Goong was one of the lucky ones; he lived to see the Central Pacific reach Promontory Point, Utah, where it joined the Union Pacific to form the first transcontinental railroad in 1869. In the celebration that followed, orators basked in the accomplishment of the "greatest monument of human labor," never mentioning the Chinese workers whose prodigious labor had built the railroad.

CHINESE RAILROAD WORKERS
*Chinese workers like this section gang pictured at Promontory Point, Utah, in 1869
made up more than 80 percent of the workforce that built America's first transcontinental railroad. Charles Crocker of the Central Pacific hired them, reasoning that the race
that built the Great Wall could build his road across the treacherous Sierra Nevada.
Besides, the Chinese workers were a bargain: Crocker paid them $10 a month less than
he paid his Irish section gangs.*
Denver Public Library, Western History Collection, photo by J. B. Silvis.

At the opposite end of the economic ladder from common laborers were skilled craftsmen like iron puddler James J. Davis, a Welsh immigrant. When he was eleven years old, he went into the iron mills in Sharon, Pennsylvania, where his father was a puddler. Using brains along with brawn, puddlers took the melted pig iron in the heat of the furnace and, with long poles, formed the cooling metal into two-hundred-pound balls, relying on eye and intuition to make each ball uniform. Davis compared the task to baking bread: "I am like some frantic baker in the inferno kneading a batch of iron bread for the devil's breakfast. My spoon weighs twenty-five pounds, my porridge is pasty iron, and the heat of my kitchen is so great that if my body was not hardened to it, the ordeal would drop me in my tracks."

Possessing such a skill meant earning good wages, up to $7 a day, when there was work. But often no work could be found. Much industry and manufacturing in the nineteenth century remained seasonal; it was a rare worker who could count on year-round pay. In addition, two major depressions only twenty years apart, in 1873 and 1893, spelled unemployment and hardship for all workers. Puddling jobs often passed from father to son, and although Davis earned the title of master puddler by the time he was sixteen, his father was not ready to turn over his hearth to his son, so in the hard times of the 1890s Davis tramped the countryside looking for work. In an era before unemployment insurance, workers' compensation, or old-age pensions, even the best worker could not guarantee security for his family. "The fear of ending in the poor-house is one of the terrors that dog a man through life," Davis confessed. Davis escaped such a fate. He gained an education, became a labor organizer, was elected to Congress, and served as secretary of labor in the 1920s.

In the iron industry, puddlers controlled the pace of work, the organization of the job, and the rate of pay. Such worker control posed a challenge to employers. As the century wore on, they attempted to limit the workers' autonomy by replacing people with machinery, breaking down skilled work into ever smaller parts, and replacing skilled workers with unskilled operatives, often young women willing to work for low wages. The textile mills provide a classic example of mechanized factory labor in the nineteenth century. Mary, a weaver at the mills in Fall River, Massachusetts, told her story to the *Independent* magazine in 1903. She had gone to work in the 1880s at the age of twelve and

had begun weaving at fourteen. Mechanization of the looms had reduced the job of the weaver to watching for breaks in the thread. "At first the noise is fierce, and you have to breathe the cotton all the time, but you get used to it," Mary told her interviewer. "When the bobbin flies out and a girl gets hurt, you can't hear her shout—not if she just screams, you can't. She's got to wait, 'till you see her. . . . Lots of us is deaf," she confessed.

The majority of factory operatives in the textile mills were young, unmarried women like Mary who were paid by the piece rather than by the day or hour. Mary worked from six in the morning to six at night, six days a week, and took home about a dollar a day. The seasonal nature of the work also drove wages down. "Like as not your mill will 'shut down' three months," and "some weeks you only get two or three days' work, when they're curtailin'," Mary recounted. After twenty years of working in the mill, Mary's family had not been able to scrape together enough money to buy a house: "We saved some, but something always comes."

Mechanization transformed the garment industry as well. With the introduction of the foot-

TEXTILE MILL WORKER
This woman weaver is typical of the factory operatives who worked in New England's textile mills. Young, unmarried women formed the majority of mill workers. The weaver's job was to watch the power looms to be sure the threads did not break. The work was both nerve-racking and unhealthy— note the lint on the floor. What can't be seen is the tremendous racket made by the huge machines—so loud that many women lost their hearing.
Courtesy George Eastman House.

COAL MINERS
Coal miners come up out of the shaft in the "cage" in Scranton, Pennsylvania. As one observer commented, "Although the mines are always cold and wet, the labor of drilling and handling the coal is so great that the miner, stripped to his shirt, soon becomes wet with sweat while the dust from the coal is at times almost stifling. The work is thirst-provoking and each miner carries with him a bottle or can, often a quart or more of strong, black coffee for the purpose of washing the dust from his throat."

Picture Research Consultants & Archives.

pedaled sewing machine in the 1850s and the use of mechanical cloth-cutting knives in the 1870s, independent tailors were replaced with workers hired by contractors to sew pieces of cloth into clothing. Working in sweatshops, small rooms hired for the season, or even the contractor's own tenement, women and children formed an important segment of garment workers.

Sadie Frowne, a sixteen-year-old Polish Jew, went to work in a Brooklyn sweatshop in the 1890s. Frowne sewed for eleven hours a day in a room twenty feet long and fourteen feet wide containing fourteen machines. "The machines go like mad all day, because the faster you work the more money you get," she recalled. Paid by the piece, she earned about $4.50 a week and, by rigid economy, tried to save $2. Young and single, Frowne typified the woman wage earner in the late nineteenth century. The largest percentage of women worked in the nee-

dle trades, but factory work ranked a close second. In 1890, the average working woman had started to work at age fifteen and was now twenty-two, working twelve hours a day, six days a week, and earning less than $6 a week. Discriminated against in the marketplace, where they earned less than men, and largely ignored by the labor unions during this period, women generally worked only eight to ten years, until they married. These women formed a unique subculture. Their youth, high spirits, and camaraderie made the hard, repetitive work they did bearable, and after hours they relished the "cheap amusements" of the day—the dance halls, social clubs, and amusement parks.

The most hazardous work and the worst working conditions existed in metal and coal mining, along with extractive industries such as lumbering. To look closely at conditions in the mines, mills, and forests, in the words of one historian, is to enter a "chamber of horrors." Ross Moudy, a miner in Cripple Creek, Colorado, recounted the dangers he faced, first in a chlorination mill. For nine or ten hours a day, he worked for $1.50 to $2, breathing sulfur dioxide or chlorine fumes and working in dust so thick that "one cannot see an object two feet away." He soon quit and went to work in a Cripple Creek gold mine. There, according to Moudy, "dangers do not seem so great to a practiced miner, who is used to climbing hundreds of feet on . . . braces put about six feet apart . . . and then walking the same distance on a couple of poles sometimes not larger than fence rails, where a misstep would mean a long drop." When a group of stockholders came to tour the mine, Moudy recounted how one man, white as a ghost after a near fall, told the miner beside him "that instead of being paid $3 per day they ought to have all the gold they could take out."

Miners died in explosions, cave-ins, and fires. New technology eliminated some dangers but often added others, for machinery could maim and kill. In the hard-rock mines of the West in the 1870s, accidents annually disabled one out of every thirty miners and killed one in eighty. Moudy's biggest worry was the carbon dioxide that often filled the tunnels because of poor ventilation. "Many times," he confessed, "I have been carried out unconscious and not able to work for two or three days after." Those who avoided accidents still breathed air so dangerous that respiratory diseases eventually disabled them. After a year on the job, Moudy joined the union "because I saw it would help me to keep in work and for protection in case of accident or sickness." The union provided good sick benefits and hired nurses, "so if one is alone and sick he is sure to be taken care of." Moudy acknowledged that there were some "hotheads" in the union, the militant Western Federation of Miners. But he insisted that most union men "believe the change will come about gradually and not by revolution."

The Family Economy: Women and Children

Although real wages (pay measured in terms of buying power) rose by 15 percent between 1873 and 1893, workers did not share equally in the improvement. African American men, for example, continued to be paid at a much lower rate than white men, as did immigrant laborers and white women. And the protracted depressions following

the panics of 1873 and 1893 undercut many of labor's gains. In 1890, the average worker earned $500 a year. Many working-class families, whether native-born or immigrant, lived in poverty or near poverty; their economic survival depended on the contributions of all, regardless of sex or age. One statistician estimated that in 1900, as many as 64 percent of working-class families relied on income other than the husband's wages to make ends meet. The paid and unpaid work of women and children were thus essential for family survival and economic advancement.

Child labor had been common in the mines and textile mills since midcentury. As other industries mechanized in the 1880s and 1890s, they hired children, girls as well as boys, who often could tend machines as efficiently as adults yet received wages considerably lower. One worker recalled his youth in the textile mills of Massachusetts: "When I began as a boy in the mill, I worked fifteen hours a day. I used to go in at a quarter past four in the morning and work until a quarter to eight at night, having thirty minutes for breakfast and the same for dinner, drinking tea after ringing out at night. . . . This I did for eleven years."

Attempts to abolish child labor began before the Civil War. By 1863, seven states had passed laws limiting the hours of child workers to forty-eight a week, but often the laws were not strictly enforced. Most southern states refused to regulate child labor, and children as young as six or seven years old continued to be widely employed in southern mills. In the nation's mines, particularly in Appalachia, young boys were recruited to pick out the slate and waste from coal as it passed along chutes. Suspended on wooden boards over the moving coal, these "breaker boys" engaged in dangerous, physically demanding work. A boy who slipped into the coal had little chance of surviving without serious injury. When a child labor committee investigated conditions in Pennsylvania, it found that more than ten thousand children were illegally employed in the coalfields. Child labor increased decade by decade, with the percentage of children under fifteen engaged in paid labor not dropping until after World War I. The 1900 census showed that 1,750,178 children ages ten to fifteen were employed, an increase of more than a million since 1870. Children in this age range constituted over 18 percent of the labor force and 7 percent of all nonagricultural workers.

"BREAKER BOYS"
Child labor in America's mines and mills was common at the turn of the century, despite state laws that attempted to restrict it. Here "breaker boys" in the 1890s take a rest from their twelve-hour day in the coal mines of Appalachia. Their unsmiling faces bear testimony to their hard and dangerous work. A committee investigating child labor found more than ten thousand children illegally employed in the Pennsylvania coalfields.
Brown Brothers.

Many working-class families, whether native-born or immigrant, lived in poverty or near poverty; their economic survival depended on the contributions of all, regardless of sex or age.

Even children who did not work for wages contributed to the family economy by scavenging firewood and coal. Gangs of children patrolled the railroad tracks, picking up whatever fell from the coal cars that fueled the locomotives. Other children worked as street vendors, newsboys, and bootblacks. Although laws in many states mandated school attendance, harried truant officers found it hard to collar children whose parents insisted they work rather than go to school.

In the late nineteenth century, the number of women workers rose sharply, with their most common occupation changing slowly from domestic service to factory work and then to office work. The typical factory operative in the late nineteenth century was a teenage girl. In 1870, the census listed 1.5 million women working in nonagricultural occupations. By 1890, more than 3.7 million women earned wages, although they were paid less than men (Figure 18.1). Women's working patterns varied considerably according to race and ethnicity. White married women, even among the working class, rarely worked outside the home; in 1890, only 3 percent were employed. Nevertheless, married women found ways to contribute to the family economy. Families often took in boarders, which meant extra housework. In many Italian families, piecework such as making artificial flowers allowed married women to contribute to the family economy without leaving their homes. Black women, married and unmarried, worked for wages outside their homes at a much higher rate than white women. The 1890 census showed that 25 percent of African American married women worked outside the home, often as domestics in the houses of white families.

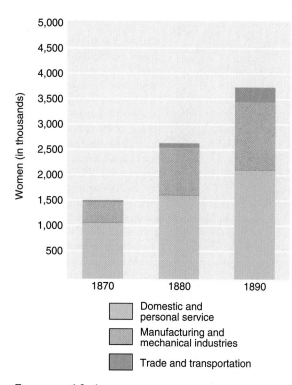

FIGURE 18.1

Women and Work, 1870–1890

In 1870, close to 1.5 million women worked in non-agricultural occupations. By 1890, that number had more than doubled to 3.7 million. The total number of women workers rose sharply while the most common occupation changed from domestic work to industry and later to office work.

Managers and White Collars

In the late nineteenth century, business expansion and consolidation led to a managerial revolution, creating a need for a new class of managers. As skilled workers saw their crafts replaced by mechanization, some moved into management positions. At the same time, new white-collar jobs in offices and department stores attracted a growing number of women workers.

The New Managerial Class

"The middle class is becoming a salaried class," a writer for the *Independent* magazine observed, "and is rapidly losing the economic and moral independence of former days." As large business organizations consolidated and created national markets,

they replaced what the eighteenth-century economist Adam Smith had called "the invisible hand" of market forces with the "visible hand" of salaried managers.

At the same time, corporate development separated management from ownership, and the job of directing the firm became the province of salaried managers and executives. The majority of these new middle managers were white men drawn from the 8 percent of Americans who held high school diplomas. In 1880, the middle managers at the Chicago, Burlington, and Quincy Railroad earned between $1,500 and $4,000 a year, while senior executives, generally recruited from the college-educated elite, took home $4,000 or more, and the company's general manager made $15,000 a year, approximately thirty times what the average worker earned.

In the late nineteenth century, business expansion and consolidation led to a managerial revolution, creating a need for a new class of managers.

Until late in the century, when engineering schools began to supply recruits, skilled workers trained on the job often moved from the shop floor to positions of considerable responsibility. The career of Captain William "Billy" Jones provides a glimpse of a skilled ironworker turned manager. Jones, the son of a Welsh immigrant, grew up in the heat of the blast furnaces, where he started working as an apprentice at the age of ten. During the Civil War, he served in the Union army and earned the rank of captain, a title he used for the rest of his life. When Andrew Carnegie opened his steelworks on the outskirts of Pittsburgh in 1872, he hired Jones as his plant superintendent. By all accounts, Jones was the best steel man in the industry. "Good wages and good workmen" was his motto. Carnegie constantly tried to force down wages, but Jones fought for his men: In 1881, he succeeded in shortening the shift from twelve to eight hours a day by convincing Carnegie that shorter hours would reduce absenteeism and accidents. Jones himself demanded and received a "hell of a big salary." Carnegie paid him $25,000—the same salary as the president of the United States—a stupendous sum in 1881 and one that testified to the value the tightfisted Carnegie placed on his superintendent. Captain

Jones did not have long to enjoy his newfound wealth. He died in 1889 when a blast furnace exploded, adding his name to the estimated thirty-five thousand killed each year in industrial accidents.

Office Work and Women "Typewriters"

As businesses became larger and more far-flung in the decades after the Civil War, the need for more elaborate and exact records as well as the greater volume of correspondence led to the hiring of more office workers. Mechanization soon transformed business as it had industry and manufacturing. The adding machine, the cash register, and the typewriter came into general use in the 1880s. Employers seeking literate workers soon turned to women. Educated men had many other career choices, while for middle class, white women secretarial work constituted one of the few areas where they could put their literacy to use for wages.

Sylvie Thygeson was typical of the young women who went to work as secretaries. Thygeson grew up in an Illinois prairie town. When her father died in 1884, she went to work as a country schoolteacher at the age of sixteen, immediately after graduating high school. Quickly learning that teaching school did not pay, she mastered typing and stenography and found work as a secretary to help support her family. According to her account, she made "a fabulous sum of money." Nevertheless, she gave up her job after a few years when she met and married her husband.

Far from seeing their work as dehumanizing, women "typewriters" viewed it with pride and relished the economic independence it afforded them.

Called "typewriters," women workers like Thygeson were quite literally identified as indistinguishable from the machines they operated. Far from seeing their work as dehumanizing, women "typewriters" viewed it with pride and relished the economic independence it afforded them. By the 1890s, secretarial work was the overwhelming choice of white, native-born women, who constituted over 90 percent of the female clerical force. Not only considered more genteel than factory work

CLERICAL WORKER
A stenographer takes dictation in an 1890s office. Note that the apron, a symbol of feminine domesticity, has accompanied the woman into the workplace. In the 1880s, with the invention of the typewriter, many women were able to put their literacy skills to use for wages in the nation's offices.
Brown Brothers.

or domestic labor, office work also meant more money for shorter hours. Boston's clerical workers made more than $6 a week in 1883, compared with less than $5 for women working in manufacturing. For Sylvie Thygeson and thousands of women like her, the office provided a welcome alternative to the limited options available to women workers.

The Department Store

A new consumer culture came to dominate American life in the late nineteenth century as men and women increasingly sought security, comfort, material well-being, and pleasure. Department stores became the symbol of this new consumer culture. Boasting ornate facades, large plate-glass display windows, marble and brass fixtures, and elegant skylights and galleries, department stores like Macy's in New York, Wanamaker's in Philadelphia, and Marshall Field in Chicago stood as monuments to the material promise of the era.

Within these palaces of consumption, one could find cash girls, stock clerks, and wrappers who earned as little as $3 a week. At the top of the scale,

THE LURE OF THE DEPARTMENT STORE
Grand department stores like Marshall Field in Chicago, pictured here in the 1890s, became monuments to the new art of consumption. Occupying an entire city block and featuring as many as seven to ten stories of goods, not counting the main floor and the bargain basement, the stores attracted shoppers to their lavishly decorated display windows. Notice how men in straw "boaters" and women in elaborate hats are drawn like magnets to the displays, where they indulge in a favorite new pastime—window shopping.
Chicago Historical Society.

buyers like Belle Cushman of the fancy goods department at Macy's earned $25 a week, an unusually high salary for a woman in the 1870s. But the gender segregation that kept women's wages low in the office and the factory also prevailed in the department stores. Male supervisors, called floorwalkers, commanded salaries of $10 to $16 per week at a time when the typical Macy's saleswoman received $5 to $6. In all stores, saleswomen were subject to harsh and arbitrary discipline. Sitting was forbidden, and conversation with other clerks led to instant dismissal. Fines for tardiness or gum chewing pared down already meager wages. Yet white-collar workers counted themselves a cut above factory workers, even when their pay envelopes were thinner and did not justify the sense of superiority.

At Home and at Play

The growth of American industrial capitalism not only dramatically altered the workplace but also transformed home and family life and gave rise to new forms of commercialized leisure. Industrialization redefined the very concepts of work and home. Increasingly, men went out to work for wages, while most white married women stayed home, either working in the home without pay—cleaning, cooking, and rearing children—or supervising paid domestic servants who did the housework. The growing separation of workplace and home led to a new ideology, one that sentimentalized the home and women's role in it.

Domesticity and "Domestics"

The separation of the workplace and the home that marked the shift to industrial society in the early nineteenth century redefined the home as a "haven in the heartless world," presided over by a wife and mother who made the household her "separate sphere." The cultural ideology that dictated woman's place to be in the home has been called the "cult of domesticity," a phrase used to prescribe an ideal of womanhood that dominated the period from 1820 to the end of the nineteenth century.

In the decades after the Civil War, the typical middle-class dwelling in which women were to find their place became more embellished architecturally and its interiors more cluttered. Possession of such a home, indeed of any home at all, marked the gulf between the working poor and the middle class. Home owners constituted only 36 percent of the U.S. housing population in 1900, compared with 66 percent today.

SUNDAY DINNER
Sunday dinner at the home of the S. H. Fairfield family of Topeka, Kansas, is served by their African American domestic servant. Middle-class families as well as the wealthy relied on domestic help in the nineteenth century. Unlike white women, who rarely worked after marriage, more than 25 percent of African American married women worked for wages outside their homes, many as domestics. Often they had to leave their own homes and children and live in the homes of their white employers.
The Kansas State Historical Society, Topeka, Kansas.

The cult of domesticity and the elaboration of the middle-class home in the nineteenth century led to a major change in patterns of hiring household help in the North. (The South continued to rely on black female labor, first slave and later free.) Domestic labor changed over the course of the nineteenth century; the so-called hired girl, who worked beside the housewife/employer, became the live-in servant, or domestic, who increasingly carried the main burden of the housework. In American cities by 1870, from 15 to 30 percent of all households included live-in domestic servants, more than 90 percent of whom were women. As the cult of domesticity and growing consumerism raised the expectations of the urban middle and upper classes, domestic servants not only worked longer hours than any other women workers but also spent their supposedly free time on call. "She is liable to be rung up at all hours," one study reported. "Her very meals are not secure from interruption, and even her sleep is not sacred."

The growing separation of workplace and home led to a new ideology, one that sentimentalized the home and women's role in it.

By the mid-nineteenth century, native-born women increasingly took up other work and left domestic service to immigrants. The maid was so often Irish that "Bridget" became a generic term for female domestics. Domestic servants by all accounts resented their lack of privacy and their limited opportunities for socializing. Furthermore, going into service carried a social stigma. As one young woman observed, "If a girl goes into the kitchen she is sneered at and called 'the Bridget,' but if she goes behind the counter she is escorted by gentlemen." No wonder domestic service was the occupation of last resort, a "hard and lonely life" in the words of one servant girl.

PULLMAN, ILLINOIS
An early photograph of a street scene in the town of Pullman, taken when the town was so new its trees were no more than saplings, illustrates the order and comfort of the company's housing, with wide streets, white wooden fencing, front steps, and window awnings. Note the neat wooden walkways over the drainage ditches on each side of the street. George Pullman's model town took into account everything but the desire of the workers to own their own houses and to have some say in the design of their community.
Chicago Historical Society.

For women of the white middle class, domestics were a boon, freeing them from household drudgery and giving them more time to spend with their children or to pursue club work or reform. Thus, while it supported the cult of domesticity, domestic service created for those women who could afford it opportunities that expanded their horizons outside the home.

Mill Towns and Company Towns

In the mill towns and company towns that sprang up across America, industrial capitalism redefined the concept of the home for the working class. Homestead, the Carnegie mill town outside Pittsburgh, grew up haphazardly. By 1892, eight thousand people lived in Homestead, transforming what had been a rural village into a bustling mill town that belied its pastoral name. As the Carnegie steelworks expanded, they encroached on the residential area, pushing the homes out of the flatlands along the Monongahela River. Workers moved into the hills and ravines. In an area called the Hollow, shanties hung precariously on the hillsides. These small, boxlike dwellings—many no larger than two rooms—housed the unskilled laborers from the mills.

Elsewhere, particularly in New England and the South, the company itself planned and built the town. The Amoskeag textile mill in Manchester, New Hampshire, was a self-contained world laid out according to a master plan conceived in the 1830s. Such planned communities rested on the notion of benevolent corporate paternalism. Viewing the workers as the "corporation's children," Amoskeag's owners sought to socialize their increasingly immigrant workforce to the patterns of industrial work and to instill loyalty to the company, curb labor unrest, and prevent unionization.

Perhaps the most famous company town in the United States was built by sleeping-car magnate George M. Pullman nine miles south of Chicago on the shores of Lake Calumet. In the wake of the Great Railroad Strike of 1877, Pullman determined to remove his plant and workers from the "snares of the great city." In 1880, he purchased forty-three hundred acres of bare prairie and built his model town according to the principle on which he built the Pullman Palace cars that made his fortune—to be orderly, clean, and with the appearance of luxury. It was "to the employer's interest," he determined, "to see that his men are clean, contented, sober, educated, and happy."

When the first family moved in on January 1, 1881, the model town of Pullman boasted parks, artificial lakes, fountains, playgrounds, an auditorium, a library, a hotel, shops and markets, a men's club, and eighteen hundred units of housing. Noticeably absent was a saloon. One worker lamented that he frequently walked by and "looked at but dared not enter Pullman's hotel with its private bar." The intimidation the workers felt underscored a major flaw in Pullman's plan. In his eagerness to inculcate what he referred to as the "habits of respectability," Pullman consulted his own wishes and tastes rather than those of his workers. The town offered housing that was clearly superior to that in neighboring towns, but workers paid for the eye appeal. Pullman intended the town to support itself and expected a 6 percent return on his investment. As a result,

Pullman's Model Town
"Pullman's Company Town."
NG MAPS/NGS Image Collection.

Pullman's rents ran 10 to 20 percent higher than housing costs in nearby communities. And a family in Pullman could not own its own home. George Pullman refused to "sell an acre under any circumstances" because as long as he controlled the town absolutely, he held the powerful whip of eviction over his employees and could quickly get rid of troublemakers. Although observers were at first dazzled by its beauty and order, critics were soon comparing Pullman's model town to a "gilded cage" for workers. In 1884, the economist Richard T. Ely went to the heart of what most concerned workers and critics alike: "The idea of Pullman is un-American. . . . It is benevolent, well wishing feudalism, which desires the happiness of the people, but in such way as shall please the authorities."

The autocracy that many feared in Pullman was realized both in textile mill towns south of the Mason-Dixon line and in mining towns in the West. "Practically speaking," a federal investigator travel-

A PULLMAN CRAFTSWORKER
Pullman palace cars were known for their luxurious details. Here a painter working in the 1890s applies elaborate decoration to a Pullman car while in the foreground we see examples of carved doors and hand detailing. Pullman workers struck in 1894 (see page 697) to protest the company's efforts to undermine their status as craftsworkers and put them on piecework for lower wages.
Chicago Historical Society.

ing in the South observed, "the company owns everything and controls everything, and to a large extent controls everybody in the mill village." These largely nameless southern company towns, with their company-controlled stores, churches, schools, and houses, provide a classic example of social con-

trol over workers. Paid in company currency, or scrip, workers had no choice but to patronize the company store, where high prices led to a mounting spiral of debt that reduced the workers to virtual captives of the company. By 1890, 92 percent of southern textile workers' families lived in company towns.

The autocracy that many feared in Pullman was realized both in textile mill towns south of the Mason-Dixon line and in mining towns in the West. "Practically speaking," a federal investigator observed, "the company owns everything and controls everything, and to a large extent controls everybody in the mill village."

In western mining towns, companies exerted control not only over the housing of the employees but over their religious and social lives as well. In Ludlow, a mining town in Colorado controlled by the Rockefeller family, the local minister was hired and supported by the company. Such ironfisted control was designed to prevent labor unions from gaining a foothold. Rockefeller hired paid spies to infiltrate the town, hang out at the local saloons, and report on any union activity.

The mill towns and company towns of America provide only the most dramatic examples of the ways in which industrialization and the rise of corporate capitalism changed the landscape of the United States and altered traditional patterns of work and home life. After the Civil War, communities where men and women of different classes knew and dealt with one another personally became more and more rare. In the face of increasing business consolidation and impersonality, traditional ideas about equal competition in the marketplace and the relative independence of employers and employees lost much of their hold.

Cheap Amusements

Growing class divisions manifested themselves in patterns of leisure as well as in work. The poor and working class took their leisure, when they had it, in the streets, the dance halls, the music houses, the ballparks, and the amusement arcades, which by the 1890s formed a familiar part of the landscape. (See "The Promise of Technology," page 669.) Saloons

The Nickelodeon

THE ADVENT OF PROJECTED MOTION PICTURES marked the culmination of the efforts of many inventors to present lifelike moving pictures on the screen. During the second half of the nineteenth century, a host of inventions, including the kinematoscope, the choreutoscope, the phasmatrope, and the zoopraxiscope, were designed to make pictures move. But it was Thomas Alva Edison's invention in 1889 of the motion picture camera (kinetograph) and a peephole device to display the moving pictures (kinetoscope) that led to the commercial development of the cinema and the rise of the first moving picture theaters, the nickelodeons.

Edison presented the first of his kinetoscope "peep shows" in 1894 and they quickly became popular in hotel lobbies, amusement parks, and arcades where viewers peered into the machine one at a time. By the century's close projectors replaced peep shows and audiences watched moving pictures together in nickelodeons. The name came from combining *nickel,* the price of admission, with *melodeon*, the old reed organ sometimes played to accompany the silent films. By 1907, there were some five thousand nickelodeons across the United States. A viewer described the early shows: "A picture about 2×4 feet was projected from an Edison machine and a reel of film 300 to 400 feet in length was a complete show, lasting for four or five minutes. After each show the house was cleared and filled again."

At first viewers marveled at the moving images—horses, dancers, waves on a beach. But the novelty soon wore off and audiences wanted a story. In 1903, *The Great Train Robbery*, an eleven-minute movie with a simple cops-and-robbers plot, proved such a hit that silent movies soon challenged the popularity of music halls, vaudeville houses, and penny arcades. To supply the public's growing taste for films, Edison opened a motion picture studio in

Corbis-Bettmann.

West Orange, New Jersey. By 1900 about a dozen producers operated out of New York and Chicago.

Edison's hope that the motion picture could be coordinated with the phonograph proved frustrating. Most theaters and all major studios remained uninterested in experimenting with "talkies" until radio technology developed in the 1920s.

Yet it is not too much to say that modern cinema began with the nickelodeons, for their sudden growth stimulated a motion picture industry that soon became one of the fastest growing industries in the nation.

played a central role in workers' lives, often serving informally as political headquarters, employment agencies, and union halls. But not all the working class thronged to the saloons. Recreation varied according to ethnicity, religion, gender, and age. For many new immigrants, social life revolved

around the family; weddings, baptisms, birthdays, and bar mitzvahs constituted the chief celebrations. Generally, older-stock American men spent more time away from home in neighborhood clubs, saloons, and fraternal orders than did their immigrant counterparts. German beer gardens, for example,

included the whole family. But more often, men and women took their leisure separately, except during youth and courtship.

The growing anonymity of urban industrial society posed a challenge to traditional rituals of courtship. Adolescent working girls, immigrant and old stock, no longer met prospective husbands only through their families. Fleeing crowded tenements, the young sought each other's company in dance halls and other commercial retreats. Reformers worried that the dance halls served as a breeding ground for drunkenness and prostitution. In 1884, millionaire heiress Grace Dodge, determined to help young working women find respectability, set up a Working Girl's Club in New York City. Members contributed twenty-five cents a month to rent and furnish a comfortable club room where young women could relax and entertain. Designed as an alternative to dance halls and amusement resorts, the Working Girl's Club sought to replicate patterns of middle-class courtship, where the young met under the watchful eye of older adults. By 1885, branches had sprung up in Brooklyn, Philadelphia, and Boston. But by far the majority of young working women seemed to prefer the pleasure (and danger) of the dance halls.

Speiling, a form of dancing in which a tightly clinched couple spun around and around, promoted a sexually charged atmosphere. "Vulgar dancing exists everywhere," observed one social reformer, noting "the easy familiarity in the dance practiced by nearly all the men in the way they handle the girls." Scorning proper introductions, working-class youth "picked up" partners at the dance halls, where drinking and smoking were part of the evening's entertainment. Young working women, who rarely could afford more than trolley fare when they went out, counted on being "treated" by men, a transaction that often implied sexual payback. The need to negotiate sexual encounters if they wished to participate in commercial amusements blurred the line between respectability and promiscuity, and made the dance halls a potent symbol for reformers who feared they lured girls into prostitution.

For men, baseball became a national pastime in the 1870s—then, as now, one force in urban life that was capable of uniting a city across class lines. Cincinnati mounted the first professional team, the Red Stockings, in 1869. Teams proliferated in cities across the nation, and Mark Twain hailed baseball as "the very symbol, the outward and visible expression, of the drive and push and rush and struggle of the raging, tearing, booming nineteenth century."

CONEY ISLAND
Coney Island became a pleasure resort in the 1870s, but it was not until the turn of the century, with the development of elaborate amusement parks like Steeplechase, Luna, and Dreamland, that Coney Island came into its own as the capital of commercialized leisure. This official guide highlighted the beach, the vaudeville hall, and the midway with its rides and its risqué harem dancers. In the foreground a barker gesticulates and a hawker urges a young man in a straw hat to buy souvenir photographs for his companion.
Brooklyn Historical Society.

The increasing commercialization of entertainment in the late nineteenth century can best be seen at Coney Island. A two-mile stretch of sand close to Manhattan by trolley or steamship, Coney Island in the 1870s and 1880s attracted visitors to its beaches, dance pavilions, and penny arcades—all connected by its famous boardwalk. In the 1890s, Coney Island was transformed into the site of some of the largest and most elaborate amusement parks in the country. Promoter George Tilyou built Steeplechase Park

For men, baseball became a national pastime in the 1870s—then, as now, one force in urban life that was capable of uniting a city across class lines.

in 1897, advertising "10 hours of fun for 10 cents." With its mechanical thrills and funhouse laughs, the amusement park encouraged behavior one schoolteacher aptly described as "everyone with the brakes off." By 1900, as many as half a million New Yorkers flocked to Coney Island on any given weekend. Other cities rushed to build their own playgrounds—Boston's Paragon Park and Revere Beach, Philadelphia's Willow Grove, Cleveland's Euclid Beach—but none rivaled Coney Island. Its popularity signaled the rise of mass entertainment, making the New York amusement park the unofficial capital of a new mass culture.

The Labor Movement

By the late nineteenth century, workers were losing control in the workplace. In the fierce competition to lower prices and cut costs, industrialists like Andrew Carnegie invested heavily in new machinery that enabled managers to replace skilled workers with unskilled workers. The erosion of skill and the redefinition of labor as mere "machine tending" left the worker with a growing sense of individual helplessness that served as a spur to collective action. Alone, the worker might be helpless in the face of the anonymous corporation, but together, workers could challenge the bosses and reassert their power in the workplace.

The Great Railroad Strike of 1877

Labor flexed its muscle with notable results during the summer of 1877 in the Great Railroad Strike. The strike, which began on the Baltimore and Ohio Railroad in West Virginia on July 16, quickly swept across the nation's rails until it involved nearly 100,000 railroad workers (Map 18.3). The strikers, whose wages had been repeatedly cut, aroused a good deal of public sympathy, even among the militia sent to put them down. In Reading, Pennsylva-

nia, militiamen refused to fire on the strikers, saying, "We may be militiamen, but we are workmen first." Rail traffic ground to a halt, and the nation lay paralyzed by the strike.

Violence erupted as the strike spread. In Pittsburgh, striking Pennsylvania Railroad workers were joined in the streets by steel rollers, mechanics, the unemployed, and women and children who were determined to make a common fight against the corporations. Militiamen recruited from Philadelphia marched into Pittsburgh arrogantly boasting that they would clean up what they described as "the workingmen's town." Opening fire on the crowd, they killed twenty people. Predictably, angry workers retaliated, and the resulting conflagration reduced an area of two miles along the track to smoldering rubble. Before the day ended, twenty more workers had been shot and the railroad had sustained property damage totaling $2 million.

Within the space of eight days, the governors of nine states, acting at the prompting of the railroad owners and managers, defined the strike as an insurrection and called for federal troops. President Rutherford B. Hayes (who, according to the New York *World*, owed his contested election in 1876 to the influence of Pennsylvania Railroad president Tom Scott) hesitated briefly and then called up the troops. By the time federal troops arrived, the violence had run its course. The army did not shoot a single striker in 1877. Its primary task consisted of acting as strikebreaker—opening rail traffic, protecting nonstriking "scab" train crews, and maintaining peace along the line.

Although the Great Railroad Strike was spontaneous and unorganized, it frightened the authorities and upper classes like nothing before in U.S. history. They quickly tried to blame the tiny, radical Workingman's Party and predicted a bloody uprising. "Any hour the mob chooses it can destroy any city in the country—that is the simple truth," wrote future secretary of state John Hay to his wealthy father-in-law. The *New York Times* editorialized about the "dangerous classes," and the *Independent* magazine offered the following advice on how to deal with "rioters":

> If the club of a policeman, knocking out the brains of the rioter, will answer, then well and good; but if it does not promptly meet the exigency, then bullets and bayonets, canister and grape[shot] . . . constitutes the one remedy and one duty of the hour.

MAP 18.3
The Great Railroad Strike of 1877
Starting in West Virginia and Pennsylvania, the Great Railway Strike of 1877 spread as far north as Buffalo and as far west as San Francisco, bringing rail traffic to a standstill.

Although large numbers of middle-class Americans had initially sympathized with the conditions that led the workers to strike, they turned against the strikers, blaming them for the violence and property damage that occurred.

In the end, the strikers, whose united action had raised the specter of revolution, won few concrete gains. Wage cuts remained in force on most railroads, hundreds of strikers were fired, and strikers' names were circulated on a blacklist to prevent them from ever being rehired. But the workers were far from demoralized. They had learned the power of concerted action and would use it in the future. As labor leader Samuel Gompers acknowledged fifty years later, "The railroad strike of 1877 was the tocsin [alarm bell] that sounded a ringing message of hope to us all."

The Knights of Labor and the American Federation of Labor

The Knights of Labor, the first mass organization of America's working class, proved the chief beneficiary of labor's newfound consciousness. The Noble and Holy Order of the Knights of Labor had been founded in 1869 by Uriah Stephens, a Philadelphia garment cutter. A secret but peaceable society of workers, the Knights envisioned a "universal brotherhood" of all laborers, from the common laborer to the master craftsman. Although the Knights played no active role in the 1877 strike, membership swelled as a result of the growing interest in unionism. In 1878, the organization dropped the trappings of secrecy and launched an ambitious campaign to organize workers regardless of skill, sex, race, or nationality.

Under the direction of Grand Master Workman Terence V. Powderly, the Knights of Labor became the dominant force in labor during the 1880s. The Knights advocated a kind of workers' democracy that embraced reforms including free land, income tax, public ownership of the railroads, equal pay for work by women, and the abolition of child labor. The Knights sought to remove class distinctions and encouraged local assemblies to welcome all comers, employees and employers alike. "I hate the word 'class' and would drive it from the English language if I could," Powderly stated. Only the "parasitic" members of society—gamblers, stockbrokers, lawyers, bankers, and liquor dealers—were denied membership.

In theory, the Knights of Labor opposed strikes. Powderly championed arbitration and preferred to use boycotts. But in practice, much of the organization's appeal came from the successful strike the Knights mounted in 1885 against three railroads controlled by Jay Gould. The Knights won a sweeping victory, including the revocation of a 15 percent pay cut. Despite the reservations of its leadership, the Knights of Labor was quickly becoming a militant labor organization that excited passionate support from working people.

The Knights advocated a kind of workers' democracy that embraced reforms including free land, income tax, public ownership of the railroads, equal pay for work by women, and the abolition of child labor.

The Knights of Labor was not without rivals. Other trade unionists disliked the broad reform goals of the Knights and sought to focus on workplace issues. Samuel Gompers, a cigar maker born in London of Dutch Jewish ancestry, promoted what he called "pure and simple" unionism. Gompers founded the Organized Trades and Labor Unions in 1881 and reorganized it in 1886 into the American Federation of Labor (AFL), which coordinated the activities of craft unions throughout the United States. His plan was simple: Organize skilled craftworkers like machinists, locomotive engineers, and iron puddlers—those with the most bargaining power—and use strikes to gain immediate objectives such as higher pay and better working conditions. Gompers at first drew few converts. The AFL had only 138,000 members in 1886, compared with 730,000 for the Knights of Labor. But events soon brought down the Knights and enabled Gompers to take control of the labor movement.

Haymarket and the Specter of Labor Radicalism

While the AFL and the Knights of Labor competed for members, radical socialists and anarchists offered different visions of labor's true path. The rad-

SAMUEL GOMPERS
Samuel Gompers, pictured here in 1895, founded the American Federation of Labor in 1886 and served as its president continuously (except for 1895) until his death in 1924. Unlike the Knights of Labor, who supported the Populist Party in the 1890s, the AFL advocated "pure and simple unionism." Gompers, convinced that workers could gain little from politics, organized only skilled workers and focused on bread-and-butter issues.
The George Meany Memorial Archives.

icals, many of whom were immigrants steeped in the tradition of European socialism, believed that reform was futile; they called instead for social revolution, in theory if not in practice. Anarchists also wanted revolutionary change but envisioned a smaller role for the state than the socialists did. Both groups, sensitive to criticism that they preferred revolution in theory to improvements here and now, rallied around the popular issue of the eight-hour day.

Since the 1840s, labor had sought to end the twelve-hour workday, which was standard in industry and manufacturing. By the mid-1880s, it seemed clear to many workers that labor shared too little in the new prosperity of the decade, and once again pressure mounted for the eight-hour day. The radicals seized on the popular issue and launched major rallies in cities across the nation. Supporters of the movement set May 1, 1886, as the date for a nationwide general strike in support of the eight-hour day.

The radicals believed that reform was futile; they called instead for social revolution, in theory if not in practice.

All factions of the nascent labor movement came together in Chicago on May Day, for what was billed as the largest demonstration in history in support of the eight-hour day. A group of radicals led by anarchist Albert Parsons, a *Mayflower* descendant, and August Spies, a German immigrant, spearheaded the eight-hour movement in Chicago. Chicago's Knights of Labor rallied to the cause even though Powderly and the union's leadership, worried by the increasing activism of the rank and file, refused to champion the movement for shorter hours.

Samuel Gompers was on hand, too, to lead the city's trade unionists, although he privately urged the AFL assemblies not to participate in a general strike. Gompers's skilled workers were labor's elite. Many still worked in small shops where negotiations between workers and employers took place in an environment tempered by personal relationships. Well dressed in their Prince Albert coats and starched shirts, they stood in sharp contrast to the dispossessed workers out on strike across town at Chicago's huge McCormick reaper works. There, strikers watched helplessly as the company brought in strikebreakers to take their jobs and marched the scabs to work under the protection of the Chicago police and security guards supplied by the Pinkerton Detective Agency. Cyrus McCormick Jr., son of the inventor of the mechanical reaper, viewed labor organization as a threat to his power as well as to his profits; he was determined to smash the union.

During the May Day rally, forty-five thousand workers paraded peacefully down Michigan Avenue in support of the eight-hour day, many singing the song that had become the movement's anthem:

> We mean to make things over;
>   we're tired of toil for naught
> But bare enough to live on: never
>   an hour for thought.

> We want to feel the sunshine; we
>   want to smell the flowers;
> We're sure that God has willed it,
>   and we mean to have eight hours.
> We're summoning our forces from
>   shipyard, shop, and mill:
> Eight hours for work, eight hours for rest,
>   eight hours for what we will!

Trouble came two days later, when strikers attacked scabs outside the McCormick works and police opened fire, killing or wounding six men. Angry radicals rushed out a circular urging workers to "arm yourselves and appear in full force" at a rally in Haymarket Square. On the evening of May 4, the turnout at Haymarket was disappointing. No more than two or three thousand gathered in the drizzle to hear Spies, Parsons, and the other anarchist speakers. Mayor Carter Harrison, known as a friend of labor, mingled conspicuously in the crowd, pronounced the meeting peaceable, and went home to bed. A short time later, police captain John "Blackjack" Bonfield, who had made his reputation cracking skulls, marched his men into the crowd, by now fewer than three hundred people, and demanded that they disperse.

Suddenly, someone threw a bomb into the police ranks. After a moment of stunned silence, the police drew their revolvers. "Fire and kill all you can," shouted a police lieutenant. When the melee ended, seven policemen and an unknown number of civilians lay dead. An additional sixty policemen and thirty or forty civilians suffered injuries. News of the "Haymarket riot" (a misnomer for what was more properly called the Haymarket affair) provoked a nationwide convulsion of fear, followed by blind rage directed at anarchists, labor unions, strikers, immigrants, and the working class in general. The hysteria ran deepest in Chicago. The police rounded up Spies and the other Haymarket speakers and jailed hundreds of radicals. Parsons managed to escape but later turned himself in to stand trial with his fellows.

Eight men went on trial in Chicago, although witnesses could testify that none of them had thrown the bomb. It was clear from the start that the men were on trial for their ideas, not their actions. "Convict these men," cried State's Attorney Julius S. Grinnell, "make examples of them, hang them, and you save our institutions." Although the state could not link any of the defendants with the

THE CHICAGO RIOT
Inflammatory pamphlets like this one published in the wake of the Haymarket affair presented a one-sided view of the incident and stirred public passion. The anarchist speakers were tried and convicted for the bombing, even though the identity and motivation of the bomb thrower remained undiscovered.
Chicago Historical Society.

Haymarket bomb, the jury nevertheless found them all guilty. Four were executed, one committed suicide, and three received prison sentences. On the gallows, August Spies spoke for the Haymarket martyrs: "The time will come when our silence will be more powerful than the voices you throttle today."

In 1893, Governor John Peter Altgeld, after a thorough investigation, pardoned the three remaining Haymarket anarchists. He denounced the trial as a shameless travesty of justice and concluded that Captain Bonfield was "the man really responsible for the death of the police officers." The governor's action brought on a storm of protest and cost him his political career. But through the entire process, Altgeld never wavered. "If I decide they are innocent, I will pardon them," he promised, "even if I never hold office another day." He did, and he didn't.

The bomb blast at Haymarket had lasting repercussions. To commemorate the death of the Haymarket martyrs, labor would make May 1 an international celebration of the worker. But the Haymarket bomb, in the eyes of one observer, proved "a godsend to all enemies of the labor movement." It effectively scotched the eight-hour day and dealt a fatal blow to the Knights of Labor.

With the labor movement everywhere under attack, many workers severed their radical connections, and many skilled workers turned to the American Federation of Labor. Under the leadership of Samuel Gompers, the AFL soon became the dominant voice of American labor. In the aftermath of Haymarket, Gompers urged workers to focus on concrete gains—higher wages, shorter hours—and use strikes and boycotts judiciously to win its demands. Gompers's narrow economic strategy made sense at the time and enabled one segment of the workforce—the skilled—to organize effectively and achieve tangible gains. But the majority of unskilled workers remained largely untouched by the AFL's brand of "pure and simple" trade unionism.

Visions of a Better Life

Fear of social upheaval generated by the uprisings of workers in the 1870s and 1880s led to a search for social solutions. Liberal reformers, sympathetic to labor's plight but fearful of violence, sought schemes that would mitigate economic injustice without threatening bloodshed or class warfare. Two journalists, Henry George and Edward Bellamy, put forward visions of a better life that captured the imagination of their times. The utopian plans of George and Bellamy expressed both fears about the present and hopes for a better future.

Henry George and the Single Tax

The Great Railroad Strike of 1877 inspired San Francisco journalist Henry George to write a book that

From Rags to Riches: What Is "Making It" in America?

THE RAGS-TO-RICHES FABLES of novelists like Horatio Alger fueled the dreams of countless young people at the end of the nineteenth century. Alger's formulaic novels feature fatherless young men who through the right combination of "pluck and luck" move ahead in the world. Yet despite the myth, few Americans rose from rags to riches. Even Alger's heroes, like his popular Ragged Dick, more often traded rags for respectability.

Without exception, Alger's characters came from old stock and were not the new immigrants who poured through the "golden door" into the United States at the turn of the century. What were *their* chances of success? Literature written by the new immigrants themselves tells different stories. Abraham Cahan's *The Rise of David Levinsky* (1917) describes the experience of an eastern European Jewish immigrant who, as the title indicates, rises to gain material success. But while the theme of success is distinctively American, the treatment is not. The author laments that Levinsky's "rise" is paralleled by a spiritual loss. "I cannot escape from my old self," Levinsky confesses at the end of the novel. "David, the poor lad swinging over a Talmud volume at the Preacher's Synagogue, seems to have more in common with my inner identity than David Levinsky the well-known cloak manufacturer." Having sacrificed all to material gain, Levinsky acknowledges, "At the height of my business success I feel that if I had my life to live over again I should never think of a business career."

Mike Gold tells a darker story of immigrant life in *Jews without Money* (1930), an autobiographical tale of the implacable economic forces that devastated Gold's fictional family and turned its young protagonist to communism. Gold's characters inhabit a world of grinding poverty and ignorance, a landscape so bleak that one character comes to doubt the existence of a benevolent God, asking plaintively, "Did God make bedbugs?" Determined to "write a truthful book of Poverty," Gold pledged, "I will mention bedbugs":

It wasn't a lack of cleanliness in our home. My mother was as clean as any German housewife; she slaved, she worked herself to the bone keeping us fresh and neat. The bedbugs were a torment to her. She doused the beds with kerosene, changed the sheets, sprayed the mattresses in an endless frantic war with the bedbugs. What was the use; nothing could help. It was Poverty; it was the Tenement.

Yet Gold's own success belied the grim economic determinism of his fiction. He made it out of the ghetto and into the world of literature and social activism.

Historians have been fascinated by the question of "making it" in America. Repeatedly they have attempted to measure economic and social mobility, from colonial times to the twentieth century. Looking at the lives of common folk, scholars have struggled to determine who made it, who did not, and why. Was America a land of boundless opportunity where the poor could rise? Or did the rich stay rich and the poor stay poor-to-middling, as pioneering studies of social mobility in the 1950s indicated?

By the 1960s, quantitative methods made possible by advances in computer technology promised to move history away from the "impressionistic," anecdotal evidence of fiction and memoirs and provide a statistical framework in which to measure success. But just what could historians measure with their new tools? Comparing Jewish and Italian immigrants in New York City at the turn of the century, one historian concluded that the Jews had done a better job of making it. By employing a table that categorized occupations, ranking them from professional, white-collar jobs to unskilled labor, the historian duly noted the movement from one category to another, concluding from his data that Jews moved more quickly than Italians into the white-collar class.

Studies of occupational mobility, however, contained major flaws. In a country where money has been and continues to be the common measure of success, historians' decision to use occupational categories and not income as the yardstick of mobility and success seemed to beg the question. Yet the choice was not surprising, given that census data, the staple of quantitative studies, provide information on occupation but not on income. Even occupational mobility proved difficult to measure accurately. For example, in the study cited, peddlers somewhat arbitrarily ranked at low-white-collar

RAGS TO RICHES

Horatio Alger's novels like **Ragged Dick** *(1868) invariably end with the young hero on the road to success. Contrast Alger's cheerful message with the bathos of the 1900 song "No One Cares for Me," in which the young newsboy in his rags replicates Alger's hero. Instead of getting ahead, the newsboy is portrayed as a victim of cruel neglect. Which portrait is more accurate? Historians for decades have wrestled with the question of social mobility and success.*

Culver Pictures; Picture Research Consultants & Archives.

status because they were self-employed. Yet the pushcart peddler and the Italian street vendor could hardly be said to have enjoyed white-collar status in the larger society in which they moved. Students must look carefully at what historians are measuring, recognizing that occupational mobility may not equate with social mobility or economic success.

The larger questions remain: What is "making it" in America? How best can it be measured—in dollars and cents, job satisfaction, occupational status, comparison with the lives of one's parents or neighbors? And what of the immigrants themselves? How did they define it? If becoming a bricklayer spelled success to the Italian immigrant and

his family, do studies of occupational mobility based on statisticians' categories and job rankings distort his lived reality? In dealing with the issue of "making it" in America, historians have increasingly come to recognize that each immigrant group had its own unique definition of success. Not all immigrants sought upward mobility, whether economic or occupational. Cultural factors, such as the value Italians placed on loyalty to the family, also played a key role. Ultimately, questions of success and mobility cannot easily be quantified, and they demand attention to the larger cultural context that shaped individual economic and occupational choices.

soon became a classic of American political economy: *Progress and Poverty* (1879). George knew poverty firsthand and harbored a deep sympathy for the underdog. In this spirit, he dedicated his book "to those who, seeing the vice and misery that spring from the unequal distribution of wealth and privilege, feel the possibility of a higher social state and would strive for its attainment." In *Progress and Poverty,* George explored the paradox central to American life: Why, in a land so rich, was there such inequality? (See "Historical Question," page 676.) He elaborated a theory that tied increasing inequality and growing monopoly to the scarcity of land caused by speculation (the practice of buying land and holding it until the price went up). Land speculators, he charged, contributed nothing to the economy yet made huge profits in "unearned increment."

George championed a single tax on unimproved land as a cure-all for the nation's industrial problems. Once speculators could no longer turn large profits on the land they held, George reasoned, the way lay open to utopia. Land would become available for farming. Industrial workers would leave the factories for the farms. Wages would naturally increase, and the life of industrial laborers would become more secure. Government, and with it the political corruption of the Gilded Age, would virtually disappear.

Liberal reformers, sympathetic to labor's plight but fearful of violence, sought schemes that would mitigate economic injustice without threatening bloodshed or class warfare.

To underscore the urgent need for change, George ended his book with an apocalyptic vision of what would befall the United States if action were not taken: disease, pauperism, and an atmosphere of "brooding revolution." His single tax offered a way out, an alternative to class warfare. In George's view, venturesome capitalists and honest laboring people were not class enemies. The real villain was the grasping land speculator. The single tax, then, promised to bring America back from the brink of disaster and usher in a golden age.

George's message found many ready adherents who made the single tax a rallying cry for reform. George moved east after the publication of *Progress and Poverty* and in 1886, in the aftermath of the Hay-

market affair, ran for mayor of New York City on the United Labor Party ticket. A member of the Knights of Labor, George appealed to laborers, who saw him as one of their own. Tammany Hall attempted to buy him off, promising to run him for Congress on the Democratic ticket. "You cannot be elected," a Tammany pol told George, "but your running will raise hell." To which George replied, "I do not want the responsibility and the work of the Mayor of New York, but I do want to raise hell."

At first, George's opponents dismissed him as a "humbug" and a "busybody" with no real chance. But when thirty-four thousand laborers signed a petition endorsing him, Democrats and Republicans began to take him seriously. Samuel Gompers himself became the chair of George's city organization and headed the speakers' bureau. Staunch Republican liberals, fearful of class war, threw their support to the Democrats and tarred George as "an apostle of anarchy and destruction." At the prompting of Tammany Hall, the Catholic archbishop of New York warned his flock not to "be deluded by men who advocate revolutionary doctrines." In what George accurately described as "one of the fiercest contests that ever took place in this or any other city," he lost the election by twenty thousand votes, despite strong working-class support. The Democratic candidate beat George, who in turn nosed out his Republican rival, a political newcomer named Theodore Roosevelt.

Edward Bellamy's Nationalist Utopia

While Henry George campaigned for mayor of New York and the country awaited the execution of the Haymarket anarchists, Edward Bellamy took up his pen to write a novel that ranks with Harriet Beecher Stowe's antislavery novel *Uncle Tom's Cabin* in terms of sales and influence. In 1888, Bellamy, a Massachusetts newspaper writer forced by tuberculosis to give up his editorial career, published *Looking Backward: 2000–1887,* a combination of utopian fantasy and genteel romance that spoke to the concerns of millions in the United States who were looking for a peaceful solution to the labor problem.

In *Looking Backward,* Bellamy's upper-crust hero, Julian West, falls asleep in Boston in 1887 and wakes in the year 2000 to find the world transformed. No labor strife, no class antagonism, no extremes of poverty and wealth exist in the twenty-first century. Instead, the people are organized into an efficient industrial army in which all men and women between the ages of twenty-one and forty-five work for the same guaranteed annual income. In Bellamy's highly centralized state, the disharmony, corruption, and party strife of the Gilded Age have vanished, replaced by benevolent bureaucracy.

Bellamy's utopia came complete with visions of technological marvels that were unheard of in the 1880s—the radio and moving sidewalks. But although the material conditions of the people have improved, Bellamy makes it clear that the new world came about from a spiritual and not a material transformation. The Religion of Solidarity, or "nationalism," transformed society, eliminating the destructive energies of both capitalist greed and proletarian envy and hatred. All society had to do was recognize and cooperate in the inevitable evolutionary process from competition to cooperation.

Julian himself experiences a conversion and, by the book's end, overcomes the smug selfishness that was the hallmark of his class. Looking back at his old life, he compares society in the late nineteenth century to "a prodigious coach which the masses of humanity were harnessed to and dragged toilsomely along a very hilly and sandy road." The driver of the coach is hunger, and his whips cut deep into the backs of the struggling team below. On top of the coach, "well up out of the dust," perch the passengers, who occasionally call down encouragement to the toilers below, "exhorting them to patience, and holding out hopes of possible compensation in another world for the hardness of their lot." Such inhumanity, Julian patiently explains to his twenty-first-century audience, could be explained by the conviction that "there was no other way in which Society could get along, except that the many pulled at the rope and the few rode." Besides, the riders suffer from the hallucination that "they [are] not exactly like their brothers and sisters" but are made "of finer clay." "This seems unaccountable," Julian confesses, "but, as I once rode this very coach and shared that very hallucination, I ought to be believed."

In the parable of the stagecoach, Bellamy offered a scathing critique of social Darwinism and a call to action. The book caused a sensation. Within three years, over a million copies had been sold, and enthusiastic readers launched more than 160 Bellamy Clubs devoted to discussing nationalism and implementing the social goals expressed in *Looking Backward*. While neither George's single tax nor Bellamy's nationalist utopia produced the kind of mass movement for social change envisioned by the two authors, the enthusiastic response to both books indicated that many Americans feared social cataclysm and were ready to take action.

Conclusion: The Workers' Own Struggle

The late nineteenth century witnessed many competing visions of a better life as Americans sought solutions to the problems attending urban industrialization and corporate capitalism. Henry George's single tax won supporters across the country and rallied New York's laborers to support him for mayor. Bellamy's nationalist utopia attracted followers drawn largely from the "sensible middle class." President Hayes called for "education" and a "wise judicious policy" to avoid labor upheavals like the Great Railroad Strike of 1877. American workers themselves had their own vision of what a better life might be—a life in which the independence eroded by industrialization could be countered by collective action, workers could regain some control of the workplace, and a shorter day and a higher wage promised escape from a brutal life of toil. Their vision and their willingness to fight for it made them active agents of social change, willing to risk their livelihood and sometimes their very lives in the struggle.

Looking at the impact on his life occasioned by industrialization, a Massachusetts machinist declared in the 1890s:

> The workers of Massachusetts have always been law and order men. We loved our country and respected the laws. For the last five years the times have been growing worse every year, until we have been brought down so far that we have not much farther to go. What do the Mechanics of Massachusetts say to each other? I will tell you: "We must have a change. Any thing is better than this. We cannot be worse off, no matter what the change is."

Mounting anger and frustration would lead American workers and farmers to join forces in the 1890s and create a grassroots movement to fight for change under the banner of a new People's Party.

www.bedfordstmartins.com/tap   SEE THE ONLINE STUDY GUIDE to assess your mastery of the material covered in this chapter.

CHRONOLOGY

1869 Uriah Stephens founds Knights of Labor.

Cincinnati mounts first professional baseball team, the Red Stockings.

1870 Wage earners account for over half of those employed in 1870 census.

1872 Andrew Carnegie opens his steelworks outside Pittsburgh.

1873 Panic on Wall Street touches off depression.

1877 Great Railroad Strike paralyzes nation.

1878 Knights of Labor campaigns to organize workers regardless of skill, sex, or race.

1879 Henry George publishes *Progress and Poverty*.

1880 George M. Pullman builds model town near Chicago.

1881 Samuel Gompers founds Organized Trades and Labor Unions.

1882 Chinese Exclusion Act prohibits immigration of Chinese to the United States.

1884 Grace Dodge organizes Working Girl's Club in New York City.

1886 Organized Trades and Labor Unions reorganized as the American Federation of Labor (AFL).

Massive rally in support of eight-hour workday takes place in Chicago on May 1; Haymarket bombing on May 4 results in widening fear of anarchy and a blow to the labor movement.

Henry George campaigns for mayor of New York City on United Labor Party ticket and loses in close election.

1888 Edward Bellamy publishes *Looking Backward: 2000–1887*.

1890 Average worker earns $500 per year.

1893 Illinois Governor John Peter Altgeld pardons three remaining Haymarket anarchists.

1893 Panic on Wall Street touches off major depression.

1897 Steeplechase amusement park opens on Coney Island.

BIBLIOGRAPHY

GENERAL

Edward L. Ayers, *The Promise of the New South: Life after Reconstruction* (1992).

John B. Boles, *The South through Time*, vol. 2 (1995).

Alan Dawley, *Struggles for Justice: Social Responsibility and the Liberal State* (1991).

Sara M. Evans, *Born for Liberty: A History of Women in America* (1989).

Alice Kessler-Harris, *Out to Work: The History of Wage-Earning Women in the United States* (1982).

Julie A. Matthaei, *An Economic History of Women in America: Women's Work, the Sexual Division of Labor, and the Development of Capitalism* (1982).

David Montgomery, *The Fall of the House of Labor: The Workplace, the State, and American Labor Activism, 1865–1925* (1987).

Nell Irwin Painter, *Standing at Armageddon: The United States, 1877–1919* (1987).

AMERICAN WORKERS

William Adelman, *Touring Pullman: A Study in Company Paternalism* (1977).

Stephen E. Ambrose, *Nothing Like It in the World: The Men Who Built the Transcontinental Railroad, 1863–1869* (2000).

Paul Avrich, *The Haymarket Tragedy* (1984).

David Haward Bain, *Empire Express: Building the First Transcontinental Railroad* (1999).

Charles Albro Barker, *Henry George* (1991).

Gunther Barth, *Bitter Strength: The History of the Chinese in the United States, 1850–1870* (1964).

Henry F. Bedford, ed., *Their Lives and Numbers: The Condition of Working People in Massachusetts, 1870–1900* (1995).

Susan Porter Benson, *Counter Cultures: Saleswomen, Managers, and Customers in American Department Stores, 1890–1940* (1986).

David Brody, *Workers in Industrial America: Essays on the Twentieth-Century Struggle* (1980).

Robert V. Bruce, *1877: Year of Violence* (1959).

Stanley Buder, *Pullman: An Experiment in Industrial Order and Community Planning, 1880–1930* (1967).

Patricia A. Cooper, *Once a Cigar Maker: Men, Women, and Work Culture in American Cigar Factories* (1987).

Henry David, *The History of the Haymarket Affair* (1963).

Margery W. Davies, *Woman's Place Is at the Typewriter: Office Work and Office Workers, 1870–1930* (1982).

James J. Davis, *The Iron Puddler: My Life in the Rolling Mills and What Became of It* (1922).

Melvyn Dubofsky, *Industrialism and the American Worker, 1865–1920* (1975).

Faye E. Dudden, *Serving Women: Household Service in Nineteenth-Century America* (1983).

Lani Ah Tye Farkas, *Bury My Bones in America: The Saga of a Chinese Family in California, 1852–1996: From San Francisco to the Sierra Gold Mines* (1998).

Philip S. Foner, *The Great Labor Uprising of 1877* (1977).

Philip S. Foner, *Women and the American Labor Movement: From the First Trade Unions to the Present* (1979).

William E. Forbath, *Law and the Shaping of the American Labor Movement* (1991).

Michael H. Frisch and Daniel J. Walkowitz, eds., *Working-Class America: Essays on Labor, Community, and American Society* (1983).

John S. Garner, *The Company Town: Architecture and Society in the Early Industrial Age* (1992).

Sherna Gluck, *From Parlor to Prison: Five American Suffragists Talk about Their Lives* (1976).

David M. Gordon, Richard Edwards, and Michael Reich, eds., *Segmented Work, Divided Workers: The Historical Transformation of Labor in the United States* (1982).

Herbert C. Gutman, *Work, Culture, and Society in Industrializing America: Essays in American Working-Class and Social History* (1976).

Jacquelyn Dowd Hall, James Leloudis, Robert Korstad, Mary Murphy, Lu Ann Jones, and Christopher B. Daly, *Like a Family: The Making of a Southern Mill World* (1987).

Tamara K. Hareven, *Family Life and Industrial Time: The Relationship between the Family and Work in a New England Industrial Community* (1982).

Tamara K. Hareven and Randolph Langenbach, *Amoskeag: Life and Work in an American Factory-City* (1978).

Robert Hendrickson, *The Grand Emporiums* (1979).

Jacobson, Matthew Frye, *Whiteness of a Different Color: European Immigrants and the Alchemy of Race* (1998).

Elizabeth Jameson, *All That Glitters: Class, Conflict, and Community in Cripple Creek* (1998).

Jacqueline Jones, *The Dispossessed: America's Underclasses from the Civil War to the Present* (1992).

David M. Katzman, *Seven Days a Week: Women and Domestic Service in Industrializing America* (1978).

David M. Katzman and William M. Tuttle Jr., eds., *Plain Folk: The Life Stories of Undistinguished Americans* (1982).

Larry Lankton, *Cradle to Grave: Life, Work, and Death at Lake Superior Copper Mines* (1991).

Janet Lecompte, ed., *Emily: The Diary of a Hard-Worked Woman* (1987).

Sidney Lens, *The Labor Wars: From the Molly Maguires to the Sitdowns* (1974).

Huping Ling, *Surviving on the Gold Mountain: A History of Chinese American Women and Their Lives* (1998).

Cathy L. McHugh, *Mill Family: The Labor System in the Southern Cotton Textile Industry, 1880–1915* (1988).

Milton Meltzer, *Bread and Roses: The Struggle of American Labor, 1865–1915* (1967).

Joanne J. Meyerowitz, *Women Adrift: Independent Wage Earners in Chicago, 1880–1930* (1988).

Daniel Nelson, *Farm and Factory: Workers in the Midwest, 1880–1900* (1995).

Lynn Pan, *Sons of the Yellow Emperor: The Story of the Overseas Chinese* (1990).

Cornelia Stratton Parker, *Working with the Working Women* (1922).

Samuel H. Preston and Michael R. Haines, *Fatal Years: Child Mortality in Late-Nineteenth-Century America* (1991).

Richard B. Rice, William A. Bullough, and Richard J. Orsi, *The Elusive Eden: A New History of California* (1988).

Edward J. Rose, *Henry George* (1968).

Leon Stein and Philip Taft, eds., *Workers Speak* (1971).

David O. Stowell, *Streets, Railroads, and the Great Strike of 1877* (1999).

Sharon Hartman Strom, *Beyond the Typewriter: Gender, Class, and the Origins of Modern American Office Work, 1900–1930* (1992).

Ronald Takaki, *Strangers from a Different Shore: A History of Asian Americans* (1989).

Leslie Woodcock Tentler, *Wage-Earning Women: Industrial Work and Family Life in the United States, 1900–1930* (1979).

John L. Thomas, *Alternative America: Henry George, Edward Bellamy, Henry Demarest Lloyd and the Adversary Tradition* (1983).

Christopher L. Tomlins, *The State and the Unions: Labor Relations, Law, and the Organized Labor Movement in America, 1880–1960* (1985).

Carole Turbin, *Working Women of Collar City: Gender, Class, and Community in Troy, New York, 1864–1886* (1992).

Jules Tygiel, *Workingmen in San Francisco, 1880–1901* (1992).

Richard White, *"It's Your Misfortune and None of My Own": A New History of the American West* (1991).

Samuel Yellen, *American Labor Struggles* (1936).

Irwin Yellowitz, *Industrialization and the American Labor Movement, 1850–1900* (1977).

POPULAR CULTURE

Elaine Abelson, *When Ladies Go A'Thieving: Middle-Class Shoplifters in the Victorian Department Store* (1989).

Charles Albro Barker, *Henry George* (1991).

Sylvia E. Bowman, *Edward Bellamy* (1986).

Lewis A. Erenberg, *Steppin' Out: New York Nightlife and the Transformation of American Culture, 1890–1930* (1981).

Michael Kammen, *American Culture, American Tastes* (1999).

William Leach, *Land of Desire: Merchants, Power, and the Rise of a New American Culture* (1993).

Kathryn J. Oberdeck, *The Evangelist and the Impresario: Religion, Entertainment, and Cultural Politics in America, 1884–1914* (1999).

Kathy Peiss, *Cheap Amusements: Working Women and Leisure in Turn-of-the-Century New York* (1986).

Ellen M. Plante, *Women at Home in Victorian America: A Social History* (1997).

Thomas J. Schlereth, *Victorian America: Transformations in Everyday Life, 1876–1915* (1992).

Daniel E. Sutherland, *The Expansion of Everyday Life, 1860–1876* (1989).

FARMERS ALLIANCE SONGBOOK

In the 1880s, the Farmers Alliance recruited followers in the South and Midwest at the rate of twenty thousand a month, using lectures, camp meetings, and even songs to educate and organize. Copies of this Farmers Alliance songbook sold by the hundreds—testimony to the growing movement. In the cover picture, an Alliance farmer shakes the hand of a blacksmith, who bears a not coincidental resemblance to Abraham Lincoln. The handshake symbolizes the willingness of the alliance to make common cause with laborers of every stripe, a message reiterated in the four corners with images of school, farm, factory, and ship.

East Carolina Manuscript Collection, J. Y. Joyner Library, East Carolina University, Greenville, North Carolina. Photo by Dewan Frentger.

FIGHTING FOR CHANGE IN THE TURBULENT NINETIES

1890–1900

19

S T. LOUIS IN FEBRUARY 1892 played host to one of the most striking political gatherings of the century. Thousands of farmers, laborers, reformers, and common people flocked to Missouri to attend a meeting that was, in the words of one reporter, "different from any other political meeting ever witnessed in St. Louis." The cigar-smoking politicians who generally worked the convention circuit were nowhere to be found. In their place were "mostly gray-haired, sunburned and roughly clothed men" assembled under a banner that proclaimed, "We do not ask for sympathy or pity. We ask for justice."

Exposition Music Hall presented a colorful spectacle. "The banners of the different states rose above the delegates throughout the hall, fluttering like the flags over an army encamped," wrote one reporter. Ignatius Donnelly, a fiery orator, attacked the money kings of Wall Street. Mary Elizabeth Lease, a veteran campaigner from Kansas known for exhorting farmers to "raise less corn and more hell," lent her powerful voice to the cause. Terence V. Powderly, head of the Knights of Labor, called on workers to join hands with farmers against the "nonproducing classes." And Frances Willard of the Woman's Christian Temperance Union argued against liquor and for woman suffrage. Between speeches the crowd sang labor songs like "Hurrah for the Toiler," "All Hail the Power of Laboring Men," and "Justice for the Farmer."

In the course of the next few days, delegates hammered out a series of demands breathtaking in their scope. They tackled the tough questions of the day—the regulation of business, the need for banking and currency reform, the right of labor to organize and bargain collectively, and the role of the federal government in regulating business, curbing monopoly, and guaranteeing democracy. The convention ended its work amid a chorus of cheers. "As if by magic, everyone was upon his feet in an instant. Thundering cheers from 10,000 throats greeted these demands as the road to liberty," one eyewitness observed. "Hats, paper, handkerchiefs, etc., were thrown into the air; wraps, umbrellas and parasols waved; cheer after cheer thundered and reverberated through the vast hall reaching the outside of the building where thousands who had been waiting the outcome joined in the applause till for blocks in every direction the exultation made the din indescribable."

What was all the shouting about? People were building a new political party, officially named the People's Party but often called the Populist Party, and its members Populists. Dissatisfied with the Democrats and Republicans, a broad coalition

PEOPLE'S PARTY BADGE, 1896
Delegates to the People's Party National Convention in St. Louis in 1896 sported ribbons like this one worn by a member of the Massachusetts delegation. As in 1896, the party's 1892 gathering in St. Louis had all the trappings of other political conventions, but the People's Party marked a new political alliance as farmers, laborers, and reformers came together to fight for change.
Collection of Janice L. and David J. Frent.

of groups came together in St. Louis to fight for change. They determined to reconvene in Omaha in July to nominate candidates for the upcoming presidential election.

The 1890s witnessed one of the most turbulent decades in U.S. history. Unrest, agitation, agrarian revolt, labor strikes, a severe financial panic and depression, and a war of expansion characterized the decade. While the major political parties continued to do business as usual, Americans flocked to organizations like the Knights of Labor, the Farmers Alliance, and the Woman's Christian Temperance Union and worked together to create new political alliances. The St. Louis gathering marked just one milestone on the road to a new politics. The Peo-

ple's Party challenged laissez-faire economics by insisting that the federal government play a more active role to ensure greater economic equity in industrial America. This challenge to the status quo would culminate in 1896 in one of the most hotly contested presidential elections in the nation's history. At the close of this tumultuous decade, the Spanish-American War helped to bring the United States together even as it raised questions about the country's new role on the world stage at the start of the twentieth century.

Women's Activism

"Do everything," Frances Willard urged her followers in 1881. The new president of the Woman's Christian Temperance Union (WCTU) meant what she said. The WCTU followed a trajectory that was common for women in the late nineteenth century. As women organized to deal with issues that touched their homes and families, they moved almost inevitably into politics, lending a new urgency to the cause of woman suffrage (the vote for women). Elizabeth Cady Stanton had advocated woman suffrage since the Woman's Rights Convention in Seneca Falls in 1848 and, together with Susan B. Anthony, she had formed the first independent women's movement in 1867 with the creation of the National Woman Suffrage Association. By the 1890s, Stanton and Anthony were coming to the end of their public careers, yet their goal still eluded them. For African American women, the intimidation and lynching of blacks in the South and the desire to improve their own lives and those of their community led to activism, as Ida B. Wells's antilynching campaign forcefully demonstrated.

Frances Willard and the Woman's Christian Temperance Union

Frances Willard, the visionary leader of the WCTU, spoke for a group that was left almost entirely out of the U.S. electoral process—women. In 1881, only two territories, Utah and Wyoming, allowed women to vote. But lack of the franchise did not mean that women were apolitical. The WCTU demonstrates the breadth of women's political activity in the late nineteenth century.

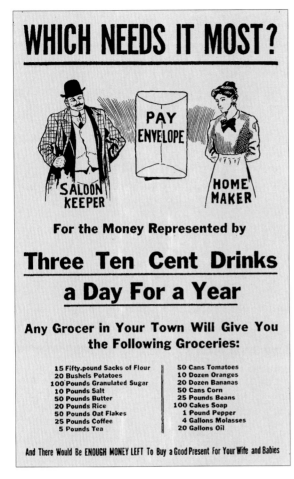

WCTU FLYER

This Woman's Christian Temperance Union flyer shows the wife pitted against the saloon keeper for her husband's pay. The economic consequences to the family of a drinker were a serious matter. At a time when the average worker made only $500 a year, the money spent on alcohol meant less to eat for the family. As the poster indicates, thirty cents a day for a year paid for a substantial amount of family staples. Beer and liquor lobbyists worked hard not only to counter the WCTU but to fight woman suffrage because they feared when women got the vote they would enact prohibition.

Culver Pictures.

The WCTU was created in 1874 following a spontaneous uprising in the Midwest known as the Woman's Crusade. During the winter of 1873–74, women, armed with Bibles and singing hymns, marched on taverns and saloons and refused to leave until the proprietors signed a pledge to quit selling liquor. The crusade spread like a prairie fire through small towns in Ohio, Indiana, Michigan, and Illinois and soon moved east into New York, New England, and Pennsylvania. Before it was over, more than 100,000 women marched in over 450 cities and towns. For the first time since the days of the antislavery movement, middle-class, respectable churchwomen took to the streets to demand change.

The women's tactics were new, but temperance (the movement to ban the sale of alcoholic beverages and eliminate drunkenness) dated back to the 1820s. Temperance was an especially explosive issue that divided communities, pitting middle class against working class, native-born against immigrant, Protestant against Catholic, and women against men. Temperance advocates had won significant victories in the 1850s when several states, starting with Maine, passed laws to prohibit the sale of liquor (the laws became known as "Maine laws"). But by the late 1860s and 1870s, the liquor business was on the rise, with about one saloon for every fifty males over the age of fifteen. Willing to spend as much money as it took, the liquor interests mounted a powerful lobby to fight temperance while both the Democratic and Republican Parties sought to avoid the divisive issue by leaving it up to counties and towns to decide whether to ban the sale of liquor.

Temperance was an especially explosive issue that divided communities, pitting middle class against working class, native-born against immigrant, Protestant against Catholic, and women against men.

Women supported the temperance movement because they felt particularly vulnerable in society. Alcoholism in a family could mean destitution, wife and child abuse, desertion, and even death. The drunken, abusive husband epitomized the evils of a nation in which women remained second-class citizens. The temperance movement provided women with a respectable outlet for their increasing resentment of women's inferior status and their growing recognition of women's capabilities. Composed entirely of women, the WCTU viewed all women's interests as essentially the same—crossing class, ethnic, and racial lines—and therefore did not hesitate to use the singular word *woman* to empha-size gender solidarity. Although largely white and middle class, the WCTU members resolved to speak for their entire sex.

In its first five years, under the leadership of Annie Wittenmyer, the WCTU relied on education and persuasion in trying to achieve its goal of total abstinence from alcohol. When Frances Willard be-came president in 1879, she radically changed the direction of the organization. Under her leadership, the WCTU moved toward viewing alcoholism as a disease rather than a sin, and poverty as a cause rather than a result of drink. Accordingly, social ac-tion replaced prayer as women's answer to the threat of drunkenness.

By 1896, twenty-five of the WCTU's depart-ments dealt with nontemperance issues. The orga-nization worked to establish women's reformatories and promoted the hiring of female police officers. The Chicago branch sponsored day nurseries, Sun-day schools, an industrial training school, a mission for homeless women, a free medical dispensary, and a lodging house for men. At the same time, the WCTU turned its attention to labor issues, joining with the Knights of Labor to press for better work-ing conditions. One WCTU member described the condition of factory operatives in a textile mill. "It is dreadful to see those girls stripped almost to the skin, wearing only the kind of loose wrapper, and running like racehorses from the beginning to the end of the day," she wrote in the *Union Signal*, the WCTU's monthly magazine. "The hard slavish work," she concluded, "is drawing the girls into the saloon."

Using "home protection" as her watchword, Willard capitalized on the cult of domesticity to move women into public life, arguing that they needed to attack the saloon to protect the home and family. In its pursuit of temperance, the WCTU soon moved toward advocacy of woman suffrage, which Willard supported as early as 1875 and which the WCTU formally embraced in 1884 by calling for the "home protection ballot." By the 1890s, the WCTU's grassroots network of local unions had spread to all but the most isolated rural areas of the country. Strong and rich, with over 150,000 dues-paying members, the WCTU was a formidable group.

Willard worked to create a broad reform coali-tion in the 1890s, embracing the Knights of Labor, the People's Party, and the Prohibition Party. Until her death in 1898, she led, if not a women's rights movement, then the first organized mass movement

of women united around a women's issue. By 1900, women could claim a generation of experience in political action—speaking, lobbying, organizing, drafting legislation, and running private charitable institutions. As Willard observed, "All this work has tended more toward the liberation of women than it has toward the extinction of the saloon."

Elizabeth Cady Stanton, Susan B. Anthony, and the Movement for Woman Suffrage

Unlike the WCTU, the organized movement for woman suffrage was small and relatively weak in the late nineteenth century. But ardent suffragists, like the temperance women, fought aggressively for change. The women's rights movement begun at Seneca Falls in 1848 had split over the issue of the Fourteenth Amendment, which granted voting rights to African American men. Women's rights ac-tivists like Elizabeth Cady Stanton and Susan B. An-thony had wanted the amendment, ratified in 1868, to apply to women as well as to African Americans newly freed from slavery. But Frederick Douglass and other advocates of black suffrage urged the women to wait, insisting that it was "the Negro's hour."

The split among women's rights activists produced two rival woman suffrage organizations. Stanton and Anthony formed the National Woman Suffrage Association (NWSA) in 1869, launching the first independent women's rights movement in the United States. The more conservative American Woman Suffrage Association formed the same year. Unlike the NWSA, this group included men as well as women and welcomed many members who be-lieved that women should vote in local but not na-tional elections.

In 1890, the two groups united under the rubric of the National American Woman Suffrage Associ-ation (NAWSA). Twenty years had made a great change. Woman suffrage was not yet generally sup-ported, but it was no longer considered a crackpot idea. Thanks to the WCTU's support of the "home protection ballot," suffrage had become accepted as a means to an end even when it was not embraced as woman's natural right. The NAWSA honored Elizabeth Cady Stanton by electing her its first pres-ident, but Susan B. Anthony, who took the helm in 1892, emerged as the leading figure in the new united organization.

Thanks to the WCTU's support of the "home protection ballot," suffrage had become accepted as a means to an end even when it was not embraced as woman's natural right.

Beginning in the 1890s, the NAWSA launched campaigns on the state level to gain the vote for women. Suffragists won victories in Colorado in 1893 and Idaho in 1896. Two more states joined the suffrage column when the territories of Wyoming and Utah entered the union in 1890 and 1996, respectively. But women suffered a bitter defeat in a California referendum in 1896. Although it would take almost three decades for all women to gain the vote with the ratification of the Nineteenth Amendment in 1920, the unification of the two woman suffrage groups in 1890 signaled a new era in women's fight for the vote, just as Frances Willard's place on the platform in 1892 at the founding of the People's Party in St. Louis symbolized women's growing role in politics and reform.

Ida B. Wells and the Antilynching Campaign

While most white women focused on reforms designed to counter the impact of urban industrialism in the North, black women followed a different path. The majority of African Americans were neither urban nor industrial. As late as 1890, more than 90 percent of the black population remained in the South. As a result, African American women activists organized around issues that affected life in the rural South. Foremost among their activities was the antilynching campaign mounted by Ida B. Wells.

In 1892, after a white mob lynched a friend of Wells's whose only crime was that his grocery business competed too successfully against one owned by a white man, Wells concluded that lynching served "as an excuse to get rid of Negroes who were acquiring wealth and property and thus keep the race terrorized." Determined to do something, she began systematically to collect data on lynching. In the decade between 1882 and 1892, she discovered lynching had risen in the South by an overwhelming 200 percent, with more than 241 people killed. The vast increase in lynchings testified to the retreat

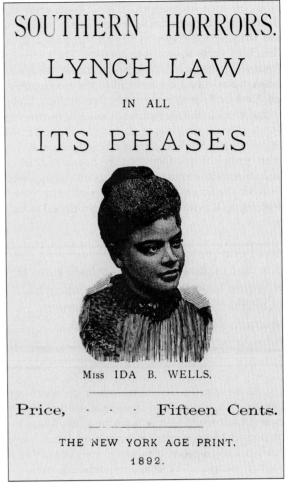

SOUTHERN HORRORS.
LYNCH LAW
IN ALL
ITS PHASES

Miss IDA B. WELLS,

Price, · · · Fifteen Cents.

THE NEW YORK AGE PRINT,
1892.

IDA B. WELLS
Ida B. Wells began her antilynching campaign at the age of thirty after the murder of a friend in 1892 led her to examine the extent of lynching in the South. She spread her message in lectures and pamphlets like this one distributed for fifteen cents. Wells brought the horror of lynching to a national and international audience and mobilized other African American women to undertake social action under the auspices of the National Association of Colored Women.
Miriam and Ira D. Wallach Division of Art, Prints and Photographs, The New York Public Library. Astor, Lenox and Tilden.

of the federal government following reconstruction and to white Southerners' determination to maintain supremacy through terrorism and intimidation.

At the time Wells began her antilynching campaign, she had already earned a reputation as an activist for African American rights. Born a slave in

Holly Springs, Mississippi, in 1862, Wells grew up during reconstruction. Her parents were active in the struggle for Negro rights and provided their daughter with strong role models. Their deaths from yellow fever left Wells an orphan at the age of sixteen. She took over as head of the family, leaving Rust College to support her five siblings. Wells found work in the Memphis schools and became an active member in the local African Methodist Episcopal church. She also joined a local lyceum, or literary group. It was there that she began her career as a journalist, writing for the lyceum's newspaper. In 1889, she became the co-owner of the *Free Speech and Headlight,* whose title was later shortened to *Free Speech.*

The vast increase in lynchings testified to the retreat of the federal government following reconstruction and to white Southerners' determination to maintain supremacy through terrorism and intimidation.

As the first salvo in her attack on lynching, Wells put to rest the "old threadbare lie that Negro men assault white women." As she pointed out, violations of black women by white men, which were much more frequent than black attacks on white women, went unnoticed and unpunished. Wells articulated lynching as a problem of race and gender, with the myth of black attacks on white southern womanhood masking the reality that mob violence had more to do with economics and the shifting social structure of the South than with rape. She demonstrated in a sophisticated way how the southern patriarchal system, having lost its control over blacks with the end of slavery, used its control over women to circumscribe the liberty of black men.

Wells's strong stance immediately resulted in reprisal. While she was traveling in the North, her office in Tennessee was ransacked and her printing equipment destroyed. Yet the warning that she would be killed on sight if she ever returned to Memphis only stiffened her resolve. As she wrote in her autobiography, *Crusade for Justice,* "Having lost my paper, had a price put on my life and been made an exile . . . , I felt that I owed it to myself and to my race to tell the whole truth now that I was where I could do so freely." Antilynching became a

lifelong commitment that took Wells twice to Britain, where she placed lynching on the international agenda. As a reporter, first for the *New York Age* and later for the Chicago *Inter-Ocean,* she used every opportunity to hammer home her message.

Wells's activities mobilized other black women, including Victoria Earle Matthews and Maritcha Lyons, who were already engaged in social reform and self-improvement. They hosted a testimonial dinner for Wells in New York in 1892 that led to the organization of a black women's club, the Women's Loyal Union. The club became a spearhead for the creation of the National Association of Colored Women (NACW) in 1896. The organization's first president, Mary Church Terrell of Washington, D.C., urged her followers to "promote the welfare of our race, along all the lines that tend to its development and advancement." Taking as their motto "Lifting As We Climb," the women of the NACW shouldered the double burden of self-improvement and social reform. They attacked myriad issues, including health care, housing, education, and the promotion of a positive image of the Negro race. In their efforts, African American club women enjoyed little help from white women's clubs. At the insistence of its southern constituency, the General Federation of Women's Clubs remained largely segregated. The NACW played a critical role in Wells's antilynching campaign by lobbying for legislation that would make lynching a federal crime. Beginning in 1894 and continuing for decades, antilynching bills were introduced in Congress only to be defeated by southern opposition.

Lynching did not end during Ida B. Wells's lifetime, nor did antilynching legislation gain passage in Congress; but Wells's forceful voice brought the issue to national prominence. At her funeral in 1931, black leader W. E. B. Du Bois eulogized Wells as the woman who "began the awakening of the conscience of the nation."

The Farmers' Revolt and the Labor Wars

Farmers counted themselves among the most disaffected Americans in the country. Hard times in the 1880s and 1890s created a groundswell of agrarian revolt. Everywhere, the farmer seemed to be the victim of rules, such as the gold standard and the protective tariff, that worked to the advantage of big business. In the face of their grievances, angry farmers across the United States raised a chorus of protest. While the farmers united to fight for change, industrial laborers fought their own battles in a series of bloody strikes so fiercely waged on both sides that one historian has called them the "labor wars."

The Farmers Alliance and the Populist Movement

Farm prices fell, decade after decade. Wheat that sold for a dollar a bushel in 1870 dropped to sixty cents in the 1890s. Cotton plummeted from fifteen cents to five cents a pound. Corn started at forty-five cents and fell to thirty cents a bushel by the 1890s (Figure 19.1). By 1894, in Kansas alone almost half the farms had fallen into the hands of the banks through foreclosure because poor farmers could not make enough money to pay their mortgages.

In the West, farmers rankled under a system in which railroads charged them exorbitant freight rates while granting discounts to large shippers. Also, the railroads' policy of charging higher rates for a short haul than for a long haul meant that large

grain elevator companies could ship their wheat from Chicago to New York and across the ocean to England for less money than it cost a Dakota farmer to send a crop to mills in nearby Minneapolis. In the South, lack of currency and credit had driven farmers to the stopgap credit system of the crop lien. The combined southern states actually had less money in circulation than did the state of Massachusetts. At the heart of the problem stood a banking system that was rooted in the gold standard and dominated by eastern commercial banks, a railroad rate system capricious and unfair, and speculation that drove up the price of land.

Farm protest was not new. In the 1870s, farmers had supported the Grange and the Greenback Labor Party. But with the farmers' situation growing more desperate, the 1880s witnessed a spontaneous outbreak as farmers organized into alliances. The first group of farmers gathered at a Lampasas County farm in Texas and banded together into the Farmers Alliance to fight "landsharks and horse thieves." In frontier farmhouses in Texas, in log cabins in backwoods Arkansas, in the rural parishes of Louisiana, separate groups formed similar alliances for self-help.

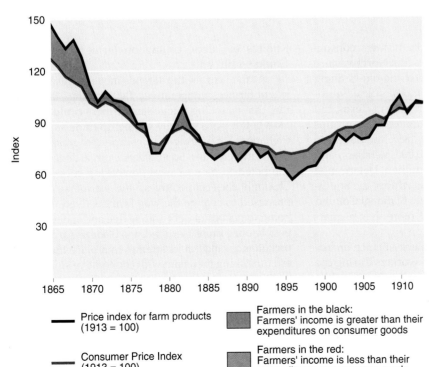

FIGURE 19.1

Consumer Prices and Farm Income, 1865–1910
Around 1870, consumer prices and farm income were about equal. During the 1880s and 1890s, however, farmers suffered great hardships as prices for their crops declined steadily and the cost of consumer goods continued to rise.

Price index for farm products (1913 = 100)

Consumer Price Index (1913 = 100)

Farmers in the black: Farmers' income is greater than their expenditures on consumer goods

Farmers in the red: Farmers' income is less than their expenditures on consumer goods

KANSAS FAMILY FORCED OFF THEIR FARM
Hard times in the 1890s sent farmers reeling back from the plains. In 1894, almost half the farmers in Kansas lost their land because they could not make mortgage payments. The Owens family of Greeley County, Kansas, pictured here, was one of the many families forced to pack up their belongings and head east. The simple writing on their wagon tells the chronology of their retreat.
Kansas State Historical Society.

As the movement grew, the farmers consolidated into two regional alliances, the Northwestern Farmers Alliance, which included the old Granger states of the Midwest, and the more radical Southern Farmers Alliance, which began in Texas but soon spread into Georgia and united with groups in Louisiana and Arkansas. By 1887, the Southern Alliance boasted more than 200,000 members, and by 1890 it counted more than 3 million. Determined to reach black farmers as well as whites, the Southern Alliance sponsored a separate National Colored Farmers Alliance that recruited more than a quarter of a million members.

At the same time, the Farmers Alliance broadened its base by reaching out to workers during the Great Southwestern Strike against Jay Gould's Texas and Pacific Railroad in 1886. The alliance insisted that the farmer, too, was a worker and that the labor question was a crucial issue for both the farmer and the wage laborer. The Southern Farmers Alliance rushed food and supplies to the strikers and issued a proclamation in support of the Knights of Labor, calling on farmers to boycott Gould's railroad.

At the heart of the alliance movement was a series of farmers' cooperatives. By "bulking" their cotton, that is, selling it together, farmers could negotiate a better price. And by setting up trade stores and exchanges, they sought to escape the grasp of the merchant/creditor. Soon alliances in a dozen states competed to pioneer new purchasing cooperatives. Through the cooperatives, the Farmers Alliance promised to change the way farmers lived. "We are going to get out of debt and be free and independent people once more," exulted one Georgia farmer. But the alliance failed in its attempt to replace the southern furnishing merchant with cooperative stores. Opposition by merchants, bankers, wholesalers, and manufacturers made it impossible for the cooperatives to get credit. The Texas exchange survived only one season. Farmers soon realized that the alliance cooperatives stood little chance of working unless fundamental changes were made in the American money and credit system.

THE FIRST FARMERS ALLIANCE FLAG
The first group of farmers to band together into the Farmers Alliance met in Texas, in 1878, vowing to fight "landsharks and horse thieves." Their movement spread in the next decade until over three million people in the South alone counted themselves members of the Alliance. This flag commemorates the organization's founding and spells out what the Alliance stood for—free trade, "the most good for the most people," and Wisdom, Justice, and Moderation. The last claim many would judge a misnomer, viewing the Alliance not as a moderate group, but as a force for sweeping change.
Torreyson Library, University of Central Arkansas.

As the cooperative movement died, a new culture of politics was born. What had begun as an organization for self-help moved toward direct political action. Texas farmers drafted a set of demands in 1886 and pressured political candidates to endorse them. These demands became the basis of a platform proposed by the Southern Alliance in 1890 calling for railroad regulation and control, laws against land speculation, and currency and credit reform. But it proved easier to get politicians to make promises than to persuade them to enact reform legislation. Confounded by the failure of the Democrats and Republicans to break with commercial interests and support the farmer, the alliance moved, often reluctantly, in the direction of a third party.

At the start of the Farmers Alliance in 1877, leader C. W. Macune had insisted, "The Alliance is a strictly white man's nonpolitical, secret business association." But by 1892, after more than a decade of organization, education, and politicization, the alliance was none of those things. Although some southern leaders, like Macune, made it clear that they would never threaten the unity of the white vote in the South by leaving the Democratic Party, advocates of a third party carried the day at the convention of laborers, farmers, and common folk in St. Louis. There, the Farmers Alliance gave birth to the People's Party and launched the Populist movement.

"There is something at the back of all this turmoil more than the failure of crops or the scarcity of ready cash," a journalist observed in 1892. Populism was more than a set of demands and a list of economic grievances. At its heart were the emotion and the promise of a religious revival. Wagon trains carrying ten thousand farmers gathered at camp meetings to listen to speeches by the angry prophets of the movement. Populism was a mass movement with its own political language and its own slogan: "The alliance is the people and the people are together."

The Populists mounted a critique of industrial society and a call for action. Convinced that the money and banking systems worked to the advantage of the few and not the many, they demanded economic democracy. To solve the farmers' credit problem, C. W. Macune hit on the ingenious idea of the subtreasury, a plan that would allow farmers to store nonperishable crops in government storehouses until the market was advantageous. At the same time, they would receive commodity credit from the federal government that would enable them to buy needed supplies and seed for the coming year's crops. The subtreasury became an article of faith in the South, where it promised to eliminate the crop lien system once and for all. Although Macune's idea would be enacted piecemeal in Progressive and New Deal legislation after the start of the twentieth century, conservatives in the 1890s dismissed it as far-fetched and communistic.

Populism was more than a set of demands and a list of economic grievances. At its heart were the emotion and the promise of a religious revival.

For the western farmer, whose enemy was not the merchant but the mortgage, Populism promised land reform. The Populists called for a plan that would reclaim excessive lands granted or sold to

ON THE WAY TO A POPULIST MEETING IN KANSAS
Populism was more than a political movement; it was a culture unto itself. For farmers in sparsely settled regions, the movement provided reassurance that they were not alone, that others shared their problems, and that solutions could be found. When the Populists called a meeting, wagons came from miles around, as in this gathering in Dickinson County, Kansas. Men, women, and children were embraced by the Populist movement, which recognized that a strong economic and political movement could be a social force.
Kansas State Historical Society, Topeka, Kansas.

railroads and foreign investors. The Populists' boldest proposal called for government ownership of the railroads and telegraphs to put an end to discriminatory rate practices. With the powerful railroads dominating politics and effectively nullifying the Interstate Commerce Act of 1887, Populists did not shrink from advocating what their opponents called state socialism.

Money joined transportation and land as the third major thrust of the Populist movement. Farmers in all sections rallied to the cry for cheaper currency, endorsing platform planks calling for free silver and greenbacks (see Chapter 17, p. 643). To show their support for labor, Populists supported the eight-hour day and an end to contract labor. And to empower the common people, their platform called for the direct election of senators and electoral reforms including the secret ballot and the right to initiate legislation, to recall elected officials, and to submit issues to the people via referendum. More than just a response to hard times, Populism pre-

sented an alternative vision of what America could become. As journalist Henry Demarest Lloyd, an enthusiastic supporter of Populism, observed, "The People's Party is more than the organized discontent of the people. It is the organized aspiration of the people for a fuller, nobler, richer, kindlier life for every man, woman, and child in the ranks of humanity." It represented, in Lloyd's words, "an uprising of principle."

The Homestead Lockout and Strike

By the 1890s labor, too, was in crisis. The year 1892 witnessed a decisive struggle as steelworkers in Pennsylvania squared off against Andrew Carnegie for the right to organize in the Homestead mills. At first glance it seemed ironic that Carnegie became the adversary in the workers' fight for the right to unionize. Andrew Carnegie was unique among industrialists as a self-styled friend of labor. In 1886 he had written, "The right of the workingmen to combine and to form trades unions is no less sacred than the right of the manufacturer to enter into associations and conferences with his fellows." Yet six years later at Homestead, Carnegie set out to crush a union in one of labor's legendary confrontations.

As much as he cherished his liberal beliefs, Carnegie cherished his profits more. Labor unions had worked well for him during the years when he was building his empire. Labor strife at Homestead during the 1870s had enabled Carnegie to buy the plant from his competitors at cost and to take over the steel industry. And during the 1880s, strong national craft unions ensured that competing mills could not undercut his labor costs. By the 1890s, Carnegie held nearly total control of the steel business. The only thing standing in his way was the Amalgamated Association of Iron and Steel Workers, one of the largest and richest of the craft unions that made up the American Federation of Labor.

In 1892, when the Amalgamated attempted to renew its contract at Carnegie's Homestead mill, its leaders were told that since "the vast majority of our employees are Non union, the Firm has decided that the minority must give place to the majority." While it was true that only eight hundred skilled workers belonged to the elite Amalgamated, the union had long enjoyed the support of the plant's three thousand nonunion workers. Slavs, who did much of the unskilled work, made common cause with the Welsh, Scots, and Irish who belonged to the union. Never before had the Amalgamated been denied a contract.

As the situation built toward a showdown, Carnegie sailed to Scotland in the spring. No doubt aware of his hypocrisy, he preferred not to be directly involved in the union busting that lay on the horizon. He left Henry Clay Frick, the toughest antilabor man in the industry, in charge of the Homestead plant. By summer, a strike looked inevitable. Frick prepared for the showdown by erecting a fifteen-foot fence around the plant and topping it with barbed wire. With platforms for searchlights and holes for rifles, the fence gave the mill a distinctly military look. Workers aptly dubbed it "Fort Frick." To defend his fort, Frick hired 316 mercenaries from the Pinkerton Detective Agency at the rate of $5 per day, more than double the wage of the average Homestead worker.

On June 28, Frick locked the workers out of the mills. They immediately rallied to the support of the Amalgamated and declared a strike. Hugh O'Donnell, the young Irishman who led the union, vowed

to prevent strikebreakers from entering the plant. On July 6 at four in the morning, a lookout spotted two barges moving up the Monongahela River in the fog. Frick was attempting to smuggle his Pinkertons into Homestead. Workers sounded the alarm, and within minutes a crowd of more than a thousand, hastily armed with rifles, hoes, and fence posts, rushed to the riverbank to meet the enemy. When the Pinkertons attempted to come ashore, gunfire broke out, and more than a dozen Pinkertons and some thirty strikers fell, killed or wounded. The Pinkertons retreated back onto the barges.

For twelve hours, the strikers (joined by their family members) threw everything they had at the barges. Finally, the Pinkertons hoisted a white flag and arranged with O'Donnell to surrender. With eight strikers dead or dying and scores wounded, the crowd, now numbering perhaps ten thousand, was in no mood for conciliation. As the hated "Pinks" came up the hill, they were forced to run a gauntlet of screaming, cursing men, women, and children. When a young guard dropped to his knees, weeping for mercy, a woman used her umbrella to poke out his eye. Only one Pinkerton had been killed in the siege on the barges, but in the grim rout that followed their surrender, three men died as a result of the beatings, and not one avoided injury.

The "battle of Fort Frick" ended in a dubious victory for the workers. They took control of the plant and elected a council to run the community. At first, public opinion favored their cause. Newspapers urged Frick to negotiate or submit to arbitration. A congressman castigated Carnegie for "skulking in his castle in Scotland," and the Populists, meeting in St. Louis, condemned the use of "hireling armies."

But the action of the strikers struck at the heart of the capitalist system, pitting the workers' right to their jobs against the rights of private property. Four days after the confrontation, the Pennsylvania governor, who sympathized with the workers, nonetheless yielded to pressure from Frick and ordered eight thousand National Guard troops into Homestead to protect Carnegie's mills. The strikers, thinking they had won the day, welcomed the troops with a brass band. But they soon understood the reality. The troops' ninety-five-day occupation not only protected Carnegie's property but also enabled Frick to reopen the mills using strikebreakers. "We have been deceived," one worker bitterly com-

LABOR TROUBLE AT HOMESTEAD
The nation's attention was riveted on the labor strife at Homestead in the summer of 1892. **Frank Leslie's Illustrated** *weekly magazine ran a cover story on the violence Pinkerton agents faced from a crowd of men, women, and children armed with clubs, guns, and ax handles. The workers, who had been locked out by Henry Clay Frick, were enraged because Frick had hired the Pinkertons to bring in strikebreakers.*
The New York Society Library.

plained. "We have stood idly by and let the town be occupied by soldiers who come here, not as our protectors, but as the protectors of non-union men. . . . If we undertake to resist the seizure of our jobs, we will be shot down like dogs."

Then, in a misguided effort to ignite a general uprising, Alexander Berkman, a Russian immigrant and anarchist, attempted to assassinate Frick. Berkman's ally in his undertaking was the noted anarchist Emma Goldman, a Russian Jewish immigrant who had won a national reputation for her fiery speeches against capitalism and in favor of birth control. Berkman bungled his attempt. Frick, shot twice, survived and showed considerable courage, allowing doctors to remove the bullets from his neck but refusing to leave his desk until the day's work was completed. "I do not think that I shall die," Frick remarked coolly, "but whether I do or not, the Company will pursue the same policy and it will win."

The action of the Homestead strikers struck at the heart of the capitalist system, pitting the workers' right to their jobs against the rights of private property.

After the assassination attempt, public opinion turned against the workers. Berkman was quickly tried and sentenced to prison. Although the Amalgamated and the AFL denounced his action, the incident linked anarchism and unionism, already associated in the public mind as a result of the Haymarket bombing in 1886. Hugh O'Donnell later wrote that "the bullet from Berkman's pistol, failing in its foul intent, went straight through the heart of the Homestead strike."

In the end, the workers' resistance was crushed. The strike collapsed after four and a half months. The Homestead mill reopened in November and the men returned to work, except for the union leaders, who were blacklisted in every steel and iron mill in the country. In the drama and melodrama of events surrounding Homestead, the ideological and political significance of what occurred often remained obscured: The workers at Homestead had been taught a lesson. They would never again, in the words of the National Guard commander, "believe the works are their's [*sic*] quite as much as Carnegie's."

With the owners firmly in charge, the mills reopened. The company slashed wages, reinstated the twelve-hour day, and eliminated five hundred jobs. The workers lapsed into a demoralized and hopeless state. It would take another forty-five years before steelworkers successfully unionized. In the meantime, Carnegie's production tripled, even in the midst of a depression. "Ashamed to tell you profits these days," Carnegie wrote a friend in 1899. And no wonder: Carnegie's profits had grown from $4 million in 1892 to $40 million in 1900.

Eugene V. Debs and the Pullman Strike

A year after the Homestead lockout, a major panic and depression hit the nation. A stock market crash on Wall Street in the spring of 1893 led to bitter hard times. The ranks of the unemployed swelled to three million, almost half of the working population. "A fearful crisis is upon us," wrote a labor publication. "Countless thousands of our fellow men are unemployed; men, women and children are suffering the pangs of hunger." Nowhere were workers more demoralized than in the model town of Pullman on the outskirts of Chicago. George M. Pullman, who made his millions by building Pullman Palace cars and leasing them to the railroads, prided himself on his enlightened approach to labor. But in 1893, Pullman's workers saw their pay sliced five times between May and December, with cuts totaling at least 28 percent.

At the same time, Pullman refused to lower the rents in his model town, insisting that "the renting of the dwellings and the employment of workmen at Pullman are in no way tied together." When workers went to the bank to cash their checks, the rent was taken out. One worker found that he had only forty-seven cents to live on for two weeks. When the bank teller asked him whether he wanted to apply it to his back rent, he retorted, "If Mr. Pullman needs that forty-seven cents worse than I do, let him have it." In the meantime, Pullman continued to pay his stockholders an 8 percent dividend, and the company accumulated a $25 million surplus.

At the heart of the labor problems at Pullman lay not only economic inequity but the company's attempt to control the work process, substituting piecework for day wages and undermining the skilled craftsworkers. The Pullman workers rebelled. During the spring of 1894, they flocked to the ranks of the American Railway Union (ARU), a new organization led by Eugene Victor Debs. The ARU, unlike the skilled craft unions of the AFL, pledged to organize all railway workers from the engineers down to the engine wipers.

George Pullman responded to his workers' grievances by firing three of the union's leaders the day after they led a delegation to protest wage cuts. Angry men and women walked off the job in disgust. What began as a spontaneous protest in May 1894 blossomed into a strike that involved more than 90 percent of Pullman's thirty-three hundred workers. "We do not know what the outcome will be, and in fact we do not much care," one worker confessed. "We do know that we are working for less wages than will maintain ourselves and families in the necessaries of life, and on that proposition we refuse to work any longer." Pullman countered by shutting down the plant.

In June, the Pullman strikers appealed to the ARU to come to their aid. Debs sympathized with the strikers, but he hesitated to commit his fledgling union to a major strike in the midst of a depression. He pleaded with the workers to find another solution. When Pullman adamantly refused to arbitrate, the ARU membership, brushing aside Debs's call for caution, voted to boycott all Pullman cars. Beginning on June 29, switchmen refused to handle any train that carried Pullman cars.

The conflict escalated quickly. The General Managers Association (GMA), a combination of managers from twenty-four different railroads, acted in concert to quash the boycott. Determined to kill the ARU, they recruited strikebreakers and fired all the protesting switchmen. Their tactics set off a chain reaction. Entire train crews walked off the job in a show of solidarity with the Pullman workers and the ARU. In a matter of days the boycott/strike spread to more than fifteen railroads and affected twenty-seven states and territories. By July 2, rail lines from New York to California lay paralyzed. Even the GMA was forced to concede that the railroads had been "fought to a standstill."

The strike remained surprisingly peaceful. Mobs stopped trains carrying Pullman cars and forced their crews to uncouple the cars and leave them on the sidings. But no major riots broke out, and no serious damage was done to railroad property. Debs, in a whirlwind of activity, fired off telegrams to all parts of the country advising his followers to avoid violence, to use no force to stop trains, and to respect law and order. But the nation's newspapers, fed press releases by the GMA, distorted and misrepresented the strike. Across the country, papers ran headlines like WILD RIOT IN CHICAGO and MOB IS IN CONTROL. Editors rushed to denounce "Dictator Debs."

In Washington, Attorney General Richard B. Olney, a lawyer with strong ties to the railroads, determined to put down the strike. When Illinois governor John Peter Altgeld refused to call out troops, Olney, acting in concert with the GMA, convinced

NATIONAL GUARD OCCUPYING PULLMAN
After President Grover Cleveland called out the troops to put down the Pullman strike
in 1894, the National Guard occupied the town of Pullman to protect George M. Pullman's
property. Here the guard rings the Arcade Building, the town's shopping center, while
curious men and women look on.
Chicago Historical Society.

President Grover Cleveland that federal troops should intervene to protect the mails. To further cripple the strike, two Chicago judges issued an injunction against the boycott so sweeping that it prohibited Debs from speaking in public. By issuing the injunction, the court in effect made the strike a crime punishable by jail sentence for contempt of court, a civil process that did not require trial by jury. Even the conservative *Chicago Tribune* judged the injunction "a menace to liberty . . . a weapon ever ready for the capitalist." Furious, Debs risked jail by refusing to honor it.

Olney's strategy worked. With the strikers violating a federal injunction and with the mails in jeopardy (the GMA made sure that Pullman cars were put on every mail train), Cleveland called out the army. On July 5, nearly eight thousand troops marched into Chicago. Violence immediately erupted. In one day, more than $340,000 worth of property was destroyed, twenty-five workers were

shot, and more than sixty were wounded. In the face of bullets and bayonets, the strikers held firm. "Troops cannot move trains," Debs reminded the strikers, a fact that was borne out as the railroads remained paralyzed despite the military intervention. But if the army could not put down the strike, the injunction could and did. Debs was arrested and imprisoned for contempt of court. With its leader in jail, its headquarters raided and ransacked, and its members demoralized, the ARU was defeated along with the strike. Pullman reopened his factory, hiring new workers to replace many of the strikers and leaving sixteen hundred workers without jobs and without the means to relocate.

In the aftermath of the strike, a special commission investigated the events at Pullman, taking testimony from 107 witnesses, including workers and George M. Pullman himself. Stubborn and self-righteous, Pullman spoke for the business orthodoxy of his era, steadfastly affirming the right of business to safeguard its interests through confederacies like the General Managers Association and at the same time denying labor's right to organize. "If we were to receive these men as representatives of the union," he stated, "they could probably force us to pay any wages which they saw fit."

Stubborn and self-righteous, Pullman spoke for the business orthodoxy of his era, steadfastly affirming the right of business to safeguard its interests.

In his jail cell, Eugene Debs reviewed the events of the Pullman strike. With the courts and the army ready to come to the aid of property, labor had little recourse, Debs realized. Strikes seemed futile, and unions remained helpless; workers must take control of the state itself. Debs went into jail a trade unionist and came out six months later a socialist. After a brief flirtation with Populism, he would go on to form the Socialist Party in 1900 and run for president on its ticket five times.

Depression Politics

The depression that began in the spring of 1893 and lasted for more than four years put nearly half of the labor force out of work. Untold numbers of farmers lost their land to bank foreclosures. The human cost was staggering. "I Take my pen in hand to let you know that we are Starving to death," a Kansas farm woman wrote to the governor in 1894. The country swarmed with people looking for jobs. They rode the rails, slept in barns, begged for work, and, when they could not get work, begged for food.

The burden of feeding and sheltering the unemployed and their families fell to private charity, city government, and some of the stronger trade unions. The states and the federal government appropriated not a cent for aid. Following the harsh dictates of social Darwinism and laissez-faire, the majority of Americans believed that it was inappropriate for the government to intervene. But the scope of the depression made it impossible for local agencies to supply sufficient relief, and increasingly voices called on the federal government to take action. The American Federation of Labor declared that the "right to

work is the right to life" and argued that "when the private employer cannot or will not give work, the municipality, state or nation must." Demands for government intervention mounted throughout the decade as poverty created its own politics.

Coxey's "Army"

Masses of unemployed Americans marched to Washington, D.C., in the spring of 1894 to call attention to their plight and to urge Congress to take action. From as far away as Seattle, San Francisco, Los Angeles, and Denver, hundreds joined the march. Jacob S. Coxey of Massilon, Ohio, led the most publicized contingent. Coxey, a wealthy manufacturer, had a plan to end unemployment. He proposed to put the jobless to work building badly needed roads. Coxey had been an ardent Greenbacker (he named his son Legal Tender), and he planned to finance his program of public works by an issue of paper currency (greenbacks) and no-interest bonds. His plan won the support of the AFL and the Populists.

Starting out from Ohio with one hundred men, Coxey's "army," as it was dubbed by journalists, swelled as it marched east through the spring snows of the Alleghenies. In Pennsylvania, Coxey recruited several hundred from the ranks of those left unemployed by the Homestead lockout. Called by Coxey the Commonweal of Christ, the army advanced to the tune of "Marching through Georgia":

> We are not tramps nor vagabonds,
> that's shirking honest toil,
> But miners, clerks, skilled artisans,
> and tillers of the soil
> Now forced to beg our brother worms
> to give us leave to toil,
> While we are marching with Coxey.
>
> Hurrah! hurrah! for the unemployed's appeal
> Hurrah! hurrah! for the marching commonweal!

On May 1, Coxey's army arrived in Washington. Given permission to parade but forbidden to speak from the Capitol, Coxey defiantly marched his men onto the Capitol grounds. Police set upon the band, cracking heads and arresting Coxey and his lieutenants. Coxey went to jail for twenty days and was fined five dollars for "walking on the grass."

Mass demonstrations of the unemployed served only to frighten comfortable Americans, who saw the specter of insurrection and rebellion every-

COXEY'S ARMY
Coxey's army called itself a "petition in boots." Here a group of Coxeyites in coats, ties, and bowler hats march behind the American flag as women and children join the curious crowd that greets the marchers as they pass. These well-dressed marchers hardly seem like a menacing army. But many feared Coxey and his followers, and the military rhetoric of the press only fueled their fears. Coxey dramatized the plight of millions of workers left unemployed in the wake of the panic of 1893.
Library of Congress.

where in 1894. Those who had trembled for the safety of the Republic heaved a sigh of relief after Coxey's arrest, hoping that it would halt the march on Washington. But other armies of the unemployed, totaling possibly as many as five thousand people, were still on their way. Too poor to pay for railway tickets, they rode the rails as "freeloaders." The more daring contingents commandeered entire trains, stirring fears of revolution. Nervous midwestern governors put trains at the marchers' disposal to speed them quickly out of the state. Journalists who covered the march did little to quiet the nation's fears. They delighted in military terminology, dubbing the marchers "armies" and describing themselves as "war correspondents." Their writing gave to the episode a tone of urgency and heightened the sense of a nation imperiled.

By August, the tattered armies dissolved. Although the "On to Washington" movement proved ineffective in forcing federal relief legislation,

Coxey's army dramatized the plight of the unemployed and acted, in the words of one participant, as a "living, moving object lesson." Like the Populists, Coxey's army called into question the underlying values of the new industrial order and demonstrated how ordinary citizens turned to means outside the regular party system to influence politics in the 1890s.

The People's Party

Even before the depression of 1893 gave added impetus to their cause, the Populists had railed against the status quo. "We meet in the midst of a nation brought to the verge of moral, political, and material ruin," Ignatius Donnelly had declared in the preamble to the St. Louis platform in 1892.

> Corruption dominates the ballot-box, the legislatures, the Congress, and touches even the ermine of

CAMPAIGN RIBBONS

*Political paraphernalia from the election of 1892 tells a good deal about each party's
candidates and beliefs. The People's Party standard-bearer, General James B. Weaver,
and his running mate are pictured on a banner promising "HOMES FOR THE TOILERS,
EQUAL RIGHTS TO ALL, SPECIAL PRIVILEGES TO NONE." Populist issues are clearly spelled
out—"MONEY, LAND, AND TRANSPORTATION." The Populists' hope that these economic
issues would replace sectional loyalties is evident in the symbolism of the blue Union
and gray Confederate hands shaking. The beliefs of Democratic candidate Grover Cleveland are summed up in the phrase that became his motto: "PUBLIC OFFICE IS A PUBLIC
TRUST." Republican Benjamin Harrison, who enjoyed the support of the business community, is aptly portrayed as sponsored by the Bankers and Brokers Republican Club.*
Collection of Janice L. and David J. Frent.

the bench. . . . The fruits of the toil of millions are
boldly stolen to build up colossal fortunes for a few.
. . . From the same prolific womb of governmental
injustice we breed the two great classes—tramps
and millionaires.

The fiery rhetoric frightened many who saw in the
People's Party a call not to reform but to revolution.
Throughout the country, the press denounced the
Populists as "cranks, lunatics, and idiots." When
one righteous editor dismissed them as "calamity

howlers," Populist Lorenzo Lewelling of Kansas
shot back, "If that is so I want to continue to howl
until those conditions are improved." And Mary
Elizabeth Lease, accused of being a communist because of the Populists' advocacy of government
ownership of railroads, responded unperturbed,
"You may call me an anarchist, a socialist or a communist, I care not, but I hold to the theory that if
one man has not enough to eat three times a day
and another man has $25 million, that last man has
something that belongs to the first."

Even before the depression of 1893 gave added impetus to their cause, the Populists had railed against the status quo.

The People's Party had captured more than a million votes in the presidential election of 1892, a respectable showing for a new party. The Populists might have done better, but on the eve of the convention they lost their standard bearer when Leonidis L. Polk, president of the Southern Farmers Alliance, died. Scrambling to find a replacement, the convention nominated General James B. Weaver of Iowa, a former Union general who had headed the Greenback Labor ticket in 1880. Many southern Populists could not bring themselves to vote for a Union general and stayed away from the polls.

More than their alliance with the Yankee North, it was the Populists' willingness to form common cause with black farmers that made them anathema in the South. Tom Watson of Georgia had tackled the "Negro question" head-on in 1892. Realizing that race prejudice obscured the common interests of black and white farmers, Watson openly courted African Americans, appearing on platforms with black speakers and promising "to wipe out the color line." When angry Georgia whites threatened to lynch a black Populist preacher, Watson rallied two thousand gun-toting Populists to the man's defense. The spectacle of white Georgians protecting a black man from lynching was symptomatic of the enormous changes Populism promised in the South.

The People's Party fared better in the 1894 congressional elections, when, unencumbered by a Yankee general, the Populists added half a million voters to their column. With the depression swelling the ranks of the disaffected, the Populists looked forward to the election of 1896.

The Election of 1896

As the election of 1896 approached, depression intensified cries for reform not only from the Populists but throughout the electorate. Depression worsened the tight money problem caused by the deflationary pressures of the gold standard. Once again, proponents of free silver (the coinage of silver in addition to gold) stirred rebellion in the ranks of both the Democratic and Republican Parties. When the Republicans nominated Ohio governor William

McKinley on a platform pledging the preservation of the gold standard, western advocates of free silver walked out of the convention. Open rebellion also split the Democratic Party as vast segments in the West and South repudiated President Grover Cleveland because of his support for the gold standard. In South Carolina, Benjamin Tillman won his race for Congress by promising, "Send me to Washington and I'll stick my pitchfork into [Cleveland's] old ribs!"

The spirit of revolt animated the Democratic National Convention in Chicago in the summer of 1896. "Pitchfork Ben" Tillman set the tone by attacking the party's president, denouncing the Cleveland administration as "undemocratic and tyrannical." But the man of the hour was William Jennings Bryan of Nebraska, the thirty-six-year-old "boy orator from the Platte," who whipped the convention into a frenzy with his passionate call for free silver. In his keynote address, Bryan masterfully cataloged the grievances of farmers and laborers, closing his dramatic speech with the ringing exhortation "Do not crucify mankind upon a cross of gold." Pandemonium immediately broke loose as delegates stampeded to nominate Bryan, the youngest candidate ever to run for the presidency.

The juggernaut of free silver rolled out of Chicago and on to St. Louis, where the People's Party met a week after the Democrats adjourned. Smelling victory, many western Populists urged the party to endorse Bryan. A note of warning came from Populists like Tom Watson, who denounced the Bryanites as opportunists and urged the Populists to steer clear of both major parties and stick to "the middle of the road." In the South, where Democrats had resorted to fraud and violence to steal elections from the Populists in 1892 and 1894, support for a Democratic ticket proved especially hard for Populists to swallow. Another obstacle in the path of fusion was Arthur M. Sewall, Bryan's running mate. A Maine railway director and bank president, Sewall had been placed on the ticket to appease conservative Democrats. But to the Populists, Sewall symbolized everything they opposed.

Populist delegates tried to remain true to their principles and their platform when they met in St. Louis in 1896. They voted to support all the planks of the 1892 platform, added to it a call for public works projects for the unemployed, and narrowly defeated a plank for woman suffrage. Only deceit and trickery enabled the fusionists (those who wished to join ranks with the Democrats) to

GOLD ELEPHANT CAMPAIGN BUTTONS, 1896
Mechanical elephant badges that opened to show
portraits of William McKinley and his running
mate, Garret Hobart, were popular campaign novel-
ties in the election of 1896. The elephant, the mascot
of the Republican Party, is gilded gold to indicate
the party's support of the gold standard.
Collection of Janice L. and David J. Frent.

carry the day. In an unorthodox turn of events, the convention selected the vice presidential candidate first. By nominating Tom Watson to replace Sewall, the party undercut opposition to fusing with the Democrats. Bryan quickly wired the chairman of the convention, protesting that he would not drop Sewall as his running mate or run on a Populist ticket with Watson. Mysteriously, his message never reached the convention floor. Watson's nomination paved the way for the selection of Bryan by a lopsided vote. The Populists did not know it, but their cheers for Bryan in St. Louis signaled not a chorus of victory, but the death knell of the People's Party.

Few contests in the nation's history have been as fiercely fought and as full of emotion as the presidential election of 1896. On one side stood Republican William McKinley, backed by the wealthy industrialist and party boss Marcus Alonzo Hanna. Hanna played on the business community's fears of free silver to raise more than $4 million for the Republican war chest, double that of any previous campaign. On the other side, William Jennings Bryan, with few assets beyond his silver tongue, struggled

to make up in energy and eloquence what his party lacked in campaign funds. He set a new style for presidential campaigning, crossing and recrossing the country in a whirlwind tour, traveling more than eighteen thousand miles and delivering more than six hundred speeches in three months. According to his own reckoning, he visited twenty-seven states and spoke to more than five million Americans.

As election day approached, the silver states of the Rocky Mountains lined up for Bryan. The Northeast stood solidly for McKinley. Much of the South, with the exception of the border states, came back to the Democratic fold, leaving Tom Watson to lament that, in the politics of fusion, "we play Jonah while they play the whale." The Midwest was in the balance. Bryan intensified his campaign in Illinois, Michigan, Ohio, and Indiana. But midwestern farmers could smell economic recovery and were less receptive to the blandishments of free silver than were voters farther west. In the cities, Democrats charged the Republicans with mass intimidation. "Men, vote as you please," the head of Brooklyn's Steinway Piano Company reportedly announced on the eve of the election, "but if Bryan is elected tomorrow the whistle will not blow Wednesday morning."

The Populists did not know it, but their
cheers for Bryan in St. Louis signaled not a
chorus of victory, but the death knell of the
People's Party.

Intimidation alone did not explain the failure of urban labor to rally to Bryan. Republicans repeatedly warned workers that if the Democrats won, the inflated silver dollar would be worth only fifty cents. However much farmers and laborers might insist that they were united as producers against the nonproducing bosses, it was equally true that inflation did not promise the boon to urban laborers that it did to western debtors.

On election day, four out of every five voters went to the polls in an unprecedented turnout. In the critical midwestern states, as many as 95 percent of the eligible voters cast their ballots. In the end, the election outcome hinged on as few as one hundred to one thousand votes in several key states. Although McKinley won twenty-three states to Bryan's twenty-two, the electoral vote showed a lopsided 271–176 (Map 19.1).

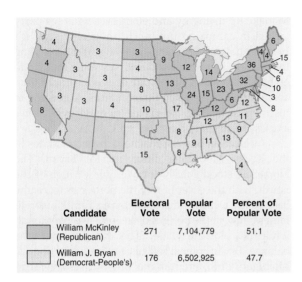

Candidate	Electoral Vote	Popular Vote	Percent of Popular Vote
William McKinley (Republican)	271	7,104,779	51.1
William J. Bryan (Democrat-People's)	176	6,502,925	47.7

MAP 19.1
The Election of 1896

The biggest losers in 1896 turned out to be the Populists. On the national level, they polled less than 300,000 votes, over a million less than in 1894. In the clamor to support Bryan, Populists in the South drifted back to the Democratic Party. The People's Party was crushed, and with it died the agrarian revolt.

But if Populism proved unsuccessful, it set the political agenda for the United States in the next decades, highlighting issues such as banking and currency reform, electoral reforms, and an enlarged role for the federal government in the economy. As the decade ended, the bugle call to arms drowned out the trumpet of reform: American expansionism spawned a "splendid little war" that whipped up patriotic fervor, uniting the country and confirming the emergence of the United States as a major world power.

American Foreign Policy at the End of a Tumultuous Decade

In the last decade of the nineteenth century, American foreign policy consisted of two currents—isolation and expansion. The determination to remain aloof from European politics had been a hallmark of policy since President George Washington,

in his farewell address, had warned Americans to "steer clear" of permanent alliances. Simultaneously, Americans believed in "manifest destiny"—the "obvious" right to expand the country from ocean to ocean and possibly on a continental scale, taking in Canada and Mexico. The Union's victory in the Civil War had uncoupled the knot of slavery and western expansion, allowing the country to resume its march across the continent and the dispossession of the Native Americans who stood in its path. The treatment of Native Americans in the Indian Wars of 1870–1890 set a precedent for the treatment of other nonwhite groups in the path of American expansion, from the Hawaiian islanders to Cubans and Filipinos.

The Monroe Doctrine and the Open Door Policy

Throughout much of the last half of the nineteenth century, U.S. interest in foreign policy took a backseat to domestic developments. "Foreign relations," one historian has written, "were composed of incidents, not policies." Intent on its own manifest destiny, the United States stood aloof while the European powers—Great Britain, France, Germany, Spain, and Belgium—as well as an increasingly powerful Japan competed for empires abroad, gobbling up what they liked to call the great "empty spaces" on the globe in Asia, Africa, Latin America, and the Pacific. Between 1870 and 1900, European nations gained control of more than 20 percent of the land and 10 percent of the earth's population.

Its emergence as a world power pitted the United States against the colonial powers, particularly Germany and Japan, who posed a threat to the twin pillars of America's expansionist foreign policy, one that dated back to President James Monroe in the 1820s and another formalized in 1900 under William McKinley. The first, the Monroe Doctrine, proclaimed the Western Hemisphere an American "sphere of influence" and warned European powers to keep their hands off or risk war. The second, the Open Door, dealt with Asia, an area coveted by American merchants since the 1840s, the heyday of the clipper ships and the China trade. In the 1890s, China, weakened by years of warfare, looked as if it might be partitioned into spheres of influence by England, Japan, Germany, France, and Russia. Concerned about American trade and the integrity of China, Secretary of State John Hay in 1899–1900 hastily wrote a series of notes calling for an "open

THE OPEN DOOR

The trade advantage gained by the United States through the Open Door policy enunci-
ated by Secretary of State John Hay in 1900 is portrayed graphically in this political car-
toon. Uncle Sam stands prominently in the "open door" while representatives of the other
great powers seek admittance to the "Flowery Kingdom" of China. Great Britain is sym-
bolized by the stocky figure of John Bull; czarist Russia is portrayed by the bearded figure
with the hat sporting the imperial double eagle. Other imperialist powers variously repre-
sented have yielded to Uncle Sam, who holds the golden key of "American Diplomacy"
while the Chinese beam with pleasure. In fact, the Open Door policy promised only equal
access for all powers to the China trade, not U.S. preeminence as the cartoon implies.
Culver Pictures.

www.bedfordstmartins.com/tap   SEE THE ONLINE STUDY GUIDE for more help in analyzing
this image.

door" policy that would ensure trade access to all
and maintain the semblance of Chinese sovereignty.
The notes—sent to Britain, Germany, and Russia
and later to France, Japan, and Italy—were greeted
by the major powers with polite evasions. Nevertheless, Hay skillfully managed to maneuver the
powers into doing his bidding and boldly an-

nounced in 1900 the Open Door as international
policy.

American foreign policy reflected a curious
paradox. Just as the United States wished to keep
the Western Hemisphere (particularly Latin America and the Caribbean) closed to foreign influences,
it wished to keep the Eastern Hemisphere (espe-

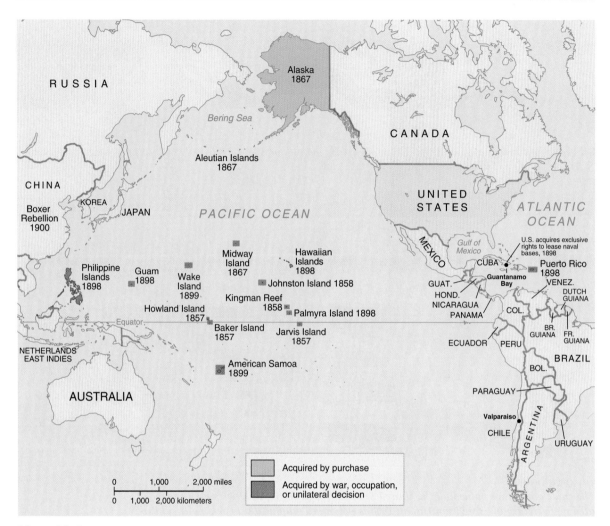

MAP 19.2
U.S. Territorial Expansion through 1900
The United States extended its interests abroad with a series of territorial acquisitions. Although Cuba was granted independence, the Platt Amendment kept the new nation firmly under U.S. control. In the wake of the Spanish-American War, the United States woke up to find that it held an empire extending halfway around the globe.

READING THE MAP: Does the map reflect more territory acquired (1) by purchase or (2) by war, occupation, or unilateral decision? How many purchases of land outside the continental United States did the government make?

CONNECTIONS: What foreign policy developments occurred in the 1890s? How did American political leaders react to them? Where was U.S. expansion headed, and why?

www.bedfordstmartins.com/tap   SEE THE ONLINE STUDY GUIDE for more help in analyzing this map.

cially Asia) open for its own purposes. In short, Americans wanted to protect their backdoor "sphere of influence" and keep it closed to control by the European powers, at the same time insisting that no other country declare Asia, especially China, its exclusive sphere. The twin pillars of U.S. foreign policy may not have been consistent, but they worked effectively to further the country's economic interests. By holding to its Open Door policy in Asia, the United States largely avoided the problems of maintaining a far-flung colonial empire while also exerting and expanding its economic power.

To defend the Monroe Doctrine, the United States was willing to risk war with Germany in 1889. Eleven years after a treaty gave the United States the right to the harbor at the Pacific port of Pago Pago in the Samoan Islands, Germany, seeking dominance over the islands, sent warships to support its honor and its claims. But before any fighting broke out, a great typhoon destroyed the German and American ships. Acceding to the will of nature, the potential combatants divided the islands amicably between themselves (Map 19.2).

American foreign policy reflected a curious paradox. Just as the United States wished to keep the Western Hemisphere closed to foreign influences, it wished to keep the Eastern Hemisphere open for its own purposes.

Elsewhere, America's foreign adventures appeared little more than a sidelight to business development. In Hawaii (first called the Sandwich Islands), American sugar interests fomented a rebellion in 1893, toppling the increasingly anti-American Queen Liliuokalani. But before they could get Congress to annex the islands, a move that would allow the planters to avoid the high tariff on sugar, Grover Cleveland replaced the more pliant Benjamin Harrison as president. When Cleveland learned that the Hawaiian population opposed annexation, he withdrew the proposal from Senate consideration. Nevertheless, expansionists continued to covet the islands, and their leaders in Congress would use the first excuse to push through annexation in 1898.

Closer to home, the United States actively worked to buttress the Monroe Doctrine, with its assertion of American hegemony (domination) in the Western Hemisphere. In the 1880s, Republican secretary of state James G. Blaine promoted hemispheric peace and trade through Pan-American cooperation at the same time that he used American troops to intervene in Latin American border disputes. In 1891, war with Chile almost erupted after two American sailors were killed and several in-

jured in a barroom brawl in Valparaiso. President Benjamin Harrison threatened war but backed down after Chile apologized and paid a $75,000 indemnity. He was wise to do so, for Chile had a better-equipped navy than the United States. Late in the century, the United States began to strengthen its navy, but its army remained little more than a token force of twenty-five thousand, barely large enough to handle disturbances at home, let alone fight abroad.

Nevertheless, in 1895 Americans risked war with Great Britain to enforce the Monroe Doctrine. When a border dispute arose between Venezuela and British Guiana over lands where gold had been discovered, President Cleveland asserted the U.S. prerogative to step in and mediate, reducing Venezuela to the role of mere onlooker. At first, Britain refused to accept U.S. mediation and conflict seemed imminent. "Let the fight come if it must," wrote Theodore Roosevelt, always itching to do battle. "I don't care whether our sea coast cities are bombarded or not." Seeing war with Britain as an opportunity to fulfill a long-held goal of extending manifest destiny to the North as well as to the West, Roosevelt promised that "we would take Canada." Cleveland, less bellicose than Roosevelt, wished only to see America's presence in the hemisphere respected and its solution for peace accepted. He was relieved when the British, who saw Germany as a greater threat and wished to avoid war in Latin America, accepted the terms of U.S. mediation.

In Central America, U.S. business triumphed in a bloodless takeover that saw French and British interests routed by behemoths like the United Fruit Company of Boston. United Fruit virtually dominated Costa Rica and Guatemala while an importer from New Orleans turned Honduras into a "banana republic." Thus, by 1895, the Venezuelan crisis signaled the extent to which the United States, through business as well as diplomacy, had successfully achieved hegemony in Latin America and the Caribbean, forcing even the British to concur with the secretary of state that "the infinite resources [of the United States] combined with its isolated position render it master of the situation and practically invulnerable as against any or all other powers."

Markets and Missionaries

The depression of the 1890s provided a powerful impetus to American commercial expansion. As markets weakened at home, American businesses looked abroad for profits. As early as 1890, Captain Alfred Thayer Mahan, leader of a growing group of American expansionists that included Henry Cabot Lodge, John Hay, and Theodore Roosevelt, prophesied, "Whether they will or not, Americans must now begin to look outward. The growing production of the country requires it." Although not all U.S. business leaders thought it advantageous to undertake adventures abroad, the logic of acquiring new markets to absorb the nation's growing capacity for production proved convincing to many. As the depression deepened, one diplomat warned that Americans "must turn [their] eyes abroad, or they will soon look inward upon discontent." Enthusiasts of expansion spoke glowingly of Asian markets: "Four hundred million Chinese without shoes."

Exports of cloth, kerosene, flour, and steel already constituted a small but significant percentage of the profits of American business in the 1890s. And where American interests led, businessmen expected American power and influence to follow to protect their investments (Figure 19.2). Companies like Standard Oil actively sought to use the government as their agent, often putting foreign service employees on the payroll. "Our ambassadors and ministers and consuls," wrote John D. Rockefeller appreciatively, "have aided to push our way into new markets to the utmost corners of the world." Whether by "our" he meant the United States or

Standard Oil remained ambiguous; in practice, the distinction was of little importance in late-nineteenth-century foreign policy.

However compelling the economic arguments about overseas markets proved, business interests alone did not account for the new expansionism that seized the nation during the 1890s. As Mahan confessed, "Even when material interests are the original exciting cause, it is the sentiment to which they give rise, the moral tone which emotion takes that constitutes the greater force." Much of that moral tone was set by American missionaries intent on spreading the gospel of Christianity to the "heathen." No area on the globe constituted a greater challenge than China. In 1858, the Tientsin treaty admitted foreign missionaries—Roman Catholics from France, Protestants from Britain, Germany, and the United States—to spread the gospel to the hinterlands.

Young women particularly were attracted to the independence and excitement promised by mission work. Missions accepted single women over twenty-six years of age. By 1890, women constituted more than 60 percent of foreign missionaries. Young women from the rural Midwest, many of whom would not have ventured into Chicago alone, set off for China. Foreign mission work promised adventure and autonomy few other callings for women could match. Although they never lost their opti-

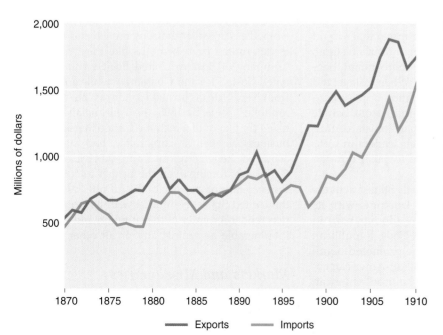

FIGURE **19.2**

Expansion in U.S. Trade, 1870–1910
Between 1870 and 1910, American exports nearly tripled. Although imports rose, they were held in check by the high protective tariff championed by Republican presidents from Ulysses Grant to William Howard Taft. A decline in imports is particularly noticeable after passage of the prohibitive McKinley tariff in 1890.

WOMEN MISSIONARIES IN CHINA
Methodist women missionaries in the Szechuan province of China relied on traditional means of transportation, in this case "back chairs." The independence enjoyed by women missionaries stood in marked contrast to the restrictions placed on young, unmarried women of their class at home.
Courtesy of the Yale Divinity School Library.

mism, the missionaries' success proved limited and their converts in China few. By the turn of the century, an estimated 100,000 converts existed in a total population of 400 million Chinese. Nevertheless, as the missionaries pointed out, the number marked a significant increase over the 8,000 Christian converts counted in 1870.

Increased missionary activity and Western enterprise touched off a series of antiforeign uprisings in China that culminated in the Boxer Rebellion of 1900–1901. The Chinese resented the interference of missionaries in village life and the preference and protection they afforded their Christian converts. Opposition to foreign missionaries took the form of antiforeign secret societies, most notably the Boxers, whose Chinese name translated literally into "Righteous Harmonious Fist." No simple pugilists, the Boxers believed that through ritual they could induce a trance that would make them invincible to Western weapons. Under the slogan "Uphold the Ch'ing Dynasty, Exterminate the Foreigners," they began to terrorize Chinese Christians and later missionaries in northern China. As they became bolder, they attacked railroads and telegraph lines, the twin symbols of Western imperialism. Their rampage eventually led to the massacre of some 2,000

Chinese converts and 250 missionaries and their families.

The missionaries clamored for the American government to protect and avenge them. Fearing for their lives, they showed little toleration for the cautious diplomatic approach favored by Secretary of State John Hay. In the end, twenty-five hundred U.S. troops joined an allied force including British and German troops sent to save the besieged foreigners in Peking (now Beijing). The arrival of foreign troops chastened the imperial government, which adopted a tougher stance against the Boxers and a more accommodationist policy toward foreign missionaries.

In their fight against the Boxers, the missionaries saw no paradox in bringing Christianity to China at gunpoint. "It is worth any cost in money, worth any cost in bloodshed," argued one bishop, "if we can make millions of Chinese true and intelligent Christians." In truth, expansionists and missionaries worked hand in hand; trade and Christianity marched into China together. "Missionaries," admitted the American clergyman Charles Denby, "are the pioneers of trade and commerce. . . . The missionary, inspired by holy zeal, goes everywhere and by degrees foreign commerce and trade follow."

In truth, expansionists and missionaries worked hand in hand; trade and Christianity marched into China together.

The moral tone of the age, set by social Darwinism with its emphasis on survival of the fittest and Anglo-Saxon racial superiority, proved ideally suited to imperialism. Congregational minister Josiah Strong revealed the mixture of racism and missionary zeal that fueled American adventurism abroad when he remarked, "It seems to me that God, with infinite wisdom and skill, is training the Anglo Saxon race for an hour sure to come in the world's future." British poet Rudyard Kipling cynically expressed the new mandate in verse:

> Take up the white man's burden
>   Send forth the best ye breed—
> Go bind your sons to exile
>   To serve your captive's need;
> To wait, in heavy harness,
>   On fluttered folk and wild—
> Your new-caught sullen people,
>   Half devil and half child.

The irony that is apparent in Kipling's poem evidently escaped those Americans who rushed to champion U.S. expansionism. No one exemplified the new jingoism (extreme nationalism tinged with belligerency) better than Theodore Roosevelt, the rising young Republican from New York. Always more concerned with manliness than with money, Roosevelt believed that nations and individuals needed the test of combat to maintain their virility. "This country needs a war," Roosevelt asserted in 1895. Power, not profits, motivated expansionists of Roosevelt's stripe. Intent on asserting the United States' place in the world of nations, they pressed for a more expansionist policy, judging imperialism "a fine expression of the American spirit."

War and Empire

As the leading industrial nation in the world, the United States seemed destined to play a significant role in global politics. Yet not until 1898 did the country take its place on the world stage by confronting

and easily defeating a European power. On the surface, the Spanish-American War seemed a giant contradiction: A war begun as a humanitarian effort to free Cuba from Spain's colonial grasp ended with the United States itself becoming a colonial power. After the war was over, American troops fought a dirty guerrilla war in the jungles of the Pacific with Filipino nationalists, who, like the Cubans, sought independence. Yet behind the contradiction stood the twin pillars of American foreign policy. The Monroe Doctrine's insistence on American control in the Western Hemisphere made Spain's presence in Cuba unacceptable, while the determination to keep an open door in Asia rendered the Philippines a convenient stepping-stone to China.

"A Splendid Little War"

Looking back on the Spanish-American War of 1898, Secretary of State John Hay judged it "a splendid little war; begun with the highest motives, carried on with magnificent intelligence and spirit, favored by that fortune which loves the brave." At the close of a decade marred by bitter depression, social unrest, and political upheaval, the war offered Americans a chance to wave the flag and march in unison. War fever proved as infectious as the tune of a John Philip Sousa march. Few argued the merits of the conflict until it was over and the time came to divide the spoils. (See "Documenting the American Promise," page 716.)

The war began with moral outrage over the treatment of Cuban revolutionaries, who had launched a fight for independence against the Spanish colonial regime in 1895. In an attempt to isolate the guerrillas, Spanish general Valeriano Weyler herded Cubans into crowded and unsanitary concentration camps, where thousands died of hunger, disease, and exposure. Starvation soon spread to the cities. Tens of thousands of Cubans died, and countless others were left without food, clothing, or shelter. By 1898, fully a quarter of the island's population had perished in the revolution.

As the Cuban war dragged on, pressure for American intervention mounted. Public outrage at Spain was fueled by American newspapers. A fierce circulation war raged in New York City between William Randolph Hearst's *Evening Journal* and Joseph Pulitzer's *World*. Their competition provoked what came to be called "yellow journalism," named for the color of ink Hearst used in his most popular comic strip, "The Yellow Kid," drawn by

THE BIG TYPE WAR OF THE YELLOW KIDS.

YELLOW JOURNALISM
Newspaper publishers Joseph Pulitzer and William Randolph Hearst square off in "The Big Type War." As the cartoon indicates, Hearst insisted he had the better right to cover the Spanish-American War because he "bought and paid for it." In their 1890s circulation war, Hearst and Pulitzer not only used big type in sensational headlines, but employed color in new comic sections. Hearst's Sunday **American** *promised "eight pages of polychromatic effulgence that make the rainbow look like a lead pipe." Hearst also stole the era's most famous cartoon character, the "Yellow Kid," from Pulitzer after a bidding war for the cartoonist's talents. Soon all forms of sensational writing were labeled "yellow journalism."*
Library of Congress.

Richard Felton Outcault. This new style of journalism, which pandered to the public's appetite for violence and sensationalism, found in the Cuban war a wealth of dramatic copy. The papers fed the American people a daily diet of "Butcher" Weyler and Spanish atrocities. Hearst sent artist Frederic Remington to document the horror, and when Remington wired home, "There is no trouble here. There will be no war," Hearst shot back, "You furnish the pictures and I'll furnish the war."

Business also played a role in U.S. intervention. American interests, in the words of the U.S. minister to Spain, were more than "merely theoretical or sentimental." American business had more than $50 million invested in Cuban sugar, and American trade with Cuba, a brisk $100 million a year before the war, had dropped to near zero as a result of the revolution. Nevertheless, the business community balked, wary of a war with Spain. When industrialist Mark Hanna, the Republican kingmaker and

What Sank the Maine?

AT 9:40 P.M. ON THE EVENING OF FEBRUARY 15, 1898, the U.S. battleship *Maine* blew up in Havana harbor. Eyewitness accounts differed, but most reported hearing a small concussion followed by a ferocious blast. American Martin Bunting, who witnessed the explosion from the wharf, reported "The shock threw us backward. From the deck forward of amidships shot a streak of fire as high as the tall buildings on Broadway. Then the glare of light widened out like a funnel at the top, and down through this bright circle fell showers of wreckage and mangled sailors." Two hundred and sixty-seven sailors drowned or burned to death in one of the worst naval catastrophes during peacetime.

Captain Charles Dwight Sigsbee, the last man to leave the burning ship, filed a terse report, saying the *Maine* had blown up and "urging [that] public opinion should be suspended until further report." Within two days, however, the yellow press led by William Randolph Hearst's *New York Journal* and Joseph Pulitzer's *World* carried banner headlines announcing "The War Ship *Maine* Was Split in Two by an Enemy's Secret Infernal Machine!" Such sensational headlines more than doubled the *Journal*'s circulation in the weeks following the disaster.

Public opinion quickly divided between those who suspected foul play and those who believed the cause was accidental. Foremost among the accident theorists of course was the Spanish government, but the English press and business groups in the United States who hoped to avoid war with Spain also favored this view. Among the "jingo's," as proponents of war were called, was Assistant Secretary of the Navy Theodore Roosevelt, who wrote even before the details were known "The *Maine* was sunk by an act of dirty treachery on the part of the Spaniards *I* believe; though we shall never find out definitely, and officially it will go down as an accident."

In less than a week the navy formed a court of inquiry and although the *Maine* could not be brought to the surface for inspection, divers examined the wreckage and the panel reported on March 25 that a mine had burst under the bottom of the ship igniting gunpowder in the forward magazine.

No guilty party was named, since the panel could not be sure whether the mine was planted by the Spanish government or by recalcitrant followers of General Valeriano Weyler, who had been recalled to Spain after the yellow press dubbed him "the Butcher" for his harsh treatment of the Cubans. The U.S. Senate carried on its own investigation, concluding that whether by intent or by negligence the Spanish government was responsible for the catastrophe. The stage was set for war. To cries of "Remember the *Maine,*" Congress passed a war resolution. President William McKinley yielded to the inevitable and signed it on April 20, 1898.

In the "splendid little war" that followed, the United States defeated Spain in a matter of months. Only ten sailors were killed in the entire war, compared to the 267 who died aboard the *Maine*. In the years following the war, however, more people came to view the explosion of the *Maine* as an accident, possibly the result of a fire in the ship's coal bins that ignited the gunpowder stored in the magazines nearby. A Spanish court of inquiry had reached the same conclusion prior to the war. European naval authorities analyzed the U.S. naval court report and proved that it had made a gross error: The explosion had not occurred at the location named in the report. In addition, European experts demonstrated the *Maine* had exploded accidentally, from a fire in the coal bunker adjacent to the reserve gunpowder and shell magazine. Many came to believe that poor design, not treachery, had sunk the *Maine*.

In 1910, the *Maine* still lay in the mud of Havana harbor, a sunken tomb containing the remains of many sailors. The Cuban government asked for the removal of the wreck. Veterans demanded a decent burial for the sailors entombed in the sunken hulk. With so many questions raised about the naval court of inquiry's conclusions, American public opinion urged further investigation. New York Congressman William Sultzer put it succinctly, "The day after the ship was sunk, you could hardly find an American who did not believe that she had been foully done to death by a treacherous enemy. Today you can hardly find an American who believes Spain had anything to do with it." So in March 1910 Congress voted to raise the *Maine*.

The "Final Report on Removing the Wreck of Battleship *Maine* from the Harbor of Habana, Cuba," was issued in April 1913. The Vreeland report, named for Admiral Charles Vreeland, who

U.S. BATTLESHIP *MAINE* SUNK IN HAVANA HARBOR

This photograph of the battleship **Maine,** *sunk in the mud of Havana harbor, ran in New York newspapers February 16, 1898, the morning after the blast. The extent of the destruction and the consequent death of 267 sailors fueled war fever. The yellow press in short order ran eight-inch headlines proclaiming "THE MAINE WAS DESTROYED BY TREACHERY," although there was no evidence to back up the assertion.*

National Archives.

chaired the investigation, noted that the original naval inquiry had, as previously reported, erred in the location of the initial explosion. The Vreeland report nevertheless failed to endorse the accident theory, determining instead that the destruction of the *Maine* was "caused by the explosion of a charge of a low form of explosive exterior to the ship" which in turn had led to a massive explosion as the ship's magazine ignited. The nature of the initial explosion indicated a home-made bomb, not a Spanish naval mine—casting suspicion on Weyler's fanatic followers. Following the investigation and removal of human remains, the wreckage of the *Maine* was towed out to sea and with full funereal honors sunk in 600 fathoms of water.

Controversy over the *Maine* proved more difficult to sink. The cause of the *Maine* disaster became a litmus test for subsequent generations as they worked through the issues of their time. In the Vietnam era, when faith in "the military establishment" reached an all-time low point, Admiral

Hyman Rickover launched yet another investigation. Many critics had come to believe that the Vreeland report was little more than a cover-up and to prove their point they noted that the ship had been sunk so deep "that there will be no chance of the true facts being revealed." Rickover, a maverick who held the naval brass in low esteem, hired experts to pour over the evidence cataloged in previous investigations. Rickover started from the position that neither of the navy's earlier investigations had yielded the truth. He noted that "the warlike atmosphere in Congress and the press, and the natural tendency to look for reasons for the loss that did not reflect on the Navy," made the previous findings highly suspect. Refuting claims that the initial explosion had been caused by a mine, Rickover insisted that self-ignition in the coal bunker triggered an explosion in the reserve magazine. Reading the past in the jaundiced light of the present, Rickover concluded "[W]e must make sure that those in 'high places' do not without most careful *(Continued)* consideration of the consequences, exert our prestige and might," presumably in unnecessary and immoral wars. Published in book form in 1976, Rickover's report, entitled *How the Battleship Maine Was Destroyed,* became the accepted version of the event.

Today the pendulum has swung back. In an era when terrorist attacks have become all too commonplace it is no surprise that a 1995 study of the *Maine* incident published by the Smithsonian Institution concludes that the battleship was sunk by zealot followers of General Weyler. "They had the opportunity, the means, and the motivation, and they blew up the *Maine* with a small low-strength mine they made themselves." According to this theory the terrorists' homemade bomb burst the *Maine's* hull and triggered a massive explosion in the ammunition magazines.

In looking at the now hundred-year-old history of controversy regarding the sinking of the *Maine,* only one thing seems certain: The "lessons" of the *Maine* have changed with the times and will no doubt continue to be drawn again as each new era questions history.

---

senator from Ohio, urged restraint, a hot-headed Theodore Roosevelt, appointed assistant secretary of the navy in 1897, exploded, "We will have this war for the freedom of Cuba, Senator Hanna, in spite of the timidity of commercial interests."

At the close of a decade marred by bitter depression, social unrest, and political upheaval, the Spanish-American War offered Americans a chance to wave the flag and march in unison.

To expansionists like Roosevelt, more than Cuban independence was at stake. War with Spain opened up the prospect of expansion into Asia as well, since Spain controlled not only Cuba and Puerto Rico but also Guam and the Philippine Islands. As assistant secretary of the navy, Roosevelt worked for preparedness whenever his boss's back was turned. During the summer of 1897, while Navy Secretary John D. Long was vacationing, Roosevelt audaciously ordered the U.S. fleet to Manila in the Philippines. In the event of conflict with Spain, he put the navy in a position to capture the islands and gain an entry point to China.

President McKinley slowly moved toward intervention. In a show of American force, he dispatched the armored cruiser *Maine* to Cuba. On the night of February 15, 1898, a mysterious explosion destroyed the *Maine,* killing 267 crew members. (See "Historical Question," page 712.) While the source of the explosion remained unclear, enraged Americans immediately blamed the Spanish government. Rallying to the cry "Remember the *Maine,*" Congress declared war in April. In the surge of patriotism that followed, more than 235,000 men enlisted. War brought with it a unity of purpose and national harmony that ended a decade of internal strife. "In April, everywhere over this good fair land, flags were flying," wrote the Kansas editor William Allen White. "At the stations, crowds gathered to hurrah for the soldiers, and to throw hats into the air, and to unfurl flags."

They soon had something to cheer about. Five days after McKinley signed the war resolution, the U.S. navy, under Commodore George Dewey, destroyed the Spanish fleet in Manila Bay (Map 19.3). Dewey's stunning victory caught the nation by surprise. Although naval strategists had been orchestrating the move for some time, few Americans had ever heard of the Philippines. Even McKinley confessed that he could not immediately locate the archipelago on the map. He nevertheless recognized the Philippines as a convenient stepping stone to China and dispatched U.S. troops to secure the islands.

The war in Cuba ended almost as quickly as it had begun. The first troops landed on June 22, and after a handful of battles the Spanish surrendered on July 17. The war lasted just long enough to elevate Theodore Roosevelt to the status of bona fide war hero. Roosevelt, sensitive to charges that he and his friends were no more than "armchair or parlor jingoes," resigned his navy post and formed the Rough Riders, a regiment composed about equally of Ivy League polo players and cowboys Roosevelt had met during his stint as a cattle rancher in the Dakotas in

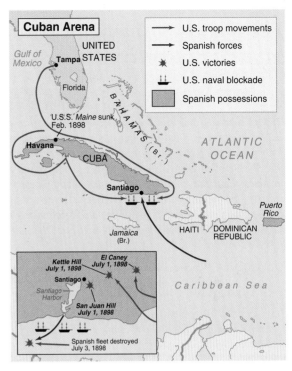

M A P **19.3**

The Spanish-American War, 1898
*The Spanish-American War of 1898 was fought in two theaters, the Philippine Islands
and Cuba. Commodore George Dewey captured Manila without the loss of a single
American sailor five days after President William McKinley called for a declaration of
war. The war lasted only a matter of months. U.S. troops landed in Cuba in mid-June,
and by mid-July they had taken Santiago and Havana and the Spanish fleet had been
destroyed off Santiago.*

the 1880s. While the troops languished in Tampa
awaiting their orders, Roosevelt and his men staged
daily rodeos for the press, with the likes of New York
blueblood William Tiffany busting broncs in competition with Dakota cowboy Jim "Dead Shot" Simpson. When the Rough Riders shipped out to Cuba,
journalists fought for a berth with the colorful regiment. Roosevelt's charge up Kettle Hill and his role
in the decisive battle of San Juan Hill made front-page
news. Overnight, Roosevelt became the most famous
man in America. By the time he sailed home from
Cuba, a coalition of independent Republicans was already busy making plans to nominate him for governor of New York. Tom Platt, nicknamed New York's
"Easy Boss," voiced the only reservation. "If he becomes governor," Platt remarked, "sooner or later,
with his personality, he will have to be President."

The Debate over American Imperialism

After a few brief campaigns in Cuba and Puerto Rico
and Dewey's stunning naval victory in the Philippines, the American people woke up in possession
of an empire that stretched halfway around the
globe. While Cuba escaped Spanish colonialism, the
United States stopped short of granting the island
the full autonomy it had promised. Contemptuous
of the Cubans, whom General William Shafter, commander of U.S. troops, declared "no more fit for self-
government than gun-powder is for hell," the U.S.
government dictated a Cuban constitution that included the so-called Platt Amendment—a series of
provisions that granted the United States the right
to intervene to protect Cuba's "independence" as

The Spanish-American War: Myth and Reality

*T*he Spanish-American War received more eyewitness
news coverage than any previous war in American
history. Hearst's papers had fanned the flames of war and,
after it started in earnest, reporters fed a public hungry
for news about the conflict. In addition to daily newspapers, weekly illustrated papers like Collier's, Leslie's, and
Harper's covered the war, using dispatches wired from
the front and illustrations by leading artists of the day.

DOCUMENT 1. Roosevelt and the Rough Riders at San Juan Hill, July 1, 1898

*The idealized lithograph on page 717 portrays a highly
romantic version of the Battle of San Juan Hill. Roosevelt
and the Rough Riders charge on horseback against the
enemy while artillery shells burst around them. Colonel
Roosevelt, mounted on his horse, Little Texas, leads the
charge with saber waving.*

SOURCE: Library of Congress.

DOCUMENT 2. Richard Harding Davis at San Juan Hill

*The press shared the country's enthusiasm for battle.
Richard Harding Davis, a star correspondent, traveled
with Roosevelt's Rough Riders and was so close to the
action that he was almost a commander himself. He was
the first to spot Spanish troops and point them out. At
one point, Davis picked up a rifle and fired a few shots
at the enemy. Here is his eyewitness account of the charge
up San Juan Hill, which took place on July 1, 1898.*

They had no glittering bayonets, they were not
massed in regular array. There were a few men in
advance, bunched together, and creeping up a steep,
sunny hill, the tops of which roared and flashed
with flame. The men held their guns pressed across
their breasts and stepped heavily as they climbed.
Behind these first few, spreading out like a fan, were
single lines of men, slipping and scrambling in the
smooth grass, moving forward with difficulty, as
though they were wading waist high through water,
moving slowly and carefully, with strenuous effort.
It was much more wonderful than any swinging
charge could have been. They walked to greet death
at every step, many of them, as they advanced, sinking suddenly or pitching forward and disappearing
in the high grass, but the others waded on, stubbornly, forming a thin blue line that kept creeping
higher and higher up the hill. It was inevitable as
the rising tide. It was a miracle of self-sacrifice, a
triumph of bull-dog courage, which one watched
with breathless wonder.

[The journalist later recollected:]
I have seen many illustrations and pictures of
this charge on the San Juan hills, but none of them
seem to show it just as I remember it. In the picture-
papers, the men are running up a hill swiftly and
gallantly, in regular formation, rank after rank, with
flags flying, their eyes aflame, and their hair streaming, their bayonets fixed, in long, brilliant lines, an
invincible overpowering weight of numbers.

Instead of which I think the thing which impressed one the most, when our men started from
cover, was they were so few. It seemed as if someone had made an awful and terrible mistake. One's
instinct was to call them to come back.

SOURCE: Frank Friedel, *The Splendid Little War* (Little,
Brown, 1958), 95–97.

DOCUMENT 3. Theodore Roosevelt Charges San Juan Hill

*Colonel Theodore Roosevelt himself kept diaries and later
published his own account of the battle. He did charge
on horseback, but it was Kettle Hill he took. After turning loose his horse, he called the Rough Riders, who were
on foot throughout the battle, to charge the line of Spanish trenches on San Juan Hill.*

Thinking that the men would all come, I jumped
over the wire fence in front of us and started at the
double; but, as a matter of fact, the troopers were
so excited, what with shooting and being shot, and
shouting and cheering, that they did not hear, or
did not heed me; and after running about a hundred
yards I found I had only five men along with me.
Bullets were ripping the grass all around us. . . .
There was no use going on. . . . Meanwhile, I ran

THE BATTLE OF SAN JUAN HILL

This idealized 1898 lithograph portrays a highly romantic version of the Battle of San Juan Hill, far from the truth. The famous charge was much less glamorous than pictured here. Theodore Roosevelt, whose Rough Riders had taken nearby Kettle Hill, called to his men to charge the next line of Spanish trenches in the San Juan hills. But in the excitement of the battle, they didn't hear him and Roosevelt found himself charging virtually alone. He had to go back and rally the Rough Riders, who then charged the hill on foot. The illustration does get one thing right: Theodore Roosevelt led the charge wearing his spectacles. Roosevelt was so myopic he feared he might lose his glasses in battle and had Brooks Brothers, who custom-made his uniform, include a dozen pockets for extra eyeglasses.

Library of Congress.

back, jumped over the wire fence, and went over the crest of the hill, filled with anger against the troopers, and especially those of my own regiment, for not having accompanied me. They, of course, were quite innocent of wrong-doing; and even while I taunted them bitterly for not having followed me, it was all I could do not to smile at the look of injury and surprise that came over their faces, while they cried out, "We didn't hear you, we didn't see you go, Colonel; lead on now and we'll sure follow you."

. . . The men of the various regiments which were already on the hill came with a rush, and we started across the wide valley which lay between us and the Spanish intrenchments. . . . Long before we got near them the Spaniards ran, save a few here and there, who either surrendered or were shot down. When we reached the trenches we found *(Continued)*

717

them filled with dead bodies in the light blue and white uniforms of the Spanish regular army. . . .

. . . I was with Henry Bardshar, running up at the double, and two Spaniards leaped from the trenches and fired at us, not ten yards away. As they turned to run I closed in and fired twice, missing the first and killing the second. My revolver was from the sunken battleship *Maine*. . . .

There was very great confusion at this time, the different regiments being completely intermingled—white regulars, colored regulars [African American soldiers in the 21st Infantry], and Rough Riders. . . . We were still under heavy fire, and I got together a mixed lot of men and pushed on from the trenches and ranch-houses which we had just taken, driving the Spaniards through a line of palm-trees, and over the crest of a chain of hills. When we reached these crests we found ourselves over-looking Santiago.

SOURCE: Theodore Roosevelt, *The Rough Riders* (Charles Scribner's Sons, 1899), 142–46.

QUESTIONS FOR ANALYSIS AND DEBATE

1. With eyewitness accounts readily available, why do you think the artist chose to represent the charge up San Juan Hill in the manner depicted in the lithograph?
2. Which do you think is more dramatic, the illustration or the eyewitness accounts? Explain your position.
3. Compare Roosevelt's account to that of Richard Harding Davis. Which do you think more effectively conveys the sense of the battle? Why?

---

well as the power to oversee Cuban debt so that European creditors could not use it as an excuse for intervention. For good measure, the United States gave itself a ninety-nine-year lease on a naval base at Guantanamo. In return, it promised to implement an extensive sanitation program to clean up the island both for its residents and not coincidentally to make it more attractive to American investors.

The formal Treaty of Paris ending the war with Spain also ceded to the United States control of Puerto Rico and Guam, former Spanish colonies. McKinley added Hawaii for good measure, annexing the islands in July 1898. But what to do with the Philippines? McKinley later claimed, somewhat disingenuously, that only after much prayer and debate did he resolve to keep the islands. Finley Peter Dunne, a popular humorist of the era, commented wryly on the situation through his mouthpieces the barroom philosophers Hennessy and Mr. Dooley: "I know what I'd do if I was Mack," Hennessy insisted. "I'd hist a flag over th' Ph'lippeens, and I'd take in th' whole lot iv them." "An yet," Mr. Dooley mused, "tis not more thin two months since ye larned whether they were islands or canned goods."

America would soon feel the weight of the "white man's burden" in the Philippines. Empire did not come cheap. When Spain balked, the United States agreed to pay an indemnity of $20 million for the islands. Nor was the cost measured in money alone. Filipino revolutionaries under Emilio Aguinaldo, who had greeted U.S. troops as liberators, bitterly fought the new masters. It would take seven years and four thousand American dead—almost ten times the number killed in Cuba—not to mention an estimated twenty thousand Filipino casualties, to defeat Aguinaldo and secure American control of the Philippines.

Americans would soon feel the weight of "the white man's burden" in the Philippines. Empire did not come cheap.

At home, a vocal minority composed largely of Democrats and former Populists resisted the country's foray into empire, judging it unwise, immoral, and unconstitutional. William Jennings Bryan, who had enlisted in the army along with Roosevelt but contracted typhoid fever and never saw action, came to the conclusion that American expansionism served only to distract the nation from its real problems at home. What did imperialism offer the ordi-

PRESIDENT MCKINLEY SIGNING THE PEACE PROTOCOL
In this contemporary painting President William McKinley officiates over the signing of the peace protocol between Spain and the United States on August 12, 1898. The terms of the protocol gave independence to Cuba, ceded Puerto Rico to the United States, and permitted American occupation of the Philippines. The Spanish lamented that the treaty "strips us of the very last memory of a glorious past, and expels us . . . from the Western Hemisphere which became peopled and civilized through the proud deeds of our ancestors."
The White House, gift of Henry Clay Frick, 1902.

nary American? Bryan asked. His answer: "Heavier taxes, Asiatic emigration and an opportunity to furnish more sons for the army." Mark Twain, lending his bitter eloquence to the cause of anti-imperialism, lamented that the United States had indeed become "yet another Civilized Power, with its banner of the Prince of Peace in one hand and its loot-basket and its butcher-knife in the other."

In the end the anti-imperialists would prove prophetic, and Hay's Open Door notes would demonstrate the principle that it was more effective for the United States to spread its influence abroad through economic power than by conquest. But in 1898, as the *Washington Post* trumpeted, "The taste of empire is in the mouth of the people," and Amer-

icans thrilled at the prospect of "an imperial policy, the Republic renascent, taking her place with the armed nations."

Conclusion: The End of a Tumultuous Decade

The Spanish-American War of 1898 symbolized America's rise as a significant player in global politics. A decade of domestic strife ended amid the blare of martial music and the waving of flags. During the 1890s, Americans, poised on the brink of the twentieth century, not only searched for order but also fought for competing visions of who should manage the new industrial society. Women fought drunkenness and the conditions that fostered it, and mounted a suffrage movement to secure their basic political rights. Ida B. Wells brought the brutality of lynching into the public spotlight. Disaffected farmers facing hard times formed the Farmers Alliance and in 1892 met in St. Louis to found the People's Party to fight for economic democracy. Laborers staged bloody strikes to determine once and for all who controlled the workplace, the workers who toiled there or the bosses who owned the machines and made the profits. The Homestead lockout and the Pullman boycott demonstrated the power of property and the conservatism of the laissez-faire state but also attested to labor's growing unity and strength. Social Darwinism, with its emphasis on white superiority, fueled overseas expansionism. Missionaries seeking converts opened up new markets, and American business, suffering from the depression that followed the panic of 1893, hungrily looked abroad for customers. Patriots and jingoes, like Theodore Roosevelt, who itched for an opportunity to show America's military muscle fought their "splendid little war" and launched the United States onto the world stage as a major power.

All in all, the 1890s witnessed more than its share of sound and fury. While none of the protest movements launched in that decade succeeded as the century waned, they laid the groundwork for what would come in the twentieth century. Women activists, rebellious farmers, and angry strikers all fought for change and, in doing so, contributed to the forging of a new politics. Their struggles added up to a decade of strife the likes of which the country would not see again for another seventy years.

www.bedfordstmartins.com/tap See the Online Study Guide to assess your mastery of the material covered in this chapter.

CHRONOLOGY

1884 The Woman's Christian Temperance Union (WCTU), under Frances Willard, calls for "home protection ballot" (suffrage for women).

1887 Southern Farmers Alliance recruits 200,000 members.

1889 United States avoids war with Germany over Pago Pago in the Samoan Islands when typhoon strikes.

1890 National American Woman Suffrage Association (NAWSA) forms, electing Elizabeth Cady Stanton president.

Wyoming enters Union with woman suffrage.

Women constitute 60 percent of foreign missionaries.

1891 President Benjamin Harrison threatens war with Chile over death of two U.S. sailors in Valparaiso; Chile apologizes and pays indemnity.

1892 Ida B. Wells begins antilynching crusade.

People's Party (also known as Populist Party) founded in St. Louis.

Homestead lockout pits Carnegie steelworkers against hired Pinkertons.

Anarchist Alexander Berkman's attempt to assassinate Henry Clay Frick turns public opinion against Homestead workers.

The National Guard of Pennsylvania takes over the Homestead mills, ending the workers' strike.

People's Party wins more than one million votes for its presidential candidate, James B. Weaver.

Susan B. Anthony becomes president of NAWSA.

1893 Severe economic depression touched off by panic on Wall Street.

President Grover Cleveland nixes attempt to annex Hawaii after Americans foment overthrow of Queen Liliuokalani.

1894 Coxey's "army" marches to Washington, D.C., to dramatize plight of unemployed.

Federal troops crush Pullman strike.

Union leader Eugene V. Debs jailed for violating court injunction.

People's Party scores victories in state elections.

1895 President Grover Cleveland risks war with Great Britain to defend Monroe Doctrine in border dispute between British Guiana and Venezuela.

1896 Democrats stampede to support William Jennings Bryan for president on free silver platform; People's Party also nominates Bryan but spurns his running mate, substituting Populist Tom Watson as vice presidential nominee.

Republican William McKinley defeats Democrat William Jennings Bryan for presidency.

National Association of Colored Women (NACW) formed, with Mary Church Terrell as president.

1897 Theodore Roosevelt appointed assistant secretary of the navy; dispatches fleet to Manila in preparation for war with Spain.

1898 U.S. battleship *Maine* mysteriously explodes in Havana harbor.

Congress declares war on Spain.

Commodore George Dewey destroys Spanish fleet in Manila Bay, the Philippines.

U.S. troops arrive in Cuba and defeat Spanish forces.

Treaty of Paris ends Spanish-American War; under treaty, United States acquires Puerto Rico, Guam, and the Philippines.

United States annexes Hawaii.

Platt Amendment gives United States oversight of liberated Cuba.

1899– Secretary of State John Hay enunciates
1900 Open Door policy in China to guarantee trade access.

1900– Boxer Rebellion in China leads to
1901 deaths of more than 250 missionaries and their families.

BIBLIOGRAPHY

GENERAL

H. W. Brands, *The Reckless Decade: America in the 1890s* (1995).

Alan Dawley, *Struggles for Justice: Social Responsibility and the Liberal State* (1991).

Sara M. Evans, *Born for Liberty: A History of Women in America* (1989).

David Montgomery, *The Fall of the House of Labor: The Workplace, the State, and American Labor Activism, 1865–1925* (1987).

Nell Irvin Painter, *Standing at Armageddon: The United States, 1877–1919* (1987).

WOMEN'S ACTIVISM

Karen J. Blair, *The Clubwoman as Feminist: True Womanhood Redefined, 1868–1914* (1980).

Jack S. Blocker Jr., *"Give to the Winds Thy Fears": The Women's Temperance Crusade, 1873–1874* (1985).

Ruth Bordin, *Women and Temperance: The Quest for Power and Liberty, 1873–1900* (1981).

Ruth Bordin, *Frances Willard: A Biography* (1986).

Ellen Carol DuBois, *Feminism and Suffrage: The Emergence of an Independent Women's Movement in America, 1848–1869* (1978).

Barbara Leslie Epstein, *The Politics of Domesticity: Women, Evangelism, and Temperance in Nineteenth-Century America* (1981).

Eleanor Flexner, *Century of Struggle: The Women's Rights Movement in the United States* (1973).

Glenda Elizabeth Gilmore, *Gender and Jim Crow: Women and the Politics of White Supremacy in North Carolina, 1896–1920* (1996).

Michael Lewis Goldberg, *An Army of Women: Gender and Politics in Gilded Age Kansas* (1997).

Gayle Anne Gullett, *Becoming Citizens: The Emergence and Development of the California Women's Movement, 1880–1911* (2000).

Darlene Clark Hine, ed., *Black Women in America* (1993).

Beverly Washington Jones, *Quest for Equality: The Life and Writings of Mary Eliza Church Terrell* (1990).

Glenda Riley, *Inventing the American Woman: A Perspective on Women's History, 1865 to the Present* (1986).

Jacqueline Jones Royster, *Southern Horrors and Other Writings: The Anti-Lynching Campaign of Ida B. Wells, 1892–1900* (1996).

Dorothy Salem, *To Better Our World: Black Women in Organized Reform, 1890–1920* (1990).

Anne Firor Scott, *Natural Allies: Women's Associations in American History* (1991).

Kathryn Kish Sklar, *Florence Kelley and the Nation's Work: The Rise of Women's Political Culture, 1830–1900* (1995).

Ian Tyrell, *Woman's World, Woman's Empire: The Woman's Christian Temperance Union in International Perspective, 1880–1930* (1991).

Charles Harris Wesley, *The History of the National Association of Colored Women's Clubs: A Legacy of Service* (1984).

THE FARMERS' REVOLT AND THE LABOR WARS

Edward L. Ayers, *The Promise of the New South: Life after Reconstruction* (1992).

Donna A. Barnes, *Farmers in Rebellion, The Rise and Fall of the Southern Farmers Alliance and People's Party in Texas* (1984).

Stanley Buder, *Pullman: An Experiment in Industrial Order and Community Planning* (1976).

Arthur G. Burgoyne, with afterword by David P. Demarest Jr., *The Homestead Strike of 1892* (1979).

Leon Fink, *Workingman's Democracy: The Knights of Labor and American Politics* (1983).

Philip S. Foner, *History of the Labor Movement in the United States*, vol. 2, *From the Founding of the American Federation of Labor to the Emergence of American Imperialism* (1955).

Lawrence Goodwyn, *The Populist Moment: A Short History of the Agrarian Revolt in America* (1978).

Steven Hahn, *The Roots of Southern Populism: Yeoman Farmers and the Transformation of the Georgia Upcountry, 1850–1890* (1983).

John D. Hicks, *The Populist Revolt: A History of the Farmers' Alliance and the People's Party* (1961).

Elizabeth Jameson, *All That Glitters: Class, Conflict, and Community in Cripple Creek* (1998).

Sidney Lens, *The Labor Wars: From the Molly Maguires to the Sitdowns* (1974).

Thomas G. Manning, ed., *The Chicago Strike of 1894: Industrial Labor in the Nineteenth Century* (1960).

Robert McMath, *Populist Vanguard* (1975).

Scott G. McNall, *The Road to Rebellion: Class Formation and Kansas Populism, 1865–1900* (1988).

Milton Meltzer, *Bread and Roses: The Struggle of American Labor, 1865–1915* (1967).

Theodore R. Mitchell, *Political Education in the Southern Farmers' Alliance, 1887–1900* (1987).

Norman Pollack, *The Just Polity: Populism, Law, and Human Welfare* (1987).

Nick Salvatore, *Eugene V. Debs: Citizen and Socialist* (1982).

William Serrin, *Homestead: The Glory and Tragedy of an American Steel Town* (1992).

Barton Shaw, *The Wool-Hat Boys: Georgia's Populist Party* (1984).

Carl Smith, *Urban Disorder and the Shape of Belief: The Great Chicago Fire, the Haymarket Bomb, and the Model Town of Pullman* (1995).

Lala Carr Steelman, *The North Carolina Farmers' Alliance* (1985).

Leon Stein, ed., *The Pullman Strike* (1969).

George Brown Tindall, ed., *A Populist Reader: Selections from the Works of American Populist Leaders* (1966).

Urwin Unger, *The Greenback Era: A Social and Political History of American Finance, 1865–1879* (1964).

Joseph Frazier Wall, *Andrew Carnegie* (1970).

Alice Wexler, *Emma Goldman: An Intimate Life* (1984).

Leon Wolff, *Lockout: The Story of the Homestead Strike of 1892* (1965).

C. Vann Woodward, *Tom Watson: Agrarian Rebel* (1963).

DEPRESSION POLITICS

Robert A. Allen, *Reluctant Reformers: Racism and Social Reform Movements in the United States* (1974).

Robert W. Cherny, *A Righteous Cause: The Life of William Jennings Bryan* (1985).

Gene Clanton, *Populism, The Humane Preference in America, 1890–1900* (1991).

Paolo Coletta, *William Jennings Bryan*, 3 vols. (1964–1969).

Robert F. Durden, *The Climax of Populism: The Election of 1896* (1969).

Paul W. Glad, *McKinley, Bryan, and the People* (1964).

Lewis L. Gould, *The Presidency of William McKinley* (1981).

Stephen Kantrowitz, *Ben Tillman and the Reconstruction of White Supremacy* (2000).

Louis W. Koenig, *Bryan: A Political Biography of William Jennings Bryan* (1971).

Donald L. McMurry, *Coxey's Army: A Study of the Industrial Army Movement of 1894* (1968).

Samuel McSeveney, *The Politics of Depression* (1972).

Carol A. Schwantes, *Coxey's Army: An American Odyssey* (1985).

AMERICAN FOREIGN POLICY

David Anderson, *Imperialism and Idealism: American Diplomacy in China, 1861–1898* (1985).

William Becker, *The Dynamics of Business-Government Relations* (1982).

Robert Beisner, *From the Old Diplomacy to the New, 1865–1900* (1975).

Charles Campbell, *The Transformation of American Foreign Relations, 1865–1900* (1976).

Edward P. Crapol, *James G. Blaine: Architect of Empire* (1999).

John Dobson, *America's Ascent: The United States Becomes a Great Power, 1880–1914* (1978).

Harold U. Faulkner, *Politics, Reform, and Expansionism, 1890–1900* (1959).

Willard Gatewood Jr., *Black Americans and the White Man's Burden* (1975).

Kenneth Hagen, *American Gun-Boat Diplomacy* (1973).

Michael H. Hunt, *The Making of a Special Relationship: The United States and China to 1914* (1983).

Jane Hunter, *The Gospel of Gentility: American Women Missionaries in Turn-of-the-Century China* (1984).

Walter LaFeber, *The New Empire: An Interpretation of American Expansion, 1860–1898* (1963).

Walter LaFeber, *The American Age* (1989).

Edmund Morris, *The Rise of Theodore Roosevelt* (1979).

Ivan Musicant, *The Banana Wars: A History of U.S. Military Intervention from the Spanish-American War to the Invasion of Panama* (1990).

Emily S. Rosenberg, *Spreading the American Dream: American Economic and Cultural Expansion, 1890–1945* (1982).

James C. Thompson Jr., Peter W. Stanley, and John Curtis Perry, *Sentimental Imperialists: The American Experience in East Asia* (1981).

Richard Turk, *The Ambiguous Relationship: Theodore Roosevelt and Alfred Thayer Mahan* (1987).

William Appleman Williams, *The Tragedy of American Diplomacy,* rev. ed. (1962).

THE SPANISH-AMERICAN WAR

Charles H. Brown, *The Correspondents' War: Journalists in the Spanish-American War* (1967).

Stan Cohen, *Images of the Spanish-American War, April–August 1898* (1997).

John A. Corry, *1898: Prelude to a Century* (1998).

Brian P. Damiani, *Avocates of Empire: William McKinley, the Senate, and American Expansion, 1898–1899* (1987).

Philip S. Foner, *The Spanish-Cuban-American War and the Birth of American Imperialism,* 2 vols. (1972).

Frank Friedel, *The Splendid Little War* (1958).

Lewis W. Gould, *The Spanish-American War and President McKinley* (1982).

Louis J. Halle, *The United States Acquires the Philippines: Consensus vs. Reality* (1985).

Stanley Karnow, *In Our Image: America's Empire in the Philippines* (1989).

Gerald F. Linderman, *The Mirror of War: American Society and the Spanish-American War* (1974).

Joyce Milton, *The Yellow Kids: Foreign Correspondents in the Heyday of Yellow Journalism* (1989).

H. Wayne Morgan, *America's Road to Empire: The War with Spain and Overseas Expansion* (1965).

Ivan Musicant, *Empire by Default: The Spanish-American War and the Dawn of the American Century* (1998).

Albert A. Nofi, *The Spanish-American War, 1898* (1997).

John L. Offner, *An Unwanted War: The Diplomacy of the United States and Spain over Cuba, 1895–1898* (1992).

George J. A. O'Toole, *The Spanish War: An American Epic—1898* (1986).

Thomas Patterson, ed., *Imperialism and Anti-Imperialism* (1973).

Louis A. Perez Jr., *The War of 1898: The United States and Cuba in History and Historiography* (1998).

David F. Trask, *The War with Spain in 1898* (1981).

David Traxel, *1898: The Birth of the American Century* (1999).

PROGRESSIVE POSTER CONDEMNING CHILD LABOR

This poster attacks child labor, borrowing the convention of the business flow chart to portray graphically how industries employing children are "making human junk." Progressives' concern for the plight of poor children won them the label "the child savers." Although activists worked hard to enact federal legislation prohibiting child labor in 1916, the Supreme Court declared the law unconstitutional two years later on the grounds that Congress had no right to regulate manufacturing within states.
Library of Congress.

PROGRESSIVE REFORM FROM THE GRASS ROOTS TO THE WHITE HOUSE

20

1890–1916

IN THE SUMMER OF 1889, A YOUNG WOMAN leased the upper floor of a dilapidated mansion on Chicago's West Side in the heart of a burgeoning immigrant population of Italians, Russian Jews, and Greeks. Watching the preparations at number 335, the neighbors scratched their heads, wondering why the well-dressed woman, who surely could afford a better house in a better neighborhood, had chosen to live on South Halsted Street. Yet the house built by Charles Hull precisely suited the needs of Jane Addams. In September, she and her college friend Ellen Gates Starr moved in. "Probably no young matron ever placed her own things in her own house with more pleasure," Addams wrote.

For Jane Addams, personal action marked the first step in the search for solutions to the social problems fostered by urban industrialism. Her object was twofold: She wanted to help her immigrant neighbors and she wanted to offer an opportunity for educated women like herself to find meaningful work. As she later wrote in her autobiography, *Twenty Years at Hull-House* (1910), "I gradually became convinced that it would be a good thing to rent a house in a part of the city where many primitive and actual needs are found, in which young women who had been given over too exclusively to study might restore a balance of activity along traditional lines and learn of life from life itself." Addams's emphasis on the reciprocal relationship between the classes made Hull House different from other philanthropic enterprises. She wished to do things with, not just for, Chicago's poor.

By 1907, Hull House had expanded from one rented floor in the old brick mansion to some thirteen buildings that housed a remarkable variety of activities. The bathrooms in the basement had been converted into public baths, a coffee shop and restaurant sold take-out food to working women too tired to cook after their long shifts, and a nursery and kindergarten provided care for neighborhood children. Hull House offered classes, lectures, art exhibits, musical instruction, and college extension courses. It boasted a gymnasium, a theater, a manual training workshop, a labor museum, and the first public playground in Chicago.

But Hull House was more than a group of buildings. From the first, it attracted an extraordinary set of reformers. Some stayed for decades, as did Julia Lathrop before she went to Washington, D.C., in 1912 to head the Children's Bureau. Others, like Gerard Swope, who later became president of the General Electric Company, came for only a short while. Most had jobs, paid room and board, and devoted time to research and reform. The people who lived at Hull House were

JANE ADDAMS
Jane Addams was twenty-nine years old when she founded Hull House on Halsted Street in Chicago. Her desire to live among the poor and her insistence that settlement house work provide benefits for educated women like herself as well as for the poor neighborhood residents separated her from the charity workers who had come before her and marked the distance from philanthropy to progressive reform.

Jane Addams Memorial Collection, Special Collection, University Library, University of Illinois at Chicago.

among the first to investigate the problems of the city with scientific precision. Armed with statistics, they launched campaigns to improve housing, end child labor, fund playgrounds, mediate between labor and management, and lobby for protective legislation.

Addams quickly learned that it was impossible to deal with urban problems without becoming involved in political action. Alarmed at the piles of decaying garbage that overflowed the trash bins, breeding flies and disease, she discovered that the

garbage contract was a political plum awarded to a contractor who felt under no obligation to provide adequate service. When she complained, the mayor appointed her garbage inspector for the nineteenth ward. Out on the streets at dawn, Addams rode atop the garbage wagon as it made its rounds to be sure the men did their work. After a year, the ward boss managed to have her removed. What had begun as an attempt to clean up Halsted Street developed into a campaign for municipal reform as Addams squared off against the boss. After backing several unsuccessful electoral campaigns to unseat him, Addams learned just how the machine worked among its constituency to provide jobs and favors. Judging the boss a symptom and not a cause of urban problems, Addams moved on to press for legislation to better the condition of the urban poor. Her path led her not only to city hall but also to the state capitol and even further to Washington, D.C. A strong advocate of woman suffrage, she argued that city women needed the ballot, not the broom, to keep their neighborhoods clean.

Under Jane Addams's leadership, Hull House, the premier settlement house in the United States, became a "spearhead for reform," part of a broader movement that contemporaries called the progressive movement. The transition from personal action to political activism that Addams personified became one of the hallmarks of this reform period, which lasted for almost three decades, from the 1890s to World War I.

What motivated comfortable, middle-class women and men to launch one of the major movements for social and political reform in U.S. history? There is no one answer because there is no single progressive profile. The progressives were a diverse group with a variety of goals. A sense of Christian mission inspired some. Others, frightened by the political tensions of the 1890s, feared social upheaval unless conditions were improved. Progressives shared a growing concern about the power of wealthy individuals and corporations, and a strong dislike of the trusts. But often they feared the new immigrants as well and sought to control and Americanize them. Along with moral fervor, a belief in technical expertise and scientific principles informed progressivism and made the cult of efficiency part and parcel of the movement. All of these elements—uplift and efficiency, social justice and social control—came together in the Progressive Era.

Grassroots Progressivism

Progressive reform began at the grassroots level and percolated upward into local, state, and eventually national politics as the reformers attacked the social problems fostered by urban industrialism. While reform flourished in many different settings across the country, the problems of urban America called forth the greatest efforts of the women and men who styled themselves progressives. In their zeal to "civilize the city," reformers founded settlement houses, professed a new Christian social gospel, and campaigned against vice and crime in the name of "social purity." Allying with the working class, they sought to better the lot of sweatshop garment workers and to end child labor. While their reform efforts often began on the local level, they just as often ended up being debated in state legislatures, in Congress, and in the Oval Office. From Hull House to the White House, progressivism became a major political force in the first decade of the twentieth century.

Civilizing the City

Typically, progressives attacked the problems of the city on many fronts. The settlement house movement attempted to bridge the distance between the classes. The social gospel called for the churches to play a new role in social reformation. And the social purity movement campaigned to clean up vice, particularly prostitution.

The settlement house movement began in England and came to the United States in 1886 with the opening of the University Settlement House in New York City. Americans modified the settlement significantly, abandoning the strong religious overtones of the English movement. Settlement house workers quickly recognized that it would be divisive and counterproductive to promote Protestantism among their largely Catholic and Jewish neighbors. Another significant change from the English model was the substantial role of women, particularly college-educated women, who formed the backbone of the settlement house movement and helped it to grow from six settlements in 1891 to more than four hundred in 1911. Eager to use their knowledge, educated women found themselves blocked from medicine, law, and the clergy (fewer than fifteen hundred women practiced law in 1900, and women constituted only 6 percent of the medical profession), college-educated women

like Jane Addams became a part of Hull House and other settlements to use their talents in the service of society. In the process, they created the new profession of social work. Florence Kelley, Julia Lathrop, Alice Hamilton, and Grace and Edith Abbott are only a few of the best known of these influential settlement house residents.

For their part, the churches confronted the social problems raised in the cities by enunciating a new social gospel, one that saw its mission not simply to reform individuals but to reform society. On a basic level, the social gospel offered a powerful corrective to the gospel of wealth, as outlined by Andrew Carnegie, with its belief that riches somehow signaled divine favor. Washington Gladden, a prominent social gospel minister, challenged that view when he urged Congregationalists to turn down a gift from John D. Rockefeller, arguing that it was "tainted money." In place of the gospel of wealth, the clergy urged their congregations to put Christ's teachings to work in their daily lives. For Walter Rauschenbusch, a Baptist minister working in New York's infamous Hell's Kitchen neighborhood, the social gospel grew out of the depression of the 1890s that left hundreds of thousands of people unemployed. "They wore down our threshold and they wore away our hearts," he later wrote. "One could hear human virtue cracking and crumbling all around." In *Christianity and the Social Crisis* (1907), Rauschenbusch called for the church to play a new role in promoting social justice.

College-educated women like Jane Addams became a part of Hull House and other settlements to use their talents in the service of society. In the process, they created the new profession of social work.

Ministers also played an active role in the social purity movement, the campaign to attack vice. The Reverend Charles Parkhurst shocked his New York congregation in the 1890s by donning a disguise and touring the city's brothels, asking at each dive, "Show me something worse." Progressives insisted that poverty bred prostitution and argued for higher wages. "Is it any wonder," asked the Chicago Vice Commission, "that a tempted girl who receives only six dollars per week working with her hands sells her body for twenty-five dollars per week

KINDERGARTEN AT HULL HOUSE
As Hull House expanded to meet the needs of its neighbors it grew from a rented floor in an old brick mansion to encompass thirteen buildings, including a gymnasium, a vocational training school, and a nursery and kindergarten. Here an early kindergarten class meets on the roof in the open air under the watchful eye of one of the women of Hull House. Note the clothing of the immigrant children—the girls' dresses, pinafores, and hats and the boys' boots and hats. The children's poverty is hinted at only by their short stature and deferential, downcast eyes.
University of Illinois at Chicago, the University Library, Jane Addams Memorial Collection.

when she learns there is a demand for it and men are willing to pay the price?"

To end the "social evil," as reformers euphemistically called prostitution, the social purity movement brought together ministers like Parkhurst who wished to stamp out sin, doctors who were concerned about the spread of venereal disease, and women reformers who were determined to fight the double standard that made it acceptable for men to engage in premarital and extramarital sex but punished women who strayed. Together, they waged campaigns to close red-light districts in cities across the country and lobbied for

the Mann Act, passed in 1910, which made it illegal to transport women across state lines for immoral purposes. Moreover, on the state level, they struck at venereal disease by securing legislation to require a blood test for syphilis before marriage.

Attacks on alcohol went hand in hand with the push for social purity. The temperance campaign launched by the Woman's Christian Temperance Union (WCTU) heated up in the early twentieth century. The Anti-Saloon League, formed in 1895 under the leadership of Protestant clergy, campaigned for an end to the sale of liquor. Reformers pointed to the links connecting drink with prostitution, wife and child abuse, unemployment, and industrial accidents. The powerful liquor lobby fought back, spending liberally in election campaigns to defeat not only prohibition but also woman suffrage and, in the process, fueling the charge that liquor corrupted the political process.

An element of nativism (dislike of foreigners) ran through the move for prohibition. The Irish, the Italians, and the Germans were among the groups stigmatized by temperance reformers for their drinking. Progressives often failed to see the important role the tavern played in many ethnic communities. Unlike the American saloon, an almost exclusively male domain, the tavern or beer garden was often a family retreat. German Americans of all ages socialized at the beer garden after church on Sunday. Even though most workers toiled six days a week and had only Sunday for recreation and relaxation, progressives campaigned on the local level to enforce Sunday closings of taverns. To deny the working class access to alcohol, progressives pushed for state legislation to outlaw the liquor traffic; by 1912, seven states were "dry."

Progressives' efforts to civilize the city, whether by launching social settlements or campaigning against prostitution and alcohol, demonstrated their willingness to take action, their belief that environment, not heredity alone, determined human behavior, and their optimism that conditions could be corrected through government action without radically altering America's economy or institutions. All of these attitudes characterized the progressive movement.

Progressives and the Working Class

Day-to-day contact with their neighbors made settlement house workers particularly sympathetic to labor unions. When Mary Kenney O'Sullivan complained that her bookbinders' union met in a dirty, noisy saloon, Jane Addams invited the union to meet at Hull House. And during the Pullman strike in 1894, Hull House residents organized strike relief and lent their prestige and financial resources. "Hull-House has been so unionized," grumbled one Chicago businessman, "that it has lost its usefulness and become a detriment and harm to the community." But to the working class, the support of middle-class reformers marked a significant gain.

Attempts to forge a cross-class alliance became institutionalized in 1903 with the creation of the Women's Trade Union League (WTUL). The WTUL brought together middle-class "allies" and women workers. Its goal was to organize working women into unions under the auspices of the American Federation of Labor (AFL). However, the AFL provided little more than lip service to the organization of women workers. As one working woman confided, "The men think that the girls should not get as good work as the men and should not make half as much money as a man." When it came to women, the AFL's main concern seemed to be to protect men from female competition. Samuel Gompers, president of the AFL, endorsed the principle of equal pay for equal work, shrewdly observing that it would help male workers more than women, since many employers hired women precisely because they could be paid less. Given the AFL's attitude, it was not surprising that the money and leadership to organize women came largely from wealthy allies in the WTUL.

The league's most notable success came in 1909 in the "uprising of twenty thousand." In November, hundreds of women employees of the Triangle Shirtwaist Company in New York City went on strike to protest low wages, dangerous and demeaning working conditions, and management's refusal to recognize their union, the International Ladies' Garment Workers Union (ILGWU). In support of the walkout, the ILGWU called for a general strike of all garment workers. An estimated twenty thousand workers, most of them teenage girls and many of them Jewish and Italian immigrants, went out on strike and stayed out through the winter, picketing in the bitter cold. More than six hundred were arrested, and many were sent to jail for "streetwalking," a move by the authorities to try to impugn the morals of the striking women. By the time the strike ended in February 1910, the workers had won important demands in many shops. But they lost their bid to gain recognition for the ILGWU. The solidarity shown by the women proved to be the strike's greatest achievement. As Clara Lemlich, one of the strike's leaders, exclaimed, "They used to say that you couldn't even organize women. They wouldn't come to union meetings. They were 'temporary' workers. Well we showed them!"

The WTUL made enormous contributions to the success of the strike. The league provided volunteers for the picket lines, posted more than $29,000 in bail, protested police brutality, organized almost overnight a massive parade of ten thousand strikers, took part in the arbitration conference, arranged mass meetings, appealed for funds, and

WOMEN STRIKERS
The "uprising of twenty thousand" pitted garment workers against their employers in a strike that lasted throughout the bitter winter of 1909–10. The strikers, primarily young women from the Jewish and Italian immigrant communities, joined the International Ladies' Garment Workers Union and showed that women could be unionized and mount an effective strike.
Labor-Management Documentation Center, Cornell University.

generated publicity for the strike. Under the leadership of the WTUL, women from every class of society, from J. P. Morgan's daughter Anne to socialists on New York's Lower East Side, joined the strikers in a dramatic demonstration of cross-class alliance.

***

By the time the strike ended in February 1910, the workers had won important demands in many shops. But the solidarity shown by the women proved to be the strike's greatest achievement.

***

For all its success, the uprising of twenty thousand failed fundamentally to change conditions for women workers. In 1911, a little over a year after the shirtwaist makers' strike ended, fire alarms sounded at the Triangle factory. The ramshackle building, full of lint and combustible cloth, went up in flames in minutes. A WTUL member described the scene below on the street: "Two young girls whom I knew to be working in the vicinity came rushing toward me, tears were running from their eyes and they were white and shaking as they caught me by the arm. 'Oh,' shrieked one of them, 'they are jumping. Jumping from ten stories up! They are going through the air like bundles of clothes.'"

The terrified Triangle workers had little choice but to jump. One door was blocked by flames, and the door to the fire escape had been locked to prevent the girls from sneaking out on breaks. Of 500 workers, 146 died and scores of others were injured. The owners of the Triangle firm were later tried for negligence, but they avoided conviction when authorities determined that the fire had been started by a careless smoker. The Triangle Shirtwaist Company reopened in another firetrap within a matter of weeks.

Outrage and a sense of futility overwhelmed Rose Schneiderman, a leading WTUL organizer who made a bitter speech at the memorial service for the dead Triangle workers. "I would be a traitor to those poor burned bodies if I came here to talk good fellowship," she told her audience. "We have tried you good people of the public and we have found you wanting. . . . I know from my experience it is up to the working people to save themselves . . . by a strong working class movement."

THE NEW YORK HERALD.

++++c NEW YORK, SUNDAY, MARCH 26, 1911.—112 PAGES.— BY THE NEW YORK HERALD COMPANY.] [COPYRIGHT, 1911, PRICE FIVE CENTS.

ONE HUNDRED AND FIFTY PERISH IN FACTORY FIRE; WOMEN AND GIRLS, TRAPPED IN TEN STORY BUILDING, LOST IN FLAMES OR HURL THEMSELVES TO DEATH

IDENTIFYING BODIES OF THOSE WHO JUMPED TO THE SIDEWALK.

OFFICES SHOW ROOMS AND SHIPPING DEPARTMENTS

MACHINE OPERATORS

WHERE FIRE STARTED

BUILDING AT NORTHWEST CORNER OF EAST WASHINGTON PLACE AND GREENE STREET, THREE TOP FLOORS IN WHICH LOSS OF LIFE OCCURRED, WERE COMPLETELY DESTROYED.

THE TRIANGLE SHIRTWAIST FACTORY FIRE
The **New York Herald** *carried the story of the fire at the Triangle Shirtwaist factory with bold headlines and a grim photo. A policeman stoops to identify the broken bodies of two of the workers who leapt to their death to escape the flames.*
The *New York Herald,* March 26, 1911.

www.bedfordstmartins.com/tap SEE THE ONLINE STUDY GUIDE for more help in analyzing this image.

The Triangle fire tested severely the bonds of the cross-class alliance. Along with Schneiderman, WTUL leaders experienced a growing sense of futility. It seemed not enough to organize and to strike, particularly when the AFL paid so little attention to women workers. Increasingly, the WTUL turned its efforts to lobbying for protective legislation—laws that would limit hours and regulate working conditions.

The principle of protective legislation won a major victory in 1908 when the U.S. Supreme Court, in *Muller v. Oregon,* reversed its previous rulings and upheld an Oregon law that limited the hours women could work to ten a day. A mass of sociological evidence put together by Florence Kelley of the National Consumers League and Josephine Goldmark of the WTUL and presented by Goldmark's brother-in-law, lawyer Louis Brandeis, demonstrated the ill effects of long hours on the health and safety of women. The "Brandeis brief" convinced the Court that long hours endangered women and therefore the entire race. The Court's ruling set a precedent, but one that separated the well-being of women workers from that of men by arguing that women's reproductive role justified special treatment. Later generations of women fighting for equality would question the effectiveness of this strategy and argue that it ultimately closed good jobs to women. But for the WTUL, protective legislation was greeted as a first stage in the attempt to ensure the safety not just of women but of all workers.

The National Consumers League (NCL), like the WTUL, fostered cross-class alliance. Formed in 1899 and led by Florence Kelley, the NCL urged middle-class women to boycott stores and exert pressure for decent wages and working conditions for women employees, primarily saleswomen. But like the WTUL, the NCL turned increasingly to protective legislation to achieve its goals in the first decade of the twentieth century. Frustrated by the reluctance of the private sector to respond to the need for reform, progressives turned to government at all levels. Critics would later charge that the progressives assumed too easily that government regulation could best solve social problems.

Progressivism: Theory and Practice

Progressive reformers developed a theoretical basis for their activist approach by countering social Darwinism with a dynamic new reform Darwinism and by championing the uniquely American philosophy of pragmatism. The progressives emphasized action and experimentation. They saw the universe not as a massive, slow-moving machine but as a system amenable to tinkering by human intelligence. An unchecked admiration for speed and efficiency also inspired enthusiasm for scientific management and a new cult of efficiency. These varied strands of progressive theory found practical application in state and local politics.

The politicians who became premier progressives were generally the followers, not the leaders, in a movement that was already well advanced at the grassroots level. Yet they left their stamp on progressivism. Among the most preeminent progressive politicians were Thomas Lofton Johnson, who made Cleveland, Ohio, "the best governed city in America"; Robert La Follette, who turned Wisconsin into a laboratory for progressivism; and Hiram Johnson, who ended the domination of the Southern Pacific railroad in California politics.

Reform Darwinism and Social Engineering

The active, interventionist approach of the progressives directly challenged social Darwinism, with its insistence that the world operated on the principle of survival of the fittest and that human beings were powerless in the face of the law of natural selection. Without abandoning the evolutionary framework of Darwinism, a new group of sociologists argued that evolution could be advanced more rapidly if men and women used their intellects to alter the environment. Dubbed "reform Darwinism," the new sociological theory condemned laissez-faire, insisting that the liberal state should play a more active role in solving social problems. Reform Darwinism provided a rationale for attacking social ills and became the ideological basis for progressive reform.

In their pursuit of reform, progressives were influenced by the work of two philosophers, William James and John Dewey, who argued for a new test for truth, insisting that there were no eternal verities and that the real worth of any idea was in its consequences. They called their pluralistic, relativistic philosophy *pragmatism*. Dewey put his theories to the test in the classroom of his laboratory school at the University of Chicago. A pioneer in American education, he emphasized process rather than content and encouraged child-centered schools where students learned by doing. By championing social experimentation, the American pragmatists provided an important impetus for progressive reform.

Increased emphasis on means as well as ends marked progressive reform. Efficiency and expertise became watchwords in the progressive vocabulary. The journalist and critic Walter Lippmann, in *Drift and Mastery* (1914), a classic statement of the progressive agenda, called for skilled technocrats who would use scientific techniques to control social change, substituting mastery for aimless drift. Progressive reformers' emphasis on expertise inevitably fostered a kind of elitism. Whereas Populism had called for a greater voice for the masses, progressivism, for all its emphasis on social justice, insisted that experts be put in charge.

At its extreme, the application of expertise and social engineering took the form of scientific management, which alienated the working class while elevating productivity and efficiency above all. Frederick Winslow Taylor, who after a nervous breakdown left Harvard to become a machinist, pioneered "systematized shop management." Taylor was obsessed with making humans and machines produce more and faster. Earning a master of engineering degree in 1885, he went back to work at Midvale Steel in Pennsylvania. With his stopwatch, he carefully timed workers and attempted to break their work down into its simplest components, one repetitious action after another, on the theory that productivity would increase if tasks were reduced to their simplest parts. When he died in 1915, stopwatch in hand, workers bitterly pointed to the speedup—pushing workers to produce more in less time and for less pay—as his legacy. But Taylor's many advocates included progressives like Louis Brandeis, who applauded the increased productivity and efficiency of Taylor's system.

Whereas Populism had called for a greater voice for the masses, progressivism, for all its emphasis on social justice, insisted that experts be put in charge.

The progressive reformers who championed scientific management and social engineering never faced the contradiction between the means they advocated and the ends they desired. The central paradox of progressivism was its insistence that social justice could be brought about by social engineering—that a just society could be achieved by applying objective scientific principles to the highly subjective experience of human life.

Progressivism at the Local and State Levels

Progressivism burst forth at every level in 1901, but nowhere more forcefully than in Cleveland, Ohio, where the voters elected Thomas Lofton Johnson mayor. Johnson, a self-made millionaire by the age of forty, had earned his money in the street railroad business in Detroit, where he had clashed frequently with reform mayor Hazen Pingree. Johnson turned his back on business in 1899 and moved to Cleveland, where he determined to seek election as a reform mayor. "I embarked on this new field for purely selfish motives," he later wrote. A flamboyant man who craved power and acclaim, Johnson pledged during the campaign to reduce the streetcar fare from five cents to three cents. His election touched off a seven-year war between advocates of the lower fare, who believed that workers paid a disproportionate share of their meager earnings for transportation, and the streetcar moguls, who ar-

gued that they couldn't meet costs with the lower fare. When Johnson responded by building his own streetcar line, his foes tore up the tracks or blocked him with court injunctions and legal delays. At the prompting of his opponents, the Ohio legislature sought to limit Johnson's mayoral power by revoking the charters of every city in the state, replacing home rule with central control from the capital, Columbus.

During his tenure as mayor, Johnson fought for home rule and fair taxation even as he called for greater democracy through the use of the initiative, referendum, and recall—devices that allowed the voters to have a direct say in legislative and judicial matters. Frustrated in his attempt to bring the streetcar industry to heel, he successfully championed municipal ownership of street railways and public utilities, a tactic that progressives called "gas and water socialism." The city bought the streetcar system and instituted the three-cent fare. Under

THREE-CENT STREETCAR TOKEN
Tom Johnson, the reform mayor of Cleveland, Ohio, from 1901 to 1909, fought for a three-cent streetcar fare for more than seven years, winning the support of the working class and angering the business interests who ran the city's streetcars. To get his cheaper fare, Johnson finally instituted municipal ownership of the transit system. Johnson used a three-cent token in his reelection campaign in 1907.
The Western Reserve Historical Society, Cleveland, Ohio.

Johnson's administration, Cleveland became, in the words of journalist Lincoln Steffens, the "best governed city in America."

In Wisconsin, Robert M. La Follette, who as a young congressional representative had supported William McKinley, abandoned Republican conservatism and converted to the progressive cause early in the 1900s. An astute politician, La Follette capitalized on the grassroots movement for reform to launch his long political career, first as governor (1901–1905) and later as senator (1906–1925). A graduate of the University of Wisconsin, La Follette brought scientists and professors into his administration and used the university, only a few blocks from the state house in Madison, as a resource in drafting legislation. As governor, he lowered railroad rates, raised railroad taxes, improved education, championed conservation, established factory regulation and workers' compensation, instituted the first direct primary in the country, and inaugurated the first state income tax. Under his leadership, Wisconsin earned the title "laboratory of democracy."

A fiery orator, "Fighting Bob" La Follette united his supporters around issues that transcended old party loyalties. This emphasis on reform rather than party loyalty became a characteristic of progressivism, which attracted followers from both major parties. Democrats like Tom Johnson and Republicans like Robert La Follette could lay equal claim to the label "progressive."

West of the Rockies, progressivism arrived somewhat later and found a champion in Hiram Johnson of California, who served as governor from 1911 to 1917 and U.S. senator from 1917 to 1945. Since the 1870s, California politics had been dominated by the Southern Pacific railroad, a corporation whose rapaciousness was detailed in Frank Norris's novel *The Octopus* (1901). Johnson ran for governor in 1910 on the promise to "kick the Southern Pacific out of politics." With the support of the reform wing of the Republican Party, he handily won. Efficiency and rationalization became the watchwords of Hiram Johnson's administration. He promised to "return the government to the people"—to give them honest public service untarnished by corruption and corporate influence. As governor, he introduced the direct primary; supported the initiative, referendum, and recall; strengthened the state's railroad commission; endorsed conservation; and signed an employer's liability law.

Who benefited from Johnson's progressivism? California's entrepreneurs—large farmers, independent oil producers, and other rising businessmen who could make money more easily once Johnson curtailed the influence of the Southern Pacific. A vigorous, compelling personality with a reputation for his towering temper, Hiram Johnson proved an able governor. In 1912, he could boast that by regulating the Southern Pacific railroad he had saved shippers more than $2 million.

Progressivism Finds a President: Theodore Roosevelt

On September 6, 1901, President William McKinley was shot twice by Leon Czolgosz, an anarchist, while attending the Pan American Exposition in Buffalo, New York. After lingering for a week, McKinley died on September 14. When news of his assassination reached his friend and political mentor Marcus Alonzo Hanna, Hanna is said to have growled, "Now that damned cowboy is president." Hanna was speaking of Vice President Theodore Roosevelt, the colorful hero of San Juan Hill, who had indeed punched cattle in the Dakotas in the 1880s.

Roosevelt's status as a Spanish-American War hero had propelled him to the governorship of New York in 1898. A moderate reformer, he clashed with party bosses, who were happy to "kick him upstairs" to the vice presidency in 1900, where he added luster to the ticket and helped reelect McKinley to a second term. As vice president, party leaders reasoned, Roosevelt could do little harm. But one bullet proved the error of their logic. Overnight, Roosevelt was president, and Mark Hanna was not alone in his concern that the conservative politics of McKinley had died with him. An activist and a moralist, imbued with progressive spirit, Roosevelt would turn the White House into a "bully pulpit" and, in the process, shift the nation's center of power from Wall Street to Washington.

The Square Deal

At the age of forty-two, Roosevelt was the youngest man ever to move into the White House. A patrician by birth and an activist by temperament, Roosevelt brought to the job enormous talent and energy. By the time he graduated from Harvard, he was already an accomplished naturalist, an enthusiastic historian, and a naval strategist. He could have picked from any of these promising careers. Instead, he chose politics. He went from the New York state assembly at the age of twenty-three to the presidency in twenty years, with time out to be a cowboy in the Dakotas, police commissioner of New York City, and colonel of the Rough Riders.

The "absolutely vital question" facing the country, Roosevelt wrote to a friend in 1901, was "whether or not the government has the power to control the trusts." The Sherman Antitrust Act of 1890 had been badly weakened by a conservative Supreme Court and by attorneys general more willing to use it against labor unions than against monopolies. To determine if the law had any teeth left, Roosevelt, in one of his first acts as president, ordered his attorney general to begin a secret antitrust investigation of the Northern Securities Company.

The "absolutely vital question" facing the country, Roosevelt wrote a friend in 1901, was "whether or not the government has the power to control the trusts."

Roosevelt trained his sights on a good target. Northern Securities resulted from one of the most controversial mergers in American history. When Edward C. Harriman, who controlled the Union Pacific and the Southern Pacific Railroads, attempted to add the Northern Pacific to his holdings, James J. Hill of the Great Northern squared off against him. The result was a ruinous railroad war that precipitated a panic on Wall Street, bankrupting thousands of small investors. To bring peace, financier J. P. Morgan created the Northern Securities Company in 1901, combining under one management three competing railroads. This new giant monopolized railroad traffic in the Northwest. Small investors still smarting from their losses, farmers worried about freight rates, and the public in general saw in Northern Securities the symbol of corporate high-handedness.

In February 1902, Wall Street rocked with the news that the government had filed an antitrust suit against Northern Securities. As one newspaper editor sarcastically observed, "Wall Street is paralyzed at the thought that a President of the United States

would sink so low as to try to enforce the law." An indignant J. P. Morgan demanded to know why he had not been consulted. "If we have done anything wrong," he told the president, "send your man to my man and they can fix it up." Roosevelt, amused, later noted that Morgan "could not help regarding me as a big rival operator." In a sense, that was just what Roosevelt intended. Roosevelt's thunderbolt put Wall Street on notice that the money men were dealing with a president who demanded to be treated as an equal and who was willing to use government as an instrument to control business. Perhaps sensing the new mood, the Supreme Court, in a significant turnaround, upheld the Sherman Act and called for the dissolution of Northern Securities in 1904.

"Hurrah for Teddy the Trustbuster," cheered the papers. Roosevelt went on to use the Sherman Act against forty-three trusts, including such giants as the American Tobacco Company, Du Pont, and Standard Oil. Always the moralist, he insisted on a "rule of reason." He would punish the "bad" trusts (those that broke the law) and leave the "good" ones alone. In practice, he preferred regulation to antitrust suits. In 1903, he pressured Congress to pass the Elkins Act, outlawing railroad rebates (money returned to a shipper to guarantee his business). And he created the new cabinet department of Commerce and Labor with a subsidiary Bureau of Corporations to act as a corporate watchdog.

In his handling of the anthracite coal strike in 1902, Roosevelt again demonstrated his willingness to assert the moral and political authority of the presidency, this time to mediate between labor and management. In May, more than fifty thousand coal miners in Pennsylvania went out on strike, demanding higher wages, shorter hours, and recognition of the United Mine Workers (UMW) union. "The miners don't suffer," scoffed George Baer, the mine operators' spokesman, "why they can't even speak English." Six eastern railroads owned over 70 percent of the anthracite mines. With the power of the railroads behind them, the mine owners refused to budge.

The strike dragged on through the summer and into the fall. Hoarding and profiteering drove up the price of coal from $2.50 to $6.00 a ton. Most American homes were heated with coal, and, with winter approaching, near riots broke out in big cities. In the face of mounting tension, Roosevelt issued a personal invitation to representatives from both sides to meet in Washington in October. At the meeting, Baer and the mine owners refused to talk to the union representatives, insulting both the president and the attorney general. Angered by the "wooden-headed obstinacy and stupidity" of management, Roosevelt threatened to seize the mines and run them with federal troops. It was a powerful bluff that called into question not only the supremacy of private property but also the rule of law. The specter of federal troops being used to operate the mines quickly brought management around. At the prompting of J. P. Morgan, the mine owners agreed to arbitration. In the end, the miners won a reduction in hours and a wage increase, but the owners succeeded in preventing formal recognition of the UMW.

Taken together, Roosevelt's actions in the Northern Securities case and the anthracite coal strike marked a dramatic departure from the tradition of William McKinley. Roosevelt demonstrated conclusively that government intended to act as a force independent of big business. Pleased with his role in the anthracite strike, Roosevelt announced that all he had tried to do was give labor and capital a "square deal."

The phrase became his slogan in the 1904 election campaign. To win the presidency in his own right, Roosevelt moved to wrest control of the Republican Party from Mark Hanna, the only man who stood between him and the nomination. Roosevelt adroitly used patronage to win supporters so that even before Hanna died of typhoid fever in 1904, Roosevelt was the undisputed leader of the party.

In the presidential election of 1904, the Democrats moved to the center, abandoning William Jennings Bryan, their candidate in the previous two elections, to support Judge Alton B. Parker, a "safe" candidate they hoped would win business votes away from Roosevelt. In the months before the election, the president prudently toned down his criticism of big business. Wealthy Republicans like J. P. Morgan, while privately branding Roosevelt a class traitor, remained loyal to the party and gave it their money and their votes. In November 1904, Roosevelt swept into office with the largest popular majority—57.9 percent—any candidate had polled to that time.

Roosevelt the Reformer

"Tomorrow I shall come into my office in my own right," Roosevelt is said to have remarked on the eve of his election. "Then watch out for me!" Roosevelt's stunning victory gave him a mandate for reform. He would need all the popularity and political savvy he could muster, however, to guide his reform measures through Congress, which was controlled by a staunchly conservative Republican "old guard" in the Senate. Roosevelt's pet project remained railroad regulation. The Elkins Act prohibiting rebates had not worked. No one could stop big shippers like Standard Oil from wringing concessions from the railroads. The Interstate Commerce Commission (ICC), created in 1887 to regulate the railroads, had been stripped of its powers by the Supreme Court. In the face of a widespread call for railroad reform, Roosevelt determined that the only solution lay in giving the ICC real power to set rates and prevent discriminatory practices.

THEODORE ROOSEVELT

Described aptly by a contemporary observer as "a steam engine in trousers," Theodore Roosevelt at forty-two was the youngest president to occupy the White House. He brought to the office energy, intellect, and activism in equal measure. Roosevelt boasted that he used the presidency as a "bully pulpit"—a forum from which he advocated reforms ranging from trust-busting to simplified spelling.
Library of Congress.

But business remained adamant in its opposition to federal rate setting. The right to determine the price of goods or services was an age-old prerogative of private enterprise, and one that business had no intention of yielding to government.

To ensure passage of the Hepburn Railway Act, a bill increasing the power of the ICC, Roosevelt worked skillfully behind the scenes. Once again, he showed his power to bluff. By threatening to call for tariff reform, a volatile issue that might split the party, he succeeded in getting a recalcitrant House of Representatives to pass the Hepburn Act. But the bill bogged down in the Senate, where Nelson Aldrich of Rhode Island, aptly dubbed "the senator from Standard Oil," attempted to amend it to death. To get the best bill possible, Roosevelt first worked with insurgent progressives and then, when they could not muster the needed votes, switched sides and succeeded in getting Aldrich and the Republican regulars to accept a compromise. In its final form, the Hepburn Act, passed in May 1906, gave the ICC power to set rates subject to court review. Committed progressives like La Follette judged the bill a defeat for reform. Die-hard conservatives branded it a "piece of populism." Both sides exaggerated. The bill left the courts too much power, and it failed to provide adequate means for the ICC to determine rates realistically, but its passage was a landmark in the evolution of federal control of private industry. For the first time, a government commission had the power to investigate private business records and to set rates.

Passage of the Hepburn Act marked the high point of Roosevelt's presidency. In a serious political blunder, Roosevelt had announced on the eve of his election in 1904 that he would not run again. By 1906, his term was starting to run out and his influence on Congress and his party was waning. Ironically, he had become a "lame duck" at the very moment he was not only enjoying his greatest public popularity but also wanted to press for more reform.

Always an apt reader of the public temper, Roosevelt witnessed a growing appetite for reform fed by the revelations of corporate and political wrongdoing that filled the papers and boosted the sales of popular periodicals. (See "The Promise of Technology," page 738.) In October 1902, Lincoln Steffens's "Tweed Days in St. Louis" appeared in *McClure's Magazine,* the first part of a series entitled "The Shame of the Cities" (later published as a book). The next month, Ida Tarbell, a schoolteacher turned journalist, began her sharply critical series on Standard Oil in *McClure's.* Soon other journalists, such as Ray Stannard Baker and Robert Hunter, tried their hand at the new brand of investigative reporting. Their hard-hitting exposés swelled magazine circulation and touched off a public clamor for reform.

Roosevelt, who wielded publicity like a weapon in reform, counted many of these new journalists, notably Jacob Riis and Lincoln Steffens, as friends. But when David Graham Phillips attacked the Republican old guard in 1906 in a series of articles entitled "The Treason of the Senate," the character assassination of his fellow Republicans offended the president. Roosevelt warned journalists that they should not be like the allegorical character in *Pilgrim's Progress* who was so busy raking up muck that he took no notice of higher things. Roosevelt's criticism gave the American vocabulary a new word: *muckraker.* Journalists soon appropriated the term and turned it into a badge of honor.

Muckraking, as Roosevelt was keenly aware, had been of enormous help in securing progressive legislation. The passage of the Pure Food and Drug Act and the Meat Inspection Act provided powerful examples. In 1905, the president had belatedly thrown his support behind legislation to outlaw misbranded and adulterated foods, drinks, and drugs. For years, Dr. Harvey Washington Wiley, chief chemist in the Department of Agriculture, had agitated for a federal law requiring accurate labeling of foods and drugs. Mark Sullivan's exposés of patent medicines in the *Ladies' Home Journal* and Samuel Hopkins Adams's "Great American Fraud" series in *Collier's* kept the issue before the public. "Gullible America," Adams announced in 1905, "will swallow huge quantities of alcohol, an appalling amount of opiates and narcotics, a wide assortment of varied drugs . . . and far in excess of all other ingredients, undiluted fraud."

In the spring of 1906, the publicity generated by the muckrakers goaded Congress into action. With Roosevelt's backing, a pure food and drug bill passed the Senate and went to the House, where its opponents hoped to keep it locked up in committee. There it would have died, were it not for publication of Upton Sinclair's novel *The Jungle,* with its sensational account of the filthy conditions in the meatpacking industry. A massive public outcry led to the passage of a tough Pure Food and Drug Act and a bill mandating federal inspection of meat.

In the waning years of his administration, Roosevelt moved to the left, allying with the more

Flash Photography and the Birth of Photojournalism

T HE CAMERA WAS NOT NEW at the turn of the twentieth century. Americans had eagerly imported the technology developed by Frenchman L. J. M. Daguerre to make portraits called daguerreotypes as early as the 1840s. By the 1880s the invention of dry plates had simplified photography, and by the 1890s Americans could purchase a Kodak camera marketed by George Eastman.

But for Jacob Riis, who wished to document the horrors of tenement life, photography was useless because it required daylight or careful studio lighting. Riis, a progressive reformer and journalist who covered the police beat for the New York *Tribune,* never thought of buying a camera. He could only rudely sketch the dim hovels, the criminal nightlife, and the windowless tenement rooms of New York. Then came the breakthrough. "One morning scanning my newspaper at the breakfast table," he wrote, "I put it down with an outcry. . . . There it was, the thing I had been looking for all these years. . . . A way had been discovered . . . to take pictures by flashlight. The darkest corner might be photographed that way."

The new technology involved a pistol lamp that fired magnesium cartridges to provide light for instantaneous photography. Armed with the new flash pistols, Riis and a band of amateur photographers soon set out to shine light in the dark corners of New York. "Our party carried terror wherever it went," Riis later recounted. "The spectacle of strange men invading a house in the mid-night hours armed with [flash] pistols which they shot off recklessly was hardly reassuring . . . and it was not to be wondered at if the tenants bolted through the windows and down fire-escapes."

Unhappy with the photographers he hired to follow him on his nighttime forays into the slums,

Riis determined to try his own hand at taking pictures and laid out $25 for his first photographic equipment in 1888. It consisted of a four-by-five-inch wooden box camera, glass plates, a tripod, a safety lantern, flash pistols, developing trays, and a printing frame. He soon replaced the pistols with a newer flash technology developed in 1887 that used magnesium powder blown through an alcohol flame. Riis carried a frying pan to ignite the powder, observing "It seemed more homelike."

Flash photography was dangerous. The pistol lamp cartridges contained highly explosive chemicals that could seriously burn the photographer. The newer technology employing magnesium powder was also risky. Riis once blew the flash into his own eyes and only his glasses saved him from being blinded. Nor was Riis the only one in peril. When he photographed the residents of a tenement on "Blind Man's Alley," he set the place on fire when he ignited the flash. He later claimed the tenement, nicknamed the "Dirty Spoon," was so filthy it wouldn't burn. He was able to douse the flames without his blind subjects ever realizing their danger.

Riis turned his photographs into magic lantern slides that he used to illustrate his lectures on tenement life. They helped spread his message, but not until *Scribner's* magazine printed his story entitled "How the Other Half Lives" in December 1889 did he begin to develop a mass audience. The article, illustrated with line drawings of Riis's photographs, became the basis for his best-selling book of the same title published in 1890.

How the Other Half Lives made photographic history. It contained, along with Riis's text and the line drawings that had appeared in *Scribner's,* seventeen halftone prints of Riis's photographs. Riis's text and pictures shined the light on New York's darkest corners—vagrants in the filthy lodging houses; "street arabs," homeless boys who lived by their wits on the streets; the saloons and dives of lower New York; the evil smelling tenement yards; the stifling sweatshops. For the first time unposed action pictures taken with a flash documented social conditions. Riis's pioneering photojournalism shocked the nation and led not only to tenement reform, but also to the development of city playgrounds, neighborhood parks, and child labor laws.

JACOB RIIS AND BAXTER STREET COURT

Jacob Riis (inset), a Danish immigrant who knew the squalor of New York's lodging houses and slums from his early days in New York, vigorously campaigned for tenement reform. He warned slum landlords (some of them prominent in New York society) that their greed bred crime, disease, and, potentially, class warfare. Flash photography enabled Riis to show the dark alleys and tenements of New York. He took his camera into Baxter Street Court, then recorded these observations: "I counted the other day the little ones, up to ten years old in a . . . tenement that for a yard has a . . . space in the center with sides fourteen or fifteen feet long, just enough for a row of ill-smelling [water] closets . . . and a hydrant. . . . There was about as much light in the 'yard' as in the average cellar. . . . I counted one hundred twenty eight [children] in forty families."

National Portrait Gallery, Smithsonian Institution / Art Resources, N.Y.; Museum of the City of New York.

progressive elements of the Republican Party. In speech after speech he attacked the "malefactors of great wealth." Styling himself a "radical," he claimed credit for leading the "ultra conservative" party of McKinley to a position of "progressive conservatism and conservative radicalism." His rhetoric led John D. Rockefeller to predict early in 1907 that Roosevelt's attacks on big business would precipitate a depression.

When a business panic developed in the fall of 1907, business interests quickly blamed the president. The panic of 1907 proved to be severe but short. As he had done in 1895, J. P. Morgan stepped in to avert disaster, this time switching funds from one bank to another to prop up weak institutions and keep them from failing. For his services, he claimed the Tennessee Coal and Iron Company, an independent steel business that had long been coveted by his U.S. Steel. Morgan dispatched his lieutenants to

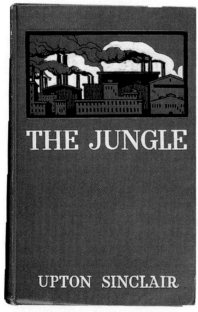

THE JUNGLE
Novelist Upton Sinclair, a lifelong socialist, wrote **The Jungle** *to expose the evils of capitalism. But readers were more horrified by the unsanitary conditions he described in the meatpacking industry, where Sinclair's hapless hero encountered rats, filth, and diseased animals processed into potted beef. It was rumored that after reading the book, President Theodore Roosevelt could no longer stomach sausage for breakfast. The president immediately ordered a thorough study of conditions in the meatpacking industry. The public outcry surrounding* **The Jungle** *contributed to the enactment of pure food and drug legislation and federal meat inspection. Sinclair ruefully remarked, "I aimed at the public's heart, but I hit them in the stomach."*
By permission of the Houghton Library, Harvard University.

Washington, where they told Roosevelt that the sale of the company would aid the economy "but little benefit" U.S. Steel. Roosevelt, willing to take the word of a gentleman, tacitly agreed not to institute antitrust proceedings against U.S. Steel. As Roosevelt later learned, Morgan and his men had been less than candid. The acquisition of Tennessee Coal and Iron for a price below market value greatly strengthened U.S. Steel and undercut the economy of the Southeast. The episode would come back to haunt Roosevelt, as it gave rise to the charge that he acted as a tool of the Morgan interests.

The charge of collusion between business and government underscored the extent to which business leaders like Morgan and his partner George W. Perkins found federal regulation preferable to unbridled competition or harsher state measures. During the Progressive Era, enlightened business leaders cooperated with government in the hope of avoiding antitrust prosecution. Roosevelt, convinced that regulation and not trust-busting was the best way to deal with big business, never acknowledged that, for all his strong rhetoric, his regulatory policies fostered an alliance between business and government. As Roosevelt's actions in the panic of 1907 demonstrated, despite his harsh attacks on the "malefactors of great wealth," the president remained indebted to Morgan, who still functioned as the national bank and would continue to do so until the passage of the Federal Reserve Act six years later.

In at least one area, Roosevelt was well ahead of his time. Robert La Follette, who found much to criticize in Roosevelt's presidency, called his efforts in conservation of natural resources the progressive president's "greatest work." When Roosevelt took office, some 45 million acres of land remained as government reserves. He more than tripled that number to 150 million acres, buying land and creating national parks and wildlife preserves by executive order. To conserve natural resources, he fought not only western cattle barons, lumber kings, and mining interests but also powerful leaders in Congress, including Speaker of the House Joseph Cannon, who was determined to spend "not one cent for scenery."

Roosevelt had no sooner entered the White House than he launched his conservation campaign, naming the able Gifford Pinchot his chief forester. In one of their most effective ploys, they fought private utilities that were intent on gobbling up waterpower sites and creating a monopoly of hydroelectric power. Pinchot protected 2,565 sites, often on the pretext that he planned to establish

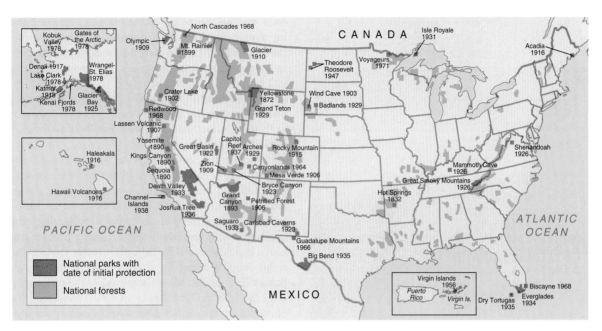

M A P 20.1

National Parks and Forests
The national park system in the West began with Yellowstone in 1872, followed in the 1890s by Grand Canyon, Yosemite, Kings Canyon, and Sequoia. During his presidency, Theodore Roosevelt added six new parks—Crater Lake, Wind Cave, Petrified Forest, Lassen Volcanic, Mesa Verde, and Zion.

ranger stations on the lands. "Public rights come first and private interest second," Roosevelt insisted.

> *Roosevelt, convinced that regulation and not trust-busting was the best way to deal with big business, never acknowledged that, for all his strong rhetoric, his regulatory policies fostered an alliance between business and government.*

By 1907, Roosevelt had stepped on the toes of every major interest in the West. To curb the president, Congress added a rider to an appropriations bill that barred the creation of any new reserves in six western states. Roosevelt could not veto the bill, but he worked feverishly in the ten days before it became law to establish twenty-one new reserves and save 16 million acres for posterity (Map 20.1). Today, six national parks, sixteen national monuments, and fifty-one wildlife refuges stand as witnesses to Roosevelt's substantial accomplishments as a conservationist.

Roosevelt the Diplomat

Roosevelt took a keen interest in shaping foreign policy and actively worked to buttress the United States' newly won place among world leaders. A fierce proponent of America's interests abroad, he was convinced that Congress was inept in foreign affairs, and he relied on executive power to effect a vigorous foreign policy, sometimes stretching his powers beyond legal limits in his pursuit of American interests. A man who relished military discipline and viewed life as a constant conflict for supremacy, Roosevelt believed that the "civilized nations" should police the world and hold the "backward" countries in line. In his relations with the great European powers, he relied on military strength and diplomacy, a combination he aptly described with the aphorism "Speak softly but carry a big stick."

In the Caribbean, Roosevelt jealously guarded the Monroe Doctrine's American sphere of influ-

ence. In 1902, he risked war to keep Germany from intervening in Venezuela when that country's dictator, Cipriano Castro (whom Roosevelt dismissed as "a villainous little monkey"), borrowed money in Europe and could not pay it back. Roosevelt issued an ultimatum to the German Kaiser, warning him to stay out of Latin American affairs or face war with the United States. The matter was eventually settled by arbitration.

Roosevelt's proprietary attitude toward the hemisphere became evident in the infamous case of the Panama Canal. A firm advocate of naval power and an astute naval strategist, Roosevelt had long been a supporter of a canal connecting the Caribbean and the Pacific. By enabling the navy to move quickly from the Atlantic to the Pacific, the canal would, in effect, double the nation's naval power. The United States began a joint venture with England to build a canal but in 1901 abandoned the partnership and moved forward alone. Two sites were possible, one in Nicaragua, which had the advantage of being at sea level, the other in Panama, where the rough and hilly terrain required a system of locks. In the end, the choice was made not by logic but by politics. Private investors who held rights to build in Panama lobbied Congress shamelessly until they won approval for the route.

The Panamanian isthmus (the narrow strip of land connecting North and South America) was at this time part of Colombia, so in 1902 Roosevelt began negotiations with that nation to gain access to the land. He offered the Colombian government a one-time sum of $10 million and an annual rent of $250,000. When the government in Bogotá refused to accept the offer, Roosevelt became incensed at what he called the "homicidal corruptionists" in Colombia for trying to "blackmail" the United States. The result was an uprising in Panama in 1903

ROOSEVELT AND MUIR IN YOSEMITE
In 1903, President Roosevelt took a camping trip to Yosemite, California, with John Muir, naturalist and founder of the Sierra Club. Roosevelt's experience as a rancher in the Dakotas made him the first president to have experienced firsthand the American West. As president, he acted vigorously to protect the beauty and resources of the West for posterity, using executive power to set aside more than a hundred million acres in government reserves and to create six national parks.
Theodore Roosevelt Collection, Harvard College Library.

arranged by New York investors. The U.S. government aided and protected the "revolution" by placing the warship *Nashville* off the isthmus, and the State Department recognized the new government of Panama within twenty-four hours. The new Panamanian government promptly accepted the $10 million, and the building got under way (Map 20.2). The canal would take eleven years and $375 million to complete but would literally double the strength of the U.S. navy by allowing it to move quickly from Atlantic to Pacific.

Roosevelt later boasted that he "took Panama"; although most Americans applauded his action, to some the episode became a national disgrace. President Woodrow Wilson would later offer to apologize and to pay the Colombian government $25 million. Furious and disgusted, Roosevelt and his friends managed to block the agreement. But in 1921, after Roosevelt had died, the U.S. made the payment without the apology.

In the wake of the Panama affair, the confrontation with Germany over Venezuela, and yet another

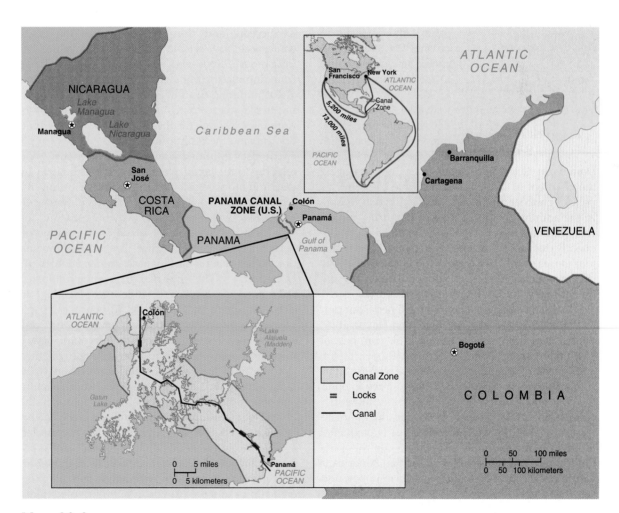

M A P   20.2

The Panama Canal, 1914

The Panama Canal, completed in 1914, bisected the isthmus in a series of massive locks and dams. As Theodore Roosevelt had planned, the canal greatly strengthened the navy by allowing ships to move from the Atlantic to the Pacific in a matter of days.

www.bedfordstmartins.com/tap   SEE THE ONLINE STUDY GUIDE for more help in analyzing this map.

default on a European debt, this time in the Dominican Republic, Roosevelt announced in 1904 what became known as the Roosevelt Corollary to the Monroe Doctrine. The United States would not intervene in Latin America as long as nations conducted their affairs with "decency." But Roosevelt warned that if any Latin American nation proved guilty of "brutal wrongdoing," as in the case of defaulting on debts to European nations, the United States would insist on stepping in. The Roosevelt Corollary in effect made the United States the policeman of the Western Hemisphere and served notice to the European powers to keep out. Roosevelt immediately put the doctrine into practice by intervening in Costa Rica and taking over the Dominican Republic's customhouse and ensuring the payment of its debts. Critics called Roosevelt's policy "gunboat diplomacy," and with good reason. In the administrations of Roosevelt and his successor, William Howard Taft, U.S. marines were frequently dispatched to the Caribbean to take over customhouses or otherwise show U.S. force. The legacy of gunboat diplomacy was bitter anti-American sentiment that would last through the century.

Roosevelt's "Gunboat Diplomacy"

In Asia, Roosevelt inherited the Open Door policy initiated by Secretary of State John Hay in 1899, which was designed to ensure U.S. commercial entry into China. As Britain, France, Russia, Japan, and Germany raced to secure Chinese trade and territory, Roosevelt was tempted to use force to enter the fray and gain economic or possibly territorial concessions. As a result of victory in the Spanish-American War, the United States already enjoyed a foothold in the region by virtue of its control of the Philippines. But Roosevelt realized that Americans would not support an aggressive Asian policy, and sensibly he held back.

In his relations with Europe, Roosevelt sought to establish the United States, fresh from its victory over Spain, as a rising force in world affairs. When tensions flared between France and Germany in Morocco in 1905, Roosevelt set up a conference in Algeciras, Spain, where he worked to maintain a balance of power to help neutralize German ambitions. His skillful mediation of the dispute gained him a reputation as an astute player on the world stage and demonstrated the United States' new presence in world affairs.

Roosevelt earned the Nobel Peace Prize in 1906 for his role in negotiating an end to the Russo-Japanese War, which had broken out when the Japanese invaded Chinese Manchuria, threatening Russia's sphere of influence in the area. Once again, Roosevelt sought to maintain a balance of power, in this case working to curb Japanese expansionism. Roosevelt admired the Japanese, judging them "the most dashing fighters in the world," but he did not want Japan to become too strong in Asia. He offered to mediate and thus presided over the peace conference at Portsmouth, New Hampshire. At Portsmouth, Roosevelt was able to prevent Japan from dominating Manchuria, but he had no qualms about initiating the Taft-Katsura agreement, granting the Japanese control of the sovereign nation of Korea in exchange for the pledge that Japan would not threaten the Philippines.

Roosevelt fumed when the United States' good relations with Japan were jeopardized in 1906 by discriminatory legislation in California calling for segregated public schools for "Orientals." Roosevelt smoothed over the incident by negotiating the "Gentlemen's Agreement" in 1907 whereby he reversed the segregation order in exchange for voluntary restrictions on Japanese immigration to the United States. This informal arrangement allowed the Japanese to save face while also placating nativist sentiment in California. To counter Japan's growing bellicosity, Roosevelt immediately dispatched the Great White Fleet, sixteen of the navy's most up-to-date battleships, on a "goodwill mission" around the world. American relations with Japan improved, and in the 1908 Root-Takahira agreement the two nations pledged to maintain the Open Door and support the status quo in the Pacific.

Roosevelt's show of American force constituted a classic example of his dictum "Speak softly but carry a big stick." Political cartoonists delighted in caricaturing the president wielding a cudgel in foreign affairs, and the American public seemed to relish the image.

The Troubled Presidency of William Howard Taft

When Roosevelt retired from the presidency in 1909 at the age of fifty to go on safari and shoot big game

THE BIG STICK IN THE CARIBBEAN SEA

THEODORE ROOSEVELT AND THE BIG STICK
In this political cartoon from 1904, President Theodore Roosevelt, dressed in his Rough Rider uniform and carrying his "big stick," turns the Caribbean into a Yankee pond. His Roosevelt Corollary to the Monroe Doctrine did just that.
Granger Collection.

in Africa, he turned the White House over to his handpicked successor, William Howard Taft. In the presidential election of 1908, Taft soundly defeated the perennial Democratic candidate, William Jennings Bryan, who had come to be known as the "Great Commoner." But Taft's popular majority amounted to only half of Roosevelt's record win in 1904. On the eve of his inauguration, Taft showed little enthusiasm about his triumph and little zest for the future. In fact, the presidency for Taft proved an ordeal. As a symptom of his discomfort in office, his weight ballooned from an already hefty 297 pounds to over 350 pounds.

Any man would have found it difficult to follow in Roosevelt's footsteps, but Taft proved hopelessly ill suited to the task. A genial man with a talent for law, Taft had no experience in elective office,

no feel for politics, no ability to compromise, and no nerve for controversy. His ambitious wife coveted the office and had urged him to take it. He would have been better off listening to his mother, who warned, "Roosevelt is a good fighter and enjoys it, but the malice of politics would make you miserable."

Once in office, Taft proved a perfect tool in the hands of Republicans who yearned for a return to the days of McKinley. A lawyer by training and instinct, he believed that it was up to the courts, not the president, to arbitrate social issues. Roosevelt had carried presidential power to a new level, often castigating the judiciary and flouting the separation of powers. Taft the legalist found it difficult to condone such actions. Wary of the progressive insurgents in his own party and without Roosevelt to guide him, Taft relied increasingly on conservatives in the Republican Party. As a progressive senator lamented, "Taft is a ponderous and amiable man completely surrounded by men who know exactly what they want."

Taft's troubles began on the eve of his inaugural when he called a special session of Congress to deal with the tariff. Roosevelt had been too politically astute to tackle the troublesome tariff issue, even though he knew that rates needed to be lowered. Taft, with his stubborn courage, blundered into the fray. The House of Representatives passed a modest downward revision and, to make up for lost revenue, imposed a small inheritance tax. Led by Senator Nelson Aldrich, the conservative Senate struck down the tax and added more than eight hundred crippling amendments to the tariff. The Payne-Aldrich bill that emerged actually raised the tariff. As if paralyzed, Taft neither fought for changes nor vetoed the measure. On a tour of the Midwest in 1909, he was greeted with jeers when he claimed, "I think the Payne bill is the best bill that the Republican Party ever passed." In the eyes of a growing number of Americans, his praise of the tariff made him either a fool or a liar.

Once in office, Taft proved a perfect tool in the hands of Republicans who yearned for a return to the days of McKinley. As a progressive senator lamented, "Taft is a ponderous and amiable man completely surrounded by men who know exactly what they want."

Taft's legalism got him into hot water over conservation. He refused to endorse his predecessor's methods of bending the law to protect the wilderness. He undid Roosevelt's work to preserve waterpower sites when he learned that they had been improperly designated as ranger stations. And when Gifford Pinchot publicly denounced Taft's secretary of the interior, Richard Ballinger, as a tool of western land-grabbers, Taft fired Pinchot, touching off a storm of controversy that damaged Taft and alienated Roosevelt.

Talk of substituting Roosevelt on the ticket in 1912 grew as Republican progressives became increasingly dissatisfied with Taft's policies. In June 1910, Roosevelt returned to New York, where he received a hero's welcome and attracted a stream of

visitors and reporters seeking his advice and opinions. Hurt, Taft kept his distance. By late summer, Roosevelt had taken sides with the progressive insurgents in his party. "Taft is utterly hopeless as a leader," Roosevelt confided to his son as he set out on a speaking tour of the West. Reading the mood of the country, Roosevelt began to sound more and more like a candidate.

With the Republican Party divided, the Democrats swept the congressional elections of 1910. Branding the Payne-Aldrich tariff "the mother of trusts," they captured a majority in the House of

WILLIAM HOWARD TAFT
William Howard Taft had little aptitude for politics. When Theodore Roosevelt tapped him as his successor in 1908, Taft had never held an elected office. A legalist by training and temperament, Taft moved congenially in the conservative circles of the Republican Party. His actions dismayed progressives and eventually led Roosevelt to challenge him for the presidency in 1912. The break with Roosevelt saddened and embittered Taft, who heartily disliked the presidency and was glad to leave it.
Library of Congress.

Representatives and won several key governorships. The revitalized Democratic Party could look to new leaders, among them the progressive governor of New Jersey, Woodrow Wilson.

With a Democratic majority in the House and progressive Republicans holding the balance of power in the Senate, Congress enacted a number of key reforms, including legislation to regulate mine and railroad safety, to create a Children's Bureau in the Department of Labor, and to establish an eight-hour day for federal workers. Two significant constitutional amendments—the Sixteenth Amendment, which provided for a modest graduated income tax, and the Seventeenth Amendment, which called for the direct election of senators (who had formerly been chosen by their state legislatures)—went to the states, where they would later win ratification in 1913. While Congress rode the high tide of progressive reform, Taft sat on the sidelines.

In foreign policy as well as in the domestic arena, Taft had a difficult time following in Roosevelt's footsteps. In the Caribbean he pursued a policy of "dollar diplomacy," championing commercial goals rather than the strategic aims that Roosevelt had advocated. He provoked anti-American feeling by attempting to force commercial treaties on Nicaragua and Honduras and by dispatching the U.S. marines to Nicaragua and Santo Domingo in 1912.

In Asia, Taft's foreign policy proved equally inept. He openly avowed his intent to promote in China "active intervention to secure for . . . our capitalists opportunity for profitable investment." Lacking Roosevelt's understanding of power politics, Taft naively believed that he could substitute "dollars for bullets." He never recognized that an aggressive commercial policy could not exist without military might. As a result, dollar diplomacy was doomed to failure. Even Taft was forced to recognize its limits when revolution broke out in Mexico in 1911. Under pressure to protect American investment, which amounted to

Taft's "Dollar Diplomacy"

more than $4 billion, he mobilized troops along the border. But in the end, he relied on diplomatic pressure to salvage American interests.

Always a legalist at heart, Taft hoped to encourage world peace through the use of a world court and arbitration. He unsuccessfully sponsored a series of arbitration treaties that Roosevelt, who prized national honor more than international law, vehemently opposed. By 1910, Roosevelt had become a vocal critic of Taft's foreign policy, which he dismissed as "maudlin folly."

The final breach between Taft and Roosevelt came in 1911, when Taft's attorney general filed an antitrust suit against U.S. Steel. In its brief against the steel giant, the government cited Roosevelt's agreement with the Morgan interests in the 1907 acquisition of Tennessee Coal and Iron by U.S. Steel. The incident greatly embarrassed Roosevelt by making it clear that he either had been hoodwinked or had acted as a tool of Wall Street. Thoroughly enraged, Roosevelt first lambasted Taft's "archaic" antitrust policy and then began to hint that he might be persuaded to run for president again.

The Election of 1912

In February 1912, Roosevelt announced, "My hat is in the ring." But for all his popularity, Roosevelt no longer controlled the party machinery. Taft, with uncharacteristic strength, refused to step aside. As he bitterly told a journalist, "Even a rat in a corner will fight." Roosevelt took advantage of newly passed primary election laws and ran in thirteen states, winning 278 delegates to Taft's 48. But at the Chicago convention, Taft's bosses refused to seat the Roosevelt delegates. Fistfights broke out on the convention floor as Taft won renomination on the first ballot. Crying robbery, Roosevelt's supporters bolted the party.

Seven weeks later, in the same Chicago auditorium, a hastily organized Progressive Party met to nominate Roosevelt. Few Republican officeholders joined the new party, but the advance guard of progressivism turned out in full force. Amid a thunder of applause, Jane Addams seconded Roosevelt's nomination. Full of reforming zeal, the delegates chose Roosevelt and Hiram Johnson to head the new party and approved the most advanced platform since the Populists' in 1892. Planks called for woman suffrage, the direct election of senators, presidential primaries, conservation of natural resources, minimum wages for women, an end to

PASS PROSPERITY AROUND

BULL MOOSE POSTER
Accepting the nomination of the Progressive Party in 1912, Theodore Roosevelt exclaimed, "I feel as strong as a bull moose." Instantly the new party had a mascot and a nickname. The Bull Moose soon decorated party emblems, as in this poster where the animal is featured more prominently than Roosevelt or his vice presidential candidate, Hiram Johnson. The slogan "PASS PROSPERITY AROUND" may refer to the party's platform, which pledged to tax the great fortunes of the day by ratifying the country's first graduated income tax.
Collection of Janice L. and David J. Frent.

child labor, workers' compensation, social security, and a federal income tax.

Roosevelt arrived in Chicago to accept the nomination and announced that he felt "as strong as a bull moose," giving the new party a nickname and a mascot. But for all the excitement and the cheering, the new Progressive Party was doomed, and the candidate knew it. The people may have supported the party, but the politicians, even insurgents like La Follette, stayed within the Republican fold. "I am under no illusion about it," Roosevelt con-

fessed to a friend. "It is a forlorn hope." But he had gone too far to turn back. He led the Bull Moose Party into the fray, exhorting his followers in ringing biblical tones, "We shall not falter, we stand at Armageddon and do battle for the Lord."

The Democrats, delighted at the split in the Republican ranks, smelled victory for the first time since 1892. Their convention turned into a bitter fight for the nomination. After forty-six ballots, William Jennings Bryan threw his support to Woodrow Wilson, who became the party's nominee. Wilson's career in politics was nothing short of astounding. After only eighteen months in office as governor of New Jersey, the former professor of political science and president of Princeton University found himself running for president of the United States.

Wilson ran on a platform designed to appeal to the diverse constituents of the Democratic Party. To the farmers, the platform promised a lower tariff and cheaper agricultural loans; to labor unions, it promised to limit the use of injunctions and antitrust laws against labor; and to small business owners, it vowed to return to competition through the breakup of the trusts. As if that were not enough, Wilson's vice presidential candidate, Thomas R. Marshall, went on record avowing, "What America needs is a good five-cent cigar."

Voters in 1912 could choose from three candidates, each of whom claimed to be a progressive. That the term could stretch to cover all three underscored some major disagreements in progressive thinking about the relation between business and government. Taft, for all his trust-busting, was generally conceded to be the candidate of the old guard. The real contest for the presidency was between Roosevelt and Wilson and the two political philosophies summed up in their campaign slogans: "The New Nationalism" and "The New Freedom."

Roosevelt's New Nationalism enunciated his belief in federal planning and regulation. He accepted big business as inevitable but demanded that government supervise it and act as "a steward of the people." Roosevelt called for an increase in the power of the federal government, a decrease in the power of the courts, and an active role for the president. As political theorist Herbert Croly pointed out in his influential book *The Promise of American Life* (1909), Roosevelt hoped to use the Hamiltonian means of a centralized federal government to further the Jeffersonian end of greater democracy.

The real contest for the presidency in 1912 was between Roosevelt and Wilson and the two political philosophies summed up in their campaign slogans: "The New Nationalism" and "The New Freedom."

Wilson, schooled in the Democratic principles of limited government and states' rights, set a markedly different course with his New Freedom. Tutored in economics by *Muller v. Oregon* lawyer Louis Brandeis, who railed against the "curse of bigness," Wilson promised to use antitrust legislation to get rid of big corporations and to give small businesses and farmers better opportunities in the marketplace.

Wilson and Roosevelt fought it out, but in the end only the energy and emotional enthusiasm of the Bull Moosers obscured the inevitable outcome of a race in which the Republican vote was split while the Democrats remained united. No candidate could claim a majority in the three-way race. Wilson captured a bare 42 percent of the popular vote, polling fewer votes than Bryan had received

when he lost to Taft in 1908. Roosevelt and his Bull Moose Party won 27 percent of the vote, an unprecedented tally for a new party. The incumbent Taft came in third with 23 percent. But in the electoral college, Wilson won a decisive 435, with 88 going to Roosevelt and only 8 to Taft (Map 20.3). The real loser in 1912 was not Taft but the Bull Moose Party, which essentially collapsed after Roosevelt's defeat. It had always been, in the words of one astute observer, "a house divided against itself and already mortgaged."

Woodrow Wilson and Progressivism at High Tide

Born in Virginia and raised in Georgia, Woodrow Wilson was the first Southerner to be elected president since James K. Polk in 1844 and only the second Democrat to occupy the White House since Reconstruction. Democrats who anticipated a wild celebration when Wilson took office soon had their hopes dashed. The son of a Presbyterian minister, Wilson was a teetotaler more given to Scripture than to celebration. He canceled the inaugural ball and called instead for a day of prayer.

This lean, ascetic man with an otherworldly gaze had come to politics by a strange route. A scholar and an academician, he had earned his doctorate at Johns Hopkins University and had taught at Bryn Mawr, Wesleyan, and Princeton, serving as president of the latter for eight years. In 1910, the New Jersey Democratic machine, looking for a respectable candidate, tapped him for governor. Once in office, he quickly cut his ties with the bosses and went over to the progressive camp. He was a man, as one biographer conceded, whose "political convictions were never as fixed as his ambition."

As governor, Wilson put New Jersey in the vanguard of progressivism by signing laws to reform the election process, to provide workers' compensation, to end corrupt practices in state government, and to regulate railroads and public utilities. A year into his term, Wilson already had his eye on the presidency. Even though he loathed William Jennings Bryan, he courted him until he won Bryan's political blessing; afterward, he rewarded the Great Commoner by naming him secretary of state.

Always able to equivocate, Wilson proved rarely able to compromise. He brought to the White House a gift for oratory, a stern will, and a set of

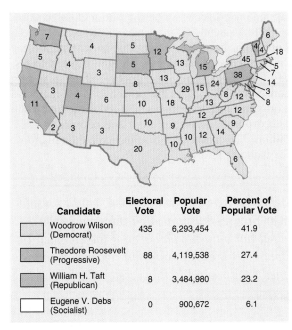

Candidate	Electoral Vote	Popular Vote	Percent of Popular Vote
Woodrow Wilson (Democrat)	435	6,293,454	41.9
Theodore Roosevelt (Progressive)	88	4,119,538	27.4
William H. Taft (Republican)	8	3,484,980	23.2
Eugene V. Debs (Socialist)	0	900,672	6.1

MAP 20.3
The Election of 1912

FOR GOVERNOR

WOODROW WILSON

WOODROW WILSON
Woodrow Wilson's political career was meteoric, propelling him from the presidency of Princeton University to the presidency of the United States in three years. As governor of New Jersey from 1910 to 1912, Wilson turned against the Democratic machine that had backed him and made a reputation as a champion of progressive reform. Elected to the White House in 1912, he presided over the high tide of progressive reform.
Collection of Janice L. and David J. Frent.

fixed beliefs. His tendency to turn differences of opinion into personal hatreds would impair his leadership and damage his presidency. Fortunately for Wilson, he came to power with a Democratic Congress eager to do his bidding.

Although he opposed big government in his campaign, Wilson viewed himself as the only leader who could speak for the country. He was prepared to work on the base built by Roosevelt to strengthen presidential power, exerting leadership and working through his party in Congress to accomplish the Democratic agenda. Before he was finished, Wilson would preside over progressivism at high tide and see enacted not only the platform of the Democratic Party but the humanitarian reforms championed by Roosevelt's Progressive Party as well.

Wilson's Reforms: Tariff, Banking, and the Trusts

In March 1913, Wilson became the first president since John Adams to go to Capitol Hill and speak directly to Congress, calling for tariff reform. "The object of the tariff," Wilson told Congress, "must be effective competition." Eager to topple the high tariff, the Democratic House of Representatives hastily passed the Underwood tariff, which lowered rates by 15 percent. To compensate for lost revenue, Congress approved a moderate income tax made possible by ratification of the Sixteenth Amendment a month earlier. In the Senate, lobbyists for industries quietly went to work to get the tariff raised, but Wilson rallied public opinion by attacking the "industrious and insidious lobby." Robert La Follette went further and demanded an investigation of the ties between business and the legislature. When senators for the first time had to disclose their finances, the public learned that more than a few were on the payrolls of big corporations. In the harsh glare of publicity, the Senate passed the Underwood tariff, which earned praise as "the most honest tariff since the Civil War."

Wilson turned his attention next to banking. The panic of 1907 had dramatically testified to the failure of the banking system. Once again, a president had had to turn to J. P. Morgan. But Morgan's legendary power was coming under close scrutiny. In 1913, Arsène Pujo, a Democratic senator from Louisiana, headed a committee to investigate the "money trust," calling J. P. Morgan himself to testify. The Pujo committee uncovered an alarming concentration of banking power. J. P. Morgan and Company and its affiliates held 341 directorships in 112 corporations, controlling assets of more than $22 billion. The sensational findings created a mandate for banking reform.

Before he was finished, Wilson would preside over progressivism at high tide and see enacted not only the platform of the Democratic Party but the humanitarian reforms championed by Roosevelt's Progressive Party.

The Federal Reserve Act of 1913 was the most significant piece of domestic legislation in Wilson's presidency. It established a national banking system composed of twelve regional banks, privately controlled but regulated and supervised by a Federal Reserve Board appointed by the president. It gave the United States its first efficient banking and currency system and, at the same time, provided for a larger degree of government control over banking than had ever existed before. The new system made currency more elastic and credit adequate for the needs of business and agriculture. It did not, however, attempt to take control of the boom and bust cycles in the U.S. economy that would produce another major depression in the 1930s.

Flushed with success, Wilson tackled the trust issue. When Congress reconvened in January 1914, Wilson supported the Clayton bill to outlaw "unfair competition"—practices such as price discrimination and interlocking directorates (directors from one corporation sitting on the board of another). By spelling out which practices were unfair, Wilson hoped to guide business activity back to healthy competition without resorting to regulation. Despite a grandiose preamble that stated, "The labor of human beings is not a commodity or article of commerce," the Clayton Act did not succeed in improving labor's position. Although AFL president Samuel Gompers hailed the act as the "Magna Carta of labor," the conservative courts continued to issue injunctions and to use antitrust legislation against labor unions.

In the midst of the fight for the Clayton Act, Wilson, at the prompting of Louis Brandeis, threw his support behind the creation of the Federal Trade Commission (FTC), precisely the kind of federal regulatory agency that Roosevelt had advocated under his New Nationalism. The FTC, created in 1913, had not only wide investigatory powers but the authority to prosecute corporations for "unfair trade practices" and to enforce its judgments by issuing "cease and desist" orders. Along with the Clayton Act, Wilson's antitrust program worked to regulate rather than to break up big business.

By the fall of 1914, Wilson had exhausted the stock of ideas that made up the New Freedom. He alarmed progressives by declaring that the progressive movement had fulfilled its mission and that the country needed "a time of healing." Disgruntled progressives also disapproved of Wilson's conservative appointments. Having fought provisions in the Federal Reserve Act that would give bankers control, Wilson promptly named a banker, Paul Warburg, as the first chief of the Federal Reserve Board. Appointments to the new FTC also

went to conservative businessmen. The progressive penchant for expertise helps explain Wilson's choices. Believing that experts in the field could best understand the complex issues at stake, Wilson appointed bankers to oversee the banks and businessmen to regulate business.

Wilson, Reluctant Progressive

Progressives watched in dismay as Wilson repeatedly obstructed or obstinately refused to encourage further progressive reforms. He failed to support labor's demand for an end to injunctions. He twice threatened to veto legislation providing for farm credits on nonperishable crops. He refused to support child labor legislation or woman suffrage. Wilson justified his actions in the rhetoric of the New Freedom by claiming that his administration would condone "special privileges to none." Virtually the only progressive measure that passed was the Seaman's Bill in 1915, a long overdue measure to improve the working conditions of sailors.

In the face of Wilson's obstinacy, reform might have ended in 1913 had not politics intruded. In the congressional elections of 1914, the Republican Party, no longer split by Roosevelt's Bull Moose faction, won substantial gains. Democratic strategists, with their eyes on the 1916 presidential race, recognized that Wilson needed to pick up support in the Midwest and the West by capturing votes from former Bull Moose progressives.

Wilson responded belatedly to this political pressure by championing reform in 1916. In a sharp about-face, he cultivated union labor, farmers, and social reformers. To please labor, he appointed Louis Brandeis to the Supreme Court. To woo farmers, he threw his support behind legislation to obtain rural credits. And he won support from advanced progressives such as Jane Addams by supporting workers' compensation and the Keating-Owen child labor law. When a railroad strike threatened in the months before the election, Wilson virtually ordered Congress to establish an eight-hour day at ten-hour pay on the railroads. He had moved a long way from his position in 1912 to embrace many of the social reforms championed by Theodore Roosevelt. (See "Documenting the American Promise," page 754.) As Wilson boasted, the Democrats had "opened their hearts to the demands of social justice" and had "come very near to carrying out the platform of the Progressive Party."

The Limits of Progressive Reform

Progressivism was never a radical movement. Its goal remained the preservation of the existing system—by government intervention if necessary, but without uprooting any of the traditional American political, economic, or social institutions. As Theodore Roosevelt, the bellwether of the movement, insisted, "The only true conservative is the man who resolutely sets his face toward the future." Roosevelt was such a man, and progressivism was such a movement. Its basic conservatism can be seen by comparing it to more radical movements of the era and by looking at the groups progressive reform left behind.

Radical Alternatives

The year 1900 witnessed the birth of the Social Democratic Party in America, later called simply the Socialist Party. Like the progressives, the socialists were middle class and native-born. They had broken with the older, more militant Socialist Labor Party precisely because of its dogmatic approach and immigrant constituency. The new group of socialists, men such as Upton Sinclair, Walter Lippmann, and John Reed, were eager to appeal to a broad mass of Americans.

The Socialist Party chose as its standard-bearer Eugene V. Debs, whose experience in the Pullman strike of 1894 convinced him that "there is no hope for the toiling masses of my countrymen, except by the pathways mapped out by Socialism." Debs's

"WE WANT DEBS"
Eugene Victor Debs, shown wearing a bow tie in a train window, poses with Socialist Party campaign workers on a whistle-stop tour during the presidential campaign of 1912. Arguing that Roosevelt and Wilson were as alike as "Tweedledee and Tweedledum," Debs saw the Socialist Party as the only hope for the working class. Over a million voters agreed and cast their votes for him in 1912.
Brown Brothers; Collection of Janice L. and David J. Frent.

brand of socialism, which owed as much to the social gospel as to the theories of Karl Marx, advocated cooperation over competition and urged men and women to liberate themselves from "the barbarism of private ownership and wage slavery." He was described by his followers as "a poet, a saint, a sweetly strong man." Debs declared, "While there is a lower class I am of it, while there is a criminal class I am of it, while there is a soul in prison I am not free."

Roosevelt labeled Debs a "mere inciter to murder and preacher of applied anarchy." Debs, for his part, pointed to the conservatism that underlay Roosevelt's fiery rhetoric. In the 1912 election, Debs indicted both parties as "Tweedledee and Tweedledum," each dedicated to the preservation of capitalism and the continuation of the wage system. The Socialist Party alone, he argued, was the "revolutionary party of the working class." Debs would run for president five times, in every election (except 1916) from 1900 to 1920. His best showing came in 1912, when he polled 6 percent of the popular vote, capturing almost a million votes.

Farther to the left of the socialists stood the Industrial Workers of the World (IWW), nicknamed the Wobblies. In 1905, Debs, along with William Dudley "Big Bill" Haywood, created the IWW, "one big union" dedicated to organizing the most destitute segment of the workforce, the unskilled workers disdained by Samuel Gompers's AFL—western miners, migrant farmworkers, lumbermen, and immigrant textile workers. Haywood, a craggy-faced miner with one eye (he had lost the other in a childhood accident), was a charismatic leader and a proletarian intellectual. While Debs insisted that change could come from ballots, not bullets, the IWW unhesitatingly advocated direct action, sabotage, and the general strike—tactics designed to trigger a workers' uprising.

In contrast to political radicals like Debs and Haywood, Margaret Sanger, a nurse and social activist, promoted birth control as a movement for change. Sanger, the daughter of a radical Irish father and a mother who died at fifty after bearing eleven children, coined the term *birth control* in 1915 and launched a movement with broad social implications. Sanger and her followers saw birth control not only as a sexual and medical reform but also as a means to alter social and political power relationships and to alleviate human misery.

The movement for birth control during the Progressive Era was another example of a cross-class alliance, in which middle-class women like Sanger made common cause with the working class. The leading advocates of birth control from 1914 to 1920 came from the ranks of anarchists, feminists, and socialists. Radicals such as the anarchist Emma Goldman were among the first to advocate birth control. They saw it as a way to improve the plight of the workers and urged working-class women to quit producing recruits for the factory and the army.

Sanger and her followers saw birth control not only as a sexual and medical reform but also as a means to alter social and political power relationships and to alleviate human misery.

Although birth control became a public issue only in the early twentieth century, the birthrate in the United States had been falling consistently throughout the nineteenth century, with the average number of children per family falling from 7.0 in 1800 to 3.6 by 1900. The desire for family limitation was widespread, and, in this sense, birth control was nothing new. But the open advocacy of contraception, the use of artificial means to prevent pregnancy, seemed to many people both new and shocking. Theodore Roosevelt fulminated against birth control as "race suicide," warning that the "white" population was declining while immigrants and "undesirables" continued to breed.

Convinced that women needed to be able to control their pregnancies but unsure of the best methods for doing so, Sanger traveled to Europe in 1913 to learn more about contraceptive techniques. On her return in 1914, she promoted birth control in her newspaper, *The Woman Rebel.* Purity laws passed in the 1870s made it illegal to distribute information on birth control or contraceptive devices, classing both as pornographic. When the post office declared Sanger's publication obscene and brought charges against her, she responded defiantly by drafting a detailed pamphlet called "Family Limitation" and getting the IWW to distribute 100,000 copies. Facing arrest, she fled to Europe only to return in 1916 something of a national celebrity. In her absence, birth control had become linked with free speech and had been taken up as a liberal cause. Under public pressure, the government dropped

The Issue of Child Labor

By the early years of the twentieth century, as many as four million children between the ages of ten and fifteen toiled long hours at low pay. They could be found in the depths of coal mines, in the searing heat of glass factories, in canneries and textile mills, in cotton fields—wherever employers coveted small size and nimble fingers. Progressive reformers, often called the "child savers," attempted to curb exploitation of children under the age of fourteen in sweatshops, mines, and mills across America. But they ran into solid opposition not only from employers, who had a vested interest in the cheap labor children performed, but also from parents, who counted on the wages of their children, however meager. In rural America, no one had questioned parents' right to put children to hard tasks in the fields and on the farm. Similarly, immigrants from rural Italy, Germany, or Russia could see no harm in putting children to work in factories or sweatshops in America's industrial cities and viewed it as the parents' prerogative to command their children's wages.

DOCUMENT 1. Lewis W. Parker, Testimony before the Congressional Committee on Labor, 1914

Not just immigrants but old-stock Americans relied on child labor, particularly in the South, where entire families of poor whites left the land to work side by side in the textile mills. On May 22, 1914, a South Carolina mill owner testified before the House of Representatives Committee on Labor on why child labor was necessary in the South.

It is not possible for a man who has been working on a farm who is an adult—after the age of 21 years, for instance—to become a skilled employee in a cotton mill. His fingers are knotted and gnarled; he is slow in action, whereas activity is required in working in the cotton mills. Therefore, as a matter of necessity, the adult of the family had to come to the cotton mill as an unskilled employee, and it was the children of the family who became the skilled employees in the cotton mills. For that reason it was

the children who had to support the families for the time being. I have seen instances in which a child of 12 years of age, working in the cotton mills, is earning one and one-half times as much as his father of 40 or 50 years of age.

SOURCE: *House of Representatives Hearings before the Committee on Labor* (1914), 93.

DOCUMENT 2. Florence Kelley, Testimony before the Congressional Committee on Labor, 1914

Progressives countered these arguments with poignant testimony about the plight of young workers and the failure of the states to enforce child labor laws. At the same 1914 committee hearings, reformer Florence Kelley described her experiences investigating child labor practices in Illinois.

I was at one time chief inspector of factories and workshops in the State of Illinois. I found great numbers of children working at night—working illegally. The superintendent of a glass-bottle company told me himself that this occurred once when he was rushed with work: A widow had come to him bringing two little boys, one still in kilts [baby skirts worn by small boys] and one in knee breeches. She told him that their father had just been killed on the railroad, and that they were penniless; and she wanted the older little boy to go to work in the glassworks, where he would get 40 cents a day. The superintendent was pressed for boys, and said, "I won't take the bigger fellow alone, but if you will take the baby back home and put him into knee pants, and then bring them both back in trousers, I will take them both." She did so, and those two little fellows, aged 9 and 7 years, began their work on the night shift.

SOURCE: *House of Representatives Hearings before the Committee on Labor* (1914), 35–36.

DOCUMENT 3. Lowell Mellett, Interview with Reuben Dagenhart, 1923

Despite heavy odds against them, progressives achieved victory in 1916 when the National Child Labor Committee finally convinced Congress and President Woodrow

Wilson to enact the Keating-Owen bill forbidding the regular employment of children under sixteen. The child savers' victory proved short-lived, however. Powerful business interests and a Supreme Court sympathetic to their views took advantage of the waning fervor for reform and in Hammer v. Dagenhart (1918) struck down the child labor law on the grounds that Congress could not regulate manufacturing within states. This decision made it legal for the chief plaintiff in the case, Roland Dagenhart, to continue having his young sons, ages thirteen and seven, work in a North Carolina cotton mill. It also protected the boys' "constitutional right" to continue to work at the mill, where they put in twelve-hour days and sometimes worked night shifts as well.

Ironically, one of the plaintiffs in the Dagenhart case had a very negative view of its outcome. In 1923, reporter Lowell Mellett tracked down Reuben Dagenhart, one of the boys in whose favor the Supreme Court had ruled six years earlier. In an article published in Labor in November 1923, Mellett recounted his meeting with Dagenhart.

I found him at his home in Charlotte. He is about the size of the office boy—weighs 105 pounds, he told me. But he is a married man with a child. He is 20 years old.

"What benefit," I asked him, "did you get out of the suit which you won in the United States Supreme Court?"

"You mean the suit the Fidelity Manufacturing Company won? [It was the Fidelity Company for which the Dagenharts were working.] I don't see that I got any benefit. I guess I'd been alot better off if they hadn't won it. . . .

"Look at me! A hundred and five pounds, a grown man and no education. I may be mistaken, but I think the years I've put in in the cotton mills have stunted my growth. They kept me from getting any schooling. I had to stop school after the third grade and now I need the education I didn't get."

"How was your growth stunted?"

"I don't know—the dust and the lint, maybe. But from 12 years old on, I was working 12 hours a day—from 6 in the morning till 7 at night, with time out for meals. And sometimes I worked nights besides. Lifting a hundred pounds and I only weighed 65 pounds myself."

He explained that he and his sister worked together, "on section," spinning. They each made about a dollar a day, though later he worked up to where he could make $2. His father made $15 a week and infant John, at the time the suit was brought, was making close to $1 a day.

"Just what did you and John get out of that suit, then?"

"Why, we got some automobile rides when them big lawyers from the North was down here. Oh, yes, and they brought both of us a coca-cola! That's all we got out of it."

"What did you tell the judge when you were in court?"

"Oh, John and me never was in court! Just Paw was there. John and me was just little kids in short pants. I guess we wouldn't have looked like much in court. We were working in the mill while the case was going on. But Paw went up to Washington."

Reuben hasn't been to school, but his mind has not been idle.

"It would have been a good thing for all the kids in this state if that law they passed had been kept. . . . I know one thing. I ain't going to let them put my kid sister in the mill. . . . She's only 15 and she's crippled and I bet I stop that!"

Source: *Labor*, November 17, 1923.

QUESTIONS FOR ANALYSIS AND DEBATE

1. After reading the testimony of Lewis W. Parker, do you think a parent has the right to require a child to work? Who do you think should decide whether and at what age a child should work?

2. According to Parker's testimony, why did employers hire children to work in mills and factories? Why weren't adults hired?

3. As a factory inspector for the state of Illinois, Florence Kelley saw child labor first hand. Do you think she effectively makes an argument against child labor? Why or why not?

4. In *Hammer v. Dagenhart* (1918), the Supreme Court ruled that the federal government could not regulate manufacturing in the states, and that everyone had a constitutional right to work. How does Reuben Dagenhart's interview with Lowell Mellett challenge this argument?

PICTURING CHILD LABOR

Each of the photographs of children pictured here was designed consciously to carry a message. Jacob Riis intended his photograph of homeless newsboys sleeping in an alley to be emblematic of the plight of the city's poor children. The boy miner, photographed by the mining company he worked for, was intended to counter criticism of child labor. Entitled **A Youthful Gold Digger,** *the photograph carried the caption "Eight-year-old Bill Scott of [Clarksburg, West Virginia] is all set to go to work in the mines. He's fully outfitted for his day's labor—with pipe, head-light, pick axe, lunch can, high shoes, overall coat and bandanna." Ironically, the pictures evoke in a modern audience the opposite responses from those the photographer intended. The staged, melodramatic poses of Riis's photo work against the grim reality Riis intended it to convey, while the mine's blatant promotion of child labor is shocking, and the plucky eight-year-old evokes our pity and horror.*

Homeless boys: The Jacob A. Riis Collection, #121, Museum of the City of New York; miner: Library of Congress.

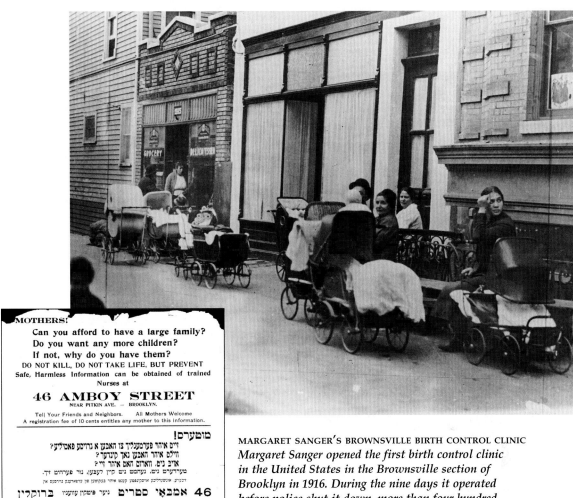

MOTHERS!

Can you afford to have a large family?
Do you want any more children?
If not, why do you have them?
DO NOT KILL, DO NOT TAKE LIFE, BUT PREVENT
Safe, Harmless Information can be obtained of trained
Nurses at

46 AMBOY STREET

NEAR PITKIN AVE. — BROOKLYN.

Tell Your Friends and Neighbors.   All Mothers Welcome
A registration fee of 10 cents entitles any mother to this information.

מוטערס!

זייט איהר פערמעגליך צו האבען א גרויסע פאמיליע?
ווילם איהר האבען נאך קינדער?
אויב ניט, ווארום האם איהר זיי?

מערדערט ניט, נעהמט ניט קיין לעבען, נור פערהיט זיך.
דעקט, אונשעדליכע אינפארמאציע קענט איהר בעקומען פון טרעאירטע נוירסעס אין

46 אמבאי סטריט ניער פיטקין עוועניו ברוקלין

זאגט דאם בעקאנט צו אייערע פריינד און שכנות.
פער 10 סענט אינשרייבנעלד קען אזוי אזוי בעקומט אזוי צו דיעזע אינפארמיישאן.

MADRI!

Potete permettervi il lusso d'avere altri bambini?
Ne volete ancora?
Se non ne volete piu', perche' continuate a metterli
al mondo?

NON UCCIDETE MA PREVENITE!

Informazioni sicure ed innocue saranno fornite da infermiere autorizzate a
46 AMBOY STREET   Near Pitkin Ave. Brooklyn
a cominciare dal 12 Ottobre.   Avvertite le vostre amiche e vicine.
Tutte le madri sono ben accette. La tassa d'iscrizione di 10 cents da diritto
a qualunque madre di ricevere consigli ed informazioni gratis.

Margaret H. Sanger

MARGARET SANGER'S BROWNSVILLE BIRTH CONTROL CLINIC
*Margaret Sanger opened the first birth control clinic
in the United States in the Brownsville section of
Brooklyn in 1916. During the nine days it operated
before police shut it down, more than four hundred
women visited the clinic. Here they are shown waiting patiently in line with their baby carriages.
Sanger published her flyers in English, Yiddish, and
Italian, and her clinic attracted immigrant women,
proving that Italian Catholics and Russian Jews
wanted birth control information as much as their
middle- and upper-class Protestant counterparts did.*
Sophia Smith Collection, Smith College.

the charges against Sanger, who undertook a nationwide tour to publicize the birth control cause.

Sanger then turned to direct action, opening the
nation's first birth control clinic in the Brownsville
section of Brooklyn, New York. Located in the heart
of a Jewish and Italian immigrant neighborhood,
the clinic attracted 464 clients in the nine days it was
open. On the tenth day, police shut down the clinic
and put Sanger in jail. By then she had become a

national figure, and the cause she championed had
gained legitimacy, if not legality. After World War I,
the birth control movement would become much
less radical as Sanger turned to doctors for support.
But in its infancy, the movement that Sanger led was
part of radical vision for reforming the world that
made common cause with the socialists and the
IWW in challenging the limits of progressive
reform.

Progressivism for Men Only

The day before President Woodrow Wilson's inauguration in March 1913, more than five thousand demonstrators marched in Washington to demand the vote for women. A rowdy crowd on hand to celebrate the Democrats' triumph heckled the marchers, as did the police. "If my wife were where you are," a burly cop told one suffragist, "I'd break her head." But for all the marching, Wilson, who didn't believe that a "lady" should vote, pointedly ignored woman suffrage in his inaugural address the next day.

The march served as a reminder that the political gains of progressivism were not spread equally in the population. When the twentieth century dawned, women still could not vote in most states. Increasingly, however, woman suffrage had become an international movement. In Great Britain, Emmeline Pankhurst and her daughters Cristabel and Sylvia promoted a new, militant suffragism. They seized the spotlight in a series of marches, mass meetings, and acts of civil disobedience, which sometimes escalated into violence, riots, and arson.

The activism of the British suffragists sparked new action in the United States, where progress toward full suffrage had moved slowly. Washington State voted for suffrage in 1910, and the next year suffragists, who had suffered a stinging defeat in California in 1896, captured the state and won significant posts in Governor Hiram Johnson's administration. Kansas, Oregon, and Arizona joined the suffrage column in 1912, evidence that suffragists were perfecting their lobbying techniques. Yet some suffragists, attracted to the flamboyance of the British movement, urged more direct action. Alice Paul, a Quaker social worker who had visited England and participated in suffrage activism there, returned to the United States in 1910 in time to plan the mass march on the eve of Wilson's inauguration and to lobby for a federal amendment to give women the vote. Paul's dramatic tactics alienated many in the National American Woman Suffrage Association (NAWSA). In 1916, she founded the

SUFFRAGE PARADE
Suffragist Inez Hayes Mulholland led the 1913 Washington march on a white horse. A daring new tactic, the women's mass march was greeted with noticeable silence by the new president, Woodrow Wilson.
Library of Congress.

militant National Woman's Party (NWP), which became the radical voice of the suffrage movement, advocating direct action and civil disobedience. Paul and her followers rejected the state-by-state strategy of the NAWSA and continued to press for a constitutional suffrage amendment, called by its supporters the Susan B. Anthony amendment.

The NAWSA, spurred by the actions of Paul and her followers, gained new direction when Carrie Chapman Catt became president in 1915. Catt revitalized the organization with a carefully crafted "winning plan" designed to achieve suffrage in six years. While Paul and her NWP held a six-month vigil outside the White House with banners that read "Mr. Wilson, What Will You Do for Woman Suffrage?" Catt led a centrally directed effort that worked on several levels. In states where women already voted, Catt lobbied for a federal amendment. Where state referenda could be won, she launched campaigns to maintain the suffrage momentum. Catt's strategy was to "keep so much 'suffrage noise' going all over the country that neither the enemy [n]or friends will discover where the real battle is." Catt's "winning plan" worked effectively, taking only four years instead of the six Catt had predicted.

World War I would provide the final impetus for woman suffrage. Paul and the NWP refused to work for the war, insisting "democracy should begin at home." In contrast, Catt seized the mantle of patriotism, arguing that there was no conflict between fighting for suffrage and aiding the war effort. It would take several more years before the Nineteenth Amendment became part of the U.S. Constitution, but when it was ratified in August 1920, the victory belonged both to Catt and to Paul, for without the militancy of the NWP, the NAWSA would not have seemed so moderate and respectable.

Racism as "Reform"

It was one of the great ironies of progressivism that, as it was practiced in the West and South, it viewed racism as reform. Anti-Asian bigotry in the West had led to a renewal of the Chinese Exclusion Act in 1902. As governor, Hiram Johnson at first stood against the strong anti-Asian prejudice of his state. But as California's Japanese population moved from urban to rural areas, an outcry arose to keep California land in "white" hands. In 1911, Johnson bottled up such legislation, but in 1913 he caved in

to near unanimous pressure and signed the Alien Land Law. His support of the legislation amounted to little more than a cynical piece of demagoguery. As Johnson well knew, the law was largely symbolic—ineffectual in practice, since Japanese children born in the United States were citizens and property could be purchased in their names. Progressive politicians like Johnson, dedicated to democracy and opposed to special interests, proved willing to undermine their own principles to maintain their popularity.

South of the Mason-Dixon line, the progressives' racism targeted African Americans. Progressives preached the disfranchisement of black voters as a "reform." During the bitter electoral fights that had pitted Populists against Democrats in the 1890s, the charge was often made that the party of white supremacy held its power only by the votes of the blacks. Since it was alleged that African American votes were purchased by money or threats of coercion, southern progressives proposed to "reform" the electoral system by eliminating black voters. Southern states, beginning in 1890 with Mississippi, sought to curtail the African American vote through devices like the poll tax (a fee required to vote) and the literacy test. Not coincidentally, these measures also denied access to poor, illiterate whites likely to vote against the reigning Democrats and for the Populist Party in the 1890s. But the racist intention of southern voting legislation became clear after 1900 when states resorted to such transparent ruses as the "grandfather clause," a legal device that allowed anyone to vote whose grandparent had cast a ballot, thus including virtually all southern whites and excluding blacks, whose grandparents had most likely been slaves.

It was one of the great ironies of progressivism that, as it was practiced in the West and South, it viewed racism as reform.

The Progressive Era witnessed not only the systematic disfranchisement of black voters but also the rise of Jim Crow laws to segregate public facilities. (The name "Jim Crow" derived from a character in a popular minstrel song.) The new railroads precipitated segregation in the South where before it had rarely existed, at least on paper. Blacks were segregated in Jim Crow train coaches, even when they paid a first-class fare. Soon separate waiting rooms, separate bathrooms, and separate dining facilities sprang up across the South. In courtrooms in the state of Mississippi, blacks were even required to swear on a separate Bible.

In the face of this growing repression, Booker T. Washington, the preeminent black leader of the day, urged caution and restraint. A former slave, Washington opened the Tuskegee Institute in Alabama in 1881 to teach vocational skills to African Americans. Washington emphasized education and economic progress for his race and urged African Americans to put aside issues of political and social equality. In an 1895 speech in Atlanta, which came to be known as the "Atlanta Compromise," he stated, "In all things that are purely social we can be as separate as the fingers, yet one as the hand in all things essential to mutual progress." Washington's accommodationist policy appealed to whites in all sections, who elevated "the wizard of Tuskegee" to the role of national spokesman for African Americans.

The year after Washington proclaimed the Atlanta Compromise, the Supreme Court upheld the

BOOKER T. WASHINGTON AND THEODORE ROOSEVELT DINE AT THE WHITE HOUSE
When Theodore Roosevelt invited Booker T. Washington to the White House in 1901, he stirred up a hornet's nest of controversy that continued into the election of 1904. This Republican campaign piece gives the meeting a positive slant, with Roosevelt and Washington sitting under a portrait of Abraham Lincoln, a symbol of the party's historic commitment to African Americans. Democrats portrayed the meeting in a very different light; their campaign buttons pictured Washington with darker skin and implied that Roosevelt favored "race mingling."
Collection of Janice L. and David J. Frent.

legality of racial segregation, affirming in *Plessy v. Ferguson* (1896) the constitutionality of the doctrine of "separate but equal." Blacks could be segregated in separate facilities, from schools to rest rooms, as long as the facilities were "equal." In actuality, facilities rarely were equal. In the North, where the growing tide of new immigrants led to a clamor for restrictive legislation, support for African American rights found few advocates. And with anti-Asian bigotry in the West, increasingly the doctrine of "white supremacy" found support in all sections of the country.

When Theodore Roosevelt invited Booker T. Washington to dine at the White House in 1901, a storm of racist criticism erupted. One southern editor fumed that the White House "had been painted black." But Roosevelt summoned Washington to talk politics and patronage, not African American rights. Busy tearing apart Mark Hanna's Republican machine and creating his own, Roosevelt wanted Washington's counsel in selecting black Republicans for party posts in the South. The president remained more interested in his own political fortunes than in those of African Americans.

When Woodrow Wilson came to power, he brought with him southern attitudes toward race and racial segregation. He allowed his postmaster general to segregate facilities, including drinking fountains and rest rooms, in the nation's capital. When critics attacked the policy, Wilson insisted that segregation was "in the interest of the Negro."

Faced with intolerance and open persecution, educated blacks in the North rebelled against the conservative leadership of Booker T. Washington. In *The Souls of Black Folk* (1903), Harvard graduate W. E. B. Du Bois attacked the "Tuskegee Machine," comparing Booker T. Washington to a political boss who used his influence to silence his critics and reward his followers. Du Bois founded the Niagara movement in 1905, calling for universal suffrage, civil rights, and leadership by a black intellectual elite. In 1909, the Niagara movement helped found the National Association for the Advancement of Colored People (NAACP), a coalition of blacks and whites that sought legal and political rights for

African Americans through the courts. Like many progressive reform coalitions, the NAACP contained a diverse group—social workers, socialists, and black intellectuals. In the decades that followed, the NAACP came to represent the future for African Americans, while Booker T. Washington, who died in 1915, represented the past.

Conclusion: Progressivism in Perspective

The limitations of progressive reform should not obscure its very real achievements. The progressive movement brought significant gains as government moved away from social Darwinism and laissez-faire to embrace a more active role designed to deal with the problems accompanying urban industrialism, to bring about greater social justice, and to achieve a better balance between business and government. Both Jane Addams and Theodore Roosevelt could lay equal claim to a movement that brought American politics into the twentieth century. Progressivism contained many paradoxes. A diverse coalition of individuals and interests, the progressive movement began at the grass roots but left as its legacy a stronger presidency and an unprecedented federal involvement in the economy and social welfare. A movement that believed in social justice, progressivism often promoted social control. And while progressives called for greater democracy, they worshiped experts and efficiency.

But whatever its inconsistencies, progressivism attempted to deal with the problems posed by urban industrialism and, by increasing the power of the presidency and expanding the power of the government, helped to launch the liberal state of the twentieth century. War on a global scale would provide progressivism with yet another challenge even before it had completed its ambitious agenda.

www.bedfordstmartins.com/tap SEE THE ONLINE STUDY GUIDE to assess your mastery of the material covered in this chapter.

CHRONOLOGY

1889 Jane Addams opens Hull House in Chicago.

1895 Booker T. Washington enunciates "Atlanta Compromise."

Anti-Saloon League founded by Protestant clergy.

1896 U.S. Supreme Court upholds doctrine of "separate but equal" in *Plessy v. Ferguson*.

1899 Florence Kelley launches the National Consumers League.

1900 Socialist Party founded with Eugene V. Debs as standard-bearer.

1901 Thomas Lofton Johnson elected mayor of Cleveland, Ohio.

Robert M. La Follette elected governor of Wisconsin.

Theodore Roosevelt succeeds to presidency following assassination of William McKinley.

1902 Roosevelt brings labor and management to bargaining table in anthracite coal strike.

Lincoln Steffens's muckraking series "The Shame of the Cities" begins in *McClure's Magazine*.

Ida Tarbell begins her "History of the Standard Oil Company" in serial form in *McClure's Magazine*.

U.S. government files antitrust lawsuit against Northern Securities Company.

1903 Women's Trade Union League founded.

Uprising in Panama leads to Panamanian independence; United States begins construction of Panama canal.

W. E. B. Du Bois challenges Booker T. Washington in his book *The Souls of Black Folk*.

1904 Roosevelt wins presidential election in landslide.

Roosevelt Corollary to the Monroe Doctrine effectively makes United States "the policeman" of the Western Hemisphere.

1905 Industrial Workers of the World (IWW) founded by Big Bill Haywood.

W. E. B. Du Bois founds the Niagara movement.

Taft-Katsura Agreement gives Japan control over Korea.

1906 Pure Food and Drug Act and meat inspection legislation passed.

Congress passes Hepburn Act to regulate railroads and strengthen Interstate Commerce Commission.

Roosevelt receives Nobel Peace Prize for his role in mediating Russo-Japanese War.

1907 Panic on Wall Street.

Roosevelt signs "Gentlemen's Agreement" with Japan restricting immigration.

Walter Rauschenbusch publishes *Christianity and the Social Crisis*.

1908 Supreme Court upholds Oregon state law limiting women's working hours to ten a day (*Muller v. Oregon*).

Root-Takahira agreement regularizes relations between United States and Japan.

William Howard Taft elected president to succeed Theodore Roosevelt.

1909 "Uprising of twenty thousand" in New York City, a garment workers strike backed by the WTUL.

National Association for the Advancement of Colored People (NAACP) formed.

President Taft defends Payne-Aldrich tariff.

1910 Hiram Johnson elected governor of California.

Woodrow Wilson elected governor of New Jersey.

Wyoming enacts woman suffrage.

Jane Addams publishes *Twenty Years at Hull-House.*

1911 Triangle fire in New York City kills 146 workers.

Taft launches antitrust suit against U.S. Steel.

California votes for woman suffrage.

1912 President Taft sends marines into Nicaragua and Santo Domingo.

Republicans nominate incumbent William Howard Taft.

Theodore Roosevelt runs for president on Progressive Party ticket.

Democrat Woodrow Wilson elected president, defeating Taft and Roosevelt.

Socialist Eugene V. Debs garners 6 percent of the vote.

Kansas, Oregon, and Arizona grant the vote to women.

1913 Suffragists march on eve of Wilson's inauguration to demand the vote.

Wilson signs legislation establishing Federal Trade Commission (FTC).

Sixteenth Amendment (income tax) and Seventeenth Amendment (direct election of senators) ratified.

1914 Congress passes Clayton Antitrust Act.

Walter Lippmann publishes *Drift and Mastery,* a statement of the progressive philosophy.

Panama Canal opens.

1915 Carrie Chapman Catt takes over leadership of national woman suffrage movement.

1916 Alice Paul launches National Woman's Party.

Margaret Sanger opens first U.S. birth control clinic in Brooklyn, New York.

Keating-Owen bill passed, outlawing child labor.

1918 Supreme Court strikes down child labor law in *Hammer v. Dagenhart.*

BIBLIOGRAPHY

GENERAL WORKS

Sean Dennis Cashman, *America in the Age of the Titans: The Progressive Era and World War I* (1988).

Alan Dawley, *Struggles for Justice: Social Responsibility and the Liberal State* (1991).

Vincent P. DeSantis, *The Shaping of Modern America, 1877–1920* (2nd ed., 1989).

Sara M. Evans, *Born for Liberty: A History of Women in America* (1989).

Samuel P. Hays, *The Response to Industrialism, 1885–1914* (1957).

Richard Hofstadter, *The Age of Reform* (1955).

Linda K. Kerber, Alice Kessler-Harris, and Katherine Kish Sklar, *U.S. History as Women's History* (1995).

Gabriel Kolko, *The Triumph of Conservatism* (1963).

George Mowry, *The Era of Theodore Roosevelt* (1958).

Nell Irvin Painter, *Standing at Armageddon: The United States, 1877–1919* (1987).

James Weinstein, *The Corporate Ideal in the Liberal State, 1900–1918* (1969).

Robert H. Wiebe, *The Search for Order, 1877–1920* (1967).

GRASSROOTS PROGRESSIVISM

Joyce Antler, *Lucy Sprague Mitchell* (1987).

Karen J. Blair, *The Clubwoman as Feminist: True Womanhood Redefined, 1868–1914* (1980).

Steven Boyer, *Urban Masses and Moral Order in America, 1820–1920* (1978).

Kathleen Brady, *Ida Tarbell: Portrait of a Muckraker* (1984).

John D. Buenker, *Urban Liberalism and Progressive Reform* (1973).

Mina Carson, *Settlement Folk: Social Thought and the American Settlement Movement, 1885–1930* (1990).

Robert M. Crunden, *Ministers of Reform: The Progressive Achievement in American Civilization, 1889–1920* (1982).

Allen F. Davis, *Spearheads for Reform: The Social Settlements and the Progressive Movement, 1890–1914* (1967).

Allen F. Davis, *American Heroine: The Life and Legend of Jane Addams* (1973).

Nancy Schrom Dye, *As Equals and as Sisters: Feminism, Unionism, and the Women's Trade Union League of New York* (1980).

John H. Ehrenreich, *The Altruistic Imagination: A History of Social Work and Social Policy in the United States* (1985).

Ellen Fitzpatrick, *Endless Crusade: Women, Social Scientists, and Progressive Reform* (1990).

Philip S. Foner, *Women and the American Labor Movement,* vol. 1, *From Colonial Times to the Eve of World War I* (1979).

Lynn D. Gordon, *Gender and Higher Education in the Progressive Era* (1989).

Samuel Haber, *Efficiency and Uplift: Scientific Management in the Progressive Era, 1899–1920* (1964).

Alice Kessler Harris, *Out to Work: A History of Wage Earning Women in the United States* (1982).

Melvin Holli, *The American Mayor: The Best and Worst Big-City Leaders* (1999).

Michael B. Katz, *In the Shadow of the Poorhouse: A Social History of Welfare in America* (1986).

Seth Koven and Sonya Michel, eds., *Mothers of a New World: Maternalist Politics and the Origins of the Welfare State* (1993).

Rivka Lissak, *Pluralism and Progressives: Hull House and the New Immigrants, 1890–1919* (1989).

Roy M. Lubove, *The Progressives and the Slums* (1962).

Kathleen McCarthy, ed., *Lady Bountiful Revisited: Women, Philanthropy, and Power* (1990).

David Montgomery, *Workers' Control in America* (1979).

Robyn Muncy, *Creating a Female Dominion in American Reform* (1991).

Donald Nelson, *Frederick W. Taylor and the Rise of Scientific Management* (1980).

Elizabeth Payne, *Reform, Labor, and Feminism: Margaret Dreier Robins and the Women's Trade Union League* (1988).

David Pivar, *The Purity Crusade: Sexual Morality and Social Control* (1973).

Jean B. Quandt, *The Social Thought of Progressive Intellectuals* (1970).

Anne Firor Scott, *Natural Allies: Women's Associations in American History* (1991).

Peter R. Shergold, *Working Class Life: The "American Standard" in Comparative Perspective, 1899–1913* (1982).

Kathryn Kish Sklar, *Florence Kelley and the Nation's Work: The Rise of Women's Political Culture, 1830–1900* (1995).

Theda Skocpol, *Protecting Soldiers and Mothers* (1992).

Barbara Miller Solomon, *In the Company of Educated Women* (1985).

Landon R. Y. Storre, *Civilizing Capitalism, The National Consumers' League, Women's Activism, and Labor Standards in the New Deal Era* (2000).

Meredith Tax, *The Rising of the Women* (1980).

Barbara Mayer Wertheimer, *We Were There: The Story of Working Women in America* (1977).

Harold S. Wilson, *McClure's Magazine and the Muckrakers* (1970).

PROGRESSIVISM: THEORY AND PRACTICE

Andrew Feffer, *The Chicago Pragmatists and American Progressivism* (1993).

William A. Link, *The Paradox of Southern Progressivism, 1880–1930* (1992).

Richard Coke Lower, *A Bloc of One: The Political Career of Hiram W. Johnson* (1993).

Richard L. McCormick, *From Realignment to Reform: Political Change in New York State* (1981).

George Mowry, *The California Progressives* (1951).

Spencer Olin Jr., *California's Prodigal Sons: Hiram Johnson and the Progressives, 1911–1917* (1968).

Judith Sealander, *Grand Plans: Business Progressivism and Social Change in Ohio's Miami Valley, 1890–1919* (1988).

David P. Thelen, *The New Citizenship: Origins of Progressivism in Wisconsin, 1885–1900* (1972).

David P. Thelen, *Robert M. La Follette and the Insurgent Spirit* (1985).

Nancy C. Unger, *Fighting Bob La Follette: The Righteous Reformer* (2000).

Michael A. Weatherson and Hal W. Bochin, *Hiram Johnson, Political Revivalist* (1995).

C. Vann Woodward, *The Origins of the New South* (1951).

James Wright, *The Progressive Yankees* (1987).

PROGRESSIVISM AND NATIONAL POLITICS

Donald E. Anderson, *William Howard Taft* (1973).

Howard K. Beale, *Theodore Roosevelt and the Rise of America to World Power* (1956).

John Morton Blum, *The Republican Roosevelt* (2nd ed., 1977).

John D. Buenker, *Urban Liberalism and Progressive Reform* (1973).

David Mark Chalmers, *The Muckrake Years* (1980).

Kendrick A. Clements, *The Presidency of Woodrow Wilson* (1992).

John Milton Cooper Jr., *The Warrior and the Priest: Woodrow Wilson and Theodore Roosevelt* (1983).

Louis Filler, *Muckraking and Progressivism in the American Tradition* (rev. ed., 1996).

Lewis L. Gould, *Reform and Regulation: American Politics from Roosevelt to Wilson* (2nd ed., 1986).

Lewis L. Gould, *The Presidency of Theodore Roosevelt* (1991).

William H. Harbaugh, *The Life and Times of Theodore Roosevelt* (rev. ed., 1982).

Samuel P. Hays, *Conservation and the Gospel of Efficiency* (1959).

James Kloppenberg, *Uncertain Victory: Social Democracy and Progressivism in European and American Thought, 1870–1920* (1986).

Richard L. McCormick, *The Party Period and Public Policy* (1986).

Emily S. Rosenberg, *Spreading the American Dream: American Economic and Cultural Expansion, 1890–1945* (1982).

Phillipa Strum, *Louis D. Brandeis* (1984).

David P. Thelen, *Robert M. La Follette and the Insurgent Spirit* (2nd ed., 1985).

Clarence E. Wunderlin Jr., *Visions of a New Industrial Order: Social Science and Labor Theory in America's Progressive Era* (1992).

James Harvey Young, *Securing the Federal Food and Drug Act of 1906* (1989).

RADICAL ALTERNATIVES

Mary Jo Buhl, *Women and American Socialism, 1870–1920* (1981).

Ellen Chesler, *Woman of Valor: Margaret Sanger and the Birth Control Movement in America* (1993).

Melvyn Dubofsky, *"Big Bill" Haywood* (1987).

Melvyn Dubofsky, *We Shall Be All: A History of the Industrial Workers of the World* (2nd ed., 1988).

Leslie Fishbein, *Rebels in Bohemia: The Radicals of the Masses, 1911–1917* (1982).

David J. Goldberg, *A Tale of Three Cities: Labor Organization and Protest in Paterson, Passaic, and Lawrence, 1916–1921* (1988).

Anthony Lukas, *Big Trouble: A Murder in a Small Western Town Sets Off a Struggle for the Soul of America* (1998).

Janice Jacqueline Miller, *Challenge from the Left: The Socialist Press and the Progressive Reform Movement, 1900–1917* (1989).

Bruno Ramirez, *When Workers Fight: The Politics of Industrial Relations in the Progressive Era, 1898–1916* (1978).

Salvatore Salerno, *Red November, Black November: Culture and Community in the Industrial Workers of the World* (1989).

Nick Salvatore, *Eugene V. Debs: Citizen and Socialist* (1982).

Ann Huber Tripp, *The IWW and the Paterson Silk Strike of 1913* (1987).

Alice Wexler, *Emma Goldman: An Intimate Life* (1984).

RACE RELATIONS AND WOMAN SUFFRAGE

Kevin K. Gaines, *Uplifting the Race, Black Leadership Politics, and Culture in the Twentieth Century* (1996).

Glenda Elizabeth Gilmore, *Gender and Jim Crow: Women and the Politics of White Supremacy in North Carolina, 1896–1920* (1996).

Louis R. Harlan, *Booker T. Washington: The Making of a Black Leader, 1856–1901* (1972).

Louis R. Harlan, *Booker T. Washington: The Wizard of Tuskegee, 1901–1915* (1983).

Charles F. Kellogg, *NAACP: A History of the National Association for the Advancement of Colored People, 1909–1920* (1967).

Jack Temple Kirby, *Darkness at the Dawning: Race and Reform in the Progressive South* (1972).

David Levering Lewis, *W. E. B. Du Bois: Biography of a Race, 1868–1919* (1993).

Alessandra Lorini, *Rituals of Race: American Public Culture and the Search for Racial Democracy* (1999).

Christine Lunardini, *From Equal Suffrage to Equal Rights: Alice Paul and the National Woman's Party, 1910–1928* (1986).

Neil R. McMillen, *Dark Journey: Black Mississippians in the Age of Jim Crow* (1989).

Joel Williamson, *The Crucible of Race* (1984).

WAR

Which Bird?

As viewed by Life

LIFE MAGAZINE COVER

This 1914 magazine cover provides a vivid visual demonstration of the early tendency of the American press to support U.S. entry into World War I. The image makes no bones about the way a viewer should answer the question posed below it. The American eagle in the center, wings spread and screaming for action, dominates the picture and makes the dove holding an olive branch appear pathetically weak. Considering the stereotyped knife-, gun-, and bomb-wielding foreigners lurking in the background, the sailor has understandably turned toward the eagle for inspiration to resist the enemies of democracy.

Picture Research Consultants & Archives.

THE UNITED STATES AND THE "GREAT WAR"

21

1914–1920

BEYOND HIS STANDING AS THE RICHEST MAN IN THE WORLD, Andrew Carnegie had reason to be ebullient in his 1914 New Year's message to friends and national leaders. Proclaiming himself "strong in the faith that International Peace is soon to prevail," Carnegie urged those he greeted to "be of good cheer" and expect delivery on the promise his beloved poetic hero Robert Burns had made long ago:

It's coming yet for a' that
When man to man the world o'er
Shall brothers be and a' that

Carnegie's optimism reflected the encouraging developments he had seen in the ten years since he had decided to focus his philanthropic conscience on the cause of peace. Carnegie money had built three centers for the advancement of peace in Europe and Latin America and endowed four trusts, most important the Carnegie Endowment for International Peace in 1910, with over $25 million. Following Carnegie's example and sharing his confidence in the enlightened progress of the nineteenth century, forty-five peace societies came into being in the United States during the first decade of the twentieth century. By 1914 the total had reached sixty-three.

That same year Carnegie founded the Church Peace Union and financed its plans to meet on August 1 in Konstanz, Germany. Carnegie hoped that the nation's ruler, Kaiser Wilhelm II, might make an appearance. He had met the German leader a few years before and had been charmed by the kaiser's positive reception to his idea of a peace league to arbitrate international disputes. In 1913, Carnegie had presented a memorial to the kaiser, signed by seventy American civic and corporate leaders, offering "congratulations upon your twenty-five years of peaceful and prosperous reign." In Carnegie's eyes, the kaiser stood out as the "foremost apostle of peace in our time."

So it was that Carnegie spent the unusually beautiful summer at Skibo, his castle in Scotland, serenely anticipating good news from the Church Peace Union meeting in Konstanz. On the opening morning of the conference he decided to conclude years of labor on his autobiography with a tribute to "The Kaiser and World Peace." It seemed a perfect moment of completion; but it proved instead to be the end of illusion. Early in the afternoon, Carnegie learned that Germany had just declared war on Russia, the act that would touch off what came to be called the Great War (World War I). Thunderstruck, Carnegie felt obliged to add a passage reversing the cheerful tone of his memoir: "What a change!" he wrote. "The world convulsed

CARNEGIE, THE PEACEMAKER
Andrew Carnegie hoped that his association with English and German leaders would help persuade them to a policy of peace. Here Carnegie (left) displays his ebullient confidence in 1913 as he takes the arm of British diplomat Lord Resdale to stroll near the headquarters of the Carnegie Endowment for International Peace in Washington. In turn, Liberal leaders in England, like Resdale, and the kaiser in Germany hoped the richest man in the world would underwrite efforts to keep the increasingly dangerous armed standoff between their nations from exploding into war. As Carnegie and his allies saw it, reason and humaneness must transcend each separate national interest. The rulers of nation states, however, had doubts about how such a reversal of policy as usual could take place and fears about the weakness that would follow.
Library of Congress.

by war as never before! Men slaying each other like wild beasts."

After that day, Carnegie was unable to write a single word more in his memoir. Nor could he any longer rely on his lifelong motto: "All is well since all grows better." Like many others who had be-

lieved that the Western world had become rational and humane, Carnegie lost his grip on old attachments and hopes. He left Skibo in September on the *Mauretania*, zigzagging its way anxiously through German submarines, and never returned to Europe. Pacifist ideals and religious injunctions against violence had failed, and Carnegie retreated to an America faced with the new dilemma of how to understand why the masses, who had been counted on to favor peace, had turned ferociously to cheer for war.

Carnegie also needed a new hero to take the place of the discredited Kaiser Wilhelm II. At the end of his memoir addendum, he rallied enough to express a vague hope: "In recent days I see another ruler coming forward upon the world stage, who may prove himself the immortal one. . . . Nothing is impossible to genius! Watch President Wilson! He has Scotch blood in his veins."

At that moment, however, Wilson was feeling all too mortal and helpless. He was sunk in a grieving vigil at the bedside of his dying wife, Ellen, and it was there that he learned the nations of Europe were mobilizing their forces against one another. The tragedy of war was thus magnified for Wilson by his own tragedy. When Ellen's death and the end of peace finally struck on the same day, Wilson seemed to his White House physician a "man with his heart torn out."

Hardening himself to grief and disillusionment, as Carnegie and other peace idealists also struggled to do, Wilson formulated a national response to the war in Europe. He never had any doubt that the only virtuous course was absolute neutrality. Even though his sympathies were with Great Britain and France, Wilson concluded that blame for the war did not lie entirely with Germany. Moreover, he believed that the United States had no vital stake in a European power struggle. Wilson agreed with the American ambassador in London, who declared, "Again and ever I thank heaven for the Atlantic Ocean." Wilson also had to consider that the United States was a nation of immigrants, millions of whom had only recently come from countries on both sides of the war. As Wilson told the German ambassador, "We definitely have to be neutral, since otherwise our mixed populations would wage war on each other."

There was another idealistic reason to stay out of the European struggle. As Wilson explained less than two weeks after the war started, the United States could offer "impartial mediation" and show the world the way to reconciliation and a healing peace. To make the most of this opportunity for service, Wilson told the American people, they must restrain their tendency to favor one side or the other and remain "impartial in thought as well as action."

Most Americans agreed with Wilson that the country should stay neutral, but they were less eager to use that neutrality to broker a peace. Essentially, the nation tried to distance itself from the conflict and just go about its business. Americans showed less interest in the spectacular explosion of European warfare in August 1914 than in the grand opening of the Panama Canal that same month. But events were to prove that the Atlantic was no moat. Trade and travel webbed the modern world and eventually entangled the United States in the war's violence and the arguments advanced to justify it. Step by step, Europe's troubles became America's, and the forces that undermined Europeans' self-confident belief in progress also ended America's Progressive Era. After nearly three years of trying to steer a neutral course, Woodrow Wilson went before Congress on April 2, 1917, to ask for a declaration of war against Germany. America's participation would be a crusade to make the Great War the war to end all wars, Wilson vowed. And America's goodness and disinterestedness would ensure a just peace "to make the world safe for democracy."

The conflict in which America finally came to have a vital stake was rightly named the Great War by the contemporaries who witnessed it, for it engendered great destruction and drastically altered the structure of international order. War stretched across continents, and nations measured their casualties in the millions. When peace arrived in 1919, both the victors and the vanquished were not merely exhausted but decimated.

America's experience was exceptional. At home, war and prosperity went hand in hand. But America paid a price as citizens and the government cracked down on dissent and demanded conformity. "Over there," as Americans called the war theater in Europe, the nation lost 112,000 soldiers, and the performance of U.S. troops on the battlefields affected the outcome of the war. In the peace negotiations that followed the armistice, Woodrow Wilson played a principal role, but the results did not confirm the president's impossible vision of himself as personal savior of the world. He had promised more than anyone could deliver, and the nation turned bitter and disillusioned.

In December 1919, Wilson's personal friend and chief foreign policy adviser, Colonel Edward House, summarized the nation's ordeal: "We came near doing a great thing in a great way, but Fate ordained otherwise and while something may still be done, it will be done in a small way and in a way full of humiliation for those who wished to see the United States lead in a new world movement."

Woodrow Wilson and the World

Shortly after winning election to the presidency in 1912, Woodrow Wilson confided to a friend: "It would be an irony of fate if my administration had to deal chiefly with foreign affairs." Indeed, Wilson had based his life and career on local attachments. He had never shown an interest in venturing far from home and had traveled abroad only on brief vacations. As president of Princeton University and then governor of New Jersey, he had remained rooted in domestic concerns. During his campaign for the presidency, Wilson had argued passionately for domestic reform, referring only rarely to foreign affairs.

But Wilson could not avoid the world. The Wilsonian foreign policy that emerged in 1913–1914 reflected his conviction that the United States should set the example in international affairs by championing the principles of liberal democracy: individual liberty, the right of national self-determination, peaceful free trade, and political democracy. Support for these principles meant opposing imperialism, large armed forces, and trade barriers. Above all, it meant righteous behavior. "We dare not turn from the principle that morality and not expediency is the thing that must guide us," Wilson announced loftily.

Taming the Americas

The rising tide of militarism, nationalism, and violence severely tested Wilson's principles. When he

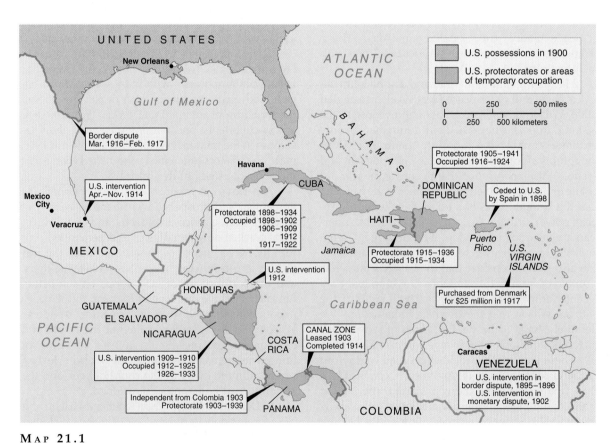

MAP 21.1
U.S. Involvement in Latin America and the Caribbean, 1895–1941
Victory against Spain in 1898 made Puerto Rico an American possession and Cuba a protectorate. America also gained control over the Panama Canal and was quick to protect expanding economic interests with military force to make sure that stable, if not necessarily democratic, governments prevailed.

came to office, Wilson sought to distinguish his foreign policy from that of his Republican predecessors. To Wilson, Theodore Roosevelt's "big stick" smacked of the blatant use of military force, and William Howard Taft's "dollar diplomacy" appeared to be a similarly crude flexing of economic muscle. Seeking a morally superior alternative, Wilson appointed William Jennings Bryan as secretary of state. A pacifist on religious grounds, Bryan immediately turned his attention to making agreements with thirty nations for the peaceful settlement of disputes.

But Wilson and Bryan, like Roosevelt and Taft, also believed that the Monroe Doctrine gave the United States special rights and responsibilities in the Western Hemisphere. The Wilson administration had the dubious goal of encouraging justice and democracy in the Western Hemisphere while protecting and expanding American investments there. Wilson thus accepted the 1912 occupation of Nicaragua by U.S. marines to thwart a radical revolution that threatened American property. In 1915, he sent marines into Haiti to quell lawlessness and to protect American interests, and in 1916 followed a similar course in the Dominican Republic. So firm was Wilson's view of American dominance in the hemisphere that when the Central American court of justice issued a ruling against American presence as a violation of national sovereignty, he simply ignored it (Map 21.1).

The Wilson administration had the dubious goal of encouraging justice and democracy in the Western Hemisphere while protecting and expanding American investments there.

Wilson's most serious and controversial involvement in Latin America came in Mexico. Just weeks before Wilson was elected, General Victoriano Huerta seized power by violent means. Most European nations promptly recognized Huerta as the new president, but Wilson balked, declaring that he would not support a "government of butchers." In April 1914, Huerta's refusal to apologize for briefly detaining American sailors in Tampico prompted Wilson to declare that it was time "to teach the South American republics to elect good men!" The president ordered eight hundred marines to seize the port of Veracruz and prevent the unloading of a large shipment of arms for Huerta, who was by then involved in a civil war of his own. After brief resistance, Huerta fled to Spain, and the United States welcomed a more compliant government.

Wilson was not able to subdue Mexico that easily, however. A rebellion erupted among desperately poor farmers who believed that the new government, aided by American business interests, had betrayed the revolution's promise to help the common people. Their leader, Francisco "Pancho" Villa, had instilled in his followers a brutal willingness to strike back at their oppressors. In January 1916, Villa's soldiers seized a trainload of gold from an American-owned mine deep within Mexico and killed the seventeen American engineers who were carrying the gold to Texas. Another band of Villa's men crossed the border on March 9 for a predawn raid on Columbus, New Mexico, that cost several lives and left the town in flames. Wilson promptly dispatched twelve thousand troops, led by General John J. Pershing, who years earlier had chased the Apache chief Geronimo through the same Mexican desert and now

U.S. Intervention in Mexico, 1916–1917

hoped that his second foray might lead to the annexation of Mexico by the United States. Instead, after a futile chase of the wily Villa, Pershing was recalled by Wilson in January of 1917 so that he might prepare the army for the possibility of fighting in the Great War. As American attention shifted toward Europe, the Mexican revolution was left to rage on until 1920, ending only after the death of about two million people, one out of every eight Mexicans.

The European Crisis

Early in the twentieth century, European leaders often proclaimed proudly that they had done away with war. But the many years of peace enjoyed by the great powers before 1914 masked profound tensions caused by nationalist desires and imperial

"Pancho" Villa and General Pershing *Here in 1914, Mexican revolutionary Francisco "Pancho" Villa (center) and American general John J. Pershing (right) pose genially as allies in the struggle to overthrow the dictatorial ruler of Mexico, Victoriano Huerta. Soon afterward Villa and Pershing would be adversaries. After a raid by Villa across the New Mexico border in 1915 to punish Americans for aiding Villa's revolutionary rivals, Pershing pursued Villa into Mexico.* Corbis-Bettmann.

rivalries. The consolidation of the German and Italian states into unified nations and the similar ambition of Russia to create a "Pan-Slavic" union initiated new rivalries throughout Europe. As the conviction spread that colonial possessions were a mark of national greatness, competition expanded onto the world stage. In particular, Germany's efforts, under Kaiser Wilhelm II, to create an empire abroad, to build industrial muscle at home, and to challenge Britain's domination of the sea threatened the balance of power in Europe and stimulated competition among nations.

Within this explosive atmosphere, a complex web of military and diplomatic alliances grew. By 1914, Germany, Austria-Hungary, and Italy (the Triple Alliance) stood opposed to Great Britain, France, and Russia (the Triple Entente). In their effort to prevent war through a balance of power, the nations of Europe had actually magnified the possibility of conflict by creating national borders that were in effect trip wires between two heavily armed power blocs (Map 21.2).

The fatal sequence started in southeastern Europe, in the Balkans. On June 28, 1914, a Bosnian Serb terrorist demonstrated Serbia's persistent desire to extend its territory to the Adriatic Sea by killing Archduke Franz Ferdinand of Austria as he toured the Bosnian coastal city of Sarajevo, then

part of the Austro-Hungarian Empire. Austria-Hungary, holding Serbia to account for the assassination, declared war on that nation on July 28. The alliance system then swung into action. Russia, determined to protect its Slavic kin, announced that it would back the Serbs. Germany, feeling compelled to support Austria-Hungary, then declared war on Russia and on France. In response, Great Britain, upholding its pact with France, declared war on Germany. The conflict became a world war when Japan, seeing an opportunity to rid itself of competition in China, joined the Allied cause against Germany.

Recognizing how terrible the situation had become for the civilization he had known, England's foreign secretary, Edward Grey, said: "The lamps are going out all over Europe. We shall not see them lit again in our lifetime." But with his usual grave dignity, Grey assured Parliament that Great Britain would rally to the cause of war when it "realizes what is at stake, what the real issues are." The next day, the German imperial chancellor, Theobald von Bethmann Hollweg, insisted that Germany had grown strong "in the works of peace" and that "only in defense of a just cause shall our sword fly from its scabbard." But beyond vague assertions from each side that aggression must be halted and honor upheld, little was done to define "just cause."

MAP 21.2

European Alliances after the Outbreak of World War I
With Germany and the Austro-Hungarian Empire wedged between their Entente rivals, and all parties fully armed, Europe was poised for war when the Archduke Franz Ferdinand of Austria was assassinated in Sarajevo in July 1914.

Central Powers (Triple Alliance, except Italy, and allies)

Allied Powers (Triple Entente and allies)

Neutral nations

The Ordeal of Neutrality

The concept of neutrality was fuzzy in international law, but the United States had traditionally insisted on the broadest possible definition. In the American view, "free ships made free goods"; that is, neutral nations had the right to trade freely with all nations at war, to send their ships safely through the open seas, and to demand the safe passage of their citizens on the merchant and passenger ships of all belligerents. More was involved in upholding neutral rights than principle. The year before Europe went to war, the American economy had started to slide into a recession that threatened to rival the depression of the 1890s. American trade with Europe offered hope of ending hardship at home; a disruption of European trade would add greatly to the distress.

Great Britain was the first to step on America's neutral rights. Britain's powerful fleet controlled the seas, and it quickly set up a blockade against Germany. The United States vigorously protested British action, but Britain refused to give up its naval advantage. In the fall of 1914, the Wilson administration reluctantly accepted the British blockade, thus indicating the widespread sympathy for Britain within the State Department and beginning the fateful process of alienation from Germany. But the huge volume of war-related trade that sprang up between the United States and Britain was enough to pull the American economy out of its prewar slump. Between 1914 and the spring of 1917, exports to Britain escalated by some 300 percent, while trade with Germany and its allies was reduced to the vanishing point.

Germany retaliated with a submarine blockade. This new form of combat by *Unterseebooten,* or U-boats, posed a disturbing threat to the traditional rules of war. Unlike surface warships that could harmlessly confiscate freighters or prevent them from entering a war zone, submarines relied on surprising and sinking their quarry. And once they sank a ship, the tiny, cramped U-boats could not possibly pick up the survivors. To much of the world, submarine warfare violated notions of how a "civilized" nation should behave. Nevertheless, in

February 1915, the German high command declared the waters around Britain a war zone and warned that any ship in the area would be subject to attack.

Woodrow Wilson responded harshly, declaring that the United States would regard the loss of an American ship or the loss of American lives on a belligerent ship as "a flagrant violation of neutral rights" and would hold Germany to "strict accountability." What "strict accountability" meant was still unclear when Wilson received the shocking news of the sinking of the British liner *Lusitania* off the coast of Ireland on May 7, 1915, with the loss of 1,198 lives, including 128 Americans.

American newspapers appeared with drawings of drowning women and children, and some editorial writers called for war. Most Americans, however, did not want to break relations with Germany. Some pointed out that the German embassy had warned prospective passengers that the *Lusitania* carried millions of rounds of ammunition and so was a legitimate target. Secretary of State Bryan, speaking for the peace movement within the administration, said that a ship carrying war materiel "should not rely on passengers to protect her from attack—it would be like putting women and children in front of an army." He argued that Wilson should instead warn American citizens using ships of belligerent countries that they traveled at their own risk.

Sinking of the *Lusitania*, 1915

Wilson sought a middle course that would retain his commitment to peace and neutrality without condoning German attacks on passenger ships. On May 10, he distanced himself from the interventionists by declaring that "there is such a thing as a man being too proud to fight," for which former president Theodore Roosevelt raged at him for being a "flub dub and mollycoddle" who should be too proud *not* to fight. But Wilson also rejected Bryan's position. Any further destruction of ships, Wilson warned, would be regarded as "deliberately unfriendly" and might lead the United States to

break diplomatic relations with Germany. Wilson's insistence that Americans had the right to travel unharmed made Bryan realize that his pacifist hopes were doomed. When the secretary of state resigned, Wilson quickly replaced him with Robert Lansing, a veteran State Department officer and a strong advocate of the Allied cause.

For a while after the *Lusitania* crisis, the tension subsided. Germany, anxious not to provoke the United States, apologized for civilian deaths and offered an indemnity. After the sinking of the English steamer *Sussex* in 1916, at the cost of two more American lives, the German government quickly acted to head off war by promising no more submarine attacks without warning and without provisions for the safety of civilians. Observers hailed the pledge as a victory for Wilson's policy of careful negotiation between the poles of Bryan's pacifism and Roosevelt's bellicosity.

Wilson's efforts for peace served him well in his bid for reelection in 1916. Still, controversies over neutrality, intervention in Mexico, and the government's role in regulating the economy made Wilson's chances uncertain. Unlike the situation in 1912, Wilson faced a united Republican challenge after Theodore Roosevelt declined to run for the Progressive Party. Wilson's opponent was the able associate justice of the Supreme Court Charles Evans Hughes, former governor of New York. The Democratic Party ran Wilson under the slogan "He kept us out of war," but Wilson shied away from the claim, protesting that "they talk of me as though I were a god. Any little German lieutenant can push us into the war at any time by some calculated outrage." Wilson did not disagree, however, when the Democrats argued that the Republican candidate was more likely to lead the nation into war. Ultimately, Wilson's case for neutrality appealed to the majority in favor of peace. Wilson won, but by only 600,000 popular and 23 electoral votes, leaving in doubt whether he spoke for a unified nation in foreign policy.

The United States Enters the War

In the end, the determination by the warring sides to achieve peace on their own terms scuttled any chance for a negotiated peace. The Germans refused to specify their war aims, and the Allies made mediation difficult by announcing aims that would have broken up the Austro-Hungarian Empire and required the Germans to pay damages for the war.

In early January 1917, the German military high command persuaded the kaiser that the country could no longer afford to allow neutral shipping to reach Great Britain while the enemy blockade threatened to starve Germany. Germany would resume unrestricted submarine warfare at the end of the month and sink without warning any ship found in the waters off Great Britain. The German military understood that it risked war with the United States but gambled that Germany would achieve a quick military victory before the United States could bring its armed might to bear.

Most of Wilson's advisers joined Theodore Roosevelt in demanding a declaration of war, but Wilson, still hoping for a peaceful way out, would only sever diplomatic relations with Germany. Then on February 25, 1917, British authorities informed Wilson of a secret telegram sent by the German foreign secretary, Arthur Zimmermann, to the German minister in Mexico. It promised that in the event of war between Germany and the United States, Germany would see that Mexico regained the territories in the Southwest it had lost in the Mexican War if Mexico would declare war against the United States. Wilson angrily responded to the Zimmermann telegram by asking Congress to approve a policy of "armed neutrality" that would allow merchant ships to fight back against any attackers. It was this wicked attempt to penetrate the Western Hemisphere, Wilson confided, that finally con-

SINKING OF THE LUSITANIA *Military prowess and civilian tragedy came together with shocking effect in the sinking of the British passenger liner* **Lusitania** *on May 7, 1915. Captain Walter Schwieger, commander of the German submarine U-20, who spotted the ship off the coast of Ireland, skillfully sank the great liner with a single torpedo. After watching the chaos that ensued, in which more than twelve hundred people lost their lives, he remembered the scene as the most awful one he had ever witnessed. For Americans, the fate of the* **Lusitania** *was crucial in turning public sentiment against Germany. This poster by Fred Spear captured the outrage people felt at the loss of many women and almost one hundred children. Nearly two years before the United States entered the war, posters like this urged Americans to enlist as preparation for the day when they must surely save civilization from German barbarism.* Corbis; Library of Congress.

WAR PROTEST IN SONG
The most popular antiwar song came from Tin Pan Alley just after the outbreak of the Great War. "I Didn't Raise My Boy to Be a Soldier" took the pacifist line that all who perish in war will have "died in vain." The cover image of mother and child clinging to each other in terror was widely acceptable until Americans began losing their lives on ships torpedoed by the Germans. Then mama's boy had to be transformed into a knight errant sent by proud parents to rescue Europe from its wicked ways. The clash between views of war as a failure of civilization and war as a crusade to save civilization was too great to be reconciled and continued to divide the nation's judgment after victory in 1918.
Collection of Colonel Stuart S. Corning Jr./Picture Research Consultants, Inc.

vinced him that the war was, indeed, a defense of democracy against autocratic German aggression.

In the end, the determination by the warring sides to achieve peace on their own terms scuttled any chance for a negotiated peace.

In mid-March, German submarines sank five American vessels in the sea lanes to Britain. After agonizing over the probable consequences, the pres-ident prevailed on Congress to issue a declaration of war on April 6. No longer too proud to fight, Wilson accused Germany of "warfare against mankind." But he insisted that the destruction of Germany was not the U.S. goal. Instead, the United States fought to make the world "safe for democracy" and to "vindicate the principles of peace and justice" in which a reconstructed Germany would find a democratic place.

Wilson did not overlook the tragic difference between those lofty aims and the brutal means chosen to achieve them. He spoke despairingly to a friend just prior to his appearance before Congress:

"Once lead this people into war, and they'll forget there ever was such a thing as tolerance. To fight you must be brutal and ruthless, and the spirit of ruthless brutality will infect Congress, the courts, the policeman on the beat, the man in the street."

The Crusade for Democracy

Despite Wilson's misgivings, progressives hoped that war would improve the quality of American life as well as free Europe from its bondage to tyranny and militarism. The American Expeditionary Force (AEF) that eventually carried two million troops to Europe, by far the largest military venture the United States had ever undertaken on foreign soil, was trained to be morally straight and knowledgeable about the civilization it was to save. Progressive enthusiasm also powered the mobilization of industrial and agricultural production. Moreover, labor shortages caused by workers leaving the labor force for military service provided new opportunities in the booming wartime economy. Where once they had been excluded, African Americans and women found work and also gained new respect and recognition for their wartime endeavors.

To instill loyalty in a public whose ancestry was rooted in all the belligerent nations, Wilson supported indoctrination in the schools, set up a government agent to promote official propaganda, and sponsored parades, rallies, films, and other forms of patriotic expression. But with commitment to patriotism also went suppression of dissent. The government launched a harsh assault on civil liberties. In addition, mobs attacked those whom they considered disloyal. Increasingly, attachment to the war stressed emotion rather than reason, and, as Wilson predicted, the progressive ideals of rational progress and free expression suffered grievous loss as the nation undertook its crusade for democracy.

The Call to Arms

When the United States entered the war in April 1917, the nation was woefully unprepared, even as it had become clear that the Allies could win only with massive and swift American involvement. War-weary Britain and France were virtually exhausted after almost three years of conflict. Hundreds of thousands of their soldiers had perished in the trenches; morale and food supplies were dangerously low. Russia was in turmoil: A democratic revolution had forced Czar Nicholas II's abdication in March 1917, and eight months later the Bolshevik Revolution removed Russia from the war. To meet the demand for fighting men, food, and war materiel, the United States would have to mobilize not only an army but its economy as well.

On May 18, 1917, Wilson signed a sweeping Selective Service Act, authorizing a draft of all young men into the armed forces. Conscription soon transformed a tiny volunteer armed force of 80,000 men, spread thinly around the United States and in outposts from the Caribbean to China, into a vast army and navy. Although almost 350,000 inductees either failed to report or claimed conscientious objector status, the draft boards eventually inducted 2.8 million men into the armed services, in addition to the 2 million who volunteered.

Eventually, almost half of the 4.8 million U.S. armed forces served in Europe. In the training camps that transformed raw recruits into fighting men, medical examinations, along with recently developed sociological and psychological techniques, took the measure of American youth. The shocking news that almost 30 percent of those drafted were rejected on physical grounds acted as a stimulus to the public health and physical education movements. Secretary of War Newton D. Baker, whose outlook had been shaped by reform crusades as mayor of Cleveland, created a Commission on Training Camp Activities staffed by YMCA workers and veterans of the settlement house and playground movements. They merged military training with games, singing, and college extension courses. The Military Draft Act of 1917 prohibited prostitution and alcohol near training camps. Never before had there been such armed encampments, which Baker described in full progressive fervor as "national universities—training schools to which the flower of American youth is being sent" to fit them with an "invisible armor" of education, comradeship, and moral fitness.

Wilson's selection of General John J. Pershing to command the new American Expeditionary Force recognized the need for hard professionalism in the lead, not the sort of romantic patriotism that had given amateurs like Theodore Roosevelt the chance to command combat troops in the Spanish-American War. Pershing had graduated from West Point in the 1880s and then seen combat in the Indian wars on the American plains and against the

Spanish in Cuba, where his command of black troops had earned him the nickname "Black Jack." Pershing's impeccable military bearing and professional standing gave promise that he would carry out his duties in the cool, efficient way required of modern war on a vast scale. His stoic ability to face adversity had hardened to steel when, in the midst of chasing Villa's men in Mexico, he was informed that his wife and daughters had perished in a fire.

When Pershing and the wide-eyed troops of the AEF marched through Paris on the Fourth of July 1917, just a week after the first troopship landed, a grateful populace showered them with flowers. At the statue of the hero who symbolized France's aid to the American Revolution, an officer stepped out and proclaimed in an inspired phrase that summed up the spirit of the occasion, "Lafayette, we are here!"

The Progressive Stake in the War

The idea of the war as an agent of social improvement fanned the old zeal and earnestness of the progressive movement. In particular, the war captivated progressives who were believers in strong government and who had been lukewarm about Wilson's cautious New Freedom, his campaign slogan from 1912 that stood for limitations on big business. The Wilson administration realized that Washington would have to assert greater control to mobilize the nation's resources and to avoid chaos. To oversee the transformation of the economy, the administration established a multitude of new federal war agencies to deal with specific needs.

The War Industries Board (WIB), created to direct and stimulate industrial production, was fortunate in the choice of Bernard Baruch to head it. At once a wealthy southern gentleman, a Jewish Wall Street stockbroker, and a reform Democrat, Baruch could speak to many constituencies. Shrewdly bullying and wheedling scientists, industrialists, public administrators, and public relations experts into efficient teams, he oversaw production of everything from boots to bullets and thus made the American soldier the most fully equipped in the world. Only in the vital area of weaponry did the quality of American equipment lag behind that of the Europeans who had long fielded large armies.

Herbert Hoover, a self-made millionaire engineer, headed the Food Administration. Sober and tireless, he led remarkably successful "Hooverizing" campaigns for "wheatless" Mondays, "meat-less" Tuesdays, and other means of conserving resources. Guaranteed high prices for wheat and other staples, the American heartland not only supplied the needs of U.S. citizens and armed forces but also became the breadbasket of America's allies. Even the First Family, including Wilson's new wife, Edith Galt, did its part with a White House "victory garden" and sheep on the White House lawn in place of the gardeners, who had moved on to new work in the war effort.

> *The idea of the war as an agent of social improvement fanned the old zeal and earnestness of the progressive movement.*

Washington soon bristled with hastily created agencies charged with managing the war effort. The Railroads' War Board directed railroad traffic, the Fuel Administration coordinated the coal industry and other fuel suppliers, the Shipping Board organized the merchant marine, and the National War Labor Policies Board resolved labor disputes. The administration gave progressives reason to believe that the new agencies would mediate between business and government and encourage harmony in the public interest. Buoyed by these developments, influential voices like those of philosopher-educator John Dewey and journalist-critic Walter Lippmann argued for public support of the war as a means of progressive reform at home and abroad. Industrial leaders were also cheered that, in achieving feats of production and efficiency, wartime agencies helped corporate profits triple.

To raise the $33 billion it cost to wage the war (more than the federal government's total expenses from 1789 to 1917), imaginative fund-raising strategies were needed as well. Secretary of the Treasury William G. McAdoo, who happened to be Wilson's son-in-law, became the principal cheerleader for the purchase of war bonds, called Liberty Bonds.

Reformers also had cause to celebrate the effect of the war on the labor front. Full mobilization meant high prices for farmers and plentiful jobs in the new war industries (Figure 21.1). Aware that increased industrial production required peaceful labor relations and the avoidance of strikes, the National War Labor Policies Board and other agencies enacted the eight-hour day, a living minimum

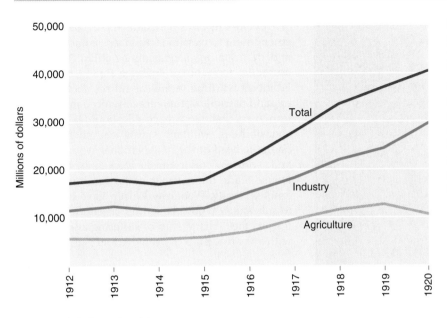

FIGURE **21.1**

Industrial Wages, 1912–1920
With help from unions and Progressive reformers, wage workers gradually improved their economic condition. The entry of millions of young men into the armed forces caused labor shortages and led to a rapid surge in wages.

Agriculture: cash receipts.
Industry: includes mining, electric power, manufacturing, construction, and communications.

wage, and collective bargaining rights in industries that had long resisted them. Wages rose sharply during the war, and the American Federation of Labor saw its membership soar from 2.7 million to more than 5 million. After long insisting that health was a private matter, Congress bowed to the patriotic cause of providing death and disability insurance for the armed forces.

The war also provided a huge boost to the stalled moral crusade to ban alcohol. Before the war, prohibitionists had campaigned fervently for a constitutional amendment to ban the manufacture and sale of alcoholic beverages, and by 1917, nineteen states had gone dry. Liquor's opponents could now cite the war as a reason for national prohibition, which would make the cause of democracy powerful and pure. At the same time, shutting down the distilleries would save millions of bushels of grain that could feed the United States and its allies. Prohibitionists also claimed that closing breweries with German names like Schlitz, Pabst, and Anheuser-Busch would deal a blow to Kaiser Wilhelm II and the German cause. Swept along by these arguments, Congress passed the Eighteenth Amendment, which banned the manufacture, transportation, and sale of alcohol, in December 1917; after swift ratification by all the states, the amendment went into effect on January 1, 1920.

The Advance to Woman Suffrage

The war also presented new opportunities for women. More than twenty thousand women served with the armed forces, a large number of them as nurses in France. In the private sector, long-standing barriers against hiring women fell when millions of working men became soldiers and few new immigrant workers found safe passage across the Atlantic. The new Women's Bureau of the Department of Labor along with the Women's Trade Union League (WTUL) helped open jobs to women, often against the opposition of the major trade organization, the American Federation of Labor (AFL). For the first time, women in sizable numbers found work with the railroads and in defense plants as welders and heavy machine operators. Some gained entry to labor unions, whose members usually earned far higher wages than nonunion workers. "This is the women's age," exulted Margaret Dreier Robins, president of the WTUL. "At last . . . women are coming into the labor and festival of life on equal terms with men."

The war effort spurred women to victory in the political arena as well. Since the Seneca Falls convention of 1848, where women voiced their first formal demand for the ballot, the struggle for woman suffrage had inched forward. Using a state-by-state approach, suffragists had achieved success in

PICKETING THE WHITE HOUSE FOR THE VOTE
Facing the growing clamor for women's right to vote, Woodrow Wilson remarked that he could neither fault the case women made nor bring himself to accept it. Here Mrs. William L. Colt stands as one of many picketers at the White House gate bringing the faultless case to the president's own home. Under such direct pressure and in recognition of women's service in the defense industry and near the battlefields as nurses and Red Cross workers, Wilson finally pledged himself to support the Suffrage Amendment. As a southern gentleman who admired women as tamers of men's aggressive tendencies, Wilson also could hope that women's moderating influence would help achieve his aim that the Great War be the war to end all wars.
Corbis.

Wyoming in 1890 and in several other western states in the following years, but elsewhere they met defeat. In New York, for example, suffragists waged a massive door-to-door referendum campaign in 1915 for an amendment to the state constitution, only to have the male electorate reject woman suffrage resoundingly. Two years later, suffragists met a similar fate in Ohio (Map 21.3).

By linking their crusade for a constitutional amendment to wartime emphasis on national unity and by adopting increasingly militant tactics, the crusaders for woman suffrage finally triumphed. Women's wartime service as nurses, factory workers, and patriotic volunteers convinced many American men that women could shoulder public responsibilities. Militant suffragists, such as Alice Paul, the head of the new National Woman's Party, and women continuously picketing the White House made the suffrage campaign impossible to ignore. Finally, Woodrow Wilson gave his support to suffrage. It would be wrong, he conceded, not to reward the "partnership of suffering and sacrifice" with a "partnership of privilege and right." In 1919,

WORLD WAR I RED CROSS WORKER
An American Red Cross worker gives water to a badly wounded British soldier on a French railway platform in May 1918. More than twenty thousand women served with the armed forces, many of them as nurses in France.
National Archives.

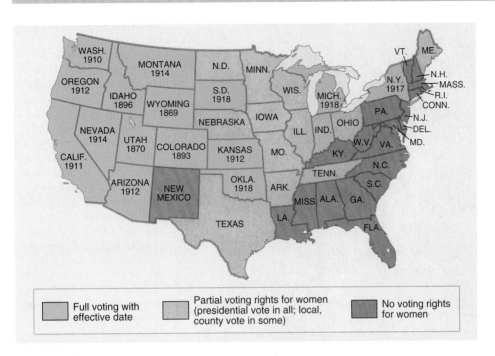

MAP 21.3

Women's Voting Rights before the Nineteenth Amendment
*The long campaign for women's voting rights reversed the pioneer epic—rolling east-
ward from its first successes in the new democratic openness of the West toward the
entrenched, male-dominated public life of the Northeast and the South.*

READING THE MAP: What was the first state to grant woman suffrage? How many states
extended full voting rights to women before the World War I years (1914–1918)? During
World War I?
CONNECTIONS: Suffragists redirected their focus during World War I. What strategies did
they use during the war? In which states was the struggle for woman suffrage fiercest,
and why?

www.bedfordstmartins.com/tap   SEE THE ONLINE STUDY GUIDE for more help in analyzing
this map.

Congress passed the Nineteenth Amendment,
granting women the vote, and by 1920 it had been
ratified by the required two-thirds of the states.
Looking back on the struggle, two suffrage leaders
remarked: "How much time and patience, how
much work, energy and aspiration, how much faith,
how much hope, how much despair went into it."

The "Great Migration" of African Americans

In 1900, thirty-five years after emancipation, African
Americans had made little progress toward achieving full citizenship. Nine of every ten African Amer-

icans were Southerners, and disfranchisement, segregation, and violence dominated their lives. The
majority of black men still toiled in agriculture, either mired in tenancy or working for wages of sixty
cents a day. Black women worked in the homes of
whites as domestics for $2 or less a week. Racial vi-
olence descended on anyone whites considered
"uppity." "If we own a good farm or horse, or cow,
or bird-dog, or yoke of oxen," a black Mississippian
observed in 1913, "we are harassed until we are
bound to sell, give away, or run away, before we can
have any peace in our lives."

The First World War provided African Americans with the opportunity to escape the South's

AFRICAN AMERICANS MIGRATE NORTH
These newcomers to a northern city in 1912 pose in their best dress on the threshold of a changed life. Several factors combined to prompt almost four and a half million African Americans to leave the South by midcentury. To the burden of racism was added the steady erosion of opportunities to make a living. In the 1920s, many rural blacks lost work when a boll weevil invasion reduced the cotton crop drastically. Subsequently, mechanization and government programs to support crop prices by reducing acreage drove many more people off the land.
Schomburg Center for Research in Black Culture, New York Public Library.

cotton fields and kitchens. Blacks who were once welcome in the urban North only in personal service occupations now found work as unskilled and semiskilled industrial workers. Young black men, who made up the bulk of the migrants, found jobs in steel mills, shipyards, munitions plants, railroad yards, and mines. From 1915 to 1920, half a million blacks (approximately 10 percent of the South's black population) boarded trains bound for Philadelphia, Detroit, Cleveland, Chicago, St. Louis, and other industrial cities.

Blacks who joined the "great migration" were not just moving north. They were fleeing the South. Whole churches, almost entire communities, sometimes transplanted themselves to northern cities. By 1930, for example, Chicago claimed nearly forty thousand black Mississippians, almost as many as Jackson, Meridian, and Greenville combined. One man, writing to a church congregation he'd left behind, announced proudly that he had recently been elevated to "first assistant to the head carpenter": "I should have been here twenty years ago. I just begin to feel like a man. It's a great deal of pleasure in knowing that you got some privileges. My chil-

dren are going to the same school with the whites and I don't have to [h]umble to no one. I have registered—will vote the next election and there ain't any 'yes sir'—it's all yes and no and Sam and Bill."

But the North was not all milk and honey. Whites fearful of losing jobs and status lashed out against the latest immigrants. In 1918, the nation witnessed ninety-six lynchings of blacks, some of them veterans still wearing their military uniforms. Race riots ripped two dozen northern cities. One of the worst occurred on a hot July night in 1917 in East St. Louis, Illinois. A mob of whites invaded a section of the city crowded with blacks who had been recruited to help break a strike; the rioters killed at least thirty-nine people and left most of the black district in flames.

African Americans in the military also experienced racial violence. The most disastrous episode occurred in August 1917 when a group of armed black soldiers went to Houston, Texas, to avenge incidents of harassment by the police. In the clash that followed, thirteen whites, including several policemen, and one black soldier were killed. With vengeful swiftness that denied any appeal to the War Department, thirteen of the black soldiers were hanged and forty-one others sentenced to life imprisonment. Black leaders charged grimly that the incident demonstrated the tragic shortcomings of America's crusade for democracy. (See "Historical Question," page 786.)

The Struggle over National Purpose

From the moment war broke out in Europe in 1914, Wilson's foreign policy became a lightning rod for interventionists and noninterventionists alike. When Wilson finally did commit the nation to war, most peace advocates rallied around the flag. The Carnegie Endowment for International Peace, for example, adopted new stationery with the heading "Peace through Victory" and issued a resolution saying that "the most effectual means of promoting peace is to prosecute the war against the Imperial German Government." In a similar shift of view, several business and civic leaders who had been prewar advocates of peaceful means of settling disputes created the League to Enforce Peace in support of Wilson's insistence that military force had become the only means to peaceful ends.

Against the tide of that conversion from pacifism to patriotism, a handful of new groups took up the cause of peace. Soon after the guns began booming in 1914, a group of professional women, led by settlement house leader Jane Addams and economics professor Emily Greene Balch, convened to resist what Addams described as "the pathetic belief in the regenerative results of war." The Women's Peace Party that emerged in 1915 and its foreign affiliates in the Women's International League for Peace and Freedom (WILPF) led the struggle to persuade governments to negotiate peace and spare dissenters from harsh punishment. It was discouraging, unpopular work. Participants were routinely labeled cowards and traitors, their efforts crushed by the steamroller of war enthusiasm.

Wilson's major strategy for fending off criticism of the war was to stir up patriotism with fervent flag-waving. In 1917, the president created the Committee on Public Information (CPI) under the direction of George Creel, a progressive journalist who thumped for the war like a cheerleader at the big game. The eclipse of peace by war was symbolized by the willingness of the Carnegie Endowment to let Creel's propagandists take over its building in Washington. From that imposing headquarters, Creel sent "Four-Minute Men," a squad of seventy-five thousand volunteers, around the country to give brief pep talks and distribute millions of press releases that described successes on the battlefields and in the factories. But information and education slid easily into propaganda. The CPI created a stream of posters, pamphlets, and cartoons

THE LIBERTY LOAN CHOIR
In promoting the war as a moral crusade, religion and patriotism often fused in the spirit of the popular hymn "Onward Christian Soldiers." On the steps of New York's City Hall in April 1918, the Liberty Loan Choir add their voices to the chorus of opera singers, movie stars, and political celebrities who were used throughout the war to rally the public to buy bonds to finance the war.
NA, US Army Signal Corps, AU, 1651, Paul Thompson.

What Did the War Mean to African Americans?

WHEN THE UNITED STATES ENTERED the First World War, some black leaders remembered the crucial role of African American soldiers in the Civil War. They rejoiced that military service would again offer blacks a chance to prove their worth. Robert Moton, president of the nation's foremost black college, Tuskegee Institute, recollected clearly when that thought had come to him. He was sitting in the midst of "dignified bankers [and] merchants" gathered in the Waldorf-Astoria Hotel in New York City to promote the sale of Liberty Bonds. At that moment of patriotic inclusion, Moton "could not but feel that my people by their contribution, their loyalty, and their spirit . . . realized fully that they are heirs of America, and that as such they must be sharers of her struggles as well as partakers of her glory."

More surprising was the support for the war voiced by W. E. B. Du Bois. Known for his bold dissent against the white power structure, Du Bois shocked many readers with his editorial in the NAACP's journal *Crisis,* urging blacks to "close ranks" and "forget our special grievances" until after a unified nation had won the war. The enemy of the moment, Du Bois insisted, was German "military despotism." Unchecked, that despotism "spells death to the aspirations of Negroes and all darker races for equality, freedom, and democracy."

Although critics bitterly assailed Du Bois for not demanding equal treatment for blacks who fought for their country, African Americans generally followed his advice and closed ranks. On the first day of registration for military service, more than 700,000 black men signed in at their draft boards. By war's end, 370,000 blacks had been inducted, some 31 percent of the total registered. The figure for whites was 26 percent.

During training, black recruits suffered the same prejudices that they had encountered in civilian life. Rigidly segregated, they were usually assigned to labor battalions. They faced crude abuse and miserable conditions. One base in Virginia that trained blacks as cargo handlers quartered troops in tents without floors or stoves and provided no changes of clothes, no blankets for the winter—not even facilities for bathing. Only several deaths from disease and exposure moved the authorities to make conditions barely tolerable.

When black soldiers began arriving in Europe, white commanders made a point of maintaining racial distinctions. A special report from the headquarters of the American commander, General John J. Pershing, advised the French that their failure to draw the color line threatened Franco-American relations. They should resist the urge, the report declared, to accept blacks as equals or to thank them for their efforts, for fear of "spoiling the Negroes."

Under such circumstances, German propagandists raised some painful questions. One leaflet distributed by the Germans to black troops reminded them that they lacked the rights that whites enjoyed and that they were segregated and were often lynched. "Why, then, fight the Germans," the leaflet asked, "only for the benefit of the Wall Street robbers and to protect the millions they have loaned to the British, French, and Italians?" Why, indeed?

Black soldiers hoped to prove a point. While they worked at first mainly as laborers and stevedores, before long they had their chance to fight. In February 1918, General Pershing received an urgent call from the French for help in the Meuse-Argonne sector. Reluctant to lose command over the white troops he valued the most, he sent black soldiers—the 369th, 370th, 371st, and 372nd Regiments of the 92nd Division—to the front, where they were integrated into units of the French army. In the 191 days spent in battle—longer than the time spent by any other American outfit—the 369th Regiment won the most medals of any American combat unit, more than one hundred Croix de Guerre (crosses given by the French for gallantry in war) alone, and had no prisoners taken. In June 1918, the French high command paid its highest respect by asking the Americans to send all the black troops they could spare.

When the battle-scarred survivors of the 92nd Division returned home, they marched proudly past cheering crowds in Manhattan and Chicago. Black spokesmen proclaimed a new era for black Americans. In May 1919, Du Bois argued that it was time for African Americans to collect what was due them. "We return from fighting," Du Bois declared. "We return fighting. Make way for Democracy. We saved it in France, and by the Great Jehovah, we will save it in the U.S.A., or know the reason why."

Reasons soon presented themselves. Segregation remained entrenched, and its defenders con-

AFRICAN AMERICAN MACHINE GUN COMPANY
This company from the 370th Regiment of the Illinois National Guard, shown early in their training, exemplifies the proud determination of black soldiers to prove their worth in battle. Once in France, the 370th encountered resistance from American commanders reluctant to use combat-ready black troops for anything but hard labor behind the lines. When desperation in the face of a German offensive in the spring of 1918 gave them the chance to fight with French units, the 370th showed its mettle and received the Croix de Guerre. Adding to the irony of black soldiers having to gain respect as Americans by serving with the French was the fact that the first black soldier from Lincoln's state of Illinois to fall in battle was a private named Robert E. Lee.
William Gladstone.

tinued to hold power in Congress and in the White House. Postwar recession left blacks worse off economically than before their wartime glory and also made them scapegoats for white resentments. Whites launched race riots against blacks in two dozen cities. The willingness of blacks to stand their ground showed a more determined self-esteem, but it also meant more suffering from escalating violence. Nor did the armed services permanently offer new opportunities. Until the late 1940s, after the next world war, the American military remained not only segregated but also almost devoid of black officers. Discrimination extended even beyond the ultimate sacrifice. When the organizers of a trip to France for parents of soldiers lost in the First World War announced that the boat would be segregated, black mothers felt honor-bound to decline the offer to visit the cemeteries where their sons lay.

It took decades for the nation to recognize the sacrifice and heroism of black soldiers in France. As one critic observed about the 92nd Division, "The example [they set] was so bright that most eyes closed against it." But in 1991, as the nation cheered U.S. success in the Persian Gulf War, Americans began to see the light. A Defense Department investigating team, though insisting it had found no evidence of discrimination in the fact that none of the 127 Medals of Honor awarded during World War I had gone to blacks, declared that the time had come to correct an "administrative oversight." For leading a charge on September 28, 1918, up a German-held hill that cost him and 40 percent of his company their lives, Corporal Freddie Stowers would receive the Medal of Honor—until then the only one attained by an African American in the world wars. The slain soldier's elderly sister, who had survived seventy-three years to accept the award for her hero brother, could take solace that recognition came under the command of General Colin Powell, the first black chairman of the Joint Chiefs of Staff.

that depicted brave American soldiers and sailors defending freedom and democracy against the "evil Hun."

To help Creel's campaign, the film industry cranked out reels of melodrama about battle-line and home-front heroes and induced audiences to hiss at the German kaiser as "the Beast of Berlin." Colleges and universities churned out war propaganda in the guise of scholarship and added courses presenting the war as a culmination of the age-old struggle for civilization. When Professor James McKeen Cattell of Columbia University in New York made known his view that America should seek peace with Germany short of victory, university president Nicholas Murray Butler fired him. In a blunt summation of the campaign for patriotic conformity, Butler declared in his 1917 commencement address that "what had been folly is now treason."

A firestorm of anti-German passion swept the nation. Campaigns with the slogan "100% American" enlisted ordinary people to act as vigilantes sniffing out disloyalty. German, the most widely taught foreign language in 1914, virtually disappeared from the high school and college curriculum. Patriotic fervor turned against German-born Americans, including Karl Muck, conductor of the Boston Symphony Orchestra, and the renowned violinist Fritz Kreisler, who were driven from the concert stage. The rabid attempt to punish the enemy reached its extreme with the lynching of Robert Prager in Collinsville, Illinois. In the atmosphere of mob rule, it was enough that Prager was German-born and had socialist leanings, even though he had not opposed American participation in the war. The defense lawyer for the drunken men who attacked Prager praised what he called a "patriotic murder." The local jury took only twenty-five minutes to acquit.

As hysteria increased, absurdity mingled with cruelty. In Montana, a school board barred a history text that had good things to say about medieval Germany. Menus across the nation changed German toast to French toast and sauerkraut to liberty cabbage. The fearful saw evidence of the enemy everywhere. One vigilant citizen claimed to see a periscope in the Great Lakes, and on the dunes of Cape Cod the fiancée of one of the war's leading critics was caught dancing and was held on suspicion of signaling to German submarines.

The Wilson administration suppressed dissent with a zeal that contrasted ironically with its com-

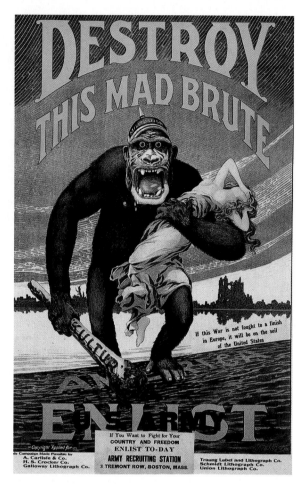

PROPAGANDA POSTER
All the primal fears of rape, invasion, and violence at the hands of a monster wielding the weapon of "KULTUR" are brought together in this 1916 scare poster. Germans so resented the dehumanizing portrait of themselves that in World War II, Nazi propagandists reproduced the poster with the warning that it had really been telling Americans to "destroy the German people."
Library of Congress.

www.bedfordstmartins.com/tap SEE THE ONLINE STUDY GUIDE for more help in analyzing this image.

mitment to defend democracy. In the name of self-defense, the Espionage Act (June 1917), the Trading with the Enemy Act (October 1917), and the Sedition Act (May 1918) gave the government sweeping powers to punish any opinion it considered "disloyal, profane, scurrilous, or abusive" of the American flag or uniform. Postmaster General Albert

ANTI-GERMAN SENTIMENT
Patriotic fervor during World War I condemned all things German—even in Cincinnati, long a center of German "Kultur." The photograph shows Dr. Ernst Kunwald, who had been driven from his post as conductor of the Cincinnati Symphony Orchestra in 1917, being escorted into custody as a prisoner of war.

War Dept., National Archives.

Burleson, a zealot of such self-importance that Wilson dubbed him "the Cardinal," blocked mailing privileges for publications he personally considered disloyal; a number of independent-minded journals were forced to close down, including the leading literary magazine *Seven Arts*. Of the fifteen hundred individuals eventually charged with sedition, all but a dozen had merely spoken words the government found objectionable. One of them was Eugene V. Debs, the leader of the Socialist Party, who was convicted under the Espionage Act for speeches condemning the war as a capitalist plot and was sent to the Atlanta penitentiary.

A firestorm of anti-German passion swept the nation.

The president also hoped that national commitment to the war would subdue partisan politics. He could not legitimately repress his Republican rivals, however, and they found many opportunities to use the war as a weapon against the Democrats. The trick was to oppose Wilson's conduct of the war but not the war itself. For example, Republicans outshouted Wilson on the nation's need to mobilize for war but then complained that Wilson's War Industries Board was a tyrannical agency that crushed free enterprise. Republican attacks appealed to widely diverse business, labor, and patriotic groups. With each month of the war, Republicans gathered power against the coalition of Democrats and progressives that had narrowly reelected Wilson in 1916.

Wilson erred when he attempted to make the off-year congressional elections of 1918 a referendum on his leadership. Instead, amid criticism of the White House for playing politics with the war, Republicans gained a narrow majority in both the House and the Senate. The end of Democratic control of Congress not only suspended any possibility of further domestic reform but also meant that the United States would advance toward military victory with authority divided between a Democratic presidency and a Republican Congress.

Over There

As the struggle over leadership and war aims unfolded at home, the American Expeditionary Force

REAL AND IDEAL WAR
The photograph of soldiers in a rat-infested trench, either tensely looking out for danger or slumped in exhausted sleep, offers a glimpse at the reality of the Great War, minus the noise and stench. But right to the end of that most destructive war, mainstream American public opinion clung to sentimental images like that on the cover of **The Ladies' Home Journal,** *the most popular source of comment and opinion on middle-class domestic life. Returning soldiers had to find ways of adjusting to a hero's welcome that did not square with the experiences they carried back with them in memory.*

Imperial War Museum/Picture Research Consultants & Archives.

gathered strength in Europe. At the front, however, the AEF discovered a desperate situation. The three-year-old war had degenerated into a stalemate of armies dug defensively into miles of trenches across France. Huddling in the mud among the bodies and rats it contained, soldiers were separated from the enemy by only a few hundred yards of "no-man's-land." When ordered "over the top," troops raced desperately toward the enemy's trenches, merely to be entangled in barbed wire, enveloped in poison gas, and mowed down by machine guns. Only with tragic slowness did commanders realize the im-

passe of modern warfare. After three days of futile attempts to mount an assault at the Battle of the Somme in 1916, French and British forces lost 600,000 (dead and wounded), while German losses reached 500,000. At the end of the ghastly campaign, the French and British had advanced their trenches only a few miles across devastated land.

To General Pershing, the tactics of stalemate violated the lessons that Civil War veterans had given him at West Point and that he had put in practice in swift, mobile warfare on the American plains and in Cuba. His commitment was to what has been termed the "American way of war"—heavy frontal pressure through weight of numbers combined with swift surprise attacks on the flanks by infantry and cavalry. Pershing thus refused to allow his fresh new army to merge with French and British units, despite the protests of the Allied commander in chief, General Ferdinand Foch. Pershing would save his soldiers for the moment when a series of lightning strikes might prove decisive.

In the best army fashion, then, American troops hurried to France, only to wait. They saw almost no combat in 1917, instead using most of their free time to explore places most could otherwise never have hoped to see. True to the crusader image, American officials allowed only uplifting tourism. Paris temptations were off-limits, and when French premier Georges Clemenceau offered to supply American troops with licensed prostitutes, the offer was declined with the half-serious remark that, if Wilson found out, he would stop the war.

Most of the sightseeing ended abruptly in March 1918 when the Germans launched a massive offensive aimed at French ports on the Atlantic. After six thousand cannons let loose the heaviest barrage in history, a million German soldiers smashed a hole forty miles deep into the French and British lines west of the Somme River at a cost of 250,000 casualties on each side. Paris became gripped with the greatest terror of the war when shells fired eighty miles away by "Big Bertha" cannons began falling on the city. More than a thousand civilians died, and a mood of defeatism began to settle in. Pershing, who believed the right moment for his crusades had come, visited Foch to ask for the "great honor" of becoming "engaged in the greatest battle in history." Foch agreed to Pershing's terms of a separate American command and in May assigned a combined army and marine force to the central sector.

Once committed, the Americans remained true to their way of war. At Cantigny and then at Château-Thierry, the fresh but green Americans checked the German advance with a series of dashing assaults (Map 21.4, page 795). Then they headed toward the forest stronghold of Belleau Wood. The American force, with the Fifth and Sixth Marine Regiments in the lead, made its way against streams of refugees and retreating Allied soldiers who cried that the Germans had won: *"La guerre est finie!"* (The war is over!) But when a French officer commanded the marines to turn and retreat with them, the American commander replied sharply, "Retreat, hell. We just got here." After charging through a wheat field against withering machine-gun fire, the marines plunged into a hand-to-hand forest battle of stalking and ambush. Victory came hard. On the single day of June 6, 1918, the marine spearhead lost 1,087 men, more than had been killed in the previous 143 years of marine corps history. In praise of the enemy's spirit, a German report noted that "the Americans' nerves are not yet worn out." Indeed, it was German morale that was on the verge of cracking.

In July 1918, the Allies launched a massive counteroffensive that would end the war. A quarter of a million American troops joined in the rout of German forces along the Marne River. In September, more than a million Americans joined the assault that threw the Germans back from positions along the Meuse River. American forces drove toward the town of Sedan, where the French had lost a war to Germany in 1870 and whose capture was thus of great symbolic importance. In early November, the Allies overran stubborn German resistance around Sedan and sent the survivors trudging northward. Soon after, a revolt against the German government sent Kaiser Wilhelm II fleeing to Holland. On November 11, 1918, a delegation from the newly established German republic met with the French high command in a railroad car in Compiègne to sign an armistice that brought the fighting to an end.

The adventure of the AEF was brief, bloody, and victorious—just the right combination to fix vivid memories of a successful crusade. When Germany resumed unrestricted U-boat warfare in 1917, it had gambled that it could defeat Britain and France before the Americans could raise and train an army and ship it to France. The German military had miscalculated. Of the 2 million American troops in Europe, 1.3 million saw at least some action. Some 112,000 soldiers of the AEF perished, their deaths divided equally between wounds and disease. Another 230,000 Americans suffered casualties but survived, many of them with permanent physical and psychological disabilities. Only the Civil War, lasting for a much longer period, had been more costly in American lives. European nations suffered much greater losses, however: 2.2 million Germans, 1.9 million Russians, 1.4 million French, and 900,000 Britons. Where they had fought and died, the landscape was as blasted and barren as the moon. Those who gazed upon it could appreciate the grim joke that the war would last one hundred years—four years of fighting and ninety-six more of rolling up the barbed wire. (See "Documenting the American Promise," page 792.)

For and Against World War I

*W*orld War I became a battleground of loyalties as well as of guns. Through the Committee on Public Information (CPI), the Wilson administration developed the art of propaganda far beyond anything known before. The CPI promoted the war by organizing rallies and parades, blanketing the country with posters and cartoons, publishing a daily Official Bulletin, and mobilizing seventy-five thousand volunteers to give speeches to hometown audiences. Only a few conscientious objectors, socialists, and disillusioned idealists were left to argue that war could not produce democracy but would instead destroy many lives and perhaps cherished values of progress and reform as well.

DOCUMENT 1. A "Four-Minute Man" Speech

The Committee on Public Information recruited volunteers in local communities to carry the official version of the war directly to their neighbors. Called "Four-Minute Men" because their speeches were supposed to be only four minutes long, these enthusiasts spoke from carefully crafted scripts. The following example indicates how audiences were encouraged to buy war bonds by rousing their indignation against the Germans.

While we are sitting here tonight enjoying a picture show, do you realize that thousands and thousands of Belgians, people just like ourselves, are *languishing in slavery* under Prussian masters? . . .

Prussian "Schrecklichkeit" (the deliberate policy of terrorism) leads to almost unbelievable besotten brutality. The German soldiers—their letters are reprinted—were often forced against their wills, they themselves weeping, to carry out unspeakable orders against defenseless old men, women, and children, so that "*respect*" might grow for German "efficiency." For instance, at Dinant the wives and children of 40 men were forced to witness the execution of their husbands and fathers.

Now, then, do you want to take the *slightest* chance of meeting Prussianism here in America? If not, then you'll have to help in summoning

all the resources of this country for the giant struggle. For resources will win the war.

Here's the way you can help save our resources. Instead of throwing money away on unnecessary things, buy Thrift Stamps, 25 cents, and War-Savings-Stamps, $4.12, worth $5 in five years, 4 percent compound interest. They're good as government money; like a mortgage on the U.S.A.

SOURCE: James R. Mock and Cedric Larson, excerpt (pp. 123–24) from *Words That Won the War.* Copyright © 1939 by Princeton University Press. Reprinted with permission of Princeton University Press. All rights reserved.

DOCUMENT 2. John S. P. Tatlock, "Why America Fights Germany," 1918

To influence public opinion, the War Department enlisted journalists and professors to write a series of "war information pamphlets." In the following example, history professor John S. P. Tatlock of Stanford University describes the sort of invasion that could be expected if the German hordes were not checked.

Now let us picture what a sudden invasion of the United States by these Germans would mean; sudden, because their settled way is always to attack suddenly. First they set themselves to capture New York City. While their fleet blockades the harbor and shells the city and the forts from far at sea, their troops land somewhere near and advance toward the city in order to cut its rail communications, starve it into surrender and then plunder it. One body of from 50,000 to 100,000 men lands, let us suppose, at Barnegat Bay, New Jersey, and advances without meeting resistance, for the brave but small American army is scattered elsewhere. They pass through Lakewood, a station on the Central Railroad of New Jersey. They first demand wine for the officers and beer for the men. Angered to find that an American town does not contain large quantities of either, they pillage and burn the post office and most of the hotels and stores. Then they demand $1,000,000 from the residents. One feeble old woman tries to conceal $20 which she has been hoarding in her desk drawer; she is taken out and hanged (to save a cartridge). Some of the teachers in two district schools meet a fate which makes them envy her. The Catholic priest and Methodist minister are thrown into a pig-sty, while the German soldiers look on and laugh. Some of the officers quarter themselves in a handsome house on the edge of the town, insult the ladies of the family, and destroy and defile the contents of the house. By this time some of the soldiers have managed to get drunk . . . and then hell breaks loose. Robbery, murder and outrage run riot. Fifty leading citizens are lined up against the First National Bank building, and shot. Most of the town and the beautiful pinewoods are burned, and then the troops move on to treat New Brunswick in the same way—if they get there.

This is not just a snappy story. It is not fancy. The general plan of campaign against America has been announced repeatedly by German military men. And every horrible detail is just what the German troops have done in Belgium and France.

SOURCE: John S. P. Tatlock, "Why America Fights Germany," War Information Series pamphlet no. 15, War Department, 1918.

DOCUMENT 3. Jane Addams, Address at Carnegie Hall, New York City, July 9, 1915

True to her belief in reason, not force, the leader of the settlement house movement, Jane Addams, helped form the Women's Peace Party in 1915. Soon afterward, Addams participated in the Hague Conference of Women in Holland and then, with a group of the delegates, visited the capitals of six warring nations to urge the leaders of those countries to seek peaceful resolution of the conflict. In this address to a New York City audience, Addams spoke about the conclusions she had drawn from her tour of Europe.

The first thing which was striking is this, that the same causes and reasons for the war were heard everywhere. Each warring nation solemnly assured you it is fighting under the impulse of self-defense. . . .

In each of the warring nations there is this other point of similarity. Generally speaking, we heard everywhere that this war was an old man's war; that the young men who were dying, the young men who were doing the fighting, were not the men who wanted the war, and were not the men who believed in the war; that somewhere in church and state, somewhere in the high places of society, the elderly people, the middle-aged people, had established

themselves and had convinced themselves that this was a righteous war. . . .

I quote a letter published in the *Cambridge Magazine* at Cambridge University and written by a young man who had gone to the front. . . .

" . . . Just when the younger generation was beginning to take its share in the affairs of the world, and was hoping to counteract the Victorian influences of the older generation, this war has come to silence us,—permanently or temporarily as the case may be. Meanwhile, the old men are having field days on their own. In our name, and for our sakes as they pathetically imagine, they are doing their very utmost, it would seem, to perpetuate, by their appeals to hate, intolerance and revenge, those very follies which have produced the present conflagration." . . .

It seemed to me . . . that the older men believed more in abstractions, shall I say; that when they talked of patriotism, when they used certain theological or nationalistic words, these meant more to them than they did to the young men; that the young men had come to take life much more from the point of view of experience . . . and when they went to the trenches and tested it out, they concluded that it did not pay, that it was not what they wanted to do with their lives.

Perhaps the most shocking impression left upon one's mind is this, that in the various countries the temper necessary for continuing the war is worked up and fed largely by the things which have occurred in the war itself. . . .

Let us say that there are two groups of boys in a boys' club, and I have much experience of that sort in boys' clubs to draw upon. If one says, "We did this because the other fellows did that," you will simply have to say, "I won't go into the rights and wrongs of this, but this thing must stop, because it leads nowhere and gets nowhere." . . .

. . . And what it needs, it seems to me, and to many of us, is a certain touch of human nature. . . . When you find that you can't talk to a woman on any subject, however remote from the war, without finding at once that she is in the deepest perplexity,—that while she is carrying herself bravely and going on with her accustomed activities because she thinks thereby that she is serving her country, her heart is being torn all the time,—it is borne in upon you that at last human nature must revolt. . . . Then men must see the horrible things which (*Continued*) have happened; they will have to soberly count up the loss of life, and the debt they have settled upon themselves for years to come.

SOURCE: Jane Addams, "The Revolt against War," *Survey,* July 17, 1915.

DOCUMENT 4. Diary of an Anonymous American Soldier, 1918

Encouraged by civilian and military officials to make their crusade in Europe an enlightening experience, many soldiers recorded their impressions in diaries and letters. In the case of one anonymous soldier, the task became so absorbing that it eventually found its way into print as Wine, Women, and War: A Diary of Disillusionment *(1926). As time in combat dragged on, the diary changed its tone and looked critically at war aims and their probable outcome.*

25 August 1918: Base Hospital at Neuilly. Has the Lord ordained that from hideous mangling of flesh beautiful things should come? . . . Can't evade it—there is sublimity in war. Man made in mold of divinity, and more than a flavor of his origin still clinging to his soul. The cheer of these lads, their quiet grave resignation, too beautiful for marring touch of praise. . . .

One comes away from this eddy of human wreckage, a little sick at heart. But one presently forgets the bodies shattered, the faces marred, the freshness of lives become stale and useless, and remembers only that "God fulfills himself in many ways." The singular evangelism of blood. . . .

18 October 1918: Three hundredth day from Hoboken! Damned cold. Shivering, fingers numb as lead, and not even November yet. . . . Race between Kaiser and my pants still on. Vital interest in early termination of conflict! Each day another seam opens or another button drops from fatigue—and can't keep pants up by merely gritting teeth. Each morning, scan communiques first—then breeches. Strain beginning to tell.

After the war problems of readjustment, hitherto kept in background, going to make all sorts of trouble. League of Nations, not mere imaginative sentimental Utopia, but only practicable solution of world in chaos. . . . The real victors in this war will be determined 10 or 20 years afterwards, and they will be the nation who will be the best able to face the growing discontent of a disillusioned people, to ward off impending famine, and to save their people from the appalling consequences of the universal bankruptcy to which Europe is speeding every day with increasing pace.

Vast amount of nonsense about Germany. Silly idea of demanding huge indemnities, and in same breath refusing to allow access to raw material, i.e., ask tree to give fruit, but shut off sun and air. . . . Either slaughter entire Teutonic race, or take them back and try to make something of them. No middle ground. No sense hating Germans. Only proper object for hate, to anyone with brains God gave little snails, is an idea. And can't destroy ideas, or crush them, or punish them. Can only substitute good ideas for bad ones.

This life hard on illusions. Not many left. A hell of a way from best of all possible worlds, and man certainly a son-of-a-bitch when he puts his mind to it. But hope not to travel too far along road on which so many realists stub their silly toes, of believing there is no angel worth mentioning in poor, complex human heart. Heaven and hell both there.

SOURCE: Anonymous, *Wine, Women, and War: A Diary of Disillusionment* (New York, 1926).

QUESTIONS FOR ANALYSIS AND DEBATE

1. What did the Committee on Public Information mean by, "Prussianism," and in what ways did the Committee suppose it might be present in American life?

2. How likely were Americans to be convinced by Professor Tatlock's warning of a German invasion? What estimate does Tatlock seem to be making of the general awareness and intelligence of the American public?

3. How plausible is Jane Addams's contention that war is the disastrous result of old men's abstractions, which are then refuted by young men's experience?

4. Has the anonymous soldier in Document 4 become more at peace with the world, or less, as a result of his war experience? Why?

MAP 21.4
The American Expeditionary Force, 1917–1918
In the last year of the war, the American Expeditionary Force joined the French army on the western front to counterattack the final German offensive and pursue the retreating enemy until surrender.

A Compromised Peace

Wilson decided to reaffirm his noble war aims by announcing his peace aims before the end of hostilities was in sight. He hoped that America's allies would rally around his generous ideas. He soon discovered, however, that his plan for international democracy did not receive ready acceptance by European heads of state. The leaders of England, France, and Italy understood that Wilson's principles jeopardized their own postwar plans for the acquisition of enemy territory, new colonial empires, and reparations. In his effort to draw public opinion to his side, Wilson also had to confront bitter political opposition at home.

Wilson's Fourteen Points

On January 8, 1918, ten months before the armistice in Europe, President Wilson delivered a speech to Congress that summarized American war aims and revealed his vision of a liberal peace. Wilson's famous Fourteen Points provided a blueprint for a new democratic world order. The first five points affirmed basic liberal ideals: "open covenants of peace, openly arrived at," that is, an end to secret treaties; freedom of the seas in war and peace; removal of economic barriers to free trade; reduction of weapons of war; and recognition of the rights of colonized peoples. The next eight points supported the right to self-determination of European peoples who had been dominated by Germany or its allies.

Wilson's final point called for a "general association of nations"—a League of Nations—to provide "mutual guarantees of political independence and territorial integrity to great and small states alike." The insistence on a League of Nations reflected Wilson's lifelong dream of a "parliament of man." Only such an organization, he believed, could resolve and justify the war. Wilson concluded his speech by pledging that the United States would welcome Germany into the family of "peace-loving nations," if it would renounce its militarism and imperialism.

Wilson's famous Fourteen Points provided a blueprint for a new democratic world order.

The Fourteen Points roused popular enthusiasm in the United States and every Allied country. Armed with such public support, Wilson felt confident that he could prevail against undemocratic forces at the peace table. During the final year of the war, he pressured the Allies to accept the Fourteen Points as the basis of the settlement. But he also conveyed his willingness, if necessary, to speak over the heads of government leaders directly to the people and so expand his role as spokesman for American citizens to the grand role of champion of all the world's people. The Allies had won the war; Wilson would win the peace.

The Paris Peace Conference

Buoyed by his sense of mission, Wilson decided to attend the Paris peace conference in 1919 as head of the American delegation himself. The decision to leave the country at a time when his opponents were sharply contesting his leadership was risky enough, but his stubborn refusal to include prominent Republicans in the delegation proved foolhardy.

The peace venture began well. As Wilson's motorcade made its way from the port of Le Havre to Paris, huge crowds cheered the American president. After four terrible years of war, Europeans looked upon Wilson as someone who would create a safer, more decent world. When the peace conference convened at Louis XIV's palace at Versailles, however, Wilson encountered a very different reception. Representing the Allies were the decidedly unidealistic David Lloyd George of Britain, Georges

LEADERS OF THE PARIS PEACE CONFERENCE
The three leaders in charge of putting the world back together after the Great War—from left to right, David Lloyd George, prime minister of Great Britain; Georges Clemenceau, premier of France; and U.S. president Woodrow Wilson—show a confident stride in approaching the peace conference in the palace of Versailles. Clemenceau is caught here displaying his frequent inclination to offer animated instruction to Wilson, whom he considered naively idealistic. Indeed, in an unguarded moment Clemenceau expressed his contempt for the entire United States as a country that was unique in having passed directly from barbarism to decadence without an intervening period of civilization. Walking silently alongside, Lloyd George maintains the poker face that helped keep his views carefully guarded throughout the conference.
Getty Images.

Clemenceau of France, and Vittorio Orlando of Italy. To them, Wilson was a naive and impractical man whose desire to reconcile former foes within a new international democratic order showed that he understood little about hard European realities. The Allies wanted to fasten blame for the war on Germany, totally disarm it, and make it pay so dearly that it would never threaten its neighbors again. The French, in particular, demanded retribution in the form of territory containing some of Germany's richest mineral resources.

Wilson was forced to make drastic compromises. In return for French moderation of territorial claims, Wilson agreed to support Article 231 of the peace treaty, assigning war guilt to Germany. Though saved from the permanent loss of Rhineland territory occupied by the French, Germany was outraged at being singled out as the instigator of the war and saddled with more than $33 billion in damages. Many Germans felt that their nation had been stabbed in the back. After agreeing to an armistice on the belief that peace terms would be based on Wilson's generous Fourteen Points, they faced hardship and humiliation instead.

Wilson had better success in establishing the principle of self-determination. On that basis the conference redrew the map of Europe. Portions of the Austro-Hungarian Empire were ceded to Italy, Poland, and Romania, and the remainder was reassembled into Austria, Hungary, Czechoslovakia, and Yugoslavia—independent republics with boundaries determined according to concentrations of ethnic groups. More arbitrarily, the Ottoman Empire was carved up into small mandates (including Palestine) under the control of France and Great Britain, partly to meet Allied concerns about stability in the Middle East and partly in accord with historical patterns of national sovereignty. Thus, with varying degrees of danger from ethnic and nationalist rivalries, each reconstructed nation faced the challenge of trying to make a new democratic government work (Map 21.5).

Wilson hoped that self-determination would also be the fate of Germany's colonies in Asia and Africa. But the Allies who had taken over the colonies during the war would go no further than allowing the League of Nations a mandate to administer them. Technically, the mandate system rejected imperialism. But it also denied self-determination to the former German colonies, even as the Allies retained their own colonial empires.

The cause of democratic equality suffered another setback when the peace conference refused to endorse Japan's proposal for a clause proclaiming the principle of racial equality. Wilson's belief in the superiority of whites, as well as his apprehension about how Americans would respond to such a declaration, led him to oppose the clause. To soothe

MAP 21.5

Europe after World War I
The post–World War I settlement redrew boundaries to create new nations based on ethnic groupings. This left bitter peoples within defeated Germany and Russia who resolved to recover territory that the new arrangements took from their homelands.

hurt feelings, Wilson agreed to grant Japan a mandate over the Shantung Peninsula in northern China, which had formerly been controlled by Germany. The gesture mollified Japan's moderate leaders, but the military faction getting ready to take over the country used bitterness toward racist Western colonialism to build support for expanding Japanese power throughout Asia.

Revolutionary upheaval also affected the dream to make the world safe for democracy. Most important was the revolution in Russia in March 1917, after terrible defeats in the war, that forced Czar Nicholas II to abdicate. Wilson, who was just then leading his country into war, greeted the Russian Revolution as confirmation that democracy would rise from the ashes of war's destruction. In reckless enthusiasm, Wilson declared that Russia had always been "democratic at heart." A very different reality soon emerged, however. Marxist radicals calling themselves Bolsheviks seized control of the nation in November 1917 and made their leader, Vladimir Ilyich Lenin, ruler of the revolutionary state that came to be known as the Soviet Union. On December 15, 1917, Lenin concluded a separate peace with Germany. To make matters worse for Wilsonian idealists, Lenin insisted that the war was being fought not for democracy but to extend capitalist power. Outraged by what he considered the Bolsheviks' betrayal of the Russian Revolution and the war for democracy, Wilson reacted as he had to the Mexican revolution by refusing to recognize the new Russian government.

Respect for self-determination kept Wilson from agreeing with British leader Winston Churchill that "the Bolshevik infant should be strangled in its cradle" by direct military action. Nonetheless, in September 1918 the president did send fourteen thousand troops to Siberia to join British and French forces assisting a Russian army loyal to the czar that was battling to overthrow Lenin and annul the Bolshevik Revolution. American opinion divided significantly. A few observers believed that the war had created possibilities for suffering millions to overthrow the tyrants who had oppressed them. Most Americans, however, saw the outcome as evidence that the cause of democracy had fallen short and left the world full of radical menace. The depth of their aversion to communism was reflected by the national government's continuation of Wilson's refusal to recognize the Soviet Union until 1993.

To many Europeans and Americans whose hopes had been stirred by Wilson's lofty aims, the Versailles treaty came as a bitter disappointment. Wilson's admirers were shocked that the president dealt in compromise, like any other politician. But without Wilson's presence, the treaty that was signed on June 28, 1919, would surely have been more vindictive. Wilson returned home in July 1919 consoled that, despite his many frustrations, he had gained what he most wanted—creation of the League of Nations. His hopes rested on the belief that the league could remedy the imperfections born of compromise and provide peace its strongest ally.

The Fight for the Treaty

The tumultuous reception Wilson received when he arrived home persuaded him, probably correctly, that the American people supported the treaty. On July 10, 1919, the president submitted the treaty to the Senate, warning that failure to ratify it would "break the heart of the world." By then, news of the treaty's provisions had spread, and criticism was mounting, especially from Americans concerned that their countries of ethnic origin had not been given fair treatment. Even Wilson's liberal supporters worried that the president's concessions at Versailles had jeopardized the treaty's capacity to provide a generous plan for rebuilding Europe and to guarantee the peace.

To many Europeans and Americans whose hopes had been stirred by Wilson's lofty aims, the Versailles treaty came as a bitter disappointment.

Some of the most potent critics were found in the Senate. Bolstered by a slight Republican majority in Congress, a group of Republican "irreconcilables," which included such powerful isolationist senators as Hiram Johnson of California and William Borah of Idaho, condemned the treaty for entangling the United States in world affairs. A larger group of Republicans did not object to U.S. participation in world politics but feared that membership in the League of Nations would jeopardize the nation's independence in foreign affairs. No Republican, in any case, was eager to hand Wilson and the Democrats a foreign policy victory with the 1920 presidential election little more than a year away.

At the center of Republican opposition was Wilson's archenemy, Senator Henry Cabot Lodge of Massachusetts. A spare man of sixty-nine whose piercing eyes and pointed beard gave him the air of an imperious Renaissance aristocrat, Lodge found himself at odds with Wilson on many fronts. The senator believed in the moral superiority of the New England Republican tradition and disdained Democratic reformers like Wilson as tools of immigrants and corrupt city bosses. To exclude foreigners who did not conform to educated Anglo-Saxon ways, Lodge helped persuade Congress to vote for a literacy test for immigrants. Wilson's veto of the bill roused bitter fury from Lodge. There was also a personal factor: Before Wilson had entered politics, Lodge, with his Ph.D. and historical publica-

tions, had become known as "the Scholar of the Senate." It rankled Lodge to be eclipsed by a rival of greater intellectual eminence who had also risen above him politically to become president. That injured pride tended to inflame Lodge's opposition to Wilson's Democratic reforms and to deepen Lodge's resentment at being left off the peace delegation. Lodge was no isolationist, however. Like his friend Theodore Roosevelt, who had died in January 1919, Lodge expected the United States' economic might and strong army and navy to propel the nation into a major role in world affairs. But Lodge insisted that membership in the League of Nations, which would require collective action to maintain peace, threatened the nation's freedom of choice in foreign relations.

WOODROW WILSON
An exhausted Wilson shows the flag in San Francisco during his 1919 cross-country tour to rouse support for the Versailles treaty. Reaction on the West Coast was mixed. Bitter labor unrest brought hecklers into the San Francisco crowds; before that, in Seattle, where a general strike had recently been crushed, the IWW lined the streets with protesters who stood in stony silence as the rattled president drove by. A week after this photograph was taken, a stroke felled Wilson and brought this mission to an end.
Corbis.

To undermine public support of Wilson, Lodge used his position as chairman of the Senate Foreign Relations Committee to air every sort of complaint. Out of the committee hearings came several amendments, or "reservations," that sought to limit the consequences of American membership in the league. For example, several reservations required approval of both the House and the Senate before the United States could participate in league-sponsored economic sanctions or military action. Eventually, it became clear that ratification of the treaty depended on acceptance of the Lodge reservations. Democratic senators, who overwhelmingly supported the treaty, urged Wilson to accept the reservations, arguing that they left the essentials of the treaty intact. Wilson, however, insisted that the reservations amounted to a "nullification" of the treaty. He expressed personal frustration as well. "*Lodge* reservations?" he thundered. "Never! I'll never consent to adopt any policy with which that impossible name is so prominently identified."

With the treaty about to be reported from the Foreign Relations Committee to the full Senate with reservations attached, Wilson decided to take his case directly to the people. On September 3, 1919, he set out by train on the most ambitious speaking tour ever undertaken by a president. Always uncomfortable with stump speaking and warned by his doctors that his health would not stand the strain, Wilson nevertheless became more eloquent, more forceful each week. But in Pueblo, Colorado, on September 25, just as his appeal seemed to be gaining momentum, Wilson collapsed and had to return to Washington. There he suffered a massive stroke that partially paralyzed him. From his bedroom, Wilson sent messages through his wife and cabinet instructing Democrats in the Senate to hold firm against any and all reservations. In the end, Wilson commanded enough loyalty to ensure a vote against the Lodge reservations. But when the treaty came up for a vote in the Senate in March 1920, the combined opposition of the Republican irreconcilables and Republican reservationists left Wilson six votes short of the two-thirds majority needed for passage.

The nations of Europe then went about organizing the league at Geneva, Switzerland, but the United States never became a member. Whether American membership could have prevented the war that began in Europe in 1939 is debatable, but America's failure to join certainly left the league a much weaker institution. Brought low by their feud, Woodrow Wilson and Henry Cabot Lodge both died in 1924, never seeing international order or security, never knowing the whirlwind that would eventually follow the Great War's failure to make the world safe for democracy.

Postwar Change

The defeat of Wilson's idealistic hopes for international democracy was the crowning blow to progressives and to peace advocates who had abandoned their cause in the hope that the war could serve as a vehicle for reform. The reaction against disappointed idealism included an urge to demobilize swiftly. In the process, servicemen, defense workers, and farmers lost their connection to national purpose and much of their economic security. The combination of displaced veterans returning home, a stalled economy, and leftover wartime patriotism looking for a new cause was so volatile that it could hardly fail to explode.

Economic Hardship and Labor Upheaval

With the armistice came the need to convert the United States back to a peacetime economy. The impulse to end the wartime experiment in government-business cooperation, dismantle the federal agencies responsible for war production, and return to free enterprise proved irresistible to economic and political leaders. Restoration of the economy to peacetime pursuits and demobilization of the armed forces came swiftly and was largely unplanned. The government simply abandoned its wartime controls on the economy and almost overnight canceled millions of dollars in orders for war materiel. In a matter of months, more than three million soldiers were mustered out of the military with only sixty dollars and a one-way ticket home. When war production ceased and veterans flooded the job market, unemployment rose sharply. At the same time, as consumers went on a postwar spending spree, inflation soared. In 1919, prices rose an astonishing 75 percent over prewar levels, and in 1920, while inflation slowed, prices rose another 28 percent.

Labor had enjoyed a share of wartime prosperity, but most of the gains for workers evaporated in the postwar period. Business, freed from control

After the Welcome Home — a JOB!

U.S. EMPLOYMENT SERVICE *Dep't of Labor*

RETURNING VETERANS AND WORK

After the triumphal parades passed by, attention turned to the question of what the heroes would do at home. The Department of Labor poster at left tries to convey a strong image of purposefulness and prosperity by framing a soldier in a victory arch in front of a booming industrial landscape. Under the circumstances, though, the soldier can best be regarded as a displaced person, teetering on a windowsill, dangerously high in the air. The U.S. Employment Service had little to offer veterans beyond posters such as this; and unions were unprepared to cope with the massive numbers of former soldiers who needed retraining. As workplace conditions deteriorated, the largest number of strikes in the nation's history broke out in 1919. The Chicago steel strikers in the photograph above look very different from the returning soldier in the poster. Their fate was to lose the strike and return to harsh conditions. No record was kept of ex-servicemen, left to find their own way in the postwar world.

Library of Congress; Corbis.

and eager to restore the more favorable position it held before the war, turned against the eight-hour day and attacked labor unions. Rather than sit back and watch inflation eat up their paychecks and bosses destroy their unions, workers fought back. The year 1919 witnessed nearly thirty-six hundred strikes involving four million workers.

The most spectacular strike occurred in February 1919 in Seattle, where large numbers of metalworkers and shipbuilders had been put out of work by demobilization. When a coalition of the radical Industrial Workers of the World (IWW) and the moderate American Federation of Labor (AFL) called a general strike, the largest work stoppage in American history shut down the city for several days. Nationwide, elected officials and newspaper editorials echoed claims in the *Seattle Times* that the walkout was "a Bolshevik effort to start a revolution" engineered by "Seattle labor criminals." An effort to deport strike leaders failed because they were citizens, not aliens, but the suppression of the strike by Seattle's anti-union mayor, Ole Hanson, and widespread alarm about radicalism cost the AFL much of the support it had gained through the war and contributed to the destruction of the IWW soon afterward.

A strike by Boston policemen in the fall of 1919 brought out postwar hostility toward labor militancy in the public sector. Though they were paid less than pick-and-shovel laborers and had received no raise since before the war, the police won little public sympathy. Once the officers stopped walking their beats, looters sacked the city. After two days of near anarchy, only slightly tamed by a volunteer police force of Harvard students and recently discharged soldiers, Massachusetts governor Calvin Coolidge called in the National Guard to restore order. The public, yearning for peace and security in the wake of war, fervently welcomed Coolidge's anti-union assurance that "there is no right to strike against the public safety by anybody, anywhere, any time." A Philadelphia newspaper echoed another popular fear about radicalism: "Wherein do the police of the New England metropolis differ from the mad minority which . . . ruined Russia . . . ? Bolshevism in the United States is no longer a specter. Boston in chaos reveals its sinister substance."

The ludicrous charge against policemen who were simply trying to get a living wage foreshadowed the alarm generated by the largest and fiercest strike of the period, which erupted in the steel industry just days after the Boston confrontation. Steelworkers had serious grievances, but for decades the industry had succeeded in beating back all their efforts to unionize. In 1919, however, the AFL, still led by its founding father, Samuel Gompers, decided it was time to try again in the face of the industry's plan to revert to seven-day weeks, twelve-hour days, and weekly wages of about $20. Having loyally supported the government's war effort, the AFL expected federal support for unionization. When Gompers began to recruit union members, however, he learned that he faced the steel barons alone. Faced with the refusal of U.S. Steel and Bethlehem Steel to negotiate, Gompers called for a strike; 350,000 workers in fifteen states walked out in September 1919.

The steel industry hired thirty thousand strikebreakers (many of them African Americans) and turned public opinion against the strikers by portraying them as radicals bent on subverting the Republic. In doing so, they drew on the wartime legacy of hostility toward foreigners. Just as propaganda turned Germans into Huns, the steel barons sought public favor by pinning the label of Red, or communist, on the strikers by playing up the recent arrival of many of them from the hated Austro-Hungarian Empire. The strike leader, William Z. Foster, though born in Philadelphia, was lumped in with radical foreigners for having once been a member of the IWW and uttering the conviction that the government was an agent of capitalist oppression.

Allied with the management view, state and federal troops blocked union members from getting close to the steel mills so they could discourage scabs from crossing their picket line. In January 1920, after eighteen workers had been killed, the strike collapsed. That devastating defeat initiated a sharp decline in the fortunes of the labor movement, a trend that would continue for almost twenty years.

The Red Scare

Response to labor strikes was one manifestation of a general fear of internal subversion that swept the nation in 1919. The "Red scare" of that time, which far outstripped the assault on civil liberties during the war, had homegrown causes in the postwar recession, labor unrest, and the difficulties of reintegrating millions of returning veterans. But unsettling events abroad also added to Americans' anxieties. Russian bolshevism became even more menacing in March 1919 when the new Soviet leaders created an association of communist leaders throughout the world it called the Third International in order to foment revolution in capitalist countries. The chance of a communist revolution in the United States was zero, but a flurry of isolated terrorist acts in 1919, most notably thirty-eight bombs mailed to prominent Americans, made it seem to edgy Americans that revolutionaries were at the door. Although the post office intercepted all but one of the bombs, fear, anger, and uncertainty about the motives of terrorists led swiftly to a hunt for scapegoats. On the grounds that "there could be no nice distinctions drawn between the theoretical ideals of the radicals and their actual violations of our national laws," Attorney General A. Mitchell Palmer led an assault on alleged conspirators. Targeting men and women who harbored what Palmer considered ideas that could lead to violence, even though they may not have done anything illegal, the Justice Department sought to purge the supposed enemies of America.

In January 1920, Palmer ordered a series of raids that netted six thousand alleged subversives. Though the plans for revolution he expected to find did not turn up, and the three pistols he confiscated did not amount to a revolutionary armory, Palmer nevertheless ordered five hundred of the suspects deported. His action came in the midst of a campaign against the most notorious radical alien, Russian-born Emma Goldman. Before the war, Goldman's passionate support of labor strikes, women's rights, and birth control had made her a leading symbol of outspoken disrespect for mainstream opinion. Finally, after a stay in prison for attacking military conscription, she was ordered deported by the fervent young director of the Radical Division of the Justice Department, J. Edgar Hoover. In December 1919, as Goldman and 250 others boarded a ship for exile in the Soviet Union, the unchastened rebel turned on the gangplank to thumb her nose at a jeering crowd and disappeared onto the deck. Anticipating timid conformity in the next decade, one observer remarked, "With Prohibition coming in and Emma Goldman goin' out, 'twill be a dull country."

The effort to rid the country of alien radicals was matched by efforts to crush radicals entitled to remain. The climax was reached on Armistice Day, November 11, 1919, in Centralia, Washington. A rugged lumber town, Centralia contained one of only two IWW halls left in the state. Rumors circulated that the hall would be raided on the first an-

RED SCARE IMAGES
The bearded anarchist, sour radical, and alien draft dodger make up the usual cartoon cast of "reds" whom zealous patriots sought to drive out of American life. The aura of "American Legion" hanging over the city indicates the central role played by that veterans organization in purging those who had opposed U.S. participation in the war and who in the Legion view posed a threat to basic American institutions. Comment from a dog about the radicals going away for their health wryly makes the point that American Legionnaires had shown a willingness to use violence against those they targeted.
Granger Collection.

niversary of the end of the war. When a menacing crowd gathered in front of the hall, nervous IWW members fired into the crowd, killing three people. Three IWW members were arrested and later convicted of murder, but another, an ex-soldier, was carried off by a mob who castrated him and then, after hanging him from a bridge, riddled his body with bullets. His death was officially ruled a suicide. A scattering of law enforcement officials, taking to that style of vigilante patriotism, also staged raids to rid their cities and towns of so-called Reds.

Public institutions joined the attack on civil liberties. Local libraries removed dissenting books.

Schools and colleges fired unorthodox teachers. Police shut down radical newspapers. State legislatures refused to seat elected representatives who professed socialist ideas. In 1919, Congress removed its lone socialist representative, Victor Berger, on the grounds that he was a threat to national safety. That same year, the Supreme Court provided a formula for restricting free speech. In upholding the conviction of socialist Charles Schenck for publishing a pamphlet urging resistance to the draft during wartime (*Schenck v. United States*), Justice Oliver Wendell Holmes, writing for the Court, established a "clear and present danger" test. Such utterances as Schenck's during a time of national peril, Holmes wrote, were equivalent to shouting "Fire!" in a crowded theater. But the analogy was false. Schenck's pamphlet echoed faintly in the open air, not in a crowded theater, and had little power to provoke a public firmly opposed to its message.

The chance of a communist revolution in the United States was zero, but a flurry of isolated terrorist acts in 1919 made it seem to edgy Americans that revolutionaries were at the door.

In time, the Red scare lost credibility. The lack of any real radical menace became clear after newspaper headlines carried Attorney General Palmer's warning that radicals were planning to celebrate the Bolshevik Revolution with a nationwide wave of violence on May 1, 1920. Officials responded by calling out state militia, fortifying public buildings and churches, mobilizing bomb squads, even putting machine-gun nests at major city intersections. When May 1 came and went without a single disturbance, the public mood turned from fear to scorn, and Palmer, who had taken to calling himself the "Fighting Quaker," was jeered as the "Quaking Fighter."

Conclusion: Troubled Crusade

At home and abroad, the First World War was a traumatic experience for the American people. Woodrow Wilson sought to keep the nation out of the conflict, but when the country entered the war in 1917, he promised that American intervention would further the noble cause of worldwide democracy. Though serving under idealistic banners, American soldiers and sailors encountered unprecedented horrors—submarines, poison gas, machine guns—and more than 100,000 died. Rather than redeeming their sacrifice, the peace that followed the armistice tarnished it. Few found consolation in the fact that the war thrust the nation into a position of international preeminence. At home, war brought prosperity, but rather than permanently improving working conditions, advancing public health, and spreading educational opportunity as progressives had hoped, the war threatened to undermine the achievements of the previous two decades.

In 1920, a bruised and disillusioned society stumbled into a new decade. The era coming to an end had called on Americans to crusade and sacrifice. Now whoever could promise them peace, prosperity, and a good time would have the best chance to win their hearts.

www.bedfordstmartins.com/tap   SEE THE ONLINE STUDY GUIDE to assess your mastery of the material covered in this chapter.

CHRONOLOGY

1914 Attempting to impose democracy on Mexico, President Woodrow Wilson sends marines to occupy the port of Veracruz.

August 6. All-out conflict erupts when Germany declares war on Russia.

1915 German submarine sinks British liner *Lusitania,* with loss of 1,198 lives, including 128 Americans.

Settlement house reformer Jane Addams helps form Women's Peace Party to seek peaceful resolution of war.

1916 General Pershing leads military expedition into Mexico in pursuit of rebel leader Pancho Villa.

1917 British authorities inform Wilson of Zimmermann telegram, prompting Wilson to ask Congress to approve "armed neutrality" policy.

April 6. Submarine attacks on American vessels convince Wilson to declare war on Germany.

Wilson creates Committee on Public Information to promote U.S. war aims.

Selective Service Act authorizes military draft that brings 2.8 million men into armed services; in addition, 2 million volunteer.

Espionage Act passed, limiting First Amendment rights.

Resentment against blacks migrating northward in search of work ignites violent race riot in East St. Louis, Illinois.

Armed action by black soldiers against racial discrimination in Houston results in execution of thirteen of the soldiers and life sentences for forty-one more.

Bolshevik Revolution ends Russian participation in war.

1918 **January 8.** President Wilson gives Fourteen Points speech, outlining his plan for peace.

May–June. American marines succeed in their first major combat with Germans at Cantigny and Château-Thierry.

November 11. Armistice signed ending World War I.

1918–1920 American forces deployed in Russia to protect Allied supplies and ports from Germany and then to support Russian efforts to undo Bolshevik Revolution.

1919 **January 18.** Paris peace conference begins, with President Wilson as head of U.S. delegation.

June 28. Versailles peace treaty signed.

Wilson undertakes speaking tour to rally support for ratification of Versailles treaty and League of Nations; the tour ends when a stroke incapacitates him. Postwar recession and ending of wartime support for labor unions lead to wave of strikes.

1919–1920 Attorney General A. Mitchell Palmer leads effort, known as Red scare, to rid country of anarchists and aliens.

1920 **January 1.** Prohibition goes into effect, following ratification of Eighteenth Amendment.

Organized labor suffers its greatest defeat by ending steel strike without settlement.

Senate votes against ratification of Versailles peace treaty.

August 18. Nineteenth Amendment, granting women the vote, ratified by states.

BIBLIOGRAPHY

GENERAL WORKS

Byron Farwell, *Over There: The United States in the Great War, 1917–1918* (1999).

Niall Ferguson, *The Pity of War: Explaining World War I* (1999).

Ellis W. Hawley, *The Great War and the Search for a Modern Order: A History of the American People and Their Institutions, 1917–1933* (1979).

Derek Heater, *National Self-Determination: Woodrow Wilson and His Legacy* (1994).

John Keegan, *The First World War* (1999).

David Kennedy, *Over Here: The First World War and American Society* (1980).

Nell Painter, *Standing at Armageddon: The United States, 1877–1919* (1987).

Robert D. Schulzinger, *American Diplomacy in the Twentieth Century* (1984).

David Steigerwald, *Wilsonian Idealism in America* (1994).

David Stevenson, *The First World War and International Politics* (1988).

J. M. Winter, *The Experience of World War I* (1989).

Neil A. Wynn, *From Progressivism to Prosperity: World War I and American Society* (1986).

EUROPEAN CONTEXT

Modris Ecksteins, *Rites of Spring: The Great War and the Birth of the Modern Age* (1990).

James Joll, *The Origins of the First World War* (1992).

Dwight Lee, *Europe's Crucial Years: The Diplomatic Background of World War I, 1902–1914* (1974).

George L. Mosse, *Fallen Soldiers: Reshaping the Memory of the World Wars* (1991).

Roland Stromberg, *Redemption by War: The Intellectuals and 1914* (1982).

Barbara W. Tuchman, *The Guns of August* (1962).

WOODROW WILSON AND THE WORLD

Kendrick A. Clement, *William Jennings Bryan, Missionary Isolationist* (1982).

Kendrick A. Clement, *Woodrow Wilson, World Statesman* (1987).

Patrick Devlin, *Too Proud to Fight: Woodrow Wilson's Neutrality* (1974).

John S. D. Eisenhower, *Intervention! The United States and the Mexican Revolution, 1913–1917* (1993).

Lloyd C. Gardner, *Safe for Democracy: The Anglo-American Response to Revolution, 1913–1923* (1987).

Friedrich Katz, *The Life and Times of Pancho Villa* (1998).

Burton I. Kaufman, *Efficiency and Expansion: Foreign Trade Organization in the Wilson Administration, 1913–1921* (1974).

Thomas Knock, *To End All Wars: Woodrow Wilson and the Quest for a New World Order* (1992).

Gordon N. Levin, *Woodrow Wilson and World Politics: America's Response to War and Revolution* (1970).

Arthur S. Link, *Wilson,* 5 vols. (1947–1965).

THE CRUSADE FOR DEMOCRACY

Daniel Beaver, *Newton D. Baker and the American War Effort, 1917–1919* (1966).

William T. Breen, *Uncle Sam at Home: Civilian Mobilization, Wartime Federalism, and the Council of National Defense, 1917–1919* (1984).

Jean Conner, *The National War Labor Board: Stability, Social Justice, and the Voluntary State in World War I* (1983).

Robert D. Cuff, *The War Industries Board: Business-Government Relations during World War I* (1973).

Carol S. Gruber, *Mars and Minerva* (1975).

John F. McClymer, *War and Welfare: Social Engineering in America, 1890–1925* (1980).

Ronald Schaffer, *America in the Great War: The Rise of the War Welfare State* (1991).

Stephen Vaughn, *Holding Fast the Inner Lines: Democracy, Nationalism, and the Committee for Public Information* (1980).

PACIFISM AND DISSENT

Charles Chatfield, *For Peace and Justice: Pacifism in America, 1914–1941* (1971).

Carrie A. Foster, *The Women and the Warriors: The U.S. Section of the Women's International League for Peace and Freedom, 1915–1946* (1995).

Emma Goldman, *Living My Life* (1931).

Frederick C. Griffin, *Six Who Protested: Radical Opposition to the First World War* (1977).

C. Roland Marchand, *The American Peace Movement and Social Reform* (1973).

Marian J. Morton, *Emma Goldman and the American Left* (1992).

Paul L. Murphy, *World War I and the Origin of Civil Liberties in the United States* (1979).

Cass Sunstein, *Democracy and the Problem of Free Speech* (1993).

WORLD WAR I IN MEMORY AND IMAGINATION

Peter Aichinger, *The American Soldier in Fiction, 1880–1963: A History of Attitudes towards Warfare and the Military Establishment* (1975).

Stanley Cooperman, *World War I and the American Novel* (1970).

Richard Cork, *The Bitter Truth: Avant-Garde Art and the Great War* (1994).

Leslie Midkiff DeBauche, *Reel Patriotism: The Movies and World War I* (1997).

Paul Fussell, *The Great War and Modern Memory* (1975).

Jon Glover and Jon Silkin, eds., *The Penguin Book of First World War Prose* (1979).

Ernest Hemingway, *A Farewell to Arms* (1929).

William S. Triplet, *A Youth in the Meuse-Argonne: A Memoir, 1917–1918* (2000).

BLACK AMERICA

Gerald Astor, *The Right to Fight: A History of African Americans in the Military* (1998).

Arthur E. Barbeau and Florette Henri, *The Unknown Soldiers: Black American Troops in World War I* (1974).

Carole Marks, *Farewell—We're Good and Gone: The Great Black Migration* (1989).

Bernard C. Nalty, *Strength for the Fight: A History of Black Americans in the Military* (1986).

Gerald Wilson Patton, *War and Race: The Black Officer in the American Military, 1915–1941* (1981).

Joe William Trotter Jr., ed., *The Great Migration in Historical Perspective* (1991).

GENDER AND SOCIETY

Nancy F. Cott, *The Grounding of American Feminism* (1987).

Sara Evans, *Born for Liberty: A History of Women in America* (1989).

Maurine Weiner Greenwald, *Women, War, and Work: The Impact of World War I on Women Workers in the United States* (1980).

Margaret Randolph Higonnet, Jane Jenson, Sonya Michel, and Margaret Collins Weitz, eds., *Behind the Lines: Gender and the Two World Wars* (1987).

Barbara J. Steinson, *American Women's Activism in World War I* (1982).

Susan Zeiger, *In Uncle Sam's Service: Women with the AEF, 1917–1919* (1999).

MILITARY ORGANIZATION AND EXPERIENCE

Michael C. C. Adams, *The Great Adventure: Male Desire and the Coming of World War I* (1990).

Thomas A. Britten, *American Indians in World War I: At Home and at War* (1997).

John Whiteclay Chambers II, *To Raise an Army: The Draft Comes to Modern America* (1987).

J. Garry Clifford, *The Citizen Soldiers* (1972).

Edward M. Coffman, *The War to End All Wars: The American Military Experience in World War I* (1968).

Kenneth J. Hagan, *This People's Navy: The Making of American Sea Power* (1990).

Lee Kennett, *The First Air War, 1914–1918* (1990).

Albert Marrin, *The Yanks Are Coming* (1986).

Allan R. Millett and Peter Maslowski, *For the Common Defense: A Military History of the United States of America* (1984).

G. Kurt Piehler, *Remembering War the American Way* (1995).

Dominick A. Pisano, Thomas J. Dietz, Joanne M. Gernstein, and Karl S. Schneide, *Legend, Memory, and the Great War in the Air* (1992).

Daniel M. Smith, *The Great Departure: The United States and World War I* (1965).

Donald Smythe, *Pershing* (1986).

Russell F. Weigley, *The American Way of War: A History of United States Military Strategy and Policy* (1977).

Stanley Weintraub, *A Stillness Heard Round the World: The End of the Great War, November 1918* (1985).

PEACE AND POSTWAR CHANGE

Peter G. Boyle, *American-Soviet Relations: From the Russian Revolution to the Fall of Communism* (1993).

David Brody, *Labor in Crisis: The Steel Strike of 1919* (1965).

Melvyn Dubofsky, *We Shall Be All: A History of the Industrial Workers of the World* (1969, 1988).

Melvyn Dubofsky, *The State and Labor in Modern America* (1994).

John L. Gaddis, *Russia, the Soviet Union, and the United States* (1978).

John Maynard Keynes, *The Economic Consequences of the Peace* (1920).

Charles L. May Jr., *The End of Order: Versailles, 1919* (1980).

Joseph A. McCartin, *Labor's Great War: The Struggle for Industrial Democracy and the Origins of Modern American Labor Relations, 1912–1921* (1977).

Robert K. Murray, *Red Scare: A Study in National Hysteria, 1919–1920* (1955).

William Pencak, *For God and Country* (1989).

Richard Polenberg, *Fighting Faiths: The Abrams Case, the Supreme Court, and Free Speech* (1987).

William G. Ross, *Forging New Freedoms: Nativism, Education, and the Constitution, 1917–1927* (1994).

Francis Russell, *A City in Terror: 1919, the Boston Police Strike* (1975).

Richard Severo and Lewis Milford, *The Wages of War: When America's Soldiers Came Home—from Valley Forge to Vietnam* (1989).

Ralph A. Stone, *The Irreconcilables: The Fight against the League of Nations* (1970).

William Tuttle Jr., *Race Riot: Chicago and the Red Summer of 1919* (1970).

Arthur Walworth, *Wilson and His Peacemakers: American Diplomacy at the Paris Peace Conference, 1919* (1986).

William C. Widenor, *Henry Cabot Lodge and the Search for an American Foreign Policy* (1980).

BOXING IN STYLE

In the 1920s boxing enjoyed such acclaim that lyrical sportswriter A. J. Liebling called it the "sweet science." To capitalize on that golden era's climactic rematch on September 27, 1927, between heavyweight champion Gene Tunney and former champion Jack Dempsey, the stylish New York City department store Peck & Peck produced this tie. Fighters and ties were not often associated, but in this case "Gentleman Gene" Tunney had displayed a certain cultivated taste and even made a news splash when he went to Yale to read Shakespeare with the students. By contrast, his opponent, Jack Dempsey, was a brawler from the wrong side of the tracks. The class and character contrast between champion and challenger broadened the appeal of the fight; but one cannot be sure how many up-scale purchasers of this tie were glad when Gentle-man Gene managed to beat the Manassa Mauler on a disputed referee's call.

Allentown Art Museum, Gift of Kate Fowler Merle-Smith, 1978.

FROM NEW ERA TO GREAT DEPRESSION

22

1920–1932

O N A GRAY CHRISTMAS MORNING IN 1922, Federal Prisoner #9653 began his last day at the Atlanta penitentiary. The frail old man glanced at the crucifix on his cell wall before exchanging his jailhouse fatigues for a cheap new suit the guard had brought. For Eugene Victor Debs, the leader and five-time presidential candidate of the Socialist Party, a long ordeal was over. President Warren Harding had granted him the pardon Woodrow Wilson had bitterly refused. After three long years in prison for opposition to World War I, Debs was at last a free man.

As he neared the main prison gate, Debs remembered, he heard behind him "what seemed a rumbling of the earth as if shaken by some violent explosion." Against every rule, the warden had allowed all twenty-three hundred inmates out of their cells to cheer the departure of the man they had come to know as a sympathetic friend. Debs had an uncanny hold on the hopes and feelings of downtrodden people. One such person was his cell mate, Sam Moore, who recalled many years later how much Debs's compassionate character had meant to him: "As miserable as I was I would defy fate with all its cruelty as long as Debs held my hand, and I was the most miserably happiest man on earth when I knew he was going home Christmas."

Debs's first stop was the White House, where his benefactor, President Harding, curious to meet America's most famous political prisoner, had invited him for a visit. The genial Harding bounded from behind his desk to shake Debs's hand, exclaiming, "Well, I have heard so damned much about you, Mr. Debs, that I am now very glad to meet you personally."

At the end of his journey, in Terre Haute, Indiana, a crowd estimated at twenty-five thousand met Debs at the train station. They lifted the old warrior into the same horse-drawn wagon that had carried him back from his first imprisonment in 1895, when he had gone to jail for defying a federal injunction during the Pullman strike. When the parade arrived at the family home near the railroad tracks, Debs gave an impromptu speech from the porch, urging his cheering supporters to view his release as a step toward the ultimate victory of socialism and the working class.

It was a touching moment, but Debs's show of the old revolutionary fire would not be able to ignite a society very different from the one he envisioned. The Harding administration shrewdly realized that pardoning America's leading antiwar martyr, along with others who had opposed the war, would reduce tensions caused by wartime repression with little risk to its conservative policies. The public, bitterly disillusioned with the outcome of World War I, no longer thrilled to the Christian moralism and idealism that had fueled the crusades of socialists and

CAMPAIGNING FROM PRISON
In the summer of 1920, jail-bird Eugene Debs receives word of his nomination as Socialist Party presidential candidate from Seymour Stedman, who was selected to be his vice presidential running mate. Debs, who had been imprisoned for opposing America's involvement in World War I, received a dying gasp of support from over 900,000 voters, but then he, Stedman, and their Socialist Party were relegated to the shade during the capitalist sunshine of the 1920s.
Dept. of Rare Books & Special Collections, Cunningham Memorial Library, Indiana State University.

progressives. Although Debs's stature as a jailed hero had won him 919,000 votes (the most ever for a socialist candidate) when he ran for president from his cell in 1920, the Socialist Party itself was in drastic decline. By the time Debs left prison, membership had fallen to 120,000. Nearly broke, the party would soon have to sell its headquarters in Chicago and move into an attic.

The New Era

The nation had turned a corner, and a spectacular burst of economic prosperity eclipsed progressive reform. Without a central focus on national crusades, once Woodrow Wilson's leadership ended, the energy generated by the war flowed away from civic unity and toward private economic enterprise and personal creativity. The rise of a freewheeling economy and a heightened sense of individual liberty caused Secretary of Commerce Herbert Hoover to declare that Americans had entered a "New Era."

This declaration of newness on behalf of a revival of old free enterprise individualism was one of several factors that made the 1920s a time of con-

tradiction and ambivalence. Stress between tradition and modern conditions was most often at issue. For the first time, according to the census of 1920, Americans lived in urban rather than rural areas, yet nostalgia idealized the farm and the small town. Although the nation prospered as a whole, the new wealth widened the gap between rich and poor. The more city life and cultural diversity flourished, the stronger pressures for conformity became. While millions admired the sophisticated new style, millions of others condemned postwar society for its vulgar materialism. And the greatest outpouring of creative talent in the nation's history produced artists of all types who indicted the United States for being aesthetically barren.

The ambivalence of the 1920s finds expression in the competing myths and labels attached to the age. Some terms focus on the era's high-spirited energy: Roaring Twenties, Jazz Age, Flaming Youth, Age of the Flapper. Others echo the rising importance of money—Dollar Decade, Golden Twenties, Prosperity Decade—or reflect the sinister side of gangster profiteering—Lawless Decade. Still other terms emphasize fragile dreams and loneliness: Lost Generation, Beautiful and the Damned. In contrast to these romantic images of the twenties, President

Calvin Coolidge aptly characterized the situation for those who wielded power and prestige when he declared, "The business of America is business." For the hopes and fortunes of the era rose, and then crashed, according to the values and ideology of the business community.

Postwar Politics and the Election of 1920

The economic chaos that accompanied the return to a peacetime economy was crucial in making Americans yearn for security rather than for more progressive adventures. People on fixed salaries—many of them middle-class progressive supporters of Wilson—lost heart as inflation shrank their purchasing power. Organized labor faced grim prospects after its defeats in 1919. During the winter of 1920–21, the national unemployment rate hit 20 percent, the highest ever suffered up to that time. Farmers fared the worst, as their bankruptcy rate increased tenfold and real farm income fell far below wartime levels.

President Woodrow Wilson, bedridden and partially paralyzed from his 1919 stroke, squandered his party's chances by refusing to allow anyone within his administration to construct a program for the postwar era. Instead, Wilson insisted that the 1920 election would be a "solemn referendum" on the League of Nations. The Democratic nominees for president, James M. Cox, three-time governor of Ohio, and for vice president, the New York aristocrat Franklin Delano Roosevelt, bearer of "Uncle Ted's" famous name, dutifully campaigned on Wilson's international ideals.

In tune with the national need for reassurance, the Republican Party chose handsome, gregarious Warren Gamaliel Harding, senator from Ohio, as its presidential candidate. Unlike the many of his generation who left the countryside to make their fortunes in the city, Harding stayed home in Marion, Ohio, to edit a newspaper and enjoy the pleasures of small-town life. His subsequent rise in party politics was a tribute to his amiable ability to connect with grassroots sentiment rather than to any political commitment. Harding vaguely opposed the

REPUBLICAN CAMPAIGN DECAL
Looking grimly dignified, these 1920 Republican candidates seek to persuade voters that they can put an end to radical and alien disruption and restore old-fashioned American values. Warren G. Harding, the Washington insider from the traditional Republican stronghold of Ohio, promises to get the country "back to normal"; his running mate, Calvin Coolidge, the Massachusetts governor who gained national fame by crushing the Boston police strike, appears as the exemplar of "law and order."
Collection of Janice L. and David J. Frent.

progressive policies of economic regulation, agricultural subsidies, and graduated income taxes. Wanting to succeed in an atmosphere of goodwill, he developed an ability to land on the winning side of an argument without having to grapple with conscience or complexity. On the two most heated domestic issues of the day—woman suffrage and prohibition—Harding showed little knowledge or conviction. He remarked that he saw no good reason for the reforms, but eventually he voted for them in a nod to public opinion.

In tune with the national need for reassurance, the Republican Party chose handsome, gregarious Warren Gamaliel Harding, senator from Ohio, as its presidential candidate.

Harding struck upon the winning formula in one of his campaign speeches by declaring that "America's present need is not heroics, but healing; not nostrums [questionable remedies] but normalcy." But what was "normalcy"? Harding explained: "By 'normalcy' I don't mean the old order but a regular steady order of things. I mean normal procedure, the natural way, without excess." The urbane *New York Times* understood the word's appeal, observing, "Mr. Harding is not writing for the super-fine weighers of verbs and adjectives but for the men and women who see in his expressions their own ideas."

Eager to put the labor strife of 1919 and the poisonous atmosphere of the Red scare behind them, the voters responded by giving Harding the largest margin of victory any presidential candidate had ever received: 60.5 percent of the popular vote and 76 percent of the electoral vote (Map 22.1). On his coattails rode Republican majorities in both houses of Congress. In early March, the Hardings arrived at the White House and threw open the barred gates, which had been closed since the declaration of war in 1917, and raised the window blinds. Bright flowers, birdhouses on the lawn, and, above all, a welcome to the public, who came by the thousands, lifted the national pall and signified a new era of easygoing good cheer.

In accord with his promise to have a government run by the best minds, Harding chose some men of stature for his cabinet. Charles Evans Hughes, for-

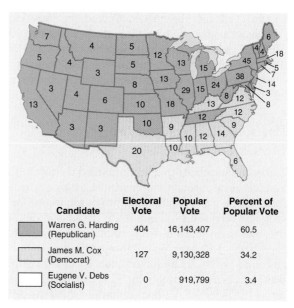

Candidate	Electoral Vote	Popular Vote	Percent of Popular Vote
Warren G. Harding (Republican)	404	16,143,407	60.5
James M. Cox (Democrat)	127	9,130,328	34.2
Eugene V. Debs (Socialist)	0	919,799	3.4

M A P   2 2 . 1
The Election of 1920

mer associate justice of the Supreme Court and Republican presidential candidate in 1916, became secretary of state; Herbert Hoover, the self-made millionaire and former head of the wartime Food Administration, was tapped for secretary of commerce; and the leading champion of scientific agriculture, Henry C. Wallace, took over as secretary of agriculture. But wealth also counted. Most significantly, Harding answered the call of conservatives to name Andrew Mellon, one of the richest men in America, secretary of the treasury. And then there was friendship. Loyally, Harding handed out jobs to acquaintances even though some of their qualifications were suspect. This curious combination of merit and cronyism made for a disjointed administration in which a few "best minds" debated national needs, while much lesser men looked for ways to advance their own interests.

Prohibition and Woman Suffrage

The shift from reform earnestness to normalcy showed in the public reaction to the last two great progressive achievements passed prior to Harding's inauguration: prohibition and woman suffrage. In January 1920, the Eighteenth Amendment took effect, banning the sale of alcohol. Prohibition—or the "noble experiment," as admirers called it—succeeded in lowering the consumption of alcohol, at least in rural America, but it also led to widespread disregard for the law. (See "Historical Question," page 816.) The "speakeasy," a place where men (and, increasingly, women) drank publicly, became a common feature of the urban landscape. There "bootleggers," so named a century before because they put bottles in their tall boots to sneak past the tax collectors, provided liquor smuggled down from Canada or concocted in makeshift stills. Otherwise upright people discovered the thrill of breaking the law; one dealer, trading on common knowledge that whiskey still flowed in the White House, distributed cards advertising himself as the "President's Bootlegger."

Eventually, serious criminals took over most of the liquor trade. Al Capone became the era's most notorious gang lord by establishing a bootlegging empire in Chicago that reputedly grossed more than $60 million in a single year. The gang-war slayings that marked the struggle for control of the lucrative market prompted public cynicism about the noble experiment. Each year, support for the Eighteenth Amendment shrank, until in 1933 it was repealed.

The Nineteenth Amendment, fulfilling nearly a century of struggle to achieve political rights for women, finally provided the chance to answer the question of how women would vote. The militant National Woman's Party, headed by Alice Paul,

SATURDAY NIGHT
With a sly wink, the young dandy dips for movie money while his date looks dubious about what will go on in the dark of that dry night. With this title, Harry Ruby, the popular songwriter, capitalizes on the expectation that resourceful Americans out for a good time will find ways around the prohibition amendment's attempt to enforce sober morality.
Picture Research Consultants & Archives.

WOMEN VOTING IN NEW YORK CITY
Sharply attired New York City officials look wearily resigned or bemused as one of them hands ballots to two women voting for the first time in 1920. The contrast in appearance and demeanor of the two groups facing each other is strikingly reminiscent of photographs of apprehensive new immigrants applying for entry.
Corbis.

Was Prohibition a Bad Idea?

GETTING HIGH has always been a part of human experience, so much so that the cultural psychologist R. K. Siegel has called intoxication "the fourth drive," after hunger, thirst, and sex. Fuel for that fourth drive has varied luxuriantly, from the caapi powder Indians in the Amazon jungle traditionally blew into one another's noses to the magic mushrooms a shaman on the frozen Siberian plains would eat so that he could pass on their essence in his urine for the rest of the community to drink.

In America, the intoxicant of choice has always been alcohol. Abundantly so. By the 1830s, the average adult was consuming a yearly total of fourteen gallons of hard liquor, mostly whiskey and rum. Alarm over what one historian has called the "alcoholic republic" soon produced two unique developments. First, the United States became the world's only society ever to outlaw its customary intoxicant. Second, to accomplish that feat, Americans passed the only constitutional amendment to be subsequently repealed.

Temperance campaigns in the nineteenth century anticipated the fate of the prohibition amendment in the twentieth century. Within an aura of general enthusiasm for reform, abstention from drink became respectable, even urgent, and by 1845 annual per capita consumption dropped to 1.8 gallons, the lowest level to that time. Yet even such sobering success could not contain the classic American insistence on free choice. Within a decade, many states repealed their laws against drinking and consumption began to climb, though not to the oceanic levels of the years before temperance consciousness-raising.

Prohibitionists rallied again at the end of the century in opposition to the thousands of saloons that were springing up alongside factories and immigrant quarters. Prominent dry champion Reverend Mark Matthews conveyed the moral intensity of the cause when he asserted that the saloon was "the most fiendish, corrupt and hell-soaked institution that ever crawled out of the slime of the eternal pit." To back up such extreme claims, the Anti-Saloon League (ASL) produced statistics and scientific studies of drunkenness, vividly touched up with horror stories of its destructive results. An irresistible coalition followed. Because saloons were mostly male preserves—awash with gambling and prostitution as well as beer—they tended to rouse strong resistance from advocates for women and children, who suffered most of the saloon's bad side effects. Out of their common concerns, women's rights activists and the ASL joined forces to battle for the prohibition amendment. Mobilization for

THE SALOON AND ITS CHILDREN

Here in 1910, in the Polish district of Chicago's South Side, children play in the dirt street in front of a saloon. This scene must have been quite typical, for the crowded city of Chicago had many saloons at the turn of the century but almost no playgrounds. Both children's advocates and supporters of the rising prohibition movement noticed the contrast and forged an alliance that helped empower Progressive campaigns for children's welfare and drive the prohibition amendment to victory.
Chicago Historical Society.

PROHIBITION ACTION

Prohibition agents sometimes liked to make sport of their work before appreciative audiences. The wastefulness of pouring nine hundred gallons of perfectly good wine down a drain in Los Angeles amuses some spectators and troubles others. Of course, those who had an interest in drinking despite the law could witness the disposal of bootleg wine and liquor serenely confident that more could easily be found.

Corbis.

World War I added a further boost in the army's insistence on soldiers remaining pure in spirit and free of drink. Hitching the profit motive to patriotism, many industrialists, including John D. Rockefeller and Henry Ford, took the advice of their efficiency experts that alcohol was the enemy of a productive workplace and thus of a successful war effort. With such broad support, the amendment was easily ratified in 1919.

Prohibition had a measure of success. F. Scott Fitzgerald famously misled his readers when he described the depression as a kind of hangover from the Jazz Age. In fact, at the start of the Jazz Age saloons disappeared from American street corners, and Americans emerged from prohibition drinking less than ever. The annual per capita consumption of alcoholic beverages declined from 2.60 gallons per capita just before prohibition to 0.97 gallons in 1934, the year after prohibition ended. Down as well were arrests for drunken disorder, along with alcohol-related deaths and psychoses.

Nonetheless, the "noble experiment," as Herbert Hoover called prohibition, was discredited. To skeptical critics, prohibition was a violation of human nature by puritanical busybodies. H. L. Mencken, the leading journalistic cynic of the time and a devotee of German beer halls in his native Baltimore, made the most savage cut against the ideal of a sober republic. Given the depth of human depravity, he remarked, society would be safer if the people in it were drunk all the time.

An avalanche of other objections joined cynicism and rebelliousness in overthrowing prohibition. As gangsters moved into bootlegging and bodies began to pile up, the public became convinced that prohibition was more about crime than redemption. Believers in individual and states' rights joined the clamor by opposing the federal government's attempt to control private behavior; and even stalwart "drys" were inclined to think that prohibition was not such a noble experiment once it was taken up by the Ku Klux Klan as a justification for a brutal campaign against minorities. At the head of the parade to repeal the Eighteenth Amendment marched a group of practical businessmen. Although business leaders had originally supported prohibition as an aid to productivity, most concluded by 1930 that banning alcohol was more apt to produce an unruly lower class, angry over losing their saloons, than a dry and docile workforce.

The repeal of prohibition in 1933 set off a rush of profit seekers, including gangsters who converted their bootlegging empires into legitimate businesses. A heavy advertising campaign, along with story lines on radio and the movies, promoted drinking and smoking as signs of sophistication and success. Making the old vices respectable and glamorous reversed the decline in drinking; by the 1970s, Americans had reached the pre-prohibition levels of consumption. By 1996, 52 percent of the population, or 111 million persons, used alcohol; of these, 32 million were part of the new binge-drinking trend and about 11 million were alcoholics. A quarter of the alcoholics followed another new trend by also being drug abusers. In the mayhem that followed, over 100,000 people were killed in (*Continued*) alcohol- and drug-related incidents each year during the 1990s, mostly in traffic accidents.

Alarm over substance abuse in the latter part of the twentieth century led to sharply divided action. Memory of the prohibition fiasco prevented any serious consideration of outlawing alcohol beyond its use by minors. The government's hands-off policy also meant that rescue of the expanding number of alcoholics was left mainly to the self-help of Alcoholics Anonymous (AA), a group founded in 1935. Drugs other than alcohol, however, were strictly prohibited. In 1956, Congress passed the Narcotic Drug Control Act, mandating jail sentences for second offenses by drug dealers and making sale to minors a capital crime. Successive broadening and tightening of drug laws culminated in the Anti–Drug Abuse Acts of 1986 and 1988, which set mandatory minimum sentences for using as well as dealing controlled substances, and established the nation's first "drug czar" to coordinate several federal agencies into an all-out "war on drugs."

The results were the worst prohibitionists of any kind had ever experienced. Ten years after passage of the first Anti–Drug Abuse Act, the United States stood out in the world as the country with the largest proportion of its population in jail. The number of newly admitted prisoners, most of them in on drug charges, rose by 120 percent between 1986 and 1996, bringing the total incarcerated to a record one million, at an estimated increase in cost from $45.6 billion to $93.8 billion. By 2000, the number of persons behind bars in America for nonviolent drug offenses alone, a very disproportionate percentage of them black and Hispanic, exceeded the prison population of all European nations combined. To extend the reach of punitive measures against drugs even further, American foreign policy exerted strong pressure on supplier nations to take action against drug cartels, even to the point of triggering civil war. Yet, despite the crackdown and a corresponding wave of antidrug propaganda, an estimated twenty-five million Americans continued to use hard drugs and double that number smoked marijuana.

The unwelcome ghost of the noble experiment has hovered confusingly around subsequent efforts to prohibit. The Eighteenth Amendment was repealed on the grounds that outlawing drink had been a spectacular failure that bred disrespect for the law. America today, however, has not seen fit to acknowledge an even greater defeat—greater because, unlike prohibition, the current war on drugs has not produced a decline in the use of forbidden substances. Perhaps the ironic lesson of the fight to repeal the Eighteenth Amendment is that the weapon of ridicule was all too successful. Looking around at today's active drug and alcohol scene, one can readily agree with the common perception that prohibition has been a joke. Not so easy to figure out, however, is whom the joke is on and who really has cause to laugh.

wanted women to form a progressive reform bloc and fight for an Equal Rights Amendment, which the party put before Congress in 1923. The more moderate League of Women Voters, formed out of the National American Woman Suffrage Association after it had achieved its goal, had the less partisan aim of educating the new electorate on the issues. Activists in both groups looked to woman suffrage, the greatest single change ever made in voting eligibility, to reshape the political landscape, starting with passage of protective legislation for women and children that had long been high on their reform agenda.

But as with prohibition, reality did not bear out expectations. Male domination and lack of experience in voting, especially among recent immigrants and Southerners, kept many women away from the polls or voting as their husbands instructed. Partly for those reasons, in 1920 and 1924, for the first time in American history, less than a majority of eligible voters cast ballots in the presidential elections. Those women who did vote showed no unified commitment to the goals of suffrage leaders. Instead, business-minded conservatives seized control of the Republican Party from the progressives and took over both the White House and Congress. In the Democratic Party, conservatives also routed Wilsonian liberals, and antifeminist, segregationist Southerners strengthened their seniority in Congress. Abe Martin, the cracker-barrel philosopher of the *Indianapolis News,* ruefully joked in 1926: "Wouldn't the way things are goin' these days make argymint in favor of woman's suffrage if we didn't already have it!"

<hr>

Activists looked to woman suffrage, the greatest single change ever made in voting eligibility, to reshape the political landscape. But as with prohibition, reality did not bear out expectations.

<hr>

It took a while for politicians to realize that they need not fear any female voting bloc. Assuming that women would have considerable political leverage, the new Congress passed the Sheppard-Towner Act in 1921, providing federal funds for maternal and infant health care. As understanding of the new voters' weak influence sank in, however, and the protests of doctors against "socialist" interference intensified, Congress reduced funds for the program and in 1928 eliminated it altogether. Those women who stuck with a progressive agenda were forced to act within a network of private agencies and reform associations to continue to press the causes of birth control, protective legislation for the workplace, legal equality for minorities, and the end of child labor. In doing so, they laid the groundwork for the time when their efforts would be supported by those in power.

The United States Retreats from the World

Harding's desire for harmony equipped him well to preside over the country's retreat from international leadership. Only four months after his inauguration, he concluded peace treaties with Germany, Austria, and Hungary that removed the United States from supervision over their affairs. To lessen tensions closer to home, he handed over $25 million to Colombia as compensation for the loss of territory that nation had suffered when President Theodore Roosevelt "took Panama" to build the canal.

Harding's most ambitious foreign policy initiative was the Washington Disarmament Conference he convened in 1921 to establish a global balance of naval power. By gaining agreement on the proportional reduction of naval might among the major powers—Britain, France, Japan, Italy, and the United States—Harding hoped to preserve peace without the bother of joining the League of Nations.

A grateful citizenry breathed a sigh of relief that the threat of war seemed so easily removed at a conference noted for its international goodwill and optimism.

The campaign to limit immigration, however, was more troubling. By the time Harding took office, worries about ethnic class differences and alien radicals had convinced the public that the time had come for drastic immigration restriction. Alongside the "100 percenters"—native-born Americans totally opposed to immigration on racist and patriotic grounds—stood union members, who feared immigrant competition for jobs, and traditionalists, who felt that the nation had completed its destined growth. In full accord, Harding made it one of his first acts to sign a quota law. The act limited the number of immigrants to no more than 357,000 per year and gave each European nation a quota, based on 3 percent of the number of people from that country listed in the U.S. census of 1910. The law effectively reversed the trend toward immigration from southern and eastern Europe, which by 1914 had amounted to 75 percent of the yearly total. Rejecting its former commitment to welcome millions of "huddled masses yearning to breathe free," the United States placed its destiny in the hands of those whose northern European ancestors had gotten there first. Congress cut the quota in half in 1923 and followed up the next year by excluding Asians and shifting the census standard back from 1910 to 1890, before the great influx of southern and eastern Europeans.

Antiforeign hysteria climaxed in the trial of two anarchist immigrants from Italy, Nicola Sacco and Bartolomeo Vanzetti. Arrested in 1920 for robbery and murder in South Braintree, Massachusetts, the men were sentenced to death by a judge who openly referred to them as "anarchist bastards." In response to doubts about the fairness of the verdict, the governor of Massachusetts named a review committee of establishment notables, including the presidents of Harvard University and the Massachusetts Institute of Technology. The panel found the trial judge guilty of a "grave breach of official decorum" but refused to recommend a motion for retrial.

For six years, critics who saw the verdict as an indication that the country was in the grip of a rich elite willing to exploit minorities and crush dissent tried vainly to save Sacco and Vanzetti from the electric chair. The condemned men cast themselves as martyrs to a cause they believed would prevail. "Never in our full life," Vanzetti cried out to his

AGITATING FOR SACCO AND VANZETTI
This image appeared in the anarchist journal that Bartolomeo Vanzetti's friend and fellow immigrant Aldino Felicani created to raise support for pardoning Sacco and Vanzetti. By writing in English under an Italian masthead, Felicani sought to make the two accused men symbols of both immigrant and working-class suffering. In the cartoon's dramatic version of events, capitalism's executioner, leaning on the electric chair like a sinister barber, summons working-class victims to their doom. In fact, deportation and mob violence were the typical weapons used against alien radicals and others deemed dangerously un-American.
L'Agitazione, August 20, 1921.

anguished admirers, "could we hope to do such work for . . . justice . . . as now we do by accident. . . . This agony is our triumph." After the anarchists were executed on August 23, 1927, however, many of their defenders saw defeat, not triumph. Novelist and critic of the ruling capitalist system John Dos Passos summed up their despair in his novel *The*

Big Money (1936). Dos Passos describes the crowd of fifty thousand mourners who followed the coffins through the rain; a bystander laments the executions as a death blow to the idea of inclusive democracy: "All right," he announces with grim resignation, "all right, we are two nations."

A Business Government

By screening out the world, the Harding administration could concentrate on prosperity at home. The American way, Harding declared, was to combine profit making and service to one's own community. Accordingly, he supported high tariffs to protect American businesses, price supports for agriculture, and the dismantling of wartime government control over industry in favor of unregulated private direction. Passage of the Fordney-McCumber tariff in 1922 raised duties on imports to unprecedented heights. Harding's policies to boost American enterprise made him a very popular president, but ultimately the small-town congeniality and trusting ways that had made his career possible did him in. The "Ohio gang"—wheeler-dealers, including some of his old friends—held forth at what became known as the "little green house on K Street," a hideaway where whiskey and poker mixed with business, some of it illegal.

The affable Harding resisted as long as he could the realization that certain of his friends were involved in lawbreaking more serious than drinking bootlegged gin. Scandal was forced upon him when Charles Forbes, an army colonel Harding had met playing poker and offhandedly appointed director of the Veterans Bureau, was caught looting his agency by selling off hospital equipment and padding expense accounts. Enraged by the betrayal of trust, Harding called Forbes into his office and, as the president told it, "shook him as a dog would a rat," before sending him on his way to jail.

Forbes was only the first crook to surface. Two other Harding appointees ended up going to prison, and several others would be indicted. When Interior Secretary Albert Fall, the highest official caught up in the scandal, was convicted of accepting bribes of more than $400,000 for leasing oil reserves on public land in Teapot Dome, Wyoming, "Teapot Dome" entered the language permanently as a label for political corruption.

Harding set off on a trip to Alaska in the summer of 1923 to escape his troubles. Baffled about how to deal with "my God-damned friends," the

COOLIDGE POSING AS A FARMER
After the labor wars subsided, the idea of Coolidge as the enforcer of law and order gave way to the more placid image of "Silent Cal." Though he knew the ways of farming from his youth, the hay and pitchfork of this image are mere props for playing a political game Coolidge does not manage to disguise. His gleaming dress shoes and the official car with Secret Service men in the background show how the old rural imagery had become window dressing for the New Era of wealth and power.
Brown Brothers.

president found no rest and his health declined. On August 2, 1923, a shocked nation learned of the fifty-eight-year-old Harding's sudden death from a heart attack. Harding himself was not involved in any financial wrongdoing, but only his death saved him from the further embarrassment of trying to cope with the corruption of those who took advantage of his trusting nature.

Vice President Calvin Coolidge was vacationing at his family's farmhouse in Plymouth Notch, Vermont, when he was wakened during the night with the news of Harding's death. The family gathered in the parlor where, by the flickering light of an oil lamp, Coolidge's father, a justice of the peace, swore his son in as president. This rustic drama had the intended effect of calming a nation confronting scandal, and the new president thereafter basked in the public's acceptance of him as a savior, wisely steeped in old-fashioned Yankee morality.

A spare, solemn man—one critic thought he must have been "weaned on a pickle"—Coolidge had won national publicity in 1919 when as governor of Massachusetts he had called out the National Guard to maintain order during the Boston police strike. The Republican old guard looked down on the drab Coolidge, as Henry Cabot Lodge made

plain in his sneer that he could never support a man who lived in a two-family house. But other delegates turned to Coolidge as a man of decisiveness to stand behind the more pliable Harding. As expected, the new administration differed from its discredited predecessor in its more formal and proper White House and close-mouthed presidential style. By altering the presidential tone, Coolidge lent new respectability to essentially unchanged policies, particularly regarding the economy.

Coolidge once expressed his belief that government should restrict itself to being the servant of business by proclaiming, "The man who builds a factory builds a temple, the man who works there worships there." Holding to that view, Coolidge rarely stirred in the White House and discouraged others in his administration from taking initiatives. His policy was to help businesses operate efficiently and profitably with a minimum of public restraint. With his approval, Secretary of the Treasury Andrew Mellon focused on reducing the role of government through tax cuts for corporations and wealthy individuals. Obligingly, Congress passed legislation that reduced its tax revenue by about half. The most active cabinet member, Secretary of Commerce Herbert Hoover, encouraged trade associations that would keep business honest and efficient through voluntary cooperation rather than government regulation.

The Supreme Court supported Coolidge's approach. It had long opposed federal regulation of hours, wages, and working conditions, arguing frequently that such legislation was the proper concern of the states. In 1916, on those grounds, the Court had struck down the federal Child Labor Act. Early in the Coolidge years, the Court found ways to curtail state regulation even though it had previously argued for states' rights to disallow such federal action. In 1923, the Court declared unconstitutional the District of Columbia's minimum-wage law for women, asserting that the law interfered with the freedom of employer and employee to make labor contracts. Soon afterward, the Court showed its partiality toward management by ruling against "closed shops," where only union members could be employed, while confirming the right of owners to form exclusive trade associations.

The election of 1924 ratified the defeat of progressive principles. To oppose Coolidge the Democrats nominated John W. Davis, a corporate lawyer whose conservative views differed little from Republican principles. In a last-gasp attempt to offer a reform alternative, the Progressive Party made Senator Robert La Follette of Wisconsin its presidential nominee. In the showdown, for which Republicans coined the slogan "Coolidge or Chaos," La Follette's fervent pledges to champion the progressive tradition of support for labor unions, regulation of business, and protection of civil liberties failed to rouse the public. The mostly silent president managed to capture more votes than his two opponents put together, and conservative Republicans strengthened their majorities in both houses of Congress. Apathy was the real winner, however: The percentage of eligible voters who bothered to go to the polls was the lowest ever.

Henry Ford and Assembly-Line Progress

With politics in eclipse, the most admired American in the 1920s was Henry Ford, the innovator of mass production who put America on wheels. Born in 1863 on a farm in Dearborn, Michigan, just outside Detroit, Ford soon rejected farmwork in favor of tinkering with machines. In 1893, he put together one of the first successful gasoline-driven carriages in

the United States. Ten years later, with $28,000 from a few backers impressed by his mechanical skills, Ford gathered twelve workers in a 250-by-50-foot shed and created the Ford Motor Company.

Ford's timing and location could not have been better. The growing country had moved to its outer limits, leaving Americans, especially those west of the Mississippi, distant from neighbors and services. With fewer than ten people to a square mile, the Midwest needed machinery to help its farmers make a living and to escape isolation. Ford's Detroit was well situated to meet these needs. Key materials for the automobile and the tractor—steel, oil, glass, and rubber— were manufactured in

Detroit and the Automobile Industry in the 1920s

Pennsylvania, Ohio, Indiana, and Illinois and were easily transported across the waterways of the Great Lakes and over the midwestern railroads. So great was the automobile industry's demand for materials that by 1929 one American in four found employment directly or indirectly in the industry. "Give us our daily bread," one commentator quipped, was no longer addressed to the Almighty, but to Detroit. Henry Ford's reward was dominance over the market. Throughout the rapid expansion of the automotive industry, the Ford Motor Company remained the industry leader, peaking in 1925 when it outsold all its rivals combined (Map 22.2).

The key to Ford's success in the factory was mass production. By installing a continuous conveyor belt, or assembly line, in his plant in 1913, Ford was able to produce a car every ninety-three minutes, in contrast to the fourteen hours it had taken before. Mass production enabled Ford to drop the price of his cars from $845 to less than $300. Soon the working class joined the wealthy on the roads. The Model T—homely and available only in black, but rugged and cheap—became a prime symbol of the New Era. Aided by the federal government's willingness to spend more on roads than on anything else, cars, trucks, and buses surged past the railroads by the end of the 1920s as the primary haulers of passengers and freight.

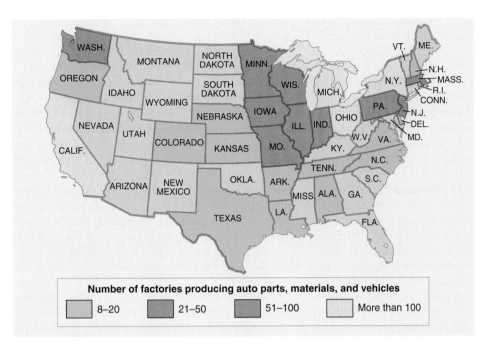

M AP 22.2

Auto Manufacturing
By the mid-1920s, the massive coal and steel industries of the Midwest had made the region the center of the new automobile industry. A major road-building program by the federal government carried the thousands of new cars produced each day to every corner of the country.

READING THE MAP: How many states had factories related to the manufacture of automobiles? In what regions was auto manufacture concentrated?
CONNECTIONS: On what related industries did auto manufacture depend? How did the integration of the automobile into everyday life affect American society?

www.bedfordstmartins.com/tap   SEE THE ONLINE STUDY GUIDE for more help in analyzing this map.

With politics in eclipse, the most admired American in the 1920s was Henry Ford, the innovator of mass production who put America on wheels.

The automobile changed the face of America. Hundreds of small towns declined or died within the decade, largely because the automobile could connect people in rural communities with distant cities and thus bypass the small towns that had formerly provided services. The one-room school-house and the crossroads church began to vanish from the landscape. At the same time, some larger towns prospered by catering to the new auto trade. "Guest cottages" were thrown up for auto tourists, and the word *motel* was coined to describe roadside accommodations. More prosperous towns paved and widened city streets, cutting down the trees on Main Street to make way for parking spaces.

Nobody entertained grander or more contradictory visions of the new America he had helped to create than Henry Ford himself. When Ford began his rise, progressive critics were vilifying the industrial giants of the nineteenth century as "robber barons" who lived in luxury while reducing their workers to wage slaves. Ford, however, was just a poor farm boy when the robber barons arose. By identifying himself with the common folk he wanted to work for him, Ford sought to claim his place as benefactor of striving Americans yearning to be free and mobile. Highly regimented automobile plants at the cutting edge of modern technology made Ford very wealthy during the 1920s. But he looked backward and moralized about the country's rural values. His pet project was to revive the past in Greenfield Village outside Detroit, where he relocated buildings from a bygone era, including his parents' farmhouse, to convey the rural simplicity of his childhood. With its exhibits of homespun family life and crafts, Greenfield Village contrasted poignantly with the roaring, racing Ford plant farther along the Detroit River at River Rouge. In the factory toiled the African American and immigrant workers left out of Ford's village idyll. Yet all would be well, Ford insisted, if Americans remained loyal to the virtues of an agrarian past and somehow managed to be modern and scientific at the same time.

With Ford's assembly-line method in ascendancy, those interested in progress looked to science and technology for guidance. Scientific management, which Frederick Winslow Taylor had pioneered at the end of the nineteenth century at Midvale Steel Company in Pennsylvania, reached its heyday during the 1920s. In an effort to become more streamlined and efficient, corporations established increasingly bureaucratic management structures. Specialized divisions sprang up—procurement, production, marketing, employee relations—each with its own team of professionally trained managers. It followed that, with approximately the same number of workers, industry produced almost twice as many goods as before. The result was vastly increased business profits and lower consumer prices, but only slightly higher wages for labor, since productivity was measured in part by how little had to be spent on the workforce. Moreover, as the assembly line became standard in almost every American factory, laborers lost many of the skills in which they had once taken pride.

To extend at least some of the benefits of scientific management to workers, industries developed paternalistic programs that came to be called "welfare capitalism." With the help of industrial psychologists and worker councils, businesses improved safety and sanitation inside factories and instituted paid vacations and contributory pension plans. In some places, company unions also gave workers a limited means of voicing grievances.

The vogue of scientific management cast a lengthening shadow over the thinking of other industrial nations as well. In France, Germany, and Britain, Ford's autobiography, *My Life and My Work* (1922), inspired manufacturers, artists, and intellectuals to ponder a future industrial system that would combine maximum economic benefit with functionally beautiful design. Democratic choice was less regarded, however. The dictatorial government of the Soviet Union could thus turn to Ford and Taylor for guidance in creating utopia. Joseph Stalin predicted that the "essence" of his country's revolutionary future lay in "the combination of the Russian revolutionary sweep with American efficiency."

Belief in scientific management helped advance the cause of higher education and the professions: Corporations needed educated managers. By the end of the decade, enrollments in colleges and universities were more than three times those at the turn of the century. During the 1920s, graduate education expanded at an even faster rate. Funding agencies such as the Rockefeller Foundation, the John Simon Guggenheim Foundation, and the Social Science Research Council were established to support scientific research and channel it into useful applications. Private business kept pace by increasing the number of industrial research laboratories from around three hundred in 1920 to more than a thousand by the end of the decade.

Welfare service also underwent professional change, especially in the growing new field of social work. Trained social workers focused more on individual psychology and less on the social justice concerns of the settlement house founders. Understanding of human behavior became more precise, but also more detached and fragmented. The aim was to adjust clients to the new, highly organized, tensely hurried business civilization all around them, not to nurture an independent sense of community and identity.

Consumer Culture

Following the recession of 1921–1922, the nation's economy grew spectacularly during the rest of the decade. Per capita income increased by a third, the cost of living stayed the same, and unemployment

TOURISM AND THE LURE OF NATIVE TRADITION
This advertisement for vacationing in the mountainous Indian country of New Mexico implies the benefits of high altitude for health. But commerce in native crafts is also an objective. Others at the time headed to New Mexico to attain quite different benefits. Attracted by anthropologists studying native culture and a coterie of painters and writers who began an artists' colony near the ancient pueblo at Taos, disillusioned strivers and other refugees from the stresses of modern life hoped to find a spiritual inner wisdom within Pueblo culture that would reconnect them with nature and the past.
Private collection.

www.bedfordstmartins.com/tap SEE THE ONLINE STUDY GUIDE for more help in analyzing this image.

fell and remained low. Americans enjoyed the highest standard of living on the globe. Although the rewards of the economic boom were not evenly distributed, white, urban Americans in the middle and upper classes had more spending money and more leisure time to spend it (Figure 22.1). Mass production created a consumer-good revolution in electric home appliances, automobiles, health and beauty aids, and gear for sport and amusement. (See "The Promise of Technology," page 826.)

No better guide exists to how the business boom and business values of the 1920s affected average Americans than the classic *Middletown* (1929). The sociologist authors, Robert Lynd, trained as a Protestant minister, and his wife, Helen, visited the small city of Muncie, Indiana, to compile data on secular and spiritual life. The almost entirely native-born, white population of Muncie (which the Lynds called "Middletown") closely approximated the national ideal in the age of normalcy. At the end of five years of study, the Lynds determined that Muncie was, above all, "a culture in which everything hinges on money."

To the Lynds, Americans—Middletowners—had been caught in a "cultural lag." Technological and organizational change had moved beyond the average citizen's comprehension. Many Middletowners had lost confidence in their ability to play an effective role in town meetings and civic organizations. Instead, they deferred to the supposed expertise of leaders in politics and economics and even in child rearing. The new passivity had a spiritual cost as well, the Lynds lamented. Religion, once a "spontaneous and pervasive part of the life of the city," had been reduced to a social ritual.

Mass production created a consumer-good revolution in electric home appliances, automobiles, health and beauty aids, and gear for sport and amusement.

The pied piper of these disturbing changes, according to the Lynds, was the rapidly expanding business of advertising, which "pounded away" to convert an independent community into a homogenized consumer aggregate. Advertising replaced the old notions of thrift, frugality, and savings with a buy-now, pay-later mentality. Newspapers, magazines, radios, and billboards told Americans what they had to have in order to be popular, secure, and successful. And installment buying—a little down, a payment each month—allowed them to buy expensive items before they had saved the money. As

Better Living through Electricity

IN THE 1920S, AFTER FORTY YEARS of technical development, visionary prophecies that electricity would be a bringer of leisure and culture seemed about to come true. Thomas Edison, America's greatest inventor of electric marvels, predicted happy electrified homes that would make night like day and free women from household drudgery. Warming to his subject, Edison suggested that some women might then be able to develop their minds as highly as men. Compulsive persons like himself could rejoice that perpetual light might eliminate the need for sleep. Perhaps, he concluded, someone might even invent electrical means for communicating with the dead.

Edison's hard-driving protégé Samuel Insull led the way in the expansion of electricity from commercial to domestic use. Insull's Chicago-based Commonwealth Edison Company, with General Electric and Westinghouse close behind, provided the power to increase the number of homes with electricity from 14 percent in 1910 to 70 percent in 1930. Now the lights that had cast their aura exclusively on the privileged rich could also shine on average Americans and their aspirations—as long as they lived in the cities.

A barrage of advertising—General Electric alone raised its annual budget from $2 million to $12 million between 1922 and 1930—fanned expectations of a better life for the masses. Without sooty gaslight, their houses would be easier to maintain, and electric vacuum cleaners would lessen whatever toil was still necessary. Electric refrigerators would keep a wide array of food available for elegant entertaining, electric washers and irons would facilitate high fashion, and radios would bring knowledge and music into comfortable, air-conditioned homes. One General Electric ad cheerily announced that, nowadays, "nobody works but ol' man river." Chiding foolish backwardness, other ads insisted that "any woman who turns the wringer [on a hand-operated clothes washer] . . . who cooks in a hot stuffy kitchen is doing work which electricity will do for a few cents per day." Rather than struggling with wringers and scrub boards, women could relax and listen to the radio "soap operas" sponsored by the laundry detergents foaming in their automatic washers.

Yet, despite $555 million in utility revenues by 1928, the promise of an idyllic electric future was hard to keep. Because America remained a market economy, rather than evolving into the engineered utopia that technological enthusiasts projected, isolated rural folk and the poor could not buy into the fully wired paradise. Most homes, for example, stayed with iceboxes until the late 1930s because they were considerably cheaper to buy and use than electric refrigerators. Freezers were so much more expensive that, although the advantages of frozen food were known in the 1920s, their use was limited to hotels and ocean liners until the late 1940s. So, too, television, another invention of the 1920s, remained undeveloped for lack of financial support, and air conditioning was sparsely used because the very people in the hottest parts of the country who needed it most were also least able to afford it.

To the extent that electric appliances found a place in American homes, they did not bear out utopian dreams of leisure. The gleaming new devices fostered expectations of higher standards of cleanliness and order that housewives could realize only by working with their appliances early and often. In some affluent homes, the burden was lightened by having servants use the appliances. For most households, however, the cost of electrification meant that less money was available for servants. Further pressure came from the fact that the number of domestic servants was declining because the booming 1920s economy offered better-paying work in offices and factories—including those that manufactured electric appliances. Electricity boosters remained unfazed. With typical unconcern about who would be left to do the work, the *Women's Home Companion* in the mid-1920s commended three housewives for saving enough money to electrify their houses by firing their hired help. These unacknowledged demands on household time and energy were made even greater by the most widely owned machine, the automobile. Not only did taking care of the family auto become a new task in the 1920s but the way people's cars enabled them to reach distant stores undermined the far more time-efficient custom of delivery vans bringing goods and services right to the doorstep.

The shortcomings of technology's promises were magnified by the 1929 stock market crash and

Westinghouse

The "COMPLETELY BALANCED"
Electric Refrigerator

A PRODUCT OF TWELVE YEARS' SCIENTIFIC RESEARCH
BY THE WESTINGHOUSE ENGINEERING STAFF

ELECTRICITY AD
The promise of electricity for modern life was frequently presented, as in this 1931 advertisement from **The Saturday Evening Post,** *in terms of the magical powers of superhuman figures drawn from ancient legends. The illustrator, Rockwell Kent, whose art tended to focus on raw nature and who later in the decade became a radical critic of capitalism, here makes the generating plant in the background puny compared with the god-like reflector of lightning and the fireball next to her. As a result the "completely balanced" electric refrigerator comes to seem a marvel created out of nature by divine genius. Probably, readers of* **The Saturday Evening Post,** *one of the most popular and conservative middle-class weeklies, were more inclined than Kent to give credit to the managerial prowess of corporate giant Westinghouse.*

Picture Research Consultants & Archives.

ensuing depression, which shattered many consumer dreams. At the same time that the means to pay for the electric promise dwindled, Insull's electric empire collapsed, revealing fraudulent use of investors' money. Insull was indicted and vilified as the bearer of technology's false hopes. In the face of such woes, one of the most popular electric inventions, the radio, was used, ironically, to provide old-fashioned reassurance. At times of special crisis, families that had been lured from their traditional closeness around the hearth by central heating and light in every room were brought back together,

huddled around the radio—technology's electronic hearth—to hear FDR pledge protection of their homes and basic values in his fireside chats (see chapter 23). Once prosperity returned, they were assured, the promise of a bright electric future would be renewed. But reassurance and revival could only go so far. Surveys showed that, alongside wide distribution of more and better appliances as hard times eased, the hours people had spent taking care of their households before the advent of electricity remained essentially unchanged until the boom years after World War II.

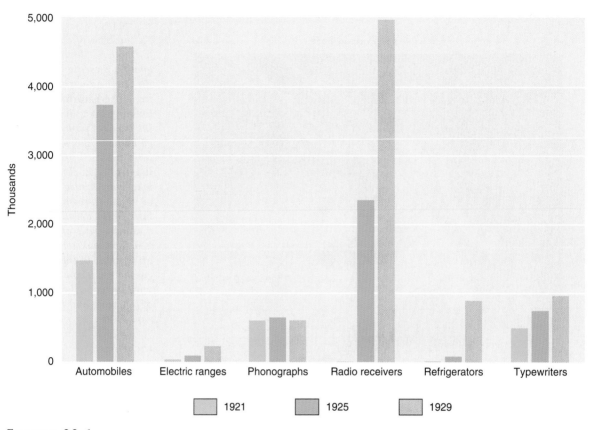

Figure 22.1

Production of Consumer Goods, 1920–1930
Transportation, communications, and entertainment changed the lives of consumers in the 1920s. While labor-saving devices for the home were popular, vastly greater sales of automobiles and radios showed that consumerism was powerful in moving people's attention beyond their homes.

one newspaper announced, "The first responsibility of an American to his country is no longer that of a citizen, but of a consumer."

The extent to which the new values overwhelmed the old became apparent in the runaway best-seller *The Man Nobody Knows,* written by a successful advertising executive, Bruce Barton, in 1925. The man nobody knew turned out to be Jesus Christ, commonly misrepresented as an unworldly enemy of the money changers in the temple. The real Jesus, Barton argued, was a crackerjack salesman whose parables were "the most powerful advertisements of all time." Jesus, Barton explained, was a genius at management who "picked up twelve men from the bottom ranks of business and forged them into an organization that conquered the world."

Society and Its Discontents

When Sigmund Freud visited the United States in 1908, the public knew little of his pioneering work in the psychology of the unconscious. But by the 1920s, Freud had become a household name. Most Americans were spared the complexity and pessimism of his works by learning about his new therapies in popular magazines that stressed self-fulfillment. Still, people realized that Freud offered a new way of looking at the world that was as radically different and important to the twentieth century as Charles Darwin's theory of evolution had been to the century before.

Freudian psychology, with its probing of the unconscious and its emphasis on the sexual origins

THE SHOPPERS
In this satirical painting, New York City scenic artist Martin Lewis shows two shoppers of the 1920s so attuned to fashion that they are wearing identical outfits and standing as if dancing the Charleston. Shown from the back to accent their anonymity, the pair look at store dummies who outdo them in style and grace, while a man nearby glances at the shoppers dully. The composition captures a certain awkward, comic yearning within the consumption boom of the 1920s for ways of purchasing elusive qualities of elegance and class.
Collection of John P. Axelrod.

of behavior, sought to break through the prudery of Victorian morality and to deal openly and honestly with human behavior. In the 1920s, much to Freud's disgust, Americans turned him on his head. If it is wrong to deny that we are sexual beings, they reasoned, then the key to health and happiness must lie in following impulse freely. Those who doubted this reasoning were simply "repressed." "I'm hipped on Freud and all that," one of F. Scott Fitzgerald's fictional flappers announced, demonstrating her commitment to personal license. The

rest of the message about the hard work of coming to terms with impulses and emotions she dismissed with the petulant complaint that "it's rotten that every bit of *real* love in the world is ninety-nine percent passion and one little soupçon of jealousy."

The new ethic excited a significant number of Americans to seek pleasure without guilt in a whirl of activity that earned the decade the name "Roaring Twenties." Others, inhibited by conscience or concern for appearances, used the words and images of vastly expanded mass communication to enjoy the spectacle from a safe distance.

At the Movies

Americans looking for happiness and escape found it most often at the movies. Starting with the construction of the Regent Theatre in New York City in 1913, thousands of movie palaces, some of them larger and more ornate than European opera houses, sprang up in cities across the country. Admission was the same for everyone, and, indistinguishable in the dark, common folk and the privileged alike could savor the same ideal of the good life.

The center of the film industry moved in the 1920s from makeshift sound stages in New York City to Hollywood, California, where producers found open space and endless sunshine. A new breed of industrial entrepreneur, the movie mogul, devised formulas combining images of opulence, sex, and adventure in thrillers, westerns, and Bible epics. Like Ford's River Rouge plant, Hollywood relied on mass production to satisfy a growing appetite for vicarious experience that by 1929 drew as many people to the movies in a single week as lived in the entire country (Figure 22.2).

To match the grand surroundings of the theater palaces, Hollywood created "movie stars," glamorous beings whose every move was tracked by fan magazines. With their perfect faces and figures wrapped in furs and tuxedos, they appeared at movie premieres as gods stepping from the screen in human form, while searchlights broadcast the event beyond the horizon and mere moviegoers stood mesmerized outside the circle of light. Actors with exotic names like Pola Negri, Rudolph Valentino, and Vilma Banky portrayed the romance of foreign lands where passion was allegedly freer. For settings closer to home, "America's Sweetheart," Mary Pickford, and her real-life husband, Douglas Fairbanks, offered more wholesome ad-

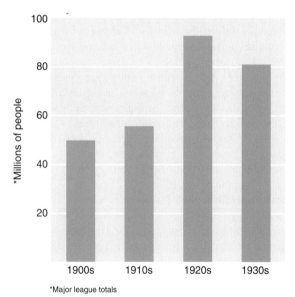

*Major league totals

FIGURE 22.2
Movie and Baseball Attendance
America's favorite pastimes, movies and baseball, served as a fever chart for the economy. The percentage of national income spent by spectators of movies and major league baseball remained nearly constant during the interwar years; the rise and fall of weekly movie attendance (top) and seasonal baseball (bottom) attendance mirrored the rise and fall of prosperity.

To match the grand surroundings of the theater palaces, Hollywood created "movie stars," glamorous beings whose every move was tracked by fan magazines.

Moralists who worried that the screen images might subvert propriety soon pressed for government regulation. To head off censorship, in 1922 the Motion Picture Producers and Directors of America hired former postmaster general Will Hays to monitor films for "decency and taste." Hays screened films and tried to balance the interests of public morality, creativity, and commerce without eliminating the raciness that made the movies so popular.

Like a magnet, the movie industry drew its leading figures from all points of the compass. Many studio owners and producers came from eastern European immigrant communities, while directors were often refugees from the stage or European film studios. Actors of color were still largely excluded (except when they were used for comic relief or as villains), but among the white majority, anyone who looked good on screen and could invent an elegant or rugged-sounding name could hope to become a star.

Sports and Hero Worship

Americans also found heroes in sports. Baseball, professionalized since 1871, solidified its place as the national pastime in the 1920s (see Figure 22.2). It remained essentially a game played by and for the working class, an outlet for raw energy and even a tinge of rebelliousness. In George Herman "Babe" Ruth, baseball had the most cherished free spirit of the time. An orphan who never really grew up, Ruth mixed his record-setting home runs with rowdy escapades, satisfying the view that sports offered a way to break out of the ordinariness of everyday life.

The public also fell in love with a young boxer from the grim mining districts of Colorado. As a teenager, Jack Dempsey had made his living hanging around saloons betting he could beat anyone in the house. When he took the heavyweight crown just after World War I, he was revered as America's equalizer, a stand-in for the average American who felt increasingly confined by bureaucracy and machine-made culture.

venture. Comedy made the closest connection with audiences, however, especially in calling sympathetic attention to the pitfalls and absurdity ordinary people faced. Most versatile of all the comics was Charlie Chaplin, whose famous character, the wistful tramp, showed an endearing inability to cope with the rules and complexities of modern life.

HEROES AND HEROINES

Within popular lore of the 1920s, two kinds of women looked up adoringly at two kinds of heroes. A wholesome image is seen at left on this 1927 cover of the **Popular Monthly Homecraft Magazine.** *Here the healthy outdoor girl type, smartly turned out in her raccoon coat and pennant, seems in flattering control of a naive college football hero. At the right, the pale, sensitive damsel Vilma Banky kneels imploringly before the hypnotic gaze of the movies' greatest heartthrob, Rudolph Valentino. The 1926 ad titillates with ambivalence. Is the pale heroine beseeching her kidnapper to release her? Or is she swooning with desire as the sheik begins to disrobe?*

Picture Research Consultants & Archives; Billy Rose Theatre Collection, The New York Public Library at Lincoln Center.

Football, essentially a college sport, held greater sway with the upper classes. The most celebrated coach, Knute Rockne of Notre Dame, was beloved for his advocacy of football as a parable of the good life of hard work and teamwork. Let the professors make learning as interesting as football, Rockne advised, and the problem of getting youth to learn would disappear. But in keeping with the times, football moved toward becoming a more public spectacle. The gridiron's greatest hero, Red Grange, a quiet, straitlaced son of the prairies, went on from the University of Illinois to apply both his skill and steady business sense to the development of a professional league.

The decade's hero worship reached its zenith in the celebration of Charles Lindbergh, a young pilot who had survived stunt flying and the equally risky pioneer air mail routes. On May 20, 1927, Lindbergh set out from Long Island in his specially built monoplane, *The Spirit of St. Louis,* to become the first person to fly nonstop across the Atlantic. Thirty-three hours later, Lindbergh landed at the Paris airport, where he was greeted by a wildly cheering crowd. Newspapers tagged Lindbergh the "Lone Eagle"—the perfect hero for an age that celebrated individual accomplishment. "Charles Lindbergh is the heir of all that we like to think is best in America," one journalist proclaimed. "He is the stuff out of which have been made the pioneers that opened up the wilderness. His are the qualities which we, as a people, must nourish." Lindbergh realized, however, that technical and organizational complexity was fast reducing chances for solitary achievement. To make the point about a new sort of heroism, he entitled his book about the flight *We* (1927) and cautioned cheering crowds not to forget the wonderful engine that made it all possible. Lindbergh reassured Americans that possibilities for human achievement remained for those with just the right technological mastery.

Women and Men of the Jazz Age

The nation's first licensed radio station, KDKA in Pittsburgh, began broadcasting in 1920, and soon American airwaves buzzed with news, sermons, soap operas, sports, comedy, and, most of all, music. Americans isolated in the high plains laughed at the latest jokes from New York. For the first time, citizens were able to listen to the voices of political candidates without leaving home. Most influentially, radio allowed advertisers to reach prospective customers in the intimacy of their own homes. Salesmen pitching their products did not have to face rebuff at the door but could come right into the nation's parlors via the airwaves. Between 1922 and 1929, the number of radio stations in the United States increased from 30 to 606. In those seven short years, the number of homes with radios jumped from 60,000 to a staggering 10,250,000.

Radio added to the growth of popular music, especially jazz. With its energetic style and its suggestion of youthful freedom and sexual openness, jazz was the product of African American artists. But in the 1920s, although a radio broadcast might occasionally feature the ragged rhythms of the King Oliver Creole Jazz Band or the "walking bass" stride piano style of James P. Johnson, white audiences for the most part embraced a classically trained musician aptly named Paul Whiteman. Although Whiteman's "symphonic jazz," with its strict tempos and avoidance of improvisation, left most black jazz fans cold, it helped bring white audiences around to a

form of music that polite society had often condemned as crude and low class.

For the first time, youth in the 1920s became a social class distinct in itself. As the traditional bonds of community, religion, and family loosened, the young felt less pressure to imitate their elders and more freedom to develop their own culture. An increasing number of college students helped the "rah-rah" style of college life become a fad, promoted in movies, songs, and advertisements. The collegiate set was the vanguard of the decade's "flaming youth."

Most stunning were the changes in the behavior of young women. In the 1920s, the "advanced" urban woman shed up to twelve yards of clothing, "parked" her corset in the cloakroom (if she wore one at all), bared her knees, smoked cigarettes, drank in speakeasies, and generally played havoc with traditionally conservative notions of female behavior. The daring "flapper," as she was called, became the symbol of youthful revolt. As her contemporary and chronicler F. Scott Fitzgerald described her in his novel *This Side of Paradise* (1920), she was "lovely and expensive and about nineteen."

For the first time, youth in the 1920s became a social class distinct in itself. As the traditional bonds of community, religion, and family loosened, the young felt less pressure to imitate their elders and more freedom to develop their own culture.

For all their spirit, rarely did the youth of the 1920s pose a threat to the status quo. For the most part, young people remained apathetic about social issues and eager to participate in the new consumer culture. Flaming youth rapidly cooled in office jobs and suburbs, and high-spirited flappers eventually settled down to become wives and mothers and employees. Yet even at home, women's lives reflected the changes of the new era. The greater availability of birth control allowed married people to remain passionate and yet have fewer children to take care of. New home appliances also lightened the load, although most rural homes were beyond the reach of power lines and urban middle-class women who had appliances still spent many hours cooking, mending, and cleaning.

HELD MAGAZINE COVER
Artist John Held lived and drew the extravagant life of the flaming youth of the Roaring Twenties. Raised in Mormon Utah, Held followed his artistic and journalistic skills to New York City and there found endless subjects to amuse himself. His caricatures of the Jazz Age came to typify it and made him a fortune. Like the high-living sorts he satirized, Held married and divorced a couple of times, dividing his time among his New York penthouse, Palm Beach cabana, and estate in Connecticut. Then, following the curve, he went broke in the Great Crash of 1929. Held gave up cartooning for landscape painting and sculpture and settled down on a small farm. Shown here is Held's inimitable style on the cover of the 1920s' leading humor magazine: sporty convertible, the flapper, and Held's signature caricature of the round-headed, almost puppetlike young man.
Culver Pictures.

For women who worked outside the home, the changing economy of the 1920s offered wider, but still limited, opportunity. Many factory jobs, such as those in the booming automobile industry, and most management positions remained male do-

mains. Women continued to become teachers and nurses, but more often found work as poorly paid secretaries, typists, file clerks, and salesclerks. By 1930, nearly eleven million women were employed, constituting 24 percent of the workforce, compared with 18 percent in 1900.

Black Assertion and the Harlem Renaissance

Cheers for the black soldiers who marched up Broadway after the First World War soon faded, and grim days of race riots and hardship followed. Still, a sense of optimism remained strong among African Americans. In New York City, the key elements of hope and talent came together to form an exceptionally dynamic moment in black history. In the years before the war, black people in New York had moved uptown from their cramped confinement in Hell's Kitchen to the spacious heights of Harlem. A highly cosmopolitan population seeking economic opportunity soon filled the new area, including poor migrants from the South and a more sophisticated wave of immigrants from the West Indies. Within that turbulent mix black artists and writers made Harlem a special place. Only with their guidance could a "New Negro," as critic and historian Alain Locke put it in a book by that name, rise from the ashes of a subjugated past and discover the race's true, creative identity.

That quest would prove more aggressive than it had been before the war. The military service of black troops raised their expectations of higher status in American society. Disillusioned with mainstream politics, many poor urban blacks turned for new leadership to a Jamaican-born visionary named Marcus Garvey. Garvey urged African Americans to rediscover the heritage of Africa and to take pride in their own culture and achievements. In 1917, Garvey launched the Universal Negro Improvement Association (UNIA) to help African Americans gain economic and political independence entirely outside of white society. By investing in their own ocean shipping company, the Black Star Line, Garvey's followers expressed the dual aim of financing their Back to Africa movement and providing the ships to carry themselves to their homeland.

Garvey's message drew enthusiastic crowds in Harlem and brought delegates from many countries to the UNIA convention of 1920. Garvey knew how to inspire followers; but he was a naive businessman, unprepared for the rough opposition he encountered. Sharp operators sold bad ships to the Black Star Line, and the federal government pinned charges of illegal practices on Garvey and deported him to Jamaica in 1927. The issues Garvey raised about black identity, racial pride, and the search for equality persisted, however, and his legacy remains at the center of black nationalist thought.

Hope for the emergence of a New Negro was also roused by an artistic outpouring in the 1920s that came to be known as the Harlem Renaissance. The poet Langston Hughes summed up the movement's central theme of self-respect in verse that shouted: "I am a Negro—and beautiful." In his music and writing, James Weldon Johnson focused on the rural southern culture that migrants brought into the streets of Harlem. In 1903, he had written the Negro national anthem, "Lift Every Voice," and in 1927, in "God's Trombones," he expressed the wisdom and beauty of black folktales. Zora Neale Hurston, as an anthropology student at Barnard College, focused on those tales. Her masterpiece, a novel called *Their Eyes Were Watching God* (1937), explores the complex passions of people within a self-governing southern black community of the rare sort she had known as a child in Florida. Langston Hughes, Claude McKay, and Countee Cullen added poetry as a way of conveying the vitality of life in Harlem amid the indifference and hostility of white America. Harlem painters, led by Aaron Douglas, sought to adapt African art, from which European modernist artists had begun taking inspiration, to the concept of the New Negro. In bold, colorful scenes Douglas combined biblical and African myths in ways that placed African Americans within a strong and unique tradition.

Hope for the emergence of a New Negro was also roused by an artistic outpouring in the 1920s that came to be known as the Harlem Renaissance.

NOAH'S ARK
The Harlem Renaissance gained its principal visual expression at the hands of Kansas-born painter Aaron Douglas. When Douglas arrived in New York City in 1925, he quickly attracted the attention of W. E. B. Du Bois, who placed great importance on the arts as a carrier of the African American soul. At Du Bois's urging, Douglas sought ways of integrating the African cultural heritage with American experience. This depiction of an African Noah commanding the loading of the ark displays a technique that became closely associated with African American art: strong silhouetted figures awash in misty color, indicating a connection between Christian faith and the vital, colorful origins of black Americans in a distant, mythologized African past.
Fisk University Art Galleries, Nashville, Tennessee.

White patrons became an important means of support for the Harlem Renaissance. But for most whites, Harlem was an exotic dark continent just up the street where they could find a lively nightlife. The most famous spot was the Cotton Club, a gangster-owned outlet for bootleggers. There, black performers hired to entertain the strictly white audience had to enter by the delivery doors and make careful preparations not to need the rest rooms, which were for whites only. For all its vigor and optimism, the Harlem Renaissance existed as an isolated demonstration of achievement in a society not yet prepared to allow African American talent full opportunity to flourish.

The Lost Generation

For many white writers and artists who felt alienated from a society they found crude and materialistic, Europe seemed the place to seek their renaissance. Young and mostly college-educated, these expatriates, as they came to be called, felt embittered by the war and renounced the progressives and patriots who had promoted it as a crusade. The poet Ezra Pound captured their view of what so many young men had died for:

> For an old bitch gone in the teeth,
> For a botched civilization.

In 1922, a young writer named Harold Stearns announced the secession of his generation through publication of a group of essays he had gathered under the ironic title *Civilization in the United States*. Relentlessly, the authors condemned the way sexual prudery and greed blighted virtually every aspect of the America they knew. Then, amid much public fanfare, Stearns and other alienated critics set sail for France, where they experienced an exhilarating sense of liberation. The American-born writer Gertrude Stein, long established in Paris, remarked famously, "They are the lost generation." Most of the expatriates, however, believed to the contrary that they had finally found themselves. The cost of living in Paris was low, and the culture receptive to free expression. Far from the complications of home and steady work, the expatriates helped launch the most creative period in American art and literature in the twentieth century.

The novelist whose spare, clean style best exemplified the expatriate efforts to reduce art to a mirror of basic reality was Ernest Hemingway. Hemingway's experience in the war, where he was wounded, convinced him that the conventional world in which he was raised, with its Christian moralism and belief in progress, was bankrupt. His own stern personal code of honor dismissed creeds, ideologies, and patriotism as pious attempts to cover up the fact that life is a losing battle with death. Hemingway's ideal of macho courage, "grace under pressure," guided a lonely, doomed struggle with the inevitable (in his case, suicide). In his novel *The Sun Also Rises* (1926), Hemingway makes the point with harrowing directness. His main character, Jake Barnes, is impotent as the result of a war wound. Bereft of conventional beliefs and romantic prospects, Barnes sets out with friends on an aimless journey through France and Spain,

the characters discovering little to sustain them except their own animal ability to appreciate sensual experience and endure suffering. Admirers of this exemplary work praised Hemingway's style because, in paring away unnecessary words, it seemed to express so perfectly a world stripped of illusions.

Writers who remained in America were often exiles in spirit who hoped that freedom from claims of duty and convention would help them explore the limits of creativity. Theater critic George Jean Nathan increased his fame when he proclaimed that "the great problems of the world—social, political, economic, and theological—do not concern me in the slightest." Within that atmosphere, novelist Sinclair Lewis in *Main Street* (1920) and *Babbitt* (1922) devastatingly satirized his native Midwest as a cultural wasteland. Humorists like James Thurber and Don Marquis created outlandish forms and characters to poke fun at taboos and inhibitions. And southern writers, led by William Faulkner, rallied against the South's reputation as a literary Sahara by exploring the dark undercurrents of that region's class and race heritage. But doubts about the new freedom surfaced as well. From the vantage of his own fame and wealth as chronicler of flaming youth, F. Scott Fitzgerald spoke with guilty brilliance in *This Side of Paradise* (1920) of a disillusioned generation "grown up to find all Gods dead, all wars fought, all faiths in man shaken."

Rural America and Resistance to Change

Rural America and urban America had eyed each other warily since the nineteenth century. Despair mounted in the 1920s when country people saw the center of American life shift from farm to city (Map 22.3). The rapid growth of cities and suburbs cost rural America its dominance over the nation's political and cultural life. It also put economic distance between city and country. Between 1918 and 1921, farm incomes and the value of farmland fell by 30 to 50 percent. Only large-scale farmers were able to afford the technological advances needed for prosperity. Others were hard pressed even to hold on to the agrarian ideal of self-reliant individualism; by the end of the decade, 40 percent of the nation's farmers had become landless. In 1930, 90 percent of rural homes had no indoor plumbing, gas, or electricity.

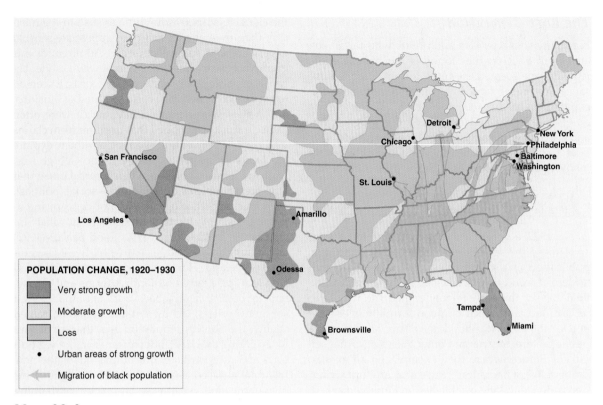

M A P 2 2 . 3

The Shift from Rural to Urban Population, 1920–1930
The movement of whites and Hispanics toward urban and agricultural opportunity made Florida, the West, and the Southwest the regions of fastest population growth. In contrast, large numbers of blacks left their traditional concentration in the South to find a better life in the North. Because almost all migrating blacks went from the countryside to cities in distant parts of the nation, while white and Hispanic migrants tended to move shorter distances toward familiar places, the population shift brought more drastic overall change to blacks than to whites and Hispanics.

In the eyes of country folk worried about their loss of status, the cities and the modern life they promoted seemed a menace to true values. Rural critics saw their communities as embodiments of an Anglo-Saxon heritage (conveniently ignoring that most blacks still lived in the rural South), while the cities filled with strangers from around the world. Rural America prided itself on being the seat of traditional Protestant values and lamented how the cities were controlled by Catholics, Jews, liberal Protestants, and atheists. Lacking in old-fashioned Puritan moral standards, modern urban culture seemed the cause of radical and blasphemous assaults on traditional values.

The Rebirth of the Ku Klux Klan

Some of those who felt forsaken by the modern world channeled their desperation into a revived Ku Klux Klan that first appeared in 1915. Although the new Klan rose once again in the South, where its predecessor had been created to curb the rights of blacks during reconstruction, it swiftly moved beyond the region. Imperial Grand Wizard Hiram Wesley Evans, a Texas dentist who styled himself as "the most average man in America," employed modern sales techniques to organize a network of klaverns (local societies) across the country. The nation, Evans argued, needed a thorough cleansing.

He promised that Klansmen would stoutly defend family, morality, and traditional values against the threat posed by blacks, immigrants, radicals, Catholics, Jews, and foreigners.

The Klan offered a certain counterfeit dignity for those who felt passed over by a changing society. It played on the decade's love of fraternal societies, with their secrecy, uniforms, and rituals, that helped counter a sense of insignificance for those outside the new world of giant corporations and large-scale farms. Like the Elks or the Odd Fellows, the Klan provided practical compensation in forging business contacts on the margins of society. At the same time, it appealed to the vengeful and brutal side of human nature, enabling its hooded members to intimidate anonymously with little fear of consequences. So many old-stock white Americans were suffering a sense of being displaced that, at its peak, the Klan attracted some three to four million members. By the mid-1920s, it virtually controlled Indiana and influenced politics in Illinois, California, Oregon, Texas, Louisiana, Oklahoma, and Kansas.

The Klan offered a certain counterfeit dignity for those who felt passed over by a changing society.

Eventually, the intolerance and lawlessness that revived the Klan caused it to wither away. Immigration restrictions eased the worry about invading foreigners, and sensational wrongdoing by Klan leaders cost it the support of radical moralists. Grand Dragon David Stephenson of Indiana, for example, went to jail for the kidnap and rape of a woman who subsequently committed suicide. Yet the social grievances and economic problems of the countryside and small towns remained, ready to be ignited by later protest movements.

The Scopes Trial

The clash between the old-time religion and the new spirit of science reached a dramatic climax in the Scopes trial in 1925. The confrontation occurred after several southern and border states passed legislation in the early 1920s against the teaching of Charles Darwin's theory of evolution in the public schools. Fundamentalist Protestants insisted that

THE LAW IS TOO SLOW
This stark depiction of a lynching by George Bellows in 1923 appeared just as the revived Ku Klux Klan was proclaiming itself the defender of traditional virtue in a sinful modern world. Bellows, an athlete as well as an artist, had gained fame as a realist and tough-minded radical before World War I and continued until his death in 1925 to spur social conscience even after doing so had gone out of fashion.

the Bible's creation story be taught as the literal truth. In answer to a clamor from scientists and civil liberties organizations for a challenge to the law, John Scopes, a young schoolteacher in Dayton, Tennessee, offered to test his state's ban on teaching evolution. When Scopes was brought to trial in the summer of 1925, Clarence Darrow, a brilliant defense lawyer from Chicago, volunteered to defend him. Darrow, an avowed agnostic, took on state's attorney William Jennings Bryan, the old war horse of the Democratic Party and symbol of rural America. Bryan, now aging and ill, prided himself on being the defender of Christian opposition to the idea that humans had evolved from apes.

The Scopes trial quickly degenerated into a media circus, despite the serious religious and philosophical issues it raised. The first trial to be covered live on radio, it attracted an avid nationwide audience. Reporters from big-city papers who converged on Dayton were largely hostile to Bryan, none more so than the cynical H. L. Mencken, who painted Bryan as a sort of Darwinian missing link ("a sweating anthropoid," a "gaping primate"). When, under relentless questioning by Darrow, Bryan declared on the witness stand that he did indeed believe the world was created in six days and that Jonah had lived in the belly of a whale, his humiliation in the eyes of most urban observers was complete. Although the Tennessee court upheld the law in defiance of modern intellectual consensus and punished Scopes with a $100 fine, Mencken had the last word in a merciless obituary for Bryan, who died just weeks after the trial ended. Portraying the "monkey trial" as a battle between the country and the city, Mencken flayed Bryan as a "charlatan, a mountebank, a zany without shame or dignity," motivated solely by "hatred of the city men who had laughed at him for so long."

As Mencken's acid prose indicated, Bryan's humiliation was not purely a victory of reason and science. It also reduced the esteem in which country people and their old values were held. The Ku Klux Klan revival and the Scopes trial dramatized and inflamed divisions between city and country, intellectuals and the unlettered, the privileged and the outcasts, the scoffers and the faithful.

Al Smith and the Election of 1928

Calvin Coolidge, who seemed a pillar of common sense and moral principle, added to the confusion by announcing in the summer of 1927 that he would not seek reelection. Who would now defuse the issues splitting the nation—prohibition, religious bigotry, and the clash between rural and urban values? Republicans chose Herbert Hoover, the energetic secretary of commerce who appeared best able to continue Coolidge's pro-business programs and bring conservative southern Democrats over to the Republican side. The Democrats nominated Governor Alfred E. Smith of New York, the son of Irish Catholic immigrant parents who had grown up on the sidewalks of New York and epitomized working-class city values. Smith, an outspoken "wet" (an opponent of prohibition), actively championed repeal of the Eighteenth Amendment.

Against these positions Republicans mobilized opposition from rural and urban conservatives.

Smith's greatest vulnerability, however, was that he was the first Catholic to run for president. An editorial in the *Baptist and Commoner* was typical of many such appeals to Protestant believers in arguing that the election of Smith "would be granting the Pope the right to dictate to this government what it should do." There would be edicts from the White House claiming that "Protestants are now living in adultery because they were not married by a priest." Are you willing, the editorial asked in its punch line, to accept a president who would tell us "our offspring are bastards"? Smith's connections with the Tammany Hall political machine also cost him support among moralists; and radio broadcasts added further to Smith's problems in the countryside, where listeners associated his New York City accent with alien and unrespectable elements.

Hoover, who neatly combined the images of morality, efficiency, service, and prosperity, won the election by a landslide (Map 22.4). He received 58 percent of the vote, taking all but eight states, and gained 444 electoral votes to Smith's 87. The Republicans managed to retain support of blacks in the South and at the same time wrenched five states loose from the formerly solid Democratic South.

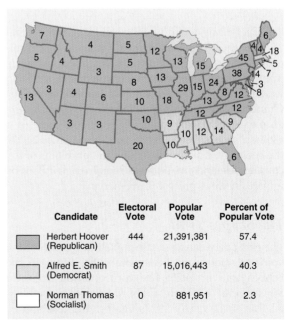

Candidate	Electoral Vote	Popular Vote	Percent of Popular Vote
Herbert Hoover (Republican)	444	21,391,381	57.4
Alfred E. Smith (Democrat)	87	15,016,443	40.3
Norman Thomas (Socialist)	0	881,951	2.3

MAP 22.4
The Election of 1928

The only dark cloud over the Republican victory, not much noted at the time, was the party's reduced support in the cities and among discontented farmers. The nation's largest cities voted Democratic in a striking reversal from 1924, indicating the rising strength of ethnic minorities, including Smith's fellow Catholics.

From the New Era to the Great Crash

At his inauguration in 1929, Herbert Hoover told the American people, "We in America today are nearer to the final triumph over poverty than ever before in the history of any land. The poorhouse is vanishing from among us." The nation had not yet reached that goal, he acknowledged, "but, given a chance to go forward with the policies of the last eight years, we shall soon with the help of God be in sight of the day when poverty will be banished from this nation." Those words came back to haunt Hoover, for in eight short months the Roaring Twenties came to a crashing halt. The prosperity Hoover touted collapsed with the stock market, and the nation fell into the most serious economic depression of all time. Hoover and his reputation were among the first casualties, along with the reverence for business that had been the hallmark of the New Era.

Herbert Hoover: The Great Engineer

It was one of the crueler ironies of the times that the Great Depression struck during Hoover's administration. Coming into office in 1929, Hoover displayed credentials that seemed to have prepared him to be a great president. From poor orphaned beginnings, Hoover had struggled upward to become one of the world's most successful mining engineers by the time he was thirty. Ten years later, having surmounted primitive conditions in Asia, labor wars, and even bombardment during China's Boxer Rebellion, he had become a millionaire with offices in New York and several European cities and a reputation as an organizational genius. His success in managing efforts to feed civilian victims of the fighting during World War I won him acclaim as "the Great Humanitarian" and led Woodrow Wilson to name him head of the Food Administration

HOOVER CAMPAIGN POSTER
Herbert Hoover's 1928 campaign poster neatly framed his major positions: middle-class prosperity in a house in the suburbs, complete with a car in every garage and, presumably, a chicken in every pot. To complete the display, smoking chimneys at a discreet distance remind voters that Hoover as secretary of commerce had promoted industry that made the suburban idyll possible.
Collection of Janice L. and David J. Frent.

after the United States entered the war. During the 1920s, Hoover's reputation soared even higher when he used his position as secretary of commerce to become the most active and accomplished cabinet member.

Hoover provided a widely read justification for the business culture he revered in a slender book titled *American Individualism* (1922). In it, he described intelligence as "a quality of the individual alone" and extolled the United States as the nation that gave the fullest opportunity to everyone who made an honest effort. Taking his own success as a benchmark, Hoover declared that a man who had not made a million dollars by the time he was forty didn't amount to much.

Hoover provided a widely read justification for the business culture he revered in a slender book titled American Individualism.

Because he was for efficiency and growth, Hoover thought of himself as a progressive, but his reluctance to use the government to force change and ameliorate bad conditions distanced him from the reform spirit of prewar progressives. Government's task, Hoover felt, was to promote private initiative and enforce rules of fair play. That hands-off approach reflected his lifetime aloofness from politics. The only elective office he had ever held was treasurer of his class at Stanford, and, having lived most of his adult life abroad, he had never voted in a presidential election. Aware of his limitations, Hoover feared the way he had been oversold. On the eve of taking office, he confided to a friend: "I have no dread of the ordinary work of the presidency. What I do fear is the . . . exaggerated idea . . . [that] I am a sort of superman, that no problem is beyond my capacity." He added prophetically, "If some unprecedented calamity should come upon the nation . . . I would be sacrificed to the unreasoning disappointment of a people who expected too much."

The Distorted Economy

Despite his fears, Hoover's belief in the prevailing economic system, reflected in his own unbroken success, led him to add to the overselling. Hoover's strong, assertive presence made it difficult for citizens to realize that the United States basked in the sunshine of a fool's paradise. Although America had become the world's leading economy, its leaders acted as though it were still a weak, developing country. American isolationism meant that European countries, devastated by the First World War, could not get the help they needed for full recovery. Rather than stepping in to help rebuild Europe's shattered economy, the Harding and Coolidge administrations demanded that European nations repay their war loans. In addition, the United States enacted tariffs that kept other nations from selling their goods to Americans. Foreign nations thus had less money to buy American goods, which were pouring out in record abundance. In a move that could work only in the short run, the United States propped up its export trade by extending credit to its foreign customers. Debt piled onto debt in an absurd pyramid. By the end of the decade, the United States accounted for 40 percent of the world's economic production and had acquired most of the world's gold in return for its exports.

The economy also suffered from skewed wealth at home. Farmers continued to suffer from low prices and chronic indebtedness; the average income of families on the land amounted to only $240 per year during the 1920s, and 54 percent earned less than $1,000. Industrial workers, though enjoying a slight rise in wages during the decade, failed to keep up with productivity and corporate profits. Overall, nearly two-thirds of all American families lived on less than the $2,000 per year that was needed to "supply only basic necessities." In sharp contrast, the top 1 percent received 15 percent of the nation's income, an amount equal to that received by the bottom 42 percent of the population. By 1929, the imbalance of wealth produced a serious problem in consumption. The rich, brilliantly portrayed in F. Scott Fitzgerald's *The Great Gatsby* (1925), gave the era much of its mythical glitter with their careless spending; but they could absorb only a tiny fraction of the nation's output. Ordinary folk, on whom the system ultimately depended, were unable to take up the slack. For a time, the new device of installment buying—buying on credit—kept consumer demand up; by the end of the decade, four out of five automobiles and two out of three radios were bought on credit. But personal indebtedness rose to an all-time high that could not be sustained.

Signs of economic trouble began to appear at mid-decade. A slowdown of new construction after

1925 indicated that the rate of business expansion had decreased. Faltering automobile sales signaled that, with nearly thirty million cars already on the road, demand had been met and producers would begin to cut back production and lay off workers. Banks followed suit. Between 1921 and 1928, as investment and loan possibilites faded, five thousand banks failed. Still, the boom went on. Confidence in fundamental soundness and eagerness to profit from it remained strong enough to conceal underlying flaws in the economy.

The Great Crash of 1929

The most spectacular example of the credit binge of the 1920s occurred in the stock market—the nerve center and symbol of the boom. Even after the economy began weakening in the mid-1920s, a get-rich-quick spirit persisted on Wall Street. There, buying stocks on margin—that is, putting up only part of the money at the time of purchase—became rampant. Many got rich in paper profits; but those who bought on credit could finance their loans only if their stock increased in value. Thus, the stock market became dependent on continued expansion, which the naive believed could go on forever. They had strong incentives to think so. Between 1924 and 1929, the values of stocks listed on the New York Stock Exchange increased by more than 400 percent. From that height, speculators could not even imagine that the market could fall and force them to meet their margin loans with cash they never had.

The stock market became dependent on continued expansion, which the naive believed could go on forever.

When stock purchased on margin rose to about 20 percent of the total by the summer of 1929, Hoover urged Richard Whitney, the head of the New York Stock Exchange, to tighten requirements. But Whitney, who later went to prison for embezzlement, gave only empty promises. Other representatives from prestigious banks and investment houses assured Hoover that all was well. Former president Calvin Coolidge stated tersely that, at current prices, stocks were a bargain. The prudent Hoover, however, decided to sell some of his own stocks. In rejecting the optimistic advice of the

boosters, Hoover took to a saying he kept repeating for the rest of his battle-scarred life: "The only trouble with capitalism is capitalists. They're too damned greedy."

Finally, in the autumn of 1929, the market hesitated. Like rabbits sniffing danger, investors nervously began to sell their overvalued stock. The dip quickly became a rush, building to panic on October 24, the day that came to be known as Black Thursday. Brokers jammed the stock exchange and overflowed into the street. Stirred by the cries of "Sell! Sell!" just outside their windows, the giants

BLACK FRIDAY
Edward Laning, a mural painter who lost his personal fortune in the stock market crash, gained a measure of revenge in this melodramatic version of panic on the Stock Exchange floor. The painting shows Stock Exchange president Richard Whitney standing firm in the center as prices and brokers collapse around him. A few years later, however, Whitney went to prison for stealing from other people's accounts to cover his own losses. Laning went on to fame for the murals he painted to adorn Ellis Island and the New York Public Library.
Collection of John P. Axelrod.

of finance gathered in the offices of J. P. Morgan Jr., son of the nineteenth-century Wall Street lion, to plot ways of restoring confidence. They injected $100 million of their assets to bolster the market and issued brave declarations of faith. But more panic selling came on Black Tuesday, October 29, the day the market suffered the greatest drop in history. In one of the few jaunty quips the panic produced, the theatrical trade journal *Variety* summed up the fiasco in its headline WALL STREET LAYS AN EGG.

It was a very large egg out of which hatched the deepest, longest-lasting economic collapse in the nation's history. The stunned public tended to believe that the Great Crash alone *caused* the Great Depression. It did not. In 1929, the national and international economies were already riddled with severe problems. But the dramatic loss of 10 percent of Americans' total personal wealth and the fear of risking what was left acted as a great brake on economic activity. With the collapse of the stock market went the New Era's aggressive confidence in America as a land of perpetually expanding prosperity.

Hoover and the Limits of Individualism

Hoover's first act in the aftermath of the crash was characteristic. He called a White House conference of business and labor leaders and urged them to join in a voluntary plan for recovery. The president asked businesses to forge ahead with their pre-crash investment plans, maintain production, and keep their workers on the job. He asked labor to accept the status quo and relinquish demands for improvements in wages, hours, or conditions. Within a few months, however, the bargain had fallen apart. As demand for their products declined, industrialists cut production, sliced wages, and laid off workers. Poorly paid or unemployed workers could not buy much, and decreased spending led to further cuts in production and further loss of jobs. Thus began the terrible spiral of economic decline.

Hoover did not just sit back and watch the depression cut its swath through American society. He worked long hours to find solutions, and, despite what people thought, felt the suffering of the American people. But his belief that the will to overcome adversity was "a quality of the individual alone" hobbled his ability to act. He resisted plans that called for direct government intervention in the economy but also disagreed with Secretary of the Treasury Andrew Mellon, who counseled that there

was nothing the administration could do but let the depression run a painful course of eliminating those too weak to compete. Hoover countered that cooperation between a free people and a sympathetic government could fix the problems and set the nation back on course.

In early 1930, Hoover got Congress to authorize $420 million for public works projects to give the unemployed something useful to do and create more purchasing power. Congress also agreed to cut taxes by $140 million to stimulate investment. To deal with the problems of rural America, Congress in 1930 passed the Agricultural Marketing Act. It created the Farm Board, which used its budget of $500 million to buy up agricultural surpluses and thus, it was hoped, raise prices. Although the Farm Board bought one-third of the nation's wheat supply, conditions worsened. To help end the decline, Hoover joined conservatives in urging protective tariffs on agricultural goods. With his approval, the Hawley-Smoot tariff of 1930 established the highest rates in history.

All to little avail. With each year of Hoover's administration, conditions worsened. Tariffs did not end the suffering of farmers because foreign nations retaliated with increased tariffs of their own that further crippled American farmers' ability to sell abroad. Even more pressing was the plight of the unemployed. Hundreds of thousands of additional workers lost their jobs each month. By 1932, one-quarter of the American workforce—more than 12 million men and women—were unemployed. There was no federal relief, and state services and private charities were swamped. Cries grew louder for the federal government to give hurting people relief, but Hoover counseled fortitude and private charity instead. Comparing federal aid to the "dole" in England, which he thought was destroying the moral fiber of the chronically unemployed, Hoover called upon the Red Cross in 1931 to distribute agricultural surpluses to the hungry. In the face of dire unmet need, he relaxed his principles enough in 1932 to offer small federal loans, not gifts, to the states to help them in their relief efforts. But these concessions were no more than Band-Aids on deep wounds.

Hoover's response to hard-pressed industry was more generous. In keeping with his previous efforts to promote cooperation between business and government, Hoover sponsored the Reconstruction Finance Corporation (RFC), a federal agency empowered to lend government funds to endangered banks, insurance companies, and railroads. It was a "trickle-down" theory: Pump money into the economy at the top, and in the long run the people at the bottom would benefit. But in the long run, as the great English economist of the day John Maynard Keynes pointed out, we are all dead. In the short run, what critics of the RFC called a "millionaires' dole" trickled very little down to the poor. One skeptic said, in earthy terms, that Hoover was trying to feed the sparrows by first feeding the horses. When it came to public welfare, however, Hoover's disapproval of federal handouts to people who should be self-reliant meant that the sparrows got very little. That was made clear by the RFC's refusal to finance welfare for the destitute in Chicago while allocating $90 million to the city's Central Republic Bank, headed by a former RFC leader.

Life in the Depression

In 1930, the nation woke up to the realization that prosperity would not soon return. The trouble was too deep, the engine too cold to restart. Suffering on a massive scale began, and a mood of cold despair settled over the land. Hollow-eyed men and women grew increasingly bewildered and angry in the face of cruel ambiguities. They saw unsellable agricultural surpluses in the countryside and knew that their children were going to bed hungry. They saw factories standing idle and knew that they and millions of others were willing to work. The gap between the American people and leaders who failed to resolve these contradictions widened as the depression deepened. By 1932, America's economic problems had become a dangerous social crisis.

The Human Toll

Statistics provide a scaffolding for understanding the human dimension of the Great Depression. When Herbert Hoover took office in 1929, the American economy stood at its peak. When he left in 1933, it had reached its twentieth-century low. More than nine thousand banks had shut their doors, and depositors had lost more than $2.5 billion. In 1929, national income was $88 billion. By 1933, it had declined to $40 billion. In 1929, unemployment was 3.1 percent, one and a half million workers. By 1933, unemployment stood at 25 percent, twelve and a half million workers.

One by one the nation's great steel mills and foundries, once the noisy centers of industrial might, had fallen quiet (Figure 22.3). U.S. Steel, the

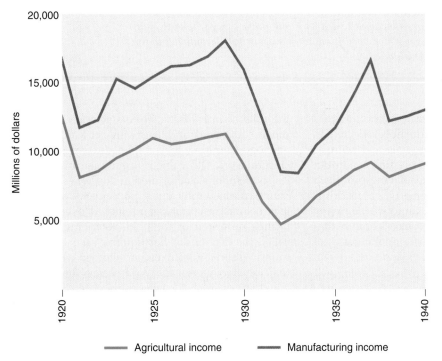

FIGURE 22.3

Manufacturing and Agricultural Income, 1920–1940

After economic collapse, recovery in the 1930s began under New Deal auspices. Sharp declines in 1937–1938, when federal spending was reduced, indicated that restoring manufacturing and agricultural income still needed New Deal stimuli.

Agricultural income   Manufacturing income

PRIVATE CAR

*In the mid-1930s, LeConte Stewart, an artist who spent most of his life painting the landscapes of his native Utah, noticed a new sight. From his remote hillside above the Union Pacific railroad tracks, he witnessed a stream of tramps heading west. The sight of one young man jauntily braced in the doorway of a boxcar made Stewart think of the elegant private cars of millionaires that used to travel along those same tracks. Stewart entitled this painting **Private Car** and achieved fame for his beautifully ironic depiction of a new wave of pioneers fleeing trouble.*

Private Car by LeConte Stewart. © The Church of Latter-Day Saints.

country's largest producer, operated at only 12 percent capacity in 1932. The reduction reflected in part the huge cutback of automobile and railroad manufacture, which also made the streets emptier and added to the stillness. After having produced an average of six hundred locomotives a year during the 1920s, the American Locomotive Company turned out only one in 1932. "Once I built a railroad," lamented one of the most popular songs of the year, "now it's done. Brother, can you spare a dime?"

Jobless, homeless victims wandered in search of work, and the tramp, or hobo, became one of the most visible figures of the decade. Young men and women unable to land their first job made up about half of the million-strong army of hoboes. Riding the rails or hitchhiking, the vagabonds tended to move southward and westward, toward the sun and opportunities, they hoped, for seasonal agricultural work. Other unemployed men and women, less hopeful or sick, huddled in doorways—human "junk," as one writer put it. Scavengers haunted alleys behind restaurants and picked over garbage dumps in search of food. In describing what he called the "American Earthquake," the writer Edmund Wilson told of an elderly woman who always took off her glasses to avoid seeing the maggots crawling over the garbage she ate. Starvation claimed its victims. Four New York City hospitals reported a total of ninety-five deaths from hunger in 1931. But enervating, rampant malnutrition posed the greater threat. The Children's Bureau announced that one of five schoolchildren did not get enough to eat.

The worst hardships hit the jobless and their families, estimated by *Fortune* magazine to include thirty-four million persons. But those at work also felt the pinch. The average weekly wage in 1932 was only $16.21. Some paychecks dwindled away to virtually nothing. In Chicago, the majority of working women received less than twenty-five cents an hour. In the lumber industry, hourly rates fell to ten cents; in general contracting to seven and a half cents; and in the sawmills to a nickel. At rock bottom, Americans had to face the painful truth that having a job did not necessarily mean avoiding hunger or destitution.

Jobless, homeless victims wandered in search of work, and the tramp, or hobo, became one of the most visible figures of the decade.

Rural poverty was most acute. Landless tenant farmers and sharecroppers, mainly in the South, came to symbolize how poverty crushed the human spirit. In 1930, eight and a half million people, three million of them black, lived in tenant and sharecropping families—amounting to one-quarter of the total southern population. Often illiterate, usually without cash incomes, they crowded into two- and three-room cabins lacking screens or even doors, without plumbing, electricity, running water, or sanitary wells. They subsisted—just barely—on salt pork, cornmeal, molasses, beans, peas, and whatever they could hunt or fish. All the diseases of dietary and vitamin deficiencies wracked them. When economist John Maynard Keynes was asked whether anything like this degradation had existed before, he replied, "Yes, it was called the Dark Ages and it lasted four hundred years."

To meet this human catastrophe, the nation was equipped with the most limited welfare system in the Western world. There was no federal assistance, only a patchwork of voluntary institutions and pinchpenny state and local agencies. For a family of four without any income, the best the city of Philadelphia could do was provide $5.50 per week. That was not enough to live on, but still comparatively generous. New York City, where the greatest number of welfare cases gathered, provided only $2.39 per week; and Detroit, devastated when the bottom fell out of the auto industry, allotted 60 cents a week before the city ran out of money altogether.

The deepening crisis roused old fears and caused some Americans to look for scapegoats. Among the most thoroughly scapegoated were Mexican Americans. During the relatively prosperous years of the 1920s, cheap agricultural labor from Mexico flowed legally across the U.S. border, welcomed by the large farmers. In the 1930s, however, public opinion turned on the newcomers, decrying them as dangerous aliens who took jobs from Americans. Government officials, most prominently those in Los Angeles County, with support from the Department of Labor, targeted all Mexican residents for deportation, regardless of citizenship status. As many as half a million Mexicans and Mexican Americans were deported or fled to Mexico. Among them were children born in the United States, American citizens from the start who had never lived outside the country.

The depression deeply affected the American family. Young people postponed marriage; when they did marry, they produced so few children that demographers warned that, for the first time, the United States was on the verge of losing population. White women, who generally worked in low-paying service areas—as cooks, salesclerks, and secretaries—did not lose their jobs as often as men who worked in industry. Unemployed men resented women workers, yet necessity drove women into the marketplace. Overall, some 25 percent more women were employed for wages in 1940 than in 1930.

Unemployed men resented women workers, yet necessity drove women into the marketplace.

As women left the home to replace their husbands as breadwinners, families experienced stress. After a decade of rising consumption, smaller incomes led to significant belt tightening. Working women became increasingly decisive and self-reliant at the same time idle men fell prey to guilt and loss of self-esteem. Yet, though family violence, alcoholism, and suicide escalated, the divorce rate went down. The desperately poor could not afford the legal expense; instead, in dramatically rising numbers, men resorted to desertion.

Denial and Escape

In the midst of the mounting crisis, J. P. Morgan Jr., the living symbol of American capitalism, testified before a congressional committee where he defended the economic importance of preserving an elite. "If you destroy the leisure class," he lectured, "you destroy civilization." When pressed to define the "leisure class," Morgan responded that it included all those who could afford a maid—about twenty-five or thirty million people, he reckoned, until informed that there were only about two million servants in the entire country. Morgan's ignorance was typical of many from his class. Under scrutiny, those who had presided over the economic collapse and now sought to lead the nation back to prosperity showed how little they had troubled to learn about the society that had made them rich. It turned out, though, that Morgan had learned enough to avoid paying income tax from 1929 to 1932.

As the economy and the reputations of its leaders sank, Hoover became an object of scorn. Makeshift shantytowns that sprang up on the edges of America's cities were called "Hoovervilles." Newspapers used as cover by those sleeping on the streets were "Hoover blankets." An empty pocket turned inside out was a "Hoover flag," and jackrabbits caught for food were "Hoover hogs." Innumerable bitter jokes circulated about Hoover. One gibe asserted that Hoover was the world's greatest engineer: "In a little more than two years he has drained, ditched, and damned the United States." Another story told of Hoover asking Andrew Mellon for a nickel to call up a friend. "Here's a dime," Mellon is said to have replied, "call up all your friends."

Hoover's effort to set an example did not help. To express his confidence in prosperity, he favored formal dress and manners in the White House and for dinner, with or without guests, he was attended by a retinue of valets and waiters. No one was starving, he calmly assured the American people from within that display of prosperity.

His administration did not consider it the business of the federal government to investigate the truth of that assertion. Walter Gifford, president of the American Telephone and Telegraph Company, appointed by Hoover to coordinate private relief efforts, acknowledged to a Senate subcommittee that he had made no attempt to compile figures on how many people were out of work and on relief. Exasperated, Senator Robert La Follette asked if Gifford

had any impulse to know the facts. Gifford's response reflected how the nation's business leadership distanced itself from the problems of failure and poverty. "Well," said Gifford genially, "I will not say that I did not make any estimate for my own interest and amusement."

While the wealthy practiced denial, other Americans sought refuge from reality at the movies. Throughout the depression, between sixty and seventy-five million people (nearly two-thirds of the nation) managed to scrounge up enough dimes to fill the movie palaces every week. Box office successes typically blended nostalgia for the lost Golden Twenties with the hope that renewed prosperity lay just around the corner. The leading musicals in 1933, *Forty-Second Street* and *Gold Diggers,* each offered a variation on the old rags-to-riches story of the chorus girl who makes the most of her big break.

"BUT HE TOOK CREDIT FOR THIS!"
This angry cartoon in a traditionally Republican newspaper poses the key dilemma for Hoover's reelection campaign in 1932. How could Hoover, the "Great Engineer," lionized as the dynamic driver of the 1920s economic boom, now plead helplessness before what he considered the European causes of economic collapse? Stunned into silence by the accusing figure, who like a graveyard specter points the bony finger of doom, Hoover's spokesman can do nothing to counter the deepening sense that the great claims for guided prosperity in the 1920s had turned out to be empty.
Franklin D. Roosevelt Library.

Grim conditions moved a few filmmakers to grapple with depression woes rather than escape them. Films such as King Vidor's *Our Daily Bread* (1932) and John Ford's *The Grapes of Wrath* (1940) expressed compassion for the down-and-out. Gangster films taught grim lessons about ill-gotten gains. Indeed, under the new production code of 1930, designed to protect public morals, all movies had to find some way to show that crime does not pay. *Public Enemy* (1931), the classic cautionary tale about the doom that awaits those who break the law found a particularly shocking way to do so when it ended with gangsters delivering the bullet-riddled body of a hoodlum to the doorstep of his saintly, long-suffering mother.

Despite Hollywood's efforts to keep Americans on the right side of the law, crime increased in the early 1930s. Away from the movie palaces, out in the countryside, the plight of people who had lost their farms to bank foreclosures cut so deep that the romantic idea took hold that bank robbers were only getting back what banks had stolen from the poor. Woody Guthrie, the populist folk singer from Oklahoma, captured the public's tolerance for outlaws in his widely admired tribute to a murderous bank robber with a choirboy face, "The Ballad of Pretty Boy Floyd":

> Yes, as through this world I ramble,
> I see lots of funny men,
> Some will rob you with a six-gun,
> Some will rob you with a pen.
> But as through your life you'll travel,
> Wherever you may roam,
> You won't never see an outlaw drive
> A family from their home.

Working-Class Militancy

Although the nation's working people bore the brunt of the economic collapse, the labor movement, including the dominant American Federation of Labor (AFL), was slow to respond. Organized labor had been hobbled during the 1920s by court injunctions curtailing the right of unions to organize and strike. Early in the depression, William Green, head of the AFL, echoed Hoover when he argued that a dole would turn the worker into "a ward of the state." But by 1931, Green had turned militant. "I warn the people who are exploiting the workers," he shouted at the AFL's annual convention, "that they can drive them only so far before they

will turn on them and destroy them. They are taking no account of the history of nations in which governments have been overturned. Revolutions grow out of the depths of hunger."

Like the labor leaders, the American people were slow to anger, then strong in protest. On the morning of March 7, 1932, several thousand unemployed autoworkers massed at the gates of Ford's River Rouge factory in Dearborn, Michigan, to demand work. Henry Ford sent out his private security forces, who told the demonstrators to disperse. The workers refused and began hurling rocks. The Ford army responded with tear gas and freezing water but quickly escalated to gunfire. When they stopped, four demonstrators were dead and dozens more wounded. An outraged public—forty thousand strong—turned out for the unemployed men's funerals. Editorials and protest rallies across the country denounced Ford's callous and brutal resort to violence.

Farmers, who desperately needed relief, mounted an uprising of their own soon afterward. When Congress refused to guarantee farm prices that would at least equal the cost of production, some three thousand farmers, led by the flamboyant Milo Reno, created the National Farmers' Holiday Association, so named because its members planned to force farmers to take a "holiday" from delivering produce to the public. Invoking the Boston Tea Party, Reno and his followers barricaded roads around Sioux City, Iowa, turned back farmers heading for market, and dumped thousands of gallons of milk in the ditches. Although the rebellion was short-lived and did not force a critical shortage of food, it raised general awareness of farm grievances. Farm militants had fuller material effect with what they called "penny sales." When farms defaulted on their mortgages and were put up for auction, neighbors packed the auctions and, after warning others not to bid, bought the foreclosed property for a few pennies and returned it to the bankrupt owners. Under this kind of pressure, some states suspended debts or reduced mortgages. Where evictions continued, farmers stepped up their protests. In early 1933, enraged Iowa farmers hauled Judge Charles Bradley out of his courtroom in midtrial. Taking him to a remote place, they smeared him with grease and released him only after he lost consciousness from being dragged with a rope around his neck.

In the vast agricultural holdings of California, resistance combined farmer and labor tactics. When landowners cut their already substandard wages to laborers in what one critic aptly called "factories in the fields," more than fifty thousand farmworkers, most of them Mexicans, went on strike. Surveying the strife mounting nationwide, John Simpson, president of the National Farmers Union, observed in 1933 that "the biggest and finest crop of revolutions you ever saw is sprouting all over the country right now."

Hard times also revived the left in America. When the crash struck, Eugene Debs was dead and so, for all purposes, was the Socialist Party. But the Great Depression—the massive failure of Western capitalism—brought socialism back to life and the Communist Party to its greatest size and influence in American history. Eventually, some 100,000 disillusioned Americans—workers, intellectuals, college students—joined the Communist Party in the belief that only an overthrow of the capitalist system could save the victims of depression. In 1931, the party, having increased membership in its National Miners Union from one hundred to twenty-five thousand, carried its convictions into Harlan County, Kentucky, to support a strike by harshly oppressed coal miners. Newspapers and newsreels riveted the attention of the public with their graphic portrayal of the violence unleashed by mine owners' thugs against the strikers. Eventually, the miners were beaten down, but the Communist Party emerged from the coalfields with a reputation as the most dedicated and fearless champion of the union cause.

Harlan County Coal Strike, 1931

The Great Depression brought socialism back to life and the Communist Party to its greatest size and influence in American history.

The left also led the fight against racism. While both major parties hesitated to challenge the system of segregation in the South, the Socialist Party, led by moral reformer Norman Thomas, sought to

SCOTTSBORO BOYS

This lithograph by black artist Prentiss Taylor was chosen for the cover of **Scottsboro Limited** *(1931), a collection by Langston Hughes of four of his poems and his play protesting the imprisonment of nine black youths in Alabama on trumped-up charges of rape. Clustered on a platform above the clamor surrounding the case, the nine boys seem like puppets suspended from telephone wires. Helpless, imploring, they could only hope that their Communist Party lawyers, who embraced the case as a way to draw blacks to the party, could defeat white extremist prosecutors insisting that conviction was necessary to defend white supremacy and Southern womanhood. Not until 1948 had appeals finally managed to lift all the boys down from their suspended state into freedom.*
Library of Congress.

break down the system of sharecropping that left many African Americans in poverty and virtual servitude. The Communist Party took action as well. When nine young black men in Scottsboro, Alabama, were arrested on trumped-up rape charges, a team of lawyers sent by the party managed to save the defendants from the electric chair. The party also opposed the efforts of Alabama plantation owners to evict their black tenants. Although Communists were unable to force much change on the deeply entrenched southern way of life, their efforts briefly attracted new recruits to the party. From only about fifty black members in 1930, party totals rose to ten thousand by the end of the decade before most of the converts returned to traditional reform movements rooted in constitutional rights and religious conviction.

The left often sparked action, but protests by workers and farmers occurred on a far greater scale. Breadlines, soup kitchens, foreclosures, unemployment, and cold despair drove patriotic men and women to question American capitalism. "I am as conservative as any man could be," a Wisconsin farmer explained, "but any economic system that has in its power to set me and my wife in the streets, at my age—what can I see but red?"

Conclusion: The Era of Boom and Bust

The decade of the 1920s defies easy generalization. During those years living standards rose, economic opportunity increased, and an image of cultural and personal liberation prevailed. For many Americans at the time, however, none of the glamour had much meaning. Instead of plunging into speculation on Wall Street, seeking thrills at speakeasies, or escaping to Paris, the vast majority went ahead as before with the struggle to attain a decent existence.

After the stock market crash swept away the aura of high living, different images emerged to fix the depression in memory: apple sellers on Broadway; empty apartment buildings alongside cardboard shantytowns; mountains of oranges rotting in the California sun while guards with shotguns chased away the hungry. Sometimes the image was of sullen apathy flaming into revolt: a line of unemployed men in New York City suddenly charging hiring agents; destitute farmers invading a small town in Arkansas to loot the food stores at gunpoint.

Eugene Debs, the most beloved socialist and friend of the common man, took from his battles in and out of prison the lesson that human happiness is never found through a solitary search. "When I rise," he liked to say, "it will be *with* the ranks, and not *from* the ranks." In the first years of the depression, however, faith in any sort of rise waned as the laboring ranks receded into hardship. The businessmen who rallied around Herbert Hoover thus faced something more desperate, more radical, than the old call for working-class solidarity and progressive reform. On a night in June 1931, a man driving a large car on the outskirts of Gary, Indiana, got a taste of what that might be when a brick crashed through his windshield. "What's the big idea?" he shouted, as he slammed on his brakes. Out of the darkness came the reply: "All rich guys ought to be strung up." "Who are you?" the driver asked. "We're the fellows that'll do the stringing."

www.bedfordstmartins.com/tap   SEE THE ONLINE STUDY GUIDE to assess your mastery of the material covered in this chapter.

CHRONOLOGY

1920 Eighteenth Amendment, prohibiting sale of liquor, goes into effect.

Nineteenth Amendment, granting women the vote, ratified.

Station KDKA in Pittsburgh begins first regular commercial radio broadcasts.

Marcus Garvey hosts Universal Negro Improvement Association convention in Harlem.

Republican Warren G. Harding elected president.

1921 Sheppard-Towner Act, providing infant health care, passes in Congress.

1922 Fordney-McCumber Act sets protective tariffs at record heights.

Principles of new business-minded era expressed in publication of Henry Ford's *My Life and Work* and Herbert Hoover's *American Individualism.*

About thirty artists and intellectuals renounce American society in *Civilization in the United States.*

New laws imposing quotas according to nationality end historical tradition of open immigration.

1923 Equal Rights Amendment introduced in Congress.

August. Harding dies in office, succeeded by Calvin Coolidge.

1924 Calvin Coolidge elected president.

1925 John Scopes convicted for violating Tennessee statute forbidding teaching of evolution.

Alain Locke expresses cultural aspirations of Harlem Renaissance in *The New Negro.*

1926 Ernest Hemingway's novel of expatriate Paris, *The Sun Also Rises,* published.

1927 Charles Lindbergh becomes America's most famous hero by flying alone across Atlantic.

Italian anarchist immigrants Sacco and Vanzetti executed.

1928 Herbert Hoover defeats Alfred E. Smith in presidential election.

1929 Robert and Helen Lynd publish their study of an average American small city, *Middletown.*

October 24. Stock market collapses on Black Thursday.

1931 Nine black men arrested in Scottsboro, Alabama, ardently defended by Communist Party lawyers.

1932 Several thousand demonstrators at Ford plant protest unemployment; security forces fire on crowd, killing four.

National Farmers' Holiday Association blocks roads and pours milk on ground to protest falling prices.

BIBLIOGRAPHY

GENERAL WORKS

Frederick Lewis Allen, *Only Yesterday: An Informal History of the Nineteen-Twenties* (1930).

Dorothy Brown, *Setting a Course: American Women in the 1920s* (1987).

Norman Cantor, *Twentieth-Century Culture: Modernism to Deconstruction* (1988).

Paul A. Carter, *Another Part of the Twenties* (1977).

Stanley Coben, *Rebellion against Victorianism: The Impetus for Cultural Change in 1920s America* (1991).

Robert Crunden, *From Self to Society: Transition in American Thought, 1919–1941* (1972).

Lynn Dumenil, *The Modern Temper: American Culture and Society in the 1920s* (1995).

David J. Goldberg, *Discontented America: The United States in the 1920s* (1999).

William E. Leuchtenburg, *The Perils of Prosperity, 1914–1932* (1958).

Robert S. Lynd and Helen M. Lynd, *Middletown: A Study in Modern American Culture* (1929).

Michael Parrish, *Anxious Decades: America in Prosperity and Depression, 1920–1941* (1992).

MAINSTREAM POLITICS, 1920–1933

Kristi Andersen, *After Suffrage: Women in Partisan and Electoral Politics before the New Deal* (1996).

David Burner, *Herbert Hoover: A Public Life* (1979).

Warren I. Cohen, *Empire without Tears: America's Foreign Relations, 1921–1933* (1987).

Frank Costigliola, *Awkward Dominion: American Political, Economic, and Cultural Relations with Europe, 1919–1933* (1984).

Paula Elder, *Governor Alfred E. Smith: The Politician as Reformer* (1983).

Lewis Ethan Ellis, *Republican Foreign Policy, 1921–1933* (1968).

Robert H. Ferrell, *The Strange Deaths of Warren Harding* (1996).

Donald R. McCoy, *Calvin Coolidge* (1967).

Michael E. McGerr, *The Decline of Popular Politics: The American North, 1865–1928* (1986).

Frances Fox Piven and Richard A. Cloward, *Why Americans Don't Vote* (1988).

William Appleman Williams, *The Tragedy of American Diplomacy* (1959).

Joan Hoff Wilson, *Herbert Hoover: Forgotten Progressive* (1975).

SCIENCE AND CONSUMPTION

Susan Porter Benson, *Counter Cultures* (1986).

Ruth Schwartz Cowan, *More Work for Mother: The Ironies of Household Technology from the Open Hearth to the Microwave* (1983).

James J. Flink, *The Automobile Age* (1988).

Louis Galambos and Joseph Pratt, *The Rise of the Corporate Commonwealth: U.S. Business and Public Policy in the Twentieth Century* (1988).

Kenneth T. Jackson, *Crabgrass Frontier: The Suburbanization of the United States* (1985).

T. J. Jackson Lears, *Fables of Abundance: A Cultural History of Advertising in America* (1994).

Roland Marchand, *Advertising the American Dream: Making Way for Modernity, 1920–1940* (1985).

David F. Noble, *America by Design: Science, Technology, and the Rise of Corporate Capitalism* (1977).

Ronald C. Tobey, *The American Ideology of National Science, 1919–1930* (1971).

Reynold M. Wik, *Henry Ford and Grass-Roots America* (1972).

LABOR

Irving Bernstein, *The Lean Years: A History of the American Worker, 1920–1933* (1960).

Colin Gordon, *New Deals: Business, Labor and Politics in America, 1920–1935* (1994).

Sanford M. Jacoby, *Employing Bureaucracy: Managers, Unions, and the Transformation of Work in American Industry, 1900–1945* (1985).

John A. Salmond, *Gastonia 1929: The Story of the Loray Mill Strike* (1995).

Winifred Wandersee, *Women's Work and Family Values, 1920–1940* (1981).

Robert H. Zieger, *Republicans and Labor, 1919–1929* (1969).

RURAL AND SMALL TOWN LIFE

Michael L. Berger, *The Devil Wagon in God's Country: The Automobile and Social Change in Rural America, 1893–1929* (1979).

James N. Gregory, *American Exodus: The Dust Bowl Migration and Okie Culture in California* (1989).

Jack Temple Kirby, *Rural Worlds Lost: The American South, 1920–1960* (1987).

Donald Worster, *Dust Bowl: The Southern Plains in the 1930s* (1979).

POPULAR CULTURE

Thomas Cripps, *Slow Fade to Black: The Negro in American Film, 1900–1942* (1977).

Ann Douglas, *Mongrel Manhattan in the 1920s* (1994).

Ronald Edsforth, *Popular Culture and Political Change in Modern America* (1991).

Lewis Erenberg, *Steppin' Out: New York City Nightlife and the Transformation of American Culture, 1890–1930* (1981).

Paula S. Fass, *The Damned and the Beautiful: American Youth in the 1920s* (1977).

Lary May, *The Big Tomorrow: Hollywood and the Politics of the American Way* (2000).

Ray Robinson, *Rockne of Notre Dame: The Making of a Football Legend* (1999).

Steven J. Ross, *Working-Class Hollywood: Silent Film and the Shaping of Class in America* (2000).

Arnold Shaw, *The Jazz Age: Popular Music in the 1920s* (1987).

Robert Sklar, *Movie-Made America* (1975).

Robert Smith, *Babe Ruth's America* (1974).

Susan Smulyan, *Selling Radio: The Commercialization of American Broadcasting, 1920–1934* (1994).

EDUCATION AND ART

Charles C. Alexander, *Here the Country Lies: Nationalism and the Arts in Twentieth-Century America* (1980).

Malcolm Cowley, *Exile's Return* (1934).

Malcolm Cowley, *The Dream of the Golden Mountains: Remembering the 1930s* (1980).

Helen Lefkowitz Horowitz, *Campus Life: Undergraduate Cultures from the End of the Eighteenth Century to the Present* (1987).

Lary May, *Outside In: Minorities and the Transformation of American Education* (1989).

Maren Stange, *Symbols of Ideal Life: Social Documentary Photography in America, 1890–1950* (1989).

William Stott, *Documentary Expression and Thirties America* (1973).

Elizabeth Hutton Turner, *American Artists in Paris, 1919–1929* (1988).

RESISTANCE TO CHANGE

David H. Bennett, *The Party of Fear: From Nativist Movements to the New Right in American History* (1988).

Kathleen M. Blee, *Women of the Klan: Racism and Gender in the 1920s* (1991).

Lyle W. Dorsett, *Billy Sunday and the Redemption of Urban America* (1991).

Ray Ginger, *Six Days or Forever? Tennessee v. John Thomas Scopes* (1958).

Nancy MacLean, *Behind the Mask of Chivalry: The Making of the Second Ku Klux Klan* (1994).

George M. Marsden, *Fundamentalism and American Culture* (1980).

Daniel Joseph Singal, *The War Within: From Victorian to Modernist Thought in the South, 1919–1945* (1982).

REFORM AND DISSENT

Daniel Aaron, *Writers on the Left* (1960).

James R. Barrett, *William Z. Foster and the Tragedy of American Radicalism* (1999).

Milton Cantor, *The Divided Left: American Radicalism, 1900–1975* (1978).

Clarke Chambers, *Seedtime of Reform, 1918–1933* (1956).

Nancy F. Cott, *The Grounding of Modern Feminism* (1977).

John P. Diggins, *The Rise and Fall of the American Left* (1992).

Thomas R. Pegram, *Battling Demon Rum: The Struggle for a Dry America, 1800–1933* (1998).

Nick Salvatore, *Eugene V. Debs: Citizen and Socialist* (1982).

David Thelen, *Robert M. La Follette and the Insurgent Spirit* (1976).

RACE AND MINORITIES

Rodolfo Acuna, *Occupied America: A History of Chicanos* (1980).

Francisco E. Balderrama and Raymond Rodriguez, *Decade of Betrayal: Mexican Repatriation in the 1930s* (1995).

William B. Barlow, *"Looking Up at Down": The Emergence of Blues Culture* (1989).

Dan T. Carter, *Scottsboro: A Tragedy of the Modern South* (1969).

John Higham, *Strangers in the Land: Patterns of American Nativism, 1860–1925* (1955).

David Levering Lewis, *When Harlem Was in Vogue* (1989).

Manning Marable, *W. E. B. Du Bois: Black Radical Democrat* (1986).

Donald L. Parman, *Indians and the American West in the Twentieth Century* (1994).

David M. Reimers, *Unwelcome Strangers: American Identity and the Turn against Immigration* (1998).

Judith Stein, *The World of Marcus Garvey* (1986).

Ronald Takaki, *A Different Mirror: A History of Multicultural America* (1993).

Cheryl A. Wall, *Women of the Harlem Renaissance* (1995).

Raymond Wolters, *Negroes and the Great Depression* (1970).

THE CRASH AND RESPONSE

William J. Barber, *From New Era to New Deal: Herbert Hoover, the Economists, and American Economic Policy, 1921–1933* (1985).

Andrew Bergman, *We're in the Money: Depression America and Its Films* (1971).

John Kenneth Galbraith, *The Great Crash, 1929* (1961).

Charles Hearn, *The American Dream in the Great Depression* (1973).

Robert McElvaine, *The Great Depression in America* (1984).

David P. Peeler, *Hope Among Us Yet: Social Criticism and Social Thought in the Depression Years* (1987).

Studs Terkel, *Hard Times: An Oral History of the Great Depression* (1979, 1986).

Tom Terrill and Jerrold Hirsch, *Such As Us* (1978).

T. H. Watkins, *The Hungry Years: America in an Age of Crisis, 1929–1939* (1999).

SOUVENIR SEWING NEEDLE BOOK

Borrowing the current popular tune "Happy Days Are Here Again" as the theme song for Roosevelt's 1932 campaign was an inspired act of wishful thinking in those dark days. By 1936, conditions had improved enough that this souvenir needle book could celebrate "happiness restored" a bit more realistically. The major places where economic recovery was to be created—farm, factory, and office—are shown operating in full swing on the cover of this little container that held sewing needles. But in accord with the New Deal emphasis on security at home, the figure of domestic happiness looms largest in the center under the arch of prosperity.

Collection of Janice L. and David J. Frent.

THE NEW DEAL ERA
1932–1939

23

I N JULY 1932, A RAGGED, DUSTY CONTINGENT of some fifteen thousand World War I veterans, calling themselves the Bonus Expeditionary Army, marched into Washington, D.C., to request immediate payment of the bonus for their military service that had been promised would be theirs in 1945. Destitute, many of these petitioners thumbed rides to Washington or came in boxcars, shipped free by sympathetic railway workers. They first camped in unfinished federal buildings just three blocks from the Capitol and then overflowed onto the mud flats along the Anacostia River.

President Hoover, angered by these disturbers of the peace and raiders of the Treasury, urged Congress to vote against the bonus because its $2.4 billion cost was more than the government could afford. To strengthen their defense of a balanced budget, which they believed necessary to restore prosperity, Hoover and his supporters vilified the bonus marchers themselves. Despite an official study showing that 94 percent of the marchers had served in the armed forces, they claimed that many in the bonus army were not veterans at all. Compounding the slander were false reports, which Hoover repeated, that the march was a revolutionary menace because its leaders were Communists. In reality, most of the marchers believed in traditional values. They had come to Washington to regain their respectability, not to overthrow the government.

Refusing to confer with men whom he thought undeserving of recognition, Hoover resorted to force. Army Chief of Staff Douglas MacArthur assured Hoover that the military would quickly get rid of the squatters and impress the public with the government's authority. Late in the afternoon of July 28, Hoover watched from the Oval Office as one thousand soldiers lobbed tear gas into the buildings occupied by the marchers. Then, in defiance of Hoover's orders to refrain from a direct attack, MacArthur commanded his troops to charge the nearby open-air encampment. In the rout that followed, several bonus marchers suffered bayonet wounds and one infant died of gas poisoning.

The following day, Franklin D. Roosevelt, Hoover's Democratic rival in the 1932 presidential campaign, read about the attack with "a feeling of horror." Were it up to him, Roosevelt declared, he would have taken coffee and doughnuts to the protesters and invited them to work on reforestation projects or to settle on vacant federal land where they could farm and regain their independence. Roosevelt's instinctive response echoed the slogan he had announced when he accepted the Democratic nomination: "I pledge you, I pledge myself, to a new deal for the American people." Like Hoover, Roosevelt thought the bonus payment was too expensive, but, unlike Hoover, he declared repeatedly that if people desperately needed help, the government should find a way to give it.

Almost a year later—after Roosevelt had been elected president—a second group of about three thousand veterans gathered in Washington to lobby for pay-

WASHINGTON BONUS MARCH
This watercolor is one of a series executed by twenty-four-year-old Lewis Rubenstein,
who in 1932 traveled as an observer with the bonus marchers. Here he depicts the march
in its early stages as a hopeful, somewhat theatrical adventure. The figure on the run-
ning board of the car, megaphone in hand, seems almost like a cheerleader encouraging
the team as it advances on its goal—in this case the steps of the United States Capitol.
Janet Marqusee Fine Arts Ltd.

ment of the bonus. Roosevelt arranged for the men to be fed and housed in military barracks at government expense while they petitioned Congress. Eleanor Roosevelt strode into their camp to express her concern and then led the men in singing favorite wartime songs. Franklin Roosevelt received a delegation at the White House and genially recalled how they had all served together in the war and reassured them that, although he could not support the bonus, the government was prepared to rescue victims of the depression. In the end, twenty-six hundred of the marchers enrolled in the government's Civilian Conservation Corps, designed to put people to work conserving the nation's natural resources, rather than accepting government transportation home.

Roosevelt's deft response to the war veterans stood in stark contrast to Hoover's refusal even to meet with the first bonus marchers. As the Second Bonus Army prepared to break camp, a reporter overheard remarks that brought into focus part of the meaning of Roosevelt's reform program that he called the New Deal. One particular rain-soaked veteran asked, "What is this bird Roosevelt up to?" Another shrugged and replied, "All I know is he's a hooman bein'."

Franklin D. Roosevelt: A Patrician in Government

The man elected president in 1932 was born into wealth and social prominence yet managed to establish an extraordinary relationship with the American people, especially the poor and dispossessed. The explanation of his success lay partly in the circumstances in which he held office. In his twelve-year reign, Roosevelt experienced two of the nation's greatest crises—the Great Depression and World War II. But simply presiding over economic catastrophe and war was no guarantee of popularity or greatness. Along with his political skills, Roosevelt's ability to convey sympathetic concern and to inspire the confidence to act against trouble made him the dominant figure of his age.

The Growth of a Politician

Born in 1882, the only child of a family with substantial inherited wealth, Franklin Delano Roosevelt grew up in a safe and secure environment that steeped him in the values of Christian service. He absorbed early a belief, which never left him, that the privileged had a duty to look after the poor and weak. At the Groton School (a prestigious prep school in Massachusetts) and Harvard University, his beliefs were fitted into an education designed to prepare him to take his place within the leadership reserved for his elite social class.

After a brief career as a reform member of the New York state legislature from 1910 to 1912 and as assistant secretary of the navy in Woodrow Wilson's administration, Roosevelt was nominated by the Democrats for the vice presidency in 1920. Despite Republican Warren Harding's landslide win, Roosevelt's spirited campaigning convinced many that he had a golden future in politics.

Fate, however, had a grim detour in store. In the summer of 1921, Roosevelt became paralyzed from the waist down, a victim of the polio virus. Despite battling the affliction with cheerful fortitude, Roosevelt would never again walk unassisted. But with the help of his devoted wife, Eleanor, and his tireless aide Louis Howe, he did regain his intense desire for an active political career. He became a student of public life and acquired an encyclopedic knowledge of local conditions and political activities. Going places and getting to know people in their own setting had always been Roosevelt's personal and political style. After the polio attack, he reversed the tactic by finding ways to draw people to him through letters, phone calls, receptions, dinner parties, cruises, and the Warm Springs, Georgia, polio sanitarium that he founded. Roosevelt's uncomplaining adjustment to his disability convinced his uncle Frederick Delano that he was "twice-born," that his ordeal had raised him above his privileged youth to help him become a strong and compassionate person. Those closest to Roosevelt—Eleanor Roosevelt and Louis Howe chief among them—insisted that the illness did not transform him but merely shifted his focus. No longer able to distract himself in physical activity, he concentrated on the art of political strategy and the use of verbal and visual symbols.

Roosevelt's chance to return to political office came sooner than he expected. When New York governor Al Smith announced his presidential candidacy in 1928, he convinced Roosevelt to run for his vacated position and so help Smith capture the state's electoral votes. The tactic did not work for Smith, who was defeated by Herbert Hoover, but Roosevelt managed a narrow upset victory. As the newly elected governor, he proposed a balanced program of conservation and scientific farming in the countryside combined with improved social services and working conditions in the cities.

Then the 1929 stock market crash forced him to take a different approach. His belief in government's prime role to respond to social need and in the idea that states could be laboratories for national policy allowed him to find democratic and humane ways of dealing with the crisis. When a noted economist visited the state house in Albany to explain that a high level of human distress was inevitable while the laws of supply and demand allowed the free market system to recover its balance, Roosevelt cut him off and scolded, "People aren't cattle, you know."

On the basis of compelling necessity, Roosevelt supported the largest state relief program in the nation's history. He played down any appearance of radical change by naming his new relief initiative the Temporary Emergency Relief Act (TERA). Using words like *temporary* and *emergency* made it possible to reassure a fearful public that the new initiatives were set securely within the established traditions of democracy and capitalism. At the head of TERA, Roosevelt placed a social worker named Harry Hopkins, who was admired as an advocate of child welfare. Hopkins knew about poverty from growing up the son of a harness maker in Iowa. At Iowa's Grinnell College, he was so moved by the social gospel fervor he found there that he went to New York City to become a resident at the Christadora settlement house in the impoverished neighborhood of the Lower East Side. Sallow and thin, with a hollow face, usually sucking on a cigarette, Hopkins resembled some of the neediest of those he sought to help. But his empathy and zestful energy provided uniquely effective leadership to New York's relief program.

On the basis of compelling necessity, Roosevelt supported the largest state relief program in the nation's history.

The other mainstay of Roosevelt's relief initiative was Frances Perkins, whom he named state labor commissioner. A veteran campaigner for improved industrial working conditions and member of Al Smith's administration, Perkins had a special relationship with the Roosevelts. When Eleanor Roosevelt first ventured into her lifelong effort to

ROOSEVELT'S COMMON TOUCH
In his campaign for reelection as governor of New York in 1930, Franklin Roosevelt boosted his vote total by 700,000 over the slender margin of 25,000 by which he won in 1928 to become the first Democratic candidate for governor to win the vote outside New York City. Sensing that his presentation of himself as a good neighbor was responsible for much of his popularity, Roosevelt arranged to have a friendly chat outside polls in his hometown of Hyde Park with working-class voter Ruben Appel. In this photograph, Appel seems unaware that Roosevelt's standing was itself a feat of stagecraft. His legs rendered useless by polio, Roosevelt could only remain upright by using the strength he had developed in his arms and shoulders to prop himself up on his cane. Rare photos like this and a taboo against showing Roosevelt in his wheelchair kept the public from thinking of Roosevelt as a cripple, unfit for office, or in many cases from even realizing he was disabled.
Franklin D. Roosevelt Library.

aid the poor and outcast, Perkins used her tough-minded experience to help the governor's wife overcome her sheltered upper-class upbringing and her psychological wounds from being considered an awkward and homely child. Perkins's plain-spoken understanding of working conditions also helped Eleanor Roosevelt direct her husband's attention to the plight of the exploited and unemployed.

Franklin Roosevelt's highly visible efforts to alleviate suffering and his argument that the nation should follow the example of World War I by mobilizing national resources to defeat the economic crisis gained him the gratitude of constituents and the attention of national politicians. In 1930, New Yorkers reelected him governor by a margin of 750,000 votes and assured his position as the Democratic Party's leading candidate in the 1932 presidential election. In an address to the New York legislature in August 1931, Roosevelt summed up his activist credo:

> The duty of the State toward the citizen is the duty of the servant to its master. . . . One of these duties of the State is that of caring for those of its citizens who find themselves the victims of such adverse circumstances as make them unable to obtain even the necessities for mere existence without the aid of others. . . . To these unfortunate citizens aid must be extended by governments, not as a matter of charity but as a matter of social duty. . . . [No one should go] unfed, unclothed, or unsheltered.

The Election of 1932

Roosevelt announced his candidacy for the presidency in January 1932. The Roosevelt name, his radiant personal charm, his earlier service in Washington, and his stature as a vice presidential candidate had made him a national figure before the 1929 crash. Afterward, his smashing reelection and leading role among governors in combating the depression gave him stature as the most active champion of recovery. In all respects, Roosevelt's record compared favorably with Hoover's dismal image as a last-ditch defender of the old order.

To supply his campaign with fresh ideas, Roosevelt assembled a group of experts on national issues that a journalist dubbed the "Brains Trust." Led by Columbia University professor Rexford Tugwell and lawyer and economist Adolf Berle, the Brains Trust plied Roosevelt with passionate arguments in favor of government planning to introduce stability and fair play into the marketplace and a welfare state to aid the helpless and end poverty. Despite support from the Brains Trust and his own personal and political strengths, Roosevelt still had to overcome the old split in the Democratic Party between the rural South and the working-class cities. Moreover, he had to avoid alienating the party faithful, who often did not agree among themselves. He added the West to his eastern and southern base through support of direct cash subsidies to farmers and commitment to the West's interest in conservation of natural resources and water development.

Roosevelt needed all his impressive political skills to overcome his rivals within the Democratic Party. He identified himself with what he described as "the forgotten man at the bottom of the pyramid" and declared that helping that forgotten man called for "bold, persistent experimentation." To win support from those who feared that change could make things worse, Roosevelt avoided any suggestion that he would tamper with established institutions. His position drew fire from both wings of the party. On the right, Al Smith, the party's 1928 presidential candidate, attacked Roosevelt as a fomenter of class conflict, while progressives chided Roosevelt for his unwillingness to offer bold plans for redistributing wealth and regulating the economy. Following the scramble for votes, Roosevelt narrowly won the nomination at the head of a peculiar new coalition. It lumped together his friends within the Democratic Party's eastern establishment, big-city machine bosses, old Wilsonian reformers, entrenched Southerners—many of them deeply conservative and racist—along with angry farmers, labor unions, and urban ethnic communities. To give that unwieldy coalition any degree of coherence, Roosevelt realized that he needed to establish a personal, symbolic presence above the fray of political battle. He also showed his awareness that he needed southern votes to enact any sort of reform program by selecting a Texan, John "Cactus Jack" Garner, Speaker of the House of Representatives, to be his running mate.

Roosevelt broke with the precedent that the nominee should stay at home during the national convention and await word of the party's choice. Instead, he flew to the convention in Chicago to deliver his acceptance speech in person. The flight, he told the delegates, signified his intention to be bold and active. He proposed to lead the party in the

direction "of liberal thought, of planned action, of enlightened international outlook, and of the greatest good to the greatest number of our citizens." Roosevelt expressed his twin allegiance to the New Freedom of Woodrow Wilson and the Square Deal of Theodore Roosevelt by forging the label for his own program: the New Deal. As the delegates' applause died away, the band struck up "Happy Days Are Here Again," a bouncy new popular tune that became the anthem of the Democratic Party for as long as New Deal enthusiasm lasted.

Roosevelt realized that he needed to establish a personal, symbolic presence above the fray of political battle.

During the presidential campaign, Roosevelt continued to balance declarations of optimistic action with hedging on specifics. In Topeka, Kansas, he promised reorganization of the Department of Agriculture to help provide a decent income to farmers. In Detroit, devastated by the slump in the auto industry, he declared his intention to eliminate poverty. The most thorough discussion of the case for an activist government came at the Commonwealth Club in San Francisco, where Roosevelt argued that the closing of the frontier meant that the limit of natural resources had been reached. The government needed to manage those resources carefully to help the nation regain and preserve its prosperity.

Frustrated that his glib opponent was trying out a variety of positions rather than committing to only one, President Hoover, the Republican nominee, attacked Roosevelt as a "chameleon on plaid" and decried the New Deal as un-American collectivism of the sort that Communists and fascists used to subdue the masses. Hoover praised the tried-and-true virtues of self-reliance, as opposed to handouts and government controls. Many voters, however, heard Hoover's appeals for individual effort and sacrifice as coldhearted rhetoric that ignored their suffering. Perturbed by the somber, silent crowds that met him everywhere, Hoover groped desperately for some way to restore the will of the public to save itself. "Perhaps," he suggested just weeks before the election, "what this country needs is a great poem . . . to raise our eyes

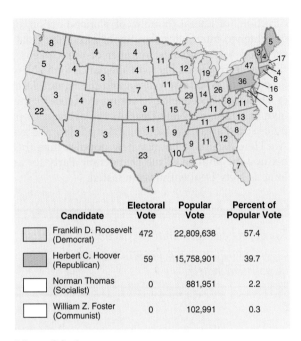

Candidate	Electoral Vote	Popular Vote	Percent of Popular Vote
Franklin D. Roosevelt (Democrat)	472	22,809,638	57.4
Herbert C. Hoover (Republican)	59	15,758,901	39.7
Norman Thomas (Socialist)	0	881,951	2.2
William Z. Foster (Communist)	0	102,991	0.3

MAP 23.1

The Election of 1932

beyond the immediate horizon . . . something simple enough for a child to put his hand on his chest and spout in school on Fridays."

Reduced to such forlorn hopes, the president soon became the scapegoat for all ills, his very name a label for poverty. New York City's Parks Department officially designated as "Hoover Valley" a gully where derelicts huddled in Central Park. When home-run king Babe Ruth was criticized for requesting a salary higher than President Hoover's, the Babe shot back with indisputable accuracy, "So what? I had a better year."

On election day, Hoover went down to utter defeat (Map 23.1). Roosevelt received 22.8 million votes, 57 percent of the total, to 15.8 million votes for Hoover. In the electoral college, Roosevelt's margin was even more lopsided, 472 to 59. Hitched to Roosevelt's star, Democrats swept into control of Congress for the first time since 1916. Democrats ruled the Senate by a margin of 59 to 36 and dominated the House by 313 to 117. Although Roosevelt had barely secured the Democrats' nomination, he won an overwhelming victory at the head of a fragmented party that had not received a majority of the votes in a presidential election since Franklin Pierce won in 1852.

The electoral switch from a landslide for Hoover and the Republicans in the 1928 election to a landslide for Roosevelt and the Democrats in 1932 was the greatest change in voter choice in the nation's history (Map 23.2). It began what political analysts have termed the "Roosevelt Revolution"—a fundamental realignment of voter allegiance that linked farmers, industrial laborers, white-collar workers, African Americans, immigrants, women, and intellectuals to the New Deal. The concept that had prevailed since the Civil War of weak central government deferring to economic free enterprise had been repudiated by a public eager to place its faith in a man who promised drastic change.

The election also showed that the left had little appeal to the voters. Arguing that recovery called for government control of the economy gained the Socialist Party only 881,951 votes and a sparse 102,991 for the Communists. Even the Farm Laborites, drawing on a half-century of Populist discontent, managed to elect only five Congressmen and a single senator.

The First New Deal in Action

At noon on March 4, 1933, Americans anxiously gathered around their radios to hear a serene and confident new president declare that the "only thing we have to fear is fear itself" and then promise "direct, vigorous action." The first months of Roosevelt's administration, called "the Hundred Days," were a blur of action that carried out that promise. The most immediate task was to offer relief to the destitute, including the 25 percent of the workforce that was unemployed. Their plight pointed toward a second need: the recovery of business and farming so that jobs would be available to all workers. And that goal led to the third challenge: reform of the system to guard against any future economic collapse.

The New Dealers

The New Deal represents the only moment in American history when a reform-minded president took office in bad times rather than good. Roosevelt's reform heroes—Andrew Jackson, Theodore Roosevelt, and Woodrow Wilson—had the advantage of serving during economic booms. Roosevelt con-

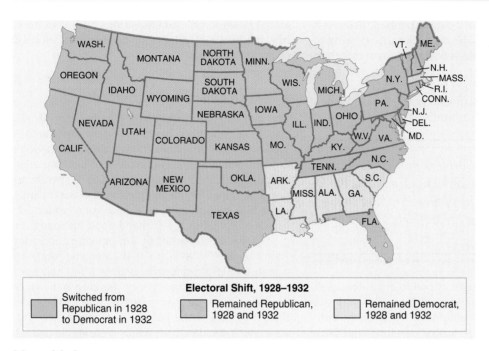

Electoral Shift, 1928–1932

Switched from Republican in 1928 to Democrat in 1932

Remained Republican, 1928 and 1932

Remained Democrat, 1928 and 1932

MAP 23.2

Electoral Shift, 1928–1932

Democratic victory in 1932 signaled the rise of a New Deal coalition within which women and minorities, many of them new voters, made the Democrats the majority party for the first time in the twentieth century.

READING THE MAP: How many states voted Democratic in 1928? How many states voted Republican in 1932? How many states shifted from Republican to Democratic between 1928 and 1932?

CONNECTIONS: What did Franklin Roosevelt's campaign slogans call for, and what past programs did he cite as influences? What factions within the Democratic party opposed Roosevelt's candidacy in 1932, and why?

www.bedfordstmartins.com/tap   SEE THE ONLINE STUDY GUIDE for more help in analyzing this map.

fronted the more daunting task of reversing an economic depression without violating the nation's allegiance to democracy and capitalism. Great numbers of reformers hurried to Washington in the spring of 1933, drawn by the combination of public desperation and the chance to serve under a president receptive to new ideas. "As for those first New Deal days," Gardiner C. Means, an economic adviser, recalled, "much of the excitement came from improvisation. Nothing was fully set in the minds of the people there. They were open to fresh ideas. Always."

In recognition of his sprawling party base, Roosevelt selected his cabinet and staff to represent important constituencies. He also chose advisers who would be loyal to him and who would be unlikely to become rivals for power. For secretary of state, Roosevelt selected an old Wilsonian Southerner and advocate of free trade, Cordell Hull, and to head the Treasury, Roosevelt called upon Will Woodin, a former industrialist and lifelong Republican who was nonetheless eager to carry out Roosevelt's experimental approach. In these appointments, Roosevelt made clear his intention to establish a friendly, cooperative relationship with businessmen and bankers yet, at the same time, to proceed openly to test ways of rescuing the economic system.

For the heads of the Labor and Agriculture Departments, whose constituencies were more fully the forgotten and the hard-pressed, Roosevelt turned to reformers. He chose Frances Perkins to become the first female secretary of labor, much to the outrage of traditional labor leaders. Henry A. Wallace of Iowa, a voice for scientific experiment and government regulation of markets, was tapped to be secretary of agriculture.

Great numbers of reformers hurried to Washington in the spring of 1933, drawn by the combination of public desperation and the chance to serve under a president receptive to new ideas.

For other, less central appointments, Roosevelt rounded out a cabinet and a set of advisers that represented virtually all sections of the country, both major parties, the three major religions, and both sexes. Through it all, Roosevelt radiated good cheer and relished his task as the impresario of a great rescue operation and the restorer of public confidence. Roosevelt wore out his assistants, picking their brains, prodding them to find fresh solutions. To communicate with the public, he began his practice of frequent news conferences, which brought him face to face with the press thirty times during the Hundred Days and at least once a week thereafter. His wide grin and infectious optimism made him the personal symbol of recovery, the emblem of hope for millions.

Banking and Finance Reform

The new administration first targeted the disaster engulfing America's banking system. By March 4, 1933, when Roosevelt was inaugurated, the nation's governors had suspended almost all banking operations within their states. That was a desperate action, but since 1930 more than five thousand banks, with $3.4 billion in assets, had gone under. On March 6, 1933, Roosevelt made good his inaugural pledge for "action now" by announcing a four-day "bank holiday" that converted emergency state action into federal policy. Three days later, Roosevelt sent Congress the Emergency Banking Act, which Congress passed in four hours (Table 23.1). Under the provisions of the bill, the secretary of the treasury could decide which banks were stable enough to reopen and could authorize the Reconstruction Finance Corporation (RFC) to supply funds for immediate circulation. Congress then created the Federal Deposit Insurance Corporation (FDIC) to insure bank customers against the loss of their deposits if their bank should fail.

The New Deal's more radical supporters were disappointed that Roosevelt did not nationalize the banks and make them a firm cornerstone for na-

TABLE 23.1
MAJOR LEGISLATION OF THE NEW DEAL'S FIRST HUNDRED DAYS

Name of Act	Date Passed	Basic Provisions
Emergency Banking Act	March 9, 1933	Provided for reopening stable banks and authorizing RFC to supply funds
Civilian Conservation Corps Act	March 31, 1933	Provided jobs for unemployed youth
Agricultural Adjustment Act	May 12, 1933	Provided funds to pay farmers for not growing surplus crops
Federal Emergency Relief Act	May 12, 1933	Provided relief funds for the destitute
Tennessee Valley Authority Act	May 18, 1933	Set up authority for development of electric power and conservation
National Industrial Recovery Act	June 16, 1933	Specified cooperation among business, government, and labor in setting fair prices and working conditions
Glass-Steagall Banking Act	June 16, 1933	Created Federal Deposit Insurance Corporation (FDIC) to insure bank deposits

tional planning. Instead, the private banking system was propped up with federal funds and subjected to federal regulation and oversight, and individual deposits were secured by the U.S. government. Within a few days, most of the nation's major banks had reopened their doors, and they remained solvent throughout the remaining depression years (Figure 23.1).

On March 12, Roosevelt broadcast his first "fireside chat" to the nation, explaining why the banking legislation was needed and how it gave good reason for confidence. That radio talk, suggesting a cozy gathering of the nation at the family hearth to discuss how much spending money was left, was a masterstroke. Roosevelt, speaking in cheerful, simple, fatherly terms, came through as a friendly savior echoing his inaugural address with his reassurance against fear. In the minds of a majority of Americans, the New Deal had established its competence and humaneness, and a glimmer of the nation's old optimism returned.

Turning to the stock market, whose scandals so vividly symbolized the 1920s, Roosevelt was eager to enact provisions that would end dubious practices such as the pyramiding of holding companies or profitable stock trading on the basis of insider in-

formation. At his insistence, Congress passed legislation in 1933 and 1934 that created the Securities and Exchange Commission (SEC) to license investment dealers, monitor all stock transactions, restrict margin buying, and require corporate officers to make full disclosures of their stock offerings and take responsibility for any claims they made about their companies.

In the minds of a majority of Americans, the New Deal had established its competence and humaneness, and a glimmer of the nation's old optimism returned.

Roosevelt named an abrasive and successful Wall Street trader, Joseph P. Kennedy, as chairman of the SEC. When critics opposed the choice of someone whose reputation had been clouded by shrewd stock manipulation, Roosevelt replied with confidence, "Set a thief to catch a thief." Kennedy proved to be tough enough to face down threats by brokers, some of them with things to hide, to boycott the exchange or even move it out of the

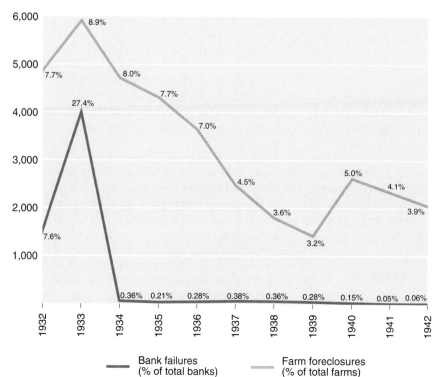

FIGURE 23.1
Bank Failures and Farm Foreclosures, 1932–1942
New Deal legislation to stabilize the economy had its most immediate and striking effect in preventing banks, along with their depositors, from going under and farmers from losing their land.

country. The most spectacular casualty turned out not to be a brash upstart like Joe Kennedy but the president of the New York Stock Exchange and symbol of the old moneyed elite, Richard Whitney, who went to jail for stealing from others' accounts to cover his own bad investments.

In addition to financial troubles at home, Roosevelt inherited a conference President Hoover had convened in London to find a way to stabilize the world's depressed monetary system. Put off by efforts to maintain the gold standard (which he believed would hamper recovery by restricting the money supply), Roosevelt brought the conference to an abrupt end. Instead, the United States would attend to its own problems before trying to renew its power and influence abroad.

Relief and Conservation Programs

Having rescued the nation's financial structure, Roosevelt took on the plight of the unemployed, the landless, the disabled, and those who were too old or too young to work. The Federal Emergency Relief Administration (FERA) Act made good on the president's promise that he would not abandon

Americans to hunger and homelessness. To publicize the terrible suffering that justified this unprecedented federal initiative, FERA director Harry Hopkins sent reporters out to describe conditions. With the backing of a public aroused by the vivid reports, FERA supported from four to five million households each month and funded thousands of work projects for the unemployed. FERA also took the lead in providing vaccinations and immunizations for millions of unprotected poor people, helped build desperately needed flood protection systems, and supported literacy classes for the most ill-prepared citizens.

The most popular work relief program was the Civilian Conservation Corps (CCC), which offered unemployed young men a chance to perform useful outdoor work and reflected Roosevelt's long-standing enthusiasm for conservation and his preference for the country over the city. Many of the recipients from the cities had good reason to agree with him. Blackie Gold remembered how as a child he had "to go out and beg for coal, buy bread that's two, three days old" in order to help support his large family. In 1937, when he was seventeen, Gold joined the CCC for $30 a month. By the time the program ended in 1942, the CCC had enrolled three million young people and achieved significant results. CCC workers erected dams to stop soil erosion and tame rivers, and planted more than two billion new trees to replenish forest preserves and check dust storms in the Southwest. They also strung 83,000 miles of telephone wires, constructed 122,000 miles of minor roads and trails, and located 23,000 new water sources in the nation's wilderness. In the end, the CCC left a legacy of magnificent outdoor recreation areas, along with the roads and communication that made them accessible to millions of people.

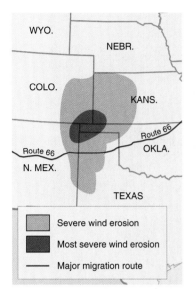

The Dust Bowl

The most spectacular accomplishment of the New Deal's conservation efforts was the Tennessee Valley Authority (TVA), established in 1933. The TVA was a regional organization designed to build hydroelectric power dams along the Tennessee River and to bring power and light to impoverished rural communities. The TVA planned to build model towns for power station workers and provide new homes for farmers who would benefit from electricity and flood control. At the same time, the TVA sponsored programs to encourage local crafts and other folkways (Map 23.3).

Following the Tennessee River across the state lines of Kentucky, Virginia, North Carolina, Tennessee, Georgia, Alabama, and Mississippi, the TVA set out to demonstrate that a partnership between the federal government and local residents could overcome traditional limitations of state boundaries and free enterprise to make efficient use of abundant resources, breaking an ancient cycle of poverty. The TVA became the most ambitious example of New Deal enthusiasm for planning. But hampered by bitter resistance from competing private power companies, the TVA never fully realized its utopian ends. It did, however, succeed in bringing electric power, flood protection, soil reclamation, and therefore sharply improved prosperity to the area it served.

Agricultural Initiatives

While the TVA aimed to make farmers in the Tennessee River valley prosperous through increased production, New Deal plans elsewhere contended with the problem of overproduction. In the hard times after World War I, farmers tried to make up for low crop prices by increasing production, thus creating

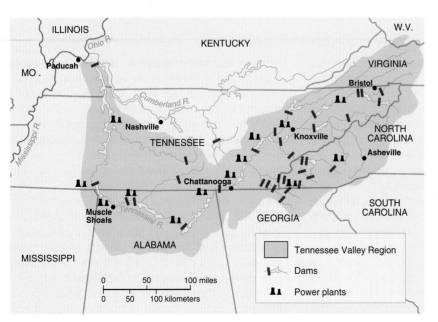

M A P   2 3 . 3

The Tennessee Valley Authority

The New Deal created the Tennessee Valley Authority to modernize a vast impoverished region with hydroelectric power dams and, at the same time, to reclaim eroded lands and preserve old folkways.

CIVILIAN CONSERVATION CORPS WORKERS
No New Deal program was more popular among its participants and the general public
than the Civilian Conservation Corps. It offered healthy outdoor work for young men
that got them out of the cities and eased their unemployment blues. To the public it
showed that the New Deal would act against the depression in a way that would repair
neglect of America's natural resources.
Forest Service Photo Collection.

surpluses that drove prices still lower. In the 1920s, congressional bills to deal with the problem by dumping the surplus abroad were vetoed by presidents fearful that foreign countries would retaliate for the harm American surpluses would do to the efforts of their own farmers to earn a living. On the eve of the New Deal, a farm economist named M. L. Wilson devised a voluntary "domestic allotment plan," which would bring prosperity without surpluses by paying farmers to leave some of their land idle. In May, Congress enthusiastically incorporated Wilson's plan within the Agricultural Adjustment Act (AAA) and soon afterward passed companion legislation, the Farm Credit Act (FCA), to provide credit on mortgaged farm property to head off foreclosures that would drive debt-ridden farmers from their land.

The security provided by the AAA and FCA dampened the urge for farm revolts and nudged prices upward. Overall results were mixed, however. In the corn, hog, and wheat region of the Mid-

west, farmers came together democratically, and a reasonably equitable distribution of benefits followed. In the South, local control meant that sharecroppers and tenant farmers on cotton plantations were denied a decent share of the benefits, while large growers reaped huge subsidies for putting land out of production—and tenants out of work. (See "The Promise of Technology," page 868.)

Nonetheless, the AAA and FCA guided agriculture toward prosperity. With almost all major crops limited, surpluses declined and gross farm income rose from $6.4 billion in 1932 to $8.5 billion in 1934. The trickle of 7,800 federal loans in 1932 rose to a flood of 287,881 in less than a year after the FCA was enacted in 1933. By the end of the decade, the federal government had financed 40 percent of farm mortgage debt, and the shadow of foreclosure had receded from most farmers' doorsteps (see Figure 23.1).

After putting both the TVA and AAA in place, the administration turned to fulfilling the old pro-

SKETCH FOR A FEDERAL ARTS PROGRAM MURAL
This sketch for a mural commissioned for Lenoir City, Tennessee, is typical of the Federal Arts Program's goal to memorialize significant moments of achievement in every region of the country. For rural folk, the sight of Rural Electrification Authority (REA) workers extending power lines was one of the more exciting symbols of the New Deal. When the REA came into existence in 1935, less than 10 percent of the nation outside the cities had electricity. By 1941, REA programs had increased that number to 40 percent; ten years later the figure had risen to 90 percent, and the gulf of silence and darkness between town and country was successfully bridged.
Public Buildings Service, General Services Administration.

gressive dream of extending electricity and all its modern benefits to rural America. When Roosevelt became president, about 90 percent of the country outside the cities and towns was without electricity. In May 1935, the New Deal created the Rural Electrification Administration (REA) to get around the reluctance of the private power industry to extend transmission lines into sparsely settled (and thus unprofitable) country. Encouraged by the successes of the AAA and TVA, the REA gave low-cost loans to farm cooperatives to bring power into their communities. By 1941, the REA succeeded in raising to 40 percent the number of farms with electricity. By 1950, nine out of every ten American farms were electrified. With the possible exception of the automobile, nothing did as much to improve the quality of rural life and close the gap between country and city.

Industrial Recovery

The New Deal's National Recovery Administration (NRA), established in June 1933 under the National

Industrial Recovery Act (NIRA), was a far less successful experiment than the agricultural programs. The NRA's objective was to coordinate management, labor, and the federal government through a network of industrial codes that governed working conditions, prices, and trade practices. To deal with the contentious issue of worker rights, the NRA struck a bargain with business leaders to ease antitrust regulations in exchange for the right of labor to engage in collective bargaining. By the end of 1933, most industries were represented within the 541 NRA codes, and the Blue Eagle symbol displayed in store windows let the public know.

The stage seemed set for a major transformation of American industry, but opinions differed widely on the direction it should take. The New Dealers emphasized the possibilities for rational management and fair competition. They hoped that coordination would produce a collective social conscience that would inhibit industry from cheating customers or destroying the environment and would make sure that workers were treated fairly. Critics, however, saw bureaucratic oppression. They claimed that

Mechanized Cotton Picking Revolutionizes a Social System

I N 1935, TWO OF THE MOST IMPORTANT farm machines of the time, the Farmall tractor and the Rust cotton picker, cut through a sea of cotton, showing how mechanization could eliminate the backbreaking work of harvesting cotton by hand. Within ten years tractors would displace horses as the main means of doing heavy farm work, but success for mechanical cotton pickers was longer in coming. For a century and a half after the invention of the cotton gin in 1793 made cotton farming feasible, inventors tried to create a device that would make picking cotton as efficient as ginning it. The first patent for a crude mechanical picker was granted in 1850 and nearly two thousand more followed before John Rust in 1931 demonstrated a machine that could pick more bales of cotton in a day than the average farmer in the deep South grew in a year.

Ironically, though Southerners had realized their dream of mechanizing cotton picking, the machine was so efficient that it was ill suited to most southern cotton farms, whose yearly crop was relatively modest. Nor could most growers afford the machinery. By 1931, cotton prices had plunged from thirty-five cents a bale in 1919 to only six cents a bale.

In the next two decades, large farms using the new mechanical cotton picker became dominant and that change shifted most cotton growing to the West, where vast agricultural holdings were the rule. Displaced by the decline of King Cotton in the South, field hands like the woman shown above migrated in thousands to the North in search of new jobs.

Cotton picking machine: Mississippi State University Libraries.
Cotton picker: Courtesy of the Harvard University Art Museums.
Gift of Bernarda B. Shahn, Estate of Ben Shahn.

because the NRA skirted antimonopoly laws and left industry subject to federal management, the economy would become rigidly controlled from the top. Some even saw the NRA as an American version of Benito Mussolini's corporate fascism in Italy, a means for controlling individuals by directing their economic lives.

In reality, neither prediction was accurate. The outcome was more an extension of conventional business practice than a radical change to either the right or the left. Poor management gave business leaders the opportunity to gain control of the code-writing mechanism, and they made sure the codes would first serve the interests of corporate profits

NATIONAL RECOVERY ADMINISTRATION QUILT
The Blue Eagle of the National Recovery Administration, fiercely clutching a machine gear and lightning bolts, symbolized the government's determination to bring American industry around to a coordinated plan for recovery. The attempt to balance the interests of producers, workers, and consumers proved too much for the Blue Eagle, however. Yet, as this back-country quilt indicates, the Blue Eagle was sometimes able to carry the spirit of cooperation far from the centers of industrial turmoil.
Franklin D. Roosevelt Library.

rather than workers or the general welfare. By the mid-1930s, prospects for a rationally coordinated business system had faded.

The stage seemed set for a major transformation of American industry, but opinions differed widely on the direction it should take.

The blizzard of new agencies and programs created in the Hundred Days succeeded in reversing the economic decline and restoring the nation's confidence, but it did not produce full recovery. The magnitude and scope of the depression and the speed of the New Deal attack ensured that the Roosevelt administration would have failures as well as successes. Inevitably, disappointment and resistance mounted.

Challenges to the New Deal

After the early rush of excitement, a discontented minority began to challenge Roosevelt's initiatives. Businesspeople expressed open hostility to the ways New Deal planning intruded on their affairs. Many conservatives insisted that New Deal changes had been too radical, that they undermined economic stability and threatened American democratic values. On the left, critics faulted the administration for not having programs radical enough to meet the people's needs.

Resistance to Business Reform

Since the New Deal sought economic recovery, New Dealers expected business leaders to come around eventually and welcome cooperative planning. But the administration was sorely disappointed. In the Tennessee River valley, private power companies battled the TVA as "creeping socialism" and unfair competition. The NRA took even greater abuse. The alliance of the New Deal with urban labor and constant feuding between business representatives and NRA officials over the industry codes caused strain from the outset. Furthermore, business leaders never reconciled themselves to the administration's planning concept. One Republican senator derided the creator of the NRA as "Frankenstein" Roosevelt and declared that the Blue Eagle was really "the Soviet duck" in disguise.

Ironically, the business community kept up its criticism even though its situation improved more steadily during the depression than did that of most other social groups, including farmers and workers. The managerial elite remained mostly intact—despite some spectacular jailings, flights from prosecution, and suicides. So did the hierarchical corporate structure that had been developed during the boom years at the turn of the century. The greatest wounds business leaders suffered were to their confidence and pride. Fearful of government regulation, higher taxes, and union organization, they created stridently anti–New Deal public relations offices and—more ominously—sometimes deployed company spies to seek out disloyal workers. The rage of business leaders toward the New Deal fastened on Franklin Roosevelt as the source of their loss of public adoration and government favor.

By 1935, the two major business organizations—the National Association of Manufacturers and the Chamber of Commerce—had become openly anti–New Deal. But their critiques were mild compared with the all-out assault of the American Liberty League, founded in 1934 as the NRA came under bitter attack. Prominent members of the league, including Al Smith and his presidential campaign manager, John Jacob Raskob, had once been leaders in the Democratic Party, but now they decried the New Deal as a betrayer of basic constitutional guarantees of freedom and individualism. To them, the AAA was a "trend toward fascist control of agriculture," relief programs marked "the end of democracy," and the NRA was a plunge into the "quicksand of visionary experimentation." Although the league's membership never exceeded 125,000, its well-financed publicity campaign led the way in widening the rift between Roosevelt and the business class.

The greatest wounds business leaders suffered were to their confidence and pride.

Planners and labor leaders who favored more worker control attacked the New Deal from the other direction. In their view, the NRA had stifled enterprise by permitting monopolistic practices.

They pointed out that industrial trade associations twisted codes to suit their aims, thwarted competition, and engaged in price gouging. Labor leaders especially resented the willingness of the NRA to allow companies to form their own unions, while blocking the organization of genuine grassroots unions that permitted workers to bargain on terms they chose for themselves.

In the midst of the crossfire, the Supreme Court in May 1935 declared that the NRA unconstitutionally conferred legislative power on an administrative agency and overstepped the limits of federal power to regulate interstate commerce. The agency lingered briefly, but its codes evaporated, and business leaders rejected most proposals for cooperation with government. In its failure, the NRA demonstrated both historic American resistance to economic planning and the refusal of the business community to yield its autonomy unless forced to do so.

Reaction against the New Deal Farm Program

The AAA weathered its battering by champions of the old order better than the NRA, and so the majority of farmers were more content with the New Deal than businessmen were. Even though farmers were reluctant to abandon their practice of increasing production as a matter of pride and survival, the allotment checks for keeping land fallow and the higher prices for farm produce created loyalty among those with enough acreage to participate.

Protest stirred, however, among those with smaller farms who did not qualify for allotments. The Southern Farm Tenants Union argued passionately that the AAA was a device for enriching large farmers at the expense of smaller ones. By taking out of production the land on which tenants lived, owners could simultaneously qualify for government subsidies and be relieved of the need to provide for the dependent tenants. Already at the bottom of the economic ladder, tenant farmers and sharecroppers faced a grave situation. One black sharecropper explained why only $75 a year from the plantation cotton subsidies made its way down to her: "De landlord think he ought to have *all* the acre p'duction checks, 'cause it his land." Bypassing the intention of New Deal programs was simple enough in her part of Arkansas because, she observed shrewdly, "de landlord is landlord, de politicians is landlord, de judge is landlord, de shurf [sheriff] is landlord, ever'body is landlord, en we

BLACK SHARECROPPERS
An unintended consequence of the New Deal plan to maintain farm prices by reducing acreage in production was the eviction of tenant farmers when the land they worked was unused. Champions of the tenant farmers, most notably the Southern Farm Tenants Union, protested in vain that federal crop subsidies should be shared between owners and those who usually worked the land. Often, however, sharecroppers like these were simply cast adrift, and lobbies for farm owners thwarted any governmental challenge. Tenant farmers' sad state continued until World War II provided opportunities for displaced tenants to escape to the cities.
Corbis.

ain' got nothin'!" Stories like this convinced critics that the New Deal was fostering just the sort of inequality and misery—among both whites and blacks—that it had set out to eliminate.

The AAA's most potent critics, however, were agricultural processors and distributors. They were unhappy that the AAA reduced the volume of production—the only source of their profits—while they were required to pay for the very program that disadvantaged them. In 1936, the Supreme Court agreed with their contention that they were the poor victims of an illegal attempt to tax one group (processors and distributors) to enrich another (farmers). Down but not out, the AAA rebounded from the Supreme Court ruling by redesigning its allotment provisions with legislation that focused more on conservation measures the Court found acceptable.

Politics on the Fringes

The New Deal also faced challenges from a small but growing minority drawn to radical movements. Socialists and Communists accused the New Deal of mounting a feeble resistance to business elites or, worse, rescuing capitalism from its self-inflicted crisis. Among those drawn to the left were many intellectuals and artists, who decided it was time to use their talents to advance the cause of radical change. Socialist author Upton Sinclair became the most prominent of the intellectuals who went directly into politics when he ran for governor of California in 1934. Rousing wide public support for his End Poverty in California plan to put the unemployed to work in idle factories, Sinclair lost by a narrow margin only because fraudulent charges that he was a Communist frightened many voters and caused Roosevelt to withdraw his support.

With that one exception, the left was never able to mount a serious electoral challenge to the New Deal. And for all the doctrinaire talk of violent overthrow of the government by the proletariat, there was no real chance of that happening in a highly modern state where the authorities had great force to bring to bear against dissenters. In any case most Americans, with varying degrees of militancy, sought inclusion, not revolution, and fundamental entitlements, not radical novelties. Accordingly, homespun populist agitators preaching old-style religion and harping on birthrights drew the biggest crowds looking for an alternative to the status quo.

The most formidable coalition of down-and-outers challenging the New Deal was led by a Catholic priest in Detroit named Charles Coughlin. Father Coughlin expressed his outrage at the depression in a series of radio broadcasts that drew a nationwide audience of forty million by 1930. The "Radio Priest" found villains in all the conventional places. He began by denouncing Communists as traditional foes of the church and soon added bankers and other "predatory capitalists," who, he increasingly insisted, were dominated by Jews. After first welcoming Roosevelt in 1932 as the nation's political savior, Coughlin soon turned against the administration for its failure to "drive the moneychangers from the temple." In 1935, Coughlin converted his grassroots coalition into the National Union for Social Justice, or the Union Party, and in 1936 called on other dissidents to join him in mounting an election challenge to Roosevelt. Drawing on the populist tradition, the Union Party called for an expanded money supply backed by silver so that the poor could be rescued from the "cross of gold" that William Jennings Bryan had so famously associated with business domination of the economy.

One of those who answered Father Coughlin's call was Dr. Francis Townsend, an elderly public health officer in Long Beach, California, angered that his retired patients existed in misery in the golden land. In late 1933, Townsend proposed the Old Age Revolving Pension, which would pay all persons over age sixty $200 a month on the condition that they spend the entire amount within thirty days and thereby stimulate the economy. Buoyed by the 90 percent of Long Beach voters who endorsed his petition to the federal government, Townsend organized pension clubs that attracted between 2 and 3.5 million paying members looking for security. When the major parties rebuffed his plan as impractical, Townsend merged his forces with Coughlin's Union Party in time for the 1936 election.

The most important of the rebellious populists came from another region ripe for protest. Huey Pierce Long, son of a backcountry farmer, had used his immense talents to become governor of Louisiana in 1928 and U.S. senator in 1932. Long reached out to the poor and dispossessed with brash rhetoric and country humor. With their support, he swept out of power a reactionary political machine that had kept Louisiana one of the poorest and most backward states. By delivering on his promises to build roads, schools, and hospitals and to provide jobs, Long shone as a beacon of hope among the desperate during the early depression years. To his relatively well-to-do enemies, he was a menace ruthlessly gathering power into his own hands. (See "Historical Question," page 874.)

Populist unrest typified by Coughlin, Townsend, and Long stirred the New Deal administration to solidify its winning coalition. An early test came in the 1934 congressional elections, normally a time when a seated president loses support. Roosevelt approached the elections as an opportunity to distance the New Deal from radical and crank causes on the right and left. In August, the president embarked on a national tour to support loyal Democratic candidates as champions of average people and traditional American values. An unusually high percentage of voters turned out to give New Dealers a landslide victory. Democrats increased their numbers in the House of Representatives from 310 to 319 out of 422; and in the Senate, the party gained 10 new seats to take a commanding two-thirds majority, the greatest margin ever achieved in that body.

The New Deal and the Rise of the Welfare State

Though Roosevelt had been "all but crowned by the people," as one journalist put it, New Dealers found the outlook at mid-decade troubling. The New Deal had begun with bold action to halt the economic decline and restore hope, yet a glance at almost any economic index—employment, production, income—revealed how anemic the economy remained. The Hundred Days had spent itself, and major programs were faltering (AAA) or had been invalidated by the Supreme Court (NRA). With criticism of insufficient action intensifying on the right and the left, Roosevelt decided it was time for a departure.

In 1935, New Dealers surged ahead with a flurry of new policies, sometimes called the Second Hundred Days, that moved away from central economic planning toward provision for the special needs of various social groups. The keystone of the emerging coalition was labor. Workers had felt overlooked in the 1920s, and Roosevelt reached out with both legislation and genuine concern and sympathy. In words of high praise, a North Carolina mill worker spoke for many by declaring that "Mr. Roosevelt is the only man we ever had in the White House who would understand that my boss is a sonofabitch." Out of the welter of legislative and executive action that made up the Second New Deal emerged the first elements of an American welfare state. Reformers who recognized that individuals were more often victims of economic forces beyond their control now looked to government as the legitimate, even sole,

power able to improve the nation's economic health and guard its citizens' well-being.

Relief for the Unemployed

Like Hoover, Roosevelt lamented that the millions of Americans who were out of work suffered a devastating blow to "their self-respect, their self-confidence and courage and determination." Unlike Hoover, in May 1935 Roosevelt set up an independent agency, the Works Progress Administration

MACBETH OPENS IN HARLEM
The New Deal Federal Theater Project, which began in 1935, had the good fortune of attracting as one of its directors a twenty-year-old genius named Orson Welles. Acting on news that Welles and an African American theater group had prepared a version of **Macbeth** *set in Haiti, an opening night crowd in 1938 mobbed the Lafayette theater in Harlem. As one reviewer put it, the play was "a classic stunt" that ensured the director's reputation and indicated new directions for the American theater.*
Library of Congress.

Huey Long:
Demagogue or Champion
of the Dispossessed?

FROM THE TIME HE WAS A SMALL CHILD, Huey Pierce Long was what one exasperated neighbor called a "pesterance." Defiant at school, artful at avoiding any disagreeable chores, ruthlessly driven to be the center of attention, Long got ahead through the shrewdness of his extraordinary intelligence and brash willingness to flout conventional rules. Though he spent only brief periods studying law at the University of Oklahoma and Tulane University, he cajoled a judge to convene a special bar examination, which he passed easily at the age of twenty-one. Declaring that he came out of that examination "running for office," Long rose swiftly from election as state railroad commissioner in 1918 to governor ten years later. Along the way, he dazzled the public with rhetorical gifts never before approached in the state and argued successfully before the Supreme Court with a skill that archconservative Chief Justice William Howard Taft—not a man to be taken in by a small-town southern lawyer—judged to be as keen as any he had ever encountered.

Circumstances and temperament dictated the political stance Long took all his life. The populist tradition of Winn Parish, where he grew up, instilled a basic loyalty to poor, rural folk. The small population of blacks in the parish and a history of blacks and whites forming a common front against rich sawmill and plantation owners meant that there never had been much race baiting in Winn. The rest of the state was very different, however. There, blacks and whites divided evenly, and the state's leaders made white supremacy the cornerstone of their rule. Out of step with majority opinion on race, Long could only hope to advance his fortunes by appealing to class division—rich against poor, rural against urban, the humble against the elite.

Long decided to focus his reform program on a more equitable distribution of income and opportunity. At St. Martinsville, deep in swampy Cajun country, he asked, "Where are the schools that you have waited for your children to have, that have never come? Where are the roads and the highways that you sent your money to build . . . ? Where are the institutions to care for the sick and dis-

abled?" When Long assumed the governorship, Louisiana had only 331 miles of paved roads outside the cities. It was also the most illiterate state in the country. In 1893, when Long was born, 45 percent of those above the age of ten could not read; by 1920, the rate of illiteracy was still 22 percent, including 38 percent of all blacks.

Long articulated the grievances and hopes of the poor people of Louisiana; he also behaved utterly ruthlessly. After overcoming an impeachment effort in 1929, Long moved to consolidate his power. "I used to try to get things done by saying 'please,'" he said. "That didn't work and now I'm a dynamiter. I dynamite 'em out of my path." By 1930, Long completely dominated the state. Journalists around the country routinely referred to him as "the dictator of Louisiana." He made no effort to hide his power. Once an angry opponent thrust a volume in his face and shouted, "Maybe you've heard of this book. It's the constitution of the state of Louisiana." Long shrugged and said, "I'm the constitution here now." He bullied and bribed the state legislature into a rubber-stamp body that passed a series of laws giving him the power to count ballots and thus determine the outcome of elections. He intimidated the courts and made them heel to his demands. Every state employee knew that his or her job depended on loyalty to "the Kingfish," as Long liked to call himself.

His grasp on Louisiana firm, Long made his leap into the national limelight by winning election to the U.S. Senate in 1932. With none of the freshman senator's expected deference to senior members, Long introduced a sweeping "soak-the-rich" tax bill that would outlaw annual personal incomes of more than $1 million and inheritances of more than $5 million. Swift rejection by the Senate triggered his long-range strategy of becoming president by mobilizing the vast numbers of low-income Americans into a Share Our Wealth protest movement. Long's plan was to mount a presidential campaign in 1936 that would take enough votes from Roosevelt to tip the election to the Republican candidate. After four years of Republican failure to alleviate the depression with conservative policies, Long would sweep into the presidency in 1940, the savior of a suffering people.

The electoral showdown never came, however. On September 8, 1935, a young physician named Carl Austin Weiss, enraged by the dishonor Long had visited on his family by removing his father from the Louisiana bench and suggesting black ancestry, fa-

HUEY LONG

Huey Long's ability to adapt his captivating stump-speech style to the radio made him the one rival politician who gave Roosevelt serious concern in the mid-1930s. Here Long is shown in 1932 campaigning in Arkansas in support of Hattie Carraway's bid for election to the United States Senate. Carraway, stigmatized as both a woman and a populist re-former, seemed a sure loser until Long crossed the border from Louisiana on her behalf. In a mere two weeks of speaking and pressing the flesh, Long brushed aside criticism that he was an interloper and boosted Carraway to victory as part of his crusade to share the wealth.

Corbis.

BADGE FOR THE FORGOTTEN MAN

An emblem in the form of a police badge lent an air of authority to Huey Long's radical Share-Our-Wealth movement, while perhaps adding to the fear of the rich that much of their wealth would be taken into custody. More darkly, the motto pro-claiming that the spirit and purpose of Huey Long would never die indicates Long's foreboding that he would be assassinated before his plans could bear fruit. He was right in fearing death, but not in sup-posing that success for Share Our Wealth would be his legacy.

Louisiana State University, Hill Memorial Library.

tally shot Long in a corridor of the Louisiana State House and was immediately gunned down by Long's bodyguards. The long lines of worn and ragged people passing by Long's coffin in the capi-tol and the smaller number of better-dressed mourn-ers at Weiss's funeral testified to the split in Louisiana along class lines. Some people at Weiss's funeral even proposed erecting a monument to Long's assassin.

Long always answered charges that he was a dictator, rather than a man of the people, by insist-ing that the polite ways of conventional democra-tic rules could never cure the nation's deepest ills. Only forceful means, he insisted, could finally break the hold of the privileged and extend opportunity to everyone. He could point to real achievements in Louisiana. As promised, he taxed the oil companies and utilities that had run Louisiana for decades and funneled the revenue into programs to benefit those who had been left out. While he built monuments to his own vanity, like the thirty-four- (*Continued*) story state capitol with his profile in bronze on the elevator doors, Long addressed some of the state's real social needs. At one time, Louisiana's road-building program was the biggest in the nation, and by 1935 the state had ten times more paved roads than when Long became governor. He made Louisiana State University a major institution of higher learning. He greatly expanded the state's pitiful public health facilities. For children, he provided free schoolbooks and new schools. For adults, he started night schools that attacked illiteracy.

Critics labeled Long a homegrown fascist and called him "the Messiah of the Rednecks," disdainful both of Long and of those who turned to him. They compared him to Mussolini or Hitler and expressed relief that his life, and thus the damage he and the rabble who supported him could do, was cut short. The bitter controversy over Long related to vital American political issues. Roosevelt had recognized that the New Deal must reach out to the "forgotten man." Long reached farther to connect with dispossessed outsiders who had never even been noticed. He gave Americans the only chance they ever had, for better or worse, to vote for a candidate with a broad national following who offered sweeping change comparable to that of parties on the radical right and left in other countries.

After Long's death, the hopes of the underclass to share the wealth lapsed into silent neglect. Most voted for Roosevelt, when they voted at all, but remained largely alienated from the prevailing system. They did achieve connection in memory, however. In 1974, a Louisiana newspaper asked citizens to name the greatest governor in the history of the state. Much to the paper's editorial dismay, the overwhelming choice was Huey Long.

(WPA), to put the unemployed to work for the public benefit. The WPA imposed few limits on the sort of work to be done; it merely specified that the projects be useful, be undertaken in places where unemployment was high, and produce results that would bring revenues back to the Treasury as soon as possible. State and municipal agencies had the responsibility to propose what needed to be done.

By 1943, when wartime needs forced Roosevelt to give the WPA an "honorable discharge," the relief effort had generated jobs costing $10 billion that provided an average of a year's worth of work for each of the thirteen million unemployed men and women put on the payroll. Construction amounted to about three-fourths of the total WPA projects, resulting in 572,000 miles of country roads, 40,000 buildings, 67,000 miles of city streets, 78,000 bridges, 8,000 parks, and 350 airports, along with a variety of smaller projects.

In a striking departure from the usual pick-and-shovel relief program, the WPA also allowed unemployed people in the arts to make use of their talents for public benefit. After all, Roosevelt pointed out in endorsing the idea, artists "have to live . . . and surely there must be some public place where paintings are wanted." At its peak, the WPA employed some six thousand artists, musicians, actors, journalists, academics, poets, and novelists. The roster included many unknowns but also towering figures such as novelist John Steinbeck and poet Conrad Aiken. WPA Theater brought sixty million people into its performances; and in the first fifteen months of the WPA Music Project, fifty million Americans heard concerts. The artist Robert Gwathmey recalled that the government imposed no restrictions: "You were a painter: Do your work. You were a sculptor: Do your work. . . . An artist could do anything he damn pleased." At a cost of only $23 million, paintings, sculptures, and prints came to grace America's courthouses, public buildings, and museums.

Empowering Labor

In 1934, a series of local uprisings, mostly by unskilled workers who had no unions to join, set in motion a labor revolution. Striking workers in Toledo, Minneapolis, and San Francisco, asserting their right to picket their employers, encountered ferocious opposition by police and the National Guard. Bloody battles in the streets and on the docks made plain the determination of militant new labor leaders to break the dominance that industrial management had achieved over workers during the 1920s.

After the violence of 1934 subsided, labor leaders focused on the National Labor Relations Act (NLRA), a bill sponsored by Senator Robert Wagner of New York that would create federal supervision of labor disputes. Justly termed a "Magna Carta for labor," the Wagner Act, as it came to be called, guaranteed workers the right to organize freely and created a National Labor Relations Board to oversee elections for union representation. If the majority of workers voted for a union, the union became the sole bargaining agent for the entire workplace, and employers were required to negotiate with the duly elected union leaders. Roosevelt was at first reluctant to have his NRA ideal of cooperative decision making replaced by adversarial collective bargaining, but he signed the Wagner Act into law in July 1935 as the best way available to protect the rights of workers and unions.

While the Wagner Act moved through Congress, unskilled workers, who had been largely unrepresented within organized labor, began to press for inclusion. Under the aggressive leadership of John L. Lewis, head of the United Mine Workers (UMW), and Sidney Hillman, head of the Amalgamated Clothing Workers, a coalition of unskilled workers gathered in 1935 to form the Committee for Industrial Organization (CIO; later the Congress of Industrial Organizations). The CIO struggled in vain with the leadership of the American Federation of Labor (AFL) to be included in a broad effort to take advantage of the New Deal's encouragement for union organization. After Lewis ended an argument on the main platform at the 1935 AFL convention in Atlantic City by dropping "Big Bill" Hutcheson of the Carpenters Union with a right cross to the jaw, the CIO went its own way. The following year, Lewis and Hillman broke with organized labor's apolitical tradition by forming the Non-Partisan League to support Roosevelt's reelection.

Justly termed a "Magna Carta for labor," the Wagner Act guaranteed workers the right to organize freely and created a National Labor Relations Board to oversee elections for union representation.

The achievements that flowed from the new militancy of labor and a sympathetic government were formidable. When Roosevelt took office in 1933, AFL membership stood at three million, down by half since the end of World War I. Once the Wag-

ner Act took hold after 1935, unions expanded almost fivefold, to fourteen million members by the time of Roosevelt's death in 1945 (Figure 23.2). Thirty percent of the workforce was then unionized, the highest union representation ever reached. During the New Deal era, large numbers of unskilled assembly-line workers, many of them African Americans or immigrants, flocked to unions, most of whose membership at the start of the 1930s, and especially its leadership, had been skilled, native-born workers of northern European ancestry. A new left-wing militancy had something to do with these expanding union memberships. The exceptional courage and organizing skill of Communists and other radicals in the CIO earned them leadership roles in the campaign to organize resistant workers in the automobile and steel industries.

The campaign by the United Auto Workers (UAW) to unionize workers at General Motors climaxed in January 1937 when workers occupied the main assembly plant in Flint, Michigan, in a "sit-down" strike that reduced the plant's production of 15,000 cars a week to a mere 150. In desperation, General Motors called on local government to evict the trespassers. When a police detachment charged the barricaded plant, strikers responded by throwing ball bearings at the "bulls" (slang for "police"); after the lawmen fled, the strikers jeeringly called the incident the "battle of bulls run." Next the company obtained injunctions against the sit-down. But neither Roosevelt nor Michigan governor Frank Murphy would act. Although they did not approve of the strikers' illegal occupation of the plant, they were unwilling to end the strike by force. Stymied, General Motors signed an agreement that made the UAW the sole bargaining agent for all of the company's workers and prohibited the company from interfering with union activity. With victory over the automobile industry's leading producer to recommend it, the UAW increased its membership almost fourfold by the summer of 1937 and decided it was ready to take on the fiercely anti-union Ford Motor Company. After four years of struggle that included beatings of labor organizers by hired thugs and finally a threat by his wife that she would divorce him if he continued to resist what the workers wanted, Henry Ford gave in and opened the way for the UAW to complete its campaign to unionize the entire automotive industry.

The CIO hoped to ride success in automobile plants to victory in the steel mills. But after unionizing the industry giant U.S. Steel, the CIO ran up

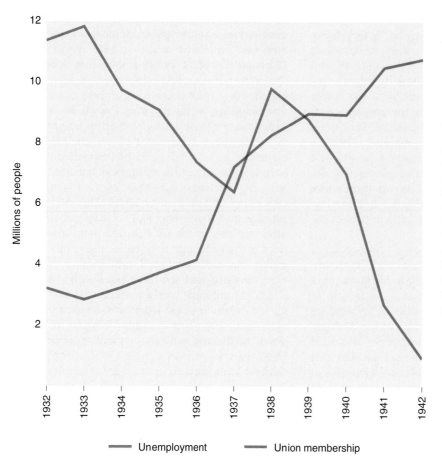

FIGURE 23.2

Unemployment and Union Membership, 1932–1942 *The intersecting lines of this graph suggest a close relationship between prosperity, unemployment, and union membership. With New Deal support and economic recovery, unions gained strength until the number of unemployed dropped far below union membership in 1942. Only when the economy dipped during the recession of 1937–1938 did the trend reverse and unemployed workers again outnumber union members.*

against fanatic opposition from smaller steel firms, led by Bethlehem Steel's Tom Girdler. The climax came in May 1937, when a crowd of strikers gathered in a field outside Chicago to organize a picket line around Republic Steel. Without warning, police who had been sent there to keep order charged the crowd, firing their sidearms and wielding clubs, killing ten and injuring scores. The battered steelworkers then halted their organizing campaign. In steel and other major industries, such as the highly resistant southern textile mills, unions would have renewed success only after 1941, when the demands of military buildup gave workers greater bargaining power.

Social Security and Tax Reform

Standing alongside the Wagner Act and the WPA as a major New Deal accomplishment was the Social Security Act, designed to provide a supplementary income for aged and retired persons. Taking care of

hard-hit elderly people during the depression became almost as desperate a necessity as providing relief to the unemployed. The population over age sixty-five had doubled between 1870 and 1930 at the same time that work for the elderly declined. Of the tiny minority who worked, only 15 percent had pension plans, and insolvent corporations and banks often could not come up with funds during the depression to pay the meager pensions they had promised. Just eighteen states provided elderly assistance, which usually amounted to about a dollar a day for impoverished individuals. With the aggressive agitation of Dr. Townsend, Father Coughlin, and Huey Long rumbling ominously in the background, Roosevelt became the first president to advocate protection for the elderly, describing it as "our plain duty to provide for that security upon which [the general] welfare depends." In 1935, he appointed Frances Perkins to chair a committee that readied the Social Security Act for his signature in August of that year.

The struggle for Social Security brought out class differences in their starkest form. Support for the measure came from a coalition of advocate groups for the elderly and the poor, traditional progressives, leftists, social workers, labor unions, and educators. Arrayed against them were economic conservatives, including the Liberty League, the National Association of Manufacturers, the Chamber of Commerce, and the American Medical Association. Enact the Social Security system, these conservatives and their representatives in the Republican Party warned, and the government will gain a whip hand over private property, destroy initiative, and reduce proud individuals to spineless loafers.

Obvious need and the large New Deal majority in Congress carried the day. Yet the strong objections to federal involvement in matters traditionally left to individual and local charity persuaded the framers of Social Security to strike a balance among federal, state, and personal responsibility. The Social Security program therefore required that pensions for the elderly be funded by tax contributions from workers and their employers. It also created unemployment insurance, paid for by employers' contributions. In a bow to traditional local responsibility for public assistance, Social Security issued grants for the states to use to support dependent mothers and children, public health services, and the blind. A Supreme Court decision in 1937 upheld the right of Congress to require all citizens to pay for Social Security through their federal taxes and allowed the Social Security Act to be expanded to include benefits for dependent survivors of deceased recipients. As a result of this momentous change in public policy, the elderly began to rise out of the lowest economic status, and the attachment of ordinary workers to the New Deal became even stronger.

Strong objections to federal involvement in matters traditionally left to individual and local charity persuaded the framers of Social Security to strike a balance among federal, state, and personal responsibility.

Opposition to Social Security struck New Dealers as evidence that the rich had learned little from the depression. Roosevelt had long felt contempt for the moneyed elite and looked for a way to redistribute wealth that would, in a single stroke, weaken conservative opposition, advance the cause of social equity, and defuse populist challenges on the fringe. In June 1935, as the Social Security Act was being debated, Roosevelt delivered a message to Congress outlining comprehensive tax reform. Charging that large fortunes put "great and undesirable concentration of control in [the hands of] relatively few individuals," Roosevelt urged a graduated tax on corporations, a similar tax on holding company dividends used to shelter corporate income, an inheritance tax, and an increase in maximum personal income taxes from 63 to 79 percent. These measures were designed to place the burden of paying for recovery programs and balancing the federal budget on the shoulders of those with the most money. Against charges that higher taxes on the rich would dampen their initiative, Roosevelt contended that the new measures would instead stimulate competition. A progressive tax would make the wealthy work harder to retain their affluence and give ordinary Americans in small, innovative enterprises a better chance to succeed.

Congress endorsed Roosevelt's basic taxation principle by enacting a slightly progressive tax on undistributed corporate profits. From there, with the Revenue Act of 1937, Roosevelt moved to close loopholes that he considered outrageous. Threatening to name names of the wealthy who were not paying their fair share of taxes, Roosevelt persuaded Congress to eliminate a number of tax shelters, including such relics from the New Era as deductions for company yachts and country estates.

Broadening the New Deal Coalition

The largest groups that had been persistently excluded from economic and political benefits were women and African Americans. Their stories were strikingly parallel. Both received wages substantially lower than those of white men and owned only a tiny sliver of the nation's property. Though constitutionally entitled to vote since reconstruction, most African Americans had been disfranchised by intimidation and legal subterfuge. Women, too, had the right to vote, but they were only starting to exercise their electoral power in numbers comparable to those of men.

Eleanor Roosevelt was determined to use her position as First Lady to increase the influence of women and minorities. At her urging, President

ELEANOR ROOSEVELT MEETING WOMEN REPORTERS
Even though about 80 percent of newspaper owners opposed the president and his wife,
both Franklin and Eleanor Roosevelt had close rapport with the working press. Making
the point that women had something important to contribute to public affairs and that
the First Lady could be more than simply a White House hostess, Eleanor Roosevelt
wrote a daily column, "My Day," and held regular news conferences to which only
women reporters were admitted. She used the occasions to reinvigorate the commitment
women had begun in the Progressive Era to education, equal rights, decent working con-
ditions, and child welfare.
Stock Montage.

Roosevelt allowed the Democratic National Committee to create a Women's Division in 1933 to define women's issues and to screen candidates for administration positions. Headed by Molly Dewson, a former leader in the suffrage movement and the National Consumers League, the Women's Division created a talent pool of eighty thousand women from which the New Deal hired an unprecedented number for government positions.

Most remarkable was the entry of women into executive positions that had always been considered for men only. Frances Perkins became the first woman cabinet officer; Ruth Bryan Owen the first woman to hold an ambassadorial post; Florence Allen the first woman judge on a district court of appeals; Nellie Tayloe Ross the first woman director of the U.S. Mint; and Marion Glass Banister the first woman assistant secretary of the treasury. Alongside these breakthroughs, women gained prominent positions within relief and welfare programs. Under the broad WPA umbrella, Ellen Woodward headed Women's and Professional Projects, Hallie Flanagan directed the Federal Theater Project, and Hilda Smith organized Workers' Education. Women also played key roles in the Division of Labor Standards, in the Children's Bureau, and in the administration of relief to the unemployed and destitute, both locally and in Washington.

These activities did not, however, result in equality between the sexes, either economically or politically. Indeed, the efforts women made within the New Deal were limited to improving conditions of children, the infirm, the unemployed, and others who lacked the ability to take care of themselves. Nonetheless, the experience of women in community organization and the design of welfare legislation established a foundation of skill and influence that buttressed future efforts to attain equal rights.

Eleanor Roosevelt also helped link the causes of gender and racial discrimination. One of her strongest allies among African American women was Mary McLeod Bethune, the founder of the Daytona Normal and Industrial Institute for Negro Women in Florida and a cofounder of the National Council on Negro Women in 1935. Bethune's accomplishments brought her to the attention of Eleanor Roosevelt and resulted in her appointment as the highest-ranking black official in the federal government as head of the Division of Negro Affairs in the National Youth Administration. Bethune used her position to guide a core group of black professionals and civil rights activists to posts within the New Deal. Nicknamed the "Black Cabinet," the group was the first sizable African American presence in the federal government. By mid-decade, their efforts helped open the way for inclusion of African Americans in New Deal relief programs to the point where about one-quarter of all blacks received some sort of federal assistance.

The conditions with which the Black Cabinet grappled were bleak in the extreme. At the outset of the New Deal, about half of urban blacks were out of work, twice the unemployment rate among whites. In the rural South, the majority of blacks had slim prospects of making a living or even retaining their place on the land as owners or tenants. Moreover, to struggle against such deepening misery proved dangerous. After years of decline, lynching increased during the depression. In Alabama, the black "Scottsboro Boys" faced the death penalty in 1931 for a rape they did not commit, and a Georgia chain gang was the fate of radical black unionist Angelo Herndon for trying to organize black workers. Up north, a riot in 1935 that focused on white owned and staffed businesses in Harlem, where the artistic Renaissance had once flourished, dramatized blacks' despair.

MARY MCLEOD BETHUNE
At the urging of Eleanor Roosevelt, Mary McLeod Bethune, a southern educational and civil rights leader, became director of the National Youth Administration's Division of Negro Affairs. The first black woman to head a federal agency, Bethune used her position to promote social change. Here Bethune takes her mission to the streets to protest the Peoples Drug Store chain's discriminatory hiring practices in the nation's capital.
Moorland Spingarn Research Center, Howard University.

The New Deal response was cautious. Roosevelt believed that, to enact ambitious New Deal reforms, he was obliged to appease powerful conservative, segregationist, southern Democrats. Reflecting these political pressures, the major New Deal programs for economic recovery—the NRA, AAA, and WPA—failed in large measure to serve African Americans. Bitter opponents of discrimination against blacks derisively charged that NRA stood for

THE NEW DEAL RACE PROBLEM
Showing even the National Recovery Administration's mighty Blue Eagle stymied by racial discrimination, this cartoon bitingly mocks the motto of business participants in the NRA, "We do our part." The task of opening up opportunities for African Americans commensurate with their talents and training would remain up in the air as long as laws enforcing fair employment practices continued to be weak or unwritten.
Chicago Historical Society.

"Negro Run Around" or "Negroes Ruined Again." Large-scale white landowners pocketed the crop reduction bonuses given out by the AAA for evicting black tenants, and in the WPA only eleven of more than ten thousand supervisors in the South were black.

Stymied administratively and legislatively, New Dealers turned to coalition building with blacks. Off the record, Roosevelt spoke of a time when politics would be realigned into opposing conservative and progressive parties, with the Re-publicans and southern Democrats making up the former and the New Deal coalition the latter. Blacks played a key role in his conception. During Roosevelt's first presidential campaign, black journalist Robert Vann called on African Americans to "turn Lincoln's picture to the wall. That debt has been paid in full." In 1934, black voters noticeably shifted from the Republican to the Democratic Party, helping elect New Deal Democrats in numerous congressional and gubernatorial races.

During Roosevelt's first two terms, the numbers of blacks in federal service tripled, and white officials showed unprecedented willingness to hear what black leaders had to say. Meetings of the president with black leaders in and out of the administration, along with Eleanor Roosevelt's many visits to black institutions, led to an identification of black reform aims with the New Deal. The symbolic climax occurred in 1939 when the superb black contralto Marian Anderson was refused permission by the Daughters of the American Revolution (DAR) to sing in the organization's Constitution Hall in Washington. Eleanor Roosevelt promptly resigned her membership in the DAR, and Interior Secretary Harold A. Ickes, former president of a chapter of the National Association for the Advancement of Colored People in Chicago, arranged to have Anderson perform on the steps of the Lincoln Memorial before an integrated throng of seventy-five thousand in an electrifying demonstration of the tie between black aspirations and the spirit of the New Deal.

By the end of Roosevelt's second term, however, African Americans still suffered severe handicaps. Most of the thirteen million black workers toiled at low-paying menial jobs. Infant mortality was half again as great as for whites, and life expectancy twelve years shorter. Segregation in the South was unmoved, nor was the equal part of "separate but equal" much advanced. Black schools had less money and worse facilities than those of whites, and only 1 percent of black students earned college degrees. In southern states, where most blacks lived, there were no black police officers or judges and hardly any black lawyers, and lynching of blacks went unpunished. By mid-decade, little had happened to refute the grim witticism that, for African Americans, the United States was "the land of the tree and the home of the grave."

Hispanic Americans and Asian Americans had even fewer voters than women and blacks, and con-

HISPANIC-AMERICAN ALLIANCE BANNER
Between 1910 and 1940, when refugees from the Mexican revolution poured across the American border, the Hispanic-American Alliance and other such organizations sought to protect Mexican Americans' rights against nativist fears and hostility. In the years between the world wars, many alliance banners such as this one flew in opposition to the deportation of Mexican aliens, an attempt in 1926 to bar Mexican Americans from city jobs in Los Angeles, and the disproportionately high use of the death penalty against Mexicans convicted of crimes. Throughout these and other trials, the alliance steadfastly emphasized the desire of Mexican Americans to receive permanent status in the United States.
The Oakland Museum.

sequently less political clout. Mexican Americans, already at the economic margins, saw their wages in California's fields plummet to not much more than a dime an hour. Even then, they had to face a new challenge from other victims of the depression.

When persistent drought raised huge dust storms and turned large areas of the plains into a "dust bowl," hundreds of thousands of ruined farmers—called "Okies" or "Arkies" because most of them came from Oklahoma or Arkansas—moved westward and competed with Mexican Americans for scarce agricultural work. In addition, local administration of many New Deal programs meant that the treatment of minorities rested in the hands of established white leadership. In the West, when Hispanics and Indians were permitted to join government work projects, they often received lower pay than their white counterparts, and less aid when out of a job.

> *By mid-decade, little had happened to refute the grim witticism that, for African Americans, the United States was "the land of the tree and the home of the grave."*

Asian Americans fared no better. Asian immigrants were still excluded from U.S. citizenship and in many states were not permitted to own land. Although more than half of Japanese Americans by 1930 had been born in the United States, they were still liable to discrimination. Even college-educated Asian Americans worked at family shops, restaurants, and laundries. As one frustrated young man said: "I am a fruitstand worker. I would much rather it were doctor or lawyer . . . but my aspirations [were] frustrated long ago by circumstances [and] I am only what I am, a professional carrot washer."

Native Americans, however, experienced a major change in their circumstances during the New Deal. Ever since the Dawes Act of 1887, the government had tried to solve the "Indian problem" by encouraging assimilation, that is, an end to a separate Indian identity. Because of the commitment of John Collier, commissioner of Indian affairs, that policy was mostly reversed in the Indian Reorganization Act of 1934. The act restored to Native Americans the right to own land communally. Though the change brought little immediate benefit and Indians remained the poorest of Americans, it did provide a foundation for economic and cultural resurgence a generation later.

JOHN COLLIER MEETS WITH NAVAJO REPRESENTATIVES *Commissioner of Indian Affairs John Collier receives a Navajo delegation protesting restrictions in the Indian Reorganization Act of 1934. The Navajos display a blanket made from the wool of their own sheep to protest limits on the number of sheep they could raise. Collier had crafted the act to revive Native American society by granting tribes an independent land base and many self-governing powers. However, his attempt to make the reservations economically viable through conservation measures, including restrictions on grass-devouring sheep, roused resistance by Indians who chose traditional ways of using resources. The tension between federal benevolence and Indian views of their own way of life has remained a painful issue.* Wide World Photos, Inc.

The New Deal's Final Phase: From Victory to Deadlock

To speed up recovery, Roosevelt shifted the emphasis of the New Deal in the mid-1930s. Having failed to build a cooperative commonwealth out of all interest groups, Roosevelt decided in his second term to rely on the New Deal coalition to force reform on bitterly resisting business groups. Support for the New Deal in the farm states and in the big cities had grown vast, mainly because of the rise in the number of women and recent immigrants inspired by the New Deal to begin voting. Roosevelt even gained some unlikely allies on the left. Throughout Roosevelt's first term, socialists and Communists had denounced the slow pace of change and charged the New Deal with failing to serve the interests of the workers who produced the nation's wealth. But in 1935 the Soviet Union, worried about the threat of fascism in Europe, instructed Communists throughout the world to join hands in a "Popular Front" to advance the fortunes of the working class. With varying degrees of enthusiasm, radicals switched from opposition to the New Deal to support for its relief programs and encouragement of unions.

The president's business and conservative opponents reacted to the massing of New Deal force by intensifying their opposition to the welfare state. To Roosevelt, the situation seemed part of a central drama that had played out since the nation's beginning, pitting a Hamiltonian faction of wealth and privilege against the heirs of Jefferson who, like Roosevelt himself, favored shared wealth and equal opportunity.

The Election of 1936

Roosevelt believed that the presidential election of 1936 would be a test of his ideals and leadership and of New Deal progressivism. Many to the right and left of the New Deal also welcomed a national referendum. Opinion polls showed that Roosevelt's popularity had dipped. Between 8.5 and 12.5 million workers were still unemployed, and most farmers remained poor. Opposition leaders took that as an indication that the American people were poised to vote against a failed experiment. From the Republican standpoint, the New Deal was undermining the traditional values that had made the country strong. Radical opponents insisted that the New Deal had missed its opportunity to displace capitalism with a socialized economy.

Republicans turned to the Kansas heartland to select Governor Alfred (Alf) Landon as their nominee for president. In what he intended to be a compliment, Henry Ford dubbed Landon the "Kansas Coolidge." But Landon offered far more than Silent

G.O.P. CONVENTION, CLEVELAND
This illustration of the 1936 Republican convention for an article in the progressive journal **Common Sense** *displays artist Thomas Hart Benton's gift for energetic satire. Benton's aged and grotesque conventiongoers underscore the article's contention that the Republican old guard is preparing "to join the Tyrannosaurus, the Pterodactyl and the Three-toed Horse." Unexpected circumstances prevented Benton's illustration from being used, however, and the GOP survived the article's prediction that "the Republican elephant [would become] as extinct as the dinosaurs," though the term "dinosaur" remained an epithet to be hurled at conservatives.*
Thomas Hart Benton, American, 1889–1973. *G.O.P. Convention, Cleveland*, 1936. Black crayon, pen and black ink, and black wash, over graphics, 37.4 × 53.4 cm. © The Cleveland Museum of Art, 1996. Leonard C. Hanna Jr., 1995. 70.

Cal. As governor, he had supported New Deal measures for conservation and farm relief. An independent oil producer, he endorsed Interior Secretary Ickes's efforts to regulate the oil industry more closely. Landon showed his loyalty to Lincoln's Republicanism by promising organized labor a fair deal and by speaking out strongly against racial prejudice to bring blacks back into the fold. Economically, however, Landon was an orthodox Republican conservative. He stoutly supported standard Republican proposals to achieve a balanced federal budget and to ease the perils of illness and old age with old-fashioned neighborliness instead of Social Security.

Roosevelt put his faith in the growing coalition of New Deal supporters, who he believed shared his conviction that the New Deal was the nation's liberator from a long period of privilege and wealth for a few and "economic slavery" for the rest. At the end of the campaign, Roosevelt struck a defiant pose before a thunderous crowd at Madison Square Garden. Assailing his "old enemies—monopoly, speculation, reckless banking, class antagonism"— he proclaimed, "Never before in all our history have these forces been so united against one candidate as they stand today. They are unanimous in their hate for me—and I welcome their hatred." When the crowd's roar subsided, Roosevelt concluded: "I should like to have it said of my first Administration that in it the forces of selfishness and of lust for power met their match. I should like to have it said of my second Administration that in it these forces met their master."

Roosevelt did not let such intensity rob him of his light touch. Toward Alf Landon he took a relaxed, amused attitude, characterizing his folksy opponent as a front for sinister interests. He pointed out that while Republicans denounced New Deal collectivism, Kansas drew 70 percent of its relief funds from New Deal programs. He further cast doubt on Landon's status as foe of big government by disclosing that, as governor, Landon had requested a federal grant of $35 million for a state-owned natural gas pipeline. Republican hypocrisy was accurately reflected, Roosevelt considered, in the Kansas state flower that Landon had adopted as his symbol: "The sunflower is yellow, has a black heart, is good only for parrot food, and dies before November."

Roosevelt triumphed spectacularly. His 60.8 percent majority and eleven million vote margin were the widest ever in a presidential race and won

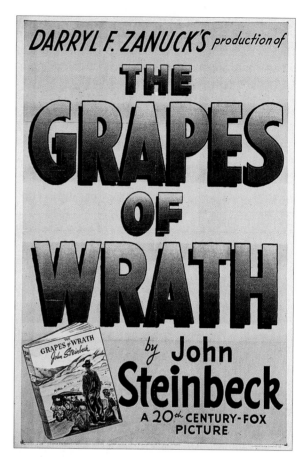

THE GRAPES OF WRATH
Movies had their greatest popularity in the depression when they offered momentary escape from the hard times outside. Through most of the 1930s, musicals like **Top Hat,** *with elegant dancers Fred Astaire and Ginger Rogers, set the pace, with comedies and costume dramas not far behind. By the end of the decade, however, years of labor strife, farm distress, and reform agitation had also created an audience for social problem films.* **The Grapes of Wrath,** *adapted in 1940 from John Steinbeck's novel of the flight of impoverished farmers from the southwestern Dust Bowl to California, made one of the most successful cinematic appeals to Americans' sympathy for the underdog and belief in social justice.*
The Oakland Museum.

him every state except the Republican strongholds of Maine and Vermont. Third parties—including the National Union for Social Justice, the Socialists, and the Communists—fell disastrously short of the support they had hoped for and never again posed a significant threat to the New Deal. Congressional results were equally lopsided, with Democrats outnumbering Republicans by more than three to one in both houses. And in the states, Democrats won twenty-six of thirty-three gubernatorial races, including the one in Landon's Kansas.

Roosevelt concluded: "I should like to have it said of my first Administration that in it the forces of selfishness and of lust for power met their match. I should like to have it said of my second Administration that in it these forces met their master."

Roosevelt's triumph was a testimony to the New Deal coalition and aroused voter interest. Whereas the 1920s saw only about 45 percent of eligible voters at the polls in national elections, 57 percent of eligible voters turned out in 1936. Northern blacks gave Roosevelt 76 percent of their votes, allowing him to wrench the key states of Illinois, Michigan, and New Jersey away from the Republicans. In the nineteen northern cities where more than half the population was composed of first- and second-generation immigrants, the crisis and Democratic encouragement had greatly increased voting participation. Overwhelmingly, the new voters tilted toward the New Deal. Democratic votes increased by 205 percent over their total in 1932, while Republicans gained only 29 percent. Roosevelt also managed to retain the support of every traditionally Democratic southern state, delaying Hoover's dream of bringing the South into the Republican Party.

Appreciative of the base of his mandate, Roosevelt made it plain that he would try to ensure a decent standard of living for all citizens. In response to news that sixty million Americans had an income of less than $1,000 per year, he declared in his inaugural address: "In this nation I see tens of millions of its citizens . . . denied . . . the necessities of life. . . . I see one third of a nation ill-housed, ill-clad, ill-nourished." With the voters' support, Roosevelt pledged his second administration to help those many disadvantaged citizens.

Court Packing

In the afterglow of his triumph, Roosevelt went on a cruise to ponder how to remove the remaining obstacles to New Deal reforms. He returned intent on targeting the Supreme Court. Laden with conservatives left over from the discredited Republican era, the Court had invalidated eleven New Deal measures as unwarranted interference with free enterprise; in more than 140 years before 1932, the Court had nullified only sixty laws. Roosevelt warned in strong terms that the Court's recent defiance of legislative will cast doubt "upon the ability of the Congress ever at any time to protect the Nation against catastrophe by squarely meeting modern social and economic maladjustment." As he spoke, Social Security, the Wagner Act, the Securities and Exchange Commission, and other New Deal innovations were moving toward an ominous rendezvous with the Court. Roosevelt concluded that he must do something to make sure the Court's "horse and buggy" notions did not nullify the popular will and demolish the New Deal.

Despite indications that more than two-thirds of Americans believed the Supreme Court should be free from political interference, Roosevelt proposed that one new justice be added to the Court for each existing judge who had already served for ten years and was over the age of seventy. In effect, the proposed law would give the president the power to overwhelm the elderly, conservative Republican justices by naming up to six New Dealers to the bench.

But the president had not reckoned with Americans' deeply rooted deference to the independent authority of the Supreme Court. Even New Deal supporters were disturbed by the "court-packing" scheme. The implication that individuals over seventy had diminished mental capacity affronted many members of Congress who were past that age. Roosevelt's proposal also aroused the ire of Louis Brandeis, the Court's oldest and most liberal justice and mentor of several key New Dealers. Roosevelt deviously insisted that the bill was intended to improve the efficiency of an "overworked" Court, although it was plain that the real purpose was to make room for supporters of New Deal initiatives. A storm of public protest, whipped up by conservatives, sank the Court bill in the Senate. Business spokesmen waxed indignant because Roosevelt's plan blatantly violated constitutional ideals and cleared the way, as the journalist Walter Lippmann claimed, "to establish the political framework for, and to destroy the safeguards against, a dictator."

Although the Court reform plan failed, it apparently sounded the alarm for Supreme Court justices. After the furor abated, Chief Justice Charles Evans Hughes and fellow moderate Owen Roberts altered their views enough to keep the Court from invalidating the Wagner Act and Social Security. Then the most resistant of the elderly justices—the "four horsemen of reaction," as New Dealer and future Supreme Court justice Felix Frankfurter called them—began to retire. Though unable to make any appointments to the Court during his first term, Roosevelt went on to name eight justices—more than any other president. His choice of liberals to fill the vacancies on the Court ultimately ensured safe passage of New Deal laws through the shoals of judicial review. But Roosevelt's error in proposing his court-packing scheme had handed conservatives a popular issue to use against the New Deal.

Reaction and Recession

Republicans and southern Democrats rallied around their common conservatism to obstruct additional reform. Factors other than the court-packing fiasco also began to work against the extension of the New Deal. The progress made in reviving the economy and alleviating hardship tended to reduce the enthusiasm of many people for new efforts. Arguments over how to proceed and how far to go weakened consensus among reformers and, as the Court fight showed, sparked antagonisms between Congress and the White House. The rise of belligerent regimes in Germany, Italy, Japan, and elsewhere also slowed reform. Some Americans began to demand that the nation concentrate on defending what it had rather than striving for change. In a surprisingly short time, these impediments made Roosevelt's 1936 landslide begin to seem like a mirage.

No action by New Deal opponents was more damaging than the administration's self-inflicted wounds. Soon after his second term began, Roosevelt accepted the view that the steady, though incomplete, economic recovery since 1933 had largely eliminated the depression crisis. He was persuaded that additional deficit spending designed to pump up the economy was no longer necessary. He also worried that inflation would reduce the value of savings and new investments the New Deal had tried to build up. Accordingly, he moved cautiously toward a balanced budget by cutting funds for relief projects, and at his urging the Federal Reserve raised interest rates to discourage borrowing on easy terms for unwise speculation. *Time* magazine

soothingly reported that "in recent weeks, [with the] Depression lapsing into memory, the portents of Boom drummed excitingly throughout the land."

Roosevelt's fiscal retrenchment soon backfired. Rather than preventing inflation, the reduction in deficit spending cooled down the economy too much. Roosevelt's anxiety about inflation had failed to take into full consideration how far the economy had to go before it would reach inflationary levels. Even at the high-water mark of recovery in the summer of 1937, unemployment remained at about 14 percent, some seven million people in all. In the next few months, national income and production slipped backward so steeply that almost two-thirds of the economic gains since 1933 were lost by June 1938. Farm prices dropped 20 percent, and unemployment rose by more than two million.

This sharp economic downturn hurt the New Deal politically. Conservatives argued that the recession proved that New Deal measures were fundamentally wrong and had produced only an illusion of progress. They maintained that the New Deal's progressive tax policy helped cause the recession by funneling money away from productive investment. Herbert Hoover had been right after all, they claimed. The way to weather the recession was to spend less, save more, and wait for the laws of the free enterprise system to restore prosperity.

Many New Dealers believed instead that the recession showed there was no going back to the orthodoxies of free enterprise. They insisted that the crash and the depression had demonstrated the shortcomings of an unregulated economy. They demanded that the administration revive federal spending and redouble efforts to stimulate the economy. In 1938, Congress heeded Roosevelt's plea to enact a massive new program of spending to revitalize the economy.

The New Deal's methods received support from new economic ideas advanced by the brilliant British economist John Maynard Keynes. In his influential work *The General Theory of Employment, Interest, and Money* (1936), Keynes made a sophisticated, theoretical argument in favor of practices that New Deal relief agencies had developed in an ad hoc, commonsense way. A nation's economy, Keynes declared, could not automatically reach its full potential in the complex, interdependent modern world. The depression had painfully illustrated that economic activity could become stalled at a level far short of a society's true potential. When that happened, only government intervention could pump enough money into the system to revive production, boost consumption, and restore prosperity. In bad times, Keynes argued, government should provide paid jobs for unemployed workers in order to spread purchasing power throughout the economy. In good times, government should restrict the supply of money to prevent the economy from producing more goods and services than consumers could absorb.

Roosevelt never had the inclination or the time to follow his economic advisers into the thicket of Keynesian theory. But the recession scare of 1938 taught the president the Keynesian lesson that economic growth had to be carefully nurtured, not left to self-regulating market forces. To make the case for renewed government intervention in the economy, Roosevelt stressed the greed and irresponsibility of "economic royalists." In April 1938, as the economy reeled and conservatives gloated over the defeat of the Court bill, Roosevelt sent a message to Congress asking for "a thorough study of the concentration of economic power in American industry." The result was a congressional study that led to the establishment of the Temporary National Economic Committee (TNEC) in June 1938.

The recession scare of 1938 taught the president the Keynesian lesson that economic growth had to be carefully nurtured, not left to self-regulating market forces.

Debates within TNEC over economic reform revived the old argument that had divided progressives since the beginning of the century. As TNEC uncovered plentiful evidence of ruthless and corrupt business practices, some New Dealers argued in the spirit of Theodore Roosevelt for increased governmental planning to make the economy more rational and efficient. Another group echoed Wilsonian Democrats and urged the government to break up monopolies that restricted competition, were too big to be efficient, and hindered the growth of new enterprises so vital for economic recovery. Neither the antimonopoly campaign nor efforts to revive central planning gained enough support to prevail. Instead, the Keynesian message gained the greatest influence within the New Deal. The notion of an active federal government freed from rigid economic doctrine and willing to engage in large-

scale spending to alleviate distress appealed to the Roosevelt administration's sense of practical adjustment to circumstances. As Harry Hopkins put it, the president's economics had always consisted of a desire to "feed the hungry, and Goddamn fast."

The Last of the New Deal Reforms

From the moment he was sworn in, Roosevelt had tinkered with the small and antiquated office of the presidency. He believed that the powers of the presidency were inadequate, especially during emergencies such as the depression. He also wanted more power over the federal bureaucracy. Arguing the need for "efficiency," Roosevelt submitted an ambitious plan of executive reorganization to Congress in 1937. The bill failed, but in September 1939 Congress passed the Administrative Reorganization Act, which gave Roosevelt part of what he desired. With a Democratic majority in Congress, a now friendly Supreme Court, and the revival of deficit spending, the newly empowered White House seemed to be in a good position to move ahead with a third New Deal.

Resistance was also on the rise, however. Conservatives argued that the New Deal had pressed its centralization too far and was bent on creating what later came to be known as "the imperial presidency." Even the New Deal's friends became weary of one emergency program after another, especially while economic recession still shadowed New Deal achievements. By the midpoint of Roosevelt's second term, restive members of Congress balked at new initiatives. Clearly, the New Deal was winding down, but enough energy remained for one last burst of reform.

The farm sector still had strong claims on New Deal attention in the face of drought, declining prices, and an impoverished class of landless hired hands. In 1937, the Agriculture Department created the Farm Security Administration (FSA) to provide housing and loans to help tenant farmers become independent. But the FSA was starved for funds and ran up against the major farm organizations, which were intent on serving the interests of the large farms. With only minor successes to show, the FSA petered out in the early 1940s. For those who owned farms, the New Deal completed its efforts to establish a secure plateau of prosperity with the Agricultural Adjustment Act (AAA) of February 1938. The plan combined production quotas on five staple crops—cotton, tobacco, wheat, corn, and rice—

NEW DEAL HOUSING GOALS
The eradication of slum housing (top) such as this in Atlanta in 1936 came to be a prime test of overcoming the depression. In his inaugural address for his second term, Roosevelt focused on the need to rescue the one-third of the nation still "ill-housed, ill-clad, and ill-nourished." The most famous attempt to point the way was the greenbelt town program run by the Resettlement Administration of the Department of Agriculture to relocate people forced off the farms. The picture of Greendale, Wisconsin (bottom), taken in 1939, offers an idea of the uniform utopia the Roosevelt administration favored but was prevented from continuing by the shifting of resources to fight World War II.
Library of Congress.

with storage loans through its Commodity Credit Corporation to moderate price swings by regulating supply. The most prosperous farmers benefited most, but the act's Federal Surplus Commodities Corporation added an element of charity by issuing food stamps so that the poor could purchase surplus food. Through that balance, the AAA of 1938 brought stability to American agriculture and ample food to the table.

Advocates for the urban underclass also had modest luck gaining attention after decades of neglect. New York senator Robert Wagner convinced Congress to pass the National Housing Act in September 1937. By 1941, some 160,000 residences had been made available at rates affordable for those below the poverty line. The project did not come close to meeting the need for affordable housing, but for the first time the federal government took an active role in providing decent urban housing.

The last major piece of New Deal labor legislation, the Fair Labor Standards Act of June 1938, reiterated the original New Deal pledge to provide workers with a decent standard of living. After unprecedented haggling and compromise that revealed the waning strength of the New Deal, Congress finally agreed to intervene in the long-sacrosanct realm of worker contracts. The act set minimum-wage and maximum-hours standards and at long last curbed the use of child labor. The minimum-wage level was modest—twenty-five cents an hour for a maximum of forty-four hours a week. And, in order to attract enough conservative votes, the act exempted merchant seamen, fishermen, domestic help, and farm laborers from these wage and hours standards. Nevertheless, the new standards were an important step toward realization of the New Deal promise to work actively to eliminate poverty.

The last major piece of New Deal labor legislation, the Fair Labor Standards Act of June 1938, reiterated the original New Deal pledge to provide workers with a decent standard of living.

The final New Deal reform effort failed to make much headway against the hidebound system of racial segregation. Although Roosevelt was willing to denounce lynching as murder, he would not jeopardize his vital base of southern political support by designating antilynching bills as "must" legislation. In 1934 and 1935, Congress voted down attempts to make lynching a federal crime, and in 1938 the last antilynching bill of the decade died in a Senate filibuster. Laws to eliminate the poll tax—used to deny blacks the opportunity to vote—encountered the same overwhelming resistance. African Americans received some meager benefit from employment opportunities in northern relief projects and federal agencies, but the New Deal refused to confront the injustice of racial segregation with the same vigor it had brought to bear on economic hardship.

By the end of 1938, the New Deal had run out of fresh ideas and into stiff opposition. As legislative initiative waned and programs played themselves out, the conservative tide rose. In the congressional elections of 1938, Republicans picked up seven seats in the Senate and eighty in the House, making them a power for the first time since 1932. New Dealers could claim unprecedented and resounding achievement since 1933 when Roosevelt entered the White House, but ten million unemployed five years later, about two-thirds as many as in 1932 under Hoover, were striking reminders that the depression had not been whipped. In his annual message to Congress in January 1939, however, Roosevelt called a halt to the great reform movement of the Second New Deal. He spoke of preserving the progress already achieved, not of extending it. As conditions dictated a pause in domestic reform, the time had come to pay more attention to America's place in a dangerous world. Roosevelt would end the decade by pointing to the threat posed by fascist aggression and proposing defense expenditures that surpassed those allocated for relief and economic revival.

Conclusion: A New Departure

Looking on ruefully as the Bonus Expeditionary Army fled the capital in 1932, humorist Will Rogers remarked that the old soldiers could get any road out of Washington, but they couldn't get a sandwich out of Congress. Into that mood of defeat and discouragement, Roosevelt brought an optimistic spirit of experimental action. An ever more inclusive majority agreed with the president that society should help those in need and that the federal government was an appropriate vehicle to deliver aid. In the process of fighting the depression, the Roosevelt administration vastly expanded the size and power of the federal government and changed the way the American people looked on Washington. It won major successes such as Social Security, labor's right to organize, and guarantees that farm prices would be maintained through controls on production and marketing.

To Hoover and many conservatives, New Deal planning appeared to be a dangerous form of socialism that threatened the foundations of democracy and capitalism. But as Frances Perkins said, Franklin Roosevelt took capitalism as much for granted as he did his family. Rather than attack capitalism, he boldly sought to save it. The daring innovation and persistent experimentation of the New Deal precluded radical and revolutionary transformation. Like his cousin Teddy, Franklin

Roosevelt understood that things would have to change in order to remain the same. Both believed that a strengthened national government was necessary to curb the destructive tendencies of increasing complexity and material power. That shift of power to the center, they believed, provided the means necessary for preserving America's democratic tradition and giving individuals full opportunity. Reflecting their belief in a militant government, New Dealers repeatedly described their programs as a kind of warfare against the adversities of the 1930s. But in the next decade, with the depression only partly overcome, the Roosevelt administration would have to turn from the symbolic New Deal war at home to test its strength in a shooting war against the enemies of democracy abroad.

www.bedfordstmartins.com/tap   SEE THE ONLINE STUDY GUIDE to assess your mastery of the material covered in this chapter.

CHRONOLOGY

1932   The Bonus Expeditionary Army marches on Washington and is routed by federal troops.

1933   Franklin D. Roosevelt assumes presidency.

March–June. New Deal established through passage of reform legislation of the Hundred Days.

Roosevelt closes nation's banks for four-day "holiday" to allow time to stabilize banking system.

The Federal Emergency Relief Administration (FERA) provides relief for unemployed.

1934   Securities and Exchange Commission licenses and regulates stock exchanges.

Upton Sinclair loses bid for governor of California and chance to enact his EPIC work relief program.

Wealthy conservatives of American Liberty League oppose New Deal.

Dr. Francis Townsend devises Old Age Revolving Pension scheme to provide money to impoverished elderly.

Congress adopts Indian Reorganization Act.

1935   Louisiana senator Huey Long assassinated.

As part of Second Hundred Days, legislation creates Works Progress Administration (WPA).

Congress passes Wagner Act to guarantee workers the right to organize unions and bargain collectively.

Committee for Industrial Organization (CIO) founded to provide union representation for unskilled workers.

Social Security Act provides supplementary income for aged and retired persons.

"Radio Priest" Father Charles Coughlin begins National Union for Social Justice.

1936   John Maynard Keynes publishes *The General Theory of Employment, Interest, and Money*, providing theoretical justification for government deficit financing.

Franklin Roosevelt reelected by landslide over Republican Alfred Landon.

1937   CIO stages successful sit-down strike at General Motors plant in Flint, Michigan. Roosevelt's "court-packing" legislation defeated in Senate.

1937–   Economic recession slows recovery
1938   from depression.

1938   Second Agricultural Adjustment Act and Fair Labor Standards Act bring New Deal legislation to an end.

Congress rejects administration's antilynching bill.

1939   Administrative Reorganization Act enlarges scope and power of presidency.

African American contralto Marian Anderson gives concert at Lincoln Memorial.

BIBLIOGRAPHY

GENERAL WORKS

Anthony Badger, *The New Deal: The Depression Years, 1933–1940* (1989).

Alan Brinkley, *The End of Reform: New Deal Liberalism in Recession and War* (1995).

Laura Browder, *Rousing the Nation: Radical Culture in Depression America* (1998).

Kenneth S. Davis, *FDR,* 4 vols. (1985–1993).

Steve Fraser and Gary Gerstle, eds., *The Rise and Fall of the New Deal Order* (1988).

William E. Leuchtenburg, *Franklin D. Roosevelt and the New Deal, 1932–1940* (1963).

William E. Leuchtenburg, *The FDR Years: On Roosevelt and His Legacy* (1995).

Katie Loucheim, ed., *The Making of the New Deal: The Insiders Speak* (1983).

Richard H. Pells, *Radical Visions and American Dreams: Culture and Social Thought in the Depression Years* (1973).

Arthur S. Schlesinger Jr., *The Coming of the New Deal* (1959).

Arthur S. Schlesinger Jr., *The Politics of Upheaval* (1960).

Harvard Sitkoff, ed., *Fifty Years Later: The New Deal Evaluated* (1985).

THE ROOSEVELT LEADERSHIP

Philip Abbott, *The Exemplary Presidency: Franklin D. Roosevelt and the American Political Tradition* (1990).

John Allswang, *The New Deal and American Politics* (1978).

Kristi Andersen, *The Creation of a Democratic Majority, 1928–1936* (1979).

James M. Burns, *Roosevelt: The Lion and the Fox* (1956).

Blanche Wiesen Cook, *Eleanor Roosevelt,* 2 vols. (1992, 1999).

Frank Friedel, *Franklin D. Roosevelt: A Rendezvous with Destiny* (1990).

Joseph Lash, *Eleanor and Franklin* (1971).

Richard Polenberg, *Reorganizing Roosevelt's Government, 1936–1939* (1966).

Albert U. Romasco, *The Politics of Recovery: Roosevelt's New Deal* (1983).

Eleanor Roosevelt, *Autobiography* (1961).

Eliot A. Rosen, *Hoover, Roosevelt, and the Brains Trust: From Depression to New Deal* (1977).

Sean J. Savage, *Roosevelt: The Party Leader, 1932–1945* (1991).

Richard W. Steele, *Propaganda in an Open Society: The Roosevelt Administration and the Media, 1933–1941* (1985).

Geoffrey C. Ward, *A First-Class Temperament: The Emergence of Franklin Roosevelt* (1989).

Susan Ware, *Beyond Suffrage: Women in the New Deal* (1981).

Susan Ware, *Partner and I: Molly Dewson, Feminism, and New Deal Politics* (1987).

ECONOMICS AND PLANNING

William J. Barber, *From New Era to New Deal: Herbert Hoover, the Economists, and American Economic Policy, 1921–1933* (1985).

Donald R. Brand, *Corporatism and the Rule of Law: A Study of the National Recovery Administration* (1988).

Mark Gelfand, *A Nation of Cities: The Federal Government and Urban America, 1933–1945* (1975).

Otis L. Graham Jr., *Toward a Planned Society: From Roosevelt to Nixon* (1976).

Erwin C. Hargrove, *Prisoners of Myth: The Leadership of the Tennessee Valley Authority, 1933–1990* (1990).

Ellis Hawley, *The New Deal and the Problem of Monopoly: A Study in Economic Ambivalence* (1966).

Susan Estabrook Kennedy, *The Banking Crisis of 1933* (1973).

Mark Leff, *The Limits of Symbolic Reform: The New Deal and Taxation, 1933–1939* (1984).

Dean May, *From New Deal to New Economics* (1981).

Michael Parrish, *Securities Regulation and the New Deal* (1970).

Eliot Rosen, *Hoover, Roosevelt, and the Brains Trust* (1977).

Theodore Rosenof, *Economics in the Long Run: New Deal Theorists and Their Legacies, 1933–1993* (1997).

REFORM AND WELFARE

W. Andrew Achenbaum, *Shades of Gray: Old Age, American Values and Federal Policies since 1920* (1983).

Edward D. Berkowitz, *America's Welfare State: From Roosevelt to Reagan* (1991).

William R. Brock, *Welfare, Democracy, and the New Deal* (1987).

John A. Clausen, *Looking Back at the Children of the Great Depression* (1993).

Phoebe Cutler, *The Public Landscape of the New Deal* (1986).

Linda Gordon, *Pitied but Not Entitled: Single Mothers and the History of Welfare* (1994).

William Graebner, *A History of Retirement: The Meaning and Function of an American Institution, 1885–1978* (1980).

Joseph Hutmacher, *Senator Robert Wagner and the Rise of American Liberalism* (1968).

Paul A. Kurzman, *Harry Hopkins and the New Deal* (1974).

Roy Lubove, *The Struggle for Social Security, 1900–1935* (1968).

Paul E. Mertz, *New Deal Policy and Southern Rural Poverty* (1978).

James T. Patterson, *America's Struggle against Poverty, 1900–1980* (1981).

John Salmond, *The Civilian Conservation Corps, 1933–1942* (1967).

Bonnie Fox Schwartz, *The Civil Works Administration, 1933–1934* (1984).

CHALLENGES TO THE NEW DEAL

Alan Brinkley, *Voices of Protest: Huey Long, Father Coughlin, and the Great Depression* (1983).

Otis L. Graham Jr., *An Encore for Reform: The Old Progressives and the New Deal* (1967).

William Ivy Hair, *The Kingfish and His Realm* (1991).

Harvey Klehr, *The Heyday of American Communism* (1984).

R. Alan Lawson, *The Failure of Independent Liberalism, 1930–1941* (1971).

Donald J. Lisio, *The President and Protest: Hoover, Conspiracy, and the Bonus Riot* (1974).

Huey Pierce Long, *Every Man a King: The Autobiography of Huey P. Long* (1933).

Huey Pierce Long, *My First Days in the White House* (1935).

James T. Patterson, *Congressional Conservatism and the New Deal* (1967).

Leo P. Ribuffo, *The Old Christian Right: The Protestant Far Right from the Great Depression to the Cold War* (1983).

Frank A. Warren, *Liberals and Communism: The "Red Decade" Revisited* (1966, 1993).

Clyde P. Weed, *The Nemesis of Reform: The Republican Party during the New Deal* (1994).

T. Harry Williams, *Huey Long* (1969).

George Wolfskill, *The Revolt of the Conservatives: A History of the American Liberty League, 1934–1940* (1962).

RURAL AMERICA, SOUTH AND WEST

David E. Conrad, *The Forgotten Farmers: The Story of the Share-Croppers in The New Deal* (1965).

Cletus E. Daniel, *Bitter Harvest: A History of California Farmworkers, 1870–1941* (1981).

David E. Hamilton, *From New Day to New Deal: American Farm Policy from Hoover to Roosevelt, 1928–1933* (1991).

Jack Temple Kirby, *Rural Worlds Lost: The American South, 1920–1960* (1987).

Richard Lowitt, *The New Deal and the West* (1984).

LABOR

John Barnard, *Walter Reuther and the Rise of the Auto Workers* (1983).

Irving Bernstein, *A Caring Society: The New Deal, the Worker, and the Great Depression* (1985).

Bert Cochran, *Labor and Communism* (1977).

Lizbeth Cohen, *Making a New Deal: Industrial Workers in Chicago, 1919–1939* (1990).

Sidney Fine, *Sitdown: The General Motors Strike of 1936–1937* (1969).

Steve Fraser, *Labor Will Rule: Sidney Hillman and the Rise of American Labor* (1991).

Gary Gerstle, *Working-Class Americanism: The Politics of Labor in a Textile City, 1914–1960* (1989).

Colin Gordon, *New Deals: Business, Labor, and Politics in America, 1920–1935* (1994).

James A. Hodges, *New Deal Labor Policy and the Southern Cotton Textile Industry, 1933–1941* (1986).

August Meier and Elliott Rudwick, *Black Detroit and the Rise of the UAW* (1979).

David Milton, *The Politics of United States Labor: From the Great Depression to the New Deal* (1980).

Judith Sealander, *As Minority Becomes Majority: Federal Reaction to the Phenomenon of Women in the Work Force, 1920–1963* (1983).

Robert H. Zieger, *John L. Lewis: Labor Leader* (1988).

RACE AND MINORITIES

Rodolfo Acuna, *Occupied America: A History of Chicanos* (1988).

Christine Bolt, *American Indian Policy and American Reform* (1987).

Dan T. Carter, *Scottsboro* (1969).

Donald L. Fixico, *The Invasion of Indian Country in the Twentieth Century: American Capitalism and Tribal Natural Resources* (1998).

Camille Guerin-Gonzales, *Mexican Workers and the American Dream: Immigration, Repatriation, and California Farm Labor, 1900–1939* (1994).

Robin D. G. Kelley, *Hammer and Hoe: Alabama Communists during the Great Depression* (1990).

John B. Kirby, *Black Americans in the Roosevelt Era: Liberalism and Race* (1980).

Doug McAdam, *Political Process and the Development of Black Insurgency, 1920–1970* (1982).

Harvard Sitkoff, *A New Deal for Blacks: The Emergence of Civil Rights As a National Issue,* vol. 1, *The Depression Decade* (1978).

Graham D. Taylor, *The New Deal and American Indian Tribalism: The Administration of the Indian Reorganization Act, 1935–1945* (1980).

Nancy J. Weiss, *Farewell to the Party of Lincoln* (1983).

Robert L. Zangrando, *The NAACP Crusade against Lynching* (1980).

PUBLIC CULTURE

E. Quita Craig, *Black Drama of the Federal Theatre Era: Beyond the Formal Horizons* (1980).

Jonathan Harris, *Federal Art and National Culture: The Politics of Identity in New Deal America* (1995).

Jerre Mangione, *The Dream and the Deal* (1972).

Karal Ann Marling, *Wall-to-Wall America: A Cultural History of Post-Office Murals in the Great Depression* (1982).

Jane DeHart Matthews, *The Federal Theatre, 1935–1939: Plays, Relief, and Politics* (1967).

Richard McKinzie, *The New Deal for Artists* (1973).

GOD BLESS AMERICA

MEMENTO OF WAR

To mark the seriousness of going to war, servicemen and their families often mounted photos in special settings, such as this painted-on-glass frame. Symbols of God and country sum up patriotic devotion to a just cause. And in the midst of these ritualized sentiments, as if looking back through a window draped in his honor, an unknown sailor seems about to tell us something more.

Private collection.

THE UNITED STATES AND THE SECOND WORLD WAR

24

1939–1945

EXCITED AND UNCERTAIN ABOUT WHAT TO EXPECT, a noisy crowd of eight thousand jostled into the America First rally in Des Moines, Iowa, on the evening of September 1, 1941, to hear Charles Lindbergh, the nation's most famous hero. A shy, private man who had resisted the media's efforts to make him a celebrity, Lindbergh dreaded the event. Only a compelling sense of duty convinced him that he must suffer the spotlight again to take a stand against President Franklin Roosevelt's order that would allow American warships to "shoot on sight" any German vessel that interfered with American ships heading to Great Britain.

Lindbergh's speech was sponsored by the America First Committee (AFC), organized in the fall of 1940 to keep the United States out of the war that had erupted in Europe the year before. The AFC's youthful organizers attracted a considerable number of followers, including two draft-age future presidents, Gerald Ford and John Kennedy. But supporters of the Allied struggle against Nazi aggression, led by the Roosevelt administration, vociferously denounced the America Firsters. Even the adored Lindbergh could not withstand ardent belief in the rightfulness of the Allied cause. Secretary of the Interior Harold Ickes referred to the doubting Lindbergh as "America's No. 1 Nazi fellow traveler." A year earlier, Roosevelt had gone even further. "I am absolutely convinced," he told Secretary of the Treasury Henry Morgenthau, "that Lindbergh is a Nazi."

Yet the man who had been the first to fly the Atlantic alone still had such a strong hold on the American imagination that the crowd in Des Moines settled down immediately when he stepped onto the stage, straight and tall, remaining at thirty-nine the godlike young aviator. In his clear, earnest voice, Lindbergh declared that war would needlessly take the lives of the nation's best young men and bleed precious resources. He then charged that "the three most important groups who have been pressing this country toward war are the British, the Jewish, and the Roosevelt administration." Lindbergh received a standing ovation. Elsewhere, however, accusations mounted that Lindbergh was anti-Semitic, if not pro-Nazi, and even close associates backed away. By the time the United States entered the war in December 1941, the "Lone Eagle" was alone again.

In 1940–1941, millions of Americans shared Lindbergh's concerns about the destructiveness of war, but few resisted involvement as hard or as long as he did. Nor did many people question the Allied cause. Torn between abhorrence of Nazism and a desire not to be drawn into another world war, Americans

CHARLES LINDBERGH

When he came home to a hero's welcome after his famous flight across the Atlantic, Charles Lindbergh told his countrymen that he hoped the feat would bring Europe and America together as friends. The outbreak of war in 1939 dashed that vision and led Lindbergh to join the isolationist America First Committee. He drew huge crowds when he spoke at rallies against intervention, such as the one shown here (left) at the Manhattan Center in April 1941. After America was attacked a few months later, Lindbergh's sense of duty shifted to all-out support of the war effort—including combat missions in the Pacific. Yet, even with victory, he never lost the sense that war meant something had gone terribly wrong with civilization.

Wide World Photos, Inc./Courtesy of McGuire Air Force Base.

reluctantly endorsed Roosevelt's support for Britain's last-ditch defense against tyranny. Only when the nation was attacked, however, did U.S. citizens throw themselves unreservedly into a struggle they were convinced was necessary to preserve democracy. With less emotion but deeper conviction than during World War I, Americans came to believe they were fighting a "good war."

Despite their sense that they were engaged in a universal cause, Americans' experience in World War II was unique. No fighting occurred on American soil, yet the nation engaged in a total war that influenced everyone in the country and almost every aspect of life. The war put Americans to work again and ended the depression. It ended the New

Deal's drive for reform and the nation's isolationism. American soldiers and sailors, many of whom had never been beyond their hometowns, fought on distant continents and seas, and came home changed. As one rifleman said of his experience abroad: "I went there a skinny, gaunt mama's boy, full of wonderment. I came back much more circumspect in my judgment of people. And of governments." Nearly four years of war also changed individuals and society at home. Women did "men's" work, minorities stepped out of their "places," and, as one woman remembered, people came out of the war "with more money than they'd had in years." But the loss of fathers, husbands, and sons left hundreds of thousands of families with wounds that would never heal. A victorious nation, grieving yet still optimistic, emerged from World War II the strongest industrial and military power in the world.

Peacetime Dilemmas

With the Japanese invasion of Manchuria in 1931, the arms buildup and talk of the glories of war in fascist Italy, and the swearing in of Adolf Hitler as chancellor of Germany in 1933, the peace structure so hopefully put into place during the Versailles Peace Conference following World War I grew more precarious. As the tide of violent nationalism rose, the United States retreated behind its ocean shield, with New Dealers determined to concentrate on domestic policies first and not to allow international complications to hinder the country's economic recovery. With few exceptions, American policy took on a peculiar polarity: In the face of crises, the nation's leaders took bold action at home but shrank from involvement abroad.

FDR and Reluctant Isolation

Nowhere was the contrast between domestic boldness and international caution more evident than in the change in Franklin Delano Roosevelt's public position on foreign policy. Roosevelt grew up within activist international circles. The Delanos on his mother's side had long been involved with China, and the family home in Hyde Park, New York, was filled with books, mementos, and talk about Asia. Moreover, his famous cousin Theodore had played a premier role in bringing the United States onto the world stage. In that heady atmosphere, Franklin Roosevelt came to believe that naval dominance determined the balance of power. His position as assistant secretary of the navy in the Wilson administration provided a splendid opportunity for him to expand that internationalist vision, and after World War I, Roosevelt advocated American membership in the League of Nations, thus remaining true to Wilson's vision that the United States should take the lead in making the world "safe for democracy." When Roosevelt reentered politics in 1928 to run for the governorship of the state of New York, he charged that Republican isolationism had undermined chances for a prosperous peace by setting high tariffs while also insisting that the exhausted Europeans pay off their loans and reparations.

The depression forced Roosevelt to retreat from his internationalism; expending effort and money on foreign ventures, he came to believe, was a risky diversion from domestic recovery. During his 1932 run for the presidency, Roosevelt sought to defuse charges that he was an international adventurer by pulling back from his endorsement of the League of Nations and reversing his position on forgiving European war debts.

Once in office, Roosevelt sought to join domestic economic recovery with a foreign policy that encouraged free trade and disarmament. He had always believed that peace, prosperity, and free trade were linked. "Foreign markets must be regained if America's producers are to rebuild a full and enduring domestic prosperity for our people," Roosevelt declared in 1935. The concept of an interdependent and open world moved Roosevelt to seek reversal of the policy that had left Russia a pariah nation since the Bolshevik Revolution of 1917. After a careful survey of American public opinion convinced him of the nation's support, Roosevelt granted formal recognition to the Soviet Union on November 17, 1933.

Other than taking this bold initiative, Roosevelt was hemmed in by circumstances. Because the New Deal needed support from isolationists in Congress, Roosevelt could not offer to help the League of Nations or the World Court curb aggression. America could only watch from the sidelines as the League of Nations gradually lost its ability to maintain peace. When rebuked for its invasion of the Chinese province of Manchuria, Japan withdrew from the league and rejected limitations on its naval strength imposed after World War I. In the fall of 1933, the new Nazi chancellor of Germany, Adolf Hitler, further dimmed the league's prospects by condemning the organization as an obstacle to Germany's national aspirations and recalling Germany's representatives to the league. Though apprehensive about the threat to world peace these moves posed, Roosevelt had to reassure Americans that support of the league's objectives would not go so far as to involve the United States in war. Under no circumstances, he declared, would the nation "use its armed forces for the settlement of any dispute anywhere."

Unable to join peacekeeping initiatives, Roosevelt turned to building U.S. defenses. In 1934, to counter the Japanese naval buildup, Roosevelt authorized the largest expansion of the U.S. navy since 1916. At the same time, he instructed the State

Department to play down Japan's expansion in China. Most citizens, absorbed in their domestic woes, paid little attention to overseas problems.

The Good Neighbor Policy

In his inaugural address in 1933, Franklin Roosevelt dedicated the United States to "the policy of the good neighbor" in foreign affairs. A few weeks later, he specifically applied the phrase to Latin America, signaling a shift from the arrogant insistence of previous administrations that they had the right to intervene in the internal affairs of Latin American nations. By offering a "helping hand" and enjoying "the cooperation of others," Roosevelt declared, the United States could engender "more order in this hemisphere and less dislike." In December 1933, Secretary of State Cordell Hull carried that message to the Inter-American Conference in Montevideo, Uruguay, where he signed a joint declaration asserting that no nation had the right to intervene in the internal or external affairs of another.

The U.S. government's commitment to nonintervention was quickly put to the test. When Mexico nationalized American oil holdings and when revolution boiled over in Nicaragua, Guatemala, and Cuba, Franklin Roosevelt refrained from his cousin Theodore's easy resort to sending in the marines to defend the interests of American corporations. Moreover, in 1934 Roosevelt withdrew American marines from Haiti, where they had exerted control since 1916. But nonintervention was a double-edged sword. While it honored the principle of national self-determination, it did not necessarily promote freedom. American business, emboldened by Roosevelt's policy, entered into lucrative arrangements with dictators like Anastasio Somoza in Nicaragua and Fulgencio Batista in Cuba that enabled those tyrants to become wealthy and powerful by exploiting and terrorizing the rest of the population.

Nonintervention was a double-edged sword. While it honored the principle of national self-determination, it did not necessarily promote freedom.

Adoption of the "good neighbor policy," therefore, did not mean that Roosevelt had abandoned Woodrow Wilson's aim of achieving economic pre-

eminence in the region. Roosevelt did not so much retreat from empire in Latin America as reject military force as the way to retain it. With Roosevelt's blessing, Hull engineered passage of the Reciprocal Trade Agreements Act of 1934. The act gave the president power to reduce the nation's high tariffs on a nation-by-nation basis with countries that would set the same tariff standards in return. By 1940, Hull's initiative persuaded twenty-two nations to sign treaties that set the pattern for most of America's foreign trade. Trade reciprocity had significant results, with American exports to Latin America doubling from 1933 to 1940. Trade reciprocity, however, did not prevent a widening of the gap between American economic power and that of the rest of the Western Hemisphere. Still, the seeds of friendship and solidarity planted in Latin America grew in importance as events in Europe and Asia eroded the hope for peace.

The Price of Noninvolvement

Increasingly in the 1930s, international order broke down. Countries beset by economic hardship, ethnic rivalries, and historic grievances turned to aggressive nationalism as the way to end their troubles. Italian strongman Benito Mussolini set the pattern. Through harsh militarist means, Mussolini constructed an authoritarian state that created a semblance of order. Even those who lamented the loss of democracy in Italy were likely to accept the myth of efficiency symbolized in the saying "At least the trains run on time." But Mussolini's philosophy of aggression eroded European resolve to settle disputes peacefully. "War is to the man what maternity is to the woman," Mussolini proclaimed with a theatrical strut. "I do not believe in perpetual peace; not only do I not believe in it, but I find it depressing and a negation of all the fundamental virtues of man."

In Germany, Hitler was feverishly rearming his nation in open defiance of the Versailles treaty. British and French leaders had the power to compel German compliance, but they contented themselves with verbal protest. In 1935, Britain concluded a treaty with the Nazis that conceded to Germany equality in submarines and the right to build a surface fleet one-third the size of the British navy. Still, Hitler ranted against the Jews as the enemies of the Aryan master race and threatened action to avenge humiliating defeat in World War I. His statements about restoring territories with

German inhabitants to the "fatherland" became harder to ignore.

Political and economic tensions in East Asia also gave rise to a militant movement in Japan that resembled European fascism in the way it subordinated the economy to a ruling caste and sought national advantage through conquest. After invading Manchuria in 1931, Japan began a military campaign to take the five northern provinces of China (see Map 24.2). What the Japanese believed would be a mere skirmish became a long and vicious war when Chinese Nationalist leader Chiang Kai-shek rallied his troops and stubbornly resisted the Japanese invasion.

At first, alarm in the United States over escalating hostility abroad played into the hands of the isolationists. Disillusionment over the failure of the Great War to make the world safe for democracy convinced many Americans that the opponents of the war had been right all along. In 1933, a senatorial committee investigated the U.S. decision to send troops to Europe in 1917. Chaired by Republican Gerald Nye of North Dakota, the committee concluded that the greed of American munitions makers, bankers, and financiers was responsible for dragging the country into war. Although it had little evidence, the Nye committee nevertheless convinced thousands of Americans that the "merchants of death" were again seeking to profit by pushing the country into a tragic mistake.

The Nye committee's report and the rapidly deteriorating international situation prodded Congress into action. Between 1935 and 1937, legislators passed a series of neutrality acts designed to prevent the recurrence of the circumstances that they now believed had involved the country in World War I. One act forbade the extension of loans to nations at war. Another gave the president the power to warn Americans about traveling on ships of belligerent nations. A third prohibited arms sales to nations at war.

But by 1937, trade in nonmilitary goods had also become an issue. Some Americans—arguing that any trade, not just in munitions, could draw the nation into war—called for a total embargo of all American products to warring countries. Most members of Congress, however, recognized that a total trade ban would devastate the shaky American economy. Congress believed that it found a way out in the Neutrality Act of 1937, which allowed nonmilitary goods to continue to flow to nations at war if the foreign nations paid cash (thus avoiding

THE QUEST FOR DISARMAMENT
With startling swoops a little white plane, meant to evoke the dove of peace, is covered by a blood-red hawk of a fighter plane, gun ablaze. The shouted cry "Disarm!" at the bottom of the poster expresses the view of peace advocates at the beginning of the 1930s that the way to make the world safe was to take weapons away from the strong, not to arm the weak. Soon after the poster appeared, the march of fascist aggression began to shift opinion toward the belief that nations could better attain collective security by using force to counter the enemies of peace. Private collection.

American loans) and shipped the goods in their own vessels (thus avoiding the use of American ships in war zones). The so-called cash-and-carry policy seemed to promise that the United States could have both peace and prosperous foreign trade.

Emboldened by democracy's presumed lack of resolve to stand firm against pressure, Germany, Italy, and Japan went from one triumphant strike to the next. In March 1936, Nazi troops marched unopposed into the Rhineland on Germany's western border in blatant violation of the Treaty of Versailles, which had placed the area under French authority. One month later, Italian armies completed their conquest of Ethiopia; a cloud of Italian bombers and poison gas against a defense of spears and old rifles prepared the way for the fascists' grand entry into the capital of Addis Ababa. Aggression in East Asia reached its climax in December 1937 when Japanese troops captured Nanking and celebrated their triumph with a murderous rampage that cost the lives of 200,000 Chinese civilians.

These brutal events occurred alongside a tragic drama in Spain that demonstrated the threat of fascist power to democracy. In 1936, the country erupted in a civil war between Loyalists, representing the existing republican government, and rebel fascists led by General Francisco Franco. In what became widely described as a rehearsal for the next world war, Germany and Italy sent troops and arms to Franco, and the Soviet Union, on a much smaller scale, came to the aid of the Loyalists. The American government and public opinion favored the Loyalists as the democratically elected government, but neither the United States nor European democracies offered assistance to either side. Neutrality meant that Loyalist forces were at a disadvantage against rebel forces amply supplied by fascist and Nazi nations that welcomed Franco as a fellow dictator. In an effort to make up for their nation's inaction, over three thousand Americans, many of them inspired by the Soviet Union's intervention, enlisted in the Russian-sponsored Abraham Lincoln Brigade to fight for the Loyalists with several thousand volunteers from other countries.

Increasingly convinced that the United States needed to play a stronger role in stopping aggres-

Spanish Civil War, 1936–1939

sion, Roosevelt spoke on October 5, 1937, in Chicago, the heartland of isolationist sentiment, in an attempt to persuade Americans that the government should be more assertive against aggression. "America hates war," he said. "America hopes for peace. Therefore, America actively engages in the search for peace." Thinking particularly of the horrors of the Japanese invasion of China, Roosevelt declared that aggressors must be "quarantined" by the international community. Otherwise the "contagion" of war would spread to every shore.

The speech advocated no specific action, but it ignited a storm of protest. Peace groups activated a letter-writing campaign to newspapers and politicians. The *Chicago Tribune* charged that the president wanted to replace "Americanism" with "internationalism." Most ominously, leaders in Congress remained silent. Roosevelt, who already had his hands full with fighting the depression, pulled back. "It's a terrible thing," he remarked to an aide, "to look over your shoulder when you are trying to lead and find no one there."

The Onset of War

Events had not spiraled far enough into disaster by the start of Roosevelt's second term to convince the public that noninvolvement would have to give way to an active role in foreign affairs, backed up by expanded armed forces. To be sure, the saber-rattling rhetoric and aggression of fascist dictators had alerted some observers to the danger. But troubles in China, Ethiopia, and Spain seemed too remote and minor to bring most Americans around to the view that it was time to take a stand.

Nazi Aggression and War in Europe

Under the spell of neutrality, Americans watched entranced as Adolf Hitler continued his campaign to dominate Europe. In the name of the fatherland's "destiny" to unite all German peoples, Hitler in 1938 bullied Austria into accepting incorporation—*Anschluss*—into the Nazi Third Reich. He then turned his attention to the German-speaking Sudetenland, granted to Czechoslovakia by the Versailles treaty. Although the Czechs were prepared to fight rather than surrender territory, the British and French wanted peace and sought to strike a deal with Hitler. British prime minister

Neville Chamberlain went to confer with the German ruler in Munich, offering terms of "appeasement," as he called it, that would turn over the Sudetenland to Germany in exchange for leaving the rest of Czechoslovakia alone. On September 29, 1938, Hitler accepted the offer, solemnly promising that he would make no more territorial claims in Europe. Chamberlain returned home convinced that he had obtained "peace in our time." In March

1939, Hitler marched the German army into weakened Czechoslovakia and took over the entire country without firing a shot (Map 24.1).

Hardly pausing for breath, Hitler in April demanded that Poland return the German territory it had been awarded after World War I. Britain and France finally recognized that the policy of appeasement was a failure. They assured Poland that they would go to its aid if Hitler attacked. Hitler

M AP 24.1

Axis Aggression through 1941

For different reasons, Hitler and Mussolini launched a series of surprise military strikes. Mussolini sought to recreate the Roman Empire in the Mediterranean. Hitler struck to reclaim German territories occupied by France after World War I and to annex Austria. When the German dictator then began his campaign to rule over "inferior" peoples beyond Germany's border by attacking Poland, World War II broke out.

then offered Premier Joseph Stalin concessions to prevent the Soviet Union from joining Germany's adversaries in the West. Despite deep enmity between Nazi Germany and the communist Soviet Union, the two powers shocked the world by signing a Nazi-Soviet treaty of nonaggression in August 1939. The agreement stipulated that the two countries would not war on each other, but also meant that the Soviet Union would stand benevolently aside should Nazi Germany commit aggression against Poland or any other countries.

Under the spell of neutrality, Americans watched entranced as Adolf Hitler continued his campaign to dominate Europe.

Hitler's only worry then was that something would interfere with his lust for war. He fretted, "I am afraid some pig-dog will make a proposal for mediation as at Munich." To prevent any such interruption, he exhorted his generals to be as ruthless as possible. "Close your hearts to pity! Act brutally! . . . In starting and waging a war it is not Right that matters, but Victory." At dawn on September 1, 1939, fully in accord with Hitler's wishes and spirit, the German army crossed the Polish border in what they called a *blitzkrieg* (literally "lightning war"), an onrush of tanks and aircraft with a mechanized force and firepower never before conceived. France and Britain kept their word by declaring war. The greatest conflict in history had begun.

From Neutrality to the Arsenal of Democracy

When war erupted, Roosevelt issued an official proclamation of American neutrality. But unlike Woodrow Wilson, he did not ask Americans to be impartial in thought as well as deed, since he and the vast majority of Americans strongly favored Britain, France, and the Allied cause. Antifascist yet neutral, the nation debated what it should do short of war to aid the Allies.

Roosevelt's immediate objective was to persuade Congress to repeal the arms embargo mandated by the neutrality legislation. He believed that France and Britain could defeat Germany only if they had access to weapons. The president's request provoked frenzied debate across the nation. Charles

". . . and the Wolf chewed up the children and spit out their bones . . . But those were Foreign Children and it really didn't matter."

DR. SEUSS TO THE RESCUE
Before he became a famous children's author, Theodor Seuss Geisel, who took the pen name "Dr. Seuss," honed the humane views that informed all his art as cartoonist for the liberal New York City journal, **PM.** *A Jew and a man of strong sympathy for those being mistreated, Dr. Seuss was particularly troubled by isolationist resistance to helping the victims of Nazism. Here in 1941, he skewers the America First Movement as a prissy, self-satisfied old lady with proper manners but a cold heart.*
Dr. Seuss Collection, Mandeville Special Collections Library, University of California, San Diego.

Lindbergh argued that the war was a European matter that the United States should stay out of. Senator William Borah of Idaho declared that Roosevelt's proposal was equivalent to taking sides and would drag the United States into war. But Congress finally consented to extend neutrality legislation and adopt a cash-and-carry policy for arms sales, as well as for nonmilitary goods, which meant that Allied, not American, ships would run the risk of transporting war goods through the German submarine blockade.

After Hitler's armies overran Poland, they paused; but the lull was shattered in the spring of 1940 by a series of Nazi hammer blows. The German blitzkrieg of dive-bombers and tanks smashed through Denmark, Norway, Belgium, and Holland and into northern France. The French made the fatal mistake of believing that they could hold out behind the Maginot Line, a massive concrete fortification that stretched from the Swiss border to the forested Ardennes region on the edge of Belgium (see Map 24.1). Reality struck in early summer when Mussolini's armies invaded France from the south, while Hitler's blitzkrieg flanked the Maginot Line in the north.

British forces in the north were then trapped by the swift German advance and forced to retreat to the port of Dunkirk, from which they were narrowly rescued by a heroic sealift that used every boat able to make it across the English Channel. Less than three weeks later, reeling from a German sweep southward, the French surrendered the largest army in the world and signed an armistice that placed three-fifths of the country under German control. In the words of a dismayed British military expert, the French sword had turned out to be a broomstick.

With the possibility of a German invasion across the Channel now looming, Parliament turned the appeaser Neville Chamberlain out of office and welcomed as prime minister the defiant Winston Churchill. Churchill had watched from the sidelines with mounting fury as Chamberlain kowtowed to Hitler. When the Germans attacked Britain itself, Churchill was ready with a vengeance to take over the last-ditch defense of the nation. His oratorical genius shone through the intensive German bombing campaign against English cities in the summer and fall of 1940. By the time the Royal Air Force won the Battle of Britain in November, ridding the skies of German bombers, Churchill (who even looked like an English bulldog when he growled that "we shall never surrender") had become the symbol of indomitable British resistance.

Roosevelt strove for a comparable role as leader and symbol by inspiring the American public to rise above its isolationist fears. In the spring of 1940, the

THE COUNTY OF LONDON ORCHESTRA
Gallant British resistance to the bombing of their cities captured American sympathy and helped to build support for U.S. entry into the war. Here in the Chelsea section of London in 1942, both the County of London Orchestra and an audience of mostly children demonstrate how to carry on in the ruins with poise and a stiff upper lip.
Getty Images.

LEND-LEASE

This button promoting the Roosevelt administration's lend-lease policy expressed one of Roosevelt's favorite themes: that helping Britain in its hour of need was essentially a neighborly act. One could not just stand by when the fellow next door was being attacked. Despite the isolationist argument that moving into the midst of a shooting war was far more dangerous than providing a neighborly hand, Lend-Lease passed Congress and received the approval of most of the American people.

Collection of Colonel Stuart S. Corning Jr./Picture Research Consultants, Inc.

president prevailed on Kansas journalist William Allen White to form the Committee to Defend America by Aiding the Allies and mount a nationwide campaign to generate public support for Roosevelt's policy of providing all aid to the Allies short of war. Noninterventionists organized in response. Within the broad tent of this ideology were America Firsters like Lindbergh, who worried about war's effect on civilized life, alongside an odd assortment of pro-Nazi spokesmen, anti-British Irish Americans, Italian American supporters of Mussolini, pacifists, and leftists who clung to the view that war was a capitalist plot.

In the midst of the vital debate about American foreign policy, the presidential election of 1940 unfolded. Having decided to run for an unprecedented third term rather than step aside in the time of crisis, Roosevelt looked forward to a campaign pitting the reformist, internationalist thrust of the New Deal against Republican isolationism and business conservatism. Instead he faced Wendell Willkie, a former Democrat who supported most of the New Deal domestic program and generally agreed with Roosevelt's foreign policy. Realizing that he trailed Roosevelt badly, Willkie veered from internationalism and attacked Roosevelt as a warmonger, forcing the president to declare, "Your boys are not going to be sent into any foreign wars." Even with mixed messages about opposing fascist aggression and staying out of war, Roosevelt claimed

a comfortable victory, although his margin was smaller than in 1936 (27.3 million votes to 22.3 million votes and 449 electoral votes to 82).

The president interpreted his victory as a mandate to continue to support Britain in every way short of war. By then, the British were in desperate straits; their treasury exhausted, they could no longer pay cash for weapons. To head off the catastrophic end of American aid, Roosevelt held a fireside chat with the American people on December 16, 1940, to explain that only the British stood between the United States and Nazi aggression. "We must be the great arsenal of democracy," he declared. As for how the British would pay, he offered the homey example of a man who lent his neighbor a garden hose when his house caught on fire: "I don't say to him . . . 'you have to pay me $15 for it.' I don't want $15— I want my garden hose back after the fire is over."

Buoyed by favorable public response, Congress approved the Lend-Lease Act in March, 1941, which allowed the British to obtain armaments from the United States so long as they returned them or their equivalent after the war was over. In reality, Lend-Lease was a charade to retain the semblance of neutrality. As one observer noted, "Lending war materiel is a little like lending chewing gum. You don't want it back." With Lend-Lease, the United States entered into full-fledged economic warfare against Germany. Moreover, since Britain could not sustain its shipping in the face of losses to German submarines, the United States inevitably would need to build and protect a vast merchant fleet. It was only a matter of time before an armed attack occurred of the sort that had precipitated World War I.

With Lend-Lease, the United States entered into full-fledged economic warfare against Germany.

The predictable series of events began on June 11, 1941, when a German U-boat (submarine) sank the American freighter *Robin Moor* off the coast of Africa. Several months later, an American destroyer and a German submarine engaged in a firefight. Roosevelt issued a "shoot on sight" policy for American escort vessels, and by September 1941 an "undeclared war" was under way. In August, as hostilities mounted, Roosevelt and Churchill met on shipboard off the coast of Newfoundland to devise what became known as the Atlantic Charter. Although the United States was still officially neutral, the joint statement looked forward to the destruction of the Nazis and set guidelines for the postwar world. In a restatement of what Wilson urged on the world after World War I, the charter called for national boundaries determined by the people living in the territory, the right of nations to choose their own form of government, economic cooperation to raise the level of disadvantaged peoples, freedom of the seas, and denial of arms to aggressor nations.

As danger in the Atlantic mounted, Hitler took a terrible gamble by launching a massive invasion of the Soviet Union on June 22, 1941. Until that violent rupture of the Nazi-Soviet pact, Americans generally thought no better of the Communists than they did of the Nazis. But the brutal facts of war called for drastic change. Churchill bluntly welcomed his old

M A P   2 4 . 2

Japanese Aggression through 1941

Beginning with the invasion of Manchuria in 1931, Japan sought to force its imperialist control over most of East Asia. Japanese aggression was driven by the need for raw materials for the country's expanding industries and by the military government's devotion to martial honor.

archenemy Joseph Stalin to the cause by stating that he would not hesitate to deal with the devil if Hitler invaded hell. Roosevelt stressed the importance of Russia's entrance in diverting German forces away from the hard-pressed British and quickly persuaded Congress to extend Lend-Lease to the Russians.

War Comes to America

Despite America's primary concern with Europe, the expansion of the Japanese empire made the danger of war for the United States most immediate in Asia. The rising tide of Japanese imperialism clashed with U.S. aspirations and commitments, especially in China. America's China policy had been set in 1899 when Secretary of State John Hay issued the Open Door notes demanding that the United States have equal access to the rich markets of China and that China maintain its territorial integrity. But the island-bound Japanese also wanted raw material and markets, and their weak neighbor China was the natural place to turn. The military invasion of Manchuria in 1931 proved to be the opening salvo of continuing Japanese aggression in China (Map 24.2). Each act of territorial conquest received a stern rebuke from the Roosevelt administration, but toothless proclamations did little to deter the Japanese. Appealing to bitterness in the region against white colonialism, the Japanese marched forward under the banner "Asia for the Asians," which in practical terms really meant China for the Japanese.

In 1940, Japan signed the Tripartite Pact, a defensive alliance with Germany and Italy. It also obtained from the Vichy government (the German puppet regime in France) the right to build airfields and station troops in northern Indochina. In 1941, U.S. naval intelligence cracked the Japanese code and learned that Tokyo had set its sights on the resource-rich Dutch East Indies (the archipelago stretching from Sumatra to New Guinea). In response, the Roosevelt administration announced a complete trade embargo, which denied Japan access to essential oil and scrap iron. Roosevelt had given Japan a choice: Japan would either have to halt its aggression and restore relations and trade with the United States, or it would have to find new sources of vital supplies, most likely by seizing British, French, and Dutch possessions in East Asia.

Most Americans did not believe they had a large stake in what went on in Asia. Neither were they apprehensive about supporting Roosevelt's increasingly bold responses to Japanese imperialism. A long history of ill-informed prejudices inclined Americans to believe that Japan would shy away from war or else be swiftly crushed by superior American might and efficiency. They felt secure, therefore, in using the economic boycott to force Japan out of China and reinstate the Open Door. Rather illogically, Americans looked upon the Japanese as comically inferior yet diabolically clever. "Made in Japan" was a term of derision for shoddy merchandise turned out by small, near-sighted people who lived in paper houses and substituted obedience to authority for creative thought. Throughout the 1930s, Japanese troops were shown in American newspapers and news-reels as horrifyingly ludicrous in their baggy uniforms, swarming into wrecked Chinese cities with a glee that seemed more fanatically simpleminded than dangerous.

Japanese nationalists were increasingly offended by the pressure against Japan's economic and territorial ambitions and by American attitudes. In October 1941, a military clique headed by General Hideki Tojo seized control and persuaded other leaders, including Emperor Hirohito, who originally called the idea "hare-brained," that swift destruction of American bases in the Pacific would leave Japan free to follow its destiny. Despite knowledge from decoded Japanese messages that an attack was imminent, the Roosevelt administration disastrously underestimated the reach of Japanese

Bombing of Pearl Harbor, December 7, 1941

military power. Consequently, American forces were unprepared for the blow that struck the Pearl Harbor naval base in Hawaii on December 7, 1941. At dawn, a swarm of Japanese carrier-borne fighters, bombers, and torpedo planes found most of the American fleet at anchor and American planes neatly crowded together at Hickam Field. In two hours, the raiders sank or damaged all eight battleships of the fleet and disabled ten other ships. The

PEARL HARBOR,
DECEMBER 7, 1941
*A rescue fireboat is hope-
lessly dwarfed by the enormous catastrophe of the
battleship* **West Virginia**
*aflame and sinking at its
mooring in Pearl Harbor.
With the dramatic force of
a vast seascape painting,
this photograph was
widely reproduced as a
graphic indication of how
great a crime the Japanese
had committed.*
U.S. Army.

bombs wrecked 340 airplanes and killed or wounded more than thirty-five hundred Americans.

Though the raid scored a stunning tactical success, in the larger sense it was a colossal blunder. Overnight, disagreement in the United States about foreign policy ended, and Americans united in their commitment to war and desire for revenge. In his message to Congress declaring war, Roosevelt said:

> Yesterday, December 7, 1941—a date which will live in infamy—the United States of America was suddenly and deliberately attacked by naval and air forces of the Empire of Japan. . . . Always will we remember the character of the onslaught against us. No matter how long it may take us to overcome this premeditated invasion, the American people in their righteous might will win through to absolute victory.

Congress endorsed the message unanimously, except for Quaker pacifist Jeannette Rankin, who had also voted against U.S. entry into World War I. Although Hitler and Mussolini had not known about the Japanese attack in advance, Germany and Italy declared war against America on December 11.

Fighting Back: 1941–1943

Never had the United States faced such a desperate military situation or so staggering a task as it did in 1941. Hitler and his armies had conquered most of Europe, and the Japanese military machine was slicing through the Pacific with amazing speed. From the beginning, American concern had centered on saving Britain and the Soviet Union from defeat so that the United States would not have to face Hitler alone. Before turning to Hitler, however, the United States and its allies would have to stop the Japanese advance through the Pacific. By 1943, the Allies had checked their enemies and were pushing them back. But the Allies could claim victory in neither Europe nor Asia. The "good war" would also be a long one.

Turning the Tide in the Pacific

Following Pearl Harbor, Japan's leading military genius, Admiral Isoroku Yamamoto, ordered an all-out offensive in the Pacific on the belief that, if his forces did not win quickly, Japan would lose the war to America's far greater manpower and resources.

With lightning speed, the Japanese attacked American airfields in the Philippines and captured the American outposts of Guam and Wake Island. Singapore, the great British naval base in Malaya, surrendered in February 1942, and most of Burma had fallen by March. All that stood in the way of Japan's total domination of the southwestern Pacific was the Philippine Islands.

Under intense attack, General Douglas MacArthur, who commanded the Philippine defenses, retreated to fortifications on the Bataan Peninsula across the harbor from Manila. In March, MacArthur escaped to Australian command headquarters, leaving General Jonathan Wainwright to hold out as long as possible. When Wainwright surrendered the Corregidor fortress in May, Japanese soldiers marched the starved and ill survivors sixty-five miles to a concentration camp. Hundreds of Americans and as many as ten thousand Filipinos died en route. Of those who survived the Bataan Death March, sixteen thousand died within weeks from disease and mistreatment in the brutal prison camp. By summer 1942, the Japanese war machine had also conquered the oil-rich Dutch East Indies and was poised to strike at Australia and New Zealand (see Map 24.5).

The dark events that followed Pearl Harbor struck hard at American confidence. Jukeboxes may have been blaring "Goodbye, Mama, I'm Off to Yokohama," but the nation had learned that the soldiers of the Rising Sun were tough, fearless, and prepared to fight to the death for honor and the emperor. At sea, the Japanese had larger, faster, heavier armored ships with bigger guns and more accurate torpedoes. And the four different kinds of airplanes that rained bombs and bullets on Pearl Harbor outperformed anything the Americans could send up against them.

The string of unbroken Japanese victories caused Americans at home to worry about their own safety. A false report that Japanese fighter planes had been spotted near Los Angeles set off an antiaircraft barrage and inspired the commander of West Coast defenses to announce that "death and destruction [from enemy planes] are likely to come at any moment." Antiaircraft guns appeared up and down the Pacific coast. In Hawaii, still shaken from the attack on Pearl Harbor, one vigilant citizen advised the authorities that he had spotted a dog on the beach "barking in Morse code to Japanese subs offshore." Clearly, Americans needed some sort of success to take the edge off panic.

The dark events that followed Pearl Harbor struck hard at American confidence. The nation had learned that the soldiers of the Rising Sun were tough, fearless, and prepared to fight to the death for honor and the emperor.

By spring of 1942, U.S. forces were ready to strike back. The new offensive began with a demonstration meant to show the Japanese that they were not safe anywhere, even in the imperial capital. On April 18, a squadron of sixteen B-25 bombers under the command of Lieutenant Colonel James H. Doolittle launched a bombing raid on Tokyo from the deck of the carrier *Hornet*. The raid did little material damage but created an authentic hero to cheer Americans at home and prompted the worry among some Japanese strategists that they should find a way to negotiate an end to the war.

The main show, however, was a mighty two-pronged offensive that the Americans hoped would stop and then reverse the Japanese advance. The plan called for an army led by General MacArthur to move north from Australia and recapture the Philippines, while forces under Admiral Chester W. Nimitz sailed west from Hawaii and retook the Japanese-held islands in the mid-Pacific. Success was not long in coming. On May 7, 1942, in the Coral Sea just north of Australia, an American fleet and carrier-based planes stopped the Japanese fleet that was sailing around the coast of New Guinea.

The Battle of the Coral Sea was a prelude to an even more significant encounter. Learning that the Japanese were sending an invasion force against Midway Island, an outpost guarding the Hawaiian Islands, Admiral Nimitz moved his carriers and cruisers into the Central Pacific. In a wild melee that raged from June 3 to June 6, American planes sank four Japanese carriers, a heavy cruiser, and two destroyers, while the American armada lost only one carrier and a destroyer. The Battle of the Coral Sea and the Battle of Midway marked the high tide of Japanese power in the Pacific.

The Campaign in Europe

With the Japanese offensive in the Pacific halted, American attention focused on defeating Germany. In the dark months after Pearl Harbor, the war news from Europe was as depressing as that from the Pacific. While imperial Japanese forces were spreading through Asia, Hitler's army drove deep into the Soviet Union and prepared for an invasion of Britain. The Germans attempted, as in World War I, to starve the British into submission by destroying their seaborne lifeline. Advances in technology made German U-boats so much more effective than in World War I that at first they sank American ships faster than new ones could be built. The toll eventually reached 4,786 merchant ships, nearly double the number in World War I, and almost 200 warships. The human cost was forty thousand Allied seamen and almost as many Germans who perished in their 781 stricken U-boats.

The Allies had done little to prepare for another battle on the Atlantic. The British had neither laid down mines to defend coastal waters nor armed merchant vessels. And, because Americans did not institute blackouts until the spring of 1942, U-boats near the Atlantic coast could spot merchant targets at night almost as easily as during the day. Using only six U-boats, the Germans sank eighty-two ships off the American East Coast and more than two hundred additional ships in the waters around Bermuda and the Caribbean islands. One bright day in June 1942, bathers at Virginia Beach watched aghast as a U-boat on the surface sank two merchant vessels. Soon afterward, the beach was awash with oily debris and bodies.

Until 1943, the war in the Atlantic remained in doubt and the British Isles hung by a precarious thread. But the use of newly invented radar detectors and production of sufficient destroyer escorts for merchant vessels made the U-boats easy prey and allowed the United States to move massive amounts of supplies to England and to the Soviet ports. The battle of the Atlantic had been won.

The big question then was when and where to open a second front against the Nazis. Stalin, desperate to keep German divisions away from his bloody doorstep, strongly urged an immediate and massive invasion of France across the English Channel. But Churchill favored something smaller, perhaps a Mediterranean target such as Europe's "soft underbelly," the Balkans. Roosevelt worried about a plan that would merely "peck on the periphery" but ultimately backed an invasion of North Africa as a first step. Since the rapidly expanding U.S. military force was clearly the vital element in any western front, Roosevelt's wishes prevailed.

The strategy targeted the one area where the Allies were having some success against the Ger-

mans. In October 1942, at El-Alamein in Egypt, the British halted General Erwin Rommel's drive to capture the Suez Canal. A few weeks later, an American army landed in French Morocco under the supreme commander of American forces in Europe, General Dwight D. Eisenhower. General George Patton, the ablest U.S. tank commander, swiftly joined the British in pursuit of the German and Italian armies, and in May 1943 Allied armies closed the jaws of a gigantic vise on the last enemy troops in North Africa. The North African campaign cost Germany and Italy dearly—some 350,000 dead and captured—and reopened the Mediterranean to Allied shipping and Italy to invasion (see Map 24.4).

As the North African campaign unfolded, Roosevelt arrived at the Moroccan city of Casablanca in January 1943 to confer with his fellow Allied leaders, Winston Churchill and General Charles de Gaulle, the leader of the Free French government in exile. Stalin, preoccupied with the desperate defense of Stalingrad, was an absent but watchful partner. Pledging to rid the world of Germany and Italy's menace, the Allied leaders announced that they would insist on "unconditional surrender." Of equal importance was their judgment that more time was needed for the buildup of enough forces in England to launch a successful cross-channel invasion of France. A strike against Italy in the meantime, the Allies decided, would capitalize on success in North Africa, a decision that meant the Soviet Union would continue to absorb the brunt of the Nazi attack for another year.

Pledging to rid the world of Germany and Italy's menace, the Allied leaders announced that they would insist on "unconditional surrender."

On July 10, 1943, a combined American and British amphibious operation, the largest in history, landed 160,000 troops in Sicily. The badly equipped Italian defenders, many of whom had lost their will to fight in the disastrous North African campaign, quickly withdrew to the mainland. When Sicily fell, the Fascist Grand Council expelled Mussolini from power, marking the end of Italian fascism. Almost immediately after the Allies invaded the mainland, the Italian government surrendered unconditionally. The Germans responded by rushing additional di-

AN ITALIAN TOWN SURRENDERS
In 1943, the Roosevelt administration authorized a special unit of "combat artists" to
present an "integrated picture of war in all its phases." Edward Reep, a trained in-
fantryman as well as an artist, achieved rare authenticity from his own combat experi-
ence. Contorted body postures and tilted buildings express the frenzied moment when
Italian partisans celebrated the liberation of their town and terrified German soldiers
ran to Reep's invading unit to escape revenge.
Courtesy of the artist, Edward Reep.

visions into the country and seizing control of Rome, at which point the military campaign in Italy became a war of liberation against German occupation.

Success came hard against the occupiers, who waited in sophisticated fortifications atop the mountainous Italian terrain. Not until June 1944, after a long and bloody campaign, did massive firepower finally breach the German lines and enable Allied forces to liberate Rome. From that time until the end of the war, the Allies struggled against German mountain defenses in northern Italy. The Italian campaign, which fell frustratingly below total victory, was the costliest of the war to the American infantry and did not satisfy the demand of an increasingly embittered Stalin for a second front. It did, however, manage to tie up twenty-five German divisions that might otherwise have been used against either the Russians or a second front in France.

The War at Home

World War II brought no physical destruction to the United States mainland; no one starved, and no civilians lost their lives in the fighting. Still, the conflagration changed the nation. Inevitably, a war as vast and as long as World War II disrupted the traditional social patterns it sought to defend. Total war meant that millions of troops went to unheard-of places to face unimaginable dangers. Conversion of the economy to war purposes also drew millions of civilians away from their roots to seize opportu-

PITCHING IN AT HOME
This poster adapts the standard children's book illustration style of the period to the war effort. White and middle class all, mother and children collect old golf clubs, cocktail shakers, and trophies—which dad, away at war, will never miss—to recycle these symbols of the American way of life into armament for defense.
Chicago Historical Society.

nities they never had before in places where they never expected to live. Women welding in the shipyards in California, men building tanks in the factories of Detroit, and children pining for their absent fathers and brothers—all felt the impact of the war and were changed by it.

From Reform to Recovery

There is partial truth in the observation that Adolf Hitler was more responsible for ending the depression in the United States than was Franklin

Roosevelt. In 1939, the federal budget was $9 billion; by 1945, at the end of total mobilization for war, it had grown to $100 billion. Within months after Pearl Harbor, unemployment, which in 1940 had stood at 14.6 percent of the nation's workforce, had virtually disappeared. Industrial cities boomed with orders for war materiel, enough not only to give work to urban dwellers but also to draw displaced farm laborers into the cities, where they enjoyed a modest prosperity far beyond anything they had known (Figure 24.1).

There was no longer much talk about social reform, however. As Roosevelt remarked, he had given up being "Dr. New Deal" in order to become "Dr. Win the War." That offhand statement spoke to a changed approach to war. In the era of progressive idealism at the start of the century, World War I struck Americans as a crusade. The disillusionment and depression experience that followed, however, made World War II less a romantic venture than a distasteful practical necessity.

By harnessing Americans' sober determination, the Roosevelt administration oversaw a miracle of

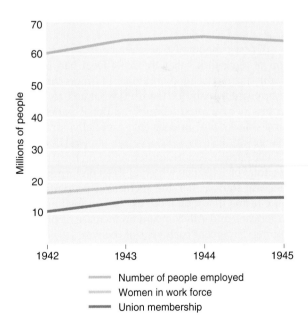

FIGURE 24.1

World War II and the Economy, 1942–1945
The end of the depression followed by war mobilization sent employment and union membership to high levels that continued into peacetime. Women lost many jobs in heavy industry after the war, but their increased numbers in the total workforce were sustained by the strong economy that followed.

production. Called to Washington by a president they had mostly opposed, "dollar-a-year" businessmen (so called because they served without pay) headed the rapidly multiplying war production agencies. Despite the confusion and chaos that accompanied the rapid conversion of the economy to war making, output was staggering. The United States produced 275,000 airplanes during the war and by 1945 was launching a new ship every twenty-four hours. The arsenal of democracy not only equipped its own gigantic armed forces but also supplied its allies in Europe and Asia with a large part of what they required. By 1942, American production equaled that of Germany, Italy, and Japan combined; by 1944, it stood at double their production. Confirmation that the depression was over came when business profit margins in 1943 soared well beyond those of 1929.

The nation's economic expansion was powered by the mobilization of its citizens. Draft boards registered 31 million men, of whom 10 million were inducted into service. In addition, more than 5 million men and women volunteered. When the war ended, 10,400,000 had served in the army, 3,900,000 in the navy, 600,000 in the marines, and 240,000 in the coast guard.

The war boom also accelerated the transformation of agriculture that the New Deal had begun. Family farms declined and tenant farmers virtually disappeared, many of them transplanted to urban centers of war production. Traditional patterns of rural black life underwent especially dramatic change. By 1950, the official census showed that only 115,000 African Americans remained on the land out of a total of 1,406,000 who had lived on farms when the war started. For the increasing proportion of large farms that remained, the task of feeding both Americans and Allies meant an increase of production by 25 percent each year of the war.

The nation's economic expansion was powered by the mobilization of its citizens.

The industrial sector broadened and prospered as well. With more than 15 million adults in the military, new workers—the old, the young, and especially women—were brought into the labor force. The cost of living increased by 30 percent from 1941 to 1945; but a 70 percent rise in weekly earnings of workers employed in manufacturing greatly outpaced inflation. Finding much to spend the new money on was another matter. Conversion of industrial plants to war purposes meant that automobiles, washing machines, refrigerators, and numerous other consumer items were no longer being manufactured. Many other civilian goods—automobile tires, gasoline, shoes, meat—were rationed because they were hard to obtain from war zones or were needed in large quantities for the military.

Political Crosscurrents

Inconveniences and dislocations notwithstanding, Americans on the home front rallied around the war effort in unprecedented unity. There were hardly any vigilante attacks on Americans suspected of being unpatriotic, because dissenters were so few. Despite the consensus on war aims, however, the Roosevelt administration struggled to hold its governing coalition together. Resentment over price controls and shortages of rationed goods, white indignation over blacks leaving their subordinate place on southern farms, and dismay that the war was not going well provoked discontent with the Democratic administration. Moreover, in the congressional elections of 1942, Democrats were denied considerable support from working-class soldiers and defense workers who were unable to cast their usual Democratic votes because the war had taken them away from the hometowns where they were registered. Low voter turnout thus helped Republicans to gain seats in the House and Senate.

Republican opponents saw the war years as an opportunity to roll back New Deal reforms in favor of traditional American free enterprise. A conservative coalition of Republicans and southern Democrats succeeded in abolishing several New Deal agencies in 1942 and 1943, including the Work Projects Administration and the Civilian Conservation Corps. But the Democratic administration did not sit idly by while Republicans mounted a threat to their congressional majority. By persuading states to ease residency requirements and Congress to guarantee absentee ballots for servicemen, they arranged to bring scattered members of the New Deal coalition back to the voting booth.

Franklin Roosevelt, though exhausted and gravely ill, decided to run for a fourth term in 1944 (breaking the record he had already set by running for a third) rather than turn the uncompleted war effort over to a new leader. "All that is within me cries out to go back to my home on the Hudson River," he declared. "But as a good soldier . . . I will accept and serve." Convinced that many Americans had soured on liberal reform, Roosevelt replaced Vice President Henry Wallace, an outspoken progressive, with a more politically viable running mate, Senator Harry S. Truman of Missouri. A reliable party man from a border state, Truman seemed likely to satisfy urban Democratic leaders while not posing a threat to Southerners who were nervous about challenges to segregation.

The Republicans, confident of a strong conservative upsurge, nominated the governor of New York, Thomas E. Dewey, who had made his reputation as a tough crime fighter. Roosevelt's failing health limited his ability to campaign and alarmed many observers. In the final reckoning, though, that weakness was outweighed by the unwillingness of the American people to change presidents at the height of a foreign war or to accept Dewey's recycling of Herbert Hoover's argument that the New Deal was a creeping socialist menace. At only 53.5 percent of the popular vote, Roosevelt's victory was his narrowest; but it virtually assured that, if he lived, he would remain commander in chief throughout the war.

Women, Family, and the War

During the depression, female workers were often accused of taking a husband's or father's job. A shortage of manpower during the war, however, reversed the trend, and millions of women found themselves being courted by the defense industry. Three-fourths of these women were married, and nearly four million had children. Often they moved from traditional jobs as domestic servants, secretaries, and waitresses to better-paying industrial work that had previously been considered beyond their skills and endurance.

The ambivalence of the women's situation, divided between home and factory, showed in the fact that the marriage rate and birth rate rose sharply once the war began, while at the same time women increased their presence in industry, especially in war production. By 1944, some eighteen million women had jobs, 50 percent more than in 1939. *Chicago Tribune* columnist Mike Royko remembered: "My sister became Rosie the Riveter. She put a bandanna on her head every day and went down to this organ company that had been converted to war work. . . . There was a sense of mission about it. Her

FEMALE DEFENSE WORKER
The war effort brought persons and activities together in unlikely ways, leading to unexpected outcomes. In this photo, the army magazine **Yank** *sought to boost morale by presenting a defense worker as pinup girl. No one could know that the young propeller technician, nineteen-year-old Norma Jean Baker Dougherty, would later remake herself as the most glamorous of movie stars, Marilyn Monroe.*
David Conover Images © Norma Jean Enterprises, a division of 733548 Ontario Limited.

husband was Over There." Along with the mission came an amazing rise in pay. A mountain woman remembered her first job after the depression at a munitions plant in Viola, Kentucky. "We made the fabulous sum of thirty-two dollars a week," she said. "To us it was just an absolute miracle. Before that, we made nothing." In the patriotic euphoria over a rise in women's weekly wages to an average of $31, it was understandable that few complained that men received $54 for comparable work.

Alongside women in the civilian workforce stood 350,000 women who joined the Nurse's Corps and the newly created military units the Women's Army Corps (WACs), the navy's Women Accepted for Volunteer Emergency Service (Waves), the coast guard's Semper Paratus (SPARs), and the Women's

Marine Corps. Women also served in the Women Air Service Pilots (WASPs). While barred from combat duty, women worked at nearly every noncombatant assignment. Women in the armed forces never achieved a secure place within the staunchly male system, but the Nurse's Corps, drawing on a respected tradition of service since the Civil War, gained officer rank and attracted many recruits.

During the depression, female workers were often accused of taking a husband's or father's job. A shortage of manpower during the war, however, reversed the trend, and millions of women found themselves being courted by the defense industry.

For women, wartime experience was stressfully divided. Their yearning in the midst of war for the peacetime joys of security and family, felt mutually by fighting men, reinforced traditional attitudes. Despite the war's dynamic social changes, most women remained at home or worked only part-time. Those attitudes gained in material strength, too. With men no longer unemployed and wages up, family survival depended less on women's earning money. The increase in consumer wealth also nurtured hopes for a comfortable home and the ability to raise children in better circumstances than during the depression. For those women who enjoyed the economic and social freedom that came with employment outside the home, a substantial number saw their work as a temporary necessity, something to set aside when the men came home.

Not all trends pointed in the direction of middle-class stability, however. The absence of millions of able-bodied young men left many families without a father in the house; other family groups traveled from one to another of the seedy fringe settlements near military bases. Poor living conditions near defense plants also made family life difficult. A desire to make the most of the moment in the face of an uncertain future prompted a rise in the number of marriages and births, but also of illegitimacy and divorce. In many cases, children compensated for the absence of fathers by doing their part for the war effort. Girl and boy scouts, for example, sponsored scrap drives collecting iron, steel, brass, bronze, tin, and wastepaper; and older teenagers took jobs formerly reserved for adults. But new responsibilities and opportunities were countered by disruptive problems. Children in the workplace faced the same hardships that caused resistance to child labor in previous times. The absence of older men also meant that young people had less guidance than usual, and juvenile delinquency, especially among girls, increased accordingly. The yearning for war's end included a desire for stability at home as well as abroad.

Prejudice and the War

Fighting against Nazism and its ideology of Aryan racial supremacy under the banner of democracy forced Americans to examine prejudice in their own society. African American leader W. E. B. Du Bois, who had welcomed World War I as a chance for black Americans to prove their worth, defined World War II as a "war for racial equality" and a struggle for "democracy not only for white folks but for yellow, brown, and black." Such aspirations squared perfectly with official proclamations of war aims. In a letter to the Southern Negro Youth Congress, Roosevelt declared that blacks were in the war "not only to defend America but . . . to establish a universal freedom under which a new basis of security and prosperity can be established for all—regardless of station, race, or creed." The *Pittsburgh Courier*, a leading black newspaper, rejoiced that, though "war may be hell for some," it appeared ready to "open up the portals of heaven for us."

Others sought to enter those portals as well. More than thirteen thousand Chinese Americans and more than twenty-five thousand Native Americans fought in the armed forces. Mexican Americans feared that for them the war would mean deportation; instead, more than 200,000 laborers were imported from Mexico to cultivate American crops in the federal government's *bracero* program. In addition, 500,000 Mexican Americans served in the U.S. armed forces. On his way to the European front, a young Mexican American soldier reflected on the dilemma of minorities: "Why fight for America when you have not been treated as an American?" His answer after he survived the war echoed Du Bois and the *Courier*: "All we wanted was a chance to prove how loyal and American we were."

Crisis also stirred old prejudices, which sometimes flared into violence. In 1943, riots occurred in Los Angeles when hundreds of white servicemen, claiming they were punishing draft dodgers, chased and beat young Chicano men who dressed in distinctive broad-shouldered, peg-legged "zoot" suits.

In an attempt to root old prejudicial patterns out of the war effort, black organizations sent a barrage of petitions to Congress and the White House demanding that the federal government require companies receiving defense contracts to integrate their workforces. A. Philip Randolph, head of the almost completely black Brotherhood of Sleeping Car Porters, promised that 100,000 marchers would descend on Washington if the president did not eliminate discrimination in defense industries. The president decided he had less to lose by offending old southern and union allies and issued Executive Order 8802, authorizing a Committee on Fair Employment Practices to investigate and prevent race discrimination in employment. Civil rights champions hailed the act as the first direct presidential intervention on behalf of black civil rights, and Randolph triumphantly called off the march.

African American leader W. E. B. Du Bois, who had welcomed World War I as a chance for black Americans to prove their worth, defined World War II as a "war for racial equality" and a struggle for "democracy not only for white folks but for yellow, brown, and black."

Actual progress developed slowly. The five and a half million blacks who flooded into industrial cities during the 1940s, making African Americans a predominantly urban population for the first time, discovered that industry policies barred them from many skilled jobs. The aircraft industry, a rapidly expanding part of the war effort and due to play a vital postwar role, provided the most striking example of exclusion. Aircraft manufacture nationwide included only 240 black employees at the start of the war; Douglas Aircraft, a major supplier to the military, had only 10 black workers. Much of organized labor, particularly the AFL craft unions, defended such exclusionary practices. At least eighteen major unions, including such vital participants in the defense industry as the machinists, ironworkers, shipbuilders, and railway workers, had explicit bans against black membership. In

time, however, severe labor shortages and government pressure opened up defense plants to African American workers. Black unemployment dropped by about 80 percent during the war, and the percentage of blacks in the defense industry doubled to a level almost equal to the percentage of blacks in the general population. Though equality of pay was still a distant hope, by the end of the war the average income of black families had risen to half that of white families.

With migration and progress went racial antagonism, which boiled over in the hot summer of 1943 when 242 racial outbreaks in forty-seven different cities far surpassed the 26 riots in the Red scare year of 1919. Worst of all were two days of mayhem in Detroit. Conflict between whites and blacks at a city park ignited a race war that saw whites smash their way with clubs through black neighborhoods and blacks retaliate by destroying and looting white-owned businesses. In the end, scores of persons suffered injury and thirty-four died, including twenty-five African Americans.

Out of the depths of violence came the stimulus for promising new strategies. The National Association for the Advancement of Colored People (NAACP) launched the "Double V" campaign—victory abroad, victory at home—and mounted legal challenges that would eventually outlaw segregation. In 1942, civil rights activists who wanted more direct confrontations founded a new organization, the Congress of Racial Equality (CORE), that organized picketing and sit-ins against Jim Crow restaurants and theaters and would achieve significant results after the war.

The military was no more free of discrimination than was the home front. Secretary of War Henry Stimson opposed any change in the segregation of blacks and whites into separate units, declaring that the military effort should not serve as a "sociological laboratory." In 1942, Stimson fumed in his diary about black reformers' claims, which he deemed absurdly presumptuous: "What these foolish leaders of the colored race are seeking is at bottom social equality." Top military brass echoed Stimson's sentiments and worked to keep African Americans in segregated units that were restricted to menial tasks. "Experiments to meet the wishes and demands of the champions of every race and creed for the solution of their problems," the army adjutant general's office warned, "are a danger to efficiency, discipline and morale, and would result in ultimate defeat."

DOUBLE V BUTTON
The Double V became African Americans' special version of the official "V for victory" symbol. Thousands of these buttons were worn as a reminder that both the Axis powers and racial discrimination should surrender unconditionally.
Private collection.

www.bedfordstmartins.com/tap SEE THE ONLINE STUDY GUIDE for more help in analyzing this image.

Denied integrated armed forces, blacks joined anyway, and by the end of the war nearly one million African American men and women had served. Segregated practices loosened as the war progressed. Blacks were trained as pilots for the first time, served on warships with white sailors, and saw extensive combat duty in the ground war in Europe and the Pacific. Yet military facilities remained segregated, and the Red Cross even segregated by race the blood it supplied to treat battlefield casualties.

In 1944, after the tide of war had turned toward victory, the Swedish sociologist Gunnar Myrdal offered a hopeful interpretation in his classic report on race in America, *The American Dilemma*. After firsthand observation all over the country, Myrdal concluded that "not since Reconstruction, has there been more reason to anticipate fundamental changes in American race relations." As Myrdal suggested, World War II was a watershed. The pressures blacks exerted against old patterns of disadvantage as they migrated out of the South and into the armed forces or defense work inspired hope and

shaped the tactics that would be used thereafter in the quest for rights and opportunity. But most of that battle lay ahead. Perhaps nothing more poignantly captured the reality of wartime race relations than the moment when Lloyd Brown, a black soldier caught in the dusty heat of a Kansas summer day, gazed past the restaurant owner denying him entry and saw a row of German prisoners of war enjoying their lunch at the counter.

A PLEA FOR INCLUSION
*This illustration, drawn by black artist E. Simms Campbell for the cover of **Opportunity**, the journal of the National Urban League, advances a theme that was central to the League: the full inclusion of African Americans in the nation's economic life. To press home the extreme absurdity of restraining black potential in times of crisis, Campbell depicted John Henry, the fabled black laborer, being held back from using his strength by a mob of puny bigots. Henry was the perfect symbol of the need for liberation and service in the creation of weapons to defeat Nazism and in the ratification of the war as a struggle for democracy against oppression and prejudice.*
Yale University Library.

World War II did not witness a repetition of the hysteria and viciousness that had characterized the home front during World War I. With almost no dissent against the war, Roosevelt felt no need to engage in a high-powered propaganda campaign such as Wilson had unleashed in 1917. This time, the government took control of the media not to stir passions against the enemy, but to suppress bad news from the war effort. Americans did worry about espionage, however. Walls were plastered with slogans such as "Loose lips sink ships" and "Enemy agents are always near; if you don't talk, they won't hear."

There was one major exception to the atmosphere of tolerance—the drastic violation of the rights of Japanese Americans, the only minority group to lose ground during the war. From the time of their first entry into the country in significant numbers in the 1890s, mainly to settle on the West Coast, the Japanese had encountered hostility as economic competitors and intruders in a "white man's country." Although they were law-abiding and successful in small businesses and farming, white prejudice prevailed. In 1907, the Japanese government was forced to accept a humiliating "gentlemen's agreement" that reduced the numbers of new Japanese immigrants in exchange for the right of Asians to attend public schools in California.

Restrictions climaxed in 1924 when federal law established that Japanese immigrants were "aliens ineligible to citizenship." In rejecting an appeal claiming that the law violated the constitutional right of all citizens to equal protection, the Supreme Court declared that the Fourteenth Amendment applied only to whites and ex-slaves. As intended, the ruling halted the influx of Japanese and left unnaturalized Japanese ("Issei") permanently in limbo as residents who could never become citizens. The absurdity of the situation was heightened by the fact that the Issei's children (called "Nisei") were automatically citizens by virtue of having been born in the United States.

Hostility did not abate with the end of Japanese immigration, however. In the 1930s, the *Los Angeles Times* led a new anti-Japanese campaign, arguing that Japanese Americans were still a threat because they would multiply endlessly and outcompete "real" Americans. Any recognition that the actual role of most Japanese was to provide cheap food—exactly what white workers, managers, and homemakers should have hailed—was swallowed up in the storm of hatred that followed the attack on Pearl Harbor. (See "Documenting the American Promise," page 920.)

Even though a military survey concluded that Japanese Americans posed no danger, General John DeWitt, army commander for the West Coast, and California law officials decided to take them into custody. "A Jap's a Jap," DeWitt explained. "It makes no difference whether he's an American or not." On February 19, 1942, President Roosevelt gave that racist premise the force of law in an executive order authorizing the roundup of all Americans of Japanese descent. Allowed little time to secure or sell their property, the victims (most of whom were American citizens) lost assets, jobs, and homes. Not a single case of subversion or sabotage was ever uncovered, yet Japanese Americans were sent to "relocation centers"—basically makeshift prison camps—in remote areas of the Southwest and Great Plains, where they were penned in by barbed wire and armed guards for more than three years (Map 24.3). Not until 1988 did Congress

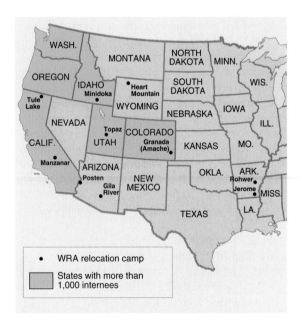

MAP 24.3

Western Relocation Authority Centers
Responding to prejudice and fear of sabotage, in 1942 President Roosevelt authorized the roundup and relocation of all Americans of Japanese descent. Taken from their homes in the cities and fertile farms of the far West, Japanese Americans were confined in desolate areas scattered as far east as the Mississippi River.

Japanese Internment

*A*ngrily determined that the bombing of Pearl Harbor would not be followed by more sneak attacks, military and political leaders on the West Coast targeted persons of Japanese descent—alien and citizen alike—as potential saboteurs.

DOCUMENT 1. Final Recommendations of the Commanding General, Western Defense Command and Fourth Army, Submitted to the Secretary of War

Early in 1942, General John DeWitt, commander of the Western Defense Command, persuaded President Franklin Roosevelt to issue an executive order authorizing the removal of the Japanese living in the United States. Subsequently, some 110,000 Japanese Americans were confined to relocation camps in remote areas, surrounded by barbed wire and armed guards. DeWitt's recommendation expressed concern for military security within racist conceptions long used to curb Asian immigration. Belying DeWitt's notion that all Japanese were the same, response on the part of detainees varied widely, from inability to understand the experience, to resistance in the courts against violations of citizen rights, to reassessment of what it meant to be of Japanese ancestry in America. In later years, after official government apology for the incident and monetary redress, the experience took its place in historical and artistic recall as a profound test of identity and assimilation.

February 14, 1942
Memorandum for the Secretary of War.
Subject: Evacuation of Japanese and Other Subversive Persons from the Pacific Coast.
1. In presenting a recommendation for the evacuation of Japanese and other subversive persons from the Pacific Coast, the following facts have been considered:
   a. Mission of the Western Defense Command and Fourth Army.
      (1) Defense of the Pacific Coast of the Western Defense Command, as extended, against attacks by sea, land, or air;
      (2) Local protection of establishment and communications vital to the National Defense for which adequate defense cannot be provided by local civilian authorities.
   b. Brief Estimate of the Situation.
      (1) ... The following are possible and probable enemy activities: ...
         (a) Naval attack on shipping on coastal waters;
         (b) Naval attack on coastal cities and vital installations;
         (c) Air raids on vital installations, particularly within two hundred miles of the coast;
         (d) Sabotage of vital installations throughout the Western Defense Command.
   Hostile Naval and air raids will be assisted by enemy agents signaling from the coastline and the vicinity thereof; and by supplying and otherwise assisting enemy vessels and by sabotage.

In the war in which we are now engaged racial affinities are severed by migration. The Japanese race is an enemy race and while many second and third generation Japanese born on United States soil, possessed of United States citizenship, have become "Americanized," the racial strains are undiluted. To conclude otherwise is to expect that children born of white parents on Japanese soil sever all racial affinity and become loyal Japanese subjects, ready to fight and, if necessary, to die for Japan in a war against the nation of their parents. ...

It, therefore, follows that along the vital Pacific Coast over 112,000 potential enemies, of Japanese extraction, are at large today. There are indications that these are organized and ready for concerted action at a favorable opportunity. The very fact that no sabotage has taken place to date is a disturbing and confirming indication that such action will be taken.

SOURCE: *Final Recommendations,* report by General John Lesesne DeWitt to the United States Secretary of War, February 14, 1942.

DOCUMENT 2. An Oral History of Life in the Japanese American Detention Camps

Imprisoned in bleak surroundings far from home, Japanese internees were prey to despair and bitterness. Looking back after forty years, Kazue Yamane recalled her confinement as a disturbing and baffling experience.

In April 1942, my husband and I and our two children left for camp, and my mother-in-law and father-in-law came about a month later. I wasn't afraid, but I kept asking in my mind, how could they? This is impossible. Even today I still think it was a nightmarish thing. I cannot reconcile myself to the fact that I had to go, that I was interned, that I was segregated, that I was taken away, even though it goes back forty years. . . .

I was separated from my husband; he went to the Santa Fe, New Mexico, camp. All our letters were censored; all our letters were cut in parts and all that. So we were not too sure what messages was getting through and not getting through, but I do know that I informed him many times of his mother's condition. He should have been allowed to come back to see her, because I thought she wouldn't live too long, but they never did allow him to come back, even for her funeral. They did not allow that. I learned that a lot of the messages didn't get to him; they were crossed out. I now have those letters with me.

In 1944 I was left with his parents and our kids. But I had no time to think of what was going to happen because my child was always sick and I had been quite sick. . . .

My son knew what was going on, and he too had many times asked me why . . . you know, why? why? Of course, I had no explanation why this was happening to us.

SOURCE: Excerpt from *And Justice for All*, by John Tateishi. Copyright © 1999 by John Tateishi. Reprinted by permission of the University of Washington Press.

DOCUMENT 3. The Kikuchi Diary

Forcibly removed from the tension between his life as a student at the University of California at Berkeley and his unassimilated family, Charles Kikuchi sought in his prison camp diary to make sense of the internment and to judge where it would lead.

December 7, 1941, Berkeley, California
Pearl Harbor. We are at war! Jesus Christ, the Japs bombed Hawaii and the entire fleet has been sunk. I just can't believe it. I don't know what in the hell is going to happen to us, but we will all be called into the Army right away.

. . . The next five years will determine the future of the Nisei [Japanese American citizens]. They are now at the crossroads. Will they be able to take it or will they go under? If we are ever going to prove our Americanism, this is the time. The Anti-Jap feeling is bound to rise to hysterical heights, and it is most likely that the Nisei will be included as Japs. I wanted to go to San Francisco tonight, but Pierre says I am crazy. He says it's best we stick on campus. In any event, we can't remain on the fence, and a positive approach must be taken if we are to have a place in fulfilling the Promise of America. I think the U.S. is in danger of going Fascist too, or maybe Socialist. . . .

I don't know what to think or do. Everybody is in a daze.

April 30, 1942, Berkeley
Today is the day that we are going to get kicked out of Berkeley. It certainly is degrading. . . .

I'm supposed to see my family at Tanforan as Jack told me to give the same family number. I wonder how it is going to be living with them as I haven't done this for years and years? I should have gone over to San Francisco and evacuated with them, but I had a last final to take. I understand that we are going to live in the horse stalls. I hope that the Army has the courtesy to remove the manure first. . . .

July 14, 1942
Marie, Ann, Mitch, Jimmy, Jack, and myself got into a long discussion about how much democracy meant to us as individuals. Mitch says that he would even go in the army and die for it, in spite of the fact that he knew he would be kept down. Marie said that although democracy was not perfect, it was the only system that offered any hope for a future, if we could fulfill its destinies. Jack was a little more skeptical. He even suggested that we [could] be in such grave danger that we would then realize that we were losing something. Where this point was he could not say. I said that this was what happened in France and they lost all. Jimmy suggested that the colored races of the world had reason to feel despair and mistrust the white man because of the past experiences. . . .

In reviewing the four months here, the chief value I got out of this forced evacuation was the strengthening of the family bonds. I never knew my family before this and this was the first chance that I have had to really get acquainted.   (*Continued*)

Document 4. Internment Poems

For some Japanese Americans who endured confinement in the desert, only artistic expression could convey their experience adequately. When poet and teacher Toyo Kawakami arrived at the internment camp in Topaz, Utah, she pondered her fate in "Barracks Home." Many years later, she visited Topaz again and distilled the experience in "Camp Memories."

Barracks Home

The floor is carpeted with dust, wind-borne
    Dry alkali, patterned by insect feet.
What peace can such a place as this impart?
We can but sense, bewildered and forlorn,
That time, disrupted by the war from neat
Routines, must now adjust within the heart.

Camp Memories

I have dredged up
Hard fragments lost
I thought, in years
Of whirlwind dust.

Exposed to light,
Silently rough
And broken shards
Confront belief.

QUESTIONS FOR ANALYSIS AND DEBATE

1. What explains General DeWitt's insistence on evacuating the Japanese after he received the report of military investigators that no acts of sabotage had occurred?

2. In what ways are the poems of Toyo Kawakami similar to the oral history of life in the camps and the Kikuchi diary? How are they different?

3. Despite the internment of their families and friends in concentration camps, the Japanese American army unit in Italy earned the largest number of citations for combat heroism of any army group. Explain this fact.

4. Court decisions many years after World War II declared internment unconstitutional and provided financial compensation to survivors. How well could these decisions be expected to reconcile Japanese Americans to the experience?

5. Could one argue that internment was beneficial because it took Japanese Americans from ethnic and family isolation to new places where they met many different people? Did that help to prepare them for entering the American mainstream after the war? Why or why not?

award modest reparations to Japanese Americans for their wartime losses.

War posed challenges for homosexual Americans in some ways comparable to those faced by other marginalized groups. The view that gays were a threat to good order and were apt to crack under stress had long dominated military thinking. After being caught trying to cover up homosexual activity in the navy during World War I, the military tightened its psychological screening process and specified criminal proceedings against homosexual acts by those who slipped through the net. Despite their broad powers, authorities showed little inclination to pursue gays in the period between the world wars when the military shrank into a small volunteer force. A few men did serve time in prison for sodomy, but psychological screening was seldom used, since officers were ill equipped to understand it. Essentially, those in charge followed what would later become an official policy of "Don't ask, don't tell."

World War II revived prejudice against homosexuals. Once the Selective Service Act of 1940 began bringing vast numbers of recruits into the

FBI SEARCHING JAPANESE AMERICAN HOME
When President Roosevelt informed military commanders that they might "from time to time" remove persons deemed dangerous, he had reason to suspect that virtually all Japanese Americans would be affected. An army "expert" on Asian culture had already advised the War Department that, "as you cannot . . . penetrate the Oriental thinking . . . the easiest course is to remove them all from the West Coast and place them . . . under guard." Intent on getting to the bottom of one Japanese American family's allegiance, an FBI agent in 1942 scrutinizes a picture album, while family members whose home has been invaded look on helplessly.
Courtesy Department of Special Collections, University Research Library, University of California (# 27.459).

armed forces, Secretary of War Henry Stimson reminded all commanding generals that they were expected to prosecute cases of sodomy. To avoid trouble by screening out gays in advance, the authorities turned to psychological experts. Brushing aside the testimony of many psychologists that homosexuality was a "maladjustment" that could be "corrected," military authorities used the definition of homosexuality as "disturbed sex development" as grounds for purging gays from the ranks. Ironically, though, the very crisis that activated prejudice also worked against enforcing it. The need to build a huge fighting force made those in charge reluctant to depart from the old policy of looking the other way. And because screening procedures had been set up with only men in mind, lesbians volunteering for the newly formed women's branches of service seldom encountered any effort to exclude them.

Thus allowed to serve, gay Americans found the war to be a special sort of transforming experience. Like other beleaguered minorities, gays sought to demonstrate their worth under fire. "I was superpatriotic," a combat veteran recalled. "And being a homosexual, I had that constant compelling need to prove how virile I was." Another gay veteran, a survivor of the brutal Iwo Jima campaign, had a more basic reaction: in the midst of life-or-death realities, "who in the hell is going to worry about this shit?"

Why Did the Allies Refuse to Bomb the Death Camps?

ONLY A FEW DAYS AFTER the German blitzkrieg swept through Poland in September 1939, Adolf Hitler traveled to the front to exult over victory. He summoned military commanders to one of the cars of his special train and instructed them to begin, as swiftly as possible, making room for Germans by "housecleaning" the territory of its clergy, aristocracy, intelligentsia, and Jews. Soon afterward, Nazi soldiers began shooting clusters of men, women, and children standing in burial pits the victims had dug themselves. Seeking faster and more efficient means to annihilate millions of people that would also relieve reluctant army forces from the bloody horror of shooting them, Nazi engineers then designed airtight vans that roamed the countryside suffocating the condemned with carbon monoxide gas.

With the implementation of Hitler's "final solution," killing became quicker and more efficient in the gas chambers of concentration camps. Though the Nazis endeavored to keep the final solution a secret, news of what was happening to Jews, gypsies, political prisoners, and others sent away in cattle cars for "resettlement" had surfaced by the summer of 1942. In July, a shaken German businessman with mines in Poland near Auschwitz, the main death camp, informed a Jewish associate in Switzerland of the plan he had discovered to exterminate 3.5 to 4 million Jews. The World Jewish Congress then led the horrified Jewish community in a campaign to get the Allies to take action.

With hope waning for the hundreds of thousands of European Jews not yet sent to their deaths, pleas mounted for the Allies to bomb the death camps and the railroad tracks leading to them in order to hamper the killing operation and block further shipments of victims. Insistence rose to frenzy in April 1944, after escapees from Auschwitz brought word to the outside world of the unimag-

THE DEAD AT BUCHENWALD
In this stark moment, all distance between official Washington and the Holocaust is breached. Soldiers and civilians pause somberly in the background as Senator Alben Barkley of Kentucky, stooped in sadness, tries to comprehend the incomprehensible.
Pentagon, U.S. Army Signal Corps.

TRAGIC BOOTY

In a shed not far from the bodies confounding Senator Barkley were these thousands of wedding rings. Nazis insisted that racial purity was their ideal goal. But the greed of jackals led them to strip these last marks of human affection from their victims.

National Archives.

inable horror of murder and starvation. The tragedy deepened on April 19, when Jews in the ghetto of Warsaw began an armed rebellion against slow death by attrition at the hands of the Nazis. For twenty-eight days, the Jewish defenders held and then suffered total annihilation.

The rising volume of proposals to bomb the railroads and camps got no farther than the desks of Assistant Secretary of War John J. McCloy in Washington and British Foreign Secretary Anthony Eden in London. Both men were seasoned members of foreign service elites, which Jews had never penetrated. Intent on achieving military victory as soon as possible without distraction, they routinely turned aside bombing requests by insisting that the air forces could not spare resources from their strictly military missions. There was an element of moral indifference, as well. Eden's Foreign Office was especially distant and patronizing, as if fending off the usual special-interest group looking for petty favors. An eloquent plea from Chaim Weizmann, one of the most imposing Jewish leaders, elicited a routine rejection letter that ended with tragic understatement: "I understand that this decision will be a disappointment to you, but be sure that the matter was considered exhaustively."

The value of bombing the death camps was not considered exhaustively, however. Tactically, there was no reason to hesitate. The German air force could offer little resistance after 1943, when the Allies gained full control of the air. The Allies had many extra planes that could have been assigned to bomb the death camps without any hindrance to the military advance into Germany. Worries expressed about loss of life were similarly hollow. Refusing to commit heavy bombers to the mission because they would kill *some* innocent people in the camps overlooked the fact that if nothing was done *all* the innocents would die. Testimony from Auschwitz survivors shows that inmates appreciated the distinction and strongly hoped the increasing number of Allied planes they saw overhead meant that their hell would soon be bombed into oblivion.

Cautious calculation of the public interest and doubt about what could be verified also prevented action. The Office of War Information (OWI) avoided the subject of death camps out of fear that charging the Germans with crimes against humanity would incite them to greater resistance that would prolong the war and cause more American casualties. Deprived of information to dispel widespread skepticism that death camps could really exist, newspapers and journals relegated news of the Holocaust to the back pages. Better to wait until the victorious armed forces could prove or refute such charges than to risk giving fake propaganda the same prominence that had so discredited journalists in World War I.

In the midst of blackout and denial, the will to disbelieve grew so strong that, when verification of the true horror did finally filter through, it tended to induce numbness. Even Supreme Court Justice Felix Frankfurter, a Jew himself and a veteran of agonizing fights against bigotry and persecution, found the truth incomprehensible. After a member of the Polish underground gave him a detailed account of the mass murder in Poland, Frankfurter denied the information as beyond the realm of possibility. "I did not say this young man is lying," he explained. "I said I cannot believe him. There is a difference." McCloy clung to the same *(Continued)* rationalization that the nightmare could not be real. At least once, though, the will to disbelieve wavered. Leon Kubowitzki of the World Jewish Congress, after repeatedly being rebuffed by false arguments masquerading as "technical reasons" for not intervening, remembered a tense meeting with the assistant secretary in December 1944. McCloy took Kubowitzki aside and said anxiously, "We are alone. Tell me the truth. Do you really believe that all those horrible things happened?"

By then it was too late. The Nazis had shut down the killing operations in Poland in November and were about to flee to Germany. When Russian troops arrived at Auschwitz in February 1945, they found only a handful of emaciated prisoners, some of them too weak to survive their liberation.

We have since learned that, aside from the Nazis' hasty attempt just before they fled to hide what they had been doing by wrecking the gas chambers and crematoria, the only destruction of killing apparatus was carried out by the victims themselves. In the fall of 1944, when the debate over bombing the death camps reached its peak, four women prisoners smuggled dynamite from the munitions plant at Auschwitz to men assigned to take ashes from the furnaces. Realizing that their deed was suicidal, the ash men managed to blow up one of the four furnaces and kill several SS guards. Immediately, the women were hanged and the men shot, their heroic act unknown to those who dared not send bombers instead.

After the war, gay veterans tended to cluster in large cities where their sense of mutual interests and loyalty shaped their communities. Toughened by the military ordeal and angry that they had been part of a successful war against oppression, including the Nazi policy of exterminating homosexuals, while remaining oppressed themselves, veterans led the way in promoting the gay liberation movement. In 1950, a group of gay veterans formed the Mattachine Society to combat discrimination, and five years later lesbians in San Francisco followed their example by founding the Daughters of Bilitis. These efforts provided the impetus for gay activism to join in the broad front of civil rights insurgency that arose in the 1960s.

The Holocaust

Throughout the 1930s, Spanish Loyalists fleeing Franco, opponents of Mussolini, and, most numerous, the targets of Hitler's maniacal racism clamored for asylum. As Hitler expanded his campaign to "purify" Germany, Jews, gypsies, religious dissenters, homosexuals, avant-garde artists, and others came under increasing pressure to flee or risk extermination. As American resolve against totalitarian oppression stiffened, a desperate contest arose between those who would rescue the victims of persecution and those who would bar the gate because of vague fears that refugees might compete

for scarce work or divert the war effort to their own purposes.

As American resolve against totalitarian oppression stiffened, a desperate contest arose between those who would rescue the victims of persecution and those who would bar the gate.

Roosevelt sympathized with the pleas for help, but only if action did not jeopardize his foreign policy or his hold on the electorate. After the German army took over Austria in March 1938, crowds of Jews besieged the American embassy in Vienna, seeking immigration visas. Roosevelt tried to raise the annual quota, which allowed only fourteen hundred Austrians into the country, but Congress, trying to keep out of war and mindful of polls showing that 82 percent of Americans were against admitting Jewish exiles, refused the request. Roosevelt then sought to persuade countries in Latin America and Africa to accept refugees. None would agree. In a last attempt before war broke out, friends of the refugees introduced legislation in Congress in 1939 that would grant asylum to twenty thousand German refugee children, most of them Jewish. Both anti-Semitism and isolationism were undoubtedly factors in the defeat of the bill, for the following year refugee English children who were not predominantly Jewish gained entry without delay.

In 1942, word leaked out that Hitler was implementing a "final solution": Jews and other "undesirables" were being sent to concentration camps in remote areas; old people, children, and others deemed too weak to work were gassed and cremated while the able-bodied were put to work until lack of food and harsh conditions killed them. Even then skeptical U.S. State Department officials stood firmly in the way. Only 152,000 Jews had managed to gain refuge in the United States prior to America's entry into the war; thereafter, the numbers dropped steadily to a mere 2,400 in 1944. Those trapped in Europe could only wait for rescue by Allied armies.

The Holocaust, 1933–1945

When Russian troops arrived at Auschwitz in Poland in February 1945, they found only a handful of emaciated prisoners, some too weak to survive their liberation. Skeletal corpses, some half burned, lay around them; nearby were ponds and pits filled with the ashes of those who had perished. The Russians discovered sheds filled with loot stripped from the dead—clothing, gold fillings, false teeth, even cloth made from human hair. At last, the truth about Nazi atrocities breached the wall of denial. But by then it was too late; Nazi extermination had reached its final toll of nine million victims. (See "Historical Question," page 924.)

Military Victory: 1943–1945

By early 1943, the defensive phase of the war was over. Having halted the German and Japanese offenses in Europe and in Asia, the Allies faced the daunting task of driving the Axis back, retaking vast conquered areas, and finally defeating Germany

and Japan on their home territory. Stalin's anger over the reluctance of the United States and Britain to relieve the Soviet Union from the brunt of Hitler's attack by opening a second front in France strained the alliance. By the time the invasion of Normandy occured, the Soviet Union had already broken German power in the east. Simultaneously in the Pacific, the United States, fighting with Australia and New Zealand, unleashed its final victorious drive toward the Japanese mainland.

From Normandy to Berlin

In November 1943, as the Italian campaign slogged on at its cold, muddy pace, Churchill, Roosevelt, and Stalin held meetings in Teheran, the capital of Iran, and Cairo to plan the final assault on Hitler. Stalin finally succeeded in getting Roosevelt and Churchill to commit to a great invasion of Europe in May 1944. The Allies had been gathering an enormous army and navy in Great Britain for nearly two years in anticipation of a return to France. General Dwight D. Eisenhower, with his great tact and organizing skills, became Supreme Commander of the Allied forces—American, British, and Free French—while General Sir Bernard Montgomery, the hero of victory in North Africa, took charge of the landing itself.

German forces, directed by the master tactician General Erwin Rommel, fortified the cliffs and mined the beaches of northwestern France. Yet, as Rommel realized more clearly than Hitler, the huge deployment of German armies in the east trying to contain the massive Soviet offensive in the spring of 1943 left Rommel without adequate troops to stop the three million Allied soldiers waiting in England. Even more of a handicap was Rommel's inability to control the air. On the eve of invasion, the Luftwaffe (German air force) had only three hundred fighter planes to face twelve thousand Allied aircraft poised for massive bombardment.

False radio signals, invented armies, and diversionary air sorties encouraged the Germans to expect an Allied invasion at the Pas de Calais area, where the English Channel is narrowest. The actual invasion took place miles to the south on the beaches of Normandy (Map 24.4). First came raging air and naval attacks, then the landing of paratroopers behind the German lines, and finally at 7:30 A.M. on June 6, 1944, referred to in military parlance as "D Day," seaborne soldiers hit the beaches. For a perilous few hours, rough seas and fortified ma-

MAP 24.4

The European Theater of World War II, 1942–1945

Russian reversal of the German offensive by breaking the sieges of Stalingrad and Leningrad, combined with Allied landings in North Africa and Normandy, placed Germany in a closing vise of armies from all sides.

READING THE MAP: By 1942, what nations or parts of nations in Europe were under Axis control? What nations had been absorbed before the war? What nations remained neutral, and what nations were members of the Allies?

CONNECTIONS: What were the three fronts in the European theater? When did the Allies initiate actions in each of them, and why did Churchill, Stalin, and Roosevelt disagree on the timing of the opening of these fronts?

D DAY INVASION
"Taxi to Hell—and Back" is what Robert Sargent called his photograph of the D Day invasion of Normandy on June 6, 1944. Amid a dense thicket of landing craft, men and equipment lucky enough to have made it through rough seas and enemy fire struggle onto the beach to open a second front in Europe. After this brief moment of safe passage, the majority of this first wave of soldiers would be cut down by withering enemy fire from the high cliffs beyond the beach.
Library of Congress.

chine guns stopped the assault in a chaos of overturned tanks, drowning men, and frantic attempts by those who made it ashore to find cover. But paratroopers coming up behind the German line and rangers scaling the cliffs to knock out enemy gun emplacements finally secured the beachhead. As General Omar N. Bradley observed, the Allies prevailed only by "guts, valor, and extreme bravery."

Within a week, Allied forces had broken out of the Normandy pocket and begun their massive sweep toward Germany. Shaken by the hammering their armies were taking on both the western and eastern fronts, some in the German military began to search for a way out. In a desperate effort to replace the Nazis with a new government that would negotiate a peace, several officers made an unsuccessful bomb attempt against Hitler in July 1944.

Suspicion fell upon Rommel, who retired to his home and committed suicide to spare his family and himself the embarrassment of trial and execution. Hitler, who now doubted the loyalty of his officer corps, retreated more and more into directing the war on the basis of his own increasingly unstable intuition. On August 25, the Allies liberated Paris from four years of Nazi occupation. Two months later, they made their first foray into Germany to capture the city of Aachen. Hitler then took a mad gamble as the giant pincers of the Allied and Soviet armies closed on German headquarters in Berlin. In December 1944, he ordered a counterattack through Belgium to recapture Antwerp and deny the Allies their major supply port. Massive German forces drove fifty-five miles into Allied lines in what was known as the Battle of the Bulge before being

YALTA CONFERENCE
In February 1945, President Roosevelt and British prime minister Winston Churchill met with Russian leader Joseph Stalin at the Black Sea resort of Yalta to plan the postwar reconstruction of Europe. Roosevelt, near the end of his life, and Churchill, soon to suffer reelection defeat, look weary next to the resolute "Man of Steel." Controversy would later arise over whether a stronger stand by the American and British leaders could have prevented the Soviet Union from imposing communist rule on eastern Europe.
U.S. Army.

stopped at Bastogne. German losses of eighty-two thousand men and hundreds of tanks proved disastrous. By committing so many of his reserves to the Bulge, Hitler left the remnant of his army, facing the Russians, close to collapse.

In February 1945, with the end in sight, Churchill, Stalin, and a seriously ill Roosevelt met secretly at the Russian Black Sea resort town of Yalta to discuss the structure of the postwar world. Talks centered on three major topics: rearranging the political map of Europe, creating a new international organization, and achieving victory over Japan. Although his stamina and mental alertness flickered, Roosevelt still managed to secure a major share of what he sought. The Soviets agreed to a declaration of self-determination for the countries their armies

In February 1945, with the end in sight, Churchill, Stalin, and a seriously ill Roosevelt met secretly at the Russian Black Sea resort town of Yalta to discuss the structure of the postwar world.

occupied in Eastern Europe. Chiang Kai-shek would receive Allied support as leader of China in the war against Japan. And the Soviet Union would have a say in the governance of Korea and Manchuria in exchange for entering the war against Japan after the defeat of Germany.

The "Big Three" also agreed on the creation of a new international organization, the United Nations (UN). All countries would have a place in the organization's General Assembly, but the Security Council would ultimately wield decisive power. The Security Council would be composed of temporary members and of permanent representatives from China, France, Great Britain, the Soviet Union, and the United States, each of which would retain the veto.

American response to the creation of the UN was startlingly different from the nation's refusal to join the League of Nations in 1919. Internationalism triumphed when Republican senator Arthur Vandenberg of Michigan, who had long been a staunch isolationist, declared that it was his mission to "end the miserable notion that the Republican Party will return to its foxhole when the last shot in this war has been fired and will blindly let the world rot in its own anarchy." The Senate ratified the United Nations charter in July by a vote of 89 to 2.

Following the Yalta agreement, the Allies began the final assault on Hitler. While American forces pounded Germany from the west, the Soviets, having swept through Poland, arrived at the outskirts of Berlin in April 1945. Hitler, who had descended into his underground bunker on January 16, signaled the end of Nazism by committing suicide on April 30. His body was burned amid the din of Russian cannons and the remains hurriedly buried under what is now the median strip of a highway deliberately placed to cover all traces of the Nazi leader. On May 7, a provisional German government surrendered unconditionally.

Franklin Roosevelt did not live to witness the end of the Nazi horror. On April 12, while resting in Warm Springs, Georgia, the president suffered a fatal stroke. Americans grieved publicly for the man who had led them through more than twelve years of depression and world war. And they worried aloud about his successor, Vice President Harry S. Truman. Truman's colleagues in Congress generally believed he would be little more than a caretaker, and Truman seemed to agree. When a reporter called him "Mr. President," he replied uneasily, "I wish you didn't have to call me that." To other reporters he pleaded, "Boys, if newspapermen pray, pray for me now." Truman showed himself to be tough-minded and a quick learner, however, with a knowledge of history deeper than that of almost any previous president. It soon became clear that he would not hesitate to make hard decisions.

The Defeat of Japan

American victories at sea in early 1942 halted the Japanese advance in the Pacific. By mid-1942, the Americans had taken the offensive. Japan had intended to use its navy to shield a vast economic empire in China and Southeast Asia. Instead, it had to fend off revived and aroused Allied forces in the Pacific while also trying to quell renewed resistance on the Asian mainland. In China, the Japanese armies had scored many victories but were unable to finish off Chiang Kai-shek. Japanese forces had advanced westward almost to India, but in 1943 British and American forces, along with Indian and Chinese troops, were preparing for a counterthrust through Burma and into China. The most decisive action, however, came in the Pacific, where the Allies moved slowly and painfully, island by island, toward the Japanese homeland (Map 24.5).

In August 1942, the island campaign began when the First Marine Division landed on Guadalcanal, where the Japanese were constructing an airfield. For the next six months, a savage battle raged for control of the strategic area. Finally, during the night of February 7, 1943, Japanese forces withdrew after terrible losses on both sides that indicated just how costly the long march to Japan would be.

In mid-1943, American, Australian, and New Zealand forces launched new offensives that penetrated the outer perimeter of Japanese defenses. Bloody campaigns in New Guinea and the Solomon Islands gradually secured the South Pacific. In the Central Pacific, amphibious forces, borne by the greatest fleet in history, took the Gilbert and Marshall Islands, which served eventually as forward positions for launching the decisive air and ground assaults on the Japanese home islands.

As the Allied offensive pressed on, resistance grew fiercer from Japanese soldiers who had been instructed to stand firm to the death. The landing on Tarawa made plain their tenacity. Stymied by a tide that grounded their landing craft far from shore, the invading marines had to wade half a mile, waist-deep, through brutal enemy fire. Survivors of that barrage then faced fortified emplacements manned by well-armed troops who had no intention of retreating. Within three days, the marines had suffered one thousand dead and another two thousand wounded—all to take a barren coral island not three square miles. Only seventeen of the three thousand Japanese defenders were left alive to surrender. Thereafter, island-to-island warfare took on an awful

MAP 24.5

The Pacific Theater of World War II, 1941–1945
To drive the Japanese from their far-flung empire, the Allies launched two combined naval and military offensives—one to recapture the Philippines and then attack Japanese forces in China, the other to hop from island to island in the Central Pacific toward the Japanese mainland.

sameness of rooting the enemy out of bunkers and caves with explosives and flamethrowers.

Both land and sea war climaxed in the fall of 1944 with the invasion of the Philippines and the battle for Leyte Gulf. The greatest naval encounter in history cost the Japanese practically their entire fleet. Before the Philippines were retaken, Allied forces captured two vital island strongholds—Iwo Jima, 750 miles from Japan, and Okinawa, only 370

miles from Tokyo. To defend Okinawa and prevent the American invaders from getting within close bombing range of their home islands, the Japanese called on thousands of suicide pilots, known as *kamikaze* ("divine wind"). Their mission was to crash bomb-laden planes into Allied ships and thus, it was hoped, make the landing forces turn back. The kamikaze made life harrowing for the American fleet but did not deter it. Rather, the suicide ges-

GUADALCANAL: *GHOST TRAIL*

This painting, **Ghost Trail** *by combat artist Kerr Eby, captures the eerie, murky quality of jungle warfare first experienced fully in the campaign to capture the Pacific island of Guadalcanal. The troops blend into a dense maze of black and green that compounds the difficulties of detecting the hidden enemy.*

Navy Art Collection/Gift of Abbott Laboratories.

ture destroyed the last vestige of the Japanese air force. By June 1945, the Japanese were virtually defenseless on sea and in the air.

Atomic Warfare

Just as the island campaigns drew to an end, American scientists were completing work on a secret weapon. The race to develop an atomic bomb had begun in 1942 after refugee scientists warned that the Nazis were working to convert nuclear energy into a superbomb. The Roosevelt administration authorized the top-secret Manhattan Project to develop the bomb before the Germans did. In thirty-seven locations across the country, coordinated by leading theorists at Los Alamos, New Mexico, 100,000 persons worked at top speed to win the race.

Germany surrendered before it produced a bomb and before the United States was ready to test its own. Then, just before dawn on July 16, 1945, a test explosion lit up the sky in an isolated corner of the Alamogordo Air Base near Los Alamos. Project

scientists had wagered in a betting pool that the blast, if the test device worked at all, would be equivalent to a few hundred tons of TNT. No one imagined the actual force of twenty thousand tons. Nor was anyone prepared for a flash of multicolored light more brilliant than ever seen before or the vast fireball and mushroom-shaped cloud of dust and debris that rose eight miles into the upper atmosphere.

A delegation of scientists and officials, troubled by the power they had unleashed, proposed a public demonstration of the bomb's doomsday force to persuade Japan to surrender. With Japanese forces incapable of offensive action and Japan totally blockaded, test proponents argued that the United States could afford to wait until the point of the demonstration sank in. The Japanese government had already sent emissaries to see if a negotiated peace could be reached. The sticking point was that the Japanese wanted to retain their emperor, while the American government remained committed to unconditional surrender.

JAPANESE KAMIKAZE
In this painting by Sentaro Iwata, Japanese suicide pilots prepare to fly to the defense of Okinawa. The pilots, some wearing ceremonial swords, look heavenward before going aloft as kamikaze, "divine wind," to deliberately crash their bomb-laden planes into enemy warships. In the fight for Okinawa, kamikaze caused over 4,000 U.S. casualties.
Painting by Sentaro Iwata, National Archives.

In the end, all reluctance to unleash the atomic monster on populated targets yielded to other urgent considerations. When President Truman heard about the bomb test, he was involved in hard bargaining with the Soviets in Potsdam, Germany, about how to reorganize the postwar world. Truman showed his distrust of the Russians by keeping the news of the test secret. Then he adjusted his strategy to take advantage of the new weapon. Clearly, the bomb made it unnecessary to call on the Russian promise to hasten victory by declaring war on Japan. Rather, a surprise use of the new superweapon might end the conflict before the Soviet Union could attack the Japanese in Korea and Manchuria. Perhaps, also, the bomb's devastation would convince the Soviets that they could not safely challenge American leadership after the war ended.

> *In the end, all reluctance to unleash the atomic monster yielded to other urgent considerations.*

A more basic motive was to save American lives. As Truman pondered his options, Americans were preparing for Operation Downfall—the invasion of the Japanese home islands in the fall. Experience with Japanese soldiers who fought to the death filled American military and civilian leaders with dread. In the battle for Okinawa alone, which ended the island-hopping campaign just before the atomic bomb test, seven thousand American fighting men lost their lives. By resisting to the end, seventy thousand Japanese soldiers and eighty

HIROSHIMA BOMBING
This rare shot taken by a news photographer in Hiroshima immediately after the atomic bomb exploded on August 6, 1945, suggests the shock and incomprehension that survivors would describe as their first reaction. Three days later another atomic bomb created similar devastation in Nagasaki.
UN photo.

thousand Okinawans also died in the two-month-long battle. Intelligence reports indicated that more than two million Japanese army troops were available for a last-ditch defense of their homeland. Behind them were twenty-eight million men, women, and boys of the civilian militia, armed with sharpened bamboo stakes, farm implements, and any other weapons they could muster.

Truman, who had been a commander of combat troops on the ground in World War I, was keenly sympathetic to the ordeal facing an invading army. He saw no reason not to use a weapon of war, even a terribly destructive one, if it would save American lives. But first he issued an ultimatum that Japan must surrender unconditionally or face utter ruin. When the Japanese failed to respond by the deadline, Truman turned to his advisory committee's recommendation that, to shock the Japanese

into surrender, the bomb be dropped without warning on cities that had not already been heavily damaged. On August 6, a single B-29, the *Enola Gay*, droned over Hiroshima and released one of the three operational atomic bombs the Americans possessed. As the plane banked sharply away, crew members could see behind them the mushroom cloud that signified the obliteration of the city and the death of seventy-eight thousand inhabitants. Three days later, a second atomic bomb devastated Nagasaki with more than a hundred thousand deaths.

In the midst of ruin, a peace faction took control of the Japanese government from diehard military leaders, and with assurance that the emperor could retain his throne under Allied control, Japan surrendered on August 14. Whether allowing the Japanese to retain their emperor before using atomic bombs would have been enough to induce surrender can never be known. Emperor Hirohito's power to shift the Japanese spirit from war to peace became clear, however, when he informed his people in a radio broadcast—the first words that the public had ever heard the emperor utter—of his divine will that they cease fighting. Loyally, his subjects laid down their arms and stood quietly by as the giant battleship *Missouri* sailed into Tokyo harbor for the formal signing of surrender on September 2, 1945.

Conclusion: Victory and Uncertainty

For Americans, the attack on Pearl Harbor was just the first shock of a war whose scope and violence was unprecedented. Never before had armies been flung across such vast stretches of the globe. And on the seas there were more battles, with more ships lost, than in all other modern wars combined. According to one estimate, the death toll reached 35 million, evenly divided between military and civilian losses. Some countries suffered much more than others. Approximately 400,000 Americans lost their lives in military service; the Soviet Union lost more in the battle of Stalingrad alone and eventually suffered nearly 20 million civilian and military deaths.

Out of war's carnage arose misgivings about human nature and the sort of world that would emerge from the ashes. The Holocaust demonstrated cruelty beyond what many had imagined possible; and the devastating use of the atomic bomb added alarm over the destructive powers of science and technology. Charles Lindbergh, who had been vilified for questioning America's intervention, found much to reinforce his forebodings during his service in both theaters of war. Just days after Germany's surrender, an assignment to study German jet planes caused Lindbergh to pass through a liberated death camp at Nordhausen. Gaunt survivors and the furnaces designed to cremate them forced memories of the savage Pacific campaign back on Lindbergh: Japanese prisoners machine-gunned on an airstrip, others pushed out of transport planes supposed to take them to safe captivity, shin bones cut for letter openers. Committing atrocities, he realized at that moment, "is not a thing confined to any nation or to any people. . . . It is not the Germans alone, or the Japs, but the men of all nations to whom this war has brought shame and degradation."

Nevertheless, most Americans emerged from the conflict convinced that they had won the "good war." The Roosevelt administration had taken the lead in creating the United Nations and had made it plain that America, as the most powerful nation on earth, would devote its resources to rebuilding worldwide political and economic stability. Although some economists expressed anxiety that the nation might return to depression after its giant military production machine was dismantled, indications were strong that war had brought firm recovery. Unemployment was negligible, and the gross national product had soared to four times what it had been when Roosevelt was elected president in 1932, while average family income had risen by half. The challenge to postwar success at home lay mainly in stabilizing the changes that had occurred during the war and reintegrating the millions of men and women who were returning from the fighting.

The postwar challenges abroad were grimmer. The United States and Western Europe soon found themselves at odds with the Communist Soviet Union and China. Efforts by Britain and France to maintain their colonial empires also violated democratic principles and met mounting resistance from national forces seeking liberation. Under these circumstances, the confidence bred of winning the good war began to give way to the anxious uncertainties of what came to be called the cold war.

www.bedfordstmartins.com/tap SEE THE ONLINE STUDY GUIDE to assess your mastery of the material covered in this chapter.

CHRONOLOGY

1933 Adolf Hitler becomes chancellor of Germany.

United States formally recognizes Soviet Union.

1935–1937 Congress seeks to shield America from world conflicts with neutrality acts.

1936 Nazi Germany occupies Rhineland.

Mussolini's fascist Italian regime conquers Ethiopia.

Civil war breaks out in Spain.

1937 Japanese troops capture Nanking.

Roosevelt delivers speech urging "quarantine" against aggressor nations.

1938 Hitler annexes Austria.

British prime minister Neville Chamberlain meets with Hitler in Munich and agrees to German seizure of Sudetenland in Czechoslovakia.

1939 German troops occupy remainder of Czechoslovakia without resistance.

Nazi Germany and Soviet Union sign nonaggression pact.

September 1. Germany's attack on Poland begins World War II.

United States and Great Britain conclude cash-and-carry agreement for arms sales.

1940 **May–June.** British troops evacuated at Dunkirk.

June. German occupation of France begins.

Isolationists, including Charles Lindbergh, create America First Committee.

Roosevelt wins reelection against Wendell Willkie.

1941 Lend-Lease Act enables Britain to obtain war materiel from United States on credit.

June. Germany invades Soviet Union.

August. Atlantic Charter devised by Roosevelt and Allies to guarantee human and international freedoms after war.

December 7. Japanese launch surprise attack on Pearl Harbor; United States declares war on Japan.

1942 Japan captures Philippines.

Civil rights activists found Congress of Racial Equality (CORE).

U.S. navy scores its first major victories in Battle of Coral Sea and at Midway.

Roosevelt authorizes top-secret Manhattan Project.

November. U.S. forces invade North Africa.

Roosevelt authorizes internment of Japanese Americans.

1943 Allied leaders agree that war will end only with unconditional surrender of Axis forces.

"Zoot suit" riots occur in Los Angeles.

U.S. forces invade Sicily.

1944 **June 6.** Combined Allied army stages successful D Day landing at Normandy.

Roosevelt wins reelection against Thomas E. Dewey.

1945 The Allies meet to plan reconstruction of Europe after defeat of Germany.

April 12. Franklin Roosevelt dies and Harry Truman becomes president.

Delegates from fifty nations, meeting in San Francisco, approve charter of United Nations.

May 7. Germany surrenders.

August 6. United States drops atomic bomb on Hiroshima.

August 9. United States drops atomic bomb on Nagasaki.

August 14. Japan surrenders, ending World War II.

BIBLIOGRAPHY

GENERAL WORKS

John Morton Blum, *V Was for Victory: Politics and American Culture during World War II* (1977).

Kenneth S. Davis, *FDR: Into the Storm, 1937–1940* (1993).

I. C. B. Dear and M. R. D. Foot, eds., *The Oxford Companion to World War II* (1995).

Paul Fussell, *Wartime* (1989).

Akira Iriye, *The Origins of the Second World War in Asia and the Pacific* (1987).

Richard Ketchum, *The Borrowed Years, 1938–1941: America on the Way to War* (1989).

Eric Larrabee, *Commander in Chief: Franklin Delano Roosevelt, His Lieutenants, and Their War* (1987).

Richard Polenberg, *War and Society: The United States, 1941–1945* (1972).

Michael S. Sherry, *In the Shadow of War: The United States since the 1930s* (1995).

Studs Terkel, *"The Good War": An Oral History of World War II* (1984).

Gerhard Weinberg, *World at Arms: A Global History of World War II* (1994).

FOREIGN POLICY

Robert Dallek, *Franklin D. Roosevelt and American Foreign Policy, 1932–1945* (1979).

Lloyd C. Gardner, *Economic Aspects of New Deal Diplomacy* (1964).

Erwin F. Gellman, *Good Neighbor Diplomacy: United States Policies in Latin America, 1933–1945* (1979).

Waldo Heinrichs, *Threshold of War: Franklin D. Roosevelt and American Entry into World War II* (1988).

Robert Hilderbrand, *Dumbarton Oaks: The Origins of the United Nations and the Search for Postwar Security* (1990).

Akira Iriye, *The Globalizing of America, 1913–1945* (1995).

Walter LaFeber, *Inevitable Revolutions* (1983).

Frederick W. Marks, *Wind over Sand: The Diplomacy of Franklin Roosevelt* (1988).

Arnold Offner, *The Origins of the Second World War* (1975).

Robert Rosenstone, *Crusade of the Left: The Lincoln Battalion in the Spanish Civil War* (1969).

David F. Schmitz, *The United States and Fascist Italy, 1922–1944* (1988).

Gaddis Smith, *American Diplomacy during the Second World War, 1941–1945* (1985).

Jonathan Utley, *Going to War with Japan, 1937–1942* (1985).

PACIFISM AND ANTI-INTERVENTIONISM

A. Scott Berg, *Lindbergh* (1999).

Wayne S. Cole, *Roosevelt and the Isolationists, 1932–1945* (1983).

Robert A. Divine, *The Illusion of Neutrality* (1982).

Charles A. Lindbergh, *The Wartime Journals* (1970).

Joyce Milton, *Loss of Eden: A Biography of Charles and Anne Morrow Lindbergh* (1994).

Geoffrey S. Smith, *To Save a Nation: American "Extremism," the New Deal, and the Coming of WWII* (1992).

John E. Wiltz, *In Search of Peace: The Senate Munitions Inquiry, 1934–1936* (1963).

MOBILIZATION AND THE HOME FRONT

Karen Anderson, *Wartime Women: Sex Roles, Family Relations, and the Status of Women during World War II* (1981).

D'Ann Campbell, *Women at War with America: Private Lives in a Patriotic Era* (1984).

Mark Jonathan Harris, Franklin D. Mitchell, and Steve J. Schechter, *The Home Front: America during World War II* (1985).

Susan Hartmann, *The Home Front and Beyond: American Women in the 1940s* (1982).

John W. Jeffries, *Wartime America: The World War II Home Front* (1996).

Clayton R. Koppes and Gregory D. Black, *Hollywood Goes to War: How Politics, Profits, and Propaganda Shaped World War II Movies* (1987).

Nelson Lichtenstein, *Labor's War at Home: The CIO in World War II* (1983).

Gerald D. Nash, *The American West Transformed: The Impact of the Second World War* (1985).

William L. O'Neill, *A Democracy at War: America's Fight at Home and Abroad in World War II* (1993).

Geoffrey Perret, *Days of Sadness, Years of Triumph: The American People, 1939–1945* (1985).

William Tuttle, *Daddy's Gone to War: The Second World War in the Lives of America's Children* (1993).

MILITARY ORGANIZATION AND CAMPAIGNS

Gar Alperovitz, *The Decision to Use the Atomic Bomb and the Architecture of an American Myth* (1995).

Stephen E. Ambrose, *D-Day, June 6, 1944* (1994).

Allan Berube, *Coming Out under Fire: The History of Gay Men and Women in World War Two* (1990).

Paul S. Boyer, *By the Bomb's Early Light: American Thought and Culture at the Dawn of the Atomic Age* (1985).

A. Russell Buchanan, *The United States and World War II*, 2 vols. (1964).

John Costello, *Virtue under Fire: How World War II Changed Our Social and Sexual Attitudes* (1986).

Albert E. Cowdrey, *Fighting for Life: American Military Medicine in World War II* (1994).

Gavan Daws, *Prisoners of the Japanese: POWs of World War II* (1992).

John Dower, *War without Mercy: Race and Power in the Pacific War* (1986).

Richard A. Gabriel and Karen S. Metz, *A History of Military Medicine*, vol. 2 (1992).

D. Clayton James, *A Time for Giants: The Politics of the American High Command in World War II* (1987).

Dan Kurzman, *Day of the Bomb: Countdown to Hiroshima* (1986).

Robert Leckie, *Delivered from Evil: The Saga of World War II* (1987).

Gerald F. Linderman, *The World within War: America's Combat Experience in World War II* (1997).

Geoffrey Perret, *Winged Victory: The Army Air Forces in World War II* (1993).

Gordon W. Prange, *At Dawn We Slept* (1981).

Richard Rhodes, *The Making of the Atomic Bomb* (1986).

Ronald Schaffer, *Wings of Judgment: American Bombing in World War II* (1988).

Michael Schaller, *Douglas MacArthur: The Far Eastern General* (1989).

Michael S. Sherry, *The Rise of American Air Power: The Creation of Armageddon* (1987).

Ronald H. Spector, *Eagle against the Sun: The American War with Japan* (1985).

Murray Williamson and Allan R. Millett, *A War to Be Won: Fighting the Second World War, 1937–1945* (2000).

RACE AND MINORITIES

Gerald Astor, *The Right to Fight: A History of African Americans in the Military* (1998).

Alison R. Bernstein, *American Indians and World War II: Toward a New Era in Indian Affairs* (1991).

Dominic Capeci, *The Harlem Race Riot of 1943* (1977).

Roger Daniels, *Concentration Camps: North American Japanese in the United States and Canada during World War II* (1971, 1989).

Jere Bishop Franco, *Crossing the Pond: The Native American Effort in World War II* (1999).

Peter H. Irons, *Justice at War: The Story of the Japanese American Internment Cases* (1983).

Daniel Kryder, *Divided Arsenal: Race and the American State during World War II* (2000).

Steven F. Lawson, *Running for Freedom: Civil Rights and Black Politics in America since 1941* (1991).

Mauricio Mazon, *The Zoot-Suit Riots: The Psychology of Symbolic Annihilation* (1984).

Bernard C. Nalty, *Strength for the Fight: A History of Black Americans in the Military* (1989).

Page Smith, *Democracy on Trial: The Japanese American Evacuation and Relocation in World War II* (1995).

Ronald Takaki, *Strangers from a Different Shore: A History of Asian Americans* (1989).

DEPICTING THE WAR

M. Joyce Baker, *Images of Women on Film: The War Years* (1981).

Thomas Doherty, *Projections of War: Hollywood, American Culture, and World War II* (1993).

William Manchester, *Goodbye Darkness: A Memoir of the Pacific War* (1980).

Karal Ann Marling and John Wetenhall, *Iwo Jima: Monuments, Memories, and the American Hero* (1991).

Peter Maslowski, *Armed with Cameras: The American Military Photographers of World War II* (1993).

Mordecai Richler, *Writers on World War II* (1991).

George H. Roeder Jr., *The Censored War: American Visual Experience during World War II* (1993).

Vernon Scannell, *Not without Glory: Poets of the Second World War* (1976).

Holly Cowan Shulman, *The Voice of America: Propaganda and Democracy, 1941–1945* (1991).

E. B. Sledge, *With the Old Breed at Peleliu and Okinawa* (1990).

Frederick S. Voss, *Reporting the War: The Journalistic Coverage of World War II* (1994).

AMERICA AND THE HOLOCAUST

Robert Abzug, *Inside the Vicious Heart: Americans and the Liberation of Nazi Concentration Camps* (1987).

Richard Breitman and Alan Kraut, *American Refugee Policy and European Jewry* (1987).

Lucy Dawidowicz, *The War against the Jews, 1933–1945* (1986).

Leonard Dinnerstein, *America and the Survivors of the Holocaust* (1982).

Lawrence L. Langer, *Admitting the Holocaust: Collected Essays* (1995).

Deborah E. Lipstadt, *Beyond Belief: The American Press and the Coming of the Holocaust, 1933–1945* (1986).

Michael Marrus, *The Holocaust in History* (1987).

Verne W. Newton, ed., *FDR and the Holocaust* (1995).

Peter Novick, *The Holocaust in American Life* (1999).

COLD WAR COMIC BOOK

Americans barely had time to celebrate the Allied victory in World War II when they perceived another threat, that posed by the Soviet Union. Fear of communism dominated much of postwar American life and politics, even invading the realm of popular culture. Four million copies of this comic book, published by a religious organization in 1947, painted a terrifying picture of what would happen to Americans if the Soviets took over the country. Such takeover stories appeared in movies, cartoons, and magazines as well as in other comic books.

Collection of Charles H. Christensen.

COLD WAR POLITICS IN THE TRUMAN YEARS

25

1945–1953

O N NOVEMBER 5, 1946, President Harry S. Truman, his wife, and his daughter boarded the train back to Washington from Truman's hometown, Independence, Missouri, where they had gone to vote in the congressional elections. During the campaigns, Republicans had blasted Truman as incapable of dealing with economic problems and the threat of communism. The president's approval rating with the public had sunk to a mere 32 percent. Many Democratic candidates had avoided mentioning his name and instead used recordings of the late Franklin Roosevelt's voice to stir voters. Playing poker with reporters on the train as the returns came in, Truman appeared unconcerned. But the results were devastating: The Republicans had captured both the House and the Senate by substantial majorities.

When Truman stepped off the train in Washington at the lowest point of his presidency, only one member of his administration showed up to greet him, Undersecretary of State Dean Acheson. Acheson's gesture signaled a developing relationship of central importance to the two men as well as to postwar history. The fifty-three-year-old Acheson shared most of Truman's political principles, even though their backgrounds differed sharply. Acheson had enjoyed a typical upper-class education at private school in Groton, Connecticut; Yale University, where classmates voted him "wittiest" and the "spiciest" dresser; and Harvard Law School. After clerking for Supreme Court justice Louis Brandeis, he earned a comfortable living as a corporate lawyer. In contrast, Truman, the son of a Missouri farmer, had not attended college and had failed in a business venture before entering local politics in the 1920s.

Despite his wealth and privilege, Acheson supported much of the New Deal and staunchly defended organized labor. He spoke out against isolationism in the late 1930s, and in 1941 he accepted President Roosevelt's offer of a job at the State Department. Shortly after Truman became president, the supremely confident Acheson wrote privately about shortcomings in Truman's "judgment and wisdom that the limitations of his experience produce," but he also found the fledgling president a man who "will learn fast and will inspire confidence." In June 1947, Acheson left the State Department, but Truman lured him back in 1949 to be secretary of state during the president's second term. Acheson appreciated Truman's willingness to make tough decisions and expressed his respect by noting that Truman's "ego never came between him and his job." Truman cherished Acheson's abiding loyalty. Relying on him as secretary of state until they both left office in January 1953, Truman called Acheson "my good right hand."

Truman needed all the help he could get. The "accidental president" lacked the charisma, experience, and political skills with which Roosevelt had transformed

DEAN ACHESON
No individual had more to do with transforming America's role in the world after World War II than Dean Acheson, President Truman's closest foreign policy adviser. Acheson, shown here with Truman in 1945, criticized those who saw the cold war in black-and-white terms and communism as an evil that the United States could expel from the earth. Rather, he advocated that American leaders learn "to limit objectives, to get ourselves away from the search for the absolute, to find out what is within our powers."
Harry S. Truman Library.

both foreign and domestic policy, won four presidential elections, and forged a Democratic Party coalition that dominated national politics. Initially criticized and abandoned by many Roosevelt loyalists, Truman faced a resurgent Republican Party as well as revolts from within his own party. Besides domestic problems left over from the New Deal—how to sustain economic growth and avoid another depression without the war to fuel the economy—Truman faced the necessity of redefining the nation's central foreign policy goals in a new international context.

Dean Acheson was instrumental in forging that foreign policy. As early as 1946, Acheson became convinced that the Soviet Union posed a major threat to U.S. security. With other officials, he helped to shape a policy designed to contain and thwart Soviet power and influence wherever they threatened to spread. By 1947, a new term had been coined to describe the intense rivalry between the superpowers—the "cold war." The containment policy worked in Western Europe, but at home it produced a wave of anti-Communist hysteria that

cost many Americans their jobs and stifled criticism of U.S. policies and institutions.

As the preeminent foreign policy official and the defender of Alger Hiss, a former colleague accused of being a Soviet spy, Acheson too reaped abuse from Republicans for being "soft on communism." At the height of the anti-Communist frenzy, Acheson received so much hate mail that guards were posted at his house. Yet he kept both his job and his sense of humor. When cab drivers asked him, "Aren't you Dean Acheson?" he would reply, "Yes. Do I have to get out?"

From the Grand Alliance to Containment

No sooner had Americans finished celebrating the victory over Japan in August 1945 than they began to besiege the government with demands to bring the troops home. Mothers sent baby booties and children's photos to the White House and the Capitol with notes pleading for the return of husbands and fathers. Throughout the world servicemen themselves staged demonstrations demanding to be sent home. Although such pressure made Truman demobilize more quickly than his advisers thought prudent, no one thought that the postwar world would require a large military establishment. Officials and civilians alike expected the Allies, led by the United States and working within the United Nations, to cooperate in the management of international peace and order.

Postwar realities quickly dashed these expectations. When the wartime alliance forged by the United States, Great Britain, and the Soviet Union crumbled, the United States began to develop the military and diplomatic means to contain the spread of Soviet power around the globe. By 1949, the nation had reestablished the military draft, embarked on a nuclear arms race, entered into its first peacetime alliance, and committed itself to a multibillion-dollar foreign aid program.

Moving from Wartime Coalition to Cold War

"The guys who came out of World War II were idealistic," reported Harold Russell, a young paratrooper who lost both hands in a training accident. "We felt the day had come when the wars were all over." Public opinion polls revealed that most Americans shared the veterans' confidence in the promise of peace. But political leaders were less optimistic. Winston Churchill had always distrusted the Soviets; in a moment of frustration during the war, he had said that the only thing worse than fighting with allies was fighting without them. Once the Allies had overcome a common enemy, the prewar mistrust and antagonism between the Soviet Union and the West resurfaced over their very different visions of the postwar world.

Soviet suspicions grew during the war when the Allies resisted Soviet leader Joseph Stalin's repeated pleas to open a second front in Western Europe. The Soviet Union had made supreme wartime sacrifices, losing more than twenty million citizens and vast portions of its agricultural and industrial capacity. At the war's end, Stalin wanted to make Germany pay for the necessary rebuilding of the Soviet economy, to eliminate future threats from neighboring countries, and to expand Soviet influence in the world. Above all, Stalin wanted to have governments friendly to the Soviet Union on its borders in Eastern Europe; he was especially concerned about Poland, through which Germany had attacked the Soviet Union twice within twenty-five years.

Once the Allies had overcome a common enemy, the prewar mistrust and antagonism between the Soviet Union and the West resurfaced over their very different visions of the postwar world.

In contrast, enemy fire had never touched the mainland of the United States, and its 405,000 dead amounted to just 2 percent of the Soviet loss. With a vastly expanded productive capacity, a monopoly on atomic weapons, and supreme confidence in American institutions, the United States emerged from the war as the most powerful nation on the planet in the unprecedented role of world leadership.

Worried about a return of the depression, U.S. officials believed that a healthy economy depended on opportunities elsewhere in the world. The United States needed access to raw materials, markets for its goods, and security for American investments in other countries. These needs could be better met in countries with economic and political systems resembling its own, not in countries whose governments imposed economic controls that interfered with the free flow of products and dollars. As Truman put it in 1947, "The American system can survive in America only if it becomes a world system."

Truman's words reflected many citizens' belief in their nation's superiority. American leaders boasted of the best economic and political system in the world and encouraged other nations to copy the United States. Convinced of the excellence of their institutions and values, Americans viewed their foreign policy not as a self-interested campaign to meet economic needs, but as the means to preserve national security and to bring freedom, democracy, and capitalism to the rest of the world.

American approaches to foreign policy also reflected the belief that World War II might have been avoided had Britain, France, and the United States resisted rather than appeased Hitler's initial aggression. In September 1945, for example, Secretary of the Navy James V. Forrestal cautioned against attempting to "buy [the Soviets'] understanding and sympathy. We tried that once with Hitler." This so-called Munich analogy (referring to the 1938 conference where Britain and France acquiesced in Hitler's annexation of Czechoslovakia) would be evoked time and again when the United States faced challenges to the international status quo.

The man with ultimate responsibility for U.S. policy came to the White House as a veteran of World War I but with little experience in international affairs. Kept in the dark by Roosevelt, Truman did not even know about the atomic bomb project. Truman hoped to maintain Soviet-American cooperation, although, like most American leaders, he had strong anti-Communist sentiments. Once he learned that America's nuclear monopoly gave him the advantage, he demanded that the Soviet Union comply with U.S. plans for the postwar world and restrain its expansionist impulses.

Soviet and American interests clashed first in Eastern Europe. Stalin insisted that the Allies' wartime agreements gave him a free hand in the countries defeated or liberated by the Red Army, just as the United States was unilaterally reconstructing governments in Italy and Japan. The Soviet dictator used harsh methods to install Communist governments in Poland and Bulgaria, countries bordering the Soviet Union. Elsewhere, the Soviets initially tolerated non-Communist governments in Hungary and Czechoslovakia. And in the spring of 1946, under pressure from the West, Stalin removed troops from Iran, the Soviet Union's neighbor to the southwest, opening the door for the United States to gain important oil concessions there.

To Stalin, U.S. officials seemed hypocritical in demanding democratic elections in Eastern Europe while supporting dictatorships friendly to U.S. interests in Cuba, Nicaragua, and other Latin American countries. The United States clung to its own sphere of influence while adamantly denying one to the Soviets. But the tough words of the Western allies were no match for the Soviet armies occupying Eastern Europe: The United States and Britain issued sharp protests but would not use military force against any of the Soviet Union's satellite countries.

In 1946, the wartime Allies contended over the future of Germany. American policymakers wanted to strip the nation of its military capacity, but they also desired a rapid industrial revival in Germany to foster European economic recovery and thus

America's own long-term prosperity. By contrast, the Soviet Union resolved to keep Germany militarily and economically weak and to exact heavy reparations that it could use to rebuild the Soviet economy. Unable to settle their differences, the Allies divided Germany. The Soviet Union installed a puppet Communist government in the eastern section, and in December 1946 Britain, France, and the United States unified their occupation zones and began the process that led to creation of the Federal Republic of Germany—West Germany—in 1949 (Map 25.1).

The war of words escalated early in 1946. Boasting of the strength of the Red Army and the superiority of the Soviet system, Stalin told a Moscow audience in February that capitalist economies inevitably produced war. One month later, Truman traveled with Winston Churchill to Westminster College in Fulton, Missouri, where the former prime minister denounced Soviet suppression of the popular will in Eastern and central Europe. "From Stettin in the Baltic to Trieste in the Adriatic, an iron curtain has descended across the continent," Churchill said. Although Truman did not officially endorse Churchill's iron curtain speech, his appearance on the platform beside Churchill implied agreement with the call for the development of joint British-American strength to combat Soviet aggression. Stalin regarded the speech as "a call to war against the USSR." (See "Documenting the American Promise," page 948.)

In February 1946, career diplomat George F. Kennan wrote a memo that furnished a comprehensive rationale for hard-line foreign policy. Kennan, who had served in U.S. embassies in Eastern Europe and Moscow, considered optimistic assumptions about Soviet-American cooperation mere pipe dreams. He downplayed the influence of Communist ideology in Soviet policy but noted the Soviets' insecurity and their need to maintain authority at home. These circumstances, Kennan argued, made it impossible to negotiate with Stalin, a conclusion shared by Secretary of State James F. Byrnes, Undersecretary Acheson, and other key Truman advisers.

Kennan predicted that the Soviet Union would try to expand its influence worldwide but would retreat "in the face of superior force." Therefore, he said, the United States should respond with "unalterable counterforce," making Russia "face frustration indefinitely," an approach that came to be called *containment*. Kennan expected that contain-

MAP 25.1

The Division of Europe after World War II

The "iron curtain," a term coined by Winston Churchill to refer to the Soviet grip on Eastern and central Europe, divided Europe for nearly fifty years. Communist governments controlled the countries along the Soviet Union's western border. The only exception was Finland, which remained neutral.

READING THE MAP: Is the division of Europe between NATO, Communist, and neutral countries about equal? Does the map of Berlin portray Soviet rule as monolithic?

CONNECTIONS: When was NATO founded and what is its purpose? How did the postwar division of Europe compare with the wartime alliances?

www.bedfordstmartins.com/tap   SEE THE ONLINE STUDY GUIDE for more help in analyzing this map.

ment would eventually end in "either the breakup or the gradual mellowing of Soviet power." This message reached a larger audience when, as "Mr. X," Kennan published an article in *Foreign Affairs* magazine in July 1947. His analysis did not so much change policy, already moving in that direction, as it marked a turning point in the development of the cold war, providing a powerful argu-

ment and intellectual framework for using U.S. power to check the spread of Soviet influence. Kennan later displayed dismay at the use of his ideas to justify what he considered an indiscriminate American response wherever communism seemed likely to succeed.

Not all public figures accepted the toughening line. Three Senate Democrats criticized Churchill's

The Emerging Cold War

Although antagonism between the Soviet Union and the West stretched back to the Russian Revolution of 1917, the United States, the Soviet Union, Britain, and other powers had cooperated to win World War II and managed to reach compromises at the Yalta and Potsdam summits in 1945. Early in 1946, however, officials in both the Soviet Union and the West publicly expressed distrust and attributed hostile motivations to each other. Within the United States, disagreement developed about how to deal with the Soviet Union.

DOCUMENT 1. Joseph Stalin Addresses an Election Rally in Moscow, February 9, 1946

At an election rally in early 1946 ("election" in name only since there was just one Communist Party candidate for each position), Premier Joseph Stalin called on the Soviet people to support his program for economic development and postwar recovery. Although Stalin did not address cold war issues, leaders in the West viewed his comments about communism and capitalism, as well as his boasts about the strength of the Red Army, as a threat to peace.

It would be incorrect to think that the [Second World] war arose accidentally or as the result of the fault of some of the statesmen. Although these faults did exist, the war arose in reality as the inevitable result of the development of the world economic and political forces on the basis of monopoly capitalism.

Our Marxists declare that the capitalist system of world economy conceals elements of crisis and war, that the development of world capitalism does not follow a steady and even course forward, but proceeds through crises and catastrophes. The uneven development of the capitalist countries leads in time to sharp disturbances in their relations and the group of countries which consider themselves inadequately provided with raw materials and export markets try usually to change this situation and to change the position in their favor by means of armed force. As a result of these factors, the capitalist world is split into two hostile camps and war follows. . . .

Now victory [in World War II] means, first of all, that our Soviet social system has won, that the Soviet social system has successfully stood the test in the fire of war and has proved its complete vitality. . . .

Now we can say that the war has refuted all the assertions of the foreign press as without foundation. The war has shown that the Soviet social system is a truly popular system, issued from the depths of the people and enjoying its mighty support. . . . The Soviet social system has proved to be more capable of life and more stable than a non-Soviet social system [and] is a better form of organization of society than any non-Soviet social system. . . .

Our victory implies that it was the Soviet armed forces that won. . . . The Red Army heroically withstood all the adversities of the war, routed completely the armies of our enemies and emerged victoriously from the war. This is recognized by everybody—friend and foe.

Now a few words on the plans for the work of the Communist party in the near future. . . . The fundamental task of the new Five-Year Plan consists in restoring the areas of the country which have suffered, restoring the prewar level in industry and agriculture, and then exceeding this level.

Apart from the fact that in the very near future the rationing system will be abolished, special attention will be focused on expanding the production of goods for mass consumption, on raising the standard of life of the working people by consistent and systematic reduction of the costs of all goods, and on wide scale construction of all kinds of scientific research institutes to enable science to develop its forces. I have no doubt that if we render the necessary assistance to our scientists they will be able not only to overtake but also in the very near future to surpass the achievements of science outside the boundaries of our country. As far as plans for a longer period are concerned, the party intends to organize a new mighty upsurge of national economy, which will enable us to increase the level of our production. [Stalin then announced goals for production of key materials.] Only under such conditions will our country be insured against any eventuality.

SOURCE: Excerpts from Joseph Stalin, *Vital Speeches of the Day,* February 9 (1946). Reprinted with permission.

DOCUMENT 2. Winston Churchill Delivers His "Iron Curtain" Speech at Westminster College, in Fulton, Missouri, March 5, 1946

Winston Churchill, former prime minister of Britain, stated that he spoke for himself alone, but President Harry Truman's presence on the platform at Westminster College suggested his approval of Churchill's assessment of Soviet actions. After reading Churchill's words, Stalin justified Soviet action in Eastern Europe as the means to "ensure its security," drew parallels between Hitler and Churchill, and called Churchill's words "a call to war with the Soviet Union."

The United States stands at this time at the pinnacle of world power. It is a solemn moment for the American democracy. With primacy in power is also joined an awe-inspiring accountability to the future. [Churchill spoke of the need to support the United Nations.]

It would nevertheless be wrong and imprudent to intrust the secret knowledge or experience of the atomic bomb, which the United States, Great Britain and Canada now share, to the world organization, while it is still in its infancy. It would be criminal madness to cast it adrift in this still agitated and ununited world. No one in any country has slept less well . . . because this knowledge and the method and the raw materials to apply it are at present largely retained in American hands. I do not believe we should all have slept so soundly had the positions been reversed and some Communist or neo-Fascist state monopolized, for the time being, these dread agencies. The fear of them alone might easily have been used to enforce totalitarian systems upon the free democratic world. . . . God has willed that this shall not be, and we have at least a breathing space before this period has to be encountered, and even then, if no effort is spared, we should still possess so formidable superiority as to impose effective deterrents upon its employment or threat of employment by others. . . .

A shadow has fallen upon the scenes so lately lighted by the Allied victory. Nobody knows what Soviet Russia and its Communist international organization intends to do in the immediate future, or what are the limits, if any, to their expansive and proselytizing tendencies. I have a strong admiration and regard for the valiant Russian people and for my wartime comrade, Marshal Stalin. . . . We understand the Russians need to be secure on her western frontiers

from all renewal of German aggression. . . . It is my duty, however, to place before you certain facts. . . .

From Stettin in the Baltic to Trieste in the Adriatic, an iron curtain has descended across the Continent. Behind that line lie all the capitals of the ancient states of central and eastern Europe. Warsaw, Berlin, Prague, Vienna, Budapest, Belgrade, Bucharest and Sofia, all these famous cities and the populations around them lie in the Soviet sphere and all are subject in one form or another, not only to Soviet influence but to a very high and increasing measure of control from Moscow. . . . The Communist parties, which were very small in all these eastern states of Europe, have been raised to preeminence and power far beyond their numbers and are seeking everywhere to obtain totalitarian control. Police governments are prevailing in nearly every case, and so far, except in Czechoslovakia, there is no true democracy. . . .

In front of the iron curtain which lies across Europe are other causes for anxiety. . . . In a great number of countries, far from the Russian frontiers and throughout the world, Communist fifth columns are established and work in complete unity and absolute obedience to the directions they receive from the Communist center.

I do not believe that Soviet Russia desires war. What they desire is the fruits of war and the indefinite expansion of their power and doctrines. . . . Our difficulties and dangers will not be removed by closing our eyes to them. They will not be removed by mere waiting to see what happens; nor will they be relieved by a policy of appeasement. . . . From what I have seen of our Russian friends and allies during the war, I am convinced that there is nothing they admire so much as strength, and there is nothing for which they have less respect than for military weakness.

SOURCE: Excerpts from Winston Churchill, *Vital Speeches of the Day,* March 5 (1946). Reprinted with permission.

DOCUMENT 3. Henry A. Wallace Addresses an Election Rally at Madison Square Garden, New York, September 12, 1946

Throughout 1946, Henry A. Wallace, Franklin D. Roosevelt's vice president from 1941 to 1945, and Harry S. Truman's secretary of commerce, urged (Continued) *the president to take a more conciliatory approach toward the Soviet Union, a position reflected in a speech Wallace gave to a rally of leftist and other liberal groups in New York City. Compared with the more pro-Soviet ones given that night, Wallace's speech was moderate and drew criticism from the U.S. Communist Party's newspaper. Nevertheless, Wallace's words in the context in which he delivered them seemed to the president to undermine his foreign policy. One week later, Truman asked for Wallace's resignation.*

Tonight I want to talk about peace—and how to get peace. Never have the common people of all lands so longed for peace. Yet, never in a time of comparative peace have they feared war so much. . . .

During the past year or so, the significance of peace has been increased immeasurably by the atomic bomb, guided missiles and airplanes which soon will travel as fast as sound. . . . We cannot rest in the assurance that we invented the atom bomb—and therefore that this agent of destruction will work best for us. He who trusts in the atom bomb will sooner or later perish by the atom bomb—or something worse. . . .

To prevent war and insure our survival in a stable world, it is essential that we look abroad through our own American eyes and not through the eyes of either the British Foreign Office or a pro-British or anti-Russian press. . . . We must not let British balance-of-power manipulations determine whether and when the United States gets into war. . . .

To achieve lasting peace, we must study in detail just how the Russian character was formed—by invasions of Tartars, Mongols, Germans, Poles, Swedes, and French; by the czarist rule based on ignorance, fear and force; by the intervention of the British, French and Americans in Russian affairs from 1919 to 1921; by the geography of the huge Russian land mass situated strategically between Europe and Asia; and by the vitality derived from the rich Russian soil and the strenuous Russian climate. Add to all this the tremendous emotional power which Marxism and Leninism gives to the Russian leaders—and then we can realize that we are reckoning with a force which cannot be handled successfully by a "Get tough with Russia" policy. "Getting tough" never bought anything real and lasting—whether for schoolyard bullies or businessmen or world powers. The tougher we get, the tougher the Russians will get. . . .

We most earnestly want peace with Russia—but we want to be met half way. We want cooperation. And I believe that we can get cooperation once Russia understands that our primary objective is neither saving the British Empire nor purchasing oil in the Near East with the lives of American soldiers. . . .

On our part we should recognize that we have no more business in the *political* affairs of Eastern

iron curtain speech as threatening to "cut the throat of the Big Three, without which the war could not have been won and without which the peace cannot be saved." But administration officials promoting a more conciliatory policy found themselves out of work. In an election campaign speech in September 1946, Secretary of Commerce Henry A. Wallace, Truman's predecessor as vice president, urged greater understanding of the Soviets' concerns about their nation's security, insisting that "we have no more business in the *political* affairs of Eastern Europe than Russia has in the *political* affairs of Latin America." (See "Documenting the American Promise," above.) State Department officials were furious. When Wallace refused to be muzzled on foreign policy topics, Truman fired him.

The Truman Doctrine and the Marshall Plan

In 1947, the United States moved from tough words to action, implementing the doctrine of containment that would guide foreign policy for the next four decades. It was not an easy transition; despite public approval of a verbal hard line, Americans wanted to keep their soldiers and tax dollars at home. In addition to selling containment to the public, Truman had to gain the support of a Republican-controlled Congress, which contained a forceful bloc, led by Ohio senator Robert A. Taft, opposed to a strong U.S. presence in Europe.

Crises in two Mediterranean countries triggered the implementation of containment. In

Europe than Russia has in the *political* affairs of Latin America, Western Europe and the United States. . . . The Russians have no more business in stirring up native communists to political activity in Western Europe, Latin America and the United States than we have in interfering in the politics of Eastern Europe and Russia. We know what Russia is up to in Eastern Europe, for example, and Russia knows what we are up to. We cannot permit the door to be closed against our trade in Eastern Europe any more than we can in China. But at the same time we have to recognize that the Balkans are closer to Russia than to us—and that Russia cannot permit either England or the United States to dominate the politics of that area. . . .

Russian ideas of social-economic justice are going to govern nearly a third of the world. Our ideas of free enterprise democracy will govern much of the rest. The two ideas will endeavor to prove which can deliver the most satisfaction to the common man in their respective areas of political dominance. But by mutual agreement, this competition should be put on a friendly basis and the Russians should stop conniving against us in certain areas of the world just as we should stop scheming against them in other parts of the world. . . . Under friendly peaceful competition the Russian world and the American world will gradually become more alike. The Russians will be forced to grant more and more of the personal freedoms; and we shall become more and more absorbed with the problems of social-economic justice.

SOURCE: Excerpts from Henry A. Wallace, *Vital Speeches of the Day*, September 12 (1946). Reprinted with permission.

QUESTIONS FOR ANALYSIS AND DEBATE

1. What lessons do these three leaders draw from World War II? What do they see as the most critical steps to preventing another war?

2. How do these three men describe the political and economic system of the Soviet Union? What differences do they see between the systems of the Soviet Union on the one hand and the United States and Western Europe on the other? How do they differ in their predictions about these systems in the future?

3. What motives do these three men ascribe to Soviet actions? How do Churchill and Wallace differ in their proposals for the Western response to the Soviet Union?

4. Which leader do you think was most optimistic about the prospects for good relationships between Russia and the West? Which was most correct? Why?

February 1947, Britain informed the United States that its crippled economy could no longer sustain military assistance to Greece and Turkey. Turkey was trying to resist Soviet pressures, and the monarchist government in Greece faced a challenge from internal leftists. Truman promptly decided to ask Congress for authority to send military and economic missions, along with $400 million in aid, to the two countries. At a private meeting that Truman called with congressional leaders, Undersecretary of State Acheson painted the issue in catastrophic terms, predicting that if Greece and Turkey fell, communism would soon consume three-fourths of the planet. After a stunned silence, Michigan senator Arthur Vandenberg, the Republican foreign policy leader and a recent convert from isolationism, warned that to get approval Truman would have to "scare hell out of the country."

In 1947, the United States moved from tough words to action, implementing the doctrine of containment that would guide foreign policy for the next four decades.

Truman did just that. To Congress, he presented what would later be called the domino theory, warning that if Greece fell to the rebels, "confusion and disorder might well spread throughout the entire Middle East . . . and would have a profound

THE MARSHALL PLAN
*World War II not only devastated European nations'
economies, but also deprived them of raw materials
and profits that they had formerly obtained from
colonies in South and Southeast Asia; in addition,
Soviet control of Eastern Europe closed that former
avenue of trade. Consequently, Marshall Plan aid
was critical in enabling European countries to purchase the raw materials, capital goods, and technology required to rebuild their economies. While economic stabilization stood at the center of Marshall
Plan goals, the plan also had a human side, expressed by the joy on the face of this Austrian boy
who has just received a new pair of shoes from Red
Cross volunteers.*
American Red Cross.

Greece and Turkey did not entail formal acceptance
of the Truman Doctrine. Yet the assumption that
American security depended on rescuing any anti-
Communist government from internal rebels or outside pressure became the cornerstone of U.S. foreign policy from 1947 until the end of the 1980s.

Aid to Greece and Turkey was a prelude to a
much larger program for Europe. In May 1947, Dean
Acheson described a war-ravaged Western Europe,
with "factories destroyed, fields impoverished,
transportation systems wrecked, populations scattered and on the borderline of starvation." American citizens were sending generous amounts of private aid, but Europe needed large-scale assistance.
It was "a matter of national self-interest," Acheson
argued, for the United States to provide aid. Only
economic recovery could halt the growth of socialist and Communist parties in France and Italy and
confine Soviet influence to Eastern Europe.

In March 1948, Congress approved the European Recovery Program—more commonly known
as the Marshall Plan, after retired general George C.
Marshall, then serving as secretary of state—and
over the next five years the United States spent $13
billion to restore the economies of Western Europe.
The Marshall Plan was also good business for the
United States, because the European nations spent
most of the dollars to buy American products
carried on American ships. Europe's economic
recovery expanded the realm of raw materials, markets, and investment opportunities available to
American capitalists. And the Truman administration could point to another victory for containment,
since every Western European government
remained non-Communist.

While Congress debated the Marshall Plan, in
February 1948 the Soviets staged a brutal coup
against the elected government of Czechoslovakia
and installed a Commu-
nist regime. Next, Soviet
leaders threatened West-
ern access to Berlin. The
former capital of Ger-
many lay within Soviet-
controlled East Ger-
many, but all four Allies
jointly occupied Berlin,
dividing it into separate
administrative units. As
the Western Allies
moved to organize West
Germany as a separate

Berlin Divided, 1948

effect upon . . . Europe." Failure to step in, he said,
"may endanger the peace of the world—and shall
surely endanger the welfare of the nation."

"I told my wife to dust off my uniform" was
one veteran's response to Truman's words. The
president's crisis rhetoric, along with its staggering
global implications, evoked dismay from Kennan
himself. According to what came to be called the
Truman Doctrine, it was not just Soviet military
power that must be resisted: The United States must
"support free peoples who are resisting attempted
subjugation by armed minorities or by outside pressures." Congressional authorization of aid for

nation, the Soviets retaliated by blocking the roads and rail lines that connected West Germany to the Western-held sections of Berlin, cutting off food, fuel, and other essentials to two million inhabitants.

"We stay in Berlin, period," Truman insisted. Yet he wanted to avoid an armed confrontation with Soviet troops. So for fifteen months, U.S. and British pilots, landing a plane every eight minutes, airlifted 2.3 million tons of goods to sustain the West Berliners. Stalin hesitated to shoot down these cargo planes, and in 1949 he lifted the blockade. The major powers then formally divided the city into East Berlin, under Soviet control, and West Berlin, which became part of West Germany. For many Americans, the Berlin airlift confirmed the wisdom of containment: When challenged, the Russians backed down, as Kennan had predicted they would.

The policy of containment reflected the dashed hopes that the major powers would cooperate through the United Nations. Instead, the new international organization served more as a propaganda body for its members. It provided a mecha-nism for discussion of disputes, and perhaps its moral authority and ability to claim world attention exercised restraints on nations. But because the United Nations could not act without unanimity on its Security Council, the Soviet-American conflict prevented effective action.

Creating a National Security State

The new policy of containment quickly acquired a military capacity to back it up. During the Truman years, the United States fashioned a five-pronged defense strategy: (1) development of atomic weapons, (2) strengthening of traditional military power, (3) military alliances with other nations, (4) military and economic aid to friendly nations, and (5) an espionage network and secret means to subvert Communist expansion.

In September 1949, the United States lost its nuclear monopoly when officials confirmed that the Soviets had detonated an atomic bomb. Even though U.S. officials had known that Soviet scientists were

THE BERLIN AIRLIFT
These German children standing on the rubble of war wave to planes carrying food and other necessities to Berlin during the Soviet blockade in 1948. Truman and his advisers were "prepared to use any means that may be necessary to stay in Berlin." To reduce the risk of war, the president decided on an airlift rather than attempting to send ground convoys through Soviet lines.
Corbis-Bettmann.

working on an A-bomb, its success came years ahead of predictions and shocked the American public. Within months, Truman approved development of an even deadlier weapon: the hydrogen bomb.

Intense debate surrounded the decision to develop a weapon based on a thermonuclear explosion equivalent to five hundred atomic bombs. Some prominent scientists and government officials who had supported the A-bomb opposed the "super bomb" on moral and practical grounds, but Truman gave it the green light. Passing its first test explosion in November 1952, a thermonuclear device left a mile-long crater in the Pacific and produced a mushroom cloud twenty-five miles high. The U.S. thermonuclear advantage was brief. By 1954, the Americans had the capability to deliver an H-bomb, but in November 1955 the Soviets exploded their own super bomb.

From the 1950s through the 1980s, the policy of deterrence formed the basis of American nuclear strategy. To deter the Soviet Union from attacking, the United States felt that it had to maintain a more powerful nuclear force than the Soviets. Because the Russians pursued a similar policy, the superpowers became locked in an ever-escalating race for nuclear dominance. Albert Einstein, whose mathematical discoveries had laid the foundations for nuclear weapons, commented grimly on the enormous destructive force now possessed by the superpowers. The war that came after World War III, he said, would be fought with stones.

The United States also beefed up its conventional military power to deter Soviet threats that might not warrant nuclear retaliation. To streamline defense planning, Congress passed the National Security Act in 1947, uniting the military branches under a single secretary of defense and creating the National Security Council (NSC) to advise the president. As the Berlin crisis simmered in 1948, Congress stepped up appropriations for the air force and enacted a peacetime draft. Urged on by military leaders, Congress also granted permanent status to the women's military branches, thereby allowing women to volunteer. With about 1.5 million men and women in uniform in 1950, the military strength of the United States had quadrupled since the 1930s.

Collective security, the third prong of postwar military strategy and the sharpest break from America's past, also developed during the Berlin showdown. In June 1948, the Senate overwhelm-ingly approved the general principle of regional military alliances. One year later, the United States joined Canada and Western European nations in its first peacetime military alliance, the North Atlantic Treaty Organization (NATO), designed to counter the Soviet threat to Western Europe (see Map 25.1). For the first time in its history, the United States pledged to go to war should one of its allies be attacked.

The fourth element of defense strategy involved foreign aid programs to strengthen friendly countries, such as the aid to Greece and Turkey in 1947. A much larger program was the $13 billion Marshall Plan that helped rebuild Western European economies. In addition, in 1949, Congress approved $1 billion of military aid to its NATO allies and began economic assistance to nations in other parts of the world.

Short of war, the United States could not stop the descent of the iron curtain, but it aggressively and successfully promoted economic recovery and a military shield for the rest of Europe.

The fifth element of the national security state was development of the government's espionage capacities and the means to deter communism through secret activities. The National Security Act of 1947 created the Central Intelligence Agency (CIA) to gather information considered necessary to the national defense and to perform any "functions and duties related to intelligence affecting the national security" that the NSC might authorize. In 1953, the United States spent $20 million on a single intelligence project in Vienna, where six hundred tape machines recorded intercepted Soviet messages and fifty CIA employees translated them. After Truman left office, CIA agents conducted secret operations that toppled legitimate foreign governments and violated the rights of U.S. citizens. In many respects, the CIA was virtually unaccountable to Congress or the public.

By 1950, the United States had abandoned age-old tenets of foreign policy. Isolationism and neutrality were replaced with not only regional military alliances but also economic and military efforts to control events far beyond U.S. borders. Short of war, the United States could not stop the descent of the iron curtain, but it aggressively and successfully promoted economic recovery and a military shield for the rest of Europe.

Superpower Rivalry around the Globe

Europe was not the only place where the Truman administration sought to implement containment. In Africa, Asia, and the Middle East, World War II furthered a tide of national liberation movements against war-weakened imperial powers. Between 1945 and 1960, forty countries, together containing more than a quarter of the world's people, won their independence. These nations came to be referred to collectively, along with Latin America, as the *third world*, a term denoting countries outside the Western (first world) and Soviet (second world) orbits that had not yet developed industrial economies.

Like Woodrow Wilson during World War I, Roosevelt and Truman promoted the ideal of self-determination: The United States granted independence to its own dominion, the Philippines, in 1946; applauded the British withdrawal from India; and encouraged France to relinquish its empire in Indochina. At the same time, both the United States and the Soviet Union cultivated governments in emerging nations that were friendly to their own interests and institutions.

Leaders of many liberation movements, impressed with the Russian Revolution and the rapid economic growth it had spawned, adopted socialist or Communist ideas, although they had few or no formal ties with the Soviet Union. But American leaders insisted on viewing these movements as a threatening extension of Soviet power and increasingly demanded that new nations take sides in the cold war, forgetting the history of neutrality in their

THE CHINESE COMMUNIST MOVEMENT
The leaders of the young Communist movement in China in 1937 exude confidence as they stand in a doorway to one of the cave dwellings where they lived and worked in Yan'an, in Northwest China. Bo Gu (right) died in a plane crash in 1946, but Zhou Enlai (left) and Mao Zedong (center) led the revolutionary forces to victory and the establishment of the People's Republic of China in 1949.
Peabody Museum, Harvard University.

own diplomatic tradition. Seeking to hold communism at bay by fostering economic development and political stability, in 1949 the Truman administration initiated the Point IV Program, providing technical aid to developing nations. Reflecting the Truman administration's cold war priorities, the modest amounts of such aid contrasted sharply with the huge sums being provided to Europe.

In Asia, civil war raged in China, where the Communists, led by Mao Zedong (Mao Tse-tung), fought the official Nationalist government under Chiang Kai-shek. While the Communists gained support among the peasants for their valiant stand against the Japanese and their land reforms, Chiang's corrupt government and poor management of the war against Japan alienated much of the population. The so-called China bloc, a lobby that included Republican members of Congress and religious groups and individuals with missionary ties to China, pressured the Truman administration not to lose that nation to the Communists. Failing in its effort to promote negotiations between Chiang and Mao, the United States provided almost $3 billion in aid to the Nationalists after the war. Yet Truman and his advisers believed that to divert further resources from Europe to China would be unwise and futile, given the ineptness of Chiang's government.

In October 1949, Mao established the People's Republic of China (PRC), and the Nationalists fled to the island of Taiwan. Some administration officials urged accommodation with Communist China, but the outbreak of war in Korea in June 1950 foreclosed that option. The United States refused to recognize the existence of the PRC, blocked its admission to the United Nations, and sent aid to the Nationalist government in Taiwan. Nothing less than a massive U.S. military commitment could have stopped the Chinese Communists, but some Republicans cried that Truman and "the pro-Communists in the State Department" had "lost" China. Thus, China became a political albatross for the Democrats, who resolved never again to be in a position where they could be accused of being soft on communism.

As it became clear that China would not be a stable capitalist ally in Asia, the administration reconsidered its plans for postwar Japan. Initially, the U.S. military occupation had aimed to prevent Japan from threatening peace again by reforming its government, purging Japanese militarists from official positions, and decentralizing its economy. But by 1948, U.S. policy had shifted to concentrate on economic recovery. The new goals were to help Japan rapidly reindustrialize and secure access to markets and natural resources in Asia. After a sluggish start, the Japanese economy flourished. American soldiers remained on military bases in Japan, but the official occupation ended when the two nations signed a peace treaty and a mutual security pact in September 1951. Like West Germany, Japan now sat squarely within the American orbit, ready to serve as an economic hub in a vital area.

The one part of the world where cold war considerations did not control American policy was Palestine. In 1943, then senator Harry Truman spoke passionately about Nazi Germany's systematic extermination of Jews, asserting, "This is not a Jewish problem, it is an American problem—and we must . . . face it squarely and honorably." As president, he had the opportunity to make good on his words. Jews had been migrating to Palestine since the nineteenth century, and one result was tension and hostilities between Palestinian Arabs and Jews. After World War II, as hundreds of thousands of European Jews sought refuge in Palestine, fighting devolved into brutal terrorism on both sides. Most of Truman's foreign policy experts saw American-Arab friendship as a critical barrier against Soviet influence in the Middle East and a means to secure U.S. access to Arabian oil. Uncharacteristically defying his advisers, the president responded instead to pressure exerted by Jewish organizations, his moral commitment to Holocaust survivors, and his interest in the American Jewish vote for the 1948 elections. When Jews in Palestine declared the independent state of Israel in May 1948, Truman quickly recognized the new country and made the defense of Israel the cornerstone of U.S. policy in the Middle East. Yet that region remained in turmoil for decades to come.

UN Partition Plan, 1947

- Proposed Jewish state
- Proposed Arab state
- Israel after the War of Independence, 1948

The Partition of Palestine and the Creation of Israel, 1947–1948

SURVIVORS OF THE HOLOCAUST IN ISRAEL *These refugees from Nazi persecution are shown doing laundry at a center for new immigrants in Palestine in June 1946. The desperation of thousands of Jews who defied immigration restrictions to get to what they hoped would be a Jewish homeland in Palestine contributed to President Truman's decision to recognize Israel as an independent state in May 1948. Isaac Halevi Herzog, the chief rabbi of Israel, later told Truman, "God put you in your mother's womb so you would be the instrument to bring the rebirth of Israel after two thousand years."* Wide World Photos, Inc.

Truman and the Fair Deal at Home

Referring to the Civil War general who coined the phrase "War is hell," Truman said in December 1945, "Sherman was wrong. I'm telling you I find peace is hell." Challenged by thorny problems abroad, Truman also faced shortages, strikes, inflation, and other problems attending the reconversion of the economy to peacetime production. At the same time, he tried to expand New Deal reform, most notably into the areas of civil rights, housing, education, and health care. Yet obstacles abounded to Truman's domestic agenda, which came to be known as the Fair Deal, and Truman had to settle for consolidation of programs that were already in place.

Reconversion and the Postwar Economic Boom

Despite deprivations and inconveniences during World War II, most Americans had enjoyed a standard of living during wartime that was higher than ever before. Economic experts as well as ordinary citizens worried about both sustaining that standard and providing jobs for millions of returning soldiers. Truman wasted no time unveiling his plan, asking Congress to enact a twenty-one-point program of economic controls and social and economic reforms. "Not even President Roosevelt ever asked for as much at one sitting," exploded Republican leader Joseph W. Martin Jr.

Congress approved only one of Truman's key proposals—full-employment legislation—and even that was watered down. The Employment Act of 1946 invested the federal government with responsibility "to promote maximum employment, production, and purchasing power," thereby formalizing what had been implicit in Roosevelt's actions to counter the depression—government's responsibility for maintaining a healthy economy. The law created a Council of Economic Advisers to assist the president in economic planning, but it authorized no new powers to translate the government's obligation into effective action.

Inflation turned out to be the most severe problem in the early postwar years. Unable to buy civilian goods during the war, in 1945 consumers had

$30 billion of savings that they now itched to spend. But shortages of meat, automobiles, housing, and a host of other items persisted. Some six million people wanted new cars in 1946, but auto manufacturers produced fewer than three million. Housing was so scarce that some returning veterans lived in basements and garages. Until industry could convert fully to civilian production and make more goods available, consumer demand could only drive up prices. The consumer price index—an official measurement of the rate of inflation—shot up by 18 percent in 1946.

Labor relations were another thorn in Truman's side. Organized labor survived the war stronger than ever, its 14.5 million adherents making up 35 percent of the civilian workforce. Yet union members feared erosion of wartime gains. With wages frozen during the war, the rising incomes enjoyed by working-class families had come largely from the availability of new, higher-paying jobs and the chance to work longer hours than before. The end of overtime meant a 30 percent cut in take-home pay for most workers. Women who had flocked into wartime jobs also saw their earnings decline; most who remained in the workforce had to settle for relatively low-paying jobs in light industry or the service sector. (See Figure 25.1, below, and "Historical Question," page 960.)

Most unions paid scant attention to the problems of women workers as they fought to preserve labor's wartime gains. More strikes took place in 1946 than at any other time in U.S. history, with five million workers disrupting production in virtually every major industry (Table 25.1). Workers saw corporate owners and executives profiting at their expense. Shortly before his union took a strike vote, a former marine read about a lavish party given by a company executive. He and his fellow carpoolers calculated that the party had cost more than their total yearly earnings in the steel mill. The veteran remembered, "That sort of stuff made us realize, hell, we *had* to bite the bullet. . . . The bosses sure didn't give a damn for us."

Although most Americans approved of unions in principle, they became fed up with labor stoppages, blamed unions for rising prices and shortages of consumer goods, and called for more government restrictions on organized labor. Truman shared the public's exasperation, although, in a letter to his mother in October 1945, he spread the

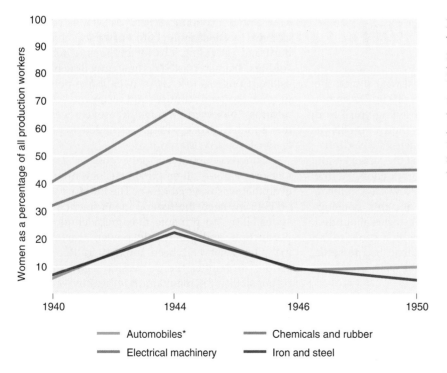

FIGURE 25.1
Women Workers in Selected Industries, 1940–1950
Women demolished the idea that some jobs were "men's work" during World War II, but they failed to maintain their gains in the manufacturing sector after the war.

*During World War II, this industry did not produce cars, but rather military transportation such as jeeps, tanks, aircraft, etc.

TABLE 25.1

WORK STOPPAGES IN THE UNITED STATES, 1936–1947

Year	Number	Average Length of Stoppage (days)	Workers Involved (in thousands)
1936	2,172	23.3	789
1937	4,740	20.3	1,860
1938	2,772	23.6	688
1939	2,613	23.4	1,170
1940	2,508	20.9	577
1941	4,288	18.3	2,360
1942	2,968	11.7	840
1943	3,752	5.0	1,980
1944	4,956	5.6	2,120
1945	4,750	9.9	3,470
1946	4,985	24.2	4,600
1947	3,693	25.6	2,170

Source: U.S. Department of Labor, *Handbook of Labor Statistics*, 1974.

blame around: "The Congress [is] balking, labor has gone crazy, and management isn't far from insane in selfishness." In May 1946, after coal miners rejected government recommendations for a settlement and their strike threatened the steel, auto, and railroad industries as well, Truman placed the mines under federal control. When the massive wave of strikes subsided at the end of 1946, workers had won wage increases of about 20 percent, but the loss of overtime along with rising prices left their purchasing power only slightly higher than in 1942.

Most unions paid scant attention to the problems of women workers as they fought to preserve labor's wartime gains. More strikes took place in 1946 than at any other time in U.S. history.

By 1947, the nation had survived the strains of reconversion and avoided a postwar depression. Wartime profits enabled businesses to invest in new plants and equipment. Consumers used their billions of dollars in wartime savings to buy the houses, cars, and appliances that had lain beyond their reach during the depression and war. Both defense spending and the $38 billion in grants and loans that enabled war-torn countries to purchase American goods also stimulated the economy. A soaring birthrate, 25 percent higher in 1949 than in 1940, further sustained consumer demand. The United States entered into a remarkable economic boom that lasted through the 1960s and flooded the American people with new consumer goods. (See Chapter 26.)

The nation's gratitude to its returning warriors provided yet another boost to the economy. Under the Servicemen's Readjustment Act (the GI Bill), passed in 1944, 16 million veterans could receive funds for job training and education; claim unemployment compensation while they looked for jobs; and take out low-interest loans to purchase homes, farms, and small businesses. By 1948, some 1.3 million veterans had bought houses with government loans, and by 1956 veterans had used $14.5 million in educational benefits. Helping 2.2 million ex-soldiers attend college, the subsidies sparked a boom in higher education.

As a form of affirmative action program for veterans, the GI Bill inadvertently disadvantaged women, who filled but a tiny portion of military slots during the war. For example, although the total number of women attending college increased, their share of degrees dropped below the prewar level. In employment, the vast majority of women could not claim the preference in hiring that veterans enjoyed from private and public employers alike. As

What Happened to Rosie the Riveter?

ALTHOUGH STUDIES HAVE BEEN MADE of the postwar lives of World War II soldiers, we know much less about another group of veterans—the women who helped fight the war on the domestic front, and who were recognized in the popular song, "Rosie the Riveter." Statistics show that women's employment fell by more than two million between 1945 and 1947. But gross statistics do not reveal which women left the labor force and why, and they obscure the experiences of women who continued to work but in different jobs.

We do know what public officials and business and labor leaders expected of women who had taken up men's work during the war. With the shadow of the depression still hovering, Americans doubted that the economy could accommodate the six million new women workers along with millions of returning veterans once wartime production had ceased. A nearly universal response to anxieties about unemployment pushed a big part of the responsibility onto women: Their wartime duty to produce the goods needed for victory was replaced with their postwar obligation to withdraw from the labor force.

The message that they should quit their jobs "for the sake of their homes as well as the labor situation" overwhelmed women. The company newspaper at Kaiser shipyards in the Pacific Northwest proclaimed in May 1945, "The Kitchen—Women's Big Post-War Goal." Putting words into the mouths of Kaiser's female employees, the article asserted, "Brothers, the tin hat and welder's torch will be yours! . . . The thing we want to do is take off these unfeminine garments and button ourselves into something starched and pretty." A General Electric ad predicted that women would welcome a return to "their old housekeeping routine" because GE intended to transform housework with new appliances. Some experts connected married women's employment to their obligations to help their husbands readjust to civilian life. A psychiatrist warned that women's economic independence might "raise problems in the future," urging women to realize that "reunion means relinquishing [independence]—to some extent at any rate."

Other evidence suggests that many women did not have to be told to give up their wartime jobs. Skyrocketing marriage rates and birthrates from that period reveal the attraction of home and family life to people compelled to postpone marriage and childbearing. Thanks to the accumulation of wartime savings, veterans' benefits, and favorable opportunities for men in the postwar economy, many families found it possible to rely on a single earner.

The double burdens placed on married women who took wartime jobs suggest another reason for women's voluntary withdrawal from the workforce. The wartime scarcity of goods had made housekeeping much more difficult, especially for women who typically worked forty-eight hours a week with one day off. Shopping became a problem because stores often sold out of goods early in the day, and few shops kept evening or Sunday hours. Washing machines, refrigerators, vacuum cleaners, and other labor-saving appliances were not produced at all during the war. Child care centers accommodated only about 10 percent of the children of employed mothers. Employed women with families to care for were simply worn out.

Yet surveys reported that 75 percent of women in wartime jobs wanted—and usually needed—to keep working. As two women employed at a Ford plant in Memphis put it, "Women didn't stop eating when the war stopped." Those who struggled to remain in the workforce experienced the most wrenching changes. The vast majority were able to find jobs; in fact, women's workforce participation began growing again in 1947 and equaled the wartime peak by 1950. But women lost the traditionally male, higher-paying jobs in durable goods industries (such as iron and steel, automobile, and machinery production) and were pushed back into the lower-paying light manufacturing and service industries that had customarily welcomed them. In the words of one historian, "Rosie the Riveter had become a file clerk."

Statistics tell part of the story of this displacement. Women virtually disappeared from shipbuilding, and their share of jobs in the auto industry fell from 25 percent in 1944 to 10 percent in 1950. In the burgeoning Los Angeles aircraft industry, the proportion of women plunged from 40 percent at its wartime height to 12 percent in 1948, rising to

Sisters under the apron—Yesterday's war worker becomes today's housewife.

What's Become of Rosie the Riveter?

WOMEN'S POSTWAR FUTURE
This photograph headed an article in the New York Times Magazine *in June 1946. The article, written by the head of the Women's Bureau of the Department of Labor, discussed the needs of women workers, stressing their right to work and to equal pay, but also assumed that they would all but vanish from heavy manufacturing.* Ellen Kaiper.

just 25 percent in the 1950s. Even in light manufacturing, such as the electrical goods industry, where women had claimed one-third of the prewar jobs, women maintained their numbers but were bumped down to lower-paying work. During the war, women had narrowed the wage gap between men and women, but in 1950, women earned only 53 percent of what men did.

How women reacted to their displacement can be pieced together to some extent from what they were willing to say to reporters and oral history interviewers and what they wrote to government agencies and labor unions. "Women do not expect or want to hold jobs at the expense of returning soldiers," proclaimed a resolution passed by the Women's Trade Union League, expressing its members' overwhelming support for veterans' claims to jobs based on seniority awarded for the years of their wartime service. Tina Hill, a black worker at North American Aircraft in Los Angeles, said, "[Being laid off] didn't bother me much. I was just glad that the war was over . . . [and] my husband had a job." Nonetheless, after doing domestic work, she accepted readily when North American called her back: "Was I a happy soul!"

When management violated women's seniority rights by hiring nonveterans, some women protested bitterly. According to one automobile worker, "We have women laid off with seniority . . . and every day they hire in new men off the street. They hire men, they say, to do the heavy work. . . . During the war they didn't care what kind of work we did." When Ford laid off women with as many as twenty-seven years' seniority, 150 women picketed with signs that read, "The Hand That Rocks the Cradle Can Build Tractors, Too." A worker infuriated by her union's failure to protect women's seniority rights told a reporter, "We are making the bullets now, and we will give the [union executive] board members a blast that will blow them out of their shoes."

Protests from a minority of women workers could not save the jobs that the "Rosies" had held during the war. Despite women's often exemplary performance, most employers still saw women and men as different species fit for different roles and deserving of different rewards. Most labor unions paid lip service to representing all their members, but even the most progressive unions gave low priority to protecting women's seniority rights. In the absence of a feminist movement that could have given both visibility and credibility to their claims for equal treatment, most Rosie the Riveters resigned themselves to "women's work."

VETERANS GO TO COLLEGE
So many World War II veterans wanted to use their GI benefits for higher education that colleges were overwhelmed; many had to turn away students. These veterans, sprinting out of the building where they have just registered, express their joy at having been admitted to Indiana University in 1947.
Indiana University Photo Services.

wives and daughters of ex-servicemen, though, women did benefit indirectly from the GI subsidies, which helped almost one of every four Americans.

Despite the postwar economic surge, prosperity was not universal. The real gains came during the war, and while wages and salaries increased by 23 percent from 1945 to 1950, prices went up by 36.2 percent. A recession in 1949 that threw 7 percent of the labor force out of work abated only when the Korean War sparked economic recovery. Moreover, the one-third of all Americans who lived in poverty failed to receive any significant benefits from the return to peacetime production.

Black Protest and the Politics of Civil Rights

"I spent four years in the army to free a bunch of Frenchmen and Dutchmen," an African American corporal declared, "and I'm hanged if I'm going to let the Alabama version of the Germans kick me around when I get home." Black men and women constituted 16 percent of military personnel in World War II, well above their 10 percent presence in the general population. African American soldiers and civilians alike resolved that the return to peace would not be a return to the racial injustices of prewar America. Their political clout had grown with the migration of 2 million African Americans to northern and western cities, where they could vote and make a difference. Even in the South, the proportion of blacks who cast ballots in local and national elections inched up from 2 percent to 12 percent in the 1940s. Pursuing civil rights through the courts and Congress, the National Association for the Advancement of Colored People (NAACP) counted half a million members.

In the postwar years, individuals broke through the color barrier, achieving several "firsts" for African Americans. Jackie Robinson integrated major league baseball when he took over second base for the Brooklyn Dodgers in 1947, braving abuse from fans and players to win the Rookie of the Year Award. In 1950, Ralph J. Bunche won the Nobel Peace Prize for his contributions to the United Nations, and Gwendolyn Brooks earned the Pulitzer Prize for poetry. A vibrant black culture, including top musicians such as Louis Armstrong, Ella Fitzgerald, and Mahalia Jackson, appealed to audiences black and white.

African American soldiers and civilians alike resolved that the return to peace would not be a return to the racial injustices of prewar America.

Still, in most respects African Americans found that little had changed. Although a number of states and cities outside the South enacted laws regarding fair employment practices in the 1940s—even as the federal government ended its wartime antidiscrimination program—African Americans struggled to

JACKIE ROBINSON
John Roosevelt Robinson slides into home in a game against the Philadelphia Phillies in 1952. Before he became, in 1947, the first African American to play major league baseball, Robinson had excelled in track as well as baseball at UCLA and had been an army officer in World War II. Even his brilliant play for the Brooklyn Dodgers did not save him from fans' and players' racial taunts or exclusion from restaurants and hotels that catered to his white teammates. Having paved the way for other black players, Robinson competed until 1956.
The Michael Barson Collection/Past Perfect.

hold on to the gains they had made during the war. Federal housing programs for the poor and non-poor alike encouraged discrimination against blacks, and violence sometimes greeted those who tried to move into white areas. Postwar Detroit saw 120 incidents of arson, cross burnings, and physical attacks in neighborhoods undergoing racial transition. As African Americans migrated to northern and western cities, they found themselves crowded into what were rapidly becoming ghettos.

Things were worse in the South, where violence greeted blacks' attempts to assert their rights. White men with guns turned back Medgar Evers (who

would become a key civil rights leader in the 1960s) and four other veterans who were trying to vote in Mississippi. A mob lynched Isaac Nixon for voting in Georgia, and an all-white jury acquitted the men accused of his murder. Governors, U.S. senators, and other southern politicians routinely intimidated potential voters with threats of economic retaliation and violence.

"My very stomach turned over when I learned that Negro soldiers just back from overseas were being dumped out of army trucks in Mississippi and beaten," Truman recalled in his memoirs. He was shaken by the violence and under pressure to act by civil rights leaders and liberals. Wrestling with the Democrats' need for northern black and

SEGREGATION
Signs like this were a normal feature of life in the South from the late nineteenth century until the 1960s. State and local laws mandated segregation in every aspect of life, literally from the cradle to the grave. African Americans could not use white hospitals, cemeteries, schools, libraries, swimming pools, playgrounds, restrooms, or drinking fountains. They were relegated to balconies in movie theaters and kept apart from whites in all public meetings.
Martin Magner/Courtesy, Center for Creative Photography, The University of Arizona.

liberal votes as well as white southern votes, Truman acted more boldly on civil rights than had any previous president. In 1946, he created the Committee on Civil Rights, and in February 1948 he asked Congress to enact the committee's recommendations. The first president to address the NAACP, Truman announced that all Americans should have equal rights to housing, education, employment, and the ballot.

Yet, as was the case with much of his domestic program, the president failed to follow up aggressively on his bold words. In the throes of the 1948 election campaign and facing threats of civil disobedience by civil rights activists, Truman did issue an executive order to desegregate the armed services. But he allowed it to lie unimplemented until the need for military personnel during the Korean War forced the military's hand. Nor did he rally much popular support for racial justice. In 1949, nearly half of the respondents to a national survey opposed federal action against job discrimination.

More quietly, Truman's Justice Department aligned the administration with the NAACP by filing *amicus curiae* (friend of the court) briefs supporting legal challenges to discrimination. In 1948, the Supreme Court struck a blow at housing discrimination, ruling in *Shelley v. Kramer* that restrictive covenants used to keep blacks—and sometimes Jews—out of certain neighborhoods could not be enforced in the courts. Two years later, it ruled that a state university could not segregate black students (*McLaurin v. Oklahoma*) and that an inferior school set up to keep African Americans out of the University of Texas Law School violated their right to equal protection (*Sweatt v. Painter*).

The Fair Deal Flounders

Republicans capitalized on the public frustrations with economic reconversion in the 1946 congressional elections. Portraying Truman as a little man in a job that was way over his head, they accused his administration of "confusion, corruption, and communism" and jeered, "To Err Is Truman." Capturing Congress for the first time in fourteen years, Republicans looked eagerly to the 1948 presidential campaign. Many Republicans campaigned against New Deal "regimentation" and "radicalism" in 1946, and the Eightieth Congress made budget cuts in some reform programs and overrode Truman's veto of tax cuts favoring higher income groups.

The most severe attack fell on organized labor, when Congress passed the Taft-Hartley Act over Truman's veto in 1947. Called a "slave labor" law and "Tuff-Heartless" by unions, Taft-Hartley imposed restrictions on the right to strike and on organizing workers. States could now pass "right-to-work" laws banning the practice of requiring all workers to join a union once a majority had voted for it. The law also compelled union leaders to swear that they were not Communists and to make public annual financial reports. While maintaining the New Deal principle of government protection for collective bargaining, Taft-Hartley put the government more squarely between labor and management and between unions and individual workers.

As the 1948 elections approached, Thomas E. Dewey, the Republican nominee who had lost to Roosevelt in 1944, was sure that his time had come, and so was nearly everyone else. Truman faced not only a resurgent Republican Party but also two revolts from within his own party. On the left, Henry Wallace, who had been pushed out of the cabinet for his foreign policy views, led a new Progressive Party. On the right, South Carolina governor J. Strom Thurmond headed the States' Rights Party—the Dixiecrats—formed by southern Democrats who walked out of the 1948 Democratic Party convention when it passed a liberal civil rights plank.

Virtually alone in believing he could win, Truman crisscrossed the country by train, answering supporters' cries of "Give 'em hell, Harry." So bleak were Truman's prospects that the confident Dewey ran a low-key campaign and, on election night, the *Chicago Daily Tribune* printed its next day's issue with the headline DEWEY DEFEATS TRUMAN. But Truman took 303 electoral votes to Dewey's 189, as his party regained control of Congress (Map 25.2). In addition to reflecting popular support for his foreign policy, Truman's unexpected victory attested to his skills as a campaigner, the enduring popularity of New Deal reform, and the booming economy.

Yet the combination of prosperity and the Democrats' control of Congress did not result in enactment of Truman's Fair Deal. Congress made modest improvements in Social Security and raised the minimum wage, but its only significant reform initiative was in housing. The Housing Act of 1949 funded 350,000 units of government-constructed housing over the next fifteen years. Although it fell far short of actual need and many projects were cheaply built with high-rise designs that created poor environments for families with children, the legisla-

TRUMAN'S WHISTLE-STOP CAMPAIGN
Harry Truman rallies a crowd from his campaign train at a stop in Bridgeport, Pennsylvania, in October 1948. His campaign theme song, "I'm Just Wild about Harry," was borrowed, with the words slightly changed, from the 1921 musical **Shuffle Along.** *This was the last presidential election in which the pollsters predicted the wrong winner. They stopped taking polls in mid-October, after which many voters apparently changed their minds. One commentator praised the American citizenry, who "couldn't be ticketed by the polls, knew its own mind and had picked the rather unlikely but courageous figure of Truman to carry on its banner."*
Photo: Truman Library; Sheet music: Collection of Janice L. and David J. Frent.

www.bedfordstmartins.com/tap SEE THE ONLINE STUDY GUIDE for more help in analyzing this image.

tion represented a landmark commitment by the government to address the housing needs of the poor.

With southern Democrats often joining the Republicans on domestic issues, Congress rejected Truman's civil rights measures and proposals for a federal health care program, federal aid to educa-

tion, and a new agriculture program for small farmers and consumers. His efforts to revise immigration policy produced the McCarran-Walter Act of 1952, ending the outright ban on immigration and citizenship for Japanese and other Asians. But the law also authorized the government to bar

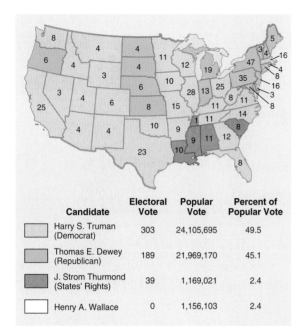

Candidate	Electoral Vote	Popular Vote	Percent of Popular Vote
Harry S. Truman (Democrat)	303	24,105,695	49.5
Thomas E. Dewey (Republican)	189	21,969,170	45.1
J. Strom Thurmond (States' Rights)	39	1,169,021	2.4
Henry A. Wallace	0	1,156,103	2.4

MAP 25.2
The Election of 1948

immigration of suspected Communists and homosexuals and, to Truman's distress, maintained the discriminatory quota system established in the 1920s.

Although Truman blamed Republicans, conservative Democrats, and interest groups such as the American Medical Association for defeating his Fair Deal, the causes of the domestic political stalemate were more complex. Truman chose to devote much more energy to foreign policy than to his domestic proposals. By late 1950, the Korean War embroiled Truman in controversy, diverted his attention from domestic affairs, and depleted his power as a legislative leader. And the anti-Communist crusade did much to discredit government reforms as well as the organizations and individuals who championed them.

The Domestic Chill: A Second Red Scare

The wave of anti-Communist hysteria that weakened left and liberal forces after the war was not new. Both "Red-baiting" (the attempt to discredit individuals or ideas by associating them with

Communists) and official retaliation against leftist critics of the government had flourished during the Red scare at the end of World War I. The second Red scare, however, was much more sweeping, more intense, and longer lasting. Born of partisan political maneuvering, collapse of the Soviet-American alliance, setbacks in U.S. foreign policy, and disclosures of Soviet espionage, the new "witch-hunt" brought personal distress to thousands of citizens and created a climate of fear, stifling expression that did not conform to mainstream beliefs.

The Politics of Anticommunism

Republicans attacked New Deal programs by equating them with communism, and they jumped at the opportunities presented by the cold war to discredit Democrats in similar ways. To Americans perplexed by the nation's inability to control events in Eastern Europe, China, and Korea, accusations of internal subversion offered simple explanations. As Wisconsin senator Joseph R. McCarthy, the nation's leading anti-Communist, charged, "The Communists within our borders have been more responsible for the success of Communism abroad than Soviet Russia."

Revelations of Soviet espionage and accusations made by former Communists furnished just enough credibility to such charges. In 1945, for example, the FBI found hundreds of secret government documents in the offices of a left-wing magazine, and in 1946 a Russian defector provided evidence of Soviet spying on atomic bomb research. A number of ex-Communists, including journalist Whittaker Chambers and Elizabeth Bentley, testified that they and others had provided secret documents to the Soviets. In 1950, Klaus Fuchs, a British physicist attached to the atomic bomb project, confessed that he was a spy. He implicated several Americans, including a New York couple, Ethel and Julius Rosenberg. The Rosenbergs pleaded innocent but were convicted of conspiracy to commit espionage and electrocuted in 1953.

To what extent did Soviet subversion and espionage threaten the United States? Although the U.S. Communist Party parroted the Soviet line on every issue, at the peak of the hysteria it counted only about twenty thousand members, some of them FBI agents. Records opened in the 1990s showed that the Soviet Union did receive secret documents from scores of Americans, but such information may

THE RED SCARE

This map, titled **The Bear Grows and Grows,** *appeared in the Sunday magazine section of the New York* **News** *in November 1947. What impact might such an image have on newspaper readers?*

The Michael Barson Collection/Past Perfect.

have, at most, sped up Soviet development of nuclear weapons. The vast majority of individuals prosecuted in the Red scare were guilty of nothing more than having at one time joined the Communist Party, associated with Communists or with groups having party members, or supported radical causes. And most of the charges involved activities that took place long before the cold war had made the Soviet Union an enemy. Red-hunters cared little for such distinctions, however. For more than ten years following World War II, the House Un-American Activities Committee (HUAC), the Senate Internal Security Subcommittee (SISS), and a host of other official bodies ordered citizens to testify about their past and present political associations.

Once witnesses admitted membership in a group that was deemed subversive, inquisitors asked them to name other members. If they tried to save their associates from a similar ordeal by refusing to identify them, they could be held in contempt of Congress. Consequently, many witnesses refused to answer any questions at all, claiming Fifth Amendment protection from self-incrimination. Anti-Communists then charged that silence was tantamount to confession, and these "unfriendly witnesses" lost their jobs and suffered public ostracism.

Nixon and McCarthy on the Attack

Richard M. Nixon was one of the Republicans who leaped at the chance to attack the Democrats for permitting subversives to operate in the United States. A member of HUAC during his first term in

Congress in 1947–1948, Nixon took up the pursuit of Alger Hiss, a former New Dealer who had served in the wartime State Department. In the 1930s, according to ex-Communist Whittaker Chambers, Hiss had belonged to a secret Communist cell that passed government documents to the Soviet Union. Hiss denied the charges, but in 1950 a jury convicted him of lying to HUAC about his connections with Chambers, and Hiss spent four years in prison. Hiss could not be tried for spying for the Soviet Union because the statute of limitations had run out, but many Americans did not distinguish between perjury and espionage, and his case invigorated the anti-Communist crusade. Prominent Democrats such as Dean Acheson and Adlai Stevenson defended Hiss, while Republicans vilified him as a prime example of "twenty years of treason" under the Democrats. Nixon's pursuit of Alger Hiss won him national fame. (U.S. and Soviet records opened in the 1990s lend some weight to Chambers's charges that Hiss gave him government documents in the 1930s, but the case continues to evoke controversy.)

No individual exceeded Joseph McCarthy in his zeal to purge the United States of nonconformists. So great was his influence that the term *McCarthyism* became synonymous with the anti-Communist crusade, even though the hysteria ranged far beyond the senator's activities. McCarthy grew up in rural Wisconsin, worked his way through college, and graduated from law school. During World War II, he served in the Marines and then, back home, lied about his unremarkable war record to appear like a heroic tail gunner. In 1946, he won election to the U.S. Senate, attacking the Truman administration with being soft on communism. McCarthy jumped into the national spotlight in 1950, when he claimed to have a list of 205 "known Communists" working in the State Department. (He later changed the number to 57, but in reality he did not have a single name.) He attacked individuals recklessly, and even though many of his charges were absurd—such as his allegation that retired general George C. Marshall belonged to a Communist conspiracy—the press covered McCarthy avidly, and his photograph appeared on the covers of *Time* and *Newsweek*.

Official Purge and Pervasive Repression

Under increasing pressure from the Republicans and with public opinion strongly against the em-

SENATOR JOSEPH R. MCCARTHY
In March 1950, McCarthy reads letters responding to his claim to have a list of 205 Communists in the State Department. Although McCarthy made his reputation from anticommunism, he seized that issue more from the need to have a campaign platform in 1950 than from genuine concern grounded in real evidence. McCarthy had loved politics from his high school days in Appleton, Wisconsin, and easily distorted the truth to promote his political ambitions.
Wide World Photos, Inc.

ployment of Communists in government jobs, in March 1947 Truman issued Executive Order 9835 requiring investigation of every federal employee. Those found guilty of Communist affiliation or even of "sympathetic association" with Communists—often interpreted as membership in groups with radical leanings—lost their jobs without a hearing. In effect, Truman's "loyalty program" violated the principles of American justice by allowing anonymous informers to make charges and then placing the burden of proof on the accused. Even so, the program extended into the mid-1950s, with the result that more than two thousand civil service employees lost their jobs and another ten thousand resigned. Years later, Truman privately admitted that the loyalty program had been a mistake.

The Truman administration also went directly after the Communist Party. Just before the 1948 elections, the Justice Department began prosecuting eleven Communist Party leaders under the Smith Act, passed in 1940, which made it a crime to "advocate the overthrow and destruction of the Government of the United States by force and violence." A jury found the eleven leaders guilty, convicting them not for their actions but for their beliefs. They were each sentenced to five years in prison. Although civil libertarians argued that the verdicts violated First Amendment rights to freedom of speech, press, and association, the Supreme Court ruled in 1951 *(Dennis v. United States)* that the Communist threat overrode the guarantees of the Constitution. Other prosecutions under the Smith Act followed, resulting in more than one hundred convictions through 1956.

No individual exceeded Joseph McCarthy in his zeal to purge the United States of nonconformists. So great was his influence that the term McCarthyism *became synonymous with the anti-Communist crusade.*

Despite his own anti-Communist actions, Truman denounced the extremism of men like Nixon and McCarthy. He vetoed the McCarran Internal Security Act in 1950, rebuking Congress for putting the government in the "thought control business." The legislation denied passports and government or defense industry jobs to Communist sympathizers and authorized the government to build concentration camps to confine "subversives" in times of national emergency. Testifying to the strength of anti-Communist sentiment, Congress easily overrode the veto.

The official purge led to pervasive repression as McCarthyism spread beyond the nation's capital. State and local governments undertook investigations, demanded loyalty oaths from everyone from teachers to professional wrestlers, fired individuals suspected of disloyalty, banned books from public libraries, and more. In addition, a 1950 Senate report claimed that homosexuals' "moral turpitude" and their susceptibility to blackmail made them unfit for government jobs. Purged from the civil service and drummed out of the military, gay

men and women also suffered surveillance and harassment at the hands of the FBI, the post office, and local police forces. Private organizations and businesses also purged dissidents and helped to create a climate of political and social conformity.

Educational institutions grilled hundreds of teachers about their past and present political associations. When individuals refused to name associates, they often lost their jobs. Rutgers, Harvard, Michigan, Fisk, and a host of other, less prominent universities dismissed professors, and public school teachers were fired in New York, Philadelphia, Los Angeles, and elsewhere. University of Chicago president Robert M. Hutchins decried the damage to freedom of inquiry: "The entire teaching profession of the U.S. is now intimidated."

Hollywood first came under HUAC's scrutiny in 1947. Ronald Reagan, president of the Screen Actors Guild, and others in the movie industry cooperated with the committee, but certain writers and directors—who became known as the Hollywood Ten—refused to testify. After serving short prison terms, they found themselves barred from work in Hollywood, as did scores of others suspected of Communist associations. The entire entertainment industry blacklisted leftists, including Pete Seeger's folksinging group, the Weavers, whose song "Goodnight Irene" had topped the record charts as recently as 1950.

Labor unions were both victims and agents in the anti-Communist crusade. Although few workers were officially Communists, the party and its sympathizers had helped to reinvigorate the labor movement in the 1930s and continued to wield influence in several unions in the Congress of Industrial Organizations (CIO). When employers used charges of communism to discredit unions, the CIO adopted a defense strategy and expelled eleven unions whose leaders refused to take the anti-Communist line. CIO president Philip Murray called Communists "dirty, filthy traitors." Unions continued to grow, but labor wasted energy in internecine battles and lost many progressive activists who had placed the CIO on the cutting edge of reform in the 1930s.

Because the Communist Party championed racial justice, civil rights activists and organizations became the prey of McCarthyism. Again, one did not have to be a party member to be a target; it was enough simply to hold views that were shared by the party. As a chairperson of a government loyalty review board put it, "Of course the fact that a person believes in racial equality doesn't *prove* that he's a Communist, but it certainly makes you look twice, doesn't it?"

McCarthyism caused untold economic and psychological harm to individuals who were innocent of breaking the law. Thousands of people found themselves humiliated and discredited, hounded from their jobs, even in some cases put behind prison bars. The anti-Communist crusade violated fundamental constitutional rights of freedom of speech and association, stifled expression of dissenting ideas, and removed unpopular causes from public contemplation.

The Cold War Becomes Hot: Korea

The cold war erupted into a shooting war in June 1950, when troops from Communist North Korea invaded South Korea. For the first time, Americans went into battle to implement containment. Con-

firming the global reach of the Truman Doctrine, U.S. involvement in Korea also marked the militarization of American foreign policy. The United States, in concert with the United Nations, ultimately held the line in Korea, but at a great cost in lives, dollars, and domestic unity.

Korea and the Military Implementation of Containment

The war grew out of the artificial division of Korea after World War II. Having expelled the Japanese, who had controlled Korea since the Russo-Japanese War of 1904, the United States and the Soviet Union divided Korea at the thirty-eighth parallel into two occupation zones (Map 25.3). The Soviets supported the Korean Communist Party in the north, while the United States backed the Korean Democratic Party in the south. With Moscow and Washington unable to agree on a unification plan, in July 1948 the United Nations sponsored elections in South Korea. The

KOREA
These demoralized U.S. soldiers reflect the grim situation for U.S. forces during the early months of the Korean War. Their North Korean captors forced them to march through Seoul in July 1950, carrying a banner proclaiming the righteousness of the Communist cause and attacking U.S. intervention.
Wide World Photos, Inc.

MAP 25.3

The Korean War, 1950–1953
After each side had plunged deep into its enemy's territory, the Korean War ended in 1953 with the dividing line between North and South Korea nearly the same as it had been before the war.

American-favored candidate, Korean nationalist Syngman Rhee, who had spent most of his life in exile in the United States, was elected president, and the United States withdrew all but five hundred troops. In the fall of 1948, the Soviets established the People's Republic of North Korea and also withdrew their occupation forces. U.S. Defense and State Department officials did not consider Korea to be of vital strategic interest, and many doubted that Rhee's conservative, repressive government could sustain popular support. But to bolster Rhee's anticommunism, Truman decided to supply a small amount of economic and military aid to the South Korean government.

Skirmishes between North and South Korean troops had occurred since 1948, with both sides crossing the thirty-eighth parallel. In June 1950, however, ninety thousand North Koreans swept into South Korea. Truman's advisers immediately assumed that either the Soviet Union, China, or both had instigated the attack. Revelations by former Soviet officials decades later indicated only that the Kremlin had acquiesced in North Korean plans.

On June 30, six days after learning of the attack, Truman decided to commit ground troops, believing that Korea was "the Greece of the Far East" and that the United States must "put up a fight [against Communism] right now." Because the Soviet Union was boycotting the UN Security Council for its refusal to seat a delegate from the People's Republic of China, the U.S. representative was able to obtain UN sponsorship of a collective effort to repel the attack. Authorized by the Security Council to appoint a commander for the UN force, Truman named General Douglas MacArthur, hero of the American victory in the Pacific and head of the Allied postwar occupation in Japan.

Sixteen nations, including many of the NATO allies, sent troops to Korea, but the United States contributed most of the personnel and weapons, deploying almost 1.8 million troops and essentially dictating military strategy. By failing to ask Congress for a declaration of war, Truman violated at least the spirit if not the letter of the Constitution. Moreover, although Congress authorized the calling up of troops and appropriated funds to fight the war, the president's political opponents called it "Truman's war" when the military situation worsened.

Truman decided to commit ground troops, believing that Korea was "the Greece of the Far East" and that the United States must "put up a fight [against Communism] right now."

The first American soldiers rushed to Korea unprepared and ill equipped. The North Koreans took the capital of Seoul and drove deep into the south between June and September, forcing UN troops to retreat south to Pusan. Then in September, General MacArthur launched a bold counteroffensive, staging an amphibious landing at Inchon, 180 miles behind the North Korean lines. By mid-October, UN forces had pushed the North Koreans back to the thirty-eighth parallel. Now Truman had to decide whether to authorize an invasion of North Korea and seek to unify Korea under UN supervision.

From Containment to Rollback to Containment

"Troops could not be expected . . . to march up to a surveyor's line and stop," remarked Dean Acheson, now secretary of state, reflecting sentiment among the public and most government officials to transform the military objective from containment to elimination of the enemy and unification of Korea. With UN approval, on September 27, 1950, Truman ordered MacArthur to move beyond the thirty-eighth parallel if necessary to destroy North Korean forces. Concerned about possible intervention by China and the Soviet Union, Truman directed the general not to send UN troops close to the Korean-Chinese border. Yet MacArthur sent UN forces to within forty miles of the border, whereupon more than 150,000 Chinese troops crossed the Yalu River into Korea. With Chinese help, by December 1950, the North Koreans had recaptured Seoul. It took three months of grueling battle for UN forces to work their way back to the thirty-eighth parallel. At that point, Truman decided to seek a negotiated settlement.

When the goal of the war reverted to containment, MacArthur vented his fury. "There is no substitute for victory," he asserted. To him, a holding action against communism represented defeat. Truman and his advisers, however, adamantly opposed a wider war in Asia. According to General Omar Bradley, chairman of the Joint Chiefs of Staff, MacArthur wanted to wage "the wrong war, at the wrong place, at the wrong time, with the wrong enemy."

MacArthur took his case public, in effect challenging the president's authority to make foreign policy and violating the principle of civilian control over the military. Fed up with MacArthur's insubordination, Truman fired him in April 1951. Three out of four Americans, however, sided with MacArthur and castigated Truman. "Quite an explosion. . . . Letters of abuse by the dozens," Truman recorded in his diary. The general came home to a hero's welcome. Millions watched his address to Congress on television, and more than seven mil-

lion people turned out for his triumphant parade in New York City. Baseball fans booed Truman when he appeared at Griffith Stadium on opening day.

Siding with MacArthur enabled Americans to hold on to their belief that the United States was all-powerful and to pin the Korean stalemate on the government's ineptitude or willingness to shelter subversives.

The adulation of MacArthur reflected Americans' frustrations with containment. Why should Americans die simply to preserve the status quo rather than destroy the enemy once and for all? Siding with MacArthur enabled Americans to hold on to their belief that the United States was all-powerful and to pin the Korean stalemate on the government's ineptitude or willingness to shelter subversives. Moreover, Truman's earlier success in "scaring the hell" out of the American people over the threat of communism in the Mediterranean came back to haunt him. If communism was so threatening, so evil, why not stamp it out as MacArthur wanted? When Congress investigated MacArthur's firing, all of the top military leaders supported the president, yet Truman never recovered from the political fallout. Nor was he able to end the war in Korea. Cease-fire negotiations began in July 1951, but peace talks dragged on for two more years, while twelve thousand more U.S. soldiers died.

Korea, Communism, and the 1952 Election

Popular discontent with Truman's war gave the Republicans a decided edge in the election battles of 1952. Their presidential candidate, General Dwight D. Eisenhower, enjoyed immense stature for his contributions to victory in World War II. Reared in modest circumstances in Abilene, Kansas, Eisenhower attended West Point and rose steadily through the army ranks. As supreme commander in Europe, he won widespread acclaim for leading the Allied armies to victory over Germany. After the war, he served as army chief of staff and then as president of Columbia University. In 1950, Truman appointed Eisenhower the first supreme commander of NATO forces.

THE 1952 REPUBLICAN TICKET
At the Republican convention in 1952, presidential nominee Dwight D. Eisenhower stands with his wife, Mamie (right), his running mate, Richard Nixon, and Nixon's wife, Patricia (left), at the start of their campaign. The campaign button featured a theme common to candidates of the party currently out of power.
Corbis-Bettmann; Collection of Janice L. and David J. Frent.

Both Republicans and Democrats had courted Eisenhower for the presidency in 1948. Although he believed that civilian control over the military worked best when professional soldiers kept out of politics, he found compelling reasons to run in 1952. Eisenhower agreed with the broad scope of Democratic foreign policy, but he deplored the Democrats' efforts to solve domestic problems with new federal programs and large expenditures. He equally disliked the foreign policy views of the leading Republican presidential contender, Senator Robert A. Taft, who attacked containment and sought to cut defense spending. Eisenhower decided to run as much to stop Taft and the conservative wing of the party as to turn the Democrats out of the White House.

Eisenhower defeated Taft for the nomination, but the old guard prevailed on the party platform. It excoriated containment as "negative, futile, and immoral" and charged the Truman administration with shielding "traitors to the Nation in high places." Eisenhower's choice of thirty-nine-year-old Senator Richard M. Nixon for his running mate helped to appease the Republican right wing and ensured that anticommunism would be a major theme of the campaign.

Richard Milhous Nixon grew up in southern California with four brothers, raised by a Quaker mother and a father who operated a grocery store. After working his way through college and law school, he served in the navy and briefly practiced law. In 1946, he entered politics, helping the Republicans recapture Congress by defeating a liberal incumbent for a seat in the House of Representatives. Nixon quickly made a name for himself as a member of HUAC. Accusing the Democrats of being soft on communism, Nixon found an issue to boost his career. In his 1950 bid for the Senate, he ran an effective smear campaign against the liberal congresswoman Helen Gahagan Douglas, charging her with being "pink [Communist] right down to her underwear."

Having decided not to run for another term, Truman persuaded Adlai E. Stevenson, governor of Illinois, to seek the Democratic nomination. Witty and eloquent, a popular governor, and acceptable to both liberals and southern Democrats, Stevenson easily won the nomination. He could not escape the domestic fallout from the Korean War, however, nor could he match the popular appeal of Eisenhower, the World War II hero.

The Republican campaign stumbled just once, over the last item of its "Korea, Communism, and Corruption" campaign. A newspaper reported that Nixon had accepted $18,000 from supporters in

California. Although such gifts were common in politics at that time, Democrats jumped on Nixon, hoping to divert attention from the scandals that involved several figures in the Truman administration and the Democratic Party. As newspaper editorials called for Nixon to withdraw from the ticket, most of Eisenhower's advisers urged him to dump his running mate.

Nixon saved himself by exploiting the new medium of television. He made an emotional appeal to a national audience, disclosing his finances and documenting his modest standard of living. Conceding that the family pet, Checkers, could be considered an illegal gift, he vowed that he would not break his daughters' hearts by returning the cocker spaniel. The overwhelming popular response to the "Checkers speech" turned the tide for Nixon. Eisenhower embraced his running mate with the words "You're my boy!" Despite this endorsement, both men bore resentments about the in-

THE CHECKERS SPEECH
Republican vice presidential nominee Richard M. Nixon poses with his wife, Patricia, just before going on radio and TV to respond to charges of having received illegal campaign funds during the 1952 campaign. In an emotional speech that he finished in tears, Nixon saved his place on the ticket and probably his political career. Pat Nixon did not like the speech, asking her husband, "Why do we have to tell people how little we have and how much we owe?"
Corbis-Bettmann.

cident and never achieved an easy or warm relationship.

With the issue of corruption neutralized, the Republicans harped on communism at home and failure to achieve victory in Korea. Less than two weeks before the election, Eisenhower made the dramatic announcement "I shall go to Korea," and voters registered their confidence in his ability to end the war. Cutting sharply into traditional Democratic territory, Eisenhower won several southern states and, overall, 55 percent of the popular vote. His coattails carried a narrow Republican majority to Congress.

An Armistice and the War's Costs

Eisenhower made good on his pledge to end the Korean War. In July 1953, the two sides reached an armistice that left Korea divided just as it had been three years earlier (see Map 25.3). The war took the lives of 54,000 Americans and wounded more than 100,000. Total UN casualties included 118,515 killed, 264,591 wounded, and 92,987 captured, most of whom did not return alive.

Korean and civilian casualties were heavier still. More than 1.6 million North Koreans and Chinese were killed or wounded, and 3 million South Koreans died of war-related causes. The nature of the war and the unpopularity of the Rhee government made it difficult for soldiers to distinguish between friends and enemies, since civilian populations sometimes harbored North Korean agents. Consequently, as one journalist reported, the situation "forced upon our men in the field, acts and attitudes of the utmost savagery . . . the blotting out of villages where the enemy *might* be hiding, the shooting and shelling of refugees who *may* be North Koreans."

The Truman administration judged the war a success for its containment policy, since the United States had supported its promise to the world to help nations that were resisting communism. Both Truman and Eisenhower managed to contain what amounted to a world war—involving twenty nations altogether—within a single country. Moreover, despite the presidents' threats to use nuclear bombs, they limited the Korean War to a conflict fought with conventional weapons.

This fact might be considered remarkable, given that, in April 1950, two months before the Korean War began, the National Security Council had given Truman a top-secret report on the nation's military strength. NSC 68, as the document was called, warned that the survival of the nation and the world required a massive military buildup. Truman read the report but took no immediate action on its recommendations to triple the current defense budget. Nearly all of the military buildup called for in NSC 68 came about during the Korean War, vastly increasing U.S. capacity to act as a global power. Using the Korean crisis to expand the American presence elsewhere, Truman persuaded Congress to approve the rearming of West Germany and the commitment of troops to NATO. Military spending shot up from $14 billion in 1950 to $50 billion in 1953 and remained above $40 billion thereafter. By 1953, defense spending claimed 60 percent of the federal budget and the size of the armed forces had tripled.

Nearly all of the military buildup called for in NSC 68 came about during the Korean War, vastly increasing U.S. capacity to act as a global power.

To General Matthew Ridgway, who succeeded MacArthur as commander of the UN forces, Korea taught the lesson that U.S. forces should never again fight a land war in Asia. Eisenhower concurred. Nevertheless, the Korean War induced the Truman administration to expand its role in Asia by increasing aid to the French, who were fighting to hang on to their colonial empire in Indochina. As U.S. marines retreated from a battle against Chinese soldiers in 1950, they sang, prophetically, "We're Harry's police force on call, / So put back your pack on, / The next step is Saigon, / Cheer up, me lads, bless 'em all."

Conclusion: Meeting the Challenges of the Postwar World

Dean Acheson chose to title his memoir about the Truman years *Present at the Creation*, aptly capturing the magnitude of change that marked the aftermath of World War II. More than any develop-

ment in the postwar world, the cold war defined American politics and society for decades to come. Truman's decision to oppose communism throughout the world marked the most momentous foreign policy initiative in the nation's history. It transformed the federal government, shifting its attention from domestic to external affairs, greatly expanding its budget, and substantially increasing the power of the president. The nuclear arms race attending the cold war put the people of the world at risk, diverted resources that might have been used to improve living standards, and skewed the economy toward dependence on military projects. While many Americans continued to debate who was responsible for the cold war and whether it could have been avoided, none could question its impact on American society or the world.

In sharp contrast to foreign policy, the domestic policies of the postwar years reflected continuity with the past. Preoccupied with foreign policy, Truman failed to mobilize support for his ambition to assist the disadvantaged with new initiatives in education, health, agriculture, and civil rights, but he successfully defended most New Deal reforms. The boost to industry from cold war spending and the reconstruction of Western Europe and Japan contributed to an economic boom that lifted the standard of living for a majority of Americans.

The anti-Communist hysteria that grew out of the cold war contributed to the domestic status quo by silencing the left, stifling debate, and narrowing the range of acceptable ideas. Partisan politics and the Truman administration's constant rhetoric about the Communist menace fueled McCarthyism, but the obsession with subversion also fed on popular frustrations over the failure of containment to produce clear-cut victories. Convulsing the nation in bitter disunity, McCarthyism reflected a loss of confidence in American power. It would be a major challenge of the next administration to restore that unity and confidence.

---

www.bedfordstmartins.com   SEE THE ONLINE STUDY GUIDE to assess your mastery of the material covered in this chapter.

CHRONOLOGY

1945 Harry S. Truman becomes president of United States upon death of Franklin D. Roosevelt.

1946 Postwar labor unrest erupts throughout United States.

Truman creates Committee on Civil Rights.

United States grants independence to Philippines.

Congress passes Employment Act signifying government's responsibility for healthy economy.

Congressional elections result in Republican control of 80th Congress.

1947 George F. Kennan's article on policy of containment appears in *Foreign Affairs*.

National Security Act of 1947 unifies military services under secretary of defense and creates National Security Council (NSC) and Central Intelligence Agency (CIA).

Truman asks Congress for aid to Greece and Turkey to counter communism and announces Truman Doctrine.

Truman establishes Federal Employees Loyalty and Security Program to eliminate Communists and their sympathizers from the government.

1948 Congress approves Marshall Plan, providing massive aid to stimulate European recovery.

Congress makes women permanent part of armed services.

Truman issues executive order to desegregate armed services.

United States recognizes state of Israel.

Truman defeats Thomas E. Dewey to win full term as president.

1948–1949 Soviets block access to West Berlin, setting off Berlin crisis and fifteen-month Western airlift.

1949 Communists under Mao Zedong win Chinese civil war and take over mainland China; Nationalists retreat to Taiwan.

The North Atlantic Treaty Organization (NATO) organizes to counter Soviet threat to Western Europe.

Truman administration initiates Point IV technical aid program to third world nations.

Soviet Union explodes atomic bomb.

1950 Senator Joseph McCarthy begins campaign against alleged Communists in United States, giving his name to period of anti-Communist hysteria.

Truman approves development of hydrogen bomb.

United States sends troops to South Korea to repel North Korean assault.

1951 Truman relieves General Douglas MacArthur of command in Korea for insubordination.

United States ends postwar occupation of Japan; the two nations sign peace treaty and mutual security pact.

1952 Republican Dwight D. Eisenhower elected president of United States.

1953 Armistice signed in Korean War.

BIBLIOGRAPHY

GENERAL WORKS

John Patrick Diggins, *The Proud Decades: America in War and Peace, 1941–1960* (1988).

Robert J. Donovan, *Conflict and Crisis: The Presidency of Harry S. Truman, 1945–1948* (1977).

Robert J. Donovan, *Tumultuous Years: The Presidency of Harry S. Truman, 1949–1953* (1982).

Alonzo L. Hamby, *Man of the People: A Life of Harry S. Truman* (1995).

Michael J. Lacy, ed., *The Truman Presidency* (1989).

Melvyn Leffler, *A Preponderance of Power: National Security, the Truman Administration, and the Cold War* (1992).

David McCullough, *Truman* (1992).

William L. O'Neill, *American High: The Years of Confidence, 1945–1960* (1986).

James T. Patterson, *Grand Expectations: The United States, 1945–1974* (1996).

William E. Pemberton, *Harry S. Truman: Fair Dealer and Cold Warrior* (1989).

Lisle A. Rose, *The Cold War Comes to Main Street: America in 1950* (1999).

Michael S. Sherry, *In the Shadow of War* (1995).

Harry S. Truman, *Year of Decisions* (1955).

Harry S. Truman, *Years of Trial and Hope* (1956).

DOMESTIC POLITICS AND POLICIES

William C. Berman, *The Politics of Civil Rights in the Truman Administration* (1970).

John C. Culver and John Hyde, *American Dreamer: The Life and Times of Henry A. Wallace* (2000).

Richard M. Dalfiume, *Desegregation of the U.S. Armed Forces: Fighting on Two Fronts* (1969).

Richard O. Davies, *Housing Reform during the Truman Administration* (1966).

Gary A. Donaldson, *Truman Defeats Dewey* (1998).

Andrew J. Dunar, *The Truman Scandals and the Politics of Morality* (1984).

John Egerton, *Speak Now against the Day: The Generation before the Civil Rights Movement in the South* (1994).

Harold I. Gullan, *The Upset That Wasn't: Harry S. Truman and the Crucial Election of 1948* (1998).

Susan M. Hartman, *Truman and the 80th Congress* (1971).

Zachary Karabell, *The Last Campaign: How Harry Truman Won the 1948 Election* (2000).

R. Alton Lee, *Truman and Taft-Hartley* (1966).

Nelson Lichtenstein, *The Most Dangerous Man in Detroit: Walter Reuther and the Fate of American Labor* (1996).

Norman D. Markowitz, *The Rise and Fall of the People's Century: Henry A. Wallace and American Liberalism, 1941–1948* (1973).

Allen J. Matusow, *Farm Policies and Politics in the Truman Years* (1967).

Donald R. McCoy and Richard T. Ruetten, *Quest and Response: Minority Rights and the Truman Administration* (1973).

Keith W. Olson, *The G.I. Bill, the Veterans, and the Colleges* (1974).

James Patterson, *Mr. Republican: A Biography of Robert A. Taft* (1974).

Monte M. Poen, *Harry S. Truman versus the Medical Lobby: The Genesis of Medicare* (1979).

David W. Reinhard, *The Republican Right since 1945* (1983).

Jules Tygiel, *Baseball's Great Experiment: Jackie Robinson and His Legacy* (1997).

Robert Zieger, *The CIO, 1935–1955* (1995).

ORIGINS OF THE COLD WAR

Gar Alperovitz, *Atomic Diplomacy* (1985).

Carolyn Eisenberg, *Drawing the Line: The American Decision to Divide Germany, 1944–1949* (1996).

John L. Gaddis, *The United States and the Origins of the Cold War* (1972).

James L. Gormly, *The Collapse of the Grand Alliance, 1945–1948* (1987).

Fraser J. Harbut, *The Iron Curtain: Churchill, America, and the Origins of the Cold War* (1986).

Joyce Kolko and Gabriel Kolko, *The Limits of Power: The World and United States Foreign Policy* (1972).

Bruce R. Kuniholm, *The Origins of the Cold War in the Near East* (1980).

Deborah W. Larson, *Origins of Containment: A Psychological Explanation* (1985).

Ernest R. May, ed., *American Cold War Strategy: Interpreting NSC 68* (1993).

Wilson D. Miscamble, *George F. Kennan and the Making of Foreign Policy, 1947–1950* (1992).

Thomas G. Patterson, *On Every Front: The Making of the Cold War* (1979).

Robert A. Pollard, *Economic Security and the Origins of the Cold War* (1985).

Michael Schaller, *The American Occupation of Japan: The Origins of the Cold War in Asia* (1985).

Hugh Thomas, *Armed Truce: The Beginnings of the Cold War, 1945–1946* (1987).

Randall B. Woods and Howard Jones, *Dawning of the Cold War: The United States' Quest for Order* (1994).

Daniel Yergin, *Shattered Peace: The Origins of the Cold War and the National Security State* (1977).

FOREIGN POLICY

Dean Acheson, *Present at the Creation* (1969).

William S. Borden, *The Pacific Alliance: United States Foreign Economic Policy and Japanese Trade Recovery, 1947–1955* (1984).

James Chace, *Acheson: The Secretary of State Who Created the American World* (1998).

Gordon H. Chang, *Friends and Enemies: The United States, China, and the Soviet Union, 1948–1972* (1990).

Michael J. Cohen, *Truman and Israel* (1990).

Peter L. Hahn, *The United States, Great Britain, and Egypt: Strategy and Diplomacy in the Early Cold War* (1991).

Gary R. Hess, *The United States' Emergence as a Southeast Asian Power, 1940–1950* (1987).

Walter L. Hixon, *George F. Kennan: Cold War Iconoclast* (1989).

Michael J. Hogan, *The Marshall Plan: America, Britain, and the Reconstruction of Western Europe, 1947–1952* (1987).

Walter Isaacson and Evan Thomas, *The Wise Men: Six Friends and the World They Made: Acheson, Bohlen, Harriman, Kennan, Lovett, McCloy* (1986).

Lawrence S. Kaplan, *The United States and NATO: The Formative Years* (1984).

Stuart W. Leslie, *The Cold War and American Science* (1993).

Thomas J. McCormick, *America's Half-Century: United States Foreign Policy in the Cold War* (1989).

David S. McLellan, *Dean Acheson: The State Department Years* (1976).

Richard Rhodes, *Dark Sun: The Making of the Hydrogen Bomb* (1995).

Michael Schaller, *Altered States: The United States and Japan since the Occupation* (1997).

Nancy B. Tucker, *Patterns in the Dust: Chinese-American Relations and the Recognition Controversy, 1949–1950* (1983).

Evan M. Wilson, *Decision on Palestine: How the U.S. Came to Recognize Israel* (1979).

Lawrence S. Wittner, *American Intervention in Greece, 1943–1949* (1982).

MCCARTHYISM

Michael R. Belknap, *Cold War Political Justice: The Smith Act, the Communist Party, and American Civil Liberties* (1977).

David Caute, *The Great Fear: The Anti-Communist Purge under Truman and Eisenhower* (1978).

Larry Ceplair and Steven Englund, *The Inquisition in Hollywood: Politics in the Film Community* (1980).

Richard M. Freeland, *The Truman Doctrine and the Origins of McCarthyism: Foreign Policy, Domestic Politics, and International Security, 1946–1948* (1972).

Richard M. Fried, *Nightmare in Red: The McCarthy Era in Perspective* (1990).

Robert Griffith, *The Politics of Fear: Joseph R. McCarthy and the Senate* (1970).

John Earl Haynes, *Red Scare or Red Menace: American Communism and Anticommunism in the Cold War Era* (1990).

John Earl Haynes and Harvey Klehr, *Venona: Decoding Soviet Espionage in America* (1999).

Stanley I. Kutler, *The American Inquisition* (1982).

Harvey Levinstein, *Communism, Anticommunism, and the CIO* (1981).

David Oshinsky, *A Conspiracy So Immense: The World of Joe McCarthy* (1983).

Richard Gid Powers, *Not without Honor: The History of American Anticommunism* (1995).

Ronald Radosh and Joyce Milton, *The Rosenberg File: A Search for the Truth* (1983).

Thomas C. Reeves, *The Life and Times of Joe McCarthy* (1983).

Ellen W. Schrecker, *No Ivory Tower: McCarthyism and the Universities* (1986).

Ellen W. Schrecker, *The Age of McCarthyism* (1994).

Peter L. Steinberg, *The Great "Red" Menace: United States Persecution of American Communists, 1947–1952* (1984).

Athan Theoharis, *Seeds of Repression: Harry S. Truman and the Origins of McCarthyism* (1971).

Allen Weinstein, *Perjury: The Hiss-Chambers Case* (1979).

Allen Weinstein and Alexander Vassiliev, *The Haunted Wood: Soviet Espionage in America* (1999).

KOREA

Bruce Cumings, *The Origins of the Korean War* (1981).

Rosemary Foot, *The Wrong War: American Policy and the Dimensions of the Korean Conflict, 1950–1953* (1984).

Gregory Henderson, *Korea: The Politics of the Vortex* (1968).

Burton I. Kaufman, *The Korean War: Challenges in Crisis, Credibility, and Command* (1986).

James I. Matray, *The Reluctant Crusade: American Foreign Policy in Korea* (1985).

Stanley Sandler, *The Korean War: No Victors, No Vanquished* (1999).

William Stueck, *The Korean War: An International History* (1995).

John Toland, *In Mortal Combat: Korea, 1950–1953* (1992).

Stanley Weintraub, *MacArthur's War: Korea and the Undoing of an American Hero* (2000).

Richard Whelan, *Drawing the Line: The Korean War, 1950–1953* (1990).

1956 CADILLAC CONVERTIBLE

The automobile reflected both corporate and family prosperity in the 1950s. This car was manufactured by General Motors, the biggest and richest corporation in the world and the first to sell a billion dollars' worth of products. Costing about $5,000, the Cadillac was GM's top-of-the-line car, one of the first purchases the McDonald brothers made when they struck it rich with their hamburger stand in California. Even the cheaper models that average Americans could afford featured the gas-guzzling size and space-age style of this Cadillac.
Ron Kimball Photography.

THE POLITICS AND CULTURE OF ABUNDANCE

26

1952–1960

TRAILED BY REPORTERS AND PHOTOGRAPHERS, U.S. vice president Richard M. Nixon led Soviet premier Nikita Khrushchev through the American National Exhibition in Moscow in July 1959. The display of American consumer goods followed an exhibition of Soviet products in New York, part of a cultural exchange between the two superpowers that reflected a slight thaw in the cold war. Both Khrushchev and Nixon seized on the propaganda potential of the moment. As they made their way through the display, their verbal sparring turned into a slugfest of words and gestures that reporters dubbed "the kitchen debate."

Showing off a new color television set, Nixon conceded to Khrushchev that the Soviet Union "may be ahead of us . . . in the thrust of your rockets for . . . outer space," but he bragged that the United States outstripped the Soviets in consumer goods. "Any steelworker could buy this house," Nixon boasted, as they walked through a six-room ranch-style model. Khrushchev retorted that in the Soviet Union, "you are entitled to housing," whereas in the United States people without money were reduced to sleeping on the pavement.

While the two leaders inspected appliances in the model kitchen, Nixon declared, "These are designed to make things easier for our women." Khrushchev responded that his country did not have "the capitalist attitude toward women"; the Soviet Union appreciated women's contributions to the economy, he said, not their domesticity. Mocking Americans' passion for buying new products, Khrushchev asked, "Don't you have a machine that puts food into the mouth and pushes it down?" The Soviet premier found many of the items on display interesting, he said, but he added that "they are not needed in life. . . . They are merely gadgets." In reply, Nixon insisted, "Isn't it far better to be talking about washing machines than machines of war?" Khrushchev agreed, yet he affirmed the persistence of cold war tensions when he later blustered, "We too are giants. You want to threaten—we will answer threats with threats."

The administration of President Dwight D. Eisenhower had in fact begun with threats to the Soviet Union. Republican campaigners vowed to roll back communism and liberate "enslaved" peoples under Soviet rule. In practice, however, Eisenhower settled for a containment policy much like that of his predecessor, Harry S. Truman, though Eisenhower relied more on nuclear weapons and on secret actions of the Central Intelligence Agency. Yet, as Nixon's visit to Moscow demonstrated, Eisenhower took advantage of changes in the government of the Soviet Union to reduce tensions in Soviet-American relations.

THE KITCHEN DEBATE
Soviet premier Nikita Khrushchev (left) and Vice President Richard M. Nixon (center)
debate the relative merits of their nations' economies at the American National
Exhibition held in Moscow in 1959.
Howard Sochurek/TimePix.

Continuity with the Truman administration also characterized domestic policy during the 1950s. Although Eisenhower favored the business community with tax cuts and opposed strong federal efforts in health care, education, and race relations, he did not propose to roll back New Deal or Fair Deal programs. A majority of Americans enjoyed prosperity under the immensely popular president and seemed content with his "moderate Republicanism."

The American display in Moscow testified to the astounding material gains savored by a majority of Americans in the postwar era. Cold war weapons production spurred the economy and contributed to the burgeoning populations and business growth of the West and Southwest. Rising incomes enabled millions of Americans to buy homes, television sets, and household appliances that transformed their patterns of living. The 1950s culture celebrated marriage, family life, and traditional gender roles, yet in one respect the United States moved closer to the Soviet model: More and more married women were taking jobs outside their homes.

Both the cold war and the economic boom helped African Americans mount a strong challenge to tradition in the 1950s. Protest took a dramatic new direction when African Americans in large numbers turned to direct action against the system of segregation and disfranchisement in the South. By the end of the decade, blacks had developed the institutions, leadership, strategies, and will to mount a civil rights movement of unprecedented size and power.

Eisenhower and the Politics of the "Middle Way"

Moderation was the guiding principle of Eisenhower's domestic agenda and leadership style. His first State of the Union message, in January 1953, pledged a "middle way between untrammeled freedom of the individual and the demands for the welfare of the whole Nation." His administration would "avoid government by bureaucracy as carefully as it avoids neglect of the helpless." Claiming that Democrats appealed to divisive class interests, Eisenhower presented himself as a leader above partisan politics and selfish interest groups who would govern by compromise and consensus. Nicknamed "Ike" by his friends and the public, the confident war hero with the winning smile remained popular throughout his presidency.

The President and McCarthy

The new president's desire to placate conservative Republicans influenced his approach to the anti-Communist fervor that had plagued the Truman administration. Eisenhower shared Senator Joseph McCarthy's goal of eliminating communism from American life. He refused to commute the death sentences of Ethel and Julius Rosenberg, despite worldwide pressure to grant clemency to these parents of young children. The couple was electrocuted in June 1953.

Although Eisenhower deplored McCarthy's method, he made little effort to silence him. Privately, Eisenhower explained that he would not demean the presidency by getting into "a pissing contest with that skunk," insisting that presidential attention would only give the senator greater publicity. Recognizing McCarthy's popularity, Eisenhower feared that to denounce him would alienate old-guard Republicans who held powerful positions in Congress. Moreover, Republicans benefited from McCarthy's attacks on the Democrats. Republican senator John Bricker of Ohio called McCarthy an "SOB" but continued, "Sometimes it's useful to have SOBs around to do the dirty work."

The changeover to a Republican administration failed to stop McCarthy's allegations that the government was rife with Communists; thousands of federal employees charged with disloyalty lost their jobs while Eisenhower was president. Drunk with power, the senator attacked several of Eisenhower's appointees and got the State Department to remove from overseas libraries books by such "subversives" as Mark Twain and John Dewey.

Eisenhower correctly predicted that McCarthy would ultimately destroy himself. With the conclusion of the Korean War, popular frustrations over containment abated, and the anti-Communist hysteria subsided. Because Eisenhower came across to

Pussyfootprints on the Sands of Time

THE PERSISTENCE OF MCCARTHYISM
This political cartoon, created in 1954, took a jab at both President Eisenhower and the U.S. Senate for allowing Senator Joseph McCarthy to destroy careers and reputations with his indiscriminate charges of communism.
Herblock © 1954/*The Washington Post.*

most Americans as a staunch anti-Communist, right-wing Republicans who continued to cry Red after he took charge of the government sounded like crackpots.

Although Eisenhower deplored McCarthy's method, he made little effort to silence him.

McCarthy tightened his own noose in 1954 when he went after alleged Communists in the army. As he hurled reckless charges during weeks of televised committee hearings, public opinion turned against him. "Have you left no sense of decency?" demanded the army's lawyer, Joseph Welch. In December 1954, the Senate voted to condemn McCarthy. After the vote, Eisenhower remarked that McCarthyism had become "McCarthywasism." But the president's inaction had allowed the senator to spread his poison longer than he might otherwise have done. Like Truman, Eisenhower lent the power of his office to the postwar Red scare and suppression of dissent.

Moderate Republicanism

For most of his two terms (1953–1961), Eisenhower presided over a divided government. In 1954, the Democrats regained control of Congress and maintained it for the rest of the decade. The moderate Republicanism of the Eisenhower years was shaped not just by Eisenhower's determination to limit the growth and size of the federal government but also by a Democratic majority in Congress that maintained the course charted by the New Deal and the Fair Deal.

Eisenhower claimed to be above interest-group politics, yet he turned for advice almost exclusively to business leaders and chose wealthy executives and attorneys for his cabinet. When he appointed Martin Durkin, president of the American Federation of Labor plumbers union, as secretary of labor, a liberal journal quipped that Eisenhower had "picked a cabinet of eight millionaires and one plumber." The "plumber" lasted less than a year and was replaced by a retail executive. Eisenhower also maintained informal ties with a group of wealthy businessmen—his "gang"—from whom he sought advice and fellowship. Eisenhower's choice of businessmen as advisers and friends furthered his goal of unifying the Republican Party, which required winning over the conservative old-guard Republicans, who opposed both New Deal programs and containment.

The president shared with the old guard a desire to restrain the role of government and leave economic decisions in the hands of private business. "If all Americans want is security, they can go to prison," Eisenhower commented about social welfare in 1949. Yet, although liberals scorned the president's conservatism by calling him "Eisen-hoover," his administration actually expanded the welfare state somewhat and involved the federal government in new projects. Eisenhower's "middle way"

POLIO VACCINE DISTRIBUTION IN THE SOUTH
In 1954, American children lined up to be inoculated with the new vaccine to prevent polio. But as this scene from Blytheville, Arkansas, shows, children waiting to receive the vaccine stood in strictly segregated lines.
Charles Bell, *Memphis Commercial Appeal.*

applied the brakes, but it did not reverse the growing federal responsibility for economic development and for the support of Americans unable to survive in the free market.

In 1954, Eisenhower signed legislation that provided higher Social Security benefits and extended coverage to some ten million workers and self-employed individuals. The Housing Act of 1954 continued the federal government's role in financing public housing. Whereas Truman had failed to win congressional approval for a new Department of Health, Education, and Welfare, Eisenhower succeeded. The second president to appoint a woman to his cabinet, Eisenhower named former Women's Army Corps commander and Texas newspaper publisher Oveta Culp Hobby to head the new department. And when the spread of polio neared epidemic proportions in the 1950s, Eisenhower obtained funds from Congress to distribute a vaccine, even though conservatives preferred that states assume that responsibility.

Eisenhower's greatest domestic initiative was the Interstate Highway and Defense System Act of 1956. Promoted as essential to the nation's cold war defense strategy and as an impetus to economic growth, the act authorized construction of a national system of highways, with the federal government paying most of the costs through increased fuel and vehicle taxes. Millions of Americans benefited from the greater ease of travel and improved transportation of goods, and the new highways also spurred growth in the fast-food and motel industries as well as the development of shopping malls. The most direct and substantial gains went to the trucking, construction, and automobile industries, which had lobbied hard for the law. The monumental highway construction project eventually exacted severe costs, unforeseen at the time, in the form of air pollution, energy consumption, declining mass transportation, and decay in central cities (Map 26.1).

Eisenhower's "middle way" applied the brakes, but it did not reverse the growing federal responsibility for economic development and for the support of Americans unable to survive in the free market.

In other areas, Eisenhower restrained the federal government in favor of state governments and private enterprise. He achieved large tax cuts, for example, that favored business and the wealthy, and he stubbornly resisted a larger federal role in the areas of health care, education, and civil rights. Moreover, whereas Democrats sought to keep nuclear power in government hands, Eisenhower not only signed legislation authorizing the private manufacture and sale of nuclear power but also directed the Atomic Energy Commission (AEC) to provide materials and services

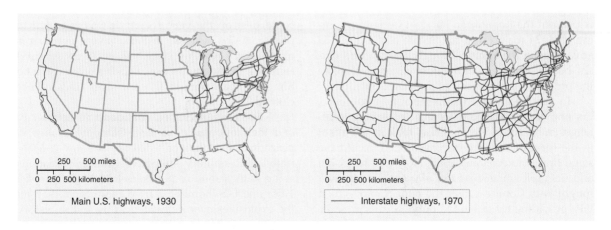

MAP 26.1
The Interstate Highway System, 1930 and 1970
Built with federal funds authorized in the Interstate Highway Act of 1956, superhighways soon crisscrossed the nation. Trucking, construction, and gasoline were among the industries that prospered, but railroads suffered from the subsidized competition.

to private utilities at cost. Workers broke ground at Shippingport, Pennsylvania, for the first commercial nuclear power plant in the fall of 1954.

The 1956 Election and the Second Term

Although Eisenhower retained his immense popularity, his health became a serious political issue in September 1955, when he suffered a heart attack that kept him away from the White House until the end of the year. The president deliberated at length whether to run for a second term. When he announced his decision in February 1956, he knew that his health made the choice of running mate even more critical than it had been in 1952.

Eisenhower worried about placing Vice President Nixon a heartbeat away from the presidency. He acknowledged Nixon's loyalty and dedication but doubted his maturity and ability to run the government. Eisenhower failed to lure Nixon off the ticket with an offer of a cabinet post but could not bring himself to dispose of Nixon forthrightly. He left the vice presidential choice up to the Republican National Convention, where conservatives led a successful drive for Nixon's renomination.

Adlai Stevenson, chosen again by the Democrats, was hard-pressed to explain why voters should abandon Eisenhower in times of peace and prosperity. With the nation at peace and the economy booming, Eisenhower lost only seven states, trouncing Stevenson with 35.6 million to 26 million votes. Two years later, however, the Democrats all but wiped out the Republican Party in Congress, gaining a 64–34 majority in the Senate and a 282–135 advantage in the House. Though Ike captured voters' hearts, a majority of them remained wedded to the programs and policies of the Democrats.

In part because of the Democratic resurgence, Eisenhower faced more serious leadership challenges in his second term. Illness took its toll again in the form of a stroke in November 1957. At the same time, the economy plunged into a recession and unemployment rose to 7 percent. Eisenhower fought with Congress over the budget and vetoed bills providing for expanded public works projects, a high level of price supports for farmers, and housing and urban development. The president and Congress did reach agreement in two important areas: enacting the first civil rights legislation in a century and establishing a new role for the government in education.

In the end, the first Republican administration after the New Deal left the size and functions of the federal government intact, though it tipped federal policy somewhat more in favor of corporate interests. Unparalleled prosperity graced the Eisenhower years, and inflation was confined to an annual average of 1.5 percent. The late-1957 recession was one of two in the 1950s, but the economy recovered without putting to a test the president's aversion to substantial federal intervention.

Liberation Rhetoric and the Practice of Containment

At his 1953 inauguration, Eisenhower warned that "forces of good and evil are massed and armed and opposed as rarely before in history." Like Truman, he saw communism as a threat to the nation's physical security and to its economic interests. Eisenhower's foreign policy differed from Truman's, though, in three areas: its rhetoric, its means, and—after Stalin's death in 1953—its movement toward accommodation with the Soviet Union.

The "New Look" in Foreign Policy

To meet his goals of balancing the federal budget and cutting taxes, Eisenhower had to control military expenditures. Moreover, he feared that massive defense spending would threaten the economic strength of the nation. A state based on warfare could destroy the very society it was intended to protect. As he declared in 1953, "Every gun that is made, every warship launched, every rocket fired signifies, in the final sense, a theft from those who hunger and are not fed, those who are cold and not clothed."

Reflecting Americans' confidence in technology and their opposition to large standing armies in peacetime, Eisenhower's defense strategy concentrated U.S. military strength in nuclear weapons along with planes and missiles to deliver them. By 1955, one U.S. bomber carried more force than all the explosives ever detonated in the entire history of humankind. Instead of spending huge amounts for large ground forces of its own, the United States would give friendly nations American weapons and back them up with an ominous nuclear arsenal. This was Eisenhower's "New Look" in foreign policy. Air power and nuclear weapons provided, in Secretary of State John Foster Dulles's words, a "maximum deterrent at bearable cost" or, as Defense Secretary Charles Wilson put it, a "bigger bang for the buck." Dulles believed that America's willingness to "go to the brink" of war with its intimidating nuclear superiority would convince the Soviets to halt any efforts to extend the territory under their control.

By 1955, one U.S. bomber carried more force than all the explosives ever detonated in the entire history of humankind.

Although the Soviets quickly developed nuclear weapons, the United States retained its superiority and deterrence capability. Nuclear bombs and missiles could not stop a Soviet attack, but they could, in return, inflict almost unimaginable destruction on the Soviet Union. The certainty of "massive retaliation" was meant to deter the Soviets from launching an attack. Because the Soviet Union could respond similarly to an American first strike, this delicately balanced nuclear standoff became known as mutually assured destruction, or MAD. Winston Churchill, once again the prime minister of Great Britain, called it a "mutual balance of terror."

Nuclear weapons were useless, however, in rolling back the iron curtain, because they would destroy the very peoples that the United States promised to liberate. When an opportunity emerged in Hungary in 1956, such promises of liberation proved to be empty rhetoric. Unwilling to risk U.S. soldiers and a possible nuclear war, Eisenhower rebuffed the Hungarian Freedom Fighters' pleas for help. Soviet troops soon suppressed the insurrection, killing thirty thousand Hungarians.

Applying Containment to Vietnam

Accepting the status quo in Europe, the Eisenhower administration sought to contain communism in other parts of the world. The major challenge to that commitment came in Southeast Asia, where in 1945 a nationalist coalition called the Vietminh, led by Ho Chi Minh, had proclaimed the independence of Vietnam from France. When France fought to maintain its colony, Ho fought back, and the area

THE NUCLEAR ARMS RACE
This **Newsweek** *cover of Soviet leader Nikita Khrushchev and President Dwight D. Eisenhower balanced on the head of a nuclear missile suggests the precarious world created by the nuclear arms race. The table on which the two men sit refers to the arms limitation negotiations under way when the magazine came off the press in 1959.*

plunged into war. Because Ho declared himself a Communist, the Truman administration had quietly begun to provide aid to the French.

Eisenhower viewed communism in Vietnam much as Truman had regarded it in Greece and Turkey. "You have a row of dominoes set up," Eisenhower said, and "you knock over the first one, and what will happen to the last one is the certainty that it will go over very quickly." The president warned that the fall of Southeast Asia to communism could well trigger the fall of Japan, Taiwan, and the Philippines. By 1954, the United States was contributing 75 percent of the cost of France's war. But the soldier-president Eisenhower also had a realistic view of American capabilities and interests. When in 1954 the French, trapped in their military base at Dien Bien Phu, asked for troops and airplanes from the United States, Eisenhower firmly said no. Conscious of the U.S. losses in the Korean War, he would not commit U.S. troops to another ground war in Asia.

Dien Bien Phu fell in May 1954 and with it the French colony of Vietnam. Two months later in Geneva, France signed a truce. The Geneva accords drew a temporary line across the seventeenth parallel of Vietnam and prohibited both the Vietminh in the north and the puppet government that the French had set up in the south from joining a military alliance or permitting foreign bases on their soil. Within two years, the Vietnamese people were to vote in elections for a unified government. The United States promised to support free elections, but it did not sign the accords.

Geneva Accords of 1954

The French defeat in Vietnam did not cause Eisenhower to abandon containment in Asia. Instead, he tried to prop up the dominoes with a new alliance. In September 1954, the United States joined with Britain, France, Australia, New Zealand, Thailand, Pakistan, and the Philippines in the Southeast Asia Treaty Organization (SEATO), committed to the defense of Cambodia, Laos, and South Vietnam.

In seeking to make South Vietnam a bulwark against communism, the United States repeated most of the mistakes that had doomed the French. The ink was barely dry on the SEATO documents when the United States began to send weapons and military advisers to South Vietnam. It put the Central Intelligence Agency (CIA) to work in efforts to cripple North Vietnam and undermine the reputation of Ho Chi Minh. Assuming that the election mandated by the Geneva accords would result in a victory for Ho Chi Minh, the United States supported the South Vietnamese prime minister Ngo Dinh Diem in his refusal to hold the election, in effect violating the Geneva agreement.

> *In seeking to make South Vietnam a bulwark against communism, the United States repeated most of the mistakes that had doomed the French.*

Between 1955 and 1961, the United States poured $1 billion into South Vietnam, 80 percent of which went to the South Vietnamese army (ARVN). Yet even with U.S. dollars, the ARVN proved to be grossly unprepared for the guerrilla warfare that began in the late 1950s. In 1959, Ho Chi Minh's government in Hanoi began sending military assistance to Vietminh rebels in the south, who stepped up their guerrilla attacks on the Diem government. The insurgents gained control over villages not only through sheer military power but also because peasants were outraged by Diem's repressive regime. Unable to reverse the growing opposition to Diem in the south and unwilling to abandon containment, Eisenhower handed over the deteriorating situation—along with a firm commitment to defend South Vietnam against communism—to his successor, John F. Kennedy, in 1961.

Interventions in Latin America and the Middle East

While attempting to buttress friendly governments in Asia, the Eisenhower administration also worked to topple unfriendly ones in Latin America and the Middle East. Much more than Truman, Eisenhower relied on behind-the-scenes efforts and covert activities against such governments through the CIA, which became an important arm of foreign policy in the 1950s. Increasingly, the administration conducted foreign policy behind the back of Congress.

Taking extreme care not to leave a paper trail, Eisenhower authorized the CIA, headed by Allen Dulles, the brother of the secretary of state, to eliminate a threat to U.S. interests in oil-rich Iran (see Map 29.2). In 1951, Iran's left-leaning prime minister, Mohammed Mossadegh, nationalized oil fields and refineries, thereby setting a precedent that threatened Western oil interests throughout the Middle East. Mossadegh also challenged the power of the shah, Mohammad Reza Pahlavi, Iran's hereditary leader, who favored foreign oil interests and the Iranian wealthy classes. Moreover, Mossadegh accepted support from the Iranian Communist Party.

For all of these reasons, Eisenhower approved a plan for CIA agents to bribe army officers and pay Iranians to demonstrate against Mossadegh's government. In August 1953, army officers took Mossadegh prisoner, and the shah's power was reestablished. Iran renegotiated oil concessions, giving U.S. companies a 40 percent share. Although the intervention worked in the short run, Americans in the 1970s and 1980s would feel the full fury of Iranian opposition to the repressive government that the United States had helped to reinstall.

Heady with the success in Iran, the Eisenhower administration soon turned to clandestine activities in Central America, where it perceived a Communist threat in Guatemala (see Map 28.1). As in Iran, the Guatemalan government was neither Communist nor Soviet-controlled, but it accepted support from the native Communist Party and threatened established economic interests. Authorized by Eisenhower, the CIA staged a coup in 1954, displacing the popularly elected government of Jacobo Arbenz with a military dictatorship. In both Guatemala and Iran, U.S. intervention thwarted the popular will, set up dictatorships, and helped American corporations.

"We're going to take care of Castro just like we took care of Arbenz," promised a CIA agent when Cubans' desire for political and economic autonomy erupted in 1959. American companies had long controlled a large portion of Cuba's major resources—especially sugar, tobacco, and mines—and decisions made in Washington directly influenced the lives and livelihoods of the Cuban people. When a 1959 uprising led by Fidel Castro drove out dictator Fulgencio Batista, who had been supported by the United States, CIA director Dulles warned Eisenhower that "Communists and other extreme radicals appear to have penetrated the Castro movement." When the United States denied Castro's requests for loans, the new Cuban leader turned for help to the Soviet Union. Also, after American companies refused Castro's offer to purchase them at their assessed value—which the Batista government had kept ridiculously low so that Americans could avoid heavy taxes—he began to nationalize their property. Many Cubans in opposition to Castro escaped to the United States and reported his atrocities, including the execution of

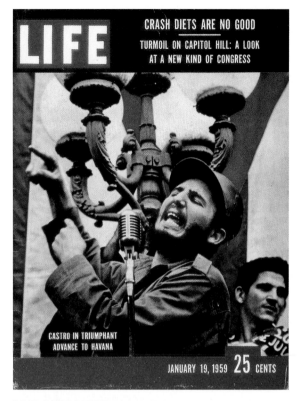

FIDEL CASTRO TRIUMPHS IN CUBA
Fidel Castro came from a privileged family and attended law school at the University of Havana, but he spent his youth working for the overthrow of Cuban dictator Fulgencio Batista. After leading an assault on Batista's soldiers in 1953, he spent two years in prison and then slowly built up an army of guerrilla fighters. He is shown here in his triumphal entrance into Havana in January 1959.
TimePix.

hundreds of Batista's supporters. Before leaving office, Eisenhower broke off diplomatic relations with Cuba and authorized the CIA to train Cuban exiles for an invasion.

Also following its involvement in Iran, elsewhere in the Middle East the Eisenhower administration turned from Truman's all-out support for Israel and attempted to foster friendships with Arab nations. But the smaller Arab nations preferred to seek aid from both the West and the Communist nations, and so rejected American insistence on complete loyalty to the United States. In 1955, Secretary of State Dulles began negotiating with Egypt about American support for building the Aswan Dam on the Nile River. But in 1956, Egypt's leader, Gamal

Abdel Nasser, declared his intention to obtain arms from Communist Czechoslovakia, formed a military alliance with other Arab nations, and recognized the People's Republic of China.

Unwilling to tolerate such independence, Dulles called off the deal for the dam. On July 26, 1956, Nasser responded boldly by seizing the Suez Canal, then owned by Britain and France. Taking the canal advanced Nasser's prestige and power because it coincided with nationalist aspirations in the Arab world, and revenue from the canal could provide capital for constructing the dam. Britain and France immediately protested the canal seizure, but Eisenhower announced that the United States would not participate in military efforts to settle the Suez crisis. He recognized that the Egyptians had claimed their own territory, and he believed that Nasser "embodie[d] the emotional demands of the people . . . for independence."

The Suez Crisis, 1956

Since the establishment of Israel in 1948, Egyptian and Israeli forces had engaged in skirmishes along their common border. When Egypt seized the Suez Canal, Israel attacked Egypt, with military support from France and Britain. Shocked and angered, Eisenhower cut off oil to Britain and France while calling on the United Nations to arrange a truce. Lacking U.S. support, the French and British soon pulled back, forcing Israel to retreat from territory it had captured in the Sinai Desert region of Egypt.

Although Eisenhower refused to intervene in the Suez crisis, he made clear that the United States would actively combat communism in the Middle East. In March 1957, Congress passed a joint resolution approving economic and military aid to any Middle Eastern nation "requesting assistance against armed aggression from any country controlled by international communism." The president invoked this "Eisenhower Doctrine" to send aid to Jordan in 1957

and troops to Lebanon in 1958 to counter anti-Western pressures on those governments.

The Nuclear Arms Race

Although Eisenhower and his aides often spoke of the Soviet Union in harsh and alarming terms, the president was determined to reduce superpower tensions. As early as 1953, he remarked to one of his aides that the armaments race would lead "at worst to atomic warfare, at best to robbing every people and nation on earth of the fruits of their own toil." A number of events made accommodation a promising prospect. After Stalin's death in 1953, a more moderate leadership under Nikita Khrushchev emerged. The Soviet Union signed a peace treaty with Austria guaranteeing Austrian neutrality and removed its troops from that country. Like Eisenhower, Khrushchev worried about the domestic costs of the cold war and wanted to reduce defense spending and check the arms race.

Eisenhower and Khrushchev met in Geneva in 1955 at the first summit conference since the end of World War II. Though it produced no significant agreements, the meeting nevertheless symbolized a lessening of tensions—as Eisenhower put it, "a new spirit of conciliation and cooperation." In 1959, Khrushchev visited the United States, and Nixon went to the Soviet Union, where he engaged in the famous kitchen debate. By 1960, the two sides were within reach of a ban on nuclear testing, and Khrushchev and Eisenhower agreed to meet again in Paris in May.

To avoid jeopardizing the summit, Eisenhower decided to cancel espionage flights over the Soviet Union, but his order came one day too late. On May 1, 1960, Soviet gunners shot down a U-2 spy plane over Soviet territory. Assuming that the pilot, Francis Gary Powers, had not survived, the State Department denied that U.S. planes had been deliberately violating Soviet air space. When the Soviets produced not only Powers but also the photos taken on his flight, they caught the United States in a lie. Eisenhower assumed responsibility but refused to apologize. He met with Khrushchev briefly in Paris, but the U-2 incident dashed all prospects for a nuclear arms agreement and ended Eisenhower's plans to visit Moscow.

Eisenhower's "more bang for the buck" defense budget enormously increased the U.S. nuclear capacity, as the stockpile of nuclear weapons more than quadrupled during his administration. By the time Eisenhower left office in 1961, the United States had installed seventy-two intercontinental ballistic missiles (ICBMs) in the United States and Britain, was prepared to deploy additional missiles in Italy and Turkey, and had several hundred more under contract. The first Polaris submarine carrying nuclear missiles was launched in November 1960.

In August 1957, the Soviets test-fired their first ICBM; two months later, they launched *Sputnik,* the first artificial satellite to circle the planet. Senate majority leader Lyndon Johnson regarded these developments as a scientific Pearl Harbor. *Sputnik's* launch spread a sense that the United States lagged behind not only in missile development and space exploration but also in science, education, economic growth, and national resolve. When the United

States tried to launch a response to *Sputnik,* its satellite exploded. Newspapers expressed the humiliation by calling it a "Stayputnik" or a "Flopnik." The United States finally launched its first satellite in January 1958.

Eisenhower correctly insisted that the United States possessed nuclear superiority, but in 1957 he could not disclose his strongest evidence: information about the Soviet arsenal obtained by the top-secret U-2 surveillance. He took steps to diminish public panic, establishing the National Aeronautics and Space Administration (NASA) in July 1958 and approving a gigantic increase in the budget for space research and development. Because some blamed American schools for the nation's inability

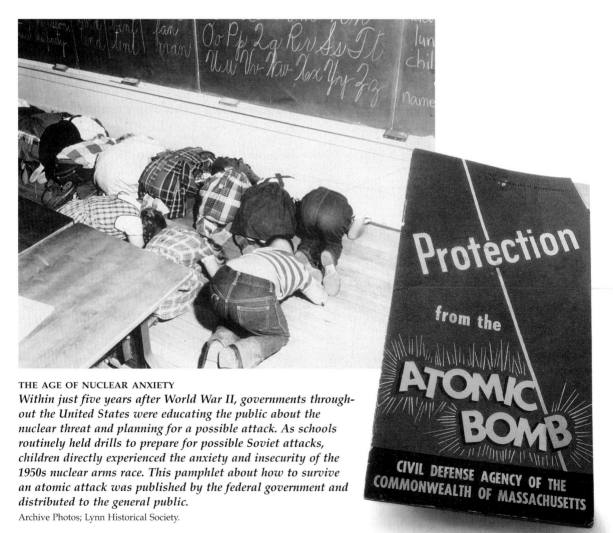

THE AGE OF NUCLEAR ANXIETY
Within just five years after World War II, governments throughout the United States were educating the public about the nuclear threat and planning for a possible attack. As schools routinely held drills to prepare for possible Soviet attacks, children directly experienced the anxiety and insecurity of the 1950s nuclear arms race. This pamphlet about how to survive an atomic attack was published by the federal government and distributed to the general public.
Archive Photos; Lynn Historical Society.

www.bedfordstmartins.com/tap SEE THE ONLINE STUDY GUIDE for more help in analyzing this image.

to beat the Soviets into space, educational reformers gained attention and new federal funds: In 1958, Eisenhower signed the National Defense Education Act, providing loans and scholarships for students in math, foreign languages, and science.

American nuclear superiority did not guarantee security. Though the Soviet Union lagged behind the United States in military technology, it nonetheless possessed sufficient nuclear weapons to devastate the United States. American schoolchildren regularly dove under their desks or crouched on the floor during drills in preparation for a nuclear attack, and the Civil Defense Administration recommended that families construct home bomb shelters. Most American families did not build shelters, but they realized how precarious nuclear weapons had made their lives. Moreover, some 200,000 Americans were exposed to radiation resulting from nuclear testing, and others were the unknowing subjects of government-sponsored experiments to see how humans reacted to radioactive materials.

Most American families did not build shelters, but they realized how precarious nuclear weapons had made their lives.

Just before he left office, Eisenhower emphasized another menace of the cold war: the growing influence of the "military-industrial complex" in American government and life. To contain the defense budget, Eisenhower had struggled against persistent pressures from defense contractors who, in tandem with the military services, sought more dollars for newer, more powerful weapons systems. In his farewell address, he warned that the "conjunction of an immense military establishment and a large arms industry . . . exercised a total influence . . . in every city, every state house, every office of the federal government." The cold war had created a warfare state.

Winners and Losers in an Economy of Abundance

U.S. military spending helped stimulate domestic prosperity. Economic productivity increased enormously in the 1950s, a multitude of new products came on the market, consumption became the order of the day, and millions of Americans moved to the suburbs. Prosperity also enabled more young people than ever before to stay in school, and higher education became the norm for the middle class. Although every section of the nation enjoyed the new prosperity, the West and Southwest especially boomed in production, commerce, and population.

The nature of work itself changed, as fewer people worked on farms, white-collar employment overtook manufacturing jobs, and women's employment grew. These economic shifts disadvantaged some segments of the population, and some forty million people—20 percent of all Americans—lived in poverty. Most Americans, however, enjoyed a higher standard of living, leading the economist John Kenneth Galbraith to call the United States "the affluent society."

Technology Transforms Agriculture and Industry

Between 1940 and 1960, the output of American farms mushroomed, while the number of farmworkers declined by nearly one-third. Farmers achieved nearly miraculous agricultural productivity through greater crop specialization, more intensive use of fertilizers, and, above all, mechanization. Tractors, mechanical pickers, and other forms of machinery increasingly replaced human labor and animal power. One mechanical cotton picker alone replaced fifty people and reduced the cost of harvesting a bale of cotton from forty dollars to five dollars.

The decline of the family farm and the growth of large commercial farming, or "agribusiness," were both causes and consequences of mechanization. Larger farmers benefited handsomely from federal price support programs begun in the New Deal, and they more easily took advantage of technological improvements, while smaller producers lacked capital to invest in the machinery that was required to compete. Consequently, although the average farm size more than doubled between 1940 and 1964, the farm population declined from thirty million to thirteen million, and the number of farms decreased by more than 40 percent.

Many small farmers who hung on constituted a core of rural poverty that escaped the attention of those who celebrated the affluence of the 1950s. Southern sharecroppers fell victim to the transformation of agriculture, forced off the land when owners replaced them with machinery. Hundreds

POVERTY IN AN ERA OF ABUNDANCE
The Whiteheads, a coal-mining family in Kentucky, represented the hidden side of the affluent postwar era. Mrs. John Whitehead, shown here, lived with her husband, their six children, and their six grandchildren in this three-room house. It had neither running water nor electricity, and the only access to the house was over a mountain trail.
National Archives.

of thousands of African Americans joined an exodus to cities in the South, North, and West, where racial discrimination and a lack of jobs for which they could qualify mired them in urban poverty. A Mississippi woman whose family had worked on a plantation since slavery recalled that when her relatives heard that "it was going to be machines now that harvest the crops," most of them went to Chicago. Worrying that "it might be worse up there," she faced an agonizing choice: "I'm afraid to leave and I'm afraid to stay, and whichever I do, I think it might be real bad for my boys and girls."

Alongside the 20 percent poverty rate, economists claimed that some 60 percent of Americans enjoyed middle-class incomes in 1960. Between 1950 and 1960, the gross national product (the value of all goods and services produced during a year)

as well as median family income grew by 25 percent in constant dollars (Figure 26.1). By the late 1950s, four of every five families owned television sets and washing machines, and nearly all had refrigerators. The number of automobiles on the road nearly doubled during the 1950s, and the great majority of American families owned at least one car.

Several forces spurred this unparalleled abundance. Even with Eisenhower's conservative fiscal policies, government spending reached $80 billion annually and stimulated the creation of jobs. A dramatic growth in population—from 152 million in 1950 to 180 million in 1960—expanded demand for products and stimulated industries ranging from baby goods to music. Nearly doubling its sales of ads during the decade, the advertising industry encouraged people to consume. Consumer borrowing

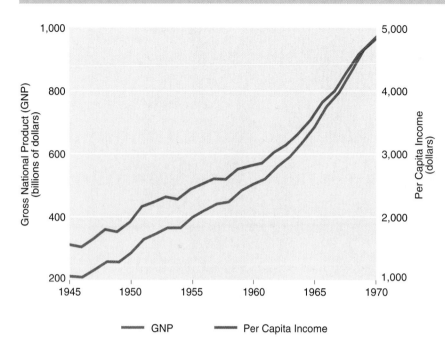

FIGURE **26.1**

The Postwar Economic Boom: GNP and Per Capita Income, 1945–1970
American dominance of the worldwide market, innovative technologies that led to new industries such as computers and plastics, population growth, and increases in worker productivity all contributed to the enormous economic growth of the United States after World War II.

also fueled the economic boom; as more and more people purchased houses, cars, and appliances on installment plans, older values of frugality and saving began to erode.

As in agriculture, technological innovation increased industrial production. In the automobile industry, for example, new technology cut the number of labor-hours needed to manufacture a car by one-half between 1945 and 1960. Technology also transformed such industries as electronics, chemicals, and air transportation and promoted the growth of newer industries, such as television, plastics, and computers. American businesses enjoyed access to cheap oil in abundance, and the nation's dominance in the international economy provided American producers ample markets abroad and relatively little foreign competition in the domestic economy.

Labor unions enjoyed their greatest success during the 1950s as production workers saw their real earnings increase by 40 percent. The merger in 1955 of the American Federation of Labor (AFL) and the Congress of Industrial Organizations (CIO) lessened jurisdictional conflicts and enabled labor to speak with one voice. Fringe benefits—pensions, health care, insurance, and paid vacations—became a staple of union contracts in most industries, though workers in the steel, automobile, and other heavy industries did much better than those in food processing, garment making, and other areas of light manufacturing. Unlike other industrial na-

tions, where government provided most of the benefits, the United States developed a mixed system in which company-funded programs—won by unions through collective bargaining—played a larger role. Sometimes referred to as the "privatization of welfare," this system resulted in wide disparities among workers, severely disadvantaging those workers not represented by unions.

While the absolute number of union members continued to increase, union membership as a percentage of the labor force peaked at 27.1 percent in 1957. Automation and innovation chipped away at jobs in heavy industry, where most union workers were concentrated. Technological advances reduced the number of workers in the steel, copper, and aluminum industries by 17 percent. Moreover, the economy as a whole was shifting from production (blue-collar jobs) to service (white-collar occupations). Instead of manufacturing products, more and more workers now distributed goods, performed services, kept records, provided education, or carried out government work. Although unions made headway in some of these fields, most white-collar employees resisted unionization, and many of the "service" workers—such as janitors, food servers, and domestics—performed hard manual labor for low wages.

The growing clerical and service occupations swelled the demand for female workers, who joined the workforce during the 1950s at a rate four times that of men. By the end of the decade, 35 percent of

Modern Farming

WITH JOHN DEERE QUALITY FARM EQUIPMENT

1955 Edition

MECHANIZING AGRICULTURE
This farm equipment ad reflects the growing application of technology to agriculture. Ever more elaborate machinery created a long-term trend in which family farms were overtaken by agribusiness. Giant farms employed the latest technology and thus reduced the need for human labor. Between 1945 and 1960, the nation's population living on farms shrank from 17.5 to 8.7 percent.
John Deere Company.

all women over age sixteen worked outside the home—twice as many as in 1940—and women held more than one-third of all jobs. Moreover, the largest increases in employment occurred for married women, who sought a second family paycheck to secure some of the new abundance for their families. As one woman remarked, "My Joe can't put five kids through college, and then Sue needed braces . . . and the washer had to be replaced, and Ann was ashamed to bring friends home because the living room furniture was such a mess, so I went to work."

Women entered a sharply segregated workplace. The vast majority worked in clerical and service jobs, light manufacturing, domestic jobs, teaching, and nursing. Union organizers neglected most of these areas, and because they were female occupations, wages were relatively low. In 1960, the average female worker, employed full-time all year, earned just 60 percent of the average wage for a male worker. At the bottom of the employment ladder, black women earned, on average, 42 percent of what white men earned.

Burgeoning Suburbs and Declining Cities

Although residential areas adjacent to cities had existed since the nineteenth century, nothing symbolized the affluent society more than the tremendous expansion of suburbs: Of the thirteen million new homes built in the 1950s, eleven million appeared in the suburbs, and more than one million Americans moved there every year of the decade. By 1960, one in every four Americans lived in the suburbs. And the suburbs were accessible to families with modest incomes. Builder William J. Levitt pioneered construction of affordable housing with his seventeen-thousand-home development, called Levittown, on Long Island, New York. Modifying the assembly-line process developed for automobiles by Henry Ford, Levitt planned nearly identical houses so that individual construction workers could move from house to house and perform the same single operation in each, such as caulking windows or installing bathtubs. Families could purchase these mass-produced houses for just under $8,000 in 1949. Developments similar to Levittown, as well as more luxurious ones, quickly went up around metropolitan areas throughout the country.

Nothing symbolized the affluent society more than the tremendous expansion of suburbs.

While private industry built the suburbs, the government made home ownership possible by guaranteeing low-interest mortgages through the Federal Housing Administration and the Veterans Administration. A veteran could buy a house in Levittown with payments of just $58 per month for twenty-five years. Moreover, thousands of

AN AFRICAN AMERICAN SUBURB
The pioneer of mass-produced suburban housing, William J. Levitt, reflected the racism that kept blacks out of suburbia when he said, "We can solve a housing problem, or we can try and solve a racial problem but we cannot combine the two." These African Americans developed their own suburb, a planned community for middle-class blacks in Richmond, California, which welcomed the first families in 1950.
Courtesy Richmond Public Library.

interstate highway miles were built through urban areas, indirectly subsidizing suburban development. Without the automobile and the freeway, the suburban explosion would not have been possible.

Although the new suburbanites enjoyed the convenience and spaciousness of their new homes and the social activities of their new neighborhoods, suburban culture was not without its detractors. Architecture critic and social philosopher Lewis Mumford blasted the suburbs as "a multitude of uniform, unidentifiable houses, lined up inflexibly, at uniform distances, on uniform roads, in a treeless communal wasteland, inhabited by people of the same class, the same income, the same age group." The growing suburbs did contribute to a more polarized society, especially along racial lines. Each Levittown homeowner signed a contract saying that "no dwelling shall be used or occupied by members of other than the Caucasian race." Although the

Supreme Court declared such covenants unenforceable in 1948, suburban America remained dramatically segregated.

As white residents joined the suburban migration, blacks moved to cities in search of economic opportunity. In most cities, the number of African American residents grew by 50 percent during the 1950s, and Washington, D.C., became the first leading city with a black majority. The newcomers in the north and east came to cities that were already in decline, losing not only population but also commerce and industry to the suburbs or to southern and western states. New manufacturing and wholesaling facilities began to ring central cities, and shoppers gradually chose suburban malls over downtown department stores. Many jobs lay beyond the reach of the recent black arrivals to the inner cities, and urban governments faced falling tax revenues at the exact time the keep their children out of work and in school longer, and the federal government subsidized the education of more than two million World War II and Korean War veterans. The cold war also sent millions of federal dollars to universities for defense-related research. Total tax dollars spent for higher education more than doubled from 1950 to 1960, as state governments vastly expanded the number of four-year colleges and universities, and municipalities began to build two-year junior or community colleges.

The GI Bill made college possible for thousands of African Americans, the majority of whom attended black institutions. College enrollments of blacks surged from thirty-seven thousand in 1941 to ninety thousand in 1961. Yet African Americans constituted only about 5 percent of all college students, less than half their percentage in the general population. Unlike their white counterparts, black men and women attended college in nearly equal numbers.

Initially, the democratization of higher education increased the educational gap between white men and women. The numbers of women college students grew, but they did not keep pace relative to those of men. In 1940, women constituted 40 percent of college graduating classes, but as veterans flocked to college campuses, women's proportion came to just 25 percent in 1950. Even by 1960, women were receiving just 33 percent of college degrees. The large veteran enrollments did, however, introduce a new feature of college life—the married student. Unlike men, however, women dropped out of college upon marriage. Reflecting gender-role norms of the 1950s, most college women responding to a survey agreed that "it is natural for a woman to be satisfied with her husband's success and not crave personal achievement."

MOVING INTO THE SUBURBS
In the Los Angeles suburb of Lakewood, families gobbled up houses as fast as they could be built. Between 1946 and 1960, an average of 400 people moved into the Los Angeles area every day, and the population of Lakewood jumped from 2,000 to 100,000. What can you tell from this photograph about the composition of the families moving into Lakewood?

J. B. Eyerman, *Life* magazine © 1953 Time, Inc.

poverty of their newer residents required greater services.

The Democratization of Higher Education

The affluent postwar years spectacularly transformed higher education. Between 1940 and 1960, enrollments leaped from 1.5 million to 3.6 million, outstripping population growth. Whereas about 15 percent of young Americans attended college in 1940, more than 40 percent did so by the mid-1960s. Higher education was no longer the domain of the privileged. Prosperity enabled many families to

The Rise of the Sun Belt

The nation seemed to be tipped westward, quipped architect Frank Lloyd Wright: Everything not bolted down was sliding toward California. No other regions experienced the postwar economic and population booms more intensely than the West and Southwest. With the number of its citizens more than doubling after World War II, California overtook New York as the most populous state in 1962. Even sports franchises moved west, beginning in 1958 when the Brooklyn Dodgers moved to Los

TABLE 26.1
THE GROWING SUN BELT CITIES, 1920–1980

	1920	1940	1960	1980
Los Angeles	879	2,916	6,039	7,478
Houston	168	529	1,418	2,905
Dallas	185	527	1,084	2,430
Atlanta	249	559	1,017	2,030
San Diego	74	289	1,033	1,862
Miami	30	268	935	1,626
Phoenix	29	186	664	1,509
New Orleans	398	552	907	1,256
San Antonio	191	338	716	1,072
Tucson	20	37	266	531

(Population in thousands)

Angeles and the New York Giants to San Francisco. A warm climate and a beautiful natural environment drew new residents to the West and Southwest, but no magnet proved stronger than the promise of economic opportunity (Table 26.1).

As railroads had fueled western growth in the nineteenth century, the automobile and the airplane helped generate the post–World War II surge, providing efficient transportation for both people and products. The technology of air-conditioning made possible industrial development in the so-called Sun Belt, which stretched from Florida to California (Map 26.2). Crucial to the region's population explosion, air-conditioning cooled nearly eight million Sun Belt homes by 1960. (See "The Promise of Technology," page 1000.)

The aerospace industry boomed in Seattle–Tacoma, Los Angeles, Tucson, and Dallas–Fort Worth, and military bases helped underwrite prosperity in such cities as San Diego and San Antonio. Although defense dollars benefited regions such as New England, with its electronics and research and development operations, the West captured the lion's share of cold war spending for research and production of bombers, missiles, other weapons, and satellites. So important was the defense industry to the growth of the South and West that some referred to the region as the "Gun Belt." In California alone, the federal government spent more than $100 billion for defense between 1945 and 1965. By the 1960s, nearly one of every three California workers held a defense-related job.

The high-technology basis of postwar economic development drew well-educated, highly skilled workers to the West. But the economic promise also attracted the poor. "We see opportunity all around us here. . . . We smell freedom here, and maybe soon we can taste it," commented a black mother in California. Between 1945 and 1960, more than one-third of the African Americans who left the South moved to the West.

A warm climate and a beautiful natural environment drew new residents to the West and Southwest, but no magnet proved stronger than the promise of economic opportunity.

The Mexican American, or Chicano, population also grew, especially in California and Texas. To supply California's vast agribusiness industry, the government continued the *bracero* program begun during World War II. Until the program ended in 1964, more than a hundred thousand Mexicans entered the United States each year to labor in the fields—and many of them stayed, legally or illegally. But while the government encouraged the use of Mexican labor, it responded to white Americans' opposition to permanent Mexican immigration, launching in 1954 a series of raids called "Operation Wetback." Designed to ferret out and deport illegal immigrants, the operation made U.S. citizens

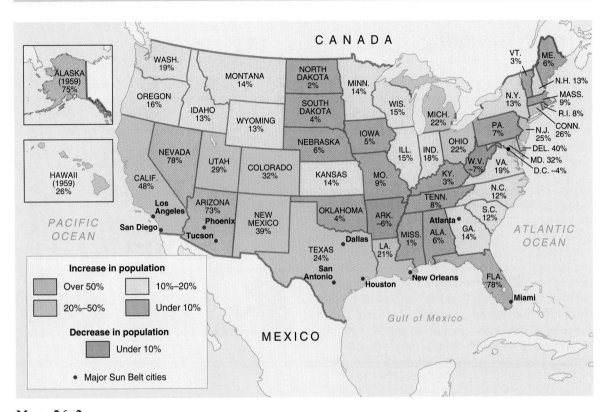

MAP 26.2

The Rise of the Sun Belt, 1940–1980

The growth of defense industries, a nonunionized labor force, and the spread of air-conditioning all helped spur economic development and population growth, which made the Sun Belt the fastest-growing region of the nation between 1940 and 1980.

READING THE MAP: What states experienced an over 20 percent growth in population? What states experienced the largest population growth?

CONNECTIONS: What stimulated the population boom in the Southwest? What role did the cold war play in this boom? What role did African Americans play in the western population boom?

www.bedfordstmartins.com/tap   SEE THE ONLINE STUDY GUIDE for more help in analyzing this map.

of Mexican descent feel unwelcome and threatened them with incidents of mistaken identity.

Native Americans increased their numbers but also suffered under new government policies. In 1953, the Eisenhower administration introduced the policy called "termination," which aimed to end the special status of American Indians, eliminate their reservations, and do away with tribal sovereignty. Termination fit well with Eisenhower's preference for a limited federal government, but it proved devastating for Native Americans. Before the policy was

abandoned in the 1960s, it moved 170,000 Indians off their reservations. Like most of the blacks who migrated from the South, the displaced Indians most typically exchanged rural poverty for urban poverty.

Free of the discrimination that denied economic opportunity to minority groups, white Americans reaped the fullest fruits of prosperity in the West. In April 1950, California developers advertised the opening of Lakewood, a large new housing development in Los Angeles County. On the first day of sales, thirty thousand people lined up to purchase

Air-Conditioning

A IR-CONDITIONING DEVELOPED PRIMARILY in response to the needs of industry. In 1902, Willis Haviland Carrier, an American engineer who formulated basic theories of air-conditioning, designed the first system to control temperature and humidity and installed it in a Brooklyn printing plant. In 1915, he founded the Carrier Corporation to manufacture air-conditioning equipment. Because fibers are sensitive to moisture, the textile industry provided an early and important market for air-conditioning. The process also helped to popularize movie theaters by making them a cool as well as an entertaining retreat during hot summer months. Room air conditioners began to appear in the 1930s. This 1950 Carrier ad promoted the clean air in homes and offices that would come with purchase of a room air conditioner. Fewer than a million homes had room air conditioners in 1950, but nearly eight million did in 1960, and more than half of all homes had some form of air conditioning by 1975, as its status changed from a luxury to a necessity.

Air-conditioning was a mixed blessing. Air-conditioned offices meant that companies no longer had to shut down and send workers home when heat and humidity became unbearable, and the machines improved air quality inside businesses, homes, and cars. But air conditioners consumed large amounts of energy and contributed to outdoor air pollution. Like other technologies such as television and, more recently, the Internet, air-conditioning had an isolating effect as people deserted front porches and backyards for closed-up houses and thus curtailed their interactions with neighbors. Perhaps its greatest impact on the nation was to make possible the population explosion in the Sun

"THAT'S MODERN AIR CONTROL!"
Ads like this one for the Carrier room air conditioner promised consumers that homes could be cool as well as clean.
Courtesy Carrier Corporation.

Belt. By facilitating the movement of commerce, industry, and tourism to the south, air-conditioning made that region more like the rest of the nation. One historian of the South, referring disparagingly to the transformation worked by air-conditioning on that region, proclaimed that "[General Electric] has proved a more devastating invader than even General Sherman."

tract houses for $8,000 to $10,000. Many of the new home owners were veterans, blue-collar and lower-level white-collar workers whose defense-based jobs at McDonnell Douglas and other aerospace corporations or at the Long Beach naval station and shipyard enabled them to fulfill the American dream of the 1950s. A huge regional shopping mall,

Lakewood Center, offered myriad products of the consumer culture. And as California's master plan for higher education went into effect, their children had access to several community colleges, four campuses of California State University, and two campuses of the University of California system—all within easy reach of Lakewood.

ROUNDING UP
UNDOCUMENTED MIGRANTS
*Not all Mexican Americans
who wanted to work in
the United States were
accommodated by the*
bracero *program. In 1953,
Los Angeles police arrested
these men who did not
have legal documents and
were hiding in a freight
train. Americans used the
crude term* **wetback** *to refer
to illegal immigrants be-
cause many of them swam
across the Rio Grande, at
the border between the
United States and Mexico.*
Corbis-Bettmann.

The Culture of Abundance

With increased prosperity in the 1950s, more people married and the birthrate soared. Religious ob-
servance quickened even as Americans sought satisfaction in material possessions. Television entered
the homes of most Americans, helping to promote
a consumer culture. Dominant values favored family life and traditional gender roles, consumption,
conformity, and "belongingness." Undercurrents of
rebellion, especially among youth, defied some of
the dominant norms but did not greatly disrupt the
complacency of the 1950s.

The Revival of Domesticity
and Religion

The entrance of married women into the workforce
in unprecedented numbers coexisted with the dominant ideology that celebrated traditional family life
and conventional gender roles. Even though more
than one-third of mothers with school-age children
left the home for work, the family ideal defined by
popular culture and public spokespersons persisted: a male breadwinner, a full-time homemaker,
and three or four children leading a safe, comfort-

able life in a new suburban home. Americans were
eager to realize a societal norm that had been disrupted by economic depression in the 1930s and
war in the 1940s.

Writer and feminist Betty Friedan gave a name
to the idealization of women's domestic roles in her
book *The Feminine Mystique,* published in 1963.
Friedan claimed that advertisers, social scientists,
educators, women's magazines, and public officials
all encouraged women to seek their ultimate ful-
fillment in serving others through marriage and
childrearing. According to the feminine mystique,
biological differences fitted men and women for entirely different roles in life. The ideal woman kept
a spotless house, cooked creative meals, raised her
children to be good citizens, served her husband's
career, and provided him emotional and sexual satisfaction. In 1956, *Life* magazine had declared, "Of
all the accomplishments of the American woman,
the one she brings off with the most spectacular success is having babies."

Although the glorification of domesticity
clashed with married women's increasing participation in the labor force, the lives of many Americans did in fact embody the family ideal. Postwar
prosperity enabled people to rush to the altar and
to have children. In 1960, some 68 percent of all

adults were married, the largest percentage in the twentieth century. Whereas its general trend over the twentieth century was downward, the American birthrate soared during the period 1945 to 1965, reaching a peak in 1957 with 4.3 million births and producing the "baby boom" generation (Figure 26.2).

Even though more than one-third of mothers with school-age children left the home for work, the family ideal persisted: a male breadwinner, a full-time homemaker, and three or four children leading a safe, comfortable life in a new suburban home.

The norms for childrearing were more demanding than ever before. Magnifying the importance of maternal attention in the child's daily development, Dr. Benjamin Spock's best-selling *Common Sense Book of Baby and Child Care* (1946) advocated a permissive approach in place of the more traditional emphasis on strictness and rigid schedules. While such an approach required that mothers devote their full time to childrearing, experts in the 1950s also urged fathers to cultivate family "togetherness" and spend more time with their children.

Along with a renewed emphasis on family life, the 1950s witnessed a surge of interest in religion. By 1960, about 63 percent of Americans belonged to churches and synagogues, up from 50 percent in 1940. Polls reported that 95 percent of all Americans professed a belief in God and 90 percent prayed. Evangelism took on new life, most notably in the nationwide crusades of Baptist minister Billy Graham, whose passionate and powerful oratory moved mass audiences to accept Christ. President-elect Eisenhower, who joined the National Presbyterian Church in Washington, expressed the enthusiasm of the religious revival when he proclaimed in 1952 that "our government makes no sense unless it is founded on a deeply felt religious faith— and I don't care what it is!" Although religious conflict did not disappear, greater cooperation was evident in Christian ecumenical movements such as the World Council of Churches, organized in 1948. Congress linked religion more closely to the state by adding "under God" to the pledge of allegiance in 1954 and by requiring in 1955 that "In God We Trust" be printed on all currency. Eisenhower's pastor attributed the renewed interest in religion to economic progress, which, he said, "provided the leisure, the energy, and the means for a level of human and spiritual values never before reached." Others suggested that Americans were turning to religious organizations for reassurance and peace of

FIGURE 26.2

U.S. Birthrate, 1900–1990
Notice the long-term trend of decline in birthrate over the twentieth century. What helps to account for the unusual plunge in the 1930s and the steep but temporary ascent in the 1950s?

EVANGELIST BILLY GRAHAM
A young Baptist minister from North Carolina, Billy Graham electrified mass audiences across the country, entreating them to find salvation in Jesus Christ and to uphold Christian moral standards. So large were his audiences that Graham extended his 1957 New York crusade from eight to sixteen weeks. Here he preaches in Madison Square Garden.
Gjon Mili/TimePix.

mind from cold war anxieties and the threat of nuclear annihilation.

Social critics questioned the depth of the religious revival, attributing the growth in church membership to a desire for conformity and a need for social outlets. One commentator, for example, noted that 53 percent of Americans could not name any book of the New Testament. The popularity of the Reverend Norman Vincent Peale, whose best-selling book *The Power of Positive Thinking* (1952) emphasized how to be successful and happy, suggested to critics the superficiality of Americans' attachment to religion.

Television Transforms Culture and Politics

Just as private family life and religion offered a respite from the anxieties of the cold war, so too did the new medium of television. In 1950, fewer than 10 percent of American homes boasted a television set, but by 1960 about 87 percent of all households owned one and on average Americans were spending more than five hours each day in front of the screen.

Television kept people at home but did not necessarily enhance family relationships. When parents and children focused their attention on the TV screen, their conversation was limited. The new medium altered eating habits when, in 1954, the frozen dinner, a complete meal in an easily portable tray, enabled families to spend the dinner hour in front of the TV set. Noticing that the heaviest water consumption took place on the hour and the half hour, civil engineers in Toledo, Ohio, recognized that television even regulated trips to the bathroom.

Especially popular were situation comedies, which projected the family ideal and the feminine mystique into millions of homes. On TV, women with families did not work outside the home and ostensibly deferred to their husbands, though they often got the upper hand through subtle manipulation. In the most popular television show of the early 1950s, *I Love Lucy,* the husband-and-wife team of Lucille Ball and Desi Arnaz played the fictional couple Lucy and Ricky Ricardo. In step with the

THE MADE-FOR-TV FAMILY
This scene is from the popular television sitcom **Father Knows Best**, *which ran from 1954 to 1963 and which, along with other shows such as* **Ozzie and Harriet** *and* **Leave It to Beaver**, *idealized white family life. In these shows, no one got divorced or became gravely ill, no one took drugs or seriously misbehaved, fathers held white-collar jobs, mothers did not work outside the home, and husbands and wives slept in twin beds.*
Culver Pictures/Rob Huntley, Lightstream/Picture Research Consultants, Inc.

trends, they moved from an apartment in the city to a house in suburbia. Ricky refused to allow his wife to work outside the home, and many of the plots depicted Lucy's zany attempts to thwart his objections.

Although TV news did not become the public's main source of news until the 1960s, television began to affect politics in the 1950s. Richard Nixon's "Checkers speech" reached a nationwide audience and kept him on the Republican ticket in 1952. The televised hearings in which Joseph McCarthy attacked army members helped to bring about the

senator's downfall. Eisenhower's 1952 presidential campaign used TV advertising spots for the first time, although Democratic candidate Adlai Stevenson refused to participate in "selling the presidency like cereal." By 1960, television played a major role in candidates' chances for success. Reflecting on his narrow victory in 1960, President-elect John F. Kennedy remarked, "We wouldn't have had a prayer without that gadget."

Television transformed politics and government in other ways as well. Money became a much larger force in politics than ever before, because candidates needed to raise huge sums for expensive TV spots. The ability to appeal directly to voters in their living rooms encouraged candidates to build their own campaign organizations and to rely less on political parties. The declining strength of parties and the growing power of money in elections were not new trends, but television did much to accelerate them.

Just as private family life and religion offered a respite from the anxieties of the cold war, so too did the new medium of television.

Unlike government-financed television in Europe, private enterprise paid for American TV through advertising, and advertisers did not hesitate to interfere with shows that might jeopardize the sale of their products. On the *Camel News Caravan,* for example, the sponsor, producer of Camel cigarettes, insisted that any film clips showing "No Smoking" signs be cut. Television became the major vehicle for selling the products of the affluent society; the soap manufacturer Procter & Gamble, for example, spent more than 90 percent of its advertising budget on TV.

In 1961, Newton Minow, chairman of the Federal Communications Commission, called television a "vast wasteland." While acknowledging some of TV's great achievements, particularly documentaries and drama, Minow depicted television programming as "a procession of game shows, . . . formula comedies about totally unbelievable families, blood and thunder, mayhem, violence, sadism, murder . . . and cartoons." But viewers kept tuning in. In little more than a decade, television came to dominate Americans' leisure time, influence their

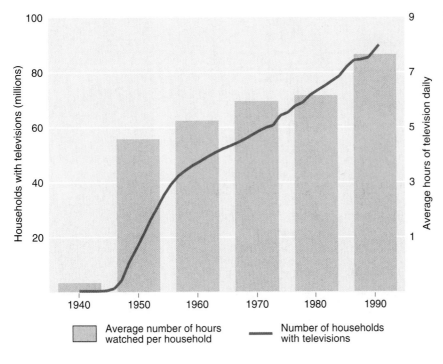

FIGURE 26.3

A Nation of Television Watchers

By the mid-1950s, television occupied a majority of U.S. homes. Set ownership and the number of hours Americans spent watching would continue to grow dramatically.

Countercurrents

Signals of unrest and dissent underlay the complacency of the 1950s. Some intellectuals took exception to the politics of consensus and to the materialism and conformity celebrated in popular culture. In *The Lonely Crowd* (1950), sociologist David Riesman expressed dismay at a shift from the "inner-directed" to the "other-directed" individual. In contrast to the independent thinking that had been at the heart of the American character in the past, Riesman found a regrettable eagerness to adapt to external standards of behavior and belief.

Other critics shared Riesman's distaste for the importance of "belonging." In his popular book *The Organization Man* (1956), William H. Whyte Jr. saw the villain as the modern corporation, whose employees had to tailor their behavior and ideas to match those of the group. According to Whyte, these "organization men" sacrificed risk taking and independence in favor of dull conformity.

Less direct challenges to mainstream culture's standards appeared in the everyday behavior of large numbers of Americans, especially youth. "Roll

over Beethoven and tell Tchaikovsky the news!" belted out Chuck Berry in his 1956 hit record. White teenagers lionized Elvis Presley, who shocked their elders with his tight pants, hip-rolling gestures, and sensuous music, a blend of country and western and black rhythm and blues. "Before there was Elvis . . . I started going crazy for 'race music,'" recalled a white man of his teenage years. "It had a beat. I loved it. . . . That got me into trouble with my parents and the schools." This man's experience illustrates African Americans' contributions to rock-and-roll music as well as the rebellion expressed by white youths' attraction to black music.

Just as rock and roll's sexual suggestiveness violated norms of middle-class respectability, the sexual behavior of many Americans departed in reality from the family ideal of the postwar era. Two books published by Alfred Kinsey and other researchers at Indiana University, *Sexual Behavior in the Human Male* (1948) and *Sexual Behavior in the Human Female* (1953), uncovered a surprising range of sexual conduct. In a survey of eighteen thousand individuals, Kinsey found that 85 percent of the men and 50 percent of the women had had sex before marriage; 50 percent of the husbands and 25 percent of the wives had engaged in extramarital sex; and one-third of the men and one-seventh of the women reported homosexual experience.

ELVIS PRESLEY
Young people seeking escape from white middle-class conformity thrilled to Elvis Presley's pulsating music, long sideburns and ducktail haircut, colorful clothing, and suggestive movements. His gyrating hips illustrated in these 1957 photographs led to the appellation "Elvis the Pelvis," while adult reviewers complained about his "grunt and groin antics" and "unnecessary bump and grind routine."
Corbis-Bettmann.

Although Kinsey's sampling procedures later cast doubt on his ability to generalize across the population, the books became best-sellers. They also drew a firestorm of outrage. Evangelist Billy Graham protested "the damage this book will do to the already deteriorating morals of America," and the Rockefeller Foundation stopped funding Kinsey's work. Critics objected most to Kinsey's refusal to make moral judgments about his findings.

The most extreme rebellion against conventionality came from the self-proclaimed Beat generation, a small group of literary figures based in New York City's Greenwich Village and in San Francisco. Rejecting nearly everything in mainstream culture—patriotism, consumerism, technology, conventional family life, discipline—the Beats insisted on spontaneity and absolute personal freedom, which included drug consumption and freewheeling sex. In his landmark poem *Howl* (1956), Allen Ginsberg in-

veighed against "Robot apartments! invisible suburbs! skeleton treasuries! blind capitals! demonic industries! . . . monstrous bombs!" and denounced the social forces that "frightened me out of my natural ecstasy!" Another leading member of the Beat generation, Jack Kerouac, wrote the best-selling novel *On the Road* (1957). The Beats' rebelliousness would provide a model for a much larger movement of youthful dissidents in the 1960s.

Rejecting nearly everything in mainstream culture, the Beats insisted on spontaneity and absolute personal freedom.

Developments in the visual arts also showed the 1950s to be more than a decade of bland con-

JACKSON POLLOCK

The leading artist in the post–World War II revolution in painting, Jackson Pollock, illustrates his technique of pouring and splattering paint onto the canvas. He worked with the canvas on the floor because, he said, "I feel nearer, more a part of the painting. . . . I can walk around it, work from the four sides and be literally 'in' the painting."

Jackson Pollock, 1950 photograph by Hans Namuth © 1991 Hans Namuth Estate. Courtesy, Center for Creative Photography, The University of Arizona.

ventionality. An artistic revolution that flowered in New York City redirected approaches to painting throughout the Western art world. Known as "action painting," "abstract expressionism," or the "New York school," this movement rejected the idea that painting should represent recognizable forms. Jackson Pollock and other abstract expressionists poured, dripped, and threw paint on canvases or substituted sticks and other implements for brushes. Their work emphasized energy and spontaneity, and it so captivated the art world that New York replaced Paris as its center.

Emergence of a Civil Rights Movement

African Americans conducted the most dramatic challenge to the status quo of the 1950s as they sought to break the chains that had replaced the literal bonds of slavery. Every southern state mandated rigid segregation in public settings ranging from hospitals and schools to drinking fountains and rest rooms. Southern voting laws and practices disfranchised the vast majority of African Americans; employment discrimination kept them at the bottom of the economic ladder.

Although black protest was as old as American racism, in the 1950s that protest developed into a grassroots movement that attracted national attention and the support of white liberals. The Supreme Court initiated significant institutional reforms, but blacks themselves directed the most important changes. Ordinary African Americans in substantial numbers sought their own liberation, building a movement that would transform race relations in the United States.

African Americans Challenge the Supreme Court and the President

A number of developments lay behind the rise of black protest in the 1950s. Between 1940 and 1960, more than three million African Americans moved out of the South into areas where they could vote and exert pressure on white politicians. White leaders also worried that the nation's dismal record in race relations disadvantaged the United States in cold war competition. In the South itself, African Americans controlled resources that were essential to a mass movement. The very system of segregation kept black talents within the African American community and encouraged the development of black churches and colleges, which developed leadership skills and provided a mass base and organizational network. Finally, both African Americans and their institutions gained a modest share of financial resources from the general postwar prosperity.

The legal strategy of the major civil rights organization, the National Association for the Advancement of Colored People (NAACP), reached its crowning achievement with the Supreme Court decision in *Brown v. Board of Education* in 1954. *Brown* was actually a consolidation of five separate suits that reflected the growing determination of black Americans to fight for their rights. The best-known suit was filed by the Reverend Oliver Brown, a welder in Topeka, Kansas, because his eight-year-old daughter had to attend a black school more than a mile away, when a white school sat just seven blocks from her house. Levi Pearson, a South Carolina farmer, brought another of the five suits and stood up against segregation despite suffering not only economic reprisals that left his crops to rot in the fields but also shots fired into his house. A third suit grew out of a strike initiated by Virginia teenagers to protest the inadequate schools set up for blacks. The lead lawyer for the NAACP, Thurgood Marshall, who would later be appointed to the Supreme Court, urged the Court to overturn the fifty-eight-year-old precedent established in *Plessy v. Ferguson* (1896), which had enshrined "separate but equal" as the law of the land. A unanimous Court, headed by Chief Justice Earl Warren, declared, "Separate educational facilities are inherently unequal" and thus violated the Fourteenth Amendment. (See "Documenting the American Promise," page 1010.)

Ordinary African Americans in substantial numbers sought their own liberation, building a movement that would transform race relations in the United States.

It was one thing to issue a decision, another matter entirely to see it enforced. The Court waited a year to deal with implementation, when its 1955 *Brown II* ruling weakly called for a "prompt and reasonable start toward full compliance" and for school systems to act "with all deliberate speed." It established no deadlines or guidelines. Ultimate responsibility for enforcement of *Brown* lay with President Eisenhower, but he would not use his enormous popularity to win acceptance for the decision. Reflecting his own racial prejudice, insensitivity to black aspirations, preference for a limited federal government, and leadership style that favored consensus and gradual progress, he refused to endorse the decision or to urge the South to comply. Such inaction fortified southern officials' determined resistance to school desegregation and contributed to the gravest constitutional crisis since the Civil War.

The crisis came in Little Rock, Arkansas, in September 1957. Local officials dutifully prepared for the integration of Central High School, but on the first day of school, Governor Orval Faubus sent National Guard troops to block the enrollment of nine black students, claiming that their presence would cause public disorder. After nearly three weeks, Faubus agreed to allow the black students to enter, but he withdrew the National Guard, leaving the nine students to face an angry mob of whites. As television cameras transmitted the ugly scene across the nation, Eisenhower was forced into action. He sent in one thousand regular army troops and took federal control of the Arkansas National Guard. In this first federal military intervention in the South since Reconstruction, Eisenhower stated clearly that he acted not to achieve integration, but to enforce the law.

Escorted by paratroopers, the black students stayed in school, and Eisenhower withdrew the army in November. Other southern cities avoided integration by closing public schools and using tax dollars to support private, white-only schools. In 1961—nearly seven years after the Supreme Court had outlawed segregation—only 6.4 percent of southern black students attended integrated schools. And forty years after Levi Pearson filed his suit in South Carolina, his town's council was all white, its high school was all black, and its white children attended school elsewhere.

Eisenhower did order the integration of public facilities in Washington, D.C., and on military bases, and he supported the first federal civil rights legislation since Reconstruction, the Civil Rights Acts of 1957 and 1960. Although they established federal bodies to focus on civil rights, the laws represented only marginal progress toward the enfranchisement of blacks. In fact, baseball star Jackie Robinson spoke for many African Americans when he wired Eisenhower, "We disagree that half a loaf is better than none. Have waited this long for bill with meaning—can wait a little longer."

Forceful and decisive in foreign affairs, Eisenhower saw no moral imperative in civil rights and moved in that arena only with the greatest reluctance. He appointed E. Frederick Morrow as the first black professional to the White House staff, but Morrow confided to his diary, "I feel ridiculous . . . trying to defend the administration's record on civil rights." Morrow later remembered Eisenhower as "a great, gentle, and noble man . . . but neither

SCHOOL INTEGRATION

In 1964, the popular artist Norman Rockwell painted **The Problem We All Live With,** *based on the experience of Ruby Bridges during the 1962 integration of the New Orleans public schools. He hoped through this painting to get people to realize what America was doing to its children. How do the composition of the scene and the characteristics of the people indicate Rockwell's intentions?*

Norman Rockwell Family Trust and Curtis Archives.

intellectually nor emotionally disposed to combat segregation."

Montgomery and Mass Protest

From individual acts of defiance and slave revolts through the legal and lobbying efforts of the NAACP, black protest had a long tradition in American society. What set the civil rights movement of the 1950s and 1960s apart from earlier protests were the great numbers of people involved, blacks' willingness to confront white institutions directly, and the use of nonviolence and passive resistance to bring about change. The Congress of Racial Equality (CORE) and other groups had experimented with these tactics in the 1940s, and African Americans had boycotted the segregated bus system in Baton Rouge, Louisiana, in 1953, but the first sus-

tained protest to claim national attention occurred in Montgomery, Alabama, in 1955 and 1956.

What set the civil rights movement of the 1950s and 1960s apart from earlier protests were the great numbers of people involved, blacks' willingness to confront white institutions directly, and the use of nonviolence and passive resistance to bring about change.

On December 1, 1955, Montgomery police arrested a forty-two-year-old black woman, Rosa Parks, for violating a local segregation ordinance. Riding the bus home from her job as a seamstress in a department store, she had not planned to challenge

The Brown Decision

B rown v. Board of Education of Topeka *was the principal Supreme Court decision in the transformation of African Americans' legal and political status during the 1950s and 1960s. Responding to lawsuits argued by NAACP lawyers, the* Brown *ruling was the culmination of a series of Supreme Court rulings between 1938 and 1950 that chipped away at an earlier Court's decision in* Plessy v. Ferguson *(1896) permitting "separate but equal" public facilities.*

DOCUMENT 1. *Brown v. Board of Education of Topeka,* May 1954

In 1954, Chief Justice Earl Warren delivered the unanimous opinion of the Supreme Court in Brown v. Board of Education of Topeka, *declaring racial segregation in public education unconstitutional and explaining why.*

In these days, it is doubtful that any child may reasonably be expected to succeed in life if he is denied the opportunity of an education. Such an opportunity, if the state has undertaken to provide it, is a right that must be made available to all on equal terms. . . .

We come then to the question presented: Does segregation of children in public schools solely on the basis of race, even though the physical facilities and other "tangible" factors may be equal, deprive the children of the minority group of equal educational opportunities? We believe that it does. . . .

In *McLaurin* [a 1950 case], the Court, in requiring that a Negro admitted to a white graduate school be treated like all other students, again resorted to intangible considerations: " . . . his ability to study, to engage in discussions and exchange views with other students, and, in general, to learn his profession." Such considerations apply with added force to children in grade and high schools. To separate them from others of similar age and qualifications solely because of their race generates a feeling of inferiority as to their status in the community that may affect their hearts and minds in a way unlikely ever to be undone.

We conclude that in the field of public education the doctrine of "separate but equal" has no place. Separate educational facilities are inherently unequal.

SOURCE: *Brown,* 347 U.S. 483 (1954).

DOCUMENT 2. Southern Manifesto on Integration, March 1956

The Brown *decision, along with a second Supreme Court ruling in 1955 about implementing desegregation, outraged many southern whites. In 1956, more than one hundred members of Congress signed a manifesto pledging resistance to the rulings.*

We regard the decision of the Supreme Court in the school cases as a clear abuse of judicial power. It climaxes a trend in the Federal judiciary undertaking to legislate . . . and to encroach upon the reserved rights of the states and the people.

The original Constitution does not mention education. Neither does the Fourteenth Amendment nor any amendment. . . . The Supreme Court of the United States, with no legal basis for such action, undertook to exercise their naked judicial power and substituted their personal political and social ideas for the established law of the land.

This unwarranted exercise of power by the court, contrary to the Constitution, is creating chaos and confusion in the states principally affected. It is destroying the amicable relations between the white and negro races that have been created through ninety years of patient effort by the good people of both races. It has planted hatred and suspicion where there has been heretofore friendship and understanding. . . .

We pledge ourselves to use all lawful means to bring about a reversal of this decision which is contrary to the Constitution and to prevent the use of force in its implementation.

SOURCE: "Southern Manifesto on Integration" (1956).

In the face of white hostility, black children carried the burden of implementing the Brown *decision. The following accounts by black students reflect varied experiences, but even those who entered white schools fairly easily found obstacles to their full participation in school activities. Nonetheless, they cherished the new opportunities, favoring integration for reasons different from those given by the Supreme Court.*

Document 3. A High School Boy in Oak Ridge, Tennessee, 1957

I like it a whole lot better than the colored school. You have a chance to learn more and you have more sports. I play forward or guard on the basketball team, only I don't get to participate in all games. Some teams don't mind my playing. Some teams object not because of the fellows on the team, but because of the people in their community. Mostly it's the fans or the board of education that decides against me. . . . The same situation occurs in baseball. I'm catcher, but the first game I didn't get to participate in. A farm club of the major league wrote the coach that they were interested in seeing me play so maybe I'll get to play the next time.

SOURCE: Dorothy Sterling, *Tender Warriors* (New York: Hill and Wang, 1958), 83. Copyright © 1958 by Dorothy Sterling. Reprinted with permission.

Document 4. A High School Girl in Louisville, Kentucky, 1957

I'm accepted now as an individual rather than as a person belonging to the Negro race. People say to me, "I'm glad I met you because if I met someone else I might not have liked them." I don't think it's fair, this individual acceptance. I feel like I was some ambassador from some foreign country.

I couldn't go out for any extracurricular activities. Cheerleading, band, drum majorettes, the people who are members of these organizations, they go to camps in the summer which are segregated. Well, what can you do? It just leaves me out. It's not the school, it's the community.

SOURCE: Dorothy Sterling, *Tender Warriors* (New York: Hill and Wang, 1958), 83. Copyright © 1958 by Dorothy Sterling. Reprinted with permission.

Document 5. A High School Girl in the Deep South, May 1966

The first day a news reporter rode the bus with us. All around us were state troopers. In front of them were federal marshals. When we got to town there were lines of people and cars all along the road. A man without a badge or anything got on the bus and started beating up the newspaper reporter. . . . He was crying and bleeding. When we got to the school the students were all around looking through the windows. The mayor said we couldn't come there because the school was already filled to capacity [and] if six of us came in it would be a fire hazard. He told us to turn around and go back. We turned around and the students started yelling and clapping. When we went back [after obtaining a court order] there were no students there at all. There were only two teachers left so they had to bring a couple of teachers from other places. [The white students did not return, so the six black students finished the year by themselves.] The shocking thing was during the graduation ceremonies. All six of the students got together to make a speech. After we finished, I looked around and saw three teachers crying. The principal had tears in his eyes and he got up to make a little speech about us. He said at first he didn't think he would enjoy being around us. You could see in his face that he was really touched. We said something like we really enjoyed school together and that we were glad they stuck it out and all that kind of stuff.

SOURCE: *In Their Own Words: A Student Appraisal of What Happened after School Desegregation* (Washington, D.C.: Department of Health, Education, and Welfare, Office of Education, 1966), 17–18.

Document 6. A High School Girl in the Deep South, May 1966

I chose to go because I felt that I could get a better education here. I knew that the [black] school that I was then attending wasn't giving me exactly what I should have had. As far as the Science Department was concerned, it just didn't have the chemicals we needed and I just decided to change. When I went over the students there weren't very friendly and when I graduated they still weren't. They didn't want us there and they made that plain, but we went there anyway and we stuck it out. The lessons there were harder, lots harder, but I studied and I managed to pass all my subjects.

SOURCE: *In Their Own Words: A Student Appraisal of What Happened after School Desegregation* (Washington, D.C.: Department of Health, Education, and Welfare, Office of Education, 1966), 44. *(Continued)*

QUESTIONS FOR ANALYSIS AND DEBATE

1. What reasons did the Supreme Court give in favor of desegregation? What reasons did black students give for wanting to attend integrated schools? How did these differ?

2. What arguments did the southern legislators make against the Supreme Court decision? Did they question its power to make the decision or the content of the decision itself?

3. What obstacles remained for African American students to confront once they had been admitted to integrated schools?

4. What conditions do you feel would be worth enduring to obtain a better education?

---

segregation. But when all the seats in the white section in the front of the bus filled up and the driver asked Parks to give up her seat at the front of the black section so that a white man could sit down, she decided that she was tired of giving in to the system. Parks had long been active in the local NAACP, headed by E. D. Nixon, who was also president of the local Brotherhood of Sleeping Car Porters. They and others had already talked about posing a legal challenge to bus segregation. A possible bus boycott by African Americans had engaged another group, the Women's Political Council (WPC). Composed of black professional women, the WPC was led by Jo Ann Robinson, an English professor at Alabama State College who had been humiliated by a bus driver when she had inadvertently sat in the white section. Parks's arrest galvanized both groups. Such local individuals and organizations, long committed to improving conditions for African Americans and well connected to various segments of the black commu-

MONTGOMERY CIVIL RIGHTS LEADERS
During the Montgomery, Alabama, bus boycott of 1955–1956, local white officials harassed African Americans with arrests and lawsuits. Here Rosa Parks, catalyst of the boycott and one of ninety-two defendants, ascends the steps of the Montgomery County courthouse in March 1956. She is accompanied by E. D. Nixon, a forceful civil rights leader and her long-time friend and associate in the Montgomery NAACP. Wide World Photos.

MARTIN LUTHER KING JR.
IN MONTGOMERY
Martin Luther King Jr. preaches at the First Baptist Church during the Montgomery bus boycott. First Baptist was the congregation of Ralph D. Abernathy, the man who would become King's close associate in the crusades to come. The crucial role that black churches played in the black freedom struggle was not lost on white racists, who bombed First Baptist and three other black churches in Montgomery during the boycott.

Dan Weiner, courtesy Sandra Weiner.

nity, laid critical foundations for the black freedom struggle throughout the South.

E. D. Nixon, who had rushed to the jail upon hearing of Parks's arrest, thought that she would be a perfect plaintiff for a suit testing the legality of bus segregation: "I knew she would stand on her feet. She was honest, she was clean, she had integrity." As Parks recalled, "The white people couldn't point to me and say that there was anything I had done to deserve such treatment except to be born black." Meanwhile, Jo Ann Robinson and other WPC members decided that Parks's arrest provided an opportune moment to mount a bus boycott. Robinson quickly mobilized fellow teachers and students, who worked through the night to copy and distribute fifty thousand flyers calling on Montgomery blacks to stay off the buses. At the same time, Nixon began calling local ministers, because, he said, they "had their hands on the black masses."

E. D. Nixon called a mass meeting for December 5 at the Holt Street Baptist Church, where so many blacks gathered that a crowd of people stretched for blocks outside the church. Those assembled founded the Montgomery Improvement Association (MIA) to organize and maintain a bus boycott among the African American community. The MIA ran an alternative transportation system of volunteer car pools and marshaled more than 90 percent of the black community to sustain the year-long boycott. It regularly held mass meetings to keep up the spirits of those who had to depend on the car pool to get to work and back, brave bad weather on foot for miles to keep a job or get to the grocery store, or face harassment from policemen. Jo Ann Robinson, though known as a most cautious driver, got seventeen traffic tickets in the space of two months.

Elected to head the MIA was Martin Luther King Jr., a newcomer to Montgomery and pastor at the Dexter Avenue Baptist Church. Only twenty-six years old, King was the son of a minister and had a doctorate in theology from Boston University. As would be true in many other centers of black protest, churches played a vital role in the movement in Montgomery, providing it not only with places to meet but also with a mass base, talented leadership, and a financial foundation. Day after day Montgomery blacks gathered at their churches to plan strategy and receive instructions and inspiration. A captivating speaker, King summoned their courage and commitment by linking racial justice to the redeeming power of Christian love. He promised, "If you will protest courageously and yet with dignity and Christian love . . . historians will have to pause and say, 'There lived a great people—a black people—who injected a new meaning and dignity into the veins of civilization.' This is our challenge and our overwhelming responsibility."

Montgomery blacks summoned their courage and determination in abundance. They continued walking miles to get to work, contributed their meager financial resources, and stood up with dignity and discipline to legal, economic, and physical intimidation. One older woman who refused a ride insisted, "I'm not walking for myself, I'm walking for my children and my grandchildren." Authorities arrested several leaders, and whites firebombed King's house. Yet the movement persisted, and Montgomery demonstrated that even without the ballot, African Americans could struggle successfully against oppression. In November 1956, the Supreme Court ruled on the suit initiated upon Parks's arrest, declaring unconstitutional Alabama's state and local laws requiring bus segregation. Although the Montgomery movement's victory came from Washington rather than the local power structure, it had demonstrated that blacks could sustain a lengthy protest and would not be intimidated.

Montgomery demonstrated that even without the ballot, African Americans could struggle successfully against oppression.

In January 1957, black clergy from across the South met to coordinate local protests against segregation and to secure the ballot for blacks. They founded the Southern Christian Leadership Conference (SCLC) and chose King to head it. Although ministers dominated the SCLC, its success owed much to Ella Baker, a seasoned activist who came from New York to set up and run its office.

King's face on the cover of *Time* magazine in February 1957 marked his rapid rise to national and international fame. He crisscrossed the nation and the world, speaking to large audiences, raising funds, and meeting with other activists. In June 1958, Eisenhower extended his first invitation to black leaders, and King and three others met with the president. Meanwhile, in the late 1950s, the SCLC, NAACP, and CORE developed centers in

several southern cities, paving the way for a mass movement that would revolutionize the racial system of the South.

Conclusion: Assessing the "Ike Age"

At the American National Exhibition in Moscow in 1959, the combination of consumer goods that Nixon proudly displayed to Khrushchev and the cold war competition that crackled through their conversation reflected two dominant themes of the 1950s: the prosperity of the U.S. economy and the superpowers' success in keeping cold war competition within the bounds of peace. The tremendous economic growth of the 1950s, which raised the standard of living for most Americans, resulted in part from the cold war: One of every ten American jobs depended directly on defense spending.

Affluence helped to change the very landscape of the United States. Suburban housing developments sprang up, interstate highways began to divide cities and connect the country, farms declined in number but grew in size, and population and industry moved south and west. Daily habits and even values of ordinary people changed as the economy became more service-oriented and the opportunity to buy a host of new products intensified the growth of a culture based on consumption. The general prosperity and seeming conformity, however, masked a number of developments and problems that Americans would face head-on in later years: rising resistance to an unjust racial system, a 20-percent poverty rate in an era of abundance, the movement of married women into the labor force, and the development of a self-conscious youth generation.

Although with its defense spending and housing, highway, and education subsidies, the federal government played a large role in the economic boom, in general Eisenhower tried to curb domestic programs and let private enterprise have its way. His administration maintained the basic structure of the welfare state inherited from the Democrats but opposed further reforms. In global affairs, Eisenhower demonstrated restraint on large issues, recognizing the limits of U.S. power. In the name of deterrence, he promoted development of more destructive atomic weapons, but he resisted pressures for even larger defense budgets. Eisenhower took from Truman the assumption that the United States must fight communism everywhere and passed it on to the next administration. He sympathized with national liberation movements, but when movements in Iran, Guatemala, Cuba, and Vietnam seemed too radical, too friendly to communism, or too inimical to American economic interests, he tried to undermine them, often with secret operations.

Thus, although Eisenhower presided over eight years of peace and prosperity, his foreign policy inspired anti-Americanism, established dangerous precedents for the expansion of executive power, and forged commitments that future generations would deem unwise. As Eisenhower's successors took on the struggle against communism and grappled with the domestic problems of race, poverty, and urban decay that he had avoided, the tranquillity and consensus of the 1950s would give way to the turbulence and conflict of the 1960s.

www.bedfordstmartins.com/tap   SEE THE ONLINE STUDY GUIDE to assess your mastery of the material covered in this chapter.

CHRONOLOGY

1952 Dwight D. Eisenhower elected president of United States.

I Love Lucy becomes number one television show.

1953 Government begins policy of termination of special status of American Indians and relocates thousands off reservations.

CIA engineers coup against government of Mohammed Mossadegh in Iran.

1954 CIA stages coup against government of Jacobo Arbenz in Guatemala.

United States organizes Southeast Asia Treaty Organization (SEATO) in wake of French defeat in Vietnam; Eisenhower administration begins aid program to government of South Vietnam.

Government launches Operation Wetback, a series of raids designed to seek out and deport illegal immigrants.

Ground broken in Pennsylvania for first commercial nuclear power plant.

U.S. Supreme Court declares segregation in public schools unconstitutional in *Brown v. Board of Education.*

1955 Eisenhower and Khrushchev meet in Geneva for first superpower summit since end of World War II.

1955–1956 Montgomery, Alabama, bus boycott by African Americans focuses national attention on civil rights.

1956 Interstate Highway and Defense System Act involves federal government in road-building activities previously done by state and local governments.

Eisenhower reelected by landslide to second term.

Allen Ginsberg publishes poem *Howl,* expressing rebelliousness of Beat generation.

1957 Southern Christian Leadership Conference (SCLC) organizes and elects Martin Luther King Jr. its president.

Soviets launch *Sputnik,* first satellite to orbit Earth.

Labor union membership peaks at 27.1 percent of labor force.

1958 United States and Soviet Union suspend nuclear testing in atmosphere.

Eisenhower establishes the National Aeronautics and Space Administration (NASA).

1958–1960 U.S. nuclear weapons stockpile triples in size.

1959 American National Exhibition in Moscow is scene of "kitchen debate" between Nixon and Khrushchev.

1960 Soviets shoot down U.S. U-2 spy plane, causing rift in U.S.-Soviet relations.

Women represent one-third of labor force; 35 percent of women work outside the home.

One-quarter of Americans live in suburbs.

BIBLIOGRAPHY

GENERAL WORKS

John Patrick Diggins, *The Proud Decades: America in War and Peace, 1941–1960* (1988).

Alan Ehrenhalt, *The Lost City: Discovering the Forgotten Virtues of Community in the Chicago of the 1950s* (1995).

David Halberstam, *The Fifties* (1993).

Marty Jezer, *The Dark Ages: Life in the United States, 1945–1960* (1982).

Douglas T. Miller and Marion Nowak, *The Fifties: The Way We Really Were* (1977).

J. Ronald Oakley, *God's Country: America in the Fifties* (1986).

William L. O'Neill, *American High: The Years of Confidence, 1945–1960* (1986).

James T. Patterson, *Grand Expectations: The United States, 1945–1974* (1996).

Michael S. Sherry, *In the Shadow of War: The United States since the 1930s* (1995).

DOMESTIC POLITICS AND POLICIES

Charles C. Alexander, *Holding the Line: The Eisenhower Era, 1952–1961* (1975).

Craig Allen, *Eisenhower and the Mass Media: Peace, Prosperity, and Prime-Time TV* (1993).

Stephen E. Ambrose, *Eisenhower*, vol. 2, *The President* (1984).

Jeff Broadwater, *Eisenhower and the Anti-Communist Crusade* (1992).

Robert F. Burk, *Dwight D. Eisenhower: Hero and Politician* (1986).

Fred I. Greenstein, *The Hidden Hand Presidency: Eisenhower as Leader* (1982).

R. Alton Lee, *Dwight D. Eisenhower: Soldier and Statesman* (1981).

Chester J. Pach Jr. and Elmo Richardson, *The Presidency of Dwight D. Eisenhower* (rev. ed., 1991).

Herbert S. Parmet, *Eisenhower and the American Crusades* (1972).

Geoffrey Perret, *Eisenhower* (1999).

Gary W. Reichard, *The Reaffirmation of Republicanism* (1975).

Mark H. Rose, *Interstate: Express Highway Politics, 1941–1956* (1979).

FOREIGN POLICY

Stephen E. Ambrose, *Ike's Spies: Eisenhower and the Espionage Establishment* (1981).

Michael R. Beschloss, *Mayday: Eisenhower, Khrushchev, and the U-2 Affair* (1986).

Blanche Weisen Cook, *The Declassified Eisenhower: A Divided Legacy of Peace and Political Warfare* (1981).

Robert A. Divine, *Eisenhower and the Cold War* (1981).

Robert A. Divine, *The Sputnik Challenge* (1993).

Steven Z. Freiberger, *Dawn over Suez: The Rise of American Power in the Middle East, 1953–1957* (1992).

George C. Herring, *America's Longest War: The United States and Vietnam, 1950–1975* (2nd rev. ed., 1986).

Richard H. Immerman, *The CIA in Guatemala* (1982).

Richard H. Immerman, *John Foster Dulles and the Diplomacy of the Cold War* (1990).

Stanley Karnow, *Vietnam: A History* (rev. ed., 1991).

Walter LaFeber, *Inevitable Revolutions: The United States in Central America* (1983).

Donald Neff, *Warriors at Suez: Eisenhower Takes America into the Middle East* (1981).

Stephen G. Rabe, *Eisenhower and Latin America: The Foreign Policy of Anticommunism* (1988).

Andrew J. Rotter, *The Path to Vietnam: Origins of the American Commitment to Southeast Asia* (1987).

David L. Snead, *The Gaither Committee, Eisenhower, and the Cold War* (1999).

Robert W. Stookey, *America and the Arab States* (1975).

Lawrence S. Wittner, *The Struggle Against the Bomb*, 2 vols. (1993, 1997).

WOMEN, GENDER ROLES, AND THE FAMILY

Wini Breines, *Young, White, and Miserable: Growing Up Female in the Fifties* (1992).

Stephanie Coontz, *The Way We Never Were: American Families and the Nostalgia Trip* (1992).

Barbara Ehrenreich, *The Hearts of Men: American Dreams and the Flight from Commitment* (1983).

Peter Filene, *Him/Her/Self: Sex Roles in Modern America* (2nd ed., 1986).

Betty Friedan, *The Feminine Mystique* (1963).

James Howard Jones, *Alfred C. Kinsey: A Public/Private Life* (1998).

Eugenia Kaledin, *Mothers and More: American Women in the 1950s* (1984).

Elaine Tyler May, *Homeward Bound: American Families in the Cold War Era* (1988).

Joanne Meyerowitz, ed., *Not June Cleaver: Women and Gender in Postwar America, 1945–1960* (1994).

Steven Mintz and Susan Kellogg, *Domestic Revolutions: A Social History of American Family Life* (1988).

Arlene Skolnick, *Embattled Paradise: The American Family in an Age of Uncertainty* (1991).

Rickie Solinger, *Wake Up Little Susie: Single Pregnancy and Race before* Roe v. Wade (1992).

ECONOMIC AND SOCIAL DEVELOPMENTS

Rosalyn Baxandall and Elizabeth Ewen, *Picture Windows: How the Suburbs Happened* (2000).

Gail Cooper, *Air-Conditioning America: Engineers and the Controlled Environment, 1900–1960* (1998).

Ruth Schwartz Cowan, *A Social History of American Technology* (1997).

Richard O. Davies, *The Age of Asphalt: The Automobile, the Freeway, and the Condition of Metropolitan America* (1975).

Scott Donaldson, *The Suburban Myth* (1969).

Herbert Gans, *The Levittowners: Ways of Life and Politics in a New Suburban Community* (2nd ed., 1982).

Kenneth T. Jackson, *Crabgrass Frontier: The Suburbanization of the United States* (1985).

Barbara Kelly, *Expanding the American Dream: Building and Rebuilding Levittown* (1993).

Michael P. Malone and Richard W. Etulain, *The American West: A Twentieth-Century History* (1989).

Raymond A. Mohl, *Searching for the Sunbelt: Historical Perspectives on a Region* (1993).

Gerald D. Nash, *The American West in the Twentieth Century* (1973).

Bruce J. Schulman, *From Cotton Belt to Sunbelt: Federal Policy, Economic Development, and the Transformation of the South, 1938–1980* (1994).

Jon C. Teaford, *The Twentieth-Century American City* (1993).

RELIGION AND CULTURE

Erik Barnouw, *Tube of Plenty: The Evolution of American Television* (rev. ed., 1982).

James L. Baughman, *The Republic of Mass Culture: Journalism, Filmmaking, and Broadcasting in America since 1941* (1997).

William Boddy, *Fifties Television: The Industry and Its Critics* (1994).

Paul Boyer, *By the Dawn's Early Light: American Thought and Culture at the Dawn of the Atomic Age* (1985).

Robert Ellwood, *The Fifties Spiritual Marketplace: American Religion in a Decade of Conflict* (1997).

Simon Frith, *Sound Effects: Youth, Leisure, and the Politics of Rock and Roll* (1981).

Serge Guilbaut, *How New York Stole the Idea of Modern Art: Abstract Expressionism, Freedom, and the Cold War* (1983).

Peter Guralnick, *Last Train to Memphis: The Rise of Elvis Presley* (1994).

Peter Guralnick, *Careless Love: The Unmaking of Elvis Presley* (1999).

James Hudnut-Beumler, *Looking for God in the Suburbs: The Religion of the American Dream and Its Critics, 1945–1965* (1994).

David Mark, *Democratic Vistas: Television in American Culture* (1984).

Karal Ann Marling, *As Seen on TV: The Visual Culture of Everyday Life in the 1950s* (1994).

Larry May, ed., *Recasting America: Culture and Politics in the Age of the Cold War* (1989).

James Miller, *Flowers in the Dustbin: The Rise of Rock and Roll, 1947–1977* (1999).

Lynn Spigel, *Make Room for TV: Television and the Family Ideal in Postwar America* (1992).

Cecelia Tichi, *Electronic Hearth: Creating an American Television Culture* (1991).

Stephen J. Whitfield, *The Culture of the Cold War* (1991).

Robert Wuthnow, *The Restructuring of American Religion: Society and Faith since World War II* (1988).

MINORITIES AND CIVIL RIGHTS

Taylor Branch, *Parting the Waters: America in the King Years, 1954–1963* (1988).

Robert Fredrick Burk, *The Eisenhower Administration and Black Civil Rights* (1984).

John Egerton, *Speak Now Against the Day: The Generation Before the Civil Rights Movement in the South* (1994).

Adam Fairclough, *To Redeem the Soul of America: The Southern Christian Leadership Conference and Martin Luther King Jr.* (1987).

David J. Garrow, *Bearing the Cross: Martin Luther King Jr. and the Southern Christian Leadership Conference* (1986).

David J. Garrow, ed., *The Montgomery Boycott and the Women Who Started It: The Memoir of Jo Ann Gibson Robinson* (1987).

Arnold R. Hirsch, *Making the Second Ghetto: Race and Housing in Chicago, 1940–1960* (1998).

Richard Kluger, *Simple Justice: The History of* Brown v. Board of Education *and Black America's Struggle for Equality* (1976).

Doug McAdam, *Political Process and the Development of Black Insurgency, 1930–1970* (1982).

Aldon D. Morris, *The Origins of the Civil Rights Movement: Black Communities Organizing for Change* (1984).

E. Frederick Morrow, *Black Man in the White House* (1963).

Thomas J. Sugrue, *The Origins of the Urban Crisis: Race and Inequality in Postwar Detroit* (1996).

Mark V. Tushnet, *Making Civil Rights Law: Thurgood Marshall and the Supreme Court, 1936–1961* (1995).

Juan Williams, *Thurgood Marshall: American Revolutionary* (1998).

"COUNTRY JOE" MCDONALD'S GUITAR *Music was an omnipresent element of protest movements in the 1960s. Civil rights demonstrators sang "We Shall Overcome," antiwar rallies featured folk singers, and hippies turned on to acid rock. The guitar was the central musical instrument for each kind of music: traditional African American, folk, and rock. This wooden acoustic guitar belonged to "Country Joe" McDonald, who started his band, Country Joe and the Fish, at a draft protest in Oakland, California, in 1965. The band was one of many that originated in the San Francisco Bay area, but its popularity soon spread across the country.* The Oakland Museum of California.

A DECADE OF REBELLION AND REFORM

27

1960–1968

ON AUGUST 31, 1962, Fannie Lou Hamer boarded a bus that took eighteen African Americans from Ruleville, Mississippi, to the county seat in Indianola, where they intended to register to vote. At that time blacks made up more than 60 percent of Sunflower County's population but only 1.2 percent of registered voters. Before young civil rights activists arrived in Ruleville to start a voter registration drive, Hamer recalled, "I didn't know that a Negro could register and vote." Her forty-five years of poverty, exploitation, and political disfranchisement typified the lives of most blacks in the rural south. Born to sharecropping parents, Hamer began working in the cotton fields at the age of six, attending school in a one-room shack only from December to March and leaving formal education entirely at the age of twelve. In her late twenties, she married Perry Hamer and moved onto the plantation where he sharecropped. She worked in the fields, did domestic work for the plantation owner, and served as record keeper when sharecroppers brought their cotton in to be weighed and recorded.

At Indianola in 1962, Hamer and her companions defied a hostile crowd of gun-carrying whites and entered the county courthouse. Using a common practice to keep blacks from voting, the registrar gave Hamer a literacy test requiring interpretation of an obscure section of the state constitution. Hamer's schooling had never exposed her to Mississippi's constitution; she, predictably, failed the test but resolved to try again. When she arrived home, her plantation-owner boss ordered her to return to Indianola and withdraw her registration application or leave his land. Refusing to back down, Hamer left the plantation. Ten days later, sixteen bullets flew into the home of friends where she was staying. White resistance and intimidation only strengthened Hamer's resolve: She not only tried again to register (and succeeded on the third attempt) but also attended a civil rights leadership training conference and began to mobilize others to vote. In 1963, she and other civil rights activists were arrested in Winona, Mississippi, and beaten so brutally while in prison that Hamer went from the jail to the hospital, refusing to show her face to her family, except for one sister, who could not recognize her.

Fannie Lou Hamer's courage and determination made her a prominent figure in a movement that shook the nation's conscience, raised hopes for the possibility of change, provided a model of protest that inspired other marginalized groups, and helped push a transformation in national domestic policy. Although the federal government often failed to protect activists in their struggle for civil rights, the two Democratic presidents of the 1960s favored a progressive government and—helped by a prosperous economy—placed efforts to solve social and economic problems high on the national agenda. After John F. Kennedy was assassinated in November 1963, Lyndon B. Johnson launched the Great Society—a multitude of

MISSISSIPPI FREEDOM DEMOCRATIC PARTY RALLY
Fannie Lou Hamer (left foreground) and other activists sing at a rally outside the Democratic National Convention hall in 1964, supporting the Mississippi Freedom Democratic Party (MFDP) in its challenge to the all-white delegation sent by the regular Mississippi Democratic Party. Next to Hamer is Eleanor Holmes Norton, a civil rights lawyer, and Ella Baker (far right), who helped organize the Southern Christian Leadership Conference and later managed MFDP headquarters in Washington, D.C.
Matt Herron.

programs aimed at promoting general economic growth, improving the conditions of racial minorities and the poor, and reforming programs related to education, health care, urban development, and the environment. Those who struggled for racial justice paid a high price in loss of property and personal safety, but by the end of the decade, law had caught up with the American ideal of equality.

Yet it did not catch up fast enough. Although Congress passed watershed legislation and the Supreme Court issued pathbreaking decisions strengthening civil rights, the law did not affect the deplorable economic conditions of African Americans, on which Hamer and others increasingly focused after 1965. Nor was the political establishment willing to promote rapid change, as Hamer

found out in 1964 when President Johnson and his allies refused to support black Democrats from Mississippi in their efforts to be represented at the Democratic National Convention. "We followed all the laws that the white people themselves made," she said, only to find that "the white man is not going to give up his power to us. . . . We have to take for ourselves." By 1966, a minority of African American activists were demanding black power; the movement soon splintered, and white support sharply declined. Radicals who formed what came to be called the New Left scorned the Great Society for failing to strike at the roots of unjustice in America's political and economic system. Conservatives cried that the Great Society went too far and expressed outrage at the wholesale challenge to

American values and institutions mounted by blacks, students, and others.

Although disillusioned and often frustrated, Fannie Lou Hamer remained an activist until her death in 1977, working to improve the material conditions of rural blacks and mingling with some of the new social movements stimulated by the black freedom struggle. She went to Mississippi Valley State College in 1969 to support students' demands for black studies courses and more autonomy from an overbearing administration. In 1972, she attended the founding conference of the National Women's Political Caucus, where she made sure that its goal of greater representation for women in government did not sanction the support of racist candidates. Feminists and other groups, including ethnic minorities, environmentalists, gays and lesbians, benefited from the visibility of the civil rights movement as well as from its ideas, tactics, and policy precedents. All of these movements aroused the moral sensibility of the nation and contributed to the greatest efforts to reconcile America's promise with reality since the New Deal.

Kennedy and the New Frontier

In his speech to the Democratic National Convention in 1960, John F. Kennedy announced that the United States stood "on the edge of a New Frontier . . . of unfulfilled hopes and threats," and he promised to confront "unsolved problems of peace and war, unconquered pockets of ignorance and prejudice, unanswered questions of poverty and surplus." Once in office, Kennedy instituted an aggressive foreign policy, but not until his final months did massive grassroots pressures spur him to launch a substantial assault on the problems of racism and poverty. Before his efforts reached fruition, an assassin ended his life.

The Style and Promise of the New Frontier

John F. Kennedy grew up in privilege, the son of an Irish Catholic businessman who served in Franklin D. Roosevelt's administration and nourished political ambitions for his sons. Helped by a distinguished World War II navy record, Kennedy won

election to the House of Representatives in 1946 and the Senate in 1952. The Massachusetts senator set his sights on the White House for 1960, using his family's fortunes to build a superb political machine directed by his brother Robert. A major challenge was to woo Democratic liberals who were put off by Kennedy's undistinguished record in Congress and his failure to speak out against McCarthyism.

Nonetheless, with his overwhelming financial advantage, handsome appearance, and dynamic style, Kennedy triumphed in a series of state primaries. A critical victory in West Virginia over Hubert H. Humphrey, the liberal senator from Minnesota, muted the question of his Catholicism, an issue that had doomed Al Smith's candidacy in 1928. After winning the nomination at the Democratic convention, Kennedy stunned nearly everyone by choosing Lyndon B. Johnson of Texas as his running mate. Although ticket balancing was a time-honored tradition, liberals detested the choice of a man whom they viewed as a typical southern conservative. The party platform, however, embodied liberal priorities, including the strongest civil rights plank the Democrats had ever endorsed.

The Republicans nominated Vice President Richard M. Nixon, who campaigned on his experience in the Eisenhower White House. With Nixon merely defending the policies of the Eisenhower administration, Kennedy seemed more dynamic, as he promised to strengthen America's position in the cold war, expand the welfare state, and increase the rate of economic growth. The two candidates actually differed little, however, on defense and foreign policy questions.

Kennedy won the excruciatingly close election, helped in large part by African American voters. He had appealed to many by expressing support for Martin Luther King Jr. after King's arrest at a demonstration in Atlanta in October. Nixon gained 52 percent of the white vote, but the black preference for Kennedy contributed to the young senator's 120,000-vote margin overall and his close victories in such key states as Illinois and Michigan. In addition, Lyndon Johnson captured most of the South for the Democrats; and a third Eisenhower recession, which pushed unemployment above 6 percent in 1960, also contributed to the incumbent party's defeat (Map 27.1). Kennedy benefited as well from the nation's first televised debates between presidential candidates: He came across as cool, confident, and in command of the issues, whereas Nixon appeared nervous, sweaty, and pale. Radio listeners declared

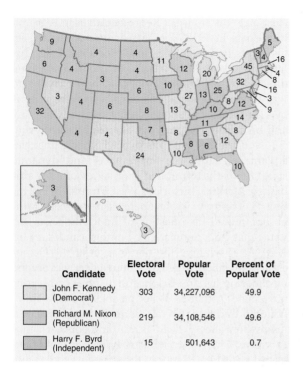

Candidate	Electoral Vote	Popular Vote	Percent of Popular Vote
John F. Kennedy (Democrat)	303	34,227,096	49.9
Richard M. Nixon (Republican)	219	34,108,546	49.6
Harry F. Byrd (Independent)	15	501,643	0.7

MAP 27.1
The Election of 1960

the debate a draw, but television viewers came away more impressed with Kennedy. Television also sparked interest in the campaign, which produced a 64 percent voter turnout, the nation's highest in the twentieth century.

The Kennedy administration projected an aura of energy, idealism, and glamour. The first president to hold live televised press conferences, Kennedy charmed the press corps and the people with his grace, vigor, and self-mocking wit. In a part of his life hidden from the public, however, Kennedy had sexual relations with several women, recklessly exposing himself to blackmail and risking the dignity of his office. Journalists at the time avoided this matter, instead projecting warm images of a youthful president playing touch football, sailing with his chic and cultured wife, Jacqueline, and romping in the executive office with his young children. The Kennedys transformed the White House into a national showcase of culture and the arts, inviting prominent writers, artists, and musicians to visit and perform.

The appointment of Robert S. McNamara as secretary of defense most reflected the style of the Kennedy administration. With his keen analytic ability and decisiveness, the hard-driving McNamara had risen to the top of the Ford Motor Company. A number of Kennedy's subcabinet and White House staff appointments shared McNamara's youth, Ivy League education, and eagerness to apply technology to problem solving. They exuded confidence, enjoyed competition, and welcomed danger and risk—characteristics that sometimes contributed to foreign policy crises under both Kennedy and Johnson. In addition, they were not well schooled in practical politics. When Lyndon Johnson told Speaker of the House Sam Rayburn how impressed he was with the brilliance of the Kennedy men, the older Texan replied, "I'd feel a whole lot better . . . if just one of them had run for sheriff once."

In 1960, John F. Kennedy announced that the United States stood "on the edge of a New Frontier."

In his inaugural address, Kennedy called on all Americans to serve the common good and to cast off the complacency and self-indulgence of the 1950s, saying, "ask not what your country can do for you—ask what you can do for your country." He declared that a "new generation" was assuming leadership and described the cold war in a tone of crisis, emphasizing America's "role of defending freedom in its hour of maximum danger." He insisted, "If a free society cannot help the many who are poor, it cannot save the few who are rich." Though his address gave domestic problems short shrift and delineated no specific programs, Kennedy's idealism inspired many, especially the young, to replace self-interest with service to a larger cause.

The Substance of the New Frontier at Home

Commenting on John F. Kennedy's actions on civil rights, Martin Luther King Jr. described the president as "committed but . . . feeling his way," a characterization that applied to Kennedy's domestic achievements in general. He failed to redeem campaign promises to expand the welfare state. Nor did he assume leadership on behalf of racial justice until near the third year of his term, when civil rights activists gave him no choice.

THE KENNEDY FAMILY
John F. Kennedy's youthful good looks, glamorous background, and attractive family added to his appeal and continue to fascinate many Americans decades after his death. Here he relaxes with his wife, Jacqueline, and their children, Caroline and John, at their vacation home in Hyannisport on Cape Cod. This photograph was taken in August 1963, a few months before Kennedy's assassination.
John F. Kennedy Library.

A number of factors account for the large gap between what Kennedy promised and what he actually achieved. Despite his party's control of Congress, conservative southern Democrats combined with Republicans to block reform. Having been elected by a slim margin, Kennedy saw no reason to go out on a limb for social justice. He displayed much more zeal for foreign policy and consigned domestic reform to a back burner.

The Kennedy administration did win support for a two-billion-dollar slum clearance and urban renewal program; the Area Redevelopment Act of 1961, which gave incentives to businesses to locate in depressed areas; and the Manpower Development and Training Act of 1962, which provided training for the unemployed. But two key items on the Democratic agenda since the Truman administration, federal aid to education and health care for the elderly, got nowhere. Referring to a book Kennedy had published, *Profiles in Courage* (1956), liberals jokingly expressed their dissatisfaction with his leadership by asking that he show "less profile and more courage."

Two initiatives of the Kennedy administration relating to women's rights received relatively little attention at the time but had important ramifications. Although Kennedy had no particular interest in women's rights, in 1961 he heeded the advice of Esther Peterson, head of the Women's Bureau in the Department of Labor, to strengthen his support among women by appointing a President's Commission on the Status of Women. Chaired by Eleanor Roosevelt and composed of leaders from the government and private organizations, the commission reported its findings in October 1963, eight months after Betty Friedan attacked sex discrimination in *The Feminine Mystique*. Although based on conservative assumptions about women's appropriate roles, the commission report, titled *American Women*, identified widespread discrimination against women and recommended remedies. Spawning counterparts at the state level, the president's commission created networks of women aware of sex discrimination and eager for action, providing an impetus for the launching of a grassroots women's movement a few years later.

The president's commission highlighted an area of discrimination that women's organizations and labor unions had been seeking to eliminate for two decades: the age-old custom of paying women less than men for doing the same work. They achieved their goal when Kennedy signed the Equal Pay Act in June 1963. Thereafter, wage disparities based solely on gender became illegal, and within a few years women began to win wage increases and back pay worth millions of dollars.

The saying "A rising tide lifts all boats" expressed Kennedy's belief that economic growth could eradicate poverty and solve most social problems. In addition, he felt that increased production would make the nation more competitive with the Soviet Union. Key economic advisers argued that infusing money into the economy by reducing taxes would increase demand, boost production, and decrease unemployment. To that end, Kennedy asked Congress to pass an enormous tax cut in 1963. This use of fiscal policy to stimulate the economy even when there was no recession gained the name "the new economics."

Kennedy did not live to see approval of his bill. Passed in February 1964, the law contributed in a small way to the greatest economic boom since World War II. Unemployment dropped to 4.1 percent, and the gross national product shot up by 7 to 9 percent annually between 1964 and 1966. Some critics of the tax cut disputed its economic impact, pointing out that the surge was already under way, stimulated by defense spending, new technology, and cheap fuel oil. Conservatives warned that cutting taxes would result in a budget deficit and spark inflation. Liberals pointed out that the tax cut favored corporations and high-income individuals and maintained that economic growth alone would not eliminate poverty, arguing instead for increased spending on social programs.

Poverty had gained the Senate's attention in 1960, when a subcommittee reported "a growing and intense problem," the poverty of eight million older Americans, whose "declining years are without dignity." That same year, Kennedy came face to face with the rural poor of Appalachia when he asked for their votes. In 1962, he read *The Other America,* Michael Harrington's devastating account of the hopelessness and wretched conditions endured by more than one in every five Americans.

The summer of 1963 marked a turning point in Kennedy's attitude toward domestic reform. In ad-dition to asking aides to plan an attack on poverty, he issued a dramatic call for passage of a comprehensive civil rights bill. Whether he could have achieved these breakthroughs in domestic policy was left unanswered by his assassination on November 22, 1963.

Assassination of a President

The murder of the president in Dallas, Texas, seared the consciousness of Americans as had no other event since the end of World War II. Within minutes of the shooting—which took place as Kennedy passed in a motorcade through Dallas, Texas—radio and television broadcast the unfolding horror to the nation. Millions watched the return of *Air Force One* to Washington bearing the president's coffin, his widow in her bloodstained suit, and the new president, Lyndon Baines Johnson, who had taken the oath of office aboard the jet.

The murder of the president in Dallas, Texas, seared the consciousness of Americans as had no other event since the end of World War II.

Stunned Americans struggled to determine what had happened and why. Soon after the assassination, police arrested Lee Harvey Oswald and concluded that he had fired the shots from a nearby building. Two days later, as a television audience watched Oswald being transferred from one jail to another, a local nightclub operator, Jack Ruby, killed him. Suspicions arose that Ruby murdered Oswald to cover up a conspiracy. Some people believed there had been a plot among ultraconservative Texans who hated Kennedy. Others, pointing to Oswald's three-year residence in the Soviet Union and his support of Castro's Cuba, suspected a Communist plot. To get at the truth and calm public fears, President Johnson appointed a commission headed by Chief Justice Earl Warren, which concluded in September 1964 that both Oswald and Ruby had acted alone. Several experts pointed to errors and omissions in the report, and later investigations alternately supported and contested the lone-killer explanation. As with Lincoln's assassination, the controversy persisted for decades, though most scholars agreed with the general conclusions of the Warren Commission.

JOHN F. KENNEDY'S FUNERAL
*For a few days following November 22, 1963, normal life stopped in the United States.
Schools and businesses were closed, while tens of thousands of Americans traveled
to Washington, D.C., to file past Kennedy's coffin in the rotunda of the Capitol. The relatively new medium of television unified the nation, as it allowed millions of viewers
to experience every moment of that long, terrible weekend, culminating in the funeral
procession, shown here. The president's widow, Jacqueline Kennedy, is escorted in the
procession by the president's brothers Robert (left) and Edward (right).*
© Henri Dauman NYC.

Debate also continued over how to assess Kennedy's domestic record. It had been unremarkable in his first two years, but his initiatives on taxes, civil rights, and poverty in 1963 suggested an important turning point. Whether Kennedy could have persuaded Congress to enact his proposals cannot be known. In the words of journalist James Reston, "What was killed was not only the president but the promise. . . . He never reached his meridian: We saw him only as a rising sun."

Johnson and the Great Society

Within six months of becoming president, Lyndon Johnson had found a theme for his administration. In May 1964, he announced the goal of a "Great Society, [which] rests on abundance and liberty for all.

It demands an end to poverty and racial injustice." In pursuing that Great Society, Johnson got Congress to pass three civil rights acts and a host of other legislation on issues ranging from antipoverty, education, and medical care to housing, consumer protection, and environmental preservation. The legislation of the 1960s constituted a remarkable record of reform yet fell short of the promise of the Great Society.

Fulfilling the Kennedy Promise

Lyndon Johnson assumed the presidency with a wealth of political experience. A self-made man from the poor Texas hill country, he had won election to the House of Representatives in 1937 and to the Senate in 1948. By 1955, he had secured the top post of Senate majority leader, which he used brilliantly to forge a Democratic consensus on the Civil Rights Acts of 1957 and 1960 and other liberal programs.

THE "JOHNSON TREATMENT"
Abe Fortas was a distinguished lawyer who had argued one of the major criminal rights cases, **Gideon v. Wainwright** *(1963), before the Supreme Court and who was a close friend and adviser to President Lyndon Johnson. When Johnson asked him to serve on the Supreme Court, he was reluctant to leave his lucrative law practice, and Johnson had to use his famous persuasive powers to secure his assent. This photograph of the president and Fortas taken in July 1965 illustrates how Johnson used his body as well as his voice to bend people to his will.*
Yoichi R. Okamoto / LBJ Library Collection.

Johnson's coarse wit, excessive vanity, intense ambition, and Texas accent put off many who were accustomed to the sophisticated Kennedy style. Lacking his predecessor's eloquent speaking style, Johnson excelled behind the scenes, where he could entice, cajole, or threaten legislators into support of his objectives. The famous "Johnson treatment" became legendary. In his ability to achieve his overriding goal of consensus—and in

the means to which he was willing to resort—he has few peers in American history.

Mobilizing emotions aroused by the assassination, he asked Congress to act so that "John Fitzgerald Kennedy did not live or die in vain." By trimming the federal budget and promising government frugality, he won over fiscal conservatives and signed Kennedy's tax cut bill in February 1964. Still more revolutionary was the Civil Rights Act of 1964, which banned discrimination in public accommodations, education, and employment. The president applied the Johnson treatment in full force to line up enough Republicans and southern Democrats to ensure passage. In July 1964, Johnson signed the strongest civil rights measure since Reconstruction.

Antipoverty legislation followed fast on the heels of the Civil Rights Act. In his first State of the Union message, Johnson called for "an unconditional war on poverty," and in August he signed the Economic Opportunity Act of 1964. The law authorized ten programs to be administered by a newly created Office of Economic Opportunity, allocating $800 million for the first year (about 1 percent of the federal budget). Many provisions were targeted at youth—from Head Start, a preschool program for poor children, to work-study grants for college students and job training programs for youth (the Job Corps). There were also loans to businesses willing to hire the long-term unemployed; aid to small farmers and rural businesses; and the Volunteers in Service to America (VISTA) program, which funded modest subsidies for volunteers working with the disadvantaged. A legal services program that provided lawyers for the poor resulted in lawsuits that enforced impoverished Americans' rights to welfare programs.

The most novel and controversial part of the law, the Community Action Program (CAP), required "maximum feasible participation" of poor people themselves in coordinating poverty programs. Unlike other aspects of the poverty program, this provision offered potential challenges to the system itself. Poor people began to organize community action programs to take control of their neighborhoods and to reform welfare agencies, school boards, police departments, housing authorities, and other agencies. Within months, mayors complained that activists were using federal funds to attack local governments and to "foster class struggle." Seeking to avoid conflict with mayors, Johnson directed federal poverty officials to back off from insistence on genuine representation for the poor. Although the Community Action Program failed to live up to its promise, for the first time people who were routinely excluded from participating in government gained a voice, an incentive to act on their own behalf, and the opportunity to develop leadership skills.

Completing the Great Society Agenda

Having steered the nation through the assassination trauma and established his capacity for national leadership, Johnson projected stability and security. With the economy booming, only a minority of voters proved willing to risk a change as dramatic as that promised by his Republican opponent in the 1964 election. Arizona senator Barry M. Goldwater represented the right wing of U.S. politics, attacking the entire framework of the welfare state and suggesting the use of nuclear weapons if necessary to crush communism in Vietnam. Although Goldwater captured five states in the Deep South, Johnson accomplished a record-breaking landslide of 61 percent of the popular vote. On his coattails came resounding Democratic majorities in the House (295–140) and Senate (68–32).

"I want to see a whole bunch of coonskins on the wall," Johnson told his aides, using a hunting analogy to stress his determination to make the most of his mandate. In the sheer amount and breadth of new legislation, Johnson succeeded extraordinarily, persuading Congress to pass three civil rights acts and measures mandating an antipoverty program, education subsidies, medical care for the aged and poor, a massive housing program, consumer protection, pollution control, environmental preservation, and more (Table 27.1). Public opinion polls gave impressively high marks to both the president and Congress. Reporters called the legislation of the Eighty-ninth Congress (1965–1966) "unprecedented" and "a political miracle."

The Economic Opportunity Act of 1964 had been just the opening shot in the War on Poverty. Congress increased the program's funding in 1965 to $2 billion and initiated two new assaults on poverty. The Appalachian Regional Development Act and the Public Works and Economic Development Act targeted depressed regions that the general economic boom had bypassed. These programs—like the tax cut of 1964—sought to help the poor indirectly by stimulating economic growth and providing jobs through road building and other public works projects.

A second approach endeavored to equip the poor with the training and skills necessary to find jobs. The largest assault on poverty through educa-

tion was the Elementary and Secondary Education Act of 1965. Ever since establishing the land-grant college system in the nineteenth century, the federal government had funded education, but only for a specific purpose, such as science education in the National Defense Education Act of 1957. The 1965 legislation provided general aid, allocating funds to public school districts based on the number of poor children they educated and providing equipment and supplies to private and parochial schools to be used for poor children. That same year Congress passed the Higher Education Act, vastly expanding federal assistance to colleges and universities, providing funds for buildings, programs, scholarships, and low-interest loans for students. In 1966, Congress renewed its commitment to education, appropriating nearly $4 billion for higher education for the next three years and $6.1 billion for a two-year extension of the elementary and secondary education program.

> *"I want to see a whole bunch of coonskins on the wall," Johnson told his aides, using a hunting analogy to stress his determination to make the most of his mandate.*

Other antipoverty efforts included a food stamp program that replaced the distribution of surplus commodities, giving poor people greater choice in obtaining food. Rent supplements also allowed some poor families more options, enabling them to avoid public housing projects, which often were massive high-rise buildings that failed to provide a positive environment for children. With the Model Cities Act, Congress authorized more than $1 billion to improve conditions in the nation's slums.

Congress also greatly increased the federal government's responsibility for health care. Trimming down the plan for government-sponsored universal care that Truman had proposed, Johnson focused his proposal on the elderly, who constituted a large portion of the nation's poor. Congress responded with the Medicare program, which provided the elderly with universal compulsory hospital insurance financed largely through Social Security taxes and a voluntary insurance program for other medical expenses funded by the government and individual contributions. A separate program, Medicaid, authorized federal grants to supplement state

TABLE 27.1
REFORMS OF THE GREAT SOCIETY, 1964–1968

1964

Twenty-fourth Amendment	Abolished poll tax as prerequisite for voting.
Tax Reduction Act	Provided $10 billion in tax cuts over 1964–1965.
Civil Rights Act	Banned discrimination in public accommodations, public education, and employment.
Economic Opportunity Act	Created programs for the disadvantaged, including Head Start, VISTA, Job Corps, and CAP.
Wilderness Preservation Act	Set aside 9.1 million acres of national forest for protection.

1965

Elementary and Secondary Education Act	Provided $1.3 billion in aid to elementary and secondary schools.
Medical Care Act	Provided health insurance (Medicare) for all citizens age 65 and over. Extended federal health benefits to welfare recipients (Medicaid).
Voting Rights Act	Banned literacy tests and other voting tests and authorized the federal government to act directly to enable African Americans to register and vote.
Executive Order 11246	Banned discrimination on the basis of race, religion, and national origin by employers awarded government contracts and required them to "take affirmative action to ensure equal opportunity."
Department of Housing and Urban Development (HUD)	New government department created to provide programs to address housing and community issues.
National Arts and Humanities Act	Created National Endowment for the Humanities (NEH) and National Endowment for the Arts (NEA) to support the work of artists, musicians, writers, and scholars.
Water Quality Act	Required states to set and enforce water quality standards.
Immigration and Nationality Act	Abolished fifty-year-old quotas based on national origins, increasing the number of non-Western and Northern European immigrants.
Air Quality Act	Imposed air pollution standards for motor vehicles.
Higher Education Act	Expanded federal assistance to colleges and universities.

1966

National Traffic and Motor Vehicle Safety Act	Established federal safety standards.
Highway Safety Act	Required federally approved safety programs at the state level.
Department of Transportation	New government department created to administer transportation programs and policies.
Model Cities Act	Authorized more than $1 billion to ameliorate nation's slums.

1967

Executive Order 11375	Extended earlier executive order banning discrimination and requiring affirmative action by federal contractors to cover women.

1968

Civil Rights Act of 1968	Banned discrimination in housing and in jury service.
National Housing Act	Subsidized the private construction of 1.7 million units of low-income housing.

programs paying for medical care for poor people below the age of sixty-five.

In response to the growing force of the civil rights movement, Johnson persuaded Congress to pass the Voting Rights Act of 1965, which banned literacy tests and authorized federal intervention to enable African Americans to register and vote. The Immigration and Nationality Act of 1965 did away with the fifty-year-old quotas based on national origins, thereby ending discrimination against immigrants from areas outside northern and western Europe. It did, however, maintain caps on the number of immigrants and for the first time placed limits on immigration from the Western Hemisphere.

The benefits of the Great Society reached well beyond the poverty-stricken. Pressures from a growing consumer movement led by liberal activist Ralph Nader and others produced legislation to make automobiles safer and to raise standards for the food, drug, and cosmetics industries. In 1965, Johnson became the first president to send Congress a special message on the environment, obtaining measures to control water and air pollution and to preserve the natural beauty of the American landscape. The National Arts and Humanities Act of 1965 created programs to support artists, musicians, writers, and scholars and to bring their work to public audiences.

The flood of reform legislation dwindled to a trickle after 1966, when midterm elections reduced the Democrats' huge majorities in Congress. Even though a sizable majority of the poor were whites, the public tended to associate antipoverty programs with African Americans. The appearance of buttons reading "I fight poverty—I work" indicated a growing backlash against the disadvantaged. The Vietnam War dealt the largest blow to domestic reform. Growing opposition to the war diverted the president's attention from domestic affairs and put his entire leadership in jeopardy. Even more damaging was the war's cost, which rose to more than $2 billion a month by 1966, increased the federal deficit, and exerted inflationary pressures on the economy.

Against these odds, Johnson in 1968 pried out of Congress one more civil rights law, which banned discrimination in housing, and he also secured a new housing program. The National Housing Act of 1968 authorized both an enormous increase in construction of low-income housing—1.7 million units over three years—and, by leaving construction and ownership in private hands, a new way of providing it. Poor people could purchase houses with low-interest loans guaranteed by the govern-ment, and developers could obtain low-interest loans to build housing for the needy.

Assessing the War on Poverty

Measured by statistics, the reduction in poverty in the 1960s was significant. The number of impoverished Americans fell from forty million in 1959 to twenty-five million in 1968, from over 20 percent of the population to around 13 percent (Figure 27.1). Equally if not more important, attitudes about poverty shifted as a growing number of people located the causes of poverty in economic and social circumstances rather than in individuals' shortcomings, and they assumed a national responsibility for alleviating it. Especially through the Community Action Programs, poor people themselves gained more control of their circumstances and a sense of their right to a fairer share of America's bounty.

Certain groups fared much better than others, however. Large numbers of the aged and members of male-headed families rose out of poverty, while the plight of female-headed families actually worsened. Although African American family income grew from 54 percent of white family income to 61 percent, whites escaped poverty at a faster rate than blacks, who constituted one-third of the poor population at the end of the decade. Moreover, despite the large increases in direct subsidies for food stamps, housing, medical care, and Aid to Families with Dependent Children (AFDC), a program launched by the New Deal, no significant redistribution of income resulted. The poorest 20 percent of the population received 5.1 percent of total national income in 1964 and 5.4 percent in 1974.

Measured by statistics, the reduction in poverty in the 1960s was significant. Equally if not more important, attitudes about poverty shifted as a growing number of people located the causes of poverty in economic and social circumstances rather than in individuals' shortcomings.

Conservatives charged that the Great Society programs discouraged initiative by giving the poor "handouts." Critics on the left claimed that the

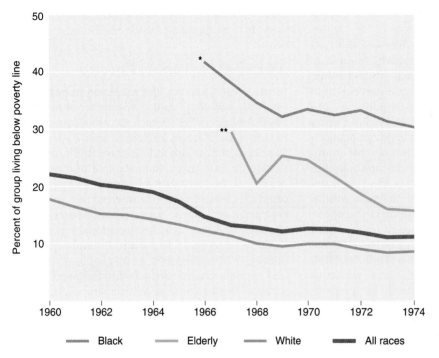

FIGURE 27.1

Poverty in the United States, 1960–1974
The short-term effects of economic growth and the Great Society's attack on poverty are seen here. Which groups experienced the sharpest decline in poverty, and what might account for the differences?

*Statistics on blacks for years 1960–1965 not available.
**Statistics on the elderly for years 1960–1966 not available.

emphasis on training and education placed the responsibility for poverty on the poor themselves rather than on an economic system that failed to provide enough decent-paying jobs. Most job training programs prepared graduates for low-level occupations and could not guarantee employment. Surveys in 1966 and 1967, for example, found 28 percent of Job Corps graduates unemployed six months after finishing their training.

Who reaped the greatest benefits from Great Society programs? Critics pointed out that most of the funds for Appalachia and other depressed areas built highways and thus helped the construction industry. Real estate developers, investors, and moderate-income families reaped the lion's share of benefits from the mortgage subsidies under the National Housing Act of 1968. Noting that in slum clearance programs, commercial development and high-income housing often displaced poor families, blacks called urban renewal "Negro removal." Physicians' fees and hospital costs soared after enactment of Medicare and Medicaid. Other beneficiaries of the Great Society programs were middle-class professionals who staffed the growing bureaucracy that ran the programs.

Some critics of the War on Poverty suggested that the solution to poverty lay in a major redistribution of income, through raising taxes and using those funds in the public sector to create jobs, overhaul social welfare systems, and rebuild slums. The Johnson administration programs did invest more heavily in the public sector, but funds for the poverty programs came from increasing revenues generated by economic growth, not from new taxes on the rich or middle class. Determined to promote consensus and avoid conflict, Johnson would not take from the advantaged to provide for the poor. Economic prosperity allowed spending for the poor to rise and significantly improved the lives of millions, but that spending never approached the amounts necessary to declare victory in the War on Poverty.

The Second Reconstruction

Unlike many of the Great Society reforms, which failed to live up to their promise and provoked widespread criticism, the civil rights movement effected a revolution in the legal status of African

Americans and won widespread acceptance. The first Reconstruction in the aftermath of the Civil War had ended slavery and written racial equality into the Constitution; the second Reconstruction a century later made the guarantee of equal status under the law a reality. That accomplishment depended heavily on the courage and determination of black people themselves. In the words of Sheyann Webb, one of the thousands of marchers in the 1965 Selma, Alabama, campaign for voting rights, "We were just people, ordinary people, and we did it."

The Flowering of the Black Freedom Struggle

The Montgomery bus boycott in the mid-1950s had given national visibility to the plight of southern blacks, produced a national leader in Martin Luther King Jr., and demonstrated the effectiveness of mass mobilization. Nevertheless, although it took enormous energy and determination, the boycott remained in a way a passive action—Montgomery blacks avoided riding the buses. In the 1960s, the form of protest underwent a major change, mobilizing blacks into direct and personal confrontation with the people and institutions that segregated and discriminated against them: lunch counters, department stores, public parks and libraries, buses and depots, and voting registrars.

Direct action as a mass movement began in February 1960, when four African American students at North Carolina A&T College in Greensboro sat at the whites-only Woolworth's lunch counter and requested service. Within days, hundreds of young people joined their demonstration. By the end of February, blacks had launched sit-ins in thirty-one cities in eight southern states. In April, Ella Baker, executive secretary of the Southern Christian Leadership Conference (SCLC), called activists together from campuses across the South. Choosing independence from the older civil rights organizations, they founded the Student Nonviolent Coordinating Committee (SNCC, pronounced "snick"), creating a decentralized, non-hierarchical structure that encouraged the development of leadership and decision making at the grassroots level.

Although rejecting organizational patterns of the older groups, SNCC embraced civil disobedience and the nonviolence principles of Martin Luther King Jr. Directly confronting the agents of oppression, students would stand up for their

rights, but they would not practice self-defense against their enemies. At SNCC's founding conference, minister James Lawson defined a strategy for blacks that he believed could change the hearts of their oppressors: "We affirm . . . nonviolence as a foundation of our purpose, the presupposition of our faith, and the manner of our action." With its appeal to human conscience, "nonviolence nurtures the atmosphere in which reconciliation and justice become actual possibilities."

Direct action as a mass movement began in February 1960, when four African American students at North Carolina A&T College in Greensboro sat at the whites-only Woolworth's lunch counter and requested service.

When students returned to the field, their optimism and commitment to nonviolence met severe testing. Although some cities quietly met student demands, more typically authorities and local citizens reacted with violence. Hostile whites poured food over demonstrators, burned them with cigarettes, called them "niggers," and pelted them with rocks. Local police went after protesters with dogs, clubs, fire hoses, and tear gas; they arrested more than thirty-six hundred civil rights demonstrators in the year following the Greensboro sit-in.

In 1961, the Congress of Racial Equality (CORE) organized Freedom Rides to integrate interstate transportation in the South. On May 4, six whites and seven blacks boarded two buses in Washington, D.C., for a thirteen-day ride to New Orleans. The riders crossed the color line unharmed in Virginia and North Carolina, but in Alabama white hoodlums bombed a bus and beat the riders with baseball bats. When some Freedom Riders turned back, SNCC members rushed in to take their places.

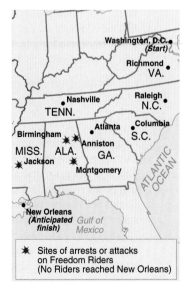

★ Sites of arrests or attacks on Freedom Riders (No Riders reached New Orleans)

Civil Rights Freedom Rides, May 1961

LUNCH COUNTER SIT-IN
John Salter Jr., a professor at Tougaloo College, and students Joan Trumpauer and Anne Moody take part in a 1963 sit-in at the Woolworth's lunch counter in Jackson, Mississippi. Shortly before this photograph was taken, whites had thrown two students to the floor and police had arrested one student. Salter was spattered with mustard and ketchup. Moody would publish a popular book in 1968 about her experiences in the black freedom struggle, **Coming of Age in Mississippi.**
State Historical Society of Wisconsin.

www.bedfordstmartins.com/tap SEE THE ONLINE STUDY GUIDE for more help in assessing this image.

After a huge mob attacked the Freedom Riders in Montgomery, Attorney General Robert Kennedy dispatched federal marshals to restore order. But when the buses reached Jackson, Mississippi, the Freedom Riders were promptly arrested, and several hundred spent part of the summer in Mississippi jails.

Encouraged in part by Kennedy administration officials who viewed voter registration as less controversial than civil disobedience (and more likely to benefit the Democratic Party), SNCC and other groups began a Voter Education Project in the summer of 1961. Yet as activists sought to register black

voters in the Deep South, they too met violence. Whites bombed black churches, threw tenant farmers out of their homes, and beat and jailed activists like Fannie Lou Hamer. When a Mississippi legislator killed Herbert Lee, one of the first blacks to attempt to register, no charges were brought. In June 1963, a white man gunned down Mississippi NAACP leader Medgar Evers in front of his house in Jackson; the murderer eluded conviction until the 1990s.

Television brought home to the entire world the brutality of southern resistance to racial equality in

BIRMINGHAM DEMONSTRATORS

In April 1963, Martin Luther King Jr. and the Southern Christian Leadership Conference initiated a campaign to integrate Birmingham, Alabama, known as the most segregated city in the nation. City officials filled the jails with demonstrators, including King himself, and nine hundred children, like these young people being attacked with powerful hoses. One police officer remarked to a colleague, "Ten or fifteen years from now, we will look back on all this and we will say, 'How stupid can you be?'" Photographs like this one evoked outrage throughout the country.

April 1963, when Martin Luther King Jr. and the SCLC launched a campaign in Birmingham, Alabama, to integrate public facilities and open jobs to African Americans. As blacks massed in demonstrations, the city's police chief, Eugene "Bull" Connor, responded with police dogs, electric cattle prods, and high-pressure hoses. Hundreds of demonstrators, including school-age children, went to jail, and firebombs exploded at King's motel and his brother's house. Four months later, a bomb killed four black children attending Sunday school in Birmingham.

The largest demonstration took place in Washington, D.C., in August 1963. Sponsored by the major civil rights organizations, the march drew 250,000 blacks and whites to the nation's capital. King put his indelible stamp on the day. Moved by the intense emotions of the crowd, King departed from his formal speech, using all the passion and skills that made him the greatest orator of his day. His words came from the Bible, Negro spirituals, and the nation's patriotic anthems. "I have a dream," he repeated again and again, spelling out a future when "the sons of former slaves and the sons of former slave owners will be able to sit down together at the table of brotherhood." With the crowd roaring in support, he imagined the day

"when all of God's children . . . will be able to join hands and sing . . . 'Free at last, free at last; thank God Almighty, we are free at last.'" (See page A-37.)

Moved by the intense emotions of the crowd, King departed from his formal speech, using all the passion and skills that made him the greatest orator of his day. "I have a dream," he repeated again and again.

Media and public response to the March on Washington was overwhelmingly positive, but the buoyant euphoria of that day quickly faded as activists returned to continued violence in the South. In 1964, the Mississippi Freedom Summer Project mobilized more than one thousand northern college students, who paid their own expenses to conduct voter education classes and help blacks register to vote in Mississippi. Resistance was fierce. By the end of the summer, only twelve hundred new voters had been allowed to register; whites had killed several activists, beaten eighty, arrested more than a thousand, and burned thirty-five black churches.

THE MARCH ON WASHINGTON
More than a quarter of a million Americans, including fifty thousand whites, gathered
on the Mall in the nation's capital on August 28, 1963, to pressure the government to
support African Americans' civil rights. After Martin Luther King Jr. mesmerized the
crowd with his "I have a dream" speech, Malcolm X said to march organizer Bayard
Rustin, "You know this dream of King's is going to be a nightmare before it's over."
James P. Blair / National Geographic Society Image Collection.

Still the movement persisted. In January 1965, the SCLC and SNCC launched a voting drive in Selma, Alabama, against brutal opposition from local authorities. In March, Alabama troopers used such fierce force to turn back a fifty-four-mile march from Selma to the state capitol in Montgomery that the incident earned the name "Bloody Sunday." After several days, President Johnson called up the Alabama National Guard to protect the marchers. Before the Selma campaign was over, whites had shot or beaten to death three demonstrators. On Bloody Sunday, John Lewis, chairman of the SNCC, was battered and hospitalized but managed to make the final march to the capitol. Looking back on that demonstration, he recalled it as one of the most meaningful events in his life: "In October of that year the Voting Rights bill was passed and we all felt we'd had a part in it."

The Response in Washington

Civil rights leaders would have to wear sneakers, Lyndon Johnson said, if they were going to keep up with him. But both Kennedy and Johnson acted more in response to events created by the black freedom struggle than on their own initiative. Both presidents moved only when events in the South gave them little choice. Kennedy sent federal marshals to Montgomery to protect the Freedom Riders; in 1962, he dispatched federal troops to enable James H. Meredith, a black air force veteran, to enroll in the all-white University of Mississippi; and he called up the Alabama National Guard during the Birmingham demonstrations in May 1963. But to activists pleading for more federal protection, Kennedy replied that law enforcement was a local matter. Well aware of the political costs of deploying federal force, the president and the attorney

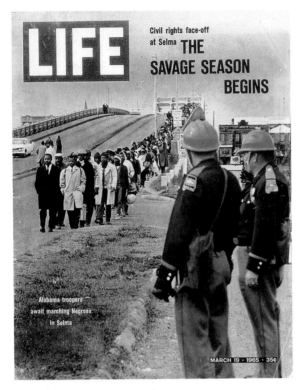

THE SELMA MARCH FOR VOTING RIGHTS

In 1963, the Student Nonviolent Coordinating Committee (SNCC) began a campaign for voting rights in Selma, Alabama, where white officials had registered only 335 of the 15,000 African Americans old enough to vote. As often happened, after younger activists had gotten things started, Martin Luther King Jr. came to Selma in January 1965 and made the city his primary focus. He planned a fifty-four-mile march from Selma to Montgomery, the state capital, to insist that blacks be registered, but, warned of a serious threat on his life, King did not lead the march. Here John Lewis of SNCC and Hosea Williams of the Southern Christian Leadership Conference head the line of marchers just before, as Lewis recalled, "They came at us like a human wave, a blur of blue uniforms, billy clubs, bullwhips and tear gas," beating him to the ground.
Life magazine © 1965 Time, Inc.

general made it clear that they intervened to enforce the law, not to support the demonstrators.

In June 1963, Kennedy finally made good on his promise to seek civil rights legislation. In a nationally televised speech, he called civil rights "a moral issue . . . as old as the scriptures and . . . as clear as the American Constitution" and specifically supported voting rights and equal access to public schools and accommodations. Pointing to the injustice suffered by blacks, Kennedy asked white Americans, "Who among us would then be content with the counsels of patience and delay?" Johnson took up Kennedy's commitment with zeal, assisted by a number of factors. Television captured the dignity and courage of African Americans and the brutal repression of southern officials, conveying scenes of violence against peaceful demonstrators that appalled many viewers across the nation. The growing public support for civil rights, the "Johnson treatment," and the president's ability to turn the measure into a memorial to the martyred Kennedy all produced the most important civil rights law since Reconstruction.

Passed in July, the Civil Rights Act of 1964 guaranteed access for all Americans to public accommodations, public education, employment, and voting, thus sounding the death knell for the South's system of segregation and discrimination. Title VII of the measure, which banned discrimination in employment, also attacked racial inequality outside the South. In addition, Title VII outlawed sex discrimination in employment. Introduced by a conservative southern opponent of civil rights in hopes of defeating the entire bill, the sex provision nonetheless had the support of some women's rights advocates, including Representative Martha Griffiths, a Michigan Democrat. Because Title VII applied not just to wages but to every aspect of employment, including hiring and promotion, it represented a giant step toward equal employment opportunity for white women as well as racial minorities.

The growing public support for civil rights, the "Johnson treatment," and the president's ability to turn the measure into a memorial to the martyred Kennedy all produced the most important civil rights law since Reconstruction.

Johnson soon demanded a new law, one that would remove "every remaining obstacle to the right and the opportunity to vote." In a televised speech before Congress, given in hopes of arousing popular support, Johnson insisted, "Should we defeat every enemy, should we double our wealth and conquer the stars [without achieving racial equality], we will have failed as a people and as a nation." The Voting Rights Act, which empowered the federal government to act directly and immediately to enable African Americans to register and vote, was signed by Johnson in August 1965. A major transformation began in southern politics. (See Map 27.2 below and "Historical Question," page 1040.)

Two more measures completed Johnson's civil rights record. A third law, the Civil Rights Act of

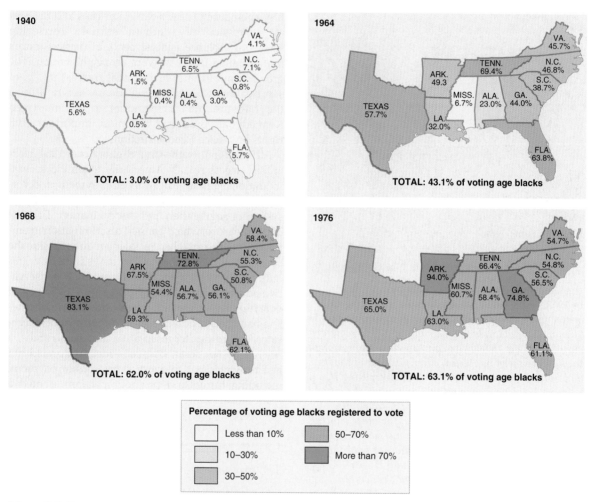

Map 27.2

The Rise of the African American Vote, 1940–1976

Voting rates of southern blacks increased gradually in the 1940s and 1950s but shot up dramatically in the Deep South after the Voting Rights Act of 1965 provided for federal agents to enforce African Americans' right to vote.

Reading the map: When did the biggest change in African American voter registration occur in the South? Which states had the highest and which had the lowest voter registration records in 1968?

Connections: What role did African American voters play in the 1960 election? What were the targets of the three major voting drives in the 1960s?

www.bedfordstmartins.com/tap See the Online Study Guide for more help in analyzing this map.

1968, banned racial discrimination in housing and jury selection and empowered the federal government to intervene to protect civil rights workers from violence. In addition, Johnson used his presidential authority in September 1965 to issue Executive Order 11246, which not only banned discrimination by employers holding government contracts (affecting about one-third of the labor force) but also required them to take affirmative action to ensure equal opportunity. Extended to cover women in 1967, the affirmative action program provoked more controversy than any of the civil rights measures. Calling it "reverse discrimination," many people thought—incorrectly—that affirmative action required absolute quotas for hiring minorities and women or employing unqualified candidates. In fact, the order required employers to counter the effects of centuries of oppression by acting forcefully to bring their labor force in line with the available pool of qualified candidates. Within a few years, most large businesses came to see affirmative action as a good employment practice.

These legal gains, however, failed to match rising aspirations, and many activists felt abandoned by white liberals. Johnson himself sided with Democratic mayors such as Richard J. Daley in Chicago when King and others began to attack discrimination in housing, education, and employment outside the South. Moreover, under Johnson the FBI continued the wiretapping and surveillance of King that had begun under Kennedy and expanded its activities to "expose, disrupt, misdirect, discredit, or otherwise neutralize" militant black protest. As the claim to racial equality moved outside the South and intensified in militancy, the president most committed to promoting civil rights became the object of bitter criticism from the black freedom movement.

Black Nationalism and the End of the Civil Rights Coalition

By 1966, civil rights activism had undergone dramatic changes. Initially focused on the South, the black freedom struggle extended its attention to racial oppression throughout the nation and broadened its goals from integration and legal equality to the elimination of poverty and miserable living conditions for millions of African Americans. In addition, many black activists had given up on white allies and the tactics of nonviolence. In part the new emphases resulted from the very success of civil

rights legislation, as one layer of oppression receded only to reveal others more subtle but just as pervasive. Equal access to public facilities and institutions did little to improve the material conditions of blacks. How valuable was the freedom to patronize a restaurant if African Americans could not afford the price of a meal?

Black rage at oppressive conditions and impatience with legal changes erupted in a wave of riots that ignited cities in the North, Midwest, and West every summer from 1964 to 1968. The Watts district of Los Angeles in 1965, Newark and Detroit in 1967, and the nation's capital in 1968 saw the most destruction and violence, but hundreds of eruptions occurred across the country, usually sparked by an incident between white police and local blacks. In Detroit, rioters swept through 14 square miles of the black ghetto; the result was 43 deaths, 7,000 arrests, 1,300 destroyed buildings, and 2,700 looted shops. "Our nation is moving toward two societies, one black, one white—separate and unequal," warned an investigating commission appointed by the president in 1967, but little was done to ameliorate the basic conditions from which riots sprang.

King and other leaders realized that legal change alone could not remedy the deplorable economic conditions of many African Americans. In 1965, the SCLC mounted a drive for better jobs, schools, and housing in Chicago. Following her drive for voter registration, Fannie Lou Hamer channeled more and more of her energy into projects to ameliorate poverty in Mississippi. King pressed the government for more adequate funding of the antipoverty program and initiated plans for a Poor People's March to the nation's capital in 1968. Yet even as his goals changed, King continued to stress the principle of nonviolence and attempted to work with white supporters and government officials. For this he came increasingly under criticism from activists in CORE and SNCC.

In the North, a powerful voice rose to challenge the dominant ethos of the civil rights movement. Malcolm Little had grown up in poverty, first in Nebraska and then in Michigan. In prison at the age of twenty-one for attempted burglary, he educated himself and joined the Nation of Islam. The Nation, whose adherents called themselves Black Muslims, drew on a long African American tradition of nationalism and separatism. Released from jail in 1952, Malcolm Little changed his name to Malcolm X, to symbolize the African identity stripped from his ancestors, and went to work for the Nation of Islam.

What Difference Did Black Voting Rights Make?

B ORN TO POOR BLACK SHARECROPPERS in the Mississippi Delta, Unita Blackwell hearkened in church one Sunday in 1964 when a SNCC worker talked about voter registration. The very next day she went to the courthouse where, as had happened to Fannie Lou Hamer and hundreds of other African Americans, officials refused her application. Undeterred, she succeeded on the third try, threw herself into activism as a SNCC organizer, and saw her share of jail cells. In fact, she and her husband planned their protest activities so that only one would risk arrest and the other would remain free to care for their child. A founder of the Mississippi Freedom Democratic Party, established to challenge the all-white state organization, Blackwell saw the challenge fall to compromise at the 1964 Democratic National Convention. But four years later, she participated in the national convention with Mississippi's reconfigured biracial delegation. Subsequently, she served as vice chair of the state Democratic Party and on the Democratic National Committee. When her small town of Mayersville incorporated in 1976, Blackwell won election as its first mayor and the first black female mayor in Mississippi.

Blackwell's career is but one measure of the transformations generated by African Americans' struggle for the most basic right of citizenship. Their determination to register to vote and the resulting resistance and violence of southern whites created a crisis that the federal government could not ignore. Its response—the Voting Rights Act of 1965 and subsequent extensions—suspended the literacy tests that had been used to disqualify blacks but not whites and brought electoral operations in most southern states under federal supervision. The law required the Justice Department to approve in advance any changes in state procedures that might disadvantage black voters, and it empowered the attorney general to send federal agents to observe registration and election processes and even to register voters in areas of continued white resistance.

"Legislation is not self-implementing," warned NAACP leader Roy Wilkins. "There is work to be done." As was the case with its passage, implementation of the Voting Rights Act depended on the efforts of African Americans themselves. More than two hundred voter registration drives between 1966 and 1968 paid off in dramatic increases in the numbers of blacks registered. Throughout the South, the proportion of African Americans on voter rolls jumped from 43 percent in 1964 to 62 percent in 1968. In Mississippi, the total leaped from just 6.7 percent in 1964 to 68 percent in 1968.

African Americans also gained political offices in unprecedented numbers. Fewer than two dozen blacks held elective office in the South in 1964. In 1970, they claimed almost five hundred elected government posts, and two years later the number reached nearly twelve hundred. Just seven years after whites bludgeoned civil rights activists during the Selma voting drive, black candidates won half of the ten seats on Selma's city council. With the victories of Barbara Jordan from Houston, Texas, and Andrew Young from Atlanta, Georgia, in 1972, the former Confederacy sent its first African Americans to the House of Representatives since Reconstruction. Black electoral success was not limited to the South. Across the nation, African Americans held fifteen hundred elected positions in 1970, and by 1990 that number exceeded seven thousand. The greatest progress came at the local level. The number of black city council members vaulted from 552 in 1970 to nearly 3,000 in 1989, and the number of black mayors grew sixfold, to more than 300, in the 1990s. The total of black representatives in Congress inched up from ten in 1970 to twenty-five in 1990 and to thirty-seven in the 1996 elections.

Electoral success translated into tangible benefits. When black officials took office, their constituents saw improvements in public facilities, police protection, roads, trash collection, and other basic services. Referring to Unita Blackwell's acernment jobs to African Americans and contracts to minority businesses. Elected mayor of Atlanta in 1973, Maynard Jackson appointed a black police chief and increased blacks' share of city jobs from 42 to 51 percent.

Most black officials had far less power than Jackson, but even when they were outnumbered by whites, they could at least introduce issues of concern to blacks that whites had ignored, and they gained access to information about behind-the-scenes government. An African American serving on a city council in Florida pointed out that "no matter what happened, [my white colleagues] knew I was listening to everything that went on." Activist Fannie Lou Hamer noted the psychological benefits of electoral progress. When blacks had no political voice, she recalled, "some white folks would drive past your house in a pickup truck with guns hanging up on the back and give you hate stares. . . . Those same people now call me Mrs. Hamer."

Yet increased political power did not guarantee African Americans economic equality or even material security. Their minority status in the population and their residential dispersion, combined with many whites' disinclination to vote for blacks, meant that even by 1990 African Americans occupied fewer than 2 percent of all elected positions in the nation. As African Americans looked to increase their political force and shape policy to meet their needs, they sought to revive grassroots activism and seek coalitions with other racial and ethnic groups. In addition, they considered a number of electoral strategies to solidify black and minority strength in a majoritarian system: reducing the number of at-large elections, which dilute minorities' power, and increasing the number of single-member district systems; monitoring electoral redistricting to ensure as many black-majority districts as possible; and proportionate or cumulative voting.

Despite the limited reach of black enfranchisement, most experts nonetheless view the voting rights revolution as the most successful of all civil rights initiatives. As Unita Blackwell put it, "We didn't have nothing, and we changed the whole world with nothing. We changed a whole outlook."

REGISTERING TO VOTE
Two civil rights volunteers during the 1964 Mississippi Freedom Summer campaign help a couple fill out voter registration forms. The form included a question asking the applicant to interpret a portion of the state's constitution, one of the ways white officials kept African Americans from voting in southern states before passage of the Voting Rights Act in 1965.

Charles Moore / Black Star.

complishments as mayor, a Mayersville resident noted, "She brought in the water tower. Mostly it was pumps then. . . . Sewage, too. There wasn't nothing but those little old outdoor houses." Another constituent pointed to "old folks' houses. And paved streets. I grew up here when they wasn't paved." Black local officials also awarded more gov-

He attracted a large following, especially in urban ghettos, calling for black pride and autonomy, separation from the "corrupt [white] society," and self-defense against white violence. In 1964, Malcolm X broke from the Black Muslims, began to cultivate a wider constituency, and expressed an openness to working with whites. At a Harlem rally in February 1965, three members of the Nation of Islam shot and killed him. Yet his ideas outlived his death and began to resonate in CORE and SNCC.

At a June 1966 rally in Greenwood, Mississippi, SNCC chairman Stokely Carmichael gave the approach advocated by Malcolm X a new name. "We want black power," he shouted again and again. "Black power" quickly became the rallying cry in SNCC and CORE. Though embraced by only a minority of African Americans, the black power movement claimed the bulk of national attention in the late 1960s.

In the North, a powerful voice rose to challenge the dominant ethos of the civil rights movement. Malcolm Little changed his name to Malcolm X, to symbolize the African identity stripped from his ancestors, and went to work for the Nation of Islam.

Carmichael and other activists issued no single systematic definition of black power. Calling integration "a subterfuge for the maintenance of white supremacy," Carmichael insisted on separation from whites, because assimilation implied the superiority of white institutions and values. African Americans were encouraged to develop independent businesses, control their own schools and other

MALCOLM X
*Malcolm X stands in front of the pyramids in Egypt during a trip to Africa and the Middle East in 1964. Partly as a result of meeting Muslims of all colors as well as whites who were committed to ending racism, he no longer equated whites with the devil. "The white man is **not** inherently evil," he concluded, "but America's racist society influences him to act evilly."*
John Launois / Black Star.

institutions, and form all-black political organizations, such as the Black Panther Party, founded in Oakland, California, in 1966. The phrase "Black is beautiful" emphasized the authenticity and worth of African American culture and racial pride.

To black power advocates, nonviolence only brought more beatings and killings. Malcolm X had once said, "If someone puts a hand on you, send him to the cemetery." Carmichael agreed: "Black people should and must fight back." The press paid an inordinate amount of attention to black radicals, and the black power movement contributed to a severe white backlash. Although the urban riots of the mid-1960s erupted spontaneously, triggered by specific incidents, horrified whites blamed them on black power militants. By 1966, a full 85 percent of the white population thought that blacks were pressing for too much too quickly; two years earlier, only 34 percent had thought so.

King agreed with black power advocates about the need for "a radical reconstruction of society," but he clung to nonviolence and integration as the means to this end. In March 1968, the thirty-nine-year-old leader took his movement to Memphis to support a strike of municipal garbage workers. There, on April 4, King was shot and killed. James Earl Ray, an escaped white convict, was arrested and confessed to the murder but later denied that he had killed King and insisted that he was a scapegoat for a wider conspiracy.

Black power advocates receded from national visibility by the end of the decade. Never able to command substantial support in the African American community, which revered King and his philosophy, black militants were harassed by the FBI, jailed, and sometimes killed by the police, some of whom were also killed. Black nationalism's emphasis on racial pride and culture and its critique of American institutions, however, resonated broadly and helped to shape the protest of other groups.

Demands for Power to the People

With its incontrovertible moral claims, the civil rights movement helped to make protest respectable, and its ability to capture national attention and move the federal government suggested possibilities for other groups with grievances. Native Americans, Latinos, college students, women, and others drew on the black freedom struggle for inspiration and models of protest. These groups engaged in direct-action protests, expressed their own cultural nationalism, and challenged dominant institutions and values.

Native American Protest

Protest was not new to the group of Americans with the oldest grievances, but Native American activism took on fresh militancy and goals in the 1960s. The cry "red power" reflected the influence of black radicalism on Native Americans who rejected the goal of assimilation. As one Indian put it, the civil rights struggle led by King "was within the System, and the System had nothing to do with Indians." Rather, American Indians sought tribal sovereignty and just treatment as independent nations.

Native Americans, Latinos, college students, women, and others drew on the black freedom struggle for inspiration and models of protest.

Native Americans demonstrated and occupied land and public buildings, claiming rights to natural resources and territory that they had owned collectively before European settlement. For example, in 1963 Northwest Indians mounted "fish-ins" to enforce fishing rights guaranteed by century-old treaties. A new, more militant generation participated in these demonstrations through the National Indian Youth Council, founded in 1961. In the most dramatic action, Indians seized Alcatraz Island in San Francisco Bay in 1969 and used it as a cultural and educational center until the federal government ran them out in 1971.

In Minneapolis in 1968, two Chippewa, Dennis Banks and George Mitchell, founded the American Indian Movement (AIM) to deal with problems in cities, where about 300,000 Indians lived. AIM focused on Native Americans who had been encouraged or forced by the relocation and termination programs of the 1950s to migrate to urban areas, only to find unemployment, poverty, and alienation from their traditions. The movement sought to protect Indians from police harassment, secure

AMERICAN INDIANS OCCUPY ALCATRAZ
In November 1969, 150 Native Americans occupied Alcatraz Island in San Francisco Bay, the site of a federal prison. Part of the Red Power movement, they were there, as one activist explained, to protest "extermination of our cultures . . . the chronic and cyclical poverty of reservations and the relocation transfer of that poverty into Red Ghettoes in the cities." The protesters, whose demand for "Land, Peace, and Freedom" is emblazoned on the water tower, offered to pay the government beads and cloth for the island in the amount that Dutch colonists had paid American Indians for Manhattan Island in 1626.
Ralph Crane / TimePix.

antipoverty program funds for Indian-controlled organizations, and establish "survival schools" to teach the history and values of Indian culture. The appeal of the new movement quickly spread beyond urban areas. AIM members "had a new look about them, not that hangdog reservation look I was used to," Mary Crow Dog wrote, and their visit to

her reservation in South Dakota "loosened a sort of earthquake inside me."

Native American protest gained attention from the Bureau of Indian Affairs, legislation to meet educational and health needs of Indians, and government decisions recognizing Indian rights to ancestral lands. Taos Indians, for example, regained land in New Mexico, and the government paid the Sioux more than $100 million for lands that were taken in gold rush days in the nineteenth century. Native Americans recovered a measure of identity and pride, greater respect for and protection of their culture, and, in the words of President Johnson's special message to Congress in 1968, a recognition of "the right of the First Americans to remain Indians while exercising their rights as Americans."

Latino Struggles for Justice

The fastest-growing minority group in the 1960s were Latinos, or Hispanic Americans, an extraordinarily varied population that includes people of Mexican, Puerto Rican, Caribbean, and other Latin American origins. (The term *Latino* stresses their common bonds as a minority group in the United States, while *Hispanic* is a less political term and also refers to those with origins in Spain.) People of Puerto Rican and Caribbean descent tended to live in urban areas on the East Coast. But more than half of the Latino population of the United States— some six million Mexican Americans—lived in California, Texas, Arizona, New Mexico, and Colorado. In addition, thousands of immigrants illegally crossed the unguarded two-thousand-mile border between Mexico and the United States in search of economic opportunity.

Throughout the twentieth century, Mexican Americans had formed organizations to push for political power and economic rights. For example, activists tried to organize farmworkers and other laborers during the depression. With more lasting results, middle-class Mexican Americans in 1929 formed the League of United Latin American Citizens (LULAC), which provided aid to newer immigrants and, like the NAACP, fought segregation and discrimination through litigation. Stressing integration, LULAC restricted membership to those who spoke English and were U.S. citizens. In the 1960s, however, young Mexican Americans, like African Americans and Native Americans, increasingly rejected traditional politics in favor of direct action. One symbol of this generational challenge was the

CESAR CHAVEZ IN
THE VINEYARDS
Cesar Chavez meets with grape pickers in California during the national grape boycott of 1965. The boycott's proclamation listed these aims: "just wages, humane working conditions, protection from the misuse of pesticides, and the fundamental right of collective bargaining."
Arthur Schatz / TimePix.

adoption of the term *Chicano* (from the Spanish word for Mexican, *mejicano*) by young activists.

Chicano activism drew national attention to California, where Cesar Chavez and Dolores Huerta organized a movement to attack the wretched living and working conditions endured by migrant agricultural workers. Chavez, whose grandfather had migrated to the United States in the nineteenth century, became part of the multiracial, multiethnic farm labor force in California when his family lost its business and farm in Arizona during the depression. Moving from farm to farm with his family, often living in soggy tents or small tarpaper cabins, exploited and cheated by labor contractors, Chavez had to change schools frequently and stopped after the eighth grade. He encountered indifference and discrimination in the educational system, where teachers forbade students to speak

Spanish. One teacher, he recalled, "hung a sign on me that said, 'I am a clown, I speak Spanish.'" After serving in the navy in World War II, marrying, and starting a family, Chavez became involved in organizing voter registration drives among Mexican Americans in California and began educating himself by reading about labor history, Catholic writers' reform ideas, and the principles of Mahatma Gandhi.

Dolores Huerta grew up in an integrated neighborhood in Stockton, California, raised by a divorced mother who ran a successful hotel, where she sometimes offered free rooms to destitute farmworkers. In contrast to Chavez, Huerta did not experience the grinding poverty and exploitation of the farmworkers, but she witnessed subtle forms of discrimination. Once, for example, a high school teacher challenged her authorship of an essay because it was so well written. She completed community college, married, bore children, and taught school, but she was driven to act directly on her growing awareness of social injustice. At the age of twenty-five, she became involved in the same organization for which Chavez worked, and by the early 1960s they both determined that a union was the key to improving the lives of farmworkers. At great personal sacrifice—both gave up paid employment, and their families barely scraped by—in 1962, they founded the United Farm Workers (UFW), which Chavez headed until his death in 1993. UFW marches and strikes gained widespread support, and a national boycott of California grapes helped the UFW to win union recognition and a wage increase for the mostly Chicano and Filipino workers in 1970. Although the union struggled and lost membership, it helped politicize Mexican Americans and improved the lives of thousands of farm workers. In 1999, California made the date of Chavez's birth a state holiday.

Chicanos mobilized elsewhere to end discrimination in employment and education, gain political power, win their share of antipoverty funds, and combat police brutality. Spreading through the Southwest in 1968 were a wave of strikes, called "Blow Outs," through which high school students protested racism in the public schools. In Denver, Colorado, Rodolfo "Corky" Gonzales organized the Crusade for Justice, setting up "freedom schools," where Chicano children learned Spanish and studied Mexican American history and culture and marched down the halls chanting, "Chicano power." The separatist and nationalist strains of Chicano protest were evident in La Raza Unida (the United Race), a political party founded by José Angel Gutierrez in Texas and based on cultural pride and brotherhood. Mexican Americans also gradually won greater representation in government and more effective enforcement of antidiscrimination legislation. With blacks and Native Americans, they continued to be overrepresented among the poor but gained a sense of their potential power and respect for their culture.

Student Rebellion and the New Left

Connections between the black freedom struggle and other protest movements were direct and immediate, as white activists returned from civil rights projects in the South to launch student protests, the

antiwar movement, and the new feminist movement. Challenging establishment institutions and traditional values, these movements, along with those of racial and ethnic minorities, formed part of a reinvigorated political left, contributed to a more intense consciousness of rights among Americans, and left their marks on higher education, the family, the national government and other key institutions.

The organizational focus of white student protest in the 1960s was Students for a Democratic Society (SDS), formed in 1960 by a small group of whites from the remains of an older socialist-oriented student organization. In 1962, some sixty students met in Port Huron, Michigan, and helped write a statement of the group's purpose and structure. "We are people of this generation, bred in at least modest comfort, housed now in universities, looking uncomfortably at the world we inherit," the statement began. The idealistic students criticized the complacency of their elders, the remoteness of decision makers from the will of the people, and the powerlessness and alienation that people experienced in a society run by impersonal bureaucratic institutions. SDS aimed to mobilize a new social movement, called the New Left, with civil rights, peace, and universal economic security as its major targets. It remained small until 1965, but other forms of student activism soon followed.

Idealistic students criticized the complacency of their elders, the remoteness of decision makers from the will of the people, and the powerlessness and alienation that people experienced in a society run by impersonal bureaucratic institutions.

The first large-scale white student protest arose in the free speech movement at the University of California, Berkeley, in the fall of 1964, when university officials banned student organizations from a campus site where they had set up tables to recruit support for civil rights and other causes. Led by white activists who had worked for civil rights in the South, the students claimed the right to freedom of expression and political action. They occupied the administration building, and more than seven hundred were arrested before the California Board of Regents overturned the new restrictions.

Hundreds of student rebellions followed on campuses of various sizes and affiliations. Opposition to the Vietnam War activated the largest number of students, who held rallies and occupied buildings to protest universities' activities linked to the war. But they also demanded curricular reforms, more financial aid for minority and poor students, independence from paternalistic rules, the freedom to hear controversial speakers on campus, and a larger voice in campus decision making. (See "Documenting the American Promise," page 1048.) Surveys in 1967 found that about 2 percent of all college students were affiliated with the SDS and nearly 13 percent called themselves radicals, but the numbers involved in protests were even larger.

These student rebels came from the baby boom generation that swelled college enrollments and gave young people a sense of power and generational solidarity. Most white students came from middle- and upper-class families; free of the immediate need to provide for themselves, they enjoyed the luxury of attacking the very system that made their rebellion possible. Such conduct bewildered and angered older Americans, as did a growing cultural revolt against nearly every conventional standard of behavior.

The Counterculture

Growing up alongside the New Left and student movements and often overlapping them was a cultural rebellion known as the counterculture, which drew on the ideas and behavior of the Beats of the 1950s and focused on personal rather than political

WOODSTOCK
The Woodstock Music Festival, held on a farm near Bethel, New York, in August 1969, featured the greatest rock and folk musicians of the era and epitomized the values and hopes of the counterculture. Despite terrible conditions created by bad weather and the failure of festival organizers to plan for so many people, the youthful crowd of 400,000 created a loving, peaceful community for three days filled with music, sex, and drugs.
Image Works.

Student Protest

T he waves of student protest that rolled across college campuses in the 1960s were all the more surprising because observers had found "the silent generation" of the 1950s so complacent and conformist. Although the majority of college students did not participate in the rebellions, a sizable number at all kinds of colleges and universities challenged traditional authorities, criticized established institutions, and demanded a voice for themselves in the decisions that affected their lives.

DOCUMENT 1. Edward Schwartz on Student Power, October 1967

This statement was written by student activist Edward Schwartz to represent the views of the National Student Association, the largest college-student organization in the 1960s. It was ironic that this association, which contributed to the student upheaval in the 1960s, had been founded a decade earlier, with secret funding from the CIA, as a liberal group to counter communism.

The educational premise behind demands for student power reflects the notion that people learn through living, through the process of integrating their thoughts with their actions, through testing their values against those of a community, through a capacity to act. College presidents who invoke legal authority to prove educational theory assume that growth is the ability to accept what the past has created. Student power is a medium through which people integrate their own experience with a slice of the past which seems appropriate, with their efforts to intensify the relationships between the community within the university.

Let this principle apply—he who must obey the rule should make it.

Students should make the rules governing dormitory hours, boy-girl visitation, student unions, student fees, clubs, newspapers, and the like. Faculty and administrators should advise—attempt to persuade, even. Yet the student should bear the burden of choice.

Students and faculty should co-decide curricular policy.

Students, faculty, and administration should co-decide admissions policy, overall college policy affecting the community, even areas like university investment. . . . Student power should not be argued on legal grounds. It is not a legal principle. It is an educational principle.

Student power is threatening to those who wield power now, but this is understandable. A student should threaten his administrators outside of class, just as bright students threaten professors inside of class. Student power ultimately challenges everyone in the university—the students who must decide; the faculty and administrators who must rethink their own view of community relations in order to persuade.

People who say that student power means anarchy imply really that students are rabble who have no ability to form community and to adhere to decisions made by community. Student power is not the negation of rules—it is the creation of a new process for the enactment of rules. Student power is not the elimination of authority, it is the development of a democratic standard of authority.

SOURCE: Edward Schwartz, "He Who Must Obey the Rule Should Make It," in Immanuel Wallerstein and Paul Starr, eds., *The University Crisis Reader*, vol. 1, *The Liberal University under Attack* (New York: Random House, 1971), 482–84. Copyright © 1971 by Random House, Inc. Reprinted with permission.

DOCUMENT 2. Demands of Howard University Students, February 1968

African American students launched campus protests even at universities where most faculty and administrators were black. Following are demands of black students at Howard University, in Washington, D.C., printed in "The Spear and Shield."

1. We demand the immediate resignation of the following Howard administrators on the grounds of their incompetence and obviously unwillingness to work toward a black Howard University. [There followed names of the president, vice president, and liberal arts dean.]
2. We demand the institution of the following curriculum changes by next semester:
   a. We demand that Howard should be the center of Afro-American thought. We demand

that the economic, government, literature and social science departments begin to place more emphasis on how these disciplines may be used to effect the liberation of black people in this country.

b. We demand the institution of non-prerequisite courses in Negro History.

c. We demand the immediate abolishment of Freshman Assembly. Black students are not culturally deprived.

3. We demand the immediate reinstatement of all Howard instructors who have been unjustifiably dismissed for their political activism.

4. We demand a Black Awareness Research Institute at Howard University.

5. Students are trained to be leaders only by learning to accept responsibility. We demand therefore . . . student control in matters that concern only students.

a. The student judiciary and codification of rules presently submitted to the Faculty Senate Steering Committee should be immediately instituted.

b. That students must be authorized to control the budgeting and expenditure of the student activity fee.

6. Howard must be made relevant to the black community. The University campus must be made more available to all black people and programs must be instituted to aid the black community in the struggle against oppression.

7. We demand that Howard personnel begin to treat students like black people should treat black people, with respect and courtesy.

SOURCE: Howard University: February 1968, "The Spear and Shield," in Immanuel Wallerstein and Paul Starr, eds., *The University Crisis Reader*, vol. 2, *Confrontation and Counterattack* (New York: Random House, 1971), 485–86. Copyright © 1971 by Random House, Inc. Reprinted with permission.

DOCUMENT 3. SDS Explanation of the Columbia Strike, September 1968

One of the longest and most violent student protests occurred in New York City at Columbia University in April and May 1968, when white and black students occupied five buildings for a week, and a subsequent student strike closed down the university for the rest of the academic year. One of the key issues arose from the university's practice of expanding by buying up land in the neighboring Harlem and evicting black tenants. The Columbia SDS chapter, one of various factions among the protesters, rationalized their actions in the following statement.

When we seized five buildings at Columbia University, we engaged the force of wealth, privilege, property—and the force of state violence that always accompanies them—with little more than our own ideals, our fears, and a vague sense of outrage at the injustices of our society. Martin Luther King had just been shot, his name demeaned by Columbia officials who refused to grant a decent wage to Puerto Rican workers, and who had recently grabbed part of Harlem for a student gym. . . .

For years Columbia Trustees had evicted tenants from their homes, taken land through city deals, and fired workers for trying to form a union. For years they had trained officers for Vietnam who, as ROTC literature indicates, killed Vietnamese peasants in their own country. In secret work for the IDA [Institute for Defense Analysis] and the CIA, in chemical-biological war research for the Department of War, the Trustees implicated their own University in genocide. They had consistently . . . lied to their own constituents and published CIA books under the guise of independent scholarship. . . . We lived in an institution that channeled us, marked us, ranked us, failed us, used us, and treated masses of humanity with class contempt. . . .

The collegiate wing of privilege could not shield us from the decay and violence in our society. The University was not, as we first believed, a sanctuary from the world; it was, in fact, a proponent of the most violent system the centuries have created—the system of capital. . . .

Columbia, standing at the top of a hill, looked down on Harlem. . . . People who survived in Harlem had been evicted by the Trustees from Morningside or still paid rent to Columbia. . . . We walked to our classrooms across land that had been privatized; we studied in buildings that had once been homes in a city that is underhoused; and we listened to the apologies for Cold War and capital in our classes.

Columbia professors often claim that the University is a neutral institution. . . . Many professors pursue all sides of a question as an end in itself. They find a certain refuge in the difficulty of *(Continued)* defining good and evil. The result is a clogging of their moral sense, their capacity for collective justice. . . . What liberals call neutrality is really one of the ways by which the faculty protects its special status in society.

A University could not, even if it wanted, choose to be really value-free. It can choose good values; it can choose bad values; or it can remain ignorant of the values on which it acts. . . . A social institution should at least articulate its own perspective, so that its own values may be consciously applied or modified. It is a typical fallacy of American teaching, that to remain silent on crucial issues is to be objective with your own constituents. Actually a "neutral" institution is far more manipulative than a University committed to avowed goals and tasks.

SOURCE: Columbia SDS, "The Columbia Statement," *The University Crisis Reader*, vol. 1, *The Liberal University under Attack* (New York: Random House, 1971), 23–47. Copyright © 1971 by Random House, Inc. Reprinted with permission.

DOCUMENT 4. Chicago Women's Liberation on Sexism in Higher Education, February 1969

In January 1969, the University of Chicago refused to reappoint Dr. Marlene Dixon, an assistant professor of sociology who had incorporated the study of women into her teaching. While officials insisted that Dixon did not meet the university's academic standards, her supporters believed that she was fired for her radical beliefs and because she was female. SDS and other factions of radical students protested for two weeks but failed to save Dixon's job. Chicago Women's Liberation, which grew out of women's activism in the New Left, issued a statement addressing broader issues.

What does women's freedom mean? . . . It means the freedom to be one's own person in an integrated life of work, love, play, motherhood: the freedoms, rights and privileges of first class citizenship, of equality in relationships of love and work: the right to choose to make decisions or not to: the right to full self-realization and to full participation in the life of the world. . . . To achieve these rights we must struggle as all other oppressed groups must struggle: one only has the rights one fights for. . . .

At the U of C we see the *first large action, the first important struggle of women's liberation.* This university—all universities—discriminate against women, impede their full intellectual development, deny them places on the faculty, exploit talented women and mistreat women students.

SOURCE: "Statement by Chicago Women's Liberation, February 1969," in Robin Morgan, ed., *Sisterhood Is Powerful: An Anthology of Writings from the Women's Liberation Movement* (New York: Vintage Books, 1970), 531. Copyright 1970 by Vintage Books, a division of Random House, Inc. Reprinted with permission.

DOCUMENT 5. Counterthrust on Student Power, Spring 1967

While the majority of students simply avoided involvement in campus rebellions, some students actively criticized the protesters. The largest conservative student organization was Young Americans for Freedom, which more than doubled in size during the 1960s. The following selection, from a leaflet entitled "Student Power Is a Farce," reflected the views of Counterthrust, a conservative group at Wayne State University in Michigan.

Our University is being treated to the insanity of Left-Wing students demanding the run of the University. . . . Wayne students are told by the Left that "student power" merely means more democracy on campus. This is an outright lie! Student power is a Left-Wing catchword symbolizing campus militancy and radicalism. In actuality, the Left-Wing, spearheaded by the SDS [Students for a Democratic Society] want to radically alter the university community. . . .

The Leftists charge a sinister plot by private enterprise to train students for jobs at taxpayers' expense. Evidently it never occurred to the SDS that private enterprise is also the biggest single taxpayer for schools. But, of course, that would require a little thought on the part of the SDS which they have already demonstrated they are incapable of. . . .

The byword of student power-union advocates is Radicalism. . . . Fraternities and student Governments will have no place in student power-unions since both are considered allies of the status quo and thus useless. . . . As responsible Wayne students, we cannot allow our University to be used by Leftists for their narrow purposes. We were invited to this campus by the Michigan Taxpayer to receive an education. Let us honor that invitation.

SOURCE: Counterthrust, "Student Power Is a Farce," *The University Crisis Reader,* vol. 1, *The Liberal University under Attack* (New York: Random House, 1971), 487–88. Copyright © 1971 by Random House, Inc. Reprinted with permission.

DOCUMENT 6. George F. Kennan's Speech on Student Protest, December 1967

George F. Kennan, the foreign policy expert who had articulated the containment policy in 1947, reflected the views of many critics of student protest when he gave this speech at Swarthmore College in Pennsylvania.

There is an ideal that has long been basic to the learning process, one that stands at the very center of our modern institutions of higher education. It is the ideal of the association of the process of learning with a certain remoteness from the contemporary scene—a certain detachment and seclusion, a certain voluntary withdrawal and renunciation of participation in contemporary life in the interests of the achievement of a better perspective on that life when the period of withdrawal is over. It is an ideal that does not predicate any total conflict between thought and action, but recognizes that there is a time for each. . . .

What strikes one first about the angry militancy [among current students] is the extraordinary degree of certainty by which it is inspired: certainty of one's own rectitude, certainty of the correctness of one's own answers, certainty of the accuracy and profundity of one's own analysis of the problems of contemporary society, certainty as to the iniquity of those who disagree. . . . One is struck to see such massive certainties already present in the minds of people who not only have not studied very much but presumably are not studying a great deal, because it is hard to imagine that the activities to which this aroused portion of our student population gives itself are ones readily compatible with quiet and successful study. . . .

I am not saying that students should not be concerned, should not have views, should not question what goes on in the field of national policy. . . . Some

of us, who are older, share many of their misgivings, many of their impulses. . . .

I have seen more harm done in this world by those who tried to storm the bastions of society in the name of utopian beliefs, who were determined to achieve the elimination of all evil . . . than by all the humble efforts of those who have tried to create a little order and civility and affection within their own intimate entourage, even at the cost of tolerating a great deal of evil in the public domain. Behind this modesty, after all, there has been the recognition of a vitally important truth—a truth that the Marxists, among others, have never brought themselves to recognize; namely that the decisive seat of evil in this world is not in social and political institutions, and not even, as a rule, in the ill will or iniquities of statesmen, but simply in the weakness and imperfection of the human soul itself.

SOURCE: George F. Kennan, "Rebels without a Program," *The University Crisis Reader,* vol. 1, *The Liberal University under Attack* (New York: Random House, 1971), 12–23. Copyright © 1971 by Random House, Inc. Reprinted with permission.

QUESTIONS FOR ANALYSIS AND DEBATE

1. What different ideas about the nature and purposes of the university do these writers present? How do they differ in their view of students' capabilities and rights?

2. Do you agree or disagree with George Kennan's insistence that universities should "maintain a certain remoteness from the contemporary scene" in order to achieve "a better perspective" on current issues? Why or why not?

3. Consider the different backgrounds and circumstances of the authors of these writings. Are factors such as age, race, gender, and economic class important to the viewpoints expressed? Why or why not?

4. To what extent do your own campus policies and practices suggest that student protest made a difference? What changes that the protesters demanded do not appear at your college? Should they?

and institutional change. Cultural radicals, or "hippies," as they were called, rejected mainstream norms that valued the work ethic, material possessions, rationality, order, and sexual control. "Do your own thing" became their motto. Hippies stood out with their long hair and wildly colorful, often ragged clothing. The Haight-Ashbury district of San Francisco harbored the most widely known hippie community, but thousands of cultural radicals established communes in cities or on farms, where they renounced private property and shared everything, often including sex partners. Seeking heightened perceptions and freedom from all inhibitions, they replaced the alcohol, nicotine, and prescription tranquilizers of their elders with illegal drugs such as marijuana and the hallucinogen lysergic acid diethylamide (LSD).

Rock music played a central role in both the counterculture and the political left. English groups such as the Beatles and the Rolling Stones and homegrown products including Bob Dylan, Janis Joplin, the Jefferson Airplane, and Jerry Garcia's Grateful Dead took American youth by storm. The 1960s music often carried insurgent political and social messages. Despairing of the violence around the world and the threat of nuclear annihilation, "Eve of Destruction," a top hit of 1965, reminded young men, "You're old enough to kill but not for votin'." Other popular songs derided authority, touted the thrills of drugs, celebrated sexual freedom, and called for peace, love, and revolution.

Cultural radicals, or "hippies," rejected mainstream norms. "Do your own thing" became their motto.

Although hippies remained a small minority, many elements of the counterculture—from rock music to jeans and long hair—filtered into the mainstream. Sexual relations outside marriage and tolerant attitudes about sexual morality spawned what came to be called a "sexual revolution." Self-fulfillment became a dominant concern of many Americans, and questioning of government and other authority became much more widespread. The hippies faded away in the early 1970s, but their legacy continued to influence American society.

Beginnings of a Feminist Movement

Both the civil rights struggle and the New Left served as inspiration and models for a new women's movement. White feminists' efforts to piggyback onto civil rights measures had gained the ban against sex discrimination in the Civil Rights Act of 1964 and the extension of affirmative action

FEMINISTS PICKET THE MISS AMERICA PAGEANT
This picketer was among the two hundred feminists who demonstrated at the Miss America pageant at Atlantic City, New Jersey, in 1968 in protest against society's exaggerated emphasis on women's appearance and its rigid beauty standards. They set up a "freedom trash can" and invited women to throw away their "bras, girdles, curlers, false eyelashes, wigs, and **Cosmopolitan,**" *which they called "objects of female torture." At right is the sheep they crowned Miss America to show that beauty contests treated women as if they were livestock at a county fair.*
Chicago Historical Society.

to women. Their expectations raised by these new policies, feminists grew impatient when the government moved slowly to enforce the law against sex discrimination in employment. Deciding that they needed a "civil rights organization for women," Betty Friedan and others founded the National Organization for Women (NOW) in 1966.

Simultaneously, a more radical feminism formed. From experiences in the civil rights movement and the New Left, women grasped a contradiction between the ideal of equality and the actual status of women. Two white women, Mary King and Casey Hayden, raised the issue in SNCC in 1964, and in 1965 they began circulating their ideas to other women active in the New Left. King and Hayden pointed out that, like blacks, women "seem[ed] to be caught up in a common-law caste system . . . forcing them to work around or outside hierarchical structures of power which may exclude them." Women, they contended, were also exploited and subordinated in personal relations. The 1965 memo struck a responsive chord among white activist women, but most male radicals reacted with indifference or ridicule. Ignored or told their cause was trivial, women began to walk out of male-dominated political meetings, and by 1967 they had created an independent women's liberation movement.

Radical white women established women's liberation groups in cities across the nation. They translated black pride into pride of womanhood, and they implemented the "participatory democracy" of SDS in their activities. Staging marches, sit-ins, and other demonstrations, they began to gain public attention, especially when one hundred women picketed the Miss America beauty pageant in 1968, protesting against being forced "to compete for male approval [and] enslaved by ludicrous 'beauty' standards." Activism by radicals and more moderate feminists surged into a mass movement that dramatically changed public policy and popular attitudes in the 1970s.

The Judicial Revolution

For more than a decade, beginning with the *Brown* school desegregation decision in 1954, the Supreme Court under Chief Justice Earl Warren (presiding from 1953 to 1969) spearheaded another form of change. Such change was not all welcome to Dwight D. Eisenhower, who referred to his appointment of Warren as "the biggest damn-fool mistake I ever made." Eisenhower was most upset about Court decisions defending the rights of Communists and accused criminals, but the Warren Court spearheaded change in a variety of areas. In expanding the Constitution's promise of equality and protection of individual rights, the Court shifted power from the states to the judicial branch of the federal government—that is, to the Supreme Court.

Civil Rights and Criminal Justice

In articulating the rights of disadvantaged groups and accused criminals, Supreme Court decisions in the 1950s and 1960s jettisoned judicial tradition and often moved ahead of public opinion. Following the pathbreaking *Brown* decision, the Warren Court ruled against all-white public facilities and struck down educational plans devised by southern states to avoid integration. The Court also upheld the constitutional rights of African Americans to freedom of assembly and freedom of speech, thereby enabling the black freedom struggle to continue sit-ins, mass marches, and other civil disobedience tactics that proved critical to its success.

In articulating the rights of disadvantaged groups and accused criminals, Supreme Court decisions in the 1950s and 1960s jettisoned judicial tradition and often moved ahead of public opinion.

Chief Justice Warren considered *Baker v. Carr* (1963) his most important decision. The case grew out of a complaint that Tennessee electoral districts were so inequitably drawn that sparsely populated rural districts had far more representatives in the state legislature than did densely populated metropolitan areas. Grounding its decisions on the Fourteenth Amendment guarantee of "equal protection of the laws," in *Baker* and companion cases the Court established the principle of "one person, one vote" both for state legislatures and for the House of Representatives. Requiring most states to redraw electoral districts, the rulings helped to make state legislatures more responsive to metropolitan interests and problems.

The egalitarian thrust of the Warren Court also touched the criminal justice system. Between 1957 and 1967, the Court overturned a series of convictions on the grounds that the accused individuals had been deprived of "life, liberty, or property, without due process of law" and thus had been denied their rights under the Fourteenth Amendment. Furthermore, the Court interpreted that amendment to require states as well as the federal government to abide by the Bill of Rights. These rulings dramatically reformed law enforcement practices and the treatment of individuals accused of crime. In *Gideon v. Wainwright* (1963), the Court ruled that states must provide lawyers to people accused of serious crime who cannot afford to pay lawyers themselves. In *Escobedo v. Illinois* (1964), the justices extended the right to counsel to the period when suspects are being questioned by police officers. Two years later, in *Miranda v. Arizona,* the Court issued guidelines requiring officers to inform suspects that they may remain silent, that anything they say can be used against them, and that they are entitled to a lawyer. And it overturned convictions resulting from evidence obtained by unlawful arrest, by electronic surveillance, and by entering property without a search warrant.

Critics accused the Supreme Court of letting criminals go free by overturning convictions and obstructing law enforcement. Liberals, however, argued that these rulings promoted equal treatment in the criminal justice system: The wealthy always had access to legal counsel, and practiced criminals were well aware of their right to remain silent. The beneficiaries of the decisions were the poor, the ignorant, and the weak as well as the general population, whose right to privacy was strengthened by the Court's stricter guidelines for admissible evidence.

Dissent and Religious Issues

The Warren Court also strengthened protections for people suspected of being Communists or subversives, setting limits, for example, on government officials who investigated and prosecuted them. Like the criminal justice cases, these rulings guaranteed the rights of people on the margins of American society and reaped their share of criticism.

The Warren Court's decisions on prayer and Bible reading in public schools provoked even greater outrage. In *Abington School District v. Schempp* (1963), the Court overturned a Pennsylvania law requiring Bible reading and recitation of the Lord's Prayer in the schools as a violation of the First Amendment principle of separation of church and state. Later decisions ruled out prayer in public schools even if students were not required to participate. An outraged Alabama legislator fumed, "They put Negroes in the schools and now they've driven God out." The Court's supporters, however, declared that the religion cases protected the rights of non-Christians and atheists.

The Warren Court's decisions on prayer and Bible reading in public schools provoked even greater outrage.

Two or three justices who believed that the Court was overstepping its authority often issued sharp dissents. Outside the Court, opponents worked to pass laws or constitutional amendments that would upset despised decisions, legal experts pleaded for the Court to exercise judicial restraint, and billboards demanded, "Impeach Earl Warren." Nonetheless, the Court's major decisions withstood Warren's retirement in 1969 and the test of time.

Conclusion: Achievements and Limitations of 1960s Liberalism

Surveying the record of the Johnson administration, Senate majority leader Mike Mansfield concluded that the president "has done more than FDR ever did, or ever thought of doing." Yet opposition to his leadership grew so strong by 1968 that Johnson abandoned hopes for reelection. As his liberal vision lay in ruins, he asked, "How was it possible that all these people could be so ungrateful to me after I have given them so much?"

Fannie Lou Hamer could have responded with a number of examples. Support from the federal government was minimal when local officials arrested and beat her and others trying to organize Mississippi blacks. A founding member of the Mississippi Freedom Democratic Party (MFDP), created in opposition to the white party that excluded blacks, Hamer felt betrayed when President Johnson and his aides refused to support the MFDP in its struggle for a significant voice at the 1964 Democratic National Convention. "We learned the hard way that even though we had all the law and all the righteousness on our side—that white man is not going to give up his power to us," Hamer concluded.

Hamer's efforts to use Johnson's antipoverty programs to help poor blacks in Mississippi eventually ended in failure. Internal problems hampered her projects, but the failures also reflected some of the more general shortcomings of the War on Poverty. Inadequately planned and funded, many antipoverty programs ended up benefiting industry and the nonpoor as much as or more than the impoverished. Because Johnson refused to ask for sacrifices from prosperous Americans, the Great Society never approached the redistribution of wealth and resources that would have been necessary for the elimination of poverty.

Black aspirations exceeded white Americans' commitment to genuine equality. It was easy for northerners to be sympathetic when the civil rights movement focused on crude and blatant forms of racism in the South. But when it attacked the subtler forms of racism that existed throughout the nation and sought equality in fact as well as in rights,

the black freedom struggle confronted a powerful backlash. By the end of the 1960s, the revolution in the legal status of African Americans was complete, but the black freedom struggle had lost much of its momentum, and African Americans remained at the bottom of the economic ladder.

Such shortcomings contributed to a rising challenge to liberalism from what came to be called the New Left. Radicalized by the black freedom struggle, a small but vocal minority of Americans emphasized the shortcomings of the Great Society and questioned whether real reform could be achieved within the framework of traditional American institutions and values. Young radicals engaged in direct confrontations with the government and universities that, together with racial conflict, escalated into political discord and social disorder not seen since the union wars of the 1930s. The war in Vietnam polarized American society as much as did the question of race or the behavior of young people. Johnson's conduct of the war undermined faith in his leadership. The war starved the Great Society, devouring revenues that might have been used for social reform and eclipsing the substantial progress that had actually been achieved.

www.bedfordstmartins.com/tap   SEE THE ONLINE STUDY GUIDE to assess your mastery of the material covered in this chapter.

CHRONOLOGY

1960   African American college students in Greensboro, North Carolina, stage sit-in at whites-only lunch counter.

John F. Kennedy elected president of United States.

Student Nonviolent Coordinating Committee (SNCC) established to mobilize young people for direct action for civil rights.

Students for a Democratic Society (SDS) founded.

1961   Congress of Racial Equality (CORE) sponsors Freedom Rides to desegregate interstate transportation in South.

President Kennedy establishes President's Commission on the Status of Women.

1962   Cesar Chavez founds United Farm Workers (UFW).

1963   *Baker v. Carr* mandates electoral redistricting to enforce "one person, one vote" principle.

Abington School District v. Schempp outlaws prayers in public schools.

Betty Friedan's best-selling book *The Feminine Mystique* published.

Equal Pay Act makes wage disparities based solely on gender illegal.

Mississippi NAACP leader Medgar Evers assassinated in Jackson.

March on Washington becomes largest civil rights demonstration in U.S. history.

President's Commission on the Status of Women issues report detailing widespread discrimination against women.

President Kennedy assassinated in Dallas, Texas; Vice President Lyndon B. Johnson becomes president.

1964   Congress enacts Civil Rights Act, the strongest such measure since Reconstruction.

Economic Opportunity Act passed.

Free speech movement, first large-scale white student protest of 1960s, organized at University of California, Berkeley.

Malcolm X breaks from Nation of Islam and attracts wide following.

President Johnson elected to full term in landslide over Republican senator Barry Goldwater.

Tax cut bill proposed by Kennedy administration passed.

1965   Malcolm X assassinated in New York City.

Selma-to-Montgomery march for voting rights; Johnson orders federal protection for marchers after they are attacked.

Congress passes Voting Rights Act.

1965–   Eighty-ninth Congress passes most of
1966   Johnson's Great Society domestic programs, including antipoverty measures, public works acts, aid to education, and Medicare/Medicaid.

1966   Black Panther Party founded, advocating African American economic and political autonomy.

In *Miranda v. Arizona,* Supreme Court requires police to inform suspects of their rights.

National Organization for Women (NOW) founded.

1968   Martin Luther King Jr. assassinated in Memphis, Tennessee.

American Indian Movement (AIM) founded.

BIBLIOGRAPHY

GENERAL WORKS

John Morton Blum, *Years of Discord: American Politics and Society, 1961–1974* (1991).

David Burner, *Making Peace with the 60s* (1996).

David Farber, *The Age of Great Dreams: America in the 1960s* (1994).

Hugh Davis Graham, *The Civil Rights Era: Origins and Development of National Policy, 1960–1972* (1990).

Jim F. Heath, *Decade of Disillusionment: The Kennedy-Johnson Years* (1975).

Maurice Isserman and Michael Kazin, *America Divided: The Civil War of the 1960s* (2000).

Allen J. Matusow, *The Unraveling of America: A History of Liberalism in the 1960s* (1984).

Douglas T. Miller, *On Our Own: Americans in the Sixties* (1996).

Edward P. Morgan, *The Sixties Experience: Hard Lessons about Modern America* (1991).

William L. O'Neill, *Coming Apart: An Informal History of America in the 1960s* (1971).

Barbara L. Tischler, ed., *Sights on the Sixties* (1992).

Irwin Unger, *The Best of Intentions: The Triumph and Failure of the Great Society* (1996).

THE BLACK FREEDOM STRUGGLE

Peter J. Albert and Ronald Hoffman, eds., *We Shall Overcome: Martin Luther King, Jr., and the Black Freedom Struggle* (1990).

Jervis Anderson, *Bayard Rustin: Troubles I've Seen* (1997).

Taylor Branch, *Parting the Waters: America in the King Years, 1954–63* (1988).

Taylor Branch, *Pillar of Fire: America in the King Years, 1963–65* (1998).

Carl M. Brauer, *John F. Kennedy and the Second Reconstruction* (1977).

James W. Button, *Black Violence: Political Impact of the 1960s Riots* (1978).

Clayborne Carson, *In Struggle: SNCC and the Black Awakening of the 1960s* (1981).

David L. Chappell, *Inside Agitators: White Southerners in the Civil Rights Movement* (1994).

Michael Eric Dyson, *Making Malcolm: The Myth and Meaning of Malcolm X* (1995).

David J. Garrow, *Protest at Selma: Martin Luther King, Jr., and the Voting Rights Act of 1965* (1978).

David J. Garrow, *Bearing the Cross: Martin Luther King, Jr., and the Southern Christian Leadership Conference* (1986).

Peter L. Goldman, *The Death and Life of Malcolm X* (1979).

Ralph G. Gomes and Linda Faye Williams, eds., *From Exclusion to Inclusion: The Long Struggle for African American Political Power* (1992).

James C. Harvey, *Black Civil Rights during the Johnson Administration* (1973).

Steven F. Lawson, *Black Ballots: Voting Rights in the South, 1944–1969* (1976).

Steven F. Lawson, *Running for Freedom: Civil Rights and Black Politics in America since 1941* (1991).

John Lewis with Michael D'Orso, *Walking with the Wind: A Memoir of the Movement* (1998).

Doug McAdam, *Freedom Summer* (1989).

August Meier and Elliott M. Rudwick, *CORE: A Study in the Civil Rights Movement, 1942–1968* (1973).

Stephen B. Oates, *Let the Trumpet Sound: The Life of Martin Luther King, Jr.* (1982).

Kenneth O'Reilly, *"Racial Matters": The FBI's Secret File on Black America, 1960–1972* (1989).

Frank R. Parker, *Black Votes Count: Political Empowerment in Mississippi after 1965* (1990).

Charles Payne, *I've Got the Light of Freedom: The Organizing Tradition and the Mississippi Freedom Struggle* (1995).

Bruce Perry, *Malcolm: The Life of a Man Who Changed Black America* (1991).

James R. Ralph Jr., *Northern Protest: Martin Luther King Jr., Chicago, and the Civil Rights Movement* (1993).

Frederick M. Wirt, *"We Ain't What We Was": Civil Rights in the New South* (1997).

POLITICS AND POLICIES OF THE NEW FRONTIER AND GREAT SOCIETY

Henry J. Aaron, *Politics and the Professors: The Great Society in Perspective* (1978).

Vaughn Davis Bornet, *The Presidency of Lyndon B. Johnson* (1983).

David Burner, *John F. Kennedy and a New Generation* (1988).

Robert Caro, *The Years of Lyndon Johnson,* vols. 1 and 2 (1982, 1990).

Paul K. Conkin, *Big Daddy from the Pedernales: Lyndon Baines Johnson* (1986).

Robert Dallek, *Flawed Giant: Lyndon B. Johnson, 1960–1973* (1998).

Robert Alan Goldberg, *Barry Goldwater* (1995).

Eric Goldman, *The Tragedy of Lyndon Johnson* (1969).

Michael B. Katz, *The Undeserving Poor: From the War on Poverty to the War on Welfare* (1989).

Doris Kearns, *Lyndon Johnson and the American Dream* (1976).

Sar Levitan and Robert Taggart, *The Promise of Greatness* (1976).

Robert Mann, *The Walls of Jericho: Lyndon Johnson, Hubert Humphrey, Richard Russell, and the Struggle for Civil Rights* (1996).

Gerald Posner, *Case Closed: Lee Harvey Oswald and the Assassination of JFK* (1993).

Jill Quadagno, *The Color of Welfare: How Racism Undermined the War on Poverty* (1994).

Richard Reeves, *President Kennedy: Profile of Power* (1993).

Mark Stern, *Calculating Visions: Kennedy, Johnson, and Civil Rights* (1992).

James L. Sundquist, *Politics and Policy: The Eisenhower, Kennedy, and Johnson Years* (1968).

PROTEST MOVEMENTS

Terry H. Anderson, *The Movement and the Sixties* (1995).

Stewart Burns, *Social Movements of the 1960s: Searching for Democracy* (1990).

David Chalmers, *And the Crooked Places Made Straight: The Struggle for Social Change in the 1960s* (1991).

Martha F. Davis, *Brutal Need: Lawyers and the Welfare Rights Movement, 1960–1973* (1993).

Vine Deloria Jr., *Behind the Trail of Broken Treaties* (1974).

Ignacio M. Garcia, *United We Win: The Rise and Fall of La Raza Unida Party* (1989).

Todd Gitlin, *The Sixties: Years of Hope, Days of Rage* (1987).

Juan Gómez-Quiñones, *Chicano Politics: Reality and Promise, 1940–1990* (1990).

Richard Griswold del Castillo and Richard A. Garcia, *Cesar Chavez: A Triumph of Spirit* (1995).

Laurence M. Hauptman, *The Iroquois Struggle for Survival: World War II to Red Power* (1986).

Maurice Isserman, *If I Had a Hammer . . . : The Death of the Old Left and the Birth of the New Left* (1987).

George Katsiaficas, *The Imagination of the New Left: A Global Analysis of 1968* (1987).

Cyril Levitt, *Children of Privilege: Student Revolt in the Sixties* (1984).

Peter B. Levy, *The New Left and Labor in the 1960s* (1994).

Peter Matthiessen, *In the Spirit of Crazy Horse* (1983).

James Miller, *"Democracy Is in the Streets": From Port Huron to the Siege of Chicago* (1987).

Joan Moore and Harry Pachon, *Hispanics in the United States* (1985).

Donald L. Parman, *Indians and the American West in the Twentieth Century* (1994).

Doug Rossinow, *The Politics of Authenticity: Liberalism, Christianity and the New Left in America* (1998).

Manuel P. Servin, *An Awakened Minority: The Mexican Americans* (2nd ed., 1974).

William Wei, *The Asian American Movement* (1993).

CULTURAL CHANGE, SEXUAL REVOLUTION, AND FEMINISM

David Allyn, *Make Love, Not War: The Sexual Revolution, an Unfettered History* (2000).

Beth Bailey, *Sex in the Heartland* (1999).

Alice Echols, *Daring to Be Bad: Radical Feminism in America, 1967–1975* (1989).

Sara Evans, *Personal Liberation: The Roots of Women's Liberation in the Civil Rights Movement and the New Left* (1978).

Jo Freeman, *The Politics of Liberation* (1975).

Cynthia Harrison, *On Account of Sex: The Politics of Women's Issues, 1945–1968* (1988).

Daniel Horowitz, *Betty Friedan and the Making of the Feminine Mystique* (1998).

James Miller, *Flowers in the Dustbin: The Rise of Rock and Roll, 1947–1977* (1999).

William L. Van Deburg, *New Day in Babylon: The Black Power Movement and American Culture, 1965–1975* (1993).

THE SUPREME COURT

Archibald Cox, *The Warren Court: Constitutional Decision as an Instrument of Reform* (1968).

Richard Y. Funston, *Constitutional Counterrevolution? The Warren Court and the Burger Court: Judicial Policy Making in Modern America* (1977).

Philip B. Kurland, *Politics and the Warren Court* (1970).

Paul L. Murphy, *The Constitution in Crisis Times, 1918–1969* (1972).

Bernard Schwartz, *Super Chief: Earl Warren and His Supreme Court, a Judicial Biography* (1983).

Bernard Schwartz, ed., *The Warren Court: A Retrospective* (1996).

Melvin I. Urofsky, *The Continuity of Change: The Supreme Court and Individual Liberties, 1953–1986* (1991).

FATIGUE HAT WITH BUTTONS
The button on this fatigue hat of a veteran who had served two tours of duty demonstrates veterans' response to the many Americans who just wanted to forget the war that the United States had failed to win. Because their war was so different from other American wars, Vietnam veterans often returned home to hostility or indifference. The POW-MIA pin refers to prisoners of war and those missing in action.
Nancy Gewitz / Antique Textile Resource / Picture Research Consultants & Archives.

VIETNAM AND THE LIMITS OF POWER

28

1961–1975

As Charles Anderson's plane prepared to land, the pilot announced, "Gentlemen, we'll be touching down in Da Nang, Vietnam, in about ten minutes. . . . Fasten your seat belts, please. On behalf of the entire crew and staff, I'd like to say we've enjoyed having you with us . . . and we hope to see all of you again next year on your way home. Goodbye and good luck." Like most soldiers after 1966, Charles Anderson went to war on a commercial jetliner, complete with stewardesses (as they were called then) in miniskirts.

Military personnel traveling to battle as if they were business executives or tourists only hints at the differences between the Vietnam War and America's previous wars. Marine infantry officer Philip Caputo landed at Da Nang in March 1965 confident that the enemy "would be quickly beaten and that we were doing something altogether noble and good." But in just a few months, "what had begun as an adventurous expedition had turned into an exhausting, indecisive war of attrition in which we fought for no other cause than our own survival."

Another soldier discovered even more quickly that "something was wrong." Wondering why the bus taking him from the air base to the compound had wire mesh over the windows, he was told, "It's the gooks man. . . . The gooks will throw grenades through the windows." Soldiers in Vietnam initially used the racist word *gook* to refer to the enemy—the North Vietnamese or their supporters in the south— but it quickly became a term used for any Vietnamese. "From one day to the next, you could see for yourself changes coming over guys on our side—decent fellows, who wouldn't dream of calling an Oriental a 'gook' back home," reported one American. The problem was that in this civil war, he said, "they couldn't tell who was their friend and who wasn't. Day after day, out on patrol we'd come to . . . a shabby village, and the elders would welcome us and the children come running with smiles on their faces, waiting for the candy we'd give them. But . . . just as we were leaving the village behind, the enemy would open up on us, and there was bitterness among us that the villagers hadn't given us warning."

Americans' horrifying and bewildering experiences in Vietnam grew out of cold war commitments made in the 1940s and 1950s by Presidents Harry S. Truman and Dwight D. Eisenhower. John F. Kennedy wholeheartedly took on those commitments, promising more innovative, flexible, and vigorous efforts to thwart communism. In the most memorable words of his 1961 inaugural address, he declared, "Let every nation know, whether it wishes us well or ill, that we shall pay any price, bear any burden, meet any hardship, support any friend, oppose any foe to assure the survival and the success of liberty."

The conflict in Vietnam became the foremost test of what the United States would or could do to "assure the survival and the success of liberty." Kennedy sent increasing amounts of American arms and personnel to help sustain the South Viet-

FIGHTING THE CLIMATE AND GEOGRAPHY
Steamy tropical conditions and inhospitable terrain were among the nonhuman enemies
U.S. troops faced in Vietnam. Soldiers like this one making his way under fire through a
rice paddy in 1966 were soaked for weeks on end. Veteran Philip Caputo wrote about
"being pounded numb by ceaseless rain" during the monsoon; "at night we squatted in
muddy holes, picked off the leeches that sucked on our veins."
Henri Gilles Huet / World Wide Photos, Inc.

namese government, and Lyndon B. Johnson dramatically escalated that commitment. By 1965, the civil war in Vietnam had become America's war.

The Americanization of the war increased the number of U.S. military personnel in Vietnam to 543,000 at peak strength in 1968 and to more than 3,000,000 total throughout the war's duration. Yet this massive intervention not only failed to defeat North Vietnam but added a new burden to the costs of fighting the cold war—intense discord among the people at home. The Vietnam War cost President Johnson another term in office and contributed to the political demise of his Republican successor, Richard M. Nixon. Some Americans lauded the U.S. goal in Vietnam and decried only the nation's unwillingness to pursue it effectively. Others believed that preserving a non-Communist South Vietnam was neither in the best interests of the United States nor within its capacity or moral right to achieve.

But none could deny the war's enormous costs. "The promises of the Great Society have been shot down on the battlefield of Vietnam," said Martin Luther King Jr. In addition to derailing domestic reform, the Vietnam War exacted a heavy toll in American lives and dollars, kindled internal conflict and disorder, and led to the violation of the rights of antiwar protesters. With the exception of the African American freedom struggle, no other post–World War II event affected Americans so intensely.

New Frontiers in Foreign Policy

John F. Kennedy moved quickly to fulfill his campaign promises of a more aggressive yet more flexible foreign policy. He embraced the goal of containment, and with his like-minded secretary of defense, Robert S. McNamara, he expanded the nation's ability to wage nuclear, conventional, or guerrilla warfare. To ensure U.S. superiority over the Soviet Union in every domain, Kennedy accelerated the nation's space exploration program and increased American attention to the third world, with new programs to promote economic development, political stability, and friendly governments. In his unflinching determination to halt communism, Kennedy took the United States to the brink of nuclear war during the 1962 Cuban missile crisis. Less dramatically, but no less tenaciously, Kennedy stepped up American contributions of arms, aid, and personnel to save the government of South Vietnam from Communist insurgents.

Meeting the "Hour of Maximum Danger"

Kennedy and other Democrats criticized the Eisenhower administration for relying too heavily on nuclear weapons, thereby denying the nation a "flexible response" to Communist expansion. They also charged that Eisenhower's desire to limit defense spending had allowed the United States to fall behind even in nuclear capability. In January 1961, Kennedy warned that the nation faced a grave peril: "Each day the crises multiply. . . . Each day we draw nearer the hour of maximum danger."

Although the president exaggerated the actual threat to national security, several developments in 1961 heightened the sense of crisis and provided rationalization for a military buildup. In a speech made shortly before Kennedy's inauguration, Soviet premier Nikita Khrushchev had encouraged "wars of national liberation," thereby aligning the Soviet Union with independence movements (usually anti-Western) in the third world. Khrushchev wanted to bolster Soviet leadership of the Communist world, then being challenged by the People's Republic of China, and to shore up his political position at home by projecting forcefulness abroad. U.S. officials, however, interpreted his words as signaling new efforts to upset the status quo of containment.

Fidel Castro's revolution had already moved Cuba—just ninety miles from the United States—into the Soviet orbit; and under Eisenhower, the CIA had been planning an invasion by anti-Castro exiles. Kennedy ordered the invasion to proceed even though his military advisers gave it only a fair

chance of success. To do otherwise, the president believed, would create an appearance of weakness.

On April 17, 1961, about thirteen hundred anti-Castro exiles, who had been trained and armed by the CIA, landed at the Bay of Pigs on the south shore of Cuba (see Map 28.1). Contrary to the anticipation of the planners, no popular uprising materialized to support the anti-Castro brigade. Kennedy refused to supply direct military support, and the invaders quickly fell to Castro's forces. The disaster was humiliating for Kennedy and the United States, posing a stark contrast to Kennedy's inaugural promise of a new, more effective foreign policy. The attempted armed interference in the affairs of another nation compromised the moral authority of the United States, evoked memories of Yankee imperialism among Latin American countries, and aligned Cuba even more closely with the Soviet Union.

Shortly before the Bay of Pigs invasion, the United States had suffered a psychological blow when a Soviet astronaut became the first human to orbit the earth. In May 1961, Kennedy called for a huge new commitment to the space race. "If we are to win the battle that is now going on around the world between freedom and tyranny," he told Congress, the United States must "take a clearly leading role in space achievement." His goal: an American on the moon within six to eight years. Congress authorized the Apollo program and substantially boosted appropriations for space exploration. In 1962, John H. Glenn orbited the earth, less than a year behind the Soviets. And in 1969, the United States surpassed the Soviet Union when two Americans, Neil A. Armstrong and Edwin E. "Buzz" Aldrin Jr., became the first humans to set foot on the moon.

═══════════════════════════════

The attempted armed interference in the affairs of another nation compromised the moral authority of the United States, evoked memories of Yankee imperialism among Latin American countries, and aligned Cuba even more closely with the Soviet Union.

═══════════════════════════════

Early in his presidency, Kennedy sought a meeting with Khrushchev, "to show him that we can be as tough as he is." The two leaders met in June 1961, in Vienna, Austria, but contrary to Kennedy's expectations, Khrushchev was belligerent and threatening and shook the president's confidence. To jour-

HUMANS REACH THE MOON
In July 1969, less than a decade after President John F. Kennedy announced the goal of "landing a man on the moon and returning him safely to earth," the space capsule Apollo 11 carried astronauts Edwin E. Aldrin Jr. and Neil A. Armstrong to the moon. As millions of people watched on television, Armstrong became the first human to step on the moon's surface, saying, "That's one small step for a man, one giant leap for mankind." Armstrong and Aldrin collected rock samples and conducted scientific experiments. Other missions to the moon followed. In this 1971 photograph of the Apollo 15 mission, astronaut James B. Irwin salutes near the lunar module and lunar roving vehicle.
NASA / Johnson Space Center.

nalist James Reston, the stunned president reported, "He just beat [the] hell out of me. . . . If he thinks I'm inexperienced and have no guts . . . we won't get anywhere with him." Khrushchev demanded an agreement recognizing the existence of two Germanys; otherwise, he warned, the Soviets would sign a separate treaty with East Germany, a move that would threaten not only America's occupation rights in West Berlin but also its access to the city, which lay some one hundred miles within East Germany. Kennedy held his ground. Returning home, he ordered more troops to Europe and a large increase in military forces.

The massive exodus of East Germans into West Berlin (which had begun shortly after Berlin was partitioned following World War II) caused the Communists a major embarrassment. To stop this flow of escapees from behind the iron curtain, on August 13, 1961, East Germany shocked the world by erecting a wall between East and West Berlin. With the Berlin Wall stemming the tide of East

German migration, Khrushchev backed off from his threats. Yet not until 1972 did the superpowers recognize East and West Germany as separate nations and guarantee Western access to West Berlin.

Kennedy used the Berlin crisis to add $3.2 billion to the defense budget, to mobilize the reserves and National Guard, and to expand the military by 300,000 troops. This buildup in conventional forces met Kennedy's demand for "a wider choice than humiliation or all-out nuclear action" by providing a "flexible response" strategy. At the same time, when the Soviet Union terminated its three-year moratorium on nuclear testing, the United States followed suit and vigorously developed new weapons and delivery systems.

New Approaches to the Third World

Kennedy administration officials sought fresh approaches to the wave of nationalism and revolutionary movements that had convulsed the world since the end of World War II. Much more than his predecessors, the president publicly supported third world democratic and nationalist aspirations. By helping to fulfill hopes for independence and democracy, he asserted, the United States could win the hearts and minds of people in the developing nations. To that end, Kennedy created the Alliance for Progress, promising $20 billion in aid for Latin America over the next decade. Like the Marshall Plan, the Alliance for Progress was designed to thwart communism and hold nations within the American sphere by fostering economic development. Likewise, the new Agency for International Development (AID) emphasized economic aid over military aid in foreign assistance programs.

With an idea borrowed from Senator Hubert H. Humphrey, in 1961 Kennedy launched his most dramatic third world initiative: the Peace Corps. Exemplifying the personal sacrifice summoned by Kennedy in his inaugural address, the program attracted many idealistic volunteers, such as one who expressed his discomfort at having been "born between clean sheets when others were issued into the dust with a birthright of hunger." After studying a country's language and culture, Peace Corps volunteers went to work directly with its people, opening schools, providing basic health care, helping establish small economic enterprises, and assisting with agriculture and nutrition projects. Some seven thousand of them by the end of Kennedy's presidency and more than sixty thousand by the mid-1970s fanned out around the globe, serving two-year stints in villages in Latin America, Africa, and Asia.

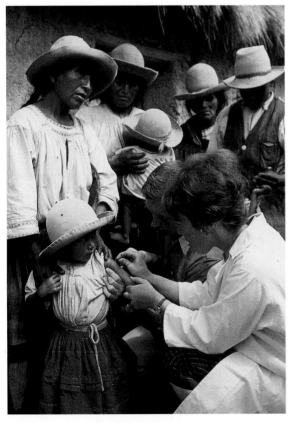

PEACE CORPS VOLUNTEERS IN BOLIVIA
The majority of Peace Corps volunteers worked on educational projects in developing countries. Others helped increase food production, build public works, and curb diseases, as did these volunteers, Rita Helmkamp and Ed Dennison, vaccinating a young Bolivian girl. President John F. Kennedy saw the Peace Corps volunteers, with their dedication to freedom, "overcoming the efforts of Mr. Khrushchev's missionaries who are dedicated to undermining that freedom." In the course of their missions, however, some volunteers came to question the single-minded focus of U.S. policy on anticommunism.
David S. Boyer © National Geographic Society.

In 1961 Kennedy launched his most dramatic third world initiative: the Peace Corps.

Nevertheless, Kennedy's foreign aid initiatives fell far short of their objectives. Though almost universally welcomed, Peace Corps projects numbered too few to make a dent in the poverty and suffering in third world countries. By 1969, the United States had provided only half of the $20 billion promised to the Alliance for Progress, and much of that went for military projects or was skimmed off by ruling elites who failed to institute meaningful reforms. In addition, a soaring birthrate in Latin America counteracted gains made in economic productivity, and these nations increasingly bore burdens of foreign indebtedness.

Kennedy also reverted to direct military means to bring political stability to the third world. Although his speeches supported popular movements' efforts to gain independence and better living conditions, he drew the line at uprisings that appeared to have Communist connections or goals. Even when a growing split between the Soviet

Union and Communist China presented an opportunity for improving U.S. relations with China, Kennedy clung to the basic tenet of the cold war: that communism was a monolithic force and had to be contained, no matter what form it took.

To that end, he promoted counterinsurgency forces to put down insurrections that smacked of communism (Map 28.1). The showcase of the administration's counterinsurgency strategy was an elite corps from the four military branches that was trained to wage guerrilla warfare. Called "special forces," the corps had been established under Eisenhower to aid groups that were sympathetic to the United States and opposed to Communist-leaning national liberation movements. Kennedy rapidly expanded the special forces, authorized their new name, the Green Berets (after their official headgear), and equipped them with the latest technology.

The Arms Race and the Nuclear Brink

The final piece of the Kennedy-McNamara defense strategy was to increase American nuclear superiority over the Soviet Union. This drive for nuclear dominance increased the number of U.S. nuclear weapons based in Europe from 2,500 to 7,200 and multiplied fivefold the supply of intercontinental ballistic missiles (ICBMs). To the Soviets, this nuclear buildup suggested that the United States wanted not just superiority but also the capacity to launch a first strike that would wipe out the Soviet missile sites before the Soviets could respond. The Kremlin therefore stepped up its own ICBM program, and thus began the most intense arms race in history.

In the fall of 1962, when Khrushchev decided to install nuclear missiles in Cuba, the super-

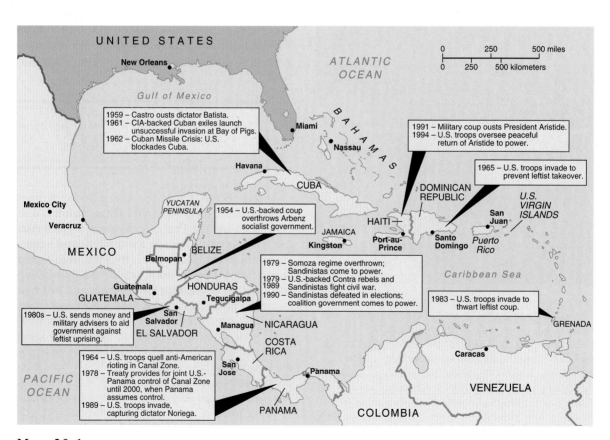

MAP 28.1

U.S. Involvement in Latin America and the Caribbean, 1954–1996
During the cold war, the United States frequently intervened in Central American and Caribbean countries to suppress Communist or leftist movements.

powers came perilously close to using their weapons of terror. On October 16, the CIA showed Kennedy photographs taken from U-2 spy planes that revealed launching sites under construction in Cuba for missiles that had ranges of 1,000 and 2,200 miles. The ensuing thirteen-day Cuban missile crisis brought the world closer to nuclear annihilation than ever before or since.

Working with a small group of top advisers meeting daily in secret, Kennedy managed the crisis. On October 22, he told a television audience that he had placed the military on full alert and was imposing a "strict quarantine on all offensive military equipment" headed from the Soviet Union to Cuba. The U.S. navy would stop, search, and turn back any Soviet vessel suspected of carrying offensive missiles to Cuba. (Only later did the United States find out that offensive missiles were already in Cuba.) Kennedy warned Khrushchev that any attack launched from Cuba would trigger a full nuclear attack against the Soviet Union.

The thirteen-day Cuban missile crisis brought the world closer to nuclear annihilation than ever before or since.

To Kennedy, projecting the appearance of toughness was paramount. According to his speechwriter, Theodore Sorensen, although the missiles did not "alter the strategic balance in fact . . . that balance would have been substantially altered in appearance; and in matters of national will and world leadership such appearances contribute to reality." But if Kennedy was willing to risk nuclear war for appearances, he also exercised considerable caution. He refused advice from the military to bomb the missile sites and instead ordered the quarantine to allow time for negotiations. On October 24, some of the Russian ships carrying nuclear warheads toward Cuba suddenly stopped and others turned back. Kennedy matched Khrushchev's restraint. When one ship crossed the blockade line, he ordered the navy to follow it rather than attempt to stop it. "We don't want to push him [Khrushchev] to a precipitous action," he said.

While Americans experienced the cold war's most fearful days, Kennedy and Khrushchev exchanged offers and counteroffers. Finally, the Soviets removed the missiles and pledged not to introduce new offensive weapons into Cuba. The United States promised not to invade the island. Secretly, Kennedy also agreed to remove U.S. missiles based in Turkey and aimed at the Soviet Union, a decision that he had made months before but had not implemented.

Even with the face-saving no-invasion promise from the United States, Khrushchev, in miscalculating Kennedy's resolution, harmed himself and his nation. The Soviets lost ground in their contest with China for the allegiance of third world countries, and his performance in the missile crisis was one element in Khrushchev's fall from power two years later. Kennedy emerged triumphant. The image of an inexperienced president fumbling the Bay of Pigs invasion and being bullied by Khrushchev in Vienna gave way to that of a brilliant leader combining firmness with restraint, bearing the United States through its "hour of maximum danger."

Having proved his toughness, Kennedy could afford to be conciliatory. After the Cuban missile crisis, he acted to prevent future confrontations. He and Khrushchev agreed to install a special telephone "hot line" to speed top-level communication at critical moments. In a major speech at the American University in June 1963, Kennedy called for a reexamination of cold war assumptions. He asked Americans "not to see only a distorted and desperate view of the other side, not to see conflict as inevitable." Acknowledging that the superpowers could not quickly resolve all their differences, Kennedy stressed what they had in common: "We all inhabit this small planet. We all breathe the same air. We all cherish our children's future and we are all mortal."

Responding to pressures from scientists and other Americans alarmed by the dangers of nuclear testing and threat of nuclear war, Kennedy also called for an end to "a vicious cycle" in which "new weapons beget counterweapons." In August 1963, the United States, the Soviet Union, and Great Britain signed a limited test ban treaty. Because France and China refused to sign, the agreement failed to stop the proliferation of nuclear weapons, and it did not apply to underground testing. Nonetheless, the limited test ban reduced the threat of radioactive fallout from nuclear testing, and it raised hopes for superpower accord on other issues.

Venturing into a Quagmire in Vietnam

The new approach to the cold war that Kennedy outlined at the American University did not mean abandoning efforts to save South Vietnam from communism. Kennedy had criticized the idea of "a Pax Americana enforced on the world by American weapons of war," but he increased the flow of those weapons into South Vietnam. His early foreign policy setbacks suggested the need to make a strong stand somewhere. "There are just so many concessions that one can make to the Communists in one year and survive politically," he remarked privately. Kennedy also remembered the political blows to the Democratic Party when China was "lost" in 1949.

Kennedy's strong anticommunism, his interpretation of the lessons of history, and his commitment to an activist foreign policy prepared him to take a stand in Vietnam. The new counterinsurgency program provided the means. Kennedy's key military adviser, General Maxwell Taylor, thought that Vietnam would be a good testing ground for the Green Berets. Author of the flexible response strategy, Taylor believed that holding firm in Vietnam would show the Soviets that wars of national liberation were "costly, dangerous, and doomed to failure."

Two major problems, however, undercut Taylor's analysis. First, the South Vietnamese insurgents—called Vietcong, short for *Vietnam Cong-san* ("Vietnamese Communists"), by the Americans—were a genuine indigenous force whose initiative came from within, not from the Soviet Union or China. Even Ho Chi Minh's Communist government in North Vietnam did not begin to supply weapons or soldiers to the rebels in the south until 1959, after those rebels had initiated guerrilla activities against the South Vietnamese government on their own. Because the government in Saigon refused to hold the elections promised in the Geneva accords and was doing everything possible to exterminate its opponents, the rebels saw no choice but to take up arms.

The second problem lay in the South Vietnamese government and army (the Army of the Republic of Vietnam, or ARVN), which proved to be ineffective vehicles for the American goal of containing communism. Ngo Dinh Diem, South Vietnamese premier from 1954 to 1963, chose self-serving military leaders merely for their personal loyalty. The government's corruption and repression of opponents alienated growing numbers of all South Vietnamese civilians, not just the Communists.

Intervention by North Vietnam made matters worse. In 1960, the Hanoi government established the National Liberation Front (NLF), composed of South Vietnamese rebels but directed by the north-

ern army. The NLF recruited most of its forces from among the South Vietnamese and fought largely with American weapons captured from the ARVN. In addition, Hanoi constructed a network of infiltration routes (called the "Ho Chi Minh Trail") in neighboring Laos, through which it sent people and supplies to help liberate the south (see Map 28.2). Violence escalated between 1960 and 1963, bringing the Saigon government close to collapse.

When Kennedy took office, more than $1 billion of aid and about seven hundred military advisers from the United States had failed to stabilize South Vietnam. He resisted pressure from some advisers for an all-out effort, but he began to escalate the American commitment in spring 1961. Within two years, military aid doubled, and nine thousand Americans served in Vietnam as military advisers, their activities occasionally going beyond training and advice to actual combat. Although the United States extracted new promises of reform from Diem with every increase of aid, the South Vietnamese government never made good on them.

Administration officials assumed that the latest military technology and sheer power could stem the Communist tide in South Vietnam. Yet the advanced weapons were ill suited to a guerrilla-type war and harmed the very people they were intended to save. Military personnel had trouble distinguishing the Vietcong and their supporters from innocent civilians. Thousands of peasants were uprooted from their land and resettled in new "strategic hamlets," supposedly out of the reach of the Communists. Those left in the countryside fell victim to bombs—containing the highly flammable substance napalm—dropped by the U.S.-backed ARVN in an effort to quell the Vietcong. In January 1962, U.S. planes began to spray herbicides to wipe out the Vietcong's jungle hideouts and destroy their food supply.

South Vietnamese military leaders effected a coup on November 2, 1963, brutally executing Premier Diem and his brother Ngo Dinh Nhu, head of the secret police. The killings shocked Kennedy, but in the next three weeks he gave no indication of any change in policy. In a speech he planned to deliver on the day he was assassinated, Kennedy intended to call Americans to their responsibilities as "the watchmen on the walls of world freedom." Referring specifically to Southeast Asia, his undelivered speech warned, "We dare not weary of the task." At his death, sixteen thousand Americans had served in Vietnam and one hundred had died there.

Lyndon Johnson's War against Communism

Lyndon Johnson followed the basic outlines of Kennedy's foreign policy, retained his key advisers, and continued the massive buildup of nuclear weapons and conventional and counterinsurgency forces that had begun in the early 1960s. At the same time, Johnson built on the less hostile U.S.-Soviet climate that had followed the Cuban missile crisis. In 1968, he signed a nuclear nonproliferation agreement with the Soviet Union, Britain, and fifty-eight nonnuclear nations, and he initiated plans for Soviet-American negotiations to control the arms race.

The cold war assumptions that shaped Kennedy's foreign policy underlay the new president's approach to Southeast Asia and Latin America as well. In 1965, when the South Vietnamese government approached collapse, Johnson made the fateful decisions to order U.S. troops into combat and initiate sustained bombing of the north. That same year, closer to home, Johnson sent U.S. marines to the Dominican Republic to crush a leftist rebellion.

Toward an All-Out Commitment in Vietnam

During his first year as president, Lyndon Johnson expanded secret raids on North Vietnam, boosted military and economic aid to the South Vietnamese, and increased the number of American advisers to twenty-three thousand. In August 1964, Johnson

seized an opportunity to increase the pressure on North Vietnam. American ships routinely engaged in espionage in the Gulf of Tonkin off the coast of North Vietnam, and on August 4, 1964, two U.S. destroyers reported that North Vietnamese gunboats had fired on them (Map 28.2). Despite uncertainty

M A P **28.2**

The Vietnam War, 1964–1975
The United States sent more than two million soldiers to Vietnam and spent more than $150 billion on the longest war in American history, but it was unable to prevent the unification of Vietnam under a Communist government.

READING THE MAP: What accord divided Vietnam into two nations? When was it signed, and where was the line of division drawn? Through what countries did the Ho Chi Minh Trail go?
CONNECTIONS: What was the Gulf of Tonkin incident and how did the United States respond? What was the Tet Offensive and how did it affect the war?

www.bedfordstmartins.com/tap SEE THE ONLINE STUDY GUIDE for more help in analyzing this map.

(expressed later by one of the ships' commanders himself) about whether the attacks had actually occurred, Johnson ordered air strikes on North Vietnamese torpedo bases and oil storage facilities.

The president also used the occasion to ask Congress for authority to take "all necessary measures to repel any armed attacks against the forces of the United States and to prevent further aggression." His portrayal of the situation was at best misleading, for he revealed neither the uncertainty about the attacks nor the provocative U.S. actions (staging covert raids and operating close to the North Vietnamese coast). Congress supported Johnson's plan by passing the Gulf of Tonkin Resolution on August 7, 1964, with just two senators voting no.

In 1965, when the South Vietnamese government approached collapse, Johnson made the fateful decisions to order U.S. troops into combat and initiate sustained bombing of the north.

Johnson's tough stance just two months before the 1964 elections helped counter the charges made by his opponent, Barry Goldwater, that he was "soft on communism." Yet the president also presented himself as the peace candidate. When Goldwater proposed massive bombing of North Vietnam, Johnson asserted that bombing would expand the war and send American forces into battle. "We are not going to send American boys nine or ten thousand miles away from home to do what Asian boys ought to be doing for themselves," Johnson insisted. Again and again he claimed, "We seek no wider war."

Soon after defeating Goldwater at the polls, however, Johnson did widen the war. He rejected peace overtures from North Vietnam, which insisted on American withdrawal and establishment of a coalition government in South Vietnam as steps toward ultimate unification of the country. Instead he accepted the advice of Robert S. McNamara, whom he had retained as secretary of defense, and other advisers to begin a bombing campaign against the north as a means to strengthen South Vietnamese morale, reduce Hanoi's ability to infiltrate personnel and equipment into the south, and break the will of what Johnson called a "raggedy-ass little fourth-rate country." In February 1965, Johnson initiated Operation Rolling Thunder, a strategy of gradually intensified bombing of North Vietnam.

Less than a month later, two battalions of marines landed near Da Nang, South Vietnam, the first U.S. combat troops to serve in Vietnam. In July, Johnson shifted U.S. troops from defensive to offensive operations and authorized the dispatch of

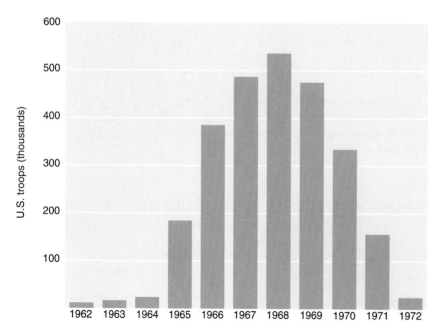

FIGURE 28.1

U.S. Troops in Vietnam, 1962–1972

The steepest increases in the American military presence in Vietnam came in 1965 and 1966. Although troop levels declined in 1971 and 1972, the U.S. continued massive bombing attacks.

fifty thousand more soldiers, ordering aides to "minimize any appearance of sudden changes of policy" (Figure 28.1). Yet those decisions, whose import was kept from Congress and the public, marked a critical turning point. Now it was genuinely America's war.

Preventing Another Castro in Latin America

Closer to home, Johnson faced perpetual problems in Latin America, despite the efforts of the Alliance for Progress. Thirteen times during the 1960s, military coups replaced Latin American governments, and local insurgencies grew apace (see Map 28.1). The administration's response to such turmoil varied from case to case but centered on the determination to prevent any more Castro-type revolutions.

In 1964, riots erupted in the Panama Canal Zone, which the United States had seized and made a U.S. territory early in the century. Instigated by Panamanian nationalists, the riots resulted in the deaths of four U.S. soldiers and more than twenty Panamanians. Johnson authorized U.S. troops to quell the disturbance, but he also initiated negotiations with Panamanian leaders. These talks dragged on until 1978, ultimately providing for Panama to assume full authority over the canal and for neutrality of the Canal Zone territory by the year 2000.

In 1965, Johnson's Latin American policy generated a new surge of anti-Americanism and cries of "Yankee imperialism." In 1961, voters in the Dominican Republic ousted a long-standing dictator and elected a constitutional government headed by Juan Bosch. But in 1963, a military coup overthrew Bosch, and two years later his supporters rallied in an uprising against the military government. When the revolt was just four days old, Johnson ordered marines to the island and eventually sent more than twenty thousand soldiers to take control. The administration said the intervention was necessary because the Boschist rebels included Communists. A special U.S. ambassador arranged a truce between the opposing sides and installed an interim government. When Dominican elections in 1966 established a constitutional government under a moderate rightist, it appeared that Johnson's policy had worked.

Yet this first outright show of Yankee force in Latin America in forty years damaged the administration at home and abroad. It quickly became clear that Communists had played no significant role in the revolt, and U.S. intervention kept the reform-

In 1965, Johnson's Latin American policy generated a new surge of anti-Americanism and cries of "Yankee imperialism."

oriented Boschists from returning to power. Moreover, the president had acted without the consent of the Dominicans or the Organization of American

U.S. TROOPS IN THE DOMINICAN REPUBLIC
These U.S. paratroopers were among the twenty thousand troops sent to the Dominican Republic in April and May 1965. The American invasion helped restore peace, but it also kept the popularly elected government of Juan Bosch from regaining office. Dominicans expressed their outrage in anti-American slogans that greeted troops throughout the capital, Santo Domingo. Bosch himself said, "This was a democratic revolution smashed by the leading democracy in the world."
Corbis-Bettmann.

Why Couldn't the United States Bomb Its Way to Victory in Vietnam?

WORLD WAR II DEMONSTRATED the critical importance of airpower in modern war. According to the official U.S. study of strategic bombing during World War II, "No nation can long survive the free exploitation of air weapons over its homeland." In the Vietnam War, U.S. planes delivered even more explosives than they had in World War II. Why, then, did strategic bombing not bring victory in Vietnam?

"Our airpower did not fail us; it was the decision makers," asserted Admiral U. S. Grant Sharp, World War II veteran and commander in chief of the Pacific Command during the Vietnam War. Military officials welcomed President Johnson's order to begin bombing North Vietnam in February 1965 as a means to destroy the north's capacity and will to support the Communist insurgents in South Vietnam. But they chafed at Johnson's strategy of gradual escalation and the restrictions he imposed on Operation Rolling Thunder, the three-and-a-half-year bombing campaign. Military officials believed that the United States should have begun Operation Rolling Thunder with all-out massive bombing and continued until the devastation brought North Vietnam to its knees. Instead, they charged, civilian decision makers compelled the military to fight with one hand tied behind its back. Their arguments echoed General Douglas MacArthur's criticism of Truman's policy during the Korean War—though these officials did not repeat MacArthur's insubordination.

Unlike military officials, who could single-mindedly focus on defeating the enemy, the president needed to balance military objectives against political considerations and found compelling reasons to limit the application of airpower. Recalling the Korean War, Johnson noted that "China is there on the [North Vietnamese] border with 700 million men," and he studiously avoided action that might provoke intervention by the Chinese, who now possessed nuclear weapons. Johnson's strategy also aimed to keep the Soviet Union out of the war, to avoid inflaming antiwar sentiment at home, and to avert international criticism of the United States.

Consequently, the president would not permit bombing of areas where high civilian casualties might result and areas near the Chinese border. He banned strikes on airfields and missile sites that were under construction and thus likely to contain Chinese or Soviet advisers, and he refused to mine North Vietnam's harbors, through which Soviet ships imported goods to North Vietnam. But Johnson did escalate the pressure, increasing the intensity of the bombing fourfold by 1968. In all, Operation Rolling Thunder rained 643,000 tons of bombs on North Vietnam between 1965 and 1968.

Military leaders agreed with Johnson's desire to spare civilians. The Joint Chiefs of Staff never proposed, for example, strikes against a system of dikes and dams that could have disrupted food production and flooded Hanoi under twenty feet of water. Rather, they focused on destroying North Vietnam's industry and transportation system. Noncombatant casualties in North Vietnam contrasted sharply with those in World War II, when Anglo-American bombing of Dresden, Germany, alone took more than 35,000 civilian lives and the firebombing of Japan caused 330,000 civilian deaths. In three and a half years, Operation Rolling Thunder's bombing claimed an estimated 52,000 civilian lives.

The relatively low level of economic development in North Vietnam and the North Vietnamese government's ability to mobilize its citizens counteracted the military superiority of the United States. Sheer man-, woman-, and child-power compensated for the demolition of transportation sources, industry sites, and electric power plants. When bombs struck a rail line, civilians rushed with bicycles to unload a train's cargo, carry it beyond the break, and load it onto a second train. Three hundred thousand full-time workers and 200,000 farmers labored in their spare time to keep the Ho Chi Minh Trail usable in spite of heavy bombing. When bridges were destroyed, the North Vietnamese resorted to ferries and pontoons made from bamboo, and they rebuilt bridges slightly underwater to make them harder to detect from the air. They dispersed oil storage facilities and production centers throughout the countryside, and when bombs knocked out electric power plants, the Vietnamese turned to more than two thousand portable generators and used oil lamps and candles in their homes.

North Vietnam's military needs were relatively small, and officials found ample means to meet them. In 1967, North Vietnam had only about 55,000 soldiers in South Vietnam, and because they waged a guerrilla war with only sporadic fighting, the insurgents in the south did not require huge amounts of supplies. Even after communist forces in the south increased, the total nonfood needs of these soldiers was estimated at just one-fifth of what a single U.S. division required. What U.S. bombs destroyed, the North Vietnamese replaced with Chinese and Soviet imports. China provided 600,000 tons of rice in 1967 alone, and it supplied small arms and ammunition, vehicles, and other goods throughout the war. Competing with China for influence in North Vietnam and favor in the third world, the Soviets contributed tanks, fighter planes, surface-to-air missiles, and other sophisticated weapons. Foreign aid substantially curtailed the effect of Operation Rolling Thunder, and the Soviet-installed modern defense systems made the bombing more difficult and dangerous for U.S. pilots.

In July 1969, Seventh Air Force commander General William W. Momyer commented on Operation Rolling Thunder to the retiring air force chief of staff, "We had the force, skill, and intelligence, but our civilian betters wouldn't turn us loose." Johnson refused to turn the military loose because in addition to the goal he shared with the military—breaking Hanoi's ability to support insurgency in the south—he also wanted to keep China and the Soviet Union (and nuclear weapons) out of the war and to contain domestic and international criticism of U.S. policy. Whether a more devastating air war would have provoked Chinese or Soviet intervention can never be known.

Nor can we know whether all-out bombing of the north could have guaranteed an independent non-Communist government in the south. We do know that Johnson's military advisers imposed their own restraints, never recommending the wholesale attacks on civilians that took place in World War II. Short of decimating the civilian population, it is questionable whether more intense bombing could have completely halted North Vietnamese support for the Vietcong, given the nature of the North Vietnamese economy, the determination and ingenuity of its people, and the plentiful assistance from China and the Soviet Union. Whether the strategic bombing that worked so well in a world war against major industrial powers could be effective in a third world guerrilla war remained in doubt after the Vietnam War.

States (OAS), to which the United States had pledged to respect national sovereignty in Latin America. Once the troops landed in the Dominican Republic, Johnson did ask for approval and joint occupation from the OAS members, but several nations, including Mexico, Chile, and Venezuela, refused to support the United States.

Johnson believed that demonstrating strength in the Caribbean would help convince the North Vietnamese that the United States was determined to resist communism. The apparent success in the Dominican Republic no doubt encouraged the president to press on in Vietnam.

The Americanized War

From Operation Rolling Thunder in 1965 to early 1968, the United States gradually escalated attacks against the North Vietnamese and their Vietcong allies, with the goal of breaking the will of the North Vietnamese while avoiding intervention by the Chinese. Johnson crudely explained the strategy to reporters as one of "seduction," from which the United States might ease off, rather than one of "rape," which might provoke China to respond as it had done in Korea. Intensely concerned with the bombing of the north, Johnson liked to boast, "They can't even bomb an outhouse without my approval."

Over the course of the war, U.S. pilots dropped 3.2 million tons of explosives, more than the United States had launched in all of World War II. (See "Historical Question," page 1072.) The intensive bombing claimed monthly death tolls of more than two thousand North Vietnamese civilians and soldiers but failed to dampen the north's commitment. The Hanoi government dispersed and concealed industrial and military facilities, taught its citizens how to protect themselves, and relied on human labor to rebuild transportation routes. Both the Soviet Union and China helped North Vietnam replace what the bombing destroyed, supplying an estimated $2 billion worth of materials between 1965 and 1968.

The United States relied even more heavily on airpower in the south, raining down more than twice the tonnage of bombs dropped on North Vietnam. Because there was no battlefront as in previous wars, military officials calculated progress not in territory seized, but in "body counts" and "kill ratios"—the number of enemies killed in relation to

the cost in American and ARVN lives. General William Westmoreland's strategy of attrition was designed to search out and kill the Vietcong and North Vietnamese regular army, but in reality American soldiers did not always take care to distinguish between military combatants and civilians. Lieutenant Philip Caputo reported that the operating rule was "If it's dead and Vietnamese, it's VC [Vietcong]." A helicopter pilot summed up the attrition strategy when, after a brutal battle, his comrade asked him, "What did we win? We don't have any more real estate, no new villages are under American control, and it took everything we had to stop them." The pilot responded, "More of them got killed than us. It's that simple."

In contrast to World War II, when the average soldier was twenty-six years old, teenagers fought the Vietnam War. Until the Twenty-sixth Amendment reduced the voting age from twenty-one to eighteen in 1971, most soldiers, whose average age was nineteen, could not even vote for the officials who sent them to Vietnam. World War II had distributed the fighting among men of various economic levels, but Vietnam was the war of the poor and working class, who constituted about 80 percent of the troops. More privileged youth found it easier to avoid the draft, usually through college deferments. Mike Clodfelter, sent to Vietnam in 1965, noticed that all of his high school buddies from Plainville, Kansas, who went to Vietnam came from working-class families: "I know of not a single middle-class son of the town's businessmen, lawyers, doctors, or ranchers who experienced the Armageddon of our generation."

World War II had distributed the fighting among men of various economic levels, but Vietnam was the war of the poor and working class.

Vietnam was the first war in which troops were fully integrated, and African Americans often chose the military over their meager opportunities in the civilian economy. They were concentrated in combat positions, however, constituting 31 percent of all combat troops in the early years of the war. Death rates among black soldiers were disproportionately high until 1966, when the military adjusted assignments of personnel to produce a more racially balanced distribution of sacrifice.

The young American troops faced extremely difficult conditions. This was a war whose purpose was unclear, a war with shifting battle sites instead of front lines. "There were no Normandies or Gettysburgs for us," wrote Philip Caputo. Soldiers fought in thick jungles and swamps filled with leeches, in oppressive heat, rain, and humidity. For Caputo the war meant "weeks of expectant waiting and, at random intervals, of conducting vicious manhunts through jungles and swamps where snipers harassed us constantly and booby traps cut us down one by one." The stress of guerrilla war, the difficulty in distinguishing Vietnamese soldiers from civilians, the desire for revenge when a comrade received savage treatment from the enemy—all of this tended to break down the moral boundaries that normally guided soldiers' actions. Caputo's marines were "not innately cruel, but . . . learned rather quickly that Vietnam was not a place where a man could expect much mercy. . . . And men who do not expect to receive mercy eventually lose their inclination to grant it."

Unlike most other wars in which Americans fought, a victory in Vietnam would depend in part on the effectiveness of the South Vietnamese government. After a series of coups and short-lived regimes, in 1965 Air Marshal Nguyen Cao Ky became prime minister, and General Nguyen Van Thieu took over as commander in chief of the military. But the Thieu-Ky government failed to rally popular support. Graft and corruption continued to flourish. In the intensified fighting and inability to distinguish friend from foe, thousands of South Vietnamese civilians were killed and wounded, their farms and villages bombed and burned. By 1968, five million people, nearly 30 percent of the population, had become refugees. Huge infusions of American dollars and goods produced rampant inflation, more opportunities for graft, the demise of local industries, and an increased dependence on foreign aid. The U.S. military inflicted great losses on the enemy, estimated at more than 200,000 by the end of 1967. Yet the United States could claim no more than a stalemate.

Americanization of the war also strained relations with the nation's most important allies. Australia, New Zealand, the Philippines, South Korea, and Thailand supported the U.S. effort by sending small military contingents to Vietnam. But French president Charles de Gaulle openly criticized U.S. policy in Vietnam, while Canadian, British, and West German leaders more quietly sought to end the war. Some allies had moral or practical reservations, and all wanted the United States to concentrate its attention and resources in areas that they deemed more critical to the West.

Johnson's cautiously made decisions flowed logically from the commitments of three presidents before him. All the same, 1965 marked a critical turning point: the rationale for involvement in the war shifted from the need to contain communism in Southeast Asia to the need to prove to the world the will and ability of the United States to make good on its commitments.

A Nation Polarized

Soon President Johnson was fighting a war on two fronts. Domestic opposition to the war grew rapidly after 1965, and the United States entered a period of internal conflict and violence unparalleled since the Civil War. Television brought the carnage of Vietnam into American homes day after day, making it the first "living-room war." Torn between his domestic critics and the military's clamor for more troops, the president in March 1968 announced restrictions on the bombing, a new effort at negotiations, and his decision not to pursue reelection. Throughout 1968, demonstrations, violence, and assassinations convulsed the nation. Vietnam took center stage in the election, and voters narrowly favored the Republican candidate, former vice president Richard Nixon, who promised to "bring Americans together again" and to achieve "peace with honor."

The Widening War at Home

Before 1965, American actions in Vietnam evoked little domestic criticism. But Johnson's authorization of Operation Rolling Thunder sparked a mass movement against the war. In April 1965, Students for a Democratic Society (SDS) launched the first major protest, recruiting twenty thousand people for a rally in Washington, D.C. SDS chapters sprang up on more than three hundred college campuses across the country, enrolling more than a hundred thousand members. Although SDS members remained a tiny minority of college students, thousands of young people joined campus protests against Reserve Officers Training Corps (ROTC) programs, recruiters from the CIA, companies that manufactured war materials, and university departments that conducted research for the Department of Defense. A new draft policy in 1967, which ended deferments for postgraduate education, gave male students a greater stake in seeing the war end. In the spring of 1968, as many as one million college and high school students participated in a nationwide strike.

Antiwar sentiment also entered society's mainstream. The *New York Times* began to question the administration's policy as early as 1965, and by 1968 media critics included the *Wall Street Journal, Life* magazine, and popular TV journalist Walter Cronkite (Figure 28.2). Clergy, businesspeople, scientists, and physicians formed their own groups to pressure Johnson to stop the bombing and start negotiations. Though most of organized labor supported the president, some unions and their leaders joined the peace movement. Increasing numbers of prominent Democratic senators, including J. William Fulbright, George McGovern, and majority leader Mike Mansfield, urged Johnson to substitute negotiation for the use of force.

Opposition to the war took diverse forms: letter-writing campaigns to officials, teach-ins on college campuses, mass marches in major cities, student strikes, withholding of federal taxes, draft card burnings, civil disobedience against military centers and manufacturers of war materials, and attempts to stop trains carrying troops. Although the peace movement never claimed a majority of the population, it brought the war to the center of media attention and severely limited the administration's options. The twenty-year-old consensus about cold war foreign policy had broken down.

Domestic opposition to the war grew rapidly after 1965, and the United States entered into a period of internal conflict and violence unparalleled since the Civil War.

Many young men would not fight in the war. When Muhammad Ali, heavyweight champion of the world, refused to serve in what he called a "white man's war," the World Boxing Association

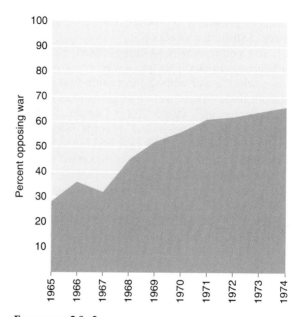

FIGURE 28.2

Public Opinion about the Vietnam War, 1965–1974
This chart reflects the percent of people answering yes to a Gallup poll question, "In view of the developments since we entered the fighting in Vietnam, do you think the United States made a mistake in sending troops to fight in Vietnam?"

stripped him of his title. More than 170,000 men who opposed the war on moral or religious grounds gained conscientious objector status (for which they had to officially apply) and performed nonmilitary duties at home or in Vietnam. About 60,000 young men fled the country to escape the draft, and more than 200,000 were accused of failing to register or committing other draft offenses.

When he got his induction notice in the summer of 1968, Tim O'Brien agonized over what to do. He opposed the war and supported Eugene McCarthy, who was campaigning for the Democratic nomination for president on an antiwar platform. Yet to avoid the draft would bring criticism and embarrassment to his family in his small-town Minnesota community, whose leaders expected young men to serve their country. In addition, he said, "I owed the prairie something. For twenty-one years I'd lived under its laws, accepted its education . . . wallowed in its luxuries, played on its Little League teams." In the end he could not bring himself to desert the country that he had never before thought of leaving. Though he held to his belief "that the

AFRICAN AMERICAN ANTIWAR PROTEST
The first expression of African American opposition to the war in Vietnam occurred in Mississippi in July 1965 when a group of civil rights workers called for draft resistance. Blacks should not fight for freedom in Vietnam "until all the Negro People are free in Mississippi," and they should not "risk our lives and kill other Colored People in Santo Domingo and Viet Nam." This protester on the West Coast in April 1967 expresses similar sentiments.
Robert LeBeck / Black Star.

war was wrong," O'Brien served in the army as an infantryman.

Opponents of the war held far from unanimous views. Some, like O'Brien, condemned the war on moral grounds, challenging the right of the United States to interfere in the affairs of another country and stressing the suffering imposed on the Vietnamese people. Their goal was total withdrawal. But as American intervention escalated with no tangible results, a larger segment of antiwar sentiment reflected practical considerations—that the war could not be won or that the cost in lives, dollars,

and the sacrifice of domestic reform would be too great to bear. Not demanding withdrawal, those activists wanted Johnson to stop bombing North Vietnam and seek a negotiated settlement.

The antiwar movement outraged the millions of Americans who supported the war. Some members of the generation who had fought against Hitler could not understand a younger generation who failed to stand behind the government. Most repellent to many Americans were peace advocates who expressed support for the enemy. "How can Americans take sides against their own young men sent to Vietnam to fight and perhaps die?" asked supporters of government policy. While working-class people expressed doubts about the war as often as other Americans, they were especially conscious of the class dimensions of both the war and the public opposition to it. A firefighter whose son had died in Vietnam said bitterly, "It's people like us who give up our sons for the country. The businesspeople, they run the country and make money from it. The college types . . . go to Washington and tell the government what to do. . . . But their sons don't end up in the swamps over there, in Vietnam."

In his domestic economic policies, President Johnson tried to avoid actions that would focus attention on the war's burdens. He avoided price and wage controls, which had been employed in other wars to control inflation, and he did not call for a tax increase until the end of 1967. Congress agreed to a 10 percent surcharge on federal income taxes in June 1968, only after Johnson pledged to reduce domestic spending. Johnson's Great Society programs suffered, but the surcharge failed to reverse the inflationary surge. Johnson reacted harshly to antiwar sentiment. He agonized over casualty reports and felt personally wounded when protesters chanted outside the White House, "Hey, hey, LBJ, how many kids have you killed today?" In addition to undertaking a public relations campaign that cast the war's progress in a deceptively optimistic light, Johnson tried to discredit opponents by labeling them "nervous Nellies" or Communists.

The administration also employed direct means to silence critics. Following Johnson's orders, the CIA spied on peace advocates, compiling secret files on more than seven thousand citizens. Law enforcement officials indicted not just draft resisters but also those like Dr. Benjamin Spock, the famous baby care expert, who counseled them. Without the president's specific authorization, the FBI infiltrated the peace movement, disrupted its work, and attempted to dis-

PRO-WAR DEMONSTRATORS
Advocates as well as opponents of the war in Vietnam took to the streets, as these New Yorkers did in support of the U.S. invasion of Cambodia in May 1970. Construction workers—called "hard hats"—and other union members marched with American flags and posters championing President Nixon's policies and blasting New York mayor John Lindsay for his antiwar position. Following the demonstration, sympathetic union leaders presented Nixon with an honorary hard hat.
Paul Fusco / Magnum Photos, Inc.

www.bedfordstmartins.com /tap   SEE THE ONLINE STUDY GUIDE for more help in analyzing this image.

credit activists by spreading false information about them. However, even the resort to illegal measures failed to subdue the opposition.

1968: Year of Upheaval

Although the majority of Americans remained detached from the peace movement and many opposed it vigorously, by late 1967 public impatience and frustration had intensified. Among the dissatisfied were the "hawks," who charged that the United States was fighting with one hand tied behind its back and called for the government to apply more power against North Vietnam. The "doves" wanted de-escalation or withdrawal. Most Americans were torn between their weariness of the war and their worry about abandoning the American commitment. As one woman said to a pollster, "I want to get out but I don't want to give up."

Grave doubts about the war penetrated the administration itself in 1967. Secretary of Defense McNamara, a principal architect of U.S. involvement, now doubted that the war was winnable. Ho Chi Minh, he believed, "won't quit no matter how much bombing we do." McNamara also feared for the image of the United States, "the world's greatest su-

perpower killing or seriously injuring 1,000 noncombatants a week, while trying to pound a tiny, backward nation into submission on an issue whose merits are hotly disputed." McNamara kept those views to himself until thirty years later, but in early 1968 he left the administration to head the World Bank.

The critical turning point for Johnson came with the Tet Offensive, which began on January 30, 1968. Just a few weeks after General Westmoreland had reported that "the enemy has been driven away from the population centers [and] has been compelled to disperse," the North Vietnamese and Vietcong attacked key cities and every major American base in South Vietnam. One band of soldiers even invaded the grounds of the U.S. embassy in Saigon, killing two Americans and holding the compound for six hours.

The Tet Offensive, named for its occurrence during the Vietnamese lunar new year celebration, Tet, was the biggest surprise of the war—and not simply because it violated a truce that both sides had generally observed during the holiday. The offensive displayed the communists' vitality and refusal to let the presence of half a million American soldiers deter them from launching a daring offensive. Militarily, the Vietcong and North Vietnamese suffered a defeat, losing more than thirty thousand men, ten times the casualty rate of ARVN and U.S. forces. Psychologically, however, the Tet Offensive was a devastating blow to the United States.

Tet highlighted the credibility gap between official statements and the actual progress of the war, in part because the press emphasized the magnitude of the attacks rather than how quickly they had been repelled. The Tet Offensive created not only one million more South Vietnamese refugees but also widespread destruction, especially in the ancient city of Hue, whose archeological treasures were reduced to rubble. Referring to a village that he had helped to defend, a U.S. army official explained, "We had to destroy the town to save it," a statement that epitomized for more and more Americans both the contradiction between means and ends in Vietnam and the brutality and senselessness of the war.

In the aftermath of the Tet Offensive, Johnson considered a request from Westmoreland for 200,000 more troops. He conferred with both his civilian advisers in the Department of Defense and an unofficial group of foreign policy experts, dubbed the "Wise Men," who had played key roles in designing cold war policies since World War II. Dean Acheson, secretary of state under Truman, summarized their conclusion: "We can no longer do the job we set out to do in the time we have left and we must begin to take steps to disengage."

Referring to a village that he had helped to defend, a U.S. army official explained, "We had to destroy the town to save it," a statement that epitomized for more and more Americans the senselessness of the war.

On March 31, 1968, Lyndon Johnson, addressing the nation on television, announced that the United States would reduce its bombing of North Vietnam and that he was prepared to begin peace talks with its leaders. Then he stunned his audience by concluding,"I shall not seek, and I will not accept, the nomination of my party for another term as your president."

Johnson's decision marked the end of the gradual escalation that had begun in 1965. What followed was a shift from "Americanization" to "Vietnamization" of the war, but it was a shift in strategy, not in policy. The United States did not abandon the goal of a non-Communist South Vietnam; it simply hoped to reach that goal by relying more heavily on the South Vietnamese. In that sense, Johnson's announcement represented a return to pre-1965 policy.

Negotiations began in Paris in May 1968. But the United States would not agree to recognition of the Hanoi government's National Liberation Front, a coalition government, and American withdrawal. The North Vietnamese would agree to nothing less. Although the talks continued, so did the fighting. The American presence neared its peak at 543,000 in mid-1968, but the cost in American lives was nearly as high after peace talks began as before.

Meanwhile, violence escalated at home. Two months after the murder of Martin Luther King Jr. and the riots that erupted in its wake, another assassination stunned the nation. In the race for the Democratic presidential nomination, Senator Robert F. Kennedy, the late president's brother, had just celebrated his triumph in the California primary when he was shot in the head by a Palestinian Arab refugee, Sirhan B. Sirhan, who was outraged by Kennedy's recent statement of support for Israel. Kennedy died twenty-six hours later, on June 6.

The spring of 1968 also saw campus demonstrations intensify in Mexico, France, Germany, and elsewhere in the world as well as in the United States, where some two hundred protests occurred in the first half of the year. The bloodiest took place at New York City's Columbia University, where students took over five buildings, demanding that the university stop uprooting African Americans in the neighboring community, do more to meet the needs of black students, stop sponsoring research for the Department of Defense, and grant amnesty to past and current student demonstrators. (See "Documenting the American Promise," page 1048.) When negotiations failed, university officials called in the New York City police, who cleared the buildings, sent more than one hundred demonstrators to the hospital, and arrested more than seven hundred others. An ensuing student strike brought the academic year to a premature end.

In August, protesters battled the police in Chicago, where the Democratic Party had convened to nominate its presidential ticket. Several thousand demonstrators had come to the city, some to show their support for Eugene McCarthy's peace candi-

PROTEST IN CHICAGO
The worst violence surrounding the 1968 Democratic National Convention in Chicago came on August 28 when protesters decided to assemble in Grant Park and march to the convention site. Mayor Daley refused them a parade permit and dispatched the police and the Illinois National Guard to the park to keep them from marching. As protesters listened to speeches in the park, a group of young men tore down the American flag and replaced it with a red T-shirt, prompting the police to go after the demonstrators with their clubs. Later that night when activists tried to march to the convention, the police struck out widely and wildly, bloodying and teargassing many people who were not connected to the radicals.
Jeffrey Blankfort / Jeroboam.

dacy, others to take a more aggressive stance. Many of the latter had been mobilized by the Youth International Party (Yippies), a splinter group of SDS. Its leaders, Abbie Hoffman and Jerry Rubin, urged students to demonstrate their hatred of the establishment by provoking the police to violence and creating chaos and disorder in the backyard of the Democratic convention.

Chicago's mayor and leading Democrat, Richard J. Daley, forbade demonstrators from holding rallies or marches, instituted a curfew, and mobilized thou-sands of police. When on August 25 police ordered demonstrators in Lincoln Park to disperse, only to be met with insults and jeers, they attacked the protesters with tear gas and clubs. Street battles continued for three days, culminating in what an official commission later termed a "police riot" on the night of August 28. Taunted by the crowd, the police fought with mace and nightsticks, clubbing not only those who had wanted to provoke violence but also reporters, peaceful demonstrators, convention delegates, and bystanders.

The bloodshed in Chicago and general upheaval across the country had little effect on the outcome of either major party's convention. Peace Democrats lost the presidential nomination, as Vice President Hubert H. Humphrey trounced Eugene McCarthy by nearly three to one. McCarthy's refusal to share the podium with Humphrey as the convention ended provided a stark illustration of the bitter split within the party. In contrast, the Republican convention produced little controversy and nominated former vice president Richard Nixon on the first ballot. For his running mate, Nixon chose Maryland governor Spiro T. Agnew, hoping to gather southern support while not alienating northern and western voters.

For the first time in nearly fifty years, a strong third party entered the electoral scene. Former Alabama governor George C. Wallace, who had gained national attention for his segregationist stance, ran on the ticket of the American Independent Party. Gaining his strongest support from the Deep South, Wallace also appealed to Americans nationwide who were alarmed and disgusted by the changes that were sweeping their society and frustrated by the nation's inability to work its will in Vietnam. His supporters included considerable numbers of working-class whites, who believed that civil rights initiatives and antipoverty programs benefited the undeserving at their expense. And he appealed to citizens outraged by the assault on traditional values—by privileged students, antiwar protesters, young people experimenting with drugs and flouting sexual mores—that had reverberated through the 1960s.

Few differences separated the two major-party candidates on the central issue of Vietnam. Nixon seized the advantage, criticizing the incumbent party for "four years in Vietnam with no end in sight." He promised to "bring an honorable end" to the war but did not indicate how he would do it. Attacking the Great Society for "pouring billions of dollars into programs that have failed" and appealing to "the forgotten Americans, the non-shouters, the non-demonstrators," Nixon more guardedly played on the resentments that fueled the Wallace campaign.

Humphrey had strong reservations about U.S. policy in Vietnam, yet as vice president he wanted to avoid a break with Johnson. At the end of October, Johnson boosted Humphrey's campaign when he announced a halt to the bombing of North

Vietnam. By election eve, Nixon and Humphrey were in a neck-and-neck race.

For the first time in nearly fifty years, a strong third party entered the electoral scene. Former Alabama governor George C. Wallace appealed to Americans nationwide who were alarmed and disgusted by the changes that were sweeping their society.

With nearly ten million votes (13 percent of the total), the American Independent Party produced the strongest third-party finish since 1924. Nixon edged out Humphrey by just half a million popular votes, prevailing more strongly in the electoral college, with 301 votes to Humphrey's 191 and Wallace's 46. The Democrats lost a few seats in Congress but kept control of both the House and the Senate (Map 28.3).

The 1968 elections revealed deep cracks in the coalition that had, with the exception of the Eisen-

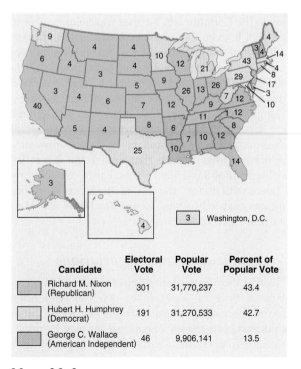

Candidate	Electoral Vote	Popular Vote	Percent of Popular Vote
Richard M. Nixon (Republican)	301	31,770,237	43.4
Hubert H. Humphrey (Democrat)	191	31,270,533	42.7
George C. Wallace (American Independent)	46	9,906,141	13.5

M A P   2 8 . 3
The Election of 1968

hower years, kept the Democrats in power for thirty years. Opposition to the Democrats' policies on race moved most of the former "Solid South" behind Nixon or Wallace, breaking a century of Democratic Party ascendency in that region. Although union leaders rallied strongly behind Humphrey, large numbers of blue-collar workers voted for Wallace or Nixon. Voters blamed the Democratic Party for its civil rights policies, the Great Society reforms, inflation, antiwar protesters, campus rebels, changing sexual mores, urban riots, and America's impotence in Vietnam. These resentments continued to simmer, later to be mobilized into a resurging right in American politics.

Nixon's Failed Search for Peace with Honor

"I'm not going to end up like LBJ, holed up in the White House afraid to show my face on the street," the new president asserted. "I'm going to stop that war. Fast." Although he began a gradual withdrawal of U.S. ground troops, Nixon was no more willing than Johnson had been to allow South Vietnam to fall to the Communists. Neither was he more able to prevent it, even though he expanded military operations into Cambodia and Laos and engaged in sporadic but ferocious bombing of North Vietnam. Instead, the Nixon administration further polarized the nation and outdid its predecessor in deceiving Congress and the public and in harassing dissenters.

Unable to marshal support at home or to defeat the enemy abroad, in January 1973 the administration concluded a truce that ended the direct involvement of the United States. Far from achieving "peace with honor," the United States accepted conditions that led to total victory for the North Vietnamese in April 1975.

Vietnamization and Negotiations

Nixon's most important adviser was not his secretary of state or secretary of defense, who often found themselves in the dark on important initiatives, but his assistant for national security, Henry A. Kissinger, a German-born refugee from Hitler's Holocaust and a Harvard professor of international relations. Nixon and Kissinger embraced the overriding goal of the three preceding administrations: a non-Communist South Vietnam. By 1969, how-

ever, that goal had become almost incidental to the larger objective of maintaining American credibility. According to Kissinger, regardless of the wisdom of the initial intervention, "the commitment of five hundred thousand Americans has settled the importance of Vietnam. For what is involved now is confidence in American promises."

From 1969 to 1972, Nixon and Kissinger pursued a four-pronged approach. First, they tried to strengthen the South Vietnamese military and government. Second, to disarm the antiwar movement at home, Nixon gradually withdrew U.S. soldiers from combat, replacing them with South Vietnamese soldiers and American technology and bombs. Third, Nixon and Kissinger negotiated with both North Vietnam and the Soviet Union. Fourth, they applied enormous firepower in an effort to get Hanoi to accept American terms at the bargaining table.

According to Kissinger, "the commitment of five hundred thousand Americans has settled the importance of Vietnam. For what is involved now is confidence in American promises."

As part of the Vietnamization of the war, ARVN forces grew to more than one million, supported with the latest American equipment, improved training, and increased pay scales and benefits. The South Vietnamese air force became the fourth largest in the world. U.S. advisers and funds also promoted land reform, village elections, and the building of schools, hospitals, and transportation facilities. Despite these improvements, whether South Vietnam could stand on its own remained doubtful.

The other side of Vietnamization was the withdrawal of U.S. forces. The number of GIs decreased to 334,600 in 1970 and to 140,000 by the end of 1971. Despite the reduced draft calls and casualties (from nearly 800 deaths a month in 1969 to 352 in 1970), more than 20,000 Americans perished in Vietnam during the last four years of the war.

Morale fell among those who were left in Vietnam. Having been exposed to the antiwar movement at home, many of these soldiers had less faith in the purpose or value of the war than their predecessors had. In addition to mounting racial tensions among soldiers, more incidents of "fragging" (attacks on officers by enlisted men) occurred than in any previous wars. A government study in 1971 reported that half of the U.S. army personnel sought escape from boredom and horror by smoking marijuana, and one-fourth used heroin, opium, and other drugs.

While reducing the U.S. presence in Vietnam, Nixon and Kissinger also endeavored to capitalize on Soviet interest in expanded trade and arms reductions by linking U.S. goals in Vietnam with Soviet concerns elsewhere. However, their breakthroughs in summit diplomacy with the Soviet Union and China (discussed in Chapter 30) failed to change the course of the war. Little that the Soviet Union or China could or would do deterred the Communist leaders in Vietnam from pursuing their twenty-year-old goal of unification and national independence.

Nor did intensification of force achieve its objective. Echoing Johnson, Kissinger believed that a "fourth-rate power like North Vietnam" had to have a "breaking point," but the hundreds of thousands of tons of bombs delivered by U.S. pilots failed to find it. Fierce application of American power bought time, but little else. (See "The Promise of Technology," page 1084.) The bombing only further inflamed passions at home, and the antiwar movement plagued the Nixon administration through 1971.

Nixon's War

In the spring of 1969, Nixon began a fierce air war in Cambodia, carefully hiding it from Congress and the public for more than a year. Designed to knock out North Vietnamese sanctuaries in Cambodia, from which the enemy launched attacks on South Vietnam, the campaign dropped more than 100,000 tons of bombs but succeeded only in sending the North Vietnamese to other hiding places. To support a new, pro-Western Cambodian government installed through a military coup in 1970 and "to show the enemy that we were still serious about our commitment in Vietnam," in

U.S. Invasion of Cambodia, 1970

April 1970 Nixon ordered a joint U.S.-ARVN invasion of Cambodia.

That order made Vietnam "Nixon's war" and provoked outrage at home. Nixon made a belligerent speech announcing his move, which he called an "incursion" because the Cambodian government acquiesced in it. He concluded by emphasizing the importance of U.S. credibility: "If when the chips are down, the world's most powerful nation acts like a pitiful helpless giant, the forces of totalitarianism and anarchy will threaten free nations . . . throughout the world."

"This will make the students puke," a cabinet member said when he read Nixon's speech. They did more. A protest in Washington drew upward of 100,000 people, and students demonstrated and boycotted classes on hundreds of campuses. At Kent State University in Ohio, where protesters had burned an ROTC building, the governor called out National Guard troops. At a peaceful rally on May 4, 1970, nervous troops fired at students, killing four and wounding ten others. "They're starting to treat their own children like they treat us," commented a black woman in Harlem. In a confrontation at Jackson State College in Mississippi on May 14, police shot into a dormitory, killing two black students. In August, a national Chicano antiwar rally held in Los Angeles erupted in violence when police used clubs and tear gas against the protesters.

Upon learning of the secret bombing and invasion of Cambodia, furious legislators attempted to curb the president. The Senate voted to terminate the Gulf of Tonkin Resolution, which had given the president virtually a blank check in Vietnam, and to cut off funds for the Cambodian operation. The House of Representatives refused to go along, but Congress was clearly becoming an obstacle to the Nixon administration's plans. By the end of June, Nixon pulled out all U.S. soldiers from Cambodia. But the following year, the United States supported an ARVN invasion of Laos (see Map 28.2).

The invasion of Cambodia failed to break the will of the North Vietnamese, but it set in motion a terrible tragedy for the Cambodian people. The North Vietnamese moved farther into Cambodia and increased their support of the Khmer Rouge, an organization of Communist insurgents attempting to overthrow the U.S.-supported government of Lon Nol. A brutal civil war lasted until 1975, when the Khmer Rouge triumphed and imposed a savage rule, slaughtering millions of Cambodians and

The Military Helicopter

REFLECTING ON HOW THE VIETNAM WAR would have been fought without helicopters, General William C. Westmoreland concluded, "We would have been fighting a different war, for a smaller area, at a greater cost, with less effectiveness." Waging war in Vietnam without helicopters, he maintained, would have been like fighting Hitler's army in Europe without tanks.

It took more than three decades after the first successful airplane flight for engineers to develop an aircraft that could take off and land vertically, move in any direction, and remain stationary in the air. The man frequently identified as the inventor of the helicopter in the United States, Russian engineer Igor Sikorsky, developed two helicopters in 1909 and 1910, but neither succeeded. After the Russian Revolution of 1917, Sikorsky emigrated to the United States and organized a company that produced airplanes, while he continued to work on the helicopter. German engineers produced the first practical helicopter in 1936, but the United States was not far behind.

As was true of much new technology in the twentieth century, federal dollars supported research and development. In 1938, Congress first appropriated funds to develop the helicopter, and Sikorsky and his associates produced the first helicopter for the Army Air Corps in 1942. During World War II, the United States used helicopters for some rescue operations in the Pacific theater, and Germany used them for artillery spotting and reconnaissance. The American military employed helicopters for medical evacuations in Korea, but not until manufacturers replaced piston engines with smaller, lighter gas-turbine engines did helicopters play a central role in military operations.

Although the army developed its plans for the use of helicopters in the 1950s within the context of nuclear warfare, once the United States began to assist with military operations of the South Vietnamese, the helicopter became a central feature of the war. The particular nature of the conflict in Vietnam—the guerrilla tactics of the enemy, the conduct of fighting all over South Vietnam rather than across a fixed battlefront, and the mountains and dense jungles, with limited landing areas—put a premium on the helicopter's mobility and maneuverability. Already in December 1961, long before U.S. troops actually saw combat in Vietnam, the army employed thirty-two of its helicopters to transfer some one thousand South Vietnamese paratroopers for an attack on suspected Vietcong headquarters.

The UH-1 Iroquois (known as "Huey") was the most widely used helicopter; thousands of them carried infantry units all over South Vietnam. One marine commented that "we commuted to and from the war," though it was hardly an ordinary commute when helicopters had to land in the midst of enemy fire. Choppers also transported artillery and ammunition, performed reconnaissance, picked up downed pilots, and evacuated the dead and wounded. Mounted with machine guns and grenade launchers, helicopters served as attack vehicles. The largest, the CH-47 ("Chinook"), could carry thirty-three soldiers or considerable amounts of cargo and even rescue smaller downed aircraft. Chinooks also dropped two and a half tons of napalm on the enemy in just one delivery.

Helicopters enabled military personnel to receive unprecedented support. In Vietnam it was not unusual for American soldiers in the field to be provided with hot meals rather than cold C rations. More important was the medical evacuation helicopter, called the "Dust-off," which could hoist to safety injured soldiers without touching land. Most of those wounded in Vietnam were promptly evacuated to hospitals, and those with grave injuries were sped to base facilities in the Pacific region or the United States. The improvements in medical evacuation, combined with advances in medicine, helped to raise the ratio of surviving wounded to dead to 6:1, in contrast to a World War II ratio of 2.6:1. So central were helicopters to a soldier's experience that, one man noted, "When the helicopters flew off, a feeling of abandonment came over us."

HELICOPTERS IN VIETNAM

This helicopter brings ammunition in 1968 to U.S. soldiers in Khe Sanh, in the far north-west region of South Vietnam. Before and during the Tet Offensive, thousands of North Vietnamese forces surrounded and shelled the garrison of six thousand Marines, making the ability to supply Khe Sanh from helicopters essential. This photo was taken by Larry Burrows, who died three years later during the invasion of Laos. The helicopter in which he and three other well-known combat photographers were traveling exploded after being hit by a North Vietnamese anti-aircraft gun.

Photograph by Larry Burrows, *Life* magazine © 1968 Time, Inc.

Journalists hitched rides on helicopters "like taxis" to see the war firsthand. Michael Herr, who wrote for *Esquire* and other magazines, flew on hundreds of them, remembering "choppers rising straight out of small cleared jungle spaces, wobbling down onto city rooftops, cartons of rations and ammunition thrown off, dead and wounded loaded on. Sometimes they were so plentiful and loose that you could touch down at five or six places a day."

The massive use of helicopters, of course, failed to defeat the enemy in Vietnam. Although air mo-bility played a key role in the successes that the U.S. and South Vietnamese armies did achieve, it could not win the war alone. In the words of one military adviser, "After all, when you come to think of it, the use of helicopters is a tacit admission that we don't control the ground. And in the long run, it's control of the ground that wins or loses the war." Helicopters remained important to the very end of the U.S. presence in Vietnam. As Saigon fell to the Communists in 1975, choppers carried the last Americans out of danger.

giving the name "killing fields" to the land of this historically peaceful people.

In 1971, Vietnam veterans themselves became a visible part of the peace movement. Although Vietnam Veterans Against the War never numbered more than about twenty-five thousand, these were the first men in U.S. history to oppose a war in which they had fought. Veterans held a public investigation of "war crimes" in Vietnam, rallied in front of the Capitol, and cast away their war medals. In May 1971, veterans numbered among the forty thousand protesters who engaged in civil disobedience in an effort to shut down Washington. Officials made more than twelve thousand arrests, which courts later ruled violations of protesters' rights.

After the spring of 1971, there were fewer massive antiwar demonstrations, but vehement protest continued. Public attention focused on the court-martial of Lieutenant William Calley, which began in November 1970 and resulted in his conviction.

During the trial, Americans learned that Calley's company had massacred more than four hundred civilians in the hamlet of My Lai in March 1968. Among those murdered were children and women, an atrocity that the military had covered up for more than a year.

Although Vietnam Veterans Against the War never numbered more than about twenty-five thousand, these were the first men in U.S. history to oppose a war in which they had fought.

Administration policy suffered another blow in June 1971 with publication of the *Pentagon Papers*, a secret, critical government study of U.S. policy in Vietnam. While working as an aide to Henry

MY LAI MASSACRE
When U.S. forces attacked the village of My Lai in March 1968, they believed that it was a Vietcong stronghold and expected a fierce fight. Even though they encountered no enemy forces, the men of Charlie Company systematically killed every inhabitant, nearly all of whom were old men, women, and children. Estimates put the death toll at more than 400 villagers. Twelve officers and enlisted men were charged with murder or assault to commit murder, but only one, First Lieutenant William Calley, was convicted. Though he was convicted of premeditated murder, Calley was paroled after serving less than four years in prison. This photograph of murdered villagers was taken by an army photographer.
Ron Haeberle, *Life* magazine © Time, Inc.

Kissinger, Daniel Ellsberg, who had previously served as a civilian adviser in Vietnam, came across the documents. Convinced that the war was futile and frustrated in his attempts to persuade officials of his view, Ellsberg copied the papers and gave them to the *New York Times*. Administration efforts to prevent publication of the papers were defeated by the Supreme Court as a violation of freedom of the press.

Ellsberg then became another victim of Nixon's obsession to punish his enemies. Instructed by the president to do anything to discredit Ellsberg, a group of men hired by Nixon aides broke into the office of Ellsberg's psychiatrist, stole confidential records, and leaked them to the press. Although these actions escaped public notice until 1973, the *Pentagon Papers* spurred disillusionment with the war by casting doubts on the government's credibility. More than 60 percent of respondents to a public opinion poll in 1971 considered it a mistake to have sent American troops to Vietnam; 58 percent believed the war to be immoral (see Figure 28.2).

The Peace Accords and the Fall of Saigon

Throughout 1972, Nixon and Kissinger continued to pursue a combined strategy of military force and negotiation. In March, responding to a strong North Vietnamese offensive, the United States resumed sustained bombing of the north, mined Haiphong and other harbors for the first time, and announced a naval blockade. With peace talks stalled in December 1972, Nixon ordered the most devastating bombing of North Vietnam yet: In twelve days, U.S. planes dropped more bombs than they had in all of 1969–1971.

On January 27, 1973, representatives of the United States, North Vietnam, the South Vietnamese government, and the Vietcong (now called the People's Revolutionary Government) signed a formal accord in Paris. The agreement required removal of all U.S. troops and military advisers but allowed North Vietnamese forces to remain in place. Both sides agreed to return prisoners of war, including hundreds of Americans, some of whom had been held since the mid-1960s. The Thieu government continued in power, and the peace treaty allowed the United States a face-saving withdrawal, but it was doubtful that South Vietnam would remain non-Communist for long.

Though the Paris agreement had established a cease-fire, fighting resumed immediately among the

Vietnamese, and the United States continued to bomb Cambodia. Nixon found his efforts to support the South Vietnamese government, and indeed his ability to govern at all, increasingly eroded by revelations of administration wrongdoing that came to be known as the Watergate scandals (discussed in Chapter 29). In June 1973, Congress passed a bill ending all military operations in Laos and Cambodia. The House sustained Nixon's veto, but public opposition compelled the president to stop the bombing.

In 1975, North Vietnam launched a new offensive in South Vietnam, achieving victory in just five months. As South Vietnam neared collapse, Congress approved funds to evacuate Americans and to serve "humanitarian" purposes but refused to authorize any more military aid. On May 1, 1975, Vietcong troops occupied Saigon and renamed it Ho Chi Minh City to honor the Communist leader, who had not lived to see his goal of Vietnamese unification and independence realized.

Confusion, humiliation, and tragedy marked the hasty evacuation of Americans and their South Vietnamese allies. The United States got its own citizens out, along with 150,000 South Vietnamese, but it lacked sufficient aircraft, ships, and time to evacuate all those who wanted to leave. U.S. marines beat back desperate Vietnamese trying to escape through the U.S. embassy. Some South Vietnamese troops, frightened and angry at being left behind, fired on departing Americans.

The Legacy of Defeat

It took Nixon four years to end the war. During that time, twenty thousand more Americans lost their lives, the conflict expanded into Cambodia and Laos, Southeast Asia endured massive bombing campaigns, and, with a Republican president now conducting it, the Vietnam War became genuinely bipartisan. And it was not only Nixon's war. Although increasing numbers of legislators criticized the war, Congress never denied the funds to fight it.

Only after the peace accords did the legislative branch stiffen its constitutional authority over the making of war. In November 1973, Congress enacted the War Powers Act over Nixon's veto. The law required the president to report to Congress within forty-eight hours of deploying military forces in places where hostilities existed or were likely to occur. If Congress failed to endorse the president's action within sixty days, the troops would have to be withdrawn.

EVACUATING SOUTH VIETNAM
As Communist troops rolled south toward Saigon in the spring of 1975, desperate South Vietnamese attempted to flee along with the departing Americans. Here an American official punches a man trying to board an already overloaded plane leaving Nha Trang on April 1. Thousands of Vietnamese who wanted to be evacuated were left behind—but not South Vietnamese President Nguyen Van Thieu, who escaped with fifteen tons of baggage on a U.S. plane to Taiwan.
Corbis-Bettmann.

Defeat in Vietnam did not become a subject of partisan political debate. Most Americans wanted simply to forget the war. Moreover, the dire predictions of three presidents did not materialize. The Communist victory in South Vietnam did not set the dominoes cascading. Although Vietnam, Laos, and Cambodia all fell within the Communist camp in the spring of 1975, Thailand, Burma, Malaysia, and the rest of Southeast Asia did not. When China and Vietnam soon reverted to their historical relationship of hostility, the myth of a monolithic Communist power overrunning Asia evaporated.

Veterans and those who lost loved ones could not so easily put the war behind them. The nation had always honored its soldiers' sacrifices, but three unique elements of the Vietnam War denied veterans the traditional homecoming: its lack of strong support at home, its character as a guerrilla war,

and its ultimate failure. As one veteran remarked, "The left hated us for killing, and the right hated us for not killing enough."

Because the Vietnam War was in large part a civil, guerrilla war, combat was especially brutal (Table 28.1). The terrors of conventional warfare were multiplied, and so were the opportunities and motivations to commit atrocities. The massacre of civilians by U.S. troops at My Lai was the most publicized war crime, but 9 percent of a sample of veterans in a government study reported that they had committed abusive violence against civilians or prisoners of war. To demonstrate the immorality of the war, peace advocates stressed the atrocities, to which the media also gave substantial coverage in the conflict's later stages. This emphasis on the cruelties contributed to an image of the Vietnam War veteran as dehumanized and

TABLE 28.1
VIETNAM WAR CASUALTIES

United States

Killed in action	47,382
Wounded	153,303
Died, non-combat	1,811
Missing, captured	10,753

South Vietnam

Killed in action	110,357
Military wounded	499,026
Civilians killed	415,000
Civilians wounded	913,000

Communist regulars and guerrillas

Killed in action	666,000

Source: U.S. Department of Defense.

violent and thus deserving of public hostility or indifference.

Veterans largely expressed two kinds of reactions to the defeat. Many felt betrayed; they regarded the commitment as an honorable one and castigated the government for not letting them and their now-dead comrades win the war. Others, sometimes expressing shame or guilt, blamed the government for sacrificing the nation's youth in an immoral or useless war. These soldiers best expressed their sense of the war's futility in the slang term they used in referring to a comrade's death: He was "wasted."

Three unique elements of the Vietnam War denied veterans the traditional homecoming: its lack of strong support at home, its character as a guerrilla war, and its ultimate failure.

"We would not return to cheering crowds, parades, and the pealing of great cathedral bells," wrote Philip Caputo. "We had done nothing more than endure." Most veterans came home to public neglect, while some faced harassment from antiwar activists who did not distinguish the war from the

warriors. A veteran remembered the "feelings of rejection and scorn that a bunch of depressed and confused young men experienced when they returned home from doing what their country told them to do." Government benefits were less generous to Vietnam War veterans than they had been to World War II and Korean War soldiers.

Much more than World War II, the Vietnam War was a men's war, and the 11,500 women who had served there felt even more isolated and ignored by the government, the public, and veterans' groups. Most of the women veterans were nurses. Although they served at much less risk to their lives than did men, they witnessed daily the devastation of young men's bodies. One nurse thought of writing her mother to ask "if she could find one whole eighteen-year-old. I didn't believe we could have any left." It took ten years and participation in a group with other female veterans for army nurse Keith Walker to deal with the nightmares and depression that she took home from Vietnam.

Yet two-thirds of Vietnam veterans said that they would serve again, and most veterans readjusted well to civilian life under difficult circumstances. Others endured the aftereffects of war for decades. The Veterans Administration (VA) estimated that nearly one-sixth of the three million veterans suffered from posttraumatic stress disorder, with its symptoms of fear, recurring nightmares, feelings of guilt and shame, violence, drug and alcohol abuse, and suicidal tendencies. More than fifteen years after the war's end, veterans remained on long waiting lists for treatment.

In the late 1970s, a larger proportion of those who had served in Vietnam than in the general population began to display a different set of symptoms: They produced deformed children and fell ill themselves with cancer, severe skin disorders, and other ailments. Veterans claimed a link between these illnesses and Agent Orange, an herbicide that contained the deadly poison dioxin, which the military had sprayed by the millions of gallons over Vietnam. Scientists disagreed about the chemical's effects on veterans, and not until 1991 did Congress enact legislation extending benefits to veterans with diseases linked to Agent Orange.

Reversal of the government's position on Agent Orange coincided with a shift in the climate surrounding Vietnam War veterans. "It wasn't until the early 1980s," one veteran observed, "that it became 'all right' to be a combat veteran." Before then, he had never seen crowds cheer Vietnam veterans who

THE VIETNAM VETERANS MEMORIAL
These Vietnam veterans honor their dead comrades at the memorial in the nation's capital. Many veterans found a healing moment in standing before the wall. As one explained at the memorial's dedication in 1982, they came "to find the names of those we lost in the war, as if by tracing the letters cut into the granite we could find what was left of ourselves."
Peter Marbottom / Magnum Photos, Inc.

marched in Fourth of July parades. The Vietnam War began to enter the realm of popular culture with novels, TV shows, and hit movies depicting a broad range of military experience—from soldiers reduced to brutality to men and women serving with courage and integrity.

The incorporation of the Vietnam War into the collective experience was symbolized most dramatically in the Vietnam Veterans Memorial, designed by Maya Lin and unveiled in Washington, D.C., in November 1982. The black, V-shaped wall inscribed with the names of fifty-eight thousand men and women lost to the war became the second most visited site in the capital, evoking emotional responses from visitors, many of whom adorned it with flowers, flags, messages, and mementos. In an article describing the memorial's dedication, a Vietnam combat veteran spoke to and for his former comrades: "Welcome home. The war is over."

Conclusion: The Limits of American Power

Vietnam was America's longest war. The United States spent $150 billion and sent more than three million of its young men and women to Southeast Asia. Fifty-eight thousand never returned, and 300,000 suffered serious injury. The war shattered consensus at home and contributed to the most severe internal disorder in a century. It not only increased presidential power at the expense of congressional authority and public accountability but also led to the downfall of two presidents.

The Vietnam War was a logical extension of the nation's post–World War II commitment to contain communism everywhere on the planet, a commitment begun when the United States had enjoyed an extraordinary margin of power, largely because

World War II had so ravaged the other major nations. As other nations recovered, the United States lost its artificial and temporary advantage. Defeat in Vietnam did not make the United States the "pitiful helpless giant" predicted by Nixon, but it did suggest the relative decline of U.S. power and the impossibility of containment on a global scale.

One of the constraints on U.S. power was the tenacity of the revolutionary movements that were determined to achieve national independence. Marine lieutenant Philip Caputo recalled the surprise at discovering "that the men we had scorned as peasant guerrillas were, in fact, a lethal, determined enemy." U.S. officials badly underestimated the sacrifices that the North Vietnamese and Vietcong were willing to make for the goal of national liberation. Policymakers overestimated the effectiveness of American technological superiority, and they failed to realize how easily the United States could be perceived as a colonial intruder, no more welcome than the French had been.

A second constraint on Eisenhower, Kennedy, Johnson, and Nixon was their resolve to avoid a major confrontation with the Soviet Union or China. Johnson, who conducted the largest escalation of the war, especially needed to be cautious to avoid provoking direct intervention by the Communist superpowers. After China exploded its first atomic bomb in 1964, the potential heightened for the Vietnam conflict to escalate into worldwide disaster.

Third, in Vietnam the United States faced the problem of containment by means of an extremely weak ally. The South Vietnamese government never won the support of its people, and the intense devastation and suffering the war brought to the civilian population only made things worse. Short of taking over the South Vietnamese government and military, the United States could do little to strengthen South Vietnam's ability to resist communism.

Finally, domestic opposition to the war constrained the options of Johnson and Nixon. From its origin in 1965, the antiwar movement grew to include significant portions of mainstream America by 1968. As the war dragged on, with increasing American casualties and growing evidence of the damage being inflicted on the Vietnamese, more and more civilians wearied of the conflict. Even some who had fought the war joined the movement, including Philip Caputo, who sent his campaign ribbons and a bitter letter of protest to the White House. By 1968, distinguished experts who had fashioned and implemented the containment policy recognized that erosion of support for the war made its continuation untenable. Yet the United States fought on for five more years before Nixon and Kissinger bowed to the resolution of the enemy and the limitations of U.S. power.

www.bedfordstmartins.com/tap SEE THE ONLINE STUDY GUIDE to assess your mastery of the material covered in this chapter.

CHRONOLOGY

1961 CIA-backed Cuban exiles launch unsuccessful invasion of Cuba at Bay of Pigs.

Berlin Wall erected, dividing East and West Berlin.

Kennedy administration increases military aid and military advisers in South Vietnam.

Kennedy administration creates Alliance for Progress and Peace Corps.

1962 Cuban missile crisis results in Soviet removal of missiles in Cuba.

1963 Limited nuclear test-ban treaty signed by United States and Soviet Union.

South Vietnamese military overthrows President Ngo Dinh Diem.

1964 U.S. troops quell anti-American rioting in Panama Canal Zone.

President Johnson uses Gulf of Tonkin incident to get congressional resolution of support for escalating the war.

1965 First major protest demonstration in Washington, D.C., against Vietnam War attracts twenty thousand people.

Johnson administration initiates Operation Rolling Thunder, intensified bombing of North Vietnam.

Johnson orders increase in number of U.S. troops in Vietnam; peak is 543,000 in 1968.

U.S. troops invade Dominican Republic to prevent leftist government from taking power.

1968 Hundreds of thousands of Americans demonstrate against war.

Vietnamese Communists' Tet Offensive leads Johnson administration to reverse its policy in Vietnam and seek negotiated settlement.

In wake of Tet Offensive, President Johnson decides not to seek second term.

Richard Nixon elected president.

1969 Nixon orders secret bombing of Cambodia.

1970 Nixon orders joint U.S.–South Vietnamese invasion of Cambodia.

Students killed by national guard members and police during campus protests at Kent State and Jackson State.

1971 *New York Times* publishes *Pentagon Papers,* a secret, critical government study of U.S. policy in Vietnam.

1973 The Paris accords between the United States, North and South Vietnam, and Vietcong bring formal end to U.S. role in Vietnam.

Congress enacts War Powers Act, limiting president's ability to send Americans to war without congressional consent.

1975 North Vietnam launches final offensive and takes over all of South Vietnam, ending war in Vietnam.

BIBLIOGRAPHY

GENERAL WORKS

David Halberstam, *The Best and the Brightest* (1972).

George C. Herring, *America's Longest War: The United States and Vietnam, 1950–1975* (1986).

Walter A. McDougall, *The Heavens and the Earth: A Political History of the Space Age* (1985).

Kim McQuaid, *The Anxious Years: America in the Vietnam and Watergate Era* (1989).

James S. Olson and Randy Roberts, *Where the Domino Fell: America and Vietnam, 1945–1990* (1996).

Irwin Unger and Debi Unger, *Turning Point: 1968* (1988).

Marilyn B. Young, *The Vietnam Wars, 1945–1990* (1991).

FOREIGN POLICY IN THE 1960s

William Bundy, *A Tangled Web: The Making of Foreign Policy in the Nixon Presidency* (1998).

Elizabeth Cobbs Hoffman, *All You Need Is Love: The Peace Corps and the Spirit of the 1960s* (1998).

Walter Isaacson, *Kissinger: A Biography* (1992).

Charles Murray and Catherine Bly Cox, *Apollo: The Race to the Moon* (1989).

James A. Nathan, ed., *The Cuban Missile Crisis Revisited* (1992).

Keith L. Nelson, *The Making of Détente: Soviet-American Relations in the Shadow of Vietnam* (1995).

Thomas G. Paterson, ed., *Kennedy's Quest for Victory: American Foreign Policy, 1961–1963* (1989).

Gerald T. Rice, *The Bold Experiment: JFK's Peace Corps* (1986).

Robert D. Schulzinger, *Henry Kissinger: Doctor of Diplomacy* (1989).

D. Michael Shafe, *Deadly Paradigms: The Failure of U.S. Counterinsurgency Policy* (1988).

Deborah Shapley, *Promise and Power: The Life and Times of Robert McNamara* (1993).

Robert Smith Thompson, *The Missiles of October: The Declassified Story of John F. Kennedy and the Cuban Missile Crisis* (1992).

Mark J. White, *Missiles in Cuba: Kennedy, Khrushchev, Castro, and the 1962 Crisis* (1997).

THE UNITED STATES AND LATIN AMERICA

Graham T. Allison, *Essence of Decision: Explaining the Cuban Crisis* (1971).

Trumbull Higgins, *The Perfect Failure: Kennedy, Eisenhower, and the CIA at the Bay of Pigs* (1987).

Jerome Levinson and Juan de Onis, *The Alliance That Lost Its Way* (1970).

Abraham Lowenthal, *The Dominican Intervention* (1972).

Thomas G. Paterson, *Contesting Castro: The United States and the Triumph of the Cuban Revolution* (1994).

THE WAR IN VIETNAM

David L. Anderson, *Shadow on the White House: Presidents and the Vietnam War* (1993).

Loren Baritz, *Backfire: A History of How American Culture Led Us into Vietnam and Made Us Fight the Way We Did* (1985).

Larry Berman, *Lyndon Johnson's War: The Road to Stalemate in Vietnam* (1989).

Robert Buzzanco, *Masters of War: Military Dissent and Politics in the Vietnam Era* (1996).

Mark Clodfelter, *The Limits of Air Power: The American Bombing of North Vietnam* (1989).

Bernard Fall, *The Two Vietnams: A Political and Military Analysis* (1967).

Frances FitzGerald, *Fire in the Lake: The Vietnamese and the Americans in Vietnam* (1972).

Lloyd C. Gardner, *Pay Any Price: Lyndon Johnson and the Wars for Vietnam* (1995).

James William Gibson, *The Perfect War: Technowar in Vietnam* (1986).

Allan E. Goodman, *The Lost Peace: America's Search for a Negotiated Settlement of the Vietnam War* (1978).

Ellen J. Hammer, *A Death in November: America in Vietnam, 1973* (1987).

Michael H. Hunt, *Lyndon Johnson's War: America's Cold War Crusade in Vietnam* (1996).

Arnold R. Isaacs, *Without Honor: Defeat in Vietnam and Cambodia* (1983).

Arnold R. Isaacs, *Vietnam Shadows: The War, Its Ghosts, and Its Legacy* (1997).

David Kaiser, *Kennedy, Johnson, and the Origins of the Vietnam War* (2000).

Stanley Karnow, *Vietnam: A History* (1983; rev. ed., 1991).

Gabriel Kolko, *Anatomy of a War: Vietnam, the United States, and the Modern Historical Experience* (1985).

Guenter Lewy, *America in Vietnam* (1978).

Michael Lind, *Vietnam, the Necessary War: A Reinterpretation of America's Most Disastrous Military Conflict* (1999).

Fredrik Logevall, *Choosing War: The Lost Chance for Peace and the Escalation of War in Vietnam* (1999).

Robert S. McNamara, *In Retrospect: The Tragedy and Lessons of Vietnam* (1995).

Robert S. McNamara, et al., *Argument without End: In Search of Answers to the Vietnam Tragedy* (1999).

Harold G. Moore, *We Were Soldiers Once—and Young: Ia Drang, the Battle That Changed the War in Vietnam* (1992).

John M. Newman, *JFK and Vietnam: Deception, Intrigue, and the Struggle for Power* (1992).

John Prados, *The Hidden History of the Vietnam War* (1995).

Jeffrey Record, *The Wrong War: Why We Lost in Vietnam* (1998).

Ronald H. Spector, *After Tet: The Bloodiest Year in Vietnam* (1993).

Roger Warner, *Shooting at the Moon: The Story of America's Clandestine War in Laos* (1997).

THOSE WHO SERVED

Christian G. Appy, *Working-Class War: American Combat Soldiers and Vietnam* (1993).

Lawrence M. Baskir and William A. Strauss, *Chance and Circumstance: The Draft, the War, and the Vietnam Generation* (1978).

Philip Caputo, *A Rumor of War* (1977).

David Donovan, *Once a Warrior King: Memories of an Officer in Vietnam* (1985).

Bernard Edelman, ed., *Dear America: Letters Home from Vietnam* (1985).

Peter Goldman, *Charlie Company: What Vietnam Did to Us* (1983).

Bob Greene, *Homecoming: When the Soldiers Returned from Vietnam* (1989).

Ron Kovic, *Born on the Fourth of July* (1976).

Myra MacPherson, *Long Time Passing: Vietnam and the Haunted Generation* (1984).

Kathryn Marshall, *In the Combat Zone: Vivid Personal Recollections of the Vietnam War from the Women Who Served There* (1987).

Harry Maurer, *Strange Ground: Americans in Vietnam, 1945–1975, an Oral History* (1998).

Steward O'Nan, ed., *The Vietnam Reader* (1998).

Al Santoli, *Everything We Had: An Oral History of the Vietnam War* (1981).

Neil Sheehan, *A Bright Shining Lie: John Paul Vann and America in Vietnam* (1988).

James E. Westheider, *Fighting on Two Fronts: African Americans and the Vietnam War* (1997).

John Wheeler, *Touched with Fire: The Future of the Vietnam Generation* (1984).

THE ANTIWAR MOVEMENT

Charles DeBenedetti, with Charles Chatfield, *An American Ordeal: The Antiwar Movement of the Vietnam Era* (1990).

Adam Garfinkle, *Telltale Hearts: The Origins and Impact of the Vietnam Antiwar Movement* (1995).

Todd Gitlin, *The Whole World Is Watching* (1980).

Andrew E. Hunt, *The Turning: A History of Vietnam Veterans Against the War* (1999).

Rhodri Jeffreys-Jones, *Peace Now! American Society and the Ending of the Vietnam War* (1999).

Thomas Powers, *Vietnam: The War at Home* (1973).

Melvin Small, *Johnson, Nixon, and the Doves* (1988).

Melvin Small and William D. Hoover, eds., *Give Peace a Chance: Exploring the Vietnam Antiwar Movement* (1992).

Amy Swerdlow, *Women Strike for Peace: Traditional Motherhood and Radical Politics in the 1960s* (1993).

Michael Useem, *Conscription, Protest, and Social Conflict: The Life and Death of a Draft Resistance Movement* (1983).

Nancy Zaroulis and Gerald Sullivan, *Who Spoke Up? American Protest against the War in Vietnam* (1984).

DOMESTIC POLITICS

Dan T. Carter, *The Politics of Race: George Wallace, the Origins of the New Conservatism, and the Transformation of American Politics* (1995).

David Halberstam, *The Unfinished Odyssey of Robert Kennedy* (1969).

Stephan Lesher, *George Wallace: American Populist* (1994).

David Rudenstine, *The Day the Presses Stopped: A History of the* Pentagon Papers *Case* (1996).

Jonathan Schell, *The Time of Illusion* (1976).

Theodore H. White, *The Making of the President, 1968* (1970).

Jules Witcover, *85 Days: The Last Campaign of Robert Kennedy* (1969).

THE ECONOMICS AND POLITICS OF CONFIDENCE
This sculpture of a bull sits on Wall Street, in the southern section of Manhattan and the financial heart of the United States, where the New York Stock Exchange, investment banks, the Federal Reserve Bank, and other financial institutions are located. In contrast to the bear, which symbolizes a declining stock market, the bull stands for investors' confidence that stock prices will continue to rise, as they did so remarkably in the 1980s and 1990s. President Ronald Reagan's ability to inspire the American people's confidence in their nation as well as its economy helped enormously in his drive to reverse the liberal direction that national politics had taken in the 1960s.

Gary Gabino / Sipa Press.

RETREAT FROM LIBERALISM 29

1968–2000

F RANKLIN DELANO REAGAN" headlined the *New York Times* editorial on Ronald Wilson Reagan's acceptance speech at the 1980 Republican convention. The presidential nominee had repeatedly quoted Roosevelt, all the while promising to reduce drastically the federal government's role in American life. Once in the White House, Reagan promptly rehung a portrait of President Calvin Coolidge—that staunch Republican believer in the virtues of big business—but he continued to grasp the mantle of Roosevelt even as his policies formed the antithesis of New Deal liberalism.

Reagan was able to pull off his identification with Roosevelt by quoting selectively and by emphasizing Roosevelt's early advocacy of government retrenchment and frugality. Reagan genuinely admired Roosevelt's dynamism and his optimism about the nation's future. But Reagan's invocation of Franklin Roosevelt also made for good politics, bolstering his appeal to traditional Democrats, who had given substantial support to George Wallace and Richard Nixon in the late 1960s. It served as well to reconcile Reagan's own history—he had once been an active Democrat and ardent Roosevelt supporter—with his present conservative Republicanism.

Reagan assumed the presidency after a decade of instability in that institution. Although Richard Nixon won reelection in a landslide victory in 1972, just two years later he resigned the office in disgrace. His successor, Gerald Ford, occupied the Oval Office for little more than two years, losing his bid for a full term, when Jimmy Carter led the Democrats back into the White House in the 1976 election. After a single term, Carter, too, was voted out of office. This rapid turnover in the presidency reflected in part a widespread loss of trust and confidence in government, expressed cynically by some Americans whose bumper stickers exhorted, "Don't vote. . . . It only encourages them." Turnout at the polls declined to just 52.3 percent in 1980, as public opinion reported a drop from 56 to 29 percent in citizens' belief that government would "do what is right most of the time."

Nixon's moral failings and Ford's and Carter's weak leadership contributed to the demise of all three, but changes in the institutions of politics and government along with new domestic and foreign challenges created obstacles that might well have defeated more talented politicians. In reaction to the expansion of presidential power by Johnson and Nixon, Congress determined to reassert its authority, yet at the same time it undercut the position of congressional party leaders. Political parties further lost influence as primary elections replaced conventions as the vehicle for nominating candidates and elected officials depended less on party support and relied more on campaign funds from special interest groups. This fragmented leadership in turn confronted critical economic problems as rising unemployment, declining productivity, and spiraling inflation replaced the rapid economic growth of the 1960s.

While restoring national optimism and presiding over an economic upturn, Reagan also sought to effect a revolution in domestic policy as striking as Roosevelt's in extent—while opposite in kind—and a new national political alignment as dominant and lasting as Roosevelt's New Deal coalition. To this end he cultivated a conservative movement that had grown through the 1970s and pursued policies to limit the role of the federal government in regulating the economy and providing for the disadvantaged. His vice president George Bush maintained the Republican hold on the White House for four more years but lost to Democrat William Jefferson Clinton in 1992.

Even though Reagan and Bush failed to achieve for the Republican Party the dominance enjoyed by the Democrats from the 1930s through the 1960s or policy changes equivalent to those of the New Deal, they did contribute mightily to moving the entire political spectrum to the right. Their successor, Bill Clinton, presented himself as a "New Democrat" and left a record in domestic policy of incremental reforms along with an abandonment of New Deal welfare policy. The Republicans' control of Congress and Clinton's own limitations, especially his recklessness in personal relations, limited the accomplishments of his administration, but that record above all reflected a development that began with Jimmy Carter, the Democratic Party's retreat from the liberalism of the 1960s. And when the 2000 elections delivered the White House to George W. Bush, son of the former president, and produced a closely divided Congress, national politics seemed likely to remain on center ground.

Politics and the Persistence of Reform in the Nixon Administration

Richard Nixon took his victory in 1968 as evidence that most Americans were fed up with social protest and government efforts to expand individual rights and opportunities and to provide for the disadvantaged. He continued to appeal to those frustrations, and the pace of reform slackened during his administration. Yet Nixon had won the Republican nomination as a centrist, and two newer reform movements—feminism and environmentalism—exerted pressures that the president could not ignore. In contrast to his public rhetoric, his adminis-

tration pursued a domestic agenda that sometimes bore marks of the very government activism that the president decried in his speeches. Nixon's domestic policies grew out of political expediency, a Democratic Congress representing a broad spectrum of political positions, the president's eye on his place in history, and serious economic problems. Nixon sustained many of the reforms of the 1960s and even expanded the government's role.

Nixon's "Southern Strategy" and Race Relations

Nixon's 1968 campaign had exploited antipathy to black protest and new civil rights policies in order to woo white southerners away from the Democratic Party. This "southern strategy" won Nixon the electoral votes of the Upper South, and Republicans hoped to make further inroads into traditional Democratic strongholds in the 1972 election by appealing to whites who thought racial progress had gone far enough. Thus the president's public rhetoric and policy proposals sought to slow the momentum of racial change and reap the political benefits of the white backlash.

Yet the Nixon administration had to answer to the courts and Congress. In 1968, fourteen years after the *Brown* decision, school desegregation had barely touched the South: Two-thirds of African American children did not have a single white schoolmate. Nixon wanted a freedom-of-choice approach that forbade discrimination but did not use federal power to compel integration. Nonetheless, when the Supreme Court overruled efforts by the Justice Department to delay court-ordered desegregation, in 1969 the administration was compelled to enforce the law. By the time Nixon left office, fewer than one in ten southern black children attended totally segregated schools.

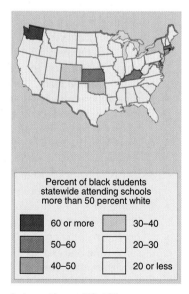

Percent of black students statewide attending schools more than 50 percent white

■ 60 or more
▨ 50–60
▧ 40–50
▥ 30–40
□ 20–30
□ 20 or less

Integration of Public Schools, 1968

School segregation was widespread also in northern and western cities, where segregated residential patterns left half of all African American children attending virtually all-black schools. By 1971, busing students between white and black neighborhoods to achieve desegregation had become one of the most inflammatory civil rights issues. That year, in *Swann v. Charlotte-Mecklenburg Board of Education*, the Supreme Court ruled unanimously that busing was an appropriate remedy to overcome segregation previously sanctioned by the city. Subsequently, federal courts approved busing plans in cities that had not officially maintained segregated schools but whose residential patterns resulted in segregation.

School segregation was widespread also in northern and western cities, where segregated residential patterns left half of all African American children attending virtually all-black schools.

Court-ordered busing for racial integration provoked outrage. When busing began at the formerly all-white South Boston High School in 1974, virtually all the white students boycotted classes while angry white crowds threw rocks at black students. The whites most affected came from working-class families, who remained in cities abandoned by more affluent whites and who felt overlooked as governments provided benefits to minorities and the poor. Moreover, white children rode buses to predominantly black schools where overcrowding and deficient facilities often meant inferior education. African Americans themselves were divided over the desirability of busing children across district lines. Nixon failed to persuade Congress to end court-ordered busing, but after he had appointed four new justices, the Supreme Court moved in the president's direction in 1974. In a five-to-four decision concerning the Detroit public schools (*Milliken v. Bradley*), the Court imposed strict limits on the use of busing to achieve racial balance.

Despite Nixon's conservative rhetoric and practice, his administration did take some steps against discrimination, requiring contractors and unions to employ more minority workers on federally funded construction projects and awarding more government contracts and loans to minority businesses. Congress took the initiative in other areas, in 1970 extending the Voting Rights Act of 1965 by five years. In March 1972, Congress strengthened the Civil Rights Act of 1964 by enlarging the jurisdiction

SCHOOL BUSING
Controversy over busing as a means to integrate public schools erupted in Boston when the school year started in autumn 1974. Opposition was especially high in white ethnic neighborhoods like South Boston, whose residents resented liberal judges from the suburbs assigning them the burden of integration. Clashes between blacks and whites in South Boston prompted authorities to dispatch police to protect black students.
Ira Wyman.

and authority of the Equal Employment Opportunity Commission, the act's enforcement agency.

Nixon believed that the Supreme Court under Chief Justice Earl Warren had been "unprecedentedly politically active . . . too often using their interpretation of the law to remake American society according to their own social, political, and ideological precepts." Through his judicial appointments, Nixon planned both to reverse the Court's direction and to implement his southern strategy. When Warren resigned in June 1969, Nixon replaced him with Warren E. Burger, a federal appeals court judge, who was seen as a more conservative, strict construction-ist. Because that approach narrowly interprets the original aims of the Constitution's authors, it limits the government's power to protect individual rights.

When Nixon tried to appoint two conservative southern judges, however, the Senate forced him to settle on more moderate candidates. The Burger Court proved more sympathetic to the president's agenda, restricting somewhat the protections of indi-vidual rights that the Warren Court had established. Yet it continued to uphold social reform, expanding the rights of welfare recipients and issuing decisions that favored victims of race and sex discrimination.

The Burger Court's approach to affirmative ac-tion reflected the middle ground it occupied. In *Re-gents of the University of California v. Bakke* (1978), the sharply divided justices ruled in favor of a white man who had been denied admission to a Univer-sity of California medical school even though his test scores were higher than those of some minor-ity applicants who were admitted. Yet the Court sanctioned affirmative action programs to attack the results of past discrimination as long as strict quo-tas or racial classifications were not involved.

The New Feminism

In contrast to the declining influence of civil rights advocates, a newer movement won significant gains in the 1970s. On August 26, 1970, fifty years after women won the right to vote, tens of thousands of women took to the streets. In nationwide protests, called Women Strike for Peace and Equality, they car-ried signs reading "Sisterhood Is Powerful," "Don't Cook Dinner—Starve a Rat Today," and "Don't Iron While the Strike Is Hot." Some of the banners pro-claimed, "The Women of Vietnam Are Our Sisters," and others demanded racial justice. But this time, women placed their own liberation at the forefront.

Feminism in the 1970s spawned hundreds of new organizations, profound shifts in how women perceived themselves and their interests, and revo-lutionary changes in women's status under the law. Women's liberation, the radical wing of feminism, erupted from women's experiences in the civil rights and antiwar movements of the 1960s. Repre-senting feminism's mainstream was the National Organization for Women (NOW), founded in 1966, an outgrowth of the work of President Kennedy's Commission on the Status of Women.

Organized largely by chapters of NOW, the strike reflected the diverse strands that constituted the new feminism of the 1970s. Participants included radical women in jeans and conservatively dressed former suffragists, peace activists and politicians, and a sprinkling of women of color. The strike cen-tered on NOW's three main demands: equality for women in employment and education; child care centers throughout the nation; and women's control over reproduction, including the right to abortion.

In contrast to civil rights, a newer movement won significant gains in the 1970s. This time, women placed their own liberation at the forefront.

Although NOW elected a black president, Aileen Hernandez, in 1970, white middle-class women in the political mainstream provided most of the national leadership and much of the con-stituency for the new feminism. They were criti-cized for their frequent indifference to the concerns of women who were unlike themselves, yet support for feminism was exceedingly multifaceted. Most African American women worked through their own groups such as the older National Council of Negro Women and the National Black Feminist Or-ganization, founded in 1973. Similarly, in the early 1970s American Indian women and Mexican Amer-ican women founded national organizations, and Asian American women formed their own local movements. Blue-collar women organized the Na-tional Coalition of Labor Union Women in 1974, and clerical workers founded 9to5. Lesbians established collectives throughout the country as well as their own caucuses in organizations such as NOW. Women formed a host of other groups that focused on single issues such as health, abortion rights, ed-ucation, and violence against women.

Common threads underlay the great diversity of organizations, issues, and activities. Above all, feminism represented the belief that women were barred from, unequally treated in, or poorly served by the male-dominated public arena, encompassing politics, medicine, law, education, and religion. Feminists challenged traditional norms that identi-fied women primarily as wives and mothers or sex objects, and they sought equality in both the private and public spheres.

The women's movement was an effect more than a cause of women's rising employment, but feminism

TITLE IX AND WOMEN'S SPORTS
The women's swim team of Brown University practice under a sign designating the "respect" women's intercollegiate athletics have won since the passage of Title IX in 1972, which banned gender discrimination in education. Nearly the entire male sports establishment resolutely opposed the law, fearing the diminished funding of football and other highly visible men's sports. Reflecting this opposition, few enforcement efforts were made during the Reagan and Bush administrations, causing women to file lawsuits against several colleges and universities. In the landmark case **Amy Brown et al. v. Brown University,** *decided in 1997, the U.S. Supreme Court let stand a lower-court decision that Brown University violated Title IX when it eliminated women's gymnastics and volleyball in 1991. Women's athletics flourished during the 1990s, so that the number of participants quadrupled from 31,000 when Title IX was passed to more than 120,000 in the late 1990s. Although the American public tends to think of athletics when they hear the term Title IX, the law applies to every aspect of education and has promoted greater equity in admissions, scholarships, housing, and more.*
Irene Perlman.

lifted female aspirations and helped lower barriers to jobs and offices historically monopolized by men. Women made some inroads into skilled crafts and management positions. Between 1970 and 2000, their share of law degrees shot up from 5 percent to nearly 50 percent, and their proportion of medical degrees from less than 10 percent to more than 35 percent. In political officeholding their gains came very slowly. Yet by the 1990s, women constituted more than 10 percent of Congress and held more than 20 percent of all state executive offices and state legislative seats.

Feminist activism produced the most sweeping changes in laws and policies concerning women since the Nineteenth Amendment in 1920 guaranteed women's right to vote. In 1972, Congress passed Title IX of the Education Amendments Act, banning sex discrimination in all aspects of education, such as admissions, athletics, and faculty hiring. Congress also outlawed sex discrimination in the granting of loans in 1974, opened U.S. military academies to women in 1976, and prohibited discrimination against pregnant workers in 1978.

At the state and local levels, radical feminists spoke out about rape and won new laws that forced more humane and just treatment of rape victims by police departments and the legal system. Groups of women set up shelters to provide safety for battered women and their children. Nearly every state passed laws affording greater protection for victims of domestic violence and more effective prosecution of offenders. Feminists pressured state legislatures to end restrictions on abortion, and many testified publicly about their own illegal abortions. In 1973, the Supreme Court issued the landmark *Roe v. Wade* decision, ruling that the Constitution protects the right to abortion and that states cannot prohibit abortion in the early stages of pregnancy. However, later decisions allowed state governments to impose restrictions on that right. Most states, for example, refused to pay for the procedure under Medicaid and other government-financed health programs, making it especially hard for poor women to obtain abortions.

The Court also struck down laws that treated men and women differently in Social Security, welfare benefits, workers' compensation, and military benefits programs. Although the Court refused to adopt the same strict standard for laws differentiating on the basis of sex as it did for those involving race, these and other rulings overturned centuries of law based on women's dependency as daughters, wives, and mothers.

Public opinion polls registered majorities in favor of most feminist goals, yet by the mid-1970s feminism faced a strong countermovement. Its

Legend:
- States that ratified the ERA
- States that did not ratify the ERA
- States that ratified and then rescinded ratification

MAP 29.1

The Fight for the Equal Rights Amendment
Many states that failed to ratify the Equal Rights Amendment had previously refused to ratify the woman suffrage amendment (or ratified it decades later, as did North Carolina in 1971).

READING THE MAP: How many states ratified the amendment, and how many did not? Did any regions overwhelmingly support or oppose the ERA?
CONNECTIONS: What was the goal of the ERA? Who were its opponents, and what were their main points of opposition?

www.bedfordstmartins.com/tap SEE THE ONLINE STUDY GUIDE for more help in analyzing this map.

leader, Phyllis Schlafly, had built her political career in the right-wing politics of fervent anticommunism and opposition to big government and social welfare programs. In the 1970s, Schlafly and other conservatives broadened their program to include a defense of conventional sex roles and the traditional family.

Antifeminism achieved its greatest victory in blocking ratification of an Equal Rights Amendment (ERA) to the Constitution that would outlaw differential treatment of men and women under all state and federal laws. Initially proposed by a small band of feminists in 1923, the ERA rode through Congress in 1972 on the wave of the new feminism. Most states rushed to ratify the amendment; yet by 1973, Schlafly and other conservative politicians, as well as a host of women at the grassroots level who feared a breakdown of traditional gender roles, had begun to organize massive resistance. When the time limit on ratification ran out in 1982, only thirty-five states had ratified the amendment, three short of the necessary three-fourths majority (Map 29.1). (See "Historical Question," page 1104.)

Opposition to the right to abortion was even more intense. Many Americans believed that human life begins with conception, and they equated abortion with murder. The Catholic Church and other religious organizations provided institutional support for their protest. Right-wing politicians and their supporters constituted another segment of the right-to-life movement. Like opponents of the ERA, the right-to-life movement mobilized thousands of women who believed that abortion devalued motherhood and saw feminism as a threat to their traditional roles.

Feminists faced a host of other challenges. For example, despite the inroads women made into male-dominated occupations, most women still worked in traditionally female jobs with low pay scales. Moreover, employed women continued to bear primary responsibility for the care of their homes and families, thereby working a "double day." As the number of female-headed families doubled from 10 percent to 20 percent of all American families by the end of the century, the situation of employed mothers became even more critical.

A New Movement to Save the Environment

Feminists were not the only activists to call attention to a new set of issues in the 1970s. In April 1970,

millions of Americans observed the first Earth Day to register their concern over the ravaging effects of industrial development on the environment. In Wisconsin, students distributed flyers on recycling, and a group of Detroit women picketed a steel plant that discharged industrial waste into a river. Girl Scouts cleaned garbage from the Potomac River, Berkeley citizens attended an environmental teach-in, and African Americans in St. Louis dramatized the effects of poisons in lead paint. Some students in Michigan smashed a Ford to protest auto emissions, and people planted trees all over the country. Inheriting their concern for the natural world from the decades-old conservation movement, the new environmentalists had a far broader agenda. Even more important than preserving portions of the natural world for aesthetic and recreational purposes was protecting human beings, wildlife, and plants from the devastating side effects of industrial development and economic growth—polluted air and water and the spread of deadly chemicals.

Biologist Rachel Carson had first drawn national attention to environmental concerns in 1962 with her best-seller *Silent Spring*, which described the harmful effects of toxic chemicals, particularly the pesticide DDT. Older conservation organizations like the Sierra Club and the Wilderness Society expanded the scope of their concerns, and a host of new organizations arose. In 1971, environmentalists founded Greenpeace, which protested nuclear testing around the world and campaigned to save whales, other ocean animals, and tropical rain forests. Even more militant was Earth First!, created in 1980 and committed to direct action and sabotage of projects injurious to the environment.

Inheriting their concern for the natural world from the decades-old conservation movement, the new environmentalists had a far broader agenda: protecting human beings, wildlife, and plants from the devastating side effects of industrial development and economic growth.

Although President Nixon asserted that the nation must begin "reclaiming the purity of its air, its waters, our living environment," he generally favored economic growth over environmental considerations. He vetoed anti–water-pollution legislation, forcing an override from Congress, and

Why Did the ERA Fail?

THE PROPOSED EQUAL RIGHTS AMENDMENT to the United States Constitution guaranteed briefly and simply that women and men would be treated equally under the law: "Equality of rights under the law shall not be denied or abridged by the United States or by any State on account of sex." Two more short sections provided that Congress would have enforcement powers and that the ERA would take effect two years after ratification. By the 1970s it had become the symbol of the late-twentieth-century women's movement.

Members of a small militant feminist organization, the National Woman's Party, first proposed an equal rights amendment to the Constitution in 1923, but it won little support either in Congress or among the public before the resurgence of feminism in the mid-1960s. In 1968, the National Organization for Women made it a key objective, and armed with support from traditional women's organizations and liberal organizations it began to pressure Congress. The pressure took many forms, including civil disobedience. In early 1970, for example, NOW members disrupted a Senate subcommittee hearing on extending the vote to eighteen-year-olds, demanding that the Senate schedule hearings on the ERA. Initially fearing arrest, according to Wilma Scott Heide, who would become NOW president in 1971, the women soon learned that "we could do almost anything and get away with it . . . they didn't want to make martyrs out of us." Feminists and their allies lobbied Congress, and women in both political parties mobilized a letter-writing campaign, flooding some congressional offices with fifteen hundred letters a month.

Despite opposition in committee hearings, both houses of Congress passed the amendment by overwhelming margins, 354 to 23 in the House and 84 to 8 in the Senate. Within three hours of Senate passage in March 1972, Hawaii rushed to become the first state to ratify. By the end of 1972, 23 states had done so. Public opinion heavily favored ratification, peaking at 74 percent in favor in 1974 and never falling below 52 percent, while the opposition never surpassed 31 percent. Yet, even after Congress ex-

tended the time period for ratification until 1982, the ERA failed. The Constitution requires approval of amendments by three-fourths of the states, and only 35 states ratified, three short of minimum needed (see Map 29.1). Why did a measure with so much congressional and popular support fail?

The ERA encountered well-organized and passionate opposition linked to the growing conservative forces in the 1970s. Opponents ranged from religious organizations, such as the National Council of Catholic Women, to local groups such as HOT-DOGS (Humanitarians Opposed to the Degradation of Our Girls), sponsored by the John Birch Society in Utah. Leading the resistance was Phyllis Schlafly, a strong antifeminist who grew up in St. Louis in a conservative Republican family, earned a master's degree in political science from Radcliffe, worked for conservative causes, and married a wealthy lawyer. While bearing and rearing six children, Schlafly ran for Congress from Alton, Illinois, published books, lectured, headed the Illinois Federation of Republican Women, and worked for Barry Goldwater's presidential campaign of 1964. In 1967, she began publishing a newsletter, *The Phyllis Schlafly Report*, from which in 1972 she launched her attack on the ERA.

Conservatives' opposition to the ERA reflected in part their traditional distaste for big government and their demand for a strong defense system to counter communism. Schlafly predicted that the amendment would transfer power from state legislatures and even from families to the federal government. Putting women in foxholes alongside men, she warned, would surely result from ratification of the ERA and that in turn would weaken the military and make the United States more vulnerable to communism. To a large extent it was this linking of antifeminist goals with issues of long-standing concern to conservatives that made the New Right "new" as it developed a "profamily" focus in the late 1970s.

The strategy of ERA opponents was to raise fears about the effects of the amendment. They could make extravagant arguments because its brevity and simplicity precluded anyone from saying with absolute certainty how courts would interpret it. Senator Samuel James Ervin Jr., nationally known and highly respected for his chairing the Watergate hearings, claimed that the ERA would eliminate laws against rape, require male and female

MARCHING FOR RATIFICATION OF THE ERA
About three thousand marchers parade down Pennsylvania Avenue in Washington, D.C., on August 26, 1977. On the fifty-seventh anniversary of ratification of the Nineteenth Amendment extending the right to vote to women, these advocates expressed their demand for ratification of the Equal Rights Amendment, carrying its words on their banner.
© Bettye Lane © Photo Researchers.

PHYLLIS SCHLAFLY (INSET)
The most prominent antifeminist, Phyllis Schlafly, is shown in her home in Alton, Illinois, in 1987. Despite time-consuming and energetic political activities that involved traveling and speaking all over the country, she insisted on calling herself a housewife. She poses here with a pillow that signals her political aim.
© Bettmann/Corbis.

prisoners to be housed together, and deprive women of alimony and child support. Others claimed that it would legalize homosexual marriages. Overall, the anti-ERA forces emphasized sex differences. By destroying the distinct sex roles on which the family was based, Erwin claimed, ERA would destroy the family and produce "increased rates of alcoholism, suicide, and possible sexual deviation."

Anti-ERA leaders were adept at framing arguments that spoke to many women's religious beliefs and their definitions of their own self-interest. In contrast to feminists who viewed traditional sex roles as constructed by society, anti-ERA men and women believed that they were God given. Evangelical minister and politician Jerry Falwell declared the ERA "a definite violation of holy Scripture" and its "mandate that 'the husband is the head of the wife.'" Many of the ERA opponents were full-time housewives who had no stake in equal treatment in the marketplace and who feared that the amendment would eliminate the duty of men (*Continued*) to support their families. They had entered traditional marriages where, in exchange for raising children and caring for home and husbands, they expected economic support. Schlafly stressed the unfairness of changing the rules in the middle of the game, noting that "ERA does not even include a 'grandmother' clause." Women in both camps recognized the precariousness of economic security; but while feminists wanted to render women self-sustaining, antifeminists wanted men to bear responsibility for their support.

Phyllis Schlafly and other conservative leaders skillfully mobilized women who saw their traditional roles threatened. In October 1972, she established a national movement, STOP (Stop Taking Our Privileges) ERA, so carefully organized that it could respond immediately when action was necessary. Thus when a state legislature began to consider ratification, STOP ERA women deluged legislators with letters and lobbied them personally in state capitals. In Illinois, for example, they gave lawmakers apple pies with notes attached that read: "My heart and my hand went into this dough / For the sake of the family please vote 'no.'" Opponents also brought baby girls to the legislature wearing signs that pled, "Please don't draft me." Another opposition group, Happiness of Womanhood (HOW), presented California legislators with mice bearing the message, "Do you want to be a man or a mouse?" And housewives in North Carolina took home-baked bread to members of the state legislature with notes reading, "To the breadwinners from the breadbakers."

ERA opponents had an easier task than supporters, for all they had to do was to convince a minority of legislators in a minority of states to preserve the status quo. The framers of the Constitution had stacked the odds against revision. Supporters, by contrast, had to persuade a majority of lawmakers in three-quarters of the states that the need to guarantee women equal rights was urgent and that it could not be accomplished without a Constitutional amendment. In addition, in contrast to the suffrage movement, which for decades gradually built up support through local and state campaigns, the ERA forces had concentrated on winning Congress and had done so in less than ten years. Amendment supporters were not prepared for the state campaigns, and the intensity of the opposition took them by surprise. By the time ERA proponents got organized on the state level, the momentum for ratification had already stalled.

Feminists still had to overcome the tendency of men to trivialize women's issues or to take them less seriously than other concerns. For example, when the House initially passed the ERA in 1970, the *New York Times* printed an editorial criticizing it under the title, "The Henpecked House." Conservative syndicated columnist James J. Kilpatrick said the ERA was "the contrivance of a gang of professional harpies" and that Congressmen had voted for it simply to "get these furies off their backs." The very gains feminists made in the 1960s and 1970s also worked against approval of the ERA. Congress had already banned sex discrimination in employment, education, credit, and other areas; and the Supreme Court used the equal protection clause of the Fourteenth Amendment to strike down several state and federal laws that treated men and women differently. Even though the Court did not ban all distinctions based on sex, its decisions made it harder for ERA advocates to demonstrate the urgency of Constitutional revision.

So why did the ERA fail? It failed because a handful of men in a handful of state legislatures voted against it. The shift of just a few votes in states such as Illinois and North Carolina would have meant ratification. Phyllis Schlafly's forces played a key role in the defeat, because men could vote no and take cover behind the many women who opposed it. And those women proved willing to commit time, energy, and money to block ratification because conservative leaders convinced them that the ERA threatened their very way of life.

Feminists did not leave the ERA battle empty-handed, however. The National Organization for Women grew enormously during the struggle for ratification. Thousands of women were mobilized across the political spectrum and participated in the political arena for the first time. Fourteen states passed their own equal rights amendments after 1970. And feminists continued to struggle in the legislative and judicial arenas for the expansion of women's rights, struggles that continued to bear fruit into the twenty-first century.

EARTH DAY
Because of its association with nature and the earth, green was the color
of the environmental movement, and environmentalists called themselves
"greens." These activists leave no doubt about their affiliation at an Earth Day celebration in
New York City in April 1970. The button, a takeoff on the antiwar slogan "Give Peace a
Chance," reflects the continuing impact of the antiwar movement.
Dennis Stock / Magnum Photos, Inc.

www.bedfordstmartins.com/tap   SEE THE ONLINE STUDY GUIDE for more help in analyzing this image.

disregarded objections from environmentalists in pushing Congress to authorize construction of a 789-mile-long pipeline to carry oil across Alaska. Yet in other respects the Nixon administration proved a friend—or at least not an enemy—of the environmental movement. In 1970, Nixon established the Environmental Protection Agency (EPA), charged with enforcing clean air and water policies and regulating pesticides. He also signed the Occupational Safety and Health Act (OSHA), which safeguarded workers against workplace accidents and disease. The strongest measure supported by the Nixon administration was the Clean Air Act of 1970, which set national standards for air quality

and restricted factory and automobile emissions. Twenty years after enactment, no major city met the new standards, but even with lenient enforcement, the Clean Air Act cut the amount of air pollutants by one-third, despite population and economic growth.

Warning of radiation leakage, the potential for accidents, and the hazards of nuclear wastes, environmentalists also targeted nuclear power plants, which by 1977 produced about 11 percent of the country's electricity. The perils of nuclear energy came into dramatic focus in March 1979, when an accident occurred at the Three Mile Island nuclear facility near Harrisburg, Pennsylvania and technicians worked for days to prevent a meltdown of the reactor core. Popular opposition and the great expense of building nuclear plants stalled further development of the nuclear power industry; but antinuclear activism endured as a part of the environmental movement, especially after the explosion of a nuclear reactor and the spread of deadly radiation in Chernobyl, Ukraine, in 1986.

Extending the Welfare State and Economic Regulation

Richard Nixon's second inaugural address in 1973 encapsulated his objections to much of Lyndon Johnson's Great Society: "Government must learn to take less from people so people can do more for themselves." Nixon's words appealed to those he labeled "middle America," people who resented government's apparent disregard for their interests while favoring individuals who they felt lacked the discipline to help themselves. Congress resisted many of Nixon's attacks on antipoverty programs, refusing, for example, to eliminate the Office of Economic Opportunity. Key programs such as Medicare and Medicaid, Head Start, Legal Services, and job training remained intact. At the same time, Nixon blocked congressional initiatives such as the child care bill passed by Congress in 1971, objecting both to the program's $2 billion cost and to its "family-weakening implications."

More significant than the Nixon administration's battle against federal programs was its extension of government assistance to the disadvantaged. The federal budget for social services exceeded defense spending for the first time since World War II. Social Security benefits increased, now required to rise with the cost of living. Subsidies for low-income housing shot up from less than $1 million in 1969 to nearly $3 billion in 1973. A new program provided $1 billion in so-called Pell grants (named for the congressman who sponsored the law) for low-income students to attend college. And in response to growing public attention to undernourishment and concern that the Democrats would capitalize on that issue, Nixon supported a huge expansion of the food stamp program; the number of recipients leapt from 2.5 to 15 million between 1969 and 1974. Nixon also acted contrary to his rhetoric against a growing federal bureaucracy in expanding government controls over the economy. Political pressures impelled him to approve new environmental controls, while economic crises and energy shortages induced him to increase the federal government's power in the marketplace.

Throughout the post–World War II economic boom, the nation's abundant oil deposits, along with access to cheap supplies of Middle Eastern oil, had encouraged the building of large cars, suburban housing developments, and glass-enclosed skyscrapers with no concern for fuel efficiency. The traditional American assumption that energy resources were boundless and the resulting wasteful practices meant that by the 1970s the United States, with just 6 percent of the world's population, consumed one-third of its fuel resources.

In the fall of 1973, the United States faced its first energy crisis when Arab nations, furious at the Nixon administration's support of Israel during the Yom Kippur War, cut off oil shipments to the United States. Nations that did not join the embargo raised prices nearly tenfold. As supplies of oil fell in the winter of 1973–74, long lines formed at gas stations, where prices had nearly doubled, many homes were cold, and some schools had to close. In response, Nixon signed legislation authorizing temporary emergency powers to allocate petroleum and establishing a national fifty-five-mile-per-hour speed limit to save gasoline. By the spring of 1974, the energy crisis had eased, thanks largely to these and other measures, voluntary conservation, a relatively mild winter, and cessation of the Arab oil embargo. But the United States had yet to come to grips with its seemingly unquenchable demand for fuel and its dependence on foreign oil.

Soaring energy prices contributed to the second serious economic problem: a rising cost of living. By 1969, the inflation rate had risen to 7 percent, an enormous increase to Americans used to rates of about 2 percent. By 1970, unemployment had joined inflation as a serious problem. This unprecedented combination of a stagnant economy and inflation soon received the name "stagflation."

Domestic troubles were compounded by the decline of American dominance in the international economy. Having fully recovered from World War II, the economies of Japan and Western Europe grew faster than the economy of the United States in the 1970s. Foreign cars, electronic equipment, and other products competed favorably with American goods throughout the world. In 1971, for the first time in decades, the United States imported more than it exported. Because the amount of dollars in foreign hands exceeded U.S. gold reserves, the nation could no longer back up its currency with gold.

Political considerations helped shape the president's response to these economic problems, a response that diverged from conventional Republican doctrine. With an eye to the 1972 election, Nixon announced a "New Economic Policy" in August 1971. He abandoned the convertibility of dollars into gold, devalued the dollar to make American goods cheaper in foreign markets and thus increase exports, and imposed a 10 percent surcharge on most imports. Nixon also froze wages and prices, thus enabling the government to stimulate the economy without fueling more inflation.

In the short run, these policies worked. Exports surged ahead of imports, inflation subsided, unemployment fell below 5 percent, and Nixon was resoundingly reelected in 1972. Yet the New Economic Policy treated the economy only superficially. The lifting of price and wage controls in 1973, the Arab oil embargo, and rising food prices sent the consumer price index soaring by 11 percent by 1974. Unemployment also crept back up, and Nixon's successor inherited the most severe economic crisis since the depression of the 1930s.

Constitutional Crisis and Restoration

In the 1972 presidential election, Richard Nixon turned his narrow victory of 1968 into a massive landslide, and his approval ratings in the polls neared 70 percent. Less than two years later, Nixon abandoned the presidency in disgrace. His abuse of presidential power and efforts to cover up crimes committed by subordinates betrayed the public trust and forced the first presidential resignation in history.

Nixon's handpicked successor, Gerald Ford, brought to the White House a reputation for decency and openness that helped to restore confidence in the presidency. Ford maintained the basic policy directions set by the Nixon administration, but he faced economic problems even more severe. In 1976, Ford lost the presidency to Democrat Jimmy Carter.

From Triumph to Disgrace: Watergate

Nixon's most spectacular foreign policy initiatives, détente with the Soviet Union and the opening of

relations with China, heightened his prospects for reelection in 1972. Although the war in Vietnam continued, antiwar protests diminished with the decrease in American ground forces and casualties. Nixon's New Economic Policy had temporarily checked both inflation and unemployment, and his attacks on busing and antiwar protesters had solidified his support on the right. At their convention in Miami Beach in August 1972, the Republicans resoundingly renominated Nixon and his vice president, Spiro Agnew.

Senator George S. McGovern of South Dakota defeated a large field of contenders for the Democratic nomination, including New York Representative Shirley Chisholm, the first African American politician to make a serious bid for the presidency. On the right, Governor George Wallace of Alabama won a series of southern primaries as well as those in Michigan and Maryland, but his campaign was cut short when a deranged man shot him, leaving Wallace paralyzed below the waist. Despite winning the nomination easily, McGovern struggled from the outset. When the press reported that his running mate, Thomas Eagleton, had undergone psychiatric treatment for nervous exhaustion and depression during the 1960s, McGovern at first refused to bow to prejudice concerning mental illness. But when he changed his mind and replaced Eagleton, he lost the public's confidence in his judgment, decisiveness, and sincerity. In addition, Republicans portrayed McGovern as an extremist on the left, and he alienated more conservative, traditional Democrats with his call for immediate withdrawal from Vietnam and his pledge to cut $30 billion from the Pentagon's budget.

Nixon received 60.7 percent of the popular vote, carrying every state except Massachusetts in a landslide victory second only to that of Johnson in 1964. Although the Democrats maintained control of the House and Senate, Nixon won a majority of votes among southerners, Catholics, urbanites, and blue-collar workers, all traditionally strong supporters of the Democratic Party. The president had little time to savor his triumph, however, as a series of revelations began to emerge about crimes and misdemeanors that had been committed to ensure the victory.

During the early morning hours of June 17, 1972, five men working for Nixon's reelection campaign crept into Democratic Party headquarters in the Watergate apartment and office complex, just a mile from the White House. Intending to repair a bugging device installed in an earlier break-in, they were discovered and arrested on the scene. In their effort to cover up the connection between those arrested and administration officials, Nixon and his aides set in motion the most serious constitutional crisis since the Civil War, which reporters dubbed "Watergate."

Nixon's abuse of presidential power and his efforts to cover up crimes committed by subordinates betrayed the public trust and forced the first presidential resignation in history.

As the events of Watergate unfolded over the next two years, Americans learned that Nixon and his associates had engaged in a host of other abuses, such as accepting illegal campaign contributions, using so-called dirty tricks to sabotage Democratic candidates, and unlawfully attempting to silence critics of the Vietnam War. Nixon was not the first president to lie to the public or to misuse presidential power. Every president since Roosevelt had enlarged the powers of the presidency, justifying his actions as necessary to protect national security in actual or cold war. This expansion of executive powers, often called the growth of the "imperial presidency," weakened some of the traditional checks and balances on the executive branch and opened the door to abuses.

Certain of Nixon's personality traits—self-righteousness, insecurity, suspiciousness, and a tendency to see opposition to his policies as a conspiracy against him—encouraged him to employ the vast powers of the executive against his enemies. Moreover, Nixon's relationships with most of his

THE WATERGATE COVER-UP UNRAVELS *Political cartoonist Jack Davis drew this cover for* **Time** *magazine. It appeared on April 30, 1973, just a few days after one of the Watergate burglars implicated high officials and Nixon asked for resignations from several members of his staff. The cartoon also makes reference to the disclosure that a taping system automatically recorded conversations in the Oval Office. The aides surrounding Nixon are (clockwise, beginning at top right): Jeb S. Magruder, H. R. Haldeman, John Dean, John Mitchell, Maurice Stans, and James McCord. Magruder, Haldeman, Dean, Mitchell, and others served prison terms for conspiracy, perjury, and other crimes.* Illustration by Jack Davis for *Time* cover, April 30, 1973 / TimePix.

closest aides rested on political calculations rather than on trust and loyalty. These men tried above all to protect themselves, and few would confront him with the truth and the opportunity to save his presidency. Faced with a grand jury investigation, a Senate inquiry, and press reports implicating his former attorney general John Mitchell and presidential aides John W. Dean, John Ehrlichman, and H. R. Haldeman, Nixon decided to act.

In a television address at the end of April 1973, Nixon accepted official responsibility for Watergate but denied any personal knowledge of the break-in or of a cover-up. He also announced the resignations of Dean, Ehrlichman, Haldeman, and Attorney General Richard Kleindienst. In May, he authorized the appointment of an independent special prosecutor, Archibald Cox, to conduct an investigation.

Meanwhile, sensational revelations exploded in the Senate investigating committee, headed by Democrat Samuel J. Ervin of North Carolina. John Dean described White House projects to harass "enemies" through income tax audits and other illegal means and asserted that the president had long known of efforts to cover up the Watergate burglary. The most damaging blow struck when a White House aide disclosed that all conversations in the Oval Office in the White House were taped. Both Cox and the Ervin committee immediately asked for tapes related to Watergate. When Nixon refused to give them up, citing executive privilege and separation of powers, Cox and Ervin took their case to federal district court.

In the midst of the battle for the tapes, more damaging disclosures revealed Nixon's misuse of federal funds and tax evasion. In August 1973, Vice President Agnew was compelled to resign after an investigation revealed that he had taken bribes as governor of Maryland. Although Nixon's choice of House minority leader Gerald Ford of Michigan to succeed Agnew won widespread approval, the vice president's resignation further tarnished the administration.

Nixon continued to hold on to the tapes. On October 19, 1973, he ordered special prosecutor Cox to cease his efforts to obtain them. When Cox refused, Nixon ordered Attorney General Elliot Richardson to fire Cox. Richardson instead resigned, as did William D. Ruckelshaus, second in line at the Justice Department. Finally, the solicitor general, Robert Bork, agreed to carry out the pres-

ident's order. The press called the series of dismissals and resignations the "Saturday night massacre," and 250,000 telegrams condemning Nixon's action flooded the White House. Nixon appointed a new special prosecutor but failed to quell demands that he resign. The president's support in public opinion polls plummeted to 27 percent.

In February 1974, the House of Representatives voted to begin an impeachment investigation. In April, Nixon began to release transcripts of the tapes that he himself had edited. As the public read passages sprinkled with "expletive deleted," the House Republican leader Hugh Scott abandoned his support of the president, calling the transcripts a "deplorable, shabby, disgusting, and immoral performance by all." The transcripts included Nixon's orders to Mitchell and Dean in March 1973: "I don't give a shit what happens. I want you all to stonewall it, let them plead the Fifth Amendment, cover up or anything else, if it'll save it—save the plan."

In July 1974, the House Judiciary Committee began debate over specific charges for impeachment: (1) obstruction of justice, (2) abuse of power, (3) contempt of Congress, (4) unconstitutional waging of war by the secret bombing of Cambodia, and (5) tax evasion and the selling of political favors. While the last two counts failed to get a majority, the committee voted to take the first three charges to the House, where a vote of impeachment seemed certain.

On July 24, a unanimous Supreme Court ordered Nixon to hand over the remaining tapes. Transcripts of new tapes released August 5 sealed his fate, revealing that just six days after the break-in Nixon and Haldeman had discussed manipulating the CIA to hinder the FBI's investigation of the burglary. This evidence was sufficient to persuade even Nixon's staunchest supporters of his guilt.

On August 8, 1974, Nixon announced his resignation to a national television audience. Acknowledging that he had made some incorrect judgments, he insisted that he had always tried to do what was best for the nation. The next morning, Nixon ended a rambling, emotional farewell to his staff with some advice: "Always give your best, never get discouraged, never get petty; always remember, others may hate you, but those who hate you don't win unless you hate them, and then you destroy yourself." Had he but practiced that advice, he might have saved his presidency.

NIXON RESIGNS

Flanked by his wife, daughter, and son-in-law, Richard Nixon becomes the first presi-
dent in American history to resign the presidency. In this televised speech on August 8,
1974, Nixon did not admit guilt, even though tapes of his conversations indicated that
he had obstructed justice, abused his power, and lied. He referred only to mistakes he
had made while trying to govern "in the best interest of the nation." In the decades
after his resignation, he gradually rehabilitated his reputation and became an elder
statesman and foreign-policy advisor. All the living presidents attended his funeral in
1994.

Harry Benson Ltd.

Backlash: The Ford Interregnum

Gerald R. Ford, who had represented Michigan in
the House of Representatives since 1948, had built
a reputation as a conservative party loyalist who
treated opponents with openness and cordiality.
Not a brilliant thinker, Ford was known for his integrity, humility, and dedication to the responsibilities of public office. Most of official Washington
and the American public looked favorably on his
succession as president.

Upon taking office, Ford announced, "Our
long nightmare is over," but he shocked many
Americans one month later when he ended the

particular nightmare of the former president. On
September 8, 1974, Ford granted Nixon a pardon
"for all offenses against the United States which
he . . . has committed or may have committed or
taken part in" during his presidency. In its uni-
versality and its promulgation even before any
charges were filed, it was the most extravagant
presidential pardon ever issued, and it saved
Nixon from nearly certain indictment and trial. It
also provoked a tremendous outcry from Congress
and the public. Capitalizing on the revulsion over
Watergate and the pardon, Democrats made impressive gains in the congressional elections in
November.

Upon taking office, Ford announced, "Our long nightmare is over," but he shocked many Americans one month later when he ended the particular nightmare of the former president.

With the Democrats in control, Congress took steps to guard against the types of abuses revealed in the Watergate investigations. The Federal Election Campaign Act of 1974, for example, established public financing of presidential campaigns, though it failed to stop the ever larger campaign chests that candidates found ways to solicit from interest groups, corporations, labor unions, and wealthy individuals. In 1978, Congress passed an independent counsel law establishing a nonpartisan procedure for the appointment of special prosecutors who could not be fired. The law was used to investigate potential criminal actions by Presidents Reagan and Clinton as well as more than a dozen lesser officials before Congress allowed it to expire in 1998.

Special investigating committees in the House and Senate discovered a host of illegal FBI and CIA activities stretching back to the 1950s. Both agencies had harassed and discredited political dissenters, and the CIA had also made plans to assassinate Fidel Castro and other foreign leaders. In response to these revelations, Ford established new controls on covert operations and Congress created permanent committees to oversee the intelligence agencies. Yet these measures did little to diminish the public cynicism and lack of trust in government that had been developing since the Johnson years and that reflected disgust with Democrats as well as Republicans.

As Ford prepared for the 1976 presidential race, he carried a number of burdens. Underlying weaknesses in the U.S. economy remained: a low rate of growth, higher than normal unemployment, a deficit in foreign trade, and high energy prices tied to dependence on oil from abroad. Ford also faced a major challenge from the Republican right. Former California governor Ronald Reagan charged that Nixon and Ford had allowed the United States to become "number two in a world where it is dangerous—if not fatal—to be second best." Attacking Ford from the right on domestic issues as well, Reagan came close to capturing the nomination.

On the Democratic side, James Earl "Jimmy" Carter Jr., a graduate of the U.S. Naval Academy and former state senator and governor of Georgia, won nomination on the first ballot. Highly intelligent and well-prepared on the issues, the soft-spoken Carter stressed his small-town roots, deep religious commitment, unpretentiousness, and distance from the popularly suspect national government. Although Carter selected liberal senator Walter F. Mondale of Minnesota as his running mate and accepted a platform that affirmed broad goals compatible with traditional Democratic principles, his nomination nonetheless represented a decided rightward turn in the party.

Carter benefited from the Watergate backlash, the economic problems that plagued the Ford administration, the damage that the Reagan challenge had done to Ford, and his own ability to attract votes from the traditional Democratic coalition of blacks, southerners, organized labor, and ethnic groups. Yet his victory over Ford was narrow. Democrats retained substantial margins in the House and Senate, but Carter received just 49.9 percent of the popular vote to Ford's 47.9 percent (Map 29.2).

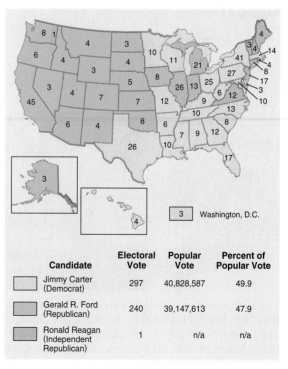

Candidate	Electoral Vote	Popular Vote	Percent of Popular Vote
Jimmy Carter (Democrat)	297	40,828,587	49.9
Gerald R. Ford (Republican)	240	39,147,613	47.9
Ronald Reagan (Independent Republican)	1	n/a	n/a

MAP 29.2
The Election of 1976

The "Outsider" Presidency of Jimmy Carter

Jimmy Carter promised "to help the poor and aged, to improve education, and to provide jobs" but at the same time "not to waste money." He wanted a humane government that would help those in need, but one that also was efficiently managed and prudent in its spending. When these two aims conflicted, especially when inflation threatened economic stability, Carter's commitment to reform took second place. Liberal Democrats accused him of deserting the Democratic reform tradition that stretched back to Franklin Roosevelt.

As president, Carter stressed his status as an "outsider" to the deals, bargaining, and inefficiency that characterized national politics. He saw his job as countering the influence of special interests by acting as the trustee of all the people. His outsider status, while helping him into office, left him without strong ties to party insiders or prominent legislators. Moreover, his desire to propose comprehensive solutions to problems went against the congressional tendency to take a piecemeal, incremental approach. Legislators complained of inadequate consultation and Carter's tendency to flood them with a mass of unprioritized proposals.

Even a president without these liabilities might not have done much better than Carter, as Congress itself weakened the ability of its party leaders to deliver a united front. While it flexed its muscles in response to Watergate and the abuse of presidential power, Congress reduced the power of its own committee chairs, weakened party control over legislators, and decentralized the decision-making process. In addition, because primary elections rather than party conventions now controlled the nominating process, candidates depended less on party support and more on campaign funds from interest groups, which they used to appeal directly to voters largely through television.

For his White House staff, Carter relied heavily on associates from Georgia—who, like him, lacked experience in national politics—but his cabinet appointments included several men from the Kennedy and Johnson administrations. Rosalynn

CARTER RECEIVES CIVIL RIGHTS AND PEACE AWARD
From left, Martin Luther King Sr., Rosalynn Carter, Andrew Young, Coretta Scott King, and Jimmy Carter join hands and sing in 1979 in the Ebenezer Baptist Church in Atlanta, which was the elder King's congregation. Carter was there to receive the Martin Luther King Non-Violent Peace Award for his role in the Camp David accords between Israel and Egypt and his efforts to promote civil rights at home.
Jimmy Carter Presidential Library.

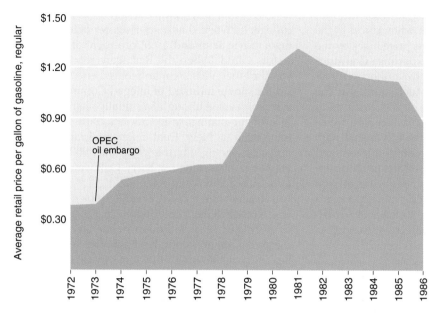

FIGURE 29.1

The Price of Gasoline, 1972–1986

The sharp increase in gasoline prices in 1973 and the even sharper one beginning in 1978 reflected price increases by the Organization of Petroleum Exporting Countries (OPEC) and contributed to inflation in the United States.

Carter, the president's wife, played a larger role in affairs of state than any First Lady since Eleanor Roosevelt. Carter involved other women in policy-making, including three at cabinet-level rank, far surpassing his predecessors in appointing women and members of minority groups to federal judgeships and high government positions. He also won congressional approval for the creation of two new departments, the Department of Education and the Department of Energy.

While it flexed its muscles in response to Watergate and the abuse of presidential power, Congress reduced the power of its own committee chairs, weakened party control over legislators, and decentralized the decision-making process.

Carter took office confident that he could solve the unusually formidable problems that had eluded the Nixon and Ford administrations—unemployment, inflation, slow economic growth, and energy shortages. With new tax cuts and federal spending, unemployment receded somewhat, but in 1978 rising inflation impelled Carter to curtail federal spending and the Federal Reserve Board to increase interest rates and tighten the money supply. These policies not only failed to halt inflation, which sur-

passed 13 percent in 1980, but also contributed to rising unemployment, reversing the progress that had been made in Carter's first two years.

The administration achieved little progress on issues traditionally central to the Democratic Party. Carter's commitment to holding down the federal budget frustrated Democratic legislators pushing for comprehensive welfare reform and a national health insurance program. To ensure solvency in the Social Security system, Carter and Congress agreed to raise employer and employee contributions, but these measures also increased the tax burden of lower- and middle-income Americans.

In contrast, corporations and wealthy individuals gained from new legislation. A sharp cut in the capital gains tax benefited high-income individuals. When the Chrysler Corporation approached bankruptcy in 1979, Congress responded with $1.5 billion worth of loan guarantees to ensure the survival of the tenth-largest corporation in the country. The government also reduced controls in several industries, deregulating airlines in 1978 and the banking, trucking, and railroad industries in 1980.

Designating the energy issue "the moral equivalent of war," Carter fought for a comprehensive energy program. But his goal to limit consumption and to reduce U.S. dependence on foreign oil fell victim to his uneasy relationship with Congress and to competing demands among energy producers and consumers. In 1979, declines in oil production abroad created the most severe energy shortage yet.

Hundreds of cars lined up at gas stations, and motorists' tempers rose even higher when prices at the pumps began to reflect enormous price hikes by the Organization of Petroleum Exporting Countries (Figure 29.1). Congress eventually authorized programs to stimulate alternative fuel sources at the same time it reduced controls on oil and gas and imposed a windfall profits tax on producers to redistribute some of the profits that would accrue with deregulation. These energy measures represented the nation's first comprehensive efforts to limit consumption and decrease its dependency on foreign oil. Still, they fell short of Carter's initial proposal and failed to curb the sinking confidence of Americans in his ability to provide effective leadership.

The Conservative Resurgence

Ronald Reagan's landslide election to the presidency in 1980 marked the most important turning point in politics since Franklin D. Roosevelt's victory in 1932. Eisenhower and Nixon had campaigned as middle-of-the-road Republicans, but Reagan's victory established conservatism's dominance in the Republican Party. Since the 1930s, the Democratic Party had defined the major issues; in the 1980s, the Republicans assumed that initiative, while the Democrats moved toward the right in their search for an effective response.

An extraordinarily adept politician, Reagan appealed to a wide spectrum of conservative groups and sentiments: free-market conservatives, militant anti-Communists, fundamentalist Christians, and white working-class Democrats disenchanted with the Great Society and suffering from the high inflation and unemployment rates of the last years of the Carter administration. On the domestic front, the Reagan administration left its most important mark on economic policies: victory over inflation, continued deregulation of industry, a moratorium on social spending, enormous tax cuts, and a staggering budget deficit.

Reagan and the Spectrum of Conservatism

The oldest candidate ever nominated for the presidency, Ronald Reagan was born in Tampico, Illinois,

in 1911. After attending Eureka, a small religious college, he worked as a sportscaster before becoming a movie actor and, later, president of the Screen Actors Guild. When the Red scare reached Hollywood in the 1940s, Reagan worked energetically to rid the movie industry of alleged Communists and sympathizers. Although he initially shared the politics of his staunchly Democratic father, who administered a New Deal relief program, Reagan moved to the right in the 1940s and 1950s. By 1964, he was campaigning for Barry Goldwater, his shift to conservatism complete.

Reagan's own political career took off when he was elected to the first of two terms as governor of California in 1966. Although he ran a conservative campaign, as governor he displayed considerable flexibility, approving a major tax increase, a strong measure to control water pollution, and a liberal abortion bill. Displaying similar flexibility in his 1980 presidential campaign, he softened his earlier attacks on the Panama Canal treaties and Social Security and chose as his running mate George Bush, a representative of the Republican center.

The poor state of the economy and the country's declining international stature provided ample weapons for Reagan's campaign. Repeatedly Reagan reminded voters of the "misery index"—the combined rates of unemployment and inflation—and asked, "Are you better off now than you were four years ago?" Reagan also accused Jimmy Carter of weakening U.S. military strength and losing the confidence of the nation's allies and the respect of its enemies. He insisted that more effective leadership and a determination to "take government off the backs of the people" would restore Americans' morale and other nations' respect.

Repeatedly Reagan reminded voters of the "misery index"—the combined rates of unemployment and inflation—and asked, "Are you better off now than you were four years ago?"

A narrow majority of voters, 51 percent, responded to Reagan's upbeat message. Carter won just 41 percent of the vote, and 7 percent went to independent candidate John R. Anderson, a Republican who reflected the views of moderates and

RONALD REAGAN NOMINATED FOR PRESIDENT
Nancy and Ronald Reagan respond to cheers at the Republican National Convention where he was nominated for president in the summer of 1980. Reagan became one of the most popular presidents of the twentieth century, though his wife did not always share his high ratings from the American people.
Lester Sloan / Woodfin Camp & Associates.

liberals in his party. The Republicans also picked up thirty-three new seats in the House and won control of the Senate.

With the election of 1980, conservatism gained greater ascendancy in American political culture than at any time since the 1920s. Reagan clearly benefited from a lingering backlash against the upheavals associated with the 1960s—the civil rights revolution, the reforms of the Johnson era, the antiwar movement, feminism, the new sexual permissiveness, and the liberalism of the Supreme Court. Much of Reagan's support came from religious conservatives with an avid interest in social

issues, who constituted a relatively new phenomenon known as the New Right. During the 1970s, evangelical Christianity claimed thousands of new adherents, abandoned the customary political neutrality of fundamentalist religion, and made adept use of new methods for mobilizing support, notably sophisticated mass-mailing techniques and the "electronic ministry." Evangelical ministers such as Jim Bakker and Pat Robertson preached to huge television audiences. Attacking feminism, abortion, homosexuality, and pornography, they called for restoration of old-fashioned "family values." They wanted prayer back in and sex education out of the schools.

Conservatives created or revitalized a raft of political organizations and journals. The religious right sought a Christian voice in government through the Moral Majority, founded by minister Jerry Falwell in 1979, and then through the Christian Coalition, which Pat Robertson created in 1989. Within a few years, the Christian Coalition claimed 1.6 million members and control of the Republican Party in more than a dozen states. The instruments of more traditional conservatives—those who advocated limited government at home and militant anticommunism abroad—likewise flourished. These included publications such as the *National Review,* edited by William F. Buckley Jr., and think tanks such as the American Enterprise Institute and the Heritage Foundation, which supported experts who developed and publicized new policy approaches.

Reagan embraced the full spectrum of conservatism, avowing agreement with the New Right on abortion, school prayer, and other social and moral issues. Yet he was careful not to alienate the more traditional conservatives, avoiding policy changes based on the moral stance of the New Right. Reagan promoted the conservative agenda most by strengthening the nation's anti-Communist posture and reducing government restraints on free enterprise. "In the present crisis," Reagan argued, "government is not the solution to our problem, government *is* the problem." Excessive government regulation and burdensome taxation crippled productivity, he claimed, while unbridled government spending was "mortgaging our future . . . for the temporary convenience of the present."

Reagan's admirers, however, reached far beyond conservatives. The extraordinarily popular president was liked even by Americans who opposed his policies and even when he made glaring mistakes. At one meeting, he failed to recognize his own secretary of housing and urban development, calling him "Mr. Mayor." On another occasion he proclaimed that vegetation caused 90 percent of all air pollution. He made so many misstatements that aides tried to keep him away from reporters. When Reagan did need to appear in public, one aide reported, "Every moment . . . was scheduled, every word was scripted, every place where Reagan was expected to stand was chalked with toe marks."

Democratic Representative Patricia Schroeder tagged Reagan the "Teflon President" because none of his administration's mistakes, even his own errors and falsehoods, seemed to stick to him. His confidence and easygoing sense of humor were a large part of his appeal, and he had the ability to ignore or recast darker aspects of the nation's past and to present a version of history that Americans could feel good about. Listeners understood Reagan's declaration that it was "morning in America" as a promise that the best was yet to come for the nation. He also gained public sympathy after being shot by a would-be assassin in March 1981. Just before surgery for removal of a bullet in his chest, Reagan joked to physicians, "I hope you're Republicans." So great was Reagan's appeal that his popularity withstood serious charges of executive branch misconduct in his second term.

Unleashing Free Enterprise

Reagan's first key objective was a massive tax cut. Although tax reduction, especially with a federal budget deficit that had been growing since the 1960s, contradicted traditional Republican economic doctrine, Reagan relied on a new theory called supply-side economics, which held that cutting taxes would actually increase revenue. In this view, high taxes had discouraged investment and weakened the economy; lower taxes would enable businesses to expand and encourage individuals to work harder because they would keep more of their earnings. Tax reduction would increase the production of goods and services, or supply, which in turn would boost demand. Supply-side economics fit perfectly with Reagan's emphasis on optimism and possibilities. In sharp contrast to Carter's talk of limitations and sacrifice, Reagan's agenda appeared to be pain free. To allay worries about the budget deficit, Reagan promised to cut federal expenditures, a position fully compatible with his antigovernment views.

Listeners understood Reagan's declaration that it was "morning in America" as a promise that the best was yet to come for the nation.

In the summer of 1981, Congress passed the Economic Recovery Tax Act, the largest tax reduction in U.S. history. Individual income taxes were cut, the lowest rate falling from 14 to 11 percent and the highest from 70 to 50 percent. Corporations also received tax breaks, and taxes on capital gains, gifts, and inheritances dropped. A second measure, the Tax Reform Act of 1986, reduced taxes even further, as the maximum tax on individual incomes fell to 28 percent and on business to 35 percent. In contrast, Social Security contributions and other taxes that affected Americans across the board increased during the 1980s. The net effect was to make the entire tax structure more regressive—that is, affluent Americans saved far more on their tax bills than did the average taxpayer, and the distribution of wealth was further skewed in favor of the rich.

"Hack, chop, crunch!" was how *Time* magazine characterized the administration's efforts to free private enterprise from government restraints. Carter had confined deregulation to particular industries such as finance and transportation while increasing regulation in areas such as health, safety, equal employment opportunity, and environmental protection. The Reagan administration, by contrast, pursued across-the-board deregulation. Reagan presided over the most lax enforcement of the Sherman Antitrust Act—the law designed to reduce monopoly and promote competition—since its early history in the 1890s. In a decade of unprecedented business mergers and takeovers, the government opposed not a single one. The Reagan administration also loosened restraints on business imposed by employee health and safety measures and helped weaken organized labor. When 13,000 members of the Professional Air Traffic Controllers Organization (PATCO) went on strike in 1981, Reagan fired them and destroyed their union.

Blaming environmental laws for the nation's sluggish economic growth, Reagan targeted them too for deregulation. His first secretary of the interior, James Watt, declared, "We will mine more, drill more, cut more timber," and released federal lands

CONTROVERSY OVER THE ENVIRONMENT
Secretary of the Interior James Watt joined the Reagan cabinet committed to dismantling much of the environmental regulation of the previous two decades. His efforts drew considerable opposition, and he failed to turn back the clock substantially. In 1983, President Reagan appointed a more moderate replacement.
Illustration by Wilson McLean. Reprinted with permission of the artist and *Newsweek* magazine.

to private exploitation, while the head of the Environmental Protection Agency eased enforcement of air and water pollution measures. Popular support for environmental protection blocked complete realization of the administration's deregulatory goals. Congress overrode vetoes of clean water legislation and of a bill establishing the Superfund for cleanup of hazardous waste sites.

Deregulation of the banking industry, supported by Democrats and Republicans alike, created a crisis in the savings and loan industry and, ultimately, a burden for taxpayers. When deregulatory laws lifted interest rate ceilings and permitted savings and loan institutions (S&Ls) to lend money more freely, some S&Ls extended enormous loans

to real estate developers and invested in other high-yield but risky ventures. With lax federal oversight, S&L owners reaped lavish profits during the early 1980s, and their depositors enjoyed high interest rates. But when real estate values began to plunge in the mid-1980s, especially in California and the Southwest, hundreds of S&Ls went bankrupt. After Congress voted to bail out the S&L industry in 1989, the burden of the largest financial scandal in U.S. history fell on American taxpayers, few of whom had profited from deregulation.

The S&L crisis deepened the federal budget deficit, which soared during the 1980s despite Reagan's pledge to pare federal spending. The administration achieved some savings in the Social Security and Aid to Families with Dependent Children programs, and it cut funds for food stamps, job training, aid to low-income students, and health services. Hundreds of thousands of people lost eligibility or some benefits, and those with incomes just around the poverty line took the hardest hits. The budget cuts, however, were overshadowed by increases in defense spending, and the budget deficit continued to climb: from $74 billion when Carter left office in 1981 to a high of $220 billion in 1986. During the Reagan administration the government had increased its debt from $834 billion to $2.3 trillion, and interest on the national debt consumed one-seventh of all federal expenditures.

After Congress voted to bail out the S&L industry in 1989, the burden of the largest financial scandal in U.S. history fell on American taxpayers, few of whom had profited from deregulation.

The problem of inflation was eliminated, but it took the severest recession since the 1930s to squeeze inflation out of the U.S. economy. Beginning in 1981, unemployment rose sharply, approaching 11 percent late in 1982. Record numbers of banks and businesses closed, and twelve million workers could not find jobs. The threat of unemployment further undermined organized labor, forcing unions to make concessions that management insisted were necessary for industry's survival. The economy recovered in 1983 and entered an unprecedented period of growth. Yet although the number of jobs increased substantially, unemployment never fell below 5 percent during the decade.

The economic upswing and Reagan's own popularity posed a formidable challenge for the Democrats in the 1984 election. Walter F. Mondale, vice president under Carter, won the Democratic nomination. Although he electrified the Democratic National Convention by choosing as his running mate New York Representative Geraldine A. Ferraro, the first woman on a major party ticket, it was not enough to save the Democrats from a humiliating defeat. Reagan charged his opponents with concentrating on America's limits and failures, while he emphasized success and possibility. Democrats, he claimed, "see an America where every day is April 15th [the due date for income tax returns] . . . we see an America where every day is the Fourth of July."

Voters responded to the president's vision and to the economic comeback, giving him 59 percent of the vote and a landslide victory in 1984, ranking close to those of Roosevelt in 1936, Johnson in 1964, and Nixon in 1972 (Map 29.3). The Democrats pondered what it would take to stem the exodus of longtime loyalists—particularly southern white males—to the Republican Party. Stung by Republican charges that the Democratic Party was captive to "special interests" such as labor, women, and minorities, some Democratic leaders urged that the party shift more toward the right.

Maintaining the Reagan Legacy: The Bush Administration

No longer burdened with Reagan's immense popularity, the Democrats did better in the 1988 election, but not enough to deny the White House to Reagan's vice president, George Herbert Walker Bush. The son of a wealthy New England senator, George Bush grew up in a privileged milieu that put a premium on public service. After fighting in World War II, he earned a Yale degree and then settled in Texas to make his own way in the oil industry and politics. Bush served in Congress during the 1960s and later represented the United States in China and headed the CIA during the Nixon-Ford years. When Ronald Reagan achieved a commanding lead in the 1980 primaries, Bush put his own aspirations on hold and accepted second place on the Republican ticket.

Michael Dukakis, governor of Massachusetts, won the Democratic party nomination after defeating a number of candidates. An important contender was the Reverend Jesse Jackson, who had fought civil rights battles alongside Martin Luther King Jr., and whose Rainbow Coalition campaign centered on the needs of blacks and other minorities, women, working-class families, and the poor. Jackson won several state primaries, gathering seven million votes, almost one-third of them from white voters. In the end, however, his race, lack of experience in public office, and position on the left wing of the Democratic Party proved to be insuperable obstacles. Half the eligible voters stayed home on election day, indicating the electorate's general disgust with a campaign that favored vitriolic attacks over serious debate. Fifty-four percent of those who did vote were satisfied with the Republican record on peace and prosperity, but the Democrats gained seats in the House and Senate.

President Bush saw himself primarily as steward and guardian of the Reagan legacy. He promised "a kinder, gentler nation" and was more inclined than Reagan to approve government activity in the private sphere. For example, he approved environmental protection legislation, the costs of which would be borne by industry and con-

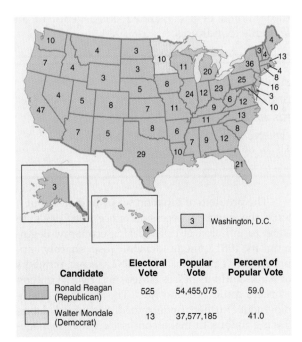

Candidate	Electoral Vote	Popular Vote	Percent of Popular Vote
Ronald Reagan (Republican)	525	54,455,075	59.0
Walter Mondale (Democrat)	13	37,577,185	41.0

MAP 29.3
The Election of 1984

sumers. The Clean Air Act of 1990 was the strongest, most comprehensive environmental law in history, requiring power plants to cut sulfur dioxide emissions by more than half by the year 2000 and oil companies to develop cleaner-burning gasoline. Some forty million disabled Americans reaped the benefits of other regulatory legislation. Reflecting the growing power of the disability rights movement, the 1991 Americans with Disabilities Act banned job discrimination against the handicapped and required that private businesses, public accommodations, and transportation be made accessible to the disabled.

Still, "If you're looking for George Bush's domestic program, and many people are, this is it: the veto pen," charged Democratic House majority leader Richard Gephardt in 1991. Bush blocked Congress thirty-six times, vetoing bills that lifted abortion restrictions, extended unemployment benefits, raised taxes, mandated family and medical leave for workers, and reformed campaign financing. By the end of his term, press reports were filled with the words *stalemate, gridlock*, and *divided government*.

Continuing a trend begun during the Reagan administration, states tried to compensate for this paralysis, and for the first time in decades state legislatures became more innovative than Washington. "Our federal politics are gridlocked, and governors have become the ones who have to have the courage to put their necks out," said a spokesperson for state governors. States passed bills to block corporate takeovers, establish parental leave policies, require equal pay for jobs of equal worth, improve food labeling, protect the environment, and promote foreign trade. Beginning in the 1980s, a few states began to pass measures protecting the rights of homosexuals. In the 1990s, dozens of cities passed ordinances requiring businesses that enjoy tax abatements, service contracts, or other benefits from cities to pay wages of $7.00 and more per hour, well above the federal minimum. And, in 1999, California passed a gun control bill that imposed much tougher restrictions on assault weapons than reformers had been able to get through Congress.

The president and Congress broke the deadlock to agree on a measure to deal with a problem inherited from the Reagan administration, the federal budget deficit. Bush reluctantly abandoned his "no new taxes" pledge and agreed to increase taxes modestly for high-income Americans and raise taxes on gasoline, cigarettes, alcoholic beverages,

and luxury items. Although the budget agreement brought in new revenues and Congress limited spending, three years later the deficit soared even higher, boosted by rising costs in entitlement programs such as Social Security and Medicare-Medicaid as well as by spending on unforeseen emergencies of war and natural disasters. The new taxes affected only slightly the massive tax reductions of the early 1980s, leaving intact a key element of Reagan's legacy.

Continuing Struggles Over Rights and Welfare

In keeping with its antigovernment philosophy, the Reagan administration tried to reverse federal protections of civil rights, particularly those of African Americans, women, and homosexuals, breaking sharply with the national commitment to equal opportunity undertaken in the 1960s. The federal courts, too, shifted to the right, limiting the government's power to enforce individual rights. Despite the more conservative climate, the women's movement and the newer gay and lesbian rights movement achieved piecemeal but significant policy reforms. As American society became increasingly diverse, the economic and political status of minority groups improved, but people of color continued to lag behind whites in opportunity, income, and political influence.

The Conservative Shift in the Federal Courts

Since the 1950s and the tenure of Earl Warren as chief justice, proponents of reform had counted on the federal judiciary as a powerful ally in their struggles for minority rights and social justice. Yet in the 1980s, liberals saw their allies slipping away as conservative justices increasingly populated the Supreme Court and the lower federal courts. With the opportunity to appoint more than half the 761 federal court judges and five new Supreme Court justices, Presidents Reagan and Bush followed Nixon's example and carefully sought candidates who would uphold the doctrine of strict construction.

Reagan used his first opportunity in 1981 to appoint the first woman to the Supreme Court, Sandra Day O'Connor, who was a moderate conservative. His next two appointments, Antonin Scalia and Anthony M. Kennedy, tipped the balance further to the right. Bush first nominated a moderate, federal appeals judge David Souter; but in 1991, when he had to replace Justice Thurgood Marshall, the only African American on the Court, he set off a national controversy. The spark was his selection of Clarence Thomas, a conservative black appeals judge, who had opposed affirmative action as head of the Equal Employment Opportunity Commission under Reagan. Charging that Thomas would not protect minority rights, the NAACP and other civil rights and women's organizations fought the nomination. Then Anita Hill, a law professor and former EEOC employee, stunned the nation by accusing Thomas of sexual harassment. Despite nationally televised hearings on the harassment charges, the Senate voted narrowly to confirm him. Although the hearings sensitized the public to sexual harassment and gave the women's movement a boost, Thomas's appointment solidified the conservative shift on the Supreme Court.

The Democrats' victory in the 1992 election gave President Bill Clinton the opportunity to put his own stamp on the courts. Whereas Reagan and Bush had appointed very few women or minorities to the federal courts, Clinton made diversity a key objective. Of his first 129 appointments to federal courts, nearly one-third were women, 31 were black, and 11 were Hispanic. In June 1993, he appointed the second woman to the Supreme Court, Ruth Bader Ginsburg, a self-identified feminist who had won key women's rights rulings from the Supreme Court before President Carter made her a federal appeals court judge in 1980.

Because of its tradition of respecting precedent, the Court did not execute an abrupt about-face in the 1980s and 1990s. It upheld important affirmative action and antidiscrimination policies, ruled that sexual harassment in the workplace constituted sex discrimination, and sustained certain rights to welfare benefits. Yet it allowed states to impose further restrictions that limited access to abortion for poor, uneducated, and rural women, weakened protections against employment discrimination, restricted application of the Americans with Disabilities Act, and whittled away at legal safeguards around the death sentence. And, in a series of cases in 1999, Reagan and Bush appointees constituted a five-to-four majority that limited federal authority in favor of state sovereignty.

Setbacks and Gains for the Women's Movement

One of the marks of the conservative resurgence in the 1980s was its capture of the Republican Party's position on women's rights. For the first time in its history, the Republican Party took an explicitly anti-feminist tone, opposing both the Equal Rights Amendment and a woman's right to abortion, key goals of women's rights activists. (See "Historical Question," page 1104.) The Reagan administration did express concerns about women, specifically about the "gender gap" in voting patterns—women's tendency throughout the 1980s to vote for liberal and Democratic candidates in larger numbers than men did. Reagan appointed three women to cabinet posts and the first woman to the Supreme Court. But these actions accompanied a general decline in the number of women and minorities in high-level positions. And with higher poverty rates than men, women suffered most from budget cuts in social programs.

For the first time in its history, the Republican Party took an explicitly antifeminist tone, opposing both the Equal Rights Amendment and a woman's right to abortion.

In this more hostile political environment, the women's movement shifted its strategies and goals. Defense of abortion rights, antidiscrimination measures, and affirmative action remained key priorities. But activists focused more on women's economic and family problems, which eluded the grasp of policies that simply banned sex discrimination. This new agenda recognized the needs of less advantaged women and acknowledged the disproportionate share of women and children among the poor, a development that some termed "the feminization of poverty." It was also clear that despite the much publicized entrance of some women into formerly male fields, the majority of employed women still filled low-paying jobs traditionally thought fit for women.

Feminists found some common ground with the Reagan administration in two measures that addressed women's economic distress. The Child Support Enforcement Amendments helped single and

CONFRONTATIONS OVER ABORTION
Failing to win a constitutional amendment banning abortion, in the late 1970s and 1980s some groups in the right-to-life movement adopted more militant tactics, picketing abortion clinics, yelling at patients and employees, and trying to block entrance into clinics. The pro-choice activists shown here defend clinic access and the right to abortion.

Paul S. Howell / Gamma Liaison.

divorced mothers by facilitating collection of court-ordered child support payments from absent parents. The Retirement Equity Act of 1984 benefited divorced and older women by strengthening their claims to their husbands' pensions and enabling women to qualify more easily for private retirement pensions.

Feminists fought successfully to retain women's right to have an abortion, but they hit a stone wall in their efforts to strengthen day care services, aid displaced homemakers, and promote pay equity—that is, equal pay for traditionally female jobs that were comparable in worth to jobs performed primarily by men. Like other pressure groups, the women's movement pursued locally what it failed to achieve at the federal level. The pay equity movement took hold in several states, and

many states strengthened their laws against rape. States also increased funding for domestic violence programs and stepped up efforts to protect victims and prosecute abusers.

Although many feminists attacked President Clinton for his policies on welfare and homosexuals' rights, his administration did ameliorate policies enacted under Reagan and Bush and advance measures that they had blocked. For example, where he could exercise executive authority, Clinton eased some of the restrictions on access to abortion. The Family and Medical Leave Act, passed in 1993, enabled workers in larger companies to take time off for childbirth, adoption, care for aging parents, or family medical emergencies. And the Violence Against Women Act of 1994 authorized $1.6 billion and new remedies for combating sexual

THE FIRST WOMAN SECRETARY OF STATE
Madeleine K. Albright is sworn in as Secretary of State in January 1997 by Vice President Albert Gore, as her three daughters and President Bill Clinton look on. Formerly a professor of international affairs at Georgetown University, Albright served in the first Clinton cabinet as U.S. representative to the United Nations.
Greg Gibson/Wide World.

assaults and domestic violence, although the Supreme Court later weakened the law by invalidating a provision that allowed victims of gender violence to sue in federal court.

Clinton also contributed to the increasing presence of women in government. In addition to his selections for the federal courts, he named women to six of twenty-three key posts in the executive branch. Janet Reno became the first female attorney general, and in his second term, Clinton appointed the first female secretary of state, Madeleine K. Albright. Using sophisticated fundraising and electioneering techniques, feminists helped elect more women to political office. By the end of the century, women had made their marks as governors of Connecticut, Kentucky, Vermont, Nebraska, New Hampshire, and New Jersey; and women had served as mayors of several large cities, including Jane Byrne of Chicago and Dianne Feinstein of San Francisco. Women continued to inch their way into Congress, holding 72 seats, or 13.5 percent of the total, in 2001. One of those women was Hillary Rodham Clinton, the new senator from New York and first First Lady to run for political office.

The Gay and Lesbian Rights Movement

Influenced by the black freedom struggle, the New Left, the counterculture, and feminism, gay men and lesbians began to claim equal rights and to express pride in their sexual identities. Although an organization for homosexual rights had existed as early as 1924, not until the 1980s did a national mass movement play a significant role in U.S. politics. The contemporary movement emerged out of the social upheaval of the 1960s, symbolized by the Stonewall riot of 1969, when gay men and lesbians fought back against a police raid on the Stonewall Inn, a gay bar in New York City's Greenwich Village.

Influenced by the black freedom struggle, the New Left, the counterculture, and feminism, gay men and lesbians began to claim equal rights for homosexuals and to express pride in their sexual identities.

The acquired immune deficiency syndrome (AIDS) epidemic further mobilized the gay and lesbian rights movement in the 1980s, because at first male homosexuals accounted for the majority of AIDS cases. As the disease swept through communities of gay men in New York, San Francisco, and elsewhere, gay men and lesbians organized for public education about AIDS and public funding for its treatment and prevention.

The gay and lesbian rights movement helped thousands of homosexuals experience the relief of being able to live openly. By "coming out" in great numbers, they helped to make homosexuality more visible, encouraging—willingly or not—acknowledgment by the larger population. Activists organized gay rights and gay pride marches throughout the country, and the movement began to win local victories, gaining some protections against discrimination. (See "Documenting the American Promise," page 1126.) Beginning with the election of Elaine Noble to the Massachusetts legislature in 1974, several openly gay politicians won election and reelec-

tion to offices from mayor to member of Congress. The Democrats began to include gay rights planks in their party platforms.

Popular attitudes about homosexuality moved toward greater tolerance but remained complex. For example, in a 1998 poll, 84 percent supported equal job opportunities for gays and lesbians, but 59 percent thought homosexuality was morally wrong. These diverse attitudes were reflected in uneven changes in policies. In some states and cities lesbians and gay men won protections that were enjoyed by heterosexual citizens. Dozens of cities banned job discrimination against homosexuals, and beginning with Wisconsin in 1982, eleven states expanded their civil rights laws to make sexual orientation a protected category. Nearly 100 cities and several large corporations began to offer health insurance and other benefits granted to employees' spouses to domestic partners. After the Vermont Supreme Court ruled that gay couples were unconstitutionally discriminated against, the Vermont legislature created the category of "civil unions" for

AIDS QUILT
An enormous quilt dedicated to AIDS victims lies spread across the Washington Mall in October 1989. Composed of patches made by individuals who lost loved ones to the fatal epidemic, the quilt was exhibited throughout the country before its arrival in the nation's capital. The quilt helped to raise money for research on and treatment of AIDS, promoted recognition of the disease, and offered a way for the bereaved to mourn and receive comfort. New AIDS quilt projects quickly followed.
Lee Snider / Image Works.

Protecting Gay and Lesbian Rights

*S*ince the 1970s, the gay and lesbian rights movement has worked for passage of laws and ordinances to protect homosexuals from discrimination. In 1982, Wisconsin became the first state to ban discrimination on the basis of sexual orientation, following the lead of several cities throughout the United States that passed gay rights ordinances in the 1970s. By the mid-1990s, nine states and more than eighty cities had such legislation on the books. These measures ignited controversy that surrounded the issue into the twenty-first century.

DOCUMENT 1. Ordinance of the City of Minneapolis, 1974

In 1974, the city council of Minneapolis amended its civil rights ordinance to cover discrimination based on sexual preference. The law provided a rationale for banning discrimination and, unlike some laws focusing exclusively on employment, encompassed a broad range of activities.

It is determined that discriminatory practices based on race, color, creed, religion, national origin, sex or affectional or sexual preference, with respect to employment, labor union membership, housing accommodations, property rights, education, public accommodations, and public services, or any of them, tend to create and intensify conditions of poverty, ill health, unrest, civil disobedience, lawlessness, and vice and adversely affect the public health, safety, order, convenience, and general welfare; such discriminatory practices threaten the rights, privileges, and opportunities of all inhabitants of the city and such rights, privileges, and opportunities are hereby to be declared civil rights, and the adoption of this Chapter is deemed to be an exercise of the policy power of the City to protect such rights.

SOURCE: Norman Dorsen and Aryeh Neier, eds., *The Rights of Gay People: The Basic ACLU Guide to a Gay Person's Rights* (New York: E. P. Dutton, 1992), 251.

DOCUMENT 2. Letter to the Editor of the *New York Times* from Paul Moore, November 23, 1981

Paul Moore, Episcopal bishop of New York, made a religious argument for gay rights in his letter to the editor of the New York Times.

I quote our diocesan resolution: "Whereas this Convention, without making any judgment on the morality of homosexuality, agrees that homosexuals are entitled to full civil rights. Now therefore be it resolved this Convention supports laws guaranteeing homosexuals all civil rights guaranteed to other citizens."

The Bible stands for justice and compassion for all of God's children. To deny civil rights to anyone for something he or she cannot help is against the clear commandment of justice and love, which is the message of the word of God.

As a New Yorker I find it incredible that this great city, populated by more gay persons than any other city in the world, still denies them basic human rights. They make an enormous contribution to the commercial, artistic, and religious life of our city.

SOURCE: Paul Moore, letter to the editor, *New York Times*, December 8, 1981.

DOCUMENT 3. Vatican Congregation for the Doctrine of the Faith, August 6, 1992

The following statement from the Roman Catholic Church reflects the views of many religious groups that take positions against gay rights.

"Sexual orientation" does not constitute a quality comparable to race, ethnic background, etc., in respect to nondiscrimination. Unlike these, homosexual orientation is an objective disorder and evokes moral concern.

There are areas in which it is not unjust discrimination to take sexual orientation into account, for example, in the placement of children for adoption or foster care, in employment of teachers or athletic coaches, and in military recruitment.

SOURCE: Vatican Congregation for the Doctrine of the Faith, *Origins*, August 6, 1992.

Document 4. Testimony of Charles Cochrane Jr. before the House Subcommittee on Employment Opportunities of the Committee on Education and Labor, January 27, 1982

Although the U.S. Congress has never enacted legislation banning discrimination on the basis of sexual orientation, it has considered a number of bills for that purpose. Charles Cochrane Jr., an army veteran and police sergeant, testified on behalf of such a bill in 1982.

I am very proud of being a New York City policeman. And I am equally proud of being gay. I have always been gay.

I have been out of the closet for 4 years. November 6 was my anniversary. It took me 34 years to muster enough courage to declare myself openly.

We gays are loathed by some, pitied by others, and misunderstood by most. We are not cruel, wicked, cursed, sick, or possessed by demons. We are artists, business people, police officers, and clergymen. We are scientists, truck drivers, politicians; we work in every field. We are loving human beings who are in some ways different. . . .

During the early years of my association with the New York City Police Department a great deal of energy did go into guarding and concealing my innermost feelings. I believed that I would be subjected to ridicule and harassment were my colleagues to learn of my sexual orientation. Happily, when I actually began to integrate the various aspects of my total self, those who knew me did not reject me.

Then what need is there for such legislation as H.R. 1454? The crying need of others, still trapped in their closets, who must be protected, who must be reassured that honesty about themselves and their lives will not cost them their homes or their jobs. . . .

The bill before you will not act as a proselytizing agent in matters of sexual orientation or preference. It will not include affirmative action provisions. Passage of this bill will protect the inherent human rights of all people of the United States, while in no way diminishing the rights of those who do not see the need for such legislation. Finally, it will signify, quite clearly, recognition and compassion for a group which is often maligned without justification.

SOURCE: U.S. House Subcommittee on Employment Opportunities of the Committee on Education and Labor, *Hearing on H.R. 1454,* 97th Cong., 2nd sess., 1982, 54–56.

Document 5. Carl F. Horowitz, "Homosexuality's Legal Revolution," May 1991

Carl Horowitz, a policy analyst at a conservative think tank, the Heritage Foundation, expresses arguments of those opposed to government protection of homosexual rights.

Homosexual activists have all but completed their campaign to persuade the nation's educational establishment that homosexuality is normal "alternative" behavior, and thus any adverse reaction to it is akin to a phobia, such as fear of heights, or an ethnic prejudice, such as anti-Semitism.

The movement now stands on the verge of fully realizing its use of law to . . . intimidate heterosexuals uncomfortable about coming into contact with it. . . .

The movement seeks to win sinecures through the state, and over any objections by "homophobic" opposition. With a cloud of a heavy fine or even a jail sentence hanging over a mortgage lender, a rental agent, or a job interviewer who might be discomforted by them, homosexuals under these laws can win employment, credit, housing, and other economic entitlements. Heterosexuals would have no right to discriminate against homosexuals, but apparently, not vice versa. . . .

These laws will create market bottlenecks. Heterosexuals and even "closeted" homosexuals will be at a competitive disadvantage for jobs and housing. . . .

The new legalism will increase heterosexual anger—and even violence—toward homosexuals.

SOURCE: Carl F. Horowitz, "Homosexuality's Legal Revolution," *Freeman,* May 1991.

QUESTIONS FOR ANALYSIS AND DEBATE

1. According to these documents, how would heterosexuals be affected by laws protecting gay and lesbian rights?
2. Which of these documents suggest that the civil rights movement influenced the authors' views on homosexual rights?
3. What do you think is the strongest argument for government protection of homosexual rights? What do you think is the strongest argument against government protection?

same-sex couples that would entitle them to rights available to married couples in areas such as inheritance, taxes, and medical decisions.

Such initiatives found less support at the national level. For example, in 1993 opposition from military leaders, enlisted men, and key legislators caused Clinton to back away from his campaign promise to lift the ban on homosexuals in the military. In June 1993, Clinton announced a compromise, quickly dubbed the "don't ask, don't tell" policy. It forbade officials from asking military personnel about their sexuality, but allowed dismissal of men and women who said they were gay or engaged in homosexual behavior. What began as an effort to promote tolerance ended in a 67 percent jump in discharges of homosexuals. In 1996, Clinton also signed the Defense of Marriage Act, prohibiting the federal government from recognizing state-licensed marriages between same-sex couples. And in 2000, the Supreme Court ruled five to four that it was constitutional under the First Amendment right of freedom of association for the Boy Scouts to exclude gay members.

Antidiscrimination Laws for Gays and Lesbians, 2000

Even as popular TV shows and movies increasingly featured gay men and lesbians, most homosexuals remained vulnerable to intolerance and sometimes violence. The New Right targeted gays and lesbians as symbols of national immorality and succeeded in overturning some homosexual rights measures. Protections against discrimination for gay men and lesbians lagged far behind the civil rights guarantees that racial minorities and women had achieved.

Minorities' Struggles and Successes

By the end of the twentieth century, the overwhelming predominance of European-Americans in American society was giving way to an increasingly diverse population. African Americans constituted about 13 percent of the population, Hispanic Americans more than 11 percent, and Asian Americans and Pacific Islanders 4 percent. Demog-raphers predicted that by the middle of the twenty-first century whites would constitute just a little over half of the population; the fastest growing groups, Latinos and Asian Americans, were projected at 24 and 9 percent respectively. Propelling this growing variety was a new wave of immigrants, the vast majority of whom came from Asia or Latin America.

The racial composition of the new immigration revived the century-old wariness of the native-born toward recent arrivals. Pressure for more restrictive policies stemmed from beliefs (generally unfounded) that immigrants took jobs from the native-born, fears that immigrants would erode the dominant culture and language, and concern about population pressures on the environment. Americans expressed particular hostility to immigrants who entered the country illegally. Primarily Latin Americans fleeing civil war and economic deprivation, illegal immigrants were estimated to number at least three million. To stem this tide, Congress passed the Immigration Reform and Control Act of 1986, which penalized employers who hired undocumented aliens but also granted amnesty to illegal immigrants who could prove residence before 1982. Some two million people took advantage of this provision (Figure 29.2). In California, where large numbers of illegal immigrants from Mexico settled, voters passed an initiative denying public schooling to their children. Nor were legal immigrants immune from nativist policy. In 1996, Congress passed a law denying food stamps, Medicaid, and other benefits to those who had not become citizens.

Although more minorities than ever attained middle-class status, in general people of color remained on the lower rungs of the economic ladder, and their situation worsened as economic conditions in the 1980s and 1990s widened the gap between rich and poor. In 1995, when the median income for white families surpassed $34,000, it stood at less than $25,000 for African American and Hispanic American households. Even in families where both parents had jobs, the median income for white families was $10,000 more than that of black families. In 1999, poverty afflicted about 23 percent of blacks and Latinos and 25 percent of American Indians, double the overall poverty rate of 11.8 percent.

The media hailed Asian Americans as "America's Super Minority" but failed to note vast differences among Asian Americans. More than 60 percent of immigrants from India, for example, came with college

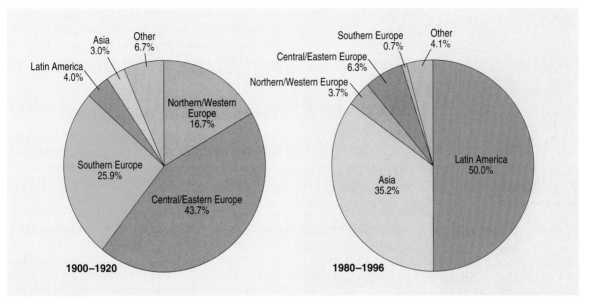

FIGURE 29.2

The Changing Profile of Immigration, 1900–1920 and 1980–1996
The United States received its largest number of immigrants during the opening and closing decades of the twentieth century, but the cultures and countries of origin of the new arrivals shifted dramatically between the two periods.

degrees, while just 20 percent of those from Vietnam did. Overall, median family income for Asian Americans surpassed that of whites, but only because Asian families had more wage earners. In contrast to 22 percent of whites, 39 percent of Asian Americans had completed college; still they lagged behind whites in per capita income and experienced greater poverty. Poor Chinese American women employed in the New York garment industry endured wages, hours, and working conditions resembling those of the early-twentieth-century sweatshops.

Although more minorities than ever attained middle-class status, in general people of color remained on the lower rungs of the economic ladder, and their situation worsened as economic conditions in the 1980s and 1990s widened the gap between rich and poor.

Minorities edged slowly into the corridors of political power. At the end of the 1980s, more than

seven thousand blacks held public office, an increase of nearly 50 percent from 1980. The most impressive gains occurred in city government, where black mayors presided over Atlanta, Chicago, Los Angeles, Philadelphia, Seattle, and other large cities. The election of David Dinkins as mayor of New York City in 1989 epitomized the rise of black leaders even in cities with predominantly white electorates.

Jesse Jackson's campaigns for the presidency in 1984 and 1988 inspired African Americans and demonstrated that many whites were willing to support a minority candidate. In 1989, Democrat L. Douglas Wilder of Virginia became the first black governor since reconstruction, joining the only Hispanic governor, Republican Bob Martinez of Florida. Minorities remained underrepresented in national politics, however. When the 107th Congress convened in January 2001, two Asian Americans and one American Indian were the only members of a minority group in the Senate. Thirty-six African Americans served in the 435-member House of Representatives, along with nineteen Hispanics and four Asian Americans.

JESSE JACKSON
Jesse Jackson was among several civil rights activists, including John Lewis, Eleanor Holmes Norton, and Andrew Young, who turned to electoral politics. A Baptist minister and dynamic speaker, Jackson mounted campaigns for the Democratic presidential nomination in 1984 and 1988, appealing to what he called a "Rainbow Coalition" of disadvantaged groups. Here he addresses an anti-apartheid demonstration in New York City in 1986.
Tom Sobolik / Black Star.

Economic Shocks

After the gravest economic crisis since the Depression, the U.S. economy recovered in the early 1980s and brought general prosperity and great fortunes to some. Making money and displaying wealth were celebrated in the 1980s, even as problems that had plagued the economy in the 1970s persisted, and growing poverty reversed the post–World War II trend toward greater economic equality. When he

left office in January 1989, Ronald Reagan could describe the nation as "More prosperous, more secure, and happier than it was eight years ago," but a recession two years later helped the Democrats win back the White House.

The Money Culture of the 1980s

Books by businesspeople climbed onto best-seller lists. The press described lavish parties costing millions of dollars. Popular magazines featured articles entitled "High Life Afloat: Superduper Yachts" and "They're Like Us, Except They're Rich." Evidence of immense fortunes and conspicuous consumption ranged from multimillion-dollar Manhattan apartments to special area codes for coastal waters to accommodate the proliferation of yachts. Fascination with wealth and consumption drew vast audiences to prime-time TV serials such as *Dallas* and *Dynasty*. College students told poll takers that their primary ambition was to make money. Even fundamentalist ministers enjoyed homes with swimming pools and travel on private jets, though none lived as extravagantly as TV evangelist Jim Bakker, whose doghouses were air-conditioned.

Most Americans profited from the economic boom of the 1980s, but those already well off enjoyed the greatest gains. Family income for the richest one-fifth of the population increased by 11.1 percent between 1979 and 1987. The number of millionaires doubled during the decade, and the number of billionaires grew from thirteen to fifty-one. Greater concentration of wealth in fewer hands had been developing since the 1970s, but Reagan's tax and spending policies intensified the trend.

Participating conspicuously in the affluence of the 1980s were members of the baby boom generation known popularly as "yuppies," short for "young urban professionals." These mostly white, well-educated young men and women tended to live in urban condominiums and to pursue fast-track careers; in their leisure time, they consumed lavishly—fancy cars, gourmet food, expensive vacations, health clubs, and the most up-to-date electronic gadgets. Though constituting a minority of their generation, they established consumption standards that many others tried to emulate.

Most of those newly wealthy in the 1980s achieved success from moving assets around rather than from producing goods. There were notable exceptions, such as Steven Jobs, who invented the Apple computer in his garage, and Liz Claiborne, who in thirteen years turned a $250,000 investment into a billion-dollar fashion enterprise. But many others got rich—or richer—by manipulating debt and restructuring corporations through corporate mergers and takeovers. Large fortunes were made by "corporate raiders" who generated the capital to take over a corporation by issuing junk bonds, so called because they were high risk and high yield. Once in control, the raiders reaped huge profits by selling off some of the corporation's valuable divisions. All too often the result was to line the financiers' pockets and leave the corporation deeply in debt.

"To say these guys are entrepreneurs is like saying Jesse James was an entrepreneur," opined Texas businessman Ross Perot, who defined entrepreneurship as making things rather than making money. Most financial entrepreneurs operated within the law, but occasionally greed led to criminal convictions. Junk bonds pioneer Michael Milken took home well over $50 million a year. But he and others landed in jail for using insider information to maximize their financial manipulations.

The Debt-Based Economy

Problems remained in the economy even as it recovered from the double-digit inflation and unemployment of the late 1970s and early 1980s. The steel, automobile, and electronics industries suffered in competition with those of countries like Germany and Japan; Americans bought more and more Volkswagens and Hondas and fewer Fords and Chevrolets. With Americans purchasing more foreign-made goods than domestic producers were able to sell abroad, the nation's trade deficit (the difference between imports and exports) soared to an all-time high of $126 billion in 1988.

International competition forced the collapse of some older companies, while others moved factories and jobs abroad to be closer to foreign markets or to benefit from the low wage standards of countries such as Mexico and Korea. The growth of service industries created new jobs at home, but former blue-collar workers who were forced to make the shift found their wages substantially lower. When David Ramos was laid off in 1982 from his $12.75-an-hour job in a steel plant, his wages fell to just $5 an hour as a security guard, and his family of six was forced to rely on food stamps. Overall, the number of full-time workers earning wages below the poverty level ($12,195 for a family of four

in 1990) rose sharply from 12 to 18 percent of all workers in the 1980s.

By contrast, corporations benefited greatly from the Reagan tax cuts. Instead of putting their tax savings into new business enterprises or machinery that would boost productivity and create new jobs, as tax cut advocates had promised, entrepreneurs used them to take over other companies or to support lavish lifestyles. As savings and investment declined, indebtedness soared among rich and poor alike, and household debt, especially credit card spending, surpassed $3 trillion. Corporate debt reached $2 trillion, twice what it had been in 1980, while the national debt grew from $834 billion to $2.3 trillion.

The economic downswing that began in 1990 made control of the federal deficit even more difficult. With higher unemployment and a drop in the economy's growth rate, federal revenues declined. Although the recession ended in 1991, the economy grew at a snail's pace. General Motors, Time Warner, Xerox, and other major corporations announced permanent reductions in their workforces. With unemployment surpassing 7 percent in 1992, economists characterized the sluggish economy as "jobless recovery" from the recession.

The Other Side of Prosperity

Even before the 1990 recession, many Americans saw the economic boom pass them by. Affluent urbanites walked past numerous men and women sleeping in subway stations, on grates over steam vents, and on park benches near city monuments. Experts debated the total number of homeless Americans—estimates ranged from 350,000 upwards—but no one doubted that homelessness had increased. Women and children constituted the fastest-growing population without shelter: One-fourth of the homeless were families with children. Those without homes included the victims of long-term unemployment, erosion of welfare benefits, and slum clearance as well as individuals suffering from mental illness, drug abuse, and alcoholism.

President Reagan insisted that a booming economy would benefit everyone. Average personal income did rise during his tenure, but the trend of income polarization that had begun in the 1970s sharpened in the 1980s, in part because of the new tax policies. The rich got richer, a portion of the middle class did well, and the poor got poorer. Personal income shot up sharply for the wealthiest 20 per-

HOMELESSNESS

The increased presence of homeless people in cities across the nation challenged the view of the 1980s as a decade of prosperity. Hundreds of homeless people could be found on the sidewalks of the nation's capital every night. In November 1987, during the first snow of the season, a homeless man sleeps in Lafayette Square across from the White House.

Corbis-Bettmann.

cent of Americans while it fell for the poorest by 9.8 percent between 1979 and 1987. No longer could all Americans expect, as they had in the two decades following World War II, that their children would do better than they had done (Figure 29.3).

Even before the 1990 recession, many Americans saw the economic boom pass them by. Affluent urbanites walked past numerous men and women sleeping in subway stations, on grates over steam vents, and on park benches near city monuments.

Poverty statistics, too, revealed a reversal of the trend toward greater equality. Between 1980 and 1988, poor people increased from 11.7 to 13.5 percent of total U.S. population—the highest poverty rate in the industrialized world. A relatively low poverty rate among the elderly testified to the lasting success of New Deal and Great Society pro-grams, especially Social Security and Medicare. Less fortunate were large segments of other groups that the economic boom had bypassed: racial minorities, female-headed families, and children. One child in every five lived in a household with income below the official poverty line.

Many Americans struggled not to lose ground. The decline in manufacturing jobs and weakening of organized labor eroded the position of blue-collar men with only high school educations. A second income was needed to stave off economic decline. By 1990, nearly 60 percent of married women with young children worked outside the home. Yet even with the growth of two-income families, fewer young families could purchase their first home. The average $10,000 per year disparity between male and female earnings made things even harder for the nearly 20 percent of families that were headed by women. One mother of two, divorced from an abusive husband, reported, "Jobs just don't pay good money." She supplemented her paycheck by selling her blood and accepting help from her church.

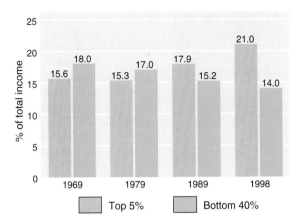

FIGURE 29.3

The Growth of Inequality: Changes in Family Income, 1969–1998

For most of the post–World War II period, income increased for all groups on the economic ladder; but after 1979, income of the poorest families actually declined, while it grew substantially for the richest 20 percent of the population.

Copyright © 1989 by the New York Times Co. Reprinted by permission.

Battling for the Center Ground: The Clinton Years

After more than two decades during which Democrats occupied the White House for only four years, Bill Clinton believed that his party could win back voters only if it moved away from liberalism and to the center of the political spectrum. This meant paying less attention to the needs of the poor and more to those of middle-class Americans, restraining federal programs and budgets, being tough on crime, and emphasizing religion and traditional family values. Yet Clinton did not completely abandon the principles that had guided the party in the 1960s. He signed some measures benefiting the working poor, delivered incremental reforms to feminists, environmentalists, and other groups, and spoke out in favor of affirmative action and gay rights.

More important than any of its domestic programs, the Clinton administration ended its eight years with a surplus in the federal budget and the longest economic boom in history. Although various factors, not just Clinton's policies, generated the prosperity, many Americans identified him with the buoyant economy and returned him to office for a second term. And a majority continued to support him even when his reckless sexual behavior disgraced the Presidency and resulted in Clinton's impeachment. Although the Senate did not find sufficient cause to remove him from office, the fallout from the scandal helped Republican George W. Bush capture the presidency in the bitterly contested election of 2000.

The 1992 Election and the Promise of Change

In 1992, the Democratic Party concluded its nominating convention in accord with tradition, as the candidates, their families, and supporters celebrated on a massive podium above the cheering delegates. This year, however, the candidates represented something new. William Jefferson "Bill" Clinton and Albert Gore Jr. were both in their mid-forties, the first baby boomers to run on a major party ticket, the first candidates not to have experienced World War II. The music, too, symbolized a new era. Instead of "Happy Days Are Here Again," the Democratic theme song since the 1930s, the band blared Fleetwood Mac's rock music. "Don't stop thinking about tomorrow," the lyrics sang. "Yesterday's gone."

Because President Bush's chances for reelection had looked so golden in 1991, the most prominent Democrats opted out of the presidential race. That, however, did not deter Bill Clinton, who at age forty-five had served as governor of Arkansas for twelve years. Like Jimmy Carter in 1976 and Michael Dukakis in 1988, Clinton and Gore presented themselves as "New Democrats." Both belonged to the Democratic Leadership Council, which Clinton had helped found in 1985 to rid the party of its liberal image. Clinton deliberately distanced himself from the Reverend Jesse Jackson and his Rainbow Coalition and appealed to voters who believed that some Americans were getting a free ride at their expense. "We're going to put an end to welfare as we know it," Clinton claimed. Disavowing the "tax and spend" label that Republicans pinned on his party, he promised a tax cut for the middle class. Portraying President Bush as a do-nothing official even while unemployment neared 8 percent, Clinton promised to reinvigorate government and the economy.

The popularity of a third candidate revealed Americans' frustrations with government and thirst

CLINTON AND GORE ON TOUR
The gregarious Bill Clinton excelled at political campaigning. During the 1992 presidential election campaign, he and his wife, Hillary—accompanied by running mate Al Gore and his wife, Tipper—went out on several bus tours as a way of demonstrating the Democrats' connection to ordinary people. Not far from this campaign stop in Sylvester, Georgia, the bus caravan passed by a handmade sign that read "Bubbas for Clinton/Gore."
Copyright © Ira Wyman / Sygma.

for change. In announcing his candidacy for president on the popular talk show *Larry King Live,* self-made Texas billionaire H. Ross Perot set the tone of his unconventional campaign. He used television extensively but gave no press conferences, and he chose an inexperienced running mate. But he had plenty of money and attracted a sizable grassroots movement with his down-to-earth personality and appeals to voters' disgust with Washington. Perot's candidacy hurt the president more than it hurt Clinton, and it established the federal budget deficit as a key campaign issue.

Americans reversed the thirty-year decline in voter turnout as 55 percent of those eligible went to the polls. They gave Clinton 43 percent of their votes, Bush 38 percent, and Perot 19 percent—the strongest third-party finish since Theodore Roosevelt's Progressive Party candidacy in 1912 (Map 29.4). The Democrats barely maintained their majority in Congress. Although casting two-thirds of their votes against Bush demonstrated a mandate for change, voters formed no majority around a particular direction that change should take.

Some Americans believed that the federal government had grown too large and powerful; they worried about the growing federal debt, which reached $4.4 trillion in 1993 and resulted in interest charges that consumed one-fifth of the federal budget. Yet most opposed higher taxes and did not want to give up the government benefits they enjoyed. As businesses tried to trim budgets and become

more competitive, victims of corporate restructuring worried about finding new jobs. Access to good health care and reversal of rising crime rates constituted other major concerns, but those goals de-

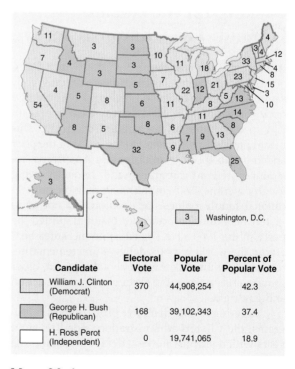

Candidate	Electoral Vote	Popular Vote	Percent of Popular Vote
William J. Clinton (Democrat)	370	44,908,254	42.3
George H. Bush (Republican)	168	39,102,343	37.4
H. Ross Perot (Independent)	0	19,741,065	18.9

MAP 29.4
The Election of 1992

pended on more federal spending or intrusion than most Americans seemed willing to accept.

Americans reversed the thirty-year decline in voter turnout as 55 percent of those eligible went to the polls. Although casting two-thirds of their votes against Bush demonstrated a mandate for change, voters formed no majority around a particular direction that change should take.

Clinton wanted to restore confidence in government as a force for good, but he did not want to alienate antigovernment voters by proposing new large federal programs, and in any case, the budget deficit precluded such spending. Just as Clinton was short on cash for using government in positive ways, he was also short on political capital, for the Republicans controlled Congress all but his first two years in office. Further, Clinton presided over a country no longer engaged in the cold war, and thus lacking the agent that had given Americans a sense of national purpose and had encouraged domestic reform to strengthen the nation at home in order to combat communism abroad.

Still, the popular mandate for change allowed the New Democrat president to exert some federal authority to solve national problems while keeping his campaign promises to limit the role of government. For example, although Clinton quickly backed away from his pledge to end discrimination against homosexuals in the military, he signed several bills that Republicans had blocked during the previous twelve years, including gun control legislation and a $30 billion anticrime program. Using his executive powers to reverse policies of Presidents Reagan and Bush, he eased restrictions on abortion counseling and paved the way for import of the French abortion pill, RU-486, which the Federal Drug Administration approved for distribution in 2000. In addition to the Family and Medical Leave Act, which allowed workers to take unpaid leave to care for family members, Clinton approved measures to increase the minimum wage, make voter registration easier, improve college students' access to federal loans, and establish Americorps, a program enabling students to pay for their education with community service. Most significantly, to fulfill his campaign promise that no full-time worker

should live in poverty, Clinton pushed through a substantial increase in the Earned Income Tax Credit for low wage earners. This meant that people who worked full-time at meager wages would receive tax reductions, or, if they paid no taxes, a government subsidy to lift their family income above the poverty line. By 2000, 15 million low-income families were benefiting from the Earned Income Tax Credit.

"The economy, stupid." During the presidential campaign, this prominent sign at Clinton's headquarters reminded staffers to keep the focus on what they thought mattered most to voters. By the election, the economy had already begun to rebound, and the boom that followed helped boost Clinton's popularity through the 1990s. Economic expansion, along with budget cuts, tax increases, and declining unemployment, reduced the federal budget deficit by about half between 1992 and 1996 and in 1998 produced the first surplus since 1969. Even after Congress in 1997 passed the largest tax cut since 1981, reducing levies on estates and capital gains and providing tax credits for families with children and for higher education, the surplus grew. The seemingly inexorable trend of increasing government debt had turned around.

Clinton stumbled badly, however, over an ambitious health care reform plan, which had two key objectives: to help the 39 million Americans without health insurance by providing universal coverage and to curb the steeply rising costs of medical care. Under the direction of First Lady Hillary Rodham Clinton, the administration presented a complex bill that much of the health care industry charged would mean higher taxes and government interference in health care decisions. Although the bill failed, private industry made strides in curtailing costs—at patients' expense, some argued. Congress enacted piecemeal reform by enabling workers who changed jobs to retain health insurance and by establishing a new health care program for 5 million uninsured children. Yet the number of Americans without health insurance surpassed 40 million, about 15 percent of the population, in 2000.

Clinton Courts the Right

If parts of President Clinton's agenda sustained the traditional Democratic emphasis on using government to help the disadvantaged, his presidency in general moved the party to the right. The 1994 elections, which swept away the Democratic majorities in both houses of Congress, contributed to Clinton's embrace of Republican issues such as welfare reform and downsizing government. Echoing Ronald Reagan, Clinton averred in his 1996 State of the Union address, "The era of big government is over."

Led by Representative Newt Gingrich of Georgia, Republicans considered the 1994 elections a mandate for their "contract with America," a conservative platform that included drastic contraction of the federal government, deep tax cuts, constitutional amendments to ban abortions, and term limits on members of Congress. Although Gingrich succeeded in moving the debate to the right, vetoes by Clinton and opposition from Democrats and more moderate Republicans stymied most of the contract pledges.

Echoing Ronald Reagan, Clinton averred in his 1996 State of the Union address, "The era of big government is over."

Far from Washington, a more extreme antigovernment movement emerged in the form of grassroots armed militias claiming patriotism and the need to defend themselves from government tyranny. Anticipating government repression, they stockpiled, according to one militia leader, "the four Bs: Bibles, bullets, beans, and bandages" and embraced a variety of sentiments, including opposition to taxes and the United Nations, anti-Semitism, and white supremacy. Their ranks grew after gun control legislation passed and after government agents stormed the headquarters of an armed religious cult in Waco, Texas, resulting in more than eighty deaths. On the second anniversary of that event, April 19, 1995, in the worst terrorist attack in the nation's history, a bomb leveled a federal building in Oklahoma City, taking 169 lives. Authorities quickly arrested two militia members, who were tried and convicted in 1997.

Clinton's reassuring handling of the Oklahoma City bombing helped restore his presidential stature. Looking toward the 1996 election, Clinton used his real and threatened veto power against what he labeled "extreme" Republican measures. Forcing the shaping of legislation along more moderate lines, he himself moved toward the center. For example, he firmly opposed deep cuts in education, environment, and welfare programs, but he cooperated with Republicans on a plan to balance the budget in seven years.

Clinton's determination to cast himself as a centrist was nowhere more apparent than in his handling of welfare reform. Since Lyndon Johnson's war on poverty in the 1960s, public sentiment had shifted. Instead of blaming poverty on a shortage of adequate jobs, poor education, and other circumstances beyond an individual's control, more people were inclined to blame the poor themselves and government welfare, which they charged kept people in cycles of dependency. Nearly everyone considered work better than welfare but disagreed about whether the nation's economy could provide sufficient jobs at decent wages and how much government assistance poor people needed in the transition from welfare to work. Most estimates showed that it cost less to support a family on welfare than to provide the job training, child care, and other supports necessary for that transition.

Clinton allowed the Republicans to take the initiative in welfare reform, though he vetoed two measures and thereby forced a less punitive bill, which he signed as the 1996 election approached. The Personal Responsibility and Work Opportunity Reconciliation Act abolished Aid to Families with Dependent Children (AFDC) and with it the nation's pledge to provide a minimum level of subsistence for all its children. In place of AFDC, the law authorized grants to the states, with the requirement to limit welfare payments to two years whether the recipient could find a job or not. The law set a lifetime limit of aid at five years, barred legal immigrants who had not become citizens from food stamps and other benefits, and allowed states to stop Medicaid to legal immigrants.

A "moment of shame," cried Marian Wright Edelman, president of the Children's Defense Fund, when Clinton signed the bill. State and local officials across the country scrambled to understand the law and how to implement it. "We certainly endorse the overall direction toward work," a Minnesota official said, while expressing grave concern about how the law would operate. "A child could very well have to go to foster care," predicted a Louisiana social worker. Critics proved wrong in their most severe predictions. By 2000, welfare rolls had been cut nearly in half, while the poverty rate fell to 11.4 percent, its lowest in more than two decades. That did not mean, however, that all former welfare recipients were now self-supporting. Forty percent of former welfare mothers were not working regularly after being cut from the rolls, and those who did have jobs earned on average only about $12,000 a year. The strong economy along with large increases in the earned income tax credit and other forms of assistance to the working poor made it possible to reduce welfare rolls without catastrophic results.

Clinton claimed that the new law meant that "welfare will no longer be a political issue," and his signature on it meant that the Republicans could not use the welfare issue against him. In the 1996 election campaign, the president ran as a moderate who would save the country from extremist Republicans. In fact, the Republican Party also moved to the center, passing over a field of conservatives to nominate Kansan Robert Dole, a World War II hero and former Senate majority leader who had served in Washington for more than two decades.

Whether out of satisfaction with a favorable economy or boredom with the candidates, about half of all voters stayed home. Fifty percent of those who voted chose Clinton, while 41 percent favored Dole, and 9 percent Perot, who ran again as a third-party candidate. The largest gender gap to date appeared in the election: Women awarded 54 percent of their votes to Clinton and 38 percent to Dole, while men split their votes between the two candidates nearly evenly. Although Clinton won reelection with room to spare, voters sent a Republican majority back to Congress.

Impeaching the President

Clinton's ability to undercut the Republicans and capture the middle ground of the electorate, along with the nation's economic successes, enabled the self-proclaimed "comeback kid" to survive a series of scandals and an impeachment trial in 1998. Early in the first Clinton administration, charges of illegalities related to firings of White House staff, political use of FBI records, and the Clintons' involvement in a real estate deal in Arkansas, nicknamed Whitewater, led to an official investigation by an independent prosecutor. Kenneth W. Starr, who took over the probe in 1994, won convictions of some Clinton associates related to Whitewater, but he could pin no illegalities on the President or the First Lady. Clinton also faced a charge of sexual harassment in a lawsuit filed in 1994 by

Paula Corbin Jones, who asserted that in 1991 when he was governor of Arkansas and she worked for the state, he had made unwanted sexual advances. A federal court threw out Jones's suit in April 1998, but Clinton's relationships with other women continued to threaten his presidency.

In January 1998, independent prosecutor Starr began to investigate the most inflammatory charge—that Clinton had had sexual relations with a twenty-one-year-old White House intern, Monica S. Lewinsky, and then had tried to cover up the affair by lying about it to a federal grand jury. Clinton first vehemently denied the charge but subsequently bowed to the mounting evidence against him. In September, Starr took his case for impeachment to the House of Representatives, and in December 1998 the House voted, mostly along party lines and by margins of 228 to 206 and 221 to 212, to impeach the president on two counts, perjury and obstruction of justice. Clinton became the second president—after Andrew Johnson, in 1868—to be impeached by the House and tried by the Senate.

Most Americans believed that the president had acted recklessly and inappropriately with Lewinsky and then lied about it, yet they continued to express approval of his presidency and to oppose impeachment. Some saw Starr as a fanatic invading individuals' privacy; most people clearly separated what they considered the president's private actions from his public duties. One man said, "Let him get a divorce from his wife. Don't take him out of office and disrupt the country." Too, Americans recognized that John F. Kennedy, among other presidents, had engaged in extramarital relations, but the press had protected them. Those favoring impeachment insisted that the president must not be above the law, that he must set a high moral standard for the nation, and that lying to a grand jury was a serious offense even if it was about a private matter.

The Senate conducted the impeachment trial with much less partisanship than that displayed in the House. A number of senators believed that Clinton had committed perjury and obstruction of justice but did not find those actions to constitute the high crimes and misdemeanors required by the Constitution for removal of a president. With a two-thirds majority needed for that result, the Senate voted 45 to 55 (with 10 Republicans supporting the president) on the perjury count and 50 to 50 (with 5 Republicans joining the Democrats) on the ob-

The Hangman

HOW DOES HE DO IT?

CLINTON'S IMPEACHMENT
This cartoon expresses the consternation of Republicans when President Clinton's approval ratings remained high despite the revelation of his affair with Monica Lewinsky and his subsequent impeachment. Many Americans, although not condoning the president's behavior, separated what they considered his private actions from his public duties and criticized prosecutor Kenneth Starr and the Republicans for not doing the same.

struction of justice count. A majority of senators seemed to agree with Clinton's advocate, former Democratic Senator Dale Bumpers of Arkansas, who called the president's behavior "indefensible, outrageous, unforgivable, shameless," but insufficient to warrant his removal from office.

The Whitewater investigation, trigger of the events leading up to impeachment, culminated in 2000 when the last independent counsel concluded that there was insufficient evidence to implicate the Clintons in the illegalities surrounding the Whitewater land deals. The investigation had lasted six years and cost almost $60 million of federal funds. Official and popular dissatisfaction with Whitewater and other investigations by special prosecutors ranged so widely and vociferously that Congress quietly declined to extend the independent counsel act when it expired in 1998.

The Booming Economy of the 1990s

President Clinton's ability to weather the impeachment crisis drew incalculable help from the prosperous economy. Beginning in 1991, Americans experienced the longest period of economic growth in U.S. history. During Clinton's years in office, the gross domestic product grew by more than one-third, 13 million new jobs were created, unemploy-

ment reached its lowest point in 25 years, inflation remained in check, and the stock market soared.

President Clinton's ability to weather the impeachment crisis drew incalculable help from the prosperous economy. Beginning in 1991, Americans experienced the longest period of economic growth in U.S. history.

Clinton eagerly took credit for the thriving economy, and his policies did contribute to the boom. He made deficit reduction a priority and in exchange the Federal Reserve Board and bond market traders lowered interest rates, which in turn encouraged economic expansion by making money easier to borrow. Major industries prospered, too, because they had squeezed down their costs through restructuring and laying off workers. Economic problems in Europe and Asia helped American firms become more competitive in the international market. Above all, the computer revolution and the application of information technology to all stages of the production and distribution of goods and services tremendously boosted productivity. By the end of the century, half the workforce used computers in their jobs.

The important role of information technology in the economic boom also meant that it had uneven effects. People at all income levels benefited from the prosperity, as median household income surpassed $40,000 for the first time in 1999 and the poverty rate fell to 11.8 percent. Yet that rate still surpassed the low of 11.1 percent reached in 1973. Moreover, in contrast to the economic expansion of the 1950s and 1960s, the gaps between rich and poor and between rich and middle class that had been growing since the 1970s failed to narrow. This persistence of inequality in a rising economy was linked in part to what fueled the boom. The growing application of information technology along with the movement of manufacturing jobs abroad increased the demand for highly skilled workers and lessened the opportunities and wages for those not trained in the requisite skills. In addition, lower-skilled workers lost power as the result of deregulation, globalization, and the continuing decline of unions; and the national minimum wage failed to keep up with inflation.

The Election of 2000

The booming economy failed to give Democratic candidate Vice President Albert Gore sufficient help to retain the White House for his party in the election of 2000. His choice of running mate, Connecticut Senator Joseph Lieberman, the first Jew to run on a major party ticket, was popular, and public opinion polls indicated that a majority of Americans agreed with the Democratic nominees on most issues. Yet Gore appeared stiff and aloof to many voters, too willing to change his positions to gain political advantage, and too inclined to shade the truth.

Texas governor George W. Bush emerged as the Republican nominee from a series of hard-fought primaries, which he financed with the most money ever raised in a presidential campaign. The oldest son of former president George H. Bush had attended Yale and Harvard and then worked in the oil industry in Texas and as managing partner of the Texas Rangers baseball team. In 1994, Texans elected him governor. Criticized for his lack of Washington and international experience and his unfamiliarity with certain policy issues, Bush chose for his running mate a seasoned official, Richard B. Cheney, who had served in the Nixon and Ford ad-

ministrations, represented Wyoming in Congress, and held the post of Secretary of Defense under the elder Bush.

Both contestants ran cautious campaigns, seeking to accommodate their positions to what polls indicated that voters wanted. Bush's strategy mirrored that of Clinton in 1992. Calling himself a "compassionate conservative," he separated himself from the extreme right wing of the Republican Party and tried to coopt Democratic issues such as education and the high cost of prescription drugs. At the same time, he promised a substantial tax cut and charged that Gore represented the party of big government.

Many observers predicted that the amazingly strong economy would give Gore the edge in the close presidential race, and he did surpass Bush by more than one-half million votes. Once the polls closed, it became clear that whoever won Florida's twenty-five electoral college votes would win the election. Bush's margin was so tiny in that state, where his brother served as governor, that it

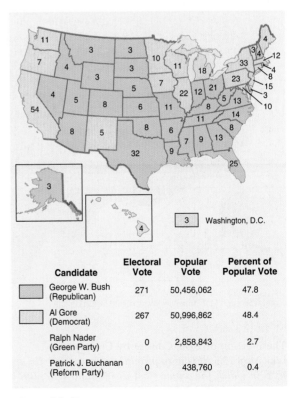

Candidate	Electoral Vote	Popular Vote	Percent of Popular Vote
George W. Bush (Republican)	271	50,456,062	47.8
Al Gore (Democrat)	267	50,996,862	48.4
Ralph Nader (Green Party)	0	2,858,843	2.7
Patrick J. Buchanan (Reform Party)	0	438,760	0.4

MAP 29.5
The Election of 2000

prompted an automatic recount of the votes, which eventually gave Bush an edge of 537 votes.

Meanwhile the Democrats asked for ballots to be counted by hand in several heavily Democratic counties where machine errors may have left hundreds of votes unrecorded. The Republicans, in turn, went to court to try to stop the hand counts. As the dispute unfolded, many Americans discovered that counties used different voting systems and that some systems were more prone to error. Punchcard ballots were most unreliable, and they were more likely to be used in counties with large numbers of minority and poor voters.

The outcome of the 2000 election hung in the balance for more than a month as the court cases went all the way up to the Supreme Court. Finally, a bitterly divided Supreme Court ruled 5–4 against further recounts of the Florida vote and Gore conceded the presidency to Bush on December 13, 2000. For the first time since 1888, a president who failed to win the popular vote took office (Maps 29.5 and 29.6). For that reason and because Republicans held a mere five-vote margin in the House of Representatives and could prevail in the evenly divided Senate only with the tie-breaking vote of Vice President Cheney, national politics seemed likely to remain on center ground and hotly contested during the first administration of the twenty-first century.

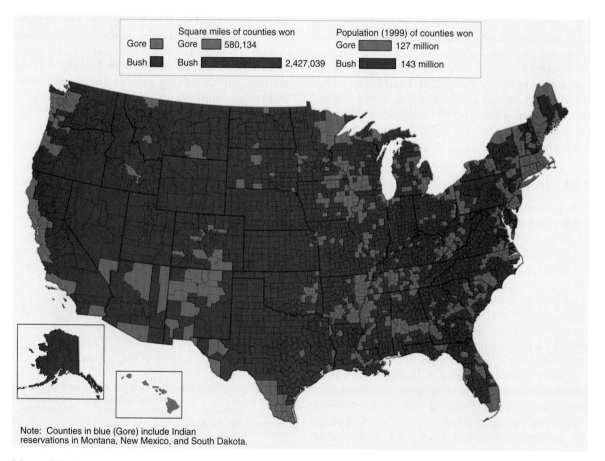

Note: Counties in blue (Gore) include Indian reservations in Montana, New Mexico, and South Dakota.

MAP 29.6

The Election of 2000, County by County

Like Map 29.5, this map provides information about the first presidential election since 1888 in which the winner lost the popular vote. But where Map 29.5 illustrates the outcome state by state, the results here are mapped county by county, to indicate the distribution of votes within as well as among states. Note especially the marked rural-urban divide that transcends state borders, revealing the strength of this traditional division at the start of a new century.

THE DISPUTED ELECTION
While lawyers representing presidential candidates George W. Bush and Al Gore
pursued lawsuits concerning the counting of ballots that would determine who won
Florida's twenty-five electoral college votes, partisan supporters took to the streets.
Here backers of both sides rally outside the Supreme Court in Washington, D.C., on
Monday, December 11, 2000, a day before the Court issued its 5–4 ruling that ended the
hand recounts of ballots and consequently secured the presidency for Bush. Critics who
charged that the five justices who voted to stop the recounts had applied partisanship
rather than objectivity to the case pointed out that the decision went against the
Court's custom of preferring state over federal authority.
Wide World Photos, Inc.

Conclusion: Reversing the Course of Government

"Ours was the first revolution in the history of mankind that truly reversed the course of government," boasted Ronald Reagan in his Farewell Address in 1989. Although he exaggerated in using the word *revolution,* his administration did stand at the center of a development that halted the expanding federal budgets, programs, and regulations that had taken off in the 1930s. Incongruously, Reagan admired and copied the political techniques of Franklin Delano Roosevelt, who had launched that expansion, but he used his comparable skills as "the Great Communicator" to cultivate antigovernment

sentiment and undo the liberal assumptions of the New Deal.

"What the people want is simple. They want an America as good as its promise." Texas Congresswoman Barbara Jordan's words at Harvard University's commencement in June 1977 recognized the decline of public confidence and trust in government in the 1970s, a disillusionment caused in part by Watergate and other revelations of deception and corruption in the Nixon administration. Presidents Ford and Carter restored morality to the White House, but both were deficient in political skills and faced the gravest economic problems since the Great Depression—a low rate of economic growth, inflation combined with unemployment, and an increasing trade deficit. Congress continued

THE STABILITY OF AMERICAN CONSTITUTIONALISM
A week after the Supreme Court stopped the recounting of votes and Gore conceded the presidency to Bush, the two met in Washington, D.C., at the vice president's residence. Their public handshake in the snow symbolized Americans' willingness to abide by the rules governing their political institutions even when the electoral process was flawed and bitterly contested.
Wide World Photos, Inc.

key domestic reforms of the 1960s and passed new legislation in response to movements for women's rights and environmental protection. Yet even the Democrat Carter gave higher priority to fiscal austerity than to social reform, and he began the government's retreat from regulation in key industries.

During the Reagan-Bush years, as a new conservative movement flourished, the United States turned explicitly away from the assumptions that had shaped domestic policy since the New Deal. Republican presidents Eisenhower and Nixon had attempted to curb the role of the federal government, but no president before Ronald Reagan had so criticized its activities. His tax cuts, combined with

hefty increases in defense spending, created a federal deficit crisis that justified cuts in social welfare spending and made new federal initiatives unthinkable. Many Americans continued to approve of specific federal programs at the end of the Reagan-Bush years, but public sentiment about the government in general had undergone a U-turn from the Roosevelt era. Instead of seeing the government as a helpful and problem-solving institution, they believed it was not only ineffective at solving national problems but often prone to make things worse. As new justices came on to the Supreme Court, that body also retreated from its earlier liberalism, in which it had upheld the government's authority to protect individual rights and regulate the economy. When the Democrats regained the White House in 1992 it was clear that the political spectrum had shifted to the right. The Clinton administration accomplished some reforms that used federal authority to solve national problems, but overall Clinton pursued a centrist strategy both in rhetoric and in practice. And in the 2000 elections for president and Congress the American electorate split its vote so evenly that the new administration of Republican George W. Bush seemed bound to continue the politics of the center.

With his optimistic rhetoric, Ronald Reagan had also lifted the confidence of Americans about their nation and its promise. The sense of American greatness, which had suffered with the economic and foreign policy blows of the 1970s, gained further strength when the United States reached a state of unparalleled prosperity in the 1990s. Yet a huge gap between rich and poor did not budge, and more than one in ten individuals continued to live in poverty. Children were disproportionately poor, as were members of minority groups, many of whom were part of the surge of immigrants that began in the 1970s. That new immigration both propelled the diversifying of American society that would stretch into the twenty-first century and reflected the process of globalization that changed American lives in manifold ways.

www.bedfordstmartins.com/tap SEE THE ONLINE STUDY GUIDE to assess your mastery of the material covered in this chapter.

CHRONOLOGY

1968 Richard Nixon elected president of United States.

1969 Warren E. Burger appointed chief justice of United States by Nixon.

1970 Earth Day demonstrations held to support environmental goals.

Congress passes Occupational Safety and Health Act.

Environmental Protection Agency established by Nixon.

Native American Women's Association founded.

Women Strike for Peace and Equality demonstrations take place nationwide.

1971 First national Mexican American women's conference held.

In *Swann*, Supreme Court upholds legality of busing to achieve integration.

Nixon announces abandonment of gold standard in his New Economic Policy.

Nixon vetoes comprehensive child care bill.

1972 Congress passes Title IX of Education Amendments Act, banning sex discrimination in education.

Ms. magazine founded by Gloria Steinem and other feminists.

Nixon campaign aides apprehended breaking into Democratic Party headquarters in Watergate apartment complex in Washington, D.C.

Richard Nixon reelected president in landslide.

1973 National Black Feminist Organization founded.

In *Roe v. Wade*, Supreme Court rules that abortion is constitutionally protected.

1974 Nixon resigns as president in face of certain impeachment by House of Representatives over his role in Watergate affair; Gerald Ford becomes president of United States.

Ford pardons Nixon of any crimes he may have committed while president.

Supreme Court imposes some limitations on use of busing to achieve racial integration in schools.

1976 Jimmy Carter elected president of United States.

1978 In *Bakke*, Supreme Court rules against racial quotas and "reverse" discrimination.

Congress passes law banning discrimination against pregnant women.

1979–1980 Congress enacts measures to conserve energy and increase its production.

1980 Ronald Reagan elected president of United States, defeating incumbent Jimmy Carter.

1981 Researchers identify cause of AIDS epidemic as virus.

Congress passes Economic Recovery Tax Act advocated by Reagan, largest tax cut in U.S. history.

Reagan appoints Sandra Day O'Connor first female justice to U.S. Supreme Court.

1982 Banking industry deregulated.

1984 Ronald Reagan reelected president.

1988 Vice President George Bush elected forty-first president of United States.

1990 Bush and Congress agree to tax increase because of mounting federal deficit.

1991 Bush's nominee Clarence Thomas becomes second African American to sit on U.S. Supreme Court.

Congress passes Americans with Disabilities Act.

1992 Bill Clinton elected forty-second president of the United States.

1993 Janet Reno appointed first female attorney general in U.S. history.

Ruth Bader Ginsburg appointed second woman to U.S. Supreme Court.

Clinton announces "don't ask, don't tell" policy for gays in military.

Gun control and anticrime bills passed.

Clinton signs Family and Medical Leave Act, enabling many workers to take time off for childbirth, adoption, or family medical emergencies.

1994 Republicans recapture both House and Senate in congressional elections.

Representative Newt Gingrich declares 1994 elections a mandate for Republicans' conservative "contract with America."

1995 Bomb destroys federal building in Oklahoma City, claiming 169 lives; two militia members convicted in 1997.

1996 Clinton signs Personal Responsibility and Work Opportunity Reconciliation Act, ending the federal welfare program begun in 1930s.

Clinton reelected president.

1997 Clinton signs largest tax cut since 1981.

1998 Federal budget shows surplus for first time since 1969.

House of Representatives votes to impeach President Clinton for perjury and obstruction of justice.

1999 Senate fails to approve articles of impeachment.

2000 George W. Bush elected forty-third president of the United States.

BIBLIOGRAPHY

ENERGY AND THE ENVIRONMENT

S. David Aviel, *The Politics of Nuclear Energy* (1982).

Thomas R. Dunlap, *DDT: Scientists, Citizens, and Public Policy* (1981).

Samuel P. Hays, *Beauty, Health, and Permanence: Environmental Politics in the United States, 1955–1985* (1987).

Michael J. Lacey, ed., *Government and Environmental Politics* (1991).

Martin V. Melosi, *Coping with Abundance: Energy and Environment in Industrial America* (1985).

Philip Shabecoff, *A Fierce Green Fire: The American Environmental Movement* (1993).

Franklin Tugwell, *The Energy Crisis and the American Political Economy: Politics and Markets in the Management of Natural Resources* (1988).

Daniel Yergin, *The Prize: The Epic Quest for Oil, Money, and Power* (1990).

THE WOMEN'S MOVEMENT

Mary Frances Berry, *Why ERA Failed* (1986).

Anne N. Costain, *Inviting Women's Rebellion* (1992).

Barbara Hinkson Craig and David M. O'Brien, *Abortion and American Politics* (1993).

Dennis Deslippe, *"Rights, Not Roses": Unions and the Rise of Working-Class Feminism* (2000).

Alice Echols, *Daring to Be Bad: Radical Feminism in America, 1967–1975* (1989).

Jo Freeman, *The Politics of Women's Liberation* (1985).

Joyce Gelb and Marion Lief Palley, *Women and Public Policies* (1987).

Susan M. Hartmann, *From Margin to Mainstream: American Women and Politics since 1960* (1989).

Susan M. Hartmann, *The Other Feminists: Activists in the Liberal Establishment* (1998).

Jane J. Mansbridge, *Why We Lost the ERA* (1986).

Donald G. Mathews and Jane Sherron De Hart, *Sex, Gender, and the Politics of ERA* (1990).

Rosalind Pollack Petchesky, *Abortion and Woman's Choice: Private Morality and Public Policy* (1981).

Ruth Rosen, *The World Split Open: How the Women's Movement Changed America* (2000).

Winifred D. Wandersee, *On the Move: American Women in the 1970s* (1988).

Guida West, *The National Welfare Rights Movement: The Social Protest of Poor Women* (1981).

Deborah Gray White, *Too Heavy a Load: Black Women in Defense of Themselves, 1894–1994* (1999).

CONSERVATISM AND RIGHT-WING MOVEMENTS

Steve Bruce, *The Rise and Fall of the New Christian Right: Conservative Protestant Politics in America, 1978–1988* (1988).

Thomas Byrd Edsall with Mary D. Edsall, *Chain Reaction: The Impact of Race, Rights, and Taxes on American Politics* (1992).

Thomas Ferguson and Joel Rogers, *Right Turn: The Decline of the Democrats and the Future of American Politics* (1986).

Godfrey Hodgson, *The World Turned Right Side Up: A History of the Conservative Ascendancy in America* (1996).

William Martin, *With God on Our Side: The Rise of the Religious Right in America* (1996).

Michael Meeropol, *Surrender: How the Clinton Administration Completed the Reagan Revolution* (1998).

Richard A. Serrano, *One of Ours: Timothy McVeigh and the Oklahoma City Bombing* (1998).

INDIVIDUAL RIGHTS AND THE SUPREME COURT

Barry D. Adam, *The Rise of a Gay and Lesbian Movement* (1987).

Norman C. Amaker, *Civil Rights and the Reagan Administration* (1988).

John D'Emilio, Urvashi Vaid, and William B. Turner, *Creating Change: Sexuality, Public Policy, and Civil Rights* (2000).

Lisa Keen and Suzanne B. Goldberg, *Strangers to the Law: Gay People on Trial* (1998).

Herman Schwartz, *Packing the Courts: The Conservative Campaign to Rewrite the Constitution* (1988).

Herman Schwartz, ed., *The Burger Years: Rights and Wrongs in the Supreme Court* (1987).

James F. Simon, *The Center Holds: The Power Struggle Inside the Rehnquist Court* (1995).

Melvin Urofsky, *A Conflict of Rights: The Supreme Court and Affirmative Action* (1991).

THE ECONOMY AND ITS CASUALTIES

Michael Bernstein, David E. Adler, and Robert Heilbroner, *Understanding American Economic Decline* (1994).

Joel Blau, *Homelessness in the United States* (1992).

Barry Bluestone and Bennett Harrison, *The Deindustrialization of America: Plant Closings, Community Abandonment, and the Dismantling of Basic Industry* (1982).

Kathleen Day, *S&L Hell: The People and the Politics behind the $1 Trillion Savings and Loan Scandal* (1993).

Martha Derthick and Paul J. Quirk, *The Politics of Deregulation* (1985).

Kathryn Marie Dudley, *The End of the Line: Lost Jobs, New Lives in Postindustrial America* (1994).

Bennett Harrison and Barry Bluestone, *The Great U-Turn: Corporate Restructuring and the Polarizing of America* (1988).

Jennifer L. Hochschild, *Facing Up to the American Dream: Race, Class, and the Soul of the Nation* (1995).

Christopher Jencks, *The Homeless* (1994).

Martin Lowy, *High Rollers: Inside the Savings and Loan Debacle* (1994).

Robert J. Samuelson, *The American Dream in the Age of Entitlement, 1945–1995* (1996).

John E. Schwarz and Thomas J. Volgy, *The Forgotten Americans* (1993).

Adam Smith, *The Roaring '80s* (1988).

A MULTICULTURAL SOCIETY

George J. Borjas, *Friends and Strangers: The Impact of Immigrants on the U.S. Economy* (1990).

L. H. Gann and Peter J. Duignan, *The Hispanics in the United States: A History* (1986).

Andrew Hacker, *Two Nations: Black and White, Separate, Hostile, Unequal* (1992).

Gerald David Jaynes and Robin M. Williams Jr., eds., *A Common Destiny: Blacks and American Society* (1989).

Sarah J. Mahler, *American Dreaming: Immigrant Life on the Margins* (1995).

David M. Reimers, *Still the Golden Door: The Third World Comes to America* (rev. ed., 1992).

David M. Reimers, *Unwelcome Strangers: American Identity and the Turn against Immigration* (1998).

Al Santoli, *New Americans: An Oral History* (1988).

Peter Skerry, *Mexican Americans: The Ambivalent Minority* (1993).

Ronald Takaki, *Strangers from a Different Shore: A History of Asian Americans* (1989).

Sanford J. Ungar, *Fresh Blood: The New American Immigrants* (1995).

William Wei, *The Asian American Movement* (1993).

THE NIXON AND FORD ADMINISTRATIONS

Stephen E. Ambrose, *Nixon: The Triumph of a Politician, 1962–1972* (1989).

Carl Bernstein and Bob Woodward, *All the President's Men* (1974).

Fred J. Cook, *The Crimes of Watergate* (1981).

Michael A. Genovese, *The Nixon Presidency: Power and Politics in Turbulent Times* (1990).

John Robert Greene, *The Limits of Power: The Nixon and Ford Administrations* (1992).

Joan Hoff, *Nixon Reconsidered* (1994).

Stanley I. Kutler, *The Wars of Watergate: The Last Crisis of Richard Nixon* (1990).

Kim McQuaid, *The Anxious Years: America in the Vietnam-Watergate Era* (1989).

Kathryn S. Olmsted, *Challenging the Secret Government: The Post-Watergate Investigations of the CIA and FBI* (1996).

Arthur M. Schlesinger, *The Imperial Presidency* (1973).

Melvin Small, *The Presidency of Richard Nixon* (1999).

Tom Wicker, *One of Us: Richard Nixon and the American Dream* (1991).

THE CARTER ADMINISTRATION

Peter G. Bourne, *Jimmy Carter: A Comprehensive Biography from Plains to Post-Presidency* (1997).

John Dumbrell, *The Carter Presidency: A Reevaluation* (1995).

Gary M. Fink and Hugh Davis Graham, eds., *The Carter Presidency: Policy Choices in the Post–New Deal Era* (1998).

Erwin C. Hargrove, *Jimmy Carter as President: Leadership and the Politics of the Public Good* (1988).

Burton I. Kaufmann, *The Presidency of James Earl Carter* (1993).

Kenneth Earl Morris, *Jimmy Carter, American Moralist* (1996).

THE REAGAN AND BUSH ADMINISTRATIONS

Lou Cannon, *President Reagan: The Role of a Lifetime* (1991).

Robert Dallek, *Ronald Reagan: The Politics of Symbolism* (1984).

John Robert Greene, *The Presidency of George Bush* (2000).

David Mervin, *George Bush and the Guardianship Presidency* (1996).

Herbert S. Parmet, *George Bush: The Life of a Lone Star Yankee* (1997).

Kevin Phillips, *The Politics of Rich and Poor: Wealth and the American Electorate in the Reagan Aftermath* (1990).

Paul Craig Roberts, *The Supply-Side Revolution* (1984).

Michael Schaller, *Reckoning with Reagan: America and Its President in the 1980s* (1992).

John W. Sloan, *The Reagan Effect: Economics and Presidential Leadership* (1999).

David Stockman, *The Triumph of Politics: How the Reagan Revolution Failed* (1986).

THE CLINTON ADMINISTRATION

James MacGregor Burns and Georgia Sorenson, *Dead Center: Clinton-Gore Leadership and the Perils of Moderation* (1999).

David Maraniss, *First in His Class: A Biography of Bill Clinton* (1995).

Roger Morris, *Partners in Power: The Clintons and Their America* (1996).

Gerald Posner, *Citizen Perot: His Life and Times* (1996).

Richard A. Posner, *An Affair of State: The Investigation, Impeachment, and Trial of President Clinton* (1999).

Jeffrey Toobin, *A Vast Conspiracy: The Real Story of the Sex Scandal that Nearly Brought Down a President* (2000).

Martin Walker, *The President We Deserve: Bill Clinton, His Rise, Falls, and Comebacks* (1996).

A SHRINKING WORLD

The videophone, a device that transmits both audio and video signals, is one of the new technologies contributing to the process of globalization that intensified with the end of the cold war in 1990. Videophones allow corporations to exchange information among operations stretching across the globe and enable their workers on several continents to "meet" face to face without traveling. These devices make possible other kinds of exchange, connecting far-flung family members as well as deaf people who use sign language to communicate. After a brutal civil war in the former Yugoslavia, videophones enabled physicians and hospitals in Britain, the United States, Saudi Arabia, and Germany to provide medical training and consultations for health-care workers in the province of Kosovo.

Frank Veronsky, Courtesy of the *Wall Street Journal*.

END OF THE COLD WAR AND RISE OF THE GLOBAL ECONOMY

30

1975–2000

A T THE END OF NOVEMBER 1999, tens of thousands of Americans went to Seattle, Washington, to protest U.S. government policy. Most of the activists marched in peaceful demonstrations and attended rallies. Hundreds of them, however, practiced civil disobedience, blocking traffic and shutting down the city's central area to prevent Secretary of State Madeleine Albright and other officials from reaching their meeting halls. Others smashed windows, spray-painted graffiti, and set fires. Police in riot gear aimed tear gas and rubber bullets at those who refused to move, and arrested more than six hundred people. Seattle's mayor Paul Schell declared a state of civil emergency and asked Governor Gary Locke to send in the National Guard. Although the vast majority of the protesters acted lawfully, such civil strife had not been seen in the United States since the antiwar demonstrations of the 1960s and 1970s.

The outward resemblances between the Seattle and anti–Vietnam War demonstrations, however, overlay acute differences demonstrating how much the world had changed by the 1990s. Citizen opposition to U.S. policy toward Vietnam dealt with political and military issues; by contrast, the Seattle protests focused on economic and environmental questions. In fact, a meeting of an international economic body, the World Trade Organization (WTO), was what had brought the demonstrators to Seattle. The WTO came into existence on January 1, 1995, replacing the General Agreement on Tariffs and Trade (GATT), which had been established in 1948 to liberalize trading policies and practices among its 23 member nations; having grown to 135 members, the WTO continued the GATT's goals and also took on the task of mediating trade disputes. Many of its critics charged that the organization promoted a global economy that undercut standards and wages for workers, destroyed the environment, and devastated the poorer, developing nations; others, who reflected an older isolationist tradition, objected to diluting American autonomy in economic decision making.

The groups represented by the Seattle protestors covered a broader political spectrum and differed in significant ways from the opponents of the Vietnam War. Young radicals appeared in both protest movements, but in Seattle they joined ranks with steelworkers, longshoremen, and other labor union members—the hard-hat workers who had largely supported administration policy in Vietnam. Environmentalists played no visible role in anti–Vietnam War activism, but they were prominent in Seattle; some dressed as sea turtles, an endangered species that symbolized for protesters the WTO's failure to uphold environmental standards.

PROTESTS AGAINST THE WTO *Environmentalists and animal protection advocates were among the varied groups demonstrating against the World Trade Organization when it attempted to meet in Seattle, Washington, in November 1999. These activists dressed as sea turtles to protest WTO agreements permitting economic actions that they believed threatened the survival of the animals.*
Wide World Photos, Inc.

Reflecting these new alliances, one protester carried a sign reading "Teamsters and Turtles—Together at Last." Other activists represented human rights groups, organizations devoted to the concerns of developing nations, and consumers. While protesters could take only part of the credit for the WTO's failure in Seattle to make progress on trade liberalization, they did achieve great visibility for their issues. California state Senator Tom Hayden, the former student radical leader from the 1960s, proclaimed, "A week ago no one even knew what the WTO was. Now these protests have made WTO a household word."

The demonstrations in Seattle in 1999 reflected massive changes that ended the cold war and transformed the world. Yet as recently as 1990, few Americans could predict the major cause for these momentous changes—the dissolution of the Soviet Union. In the 1970s, President Richard Nixon pursued less hostile relationships with both the Soviet Union and China, yet he practiced unrelenting opposition to communism in the third world. In the 1980s, President Ronald Reagan voiced the most hawkish rhetoric since the days of John Foster Dulles and promoted the nation's largest military buildup in peacetime. Even though the United States and the Soviet Union moved closer together near the end of Reagan's second term, the end of the cold war took the most astute foreign policy observers by surprise.

Eastern Europe broke free from Communist control in 1989, and the Soviet Union disintegrated in 1991. With the end of the cold war, which had been the obsession of U.S. foreign policy for forty-five years, the nation's leaders searched for a new strategy in an era no longer defined by containment of communism. Emerging from the cold war as the lone superpower, the United States deployed both military and diplomatic power during episodes of instability in the Middle East, eastern Europe, and Africa. Yet no consensus emerged around the questions of where and under what conditions the United States should act beyond its borders. And, as the demonstrations in Seattle proved, neither did Americans agree about how the United States should participate in the increasingly interconnected global economy.

New Opportunities and Dangers in a Multipolar World

The challenges and opportunities of foreign policy captured Richard M. Nixon's greatest enthusiasm, and he hoped to use his broad understanding of international relations to make his mark on history. Diverging from Republican orthodoxy, he made dramatic overtures to the Soviet Union and China and helped lessen hostilities between the United States and those two nations. In other areas of the world such as the Middle East and Latin America, however, his policies came straight out of the cold war book of anticommunism.

Détente faltered under Nixon's successors, presidents Ford and Carter, and Soviet-American relations deteriorated. Carter followed up on Nixon's initiatives by establishing normal diplomatic relations with China. In addition, he obtained ratification of treaties ending U.S. control over the Panama Canal, and his skillful diplomacy helped to secure a peace treaty between Israel and Egypt. But Middle East tensions failed to ease significantly, and his last year in office was dominated by a crisis with a new intensely anti-American government in Iran.

Moving toward Détente with the Soviet Union and China

New approaches to China and the Soviet Union formed the keystone of Nixon's foreign policy. The discord between the Soviet Union and China and the growing power of Europe and Japan, he believed, indicated that the "rigid and bipolar world of the 1940s and 1950s" was giving way to "the fluidity of a new era of multilateral diplomacy." With

his chief foreign policy adviser, Henry Kissinger, he moved to deflate ideology as the driving force behind international relations. As Kissinger put it in 1969, "We will judge other countries, including Communist countries, . . . on the basis of their actions and not on the basis of their domestic ideology." Nixon and Kissinger worked—often in secret, without consulting Congress—to exploit the deterioration in Soviet-Chinese relations that had begun in the early 1960s and had escalated into military clashes along their common border in 1969. If these two nations balanced and checked each other's power, the threat of either of them to the United States would lessen. Nixon later recalled that Soviet-Chinese hostility "served our purpose best if we maintained closer relations with each side than they did with each other."

U.S. overtures through intermediaries set the stage for Nixon's most dramatic act as president. In February 1972 (with his arrival carefully orchestrated to take advantage of prime-time television), he became the nation's first president to set foot on Chinese soil—an astonishing act by a man who had climbed the political ladder as a fervent anti-Communist. Indeed, Nixon's irreproachable anti-Communist credentials were what enabled him to conduct this shift in U.S.-Chinese relations with no significant objections at home. As he remarked to Chinese leader Mao Zedong, "Those on the right can do what those on the left only talk about."

Neither side expected immediate results from Nixon's historic but largely symbolic act. Plans proceeded for cultural and scientific exchanges, and American manufacturers began to find markets in China—small steps in the process of globalization that would take giant strides in the 1990s. The United States did not abandon the Nationalist Chinese government on Taiwan, but Nixon acknowledged that Taiwan was a part of China, its fate to be settled by the Chinese themselves. His visit brought U.S. policy more into conformity with that of other developed nations and paved the way for formal diplomatic relations by the end of the decade.

As Nixon and Kissinger hoped, the warming of U.S.-Chinese relations increased Soviet responsiveness to the Nixon-Kissinger strategy of détente, the term given to efforts to ease conflict with the Soviet Union. In pursuing détente (French for "loosening"), Nixon and Kissinger did not abandon the principle of containment but instead concentrated on issues of common concern to the two super-

NIXON IN CHINA
"This was the week that changed the world," proclaimed President Richard M. Nixon in February 1972, emphasizing the dramatic turnaround in relations with America's former enemy, the People's Republic of China. The Great Wall of China forms the setting for this photograph of Nixon and his wife, Pat.
Nixon Presidential Materials Project.

powers, such as arms control, trade, and stability in Europe. Containment would be achieved not only by military threat but also by ensuring that Russia and China had stakes in a stable international order and would therefore refrain from precipitating crises. The goal, as Nixon defined it in 1972, was "a stronger healthy United States, Europe, Soviet Union, China, Japan, each balancing the other."

In May 1972, three months after his trip to China, Nixon met with Soviet leaders in Moscow, coming away with several agreements regarding trade and cooperation in science and space. Most significantly, Soviet and U.S. leaders signed arms limitation treaties that had grown out of the Strategic Arms Limitation Talks (SALT) begun in 1969. Both sides agreed to limit antiballistic missile sys-

tems (ABMs) to two each. Giving up pursuit of a defense against nuclear weapons was a critical move, because it meant that neither nation could become so secure against a nuclear attack that it would risk a first strike. The SALT treaty also made the first advance in curbing offensive weapons, although it allowed both sides to continue weapons research and development.

Keeping Henry Kissinger as secretary of state, Gerald Ford (who took over as president when Nixon resigned in 1974) pursued foreign policy goals set by Nixon but failed to sustain widespread support of détente. The secrecy of the Nixon-Kissinger initiatives had alienated legislators, and some Democrats charged that détente ignored Soviet violations of human rights. Members of both parties worried that Soviet strength was overtaking that of the United States. In response, Congress derailed trade agreements with the Soviet Union, refusing economic favors unless the Soviets stopped their harsh treatment of internal dissidents and gave Jews who wanted to leave the country permission to emigrate.

Although negotiations continued, the superpowers achieved no further agreements to limit strategic arms. President Ford's most notable international agreement took place in 1975 in Helsinki, Finland, where he, Soviet leader Leonid Brezhnev, and European leaders formally recognized the existing post–World War II boundaries in Europe. In signing the Helsinki accords, the United States accepted the Soviets' domination over their satellite countries in eastern Europe—a condition to which it had objected so bitterly thirty years earlier as the cold war began.

Shoring Up Anticommunism in the Third World

In his second inaugural address in January 1973, Nixon promised, "The time has passed when America will make every other nation's conflict our own . . . or presume to tell the people of other nations how to manage their own affairs." Yet even while dealing with China and the Soviet Union on the basis of practical politics rather than ideology, in Vietnam and elsewhere Nixon and Kissinger continued to equate the ideology of Marxism with a threat to U.S. interests and actively resisted social revolutions that might lead to communism.

The Nixon administration found such a threat in Salvador Allende, a self-proclaimed Marxist who was elected president of Chile in 1970. Since 1964, the Central Intelligence Agency (CIA) and U.S. corporations concerned about nationalization of their Chilean properties had provided funds to Allende's opponents. When Allende nonetheless won the election, Nixon announced that the United States "accepted that decision." Yet the CIA made plans for a military coup to overthrow Allende, and the United States continued to exert political and economic pressure to destabilize the Allende government. "I don't see why we have to let a country go Marxist just because its people are irresponsible," Kissinger remarked privately. In 1973, the Chilean military engineered a coup, killed Allende, and established a brutal dictatorship under General Augusto Pinochet, who twenty-five years later was tried and found guilty of torture, murder, and terrorism by an international court.

Chile

Even while dealing with China and the Soviet Union on the basis of practical politics rather than ideology, in Vietnam and elsewhere Nixon and Kissinger continued to equate the ideology of Marxism with a threat to U.S. interests and actively resisted social revolutions that might lead to communism.

In other parts of the world, too, the Nixon administration moved closer to repressive governments. It eased pressures on white minority governments that oppressed and impoverished blacks in southern Africa, believing that, as a National Security Council memorandum put it, the "whites are here to stay. . . . There is no hope for the blacks to gain the political rights they seek through violence, which will lead only to chaos and increased opportunities for Communists." In the Middle East, since 1953, when the CIA had helped the shah of Iran regain power, the United States had supported his harsh regime as a stable anti-Communist ally with enormous petroleum reserves. In 1972, the Nixon administration secretly began to provide massive amounts of arms to the shah, cementing a relationship that would ignite a new crisis for the United States when the shah was overthrown in 1979.

Continuing Tensions in the Middle East

Like its predecessors, the Nixon administration pursued a delicate balance between defending Israel's security and seeking the goodwill of Arab nations that were strategically and economically important to the United States. Conflict between Israel and the Arab nations had escalated into the all-out Six-Day War in 1967, when Israel won a stunning victory over Egyptian, Syrian, and Jordanian forces, seizing territory that amounted to twice the original size of Israel. Its forces took control of the Sinai Peninsula and Gaza Strip from Egypt, the Golan Heights from Syria, and the West Bank from Jordan, which included the Arab sector of Jerusalem, a city sacred to Jews, Christians, and Muslims alike (Map 30.1).

That decisive victory did not quell Middle Eastern turmoil. Instead, Palestinians stepped up guerrilla attacks against Israelis, and the Soviet Union expanded military aid to Arab countries. American diplomats' efforts to reduce tensions in the Middle East had little success. The Arab countries refused to recognize Israel's right to exist, Israel would not withdraw from the territories occupied during the Six-Day War, and no solution could be found for the Palestinian refugees who had been displaced by the creation of Israel in the late 1940s.

In October 1973, on Yom Kippur, the holiest day in the Jewish calendar, Egypt and Syria surprised Israel with a full-scale attack. When the Nixon administration sided with Israel, the Arab nations imposed an oil embargo. Although the Soviet Union threatened to intervene, the United States held its ground, and Israel repulsed the attack. Shortly after the war, the United States adopted the role of mediator and Kissinger embarked on "shuttle diplomacy," moving back and forth across the Middle East. Unable to resolve the underlying conflicts, he achieved some limited disengagements between

Israeli forces and their enemies. As a result, the Arab nations lifted the oil embargo, Soviet influence in the area declined, and U.S. credibility among Arabs increased.

Idealism and Human Rights in Foreign Policy

Campaigning for president in 1976, Jimmy Carter promised that moral principles would guide his approach to foreign policy. His predecessors' obsession with protecting and expanding U.S. power by any means, Carter believed, had violated the nation's principles of freedom and human dignity. "We've seen a loss of morality . . . and we're ashamed of what our government is as we deal with other nations around the world," he said. The cynical support of dictators, the secret diplomacy, the interference in the internal affairs of other countries, and the excessive reliance on military solutions— Carter promised to reverse them all.

Human rights formed the cornerstone of Carter's approach. Led by the president, U.S. officials took every opportunity to focus attention on governments that denied their citizens basic political and civil rights or freedom of religion and expression. The administration also applied economic pressure, denying aid or trading privileges to nations that oppressed their citizens. It levied economic sanctions against a number of countries, including Argentina, Chile, and El Salvador, and the white minority governments of Rhodesia and South Africa, which blatantly violated the rights of their black majorities.

Yet the administration implemented the human rights policy with glaring inconsistencies. In 1979, the United States established formal diplomatic relations with the People's Republic of China, concluding the process that Nixon and Kissinger had begun. In this case, improved relations with China took priority over attempts to secure democratic rights for the Chinese people. Moreover, in dealing with staunch anti-Communist allies, Carter sacrificed human rights ideals to strategic and security considerations. The administration invoked no sanctions against Iran, South Korea, and the Philippines, even though official oppression was obvious in those countries.

Cold war considerations vied with concern for human rights in the administration's approach to Nicaragua, which had been ruled since 1936 by the corrupt and viciously oppressive regime led by Anastasio Somoza and, in turn, his sons. The administration complained about the Nicaraguan dictatorship's excesses and invoked some economic sanctions, but when civil war erupted there, its greatest concern was to contain Communist influence in the anti-Somoza movement. Officials were particularly uneasy about the Sandinistas, named after General Augusto César Sandino, the leader of a popular but unsuccessful insurrection in 1926. The Sandinistas were a leading element in the opposition, with ties to Cuba. Nonetheless, when the Somoza regime fell in 1979 and Sandinista leader Daniel Ortega assumed power, the United States extended recognition and economic aid to the new government. Critics on the right charged that Carter's pressuring of the Somoza regime on human rights helped to undermine his regime. These critics demanded the more typical test for U.S. support during the cold war years—whether a country was anti-Communist and friendly to American interests, not how it treated its citizens.

The president took on heavy political burdens in applying moral principles to relations with Panama concerning the Panama Canal, the most conspicuous symbol of Yankee imperialism. Carter sped up the negotiations over control of the canal that the Johnson administration had begun. In 1977, the United States and Panama completed two treaties, one providing for joint control of the canal until the end of the century and the second defining U.S. rights after Panama assumed control.

Although Carter and his supporters viewed the treaties with Panama as recompense for the blatant use of U.S. power in obtaining the canal in 1903, angry opponents insisted on maintaining control of this vital waterway.

The treaties evoked intense controversy. Although Carter and his supporters viewed the treaties with Panama as recompense for the blatant use of U.S. power in obtaining the canal in 1903, angry opponents insisted on maintaining control of this vital waterway. "We bought it, we paid for it, it's ours, and we're going to keep it," claimed Ronald Reagan in his 1976 campaign for the Republican nomination. Behind the opposition lay anxieties about the decline of U.S. power. Only after the Carter administration undertook a massive campaign to rally support did the Senate ratify the treaties by the narrowest margins.

In applying his moral authority to peace in the Middle East, Carter achieved his most brilliant victory. He seized on the courage and foresight of Egyptian president Anwar Sadat, the first Arab leader to risk his political future by talking directly with Israeli officials. When initial discussions between Sadat and Israeli prime minister Menachem Begin faltered, Carter invited them to the presidential retreat at Camp David, Maryland, in September 1978. Carter studied all the issues down to the smallest details and then spent thirteen days at Camp David mediating between Begin and Sadat, carrying proposals and counterproposals from one

cabin to the other. His enormous investment paid off in the form of a tentative agreement known popularly as the Camp David accords.

When subsequent negotiations for an official treaty bogged down, Carter flew to Jerusalem and Cairo and applied his tenacious diplomacy once more, obtaining an agreement that Begin and Sadat signed on the White House lawn in March 1979. In that pact, Egypt became the first Arab state to recognize Israel, and Israel agreed to gradual withdrawal from the Sinai Peninsula, territory that it had seized in the 1967 war (see Map 30.1). Although the issues of Palestinian self-determination in other Israeli-occupied territories—the West Bank and Gaza—and the plight of Palestinian refugees remained unresolved, the first meaningful steps toward peace in the Middle East had been taken.

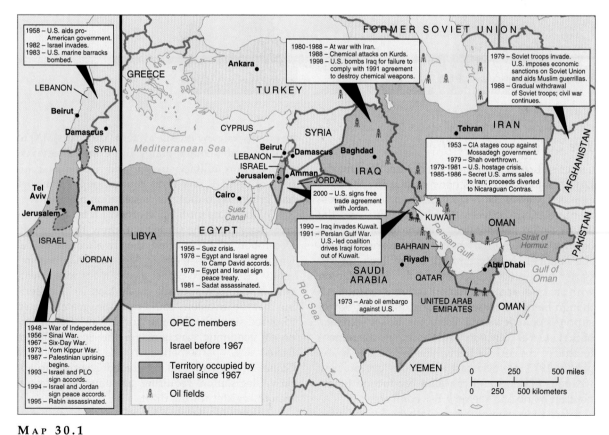

M A P   30.1

The Middle East, 1948–2000

U.S. determination to preserve access to the rich oil reserves of the Middle East and its commitment to the security of Israel were the fundamental—and sometimes conflicting—principles of U.S. foreign policy in that region.

THE CAMP DAVID ACCORDS
President Jimmy Carter oversees the meeting of Egyptian president Anwar Sadat, left, and Israeli prime minister Menachem Begin at Camp David, Maryland, in September 1978. Carter's passionate commitment to promoting peace helped produce the first easing of hostility between Arabs and Israelis in thirty years.
Corbis-Bettmann.

The Cold War Intensifies

Carter's success with the Panama treaties and the Egypt-Israel accord was not matched in other foreign policy areas. During his last two years as president, relations between the United States and the Soviet Union deteriorated, and the administration began a sizable military buildup. Preferring to pursue national security through nonmilitary means, Carter had initially approached the Soviet Union with an air of accommodation and reassurance. Although he never ceased speaking out about Soviet suppression of Jews and dissidents, he set Secretary of State Cyrus Vance to work on a new agreement to replace the SALT I treaty, which was due to expire in 1977. He also cast a cautious eye on new weapons systems and canceled production of the neutron bomb and the new B-1 bomber.

Two years of negotiations with the Soviet Union produced a SALT II treaty in 1979, but by then Carter had accepted his national security adviser Zbigniew Brzezinski's warnings about the need to counter a Soviet military buildup. The president authorized development of intermediate-range missiles to be deployed in western Europe as well as

an enormous new missile system (known as MX) to be built in the United States. But even this revived emphasis on military strength did not defuse criticism of SALT II and arms control, opposition that had grown with Carter's cancellation of the B-1.

With Senate ratification of SALT II becoming increasingly unlikely, Carter withdrew the treaty in December 1979. He acted shortly after the Soviet Union invaded its neighbor Afghanistan, whose recently installed pro-Soviet government was threatened by Muslim opposition (see Map 30.1). Asserting that the invasion "could pose the greatest threat to peace since the Second World War," Carter imposed economic sanctions on the Soviet Union, barred U.S. participation in the 1980 Olympic Games in Moscow, and persuaded Congress to approve legislation requiring all nineteen-year-old men to register for the draft.

The president claimed that Soviet actions threatened oil supplies from the Middle East and announced his own "Carter Doctrine," stating that the United States would intervene with any means necessary should an outside force try to gain control of the Persian Gulf. His human rights policy fell by the wayside as the United States stepped up aid to

Afghanistan's neighbor, Pakistan, which was controlled by a military regime that had overthrown and executed the popularly elected head of state, Zulfikar Ali Bhutto. Finally, Carter called for hefty increases in defense spending over the next five years.

Events in Iran fueled this reversion to a hard-line, militaristic approach. All the U.S. arms and support had not enabled the shah to suppress growing opposition to his regime. Iranian dissidents still resented the CIA's role in the overthrow of the Mossadegh government in 1953, and they deplored the Westernization of their country that accompanied the shah's rule as well as his savage attempts to silence opposition. In Teheran on New Year's Eve 1977, Carter toasted the shah's "great leadership," but fourteen months

later a revolution forced the shah to abandon his throne and country. By March 1979, Ayatollah Ruholla Khomeini and other Shiite Islamic fundamentalists controlled the Iranian government. They were intensely hostile to the United States, which they blamed for supporting the shah's brutalities and undermining the religious foundations of their country.

When Carter permitted the shah to enter the United States for medical treatment, anti-American demonstrations escalated in Teheran. On November 4, 1979, a crowd broke into the U.S. embassy and seized more than sixty Americans, holding them captive with demands that the United States return the shah for trial. When Khomeini supported the captors and refused to negotiate, Carter froze

AMERICAN HOSTAGES IN IRAN
Iranian militants display one of the hostages they took when they occupied the American embassy in Teheran on November 4, 1979. Until the hostages were released in January 1981, Americans regularly watched TV images of the American captives being paraded before angry Iranian crowds. The bound, blindfolded hostages served as humiliating symbols of the limitations of American power.
Ph. Ledru / Sygma.

Iranian assets in U.S. banks and placed an embargo on Iranian oil. For the next year, the hostage crisis dominated the news and absorbed vast amounts of the administration's time and energy.

After every attempt to negotiate was frustrated, in April 1980 Carter authorized force to rescue the hostages. But the small military operation ran into difficulties landing in the Iranian desert, and eight Americans died when a U.S. plane and helicopter collided during the aborted evacuation. Failure of the rescue mission further embarrassed the president, and the hostage crisis burdened Carter's campaign for reelection. Continuing efforts to reach an agreement with Iran finally produced release of the hostages on the day Carter left office.

The inability of the United States to rescue its own citizens fed Americans' feelings of impotence, which had been growing since the nation had withdrawn in defeat from Vietnam. And those frustrations in turn produced support for a more militaristic approach to foreign policy. Opposition to Soviet-American détente, combined with the Soviet invasion of Afghanistan, nullified the thaw in relations that Nixon and Kissinger had begun.

Ronald Reagan Confronts an "Evil Empire"

Campaigning for the presidency in 1980, Ronald Reagan capitalized on the Soviet invasion of Afghanistan and the Iranian hostage crisis, accusing Carter of weakening U.S. military strength and losing the confidence of the nation's allies and the respect of its enemies. Once in office, Reagan accelerated the arms buildup that Carter had begun and spoke of the Soviet Union in harsh terms, calling it "an evil empire." Yet despite the new aggressiveness—or, as some have argued, because of it—superpower conflict was confined to public rhetoric and the bargaining table throughout the 1980s. In fact, Reagan presided over the most impressive improvement in superpower relations since the shattering of the World War II alliance.

On the periphery of the cold war, however, Reagan did not waver from a militant anticommunism. He authorized aid to antileftist movements in Asia and Africa, and dispatched American troops to both the Middle East and the Caribbean. When Congress blocked Reagan's efforts to assist opponents of the leftist Sandinista government in Nicaragua, administration officials acted secretly and illegally to undermine congressional authority.

Militarization and Interventions Abroad

Reagan moved quickly to expand the military, with the objectives of enabling the nation to fight several wars at the same time and to close what the president claimed was a "window of vulnerability," through which U.S. missiles were exposed to a Soviet attack. He oversaw plans for new bombers and missiles, an enhanced nuclear force in Europe, an expanded navy, and a rapid-deployment force. Despite the implications for the growing budget deficit, Congress approved most of these programs, and military expenditures shot up by one-third in the first half of the 1980s. Throughout Reagan's presidency, defense spending averaged $216 billion a year, up from $158 billion in the Carter years and higher even than in the Vietnam era.

Despite the new aggressiveness, superpower conflict was confined to public rhetoric and the bargaining table throughout the 1980s. In fact, Reagan presided over the most impressive improvement in superpower relations since the shattering of the World War II alliance.

One justification for the arms buildup was that the United States must negotiate with the Soviets from a position of strength. The unintended effect of this buildup was to provoke an outburst of calls to halt the arms race. A rally demanding a freeze on nuclear weapons at current levels drew 700,000 people in New York City in 1982. Hundreds of thousands of Europeans demonstrated across the continent, stimulated by fears of new U.S. missiles that were scheduled for deployment in North Atlantic Treaty Organization (NATO) countries in 1983.

Reagan startled many of his own advisers in March 1983 by announcing plans for research on what was officially called the Strategic Defense Initiative (SDI). Immediately dubbed "Star Wars" by its critics, who doubted its feasibility, the project's architects envisioned deploying lasers in space to destroy enemy missiles before they could reach their targets. Reagan conceded that developing an SDI could be seen as

THE NUCLEAR FREEZE CAMPAIGN
An active movement in the United States and Europe worked to limit nuclear weapons and diminish the threat of nuclear destruction in the early 1980s. In 1982, half a million antinuclear protesters marched and rallied in New York City.
Corbis-Bettmann.

"fostering an aggressive policy," since it would allow the United States to fire first and not fear retaliation. The Soviets reacted angrily because SDI development violated the 1972 treaty restricting antiballistic missile systems and would require the Soviets to invest huge sums in their own Star Wars technology. For several years, Reagan's attachment to SDI impeded superpower agreement on strategic arms control. Even after the end of the cold war, research on Star Wars continued, supported by legislators from both parties who by 2000 had authorized more than $60 billion with still no workable results.

The U.S. military buildup placed the Soviets on the defensive, but it did not guarantee American dominance in the world. Although Iran released the American hostages the day of Reagan's inauguration, terrorism continued to plague the United States. In October 1983 in Lebanon, an Islamic extremist drove a bomb-filled truck into a marine barracks, killing 241 Americans (see Map 30.1). Faced with other incidents of murder, kidnapping, and hijacking by various Middle Eastern extremist groups,

Reagan refused to negotiate. To bargain with terrorists, he insisted, would only encourage more assaults, and he pledged never to do so.

Closer to home, the U.S. military flexed its muscles. Just two days after the Lebanon disaster, U.S. troops invaded Grenada, a small British Commonwealth island nation in the Caribbean, in response to a coup by left-wing forces. Ostensibly undertaken to protect U.S. medical students on the island, the intervention reflected administration fears that Grenada would fall into the Cuban-Soviet orbit. Margaret Thatcher, the conservative British prime minister, called the invasion a violation of international law, but a majority of Americans exulted in the display of national power.

Elsewhere, the United States sought to contain leftist movements privately and less aggressively. In Asia, Afghan rebels fighting to dislodge the Soviet-backed government received U.S. aid. In the African nation of Angola, the United States armed rebel forces against the Soviet- and Cuban-backed government. Siding with the racist South African government in the Angolan crisis did not trouble the president. In one of his most extreme misrepresentations, Reagan told reporters—at a time when the South African government was brutally suppressing black protest against apartheid—that South Africa had eliminated "the segregation that we once had in our own country." In 1985, students and other activists mounted demonstrations to pressure the United States to apply economic sanctions against South Africa, as most U.S. allies had already done, and to persuade private corporations to stop investing in the country. In response, Congress enacted legislation to ban loans to and new investments in South Africa, but only after overriding Reagan's veto.

The U.S. military buildup placed the Soviets on the defensive, but it did not guarantee American dominance in the world.

Administration officials were most fearful of left-wing movements in Central America. These movements, Reagan charged, threatened to "destabilize the entire region from the Panama Canal to Mexico." When a leftist uprising occurred in 1981 in El Salvador, the United States sent money and military advisers to prop up the government, even though it had committed murderous human rights violations and opposed social reform.

In neighboring Nicaragua, Reagan aimed to unseat the left-wing Sandinistas, who had overthrown the repressive Somoza dictatorship and assumed power in 1979. The Reagan administration threw itself into efforts to undercut the Nicaraguan government by aiding the Contras (literally, "opposers"), a coalition of armed opposition to the Sandinistas that included many individuals from the ousted regime. Many Americans feared being drawn into another Vietnam and opposed aligning the United States with reactionary forces not supported by the majority of Nicaraguans. Holding its own against unrelenting administration efforts, Congress repeatedly instructed the president to either cut off aid to the Contras or limit it to nonmilitary purposes.

Deliberately violating congressional will, the administration secretly used economic pressure to destabilize the Sandinista government and provided weapons and training to the Contras, called "freedom fighters" by Reagan. The CIA itself directed assaults on economic targets and was involved in the covert mining of Nicaraguan harbors in 1984. Through legal and illegal means, the Reagan administration helped sustain the Contras and wreck the Nicaraguan economy, thereby undermining support for the Sandinista government. After nine years of civil war, Daniel Ortega, the Sandinista president, agreed to a political settlement engineered by the leaders of the four other Central American states: Guatemala, El Salvador, Honduras, and Costa Rica. When elections were held in 1990, a coalition of all the opposition groups defeated the Sandinistas, and Ortega stepped aside.

The Iran-Contra Scandal

Secret American aid to the Contras was part of a larger project that came to be known as the Iran-Contra scandal. The affair began in 1985, when heads of the National Security Council (NSC), NSC aide marine lieutenant colonel Oliver North, and CIA director William Casey arranged to sell U.S.-made arms to Iran, which was then at war with neighboring Iraq. In exchange, Iranians were to exert pressure on Muslim terrorists to release seven American hostages who were being held in Lebanon (see Map 30.1). Funds from the arms sales were then channeled through Swiss bank accounts to aid the Nicaraguan Contras in their efforts to overthrow the Sandinista government. Over the objections of Secretary of State George Shultz and Defense Secretary Caspar Weinberger, Reagan approved the arms sales. He and his cabinet secretaries subsequently disclaimed knowledge of the diversion of the resulting funds to the Contras.

When news of the affair surfaced in November 1986, the Reagan administration faced a number of serious charges. First, the president who had consistently pledged never to bargain with terrorists was now revealed to have allowed his aides to do so, violating the U.S. government's stated neutral-

MEXICO
BELIZE
Caribbean Sea
GUATEMALA
HONDURAS
NICARAGUA
EL SALVADOR
COSTA RICA
PACIFIC OCEAN
PANAMA

0   150   300 miles
0   150   300 kilometers

El Salvador and Nicaragua

OLIVER NORTH
*The central figure in the Iran-Contra affair, Lieu-
tenant Colonel Oliver North, in his U.S. marine
uniform, testified in July 1987 for six days before a
congressional investigating committee. To many
television viewers, North came across as a handsome young patriot whose lies to Congress, destruction of public records, and other illegal actions were
justified in the fight against communism. In spite
of his later conviction for a felony, which was overturned on a technicality, North maintained a strong
following, especially among the right wing of the
Republican Party, and nearly secured a Virginia
Senate seat in 1994.*
Corbis-Bettmann.

ity in the Iran-Iraq War. Even worse, the administration had defied Congress's express ban on military aid for the Contras. Although North and others destroyed incriminating documents, enough
evidence remained to demonstrate the culpability
of seven individuals. Brought to trial by an independent prosecutor appointed by Reagan, all
pleaded guilty or were convicted of lying to Congress and destroying evidence. North's felony con-

viction was later overturned on a technicality, and
President George Bush pardoned the other six officials in December 1992.

In public statements, Reagan appeared as a detached, fumbling leader who could not remember
key events. The independent prosecutor's final report, issued in 1994, found no evidence that Reagan
had broken the law but concluded that both Reagan and Bush, vice president during the affair, had
known about the diversion of funds to the Contras.
The report stated as well that Reagan had "know-
ingly participated or at least acquiesced" in covering up the scandal—the most serious example of
executive branch misconduct since Watergate.

A Thaw in Soviet-American Relations

Reagan weathered the Iran-Contra storm in part because Americans applauded a momentous thaw that
developed in the cold war, one all the more surprising because it occurred under an administration
whose militant anticommunism exceeded that of
any previous administration. Though Reagan's flexibility was a contributing factor, the Soviet-American
accord would not have happened without the innovative Soviet head of state who recognized that his
country's domestic problems demanded a relaxation
of cold war antagonism.

Mikhail Gorbachev assumed power in 1985 determined to revitalize the Soviet economy, which
was plagued with bureaucratic inefficiencies, a massive military budget, and an inability to deliver
basic consumer goods and services. Hoping to stimulate production and streamline distribution, Gorbachev called for *perestroika* (economic restructuring), which included some elements of free
enterprise. He proclaimed a new era of *glasnost*
(greater freedom of expression), eventually allowing such challenges to Communist rule as new political parties and contested elections.

Difficulties surrounding large defense budgets
moved both Reagan and Gorbachev to the negotiating table. The Soviet premier recognized that economic revival depended on cutting the enormous
military expenditures in order to revive civilian production. Reagan, meanwhile, faced increasing congressional resistance to funding the arms race and
popular support for arms reductions. Prodded too
by First Lady Nancy Reagan, who had substantial
influence on her husband, the president made disarmament a major goal in his last years in office.

THE COLD WAR THAWS

U.S. president Ronald Reagan and Soviet premier Mikhail Gorbachev shake hands as they meet at a five-day summit in June 1988 in Moscow for a round of Strategic Arms Reduction Talks (START). Moving beyond the Strategic Arms Limitation Talks (SALT) agreements of the 1970s, these negotiations aimed to actually reduce rather than just limit nuclear warheads and the missiles and bombers that carried them. The talks culminated in a comprehensive treaty signed by Reagan's successor George Bush and Gorbachev in July 1991. After the breakup of the Soviet Union, supplementary agreements were signed by Russia, Ukraine, Belarus, and Kazakhstan.

David Burnett / Contact Press Images.

When Gorbachev took the initiative, Reagan was ready to respond.

Though Reagan's flexibility was a contributing factor, the Soviet-American accord would not have happened without the innovative Soviet head of state who recognized that his country's domestic problems demanded a relaxation of cold war antagonism.

A positive personal chemistry developed between Reagan and Gorbachev, who met four times between 1985 and 1988. Negotiations stalemated when Reagan refused to stop research and development on Star Wars, but eventually Gorbachev gave

up that demand. By December 1987, the superpowers had completed an intermediate-range nuclear forces (INF) agreement, which eliminated all short- and medium-range missiles from Europe and provided for on-site inspection for the first time. George Bush, Reagan's successor, achieved another breakthrough in arms reductions in June 1990, with a strategic arms reduction treaty (START) that actually eliminated existing nuclear weapons—about 30 percent of each superpower's nuclear arsenal.

In 1988, Gorbachev removed an element of contention between the United States and the Soviet Union when he announced a gradual withdrawal from Afghanistan, which had become the Soviet equivalent of America's Vietnam. In Africa, the Soviet Union and the United States joined Cuba in agreement on a political settlement for the civil war in Angola. And in the Middle East, both superpowers supported a cease-fire and peace talks in the eight-year war between Iran and Iraq. Although the Soviet Union had seized the initiative, Reagan could justifiably claim a share of the credit for what he called "a satisfying new closeness with the Soviet Union"—a détente that far surpassed what Nixon and Kissinger had accomplished.

Defining American Interests in a Post–Cold War World

"All the action is in Moscow and Berlin, not here," complained a former Reagan aide, referring to the Bush administration's distance from events unfolding in Europe in 1989, as one by one the Eastern bloc

nations threw out their Communist rulers, and then in 1991, when the Soviet Union fell apart. Yet, though the United States stood on the sidelines of those momentous world events, President George Bush did not hesitate to deploy military power in Latin America and the Middle East. His successor, Bill Clinton, also took military actions abroad—in Somalia, in Haiti, in the Middle East, and in eastern Europe. Even so, neither Bush nor Clinton formulated a new global strategy to replace containment of communism as the guiding principle of U.S. foreign policy.

The End of the Cold War

The forces of change that Gorbachev had both responded to and encouraged in the Soviet Union

FALL OF THE BERLIN WALL
After 1961, the Berlin Wall stood as the prime symbol of the cold war and the iron grip of communism over eastern Europe and the Soviet Union. More than 400,000 easterners were killed trying to flee. After Communist authorities opened the wall on November 9, 1989, permitting free travel between the east and west, Berliners from both sides gathered at the wall to celebrate.
Eric Bouvet / Gamma Liaison.

www.bedfordstmartins.com/tap   SEE THE ONLINE STUDY GUIDE for more help in analyzing this image.

swept through eastern Europe in 1989, where popular uprisings demanded an end to state repression, official corruption, and economic bureaucracies that failed to deliver an acceptable standard of living. Communist governments toppled like dominoes, in most cases with little bloodshed (Map 30.2). In the first multiparty elections since World War II, non-Communist governments took office in Czechoslovakia, East Germany, Hungary, Poland, and Yu-

goslavia. In the most dramatic moment of the transformation of the postwar order, East Germany opened its border with West Germany. On November 12, 1989, ecstatic Germans danced on the Berlin Wall, using whatever was at hand to begin demolishing that dominant symbol of the cold war.

West German chancellor Helmut Kohl's call for a united Germany immediately after the fall of the Berlin Wall shocked U.S. leaders. Nevertheless,

MAP 30.2

Events in Eastern Europe, 1989–1992

The overthrow of Communist governments throughout eastern and central Europe and the splintering of the Soviet Union into more than a dozen separate nations were the most momentous changes in world history since World War II.

READING THE MAP: Which country was the first to overthrow its Communist government? Which was the last? In which nations did elections usher in change in government?

CONNECTIONS: What problems did Mikhail Gorbachev try to solve, and what were his two major initiatives? What policy launched by Ronald Reagan contributed to Soviet dilemmas? Did it create any problems in the United States?

www.bedfordstmartins.com/tap SEE THE ONLINE STUDY GUIDE for more help in analyzing this map.

President Bush helped persuade Gorbachev that the Soviet Union had nothing to fear from the unification of East and West Germany, a move that sped to completion in 1990. The Warsaw Pact dissolved, and three of the former iron curtain countries—the Czech Republic, Hungary, and Poland—joined NATO in 1999. Although U.S. military forces remained in Europe as part of NATO, the commanding role of the United States had been eclipsed. The same was true of its economic clout: Western Europe, including a unified Germany, formed a common economic market in 1992. The destiny of Europe, to which the United States and the Soviet Union had held the key for forty-five years, now lay in European hands.

On November 12, 1989, ecstatic Germans danced on the Berlin Wall, using whatever was at hand to begin demolishing that dominant symbol of the cold war.

By the end of 1991, Gorbachev's initiatives had brought his own downfall. Inspired by the liberation of eastern Europe, republics within the Soviet Union sought their own independence, while the Moscow government's efforts at economic change brought widespread destitution. According to one Muscovite, "Gorbachev knew how to bring us freedom but he did not know how to make sausage." The premier survived an attempted coup in August 1991, but he could not hold the Soviet Union together. In December, Boris Yeltsin, president of the Russian Republic, announced that Russia and eleven other republics had joined a new entity, the Commonwealth of Independent States (CIS). The three Baltic republics—Estonia, Latvia, and Lithuania—and the southern republic Georgia chose not to join the CIS. With nothing left to govern, Gorbachev resigned.

The United States officially recognized Russia, but the breakup of the Soviet Union seemed to many as ominous as its existence had once appeared. "The post–cold war world is decidedly not postnuclear," declared President Clinton's first secretary of defense, Les Aspin. "During the cold war, the threat was deliberate Soviet attack. Now the bigger threat seems to be chaos in a nation with 30,000 nuclear weapons." The breakdown of the Soviet Union meant that four countries with nuclear weapons—Russia, Ukraine, Belarus, and Kazakhstan—now stood in place of one, in addition to the United States, Britain, France, China, India, Israel, Pakistan, and possibly North Korea, still under a Communist dictatorship. In 1996, the world took a small step back from the nuclear brink when the leaders of the nuclear powers signed a comprehensive test ban treaty. Yet India and Pakistan, hostile neighbors, refused to sign the pact, and both exploded atomic devices in May 1998, increasing the nuclear risk in South Asia. Moreover, in a highly partisan vote, the Republican-controlled Senate defeated U.S. ratification of the treaty in October 1999. The first rejection of a major international agreement since the Senate repudiated the Versailles treaty in 1919, the Senate's action halted, at least temporarily, a decade of progress on nuclear weapons control.

The future of Russia involved both economic and nuclear issues. In the post–cold war world, U.S. leaders promoted economic stability and political democracy in its former enemy, in no small part because Russia continued to possess large amounts of nuclear weapons. Yet despite Russia's rush to embrace capitalism, the United States continued to spend heavily—within the limits of arms reduction agreements—on defense in the 1990s. Not only was the nuclear balance tipped in favor of the Americans, but in 1999 the United States posed what Russians could construe as a further threat when it allowed entry of the Czech Republic, Hungary, and Poland into NATO after rebuffing Russian efforts to join. Plagued with corruption and ineffective leadership—and, according to some, bad advice from American economists—Russia deteriorated into widespread destitution and despair. At the same time, the United States committed far fewer resources to stabilization of the former Communist countries than it had to the nations it defeated in World War II. Even a severe economic crisis that swept through Asia in 1998 and further crippled the Russian economy did not call forth a response as systematic and sustained as the one the United States had given to the rise of communism.

The Gulf War, 1991

The end of the cold war enabled former enemies to cooperate when warfare broke out in the Middle East. In August 1990, Iraq's army invaded and quickly took over the small, oil-rich country of Kuwait (see Map 30.3). Struggling with an enor-

MAP 30.3

The Gulf War, February 1991

The heavy forty-day bombing of Iraq and the massive international mobilization on its borders enabled the U.S.-led United Nations force to defeat Iraq in just four days of ground war.

mous debt from the now ten-year-old war against Iran, Iraqi president Saddam Hussein desperately needed revenues, and control of Kuwaiti oil would give him powerful leverage over prices. Within days of invading Kuwait, Iraqi troops moved toward the Saudi Arabian border, threatening the world's largest oil reserves.

President Bush reacted quickly to the invasion. Although he invoked principles of national self-determination and international law, the need to maintain secure access to oil primarily determined the U.S. response. As the largest importer of oil, the United States consumed one-fourth of the world's annual supply. With the consent of Saudi Arabia, Bush ordered Operation Desert Shield, a massive

mobilization of land, air, and naval forces to counter the Iraqi threat. At the same time, the administration began to assemble an international coalition—ultimately involving more than thirty nations—to repel Iraqi aggression.

Reflecting the end of superpower conflict in the Middle East, the Soviet Union and the United States issued a joint condemnation of Iraq, and the Soviets cut off shipments of arms to Iraq. The United Nations instituted economic sanctions, and most of the world joined an embargo on oil from Iraq and Kuwait. In November, the United Nations (UN) authorized the use of force against Iraq if it did not withdraw from Kuwait by January 15, 1991. By early January, the United States had deployed 400,000 soldiers to Saudi Arabia, where 265,000 troops from European nations, Egypt, Syria, and several other Arab states joined them. Meanwhile, Bush asked Congress for authorization to use military force against Iraq. Considerable public and legislative sentiment favored waiting to see whether the embargo would force Hussein to back down. But after three days of solemn debate, Congress approved what amounted to a declaration of war by margins of five votes in the Senate and sixty-seven in the House. Unlike Lyndon Johnson in Vietnam, George Bush would go to war with clear congressional authorization.

On January 17, 1991, Operation Desert Shield became Operation Desert Storm, when the U.S.-led coalition began a forty-day air war against Iraq. Bombs and missiles smashed not only military targets but also power plants, oil refineries, and transportation networks. Having severely crippled Iraq through air bombardment, the coalition launched a massive ground assault against Iraqi troops on February 23. Allied forces quickly routed the Iraqi soldiers, and within one hundred hours Hussein announced that he would withdraw from Kuwait (Map 30.3).

"By God, we've kicked the Vietnam syndrome once and for all," President Bush said on March 1. Most Americans found no moral ambiguity in the Persian Gulf War and took pride in the display of military competence. The war's costs were relatively cheap: Germany and Japan (who sent no troops) and other coalition allies paid a substantial part of the bill, while 146 U.S. servicemen and women were killed in action, and 124 died outside of combat, in contrast to some 50,000 Vietnam War dead. The United States stood at the apex of global leadership, steering a massive coalition in which,

THE GULF WAR
These soldiers from the Twenty-fourth Infantry arrived in Saudi Arabia in August 1990 as part of the U.S.-led effort to drive Iraq out of Kuwait. For the first time women served in combat-support positions, with more than thirty-three thousand stationed throughout the Gulf; eleven died and two were held as prisoners of war. Among their duties, women piloted planes and helicopters, directed artillery, and fought fires.
Corbis-Bettmann.

for the first time, Arab nations fought beside their former colonial rulers.

Yet victory did not bring stability to the Middle East. Israel, which had endured Iraqi missile attacks, was more secure than before the brief war, but the Israeli-Palestinian conflict continued to simmer. Despite military losses and a continuing economic embargo, Saddam Hussein remained in power and turned the remains of his war machine on Iraqi Kurds and Shiite Muslims, ethnic and religious minority groups whom the United States had encouraged to rebel. Two million rebels became refugees; other Iraqi citizens suffered malnutrition, disease, and death caused by the embargo and the destruction of the nation's fuel, communications, and transportation systems.

Deploying American Power

In its first substantial military engagement in forty-five years that was not directed against communism, the United States demonstrated that the end of the cold war did not mean a diminution of U.S. leadership in world affairs. Yet American leaders had still not articulated an overarching vision to replace the containment of communism as the major foreign policy goal and define America's purpose in a post–cold war world of some 190 nations. Moreover, although the international context had shifted, U.S. officials faced the fundamental problems of how to promote global economic prosperity and to prevent nuclear peril.

Both before and after the Gulf War, the United States inconsistently used its diplomatic and military power in a variety of situations. Guided largely by humanitarian concern, in December 1992 President Bush attached U.S. forces to a United Nations operation in the small African country of Somalia, where famine and civil war raged. In summer 1993, President Clinton allowed the humanitarian mission to turn into "nation building," an effort to restore national stability. Eighteen U.S. soldiers were killed in the process, and an outcry at home suggested that most Americans were not prepared to sacrifice lives when they perceived no vital economic or political interests at stake. For example, the United Nations and the United States stood by when more than half a million people were massacred in a brutal civil war in the central African nation of Rwanda in 1994.

American leaders had still not articulated an overarching vision to replace the containment of communism as the major foreign policy goal and define America's purpose in a post–cold war world.

The United States was less willing to stand aside in the face of suffering and turmoil in Europe and Latin America, where the Bush administration committed U.S. soldiers in 1989. The Panamanian dictator General Manuel Noriega had long sold the CIA information about Communist activities in Cuba and Central America, but he also passed information to Fidel Castro in Cuba while amassing a fortune through dealing in illegal drugs, torturing and killing his domestic opposition. In 1988, a Miami, Florida, grand jury indicted Noriega for drug trafficking, and in December 1989 President Bush ordered twenty-five thousand troops into Panama to capture the dictator. The invasion forces quickly overcame Noriega's troops, at the cost of twenty-three Americans and hundreds of Panamanians, many of them civilians. This resort to military intervention revived the image of Yankee imperialism.

In contrast, President Clinton obtained UN authorization in 1994 for intervention in Haiti, where U.S. troops received a warmer welcome. The United States had maintained a military presence in the Caribbean nation from 1915 to 1934, and after American withdrawal, Haitians suffered under harsh dictatorships. In the country's first free election in December 1990, the Reverend Jean-Bertrand Aristide won the presidency, but nine months later a military coup overthrew the government. Thousands of Haitians tried to escape the poverty and violence of the military dictatorship, many of them building flimsy boats and heading for Florida. With anti-immigrant sentiment already high in Florida and in the nation, Clinton was pressed hard to stop the refugee flow. (See "Historical Question," page 1170.) At the same time, the Black Congressional Caucus and others insisted that the United States had a moral responsibility to end the suffering and restore democracy in Haiti.

In September 1994, Clinton dispatched twenty thousand troops but also sent a last-minute mission, led by former president Jimmy Carter, to negotiate. Hours before the invasion was to begin, the negotiating team reached an agreement under which the military leaders promised to step down. Consequently, when U.S. forces began landing on September 19 and then disarming Haitian troops, they did so peacefully. Initially a huge success, U.S. policy would continue to be tested as Haiti faced grave challenges of economic and political reconstruction.

In eastern Europe, the collapse of communism ignited the most severe crisis on the continent since the 1940s. During the cold war, the Communist government of Yugoslavia had held ethnic tensions in check, and many Muslims, Croats, and Serbs had grown accustomed to living and working with each other. After the Communists were swept out in 1989, Yugoslavia splintered into the three states of Serbia, Croatia, and Bosnia and then fell into a brutal civil war as ruthless leaders tried to use ethnic

differences to bolster their power. The Serbs' aggression against the Bosnian Muslims horrified much of the world, and people remembered how an event in Sarajevo had sparked World War I. For several years the United States joined with its European allies in NATO and the United Nations in peace efforts, but the allied nations studiously avoided direct intervention.

As reports of terror, rape, and torture in Bosnia worsened, American leaders worried about the image of the world's most powerful nation unwilling to use its power to stop the violence. In November 1995, the United States brought the leaders of Serbia, Croatia, and Bosnia to Dayton, Ohio, where they hammered out a peace treaty. President Clinton then agreed to send twenty thousand American troops to Bosnia as part of a NATO peacekeeping mission. "We won't know for some years" whether the mission would succeed, Clinton's national security adviser, Anthony Lake, predicted.

Breakup of Yugoslavia, 1991–1992

In 1998, new fighting broke out within Serbia, in its southern province of Kosovo, where ethnic Albanians, who constituted 90 percent of the population, were making a bid for independence. The Serbian army brutally retaliated, driving one-third of Kosovo's 1.8 million Albanians from their homes and into neighboring Albania, Macedonia, and Montenegro. When Serbian president Slobodan Milosevic refused to agree to a peace settlement in 1999, NATO launched a bombing attack, carried out largely by U.S. pilots and planes, on Serbian military and government targets. After three months of being bombed, Serbia agreed to a settlement, and the United States sent in soldiers as part of a NATO force whose mission was to see the terms carried out. Although the situation in Kosovo remained unstable politically and economically, Serbians voted Milosevic out of office in October 2000, an act that encouraged hopes for the return of peace and stability to the Balkans.

U.S. TROOPS IN KOSOVO

In 1999, American troops joined a NATO peacekeeping force in the former Yugoslav province of Kosovo, after a U.S.-led NATO bombing campaign forced the Serbian army to withdraw. The NATO forces were dispatched to monitor the departure of Serbian soldiers, assist the return of ethnic Albanians who had fled the Serb army, and reestablish civil governments. Here, an ethnic Albanian boy walks beside Specialist Brent Baldwin from Jonesville, Michigan, as he patrols the town of Gnjilane in southeast Kosovo in May 2000.

Wide World Photos, Inc.

President Clinton seemed less hesitant to deploy American power when he could send missiles rather than men and women; and he also proved willing to act without international support or UN sanction. In August 1998, bombs exploded in U.S. embassies in Kenya and Tanzania, killing 12 Americans and more than 250 Africans. Thirteen days later, Clinton ordered missile attacks on sites in Afghanistan suspected to be terrorist training camps and on a factory in Sudan alleged to be a chemical weapons plant. These facilities, Clinton asserted, were controlled by Osama bin Laden, a Saudi-born millionaire who financed an Islamic-extremist terrorist network and who, officials believed, directed the embassy bombings. Some U.S. experts challenged Clinton's claim, and critics charged that Clinton's use of the military was intended to distract the public from the intensifying heat of impeachment.

A few months later, in December 1998, Clinton launched Desert Fox, a series of air strikes against Iraqi military installations. At the end of the Gulf War in 1991, President Saddam Hussein had agreed to eliminate Iraq's chemical, germ, and nuclear weapons and to allow inspections by UN officials. But he resisted compliance with the agreement and tried to block inspection officials late in 1998, which prompted the U.S. attacks. Whereas Bush had acted in the Gulf War with the support of an international force that included Arab states, Clinton acted in the face of Arab opposition and without authorization from the United Nations.

Using its diplomatic rather than its military power, the Clinton administration continued the decades-long efforts to ameliorate the Israeli-Palestinian conflict. At a ceremony on the White House lawn in September 1993, Yasir Arafat, head of the Palestine Liberation Organization (PLO), and Yitzhak Rabin, Israeli prime minister, recognized for the first time existence of the other's state and agreed to Israeli withdrawal and self-government for Palestinians in the Gaza Strip and Jericho. Less than a year later, in July 1994, Clinton presided over another turning point as Rabin and King Hussein of Jordan signed a declaration of peace. Although these constituted momentous steps, negotiations between Israel and the Palestinians over control of Jerusalem, the fate of Palestinian refugees, and other issues broke down in 2000, and maintaining peace in the Middle East continued to be a challenge for American foreign policy.

The president played a more crucial role in persuading Irish and British officials in the spring of 1998 to take the first steps toward resolving the centuries-old conflict between Catholics and Protestants in Ireland. Signed on April 10, the "Good Friday Agreement" provided for the end of British rule in Northern Ireland, power sharing between Protestants and the Catholic minority living there, and closer relations between Northern Ireland and the largely Catholic Republic of Ireland to its south. Full implementation would not occur for years, but violence in the region diminished.

Still a Promised Land?

THE UNITED STATES IS OUR LAND. . . . We intend to maintain it so. The day of unalloyed welcome to all peoples, the day of indiscriminate acceptance of all races, has definitely ended." So spoke Washington senator Albert Johnson in 1924, just after Congress severely limited immigration with passage of the National Origins Act, which Johnson had sponsored. Thereafter, immigration, which had forcefully shaped American society since its beginning, ebbed for several decades as the restrictive law combined with the Great Depression and World War II to discourage potential newcomers. In fact, during the worst years of the depression, more people abandoned the United States than chose to migrate there. Yet the immigration question had not been settled at last. By the 1980s, large numbers of immigrants once more were entering the United States, reigniting old debates about whether Americans should share their promise of political freedom and economic opportunity with people from other lands.

What reopened the door to immigration after World War II? Economic considerations always loomed large in prompting migration to the United States and in determining how welcome immigrants would be: The twenty-five-year economic boom that followed World War II exerted a positive force on both ends. In fact, until 1964 the U.S. government actively encouraged the temporary migration of Mexicans by continuing the so-called *bracero* program that was begun during World War II to fill a shortage of agricultural workers. Hundreds of thousands of Mexicans established social networks in the United States and grew accustomed to crossing the border for jobs, even when the jobs were backbreaking and low-paying by U.S. standards. When the *bracero* program ended, many Mexicans continued to come north for work whether they could obtain legal authorization or not.

In addition to a prosperous economy, a growing tolerance toward people of different races and ethnic groups in the decades following World War II contributed to the increase in immigration. Like the key civil rights laws passed around the same time, the Immigration Act of 1965 reflected a more broad-minded climate of opinion based on the be-

lief that people should be treated as human beings rather than as members of a particular group. The new immigration law ended the national quotas that were so insulting to non–Western European groups, although it for the first time placed limits on newcomers from the Western Hemisphere. It made possible a tremendous rise in the volume of immigration and facilitated a huge increase in migrants from Asia and Latin America, a result that the law's sponsors did not anticipate.

The new immigration law set an annual ceiling of 270,000, but the actual volume was much higher. Besides those who came illegally, hundreds of thousands of people fell into special categories that gained them legal admission above and beyond the limit. In 1986, for example, the United States admitted 335,000 immigrants over the ceiling; about two-thirds of these were children, spouses, or parents of U.S. citizens, and the rest were political refugees and asylum seekers. Migration chains were thus established by which, once newcomers became citizens, their sisters, brothers, and adult children received special preference, while even closer relatives gained entry without regard to the limit.

The new waves of immigration also grew directly from U.S. foreign policy after World War II. The cold war spread U.S. military and other personnel throughout the world, enabling foreigners to learn about the United States and make personal contacts with Americans. Once the cold war identified communism as an unmitigated evil, the United States could hardly refuse asylum to its enemy's victims. In the twenty-five years following Fidel Castro's revolution in 1959, for example, more than 800,000 Cubans fled to the United States. The Vietnam War and its aftermath brought more than 600,000 Vietnamese, Laotians, and Cambodians to the United States in the decade following 1974.

Not all refugees entered the United States so easily, for American refugee policy bore a distinct anti-Communist bias. Haitians, Salvadorans, and others fleeing right-wing dictatorships were frequently turned back or, having reached the United States, were denied asylum and deported. "Why let Poles stay but not Salvadorans?" demanded one advocate for these refugees, pointing out the more favorable treatment given to immigrants from Communist countries.

Even though U.S. policy failed to accommodate all who wanted to immigrate, by the 1980s immi-

CUBAN REFUGEES

These Cubans are being towed by the U.S. Coast Guard into port at Miami, Florida. Their desire for the expected economic opportunity and political freedom of the United States is evinced in their willingness to flee Cuba on a crowded, makeshift vessel. Some "boat people" drowned in these risky ventures.

Jon Kral / *Miami Herald.*

gration was once more a major force in American society. During that decade, the six million legal and an estimated two million undocumented immigrants accounted for more than one-third of total population growth. Seventy-five percent of the immigrants settled in just seven states, with California, New York, Texas, and Florida receiving the most. After the 1990 census, California won five additional seats in the House of Representatives solely on the basis of immigrant additions to the population. A 1983 *Time* magazine article called Los Angeles "the new Ellis Island" because of its large Asian and Hispanic populations. A decade later, one-third of Los Angeles area residents were foreign-born.

The higher volume of immigration, its third world sources, and the economy's recession combined to reactivate nativist sentiment in the 1980s. Increasingly, Americans saw immigrants as taking jobs from the native-born and acting as a drain on schools,

health care, police, and other services; and Congress sought to reduce illegal immigration with the Immigration Reform and Control Act of 1986. In the 1990s, anti-immigrant sentiment grew especially strong in California, then reeling from an economic slump owing to the downsizing of defense production. That state took in more than one-third of the nation's immigrants in the 1980s and an estimated one-half of the undocumented ones. Congress reflected national anti-immigrant feelings when it restricted health care, food stamps, and other benefits to immigrants as part of its transformation of welfare policy in 1996.

Greatest hostility focused on immigrants who entered without legal documentation, a phenomenon that the 1986 law penalizing employers of such people had not significantly curtailed. Some states, including California, Florida, and New Jersey, filed lawsuits charging the federal government with failure to stop the flow of illegal immigration *(Continued)* and suing for the costs it added to state budgets. In 1994, California voters passed a referendum that barred the children of illegal immigrants from attending public schools, although the courts later ruled it unconstitutional.

Economic and political crises elsewhere and the continuing appeal of the United States meant that high levels of immigration—legal and illegal—persisted into the 1990s. Anti-immigrant sentiment diminished somewhat as jobs became plentiful during the spectacular economic boom at the end of the twentieth century. The chief executive of a semiconductor firm who filled more than one-third of his administrative and engineering positions with immigrants, lashed out at restrictionist legislators: "They want to send back the first-round draft choices of the intellectual world so that they can compete against us in their homelands." With labor in short supply and employers especially desperate for skilled workers, former opponents of immigration pressured the government to relax restrictions, and politicians of both parties recognized that immigrant bashing would not endear them to a rapidly rising population of Hispanic voters. America entered the twenty-first century as it had the twentieth, with a rapidly diversifying society, continuing to make itself, as sociologist Nathan Glazer put it, a "permanently unfinished country."

American Efforts to Shape Globalization

Unlike the six presidents immediately before him, whose international meetings had largely focused on arms control and national security, Bill Clinton traveled to summits where national leaders more typically discussed trade policies and other economic issues. As the United States emerged from the cold war as the only military superpower, it also became the dominant economic power by the end of the twentieth century. From that position, American leaders tried to shape the tremendous economic transformations occurring in a process that came to be called globalization.

As the tumult that engulfed the 1999 World Trade Organization meeting in Seattle demonstrated, both gains and losses attended the growing integration and interdependence of national economies. In particular, debates in the United States and elsewhere formed around the liberalization of trade. Countries argued over which trade barriers to eliminate, how fast, and under what conditions. In a world economy characterized by laissez-faire capitalism, who would protect both human rights and the environment?

Debates over Globalization

Globalization was not a new development. It began in the fifteenth century, when Europeans began to trade with and populate other parts of the world. The most recent era of globalization occurred in the period between the U.S. Civil War and World War I, when the flow of products, capital, and labor crossed national boundaries in large quantities. What distinguished the globalization at the end of the twentieth century was its scope coupled with its intensity: New communications technology connected nations, corporations, and individuals—nearly the entire planet—with much greater speed and much less cost than at any other time in history. (See "The Promise of Technology," page 1174.)

What distinguished the globalization at the end of the twentieth century was its scope coupled with its intensity: New communications technology connected nations, corporations, and individuals—nearly the entire planet—with much greater speed and much less cost than at any other time in history.

Those who wanted to slow down the growth of free trade or to attach conditions to the lifting of trade barriers expressed concerns about the impact of globalization on both the United States and the rest of the world. They pointed to how quickly, in an increasingly integrated global economy, economic disasters in one country could spread to oth-

Labor unions and their supporters emphasized the flight of manufacturing jobs to developing nations, as U.S. executives sought to lower production costs with much cheaper labor and fewer standards regarding working conditions. Critics of globalization linked it to the weakening of unions, the erosion of the "social contract" through which the American government and employers had provided a safety net for workers since the 1930s, and the growing gap between rich and poor in the United States. Both the extent of the global economy and what it could do to American jobs was exemplified by a product of one of the largest U.S. manufacturers, General Motors: The Pontiac Le Mans was actually made in Korea, with parts manufactured in Japan, Germany, Taiwan, Singapore, Britain, Ireland, and Barbados.

Most critics of globalization did not want to stop it—even if they could—but they demanded conditions in trade-reduction treaties that would make other countries enforce decent wage and labor standards. They spoke in favor of "fair trade" rather than simply free trade. Environmentalists similarly argued for provisions requiring countries that wanted to eliminate economic barriers between themselves and the United States to adopt measures that would eliminate or reduce pollution and prevent the destruction of endangered species.

Much of the controversy over globalization centered on relationships between the United States, which dominated the world's industrial core, and the developing nations on the periphery, which attracted investment because labor was cheap and environmental standards were lax. Various activist groups deplored the practices of some poorer nations, including the use of forced labor, the employment of children, the failure to establish safety standards, the dumping of industrial wastes in oceans, and the release of pollutants in the air. United Students Against Sweatshops, for example, attacked the international conglomerate Nike, which paid Chinese workers $1.50 per pair to produce shoes that sold for $100 or more in the United States. Yet many leaders of developing nations wanted foreign investment and manufacturing jobs for their workers. Wages that seemed pitiful from an American worker's perspective, they argued, offered people in these poorer nations a much better living than they could otherwise obtain.

The demonstrations in Seattle, and the protests that followed in Washington, D.C., and Prague, capital of the Czech Republic, targeted international

PROTESTS AGAINST U.S. CORPORATIONS ABROAD
Some critics of globalization charged that American corporations not only deprived U.S. residents of jobs but also exploited foreign workers with low wages and poor working conditions when they opened manufacturing plants in poorer countries. The enormous success of the athletic shoe company Nike made it a popular target of protesters. Here, United Students Against Sweatshops stage a demonstration at the Niketown store in New York City in April 2000.
Wide World Photos, Inc.

ers. Exactly that happened in 1997 when a banking crisis, caused in part by international investors and currency speculators, began in Thailand. It then spread to Malaysia, the Philippines, Indonesia, Korea, Japan, and Russia, threatening American investments in all of those countries. Observers noted that, unlike in single nations, where governments could step in to counter economic downslides, the global marketplace was beyond any single organization's or person's control.

The Internet

THE NETWORK THAT LINKS MILLIONS of computers throughout the world began to alter the lives of millions of Americans in the 1990s. Just 313,000 computers were linked to the Internet in 1990; six years later, 10 million were connected. By the year 2000, a majority of Americans logged on to the Internet at home or at work to e-mail coworkers, friends and relatives, shop, chat with strangers around the world, listen to music, play games, buy and sell stocks, do homework assignments, and more.

Like many technological innovations of the post–World War II era, the Internet was a product of federal government funding inspired by the cold war. In 1969, the U.S. Department of Defense established the Advanced Research Projects Agency Network (ARPANET), which developed a system called packet switching to route digitized messages between computers. Not only would such a system be able to handle vast amounts of information—allowing many users to share computers and communications lines—but it would provide security for military secrets and enable communication to continue even if some computers were damaged by an enemy attack. By 1971, ARPANET linked twenty-three computers, most of them at research universities.

Universities and research centers rushed to join ARPANET, but some were turned down because the military restricted access for security reasons. New networks soon developed, and the military created its own separate network in 1982. Meanwhile, the National Science Foundation (NSF) took over much of the technology and sponsored development of a civilian "backbone network," called NSFNET. With technology developed under ARPA, disparate networks could now connect with one another through Transmission Control Protocol/Internet Protocol (TCP/IP), or sets of instructions that translated each network's system for other networks' systems. In 1980, fewer than two hundred networks were connected, but by 1988 what had come to be called the Internet connected more than fifty thousand host computers.

Electronic mail had not been on the minds of defense officials when they developed packet switching, but it quickly surpassed all other forms of traffic on ARPANET. It was much faster than "snail mail," the scornful term computer users applied to mail sent via the postal service, and it was much cheaper than long-distance telephone conversations. Moreover, two people could communicate on the same day without having to be at their phones at the same time, and they could do so easily across different time zones.

As ownership of personal computers spread, people not only exchanged e-mail but also began to put entire documents on the Net. Two key inventions helped users to find and retrieve such material. In 1991, researchers at the University of Minnesota launched a retrieval system called "gopher," a slang term for one who fetches things and also the university's mascot. Then came the World Wide Web, first proposed in 1989, by researchers at a physics institute in Geneva, Switzerland. Through the Web, users gained access to billions of documents connected to each other by hyperlinks, which take the user from one text to another.

The Internet and Web were central to what journalist Thomas Friedman calls "the democratization of information." Dictatorships could no longer keep their subjects ignorant of what was going on in the rest of the world, nor restrain dissidents from communicating with one another. As President Bill Clinton asserted in 1998, "In this global information age, when economic success is built on ideas, personal freedom is essential to the greatness of any modern nation." The Internet carried the potential to empower people even in democratic nations: Organizers of the Seattle protests against globalization carried out much of their mobilization via the Internet, and the high speed and low cost of communication enabled international movements to organize around other issues much more easily than ever before. In the United States, "distance learning" via the Internet began to breach geographical and financial barriers to formal education.

By offering nearly instant, cheap communication around the globe, the Internet tremendously facilitated the growth of a global economy. It quickly spread capital around the world, made it easier for companies to manage operations abroad, and even enabled employees to work together while thousands of miles separated them. In 1997, for example, computer programmers in Beijing developing a project for IBM sent their work at the end of the day via the Internet to IBM workers in Seattle, who built on it and then passed it on to programmers in Belarus and Latvia, who did the same and relayed

THE INTERNET LINKS THE WORLD
By the end of the twentieth century, even the poorest countries in the world had some access to the Internet. These Buddhist monks stand outside an Internet café in the Cambodian capital of Phnom Penh in December 2000. President Bill Clinton displayed his fervent faith in the promise of technology to encourage democracy, claiming that, "when over 100 million people in China can get on the Net, it will be impossible to maintain a closed political and economic society."

it on to counterparts in India, who passed it on to the Beijing group, who started the process all over again until the project was finished. According to IBM executive John Patrick, "It's like we've created a forty-eight-hour day through the Internet."

Although the Internet has enabled people to exchange news, knowledge, photographs, music, and money rapidly, it is not without critics. Some observers worry that the Internet is taking the place of human relationships. A 2000 survey found that 20 percent of the people who went online five or more hours a week spent less time with family and friends or at social events than they spent before gaining access to the Net. Respondents had even more sharply reduced their time devoted to reading the newspaper or watching television. The availability of pornography on the Web and the exposure of users' personal and financial information are also concerns.

Other critics have pointed to the disparate access to information technology, a "digital divide" across class and racial lines. As costs of hardware and software plummeted during the 1990s, computers and access to the Internet grew dramatically but unevenly. By 2000, more than 50 percent of all U.S. households had computers, and 41 percent could log on to the Internet, in contrast to fewer than 25 percent of African American and Latino households. Even so, the Internet is well on its way to becoming as ubiquitous as television but with a much greater and varied impact. A computer software engineer who helped develop the Internet remarked, "It has already changed everything we do and changed it for good."

financial institutions like the World Trade Organization and the International Monetary Fund (IMF). Protesters charged that poorer nations lacked an adequate voice in trade policy decisions and that the WTO and IMF forced devastating regulations on developing nations. For example, although each of the WTO's 135 member nations had one vote, the United States could rely on much greater numbers of experts and send many more delegates to negotiations than most other countries could. And the IMF often required developing nations to which it issued loans to privatize state industries, deregulate their economies, and cut back on government spending for social welfare. While cheerleaders of globalization argued that in the long run everyone would benefit from global economic integration, critics focused on the short-term victims and decried the destruction of traditional cultures that accompanied economic modernization.

Liberalizing Foreign Trade

Building on the progress made in the Reagan and Bush administrations, Bill Clinton sought bipartisan support for new measures to ease restrictions on international trade. In November 1993, Congress approved the North American Free Trade Agreement (NAFTA), a pact eliminating all tariffs and trade barriers among the United States, Canada, and Mexico. NAFTA ran into stiff opposition from organized labor and other groups—including presidential hopeful Ross Perot and his supporters—that feared loss of jobs and industries to Mexico, where wages and labor standards were substantially lower than in the United States. Proponents argued that all three trading partners would benefit from greater export opportunities, creation of more jobs in the long run, and global clout. With 360 million people and a $6 billion economy, the NAFTA trio constituted the largest trading bloc in the world.

A year later, the Senate moved again to eliminate trade barriers by ratifying the General Agreement on Tariffs and Trade (GATT), which had already been signed by more than one hundred nations. GATT established the World Trade Organization to enforce provisions of the treaty, which included substantial tariff reductions and elimination of quotas on imports. Unlike NAFTA, GATT did not completely eliminate trade barriers, but the debates were similar in reflecting two visions of America's place in the world economy. Supporters of free trade envisioned American prosperity flowing from the increase in export opportunities. Opponents tied the nation's economic health to nurturing its established industries, thereby keeping its traditional jobs at home, and maintaining labor and environmental standards. The latter side prevailed in 1997 when Congress slowed down the liberalization of trade by refusing to renew the president's authority to negotiate "fast-track" trade agreements; such authority had allowed the president to submit trade agreements to Congress that it could not amend but that it had to vote for or against in ninety days. In 1998, Congress turned Clinton down again by refusing to allow the president to expand NAFTA to include Chile.

But in 2000, Clinton won a major victory in a controversy over whether to add China to the vast majority of countries that enjoyed normal trade relations with the United States. Liberals and conservatives alike opposed normalization. Despite the potential for opening large markets to American producers, conservatives attacked the deal with Communist China as "selling out the very moral and spiritual principles that made America great." For their part, liberals expressed concerns about labor standards and human rights violations in China and wanted evidence of reforms before granting permanent normal trading status. Supporters of the China trade bill also deplored the human rights violations and widespread inhumane working conditions, but they saw increased trade as the solution, not the problem.

In fact, Clinton promoted trade not just for its economic benefits but as a means of promoting international peace and security. Opening China to outside competition, he asserted, would "speed the information revolution there . . . speed the demise of China's huge state industries . . . spur the enterprise of private-sector involvement . . . and diminish the role of government in people's daily lives," thereby making its economy and government more like that of the United States and improving the prospects for peace in the long run. Revealing again the atypical alliances in the issue of free trade, just one-third of the Democrats in the House supported the president, who had to rely on the Republicans for his victory on the China trade bill.

Critics of globalization increasingly gained the attention of officials who had authority over international economic relationships. In 2000, for example, President Clinton issued an executive order requiring an environmental impact review before the signing of any trade agreement. He also signed the first trade agreement that had commitments to labor and environmental standards as key elements. Although the accord was negotiated with Jordan, whose trade with the United States was small, it set a precedent for requiring countries that wanted to eliminate tariffs not to try to gain a trade advantage by lowering labor and environmental standards. While some Republicans promised to defeat the agreement in Congress, AFL-CIO president John J. Sweeney hailed it as "a basic and important step forward in making globalization work for working families."

Although in smaller numbers than had gathered in Seattle, thousands of protesters showed up in Prague at a meeting of two international financial bodies, the World Bank and the International Monetary Fund, in September 2000. Officials from both bodies as well as representatives from the

United States and other wealthy nations promised to provide more debt relief to poor countries and to involve those nations more fully in decisions about loans and grants. According to James D. Wolfensohn, World Bank president and former international investment banker, "Our challenge is to make globalization an instrument of opportunity and inclusion—not fear."

The Internationalization of the United States

Although globalization was often associated with the expansion of American enterprise and culture to—or its imposition on—other countries, the

DISNEYLAND IN PARIS
Some people use the term "cultural imperialism" to describe the spread of American products and popular culture throughout the world. Since World War II, Coke and Levis, for example, as well as American movies, TV shows, and music, can be found nearly everywhere on the planet. In 1984, the Walt Disney Company opened Tokyo Disneyland, its first theme park abroad; Disneyland Paris followed in 1992, and it quickly became the leading tourist destination in Europe. While many French people expressed concern that the spreading American culture would drive out their own traditions and heritage, these employees of Disneyland Paris are striking for higher wages in 1998.
Corbis-Sygma.

United States itself was being transformed by the dynamic forces creating a global economy. Already in the 1980s, foreign investors from Japan, western Europe, and the Middle East had purchased American stocks and bonds, real estate, and corporations. Time-honored U.S. companies such as Firestone, Brooks Brothers, 20th Century-Fox, and Capitol Records passed into foreign ownership. Local communities welcomed infusions of foreign capital, and several states went to great lengths to encourage foreign companies to establish automobile plants within their boundaries. American non-union workers began to produce Hondas in Marysville, Ohio, and build BMWs in Spartanburg, South Carolina.

Globalization was transforming not just the economy but American society as well. Although the migration of labor was greater in the expanding international economy of the late nineteenth and early twentieth centuries, the United States experienced a tremendous surge of immigration in the late twentieth century. Five million new immigrants arrived in the 1980s, surpassing the totals for every decade in the twentieth century but the first and exhibiting a striking difference in country of origin. While 85 percent of the previous immigrants had come from Europe, by the 1980s Europe contributed just 11 percent of the newcomers. Almost half of the recent arrivals were Asians, and nearly 40 percent migrated from Latin America and the Caribbean. The flow of newcomers continued in the 1990s, as the Asian and Pacific Islander population grew by 43 percent, to nearly 11 million, and the number of Latinos increased by 39 percent, to 31 million. In 2000, immigrants made up more than 9 percent of the U.S. population. (See "Historical Question," page 1170, and Appendix, page A-62.)

THE NEW IMMIGRATION

These employees at UroGenesys, Inc., in Santa Monica, California provide one example of America's increasingly diverse workforce at the start of the twenty-first century, the result of the largest immigration rates in a hundred years and of the economy's increasing need for a technologically skilled workforce. This biotechnology company conducts research aimed at discovering and developing therapeutic and diagnostic products for urological cancers, especially prostate cancer.

Courtesy UroGenesys. Photo by Deidre Davidson.

The sources of the new immigration meant that America was becoming a truly international, interracial society, and not just along the coasts. American culture reflected the growing diversity: Salsa became a popular condiment, sushi bars appeared in cities across the country, cable TV companies added Spanish-speaking stations, and a truly international sport, soccer, soared in popularity. Mixed marriages also reflected a growing fusion of cultures, a fact recognized by the Census Bureau in 2000 when it let Americans check more than one racial category on their census forms. Demographers predicted, based on current trends, that the number of Americans of mixed racial ancestry would quadruple by 2050 and comprise between one-fifth and one-quarter of the population. By then, they also predicted, the American population would be just over 50 percent white, 16 percent black, 24 percent Hispanic, and 9 percent Asian.

Although globalization was often associated with the expansion of American enterprise and culture to other countries, the United States itself was being transformed by the dynamic forces creating a global economy.

Like their predecessors a hundred years earlier, the majority of post-1965 immigrants were unskilled. They took the lowest-paying jobs, providing household help, yard work, child and elder care, and cleaning services in hospitals, hotels, and businesses. Nonetheless, highly educated and trained workers constituted a significant proportion of the post-1965 immigration, and they were widely sought after by employers in the burgeoning high-tech industries. For example, in 1999 about one-third of the scientists and engineers who worked in Silicon Valley had been born abroad. One small company of thirty-one employees, a biotech firm working to invent cures for prostate diseases, employed two Vietnamese, two Canadians, one Pole, two Lebanese, three Chinese, one Korean, one Indian, one Israeli, one Scots, one English, and two Latinos—all scientists except one of the Vietnamese, who was an administrator. Emphasizing the multicultural uniqueness of American society at the turn of the twenty-first century, the company's owner boasted, "I cannot think of another country in the world where you could so easily put such a team together."

Conclusion: Entering the New Millennium

Despite the differences between the protesters of the 1960s and those who demonstrated against the current and potential damages accompanying the globalizing economy in 1999 and 2000, both groups belonged to a deep-rooted reform tradition that sought to realize the American promise of justice and human well-being. The demonstrators in Seattle sought on an international scale what the Populists and Progressives, the New Deal reformers, and many activists of the 1960s had sought for the domestic population—protection of individual rights, curbs on laissez-faire capitalism, and protection of and assistance to the victims of rapid economic change. Nonetheless, the global focus of reform impulses at the dawn of the twenty-first century did not mean that justice and material security for all groups had been achieved at home or that the question of what role the government should play in meeting those challenges had been resolved.

With a population derived to a great extent from people fleeing oppressive governments, Americans had for more than two centuries debated what the government could or should do, and what was best to leave to private enterprise, families, churches, and other voluntary institutions. Far more than other democracies, the United States had taken the path of private rather than public obligation, individual rather than collective solutions. In the twentieth century, Americans had entrusted the federal government with significantly greater powers and responsibilities than before, but the last three decades of the twentieth century had seen a turn against government, a decline of trust in the ability of federal programs to improve peoples' lives, even as a poverty rate of 20 percent among children and a growing gap between rich and poor accompanied the economic boom of the 1990s.

Americans for two centuries had also struggled over how their nation should act in the world. That question became particularly acute when the ending of the cold war eliminated containment of communism as the linchpin of U.S. foreign policy. Although post–cold war presidents dispatched military power in Latin America and the Middle East, no consensus formed around what constituted U.S. interests in the world and how those interests should be secured. Unlike their counterparts at the end of the nineteenth century, Americans displayed little taste for foreign adventures, nor did a majority want to see their tax dollars used for international purposes. Yet as it entered the twenty-first century, the United States continued to become more deeply embedded in the global economy as products, information, and people crossed borders with astonishing speed and frequency. How it would maintain and exercise its economic and military power on a rapidly changing planet constituted its greatest challenge.

www.bedfordstmartins.com/tap   See the Online Study Guide to assess your mastery of the material covered in this chapter.

CHRONOLOGY

1972 Nixon becomes first U.S. president to visit China.

Nixon visits Moscow to sign arms limitation treaties with Soviets.

1973 Arab oil embargo in retaliation for U.S. support of Israel creates energy crisis in United States.

1976 Jimmy Carter elected thirty-ninth president of the United States.

1978 Carter helps negotiate peace agreement between Israel and Egypt (Camp David accords).

1979 **November 4.** Beginning of hostage crisis in Iran.

1980 **April.** Attempt to free U.S. hostages in Iran fails.

Ronald Reagan elected fortieth president of the United States.

1982 United States invades Grenada and topples its Marxist government.

1983 U.S. involvement in Lebanon terminated after bombing of marine barracks and deaths of 241 Americans.

Reagan announces plans for Strategic Defense Initiative ("Star Wars").

1986 Iran-Contra scandal shakes Reagan administration.

1987 Soviet leader Mikhail Gorbachev visits Washington to sign INF agreement.

1988 George Bush elected forty-first president of the United States.

1989 Communism collapses in eastern Europe; Berlin Wall falls.

United States invades Panama and arrests dictator Manuel Noriega, who is jailed in United States.

1991 United States commits more than 400,000 troops to oust Iraqi army from Kuwait in Persian Gulf War.

1993 Israeli prime minister Yitzhak Rabin and PLO leader Yasir Arafat sign peace accords.

Eighteen U.S. soldiers are killed in Somalia.

Congress approves North American Free Trade Agreement (NAFTA).

1994 U.S. troops oversee peaceful return of Haitian president Jean-Bertrand Aristide to power.

Senate ratifies General Agreement on Tariffs and Trade (GATT).

1995 U.S. leaders broker peace accords among Serbia, Croatia, and Bosnia in Dayton, Ohio, temporarily ending civil war in former Yugoslavia.

1996 Leaders of nuclear powers sign comprehensive test ban treaty at United Nations.

1998 United States bombs alleged terrorist sites in Afghanistan and Sudan.

United States bombs Iraq for failure to comply with its 1991 agreement to destroy its weapons of mass destruction.

1999 United States, with NATO, bombs Serbia for more than two months to force an end to Serbian atrocities against ethnic Albanians in Kosovo.

Protesters disrupt meeting of the World Trade Organization in Seattle.

2000 Congress approves China trade bill, normalizing trade relations.

BIBLIOGRAPHY

GENERAL WORKS

Seyom Brown, *The Crisis of Power: Foreign Policy in the Kissinger Years* (1979).

Zbigniew Brzezinski, *Power and Principle: Memoirs of the National Security Adviser, 1977–1981* (1983).

Martin Campbell-Kelly and William Aspray, *Computer: A History of the Information Machine* (1996).

Seymour Hersh, *The Price of Power: Kissinger in the Nixon White House* (1983).

Bruce Hoffman, *Inside Terrorism* (1998).

William Hyland, *Clinton's World* (1999).

David E. Kyvig, ed., *Reagan and the World* (1990).

William Pfaff, *Barbarian Sentiments: How the American Century Ends* (1989).

James M. Scott, ed., *After the End: Making U.S. Foreign Policy in the Post–Cold War World* (1998).

George P. Shultz, *Turmoil and Triumph: My Years as Secretary of State* (1993).

Gaddis Smith, *Morality, Reason, and Power: American Diplomacy in the Carter Years* (1986).

Cyrus Vance, *Hard Choices: Critical Years in America's Foreign Policy* (1983).

THE UNITED STATES AND THE MIDDLE EAST

Rick Atkinson, *Crusade: The Untold Story of the Persian Gulf War* (1994).

James A. Bill, *The Eagle and the Lion: The Tragedy of American-Iranian Relations* (1988).

Theodore Draper, *A Very Thin Line: The Iran-Contra Affair* (1991).

Lawrence Freedman and Efraim Karsh, *The Gulf Conflict, 1990–1991: Diplomacy and War in the New World Order* (1993).

Mark J. Gasiorowski, *U.S. Foreign Policy and the Shah: Building a Client State in Iran* (1991).

Benny Morris, *Righteous Victims: A History of the Zionist-Arab Conflict, 1881–1999* (1999).

Donald Neff, *Fallen Pillars: U.S. Policy towards Palestine and Israel since 1945* (1995).

Elaine Sciolino, *The Outlaw State: Saddam Hussein's Quest for Power and the Gulf Crisis* (1991).

Baylis Thomas, *How Israel Was Won: A Concise History of the Arab-Israeli Conflict* (1999).

THE UNITED STATES AND LATIN AMERICA

Cynthia J. Arnson, *Crossroads: Congress, the Reagan Administration, and Central America* (1989).

Thomas Carothers, *In the Name of Democracy: U.S. Policy toward Latin America in the Reagan Years* (1991).

John Dinges, *Our Man in Panama: How General Noriega Used the United States—and Made Millions in Drugs and Arms* (1990).

J. Michael Hogan, *The Panama Canal in American Politics* (1986).

Robert Kagan, *A Twilight Struggle: American Power and Nicaragua, 1977–1990* (1996).

Frederick Kempe, *Divorcing the Dictator: America's Bungled Affair with Noriega* (1990).

William M. LeoGrande, *Our Own Backyard: The United States in Central America, 1977–1992* (1998).

THE COLD WAR AND ITS END

Michael R. Beschloss and Strobe Talbott, *At the Highest Levels: The Inside Story of the End of the Cold War* (1993).

Beth A. Fischer, *The Reagan Reversal: Foreign Policy and the End of the Cold War* (1997).

Raymond I. Garthoff, *Détente and Confrontation: American-Soviet Relations from Nixon to Reagan* (rev. ed., 1994).

Raymond I. Garthoff, *The Great Transition: American-Soviet Relations and the End of the Cold War* (1994).

Michael J. Hogan, ed., *The End of the Cold War: Its Meanings and Implications* (1992).

Robert L. Hutchings, *American Diplomacy and the End of the Cold War: An Insider's Account of U.S. Policy in Europe, 1989–1992* (1997).

Richard Ned Lebow and Janice Gross Stein, *We All Lost the Cold War* (1994).

Keith I. Nelson, *The Making of Détente: Soviet-American Relations in the Shadow of Vietnam* (1995).

Peter Schweizer, *Victory: The Reagan Administration's Secret Strategy That Hastened the Collapse of the Soviet Union* (1995).

James M. Scott, ed., *After the End: Making U.S. Foreign Policy in the Post–Cold War World* (1998).

WEAPONS AND ARMS CONTROL

Richard Butler, *The Greatest Threat: Iraq, Weapons of Mass Destruction, and the Crisis of Global Security* (2000).

Frances Fitzgerald, *Way Out There in the Blue: Reagan, Star Wars and the End of the Cold War* (2000).

Sanford Lakoff and Herbert F. York, *A Shield in Space?* (1989).

Strobe Talbott, *The Master of the Game: Paul Nitze and the Nuclear Peace* (1988).

Terry Terriff, *The Nixon Administration and the Making of U.S. Nuclear Strategy* (1995).

Daniel Wirls, *Buildup: The Politics of Defense in the Reagan Era* (1992).

GLOBALIZATION

Jeremy Brecher, Tim Costello, and Brendan Smith, *Globalization from Below* (2000).

Stephen Castles, ed., *Citizenship and Migration: Globalization and the Politics of Belonging* (2000).

Thomas L. Friedman, *The Lexus and the Olive Tree: Understanding Globalization* (1999).

John Gray, *The Delusions of Global Capitalism* (1999).

Evelyn Hu-Dehart, ed., *Across the Pacific: Asian Americans and Globalization* (1999).

John R. MacArthur, *The Selling of "Free Trade": NAFTA, Washington, and the Subversion of American Democracy* (2000).

Douglas S. Massey, *Worlds in Motion: Understanding International Migration at Century's End* (1998).

David M. Reimers, *Still the Golden Door: The Third World Comes to America* (1992).

David M. Reimers, *Unwelcome Strangers: American Identity and the Turn against Immigration* (1998).

Roberto Suro, *Strangers among Us: Latinos' Lives in a Changing America* (1999).

THE DECLARATION OF INDEPENDENCE

In Congress, July 4, 1776,

THE UNANIMOUS DECLARATION OF THE THIRTEEN UNITED STATES OF AMERICA

When in the course of human events, it becomes necessary for one people to dissolve the political bands which have connected them with another, and to assume, among the powers of the earth, the separate and equal station to which the laws of nature and of nature's God entitle them, a decent respect to the opinions of mankind requires that they should declare the causes which impel them to the separation.

We hold these truths to be self-evident, that all men are created equal; that they are endowed by their Creator with certain unalienable rights; that among these, are life, liberty, and the pursuit of happiness. That, to secure these rights, governments are instituted among men, deriving their just powers from the consent of the governed; that, whenever any form of government becomes destructive of these ends, it is the right of the people to alter or to abolish it, and to institute a new government, laying its foundation on such principles, and organizing its powers in such form, as to them shall seem most likely to effect their safety and happiness. Prudence, indeed, will dictate that governments long established, should not be changed for light and transient causes; and, accordingly, all experience hath shown, that mankind are more disposed to suffer, while evils are sufferable, than to right themselves by abolishing the forms to which they are accustomed. But, when a long train of abuses and usurpations, pursuing invariably the same object, evinces a design to reduce them under absolute despotism, it is their right, it is their duty, to throw off such government and to provide new guards for their future security. Such has been the patient sufferance of these colonies, and such is now the necessity which constrains them to alter their former systems of government. The history of the present King of Great Britain is a history of repeated injuries and usurpations, all having, in direct object, the establishment of an absolute tyranny over these States. To prove this, let facts be submitted to a candid world:

He has refused his assent to laws the most wholesome and necessary for the public good.

He has forbidden his governors to pass laws of immediate and pressing importance, unless suspended in their operation till his assent should be obtained; and, when so suspended, he has utterly neglected to attend to them.

He has refused to pass other laws for the accommodation of large districts of people, unless those people would relinquish the right of representation in the legislature; a right inestimable to them, and formidable to tyrants only.

He has called together legislative bodies at places unusual, uncomfortable, and distant from the depository of their public records, for the sole purpose of fatiguing them into compliance with his measures.

He has dissolved representative houses repeatedly for opposing, with manly firmness, his invasions on the rights of the people.

He has refused, for a long time after such dissolutions, to cause others to be elected; whereby the legislative powers, incapable of annihilation, have returned to the people at large for their exercise; the state remaining in the mean-time exposed to all the danger of invasion from without, and convulsions within.

He has endeavoured to prevent the population of these States; for that purpose, obstructing the laws for naturalization of foreigners, refusing to pass others to encourage their migration hither, and raising the conditions of new appropriations of lands.

He has obstructed the administration of justice, by refusing his assent to laws for establishing judiciary powers.

He has made judges dependent on his will alone, for the tenure of their offices, and the amount and payment of their salaries.

He has erected a multitude of new offices, and sent hither swarms of officers to harass our people, and eat out their substance.

He has kept among us, in times of peace, standing armies, without the consent of our legislature.

He has affected to render the military independent of, and superior to, the civil power.

He has combined, with others, to subject us to a jurisdiction foreign to our Constitution, and unacknowledged by our laws; giving his assent to their acts of pretended legislation:

For quartering large bodies of armed troops among us:

For protecting them by a mock trial, from punishment, for any murders which they should commit on the inhabitants of these States:

For cutting off our trade with all parts of the world:

For imposing taxes on us without our consent:

For depriving us, in many cases, of the benefit of trial by jury:

For transporting us beyond seas to be tried for pretended offences:

For abolishing the free system of English laws in a neighboring province, establishing therein an arbitrary government, and enlarging its boundaries, so as to render it at once an example and fit instrument for introducing the same absolute rule into these colonies:

For taking away our charters, abolishing our most valuable laws, and altering, fundamentally, the powers of our governments:

For suspending our own legislatures, and declaring themselves invested with power to legislate for us in all cases whatsoever.

He has abdicated government here, by declaring us out of his protection, and waging war against us.

He has plundered our seas, ravaged our coasts, burnt our towns, and destroyed the lives of our people.

He is, at this time, transporting large armies of foreign mercenaries to complete the works of death, desolation, and tyranny, already begun, with circumstances of cruelty and perfidy scarcely paralleled in the most barbarous ages, and totally unworthy the head of a civilized nation.

He has constrained our fellow citizens, taken captive on the high seas, to bear arms against their country, to become the executioners of their friends, and brethren, or to fall themselves by their hands.

He has excited domestic insurrections amongst us, and has endeavored to bring on the inhabitants of our frontiers, the merciless Indian savages, whose known rule of warfare is an undistinguished destruction of all ages, sexes, and conditions.

In every stage of these oppressions, we have petitioned for redress; in the most humble terms; our repeated petitions have been answered only by repeated injury. A prince, whose character is thus marked by every act which may define a tyrant, is unfit to be the ruler of a free people.

Nor have we been wanting in attention to our British brethren. We have warned them, from time to time, of attempts made by their legislature to extend an unwarrantable jurisdiction over us. We have reminded them of the circumstances of our emigration and settlement here. We have appealed to their native justice and magnanimity, and we have conjured them, by the ties of our common kindred, to disavow these usurpations, which would inevitably interrupt our connections and correspondence. They, too, have been deaf to the voice of justice and consanguinity. We must, therefore, acquiesce in the necessity which denounces our separation, and hold them as we hold the rest of mankind, enemies in war, in peace, friends.

We, therefore, the representatives of the United States of America, in general Congress assembled, appealing to the Supreme Judge of the world for the rectitude of our intentions, do, in the name, and by authority of the good people of these colonies, solemnly publish and declare, that these united colonies are, and of right ought to be, free and independent states: that they are absolved from all allegiance to the British Crown, and that all political connection between them and the state of Great Britain is, and ought to be, totally dissolved; and that, as free and independent states, they have full power to levy war, conclude peace, contract alliances, establish commerce, and to do all other acts and things which independent states may of right do. And, for the support of this declaration, with a firm reliance on the protection of Divine Providence, we mutually pledge to each other our lives, our fortunes, and our sacred honor.

The foregoing Declaration was, by order of Congress, engrossed, and signed by the following members:

JOHN HANCOCK

New Hampshire
Josiah Bartlett
William Whipple
Matthew Thornton

New York
William Floyd
Phillip Livingston
Francis Lewis
Lewis Morris

Massachusetts Bay
Samuel Adams
John Adams
Robert Treat Paine
Elbridge Gerry

New Jersey
Richard Stockton
John Witherspoon
Francis Hopkinson
John Hart
Abraham Clark

Rhode Island
Stephen Hopkins
William Ellery

Connecticut
Roger Sherman
Samuel Huntington
William Williams
Oliver Wolcott

Delaware
Caesar Rodney
George Read
Thomas M'Kean

Pennsylvania
Robert Morris
Benjamin Rush
Benjamin Franklin
John Morton
George Clymer
James Smith
George Taylor
James Wilson
George Ross

North Carolina
William Hooper
Joseph Hewes
John Penn

Maryland
Samuel Chase
William Paca
Thomas Stone
Charles Carroll,
   of Carrollton

Virginia
George Wythe
Richard Henry Lee
Thomas Jefferson
Benjamin Harrison
Thomas Nelson, Jr.
Francis Lightfoot Lee
Carter Braxton

South Carolina
Edward Rutledge
Thomas Heyward, Jr.
Thomas Lynch, Jr.
Arthur Middleton

Georgia
Button Gwinnett
Lyman Hall
George Walton

Resolved, That copies of the Declaration be sent to the several assemblies, conventions, and committees, or councils of safety, and to the several commanding officers of the continental troops; that it be proclaimed in each of the United States, at the head of the army.

THE ARTICLES OF CONFEDERATION AND PERPETUAL UNION

Agreed to in Congress, November 15, 1777
Ratified March 1781

BETWEEN THE STATES OF NEW HAMPSHIRE, MASSACHU-
SETTS BAY, RHODE ISLAND AND PROVIDENCE PLANTA-
TIONS, CONNECTICUT, NEW YORK, NEW JERSEY, PENN-
SYLVANIA, DELAWARE, MARYLAND, VIRGINIA, NORTH
CAROLINA, SOUTH CAROLINA, GEORGIA.*

Article 1

The stile of this confederacy shall be "The United States
of America."

Article 2

Each State retains its sovereignty, freedom and independence, and every power, jurisdiction, and right,
which is not by this confederation expressly delegated
to the United States, in Congress assembled.

Article 3

The said states hereby severally enter into a firm league
of friendship with each other for their common defence, the security of their liberties and their mutual
and general welfare; binding themselves to assist each
other against all force offered to, or attacks made upon
them, or any of them, on account of religion, sovereignty, trade, or any other pretence whatever.

Article 4

The better to secure and perpetuate mutual friendship
and intercourse among the people of the different
states in this union, the free inhabitants of each of these
states, paupers, vagabonds, and fugitives from justice
excepted, shall be entitled to all privileges and immunities of free citizens in the several states; and the people of each State shall have free ingress and regress to
and from any other State, and shall enjoy therein all
the privileges of trade and commerce, subject to the
same duties, impositions, and restrictions, as the in-

habitants thereof respectively; provided, that such restrictions shall not extend so far as to prevent the removal of property, imported into any State, to any
other State of which the owner is an inhabitant; provided also, that no imposition, duties, or restriction,
shall be laid by any State on the property of the United
States, or either of them.

If any person guilty of, or charged with treason,
felony, or other high misdemeanor in any State, shall
flee from justice and be found in any of the United
States, he shall, upon demand of the governor or executive power of the State from which he fled, be delivered up and removed to the State having jurisdiction of his offence.

Full faith and credit shall be given in each of these
states to the records, acts, and judicial proceedings of
the courts and magistrates of every other State.

Article 5

For the more convenient management of the general interests of the United States, delegates shall be annually
appointed, in such manner as the legislature of each
State shall direct, to meet in Congress, on the 1st Monday in November in every year, with a power reserved
to each State to recall its delegates, or any of them, at
any time within the year, and to send others in their
stead for the remainder of the year.

No State shall be represented in Congress by less
than two, nor by more than seven members; and no
person shall be capable of being a delegate for more
than three years in any term of six years; nor shall any
person, being a delegate, be capable of holding any office under the United States, for which he, or any other
for his benefit, receives any salary, fees, or emolument
of any kind.

Each State shall maintain its own delegates in a
meeting of the states, and while they act as members
of the committee of the states.

In determining questions in the United States, in
Congress assembled, each State shall have one vote.

Freedom of speech and debate in Congress shall
not be impeached or questioned in any court or place
out of Congress: and the members of Congress shall
be protected in their persons from arrests and impris-
onments, during the time of their going to and from,
and attendance on Congress, except for treason, felony,
or breach of the peace.

---

*This copy of the final draft of the Articles of Confederation is taken
from the *Journals*, 9:907–925, November 15, 1777.

Article 6

No State, without the consent of the United States, in Congress assembled, shall send any embassy to, or receive any embassy from, or enter into any conference, agreement, alliance, or treaty with any king, prince, or state; nor shall any person, holding any office of profit or trust under the United States, or any of them, accept of any present, emolument, office or title, of any kind whatever, from any king, prince, or foreign state; nor shall the United States, in Congress assembled, or any of them, grant any title of nobility.

No two or more states shall enter into any treaty, confederation, or alliance, whatever, between them, without the consent of the United States, in Congress assembled, specifying accurately the purposes for which the same is to be entered into, and how long it shall continue.

No state shall lay any imposts or duties which may interfere with any stipulations in treaties entered into by the United States, in Congress assembled, with any king, prince, or state, in pursuance of any treaties already proposed by Congress to the courts of France and Spain.

No vessels of war shall be kept up in time of peace by any State, except such number only as shall be deemed necessary by the United States, in Congress assembled, for the defence of such State or its trade; nor shall any body of forces be kept up by any State, in time of peace, except such number only as, in the judgment of the United States, in Congress assembled, shall be deemed requisite to garrison the forts necessary for the defence of such State; but every State shall always keep up a well regulated and disciplined militia, sufficiently armed and accoutred, and shall provide, and constantly have ready for use, in public stores, a due number of field pieces and tents, and a proper quantity of arms, ammunition and camp equipage.

No State shall engage in any war without the consent of the United States, in Congress assembled, unless such State be actually invaded by enemies, or shall have received certain advice of a resolution being formed by some nation of Indians to invade such State, and the danger is so imminent as not to admit of a delay till the United States, in Congress assembled, can be consulted; nor shall any State grant commissions to any ships or vessels of war, nor letters of marque or reprisal, except it be after a declaration of war by the United States, in Congress assembled, and then only against the kingdom or state, and the subjects thereof, against which war has been so declared, and under such regulations as shall be established by the United States, in Congress assembled, unless such State be in-

fested by pirates, in which case vessels of war may be fitted out for that occasion, and kept so long as the danger shall continue, or until the United States, in Congress assembled, shall determine otherwise.

Article 7

When land forces are raised by any State for the common defence, all officers of or under the rank of colonel, shall be appointed by the legislature of each State respectively, by whom such forces shall be raised, or in such manner as such State shall direct; and all vacancies shall be filled up by the State which first made the appointment.

Article 8

All charges of war and all other expences, that shall be incurred for the common defence or general welfare, and allowed by the United States, in Congress assembled, shall be defrayed out of a common treasury, which shall be supplied by the several states, in proportion to the value of all land within each State, granted to or surveyed for any person, as such land and the buildings and improvements thereon shall be estimated according to such mode as the United States, in Congress assembled, shall, from time to time, direct and appoint.

The taxes for paying that proportion shall be laid and levied by the authority and direction of the legislatures of the several states, within the time agreed upon by the United States, in Congress assembled.

Article 9

The United States, in Congress assembled, shall have the sole and exclusive right and power of determining on peace and war, except in the cases mentioned in the 6th article; of sending and receiving ambassadors; entering into treaties and alliances, provided that no treaty of commerce shall be made, whereby the legislative power of the respective states shall be restrained from imposing such imposts and duties on foreigners as their own people are subjected to, or from prohibiting the exportation or importation of any species of goods or commodities whatsoever; of establishing rules for deciding, in all cases, what captures on land or water shall be legal, and in what manner prizes, taken by land or naval forces in the service of the United States, shall be divided or appropriated; of granting letters of marque and reprisal in times of peace; appointing courts for the trial of piracies and felonies committed on the high seas, and establishing courts for receiving and determining, finally, appeals in all cases of captures; provided, that no member of Congress shall be appointed a judge of any of the said courts.

The United States, in Congress assembled, shall also be the last resort on appeal in all disputes and differences now subsisting, or that hereafter may arise between two or more states concerning boundary, jurisdiction or any other cause whatever; which authority shall always be exercised in the manner following: whenever the legislative or executive authority, or lawful agent of any State, in controversy with another, shall present a petition to Congress, stating the matter in question, and praying for a hearing, notice thereof shall be given, by order of Congress, to the legislative or executive authority of the other State in controversy, and a day assigned for the appearance of the parties by their lawful agents, who shall then be directed to appoint, by joint consent, commissioners or judges to constitute a court for hearing and determining the matter in question; but, if they cannot agree, Congress shall name three persons out of each of the United States, and from the list of such persons each party shall alternately strike out one, the petitioners beginning, until the number shall be reduced to thirteen; and from that number not less than seven, nor more than nine names, as Congress shall direct, shall, in the presence of Congress, be drawn out by lot; and the persons whose names shall be so drawn, or any five of them, shall be commissioners or judges to hear and finally determine the controversy, so always as a major part of the judges who shall hear the cause shall agree in the determination; and if either party shall neglect to attend at the day appointed, without shewing reasons which Congress shall judge sufficient, or, being present, shall refuse to strike, the Congress shall proceed to nominate three persons out of each State, and the secretary of Congress shall strike in behalf of such party absent or refusing; and the judgment and sentence of the court to be appointed, in the manner before prescribed, shall be final and conclusive; and if any of the parties shall refuse to submit to the authority of such court, or to appear or defend their claim or cause, the court shall nevertheless proceed to pronounce sentence or judgment, which shall, in like manner, be final and decisive, the judgment or sentence and other proceedings begin, in either case, transmitted to Congress, and lodged among the acts of Congress for the security of the parties concerned: provided, that every commissioner, before he sits in judgment, shall take an oath, to be administered by one of the judges of the supreme or superior court of the State where the cause shall be tried, "well and truly to hear and determine the matter in question, according to the best of his judgment,

without favour, affection, or hope of reward:" provided, also, that no State shall be deprived of territory for the benefit of the United States.

All controversies concerning the private right of soil, claimed under different grants of two or more states, whose jurisdictions, as they may respect such lands and the states which passed such grants, are adjusted, the said grants, or either of them, being at the same time claimed to have originated antecedent to such settlement of jurisdiction, shall, on the petition of either party to the Congress of the United States, be finally determined, as near as may be, in the same manner as is before prescribed for deciding disputes respecting territorial jurisdiction between different states.

The United States, in Congress assembled, shall also have the sole and exclusive right and power of regulating the alloy and value of coin struck by their own authority, or by that of the respective states; fixing the standard of weights and measures throughout the United States; regulating the trade and managing all affairs with the Indians not members of any of the states; provided that the legislative right of any State within its own limits be not infringed or violated; establishing and regulating post offices from one State to another throughout all the United States, and exacting such postage on the papers passing through the same as may be requisite to defray the expences of the said office; appointing all officers of the land forces in the service of the United States, excepting regimental officers; appointing all the officers of the naval forces, and commissioning all officers whatever in the service of the United States; making rules for the government and regulation of the said land and naval forces, and directing their operations.

The United States, in Congress assembled, shall have authority to appoint a committee to sit in the recess of Congress, to be denominated "a Committee of the States," and to consist of one delegate from each State, and to appoint such other committees and civil officers as may be necessary for managing the general affairs of the United States, under their direction; to appoint one of their number to preside; provided that no person be allowed to serve in the office of president more than one year in any term of three years; to ascertain the necessary sums of money to be raised for the service of the United States, and to appropriate and apply the same for defraying the public expences; to borrow money or emit bills on the credit of the United States, transmitting, every half year, to the respective states, an account of the sums of money so borrowed or emitted; to build and equip a navy; to agree upon the number of land forces, and to make requisitions from each State for its quota, in proportion to the number of white inhabitants in such State; which requisitions shall be binding; and thereupon, the legislature of each State shall appoint the regimental officers, raise the men, and cloathe, arm, and equip them in a soldier-like manner, at the expence of the United States; and the officers and men so cloathed, armed, and equipped, shall march to the place appointed and within the time agreed on by the United States, in Congress assembled; but if the United States, in Congress assembled, shall, on consideration of circumstances, judge proper that any State should not raise men, or should raise a smaller number than its quota, and that any other State should raise a greater number of men than the quota thereof, such extra number shall be raised, officered, cloathed, armed, and equipped in the same manner as the quota of such State, unless the legislature of such State shall judge that such extra number cannot be safely spared out of the same, in which case they shall raise, officer, cloathe, arm, and equip as many of such extra number as they judge can be safely spared. And the officers and men so cloathed, armed, and equipped, shall march to the place appointed and within the time agreed on by the United States, in Congress assembled.

The United States, in Congress assembled, shall never engage in a war, nor grant letters of marque and reprisal in time of peace, nor enter into any treaties or alliances, nor coin money, nor regulate the value thereof, nor ascertain the sums and expences necessary for the defence and welfare of the United States, or any of them: nor emit bills, nor borrow money on the credit of the United States, nor appropriate money, nor agree upon the number of vessels of war to be built or purchased, or the number of land or sea forces to be raised, nor appoint a commander in chief of the army or navy, unless nine states assent to the same; nor shall a question on any other point, except for adjourning from day to day, be determined, unless by the votes of a majority of the United States, in Congress assembled.

The Congress of the United States shall have power to adjourn to any time within the year, and to any place within the United States, so that no period of adjournment be for a longer duration than the space of six months, and shall publish the journal of their proceedings monthly, except such parts thereof, relating to treaties, alliances or military operations, as, in their judgment, require secrecy; and the yeas and nays of the delegates of each State on any question shall be entered on the journal, when it is desired by any delegate; and the delegates of a State, or any of them, at his, or their request, shall be furnished with a transcript of the said journal, except such parts as are above excepted, to lay before the legislatures of the several states.

Article 10

The committee of the states, or any nine of them, shall be authorized to execute, in the recess of Congress, such of the powers of Congress as the United States, in Congress assembled, by the consent of nine states, shall, from time to time, think expedient to vest them with; provided, that no power be delegated to the said committee, for the exercise of which, by the articles of confederation, the voice of nine states, in the Congress of the United States assembled, is requisite.

Article 11

Canada acceding to this confederation, and joining in the measures of the United States, shall be admitted into and entitled to all the advantages of this union; but no other colony shall be admitted into the same, unless such admission be agreed to by nine states.

Article 12

All bills of credit emitted, monies borrowed and debts contracted by, or under the authority of Congress before the assembling of the United States, in pursuance of the present confederation, shall be deemed and considered as a charge against the United States, for payment and satisfaction whereof the said United States and the public faith are hereby solemnly pledged.

Article 13

Every State shall abide by the determinations of the United States, in Congress assembled, on all questions which, by this confederation, are submitted to them. And the articles of this confederation shall be inviolably observed by every State, and the union shall be perpetual; nor shall any alteration at any time hereafter be made in any of them; unless such alteration be agreed to in a Congress of the United States, and be afterwards confirmed by the legislatures of every State.

These articles shall be proposed to the legislatures of all the United States, to be considered, and if approved of by them, they are advised to authorize their delegates to ratify the same in the Congress of the United States; which being done, the same shall become conclusive.

THE CONSTITUTION OF THE UNITED STATES*

Agreed to by Philadelphia Convention, September 17, 1787. Implemented March 4, 1789.

Preamble

We the people of the United States, in order to form a more perfect union, establish justice, insure domestic tranquility, provide for the common defense, promote the general welfare, and secure the blessings of liberty to ourselves and our posterity, do ordain and establish this Constitution for the United States of America.

Article I

Section 1   All legislative powers herein granted shall be vested in a Congress of the United States, which shall consist of a Senate and a House of Representatives.

Section 2   The House of Representatives shall be composed of members chosen every second year by the people of the several States, and the electors in each State shall have the qualifications requisite for electors of the most numerous branch of the State Legislature.

No person shall be a Representative who shall not have attained to the age of twenty-five years, and been seven years a citizen of the United States, and who shall not, when elected, be an inhabitant of that State in which he shall be chosen.

Representatives and direct taxes shall be apportioned among the several States which may be included within this Union, according to their respective numbers, *which shall be determined by adding to the whole number of free persons, including those bound to service for a term of years and excluding Indians not taxed, three-fifths of all other persons.* The actual enumeration shall be made within three years after the first meeting of the Congress of the United States, and within every subsequent term of ten years, in such manner as they shall by law direct. The number of Representatives shall not exceed one for every thirty thousand, but each State shall have at least one Representative; *and until such enumeration shall be made, the State of New Hampshire shall be entitled to choose three, Massachusetts eight, Rhode Island and Providence Plantations one, Connecticut five, New York six, New Jersey four, Pennsylvania eight, Delaware one, Maryland six, Virginia ten, North Carolina five, South Carolina five, and Georgia three.*

When vacancies happen in the representation from any State, the Executive authority thereof shall issue writs of election to fill such vacancies.

The House of Representatives shall choose their Speaker and other officers; and shall have the sole power of impeachment.

Section 3   The Senate of the United States shall be composed of two Senators from each State, *chosen by the legislature thereof,* for six years; and each Senator shall have one vote.

Immediately after they shall be assembled in consequence of the first election, they shall be divided as equally as may be into three classes. The seats of the Senators of the first class shall be vacated at the expiration of the second year, of the second class at the expiration of the fourth year, and of the third class at the expiration of the sixth year, so that one-third may be chosen every second year; *and if vacancies happen by resignation or otherwise, during the recess of the legislature of any State, the Executive thereof may make temporary appointments until the next meeting of the legislature, which shall then fill such vacancies.*

No person shall be a Senator who shall not have attained to the age of thirty years, and been nine years a citizen of the United States, and who shall not, when elected, be an inhabitant of that State for which he shall be chosen.

The Vice-President of the United States shall be President of the Senate, but shall have no vote, unless they be equally divided.

The Senate shall choose their other officers, and also a President *pro tempore*, in the absence of the Vice-President, or when he shall exercise the office of President of the United States.

The Senate shall have the sole power to try all impeachments. When sitting for that purpose, they shall be on oath or affirmation. When the President of the United States is tried, the Chief Justice shall preside: and no person shall be convicted without the concurrence of two-thirds of the members present.

Judgment in cases of impeachment shall not extend further than to removal from the office, and disqualification to hold and enjoy any office of honor, trust or profit under the United States: but the party convicted shall nevertheless be liable and subject to indictment, trial, judgment and punishment, according to law.

Section 4   The times, places and manner of holding elections for Senators and Representatives shall be prescribed in each State by the legislature thereof; but the

---

*Passages no longer in effect are in italic type.

Congress may at any time by law make or alter such regulations, except as to the places of choosing Senators.

The Congress shall assemble at least once in every year, and such meeting *shall be on the first Monday in December, unless they shall by law appoint a different day.*

Section 5 Each house shall be the judge of the elections, returns and qualifications of its own members, and a majority of each shall constitute a quorum to do business; but a smaller number may adjourn from day to day, and may be authorized to compel the attendance of absent members, in such manner, and under such penalties, as each house may provide.

Each house may determine the rules of its proceedings, punish its members for disorderly behavior, and with the concurrence of two-thirds, expel a member.

Each house shall keep a journal of its proceedings, and from time to time publish the same, excepting such parts as may in their judgment require secrecy; and the yeas and nays of the members of either house on any question shall, at the desire of one-fifth of those present, be entered on the journal.

Neither house, during the session of Congress, shall, without the consent of the other, adjourn for more than three days, nor to any other place than that in which the two houses shall be sitting.

Section 6 The Senators and Representatives shall receive a compensation for their services, to be ascertained by law and paid out of the treasury of the United States. They shall in all cases except treason, felony and breach of the peace, be privileged from arrest during their attendance at the session of their respective houses, and in going to and returning from the same; and for any speech or debate in either house, they shall not be questioned in any other place.

No Senator or Representative shall, during the time for which he was elected, be appointed to any civil office under the authority of the United States, which shall have been created, or the emoluments whereof shall have been increased, during such time; and no person holding any office under the United States shall be a member of either house during his continuance in office.

Section 7 All bills for raising revenue shall originate in the House of Representatives; but the Senate may propose or concur with amendments as on other bills.

Every bill which shall have passed the House of Representatives and the Senate, shall, before it become a law, be presented to the President of the United States; if he approve he shall sign it, but if not he shall return it with objections to that house in which it shall have originated, who shall enter the objections at large on their journal, and proceed to reconsider it. If after such reconsideration two-thirds of that house shall agree to pass the bill, it shall be sent, together with the objections, to the other house, by which it shall likewise be reconsidered, and, if approved by two-thirds of that house, it shall become a law. But in all such cases the votes of both houses shall be determined by yeas and nays, and the names of the persons voting for and against the bill shall be entered on the journal of each house respectively. If any bill shall not be returned by the President within ten days (Sundays excepted) after it shall have been presented to him, the same shall be a law, in like manner as if he had signed it, unless the Congress by their adjournment prevent its return, in which case it shall not be a law.

Every order, resolution, or vote to which the concurrence of the Senate and House of Representatives may be necessary (except on a question of adjournment) shall be presented to the President of the United States; and before the same shall take effect, shall be approved by him, or being disapproved by him, shall be repassed by two-thirds of the Senate and House of Representatives, according to the rules and limitations prescribed in the case of a bill.

Section 8 The Congress shall have power
To lay and collect taxes, duties, imposts, and excises, to pay the debts and provide for the common defense and general welfare of the United States; but all duties, imposts and excises shall be uniform throughout the United States;

To borrow money on the credit of the United States;

To regulate commerce with foreign nations, and among the several States, and with the Indian tribes;

To establish an uniform rule of naturalization, and uniform laws on the subject of bankruptcies throughout the United States;

To coin money, regulate the value thereof, and of foreign coin, and fix the standard of weights and measures;

To provide for the punishment of counterfeiting the securities and current coin of the United States;

To establish post offices and post roads;

To promote the progress of science and useful arts by securing for limited times to authors and inventors the exclusive right to their respective writings and discoveries;

To constitute tribunals inferior to the Supreme Court;

To define and punish piracies and felonies committed on the high seas and offences against the law of nations;

To declare war, grant letters of marque and reprisal, and make rules concerning captures on land and water;

To raise and support armies, but no appropriation of money to that use shall be for a longer term than two years;

To provide and maintain a navy;

To make rules for the government and regulation of the land and naval forces;

To provide for calling forth the militia to execute the laws of the Union, suppress insurrections and repel invasions;

To provide for organizing, arming, and disciplining the militia, and for governing such part of them as may be employed in the service of the United States, reserving to the States respectively the appointment of the officers, and the authority of training the militia according to the discipline prescribed by Congress;

To exercise exclusive legislation in all cases whatsoever, over such district (not exceeding ten miles square) as may, by cession of particular States, and the acceptance of Congress, become the seat of the government of the United States, and to exercise like authority over all places purchased by the consent of the legislature of the State, in which the same shall be, for erection of forts, magazines, arsenals, dock-yards, and other needful buildings;—and

To make all laws which shall be necessary and proper for carrying into execution the foregoing powers, and all other powers vested by this Constitution in the government of the United States, or in any department or officer thereof.

Section 9   *The migration or importation of such persons as any of the States now existing shall think proper to admit shall not be prohibited by the Congress prior to the year one thousand eight hundred and eight; but a tax or duty may be imposed on such importation, not exceeding ten dollars for each person.*

The privilege of the writ of habeas corpus shall not be suspended, unless when in cases of rebellion or invasion the public safety may require it.

No bill of attainder or ex post facto law shall be passed.

No capitation, or other direct, tax shall be laid, unless in proportion to the census or enumeration herein before directed to be taken.

No tax or duty shall be laid on articles exported from any State.

No preference shall be given by any regulation of commerce or revenue to the ports of one State over those of another; nor shall vessels bound to, or from, one State be obliged to enter, clear, or pay duties in another.

No money shall be drawn from the treasury, but in consequence of appropriations made by law; and a regular statement and account of the receipts and expenditures of all public money shall be published from time to time.

No title of nobility shall be granted by the United States: and no person holding any office of profit or trust under them, shall, without the consent of the Congress, accept of any present, emolument, office, or title, of any kind whatever, from any king, prince, or foreign state.

Section 10   No State shall enter into any treaty, alliance, or confederation; grant letters of marque and reprisal; coin money; emit bills of credit; make anything but gold and silver coin a tender in payment of debts; pass any bill of attainder, ex post facto law, or law impairing the obligation of contracts, or grant any title of nobility.

No State shall, without the consent of Congress, lay any imposts or duties on imports or exports, except what may be absolutely necessary for executing its inspection laws: and the net produce of all duties and imposts, laid by any State on imports or exports, shall be for the use of the treasury of the United States; and all such laws shall be subject to the revision and control of the Congress.

No State shall, without the consent of Congress, lay any duty of tonnage, keep troops, or ships of war in time of peace, enter into any agreement or compact with another State, or with a foreign power, or engage in war, unless actually invaded, or in such imminent danger as will not admit of delay.

Article II

Section 1   The executive power shall be vested in a President of the United States of America. He shall hold his office during the term of four years, and, together with the Vice-President, chosen for the same term, be elected as follows:

Each State shall appoint, in such manner as the legislature thereof may direct, a number of electors, equal to the whole number of Senators and Representatives to which the State may be entitled in the Congress; but no Senator or Representative, or person holding an office of trust or profit under the United States, shall be appointed an elector.

The electors shall meet in their respective States, and vote by ballot for two persons, of whom one at least shall not be an inhabitant of the same State with themselves. And they shall make a list of all the persons voted for, and of the number of votes for each; which list they shall sign and certify, and transmit sealed to the seat of government of the United States, directed to the President of the Senate. The President of the Senate shall, in the presence of the Senate and House of Representatives, open all the certificates, and the votes shall then be counted. The person having the greatest number of votes shall be the President, if such number be a majority of the whole number of electors appointed; and if there be more than one who have such majority, and have an equal number of votes, then the House of Representatives shall immediately choose by ballot one of them for President; and if no person have a majority, then from the five highest on the list said house shall in like manner choose the President. But in choosing the President the votes shall be taken by States, the representation from each State having one vote; a quorum for this purpose shall consist of a member or members from two-thirds of the States, and a majority of all the States shall be necessary to a choice. In every case, after the choice of the President, the person having the greatest number of votes of the electors shall be the Vice-President. But if there should remain two or more who have equal votes, the Senate shall choose from them by ballot the Vice-President.

The Congress may determine the time of choosing the electors, and the day on which they shall give their votes; which day shall be the same throughout the United States.

No person except a natural-born citizen, *or a citizen of the United States at the time of the adoption of this Constitution*, shall be eligible to the office of President; neither shall any person be eligible to that office who shall not have attained to the age of thirty-five years, and been fourteen years a resident within the United States.

In cases of the removal of the President from office or of his death, resignation, or inability to discharge the powers and duties of the said office, the same shall devolve on the Vice-President, and the Congress may by law provide for the case of removal, death, resignation, or inability, both of the President and Vice-President, declaring what officer shall then act as President, and such officer shall act accordingly, until the disability be removed, or a President shall be elected.

The President shall, at stated times, receive for his services a compensation, which shall neither be increased nor diminished during the period for which he shall have been elected, and he shall not receive within that period any other emolument from the United States, or any of them.

Before he enter on the execution of his office, he shall take the following oath or affirmation:—"I do solemnly swear (or affirm) that I will faithfully execute the office of the President of the United States, and will to the best of my ability preserve, protect and defend the Constitution of the United States."

Section 2 The President shall be commander in chief of the army and navy of the United States, and of the militia of the several States, when called into the actual service of the United States; he may require the opinion, in writing, of the principal officer in each of the executive departments, upon any subject relating to the duties of their respective offices, and he shall have power to grant reprieves and pardons for offenses against the United States, except in cases of impeachment.

He shall have power, by and with the advice and consent of the Senate, to make treaties, provided two-thirds of the Senators present concur; and he shall nominate, and by and with the advice and consent of the Senate, shall appoint ambassadors, other public ministers and consuls, judges of the Supreme Court, and all other officers of the United States, whose appointments are not herein otherwise provided for, and which shall be established by law: but Congress may by law vest the appointment of such inferior officers, as they think proper, in the President alone, in the courts of law, or in the heads of departments.

The President shall have power to fill up all vacancies that may happen during the recess of the Senate, by granting commissions which shall expire at the end of their next session.

Section 3 He shall from time to time give to the Congress information of the state of the Union, and recommend to their consideration such measures as he shall judge necessary and expedient; he may, on extraordinary occasions, convene both houses, or either of them, and in case of disagreement between them, with respect to the time of adjournment, he may adjourn them to such time as he shall think proper; he shall receive ambassadors and other public ministers; he shall take care that the laws be faithfully executed, and shall commission all the officers of the United States.

Section 4 The President, Vice-President and all civil officers of the United States shall be removed from office on impeachment for, and on conviction of, treason, bribery, or other high crimes and misdemeanors.

Article III

Section 1 The judicial power of the United States shall be vested in one Supreme Court, and in such inferior courts as the Congress may from time to time ordain and establish. The judges, both of the Supreme and inferior courts, shall hold their offices during good behavior, and shall, at stated times, receive for their services a compensation which shall not be diminished during their continuance in office.

Section 2 The judicial power shall extend to all cases, in law and equity, arising under this Constitution, the laws of the United States, and treaties made, or which shall be made, under their authority;—to all cases affecting ambassadors, other public ministers and consuls;—to all cases of admiralty and maritime jurisdiction;—to controversies to which the United States shall be a party;—to controversies between two or more States;—*between a State and citizens of another State;*—between citizens of different States;—between citizens of the same State claiming lands under grants of different States, and between a State, or the citizens thereof, and foreign states, citizens or subjects.

In all cases affecting ambassadors, other public ministers and consuls, and those in which a State shall be party, the Supreme Court shall have original jurisdiction. In all the other cases before mentioned, the Supreme Court shall have appellate jurisdiction, both as to law and fact, with such exceptions, and under such regulations, as the Congress shall make.

The trial of all crimes, except in cases of impeachment, shall be by jury; and such trial shall be held in the State where said crimes shall have been committed; but when not committed within any State, the trial shall be at such place or places as the Congress may by Law have directed.

Section 3 Treason against the United States shall consist only in levying war against them, or in adhering to their enemies, giving them aid and comfort. No person shall be convicted of treason unless on the testimony of two witnesses to the same overt act, or on confession in open court.

The Congress shall have power to declare the punishment of treason, but no attainder of treason shall work corruption of blood, or forfeiture except during the life of the person attainted.

Article IV

Section 1 Full faith and credit shall be given in each State to the public acts, records, and judicial proceedings of every other State. And the Congress may by general laws prescribe the manner in which such acts, records, and proceedings shall be proved, and the effect thereof.

Section 2 The citizens of each State shall be entitled to all privileges and immunities of citizens in the several States.

A person charged in any State with treason, felony, or other crime, who shall flee from justice, and be found in another State, shall on demand of the executive authority of the State from which he fled, be delivered up, to be removed to the State having jurisdiction of the crime.

No Person held to service or labor in one State, under the laws thereof, escaping into another, shall, in consequence of any law or regulation therein, be discharged from such service or labor, but shall be delivered up on claim of the party to whom such service or labor may be due.

Section 3 New States may be admitted by the Congress into this Union; but no new State shall be formed or erected within the jurisdiction of any other State; nor any State be formed by the junction of two or more States, or parts of States, without the consent of the legislatures of the States concerned as well as of the Congress.

The Congress shall have power to dispose of and make all needful rules and regulations respecting the territory or other property belonging to the United States; and nothing in this Constitution shall be so construed as to prejudice any claims of the United States, or of any particular State.

Section 4 The United States shall guarantee to every State in this Union a republican form of government, and shall protect each of them against invasion; and on application of the legislature, or of the executive (when the legislature cannot be convened), against domestic violence.

Article V

The Congress, whenever two-thirds of both houses shall deem it necessary, shall propose amendments to this Constitution, or, on the application of the legislatures of two-thirds of the several States, shall call a convention for proposing amendments, which, in either case, shall be valid to all intents and purposes, as part of this Constitution, when ratified by the legislatures of three-fourths of the several States, or by conventions in three-fourths thereof, as the one or the other mode of ratification may be proposed by the Congress; provided *that no amendments which may be made prior to the year one thousand eight hundred and eight shall in any manner affect the first and fourth clauses in the ninth section of the first article*; and that no State, without its consent, shall be deprived of its equal suffrage in the Senate.

Article VI

All debts contracted and engagements entered into, before the adoption of this Constitution, shall be as valid against the United States under this Constitution, as under the Confederation.

This Constitution, and the laws of the United States which shall be made in pursuance thereof; and all treaties made, or which shall be made, under the authority of the United States, shall be the supreme law of the land; and the judges in every State shall be bound thereby, anything in the Constitution or laws of any State to the contrary notwithstanding.

The Senators and Representatives before mentioned, and the members of the several State legislatures, and all executive and judicial officers, both of the United States and of the several States, shall be bound by oath or affirmation to support this Constitution; but no religious test shall ever be required as a qualification to any office or public trust under the United States.

Article VII

The ratification of the conventions of nine States shall be sufficient for the establishment of this Constitution between the States so ratifying the same.

Done in convention by the unanimous consent of the States present, the seventeenth day of September in the year of our Lord one thousand seven hundred and eighty-seven and of the Independence of the United States of America the twelfth. In witness whereof we have hereunto subscribed our names.

GEORGE WASHINGTON
PRESIDENT AND DEPUTY FROM VIRGINIA

New Hampshire
John Langdon
Nicholas Gilman

Massachusetts
Nathaniel Gorham
Rufus King

Connecticut
William Samuel
   Johnson
Roger Sherman

New York
Alexander Hamilton

New Jersey
William Livingston
David Brearley
William Paterson
Jonathan Dayton

Pennsylvania
Benjamin Franklin
Thomas Mifflin
Robert Morris
George Clymer
Thomas FitzSimons
Jared Ingersoll
James Wilson
Gouverneur Morris

Delaware
George Read
Gunning Bedford, Jr.
John Dickinson
Richard Bassett
Jacob Broom

Maryland
James McHenry
Daniel of
   St. Thomas Jenifer
Daniel Carroll

Virginia
John Blair
James Madison, Jr.

North Carolina
William Blount
Richard Dobbs
   Spaight
Hugh Williamson

South Carolina
John Rutledge
Charles Cotesworth
   Pinckney
Charles Pinckney
Pierce Butler

Georgia
William Few
Abraham Baldwin

AMENDMENTS TO THE CONSTITUTION WITH ANNOTATIONS
(Including the six unratified amendments)

IN THEIR EFFORT TO GAIN Antifederalists' support for the Constitution, Federalists frequently pointed to the inclusion of Article 5, which provides an orderly method of amending the Constitution. In contrast, the Articles of Confederation, which were universally recognized as seriously flawed, offered no means of amendment. For their part, Antifederalists argued that the amendment process was so "intricate" that one might as easily roll "sixes an hundred times in succession" as change the Constitution.

The system for amendment laid out in the Constitution requires that two-thirds of both houses of Congress agree to a proposed amendment, which must then be ratified by three-quarters of the legislatures of the states. Alternatively, an amendment may be proposed by a convention called by the legislatures of two-thirds of the states. Since 1789, members of Congress have proposed thousands of amendments. Besides the seventeen amendments added since 1789, only the six "unratified" ones included here were approved by two-thirds of both houses and sent to the states for ratification.

Among the many amendments that never made it out of Congress have been proposals to declare dueling, divorce, and interracial marriage unconstitutional as well as proposals to establish a national university, to acknowledge the sovereignty of Jesus Christ, and to prohibit any person from possessing wealth in excess of ten million dollars.[1]

Among the issues facing Americans today that might lead to constitutional amendment are efforts to balance the federal budget, to limit the number of terms elected officials may serve, to limit access to or prohibit abortion, to establish English as the official language of the United States, and to prohibit flag burning. None of these proposed amendments has yet garnered enough support in Congress to be sent to the states for ratification.

Although the first ten amendments to the Constitution are commonly known as the Bill of Rights, only Amendments 1–8 actually provide guarantees of individual rights. Amendments 9 and 10 deal with the structure of power within the constitutional system. The Bill of Rights was promised to appease Antifederalists who refused to ratify the Constitution without guarantees of individual liberties and limitations to federal power. After studying more than two hundred amendments recommended by the ratifying conventions of the states, Federalist James Madison presented a list of seventeen to Congress, which used Madison's list as the foundation for the twelve amendments that were sent to the states for ratification. Ten of the twelve were adopted in 1791. The first on the list of twelve, known as the Reapportionment Amendment, was never adopted (see p. A-17). The second proposed amendment was adopted in 1992 as Amendment 27 (see p. A-26).

Amendment I

Congress shall make no law respecting an establishment of religion, or prohibiting the free exercise thereof; or abridging the freedom of speech, or of the press; or the right of the people peaceably to assemble, and to petition the government for a redress of grievances.

The First Amendment is a potent symbol for many Americans. Most are well aware of their rights to free speech, freedom of the press, and freedom of religion and their rights to assemble and to petition, even if they cannot cite the exact words of this amendment.

The First Amendment guarantee of freedom of religion has two clauses: the "free exercise clause," which allows individuals to practice or not practice any religion, and the "establishment clause," which prevents the federal government from discriminating against or favoring any particular religion. This clause was designed to create what Thomas Jefferson referred to as "a wall of separation between church and state." In the 1960s, the Supreme Court ruled that the First Amendment prohibits prayer (see Engel v. Vitale, *p. A-51) and Bible reading in public schools.*

Although the rights to free speech and freedom of the press are established in the First Amendment, it was not until the twentieth century that the Supreme Court began to explore the full meaning of these guarantees. In 1919, the Court ruled in Schenck v. United States *(see p. A-50) that the government could suppress free expression only where it could cite a "clear and present danger." In a decision that continues to raise controversies, the Court ruled in 1990, in* Texas v. Johnson, *that flag burning is a form of symbolic speech protected by the First Amendment.*

[1]Richard B. Bernstein, *Amending America* (New York: Times Books, 1993), 177–81.

Amendment II

A well-regulated militia being necessary to the security of a free State, the right of the people to keep and bear arms shall not be infringed.

Fear of a standing army under the control of a hostile government made the Second Amendment an important part of the Bill of Rights. Advocates of gun ownership claim that the amendment prevents the government from regulating firearms. Proponents of gun control argue that the amendment is designed only to protect the right of the states to maintain militia units.

    In 1939, the Supreme Court ruled in United States v. Miller *that the Second Amendment did not protect the right of an individual to own a sawed-off shotgun, which it argued was not ordinary militia equipment. Since then, the Supreme Court has refused to hear Second Amendment cases, while lower courts have upheld firearms regulations. Several justices currently on the bench seem to favor a narrow interpretation of the Second Amendment, which would allow gun control legislation. The controversy over the impact of the Second Amendment on gun owners and gun control legislation will certainly continue.*

Amendment III

No soldier shall, in time of peace, be quartered in any house without the consent of the owner, nor in time of war, but in a manner to be prescribed by law.

The Third Amendment was extremely important to the framers of the Constitution, but today it is nearly forgotten. American colonists were especially outraged that they were forced to quarter British troops in the years before and during the American Revolution. The philosophy of the Third Amendment has been viewed by some justices and scholars as the foundation of the modern constitutional right to privacy. One example of this can be found in Justice William O. Douglas's opinion in Griswold v. Connecticut *(see p. A-52).*

Amendment IV

The right of the people to be secure in their persons, houses, papers, and effects, against unreasonable searches and seizures, shall not be violated, and no warrants shall issue but upon probable cause, supported by oath or affirmation, and particularly describing the place to be searched, and the persons or things to be seized.

In the years before the Revolution, the houses, barns, stores, and warehouses of American colonists were ransacked by British authorities under "writs of assistance" or general warrants. The British, thus empowered, searched for seditious material or smuggled goods that could then be used as evidence against colonists who were charged with a crime only after the items were found.

    The first part of the Fourth Amendment protects citizens from "unreasonable" searches and seizures. The Supreme Court has interpreted this protection as well as the words search *and* seizure *in different ways at different times. At one time, the Court did not recognize electronic eavesdropping as a form of search and seizure, though it does today. At times, an "unreasonable" search has been almost any search carried out without a warrant, but in the two decades before 1969 the Court sometimes sanctioned warrantless searches that it considered reasonable based on "the total atmosphere of the case."*

    The second part of the Fourth Amendment defines the procedure for issuing a search warrant and states the requirement of "probable cause," which is generally viewed as evidence indicating that a suspect has committed an offense.

    The Fourth Amendment has been controversial because the Court has sometimes excluded evidence that has been seized in violation of constitutional standards. The justification is that excluding such evidence deters violations of the amendment, but doing so may allow a guilty person to escape punishment.

Amendment V

No person shall be held to answer for a capital, or otherwise infamous crime, unless on a presentment or indictment of a grand jury, except in cases arising in the land or naval forces, or in the militia, when in actual service in time of war or public danger; nor shall any person be subject for the same offence to be twice put in jeopardy of life or limb; nor shall be compelled in any criminal case to be a witness against himself, nor be deprived of life, liberty, or property, without due process of law; nor shall private property be taken for public use without just compensation.

The Fifth Amendment protects people against government authority in the prosecution of criminal offenses. It prohibits the state, first, from charging a person with a serious crime without a grand jury hearing to decide whether there is sufficient evidence to support the charge and, second, from charging a person with the same crime twice. The best-known aspect of the Fifth Amendment is that it

prevents a person from being "compelled . . . to be a witness against himself." The last clause, the "takings clause," limits the power of the government to seize property.

Although invoking the Fifth Amendment is popularly viewed as a confession of guilt, a person may be innocent yet still fear prosecution. For example, during the Red-baiting era of the late 1940s and 1950s, many people who had participated in legal activities that were associated with the Communist Party claimed the Fifth Amendment privilege rather than testify before the House Un-American Activities Committee because the mood of the times cast those activities in a negative light. Since "taking the Fifth" was viewed as an admission of guilt, those people often lost their jobs or became unemployable. (See Chapter 25.) Nonetheless, the right to protect oneself against self-incrimination plays an important role in guarding against the collective power of the state.

Amendment VI

In all criminal prosecutions, the accused shall enjoy the right to a speedy and public trial, by an impartial jury of the State and district wherein the crime shall have been committed, which district shall have been previously ascertained by law, and to be informed of the nature and cause of the accusation; to be confronted with the witnesses against him; to have compulsory process for obtaining witnesses in his favor, and to have the assistance of counsel for his defence.

The original Constitution put few limits on the government's power to investigate, prosecute, and punish crime. This process was of great concern to the early Americans, however, and of the twenty-eight rights specified in the first eight amendments, fifteen have to do with it. Seven rights are specified in the Sixth Amendment. These include the right to a speedy trial, a public trial, a jury trial, a notice of accusation, confrontation by opposing witnesses, testimony by favorable witnesses, and the assistance of counsel.

Although this amendment originally guaranteed these rights only in cases involving the federal government, the adoption of the Fourteenth Amendment began a process of applying the protections of the Bill of Rights to the states through court cases such as Gideon v. Wainwright *(see p. A-51).*

Amendment VII

In suits at common law, where the value in controversy shall exceed twenty dollars, the right of trial by jury shall be preserved, and no fact tried by a jury shall be otherwise reexamined in any court of the United States, than according to the rules of the common law.

This amendment guarantees people the same right to a trial by jury as was guaranteed by English common law in 1791. Under common law, in civil trials (those involving money damages) the role of the judge was to settle questions of law and that of the jury was to settle questions of fact. The amendment does not specify the size of the jury or its role in a trial, however. The Supreme Court has generally held that those issues be determined by English common law of 1791, which stated that a jury consists of twelve people, that a trial must be conducted before a judge who instructs the jury on the law and advises it on facts, and that a verdict must be unanimous.

Amendment VIII

Excessive bail shall not be required, nor excessive fines imposed, nor cruel and unusual punishments inflicted.

The language used to guarantee the three rights in this amendment was inspired by the English Bill of Rights of 1689. The Supreme Court has not had a lot to say about "excessive fines." In recent years it has agreed that despite the provision against "excessive bail," persons who are believed to be dangerous to others can be held without bail even before they have been convicted.

Although opponents of the death penalty have not succeeded in using the Eighth Amendment to achieve the end of capital punishment, the clause regarding "cruel and unusual punishments" has been used to prohibit capital punishment in certain cases (see Furman v. Georgia, *p. A-52) and to require improved conditions in prisons.*

Amendment IX

The enumeration in the Constitution, of certain rights, shall not be construed to deny or disparage others retained by the people.

Some Federalists feared that inclusion of the Bill of Rights in the Constitution would allow later generations of interpreters to claim that the people had surrendered any rights not specifically enumerated there. To guard against this, Madison added language that became the Ninth Amendment. Interest in this heretofore largely ignored amendment revived in 1965 when it was used in a concurring opinion in Griswold v. Connecticut *(see p. A-52). While Justice William O. Douglas called on the Third Amendment to support the right to privacy in deciding that case, Justice Arthur Goldberg, in the concurring opinion, argued that the right to privacy regarding contraception was an*

unenumerated right that was protected by the Ninth Amendment.

In 1980, the Court ruled that the right of the press to attend a public trial was protected by the Ninth Amendment. While some scholars argue that modern judges cannot identify the unenumerated rights that the framers were trying to protect, others argue that the Ninth Amendment should be read as providing a constitutional "presumption of liberty" that allows people to act in any way that does not violate the rights of others.

Amendment X

The powers not delegated to the United States by the Constitution, nor prohibited by it to the States, are reserved to the States respectively, or to the people.

The Antifederalists were especially eager to see a "reserved powers clause" explicitly guaranteeing the states control over their internal affairs. Not surprisingly, the Tenth Amendment has been a frequent battleground in the struggle over states' rights and federal supremacy. Prior to the Civil War, the Democratic Republican Party and Jacksonian Democrats invoked the Tenth Amendment to prohibit the federal government from making decisions about whether people in individual states could own slaves. The Tenth Amendment was virtually suspended during Reconstruction following the Civil War. In 1883, however, the Supreme Court declared the Civil Rights Act of 1875 unconstitutional on the grounds that it violated the Tenth Amendment. Business interests also called on the amendment to block efforts at federal regulation.

The Court was inconsistent over the next several decades as it attempted to resolve the tension between the restrictions of the Tenth Amendment and the powers the Constitution granted to Congress to regulate interstate commerce and levy taxes. The Court upheld the Pure Food and Drug Act (1906), the Meat Inspection Acts (1906 and 1907), and the White Slave Traffic Act (1910), all of which affected the states, but struck down an act prohibiting interstate shipment of goods produced through child labor. Between 1934 and 1935, a number of New Deal programs created by Franklin D. Roosevelt were declared unconstitutional on the grounds that they violated the Tenth Amendment. (See Chapter 23.) As Roosevelt appointees changed the composition of the Court, the Tenth Amendment was declared to have no substantive meaning. Generally, the amendment is held to protect the rights of states to regulate internal matters such as local government, education, commerce, labor, and business, as well as matters involving families such as marriage, divorce, and inheritance within the state.

Unratified Amendment
Reapportionment Amendment (proposed by Congress September 25, 1789, along with the Bill of Rights)

After the first enumeration required by the first article of the Constitution, there shall be one Representative for every thirty thousand, until the number shall amount to one hundred, after which the proportion shall be so regulated by Congress, that there shall be not less than one hundred Representatives, nor less than one Representative for every forty thousand persons, until the number of Representatives shall amount to two hundred; after which the proportion shall be so regulated by Congress, that there shall not be less than two hundred Representatives, nor more than one Representative for every fifty thousand persons.

If the Reapportionment Amendment had passed and remained in effect, the House of Representatives today would have more than 5,000 members rather than 435.

Amendment XI
[Adopted 1798]

The judicial power of the United States shall not be construed to extend to any suit in law or equity, commenced or prosecuted against one of the United States by citizens of another State, or by citizens or subjects of any foreign state.

In 1793, the Supreme Court ruled in favor of Alexander Chisholm, executor of the estate of a deceased South Carolina merchant. Chisholm was suing the state of Georgia because the merchant had never been paid for provisions he had supplied during the Revolution. Many regarded this Court decision as an error that violated the intent of the Constitution.

Antifederalists had long feared a federal court system with the power to overrule a state court. When the Constitution was being drafted, Federalists had assured worried Antifederalists that section 2 of Article 3, which allows federal courts to hear cases "between a State and citizens of another State," did not mean that the federal courts were authorized to hear suits against a state by citizens of another state or a foreign country. Antifederalists and many other Americans feared a powerful federal court system because they worried that it would become like the British courts of this period, which were accountable only to the monarch. Furthermore, Chisholm v. Georgia prompted a series of suits against state governments by creditors and suppliers who had made loans during the war.

In addition, state legislators and Congress feared that the shaky economies of the new states, as well as the country as a whole, would be destroyed, especially if Loyalists who had fled to other countries sought reimbursement for land and property that had been seized. The day after the Supreme Court announced its decision, a resolution proposing the Eleventh Amendment, which overturned the decision in Chisholm v. Georgia, *was introduced in the U.S. Senate.*

Amendment XII
[Adopted 1804]

The electors shall meet in their respective States, and vote by ballot for President and Vice-President, one of whom, at least, shall not be an inhabitant of the same State with themselves; they shall name in their ballots the person voted for as President, and in distinct ballots the person voted for as Vice-President, and they shall make distinct lists of all persons voted for as President, and of all persons voted for as Vice-President, and of the number of votes for each, which lists they shall sign and certify, and transmit sealed to the seat of government of the United States, directed to the President of the Senate;—the President of the Senate shall, in the presence of the Senate and House of Representatives, open all the certificates and the votes shall then be counted;—the person having the greatest number of votes for President shall be the President, if such number be a majority of the whole number of electors appointed; and if no person have such majority, then from the persons having the highest numbers not exceeding three on the list of those voted for as President, the House of Representatives shall choose immediately, by ballot, the President. But in choosing the President, the votes shall be taken by States, the representation from each State having one vote; a quorum for this purpose shall consist of a member or members from two-thirds of the States, and a majority of all the States shall be necessary to a choice. And if the House of Representatives shall not choose a President whenever the right of choice shall devolve upon them, before *the fourth day of March* next following, then the Vice-President shall act as President, as in the case of the death or other constitutional disability of the President.

The person having the greatest number of votes as Vice-President shall be the Vice-President, if such number be a majority of the whole number of electors appointed; and if no person have a majority, then from the two highest numbers on the list the Senate shall choose the Vice-President; a quorum for the purpose shall consist of two-thirds of the whole number of Senators, and a majority of the whole number shall be necessary to a choice. But no person constitutionally ineligible to the office of President shall be eligible to that of Vice-President of the United States.

The framers of the Constitution disliked political parties and assumed that none would ever form. Under the original system, electors chosen by the states would each vote for two candidates. The candidate who won the most votes would become president, while the person who won the second-highest number of votes would become vice president. Rivalries between Federalists and Antifederalists led to the formation of political parties, however, even before George Washington had left office. Though Washington was elected unanimously in 1789 and 1792, the elections of 1796 and 1800 were procedural disasters because of party maneuvering (see Chapters 9 and 10). In 1796, Federalist John Adams was chosen as president, and his great rival, the Antifederalist Thomas Jefferson (whose party was called the Republican Party), became his vice president. In 1800, all the electors cast their two votes as one of two party blocs. Jefferson and his fellow Republican nominee, Aaron Burr, were tied with seventy-three votes each. The contest went to the House of Representatives, which finally elected Jefferson after thirty-six ballots. The Twelfth Amendment prevents these problems by requiring electors to vote separately for the president and vice president.

Unratified Amendment
Titles of Nobility Amendment (proposed by Congress May 1, 1810)

If any citizen of the United States shall accept, claim, receive or retain any title of nobility or honor or shall, without the consent of Congress, accept and retain any present, pension, office or emolument of any kind whatever, from any emperor, king, prince or foreign power, such person shall cease to be a citizen of the United States, and shall be incapable of holding any office of trust or profit under them, or either of them.

This amendment would have extended Article 1, section 9, clause 8 of the Constitution, which prevents the awarding of titles by the United States and the acceptance of such awards from foreign powers without congressional consent. Historians speculate that general nervousness about the power of the Emperor Napoleon, who was at that time extending France's empire throughout Europe, may have prompted the proposal. Though it fell one vote short of ratification, Congress and the American people thought the proposal had been ratified and it was included in many nineteenth-century editions of the Constitution.

The Civil War and Reconstruction Amendments (Thirteenth, Fourteenth, and Fifteenth Amendments)

In the four months between the election of Abraham Lincoln and his inauguration, more than two hundred proposed constitutional amendments were presented to Congress as part of a desperate attempt to hold the rapidly dissolving Union together. Most of these were efforts to appease the southern states by protecting the right to own slaves or by disfranchising African Americans through constitutional amendment. None were able to win the votes required from Congress to send them to the states. The relatively innocuous Corwin Amendment seemed to be the only hope for preserving the Union by amending the Constitution.

    The northern victors in the Civil War tried to restructure the Constitution just as the war had restructured the nation. Yet they were often divided in their goals. Some wanted to end slavery; others hoped for social and economic equality regardless of race; others hoped that extending the power of the ballot box to former slaves would help create a new political order. The debates over the Thirteenth, Fourteenth, and Fifteenth Amendments were bitter. Few of those who fought for these changes were satisfied with the amendments themselves; fewer still were satisfied with their interpretation. Although the amendments put an end to the legal status of slavery, it took nearly a hundred years after the amendments' passage before most of the descendants of former slaves could begin to experience the economic, social, and political equality the amendments had been intended to provide.

Unratified Amendment
Corwin Amendment (proposed by Congress March 2, 1861)

No amendment shall be made to the Constitution which will authorize or give to Congress the power to abolish or interfere, within any State, with the domestic institutions thereof, including that of persons held to labor or service by the laws of said State.

Following the election of Abraham Lincoln, Congress scrambled to try to prevent the secession of the slaveholding states. House member Thomas Corwin of Ohio proposed the "unamendable" amendment in the hope that by protecting slavery where it existed, Congress would keep the southern states in the Union. Lincoln indicated his support for the proposed amendment in his first inaugural address. Only Ohio and Maryland ratified the Corwin Amendment before it was forgotten.

Amendment XIII
[Adopted 1865]

Section 1　Neither slavery nor involuntary servitude, except as a punishment for crime whereof the party shall have been duly convicted, shall exist within the United States, or any place subject to their jurisdiction.

Section 2　Congress shall have power to enforce this article by appropriate legislation.

Although President Lincoln had abolished slavery in the Confederacy with the Emancipation Proclamation of 1863, abolitionists wanted to rid the entire country of slavery. The Thirteenth Amendment did this in a clear and straightforward manner. In February 1865, when the proposal was approved by the House, the gallery of the House was newly opened to black Americans who had a chance at last to see their government at work. Passage of the proposal was greeted by wild cheers from the gallery as well as tears on the House floor, where congressional representatives openly embraced one another.

    The problem of ratification remained, however. The Union position was that the Confederate states were part of the country of thirty-six states. Therefore, twenty-seven states were needed to ratify the amendment. When Kentucky and Delaware rejected it, backers realized that without approval from at least four former Confederate states, the amendment would fail. Lincoln's successor, President Andrew Johnson, made ratification of the Thirteenth Amendment a condition for southern states to rejoin the Union. Under those terms, all the former Confederate states except Mississippi accepted the Thirteenth Amendment, and by the end of 1865 the amendment had become part of the Constitution and slavery had been prohibited in the United States.

Amendment XIV
[Adopted 1868]

Section 1　All persons born or naturalized in the United States, and subject to the jurisdiction thereof, are citizens of the United States and of the State wherein they reside. No State shall make or enforce any law which shall abridge the privileges or immunities of citizens of the United States; nor shall any State deprive any person of life, liberty, or property, without due process of law; nor deny to any person within its jurisdiction the equal protection of the laws.

Section 2　Representatives shall be appointed among the several States according to their respective numbers, counting the whole number of persons in each

State, excluding Indians not taxed. But when the right to vote at any election for the choice of Electors for President and Vice-President of the United States, Representatives in Congress, the executive and judicial officers of a State, or the members of the legislature thereof, is denied to any of the male inhabitants of such State, being twenty-one years of age and citizens of the United States, or in any way abridged, except for participation in rebellion, or other crime, the basis of representation therein shall be reduced in the proportion which the number of such male citizens shall bear to the whole number of male citizens twenty-one years of age in such State.

Section 3 No person shall be a Senator or Representative in Congress, or Elector of President and Vice-President, or hold any office, civil or military, under the United States, or under any State, who, having previously taken an oath, as a member of Congress, or as an officer of the United States, or as a member of any State legislature, or as an executive or judicial officer of any State, to support the Constitution of the United States, shall have engaged in insurrection or rebellion against the same, or given aid or comfort to the enemies thereof. Congress may, by a vote of two-thirds of each house, remove such disability.

Section 4 The validity of the public debt of the United States, authorized by law, including debts incurred for payment of pensions and bounties for services in suppressing insurrection or rebellion, shall not be questioned. But neither the United States nor any State shall assume or pay any debt or obligation incurred in aid of insurrection or rebellion against the United States, or any claim for the loss or emancipation of any slave; but all such debts, obligations, and claims shall be held illegal and void.

Section 5 The Congress shall have power to enforce, by appropriate legislation, the provisions of this article.

◆◆◆

Without Lincoln's leadership in the reconstruction of the nation following the Civil War, it soon became clear that the Thirteenth Amendment needed additional constitutional support. Less than a year after Lincoln's assassination, Andrew Johnson was ready to bring the former Confederate states back into the Union with few changes in their governments or politics. Anxious Republicans drafted the Fourteenth Amendment to prevent that from happening. The most important provisions of this complex amendment made all native-born or naturalized persons American citizens and prohibited states from abridging the "privileges or immunities" of citizens; depriving them of "life, liberty, or

property, without due process of law"; and denying them "equal protection of the laws." In essence, it made all ex-slaves citizens and protected the rights of all citizens against violation by their own state governments.

As occurred in the case of the Thirteenth Amendment, former Confederate states were forced to ratify the amendment as a condition of representation in the House and the Senate. The intentions of the Fourteenth Amendment, and how those intentions should be enforced, have been the most debated point of constitutional history. The terms due process *and* equal protection *have been especially troublesome. Was the amendment designed to outlaw racial segregation? Or was the goal simply to prevent the leaders of the rebellious South from gaining political power?*

The framers of the Fourteenth Amendment hoped Article 2 would produce black voters who would increase the power of the Republican Party. The federal government, however, never used its power to punish states for denying blacks their right to vote. Although the Fourteenth Amendment had an immediate impact in giving black Americans citizenship, it did nothing to protect blacks from the vengeance of whites once Reconstruction ended. In the late nineteenth and early twentieth centuries, section 1 of the Fourteenth Amendment was often used to protect business interests and strike down laws protecting workers on the grounds that the rights of "persons," that is, corporations, were protected by "due process." More recently, the Fourteenth Amendment has been used to justify school desegregation and affirmative action programs, as well as to dismantle such programs.

Amendment XV
[Adopted 1870]

Section 1 The right of citizens of the United States to vote shall not be denied or abridged by the United States or by any State on account of race, color, or previous condition of servitude.

Section 2 The Congress shall have power to enforce this article by appropriate legislation.

The Fifteenth Amendment was the last major piece of Reconstruction legislation. While earlier Reconstruction acts had already required black suffrage in the South, the Fifteenth Amendment extended black voting rights to the entire nation. Some Republicans felt morally obligated to do away with the double standard between North and South since many northern states had stubbornly refused to enfranchise blacks. Others believed that the freedman's ballot required the extra protection of a constitutional amendment to shield it from white counterattack. But partisan advantage also played an important role in the amendment's

passage, since Republicans hoped that by giving the ballot to northern blacks, they could lessen their political vulnerability.

Many women's rights advocates had fought for the amendment. They had felt betrayed by the inclusion of the word male in section 2 of the Fourteenth Amendment and were further angered when the proposed Fifteenth Amendment failed to prohibit denial of the right to vote on the grounds of sex as well as "race, color, or previous condition of servitude." In this amendment, for the first time, the federal government claimed the power to regulate the franchise, or vote. It was also the first time the Constitution placed limits on the power of the states to regulate access to the franchise. Although ratified in 1870, however, the amendment was not enforced until the twentieth century.

The Progressive Amendments (Sixteenth–Nineteenth Amendments)

No amendments were added to the Constitution between the Civil War and the Progressive Era. America was changing, however, in fundamental ways. The rapid industrialization of the United States after the Civil War led to many social and economic problems. Hundreds of amendments were proposed, but none received enough support in Congress to be sent to the states. Some scholars believe that regional differences and rivalries were so strong during this period that it was almost impossible to gain a consensus on a constitutional amendment. During the Progressive Era, however, the Constitution was amended four times in seven years.

Amendment XVI
[Adopted 1913]

The Congress shall have power to lay and collect taxes on incomes, from whatever source derived, without apportionment among the several States, and without regard to any census or enumeration.

Until passage of the Sixteenth Amendment, most of the money used to run the federal government came from customs duties and taxes on specific items, such as liquor. During the Civil War, the federal government taxed incomes as an emergency measure. Pressure to enact an income tax came from those who were concerned about the growing gap between rich and poor in the United States. The Populist Party began campaigning for a graduated income tax in 1892, and support continued to grow. By 1909, thirty-three proposed income tax amendments had been presented in Congress, but lobbying by corporate and other special interests had defeated them all. In June 1909,

the growing pressure for an income tax, which had been endorsed by Presidents Roosevelt and Taft, finally pushed an amendment through the Senate. The required thirty-six states had ratified the amendment by February 1913.

Amendment XVII
[Adopted 1913]

Section 1   The Senate of the United States shall be composed of two Senators from each State, elected by the people thereof, for six years; and each Senator shall have one vote. The electors in each State shall have the qualifications requisite for electors of [voters for] the most numerous branch of the State legislatures.

Section 2   When vacancies happen in the representation of any State in the Senate, the executive authority of such State shall issue writs of election to fill such vacancies: Provided, that the Legislature of any State may empower the executive thereof to make temporary appointments until the people fill the vacancies by election as the Legislature may direct.

Section 3   This amendment shall not be so construed as to affect the election or term of any Senator chosen before it becomes valid as part of the Constitution.

The framers of the Constitution saw the members of the House as the representatives of the people and the members of the Senate as the representatives of the states. Originally senators were to be chosen by the state legislators. According to reform advocates, however, the growth of private industry and transportation conglomerates during the Gilded Age had created a network of corruption in which wealth and power were exchanged for influence and votes in the Senate. Senator Nelson Aldrich, who represented Rhode Island in the late nineteenth and early twentieth centuries, for example, was known as "the senator from Standard Oil" because of his open support of special business interests.

Efforts to amend the Constitution to allow direct election of senators had begun in 1826, but since any proposal had to be approved by the Senate, reform seemed impossible. Progressives tried to gain influence in the Senate by instituting party caucuses and primary elections, which gave citizens the chance to express their choice of a senator who could then be officially elected by the state legislature. By 1910, fourteen of the country's thirty senators received popular votes through a state primary before the state legislature made its selection. Despairing of getting a proposal through the Senate, supporters of a direct-election amendment had begun in 1893 to seek a convention of representatives from two-thirds of the states to propose an amendment that could then be ratified. By 1905, thirty-one of forty-five states had endorsed such an amendment. Finally, in 1911, despite extraordinary opposition, a proposed amendment passed the Senate; by 1913, it had been ratified.

Amendment XVIII
[Adopted 1919; Repealed 1933 by Amendment XXI]

Section 1   After one year from the ratification of this article the manufacture, sale, or transportation of intoxicating liquors within, the importation thereof into, or the exportation thereof from the United States and all territory subject to the jurisdiction thereof, for beverage purposes, is hereby prohibited.

Section 2   The Congress and the several States shall have concurrent power to enforce this article by appropriate legislation.

Section 3   This article shall be inoperative unless it shall have been ratified as an amendment to the Constitution by the legislatures of the several States, as provided by the Constitution, within seven years from the date of the submission thereof to the States by the Congress.

The Prohibition Party, formed in 1869, began calling for a constitutional amendment to outlaw alcoholic beverages in 1872. A prohibition amendment was first proposed in the Senate in 1876 and was revived eighteen times before 1913. Between 1913 and 1919, another thirty-nine attempts were made to prohibit liquor in the United States through a constitutional amendment. Prohibition became a key element of the Progressive agenda as reformers linked alcohol and drunkenness to numerous social problems, including the corruption of immigrant voters. While opponents of such an amendment argued that it was undemocratic, supporters claimed that their efforts had widespread public support. The admission of twelve "dry" western states to the Union in the early twentieth century and the spirit of sacrifice during World War I laid the groundwork for passage and ratification of the Eighteenth Amendment in 1919. Opponents added a time limit to the amendment in the hope that they could thus block ratification, but this effort failed. (See also Amendment XXI.)

Amendment XIX
[Adopted 1920]

Section 1   The right of citizens of the United States to vote shall not be denied or abridged by the United States or by any State on account of sex.

Section 2   Congress shall have the power to enforce this article by appropriate legislation.

Advocates of women's rights tried and failed to link woman suffrage to the Fourteenth and Fifteenth Amendments. Nonetheless, the effort for woman suffrage continued. Between 1878 and 1912, at least one and sometimes as many as four proposed amendments were introduced in Congress each year to grant women the right to vote. While over time women won very limited voting rights in some states, at both the state and federal levels opposition to an amendment for woman suffrage remained very strong. President Woodrow Wilson and other officials felt that the federal government should not interfere with the power of the states in this matter. Others worried that granting suffrage to women would encourage ethnic minorities to exercise their own right to vote. And many were concerned that giving women the vote would result in their abandoning traditional gender roles. In 1919, following a protracted and often bitter campaign of protest in which women went on hunger strikes and chained themselves to fences, an amendment was introduced with the backing of President Wilson. It narrowly passed the Senate (after efforts to limit the suffrage to white women failed) and was adopted in 1920 after Tennessee became the thirty-sixth state to ratify it.

Unratified Amendment
Child Labor Amendment (proposed by Congress June 2, 1924)

Section 1   The Congress shall have power to limit, regulate, and prohibit the labor of persons under eighteen years of age.

Section 2   The power of the several States is unimpaired by this article except that the operation of State laws shall be suspended to the extent necessary to give effect to legislation enacted by Congress.

Throughout the late nineteenth and early twentieth centuries, alarm over the condition of child workers grew. Opponents of child labor argued that children worked in dangerous and unhealthy conditions, that they took jobs from adult workers, that they depressed wages in certain industries, and that states that allowed child labor had an economic advantage over those that did not. Defenders of child labor claimed that children provided needed income in many families, that working at a young age developed character, and that the effort to prohibit the practice constituted an invasion of family privacy.

In 1916, Congress passed a law that made it illegal to sell goods made by children through interstate commerce. The Supreme Court, however, ruled that the law violated the limits on the power of Congress to regulate interstate commerce. Congress then tried to penalize industries that used child labor by taxing such goods. This measure was also thrown out by the courts. In response, reformers set out to amend the Constitution. The proposed amendment was ratified by twenty-eight states, but by 1925, thirteen states had rejected it. Passage of the Fair Labor Standards Act in 1938, which was upheld by the Supreme Court in 1941, made the amendment irrelevant.

Amendment XX
[Adopted 1933]

Section 1 The terms of the President and Vice-President shall end at noon on the 20th day of January, and the terms of Senators and Representatives at noon on the 3rd day of January, of the years in which such terms would have ended if this article had not been ratified; and the terms of their successors shall then begin.

Section 2 The Congress shall assemble at least once in every year, and such meeting shall begin at noon on the 3rd day of January, unless they shall by law appoint a different day.

Section 3 If, at the time fixed for the beginning of the term of the President, the President-elect shall have died, the Vice-President-elect shall become President. If a President shall not have been chosen before the time fixed for the beginning of his term, or if the President-elect shall have failed to qualify, then the Vice-President-elect shall act as President until a President shall have qualified; and the Congress may by law provide for the case wherein neither a President-elect nor a Vice-President-elect shall have qualified, declaring who shall then act as President, or the manner in which one who is to act shall be selected, and such person shall act accordingly until a President or Vice-President shall have qualified.

Section 4 The Congress may by law provide for the case of the death of any of the persons from whom the House of Representatives may choose a President whenever the right of choice shall have devolved upon them, and for the case of the death of any of the persons from whom the Senate may choose a Vice-President whenever the right of choice shall have devolved upon them.

Section 5 Sections 1 and 2 shall take effect on the 15th day of October following the ratification of this article.

Section 6 This article shall be inoperative unless it shall have been ratified as an amendment to the Constitution by the Legislatures of three-fourths of the several States within seven years from the date of its submission.

Until 1933, presidents took office on March 4. Since elections are held in early November and electoral votes are counted in mid-December, this meant that more than three months passed between the time a new president was elected and when he took office. Moving the inauguration to January shortened the transition period and allowed Congress to begin its term closer to the time of the president's inauguration. Although this seems like a minor change, an amendment was required because the Constitution specifies terms of office. This amendment also deals with questions of succession in the event that a president- or vice president-elect dies before assuming office. Section 3 also clarifies a method for resolving a deadlock in the electoral college.

Amendment XXI
[Adopted 1933]

Section 1 The eighteenth article of amendment to the Constitution of the United States is hereby repealed.

Section 2 The transportation or importation into any State, Territory, or Possession of the United States for delivery or use therein of intoxicating liquors, in violation of the laws thereof, is hereby prohibited.

Section 3 This article shall be inoperative unless it shall have been ratified as an amendment to the Constitution by conventions in the several States, as provided in the Constitution, within seven years from the date of the submission thereof to the States by the Congress.

Widespread violation of the Volstead Act, the law enacted to enforce prohibition, made the United States a nation of lawbreakers. Prohibition caused more problems than it solved by encouraging crime, bribery, and corruption. Further, a coalition of liquor and beer manufacturers, personal liberty advocates, and constitutional scholars joined forces to challenge the amendment. By 1929, thirty proposed repeal amendments had been introduced in Congress, and the Democratic Party made repeal part of its platform in the 1932 presidential campaign. The Twenty-First Amendment was proposed in February 1933 and ratified less than a year later. The failure of the effort to enforce prohibition through a constitutional amendment has often been cited by opponents to subsequent efforts to shape public virtue and private morality.

Amendment XXII
[Adopted 1951]

Section 1   No person shall be elected to the office of the President more than twice, and no person who has held the office of President, or acted as President, for more than two years of a term to which some other person was elected President shall be elected to the office of President more than once. But this article shall not apply to any person holding the office of President when this Article was proposed by the Congress, and shall not prevent any person who may be holding the office of President, or acting as President, during the term within which this Article becomes operative from holding the office of President or acting as President during the remainder of such term.

Section 2   This article shall be inoperative unless it shall have been ratified as an amendment to the Constitution by the legislatures of three-fourths of the several States within seven years from the date of its submission to the States by the Congress.

George Washington's refusal to seek a third term of office set a precedent that stood until 1912, when former President Theodore Roosevelt sought, without success, another term as an independent candidate. Democrat Franklin Roosevelt was the only president to seek and win a fourth term, though he did so amid great controversy. Roosevelt died in April 1945, a few months after the beginning of his fourth term. In 1946, Republicans won control of the House and the Senate, and early in 1947 a proposal for an amendment to limit future presidents to two four-year terms was offered to the states for ratification. Democratic critics of the Twenty-Second Amendment charged that it was a partisan posthumous jab at Roosevelt.

Since the Twenty-Second Amendment was adopted, however, the only presidents who might have been able to seek a third term, had it not existed, were Republicans Dwight Eisenhower and Ronald Reagan, and Democrat Bill Clinton. Since 1826, Congress has entertained 160 proposed amendments to limit the president to one six-year term. Such amendments have been backed by fifteen presidents, including Gerald Ford and Jimmy Carter.

Amendment XXIII
[Adopted 1961]

Section 1   The District constituting the seat of Government of the United States shall appoint in such manner as the Congress may direct: A number of electors of President and Vice-President equal to the whole number of Senators and Representatives in Congress to which the District would be entitled if it were a State, but in no event more than the least populous State; they shall be in addition to those appointed by the States, but they shall be considered for the purposes of the election of President and Vice-President, to be electors appointed by a State; and they shall meet in the District and perform such duties as provided by the twelfth article of amendment.

Section 2   The Congress shall have the power to enforce this article by appropriate legislation.

When Washington, D.C., was established as a federal district, no one expected that a significant number of people would make it their permanent and primary residence. A proposal to allow citizens of the district to vote in presidential elections was approved by Congress in June 1960 and was ratified on March 29, 1961.

Amendment XXIV
[Adopted 1964]

Section 1   The right of citizens of the United States to vote in any primary or other election for President or Vice-President, for electors for President or Vice-President, or for Senator or Representative in Congress, shall not be denied or abridged by the United States or any State by reason of failure to pay any poll tax or other tax.

Section 2   The Congress shall have the power to enforce this article by appropriate legislation.

In the colonial and Revolutionary eras, financial independence was seen as necessary to political independence, and the poll tax was used as a requirement for voting. By the twentieth century, however, the poll tax was used mostly to bar poor people, especially southern blacks, from voting. While conservatives complained that the amendment interfered with states' rights, liberals thought that the amendment did not go far enough because it barred the poll tax only in national elections and not in state or local elections. The amendment was ratified in 1964, however, and two years later, the Supreme Court ruled that poll taxes in state and local elections also violated the equal protection clause of the Fourteenth Amendment.

Amendment XXV
[Adopted 1967]

Section 1   In case of the removal of the President from office or of his death or resignation, the Vice-President shall become President.

Section 2 Whenever there is a vacancy in the office of the Vice-President, the President shall nominate a Vice-President who shall take office upon confirmation by a majority vote of both Houses of Congress.

Section 3 Whenever the President transmits to the President pro tempore of the Senate and the Speaker of the House of Representatives his written declaration that he is unable to discharge the powers and duties of his office, and until he transmits to them a written declaration to the contrary, such powers and duties shall be discharged by the Vice-President as Acting President.

Section 4 Whenever the Vice-President and a majority of either the principal officers of the executive departments or of such other body as Congress may by law provide, transmit to the President pro tempore of the Senate and the Speaker of the House of Representatives their written declaration that the President is unable to discharge the powers and duties of his office, the Vice-President shall immediately assume the powers and duties of the office as Acting President.

Thereafter, when the President transmits to the President pro tempore of the Senate and the Speaker of the House of Representatives his written declaration that no inability exists, he shall resume the powers and duties of his office unless the Vice-President and a majority of either the principal officers of the executive department[s] or of such other body as Congress may by law provide, transmit within four days to the President pro tempore of the Senate and the Speaker of the House of Representatives their written declaration that the President is unable to discharge the powers and duties of his office. Thereupon Congress shall decide the issue, assembling within forty-eight hours for that purpose if not in session. If the Congress, within twenty-one days after receipt of the latter written declaration, or, if Congress is not in session, within twenty-one days after Congress is required to assemble, determines by two-thirds vote of both Houses that the President is unable to discharge the powers and duties of his office, the Vice-President shall continue to discharge the same as Acting President; otherwise, the President shall resume the powers and duties of his office.

◆◆◆

The framers of the Constitution established the office of vice president because someone was needed to preside over the Senate. The first president to die in office was William Henry Harrison, in 1841. Vice President John Tyler had himself sworn in as president, setting a precedent that was followed when seven later presidents died in office. The assassination of President James A. Garfield in 1881

posed a new problem, however. After he was shot, the president was incapacitated for two months before he died; he was unable to lead the country, while his vice president, Chester A. Arthur, was unable to assume leadership. Efforts to resolve questions of succession in the event of a presidential disability thus began with the death of Garfield.

In 1963, the assassination of President John F. Kennedy galvanized Congress to action. Vice President Lyndon Johnson was a chain smoker with a history of heart trouble. According to the 1947 Presidential Succession Act, the two men who stood in line to succeed him were the seventy-two-year-old Speaker of the House and the eighty-six-year-old president of the Senate. There were serious concerns that any of these men might become incapacitated while serving as chief executive. The first time the Twenty-Fifth Amendment was used, however, was not in the case of presidential death or illness, but during the Watergate crisis. When Vice President Spiro T. Agnew was forced to resign following allegations of bribery and tax violations, President Richard M. Nixon appointed House Minority Leader Gerald R. Ford vice president. Ford became president following Nixon's resignation eight months later and named Nelson A. Rockefeller as his vice president. Thus, for more than two years, the two highest offices in the country were held by people who had not been elected to them.

Amendment XXVI
[Adopted 1971]

Section 1 The right of citizens of the United States, who are eighteen years of age or older, to vote shall not be denied or abridged by the United States or by any State on account of age.

Section 2 The Congress shall have power to enforce this article by appropriate legislation.

◆◆◆

Efforts to lower the voting age from twenty-one to eighteen began during World War II. Recognizing that those who were old enough to fight a war should have some say in the government policies that involved them in the war, Presidents Eisenhower, Johnson, and Nixon endorsed the idea. In 1970, the combined pressure of the antiwar movement and the demographic pressure of the baby boom generation led to a Voting Rights Act lowering the voting age in federal, state, and local elections.

In Oregon v. Mitchell (1970), the state of Oregon challenged the right of Congress to determine the age at which people could vote in state or local elections. The Supreme Court agreed with Oregon. Since the Voting Rights Act was ruled unconstitutional, the Constitution had to be amended to allow passage of a law that would lower the voting age. The amendment was ratified in a little more than three months, making it the most rapidly ratified amendment in U.S. history.

Unratified Amendment

Equal Rights Amendment (proposed by Congress March 22, 1972; seven-year deadline for ratification extended June 30, 1982)

Section 1 Equality of rights under the law shall not be denied or abridged by the United States or by any State on account of sex.

Section 2 The Congress shall have the power to enforce, by appropriate legislation, the provisions of this article.

Section 3 This amendment shall take effect two years after the date of ratification.

In 1923, soon after women had won the right to vote, Alice Paul, a leading activist in the woman suffrage movement, proposed an amendment requiring equal treatment of men and women. Opponents of the proposal argued that such an amendment would invalidate laws that protected women and would make women subject to the military draft. After the 1964 Civil Rights Act was adopted, protective workplace legislation was removed anyway.

The renewal of the women's movement, as a by-product of the civil rights and antiwar movements, led to a revival of the Equal Rights Amendment (ERA) in Congress. Disagreements over language held up congressional passage of the proposed amendment, but on March 22, 1972, the Senate approved the ERA by a vote of eighty-four to eight, and it was sent to the states. Six states ratified the amendment within two days, and by the middle of 1973 the amendment seemed well on its way to adoption, with thirty of the needed thirty-eight states having ratified it. In the mid-1970s, however, a powerful "Stop ERA" campaign developed. The campaign portrayed the ERA as a threat to "family values" and traditional relationships between men and women. Although thirty-five states ultimately ratified the ERA, five of those state legislatures voted to rescind ratification, and the amendment was never adopted.

Unratified Amendment

D.C. Statehood Amendment (proposed by Congress August 22, 1978)

Section 1 For purposes of representation in the Congress, election of the President and Vice-President, and article V of this Constitution, the District constituting

the seat of government of the United States shall be treated as though it were a State.

Section 2 The exercise of the rights and powers conferred under this article shall be by the people of the District constituting the seat of government, and as shall be provided by Congress.

Section 3 The twenty-third article of amendment to the Constitution of the United States is hereby repealed.

Section 4 This article shall be inoperative, unless it shall have been ratified as an amendment to the Constitution by the legislatures of three-fourths of the several states within seven years from the date of its submission.

The 1961 ratification of the Twenty-Third Amendment, giving residents of the District of Columbia the right to vote for a president and vice president, inspired an effort to give residents of the district full voting rights. In 1966, President Lyndon Johnson appointed a mayor and city council; in 1971, D.C. residents were allowed to name a nonvoting delegate to the House; and in 1981, residents were allowed to elect the mayor and city council. Congress retained the right to overrule laws that might affect commuters, the height of federal buildings, and selection of judges and prosecutors. The district's nonvoting delegate to Congress, Walter Fauntroy, lobbied fiercely for a congressional amendment granting statehood to the district. In 1978, a proposed amendment was approved and sent to the states. A number of states quickly ratified the amendment, but, like the ERA, the D.C. Statehood Amendment ran into trouble. Opponents argued that section 2 created a separate category of "nominal" statehood. They argued that the federal district should be eliminated and that the territory should be reabsorbed into the state of Maryland. Although these theoretical arguments were strong, some scholars believe that racist attitudes toward the predominantly black population of the city was also a factor leading to the defeat of the amendment.

Amendment XXVII
[Adopted 1992]

No law, varying the compensation for the services of the Senators and Representatives, shall take effect, until an election of Representatives shall have intervened.

While the Twenty-Sixth Amendment was the most rapidly ratified amendment in U.S. history, the Twenty-Seventh

Amendment had the longest journey to ratification. First proposed by James Madison in 1789 as part of the package that included the Bill of Rights, this amendment had been ratified by only six states by 1791. In 1873, however, it was ratified by Ohio to protest a massive retroactive salary increase by the federal government. Unlike later proposed amendments, this one came with no time limit on ratification. In the early 1980s, Gregory D. Watson, a University of Texas economics major, discovered the "lost" amendment and began a single-handed cam-paign to get state legislators to introduce it for ratification. In 1983, it was accepted by Maine. In 1984, it passed the Colorado legislature. Ratifications trickled in slowly until May 1992, when Michigan and New Jersey became the thirty-eighth and thirty-ninth states, respectively, to ratify. This amendment prevents members of Congress from raising their own salaries without giving voters a chance to vote them out of office before they can benefit from the raises.

THE CONSTITUTION OF THE CONFEDERATE STATES OF AMERICA

In framing the Constitution of the Confederate States, the authors adopted, with numerous small but significant changes and additions, the language of the Constitution of the United States, and followed the same order of arrangement of articles and sections. The revisions that they made to the original Constitution are shown here. The parts stricken out are enclosed in brackets, and the new matter added in framing the Confederate Constitution is printed in italics.

Adopted March 11, 1861

WE, the People of the [United States] *Confederated States, each State acting in its sovereign and independent character,* in order to form a [more perfect Union] *permanent Federal government,* establish Justice, insure domestic Tranquillity [provide for the common defense, promote the general Welfare], and secure the Blessings of Liberty to ourselves and our Posterity, *invoking the favor and guidance of Almighty God,* do ordain and establish this Constitution for the [United] *Confederate* States of America.

Article I

Section I All legislative Powers herein [granted] *delegated,* shall be vested in a Congress of the [United] *Confederate* States, which shall consist of a Senate and House of Representatives.

Section II The House of Representatives shall be composed of Members chosen every second Year by the People of the several States, and the Electors in each State shall *be citizens of the Confederate States, and* have the Qualifications requisite for Electors of the most numerous Branch of the State Legislature; *but no person of foreign birth, and not a citizen of the Confederate States, shall be allowed to vote for any officer, civil or political, State or federal.*

No Person shall be a Representative who shall not have attained to the Age of twenty-five Years, and [been seven Years a Citizen of the United] *be a citizen of the Confederate* States, and who shall not, when elected, be an Inhabitant of that State in which he shall be chosen.

Representatives and direct Taxes shall be apportioned among the several States which may be included within this [Union] *Confederacy,* according to their respective Numbers, which shall be determined by adding to the whole Number of free Persons, including those bound to Service for a Term of Years, and excluding Indians not taxed, three-fifths of all [other Persons] *slaves.* The actual Enumeration shall be made within three Years after the first Meeting of the Congress of the [United] *Confederate* States, and within every subsequent Term of ten Years, in such Manner as they shall by Law direct. The Number of Representatives shall not exceed one for every [thirty] *fifty* Thousand, but each State shall have at Least one Representative; and until such enumeration shall be made, the State of [New Hampshire shall be entitled to choose three, Massachusetts eight, Rhode Island and Providence Plantations one, Connecticut five, New York six, New Jersey four, Pennsylvania eight, Delaware one, Maryland six, Virginia ten, North Carolina five, South Carolina five, and Georgia three] *South Carolina shall be entitled to choose six, the State of Georgia ten, the State of Alabama nine, the State of Florida two, the State of Mississippi seven, the State of Louisiana six, and the State of Texas six.*

When vacancies happen in the Representation from any State, the Executive Authority thereof shall issue Writs of Election to fill such Vacancies.

The House of Representatives shall choose their Speaker and other Officers; and shall have the sole Power of Impeachment; *except that any judicial or other federal officer resident and acting solely within the limits of any State, may be impeached by a vote of two-thirds of both branches of the Legislature thereof.*

Section III The Senate of the [United] *Confederate* States shall be composed of two Senators from each State, chosen by the Legislature thereof, for six Years, *at the regular session next immediately preceding the commencement of the term of service;* and each Senator shall have one Vote.

Immediately after they shall be assembled in Consequence of the first Election, they shall be divided as equally as may be into three Classes. The Seats of the Senators of the first Class shall be vacated at the Expiration of the second Year, of the second Class at the Expiration of the fourth Year, and of the third Class at the Expiration of the sixth Year, so that one-third may be chosen every second Year; and if Vacancies happen by Resignation, or otherwise, during the Recess of the Legislature of any State, the Executive thereof may make temporary Appointments until the next Meeting of the Legislature, which shall then fill such Vacancies.

No Person shall be a Senator who shall not have attained to the Age of thirty Years, and [been nine Years a Citizen of the United] *be a citizen of the Confederate* States, and who shall not, when elected, be an Inhabitant of that State for which he shall be chosen.

The Vice President of the [United] *Confederate* States shall be President of the Senate, but shall have no Vote, unless they be equally divided.

The Senate shall choose their other Officers, and also a President *pro tempore,* in the Absence of the Vice President, or when he shall exercise the Office of President of the United States.

The Senate shall have the sole Power to try all Impeachments. When sitting for that Purpose, they shall be on Oath or Affirmation. When the President of the [United] *Confederate* States is tried, the Chief Justice shall preside: And no Person shall be convicted without the Concurrence of two-thirds of the Members present.

Judgment in Cases of Impeachment shall not extend further than to removal from Office, and Disqualification to hold and enjoy any Office of honour, Trust or Profit under the [United] *Confederate* States; but the Party convicted shall nevertheless be liable and subject to Indictment, Trial, Judgment and Punishment, according to Law.

Section IV   The Times, Places and Manner of holding Elections for Senators and Representatives, shall be prescribed in each State by the Legislature thereof, *subject to the provisions of this Constitution;* but the Congress may at any time by Law make or alter such Regulations, except as to the *times and* places of choosing Senators.

The Congress shall assemble at least once in every Year, and such Meeting shall be on the first Monday in December, unless they shall by Law appoint a different Day.

Section V   Each House shall be the Judge of the Elections, Returns and Qualifications of its own Members, and a Majority of each shall constitute a Quorum to do Business; but a smaller Number may adjourn from day to day, and may be authorized to compel the Attendance of absent Members, in such Manner, and under such Penalties as each House may provide.

Each House may determine the Rules of its Proceedings, punish its Members for disorderly Behaviour, and, with the Concurrence of two-thirds *of the whole number* expel a Member.

Each House shall keep a Journal of its Proceedings, and from time to time publish the same, excepting such Parts as may in their Judgment require Secrecy; and the Yeas and Nays of the Members of either House on any question shall, at the Desire of one-fifth of those Present, be entered on the Journal.

Neither House, during the Session of Congress, shall, without the Consent of the other, adjourn for more than three days, nor to any other Place than that in which the two Houses shall be sitting.

Section VI   The Senators and Representatives shall receive a Compensation for their Services, to be ascertained by Law, and paid out of the Treasury of the [United] *Confederate* States. They shall in all Cases, except Treason [Felony] and Breach of the Peace, be privileged from Arrest during their Attendance at the Session of their respective Houses, and in going to and returning from the same; and for any Speech or Debate in either House, they shall not be questioned in any other Place.

No Senator or Representative shall, during the Time for which he was elected, be appointed to any civil Office under the Authority of the [United] *Confederate* States, which shall have been created, or the Emoluments whereof shall have been increased during such time; and no Person holding any Office under the [United] *Confederate* States, shall be a Member of either House during his Continuance in Office. *But Congress may, by law, grant to the principal officers in each of the executive departments a seat upon the floor of either House, with the privilege of discussing any measures appertaining to his department.*

Section VII   All Bills for raising Revenue shall originate in the House of Representatives; but the Senate may propose or concur with Amendments as on other Bills.

Every Bill which shall have passed [the House of Representatives and the Senate] *both Houses,* shall, before it become a Law, be presented to the President of the [United] *Confederate* States; If he approve he shall sign it, but if not he shall return it, with his Objections to that House in which it shall have originated, who shall enter the Objections at large on their Journal, and proceed to reconsider it. If after such Reconsideration two-thirds of that House shall agree to pass the Bill, it shall be sent, together with the Objections, to the other House, by which it shall likewise be reconsidered, and if approved by two-thirds of that House, it shall become a Law. But in all *such* Cases the Votes of both Houses shall be determined by Yeas and Nays, and the Names of the Persons voting for and against the Bill shall be entered on the Journal of each House respectively. If any Bill shall not be returned by the President within ten Days (Sundays excepted) after it shall have been presented to him, the Same shall be a law, in like Manner as if he had signed it, unless the Congress by their Adjournment prevent its return, in which Case it shall not be a Law. *The President may approve any appropriation and disapprove any other appropriation in the same bill. In such case he shall, in signing the bill, designate the appropriation disapproved, and shall return a copy of such appropriation, with his objections, to the House in which the bill shall have originated; and the same proceedings shall then be had as in case of other bills disapproved by the President.*

Every Order, Resolution, or Vote to which the Concurrence of [the Senate and House of Representatives] *both Houses* may be necessary (except on a question of Adjournment), shall be presented to the President of the [United] *Confederate* States; and before the Same shall take Effect, shall be approved by him, or being disapproved by him, [shall] *may* be repassed by two-thirds of [the Senate and House of Representatives] *both Houses,* according to the Rules and Limitations prescribed in the Case of a Bill.

Section VIII The Congress shall have Power

To lay and collect Taxes, Duties, Imposts and *Excises, for revenue necessary* to pay the Debts [and], provide for the common Defense [and general Welfare of the United States; but], *and carry on the government of the Confederate States; but no bounties shall be granted from the treasury, nor shall any duties, or taxes, or importation from foreign nations be laid to promote or foster any branch of industry; and* all Duties, Imposts and Excises shall be uniform throughout the [United] *Confederate* States;

To borrow Money on the credit of the [United] *Confederate* States;

To regulate Commerce with foreign Nations, and among the several States, and with the Indian Tribes; *but neither this, nor any other clause contained in this Constitution, shall ever be construed to delegate the power to Congress to appropriate money for any internal improvement intended to facilitate commerce; except for the purpose of furnishing lights, beacons, and buoys, and other aids to navigation upon the coasts, and the improvement of harbors, and the removing of obstructions in river navigation; in all such cases such duties such duties shall be laid on the navigation facilitated thereby, as may be necessary to pay the costs and expenses thereof;*

To establish an uniform Rule of Naturalization, and uniform Laws on the subject of Bankruptcies throughout the [United] *Confederate* States; *but no law of Congress shall discharge any debt contracted before the passage of the same;*

To coin Money, regulate the Value thereof, and of foreign Coin, and fix the Standard of Weights and Measures;

To provide for the Punishment of counterfeiting the Securities and current Coin of the [United] *Confederate* States;

To establish Post Offices and post [Roads] *routes; but the expenses of the Postoffice Department, after the first day of March, in the year of our Lord eighteen hundred and sixty-three, shall be paid out of its own revenues;*

To promote the progress of Science and useful Arts, by securing for limited Times to Authors and Inventors the exclusive Right to their respective Writings and Discoveries;

To constitute Tribunals inferior to the supreme Court;

To define and punish Piracies and Felonies committed on the high Seas, and Offences against the Law of Nations;

To declare War, grant Letters of Marque and Reprisal, and make Rules concerning Captures on Land and Water;

To raise and support Armies, but no Appropriation of Money to that Use shall be for a longer Term than two Years;

To provide and maintain a Navy;

To make Rules for the Government and Regulation of the land and naval Forces;

To provide for calling forth the Militia to execute the Laws of the [Union] *Confederate States,* suppress Insurrections and repel Invasions;

To provide for organizing, arming, and disciplining the Militia and for governing such Part of them as may be employed in the Service of the [United] *Confederate* States, reserving to the States respectively, the Appointment of the Officers, and the Authority of training the Militia according to the Discipline prescribed by Congress;

To exercise exclusive Legislation in all Cases whatsoever, over such District (not exceeding ten Miles square) as may, by Cession of particular States, and the Acceptance of Congress, become the Seat of the Government of the [United] *Confederate* States, and to exercise like Authority over all Places purchased by the Consent of the Legislature of the State in which the Same shall be, for the Erection of Forts, Magazines, Arsenals, Dock Yards, and other needful Buildings;— And

To make all Laws which shall be necessary and proper for carrying into Execution the foregoing Powers, and all other Powers vested by this Constitution in the Government of the [United] *Confederate* States or in any Department or Officer thereof.

Section IX [The Migration or Importation of such Persons as any of the States now existing shall think proper to admit, shall not be prohibited by the Congress prior to the Year one thousand eight hundred and eight, but a Tax or Duty may be imposed on such Importation, not exceeding ten dollars for each Person.]

The importation of negroes of the African race from any foreign country other than the slaveholding States or territories of the United States of America, is hereby forbidden; and Congress is required to pass such laws as shall effectually prevent the same. Congress shall also have power to prohibit the introduction of slaves from any State not a member of, or territory not belonging to, this Confederacy.

The Privilege of the Writ of Habeas Corpus shall not be suspended, unless when in Cases of Rebellion or Invasion the public Safety may require it. No Bill of Attainder or ex post facto Law, *or law denying or impairing the right of property in negro slaves,* shall be passed.

No Capitation, or other direct, Tax shall be laid, unless in Proportion to the Census or Enumeration herein before directed to be taken.

No Tax or Duty shall be laid on Articles exported from any State, *except by a vote of two-thirds of both Houses.*

No Preference shall be given by any Regulation of Commerce or Revenue to the Ports of one State over those of another; nor shall Vessels bound to, or from, one State, be obliged to enter, clear, or pay Duties in another.

No Money shall be drawn from the Treasury, but in Consequence of Appropriations made by Law; and a regular Statement and Account of the Receipts and Expenditures of all public Money shall be published from time to time.

Congress shall appropriate no money from the Treasury except by a vote of two-thirds of both Houses, taken by yeas and nays, unless it be asked and estimated for by some one of the heads of departments and submitted to Congress by the President; or for the purpose of paying its own expenses and contingencies; or for the payment of claims against the Confederate States, the justice of which shall have been officially declared by a tribunal for the investigation of claims against the Government, which it is hereby made the duty of Congress to establish.

All bills appropriating money shall specify in Federal currency the exact amount of each appropriation and the purposes for which it is made; and Congress shall grant no extra compensation to any public contractor, officer, agent or servant, after such contract shall have been made or such service rendered.

No Title of Nobility shall be granted by the [United] *Confederate* States; and no Person holding any Office of Profit or Trust under them, shall, without the Consent of the Congress, accept of any present, Emolument, Office, or Title, of any kind whatever, from any King, Prince or foreign State.

[Here the framers of the Confederate Constitution insert the U.S. Bill of Rights.]

Congress shall make no law respecting an establishment of religion, or prohibiting the free exercise thereof; or abridging the freedom of speech, or of the press; or the right of the people peaceably to assemble, and to petition the Government for a redress of grievances.

A well-regulated Militia, being necessary to the security of a free State, the right of the people to keep and bear Arms shall not be infringed.

No Soldier shall, in time of peace, be quartered in any house, without the consent of the Owner, nor in time of war, but in a manner to be prescribed by law.

The right of the people to be secure in their persons, houses, papers, and effects, against unreasonable searches and seizures, shall not be violated, and no Warrants shall issue, but upon probable cause, supported by Oath or affirmation, and particularly describing the place to be searched, and the persons or things to be seized.

No person shall be held to answer for a capital, or otherwise infamous crime, unless on a presentment or indictment of a Grand Jury, except in cases arising in the land or naval forces, or in the Militia, when in actual service in time of War or public danger; nor shall any person be subject for the same offence to be twice put in jeopardy of life or limb; nor shall be compelled in any Criminal Case to be a witness against himself, nor be deprived of life, liberty or property without due process of law; nor shall private property be taken for public use, without just compensation.

In all criminal prosecutions, the accused shall enjoy the right to a speedy and public trial, by an impartial jury of the State and district wherein the crime shall have been committed, which district shall have been previously ascertained by law, and to be informed of the nature and cause of the accusation; to be confronted with the witnesses against him; to have Compulsory process for obtaining Witnesses in his favour, and to have the Assistance of Counsel for his defence.

In Suits at common law, where the value in controversy shall exceed twenty dollars, the right of trial by jury shall be preserved, and no fact tried by a jury shall be otherwise reexamined in any Court of the [United] *Confederate* States, than according to the rules of the common law.

Excessive bail shall not be required, nor excessive fines imposed, nor cruel and unusual punishments inflicted.

Every law or resolution having the force of law, shall relate to but one subject, and that shall be expressed in the title.

Section X No State shall enter into any Treaty, Alliance, or Confederation; grant Letters of Marque and Reprisal; coin Money; [emit Bills of Credit;] make any Thing but gold and silver Coin a Tender in Payment of Debts; pass any Bill of Attainder, *or* ex post facto Law, or Law impairing the Obligation of Contracts, or grant any Title of Nobility.

No State shall, without the consent of the Congress, lay any Imposts or Duties on Imports or Exports, except what may be absolutely necessary for executing its inspection Laws: and the net Produce of all Duties and Imposts, laid by any State on Imports or Exports, shall be for the Use of the Treasury of the [United] *Confederate* States; and all such Laws shall be subject to the Revision and Control of the Congress.

No State shall, without the Consent of Congress, lay any Duty of Tonnage, *except on sea-going vessels, for the improvement of its rivers and harbors navigated by the said vessels; but such duties shall not conflict with any treaties of the Confederate States with foreign nations; and any surplus of revenue thus derived shall, after making such improvement, be paid into the common treasury; nor shall any State* keep Troops, or Ships of War in time of Peace, enter into any Agreement or Compact with another State, or with a foreign Power, or engage in War, unless actually invaded, or in such imminent Danger as will not admit of Delay. *But when any river divides or flows through two or more States, they may enter into compacts with each other to improve the navigation thereof.*

Article II

Section I   [The executive Power shall be vested in a President of the United States of America. He shall hold his Office during the Term of four Years, and, together with the Vice President, chosen for the same Term, be elected, as follows:] *The executive power shall be vested in a President of the Confederate States of America. He and the Vice President shall hold their offices for the term of six years; but the President shall not be re-eligible. The President and Vice President shall be elected as follows:*

Each State shall appoint in such Manner as the Legislature thereof may direct, a Number of Electors, equal to the whole Number of Senators and Representatives to which the State may be entitled in the Congress; but no Senator or Representative, or Person holding an Office of Trust or Profit under the [United] *Confederate* States, shall be appointed an Elector.

The Electors shall meet in their respective States, and vote by ballot for President and Vice President, one of whom, at least, shall not be an inhabitant of the same State with themselves; they shall name in their ballots the person voted for as President, and in distinct ballots the person voted for as Vice President, and they shall make distinct lists of all persons voted for as President, and of all persons voted for as Vice President, and of the number of votes for each, which lists they

shall sign and certify, and transmit sealed to the seat of the government of the [United] *Confederate* States, directed to the President of the Senate;—The President of the Senate shall, in the presence of the Senate and House of Representatives, open all the certificates and the votes shall then be counted;—The person having the greatest number of votes for President shall be the President, if such number be a majority of the whole number of Electors appointed; and if no person have such majority, then from the persons having the highest numbers not exceeding three on the list of those voted for as President, the House of Representatives shall choose immediately, by ballot, the President. But in choosing the President, the votes shall be taken by States, the representation from each State having one vote; a quorum for this purpose shall consist of a member or members from two-thirds of the States, and a majority of all the States shall be necessary to a choice. And if the House of Representatives shall not choose a President whenever the right of choice shall devolve upon them, before the fourth day of March next following, then the Vice President shall act as President, as in the case of the death or other constitutional disability of the President. The person having the greatest number of votes as Vice President shall be the Vice President, if such number be a majority of the whole number of Electors appointed, and if no person have a majority, then from the two highest numbers on the list the Senate shall choose the Vice President; a quorum for the purpose shall consist of two-thirds of the whole number of Senators, and a majority of the whole number shall be necessary to a choice. But no person constitutionally ineligible to the office of President shall be eligible to that of Vice President of the [United] *Confederate* States.

The Congress may determine the Time of choosing the Electors, and the Day on which they shall give their Votes; which Day shall be the same throughout the [United] *Confederate* States.

No Person except a natural-born Citizen [or a Citizen of the United States] *of the Confederate States, or a citizen thereof,* at the time of the Adoption of this Constitution, *or a citizen thereof born in the United States prior to the 20th of December, 1860,* shall be eligible to the Office of President; neither shall any Person be eligible to that Office who shall not have attained to the Age of thirty-five Years, and been fourteen Years a Resident within the [United States] *limits of the Confederate States, as they may exist at the time of his election.*

In Cases of the Removal of the President from Office, or of his Death, Resignation, or Inability to discharge the Powers and Duties of the said Office, the same shall devolve on the Vice President, and the Congress may by Law provide for the Case of Removal, Death, Resignation, or Inability, both of the President and Vice President, declaring what Officer shall then act as President, and such Officer shall act accordingly, until the Disability be removed, or a President shall be elected.

The President shall, at stated Times, receive for his Services, a Compensation, which shall neither be increased nor diminished during the Period for which he shall have been elected, and he shall not receive within that Period any other Emolument from the [United] *Confederate* States or any of them.

Before he enters on the Execution of his Office, he shall take the following Oath or Affirmation:—"I do solemnly swear (or affirm) that I will faithfully execute the Office of President of the [United] *Confederate* States, and will to the best of my Ability, preserve, protect and defend the Constitution [of the United States] *thereof.*"

Section II. The President shall be Commander in Chief of the Army and Navy of the [United] *Confederate* States, and of the Militia of the several States, when called into the actual Service of the [United] *Confederate* States; he may require the Opinion, in writing, of the principal Officer in each of the executive Departments, upon any Subject relating to the Duties of their respective Offices, and he shall have Power to grant Reprieves and Pardons for Offenses against the [United] *Confederate* States, except in Cases of Impeachment.

He shall have Power, by and with the Advice and Consent of the Senate, to make Treaties, provided two-thirds of the Senators present concur; and he shall nominate, and by and with the Advice and Consent of the Senate, shall appoint Ambassadors, other public Ministers and Consuls, Judges of the supreme Court, and all other Officers of the [United] *Confederate* States, whose Appointments are not herein otherwise provided for, and which shall be established by Law: but the Congress may by Law vest the Appointment of such inferior Officers, as they think proper, in the President alone, in the Courts of Law, or in the Heads of Departments. *The principal officer in each of the executive departments, and all persons connected with the diplomatic service, may be removed from office at the pleasure of the President. All other civil officers of the executive department may be removed at any time by the President, or other appointing power, when their services are unnecessary, or for dishonesty, incapacity, inefficiency, misconduct, or neglect of duty; and when so removed, the removal shall be reported to the Senate, together with the reasons therefor.*

The President shall have Power to fill [up] all Vacancies that may happen during the Recess of the Senate, by granting Commissions which shall expire at the End of their next Session.

Section III [He] *The President* shall from time to time give to the Congress Information of the State of the [Union] *Confederacy,* and recommend to their Consideration such Measures as he shall judge necessary and expedient; he may, on extraordinary Occasions, convene both Houses, or either of them, and in Case of Disagreement between them, with Respect to the Time of Adjournment, he may adjourn them to such Time as he shall think proper; he shall receive Ambassadors and other public Ministers; he shall take Care that the Laws be faithfully executed, and shall Commission all the officers of the [United] *Confederate* States.

Section IV The President, Vice President and all civil Officers of the [United] *Confederate* States, shall be removed from Office or Impeachment for, and Conviction of, Treason, Bribery, or other high Crimes and Misdemeanors.

Article III

Section I The judicial Power of the [United] *Confederate* States shall be vested in one [supreme] *Superior* Court, and in such inferior Courts as the Congress may from time to time ordain and establish. The Judges, both of the supreme and inferior Courts, shall hold their Offices during good Behavior, and shall, at stated Times, receive for their Services a Compensation, which shall not be diminished during their Continuance in Office.

Section II The judicial Power shall extend to all cases [in Law and Equity, arising under this Constitution], *arising under this Constitution, in law and equity,* the Laws of the [United] *Confederate* States, and Treaties made, or which shall be made, under their Authority;—to all Cases affecting Ambassadors, other public Ministers, and Consuls;—to all Cases of admiralty and maritime Jurisdiction;—to Controversies to which the [United] *Confederate* States shall be a Party;—to Controversies between two or more States; —between a State and Citizens of another State *where the State is plaintiff;—between* Citizens *claiming lands under grants* of different States,—[between Citizens of the same State claiming Lands under Grants of different States,] and between a State, or the Citizens thereof, and foreign States, Citizens or Subjects; *but no State shall be sued by a citizen or subject of any foreign State.*

In all Cases affecting Ambassadors, other public Ministers and Consuls, and those in which a State shall be Party, the supreme Court shall have original Jurisdiction. In all the other Cases before mentioned, the supreme Court shall have appellate Jurisdiction, both as to Law and Fact, with such Exceptions, and under such Regulations as the Congress shall make.

The Trial of all Crimes, except in Cases of Impeachment, shall be by Jury; and such Trial shall be held in the State where the said Crime[s] shall have been committed; but when not committed within any State, the Trial shall be at such Place or Places as the Congress may by Law have directed.

Section III Treason against the [United] *Confederate* States shall consist only in levying War against them, or in adhering to their Enemies, giving them Aid and Comfort. No Person shall be convicted of Treason unless on the Testimony of two Witnesses to the same overt Act, or on Confession in open Court.

The Congress shall have Power to declare the Punishment of Treason, but no Attainder of Treason shall work Corruption of Blood, or Forfeiture except during the Life of the Person attainted.

Article IV

Section I Full Faith and Credit shall be given in each State to the public Acts, Records, and judicial Proceedings of every other State. And the Congress may by general Laws prescribe the Manner in which such Acts, Records and Proceedings shall be proved, and the Effect thereof.

Section II The Citizens of each State shall be entitled to all Privileges and Immunities of Citizens in the several States, *and shall have the right of transit and sojourn in any State of this Confederacy, with their slaves and other property; and the right of property in such slaves shall not be impaired.*

A Person charged in any State with Treason, Felony, or other Crime, who shall flee from Justice, and be found in another State, shall on Demand of the executive Authority of the State from which he fled, be delivered up, to be removed to the State having Jurisdiction of the Crime.

No *slave or* Person held to Service or Labor in [one State] *any State or Territory of the Confederate States* under the Laws thereof, escaping *or unlawfully carried* into another, shall, in Consequence of any Law or Regulation therein, be discharged from such Service or Labor, but shall be delivered up on Claim of the Party to whom such *slave belongs, or to whom such* Service or Labor may be due.

Section III [New States may be admitted by the Congress into this Union;] *Other States may be admitted into*

this Confederacy *by a vote of two-thirds of the whole House of Representatives and two-thirds of the Senate, the Senate voting by States;* but no new State shall be formed or erected within the Jurisdiction of any other State; nor any State be formed by the Junction of two or more States, or Parts of States, without the Consent of the Legislatures of the States concerned as well as of the Congress.

The Congress shall have Power to dispose of and make all needful Rules and Regulations [respecting the Territory or other Property belonging to the United States; and nothing in this Constitution shall be so construed as to Prejudice any Claims of the United States, or of any particular State] *concerning the property of the Confederate States, including the lands thereof.*

The Confederate States may acquire new territory, and Congress shall have power to legislate and provide governments for the inhabitants of all territory belonging to the Confederate States lying without the limits of the several States, and may permit them, at such times and in such manner as it may by law provide, to form States to be admitted into the Confederacy. In all such territory the institution of negro slavery as it now exists in the Confederate States shall be recognized and protected by Congress and by the territorial government, and the inhabitants of the several Confederate States and territories shall have the right to take to such territory any slaves lawfully held by them in any of the States or Territories of the Confederate States.

[Section IV] The [United] *Confederate* States shall guarantee to every State [in this Union] *that now is, or hereafter may become, a member of this Confederacy*, a Republican Form of Government, and shall protect each of them against Invasion; and on Application of the Legislature, or of the Executive (when the Legislature [cannot be convened] *is not in session*) against domestic Violence.

Article V

[The Congress, whenever two-thirds of both Houses shall deem it necessary, shall propose Amendments to this Constitution, or on the Application of the Legislatures of two-thirds of the several States, shall call a Convention for proposing Amendments, which, in either Case, shall be valid to all Intents and Purposes, as Part of this Constitution, when ratified by the Legislatures of three-fourths of the several States, or by Conventions in three-fourths thereof, as the one or the other Mode of Ratification may be proposed by the Congress; Provided that no Amendment which may be made prior to the Year one thousand eight hundred and eight shall in any Manner affect the first and fourth Clauses in the

Ninth Section of the first Article; and that no State, without its Consent, shall be deprived of its equal Suffrage in the Senate.]

Upon the demand of any three States, legally assembled in their several Conventions, the Congress shall summon a Convention of all the States, to take into consideration such amendments to the Constitution as the said States shall concur in suggesting at the time when the said demand is made; and should any of the proposed amendments to the Constitution be agreed on by the said Convention—voting by States—and the same be ratified by the Legislatures of two-thirds of the several States, or by Conventions in two-thirds thereof—as the one or the other mode of ratification may be proposed by the general Convention—they shall henceforward form a part of this Constitution. But no State shall, without its consent, be deprived of its equal representation in the Senate.

Article VI

The Government established by this Constitution is the successor of the Provisional Government of the Confederate States of America, and all laws passed by the latter shall continue in force until the same shall be repealed or modified; and all the officers appointed by the same shall remain in office until their successors are appointed and qualified or the offices abolished.

All Debts contracted and Engagements entered into, before the Adoption of this Constitution, shall be as valid against the [United] *Confederate* States under this Constitution, as under the [Confederation] *Provisional Government.*

This Constitution and the Laws of the [United] *Confederate* States [which shall be] made in Pursuance thereof; and all Treaties made, or which shall be made, under the authority of the [United] *Confederate* States, shall be the supreme Law of the Land; and the Judges in every State shall be bound thereby, any Thing in the Constitution or Laws of any State to the Contrary notwithstanding.

The Senators and Representatives before mentioned, and the Members of the several State Legislatures, and all executive and judicial Officers, both of the [United] *Confederate* States and of the several States, shall be bound by Oath or Affirmation, to support this Constitution; but no religious Test shall ever be required as a Qualification to any Office or public Trust under the [United] *Confederate* States.

The enumeration in the Constitution, of certain rights, shall not be construed to deny or disparage others retained by the people *of the several States.*

The powers not delegated to the [United] *Confederate* States by the Constitution, nor prohibited by it to the States, are reserved to the States respectively, or to the people.

Article VII

The Ratification of the Conventions of [nine] *five* States shall be sufficient for the Establishment of this Constitution between the States so ratifying the same.

When five States shall have ratified this Constitution, in the manner before specified, the Congress under the Provisional Constitution shall prescribe the time for holding the election of President and Vice President; and for the meeting of the electoral college; and for counting the votes and inaugurating the President. They shall also prescribe the time for holding the first election of members of Congress under this Constitution, and the time for assembling the same. Until the assembling of such Congress, the Congress under the Provisional Constitution shall continue to exercise the legislative powers granted them, not extending beyond the time limited by the Constitution of the Provisional Government.

[Done in Convention by the Unanimous Consent of the States present, the Seventeenth Day of September in the Year of our Lord one thousand seven hundred and eighty-seven and of the Independence of the United States of America the Twelfth.] *Adopted unanimously March 11, 1861.*

SENECA FALLS RESOLUTION

In 1848, leaders of the nascent women's movement took a critical step by calling a convention in Seneca Falls in upstate New York. Organized by Elizabeth Cady Stanton and Lucretia Mott, who had met at the World's Anti-Slavery Convention in 1840, and joined by a few sympathetic male abolitionists, the convention outlined for the first time a coherent program for women's equality. The delegates at Seneca Falls based their program on republican ideology, adopting resolutions patterned directly on the Declaration of Independence.

WHEREAS, The great precept of nature is conceded to be, that "man shall pursue his own true and substantial happiness." Blackstone in his Commentaries remarks, that this law of Nature being coeval with mankind, and dictated by God himself, is of course superior in obligation to any other. It is binding over all the globe, in all countries and at all times; no human laws are of any validity if contrary to this, and such of them as are valid, derive all their force, and all their validity, and all their authority, mediately and immediately, from this original; therefore,

Resolved, That such laws as conflict, in any way, with the true and substantial happiness of woman, are contrary to the great precept of nature and of no validity, for this is "superior in obligation to any other."

Resolved, That all laws which prevent woman from occupying such a station in society as her conscience shall dictate, or which place her in a position inferior to that of man, are contrary to the great precept of nature, and therefore of no force or authority.

Resolved, That woman is man's equal — was intended to be so by the Creator, and the highest good of the race demands that she should be recognized as such.

Resolved, That the women of this country ought to be enlightened in regard to the laws under which they live, that they may no longer publish their degradation by declaring themselves satisfied with their present position, nor their ignorance, by asserting that they have all the rights they want.

Resolved, That inasmuch as man, while claiming for himself intellectual superiority, does accord to woman moral superiority, it is pre-eminently his duty to encourage her to speak and teach, as she has an opportunity, in all religious assemblies.

Resolved, That the same amount of virtue, delicacy, and refinement of behavior that is required of woman in the social state, should also be required of man, and the same transgressions should be visited with equal severity on both man and woman.

Resolved, That the objection of indelicacy and impropriety, which is so often brought against woman when she addresses a public audience, comes with a very ill-grace from those who encourage, by their attendance, her appearance on the stage, in the concert, or in feats of the circus.

Resolved, That woman has too long rested satisfied in the circumscribed limits which corrupt customs and a perverted application of the scriptures have marked out for her, and that it is time she should move in the enlarged sphere which her great Creator has assigned her.

Resolved, That it is the duty of the women of this country to secure to themselves their sacred right to the elective franchise.

Resolved, That the equality of human rights results necessarily from the fact of the identity of the race in capabilities and responsibilities.

Resolved, therefore, That, being invested by the Creator with the same capabilities, and the same consciousness of responsibility for their exercise, it is demonstrably the right and duty of woman, equally with man, to promote every righteous cause by every righteous means, and especially in regard to the great subjects of morals and religion, it is self-evidently her right to participate with her brother in teaching them, both in private and in public, by writing and by speaking, by any instrumentalities proper to be used, and many assemblies proper to be held; and this being a self-evident truth growing out of the divinely implanted principles of human nature, any custom or authority adverse to it, whether modern or wearing the hoary sanction of antiquity, is to be regarded as a self-evident falsehood, and at war with mankind.

Resolved, That the speedy success of our cause depends upon the zealous and untiring efforts of both men and women, for the overthrow of the monopoly of the pulpit, and for the securing to woman an equal participation with men in the various trades, professions, and commerce.

"I HAVE A DREAM," MARTIN LUTHER KING JR.

On August 28, 1963, about 250,000 black and white demonstrators—the largest civil rights demonstration up to that time—gathered at the Lincoln Memorial in Washington, D.C. For many people, the speech that the Reverend Martin Luther King Jr. delivered was the high point of the March on Washington. King's eloquence and the sight of blacks and whites marching solemnly together did more than any other event to make the civil rights movement acceptable to white Americans.

Five score years ago, a great American, in whose symbolic shadow we stand signed the Emancipation Proclamation. This momentous decree came as a great beacon light of hope to millions of Negro slaves who had been seared in the flames of withering injustice. It came as a joyous daybreak to end the long night of captivity.

But one hundred years later, we must face the tragic fact that the Negro is still not free. One hundred years later, the life of the Negro is still sadly crippled by the manacles of segregation and the chains of discrimination. One hundred years later, the Negro lives on a lonely island of poverty in the midst of a vast ocean of material prosperity. One hundred years later, the Negro is still languishing in the corners of American society and finds himself an exile in his own land. So we have come here today to dramatize an appalling condition.

In a sense we have come to our nation's capital to cash a check. When the architects of our republic wrote the magnificent words of the Constitution and the Declaration of Independence, they were signing a promissory note to which every American was to fall heir. This note was a promise that all men would be guaranteed the inalienable rights of life, liberty, and the pursuit of happiness.

It is obvious today that America has defaulted on this promissory note insofar as her citizens of color are concerned. Instead of honoring this sacred obligation, America has given the Negro people a bad check which has come back marked "insufficient funds." But we refuse to believe that the bank of justice is bankrupt. We refuse to believe that there are insufficient funds in the great vaults of opportunity of this nation. So we have come to cash this check—a check that will give us upon demand the riches of freedom and the security of justice. We have also come to this hallowed spot to remind America of the fierce urgency of now. This is no time to engage in the luxury of cooling off or to take the tranquilizing drug of gradualism. Now

is the time to rise from the dark and desolate valley of segregation to the sunlit path of racial justice. Now is the time to open the doors of opportunity to all of God's children. Now is the time to lift our nation from the quicksands of racial injustice to the solid rock of brotherhood.

It would be fatal for the nation to overlook the urgency of the moment and to underestimate the determination of the Negro. This sweltering summer of the Negro's legitimate discontent will not pass until there is an invigorating autumn of freedom and equality. Nineteen sixty-three is not an end, but a beginning. Those who hope that the Negro needed to blow off steam and will now be content will have a rude awakening if the nation returns to business as usual. There will be neither rest nor tranquility in America until the Negro is granted his citizenship rights. The whirlwinds of revolt will continue to shake the foundations of our nation until the bright day of justice emerges.

But there is something that I must say to my people who stand on the warm threshold which leads into the palace of justice. In the process of gaining our rightful place we must not be guilty of wrongful deeds. Let us not seek to satisfy our thirst for freedom by drinking from the cup of bitterness and hatred.

We must forever conduct our struggle on the high plane of dignity and discipline. We must not allow our creative protest to degenerate into physical violence. Again and again we must rise to the majestic heights of meeting physical force with soul force. The marvelous new militancy which has engulfed the Negro community must not lead us to distrust of all white people, for many of our white brothers, as evidenced by their presence here today, have come to realize that their destiny is tied up with our destiny and their freedom is inextricably bound to our freedom. We cannot walk alone.

And as we walk, we must make the pledge that we shall march ahead. We cannot turn back. There are those who are asking the devotees of civil rights, "When will you be satisfied?" We can never be satisfied as long as our bodies, heavy with the fatigue of travel, cannot gain lodging in the motels of the highways and the hotels of the cities. We cannot be satisfied as long as the Negro's basic mobility is from a smaller ghetto to a larger one. We can never be satisfied as long as a Negro in Mississippi cannot vote and a Negro in New York believes he has nothing for which to vote. No, no, we are not satisfied, and we will not be satisfied until justice rolls down like waters and righteousness like a mighty stream.

I am not unmindful that some of you have come here out of great trials and tribulations. Some of you have come fresh from narrow cells. Some of you have come from areas where your quest for freedom left you battered by the storms of persecution and staggered by the winds of police brutality. You have been the veterans of creative suffering. Continue to work with the faith that unearned suffering is redemptive.

Go back to Mississippi, go back to Alabama, go back to Georgia, go back to Louisiana, go back to the slums and ghettos of our northern cities, knowing that somehow this situation can and will be changed. Let us not wallow in the valley of despair.

I say to you today, my friends, that in spite of the difficulties and frustrations of the moment, I still have a dream. It is a dream deeply rooted in the American dream.

I have a dream that one day this nation will rise up and live out the true meaning of its creed: "We hold these truths to be self-evident: that all men are created equal."

I have a dream that one day on the red hills of Georgia the sons of former slaves and the sons of former slaveowners will be able to sit down together at a table of brotherhood.

I have a dream that one day even the state of Mississippi, a desert state, sweltering with the heat of injustice and oppression, will be transformed into an oasis of freedom and justice.

I have a dream that my four children will one day live in a nation where they will not be judged by the color of their skin but by the content of their character.

I have a dream today.

I have a dream that one day the state of Alabama, whose governor's lips are presently dripping with the words of interposition and nullification, will be transformed into a situation where little black boys and black girls will be able to join hands with little white boys and white girls and walk together as sisters and brothers.

I have a dream today.

I have a dream that one day every valley shall be exalted, every hill and mountain shall be made low, the rough places will be made plain, and the crooked places will be made straight, and the glory of the Lord shall be revealed, and all flesh shall see it together.

This is our hope. This is the faith with which I return to the South. With this faith we will be able to hew out of the mountain of despair a stone of hope. With this faith we will be able to transform the jangling discords of our nation into a beautiful symphony of brotherhood. With this faith we will be able to work together, to pray together, to struggle together, to go to jail together, to stand up for freedom together, knowing that we will be free one day.

This will be the day when all of God's children will be able to sing with a new meaning, "My country, 'tis of thee, sweet land of liberty, of thee I sing. Land where my fathers died, land of the pilgrim's pride, from every mountainside, let freedom ring."

And if America is to be a great nation this must become true. So let freedom ring from the prodigious hilltops of New Hampshire. Let freedom ring from the mighty mountains of New York. Let freedom ring from the heightening Alleghenies of Pennsylvania!

Let freedom ring from the snowcapped Rockies of Colorado!

Let freedom ring from the curvaceous peaks of California!

But not only that; let freedom ring from Stone Mountain of Georgia!

Let freedom ring from Lookout Mountain of Tennessee!

Let freedom ring from every hill and every molehill of Mississippi. From every mountainside, let freedom ring.

When we let freedom ring, when we let it ring from every village and every hamlet, from every state and every city, we will be able to speed up that day when all of God's children, black men and white men, Jews and Gentiles, Protestants and Catholics, will be able to join hands and sing in the words of the old Negro spiritual, "Free at last! free at last! thank God Almighty, we are free at last!"

U.S. POLITICS AND GOVERNMENT

PRESIDENTIAL ELECTIONS

Year	Candidates	Parties	Popular Vote	Percentage of Popular Vote	Electoral Vote	Percentage of Voter Participation
1789	**GEORGE WASHINGTON (Va.)***				69	
	John Adams				34	
	Others				35	
1792	**GEORGE WASHINGTON (Va.)**				132	
	John Adams				77	
	George Clinton				50	
	Others				5	
1796	**JOHN ADAMS (Mass.)**	Federalist			71	
	Thomas Jefferson	Democratic-Republican			68	
	Thomas Pinckney	Federalist			59	
	Aaron Burr	Dem.-Rep.			30	
	Others				48	
1800	**THOMAS JEFFERSON (Va.)**	Dem.-Rep.			73	
	Aaron Burr	Dem.-Rep.			73	
	John Adams	Federalist			65	
	C. C. Pinckney	Federalist			64	
	John Jay	Federalist			1	
1804	**THOMAS JEFFERSON (Va.)**	Dem.-Rep.			162	
	C. C. Pinckney	Federalist			14	
1808	**JAMES MADISON (Va.)**	Dem.-Rep.			122	
	C. C. Pinckney	Federalist			47	
	George Clinton	Dem.-Rep.			6	
1812	**JAMES MADISON (Va.)**	Dem.-Rep.			128	
	De Witt Clinton	Federalist			89	
1816	**JAMES MONROE (Va.)**	Dem.-Rep.			183	
	Rufus King	Federalist			34	
1820	**JAMES MONROE (Va.)**	Dem.-Rep.			231	
	John Quincy Adams	Dem.-Rep.			1	
1824	**JOHN Q. ADAMS (Mass.)**	Dem.-Rep.	108,740	30.5	84	26.9
	Andrew Jackson	Dem.-Rep.	153,544	43.1	99	
	William H. Crawford	Dem.-Rep.	46,618	13.1	41	
	Henry Clay	Dem.-Rep.	47,136	13.2	37	
1828	**ANDREW JACKSON (Tenn.)**	Democratic	647,286	56.0	178	57.6
	John Quincy Adams	National Republican	508,064	44.0	83	

*State of residence when elected president.

Year	Candidates	Parties	Popular Vote	Percentage of Popular Vote	Electoral Vote	Percentage of Voter Participation
1832	**ANDREW JACKSON (Tenn.)**	Democratic	687,502	55.0	219	55.4
	Henry Clay	National Republican	530,189	42.4	49	
	John Floyd	Independent			11	
	William Wirt	Anti-Mason	33,108	2.6	7	
1836	**MARTIN VAN BUREN (N.Y.)**	Democratic	765,483	50.9	170	57.8
	W. H. Harrison	Whig			73	
	Hugh L. White	Whig	739,795	49.1	26	
	Daniel Webster	Whig			14	
	W. P. Magnum	Independent			11	
1840	**WILLIAM H. HARRISON (Ohio)**	Whig	1,274,624	53.1	234	80.2
	Martin Van Buren	Democratic	1,127,781	46.9	60	
	J. G. Birney	Liberty	7,069		—	
1844	**JAMES K. POLK (Tenn.)**	Democratic	1,338,464	49.6	170	78.9
	Henry Clay	Whig	1,300,097	48.1	105	
	J. G. Birney	Liberty	62,300	2.3	—	
1848	**ZACHARY TAYLOR (La.)**	Whig	1,360,967	47.4	163	72.7
	Lewis Cass	Democratic	1,222,342	42.5	127	
	Martin Van Buren	Free-Soil	291,263	10.1	—	
1852	**FRANKLIN PIERCE (N.H.)**	Democratic	1,601,117	50.9	254	69.6
	Winfield Scott	Whig	1,385,453	44.1	42	
	John P. Hale	Free-Soil	155,825	5.0	—	
1856	**JAMES BUCHANAN (Pa.)**	Democratic	1,832,995	45.3	174	78.9
	John C. Frémont	Republican	1,339,932	33.1	114	
	Millard Fillmore	American	871,731	21.6	8	
1860	**ABRAHAM LINCOLN (Ill.)**	Republican	1,865,593	39.8	180	81.2
	Stephen A. Douglas	Democratic	1,382,713	29.5	12	
	John C. Breckinridge	Democratic	848,356	18.1	72	
	John Bell	Union	592,906	12.6	39	
1864	**ABRAHAM LINCOLN (Ill.)**	Republican	2,206,938	55.0	212	73.8
	George B. McClellan	Democratic	1,803,787	45.0	21	
1868	**ULYSSES S. GRANT (Ill.)**	Republican	3,012,833	52.7	214	78.1
	Horatio Seymour	Democratic	2,703,249	47.3	80	
1872	**ULYSSES S. GRANT (Ill.)**	Republican	3,597,132	55.6	286	71.3
	Horace Greeley	Democratic; Liberal Republican	2,834,125	43.9	66	
1876	**RUTHERFORD B. HAYES (Ohio)**	Republican	4,036,572	48.0	185	81.8
	Samuel J. Tilden	Democratic	4,284,020	51.0	184	
1880	**JAMES A. GARFIELD (Ohio)**	Republican	4,454,416	48.5	214	79.4
	Winfield S. Hancock	Democratic	4,444,952	48.1	155	
1884	**GROVER CLEVELAND (N.Y.)**	Democratic	4,879,507	48.5	219	77.5
	James G. Blaine	Republican	4,850,293	48.2	182	
1888	**BENJAMIN HARRISON (Ind.)**	Republican	5,439,853	47.9	233	79.3
	Grover Cleveland	Democratic	5,540,309	48.6	168	
1892	**GROVER CLEVELAND (N.Y.)**	Democratic	5,555,426	46.1	277	74.7
	Benjamin Harrison	Republican	5,182,690	43.0	145	
	James B. Weaver	People's	1,029,846	8.5	22	

Year	Candidates	Parties	Popular Vote	Percentage of Popular Vote	Electoral Vote	Percentage of Voter Participation
1896	**WILLIAM McKINLEY (Ohio)**	Republican	7,104,779	51.1	271	79.3
	William J. Bryan	Democratic-People's	6,502,925	47.7	176	
1900	**WILLIAM McKINLEY (Ohio)**	Republican	7,207,923	51.7	292	73.2
	William J. Bryan	Dem.-Populist	6,358,133	45.5	155	
1904	**THEODORE ROOSEVELT (N.Y.)**	Republican	7,623,486	57.9	336	65.2
	Alton B. Parker	Democratic	5,077,911	37.6	140	
	Eugene V. Debs	Socialist	402,283	3.0	—	
1908	**WILLIAM H. TAFT (Ohio)**	Republican	7,678,908	51.6	321	65.4
	William J. Bryan	Democratic	6,409,104	43.1	162	
	Eugene V. Debs	Socialist	420,793	2.8	—	
1912	**WOODROW WILSON (N.J.)**	Democratic	6,293,454	41.9	435	58.8
	Theodore Roosevelt	Progressive	4,119,538	27.4	88	
	William H. Taft	Republican	3,484,980	23.2	8	
	Eugene V. Debs	Socialist	900,672	6.1	—	
1916	**WOODROW WILSON (N.J.)**	Democratic	9,129,606	49.4	277	61.6
	Charles E. Hughes	Republican	8,538,221	46.2	254	
	A. L. Benson	Socialist	585,113	3.2	—	
1920	**WARREN G. HARDING (Ohio)**	Republican	16,143,407	60.5	404	49.2
	James M. Cox	Democratic	9,130,328	34.2	127	
	Eugene V. Debs	Socialist	919,799	3.4	—	
1924	**CALVIN COOLIDGE (Mass.)**	Republican	15,725,016	54.0	382	48.9
	John W. Davis	Democratic	8,386,503	28.8	136	
	Robert M. LaFollette	Progressive	4,822,856	16.6	13	
1928	**HERBERT HOOVER (Calif.)**	Republican	21,391,381	58.2	444	56.9
	Alfred E. Smith	Democratic	15,016,443	40.9	87	
	Norman Thomas	Socialist	267,835	0.7	—	
1932	**FRANKLIN D. ROOSEVELT (N.Y.)**	Democratic	22,809,638	57.4	472	56.9
	Herbert Hoover	Republican	15,758,901	39.7	59	
	Norman Thomas	Socialist	881,951	2.2	—	
1936	**FRANKLIN D. ROOSEVELT (N.Y.)**	Democratic	27,751,597	60.8	523	61.0
	Alfred M. Landon	Republican	16,679,583	36.5	8	
	William Lemke	Union	882,479	1.9	—	
1940	**FRANKLIN D. ROOSEVELT (N.Y.)**	Democratic	27,244,160	54.8	449	62.5
	Wendell Willkie	Republican	22,305,198	44.8	82	
1944	**FRANKLIN D. ROOSEVELT (N.Y.)**	Democratic	25,602,504	53.5	432	55.9
	Thomas E. Dewey	Republican	22,006,285	46.0	99	
1948	**HARRY S. TRUMAN (Mo.)**	Democratic	24,105,695	49.5	303	53.0
	Thomas E. Dewey	Republican	21,969,170	45.1	189	
	J. Strom Thurmond	State-Rights Democratic	1,169,021	2.4	38	
	Henry A. Wallace	Progressive	1,156,103	2.4	—	
1952	**DWIGHT D. EISENHOWER (N.Y.)**	Republican	33,936,252	55.1	442	63.3
	Adlai Stevenson	Democratic	27,314,992	44.4	89	
1956	**DWIGHT D. EISENHOWER (N.Y.)**	Republican	35,575,420	57.6	457	60.6
	Adlai Stevenson	Democratic	26,033,066	42.1	73	
	Other	—	—		1	

Year	Candidates	Parties	Popular Vote	Percentage of Popular Vote	Electoral Vote	Percentage of Voter Participation
1960	**JOHN F. KENNEDY (Mass.)**	Democratic	34,227,096	49.9	303	62.8
	Richard M. Nixon	Republican	34,108,546	49.6	219	
	Other	—	—		15	
1964	**LYNDON B. JOHNSON (Tex.)**	Democratic	43,126,506	61.1	486	61.7
	Barry M. Goldwater	Republican	27,176,799	38.5	52	
1968	**RICHARD M. NIXON (N.Y.)**	Republican	31,770,237	43.4	301	60.9
	Hubert H. Humphrey	Democratic	31,270,533	42.7	191	
	George Wallace	American Indep.	9,906,141	13.5	46	
1972	**RICHARD M. NIXON (N.Y.)**	Republican	47,169,911	60.7	520	55.2
	George S. McGovern	Democratic	29,170,383	37.5	17	
	Other	—	—		1	
1976	**JIMMY CARTER (Ga.)**	Democratic	40,828,587	50.0	297	53.5
	Gerald R. Ford	Republican	39,147,613	47.9	241	
	Other	—	1,575,459	2.1	—	
1980	**RONALD REAGAN (Calif.)**	Republican	43,901,812	50.7	489	54.0
	Jimmy Carter	Democratic	35,483,820	41.0	49	
	John B. Anderson	Independent	5,719,722	6.6	—	
	Ed Clark	Libertarian	921,188	1.1	—	
1984	**RONALD REAGAN (Calif.)**	Republican	54,455,075	59.0	525	53.1
	Walter Mondale	Democratic	37,577,185	41.0	13	
1988	**GEORGE BUSH (Texas)**	Republican	47,946,422	54.0	426	50.2
	Michael S. Dukakis	Democratic	41,016,429	46.0	112	
1992	**WILLIAM J. CLINTON (Ark.)**	Democratic	44,908,254	42.3	370	55.9
	George Bush	Republican	39,102,282	37.4	168	
	H. Ross Perot	Independent	19,721,433	18.9	—	
1996	**WILLIAM J. CLINTON (Ark.)**	Democratic	47,401,185	49.2	379	49.0
	Robert Dole	Republican	39,197,469	40.7	159	
	H. Ross Perot	Independent	8,085,294	8.4	—	
2000	**GEORGE W. BUSH (Texas)**	Republican	50,456,062	47.8	271	51.2
	Al Gore	Democratic	50,996,862	48.4	267	
	Ralph Nader	Green Party	2,858,843	2.7	—	
	Patrick J. Buchanan	—	438,760	.4	—	

PRESIDENTS, VICE PRESIDENTS, AND SECRETARIES OF STATE

The Washington Administration (1789–1797)

Vice President	John Adams	1789–1797
Secretary of State	Thomas Jefferson	1789–1793
	Edmund Randolph	1794–1795
	Timothy Pickering	1795–1797

The John Adams Administration (1797–1801)

Vice President	Thomas Jefferson	1797–1801
Secretary of State	Timothy Pickering	1797–1800
	John Marshall	1800–1801

The Jefferson Administration (1801–1809)

Vice President	Aaron Burr	1801–1805
	George Clinton	1805–1809
Secretary of State	James Madison	1801–1809

The Madison Administration (1809–1817)

Vice President	George Clinton	1809–1813
	Elbridge Gerry	1813–1817
Secretary of State	Robert Smith	1809–1811
	James Monroe	1811–1817

The Monroe Administration (1817–1825)

Vice President	Daniel Tompkins	1817–1825
Secretary of State	John Quincy Adams	1817–1825

The John Quincy Adams Administration (1825–1829)

Vice President	John C. Calhoun	1825–1829
Secretary of State	Henry Clay	1825–1829

The Jackson Administration (1829–1837)

Vice President	John C. Calhoun	1829–1833
	Martin Van Buren	1833–1837
Secretary of State	Martin Van Buren	1829–1831
	Edward Livingston	1831–1833
	Louis McLane	1833–1834
	John Forsyth	1834–1837

The Van Buren Administration (1837–1841)

Vice President	Richard M. Johnson	1837–1841
Secretary of State	John Forsyth	1837–1841

The William Harrison Administration (1841)

Vice President	John Tyler	1841
Secretary of State	Daniel Webster	1841

The Tyler Administration (1841–1845)

Vice President	None	
Secretary of State	Daniel Webster	1841–1843
	Hugh S. Legaré	1843
	Abel P. Upshur	1843–1844
	John C. Calhoun	1844–1845

The Polk Administration (1845–1849)

Vice President	George M. Dallas	1845–1849
Secretary of State	James Buchanan	1845–1849

The Taylor Administration (1849–1850)

Vice President	Millard Fillmore	1849–1850
Secretary of State	John M. Clayton	1849–1850

The Fillmore Administration (1850–1853)

Vice President	None	
Secretary of State	Daniel Webster	1850–1852
	Edward Everett	1852–1853

The Pierce Administration (1853–1857)

Vice President	William R. King	1853–1857
Secretary of State	William L. Marcy	1853–1857

The Buchanan Administration (1857–1861)

Vice President	John C. Breckinridge	1857–1861
Secretary of State	Lewis Cass	1857–1860
	Jeremiah S. Black	1860–1861

The Lincoln Administration (1861–1865)

Vice President	Hannibal Hamlin	1861–1865
	Andrew Johnson	1865
Secretary of State	William H. Seward	1861–1865

The Andrew Johnson Administration (1865–1869)

Vice President	None	
Secretary of State	William H. Seward	1865–1869

The Grant Administration (1869–1877)

Vice President	Schuyler Colfax	1869–1873
	Henry Wilson	1873–1877
Secretary of State	Elihu B. Washburne	1869
	Hamilton Fish	1869–1877

The Hayes Administration (1877–1881)

Vice President	William A. Wheeler	1877–1881
Secretary of State	William M. Evarts	1877–1881

The Garfield Administration (1881)

Vice President	Chester A. Arthur	1881
Secretary of State	James G. Blaine	1881

The Arthur Administration (1881–1885)

Vice President	None	
Secretary of State	F. T. Frelinghuysen	1881–1885

The Cleveland Administration (1885–1889)

Vice President	Thomas A. Hendricks	1885–1889
Secretary of State	Thomas F. Bayard	1885–1889

The Benjamin Harrison Administration (1889–1893)

Vice President	Levi P. Morton	1889–1893
Secretary of State	James G. Blaine	1889–1892
	John W. Foster	1892–1893

The Cleveland Administration (1893–1897)

Vice President	Adlai E. Stevenson	1893–1897
Secretary of State	Walter Q. Gresham	1893–1895
	Richard Olney	1895–1897

The McKinley Administration (1897–1901)

Vice President	Garret A. Hobart	1897–1901
	Theodore Roosevelt	1901
Secretary of State	John Sherman	1897–1898
	William R. Day	1898
	John Hay	1898–1901

The Theodore Roosevelt Administration (1901–1909)

Vice President	Charles Fairbanks	1905–1909
Secretary of State	John Hay	1901–1905
	Elihu Root	1905–1909
	Robert Bacon	1909

The Taft Administration
(1909–1913)

Vice President	James S. Sherman	1909–1913
Secretary of State	Philander C. Knox	1909–1913

The Wilson Administration
(1913–1921)

Vice President	Thomas R. Marshall	1913–1921
Secretary of State	William J. Bryan	1913–1915
	Robert Lansing	1915–1920
	Bainbridge Colby	1920–1921

The Harding Administration
(1921–1923)

Vice President	Calvin Coolidge	1921–1923
Secretary of State	Charles E. Hughes	1921–1923

The Coolidge Administration
(1923–1929)

Vice President	Charles G. Dawes	1925–1929
Secretary of State	Charles E. Hughes	1923–1925
	Frank B. Kellogg	1925–1929

The Hoover Administration
(1929–1933)

Vice President	Charles Curtis	1929–1933
Secretary of State	Henry L. Stimson	1929–1933

The Franklin D. Roosevelt Administration (1933–1945)

Vice President	John Nance Garner	1933–1941
	Henry A. Wallace	1941–1945
	Harry S. Truman	1945
Secretary of State	Cordell Hull	1933–1944
	Edward R. Stettinius Jr.	1944–1945

The Truman Administration
(1945–1953)

Vice President	Alben W. Barkley	1949–1953
Secretary of State	Edward R. Stettinius Jr.	1945
	James F. Byrnes	1945–1947
	George C. Marshall	1947–1949
	Dean G. Acheson	1949–1953

The Eisenhower Administration
(1953–1961)

Vice President	Richard M. Nixon	1953–1961
Secretary of State	John Foster Dulles	1953–1959
	Christian A. Herter	1959–1961

The Kennedy Administration
(1961–1963)

Vice President	Lyndon B. Johnson	1961–1963
Secretary of State	Dean Rusk	1961–1963

The Lyndon Johnson Administration (1963–1969)

Vice President	Hubert H. Humphrey	1965–1969
Secretary of State	Dean Rusk	1963–1969

The Nixon Administration
(1969–1974)

Vice President	Spiro T. Agnew	1969–1973
	Gerald R. Ford	1973–1974
Secretary of State	William P. Rogers	1969–1973
	Henry A. Kissinger	1973–1974

The Ford Administration
(1974–1977)

Vice President	Nelson A. Rockefeller	1974–1977
Secretary of State	Henry A. Kissinger	1974–1977

The Carter Administration (1977–1981)

Vice President	Walter F. Mondale	1977–1981
Secretary of State	Cyrus R. Vance	1977–1980
	Edmund Muskie	1980–1981

The Reagan Administration (1981–1989)

Vice President	George H. W. Bush	1981–1989
Secretary of State	Alexander M. Haig	1981–1982
	George P. Shultz	1982–1989

The George H. W. Bush Administration (1989–1993)

Vice President	J. Danforth Quayle	1989–1993
Secretary of State	James A. Baker III	1989–1992
	Lawrence S. Eagleburger	1992–1993

The Clinton Administration (1993–2001)

Vice President	Albert Gore	1993–2001
Secretary of State	Warren M. Christopher	1993–1997
	Madeleine K. Albright	1997–2001

The George W. Bush Administration (2001–)

| Vice President | Dick Cheney | 2001– |
| Secretary of State | Colin Powell | 2001– |

ADMISSION OF STATES TO THE UNION

State	Date of Admission
Delaware	December 7, 1787
Pennsylvania	December 12, 1787
New Jersey	December 18, 1787
Georgia	January 2, 1788
Connecticut	January 9, 1788
Massachusetts	February 6, 1788
Maryland	April 28, 1788
South Carolina	May 23, 1788
New Hampshire	June 21, 1788
Virginia	June 25, 1788
New York	July 26, 1788
North Carolina	November 21, 1789
Rhode Island	May 29, 1790
Vermont	March 4, 1791
Kentucky	June 1, 1792
Tennessee	June 1, 1796
Ohio	March 1, 1803
Louisiana	April 30, 1812
Indiana	December 11, 1816
Mississippi	December 10, 1817
Illinois	December 3, 1818
Alabama	December 14, 1819
Maine	March 15, 1820
Missouri	August 10, 1821
Arkansas	June 15, 1836

State	Date of Admission
Michigan	January 16, 1837
Florida	March 3, 1845
Texas	December 29, 1845
Iowa	December 28, 1846
Wisconsin	May 29, 1848
California	September 9, 1850
Minnesota	May 11, 1858
Oregon	February 14, 1859
Kansas	January 29, 1861
West Virginia	June 19, 1863
Nevada	October 31, 1864
Nebraska	March 1, 1867
Colorado	August 1, 1876
North Dakota	November 2, 1889
South Dakota	November 2, 1889
Montana	November 8, 1889
Washington	November 11, 1889
Idaho	July 3, 1890
Wyoming	July 10, 1890
Utah	January 4, 1896
Oklahoma	November 16, 1907
New Mexico	January 6, 1912
Arizona	February 14, 1912
Alaska	January 3, 1959
Hawaii	August 21, 1959

SUPREME COURT JUSTICES

Name	Service	Appointed by
John Jay*	1789–1795	Washington
James Wilson	1789–1798	Washington
John Blair	1789–1796	Washington
John Rutledge	1790–1791	Washington
William Cushing	1790–1810	Washington
James Iredell	1790–1799	Washington
Thomas Johnson	1791–1793	Washington
William Paterson	1793–1806	Washington
John Rutledge†	1795	Washington
Samuel Chase	1796–1811	Washington
Oliver Ellsworth	1796–1799	Washington
Bushrod Washington	1798–1829	J. Adams
Alfred Moore	1799–1804	J. Adams
John Marshall	1801–1835	J. Adams
William Johnson	1804–1834	Jefferson
Henry B. Livingston	1806–1823	Jefferson
Thomas Todd	1807–1826	Jefferson
Gabriel Duval	1811–1836	Madison
Joseph Story	1811–1845	Madison
Smith Thompson	1823–1843	Monroe
Robert Trimble	1826–1828	J. Q. Adams
John McLean	1829–1861	Jackson
Henry Baldwin	1830–1844	Jackson
James M. Wayne	1835–1867	Jackson
Roger B. Taney	1836–1864	Jackson
Philip P. Barbour	1836–1841	Jackson
John Catron	1837–1865	Van Buren
John McKinley	1837–1852	Van Buren
Peter V. Daniel	1841–1860	Van Buren
Samuel Nelson	1845–1872	Tyler
Levi Woodbury	1845–1851	Polk
Robert C. Grier	1846–1870	Polk
Benjamin R. Curtis	1851–1857	Fillmore
John A. Campbell	1853–1861	Pierce
Nathan Clifford	1858–1881	Buchanan
Noah H. Swayne	1862–1881	Lincoln
Samuel F. Miller	1862–1890	Lincoln

*Chief Justices appear in bold type.

†Acting Chief Justice; Senate refused to confirm appointment.

Name	Service	Appointed by
David Davis	1862–1877	Lincoln
Stephen J. Field	1863–1897	Lincoln
Salmon P. Chase	1864–1873	Lincoln
William Strong	1870–1880	Grant
Joseph P. Bradley	1870–1892	Grant
Ward Hunt	1873–1882	Grant
Morrison R. Waite	1874–1888	Grant
John M. Harlan	1877–1911	Hayes
William B. Woods	1880–1887	Hayes
Stanley Matthews	1881–1889	Garfield
Horace Gray	1882–1902	Arthur
Samuel Blatchford	1882–1893	Arthur
Lucious Q. C. Lamar	1888–1893	Cleveland
Melville W. Fuller	1888–1910	Cleveland
David J. Brewer	1889–1910	B. Harrison
Henry B. Brown	1890–1906	B. Harrison
George Shiras	1892–1903	B. Harrison
Howell E. Jackson	1893–1895	B. Harrison
Edward D. White	1894–1910	Cleveland
Rufus W. Peckham	1896–1909	Cleveland
Joseph McKenna	1898–1925	McKinley
Oliver W. Holmes	1902–1932	T. Roosevelt
William R. Day	1903–1922	T. Roosevelt
William H. Moody	1906–1910	T. Roosevelt
Horace H. Lurton	1910–1914	Taft
Charles E. Hughes	1910–1916	Taft
Willis Van Devanter	1910–1937	Taft
Joseph R. Lamar	1911–1916	Taft
Edward D. White	1910–1921	Taft
Mahlon Pitney	1912–1922	Taft
James C. McReynolds	1914–1941	Wilson
Louis D. Brandeis	1916–1939	Wilson
John H. Clarke	1916–1922	Wilson
William H. Taft	1921–1930	Harding
George Sutherland	1922–1938	Harding

Name	Service	Appointed by
Pierce Butler	1923–1939	Harding
Edward T. Sanford	1923–1930	Harding
Harlan F. Stone	1925–1941	Coolidge
Charles E. Hughes	1930–1941	Hoover
Owen J. Roberts	1930–1945	Hoover
Benjamin N. Cardozo	1932–1938	Hoover
Hugo L. Black	1937–1971	F. Roosevelt
Stanley F. Reed	1938–1957	F. Roosevelt
Felix Frankfurter	1939–1962	F. Roosevelt
William O. Douglas	1939–1975	F. Roosevelt
Frank Murphy	1940–1949	F. Roosevelt
Harlan F. Stone	1941–1946	F. Roosevelt
James F. Byrnes	1941–1942	F. Roosevelt
Robert H. Jackson	1941–1954	F. Roosevelt
Wiley B. Rutledge	1943–1949	F. Roosevelt
Harold H. Burton	1945–1958	Truman
Frederick M. Vinson	1946–1953	Truman
Tom C. Clark	1949–1967	Truman
Sherman Minton	1949–1956	Truman
Earl Warren	1953–1969	Eisenhower
John Marshall Harlan	1955–1971	Eisenhower
William J. Brennan Jr.	1956–1990	Eisenhower
Charles E. Whittaker	1957–1962	Eisenhower
Potter Stewart	1958–1981	Eisenhower
Byron R. White	1962–1993	Kennedy
Arthur J. Goldberg	1962–1965	Kennedy
Abe Fortas	1965–1969	L. Johnson
Thurgood Marshall	1967–1991	L. Johnson
Warren E. Burger	1969–1986	Nixon
Harry A. Blackmun	1970–1994	Nixon
Lewis F. Powell Jr.	1972–1988	Nixon
William H. Rehnquist	1972–1986	Nixon
John Paul Stevens	1975–	Ford
Sandra Day O'Connor	1981–	Reagan
William H. Rehnquist	1986–	Reagan
Antonin Scalia	1986–	Reagan
Anthony M. Kennedy	1988–	Reagan
David H. Souter	1990–	Bush
Clarence Thomas	1991–	Bush
Ruth Bader Ginsburg	1993–	Clinton
Stephen Breyer	1994–	Clinton

SIGNIFICANT SUPREME COURT CASES

Marbury v. Madison (1803)

This case established the right of the Supreme Court to review the constitutionality of laws. The decision involved judicial appointments made during the last hours of the administration of President John Adams. Some commissions, including that of William Marbury, had not yet been delivered when President Thomas Jefferson took office. Infuriated by the last-minute nature of Adams's Federalist appointments, Jefferson refused to send the undelivered commissions out, and Marbury decided to sue. The Supreme Court, presided over by John Marshall, a Federalist who had assisted Adams in the judicial appointments, ruled that although Marbury's commission was valid and the new president should have delivered it, the Court could not compel him to do so. The Court based its reasoning on a finding that the grounds of Marbury's suit, resting in the Judiciary Act of 1789, were in conflict with the Constitution.

For the first time, the Court had overturned a national law on the grounds that it was unconstitutional. John Marshall had quietly established the concept of judicial review: The Supreme Court had given itself the authority to nullify acts of the other branches of the federal government. Although the Constitution provides for judicial review, the Court had not exercised this power before and did not use it again until 1857. It seems likely that if the Court had waited until 1857 to use this power, it would have been difficult to establish.

McCulloch v. Maryland (1819)

In 1816, Congress authorized the creation of a national bank. To protect its own banks from competition with a branch of the national bank in Baltimore, the state legislature of Maryland placed a tax of 2 percent on all notes issued by any bank operating in Maryland that was not chartered by the state. McCulloch, cashier of the Baltimore branch of the Bank of the United States, was convicted for refusing to pay the tax. Under the leadership of Chief Justice John Marshall, the Court ruled that the federal government had the power to establish a bank, even though that specific authority was not mentioned in the Constitution.

Marshall maintained that the authority could be reasonably implied from Article 1, section 8, which gives Congress the power to make all laws that are necessary and proper to execute the enumerated powers. Marshall also held that Maryland could not tax the national bank because in a conflict between federal and state laws, the federal law must take precedence. Thus he established the principles of implied powers and federal supremacy, both of which set a precedent for subsequent expansion of federal power at the expense of the states.

Scott v. Sandford (1857)

Dred Scott was a slave who sued for his own and his family's freedom on the grounds, that, with his master, he had traveled to and lived in free territory that did not allow slavery. When his case reached the Supreme Court, the justices saw an opportunity to settle once and for all the vexing question of slavery in the territories. The Court's decision in this case proved that it enjoyed no special immunity from the sectional and partisan passions of the time. Five of the nine justices were from the South and seven were Democrats.

Chief Justice Roger B. Taney hated Republicans and detested racial equality; his decision reflects those prejudices. He wrote an opinion not only declaring that Scott was still a slave but also claiming that the Constitution denied citizenship or rights to blacks, that Congress had no right to exclude slavery from the territories, and that the Missouri Compromise was unconstitutional. While southern Democrats gloated over this seven-to-two decision, sectional tensions were further inflamed and the young Republican Party's claim that a hostile "slave power" was conspiring to destroy northern liberties was given further credence. The decision brought the nation closer to civil war and is generally regarded as the worst decision ever rendered by the Supreme Court.

Butchers' Benevolent Association of New Orleans v. Crescent City Livestock Landing and Slaughterhouse Co. (1873)

The *Slaughterhouse* cases, as the cases docketed under the *Butchers'* title were known, were the first legal test of the Fourteenth Amendment. To cut down on cases of cholera believed to be caused by contaminated water, the state of Louisiana prohibited the slaughter of livestock in New Orleans except in one slaughterhouse, effectively giving that slaughterhouse a monopoly. Other New Orleans butchers claimed that the state had deprived them of their occupation without due process of law, thus violating the Fourteenth Amendment.

In a five-to-four decision, the Court upheld the Louisiana law, declaring that the Fourteenth Amendment protected only the rights of federal citizenship, like voting in federal elections and interstate travel. The federal government thus was not obliged to protect basic civil rights from violation by state governments. This decision would have significant implications for African Americans and their struggle for civil rights in the twentieth century.

United States v. E. C. Knight Co. (1895)

Also known as the *Sugar Trust* case, this was among the first cases to reveal the weakness of the Sherman Antitrust Act in the hands of a pro-business Supreme Court. In 1895, American Sugar Refining Company purchased four other sugar producers, including the E. C. Knight Company, and thus took control of more than 98 percent of the sugar refining in the United States. In an effort to limit monopoly, the government brought suit against all five of the companies for violating the Sherman Antitrust Act, which outlawed trusts and other business combinations in restraint of trade. The Court dismissed the suit, however, arguing that the law applied only to commerce and not to manufacturing, defining the latter as a local concern and not part of the interstate commerce that the government could regulate.

Plessy v. Ferguson (1896)

African American Homer Plessy challenged a Louisiana law that required segregation on trains passing through the state. After ensuring that the railroad and the conductor knew that he was of mixed race (Plessy appeared to be white but under the racial code of Louisiana was classified as "colored" because he was one-eighth black), he refused to move to the "colored only" section of the coach. The Court ruled against Plessy by a vote of seven to one, declaring that "separate but equal" facilities were permissible according to section 1 of the Fourteenth Amendment, which calls upon the states to provide "equal protection of the laws" to anyone within their jurisdiction. Although the case was viewed as relatively insignificant at the time, it cast a long shadow over several decades.

Initially, the decision was viewed as a victory for segregationists, but in the 1930s and 1940s civil rights advocates referred to the doctrine of "separate but equal" in their efforts to end segregation. They argued that segregated institutions and accommodations were often *not* equal to those available to whites, and finally succeeded in overturning *Plessy* in *Brown v. Board of Education* in 1954 (see p. A-51).

Lochner v. New York (1905)

In this case, the Court ruled against a New York state law that prohibited employees from working in bakeries more than ten hours a day or sixty hours a week. The purpose of the law was to protect the health of workers, but the Court ruled that it was unconstitutional because it violated "freedom of contract" implicitly protected by the due process clause of the Fourteenth Amendment. Most of the justices believed strongly in a laissez-faire economic system that favored survival of the fittest. They felt that government protection of workers interfered with this system. In a dissenting opinion, Justice Oliver Wendell Holmes accused the majority of distorting the Constitution and of deciding the case on "an economic theory which a large part of the country does not entertain."

Muller v. Oregon (1908)

In 1905, Curt Muller, owner of a Portland, Oregon, laundry, demanded that one of his employees, Mrs. Elmer Gotcher, work more than the ten hours allowed as a maximum workday for women under Oregon law. Muller argued that the law violated his "freedom of contract" as established in prior Supreme Court decisions.

Progressive lawyer Louis D. Brandeis defended the Oregon law by arguing that a state could be justified in abridging freedom of contract when the health, safety, and welfare of workers was at issue. His innovative strategy drew on ninety-five pages of excerpts from factory and medical reports to substantiate his argument that there was a direct connection between long hours and the health of women and thus the health of the nation. In a unanimous decision, the Court upheld the Oregon law, but later generations of women fighting for equality would question the strategy of arguing that women's reproductive role entitled them to special treatment.

Schenck v. United States (1919)

During World War I, Charles Schenck and other members of the Socialist Party printed and mailed out flyers urging young men who were subject to the draft to oppose the war in Europe. In upholding the conviction of Schenck for publishing a pamphlet urging draft resistance, Justice Oliver Wendell Holmes established the "clear and present danger" test for freedom of speech. Such utterances as Schenck's during a time of national peril, Holmes wrote, could be considered the equivalent of shouting "Fire!" in a crowded theater. Congress had the right to protect the public against such an incitement to panic, the Court ruled in a unanimous decision. But the analogy was a false one. Schenck's pamphlet had little power to provoke a public firmly opposed to its message. Although Holmes later modified his position to state that the danger must relate to an immediate evil and a specific action, the "clear and present danger" test laid the groundwork for those who later sought to limit First Amendment freedoms.

Schechter Poultry Corp. v. United States (1935)

During the Great Depression, the National Industrial Recovery Act (NIRA), which was passed under President Franklin D. Roosevelt, established fair competition codes that were designed to help businesses. The Schechter brothers of New York City, who sold chickens, were convicted of violating the codes. The Supreme Court ruled that the NIRA unconstitutionally conferred legislative power on an administrative agency and overstepped the limits of federal power to regulate interstate commerce. The decision was a significant blow to the New Deal recovery program, demonstrating both historic American resistance to economic planning and the refusal of the business community to yield its autonomy unless it was forced to do so.

Brown v. Board of Education (1954)

In 1950, the families of eight Topeka, Kansas, children sued the Topeka Board of Education. The children were blacks who lived within walking distance of a whites-only school. The segregated school system required them to take a time-consuming, inconvenient, and dangerous route to get to a black school, and their parents argued that there was no reason their children should not be allowed to attend the nearest school. By the time the case reached the Supreme Court, it had been joined with similar cases regarding segregated schools in other states and the District of Columbia. A team of lawyers from the National Association for the Advancement of Colored People (NAACP), led by Thurgood Marshall (who would later be appointed to the Supreme Court), urged the Court to overturn the fifty-eight-year-old precedent established in *Plessy v. Ferguson*, which had enshrined "separate but equal" as the law of the land. A unanimous Court, led by Chief Justice Earl Warren, declared that "separate educa-

tional facilities are inherently unequal" and thus violate the Fourteenth Amendment. In 1955, the Court called for desegregation "with all deliberate speed" but established no deadline.

Roth v. United States (1957)

In 1957, New Yorker Samuel Roth was convicted of sending obscene materials through the mail in a case that ultimately reached the Supreme Court. With a six-to-three vote, the Court reaffirmed the historical view that obscenity is not protected by the First Amendment. Yet it broke new ground by declaring that a work could be judged obscene only if, "taken as a whole," it appealed to the "prurient interest" of "the average person."

Prior to this case, work could be judged obscene if portions were thought able to "deprave and corrupt" the most susceptible part of an audience (such as children). Thus, serious works of literature such as Theodore Dreiser's *An American Tragedy*, which was banned in Boston when first published, had received no protection. Although this decision continued to pose problems of definition, it did help to protect most works that attempt to convey ideas, even if those ideas have to do with sex, from the threat of obscenity laws.

Engel v. Vitale (1962)

In 1959, five parents with ten children in the New Hyde Park, New York, school system sued the school board. The parents argued that the so-called Regents' Prayer that public school students in New York recited at the start of every school day violated the doctrine of separation of church and state outlined in the First Amendment. In 1962, the Supreme Court voted six to one in favor of banning the Regents' Prayer.

The decision threw the religious community into an uproar. Many religious leaders expressed dismay and even shock; others welcomed the decision. Several efforts to introduce an amendment allowing school prayer have failed. Subsequent Supreme Court decisions have banned reading of the Bible in public schools. The Court has also declared mandatory flag saluting to be an infringement of religious and personal freedoms.

Gideon v. Wainwright (1963)

When Clarence Earl Gideon was tried for breaking into a poolroom, the state of Florida rejected his demand for a court-appointed lawyer as guaranteed by the Sixth Amendment. In 1963, the Court upheld his demand in a unanimous decision that established the obligation of states to provide attorneys for indigent defendants in felony cases. Prior to this decision, the right to an attorney had applied only to federal cases, not state cases. In its ruling in *Gideon v. Wainwright*, the Supreme Court applied the Sixth through the Fourteenth Amendments to the states. In 1972, the Supreme Court extended the right to legal representation to all cases, not just felony cases, in its decision in *Argersinger v. Hamlin*.

Griswold v. Connecticut (1965)

With a vote of seven to two, the Supreme Court reversed an "uncommonly silly law" (in the words of Justice Potter Stewart) that made it a crime for anyone in the state of Connecticut to use any drug, article, or instrument to prevent conception. *Griswold* became a landmark case because here, for the first time, the Court explicitly invested with full constitutional status "fundamental personal rights," such as the right to privacy, that were not expressly enumerated in the Bill of Rights. The majority opinion in the case held that the law infringed on the constitutionally protected right to privacy of married persons.

Although the Court had previously recognized fundamental rights not expressly enumerated in the Bill of Rights (such as the right to procreate in *Skinner v. Oklahoma* in 1942), *Griswold* was the first time the Court had justified, at length, the practice of investing such unenumerated rights with full constitutional status. Writing for the majority, Justice William O. Douglas explained that the First, Third, Fourth, Fifth, and Ninth Amendments imply "zones of privacy" that are the foundation for the general right to privacy affirmed in this case.

Miranda v. Arizona (1966)

In 1966, the Supreme Court, by a vote of five to four, upheld the case of Ernesto Miranda, who appealed a murder conviction on the grounds that police had gotten him to confess without giving him access to an attorney. The *Miranda* case was the culmination of the Court's efforts to find a meaningful way of determining whether police had used due process in extracting confessions from people accused of crimes. The *Miranda* decision upholds the Fifth Amendment protection against self-incrimination outside the courtroom and requires that suspects be given what came to be known as the "Miranda warning," which advises them of their right to remain silent and warns them that anything they say might be used against them in a court of law. Suspects must also be told that they have a right to counsel.

New York Times Co. v. United States (1971)

With a six-to-three vote, the Court upheld the right of the *New York Times* and the *Washington Post* to print materials from the so-called *Pentagon Papers*, a secret government study of U.S. policy in Vietnam, leaked by dissident Pentagon official Daniel Ellsberg. Since the papers revealed deception and secrecy in the conduct of the Vietnam War, the Nixon administration had quickly obtained a court injunction against their further publication, claiming that suppression was in the interests of national security. The Supreme Court's decision overturning the injunction strengthened the First Amendment protection of freedom of the press.

Furman v. Georgia (1972)

In this case, the Supreme Court ruled five to four that the death penalty for murder or rape violated the cruel and unusual punishment clause of the Eighth Amendment because the manner in which the death penalty was meted out was irregular, "arbitrary," and "cruel." In response, most states enacted new statutes that allow the death penalty to be imposed only after a postconviction hearing at which evidence must be presented to show that "aggravating" or "mitigating" circumstances were factors in the crime. If the postconviction hearing hands down a death sentence, the case is automatically reviewed by an appellate court.

In 1976, the Court ruled in *Gregg v. Georgia* that these statutes were not unconstitutional. In 1977, the Court ruled in *Coker v. Georgia* that the death penalty for rape was "disproportionate and excessive," thus allowing the death penalty only in murder cases. Between 1977 and 1991, some 150 people were executed in the United States. Public opinion polls indicate that about 70 percent of Americans favor the death penalty for murder. Capital punishment continues to generate controversy, however, as opponents argue that there is no evidence that the death penalty deters crime and that its use reflects racial and economic bias.

Roe v. Wade (1973)

In 1973, the Court found, by a vote of seven to two, that state laws restricting access to abortion violated a woman's right to privacy guaranteed by the due process clause of the Fourteenth Amendment. The decision was based on the cases of two women living in Texas and Georgia, both states with stringent anti-abortion laws. Upholding the individual rights of both women and physicians, the Court ruled that the Constitution protects the right to abortion and that states cannot prohibit abortions in the early stages of pregnancy.

The decision stimulated great debate among legal scholars as well as the public. Critics argued that since abortion was never addressed in the Constitution, the Court could not claim that legislation violated fundamental values of the Constitution. They also argued that since abortion was a medical procedure with an acknowledged impact on a fetus, it was inappropriate to invoke the kind of "privacy" argument that was used in *Griswold v. Connecticut* (see p. A-52), which was about contraception. Defenders suggested that the case should be argued as a case of gender discrimination, which did violate the equal protection clause of the Fourteenth Amendment. Others said that the right to privacy in sexual matters was indeed a fundamental right.

Regents of the University of California v. Bakke (1978)

When Allan Bakke, a white man, was not accepted by the University of California Medical School at Davis, he filed a lawsuit alleging that the admissions program, which set up different standards for test scores and grades for members of certain minority groups, violated the Civil Rights Act of 1964, which outlawed racial or ethnic preferences in programs supported by federal funds. Bakke further argued that the university's practice of setting aside spaces for minority applicants denied him equal protection as guaranteed by the Fourteenth Amendment. In a five-to-four decision, the Court ordered that Bakke be admitted to the medical school, yet it sanctioned affirmative action programs to attack the results of past discrimination as long as strict quotas or racial classifications were not involved.

Webster v. Reproductive Health Services (1989)

By a vote of five to four, the Court upheld several restrictions on the availability of abortions as imposed by Missouri state law. It upheld restrictions on the use of state property, including public hospitals, for abortions. It also upheld a provision requiring physicians to perform tests to determine the viability of a fetus that a doctor judged to be twenty weeks of age or older. Although the justices did not go so far as to overturn the decision in *Roe v. Wade* (see p. A-52), the ruling galvanized interest groups on both sides of the abortion issue. Opponents of abortion pressured state legislatures to place greater restrictions on abortions; those who favored availability of abortion tried to mobilize public action by presenting the decision as a major threat to the right to choose abortion.

Cipollone v. Liggett (1992)

In a seven-to-two decision, the Court ruled in favor of the family of Rose Cipollone, a woman who died of lung cancer after smoking for forty-two years. The Court rejected arguments that health warnings on cigarette packages protected tobacco manufacturers from personal injury suits filed by smokers who contract cancer and other serious illnesses.

Miller v. Johnson (1995)

In a five-to-four decision, the Supreme Court ruled that voting districts created to increase the voting power of racial minorities were unconstitutional. The decision threatens dozens of congressional, state, and local voting districts that were drawn to give minorities more representation as had been required by the Justice Department under the Voting Rights Act. If states are required to redraw voting districts, the number of black members of Congress could be sharply reduced.

Romer v. Evans (1996)

In a six-to-three decision, the Court struck down a Colorado amendment that forbade local governments from banning discrimination against homosexuals. Writing for the majority, Justice Anthony Kennedy said that forbidding communities from taking action to protect the rights of homosexuals and not of other groups unlawfully deprived gays and lesbians of opportunities that were available to others. Kennedy based the decision on the guarantee of equal protection under the law as provided by the Fourteenth Amendment.

Bush v. Palm Beach County Canvassing Board (2000)

In a bitterly argued five-to-four decision, the Court reversed the Florida Supreme Court's previous order for a hand recount of contested presidential election ballots in several counties of that battleground state, effectively securing the presidency for Texas Republican Governor, George W. Bush. The ruling ended a protracted legal dispute between presidential candidates Bush and Vice President Al Gore while inflaming public opinion: For the first time since 1888, a president who failed to win the popular vote took office. Critics charged that the Supreme Court had applied partisanship rather than objectivity to the case, pointing out that the decision went against this Court's customary interpretation of the Constitution to favor state over federal authority.

THE AMERICAN ECONOMY

THESE FOUR "SNAPSHOTS" of the U.S. economy show significant changes over the past century and a half. In 1849, the agricultural sector was by far the largest contributor to the economy. By the turn of the century, with advances in technology and an abundance of cheap labor and raw materials, the country had experienced remarkable industrial expansion and the manufacturing industries dominated. By 1950, the service sector had increased significantly, fueled by the consumerism of the 1920s and the post–World War II years, and the economy was becoming more diversified. Note that by 1990, government's share in the economy was more than 10 percent and activity in both the trade and manufacturing sectors had declined, partly as a result of competition from Western Europe and Asia.

Main Sectors of the U.S. Economy: 1849, 1899, 1950, 1997

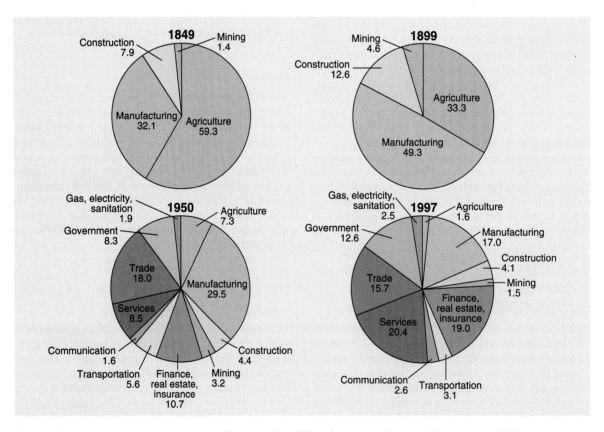

Source: Historical Statistics of the U.S., Colonial Times to 1970 (1975) and Statistical Abstract of the U.S., 1999 (1999).

Federal Spending and the Economy, 1790–1998

Year	Gross National Product (in billions)	Foreign Trade (in millions)		Federal Budget (in billions)	Federal Surplus/Deficit (in billions)	Federal Debt (in billions)
		Exports	Imports			
1790	NA	20	23	0.004	0.00015	0.076
1800	NA	71	91	0.011	0.0006	0.083
1810	NA	67	85	0.008	0.0012	0.053
1820	NA	70	74	0.018	−0.0004	0.091
1830	NA	74	71	0.015	0.100	0.049
1840	NA	132	107	0.024	−0.005	0.004
1850	NA	152	178	0.040	0.004	0.064
1860	NA	400	362	0.063	−0.01	0.065
1870	7.4	451	462	0.310	0.10	2.4
1880	11.2	853	761	0.268	0.07	2.1
1890	13.1	910	823	0.318	0.09	1.2
1900	18.7	1,499	930	0.521	0.05	1.2
1910	35.3	1,919	1,646	0.694	−0.02	1.1
1920	91.5	8,664	5,784	6.357	0.3	24.3
1930	90.4	4,013	3,500	3.320	0.7	16.3
1940	99.7	4,030	7,433	9.6	−2.7	43.0
1950	284.8	10,816	9,125	43.1	−2.2	257.4
1960	503.7	19,600	15,046	92.2	0.3	286.3
1970	977.1	42,700	40,189	195.6	−2.8	371.0
1980	2,631.7	220,600	244,871	590.9	−73.8	907.7
1990	5,764.9	393,600	495,300	1,253.2	−221.2	3,266.1
1998	8,490.5	682,100	911,900	1,652.5	69.2	5,555.5

Source: Historical Statistics of the U.S., Colonial Times to 1970 (1975), Statistical Abstract of the U.S., 1996 (1996), and Statistical Abstract of the U.S., 1999 (1999).

A DEMOGRAPHIC PROFILE OF THE UNITED STATES AND ITS PEOPLE

POPULATION

FROM AN ESTIMATED 4,600 WHITE INHABITANTS IN 1630, the country's population grew to a total of just under 250 million in 1990. It is important to note that the U.S. census, first conducted in 1790 and the source of these figures, counted blacks, both free and slave, but did not include American Indians until 1860. The years 1790 to 1900 saw the most rapid population growth, with an average increase of 25 to 35 percent per decade. In addition to "natural" growth—birthrate exceeding death rate—immigration was also a factor in that rise, especially between 1840 and 1860, 1880 and 1890, and 1900 and 1910 (see table on page A-61). The twentieth century witnessed slower growth, partly a result of 1920s immigration restrictions and a decline in the birthrate, especially during the Depression era and the 1960s and 1970s. The U.S. population is expected to reach almost 300 million by the year 2010.

Population Growth, 1630–2000

Year	Population	Percent Increase
1630	4,600	—
1640	26,600	473.3
1650	50,400	89.1
1660	75,100	49.0
1670	111,900	49.1
1680	151,500	35.4
1690	210,400	38.9
1700	250,900	19.3
1710	331,700	32.2
1720	466,200	40.5
1730	629,400	35.0
1740	905,600	43.9
1750	1,170,800	30.0
1760	1,593,600	36.1
1770	2,148,100	34.8
1780	2,780,400	29.4
1790	3,929,214	41.3
1800	5,308,483	35.1
1810	7,239,881	36.4
1820	9,638,453	33.1
1830	12,866,020	33.5
1840	17,069,453	32.7
1850	23,191,876	35.9
1860	31,443,321	35.6
1870	39,818,449	26.6
1880	50,155,783	26.0
1890	62,947,714	25.5
1900	75,994,575	20.7
1910	91,972,266	21.0
1920	105,710,620	14.9
1930	122,775,046	16.1
1940	131,669,275	7.2
1950	150,697,361	14.5
1960	179,323,175	19.0
1970	203,302,031	13.4
1980	226,542,199	11.4
1990	248,718,301	9.8
2000	281,421,906	11.0

Source: Historical Statistics of the U.S. (1960), Historical Statistics of the U.S., Colonial Times to 1970 (1975), Statistical Abstract of the U.S., 1996 (1996), and United States Census, 2000 (2000).

VITAL STATISTICS

WITH SOME MINOR FLUCTUATIONS, the birthrate has been on a downward trend throughout the past century and a half, dipping especially low during the 1930s Depression years, when many economically hard-hit Americans postponed having children. A major exception to this decline was the steep but temporary rise nicknamed the "baby boom," which occurred during the relatively affluent post–World War II period. Improvements in health care and lifestyles have contributed to a decline in the death rate over the past century, which in turn has increased life expectancy figures. Over time, as people lived longer and the birthrate declined, the median age of Americans has increased from approximately seventeen in 1820 to thirty-three in 1990 and continues to rise.

Birthrate, 1820–2000

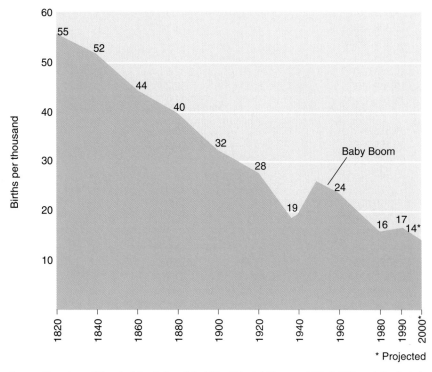

Source: Data from *Historical Statistics of the U.S., Colonial Times to 1970* (1975) and *Statistical Abstract of the U.S., 1996* (1996).

Death Rate, 1900–2000

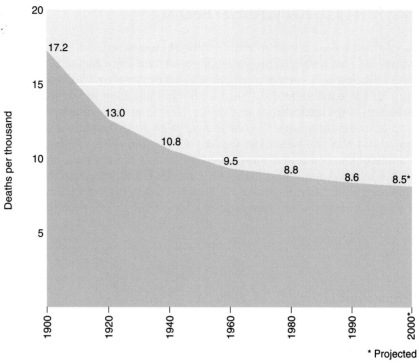

Source: Historical Statistics of the U.S., Colonial Times to 1970 (1975) and
           Statistical Abstract of the U.S., 1996 (1996).

Life Expectancy, 1900–2000

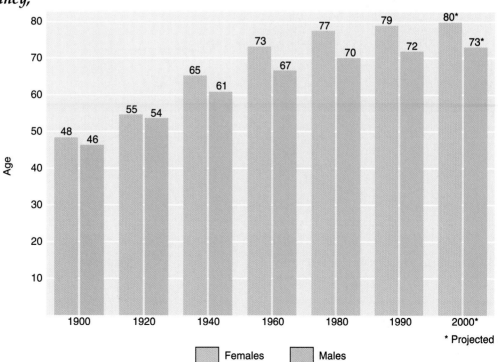

Source: Historical Statistics of the U.S., Colonial Times to 1970 (1975) and
           Statistical Abstract of the U.S., 1996 (1996).

MIGRATION AND IMMIGRATION

We tend to associate internal migration with movement westward, yet equally significant has been the movement of the nation's population from the country to the city. In 1790, the first U.S. census recorded that approximately 95 percent of the population lived in rural areas. By 1990, that figure had fallen to less than 25 percent. The decline of the agricultural way of life, late-nineteenth-century industrialization, and immigration have all contributed to increased urbanization. A more recent trend has been the migration, especially since the 1970s, of people to the Sun Belt states of the South and West, lured by factors as various as economic opportunities in the defense and high-tech industries and good weather. This migration has swelled the size of cities like Houston, Dallas, Tucson, Phoenix, and San Diego, all of which in recent years ranked among the top ten most populous U.S. cities.

Rural and Urban Population, 1750–2000

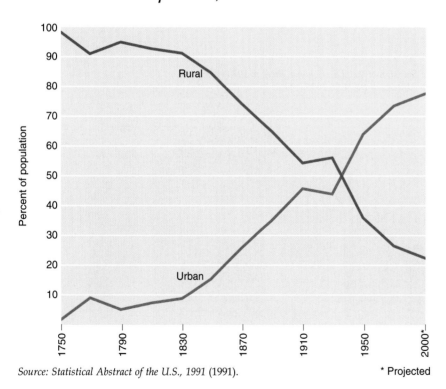

Source: *Statistical Abstract of the U.S., 1991* (1991).   * Projected

THE QUANTITY AND CHARACTER OF IMMIGRATION to the United States has varied greatly over time. During the first major influx, between 1840 and 1860, newcomers hailed primarily from northern and western Europe. From 1880 to 1915, when rates soared even more dramatically, the profile changed, with 80 percent of the "new immigration" coming from central, eastern, and southern Europe. Following World War I, strict quotas reduced the flow considerably. Note also the significant falloff during the years of the Great Depression and World War II. The sources of immigration during the last half century have changed significantly, with the majority of people coming from Latin America, the Caribbean, and Asia. The latest surge during the 1980s brought more immigrants to the United States than in any decade except 1901–1910.

Rates of Immigration, 1820–1997

Year	Number	Percent of Total Population
1821–1830	151,824	1.6
1831–1840	599,125	4.6
1841–1850	1,713,521	10.0
1851–1860	2,598,214	11.2
1861–1870	2,314,824	7.4
1871–1880	2,812,191	7.1
1881–1890	5,246,613	10.5
1891–1900	3,687,546	5.8
1901–1910	8,795,386	11.6
1911–1920	5,735,811	6.2
1921–1930	4,107,209	3.9
1931–1940	528,431	0.4
1941–1950	1,035,039	0.7
1951–1960	2,515,479	1.6
1961–1970	3,321,677	1.8
1971–1980	4,493,300	2.2
1981–1990	7,338,100	3.0
1991	1,827,167	7.2
1992	973,977	3.8
1993	904,292	3.5
1994	804,416	3.0
1995	720,461	2.7
1996	915,900	3.5
1997	798,378	3.0

Source: Historical Statistics of the U.S., Colonial Times to 1970 (1975), Statistical Abstract of the U.S., 1996 (1996), and Statistical Abstract of the U.S., 1999 (1999).

Major Trends in Immigration, 1820–1998

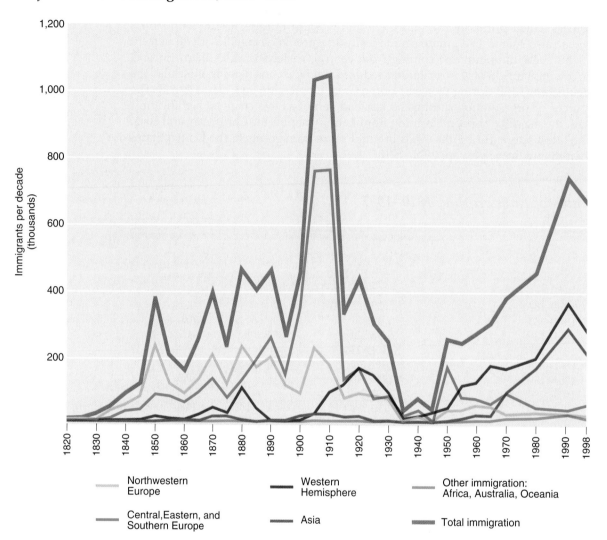

Source: *Historical Statistics of the U.S., Colonial Times to 1970* (1975) and *Statistical Abstract of the U.S., 1999* (1999).

APPENDIX III. RESEARCH RESOURCES IN U.S. HISTORY

WHILE DOING RESEARCH IN HISTORY, you will use the library to track down primary and secondary sources and to answer questions that arise as you learn more about your topic. This appendix suggests helpful indexes, references, periodicals, and sources of primary documents. It also offers an overview of electronic resources available through the Internet. The materials listed here are not carried at all libraries, but they will give you an idea of the range of sources available. Remember, too, that librarians are an extremely helpful resource. They can direct you to useful materials throughout your research process.

Bibliographies and Indexes

American Historical Association Guide to Historical Literature. 3rd ed. New York: Oxford University Press, 1995. Offers 27,000 citations to important historical literature, arranged in forty-eight sections covering theory, international history, and regional history. An indispensable guide recently updated to include current trends in historical research.

American History and Life. Santa Barbara: ABC-Clio, 1964–. Covers publications of all sorts on U.S. and Canadian history and culture in a chronological/regional format, with abstracts and alphabetical indexes. Available in computerized format. The most complete ongoing bibliography for American history.

Freidel, Frank Burt. *Harvard Guide to American History.* Cambridge: Harvard University Press, Belknap Press, 1974. Provides citations to books and articles on American history published before 1970. The first volume is arranged topically, the second chronologically. Though it does not cover current scholarship, it is a classic and remains useful for tracing older publications.

Prucha, Francis Paul. *Handbook for Research in American History: A Guide to Bibliographies and Other Reference Works.* 2nd rev. ed. Lincoln: University of Nebraska Press, 1994. Introduces a variety of research tools, including electronic ones. A good source to consult when planning an in-depth research project.

General Overviews

Dictionary of American Biography. New York: Scribner's, 1928–1937, with supplements. Gives substantial biographies of prominent Americans in history.

Dictionary of American History. New York: Scribner's, 1976. An encyclopedia of terms, places, and concepts in U.S. history; other more specialized sets include the *Encyclopedia of North American Colonies* and the *Encyclopedia of the Confederacy.*

Dictionary of Concepts in History. New York: Greenwood, 1986. Contains essays defining concepts in historiography and describing how the concepts were formed; excellent bibliographies.

Encyclopedia of American Social History. New York: Scribner's, 1993. Surveys topics such as religion, class, gender, race, popular culture, regionalism, and everyday life from pre-Columbian to modern times.

Encyclopedia of the United States in the Twentieth Century. New York: Scribner's, 1996. An ambitious overview of American cultural, social, and intellectual history in broad articles arranged topically. Each article is followed by a thorough and very useful bibliography for further research.

Specialized Information

Black Women in America: An Historical Encyclopedia. Brooklyn: Carlson, 1993. A scholarly compilation of biographical and topical articles that constitute a definitive history of African American women.

Carruth, Gordon. *The Encyclopedia of American Facts and Dates.* 10th ed. New York: HarperCollins, 1997. Covers American history chronologically from 986 to the present, offering information on treaties, battles, explorations, popular culture, philosophy, literature, and so on, mixing significant events with telling trivia. Tables allow for reviewing a year from a variety of angles. A thorough index helps pinpoint specific facts in time.

Cook, Chris. *Dictionary of Historical Terms.* 2nd ed. New York: Peter Bendrick, 1990. Covers a wide variety of terms—events, places, institutions, and topics—in history for all periods and places in a remarkably small package. A good place for quick identification of terms in the field.

Dictionary of Afro-American Slavery. New York: Greenwood, 1985. Surveys important people, events, and topics, with useful bibliographies; similar works include *Dictionary of the Vietnam War, Historical Dictionary of the New Deal*, and *Historical Dictionary of the Progressive Era.*

Knappman-Frost, Elizabeth. *The ABC-Clio Companion to Women's Progress in America.* Santa Barbara: ABC-Clio, 1994. Covers American women who were notable for their time as well as topics and organizations that have been significant in women's quest for equality. Each article is brief; there are a chronology and a bibliography at the back of the book.

United States Bureau of the Census. *Historical Statistics of the United States, Colonial Times to 1970.* Washington, D.C.: Government Printing Office, 1975. Offers vital statistics, economic figures, and social data for the United States. An index at the back helps locate tables by subject. For statistics since 1970, consult the annual *Statistical Abstract of the United States.*

Primary Resources

There are many routes to finding contemporary material for historical research. You may search your library catalog using the name of a prominent historical figure as an author; you may also find anthologies covering particular themes or periods in history. Consider also the following special materials for your research.

The Press

American Periodical Series, 1741–1900. Ann Arbor: University Microfilms, 1946–1979. Microfilm collection of periodicals from the colonial period to the turn of the century. An index identifies periodicals that focused on particular topics.

Herstory Microfilm Collection. Berkeley: Women's History Research Center, 1973. A microfilm collection of alternative feminist periodicals published between 1960 and 1980. Offers an interesting documentary history of the women's movement.

New York Times. New York: New York Times, 1851–. Many libraries have this newspaper on microfilm going back to its beginning in 1851. An index is available to locate specific dates and pages of news stories; it also provides detailed chronologies of events as they were reported in the news.

Readers' Guide to Periodical Literature. New York: Wilson, 1900–. This index to popular magazines started in 1900; an earlier index, *Poole's Index to Periodical Literature*, covers 1802–1906, though it does not provide such thorough indexing.

Diaries, Pamphlets, Books

The American Culture Series. Ann Arbor: University Microfilms, 1941–1974. A microfilm set, with a useful index, featuring books and pamphlets published between 1493 and 1875.

American Women's Diaries. New Canaan: Readex, 1984–. A collection of reproductions of women's diaries. There are different series for different regions of the country.

The March of America Facsimile Series. Ann Arbor: University Microfilms, 1966. A collection of more than ninety facsimiles of travel accounts to the New World published in English or English translation from the fifteenth through the nineteenth century.

Women in America from Colonial Times to the Twentieth Century. New York: Arno, 1974. A collection of reprints of dozens of books written by women describing women's lives and experiences in their own words.

Government Documents

Congressional Record. Washington, D.C.: Government Printing Office, 1874–. Covers daily debates and proceedings of Congress. Earlier series were called *Debates and Proceedings in the Congress of the United States* and *The Congressional Globe.*

Foreign Relations of the United States. Washington, D.C.: Department of State, 1861–. A collection of documents from 1861, including diplomatic papers, correspondence, and memoranda, that provides a documentary record of U.S. foreign policy.

Public Papers of the Presidents. Washington, D.C.: Office of the Federal Register, 1957–. Includes major documents issued by the executive branch from the Hoover administration to the present.

Serial Set. Washington, D.C.: Government Printing Office, 1789–1969. A huge collection of congressional documents, available in many libraries on microfiche, with a useful index.

Local History Collections

State and county historical societies often house a wealth of historical documents; consider their resources when planning your research—you may find yourself working with material that no one else has analyzed before.

Internet Resources

The Internet has been a useful place for scholars to communicate and publish information in recent years. Electronic discussion lists, electronic journals, and primary texts are among the resources available for historians. The following sources are good places to find historical information. You can also search the World Wide Web using any of a number of search engines. However, bear in mind that there is no board of editors screening Internet sites for accuracy or usefulness, and the search engines generally rely on free-text searches rather than subject headings. Be critical of all of your sources, particularly those found on the Internet. Note that when this book went to press, the sites listed below were active and maintained.

American Memory: Historical Collections for the National Digital Library Program. <http://rs6.loc.gov/amhome.html> An Internet site that features digitized primary source materials from the Library of Congress, among them African American pamphlets, Civil War photographs, documents from the Continental Congress and the Constitutional Convention of 1774–1790, materials on woman suffrage, and oral histories.

Supreme Court Collection. <http://supct.law.cornell.edu/supct> This database can be used to search for information on various Supreme Court cases. Although the site primarily covers cases that occurred after 1990, there is information on some earlier historic cases. The justices' opinions, as originally written, are also included.

Directory of Scholarly and Professional E-Conferences. <http://n2h2.com/KOVAKS> A good place to find out what electronic conversations are going on in a scholarly discipline. Includes a good search facility and instructions on how to connect to e-mail discussion lists, newsgroups, and interactive chat sites with academic content. Once identified, these conferences are good places to raise questions, find out what controversies are currently stirring the profession, and even find out about grants and jobs.

Douglass Archives of American Public Address. <http://douglass.speech.nwu.edu> An electronic archive of American speeches and documents by a variety of people from Jane Addams to Jonathan Edwards to Theodore Roosevelt.

Historical Text Archive. <http://www.geocities.com/djmabry/index.html> A Web interface for the oldest and largest Internet site for historical documents. Includes sections on Native American, African American, and U.S. history, in which can be found texts of the Declaration of Independence, the U.S. Constitution, the Constitution of Iroquois Nations, World War II surrender documents, photograph collections, and a great deal more. These can be used online or saved as files.

History Links from Yahoo! <http://dir.yahoo.com/Humanities/History> A categorically arranged and frequently updated site list for all types of history. Some of the sources are more useful than others, but this can be a helpful gateway to some good information.

Index of Civil War Information on the Internet. <http://www.cwc.lsu.edu/cwc/civlink.htm> Compiled by the United States Civil War Center, this index lists everything from diaries to historic battlefields to reenactments.

Index of Native American Resources on the Internet. <http://www.hanksville.org/NAresources> A vast index of Native American resources organized by category. Within the history category, links are organized under subcategories: oral history, written history, geographical areas, timelines, and photographs and photographic archives. A central place to come in the search for information on Native American history.

WWW-VL History Index. <http://www.ukans.edu/history/VL/> A vast list of more than 1,700 links to sites of interest to historians, arranged alphabetically by general topic. Some links are to sources for general reference information, but most are on historical topics. A good place to start an exploration of Internet resources.

Internet Archive of Texts and Documents. <http://history.hanover.edu/texts.html> As stated on its home page, the purpose of this site is to make primary sources available to students and faculty. Arranged chronologically, geographically, and by subject, the site lists speeches, reports, and other primary-document links. It also includes some secondary sources on each subject.

Internet Resources for Students of Afro-American History and Culture. <http://www.libraries.rutgers.edu/rul/rr_gateway/research_guides/history/afrores.shtml> A good place to begin research on topics in African American history. The site is indexed and linked to a wide variety of sources, including primary documents, text collections, and archival sources on African American history. Individual documents such as slave narratives and petitions, the Fugitive Slave Acts, and speeches by W. E. B. Du Bois, Booker T. Washington, and Martin Luther King Jr. are categorized by century.

The Martin Luther King Jr. Papers Project. <http://www.stanford.edu/group/King> Organized by Stanford University, this site gives information about Martin Luther King Jr. and offers some of his writings.

NativeWeb. <http://www.nativeweb.org> One of the best-organized and most-accessible sites available on

Native American issues, *NativeWeb* combines an events calendar and message board with history, statistics, a list of news sources, archives, new and updated related sites each week, and documents. The text is indexed and can be searched by subject, nation, and geographic region.

Perry-Castañeda Library Map Collection. <http://www.lib.utexas.edu/Libs/PCL/Map_collection/Map_collection.html> The University of Texas at Austin library has put over seven hundred United States maps on the Web for viewing by students and professors alike.

Smithsonian Institution. <http://www.si.edu> Organized by subject, such as military history or Hispanic/Latino American resources, this site offers selected links to sites hosted by Smithsonian Institution museums and organizations. Content includes graphics of museum pieces and relevant textual information, book suggestions, maps, and links.

United States History Index. <http://www.ukans.edu/~usa> Maintained by a history professor and arranged by subject, such as women's history, labor history, and agricultural history, this index provides links to a variety of other sites. Although the list is extensive, it does not include a synopsis of each site, which makes finding specific information a time-consuming process.

United States History Resources by Period. <http://www.cms.ccsd.k12.co.us/ss.history.htm> This list of links to a variety of history sites is arranged chronologically and updated periodically.

United States Holocaust Memorial Museum. <http://www.ushmm.org/learn.htm> This site contains information about the Holocaust Museum in Washington, D.C., in particular and the Holocaust in general, and it lists links to related sites.

Women's History Resources. <http://www.mcps.k12.md.us/curriculum/socialstd/Women_Bookmarks.html> An extensive listing of women's history sources available on the Internet. The site indexes resources on subjects as diverse as woman suffrage, women in the workplace, and celebrated women writers. Some of the links are to equally vast indexes, providing an overwhelming wealth of information.

A note about the index:

Names of individuals appear in boldface; biographical dates are included for major historical figures.

Letters in parentheses following pages refer to:
(i)   illustrations, including photographs and artifacts, as well as information in picture captions
(f)   figures, including charts and graphs
(t)   tables
(m)   maps
(b)   boxed features (such as "Historical Question")
(n)   notes

United Students Against Sweatshops, 1173, 1173(i)

Universal Negro Improvement Association (UNIA), 833

University of California
affirmative action and, 1100
at Berkeley, free speech movement (1964) in, 1046

University Settlement House (New York City), 727

"Uprising of twenty thousand" (1909–10), 729–730, 730(i)

Uprisings. See Rebellions, revolts, and uprisings

Urbanization, 598

Urban renewal, 1025, 1032

U.S. Steel (later USX), 634, 634(i), 740, 747, 802, 877

USX (United States Steel), 634, 634(i), 740, 747, 802, 877

Utah, 577, 587, 638
woman suffrage in, 689

Ute Indians, 590

Utopia, Bellamy's, 678–679

Vail, Theodore N., 627

Valentino, Rudolph, 831(i)

Vance, Cyrus, 1156

Vandenberg, Arthur (1884–1951), 931, 951

Vanderbilt, Alice, 604(i)

Vanderbilt, Alva (Mrs. William K. Vanderbilt I), 605

Vanderbilt, "Commodore" Cornelius (1794–1877), 605, 621

Vanderbilt, William, 605

Vanderbilt family, 605

Vann, Robert, 882

Vanzetti, Bartolomeo (1888–1927), 819–820

Vaux, Calvert (1824–1895), 609, 610(i)

Veblen, Thorstein, 604(i)

Venezuela, 707, 742

Vermont, civil unions for same-sex couples in, 1125, 1128

Versailles, Treaty of (1919), 798–800, 902

Vertical integration, 622

Veterans, 1060
Korean War, 997
Vietnam War, 1086, 1088, 1089, 1090, 1090(i)
World War I, 801(i), 855
World War II, 959, 962, 962(i)

Veterans Administration, 995

Vienna (Austria), 1961 summit meeting in, 1063–1064

Vietcong, 1068, 1074
Tet Offensive (1968), 1078–1079

Vietminh, 987

Vietnam, Geneva Accord (1954), 988, 988(m)

Vietnam Veterans Against the War, 1086

Vietnam Veterans Memorial, 1090, 1090(i)

Vietnam War (1954–1975), 1031, 1062(i), 1069(m)
1955–1961 U.S. involvement in, 988
1962–1972 troop levels, 1070(f)
Americanization of, 1062, 1074–1075
attrition strategy, 1074
bombing of North Vietnam, 1069–1070, 1072–1073(b), 1074, 1076, 1077, 1079, 1081–1083, 1087
casualties, 1089(t)
China and, 1072–1074
domestic opposition to, 1075–1082. See also Antiwar movement
1968 events, 1078–1082
end of, 1087
French defeat in, 987–988
helicopters in, 1084–1085, 1085(i)
Johnson administration and, 1069–1075
Kennedy administration and, 1061–1062, 1067–1068
legacy of defeat in, 1087–1090
My Lai massacre (1968), 1086, 1086(i)
Nixon administration and, 1078, 1082–1083, 1087–1090
Cambodia, 1083, 1083(m)
peace negotiations, 1087
Pentagon Papers, 1087
Vietnamization, 1082
Paris accords (1973), 1087
Paris peace talks, 1079
Pentagon Papers, 1086–1087
pro-war demonstrators, 1078(i)
public opinion about (1965–1974), 1076(f)
Soviet Union and, 1072–1074, 1083
Tet Offensive (1968), 1078–1079
veterans of, 1086, 1088, 1089, 1090, 1090(i)
Vietnamization of, 1079, 1082–1083
withdrawal of U.S. forces, 1082

Villa, Francisco "Pancho" (1877–1923), 773, 774(i)

Violence
domestic, 1102, 1123–1124
political. See Riots and mob violence (political violence)
in the West, 588–589

Violence Against Women Act (1994), 1123

VISTA (Volunteers in Service to America), 1028

Voter Education Project, 1034

Voter registration, 1135
1960s drives for, 1021, 1034, 1040(b), 1041(i), 1045

Voter turnout
1868–1900, 636–637, 637(f)
in 1896 election, 703
1920 and 1924, 818
in 1936 election, 887
1968–1996, 637(f)
in 1980 election, 1097
in 1992 election, 1134

Voting rights (suffrage)
of blacks, 642
1870s–1890s, 638
1940–1976, 1038(m)
in 1960s, 1040–1041(b)
Fifteenth Amendment, 688
progressivism and, 759–761
literacy tests and, 759, 1021
banned by Voting Rights Act of 1965, 1031, 1040
for immigrants, 602, 799
"one person, one vote" principle, 1053–1054
poll tax and, 759, 1030(t)
of women, 638, 815(i), 818–819
in Great Britain, 758
before the Nineteenth Amendment, 783(m)
Nineteenth Amendment and, 815, 818
organized movement for, 688–689
progressivism and, 758–759
WCTU and, 688
Wilson and, 751, 782
World War I and, 781–782

Voting Rights Act (1965), 1030(t), 1031, 1038, 1038(m), 1040, 1099

Vreeland, Charles, 712–713(b)

Vreeland report, 712

Wabash v. Illinois (1886), 643

Waco (Texas), armed religious cult in, 1136

WACs (Women's Army Corps), 915

Wages and salaries
1870s–1890s, 642, 651, 656, 657, 660, 665, 671
in 1920s, 840
in 1932, 845
gender differences in, 1026, 1132
1870s, 665
pay equity movement, 1123
industrial (1912–1920), 781(f)
male-female disparities, 1026
minimum, 822, 891, 1135
during World War I, 781, 781(f), 783
after World War II, 958, 962

Wagner, Robert, 891

THE TERRITORIAL GROWTH OF THE UNITED STATES

CANADA

MINNESOTA

WISCONSIN

MICHIGAN

Lake Superior

Lake Huron

Lake Michigan

Lake Ontario

Lake Erie

VERMONT

MAINE
(part of Mass.
until 1820)

St. Lawrence R.

NEW
HAMPSHIRE

NEW
YORK

MASS.

RHODE
ISLAND

CONNECTICUT

Hudson R.

Connecticut R.

IOWA

OHIO

PENN.

Delaware R.

Susquehanna R.

NEW JERSEY

DELAWARE

MARYLAND

Chesapeake
Bay

ILLINOIS

INDIANA

WEST
VIRGINIA

Potomac R.

James R.

KANSAS

MISSOURI

Ohio R.

KENTUCKY

VIRGINIA

NORTH
CAROLINA

Cape Fear R.

ATLANTIC
OCEAN

Missouri R.

Cumberland R.

Proclamation Line of 1763

THE ORIGINAL THIRTEEN COLONIES

ARKANSAS

Arkansas R.

TENNESSEE

Tennessee R.

SOUTH
CAROLINA

OKLAHOMA

Mississippi R.

Savannah R.

MISSISSIPPI

ALABAMA

GEORGIA

THE ORIGINAL
THIRTEEN COLONIES
IN 1776

LOUISIANA

TEXAS

0   150   300 miles
0   150   300 kilometers

FLORIDA

Gulf of Mexico

BAHAMAS

CUBA

CANADA

MINNESOTA

WISCONSIN

MICHIGAN

Lake Superior

Lake Huron

Lake Michigan

Lake Ontario

Lake Erie

St. Lawrence R.

MAINE
(part of Mass.
until 1820)

VERMONT

NEW
HAMPSHIRE

NEW YORK

MASS.

Connecticut R.

Hudson R.

RHODE
ISLAND

CONNECTICUT

PENN.

Delaware R.

Susquehanna R.

NEW JERSEY

DELAWARE

MARYLAND

Chesapeake
Bay

IOWA

Missouri R.

ILLINOIS

INDIANA

OHIO

WEST
VIRGINIA

Potomac R.

VIRGINIA

James R.

*Gained by treaty
with Britain, 1783*

KENTUCKY

Ohio R.

KANSAS

MISSOURI

NORTH
CAROLINA

Cape Fear R.

Proclamation Line of 1763

THE ORIGINAL THIRTEEN COLONIES

TENNESSEE

Cumberland R.

Tennessee R.

ARKANSAS

Arkansas R.

OKLAHOMA

Mississippi R.

SOUTH
CAROLINA

ATLANTIC
OCEAN

Savannah R.

MISSISSIPPI

ALABAMA

GEORGIA

TEXAS

LOUISIANA

**THE UNITED STATES
IN 1783**

0		150		300 miles

0	150		300 kilometers

FLORIDA

Gulf of Mexico

BAHAMAS

CUBA

WASHINGTON

Columbia R.

OREGON

IDAHO

Snake R.

MONTANA

Missouri R.

Area ceded by Great Britain, 1818

NORTH DAKOTA

SOUTH DAKOTA

LOUISIANA PURCHASE
From France, 1803

WYOMING

NEBRASKA

N. Platte R.

Platte R.

NEVADA

Sacramento R.

San Joaquin R.

UTAH

Colorado R.

COLORADO

S. Platte R.

KANSAS

CALIFORNIA

PACIFIC
OCEAN

ARIZONA

NEW
MEXICO

Red R.

TEXAS

Rio Grande

M E X I C O

CANADA

Lake Superior

MINNESOTA

WISCONSIN

MICHIGAN

Lake Michigan

Lake Huron

Lake Ontario

Lake Erie

St. Lawrence R.

MAINE
(part of Mass.
until 1820)

VERMONT

NEW
HAMPSHIRE

NEW YORK

MASS.

RHODE
ISLAND

CONNECTICUT

Connecticut R.

Hudson R.

PENN.

Susquehanna R.

Delaware R.

NEW JERSEY

IOWA

ILLINOIS

INDIANA

OHIO

WEST
VIRGINIA

Potomac R.

Proclamation Line of 1763

THE ORIGINAL THIRTEEN COLONIES

DELAWARE

MARYLAND

Chesapeake
Bay

Missouri R.

MISSOURI

KENTUCKY

*Gained by treaty
with Britain, 1783*

Ohio R.

James R.

VIRGINIA

NORTH
CAROLINA

Cape Fear R.

OKLAHOMA

ARKANSAS

Arkansas R.

Cumberland R.

Tennessee R.

TENNESSEE

Mississippi R.

SOUTH
CAROLINA

Savannah R.

ATLANTIC
OCEAN

LOUISIANA

MISSISSIPPI

ALABAMA

GEORGIA

*Areas taken from Spain
in 1810, 1813*

Gulf of Mexico

FLORIDA

*FLORIDA,
Treaty with Spain,
1819*

THE UNITED STATES
IN 1819

0   150   300 miles

0   150   300 kilometers

BAHAMAS

CUBA

WASHINGTON

OREGON COUNTRY
Agreement with Britain,
_1846_

OREGON

Columbia R.

IDAHO

Snake R.

MONTANA

Missouri R.

NORTH DAKOTA

SOUTH DAKOTA

Area ceded by
Great Britain,
_1818_

L O U I S I A N A
P U R C H A S E
From France, 1803

WYOMING

N. Platte R.

NEBRASKA

Platte R.

NEVADA

UTAH

Sacramento R.

San Joaquin R.

MEXICAN CESSION,
_1848_

CALIFORNIA

Colorado R.

S. Platte R.

COLORADO

KANSAS

PACIFIC
OCEAN

ARIZONA

NEW
MEXICO

Red R.

TEXAS
Annexed, 1845

TEXAS

GADSDEN PURCHASE
From Mexico, 1853

Rio Grande

M E X I C O

M–6

CANADA

Lake Superior

Lake Huron

Lake Michigan

Lake Ontario

Lake Erie

MINNESOTA

WISCONSIN

MICHIGAN

MAINE

VERMONT

NEW
HAMPSHIRE

NEW YORK

MASS.

RHODE
ISLAND

CONNECTICUT

IOWA

ILLINOIS

INDIANA

OHIO

PENN.

NEW JERSEY

Missouri R.

DELAWARE

MARYLAND

WEST
VIRGINIA

*Chesapeake
Bay*

VIRGINIA

MISSOURI

Ohio R.

KENTUCKY

**Gained by treaty
with Britain, 1783**

Proclamation Line of 1763

THE ORIGINAL THIRTEEN COLONIES

James R.

Potomac R.

Hudson R.

Connecticut R.

Delaware R.

Susquehanna R.

St. Lawrence R.

NORTH
CAROLINA

Cape Fear R.

Cumberland R.

TENNESSEE

Tennessee R.

Arkansas R.

OKLAHOMA

ARKANSAS

Mississippi R.

SOUTH
CAROLINA

Savannah R.

ATLANTIC
OCEAN

MISSISSIPPI

ALABAMA

GEORGIA

LOUISIANA

**Areas taken from Spain
in 1810, 1813**

FLORIDA

**FLORIDA,
Treaty with Spain,
1819**

Gulf of Mexico

BAHAMAS

CUBA

**THE UNITED STATES
IN 1853**

0   150   300 miles

0   150   300 kilometers

Area ceded by
Great Britain,
1818

WASHINGTON
★ Olympia

MONTANA
★ Helena

NORTH DAKOTA
Bismarck ★

Columbia R.
★ Salem

OREGON COUNTRY
Agreement with Britain,
1846

OREGON

IDAHO
★ Boise

Missouri R.

SOUTH DAKOTA
Pierre ★

Snake R.

WYOMING

LOUISIANA
PURCHASE
From France, 1803

N. Platte R.

NEBRASKA

Sacramento R.

★ Carson City

NEVADA

Salt Lake
City

UTAH

Cheyenne ★

S. Platte R.

Platte R.

★ Sacramento

San Joaquin R.

Colorado R.

★ Denver
COLORADO

KANSAS

MEXICAN CESSION
1848

CALIFORNIA

PACIFIC
OCEAN

ARIZONA

★ Phoenix

NEW
MEXICO

Santa Fe ★

Red R.

TEXAS
Annexed, 1845

TEXAS

GADSDEN PURCHASE
From Mexico, 1853

Rio Grande

MEXICO

ARCTIC OCEAN

RUSSIA

ALASKA
Purchased from
Russia, 1867

CANADA

Yukon R.

Bering
Sea

Gulf of
Alaska

Juneau ★

PACIFIC
OCEAN

Honolulu HAWAII
★ Annexed, 1898

0   250   500 miles

0   250   500 kilometers

0   50   100 miles

0   50   100 kilometers

M–8

CANADA

MAINE
★ Augusta

VERMONT
Montpelier ★

Concord ● NEW
HAMPSHIRE

NEW YORK
Albany ★
★ Boston
MASS.
★ Providence
RHODE
ISLAND

MINNESOTA
St. Paul ★

WISCONSIN

MICHIGAN

Lake Superior

Lake Huron

Lake Michigan

Lake Ontario

Lake Erie

Hartford ★
CONNECTICUT

PENN.

★ Madison

Lansing ●

★ Trenton
Harrisburg ★
NEW JERSEY

IOWA

INDIANA

OHIO

Des
Moines ★

Columbus ●

ILLINOIS

Indianapolis ★

Springfield ★

Lincoln ★

WEST
VIRGINIA

● Dover
Annapolis ★
DELAWARE
MARYLAND
WASHINGTON, D.C.
Chesapeake
Bay

Charleston ★

Richmond ★

VIRGINIA

Topeka ★

Jefferson
City ★

Frankfort ★

KENTUCKY

Gained by treaty
with Britain, 1783

NORTH
CAROLINA

MISSOURI

Raleigh ★

Nashville ●

Cumberland R.

TENNESSEE

SOUTH
CAROLINA

Oklahoma
City ★

ARKANSAS

Columbia ★

OKLAHOMA

Little
Rock ★

Atlanta ●

ATLANTIC
OCEAN

GEORGIA

MISSISSIPPI

ALABAMA

Austin ★

LOUISIANA

Jackson ★

Montgomery ★

Tallahassee ★

Baton
Rouge ●

Areas taken
from Spain
in 1810, 1813

FLORIDA

THE CONTEMPORARY
UNITED STATES

0   150   300 miles

0   150   300 kilometers

FLORIDA,
Treaty with Spain,
1819

U.S. Territories

ATLANTIC
OCEAN

San
Juan

VIRGIN
ISLANDS
Acquired from
Denmark,
1916–1917

PUERTO RICO
Acquired from
Spain, 1898

Caribbean Sea

Gulf of Mexico

BAHAMAS

0   50   100 miles

0   50   100 kilometers

CUBA

St. Lawrence R.

Connecticut R.

Hudson R.

Delaware R.

Susquehanna R.

Potomac R.

James R.

Ohio R.

Tennessee R.

Mississippi R.

Missouri R.

Arkansas R.

Savannah R.

Cape Fear R.

THE ORIGINAL THIRTEEN COLONIES

Proclamation Line of 1763